# Foundations of Insurance Economics
## Readings in Economics and Finance

# Huebner International Series on Risk, Insurance, and Economic Security

J. David Cummins, Editor
  The Wharton School
  University of Pennsylvania
  Philadelphia, Pennsylvania, USA

**Series Advisors:**

Dr. Phelim P. Boyle
  University of Waterloo, Canada
Dr. Jean Lemaire
  University of Pennsylvania, USA
Professor Akihiko Tsuboi
  Kagawa University, Japan
Dr. Richard Zeckhauser
  Harvard University, USA

**Other books in the series:**

Cummins, J. David; Smith, Barry D.;
  Vance, R. Neil; VanDerhei, Jack L.:
  *Risk Classification in Life Insurance*
Mintel, Judith: *Insurance Rate Litigation*
Cummins, J. David: *Strategic Planning and
  Modeling in Property-Liability Insurance*
Lemaire, Jean: *Automobile Insurance:
  Actuarial Models*
Rushing, William: *Social Functions and
  Economic Aspects of Health Insurance*
Cummins, J. David and Harrington, Scott E.:
  *Fair Rate of Return in Property-Liability Insurance*
Appel, David and Borba, Phillip S.: *Workers
  Compensation Insurance Pricing*
Cummins, J. David and Derrig, Richard A.:
  *Classical Insurance Solvency Theory*
Borba, Philip S. and Appel, David: *Benefits,
  Costs and Cycles in Workers Compensation*
Cummins, J. David and Derrig, Richard A.:
  *Financial Models of Insurance Solvency*
Williams, C. Arthur: *An International Comparison of
  Workers' Compensation*
Cummins, J. David and Derrig, Richard A.:
  *Managing the Insolvency Risk of Insurance
  Companies*

The objective of the series is to publish original research and
advanced textbooks dealing with all major aspects of risk bearing and
economic security. The emphasis is on books that will be of interest
to an international audience. Interdisciplinary topics as well as those
from traditional disciplines such as economics, risk and insurance,
and actuarial science are within the scope of the series. The goal is
to provide an outlet for imaginative approaches to problems in both
the theory and practice of risk and economic security.

# Foundations of Insurance Economics
## Readings in Economics and Finance

edited by

**Georges Dionne**
Université de Montréal

**Scott E. Harrington**
University of South Carolina

**Kluwer Academic Publishers**
Boston / Dordrecht / London

**Distributors for North America:**
Kluwer Academic Publishers
101 Philip Drive
Assinippi Park
Norwell, Massachusetts 02061 USA

**Distributors for all other countries:**
Kluwer Academic Publishers Group
Distribution Centre
Post Office Box 322
3300 AH Dordrecht, THE NETHERLANDS

**Library of Congress Cataloging-in-Publication Data**

Foundations of insurance economics : readings in economics and finance
    / edited by Georges Dionne, Scott E. Harrington.
        p.   cm. — (Huebner international series on risk, insurance,
    and economic security)
    ISBN 0-7923-9204-3 (acid-free paper)
    1. Insurance.   2. Risk (Insurance)   I. Dionne, Georges.
II. Harrington, Scott E.   III. Series.
HG8051.F58   1991
368′.01—dc20                                              91-22346
                                                             CIP

*Printed on acid-free paper.*

Printed in the United States of America

# Contents

vi

# PREFACE

Economic and financial research on insurance markets has undergone dramatic growth since its infancy in the early 1960s. Our main objective in compiling this volume was to achieve a wider dissemination of key papers in this literature. Their significance is highlighted in the introduction, which surveys major areas in insurance economics. While it was not possible to provide comprehensive coverage of insurance economics in this book, these readings provide an essential foundation to those who desire to conduct research and teach in the field. In particular, we hope that this compilation and our introduction will be useful to graduate students and to researchers in economics, finance, and insurance. Our criteria for selecting articles included significance, representativeness, pedagogical value, and our desire to include theoretical and empirical work. While the focus of the applied papers is on property-liability insurance, they illustrate issues, concepts, and methods that are applicable in many areas of insurance.

The S.S. Huebner Foundation for Insurance Education at the University of Pennsylvania's Wharton School made this book possible by financing publication costs. We are grateful for this assistance and to J. David Cummins, Executive Director of the Foundation, for his efforts and helpful advice on the contents.

We also wish to thank all of the authors and editors who provided permission to reprint articles and our respective institutions for technical and financial support. We express our debt to Michele Bergen, Danielle Blanchard, Josée Lafontaine, Andrée Mathieu, Betty McLees, and Nicos Scordis for assistance in preparation of the manuscript.

Georges Dionne
Economics Department and Center
  for Research on Transportation
Université de Montréal

Scott E. Harrington
College of Business Administration
University of South Carolina

## Acknowledgments

**The editors wish to thank the following authors and sources to reprint their articles:**

Arrow, Kenneth J. (1971) "Insurance, Risk and Resource Allocation" Chapter 5 in Essays in the Theory of Risk Bearing, Elsevier Publishing Company, Inc., pp. 134-143. Reprinted by permission of the author.

Biger, Nahum and Yehuda Kahane (1978) "Risk Considerations in Insurance Ratemaking" Journal of Risk and Insurance, Vol. XLIV, No 1, pp. 121-132. Reprinted by permission of the Editor. Copyright 1978 by the American Risk and Insurance Association.

Borch, Karl (1962) "Equilibrium in a Reinsurance Market" Econometrica, 30, pp. 424-444. Reprinted by permission of the Econometric Society.

Cook, Philip J. and Graham, Daniel A. (1977) "The Demand for Insurance and Protection : The Case of Irreplaceable Commodities" Quarterly Journal of Economics XCI, pp. 143-156. Reprinted by permission of John Wiley & Sons, Inc. Copyright 1977 by the President and Fellows of Harvard College.

Cooper, Russell and Hayes, Beth (1987) "Multi-Period Insurance Contracts" International Journal of Industrial Organization 5, pp. 211-231. Reprinted by permission of Elsevier Science Publishers.

Crocker, Keith J. and Snow, Arthur (1986) "The Efficiency Effects of Categorical Discrimination in the Insurance Industry," Journal of Political Economy, pp. 321-344. Reprinted by permission of the University of Chicago Press. Copyright 1986 by the University of Chicago.

Cummins, J. David and Vanderhei, Jack L. (1979) "A Note on the Relative Efficiency of Property-Liability Insurance Distribution Systems" Bell Journal of Economics, Autumn, pp. 709-719. Reprinted by permission of the Rand Corporation.

Cummins, J. David and Outreville, J. François (1987) "An International Analysis of Underwriting Cycles in Property-Liability Insurance", The Journal of Risk and Insurance, Vol. LIV, June, pp. 246-262. Reprinted by permission of the Editor. Copyright 1987 by the American Risk and Insurance Association.

Cummins, J. David (1988) "Risk-Based Premiums for Insurance Guaranty Funds," Journal of Finance, September, pp. 823-839. Reprinted by permission of the American Finance Association.

Dahlby, Beverly G. (1983) "Adverse Selection and Statistical Discrimination: An Analysis of Canadian Automobile Insurance" Journal of Public Economics 20, pp. 121-130. Reprinted by permission of Elsevier Science Publishers.

Dionne, Georges (1983) "Adverse Selection and Repeated Insurance Contracts" Geneva Papers on Risk and Insurance, 8, pp. 316-332. Reprinted by permission of the Geneva Association.

Doherty, Neil and Garven, James (1986) "Price Regulation in Property/Liability Insurance : A Contingent Claims Approach," Journal of Finance, pp. 1031-1050. Reprinted by permission of the American Finance Association.

Ehrlich, Isaac and Becker, Garry S. (1972) "Market Insurance, Self-Insurance and Self-Protection" Journal of Political Economy, 80, pp. 623-648. Reprinted by permission of the University of Chicago Press. Copyright 1972 by the University of Chicago.

Finsinger, Jorg and Pauly, Mark V. (1984) "Reserve Levels and Reserve Requirements for Profit-Maximizing Insurance Firms," in G. Bamberg and K. Spremann, Risk and Capital, pp. 160-180. Reprinted by permission of Springer-Verlag. Copyright 1984 by Springer Verlag.

Grossman, Sanford J. and Hart, Oliver D. (1983) "An Analysis of the Principal Agent Problem", Econometrica, January, pp. 7-45. Reprinted by permission of the Econometric Society.

Harrington, Scott E. (1987) "A Note on the Impact of Auto Insurance Rate Regulation", Review of Economics and Statistics, LXIX, pp. 166-170. Reprinted by permission of Elsevier Science Publishers.

Harrington, Scott E. (1988) "Prices and Profits in the Liability Insurance Market" in Liability : Perspectives and Policy, R. Litan and C. Winston eds., Brookings Institution, Washington, D.C., pp. 42-100. Reprinted by permission of Brookings Institution.

Joskow, Paul J. (1973) "Cartels, Competition and Regulation in the Property-Liability Insurance Industry" Bell Journal of Economics pp. 375-427. Reprinted by permission of the Rand Corporation.

Kihlstrom, Richard E. and Roth, Alvin E. (1982) "Risk Aversion and the Negotiation of Insurance Contracts" Journal of Risk and Insurance XLIX, September, pp. 372-387. Reprinted by permission of the Editor. Copyright 1982 by the American Risk and Insurance Association.

Kunreuther, Howard and Pauly, Mark V. (1985) "Market Equilibrium With Private Knowledge : An Insurance Example", Journal of Public Economics, pp. 269-288. Reprinted by permission of Elsevier Science Publishers.

Machina, Mark (1987) "Choice Under Uncertainty : Problems Solved and Unsolved" Journal of Economic Perspectives, 1, pp. 121-154. Reprinted by permission of the American Economic Association.

Mayers, David and Smith, Clifford W. (1982) "On the Corporate Demand for Insurance" Journal of Business, pp. 281-296. Reprinted by permission of the University of Chicago Press. Copyright 1982 by the University of Chicago.

Mayers, David and Smith, Clifford W. (1983) "The Interdependence of Individual Portfolio Decisions and the Demand for Insurance" Journal of Political Economy, pp. 304-311. Reprinted by permission of the University of Chicago Press. Copyright 1983 by the University of Chicago.

Mayers, David and Smith, Clifford W. (1988) "Ownership Structure across Lines of Property - Casualty Insurance", The Journal of Law and Economics, XXXI, October, pp. 351-378. Reprinted by permission of the University of Chicago Press. Copyright 1988 by the University of Chicago.

Mossin, Jan (1968) "Aspects of Rational Insurance Purchasing" Journal of Political Economy, pp. 553-568. Reprinted by permission of the University of Chicago Press. Copyright 1968 by the University of Chicago.

Munch, Patricia and Smallwood, Dennis E. (1980) "Solvency Regulation in the Property-Liability Insurance Industry : Empirical Evidence" Bell Journal of Economics, pp. 261-279. Reprinted by permission of the Rand Corporation.

Pratt, John W. (1964) "Risk Aversion in the Small and in the Large", Econometrica, 32, pp. 122-136. Reprinted by the permission of the Econometric Society.

Raviv, Arthur (1979) "The Design of an Optimal Insurance Policy", American Economic Review, 69, pp. 84-96. Reprinted by permission of the American Economic Association.

Rothschild, Michael and Stiglitz, Joseph E. (1970) "Increasing Risk I : A Definition" Journal of Economic Theory, 2, pp. 225-243. Reprinted by permission of the Acamedic Press. Copyright 1970 by Academic Press, Inc.

Rothschild, Michael and Stiglitz, Joseph E. (1976) "Equilibrium in Competitive Insurance Markets : An Essay on the Economics of Imperfect Information" Quarterly Journal of Economics, 90, pp. 629-649. Reprinted by permission of John Wiley & Sons, Inc. Copyright 1976 by the President and Fellows of Harvard College.

Schlesigner, Harris and Doherty, Neil (1985) "Incomplete Markets for Insurance : An Overview", Journal of Risk and Insurance, LII, pp. 402-423. Reprinted by the permission of the Editor. Copyright 1985 by the American Risk and Insurance Association.

Shavell, Steven (1979) "On Moral Hazard and Insurance", Quarterly Journal of Economics, 93, pp. 541-562. Reprinted by permission of John Wiley & Sons, Inc. Copyright 1979 by the President and Fellows of Harvard College.

Shavell, Steven (1986) "The Judgment Proof Problem", International Review of Law and Economics, 6, pp. 45-58. Reprinted by the permission of Butterworth Publishers. Copyright 1986 by Butterworth & Co. (Publishers) Ltd.

# Foundations of Insurance Economics
Readings in Economics and Finance

## An Introduction to Insurance Economics[*]

*Georges Dionne and Scott E. Harrington*
*April 1990*
*Revised October 1990*

[*] Respectively from the Université de Montréal and the University of South Carolina. Comments on an earlier version by L. Eeckhoudt, C. Gollier, and P. Viala were very useful.

Although the prevalence of risk in economic activity has always been recognized (Green, 1984), deterministic models dominated economic explanations of observed phenomena for many years. As a result, the economics of insurance has a relatively short history. In early work that formally introduced risk and uncertainty in economic analysis (von Neumann and Morgenstern, 1947; Friedman and Savage, 1948; Allais, 1953; Arrow, 1953; Debreu, 1953), insurance was viewed either as a contingent good or was discussed in relation to gambling. Before 1960, economic literature was largely void of analyses of the nature of insurance markets or of the economic behavior of individual agents in these markets.[1]

During the early 1960s, Kenneth Arrow and Karl Borch published several important articles (Arrow, 1963, 1965; Borch, 1960, 1961, 1962) that can be viewed as the beginning of modern economic analysis of insurance activity. Two of these papers are reprinted in this volume.[2] Arrow was a leader in the development of insurance economics, and more generally, in the development of the economics of uncertainty, information, and communication. Arrow (1965) presented a framework of analysis that explains the role of different institutional arrangements for risk-shifting, such as insurance markets, stock markets, implicit contracts, cost-plus contracts, and futures markets. All of these institutions transfer risk to parties with comparative advantage in risk bearing. In the usual insurance example, risk averse individuals confronted with risk are willing to pay a fixed price to a less risk averse

---

[1] Borch (1990, Ch. 1) reviews brief discussions of insurance contained in the works of Adam Smith and Alfred Marshall, as well as the role of uncertainty in Austrian economics.

[2] References reprinted in this volume are highlighted. Arrow (1963) is reprinted in Diamond and Rothschild (1978) and Borch (1960, 1961) are reprinted in Borch (1990).

or more diversified insurer who offers to bear the risk at that price. Since both parties agree to the contract, they are both better off.

Risk is seldom completely shifted in any market. Arrow (1963) discussed three of the main reasons that risk shifting is limited: moral hazard, adverse selection, and transaction costs. Arrow (1965) emphasized the problem of moral hazard and suggested that coinsurance arrangements in insurance contracts can be explained by this information problem.[3] Arrow (1963) showed in the absence of moral hazard that full insurance above a deductible is optimal when the premium contains a fixed-percentage loading. He also proved that risk aversion on the part of the insurer is another explanation for coinsurance. Both results were extended by Raviv (1979) and others.

Borch (1960, 1961, 1962) also made significant contributions to the theory of optimal insurance. He developed necessary and sufficient conditions for Pareto optimal exchange in risk pooling arrangements. He also showed, in a general framework, how risk aversion affects the optimal coverage (or optimal shares) of participants in the pool. Although his formal analysis was in terms of reinsurance contracts, it was shown by Moffet (1979) that the same result applies for contracts between policyholders and direct insurers. Borch's formulation of risk exchange influenced the development of principal-agent models (Ross, 1973; Holmstrom, 1979), and it has led to many other applications in the insurance literature.[4] More generally, Borch made many contributions to the application of expected utility theory to insurance and influenced the development of portfolio theory and its applicability to the insurance industry. Finally, Borch's contributions established some important links between actuarial science and insurance economics (Loubergé, 1990).[5]

*Outline of this Volume*. The remainder of this introductory essay reviews the main developments of insurance economics subsequent to the pathbreaking work of Arrow and

---

[3]In the insurance economics literature, coinsurance refers to a contract in which the insurer pays a fixed proportion of any claim amount.

[4]See Lemaire (1990) for a survey of these applications.

[5]See Boyle (1990) for a survey of Borch's scholarly contributions.

Borch. In the process, the articles included in this volume are introduced. The remaining eight sections include articles on (1) utility, risk, and risk aversion, (2) the demand for insurance, (3) insurance and resource allocation (in which we include Borch, 1962, and Arrow, 1965), (4) moral hazard, (5) adverse selection, (6) insurance market structure and organizational form, (7) insurance pricing, and (8) insurance regulation.

The selection of articles was based on several criteria including the significance of the contribution, the representativeness of the work, and the desire to include empirical as well as theoretical articles. The selection process also considered whether the level of mathematics employed was likely to be accessible to most readers. In a few instances, we showed a slight preference for articles in books that are not as readily available as those published in journals.

For the most part, neither this introductory essay nor the remainder of the volume attempts to cover the wide variety of applications of insurance economics in the areas of health insurance, life insurance and annuities, social insurance, and in the law and economics literature. Instead, we review significant applications and include several articles dealing with property-liability insurance. This approach is at least partially due to our taste (and expertise). However, these articles and our introductory discussion help to illustrate issues, concepts, and methods that are applicable in many areas of insurance.

## UTILITY, RISK, AND RISK AVERSION

*The Expected Utility Model.* Although the theory of decision making under uncertainty has frequently been criticized since its formal introduction by von Neumann and Morgenstern, it has been very useful in the study of optimal insurance decisions. Until recently, the linear expected utility model was the standard paradigm used to formally analyze economic behavior under uncertainty and to derive applications in many fields such as insurance. With objective probabilities, three basic axioms are necessary to obtain the von Neumann-Morgenstern theorem : weak order, independence, and continuity. Given these three axioms (and some other technical assumptions), insurance policy A will be chosen over policy B if and only if $E_A U > E_B U$ (where $E_i U$ is the linear expected utility associated with policy i). With subjective probabilities, additional axioms must be introduced in order to obtain a unique subjective probability measure over the set of states and a utility function that is unique up to a positive linear transformation : state-independent preferences and "reversal of order", which rules out moral hazard (Anscombe and Auman, 1963; Karni, 1985; Drèze, 1961, 1987).[6]

Linearity in probabilities is directly associated with the independence axiom (Machina, 1987). This axiom has been challenged by many researchers, including Allais (1953a) who presented a now classic example that violates linearity in probabilities (and thus the independence axiom). Nonetheless, a large number of fundamental results in insurance economics have been derived from the linear expected utility model. In fact, very few contributions use non-linear models (see, however, Karni, 1990a), and the classical expected utility model remains the most useful approach for applications in insurance. We have chosen to reprint Machina's article for two main reasons. First, the classical linear expected utility model is presented with a different perspective than in other articles on the subject (e.g., Drèze, 1974; Shoemaker, 1982). Second, and more importantly, problems with the traditional model and some of the proposed responses are discussed in detail.

*Measures of Risk Aversion.* The Arrow-Pratt measures of absolute and relative risk aversion (Arrow, 1965; Pratt, 1964) are commonly used in analyses of insurance decisions.[7] They measure both the intensity of an individual's preference to avoid risk and variation in this intensity as a function of wealth. Given a von Neumann-Morgenstern utility of wealth function, $U(W)$ with $U'(W) > 0$ and $U''(W) < 0$ for risk aversion, these measures of risk aversion are useful in calculating the certainty equivalent of a risky situation and the corresponding risk premium $\Pi^U$, which can be interpreted as the largest sum of money an

---

[6]See Drèze (1987) for an analysis of the foundations of the linear expected utility model in presence of moral hazard. For analyses of the foundations and economic implications of linear state-dependent preferences, see Karni (1985), Drèze (1987), Karni (1990), and Viscusi and Evans (1990).

[7]A concept of partial risk aversion also has been defined by Menezes and Hanson (1970) and Zeckhauser and Keeler (1970). See Dionne (1984) for an application to insurance economics and Briys and Eeckhoudt (1985) for other applications and a discussion of the relationships between the three measures of risk aversion.

insured with a given utility function is willing to pay above the expected outcome (actuarially fair premium) to avoid the risk. Moreover, an insured with utility function U is said to be more risk averse than another insured with utility function V if $\Pi^U \geq \Pi^V$ when both face the same risky situation and have identical non random initial wealth.[8] Finally, the absolute measure of risk aversion corresponding to a given utility function (- U"/U') is said to be non-increasing in wealth, W, if in the same risky situation, $\Pi^U(W_1) \geq \Pi^U(W_2)$ for $W_1 \leq W_2$. A necessary condition for decreasing absolute risk aversion is that U'''(W) > 0.[9]

*Measures of Risk.* Another important concept in the analysis of optimal insurance behavior is the measurement of risk. Let X and Y be two random variables with respective distribution functions $F_X$ and $F_Y$. $F_X$ is a mean preserving spread of $F_Y$ (Rothschild and Stiglitz, 1970) if E(X) = E(Y) and $E_X U < E_Y U$ (where $E_i U$ is the linear expected utility associated with the random variable i). Many insurance contracts with actuarially fair premiums can be interpreted in terms of a mean preserving spread since they reduce the spread of the loss distribution without affecting the mean. For example, full insurance (i.e., a contract that pays the full amount of loss) produces a global decrease in risk since it implies the comparison of a risky situation with a non-risky one (Meyer and Ormiston, 1989).

In some cases, Rothschild and Stiglitz's definition of increasing risk is too general to generate non-ambiguous comparative statics results (Meyer and Orminston, 1985). When this is the case, a particular definition of an increase in risk can be defined by imposing restrictions on the distribution functions representing the initial and final random variables in order to compare the optimal values of decision variables for each distribution function. In a recent article, Alarie, Dionne, and Eeckhoudt (1990) show how this methodology can be applied to the optimal choice of insurance coverage. Several types of increases in risk that represent particular cases of mean preserving spreads are analyzed including a strong increase in risk (Meyer and Orminston, 1985), a "squeeze of the distribution" (Eeckhoudt and

---

[8]See Ross (1981), Kihlstrom, Romer, and Williams (1981), and Doherty, Loubergé, and Schlesinger (1987) for analyses of risk aversion with random initial wealth.

[9]An equivalent condition is that - U'''/U" > 0 where - U'''/U" is a measure of absolute "prudence" (Kimball, 1990). Prudence measures how an individual's preferences affect optimal values of decision variables.

6

Hansen, 1980), "tail dominance" (Eeckhoudt and Hansen, 1984), and a relatively strong increase in risk (Black and Bulkley, 1989). Meyer and Orminston (1989) generalized another definition of increasing risk : the "stretching of a density around a constant mean" (Sandmo, 1970). This approach, which they characterized as involving "deterministic transformations of random variables", also represents a particular type of mean preserving spread. It has been applied to many economic decision problems, such as optimal output choice under uncertainty (Sandmo, 1971; Leland, 1972), optimal saving under uncertainty (Sandmo, 1970), optimal portfolio choice (Meyer and Orminston, 1989), and optimal insurance decisions (Alarie, Dionne, and Eeckhoudt, 1990).

## DEMAND FOR INSURANCE[10]

*Basic Models of Coinsurance and Deductible Choice.* Mossin, (1968) and Smith (1968) proposed a simple model of insurance demand in which a risk averse decision maker has a total wealth $(Y)$ equal to $W - L$ where $W$ is nonstochastic wealth and $L$ is an insurable loss. To illustrate this model, first assume that the individual can buy coverage $\alpha L$ ($0 \leq \alpha \leq 1$) for a premium $\alpha P$ where $\alpha$ is the rate of insurance coverage (the coinsurance rate), $\lambda$ ($\lambda \geq 1$) is the premium loading factor, $E(L)$ is the expected loss, and $P \equiv \lambda E(L)$. It can be shown that the optimal insurance coverage is such that $0 \leq \alpha^* \leq 1$ for $P \geq \bar{P} \geq E(L)$ where $\bar{P} \equiv \bar{\lambda}$ $E(L)$ solves

$$E \left[ U (Y + \alpha^* (L - \bar{\lambda} E(L)) \right] = E U (Y)$$

and where $U$ is a von Neumann-Morgenstern utility function ($U'(\cdot) > 0$, $U''(\cdot) < 0$) and $EU(Y)$ is the level of utility corresponding to no insurance. Hence, if the premium loading factor exceeds one but is less than $\bar{\lambda}$ , partial coverage ($0 < \alpha^* < 1$) is demanded.

---

[10]In this section, we limit discussion to the case where insurance premiums are exogenously determined. The general case is considered in the next section.

When $\lambda = 1$, $\alpha^*$ is equal to one and the maximum premium that a risk averse individual is willing to pay over and above the actuarially fair value of full insurance is the Arrow-Pratt risk premium ($\Pi^U$). This premium solves

$$U (W - E(L) - \Pi^U) = E U (Y)$$

As shown by Pratt (1964), a more risk averse individual with utility V such that $V = k(U)$, $k' > 0$, and $k'' < 0$ will have a risk premium $\Pi^V$ greater than $\Pi^U$.

Another important result in Mossin (1968) is that insurance coverage is an inferior good if the insured has decreasing absolute risk aversion. Under this assumption, there are two opposite effects on the demand for insurance when the loading factor ($\lambda$) increases : a negative substitution effect and a positive wealth effect. Hoy and Robson (1981) proposed an explicit theoretical condition under which insurance is a Giffen good for the class of constant relative risk aversion functions. More recently, Briys, Dionne, and Eeckhoudt (1989) generalized the Hoy and Robson (1981) analysis and provided a necessary and sufficient condition for insurance not to be a Giffen good. This condition bounds the variation of absolute risk aversion so that the wealth effect is always dominated by the substitution effect. Finally, Alarie, Dionne and Eeckhoudt (1990) present sufficient conditions to obtain the intuitive result that an insured will increase his demand for insurance when a mean preserving increase in risk is introduced in the initial loss distribution.

Another form of partial insurance is a policy with a deductible (Mossin, 1968; Gould, 1969; Pashigian, Schkade, and Menefee, 1966; Schlesinger, 1981). For the above model, consider a general indemnity function $I(L)$ and premium $P = \lambda \int I (L) \, dF (L)$ where $\lambda$ ($> 1$) is again a proportional loading factor. Then it can be shown under the constraint $I (L) \geq 0$ for all L, that for every P,

$$I^* (L) = \begin{cases} L - D^* & \text{if } L - D^* \geq 0 \\ 0 & \text{if } L - D^* < 0 \end{cases}$$

8

where D* is the optimal deductible.[11] Since an insured bears some risk with the optimal contract it is reasonable to expect that a more risk averse insured would prefer a policy with a smaller deductible and higher premium. This result was proved by Schlesinger (1981) and Karni (1985). Moreover, under decreasing absolute risk aversion, $dD^*/dW > 0$ (Mossin, 1968). Also, it is possible to infer the degree of risk aversion of insurance buyers by observing their choices of deductibles (Drèze, 1981). The above results are generated under the assumption that the contract is free of default risk. With insolvency risk the above results do not in general hold but some qualitative results can be obtained with stronger utility assumptions (Doherty and Schlesinger, 1990).

*Optimal Coverage with Random Wealth.* If W is an uninsurable random variable rather than fixed, the optimal level of coverage ($\alpha^{**}$) depends on the statistical relationship between W and L. If, for example, the correlation coefficient is a sufficient measure of the relationship between W and L, Doherty and Schlesinger (1983) have shown that the Mossin (1968) and Smith (1968) result on the optimal coinsurance rate with fixed W ($\alpha^*$) is qualitatively similar to the case in which W and L are independent. That is, $\alpha^{**} = 1$ when the premium is actuarially fair and $\alpha^{**} < 1$ when $\lambda > 1$. Moreover, Eeckhoudt and Kimball (1990) showed that $\alpha^{**} \neq \alpha^*$ when $\lambda > 1$. Specifically, they showed that $\alpha^{**} > \alpha^*$ when the degree of absolute prudence (- U'''/U'') is positive and nonincreasing in wealth. This result was proved for any pair of statistically independent risks. They also analyzed optimal deductibles and showed, under the same conditions, that $0 < D^{**} < D^*$ where $D^{**}$ is the optimal deductible when W and L are independent random variables and $D^*$ is the optimal deductible with fixed W. Hence, with independent risks, more coverage is demanded than with fixed wealth under both coinsurance and deductible contracts.

It was mentioned above that a more risk averse individual with utility V is willing to pay a greater risk premium for full insurance than a less risk averse individual with utility U when W is not random. This result also holds when W and L are independent random variables. For example, Kihlstrom, Romer, and Williams (1981) showed that a more risk averse individual with utility V will be willing to pay a higher premium than an individual with utility

---

[11]The next section considers the optimality of coinsurance and deductible contracts when the insurance premium is not exogenously specified.

U if the absolute risk aversion for either individual for realized levels of W is nonincreasing in wealth.

If W and L are negatively (positively) correlated, high losses are likely to accompany low (high) values of W. Doherty and Schlesinger (1983) showed in the case of a two-state marginal distribution that $\alpha^{**} > 1$ ($< 1$) when actuarially fair insurance is available for L. They also analyzed non-actuarially fair insurance prices. More details and more general results are outlined in Schlesinger and Doherty (1985).[12]

*Insurance, Portfolio Choice, and Saving.* Mayers and Smith (1983) and Doherty (1984) analyzed the individual demand for insurance as a special case of general portfolio hedging strategy. They introduced nonmarketable assets (such as human capital) in a capital asset pricing model to simultaneously determine the demands for insurance contracts and other assets in the portfolio.[13] Mayers and Smith (1983) proposed sufficient conditions for a separation theorem between insurance contracts and other portfolio decisions. However, their analysis suggests that portfolio and insurance decisions generally will be interdependent. Consequently, full insurance is not necessarily optimal even when insurance is available at actuarially fair prices. This result is similar to that obtained by Doherty and Schlesinger (1983).

Moffet (1975, 1977) and Dionne and Eeckhoudt (1984) provided joint analyses of the saving (consumption) and insurance decisions in a two-period model. Dionne and Eeckhoudt (1984), which generalized Moffet's results, showed that under decreasing temporal risk aversion deposits and insurance are pure substitutes in the Hicksian sense. Moreover, in their two-decision variable model, insurance is not necessarily an inferior good. They also presented two alternative conditions under which a separation theorem holds between

---

[12]See also Doherty and Schlesinger (1983a), Schulenburg (1986), Turnbull (1983), Eeckhoudt and Kimball (1990) and Lévy-Garboua and Montmarquette (1990).

[13]See Kahane and Kroll (1985) and Smith and Buser (1987) for extensions of these models.

insurance and savings:[14] actuarially fair insurance premiums or constant temporal risk aversion. The conditions differ from those of Mayers and Smith (1983) in their portfolio model of insurance decisions without consumption. This difference can be explained by the fact that Mayers and Smith considered a menu of risky assets while Dionne and Eeckhoudt (1984) considered only a safe asset. The latter study, which used a more general utility function than Mayers and Smith, is actually more closely related to the consumption-portfolio model developed by Sandmo (1969).

More recently, Briys (1988) extended these studies by jointly analyzing insurance, consumption, and portfolio decisions in a framework similar to that defined by Merton (1971). The individual's optimal insurance choice is explicitly derived for the class of isoelastic utility functions. Not surprisingly, the properties of optimal insurance coverage are much more difficult to characterize than in models where insurance is studied in isolation or in the presence of either consumption or portfolio choice alone.

*Self-Insurance and Self-Protection.* Returning to the case of a single random variable L, market insurance can be analyzed in relation to other risk-mitigation activities. Ehrlich and Becker (1972) introduced the concepts of self-insurance and self-protection. Self-insurance refers to actions (y) that reduce the size (severity) of losses (i.e., $L'(y) < 0$ with $L''(y) > 0$) while self-protection refers to actions (x) that reduce the probability (frequency) of accidents ($p'(x) < 0$ with $p''(x) > 0$). Ehrlich and Becker gave conditions under which self-insurance and market insurance are substitutes and conditions under which self-protection and market insurance are complements. In both cases, self-protection and self-insurance activities were assumed to be observable by insurers.[15]

While Ehrlich and Becker (1972) focused on the interaction between market insurance and activities involving either self-insurance or self-protection, they did not study in detail interactions between self-insurance and self-protection with and without the existence of

---

[14]See Drèze and Modigliani (1972) for another sufficient condition on utility to obtain separation between consumption, portfolio, and insurance decisions.

[15]See Winter (1990) for an analysis of self-protection and self-insurance under asymmetrical information.

market insurance. Boyer and Dionne (1983, 1989) and Chang and Ehrlich (1985) presented propositions concerning the choices among all three activities. When full insurance is not available, risk aversion affects the optimal choice of self-insurance and self-protection. While it seems intuitive that increased risk aversion should induce a risk averse decision maker to choose a higher level of both activities, Dionne and Eeckhoudt (1985) showed in a model with two states of the world that this is not always the case : more risk averse individuals may undertake less self-protection.[16]

*Corporate Demand for Insurance*. Portfolio decisions also have implications for the demand for insurance by corporations. When corporations are owned by shareholders who can reduce their investment risk at low cost through diversification of their own portfolios, risk aversion by owners is insufficient to generate demand for insurance. Specifically, if shareholders can costlessly eliminate the risk of corporate losses in their own portfolio's through portfolio diversification, the purchase of insurance by corporations can only increase shareholder wealth if it increases expected net cash flows by an amount that exceeds any loading in insurance premiums.[17] Mayers and Smith (1982) analyzed the corporate demand for insurance from the perspective of modern finance theory (also see Main, 1982; Mayers and Smith, 1990, and MacMinn, 1990). They discussed how bankruptcy costs; risk aversion by managers, employees, customers, and suppliers; efficiencies in claims administration by insurers; and a number of other factors each can provide an incentive for the purchase of insurance even when shareholders can costlessly eliminate risk through portfolio diversification. In a later study, Mayers and Smith (1987) considered the possible ability of insurance to increase shareholder wealth by mitigating the underinvestment problem that was originally analyzed by Myers (1977).

*State Dependent Utility*. The previous analyses have implicitly assumed that all commodities subject to loss can be valued in relevant markets. Examples of such insurable commodities include buildings and automobiles. For these commodities, an accident

---

[16]See Hiebert (1989) and Briys and Schlesinger (1990) for extensions of their analysis.

[17]This statement also holds if insurable risk has an undiversifiable (i.e., market) component, since insurers have no comparative advantage in bearing market risk (see Main, 1982).

primarily produces monetary losses and insurance contracts offer compensation to replace them in whole or in part. However, there are other commodities for which good market substitutes do not exist. Examples include good health, the life of a child, and family heirlooms. For these "commodities", an accident produces more than monetary losses; it also has a non-monetary component (such as "pain and suffering"). Non-monetary losses can be introduced in a two-state model (I for no-accident and II for an accident) by using state dependent utility functions (Cook and Graham, 1977; Karni, 1985). Without a monetary loss, an accident is assumed to reduce utility if $U^I(W) > U^{II}(W)$ for all W (where $U^i(Y)$, i=I, II is the utility in state i). With a monetary loss (L > 0), $U^I(W) - U^I(W - L)$ measures the disutility of the monetary loss and $U^I(W - L) - U^{II}(W - L)$ measures the disutility of the non-monetary loss.

Marginal utility of wealth also depends on the state of the world. Three cases usually are considered : (1) $U_Y^I = U_Y^{II}$ for all Y; (2) $U_Y^I > U_Y^{II}$ for all Y; and (3) $U_Y^I < U_Y^{II}$ for all Y where $U_Y^i$ denotes $\partial U^i / \partial Y$. It can be shown that $\alpha^* \gtrless 1$ for a policy with an actuarially fair premium as long as $U_Y^{II} \gtrless U_Y^I$ for all Y. That is, the individual will buy more (less) insurance than under state independent preferences when the marginal utility of wealth is greater (less) in the accident state than in the no accident state for all Y. Karni (1985) showed how an increase in risk aversion affects optimal insurance coverage when preferences are state-dependent, but the extension of measures of risk aversion to this case is not straightforward.

## INSURANCE AND RESOURCE ALLOCATION

Allais (1953) and Arrow (1953) introduced general equilibrium models of resource allocation in the presence of uncertainty at a meeting on the subject in Paris during 1952. A year later, Debreu (1953) extended Arrow's (1953) contribution to a general framework of resource allocation under uncertainty.[18] In this framework, physical goods are redefined as functions of states of the world and a consumption plan specifies the quantity of each good consumed in each state. Preferences among consumption plans reflect tastes, subjective

---

[18]This paper became a chapter in Debreu (1959).

beliefs about the likelihoods of states of the world, and attitudes towards risk.[19]  However, beliefs and attitudes towards risk do not affect producer behavior since for given contingent prices, there is no uncertainty about the present value of production plans.  The existence of a competitive equilibrium that entails a Pareto optimal allocation of goods and services can be demonstrated for this economy.

Insurance markets can be viewed as markets for contingent goods.  Borch (1962) proposed the first formal model of optimal insurance contracts.  He presented a very elegant comparison between a general model of reinsurance and the Arrow-Debreu model with pure contingent goods and contingent prices for every state of the world.  As noted earlier, Borch's insurance model can be reinterpreted in terms of standard insurance contracts.  Two of his major contributions were to provide conditions for Pareto optimal exchange of risk and to show how risk aversion by insurers can explain partial coverage.  Arrow (1963) used the same argument to introduce some element of coinsurance in optimal insurance contracts. Moreover, Arrow (1963) showed that if a risk neutral insurer offers a policy with a premium equal to the expected indemnity plus a proportional loading then the optimal contract provides full coverage of losses above a deductible.  These forms of partial insurance limit the possibilities of risk shifting between economic agents (Arrow, 1965).

Raviv (1979) extended these results and showed that a Pareto optimal contract involves both a deductible and coinsurance of losses above the deductible.[20]  He also showed that the optimal contract does not have a deductible if the administrative cost of providing insurance does not depend on the amount of coverage.  Coinsurance was explained either by insurer risk aversion or convexity of insurer costs.  Conditions for an

---

[19]In the Arrow-Debreu world each agent has incomplete information about states but all agents share the same information (Radner, 1968).  The latter implicit assumption rules out moral hazard and adverse selection problems.

[20]Also see Arrow (1974), Bühlmann and Jewell (1979), Gerber (1978), Gollier (1987a), and Marshall (1990).

optimal contract with an upper limit of coverage also were presented. All these results were obtained under the constraint that coverage be nonnegative.[21]

Kihlstrom and Roth (1982) studied the nature of negotiated insurance contracts in a non-competitive context in which there is bargaining over the amount and price of coverage. They showed that a risk neutral insurer obtains a higher expected income when bargaining against a more risk averse insured and that the competitive equilibrium allocation is not affected by the insured's risk aversion. Many of their results are represented in an Edgeworth Box diagram.

## MORAL HAZARD

The concept of moral hazard was introduced in the economics literature by Arrow (1963), Drèze (1961), and Pauly (1968) (see also Kihlstrom and Pauly, 1971, and Spence and Zechauser, 1971). Two types of moral hazard have been defined according to the timing of an individual's actions in relation to the determination of the state of nature. They can be called ex ante and ex post moral hazard. In the first case the action is taken before the realization of the state of nature while in the second case the action is taken after.

*Ex Ante Moral Hazard.* Pauly (1974), Marshall (1976), and Shavell (1979) considered the case in which the occurrence of an accident (or the output of the consumption good) can be observed by the insurer and where neither the insured's actions nor the states of nature are observed.[22] Under this structure of asymmetric information, the provision of insurance reduces (in general) the incentive to take care compared to the case of full information. Thus, there is a trade-off between risk sharing and incentives for care.

---

[21]See Gollier (1987) for an extensive analysis of this constraint and Gollier (1990) for a recent review of optimal insurance contracting.

[22]The ex ante actions can affect event probabilities, event severity, or both (see Winter, 1990, for more details).

Shavell (1979) used a simple two-state model where the individual faces either a known positive loss or no loss with probabilities that depend on effort (care) to show that partial insurance coverage is optimal in the presence of moral hazard.[23] He emphasized that the cost of care has a major impact on the optimal solution. Another important result was that moral hazard alone cannot eliminate gains to trade in insurance markets (i.e., it reduces but does not eliminate the benefits of insurance). These results were obtained assuming that the insurer has no information on an individual's level of care. In the second part of the paper, Shavell showed that moral hazard problems are reduced (but not eliminated) when actions are partially observable (also see Holmstrom, 1979).

Shavell's two-state model did not permit a detailed characterization of insurance contracts. More than two states are necessary to derive conditions under which deductibles, coinsurance, and coverage limits are optimal under moral hazard (see Holmstrom, 1979, and Winter, 1990, for detailed analysis).

Moral hazard in insurance also can be analyzed within a general principal-agent framework (Ross, 1973; Holmstrom, 1979; Grossman and Hart, 1983). However, certain conditions must be imposed to generate predictions. First, the action of the agent cannot affect the support of the distribution of outcomes, a condition naturally met in the two-state model (Shavell, 1979). The other two conditions concern the use of a first-order condition to replace the incentive compatibility constraint. The first-order approach is valid if it identifies the global optimal solution. Mirrlees (1975) and Rogerson (1985) proposed two sufficient conditions for the first-order approach to be valid when corner solutions are ruled out : (1) the distribution function must be a convex function of effort and (2) the likelihood ratio has to be monotone. If the distribution function satisfies the above conditions, optimal insurance coverage will be decreasing in the size of loss since large losses signal low effort levels to a bayesian principal. Jewitt (1988) recently questioned the intuitive economic justification of these two conditions and showed that they can be violated by reasonable examples. Specifically, he showed that most of the distributions commonly used in statistics are not

---

[23]Also see Pauly (1974) for a similar model. See Dionne (1982) for a model with state-dependent preferences. It is shown that moral hazard is still an important problem when preferences are not limited to monetary losses.

convex. He then supplied an alternative set of conditions including restrictions on the agent's utility function to validate the first-order approach (see Winter, 1990, and Arnott, 1990, for further discussion).

Grossman and Hart (1983) proposed a method to replace the first-order approach. They also showed that the two conditions proposed by Mirrlees and Rogerson are sufficient to obtain monotonicity of the optimal incentive scheme. They analyzed the principal problem without using the first-order approach and consequently did not need any restriction on the agent's utility function. As Grossman and Hart noted, many of their results were limited to a risk-neutral principal. This restriction is reasonable for many insurance problems.[24]

Long term contracts between principals and agents can increase welfare in the presence of moral hazard (Rogerson, 1985a; Radner, 1981; Rubinstein and Yaari, 1983; Boyer and Dionne, 1989a). In multiperiod insurance models, an individual's past experience eventually gives a good approximation of care. Hence insurers use the individual's past experience to determine premiums and to increase incentives for exercising care.

Moral hazard may alter the nature of competitive equilibrium by, for example, introducing nonconvexities in indifference curves. A competitive equilibrium may not exist, and when it does, insurance markets for some risks may fail to exist. More importantly, neither the first nor second theorems of welfare economics hold under moral hazard. Since market prices will not reflect social opportunity costs, theory suggests that governmental intervention in some insurance markets possibly could improve welfare if government has superior information (Arnott and Stiglitz, 1990; Arnott 1990).

Moral hazard also can affect standard analyses of government responses to externalities. An important example involves liability rules and compulsory insurance.[25] With strict liability and risk averse victims and injurers, Shavell (1982) showed with perfect

---

[24]See Dye (1986) and Mookherjee and Png (1989) for recent applications of Grossman and Hart's model.

[25]See Danzon and Harrington (1990) for a survey on the demand and supply of liability insurance.

information that both first-party and liability insurance produce an efficient allocation of risk between parties in a model of unilateral accidents (with pecuniary losses only). When insurers cannot observe defendants care, moral hazard results in a trade-off between care and risk sharing (as in the case of first-party coverage). Shavell (1982) noted that if the government has no better information than insurers, its intervention in liability insurance does not improve welfare. This conclusion assumed that defendants were not judgement proof (i.e., they had sufficient assets to fully satisfy a judgement). Otherwise, their incentives to purchase liability insurance are reduced (Keeton and Kwerel, 1984; Shavell, 1986). Under strict liability, Shavell (1986) showed that if insurers cannot observe care, insureds buy partial insurance and the level of care is not optimal. He also showed that making liability insurance compulsory under these conditions need not restore efficient incentives. In fact, compulsory insurance could reduce care, and it is even possible that prohibiting insurance coverage could improve the level of care.

*Ex Post Moral Hazard.* The second type of moral hazard was first suggested by Spence and Zeckhauser (1971) who showed that an optimal contract between a principal and agent depends on the principal's ability to monitor the state of nature, the ex ante action taken by the agent, and the nature of the accident. The previous discussion of ex ante moral hazard assumed that the principal knew the nature of the accident. Marshall (1976a), Dionne (1984), and Townsend (1979) investigated the case in which the nature of an accident is not perfectly observable by the principal. Townsend (1979) considered the case in which the nature of the accident is known by the agent and verification is costly to the principal. One interpretation of such costly verification is auditing.

Mookerjee and Png (1989) extended the Grossman and Hart (1983) model to consider optimal contracts in the presence of both ex ante and ex post moral hazard. In their model, the agent takes an unobservable action that affects accident probabilities and then reports his realized accident to the principal. The principal may audit the report at a cost. Their main result is that random audits reduce expected auditing costs without distorting the incentives of the agent provided that wealth of the agent is strictly positive in all states of the world. Their results apply when falsification is costless and verification is costly. Lacker and

Weinberg (1989) showed that partial insurance can be optimal if the nature of an accident can be falsified by the agent, but only at a cost.[26]

## ADVERSE SELECTION

Adverse selection occurs in insurance markets when information is asymmetric, i.e., when the insurer cannot observe an individual's risk at the time policies are issued and the individual has superior information about his or her risk. Akerloff (1970) proposed that if insurers have imperfect information about differences in risk for prospective insureds, then some insurance markets may fail to exist and others may be inefficient. Studies have analysed the ability of partial insurance coverage, experience rating, and risk categorization to reduce the negative effects of adverse selection.[27]

*Partial Insurance and Sorting.* Partial insurance coverage can result from two types of insurance pricing: "price only" policies (Pauly, 1974) and "price-quantity" policies (Rothschild and Stiglitz, 1976; Stiglitz, 1977). In the first case, insurers charge a uniform premium rate per unit of coverage to all applicants. Pauly's model ruled out price-quantity competition by assuming that insurers could not observe the total amount of coverage purchased by a client. In the second case, insurers offer a menu of policies with different prices and quantities so that different risks choose different insurance policies. These pricing strategies have been studied for single vs. multi-period contracts, for competition vs. monopoly, and, when assuming competition, for several different equilibrium concepts.[28]

---

[26]See Dionne and St-Michel (1988) for an empirical measure of the second type of moral hazard in the workers' compensation market.

[27]We only consider models in which uninformed agents move first (screening): uninformed insurers offer contracts and consumers choose contracts given their accident probability. Stiglitz and Weiss (1984) analyzed differences between screening and signalling models.

[28]See Cooper and Hayes (1987), Crocker and Snow (1985), and Cresta (1984) for an introduction to these models and Dionne and Doherty (1990) for a survey on adverse selection in insurance contracts.

In a single period model with competition, Rothschild and Stiglitz (1976) first showed that a pooling equilibrium cannot exist if a Nash definition of equilibrium is adopted (i.e, if each firm assumes that competitors' contract offers are independent of its own offer). Conditions under which "separating" contracts reveal information about insured risk were then studied by the authors. A major result is that when firms offer a menu of policies with different prices and quantities, policyholders may be induced to but do not necessarily reveal hidden information.[29] They showed that a separating Nash equilibrium can exist in which high risk and low risk buyers purchase separate contracts. This separating equilibrium is characterized by zero profits for each contract, by partial insurance coverage for low risk buyers, and by full insurance for the high risk buyers. However, when there exist relatively few high risk persons in the market, they showed that neither a separating nor a pooling equilibrium exist.

Other equilibrium concepts that eliminate the non-existence problem have been proposed. Wilson (1977), Miyasaki (1977), and Spence (1978) (WMS) considered the case in which firms anticipate that other insurers' policies that become unprofitable as a result of new offerings will be withdrawn.[30] A WMS equilibrium is a pair of contracts in which profits on low risk contracts offset losses on high risk contracts. A WMS equilibrium exists regardless of the number of high risk persons in the market. If a Nash equilibrium exists, it coincides with the WMS equilibrium.[31] Finally, a WMS equilibrium is always second best efficient.

---

[29]A similar analysis was provided by Stiglitz (1977) for the monopoly case. In his model there is always a separating equilibrium and the monopolist extracts all surplus subject to self-selection constraints.

[30]The anticipatory concept of equilibrium was introduced by Wilson (1977). Miyazaki (1977) (for the labor market) and Spence (1978) (for the insurance market) extended Wilson's model to the case in which each firm could break even by offering a portfolio of contracts. Riley (1979) and Grossman (1979) proposed other non-Nash equilibrium concepts. (See Crocker and Snow (1985) for a review of alternative equilibrium concepts).

[31]Each of these models either explicitly or implicitly assumed that insurers could enforce the requirement that their customers would buy coverage from only one insurer. Hellwig (1988) considered a model with endogenous sharing of information about customers' purchases and obtained an equilibrium with a reactive element that is similar to Wilson's (1977) anticipatory equilibrium.

Dahlby (1983) provided some empirical evidence of adverse selection in the Canadian automobile insurance market. He suggested that his empirical results were consistent with the WMS model with cross-subsidization between individuals in each class of risk. However, Riley (1983) argued that Dahlby's results were also consistent with Wilson's (1977) anticipatory equilibrium and Riley's (1979) reactive equilibrium. Cross-subsidization is not feasible in either of these models.

*Experience Rating.* Experience rating can be viewed as either a substitute or a complement to both risk categorization and sorting contracts with self-selection constraints when adverse selection is present.[32] One polar case is when infinite length contracts yield the same solution as with full information. In this case, ex ante risk categorization is useless. The other polar case is when costless risk categorization permits full observation of an individual risk so that information on past experience is irrelevant. While experience rating, risk categorization, and sorting contracts are used simultaneously in most markets, economic analysis to date has considered the three mechanisms independently (see Dionne and Doherty, 1990, for a more detailed review).

Dionne (1983), Dionne and Lasserre (1985), and Cooper and Hayes (1987) extended Stiglitz's monopoly model (1977) to multi-period contracts. Dionne (1983) considered infinite length contracts without discounting while Cooper and Hayes (1987) mainly dealt with a finite horizon model (without discounting). While findings in both cases suggested that experience rating induced sorting or risk disclosure, the analyses differ in many respects. In Dionne (1983), a simple statistical review strategy is proposed along with risk announcement in the first period. The insurer offers a buyer full coverage at the full information price unless the observed average loss is greater than the true expected loss plus a statistical margin of error. Otherwise, full coverage is offered at a premium that includes a penalty. Both elements — announcement of risk and penalties — are necessary to obtain the same solution as with full information. They have the same role as the self selection constraint and the premium adjustment mechanism of Cooper and Hayes (1987). In their model, the premium adjustment

---

[32]See Dalhby (1990), Dionne and Lasserre (1987), and Dionne and Vanasse (1988) for analyses of experience rating when moral hazard and adverse selection are present simultaneously.

mechanism served to relax the self-selection constraints and to increase the monopolist's profits. Finally, in both articles the monopolist commits to the terms of the contract.[33]

Cooper and Hayes (1987) also extended the Rothschild and Stiglitz (1976) model to two periods assuming that a Nash separating equilibrium exists. When consumers were assumed to be bound to a two-period contract, they obtained the same result as for the monopoly case. When the assumption that consumers sign a binding two-period contract was relaxed, they showed that competition in the second period limited but did not eliminate the use of experience rating. In both cases, the insurer was assumed to be committed to its experience rating contract.

Nilssen (1990) analyzed experience rating contracts without commitment by insurers in a competitive market. His results differed from those of Cooper and Hayes and were quite similar to those of Kunreuther and Pauly (1985), who assumed that insurers sell price-only policies (Pauly, 1974) rather than price-quantity policies. Another important assumption in Kunreuther and Pauly's model was myopic behavior by insureds, whereas firms could have foresight. With foresight, firms suffer losses in early periods, and make profits in later periods, whereas in the Cooper-Hayes (1987) model, they make profits in the initial period and losses in subsequent periods. D'arcy and Doherty (1990) provided some empirical evidence that is consistent with Kunreuther and Pauly's model.

*Risk Categorization.*[34]   In most types of insurance, insurers classify risks using many variables. In auto insurance, for example, evidence indicates that driver age and sex are significanty related to accident probabilities (Dionne and Vanasse, 1988). In particular, evidence suggests that young male drivers (less than age 25) have much higher accident probabilities than the average driver. Since age and sex can be observed at very low cost, competition will force insurers to charge higher premiums to young males. Categorization

---

[33]See Hosios and Peters (1989) for an analysis of contracts without any commitment by a monopolist in a finite-horizon environment.

[34]We limit our discussion to exogenous categorization of risks. See Bond and Crocker (1990) for an analysis of endogenous categorization of risks.

using particular variables is prohibited in many markets, and the efficiency of categorization is an important policy issue.

Is statistical classification efficient in the presence of asymmetric information and adverse selection? Crocker and Snow (1985, 1986; also see Hoy, 1982, and Rea, 1987, 1990) showed that costless imperfect categorization always enhances efficiency when efficiency is defined as in Harris and Townsend (1981): second-best efficiency given the self-selection constraints imposed by asymmetric information. However, if classification is costly, the efficiency implications were ambiguous. Crocker and Snow (1986) also considered the existence of a balanced-budget tax-subsidy policy that provides private incentives to use risk categorization. With appropriate taxes, they showed that no agent would lose from classification. In their 1986 article, the results were shown using a WMS equilibrium, but a tax system also may sustain an efficient allocation with a Nash equilibrium. Their results can also be applied to a Wilson (1977) anticipatory equilibrium, or to a Riley (1979) reactive equilibrium (see Crocker and Snow, 1985). These results suggest that prohibiting statistical discrimination will impose efficiency losses in insurance markets when classification is virtually costless (e.g., age and sex classification in auto insurance).

## MARKET STRUCTURE AND ORGANIZATIONAL FORM

The seminal study by Joskow (1973) on market structure, conduct, and performance in the U.S. property-liability insurance industry considered market concentration and barriers to entry, estimated returns to scale, analyzed direct writer (exclusive agency/salaried employee) and independent agency (multiple insurer representation) distribution systems, and discussed possible effects of rate regulation on prices and availability of coverage. While written when rate regulation was predominant and when rating bureaus had a greater impact on the market than later in the 1970s and in the 1980s, this study nonetheless provided a basis for later work on a variety of subjects.[35]

---

[35]Joskow's formal modelling of profitability and leverage also preceded and thus did not reflect developments in the theory of required compensation for risk bearing by insurance company owners.

*Concentration, Ease of Entry, and Consumer Search.* Joskow concluded that market concentration levels were low, especially for the national market, and that significant entry barriers did not exist. He estimated simple models of insurer operating expense ratios and concluded that the industry was characterized by constant returns to scale. He did find, however, that expense ratios were much lower for direct writers than for independent agency insurers. Cummins and VanDerhei (1979) estimated more elaborate models than those employed by Joskow using pooled cross-section and time-series data. Their results again indicated significantly lower expense ratios for direct writers, but they suggested increasing returns to scale throughout the range of output.[36]

While the results of other studies that have estimated cost functions with cross-sectional accounting data also suggest increasing returns to scale (e.g., Doherty, 1981; Johnson, Flanigan, and Weisbart, 1981), the use of accounting data to infer returns to scale is problematic. Among other limitations, available data on insurance company operating expenses aggregate capital (e.g., product and market development) expenditures and current costs. Firm output also cannot be measured accurately.[37] Appel, Worrall, and Butler (1985) analyzed changes in the size distribution of insurers over time. Their results were inconsistent with increasing returns for small insurers and thus more in line with evidence on entry and levels of concentration.

Joskow argued that differences in operating costs between direct writers and independent agency insurers could not be explained by differences in service.[38] In order

---

[36]Zweifel and Ghermi (1990) reported evidence of lower expense ratios for independent agency insurers than for exclusive agency insurers in Switzerland, but they included commission rates (which generally are higher for independent agents than for exclusive agents in the U.S. property-liability insurance market) as control variables. Their data also included experience for life and health insurance.

[37]See, for example, the discussion in Doherty (1981). Moreover, Braeutigam and Pauly (1986) concluded that substantive bias in cost function estimates could arise from unobservable differences in quality that could result from price regulation.

[38]Cummins and VanDerhei (1979) assumed that lower operating expenses for direct writers were prima facie evidence of superior efficiency, and concluded that regulators should take a more active role in disseminating information on prices.

to explain why direct writers had not grown more rapidly, he suggested that prior approval rate regulation had discouraged price cuts by direct writers, that difficulty in raising capital and obtaining consumer recognition slowed their expansion, and that it would be costly for independent agency insurers to become direct writers. As a result, he concluded that direct writers behaved as oligopolists subject to short-run capacity constraints and that constrained profit maximization involved selection of risks with lower than average expected claim costs.

Smallwood (1975) also suggested barriers to insurers switching to direct writer distribution. He argued that independent agency insurers were more vulnerable to adverse selection, and he developed a formal model of insurer risk selection (which did not consider asymmetric information). However, in contrast to Joskow's analysis, Pauly, Kleindorfer, and Kunreuther (1986) argued that significant barriers to raising capital for growth were highly unlikely. Instead, they suggested that direct writers and independent agency insurers produced different levels and types of services.

Joskow also conjectured that costly consumer search for low prices impeded direct writer growth.[39] Joskow and others (e.g., Kunreuther, Kleindorfer, and Pauly, 1983) have suggested that search for low prices is costly because of differences among insurers in risk selection criteria and because information provided by friends and neighbours that have different risk characteristics may convey little information. In an empirical analysis, Dahlby and West (1986) concluded that premium dispersion in Canadian auto insurance was consistent with a model of costly consumer search. This conclusion was contingent on their argument that risk classification could not account for premium variation. Berger, Kleindorfer, and Kunreuther (1989) modeled word of mouth transmission of price information in auto insurance in conjunction with consumer switch costs.

*Returns to Scale and Underwriting Risk.* The previously discussed studies of returns to scale and entry conditions focused primarily on insurer underwriting (risk selection), administrative, and commission expenses. Basic analysis of the relationship between insurer

---

[39]Costly consumer search has played a role in the literature on solvency regulation for insurers (see below). Costly search associated with other dimensions of quality, such as timing and magnitude of claim payments in the absence of insurer default, also has received attention (e.g., Smallwood, 1975).

underwriting risk and scale of operations suggests that increasing returns to scale also could be associated with capital costs. If claim costs are not perfectly correlated across insured exposures, the standard deviation of an insurer's average claim cost will decline, ceteris paribus, as the number of insured exposures increases (e.g., Houston, 1964; Cummins, 1974; Venezian, 1983). If holding financial capital to reduce insurer default risk is costly (see below), this reduction in risk implies decreasing costs per insured exposure for any given probability of default because the required amount of capital per exposure will decline as the number of exposures increases. Low levels of market concentration and evidence on entry suggest that decreasing capital costs do not produce a large minimum efficient scale relative to market size. Underwriting risk declines at a decreasing rate with increases in scale, and the marginal reduction could be small relative to risk that cannot be reduced by writing more exposures (or by writing coverage in different lines of insurance).[40]

Possible efficiency enhancing and anti-competitive aspects of institutional arrangements for pooling information among insurers have been analyzed in a number of studies (e.g., Danzon, 1983; Eisenach, 1985; also see Winter, 1988). Absent mechanisms for pooling data among insurers, claim cost forecasts might be expected to be more accurate for large firms due to their superior information.[41] The costs of ratemaking and of complying with rate regulation also are likely to have a large fixed component. Hence, arrangements for pooling information and data analysis, some of which are made possible by the insurance industry's limited antitrust exemption under federal law and the laws of many states, are likely to reduce these costs and facilitate entry.

***Alternative Organizational Forms.*** In addition to significant variation in distribution methods, insurance markets generally are characterized by a variety of organizational forms. Most important, mutual organizations commonly have a significant market share. Mayers and

---

[40]The effects of undiversifiable risk on insurance prices are discussed below. Venezian (1984) discussed equity issues associated with insurance pricing when capital costs are subadditive. Much of this discussion asserted significant barriers to entry as a result of increasing returns to scale in operating costs and costly consumer search.

[41]This result requires that small firms are unable to infer information available to large firms by observing market prices.

Smith (1981) briefly considered the ability of alternative forms of insurance company ownership to minimize the cost of conflicts between owners, policyholders, and managers (also see Fama and Jensen, 1983). Mayers and Smith argued that while mutual organization eliminates owner-policyholder conflict, it can increase the cost of controlling manager-policyholder conflict compared to stock organization. They predicted that mutuals will specialize in lines of insurance where managers have limited discretion to pursue their own interests at the expense of policyholders.

Mayers and Smith (1988) provided further discussion of the ability of stock, mutual, and other organizational forms used in property-liability insurance to control conflict efficiently, and they developed and tested hypotheses concerning product specialization and geographic concentration across ownership types (also see Mayers and Smith, 1986). They obtained some evidence consistent with their predictions, including significant variation in product mix across ownership types. In other analysis, Hansmann (1985) provided detailed discussion of the possible role of mutual ownership in reducing conflicts between owners and policyholders over the level of insurer default risk (also see Garven, 1987). He also considered the possible ability of mutual ownership to facilitate risk selection during the formative years of U.S. insurance markets.

## INSURANCE PRICING

Economic and financial analysis of insurance pricing has largely focused on two issues: (1) the determinants of long-run equilibrium prices in view of modern financial theory, and (2) the existence and possible causes of temporal volatility in insurance prices and in the availability of coverage that cannot be explained by changes in expected costs. Both areas have important policy implications.[42]

---

[42]A number of studies also have analyzed short-run determinants of prices and other aspects of insurer operations using expected profit or expected utility models of insurer decision-making (e.g., Witt, 1974; McCabe and Witt, 1980; MacMinn and Witt, 1987).

*Determinants of Long-run Equilibrium Prices*. Using the equilibrium risk-return relation implied by the Capital Asset Pricing Model (CAPM), Biger and Kahane (1978) showed that equilibrium insurance underwriting profit margins (and thus premiums) were a linear function of the riskless rate of interest and the systematic risk (beta) of underwriting in the absence of income taxes. They also provided estimates of underwriting betas using accounting data for different lines of insurance (also see Cummins and Harrington, 1985). Fairley (1979) (also see Hill, 1979, and Hill and Modigliani, 1986) developed a similar model and showed that with income taxes equilibrium premiums also increased with the tax rate and the amount of financial capital invested to support the sale of insurance.

Myers and Cohn (1986) criticized the ad hoc approach used by Fairley and others to apply the CAPM to contracts with multiperiod cash flows. They proposed a discounted cash flow model that would leave insurance company owners indifferent between selling policies and operating as an investment company. Key variables affecting equilibrium premiums again included tax rates on investment income, the amount of capital invested, and the required compensation to owners for risk bearing.[43] Kraus and Ross (1982) considered application of arbitrage pricing theory to insurance pricing using both discrete and continuous time models.

The preceding studies either ignored default risk or implicitly assumed unlimited liability for insurance company owners. Doherty and Garven (1986) analyzed long-run equilibrium premiums with limited liability using discrete time options pricing theory under conditions in which stochastic investment returns and claim costs could be valued using risk neutral valuation functions. They used numerical examples to illustrate the effects of changing various parameters. Among other implications, premiums increased and default risk declined as invested capital increased.[44] Cummins (1988) illustrated the application of continuous time options pricing theory to calculation of risk-based premiums for insurance

---

[43]Premiums depend on the amount of invested capital in these models because selling insurance (as opposed to operating as an investment fund) exposes owners to income tax on investment returns.

[44]Borch (1974) obtained a qualitatively similar result assuming limited liability and expected utility maximization by insurers.

guaranty funds. Again, numerical examples were used to illustrate the sensitivity of premiums to changes in underlying parameters.[45]

An important implication of research on long-run equilibrium prices is that variability in claim costs that cannot be eliminated by insurer diversification raises prices (premium loadings ) for any given level of default risk and thus reduces the gains from trade in insurance markets (also see Danzon, 1984, 1985; Doherty and Dionne, 1989). Hence, undiversifiable risk provides a possible explanation of why some risks may be uninsurable in addition to the effects of adverse selection, moral hazard, and insurer sales and administrative costs.

*Price Volatility and Underwriting Cycles*. Many lines of insurance appear to be characterized by "soft" markets, in which prices are stable or falling and coverage is readily available, followed by "hard" markets, in which prices rise rapidly and the number of insurers offering coverage for some types of risk declines substantially. Popular wisdom holds that soft and hard markets occur cyclically with a period of about six years. Several studies have provided empirical evidence that reported underwriting and total operating profit margins follow a second-order autoregressive process that is consistent with a cycle (Venezian, 1985; Cummins and Outreville, 1987; Doherty and Kang, 1988; also see Smith, 1989). Interest in this area was stimulated by the liability insurance "crisis" of the mid-1980s, which was characterized by dramatic increases in premiums for many commercial liability risks and by reductions in the availability of coverage.

The traditional view of underwriting cycles by insurance industry analysts emphasizes fluctuations in capacity to write coverage. According to this view, which assumes an inelastic supply of capital, competition drives prices down until capital is depleted, insurers ultimately constrain supply in order to prevent default, and attendant increases in prices and retained earnings then replenish capital until price-cutting ensues again. Berger (1988) presented a

---

[45]Several studies (e.g., Fairley, 1979; Danzon, 1985; Harrington, 1988; D'Arcy and Garven, 1990) have compared actual underwriting margins to margins predicted by theoretical models with mixed results.

simple model of this scenario that assumed that insurers were unable to add new capital and that pricing decisions were based on beginning of period surplus.

Several studies have questioned the existence of true cycles in prices. Cummins and Outreville (1987) considered whether cycles in reported underwriting results could simply reflect insurer financial reporting procedures in conjunction with information, policy renewal, and regulatory lags. They also provided evidence that reported operating margins follow a cyclical process for many lines of insurance in the United States and other countries. Doherty and Kang (1988) essentially argued that cycles in insurer operating results reflected slow adjustment of premiums to changes in the present value of expected future costs. However, the causes of slow adjustment and the influence of slow adjustment versus charges in costs were not clear in their analysis.

Harrington (1988) analyzed industry financial results surrounding the liability insurance crisis of the mid-1980s and discussed possible causes of the crisis including cyclical effects.[46] This study also provided evidence that rapid premium growth in general liability insurance was associated with upward revisions in insurer loss reserves for prior years' business and rapid growth in reported losses for new business. The results suggested that much of the total growth in premiums during 1980-86 could be explained by growth in expected losses and changes in interest rates (i.e., by determinants of long-run equilibrium premiums). However, premiums grew slower than discounted reported losses during the early 1980s and faster than discounted reported losses during 1985-86, a result that is consistent with cyclical effects.

McGee (1986) suggested that heterogeneous expectations of future claim costs among insurers could lead to price-cutting that characterizes soft markets.[47] Harrington (1988) questioned whether aggressive behavior by firms with little to lose in the event of

---

[46]This article also is included in this volume because it contains a large amount of institutional background that is useful in understanding the literature and policy debate on insurance market volatility.

[47]Venezian (1985) suggested that industry wide use of suboptimal forecasting methods could produce cycles.

default could lead to excessive price-cutting. Winter (1988 and 1989) developed a model in which undiversifiable risk and constraints on external capital flows (such as those that might arise from asymmetric information between insurer managers and investors or from income tax treatment of shareholder dividends) and solvency (which could be imposed by regulators or reflect policyholder preferences) could lead to periods of soft markets followed by sharp increases in prices. His model predicts a negative relation between price and capital. He reported (1989) some evidence consistent with this prediction using aggregate industry data prior to the crisis of 1985-86, at which time the relationship became positive.[48]

Volatility in the commercial liability insurance market during the 1980s has led to a number of recent working papers (several of which only contain preliminary analysis and results). Subjects covered include insurer responses to exogenous shocks to capital (Gron, 1989; Cummins and Danzon, 1990), the sensitivity of premiums to interest rates (Doherty and Garven, 1990), the possible effects of regulation (Winter, 1988a; Tennyson, 1989), and possible causes of price-cutting in soft markets (Harrington and Danzon, 1990).

## INSURANCE REGULATION

Most economic analyses of regulation of insurance markets have focused on solvency regulation and regulation of premium rates and the availability of coverage.[49] Theoretical work has had both positive and normative aspects. Most empirical work has focused on estimating the effects of regulation.

---

[48]Winter also analyzed the implications of his model for the availability of coverage for risks with a high degree of uncertainty about future costs. Other studies that have dealt with the effects of uncertainty on availability and contract design include Danzon (1984, 1985) and Doherty and Dionne (1989). Also see Priest (1987) and Clarke, et al. (1988).

[49]See Kunreuther, Kleindorfer, and Pauly (1983) for an overview of insurance regulation that also discusses compulsory insurance requirements. Possible conflicts between regulatory goals of reducing rates and promoting solvency have been discussed in many studies (e.g., Borch, 1974).

*Default Risk and Solvency Regulation.* Solvency regulation in the United States has three major facets: (1) direct controls on certain activities and financial reporting, (2) monitoring of insurer behavior, and (3) a system for paying claims of insolvent insurers (see Harrington and Danzon, 1986, for details). Direct controls include minimum capital requirements and limitations on investment activities. The principal monitoring system is administered by the National Association of Insurance Commissioners. Guaranty funds exist to pay claims of insolvent property-liability insurers in all states; many states have similar arrangements for other types of insurance.[50] The traditional rationale for solvency regulation is that consumers are unable to monitor the risk of insurer default.

Actuarial literature (see Kastelijn and Remmerswaal, 1986, for a survey) has analyzed default risk as a function of various operating and financial decisions or analyzed decisions necessary to achieve a given probability of default (which generally is presumed to be chosen by regulators or management). Portfolio models of property-liability insurance company behavior (e.g., Michaelsen and Goshay, 1967; Kahane and Nye, 1975; Hammond and Shilling, 1978) have either treated default risk as exogenously determined or subject to insurer choice. Economic factors that could influence this choice have not been the focus of this literature.

More recently, economic analysis of insurer default risk has focused on factors that influence insurer capital decisions under default risk. Building on the work of Borch (e.g., Borch, 1982; also see DeFinetti, 1957), Munch and Smallwood (1982) and Finsinger and Pauly (1984) model insurer default risk assuming that insurers maximize value to shareholders, that demand is inelastic with respect to default risk, and that investing financial capital to support insurance operations is costly. The principal implication is that optimal capital is positively related to the amount of loss that shareholders would suffer if claim costs were to exceed the firm's financial assets. Munch and Smallwood (1982) considered possible loss of goodwill in the event of default; Finsinger and Pauly (1984) assumed that an entry cost would be forfeited that otherwise would allow the firm to continue operating (also

---

[50]Almost all guaranty funds are financed by post-insolvency assessments on surviving insurers. The scope of coverage is limited. For example, the maximum property-liability claim payable commonly is $300,000 or less except for workers' compensation claims, which generally are fully covered.

see Tapiero, Zuckerman, and Kahane, 1978). If shareholders have nothing to lose, they will not commit any capital. If they are exposed to loss, and if it is assumed that firms cannot add capital after claims are realized, firms will commit some capital ex ante.[51]

In an empirical analysis of the effects of solvency regulation using cross-state data, Munch and Smallwood (1980) estimated the impact of minimum capital requirements and other forms of solvency regulation on the number of insurers selling coverage and the number of insolvencies. While subject to significant data limitations, their results provided some evidence that minimum capital requirements reduced insolvencies by reducing the number of small domestic insurers in the market. They also compared characteristics of solvent and insolvent firms and concluded that the results were consistent with selection of default risk to maximize firm value.

Other empirical studies generally have focused on predicting insurer defaults using financial data without closely relating the variables chosen to the theory of default risk (e.g., Pinches and Trieschmann, 1973; Harrington and Nelson, 1986; McDonald, 1988). Not much is presently known about the magnitude of the effects of regulatory monitoring and guaranty funds on default risk.

*Rate Regulation.* Regulation of rates, which is used primarily in property-liability insurance, can affect an insurer's average rate level or overall percentage change in its rates during a given period. It also can affect rate differentials between groups of consumers by

---

[51]The literature on capital decisions by banks contains similar results (e.g., Herring and Vankudre, 1987). Doherty (1989) and Tapiero, Kahane, and Jacques (1986) considered insurer capital decisions when demand for coverage depends on default risk. Following Mayers and Smith (1981, 1988), Garven (1987) analyzed default risk within an agency cost framework in which shareholders, managers, sales personnel, and policyholders have different incentives regarding default risk.

imposing limits on voluntary or involuntary market rates for particular groups or by restricting risk classification.[52]

Voluntary market rates for most U.S. property-liability lines presently are subject to prior approval regulation in about half of the states. Most states had prior approval regulation during the 1950s and 1960s, and rate regulation was likely to have encouraged insurers to use rates developed by rating bureaus (Joskow, 1973; Harrington, 1984; also see Danzon, 1983). A trend towards deregulation began in the late 1960s and continued until the early 1980s. A number of states reregulated commercial liability insurance rates following the liability insurance crisis of 1985-86. California adopted prior approval regulation for property-liability insurance with the enactment of Proposition 103 in 1988. Several additional states either have reenacted or are considering reenactment of prior approval regulation.[53]

Most studies of rate regulation have estimated the impact of voluntary market rate regulation in auto insurance on average rate levels for the overall (voluntary and involuntary) market.[54] Major hypotheses have been that regulation raises rates due to capture by industry, that regulation has short-run effects due to regulatory lag, and that regulation persistently reduces rates due to consumer pressure (see Harrington, 1984). Most studies have regressed either the statewide ratio of premiums to losses (or of losses to premiums) on a rate regulation dummy variable and on a variety of control variables. Harrington (1987) used this procedure and maximum likelihood estimation to provide evidence of cross-state

---

[52]For background information on insurance rate regulation in the United States, see Harrington (1984). Involuntary markets, which are important mainly in auto, workers' compensation, and medical malpractice insurance, include mechanisms such as assigned risk plans and joint underwriting associations. They require joint provision of coverage by insurers at a regulated rate.

[53]California and a few other states also enacted rate "rollbacks" during the last few years.

[54]Several studies have estimated the impact of prior approval regulation in other lines of business without firm conclusions (e.g., Stewart, 1987; Cummins and Harrington, 1987; D'Arcy, 1988; and Rizzo, 1989). It is very difficult to control for factors that could be expected to influence premiums (or the ratio of premiums to losses) for commercial lines in the absence of rate regulation. A priori, prior approval regulation is likely to have little or no impact in some commercial lines due to the widespread use of individual risk rating procedures (Stewart, 1987).

variation in the impact of regulation. The results of this and other studies using data from the late 1970s and early 1980s (e.g., Pauly, Kleindorfer, and Kunreuther, 1986; Grabowski, Viscusi, and Evans, 1989) suggested that on average prior approval regulation reduced the ratio of premiums to losses.

Some evidence of variation in the impact of prior approval regulation across states was provided in <u>Harrington (1987)</u> and several other studies, but causes of such variation generally were not addressed. A large amount of anecdotal evidence suggests that substantial regulatory intervention in insurance pricing tends to occur in states where the unregulated cost of coverage would be relatively high, that regulation favors high risk groups, and that exits eventually have occurred in response to restrictive regulation. Pauly, Kleindorfer, and Kunreuther (1986) provided evidence that direct writer market share was significantly lower in states with prior approval regulation. Building on the work of Ippolito (1979), they also provided evidence that restrictive rate regulation was associated with lower operating expenses (and presumably lower quality; also see Braeutigam and Pauly, 1986).

Involuntary markets in auto insurance have been found to be significantly larger in states with prior approval regulation of voluntary market rates (e.g., Ippolito, 1979; Grabowski, Viscusi, and Evans, 1989). Involuntary market rate regulation and state restrictions on risk classification (e.g, unisex rating rules) also will affect involuntary market size (as was implied by <u>Joskow, 1973</u>). The relative effects of these influences and of voluntary market rate regulation would be difficult to sort out. Voluntary and involuntary market regulation of auto liability insurance rates could reduce the number of uninsured drivers by lowering rates to drivers who otherwise would fail to buy coverage (see Kunreuther, Kleindorfer, and Pauly, 1983; Keeton and Kwerel, 1984). If so, the efficiency loss that otherwise would be expected from rate regulation would be mitigated. Not much is known about the magnitude of these effects or the effects of insurance rate regulation on decisions to drive and the frequency and severity of accidents.

# Bibliography

AKERLOF, G.A. (1970), "The Market for 'Lemons' : Quality Uncertainty and the Market Mechanism", *Quarterly Journal of Economics*, **84**, 488-500.

ALARIE, Y., DIONNE, G. AND EECKHOUDT, L. (1990), "Increases in Risk and Demand for Insurance" in G. Dionne (ed.), *Contributions to Insurance Economics*, Kluwer Academic Publishers, in press.

ALLAIS, M. (1953), "Généralisation des théories de l'équilibre économique général et du rendement social au cas du risque" in *Econométrie*, 81-110, Paris : CNRS.

ALLAIS, M. (1953a), "Le comportement de l'homme rationel devant le risque, critique des postulats et axiomes de l'École américaine", *Econometrica*, **21**, 503-46.

ANSCOMBE, F.J. AND AUMANN, R.J. (1963), "A Definition of Subjective Probability", *Mathematical Statistics*, **43**, 199-205.

APPEL, D., WORRALL, J.D. AND BUTLER, R.J. (1985), "Survivorship and the Size Distribution of the Property-Liability Insurance Industry", *Journal of Risk and Insurance*, **52**, 424-440.

ARNOTT, R. (1990), "Moral Hazard and Competitive Insurance Markets", in G. Dionne (ed.), *Contributions to Insurance Economics*, Kluwer Academic Publishers, in press.

ARNOTT, R. AND STIGLITZ, J.E. (1990), "The Welfare Economics of Moral Hazard", in H. Loubergé (ed.) *Risk, Information and Insurance : Essays in the Memory of Karl Borch*, Kluwer Academic Publishers.

ARROW, K.J. (1953), "Le rôle des valeurs boursières pour la répartition la meilleure des risques" in *Économétrie*, 41-47, Paris : CNRS. Translated as "The Role of Securities in the Optimal Allocation of Risk-Bearing", *Review of Economic Studies*, **31**, 1964, 91-96.

ARROW, K.J. (1963), "Uncertainty and the Welfare Economics of Medical Care", *American Economic Review*, **53**, 941-969.

ARROW, K.J. (1965), "Insurance, Risk and Resource Allocation" in Arrow, K.J. (1965), *Aspects of the Theory of Risk-Bearing*, Helsinki : Yrjö Jahnsson Foundation. Reprinted in Arrow, K.J. 1971), *Essays in the Theory of Risk Bearing*, Elsevier Publishing Company Inc., 134-143.

ARROW, K.J. (1974), "Optimal Insurance and Generalized Deductibles", *Scandinavian Actuarial Journal*, **1**, 1-42.

BERGER, L.A. (1988), "A Model of Underwriting Cycles in the Property-Liability Insurance Industry", *Journal of Risk and Insurance*, **55**, 298-306.

BERGER, L.A., KLEINDORFER, P.R. AND KUNREUTHER, H. (1989), "A Dynamic Model of Price Information in Auto Insurance Markets", *Journal of Risk and Insurance*, **56**, 17-33.

BIGER, N. AND KAHANE, Y. (1978), "Risk Considerations in Insurance Ratemaking", *Journal of Risk and Insurance*, **45** (1), 121-132.

BLACK, J.M. AND BULKLEY, G. (1989), "A Ratio Criterion for Signing the Effects of an Increase in Uncertainty", *International Economic Review*, **30**, 119-130.

BOND, E.W. AND CROCKER, K.J. (1990), "Smoking, Skydiving, and Knitting : The Endogenous Categorization of Risks in Insurance Markets with Asymmetric Information", *Journal of Political Economy*, in press.

BORCH, K. (1960), "The Safety Loading of Reinsurance Premiums", *Skandinavisk Aktuarietidskrift*, 163-184.

BORCH, K. (1961), "The Utility Concept Applied to the Theory of Insurance", *Astin Bulletin*, 1, 245-255.

BORCH, K. (1962), "Equilibrium in a Reinsurance Market", *Econometrica*, 30, 424-444.

BORCH, K. (1974), "Capital Markets and the Supervision of Insurance Companies", *Journal of Risk and Insurance*, 41, 397-405.

BORCH, K. (1982), "Optimal Strategies in a Game of Economic Survival", *Naval Research Logistics Quarterly*, 29, 19-27.

BORCH, K. (1990), *Economics of Insurance*, Amsterdam : North Holland.

BOYER, M. AND DIONNE, G. (1983), "Variations in the Probability and Magnitude of Loss: Their Impact on Risk", *Canadian Journal of Economics*, 16, 411-419.

BOYER, M. AND DIONNE, G. (1989), "More on Insurance, Protection and Risk", *Canadian Journal of Economics*, 22, 202-205.

BOYER, M. AND DIONNE, G. (1989a), "An Empirical Analysis of Moral Hazard and Experience Rating", *Review of Economics and Statistics*, 71, 128-134.

BOYLE, P.B. (1990), "Karl Borch's Research Contributions to Insurance", *Journal of Risk and Insurance*, 57, 307-320.

BRAEUTIGAM, R.R. AND PAULY, M.V. (1986), "Cost-Function Estimation and Quality Bias: The Regulated Automobile Insurance Industry", *Rand Journal of Economics*, 17, 606-617.

BRIYS, E. (1988), "On the Theory of Rational Insurance Purchasing in a Continuous Time Model", *Geneva Papers on Risk and Insurance*, 13, 165-177.

BRIYS, E. AND EECKHOUDT, L. (1985), "Relative Risk Aversion in Comparative Statics : Comment", *American Economic Review*, 75, 284-286.

BRIYS, E., DIONNE, G. AND EECKHOUDT, L. (1989), "More on Insurance as a Giffen Good", *Journal of Risk and Uncertainty*, 2, 420-425.

BRIYS, E. AND SCHLESINGER, H. (1990), "Risk Aversion and the Propensities for Self-Insurance and Self-Protection", *Southern Economic Journal*, in press.

BÜHLMANN, H. AND JEWELL, H. (1979), "Optimal Risk Exchanges", *Astin Bulletin*, 10, 243-262.

CHANG, Y.M. AND EHRLICH, I. (1985), "Insurance, Protection from Risk and Risk Bearing", *Canadian Journal of Economics*, 18, 574-587.

CLARKE, R.N., WARREN-BOULTON, F., SMITH, D.K. AND SIMON, M.J. (1988), "Sources of the Crisis in Liability Insurance: An Empirical Analysis", *Yale Journal on Regulation*, 5, 367-395.

COOK, P.J. AND GRAHAM, D.A. (1977), "The Demand for Insurance Protection : The Case of Irreplaceable Commodities", *Quarterly Journal of Economics*, 91, 143-156.

COOPER, R. AND HAYES, B. (1987), "Multi-period Insurance Contracts", *International Journal of Industrial Organization*, **5**, 211-231.

CRESTA, J.P. (1984), *Théorie des Marchés d'Assurance*, Collection "Approfondissement de la connaissance économique", Economica, Paris.

CROCKER, K.J. AND SNOW, A. (1985), "The Efficiency of Competitive Equilibria in Insurance Markets with Adverse Selection", *Journal of Public Economics*, **26**, 207-219.

CROCKER, K.J. AND SNOW, A. (1986), "The Efficiency Effects of Categorical Discrimination in the Insurance Industry", *Journal of Political Economy*, **94**, 321-344.

CUMMINS, J.D. (1974), "Insurer's Risk: A Restatement", *Journal of Risk and Insurance*, **41**, 147-157.

CUMMINS, J.D. (1988), "Risk-Based Premiums for Insurance Guaranty Funds", *Journal of Finance*, **43**, 823-839.

CUMMINS, J.D. AND DANZON, P.M. (1990), "Price Shocks and Capital Flows in Property-Liability Insurance", Mimeo, University of Pennsylvania.

CUMMINS, J.D. AND HARRINGTON, S.E. (1985), "Property-Liability Insurance Rate Regulation: Estimation of Underwriting Betas Using Quarterly Profit Data", *Journal of Risk and Insurance*, **52**, 16-43.

CUMMINS, J.D. AND HARRINGTON, S.E. (1987), "The Impact of Rate Regulation on Property-Liability Insurance Loss Ratios: A Cross-Sectional Analysis with Individual Firm Data", *Geneva Papers on Risk and Insurance*, **12**, 50-62.

CUMMINS, J.D. AND OUTREVILLE, J.F. (1987), "An International Analysis of Underwriting Cycles in Property-Liability Insurance", *Journal of Risk and Insurance*, **54**, 246-262.

CUMMINS, J.D. AND VANDERHEI, J.L. (1979), "A Note on the Relative Efficiency of Property-Liability Insurance Distribution System", *Bell Journal of Economics*, **10**, 709-720.

DAHLBY, B. (1983), "Adverse Selection and Statistical Discrimination : An Analysis of Canadian Automobile Insurance", *Journal of Public Economics*, **20**, 121-131.

DAHLBY, B. (1990), "Testing for Asymmetric Information in Canadian Automobile Insurance", in G. Dionne (ed.), *Contributions to Insurance Economics*, Kluwer Academic Publishers, in press.

DAHLBY, B. AND WEST, D.S. (1986), "Price Dispersion in an Automobile Insurance Market", *Journal of Political Economy*, **94**, 418-438.

DANZON, P.M. (1983), "Rating Bureaus in U.S. Property-Liability Insurance Markets: Anti or Pro-Competitive?", *Geneva Papers on Risk and Insurance*, **8**, 371-402.

DANZON, P.M. (1984), "Tort Reform and the Role of Government in Private Insurance Markets", *Journal of Legal Studies*, **13**, 517-549.

DANZON, P.M. (1985), Medical Malpractice: Theory, Evidence and Public Policy, Cambridge, Mass.: Harvard University Press.

DANZON, P.M. AND S.E. HARRINGTON (1990), "The Demand for and Supply of Liability Insurance", in Dionne G. (ed.), *Contributions to Insurance Economics*, Kluwer Academic Publishers, in press.

38

D'ARCY, S.P. (1988), "Application of Economic Theories of Regulation to the Property-Liability Insurance Industry", *Journal of Insurance Regulation*, 7, 19-52.

D'ARCY, S.P. AND N. DOHERTY (1990), "Adverse Selection, Private Information and Lowballing in Insurance Markets", *Journal of Business*, 63, 145-163.

D'ARCY, S.P. AND GARVEN, J.R. (1990), "Property-Liability Insurance Pricing Models: An Empirical Evaluation", *Journal of Risk and Insurance*, 57, 391-430.

DEBREU, G. (1953), "Une économie de l'incertain", Miméo, Électricité de France.

DEBREU, G. (1959), Theory of Value, New-York : Wiley.

DEFINETTI, B. (1957), "Su una Impostazione Altenativa delta Teoria Collettiva del Rischio", *Transactions of the XV International Congress of Actuaries*, 2, 433-443.

DIAMOND, P.A. AND ROTHSCHILD, M. (1978), *Uncertainty in Economics : Readings and Exercices*, New York : Academic Press.

DIONNE, G. (1982), "Moral Hazard and State-Dependent Utility Function", *Journal of Risk and Insurance*, 49, 405-423.

DIONNE, G. (1983), "Adverse Selection and Repeated Insurance Contracts", *Geneva papers on Risk and Insurance*, 8, 316-333.

DIONNE, G. (1984), "Search and Insurance", *International Economic Review*, 25, 357-367.

DIONNE, G. AND DOHERTY, N. (1990), "Adverse Selection in Insurance Markets : A Selective Survey", in G. Dionne (ed.), *Contributions to Insurance Economics*, Kluwer Academic Publishers, in press.

DIONNE, G. AND EECKHOUDT, L. (1984), "Insurance and Saving : Some Further Results", *Insurance : Mathematics and Economics*, 3, 101-110.

DIONNE, G. AND EECKHOUDT, L. (1985), "Self Insurance, Self Protection and Increased Risk Aversion", *Economics Letters*, 17, 39-42.

DIONNE, G. AND LASSERRE, P. (1985), "Adverse Selection, Repeated Insurance Contracts and Announcement Strategy", *Review of Economic Studies*, 52, 719-723.

DIONNE, G. AND LASSERRE, P. (1987), "Dealing with Moral Hazard and Adverse Selection Simultaneously", Working Paper, University of Pennsylvania.

DIONNE G. AND VANASSE, C. (1988), "Automobile Insurance Ratemaking in the Presence of Asymmetrical Information", Working Paper # 603. CRT, Université de Montréal.

DIONNE, G. AND ST-MICHEL, P. (1988), "Moral Hazard and Workers' Compensation", *Review of Economics and Statistics*, in press.

DOHERTY, N. (1981), "The Measurement of Output and Economies of Scale in Property-Liability Insurance", *Journal of Risk and Insurance*, 48, 390-402.

DOHERTY, N. (1984), "Portfolio Efficient Insurance Buying Strategies", *Journal of Risk and Insurance*, 51, 205-224.

DOHERTY, N. (1989), "On the Capital Structure of Insurance Firms", in J.D. Cummins and R.A. Derrig (eds.), *Financial Models of Insurer Solvency*, Kluwer Academic Publishers.

DOHERTY, N. AND DIONNE, G. (1989), "Risk Pooling, Contract Structure and Organizational Form of Insurance Firms", Working Paper 8935, Département de sciences économiques, Université de Montréal.

DOHERTY, N. AND GARVEN, J.R. (1986), "Price Regulation in Property/Liability Insurance : A Contingent Claims Approach", *Journal of Finance*, **41**, 1031-1050.

DOHERTY, N. AND GARVEN, J. (1990), "Capacity and the Cyclicality of Insurance Markets", Mimeo, University of Pennsylvia and University of Texas.

DOHERTY, N. AND KANG, H.B. (1988), "Price Instability for a Financial Intermediary: Interest Rates and Insurance Price Cycles", *Journal of Banking and Finance*, **12**, 191-214.

DOHERTY, N., LOUBERGÉ, H. AND SCHLESINGER, H. (1987), "Additive and Multiplicative Risk Premiums", *Scandinavian Actuarial Journal*, **13**, 41-49.

DOHERTY, N. AND SCHLESINGER, H. (1983), "Optimal Insurance in Incomplete Markets", *Journal of Political Economy*, **91**, 1045-1054.

DOHERTY, N. AND SCHLESINGER, H. (1983a), "The Optimal Deductible for an Insurance Policy when Initial Wealth is Random", *Journal of Business*, **56**, 555-565.

DOHERTY, N. AND SCHLESINGER, H. (1990), "Rational Insurance Purchasing : Considerations of Contract Non-Performance", *Quarterly Journal of Economics*, **105**, 243-253.

DRÈZE, J. (1961), "Les fondements logiques de l'utilité cardinale et de la probabilité subjective", *La Décision*, 73-87. Translated as Chapter 3 of Drèze (1987), *Essays on Economic Decision Under Uncertainty*, Cambridge University Press.

DRÈZE, J. (1974), "Axiomatic Theories of Choice, Cardinal Utility and Subjective Probability : A Review", in Drèze J. (ed.), *Allocation Under Uncertainty : Equilibrium and Optimality*, Wiley. Reprinted in Diamond and Rothschild (1978).

DRÈZE, J. (1981), "Inferring Risk Tolerance from Deductibles in Insurance Contracts", *Geneva Papers on Risk and Insurance*, **20**, 48-52.

DRÈZE, J. (1987), "Decision Theory with Moral Hazard and State-Dependent Preferences" in Drèze (1987), *Essays on Economic Decisions Under Uncertainty*, Cambridge University Press.

DRÈZE, J. AND MODIGLIANI, F. (1972), "Consumption Decisions Under Uncertainty", *Journal of Economic Theory*, **5**, 308-335.

DYE, R.A. (1986), "Optimal Monitoring Policies in Agencies", *The Rand Journal of Economics*, **17**, 339-350.

EECKHOUDT, L. AND KIMBALL, M. (1990), "Background Risk, Prudence and the Demand for Insurance", in G. Dionne (ed.), *Contributions to Insurance Economics*, Kluwer Academic Publishers, in press.

EECKHOUDT, L. AND HANSEN, P. (1980), "Minimum and Maximum Prices, Uncertainty and the Theory of the Competitive Firm", *American Economic Review*, **70**, 1064-1068.

EECKHOUDT, L. AND HANSEN, P. (1984), "Mean-Preserving Changes in Risk with Tail-Dominance", Working Paper 8413, Département de sciences économiques, Université de Montréal.

EHRLICH, J. AND BECKER, G. (1972), "Market Insurance, Self Insurance and Self Protection", *Journal of Political Economy*, **80**, 623-648.

EISEN, R. (1990), "Problems of Equilibria in Insurance Markets with Asymmetric Information", in H. Loubergé (ed.), *Risk, Information and Insurance*, Kluwer Academic Publishers.

EISENACH, J.A. (1985), "The Role of Collective Pricing in Auto Insurance", Ph.D. thesis, University of Virginia and Staff Report, Bureau of Economics, U.S. Federal Trade Commission.

FAIRLEY, W. (1979), "Investment Income and Profit Margins in Property-Liability Insurance: Theory and Empirical Results", *Bell Journal of Economics*, **10**, 192-210.

FAMA, E.F. AND JENSEN, M.C. (1983), "Separation of Ownership and Control", *Journal of Law and Economics*, **26**, 301-325.

FINSINGER, J. AND PAULY, M.V. (1984), "Reserve Levels and Reserve Requirements for Profit-Maximizing Insurance Firms", in G. Bamberg and K. Spremann (eds.), *Risk and Capital*, Springer-Verlag, 160-180.

FRIEDMAN, M. AND L.J. SAVAGE (1948), "The Utility Analysis of Choices Involving Risk", *Journal of Political Economy*, **56**, 279-304.

GARVEN, J.R. (1987), "On the Application of Finance Theory to the Insurance Firm", *Journal of Financial Services Research*, **1**, 57-76.

GERBER, H. (1978), "Pareto-Optimal Risk Exchanges and Related Decision Problems", *Astin Bulletin*, **10**, 25-33.

GOLLIER, C. (1987), "The Design of Optimal Insurance Contracts Without the Nonnegativity Constraint on Claims", *Journal of Risk and Insurance*, **54**, 314-324.

GOLLIER, C. (1987a), "Pareto-Optimal Risk Sharing with Fixed Costs Per Claim", *Scandinavian Actuarial Journal*, **13**, 62-73.

GOLLIER, C. (1990), "Economic Theory of Risk Exchanges : A Review", in G. Dionne (ed.), *Contributions to Insurance Economics*, Kluwer Academic Publishers, in press.

GOULD, J.P. (1969), "The Expected Utility Hypothesis and the Selection of Optimal Deductibles for a Given Insurance Policy", *Journal of Business*, **42**, 143-151.

GRABOWSKI, H., VISCUSI, W.K. AND EVANS, W.N. (1989), "Price and Availability Tradeoffs of Automobile Insurance Regulation", *Journal of Risk and Insurance*, **56**, 275-299.

GREEN, M.R. (1984), "Insurance", in *The New Encyclopedia Britannica*, 15th edition, **9**, 645-658.

GRON, A. (1989), "Capacity Constraints and Cycles in Property-Casualty Insurance Markets", Mimeo, Massachusetts Institute of Technology.

GROSSMAN, H.I. (1979), "Adverse Selection, Dissembling and Competitive Equilibrium, *Bell Journal of Economics* **10**, 330-343.

GROSSMAN, S. AND HART, O.D. (1983), "An Analysis of the Principal-Agent Problem", *Econometrica*, **51**, 7-45.

HAMMOND, J.D. AND SHILLING, N. (1978), "Some Relationships of Portfolio Theory to the Regulation of Insurer Solidity", *Journal of Risk and Insurance*, **45**, 377-400.

HANSMANN, H. (1985), "The Organization of Insurance Companies: Mutual versus Stock", *Journal of Law, Economics, and Organization*, **1**, 125-153.

HARRINGTON, S.E. (1984), "The Impact of Rate Regulation on Prices and Underwriting Results in the Property-Liability Insurance Industry: A Survey", *Journal of Risk and Insurance*, **51**, 577-617.

HARRINGTON, S.E. (1987), "A Note on the Impact of Auto Insurance Rate Regulation", *Review of Economics and Statistics*, **69**, 166-170.

HARRINGTON, S.E. (1988), "Prices and Profits in the Liability Insurance Market" in R. Litan and C. Winston (eds.), *Liability : Perspective and Policy*, The Brooking Institution, 42-100.

HARRINGTON, S.E. AND DANZON, P.M. (1986), "An Evaluation of Solvency Surveillance in the Property Liability Insurance Industry", Schaumburg, Ill.: Alliance of American Insurers.

HARRINGTON, S.E. AND DANZON, P.M. (1990), "Price-Cutting in Liability Insurance Markets", Mimeo, University of Pennsylvania and University of South Carolina.

HARRINGTON, S.E. AND NELSON, J.M. (1986), "A Regression-Based Methodology for Solvency Surveillance in the Property-Liability Insurance Industry", *Journal of Risk and Insurance*, **53**, 583-605.

HARRIS, M. AND R.M. TOWNSEND (1981), "Resource Allocation under Asymmetric Information", *Econometrica*, **49**, 33-64.

HELLWIG, M. (1988), "A Note of the Specification of Interfirm Communication in Insurance Markets with Adverse Selection", *Journal of Economic Theory*, **46**, 154-163.

HENRIET, D. AND ROCHET, J.C. (1986), "La logique des systèmes bonus-malus en assurance automobile : une approche théorique", *Annales d'Économie et de Statistique*, 133-152.

HERRING, R.J. AND VANKUDRE, P. (1987), "Growth Opportunities and Risk-Taking by Financial Intermediaries", *Journal of Finance*, **42**, 583-600.

HIEBERT, L.D. (1989), "Optimal Loss Reduction and Risk Aversion", *Journal of Risk and Insurance*, **56**, 300-306.

HILL, R.D. (1979), "Profit Regulation in Property-Liability Insurance", *Bell Journal of Economics*, **10**, 172-191.

HILL, R.D. AND MODIGLIANI, F. (1986), "The Massachusetts Model of Profit Regulation in Nonlife Insurance: Theory and Empirical Results", in J.D. Cummins and S.E. Harrington, (eds.), *Fair Rate of Return in Property-Liability Insurance*, Kluwer-Nijhoff Publishing.

HOLMSTROM, B. (1979), "Moral Hazard and Observability", *Bell Journal of Economics*, **10**, 74-91.

HOSIOS, A.J. AND PETERS, M. (1989), "Repeated Insurance Contracts with Adverse Selection and Limited Commitment", *Quarterly Journal of Economics*, **104**, 229-253.

HOUSTON, D.B. (1964), "Risk, Insurance, and Sampling", *Journal of Risk and Insurance*, **31**, 511-538.

HOY, M. (1982), "Categorizing Risks in the Insurance Industry", *Quarterly Journal of Economics*, **97**, 321-336.

HOY, M. AND ROBSON, R.J. (1981), "Insurance as a Giffen Good", *Economics Letters*, **8**, 47-51.

42

IPPOLITO, R. (1979), "The Effects of Price Regulation in the Automobile Insurance Industry", *Journal of Law and Economics*, **22**, 55-89.

JEWITT, I. (1988), "Justifying the First-Order Approach to Principal-Agent Problems", *Econometrica*, **56**, 1177-1190.

JOHNSON, J., FLANIGAN, G. AND WEISBART, S.N. (1981), "Returns to Scale in the Property and Liability Insurance Industry", *Journal of Risk and Insurance*, **48**, 18-45.

JOSKOW, P.J. (1973), "Cartels, Competition and Regulation in the Property-Liability Insurance Industry", *Bell Journal of Economics and Management Science*, **4**, 327-427.

KAHANE, Y. AND KROLL, Y. (1985), "Optimal Insurance Coverage in Situations of Pure and Speculative Risk and the Risk Free Asset", *Insurance Mathematics and Economics*, **4**, 191-199.

KAHANE, Y. AND NYE, D.J. (1975), "A Portfolio Approach to the Property-Liability Insurance Industry", *Journal of Risk and Insurance*, **42**, 579-598.

KAHANE, Y., TAPIERO, C.S. AND JACQUES, L. (1986), "Concepts and Trends in the Study of Insurer's Solvency", in J.D. Cummins and R.A. Derrig (eds.), *Financial Models of Insurance Solvency*, Kluwer Academic Publishers.

KARNI, E. (1985), *Decision Making Under Uncertainty*, Cambridge, Mass. : Harvard University Press.

KARNI, E. (1990), "A Definition of Subjective Probabilities with State-Dependent Preferences", Working Paper # 247, Johns Hopkins University.

KARNI, E. (1990a), "Optimal Insurance : A Non-Expected Utility Analysis", in G. Dionne (ed.), *Contributions to Insurance Economics*, Kluwer Academic Publishers, in press.

KASTELIJN, W.M AND REMMERSWAAL, J.C. (1986), Solvency, Surveys of Actuarial Studies No. 3, National Nederlanden N.V.

KEETON, W.R. AND KWEREL, E. (1984), "Externalities in Automobile Insurance and the Uninsured Driver Problem", *Journal of Law and Economics*, **27**, 149-180.

KIHLSTROM R.E. AND PAULY, M. (1971), "The Role of Insurance in the Allocation of Risk", *American Economic Review*, **61**, 371-379.

KIHLSTROM, R.E., ROMER, D. AND WILLIAMS, S. (1981), "Risk Aversion with Random Initial Wealth", *Econometrica*, **49**, 911-920.

KIHLSTROM, R.E. AND ROTH, A.E. (1982), "Risk Aversion and the Negotiation of Insurance Contracts", *Journal of Risk and Insurance*, **49**, 372-387.

KIMBALL, M. (1990), "Precautionary Saving in the Small and in the Large", *Econometrica*, **58**, 53-73.

KRAUS, A. AND ROSS, S.A. (1982), "The Determinants of Fair Profits for the Property-Liability Insurance Firm", *Journal of Finance*, **37**, 1015-1030.

KUNREUTHER, H. ET AL. (1978), *Disaster Insurance Protection : Public Policy Lessons*, New York : Wiley.

KUNREUTHER, H. KLEINDORFER, P.R. AND PAULY, M.V. (1983), "Insurance Regulation and Consumer Behavior in the United States", *Journal of Institutional and Theoretical Economics*, **139**, 452-472.

KUNREUTHER, H. AND PAULY, M.V. (1985), "Market Equilibrium with Private Knowledge : An Insurance Example", *Journal of Public Economics*, **26**, 269-288.

LACKER, J.M. AND WEINBERY, J.A. (1989), "Optimal Contracts under Costly State Falsification", *Journal of Political Economy*, **97**, 1343-1363.

LAFFONT, J.J. (1989), *The Economics of Uncertainty and Information*, Cambridge, Mass. : MIT Press.

LELAND, H.E. (1972), "Theory of the Firm Facing Uncertain Demand", *American Economic Review*, **62**, 278-291.

LEMAIRE, J. (1990), "Borch's Theorem : A Historical Survey of Applications" in H. Loubergé (ed.), *Risk, Information and Insurance*, Kluwer Academic Publishers, 15-37.

LÉVY-GARBOUA, L. AND MONTMARQUETTE, C. (1990), "The Demand for Insurance Against More than One Risk, With an Application to Social Insurance", Mimeo, Economics Department, Université de Montréal.

LOUBERGÉ, H. (1990), "Introduction" in H. Loubergé (ed.), *Risk, Information and Insurance*, Kluwer Academic Publishers, 1-14.

MACMINN, R. (1990), "Limited Liability, Corporate Value, and the Demand for Liability Insurance", *Journal of Risk and Insurance*, in press.

MACMINN, R.D. AND WITT, R.C. (1987), "A Financial Theory of the Insurance Firm under Uncertainty and Regulatory Constraints", *Geneva Papers on Risk and Insurance*, **12**, 3-20.

MCCABE, G. AND WITT, R.C. (1980), "Insurance Pricing and Regulation under Uncertainty: A Chance-Constrained Approach", *Journal of Risk and Insurance*, **47**, 607-635.

MCDONALD, J.B. (1988), "Predicting Insurance Insolvency Using Generalized Qualitatives Response Models", Mimeo, Brigham Young University.

MCGEE, R.T. (1986), "The Cycle in Property/Casualty Insurance", *Federal Reserve Bank of New York Quarterly Review*, 22-30.

MAIN, B. (1982), "Business Insurance and Large, Widely-Held Corporations", *Geneva Papers on Risk and Insurance*, **7**, 237-247.

MACHINA, M.J. (1987), "Choice Under Uncertainty : Problems Solved and Unsolved", *The Journal of Economic Perspectives*, **1**, 121-154.

MARSHALL, J.M. (1976), "Moral Hazard", *American Economic Review*, **66**, 880-890.

MARSHALL, J.M. (1976a), "Moral Hazard", Working paper no 18, University of California, Santa Barbara.

MARSHALL, J.M. (1990), "Optimum Insurance with Deviant Beliefs", in G. Dionne (ed.), *Contributions to Insurance Economics*, Kluwer Academic Publishers, in press.

MAYERS, D. AND SMITH, C.W. (1981), "Contractual Provisions, Organizational Structure, and Conflict Control in Insurance Markets", *Journal of Business*, **54**, 407-434.

MAYERS, D. AND SMITH, C.W. (1982), "On the Corporate Demand for Insurance", *Journal of Business*, 281-296.

44

MAYERS, D. AND SMITH, C.W. (1983), "The Interdependance of Individual Portfolio Decisions and the Demand for Insurance", *Journal of Political Economy*, **91**, 304-311.

MAYERS, D. AND SMITH, C.W. (1986), "Ownership Structure and Control: The Mutualization of Stock Life Insurance Companies", *Journal of Financial Economics*, **16**, 73-98.

MAYERS, D. AND SMITH, C.W. (1987), "Corporate Insurance and the Underinvestment Problem", *Journal of Risk and Insurance*, **54**, 45-54.

MAYERS, D. AND SMITH, C.W. (1988), "Ownership Structure Across Lines of Property — Casualty Insurance", *The Journal of Law and Economics*, **31**, 351-378.

MAYERS, D. AND SMITH, C.W. (1990), "On the Corporate Demand for Insurance: Evidence from the Reinsurance Market", *Journal of Business*, **63**, 19-40.

MERTON, R.C. (1971), "Optimum Consumption and Portfolio Rules in a Continuous-Time Model", *Journal of Economic Theory*, **3**, 373-413.

MEYER, J. AND ORMISTON, M. (1985), "Strong Increases in Risk and Their Comparative Statics", *International Economic Review*, **17**, 425-437.

MEYER, J. AND ORMISTON, M. (1989), "Deterministic Transformations of Random Variables and the Comparative Statics of Risks", *Journal of Risk and Uncertainty*, **2**, 179-188.

MENEZES, C. AND HANSON, D. (1970), "On the Theory of Risk Aversion", *International Economic Review*, **2**, 481-487.

MICHAELSON, J.B. AND GOSHAY, R.C. (1967), "Portfolio Selection in Financial Intermediaries: A New Approach", *Journal of Financial and Quantitative Analysis*, **2**, 166-199.

MIRRLEES, J. (1975), "The Theory of Moral Hazard and Unobservable Behavior — Part I", Mimeo, Nuffield College, Oxford.

MIYAZAKI, H. (1977), "The Rat Race and Internal Labor Markets", *Bell Journal of Economics*, **8**, 394-418.

MOFFET, D. (1975), "Risk Bearing and Consumption Theory", *Astin Bulletin*, **8**, 342-358.

MOFFET, D. (1977), "Optimal Deductible and Consumption Theory", *Journal of Risk and Insurance*, **44**, 669-683.

MOFFET, D. (1979), "The Risk Sharing Problem", *Geneva Papers on Risk and Insurance*, **11**, 5-13.

MOOKHERJEE, D. AND PNG, I. (1989), "Optimal Auditing Insurance and Redistribution", *Quarterly Journal of Economics*, **104**, 205-228.

MOSSIN, J. (1968), "Aspects of Rational Insurance Purchasing", *Journal of Political Economy*, **79**, 553-568.

MUNCH, P. AND SMALLWOOD, D.E. (1980), "Solvency Regulation in the Property-Liability Insurance Industry : Empirical Evidence", *Bell Journal of Economics*, **11**, 261-282.

MUNCH, P. AND SMALLWOOD, D.E. (1982), "Theory of Solvency Regulation in the Property and Casualty Insurance Industry", in Gary Fromm (ed.), *Studies in Public Regulation*, MIT Press.

MYERS, S. (1977), "Determinants of Corporate Borrowing", *Journal of Financial Economics*, **5**, 147-175.

MYERS, S.C. AND COHN, R.A. (1986), "A Discounted Cash Flow Approach to Property-Liability Insurance Rate Regulation", in J.D. Cummins and S.E. Harrington (eds.), *Fair Rate of Return in Property-Liability Insurance*, Kluwer-Nijhoff Publishing.

NILSSEN, T. (1990), "Consumer Lock-in with Asymmetric Information", Working paper, Norvegian School of Economics and Business.

PASHIGIAN, B. SCHKADE, L. AND MENEFEE, G. (1966), "The Selection of an Optimal Deductible for a Given Insurance Policy", *Journal of Business*, **39**, 35-44.

PAULY, M.V. (1968), "The Economics of Moral Hazard : Comment", *American Economic Review*, **58**, 531-36.

PAULY, M.V. (1974), "Overinsurance and Public Provision of Insurance : The Role of Moral Hazard and Adverse Selection", *Quarterly Journal of Economics*, **88**, 44-62.

PAULY, M.V., KLEINDORFER, P.R. AND KUNREUTHER, H. (1986), "Regulation and Quality Competition in the U.S. Insurance Industry", in J. Finsinger and M.V. Pauly (eds.), *The Economics of Insurance Regulation*, MacMillan Press.

PINCHES, G.E. AND TRIESCHMANN, J.S. (1973), "A Multivariate Model for Predicting Financially Distressed Property-Liability Insurers", *Journal of Risk and Insurance*, **40**, 327-338.

PRATT, J.W. (1964), "Risk Aversion in the Small and in the Large", *Econometrica*, **32**, 122-136.

PRIEST, G. (1987), "The Current Insurance Crisis and Modern Tort Law", *Yale Law Journal*, **96**, 1521-1590.

RADNER, R. (1968), "Competitive Equilibrium Under Uncertainty", *Econometrica*, **36**, 31-58.

RADNER, R. (1981), "Monitoring Cooperative Agreements in a Repeated Principal-Agent Relationship", *Econometrica*, **49**, 1127-1148.

RAVIV, A. (1979), "The Design of an Optimal Insurance Policy", *American Economic Review*, **69**, 84-86.

REA, S.A. (1987), "The Market Response to the Elimination of Sex-Based Annuities", *Southern Economic Journal*, **54**, 55-63.

REA, S.A. (1990), "Insurance Classifications and Social Welfare", in G. Dionne (ed.), *Contributions to Insurance Economics*, Kluwer Academic Publishers, in press.

RILEY, J.G. (1979), "Informational Equilibrium", *Econometrica*, **47**, 331-359.

RILEY, J.G. (1983), "Adverse Selection and Statistical Discrimination : Further Comments", *Journal of Public Economics*, **20**, 131-137.

RIZZO, J.A. (1989), "The Impact of Medical Malpractice Insurance Rate Regulation", *Journal of Risk and Insurance*, **56**, 482-500.

ROGERSON, W.P. (1985), "The First-Order Approach to Principal-Agent Problems", *Econometrica*, **53**, 1357-1367.

ROGERSON, W.P. (1985a), "Repeated Moral Hazard", *Econometrica*, **53**, 69-76.

ROSS, S. (1973), "The Economic Theory of Agency : The Principal's Problem", *American Economic Review*, **63**, 134-139.

46

Ross, S. (1981), "Some Stronger Measures of Risk Aversion in the Small and in the Large with Applications", *Econometrica*, **49**, 621-638.

Rothschild, M. and Stiglitz, J.E. (1970), "Increasing Risk, I : A Definition", *Journal of Economic Theory*, **2**, 225-243.

Rothschild, M. and Stiglitz, J.E. (1976), "Equilibrium in Competitive Insurance Markets : The Economics of Markets with Imperfect Information", *Quarterly Journal of Economics*, **90**, 629-650.

Rubinstein, A. and Yaari, M.E. (1983), "Repeated Insurance Contracts and Moral Hazard", *Journal of Economic Theory*, **30**, 74-97.

Sandmo, A. (1969), "Capital Risk, Consumption and Portfolio Choice", *Econometrica*, **37**, 568-599.

Sandmo, A. (1970), "The Effect of Uncertainty on Saving Decisions", *Review of Economic Studies*, **37**, 353-360.

Sandmo, A. (1971), "On the Theory of the Competitive Firms under Price Uncertainty, *American Economic Review*, **61**, 65-73.

Schlesinger, H. (1981), "The Optimal Level of Deductibility in Insurance Contracts", *Journal of Risk and Insurance*, **48**, 465-481.

Schlesinger, H. and Doherty, N. (1985), "Incomplete Markets for Insurance : An Overview", *Journal of Risk and Insurance*, **52**, 402-423.

Schoemaker, P.J. (1982), "The Expected Utility Model : Its Variants, Evidence and Limitations", *Journal of Economic Literature*, **20**, 529-563.

Schulenburg, J.M. (1986), "Optimal Insurance Purchasing in the Presence of Compulsory Insurance and Insurable Risks", *Geneva Papers on Risk and Insurance*, **38**, 5-16.

Shavell, S. (1979), "On Moral Hazard and Insurance", *Quarterly Journal of Economics*, **93**, 541-562.

Shavell, S. (1982), "On Liability and Insurance", *Bell Journal of Economics*, **13**, 120-132.

Shavell, S. (1986), "The Judgement Proof Problem", *International Review of Law and Economics*, **6**, 45-58.

Smallwood, D. (1975), "Regulation, and Product Quality in the Automobile Insurance Industry", in Almarin Phillips (ed.), *Promoting Competition in Regulated Markets*, The Brooking Institution.

Smith, M.L. (1989), "Investment Returns and Yields to Holders of Insurance", *Journal of Business*, **62**, 81-98.

Smith, M.L. and Buser, S.A. (1987), "Risk Aversion, Insurance Costs and Optimal Property-Liability Coverages", *Journal of Risk and Insurance*, **54**, 225-245.

Smith, V. (1968), "Optimal Insurance Coverage", *Journal of Political Economy*, **79**, 68-77.

Spence, M. (1978), "Product Differentiation and Performance in Insurance Markets", *Journal of Public Economics*, **10**, 427-447.

Spence, M. and Zeckhauser, R. (1971), "Insurance, Information and Individual Action", *American Economic Review*, **61**, 380-387.

Stewart, R.E. (1987), Remembering a Stable Future: Why Flex Rating Cannot Work, New York: Insurance Services Office and Insurance Information Institute.

STIGLITZ, G.J. (1977), "Monopoly, Non-Linear Pricing and Imperfect Information : The Insurance Market", *Review of Economic Studies*, **44**, 407-430.

STIGLITZ, G.J. AND WEISS, A. (1984), "Sorting Out the Differences Between Screening and Signaling Models", Mimeo, Princeton University.

TAPIERO, C.S., KAHANE, Y. AND JACQUES, L. (1986), "Insurance Premiums and Default Risk in Mutual Insurance", *Scandinavian Actuarial Journal*, 82-97.

TAPIERO, C.S. ZUCKERMAN, D. AND KAHANE, Y., (1978), "Regulation of an Insurance Firm with a Compound Poisson Claim Process", in Y. Kahane (ed.), *New Frontiers in Insurance*, Papirus Press.

TENNYSON, S. (1989), "The Dynamics of Insurance Supply: Testing Competiting Hypotheses", Mimeo, Northwestern University.

TOWNSEND, R. (1979), "Optimal Contracts and Competitive Contracts with Costly State Verification", *Journal of Economic Theory*, **22**, 265-293.

TURNBULL, S. (1983), "Additional Aspects of Rational Insurance Purchasing", *Journal of Business*, **56**, 217-229.

VENEZIAN, E.C. (1983), "Insurer Parameter Needs under Parameter Uncertainty", *Journal of Risk and Insurance*, **50**, 19-32.

VENEZIAN, E.C. (1984), "Efficiency and Equity in Insurance", *Journal of Risk and Insurance*, **51**, 190-204.

VENEZIAN, E.C. (1985), "Ratemaking Methods and Profit Cycles in Property and Liability Insurance", *Journal of Risk and Insurance*, **52**, 477-500.

VISCUSI, W. KIP AND EVANS, W.N. (1990), "Utility Functions that Depend on Health Status : Estimates and Economic Implications", *American Economic Review*, **80**, 353-374.

VON NEUMANN, J. AND MORGENSTERN, O. (1947), *Theory of Games and Economic Behavior*, Princeton University Press.

WILSON, C. (1977), "A Model of Insurance Markets with Incomplete Information", *Journal of Economic Theory*, **12**, 167-207.

WINTER, R.A. (1988), "The Liability Crisis and the Dynamics of Competitive Insurance Markets", *Yale Journal on Regulation*, **5**, 455-499.

WINTER, R.A. (1988a), "Solvency Regulation and the Property-Liability Insurance Cycle", Mimeo, Yale Law School and University of Toronto.

WINTER, R.A. (1989), "The Dynamics of Competitive Insurance Contracts", Mimeo, University of Toronto.

WINTER, R.A. (1990), "Moral Hazard in Insurance Contracts", in G. Dionne (ed.), *Contributions to Insurance Economics*, Kluwer Academic Publishers, in press.

WITT, R.C. (1974), "Pricing, Investment Income and Underwriting Risk: A Stochastic View", *Journal of Risk and Insurance*, **41**, 109-133.

ZECKHAUSER, R. AND KEELER, E. (1970), "Another Type of Risk Aversion", *Econometrica*, **38**, 661-665.

ZWEIFEL, P. AND GHERMI, P. (1990), "Exclusive vs. Independent Agencies: A Comparison of Performance", *Geneva Papers on Risk and Insurance Theory*, **2**, 171-192.

# Choice Under Uncertainty: Problems Solved and Unsolved

## Mark J. Machina

F ifteen years ago, the theory of choice under uncertainty could be considered one of the "success stories" of economic analysis: it rested on solid axiomatic foundations, it had seen important breakthroughs in the analytics of risk, risk aversion and their applications to economic issues, and it stood ready to provide the theoretical underpinnings for the newly emerging "information revolution" in economics.[1] Today choice under uncertainty is a field in flux: the standard theory is being challenged on several grounds from both within and outside economics. The nature of these challenges, and of our profession's responses to them, is the topic of this paper.

The following section provides a brief description of the economist's canonical model of choice under uncertainty, the expected utility model of preferences over random prospects. I shall present this model from two different perspectives. The first perspective is the most familiar, and has traditionally been the most useful for addressing standard economic questions. However the second, more modern perspective will be the most useful for illustrating some of the problems which have beset the model, as well as some of the proposed responses.

Each of the subsequent sections is devoted to one of these problems. All are important, some are more completely "solved" than others. In each case I shall begin with an example or description of the phenomenon in question. I shall then review the empirical evidence regarding the uniformity and extent of the phenomenon. Finally, I shall report on how these findings have changed, or are likely to change, or ought to

---

[1]E.g. von Neumann and Morgenstern (1947) and Savage (1954) (axiomatics); Arrow (1965), Pratt (1964) and Rothschild and Stiglitz (1970) (analytics); Akerlof (1970) and Spence and Zeckhauser (1971) (information).

■ *Mark J. Machina is Associate Professor of Economics, University of California, San Diego, La Jolla, California.*

change, the way we view and model economic behavior under uncertainty. On this last topic, the disclaimer that "my opinions are my own" has more than the usual significance.[2]

## The Expected Utility Model

### The Classical Perspective: Cardinal Utility and Attitudes Toward Risk

In light of current trends toward generalizing this model, it is useful to note that the expected utility hypothesis was itself first proposed as an alternative to an earlier, more restrictive theory of risk-bearing. During the development of modern probability theory in the 17th century, mathematicians such as Blaise Pascal and Pierre de Fermat assumed that the attractiveness of a gamble offering the payoffs $(x_1, \ldots, x_n)$ with probabilities $(p_1, \ldots, p_n)$ was given by its expected value $\bar{x} = \Sigma x_i p_i$. The fact that individuals consider more than just expected value, however, was dramatically illustrated by an example posed by Nicholas Bernoulli in 1728 and now known as the *St. Petersburg Paradox*:

> Suppose someone offers to toss a fair coin repeatedly until it comes up heads, and to pay you $1 if this happens on the first toss, $2 if it takes two tosses to land a head, $4 if it takes three tosses, $8 if it takes four tosses, etc. What is the largest sure gain you would be willing to forgo in order to undertake a single play of this game?

Since this gamble offers a $1/2$ chance of winning $1, a $1/4$ chance of winning $2, etc., its expected value is $(1/2) \cdot \$1 + (1/4) \cdot \$2 + (1/8) \cdot \$4 + \cdots = \$1/2 + \$1/2 + \$1/2 + \cdots = \$\infty$, so it should be preferred to any finite sure gain. However, it is clear that few individuals would forgo more than a moderate amount for a one-shot play. Although the unlimited financial backing needed to actually make this offer is somewhat unrealistic, it is not essential for making the point: agreeing to limit the game to at most one million tosses will still lead to a striking discrepancy between most individuals' valuations of the modified gamble and its expected value of $500,000.

The resolution of this paradox was proposed independently by Gabriel Cramer and Nicholas's cousin Daniel Bernoulli (Bernoulli, 1738/1954). Arguing that a gain of $200 was not necessarily "worth" twice as much as a gain of $100, they hypothesized that the individual possesses what is now termed a *von Neumann-Morgenstern utility function* $U(\cdot)$, and rather than using expected value $\bar{x} = \Sigma x_i p_i$, will evaluate gambles on the basis of expected utility $\bar{u} = \Sigma U(x_i) p_i$. Thus the sure gain $\xi$ which would yield the same utility as the Petersburg gamble, i.e. the certainty equivalent of this gamble,

---

[2]In keeping with the spirit of this journal, references have been limited to the most significant examples of and/or most useful introductions to the literature in each area. For further discussions of these issues see Arrow (1982), Machina (1983a, 1983b), Sugden (1986) and Tversky and Kahneman (1986).

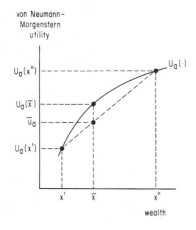

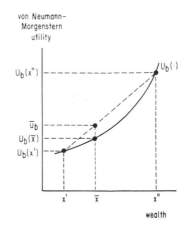

Fig. 1a. Concave utility function of a risk averter   Fig. 1b. Convex utility function of a risk lover

is determined by the equation

$$(1) \qquad U(W + \xi) = (1/2) \cdot U(W + 1) + (1/4) \cdot U(W + 2)$$

$$+ (1/8) \cdot U(W + 4) + \cdots$$

where $W$ is the individual's current wealth. If utility took the logarithmic form $U(x) \equiv \ln(x)$ and $W = \$50,000$, for example, the individual's certainty equivalent $\xi$ would only be about \$9, even though the gamble has an infinite expected value.

Although it shares the name "utility," $U(\cdot)$ is quite distinct from the ordinal utility function of standard consumer theory. While the latter can be subjected to any monotonic transformation, a von Neumann-Morgenstern utility function is cardinal in that it can only be subjected to transformations of the form $a \cdot U(x) + b$ ($a > 0$), i.e. transformations which change the origin and/or scale of the vertical axis, but do not affect the "shape" of the function.[3]

To see how this shape determines risk attitudes, consider Figures 1a and 1b. The monotonicity of $U_a(\cdot)$ and $U_b(\cdot)$ in the figures reflects the property of stochastic dominance preference, where one lottery is said to stochastically dominate another one if it can be obtained from it by shifting probability from lower to higher outcome levels.[4] Stochastic dominance preference is thus the probabilistic analogue of the attitude that "more is better."

Consider a gamble offering a $2/3 : 1/3$ chance of the outcomes $x'$ or $x''$. The points $\bar{x} = (2/3) \cdot x' + (1/3) \cdot x''$ in the figures give the expected value of this

[3] Such transformations are often used to normalize the utility function, for example to set $U(0) = 0$ and $U(M) = 1$ for some large value $M$.
[4] Thus, for example, a $2/3 : 1/3$ chance of \$100 or \$20 and a $1/2 : 1/2$ chance of \$100 or \$30 both stochastically dominate a $1/2 : 1/2$ chance of \$100 or \$20.

gamble, and $\bar{u}_a = (2/3) \cdot U_a(x') + (1/3) \cdot U_a(x'')$ and $\bar{u}_b = (2/3) \cdot U_b(x') + (1/3) \cdot U_b(x'')$ give its expected utilities for $U_a(\cdot)$ and $U_b(\cdot)$. For the concave utility function $U_a(\cdot)$ we have $U_a(\bar{x}) > \bar{u}_a$, which implies that this individual would prefer a sure gain of $\bar{x}$ (which would yield utility $U_a(\bar{x})$) to the gamble. Since someone with a concave utility function will in fact always prefer receiving the expected value of a gamble to the gamble itself, concave utility functions are termed risk averse. For the convex utility function $U_b(\cdot)$ we have $\bar{u}_b > U_b(\bar{x})$, and since this preference for bearing the risk rather than receiving the expected value will also extend to all gambles, $U_b(\cdot)$ is termed risk loving. In their famous article, Friedman and Savage (1948) showed how a utility function which was concave at low wealth levels and convex at high wealth levels could explain the behavior of individuals who both incur risk by purchasing lottery tickets as well as avoid risk by purchasing insurance. Algebraically, Arrow (1965) and Pratt (1964) have shown how the degree of concavity of a utility function, as measured by the curvature index $-U'''(x)/U'(x)$, determines how risk attitudes, and hence behavior, will vary with wealth or across individuals in a variety of situations. If $U_c(\cdot)$ is at least as risk averse as $U_d(\cdot)$ in the sense that $-U_c'''(x)/U_c'(x) \geq -U_d''(x)/U_d'(x)$ for all $x$, then an individual with utility function $U_c(\cdot)$ would be willing to pay at least as much for insurance against any risk as would someone with utility function $U_d(\cdot)$.

Since a knowledge of $U(\cdot)$ would allow us to predict preferences (and hence behavior) in any risky situation, experimenters and applied decision analysts are frequently interested in eliciting or recovering their subjects' (or clients') von Neumann-Morgenstern utility functions. One method of doing so is termed the fractile method. This approach begins by adopting the normalization $U(0) = 0$ and $U(M) = 1$ (see Note 3) and fixing a "mixture probability" $\bar{p}$, say $\bar{p} = 1/2$. The next step involves finding the individual's certainty equivalent $\xi_1$ of a $1/2 : 1/2$ chance of $M$ or 0, which implies that $U(\xi_1) = (1/2) \cdot U(M) + (1/2) \cdot U(0) = 1/2$. Finding the certainty equivalents of the $1/2 : 1/2$ chances of $\xi_1$ or 0 and of $M$ or $\xi_1$ yields the values $\xi_2$ and $\xi_3$ which solve $U(\xi_2) = 1/4$ and $U(\xi_3) = 3/4$. By repeating this procedure (i.e. $1/8, 3/8, 5/8, 7/8, 1/16, 3/16$, etc.), the utility function can (in the limit) be completely assessed.

Our discussion so far has paralleled the economic literature of the 1960s and 1970s by emphasizing the flexibility of the expected utility model compared to the Pascal-Fermat expected value approach. However, the need to analyze and respond to growing empirical challenges has led economists in the 1980's to concentrate on the behavioral restrictions implied by the expected utility hypothesis. It is to these restrictions that we now turn.

## A Modern Perspective: Linearity in the Probabilities as a Testable Hypothesis

As a theory of individual behavior, the expected utility model shares many of the underlying assumptions of standard consumer theory. In each case we assume that the objects of choice, either commodity bundles or lotteries, can be unambiguously and objectively described, and that situations which ultimately imply the same set of availabilities (e.g. the same budget set) will lead to the same choice. In each case we

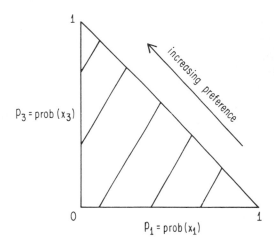

Fig. 2. Expected utility indifference curves in the triangle diagram

also assume that the individual is able to perform the mathematical operations necessary to actually determine the set of availabilities, e.g. to add up the quantities in different sized containers or calculate the probabilities of compound or conditional events. Finally, in each case we assume that preferences are transitive, so that if an individual prefers one object (either a commodity bundle or a risky prospect) to a second, and prefers this second object to a third, he or she will prefer the first object to the third. We shall examine the validity of these assumptions for choice under uncertainty in some of the following sections.

However, the strongest implication of the expected utility hypothesis stems from the form of the expected utility maximand or preference function $\sum U(x_i)p_i$. Although this preference function generalizes the expected value form $\sum x_i p_i$ by dropping the property of linearity in the payoffs (the $x_i$'s), it retains the other key property of this form, namely linearity in the probabilities.

Graphically, we may illustrate the property of linearity in the probabilities by considering the set of all lotteries or prospects over the fixed outcome levels $x_1 < x_2 < x_3$, which can be represented by the set of all probability triples of the form $P = (p_1, p_2, p_3)$ where $p_i = \text{prob}(x_i)$ and $\sum p_i = 1$. Since $p_2 = 1 - p_1 - p_3$, we can represent these lotteries by the points in the unit triangle in the $(p_1, p_3)$ plane, as in Figure 2.[5] Since upward movements in the triangle increase $p_3$ at the expense of $p_2$ (i.e. shift probability from the outcome $x_2$ up to $x_3$) and leftward movements reduce $p_1$ to the benefit of $p_2$ (shift probability from $x_1$ up to $x_2$), these movements (and more generally, all northwest movements) lead to stochastically dominating lotteries

[5] Thus if $x_1 = \$20$, $x_2 = \$30$ and $x_3 = \$100$, the prospects in Note 4 would be represented by the points $(p_1, p_3) = (1/3, 2/3)$, $(p_1, p_3) = (0, 1/2)$ and $(p_1, p_3) = (1/2, 1/2)$ respectively. Although it is fair to describe the renewal of interest in this approach as "modern," versions of this diagram go back at least to Marschak (1950).

54

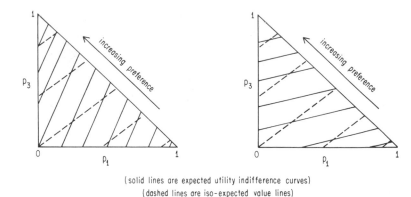

(solid lines are expected utility indifference curves)
(dashed lines are iso-expected value lines)

Fig. 3a. Relatively steep indifference curves of a   Fig. 3b. Relatively flat indifference curves of a risk
risk averter                                                                        lover

and would accordingly be preferred. Finally, since the individual's indifference curves
in the $(p_1, p_3)$ diagram are given by the solutions to the linear equation

$$(2) \quad \bar{u} = \sum_{i=1}^{3} U(x_i)p_i = U(x_1)p_1 + U(x_2)(1 - p_1 - p_3) + U(x_3)p_3 = \text{constant}$$

they will consist of parallel straight lines of slope $[U(x_2) - U(x_1)]/[U(x_3) - U(x_2)]$,
with more preferred indifference curves lying to the northwest. This implies that in
order to know an expected utility maximizer's preferences over the entire triangle, it
suffices to know the slope of a single indifference curve.

To see how this diagram can be used to illustrate attitudes toward risk, consider
Figures 3a and 3b. The dashed lines in the figures are not indifference curves but
rather *iso-expected value lines*, i.e. solutions to

$$(3) \quad \bar{x} = \sum_{i=1}^{3} x_i p_i = x_1 p_1 + x_2(1 - p_1 - p_3) + x_3 p_3 = \text{constant}$$

Since northeast movements along these lines do not change the expected value of the
prospect but do increase the probabilities of the tail outcomes $x_1$ and $x_3$ at the
expense of the middle outcome $x_2$, they are examples of *mean preserving spreads* or
"pure" increases in risk (Rothschild and Stiglitz, 1970). When the utility function $U(\cdot)$
is concave (i.e. risk averse), its indifference curves can be shown to be steeper than the
iso-expected value lines as in Figure 3a,[6] and such increases in risk will lead to lower
indifference curves. When $U(\cdot)$ is convex (risk loving), its indifference curves will be
flatter than the iso-expected value lines (as in Figure 3b) and increases in risk will lead

[6] This follows since the slope of the indifference curves is $[U(x_2) - U(x_1)]/[U(x_3) - U(x_2)]$, the slope of
the iso-expected value lines is $[x_2 - x_1]/[x_3 - x_2]$, and concavity of $U(\cdot)$ implies $[U(x_2) - U(x_1)]/$
$[x_2 - x_1] > [U(x_3) - U(x_2)]/[x_3 - x_2]$ whenever $x_1 < x_2 < x_3$.

to higher indifference curves. If we compare two different utility functions, the one which is more risk averse (in the above Arrow-Pratt sense) will possess the steeper indifference curves.

Behaviorally, we can view the property of linearity in the probabilities as a restriction on the individual's preferences over probability mixtures of lotteries. If $P^* = (p_1^*, \ldots, p_n^*)$ and $P = (p_1, \ldots, p_n)$ are two lotteries over a common outcome set $\{x_1, \ldots, x_n\}$, the $\alpha : (1 - \alpha)$ probability mixture of $P^*$ and $P$ is the lottery $\alpha P^* + (1 - \alpha)P = (\alpha p_1^* + (1 - \alpha)p_1, \ldots, \alpha p_n^* + (1 - \alpha)p_n)$. This may be thought of as that prospect which yields the same ultimate probabilities over $\{x_1, \ldots, x_n\}$ as the two-stage lottery which offers an $\alpha : (1 - \alpha)$ chance of winning either $P^*$ or $P$. Since linearity in the probabilities implies that $\Sigma U(x_i)(\alpha p_i^* + (1 - \alpha)p_i) = \alpha \cdot \Sigma U(x_i)p_i^* + (1 - \alpha) \cdot \Sigma U(x_i)p_i$, expected utility maximizers will exhibit the following property, known as the *Independence Axiom* (Samuelson, 1952):

> If the lottery $P^*$ is preferred (resp. indifferent) to the lottery $P$, then the mixture $\alpha P^* + (1 - \alpha)P^{**}$ will be preferred (resp. indifferent) to the mixture $\alpha P + (1 - \alpha)P^{**}$ for all $\alpha > 0$ and $P^{**}$.

This property, which is in fact equivalent to linearity in the probabilities, can be interpreted as follows:

> In terms of the ultimate probabilities over the outcomes $\{x_1, \ldots, x_n\}$, choosing between the mixtures $\alpha P^* + (1 - \alpha)P^{**}$ and $\alpha P + (1 - \alpha)P^{**}$ is the same as being offered a coin with a probability of $1 - \alpha$ of landing tails, in which case you will obtain the lottery $P^{**}$, and being asked before the flip whether you would rather have $P^*$ or $P$ in the event of a head. Now either the coin will land tails, in which case your choice won't have mattered, or else it will land heads, in which case you are 'in effect' back to a choice between $P^*$ or $P$, and it is only 'rational' to make the same choice as you would before.

Although this is a prescriptive argument, it has played a key role in economists' adoption of expected utility as a descriptive theory of choice under uncertainty. As the evidence against the model mounts, this has lead to a growing tension between those who view economic analysis as the description and prediction of what they consider to be rational behavior and those who view it as the description and prediction of observed behavior. We turn now to this evidence.

## Violations of Linearity in the Probabilities

### The Allais Paradox and "Fanning Out"

One of the earliest and best known examples of systematic violation of linearity in the probabilities (or equivalently, of the independence axiom) is the well-known *Allais Paradox* (Allais, 1953, 1979). This problem involves obtaining the individual's

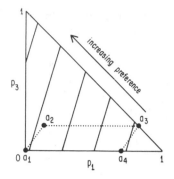
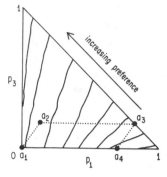

Fig. 4a. Expected utility indifference curves and the
Allais Paradox

Fig. 4b. Indifference curves which 'fan out' and the
Allais Paradox

preferred option from each of the following two pairs of gambles (readers who have never seen this problem may want to circle their own choice from each pair before proceeding):

$$a_1: \left\{ 1.00 \text{ chance of } \$1,000,000 \right. \quad \text{versus} \quad a_2: \left\{ \begin{array}{l} .10 \text{ chance of } \$5,000,000 \\ .89 \text{ chance of } \$1,000,000 \\ .01 \text{ chance of } \$0 \end{array} \right.$$

and

$$a_3: \left\{ \begin{array}{l} .10 \text{ chance of } \$5,000,000 \\ .90 \text{ chance of } \$0 \end{array} \right. \quad \text{versus} \quad a_4: \left\{ \begin{array}{l} .11 \text{ chance of } \$1,000,000 \\ .89 \text{ chance of } \$0 \end{array} \right.$$

Defining $\{x_1, x_2, x_3\} = \{\$0; \$1,000,000; \$5,000,000\}$, these four gambles are seen form a parallelogram in the $(p_1, p_3)$ triangle, as in Figures 4a and 4b. Under the expected utility hypothesis, therefore, a preference for $a_1$ in the first pair would indicate that the individual's indifference curves were relatively steep (as in Figure 4a), and hence a preference for $a_4$ in the second pair. In the alternative case of relatively flat indifference curves, the gambles $a_2$ and $a_3$ would be preferred.[7] However, researchers such as Allais (1953), Morrison (1967), Raiffa (1968) and Slovic and Tversky (1974) have found that the modal if not majority preferences of subjects has been for $a_1$ in the first pair and $a_3$ in the second, which implies that indifference curves are not parallel but rather fan out, as in Figure 4b.

One of the criticisms of this evidence has been that individuals whose choices violated the independence axiom would "correct" themselves once the nature of their violation was revealed by an application of the above coin-flip argument. Thus, while even Savage chose $a_1$ and $a_3$ when first presented with this example, he concluded upon reflection that these preferences were in error (Savage, 1954, pp. 101–103).

[7]Algebraically, these cases are equivalent to the expression $[.10 \cdot U(5,000,000) - .11 \cdot U(1,000,000) + .01 \cdot U(0)]$ being negative or positive, respectively.

Although his own reaction was undoubtedly sincere, the hypothesis that individuals would invariably react in such a manner has not been sustained in direct empirical testing. In experiments where subjects were asked to respond to Allais-type problems and then presented with arguments both for and against the expected utility position, neither MacCrimmon (1968), Moskowitz (1974) nor Slovic and Tversky (1974) found predominant net swings toward the expected utility choices.

### Additional Evidence of Fanning Out

Although the Allais Paradox was originally dismissed as an isolated example, it is now known to be a special case of a general empirical pattern termed the *common consequence effect*. This effect involves pairs of probability mixtures of the form:

$$b_1: \alpha\delta_x + (1 - \alpha)P^{**} \quad \text{versus} \quad b_2: \alpha P + (1 - \alpha)P^{**}$$

and

$$b_3: \alpha\delta_x + (1 - \alpha)P^* \quad \text{versus} \quad b_4: \alpha P + (1 - \alpha)P^*$$

where $\delta_x$ denotes the prospect which yields $x$ with certainty, $P$ involves outcomes both greater and less than $x$, and $P^{**}$ stochastically dominates $P^*$.[8] Although the independence axiom clearly implies choices of either $b_1$ and $b_3$ (if $\delta_x$ is preferred to $P$) or else $b_2$ and $b_4$ (if $P$ is preferred to $\delta_x$), researchers have found a tendency for subjects to choose $b_1$ in the first pair and $b_4$ in the second (MacCrimmon, 1968; MacCrimmon and Larsson, 1979; Kahneman and Tversky, 1979; Chew and Waller, 1986). When the distributions $\delta_x$, $P$, $P^*$ and $P^{**}$ are each over a common outcome set $\{x_1, x_2, x_3\}$, the prospects $b_1$, $b_2$, $b_3$ and $b_4$ will again form a parallelogram in the $(p_1, p_3)$ triangle, and a choice of $b_1$ and $b_4$ again implies indifference curves which fan out, as in Figure 4b.

The intuition behind this phenomenon can be described in terms of the above "coin-flip" scenario. According to the independence axiom, preferences over what would occur in the event of a head should not depend upon what would occur in the event of a tail. In fact, however, they may well depend upon what would otherwise happen.[9] The common consequence effect states that the better off individuals would be in the event of a tail (in the sense of stochastic dominance), the more risk averse they become over what they would receive in the event of a head. Intuitively, if the distribution $P^{**}$ in the pair $\{b_1, b_2\}$ involves very high outcomes, I may prefer not to bear further risk in the unlucky event that I don't receive it, and prefer the sure outcome $x$ over the distribution $P$ in this event (i.e. choose $b_1$ over $b_2$). But if $P^*$ in $\{b_3, b_4\}$ involves very low outcomes, I may be more willing to bear risk in the (lucky)

---

[8]The Allais Paradox choices $a_1$, $a_2$, $a_3$, and $a_4$ correspond to $b_1$, $b_2$, $b_4$ and $b_3$, where $\alpha = .11$, $x = \$1,000,000$, $P$ is a $10/11 : 1/11$ chance of $\$5,000,000$ or $\$0$, $P^*$ is a sure chance of $\$0$, and $P^{**}$ is a sure chance of $\$1,000,000$. The name of this phenomenon comes from the "common consequence" $P^{**}$ in $\{b_1, b_2\}$ and $P^*$ in $\{b_3, b_4\}$.

[9]As Bell (1985) notes, "winning the top prize of $10,000 in a lottery may leave one much happier than receiving $10,000 as the lowest prize in a lottery."

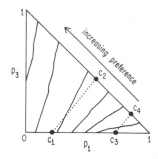
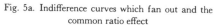

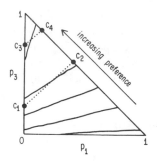

Fig. 5a. Indifference curves which fan out and the common ratio effect

Fig. 5b. Indifference curves which fan out and the common ratio effect with negative payoffs

event that I don't receive it, and prefer the lottery $P$ to the outcome $x$ in this case (i.e. choose $b_4$ over $b_3$). Note that it is not my beliefs regarding the probabilities in $P$ which are affected here, merely my willingness to bear them.[10]

A second class of systematic violations, stemming from another early example of Allais (1953), is known as the *common ratio effect*. This phenomenon involves pairs of prospects of the form:

$$c_1 : \begin{cases} p \text{ chance of } \$X \\ 1 - p \text{ chance of } \$0 \end{cases} \quad \text{versus} \quad c_2 : \begin{cases} q \text{ chance of } \$Y \\ 1 - q \text{ chance of } \$0, \end{cases}$$

and

$$c_3 : \begin{cases} rp \text{ chance of } \$X \\ 1 - rp \text{ chance of } \$0 \end{cases} \quad \text{versus} \quad c_4 : \begin{cases} rq \text{ chance of } \$Y \\ 1 - rq \text{ chance of } \$0, \end{cases}$$

where $p > q$, $0 < X < Y$ and $r \in (0, 1)$, and includes the "certainty effect" of Kahneman and Tversky (1979) and the ingenious "Bergen Paradox" of Hagen (1979) as special cases.[11] Setting $\{x_1, x_2, x_3\} = \{0, X, Y\}$ and plotting these prospects in the $(p_1, p_3)$ triangle, the segments $\overline{c_1 c_2}$ and $\overline{c_3 c_4}$ are seen to be parallel (as in Figure 5a), so that the expected utility model again predicts choices of $c_1$ and $c_3$ (if the individual's indifference curves are steep) or else $c_2$ and $c_4$ (if they are flat). However, experimental studies have found a systematic tendency for choices to depart from these predictions

[10] In a conversation with the author, Kenneth Arrow has offered an alternative phrasing of this argument: The widely maintained hypothesis of decreasing absolute risk aversion asserts that individuals will display more risk aversion in the event of a loss, and less risk aversion in the event of a gain. In the common consequence effect, individuals display more risk aversion in the event of an opportunity loss, and less risk aversion in the event of an opportunity gain.

[11] The former involves setting $p = 1$, and the latter consists of a two-step choice problem where individuals exhibit the effect with $Y = 2X$ and $p = 2q$. The name "common ratio effect" comes from the common value of $\text{prob}(X)/\text{prob}(Y)$ in the pairs $\{c_1, c_2\}$ and $\{c_3, c_4\}$.

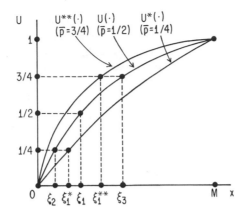

Fig. 6a. 'Recovered' utility functions for mixture probabilities 1/4, 1/2 and 3/4

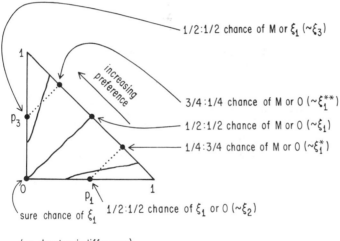

( ~ denotes indifference )

Fig. 6b. Fanning out indifference curves which generate the responses of Figure 6a

and de Neufville (1983, 1984) have found a tendency for higher values of $\bar{p}$ to lead to the "recovery" of higher valued utility functions, as in Figure 6a. By illustrating the gambles used to obtain the values $\xi_1$, $\xi_2$ and $\xi_3$ for $\bar{p} = 1/2$, $\xi_1^*$ for $\bar{p} = 1/4$ and $\xi_1^{**}$ for $\bar{p} = 3/4$, Figure 6b shows that, as with the common consequence and common ratio effects, this *utility evaluation effect* is precisely what would be expected

---

[12] Kahneman and Tversky (1979), for example, found that 80 percent of their subjects preferred a sure gain of 3,000 Israeli pounds to a .80 chance of winning 4,000, but 65 percent preferred a .20 chance of winning 4,000 to a .25 chance of winning 3,000.

in the direction of preferring $c_1$ and $c_4$,[12] which again suggests that indifference curves fan out, as in the figure (Tversky, 1975; MacCrimmon and Larsson, 1979; Chew and Waller, 1986). In a variation on this approach, Kahneman and Tversky (1979) replaced the gains of $\$X$ and $\$Y$ in the above gambles with losses of these magnitudes, and found a tendency to depart from expected utility in the direction of $c_2$ and $c_3$. Defining $\{x_1, x_2, x_3\}$ as $\{-Y, -X, 0\}$ (to maintain the condition $x_1 < x_2 < x_3$) and plotting these gambles in Figure 5b, a choice of $c_2$ and $c_3$ is again seen to imply that indifference curves fan out. Finally, Battalio, Kagel and MacDonald (1985) found that laboratory rats choosing among gambles which involved substantial variations in their actual daily food intake also exhibited this pattern of choices.

A third class of evidence stems from the elicitation method described in the previous section. In particular, note that there is no reason why the mixture probability $\bar{p}$ must be $1/2$ in this procedure. Picking any other $\bar{p}$ and defining $\xi_1^*$, $\xi_2^*$ and $\xi_3^*$ as the certainty equivalents of the $\bar{p}$: $(1 - \bar{p})$ chances of $M$ or 0, $\xi_1^*$ or 0, and $M$ or $\xi_1^*$ yields the equations $U(\xi_1^*) = \bar{p}$, $U(\xi_2^*) = \bar{p}^2$, $U(\xi_3^*) = \bar{p} + (1 - \bar{p})\bar{p}$, etc., and such a procedure can also be used to recover $U(\cdot)$.

Although this procedure should recover the same (normalized) utility function for any mixture probability $\bar{p}$, researchers such as Karmarkar (1974, 1978) and McCord from an individual whose indifference curves departed from expected utility by fanning out.[13]

**Non-Expected Utility Models of Preferences**

The systematic nature of these departures from linearity in the probabilities have led several researchers to generalize the expected utility model by positing nonlinear functional forms for the individual preference function. Examples of such forms and researchers who have studied them include:

(4)  $\quad\quad\quad \sum \nu(x_i)\pi(p_i) \quad\quad\quad$ Edwards (1955)

Kahneman and Tversky (1979)

(5)  $\quad\quad\quad \dfrac{\sum \nu(x_i)\pi(p_i)}{\sum \pi(p_i)} \quad\quad\quad$ Karmarkar (1978)

(6)  $\quad\quad\quad \dfrac{\sum \nu(x_i)p_i}{\sum \tau(x_i)p_i} \quad\quad\quad$ Chew (1983)

Fishburn (1983)

(7)  $\sum \nu(x_i)[g(p_1 + \cdots + p_i) - g(p_1 + \cdots + p_{i-1})]$  Quiggin (1982)

(8)  $\quad\quad\quad \sum \nu(x_i)p_i + [\sum \tau(x_i)p_i]^2 \quad\quad\quad$ Machina (1982)

[13] Having found that $\xi_1$ which solves $U(\xi_1) = (1/2) \cdot U(M) + (1/2) \cdot U(0)$, choose $\{x_1, x_2, x_3\} = \{0, \xi_1, M\}$, so that the indifference curve through $(0,0)$ (i.e. a sure gain of $\xi_1$) also passes through $(1/2, 1/2)$ (a $1/2 : 1/2$ chance of $M$ or 0). The order of $\xi_1$, $\xi_2$, $\xi_3$, $\xi_1^*$ and $\xi_1^{**}$ in Figure 6a is derived from the individual's preference ordering over the five distributions in Figure 6b for which they are the respective certainty equivalents.

Many (though not all) of these forms are flexible enough to exhibit the properties of stochastic dominance preference, risk aversion/risk preference and fanning out, and (6) and (7) have proven to be particularly useful both theoretically and empirically. Additional analyses of these forms can be found in Chew, Karni and Safra (1987), Fishburn (1964), Segal (1984) and Yaari (1987).

Although such forms allow for the modelling of preferences which are more general than those allowed by the expected utility hypothesis, each requires a different set of conditions on its component functions $\nu(\cdot)$, $\pi(\cdot)$, $\tau(\cdot)$ or $g(\cdot)$ for the properties of stochastic dominance preference, risk aversion/risk preference, comparative risk aversion, etc. In particular, the standard expected utility results linking properties of the function $U(\cdot)$ to such aspects of behavior will generally not extend to the corresponding properties of the function $\nu(\cdot)$ in the above forms. Does this mean that the study of non-expected utility preferences requires us to abandon the vast body of theoretical results and intuition we have developed within the expected utility framework?

Fortunately, the answer is no. An alternative approach to the analysis of non-expected utility preferences proceeds not by adopting a specific nonlinear function, but rather by considering nonlinear functions in general, and using calculus to extend the results from expected utility theory in the same manner in which it is typically used to extend results involving linear functions.[14]

Specifically, consider the set of all probability distributions $P = (p_1, \ldots, p_n)$ over a fixed outcome set $\{x_1, \ldots, x_n\}$, so that the expected utility preference function can be written as $V(P) = V(p_1, \ldots, p_n) \equiv \Sigma U(x_i) p_i$, and think of $U(x_i)$ not as a "utility level" but rather as the coefficient of $p_i = \text{prob}(x_i)$ in this linear function. If we plot these coefficients against $x_i$ as in Figure 7, the expected utility results of the previous section can be stated as:

*Stochastic Dominance Preference:* $V(\cdot)$ will exhibit global stochastic dominance preference if and only if the coefficients $\{U(x_i)\}$ are increasing in $x_i$, as in the figure.

*Risk Aversion:* $V(\cdot)$ will exhibit global risk aversion if and only if the coefficients $\{U(x_i)\}$ are concave in $x_i$,[15] as in the figure.

*Comparative Risk Aversion:* The expected utility preference function $V^*(P) \equiv \Sigma U^*(x_i) p_i$ will be at least as risk averse as $V(\cdot)$ if and only if the coefficients $\{U^*(x_i)\}$ are at least as concave in $x_i$ as $\{U(x_i)\}$.[16]

Now take the case where the individual's preference function $\mathcal{V}(P) = \mathcal{V}(p_1, \ldots, p_n)$ is not linear (i.e. not expected utility) but at least differentiable, and consider its partial derivatives $\mathcal{U}(x_i; P) \equiv \partial \mathcal{V}(P)/\partial p_i = \partial \mathcal{V}(P)/\partial \text{prob}(x_i)$. Pick some probability distribution $P_0$ and plot these $\mathcal{U}(x_i; P_0)$ values against $x_i$. If they

---

[14] Readers who wish to skip the details of this approach may proceed to the next section.

[15] As in Note 6, this is equivalent to the condition that $[U(x_{i+1}) - U(x_i)]/[x_{i+1} - x_i] < [U(x_i) - U(x_{i-1})]/[x_i - x_{i-1}]$ for all $i$.

[16] This is equivalent to the condition that $U^*(x_i) \equiv \rho(U(x_i))$ for some increasing concave function $\rho(\cdot)$.

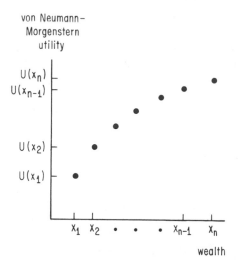

von Neumann–
Morgenstern
utility

wealth

Fig. 7. von Neumann-Morgenstern utilities as coefficients of the expected utility preference function
$V(p_1, \ldots, p_n) \equiv \Sigma U(x_i) p_i$

are again increasing in $x_i$, it is clear that any infinitesimal stochastically dominating shift from $P_0$, such as a decrease in some $p_i$ and matching increase in $p_{i+1}$, will be preferred. If they are again concave in $x_i$, any infinitesimal mean preserving spread, such as a drop in $p_i$ and (mean preserving) rise in $p_{i-1}$ and $p_{i+1}$, will make the individual worse off. In light of this correspondence between the coefficients $\{U(x_i)\}$ of an expected utility preference function $V(\cdot)$ and the partial derivatives $\{\mathcal{U}(x_i; P_0)\}$ of the non-expected utility preference function $\mathcal{V}(\cdot)$, we refer to $\{\mathcal{U}(x_i; P_0)\}$ as the individual's local utility indices at $P_0$.

Of course, the above results will only hold precisely for infinitesimal shifts from the distribution $P_0$. However, we can exploit another result from standard calculus to show how "expected utility" results may be applied to the exact global analysis of non-expected utility preferences. Recall that in many cases, a differentiable function will exhibit a specific global property if and only if that property is exhibited by its linear approximations at each point. For example, a differentiable function will be globally nondecreasing if and only if its linear approximations are non-decreasing at each point. In fact, most of the fundamental properties of risk attitudes and their expected utility characterizations are precisely of this type. In particular, it can be shown that:

*Stochastic Dominance Preference:* A non-expected utility preference function $\mathcal{V}(\cdot)$ will exhibit global stochastic dominance preference if and only if its local utility indices $\{\mathcal{U}(x_i; P)\}$ are increasing in $x_i$ at each distribution $P$.

*Risk Aversion:* $\mathcal{V}(\cdot)$ will exhibit global risk aversion if and only if its local utility indices $\{\mathcal{U}(x_i; P)\}$ are concave in $x_i$ at each distribution $P$.

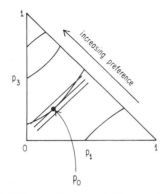

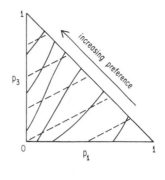

(solid lines are local expected utility approximation to non-expected utility indifference curves at $P_0$)

(dashed lines are iso-expected value lines)

Fig. 8a. Tangent 'expected utility' approximation to non-expected utility indifference curves

Fig. 8b. Risk aversion of every local expected utility approximation is equivalent to global risk aversion

*Comparative Risk Aversion:* The preference function $\mathcal{V}^*(\cdot)$ will be globally at least as risk averse as $\mathcal{V}(\cdot)$[17] if and only if its local utility indices $\{\mathcal{U}^*(x_i; P)\}$ are at least as concave in $x_i$ as $\{\mathcal{U}(x_i; P)\}$ at each $P$.

Figures 8a and 8b give a graphical illustration of this approach for the outcome set $\{x_1, x_2, x_3\}$. Here the solid curves denote the indifference curves of the non-expected utility preference function $\mathcal{V}(P)$. The parallel lines near the lottery $P_0$ denote the tangent "expected utility" indifference curves that correspond to the local utility indices $\{\mathcal{U}(x_i; P_0)\}$ at $P_0$. As always with differentiable functions, an infinitesimal change in the probabilities at $P_0$ will be preferred if and only if they would be preferred by this tangent linear (i.e. expected utility) approximation. Figure 8b illustrates the above "risk aversion" result: It is clear that these indifference curves will be globally risk averse (averse to mean preserving spreads) if and only if they are everywhere steeper than the dashed iso-expected value lines. However, this is equivalent to all of their *tangents* being steeper than these lines, which is in turn equivalent to all of their local expected utility approximations being risk averse, or in other words, to the local utility indices $\{\mathcal{U}(x_i; P)\}$ being concave in $x_i$ at each distribution $P$.

My fellow researchers and I have shown how this and similar techniques can be applied to further extend the results of expected utility theory to the case of non-expected utility preferences, to characterize and explore the implications of preferences which "fan out," and to conduct new and more general analyses of economic behavior under uncertainty (Machina, 1982; Chew, 1983; Fishburn, 1984; Epstein, 1985; Allen, 1987; Chew, Karni and Safra, 1987). However, while I feel that

---

[17]For the appropriate generalizations of the expected utility concepts of "at least as risk averse" in this context, see Machina (1982, 1984).

they constitute a useful and promising response to the phenomenon of non-linearities in the probabilities, these models do not provide solutions to the more problematic empirical phenomena of the following sections.

## The Preference Reversal Phenomenon

### The Evidence

The finding now known as the preference reversal phenomenon was first reported by psychologists Lichtenstein and Slovic (1971). In this study, subjects were first presented with a number of pairs of bets and asked to choose one bet out of each pair. Each of these pairs took the following form:

$$P\text{-bet}: \begin{cases} p \text{ chance of } \$X \\ 1 - p \text{ chance of } \$x \end{cases} \quad \text{versus} \quad \$\text{-bet}: \begin{cases} q \text{ chance of } \$Y \\ 1 - q \text{ chance of } \$y, \end{cases}$$

where $X$ and $Y$ are respectively greater than $x$ and $y$, $p$ is greater than $q$, and $Y$ is greater than $X$ (the names "$P$-bet" and "$\$$-bet" come from the greater probability of winning in the first bet and greater possible gain in the second). In some cases, $x$ and $y$ took on small negative values. The subjects were next asked to "value" (state certainty equivalents for) each of these bets. The different valuation methods used consisted of (1) asking subjects to state their minimum selling price for each bet if they were to own it, (2) asking them to state their maximum bid price for each bet if they were to buy it, and (3) the elicitation procedure of Becker, DeGroot and Marschak (1964), in which it is in a subject's best interest to reveal his or her true certainty equivalents.[18] In the latter case, real money was used.

The expected utility model, as well as each of the non-expected utility models of the previous section, clearly implies that the bet which is actually chosen out of each pair will also be the one which is assigned the higher certainty equivalent.[19] However, Lichtenstein and Slovic found a systematic tendency for subjects to violate this prediction by choosing the $P$-bet in a direct choice but assigning a higher value to the $\$$-bet. In one experiment, for example, 127 out of 173 subjects assigned a higher sell price to the $\$$-bet in every pair in which the $P$-bet was chosen. Similar findings were obtained by Lindman (1971), and in an interesting variation on the usual experimental setting, by Lichtenstein and Slovic (1973) in a Las Vegas casino where customers actually staked (and hence sometimes lost) their own money. In another real-money

[18] Roughly speaking, the subject states a value for the item, and then the experimenter draws a random price. If the price is above the stated value, the subject forgoes the item and receives the price. If the drawn price is below the state value, the subject keeps the item. The reader can verify that under such a scheme it can never be in a subject's best interest to report anything other than his or her true value.

[19] Economic theory tells us that income effects could cause an individual to assign a lower bid price to the object which, if both were free, would actually be preferred. However, this reversal should not occur for either selling prices or the Becker, DeGroot and Marschak elicitations. For evidence on sell price/bid price disparities, see Knetsch and Sinden (1984) and the references cited there.

experiment, Mowen and Gentry (1980) found that groups who could discuss their (joint) decisions were, if anything, more likely than individuals to exhibit the phenomenon.

Although the above studies involved deliberate variations in design in order to check for the robustness of this phenomenon, they were nevertheless received skeptically by economists, who perhaps not unnaturally felt they had more at stake than psychologists in this type of finding. In an admitted attempt to "discredit" this work, economists Grether and Plott (1979) designed a pair of experiments which, by correcting for issues of incentives, income effects, strategic considerations, ability to indicate indifference and other items, would presumably not generate this phenomenon. They nonetheless found it in both experiments. Further design modifications by Pommerehne, Schneider and Zweifel (1982) and Reilly (1982) yielded the same results. Finally, the phenomenon has been found to persist (although in mitigated form) even when subjects are allowed to engage in experimental market transactions involving the gambles (Knez and Smith, 1986), or when the experimenter is able to act as an arbitrageur and make money off of such reversals (Berg, Dickhaut and O'Brien, 1983).

### Two Interpretations of this Phenomenon

How you interpret these findings depends on whether you adopt the worldview of an economist or a psychologist. An economist would reason as follows: Each individual possesses a well-defined preference relation over objects (in this case lotteries), and information about this relation can be gleaned from either direct choice questions or (properly designed) valuation questions. Someone exhibiting the preference reversal phenomenon is therefore telling us that he or she (1) is indifferent between the $P$-bet and some sure amount $\xi_P$, (2) strictly prefers the $P$-bet to the $-bet, and (3) is indifferent between the $-bet and an amount $\xi_\$$ greater than $\xi_P$. Assuming they prefer $\xi_\$$ to the lesser amount $\xi_P$, this implies that their preferences over these four objects are cyclic or intransitive.

Psychologists on the other hand would deny the premise of a common underlying mechanism generating both choice and valuation behavior. Rather, they view choice and valuation (even different forms of valuation) as distinct processes, subject to possibly different influences. In other words, individuals exhibit what are termed *response mode effects*. Excellent discussions and empirical examinations of this phenomenon and its implications for the elicitation of probabilistic beliefs and utility functions can be found in Hogarth (1975), Slovic, Fischhoff and Lichtenstein (1982), Hershey and Schoemaker (1985) and MacCrimmon and Wehrung (1986). In reporting how the response mode study of Slovic and Lichtenstein (1968) led them to actually predict the preference reversal phenomenon, I can do no better than quote the authors themselves:

"The impetus for this study [Lichtenstein and Slovic (1971)] was our observation in our earlier 1968 article that choices among pairs of gambles appeared to be influenced primarily by probabilities of winning and losing, whereas buying and selling prices were primarily determined by the dollar amounts that could be won or lost. ... In our 1971 article, we argued that, if the information in a gamble is processed differently when making choices and setting prices, it should be possible to construct pairs of gambles such that people would choose one member of the pair but set a higher price on the other."

Slovic and Lichtenstein (1983)

## Implications of the Economic Worldview

The issue of intransitivity is new neither to economics nor to choice under uncertainty. May (1954), for example, observed intransitivities in pairwise rankings of three alternative marriage partners, where each candidate was rated highly in two of three attributes (intelligence, looks, wealth) and low in the third. In an uncertain context, Blyth (1972) has adapted this approach to construct a set of random variables $(\tilde{x}, \tilde{y}, \tilde{z})$ such that $\text{prob}(\tilde{x} > \tilde{y}) = \text{prob}(\tilde{y} > \tilde{z}) = \text{prob}(\tilde{z} > \tilde{x}) = 2/3$, so that individuals making pairwise choices on the basis of these probabilities would also be intransitive. In addition to the preference reversal phenomenon, Edwards (1954, pp. 404–405) and Tversky (1969) have also observed intransitivities in preferences over risky prospects. On the other hand, researchers have shown that many aspects of economic theory, in particular the existence of demand functions and of general equilibrium, are surprisingly robust to dropping the assumption of transitivity (Sonnenschein, 1971; Mas-Colell, 1974; Shafer, 1974).

In any event, economists have begun to develop and analyze models of nontransitive preferences over lotteries. The leading example of this is the "expected regret" model developed independently by Bell (1982), Fishburn (1982) and Loomes and Sugden (1982). In this model of pairwise choice, the von Neumann-Morgenstern utility function $U(x)$ is replaced by a *regret/rejoice function* $r(x, y)$ which represents the level of satisfaction (or if negative, dissatisfaction) the individual would experience if he or she were to receive the outcome $x$ when the alternative choice would have yielded the outcome $y$ (this function is assumed to satisfy $r(x, y) \equiv -r(y, x)$). In choosing between statistically independent gambles $P^* = (p_1^*, \ldots, p_n^*)$ and $P = (p_1, \ldots, p_n)$ over a common outcome set $\{x_1, \ldots, x_n\}$, the individual will choose $P^*$ if the expectation $\sum_i \sum_j r(x_i, x_j) p_i^* p_j$ is positive, and $P$ if it is negative.

Note that when the regret/rejoice function takes the special form $r(x, y) \equiv U(x) - U(y)$ this model reduces to the expected utility model, since we have

$$(9) \qquad \sum_i \sum_j r(x_i, x_j) p_i^* p_j$$

$$\equiv \sum_i \sum_j \left[ U(x_i) - U(x_j) \right] p_i^* p_j \equiv \sum_i U(x_i) p_i^* - \sum_j U(x_j) p_j$$

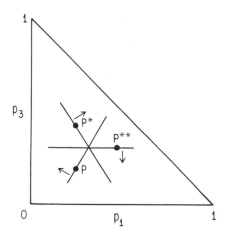

Fig. 9. 'Indifference curves' for the expected regret model

so that the individual will prefer $P^*$ to $P$ if and only if $\sum_i U(x_i)p_i^* > \sum_j U(x_j)p_j$.[20]
However, in general such an individual will neither be an expected utility maximizer nor have transitive preferences.

However, this intransitivity does not prevent us from graphing such preferences, or even applying "expected utility" analysis to them. To see the former, consider the case when the individual is facing alternative independent lotteries over a common outcome set $\{x_1, x_2, x_3\}$, so that we may again use the triangle diagram to illustrate their "indifference curves," which will appear as in Figure 9. In such a case it is important to understand what is and is not still true of these indifference curves. The curve through $P$ will still correspond to the set of lotteries that are indifferent to $P$, and it will still divide the set of lotteries that are strictly preferred to $P$ (the points in the direction of the arrow) from the ones to which $P$ is strictly preferred. Furthermore, if (as in the figure) $P^*$ lies above the indifference curve through $P$, then $P$ will lie below the indifference curve through $P^*$ (i.e. the individual's ranking of $P$ and $P^*$ will be unambiguous). However, unlike indifference curves for transitive preferences, these curves will cross,[21] and preferences over the lotteries $P$, $P^*$ and $P^{**}$ are seen to form an intransitive cycle. But in regions where the indifference curves do not cross (such as near the origin) the individual will be indistinguishable from someone with transitive (albeit non-expected utility) preferences.

To see how expected utility results can be extended to this nontransitive framework, fix a lottery $P = (p_1, \ldots, p_n)$ and consider the question of when an (independent) lottery $P^* = (p_1^*, \ldots, p_n^*)$ will be preferred or not preferred to $P$. Since

---

[20] When $r(x, y)$ takes the form $r(x, y) \equiv \nu(x)\tau(y) - \nu(y)\tau(x)$, this model will reduce to the (transitive) model of equation (6). This is the most general form of the model which is compatible with transitivity.
[21] In this model the indifference curves will all cross at the same point. This point will thus be indifferent to all lotteries in the triangle.

$r(x, y) \equiv -r(y, x)$ implies $\sum_i \sum_j r(x_i, x_j) p_i p_j \equiv 0$, we have that $P^*$ will be preferred to $P$ if and only if

$$
(10) \quad 0 < \sum_i \sum_j r(x_i, x_j) p_i^* p_j = \sum_i \sum_j r(x_i, x_j) p_i^* p_j - \sum_i \sum_j r(x_i, x_j) p_i p_j
$$

$$
= \sum_i \left[ \sum_j r(x_i, x_j) p_j \right] p_i^* - \sum_i \left[ \sum_j r(x_i, x_j) p_j \right] p_i
$$

$$
= \sum_i \phi(x_i; P) p_i^* - \sum_i \phi(x_i; P) p_i
$$

In other words, $P^*$ will be preferred to $P$ if and only if it implies a higher expectation of the "utility function" $\phi(x_i; P) \equiv \sum_j r(x_i, x_j) p_j$ than $P$. Thus if $\phi(x_i; P)$ is increasing in $x_i$ for all lotteries $P$ the individual will exhibit global stochastic dominance preference, and if $\phi(x_i; P)$ is concave in $x_i$ for all $P$ the individual will exhibit global risk aversion, even though he or she is not necessarily transitive (these conditions will clearly be satisfied if $r(x, y)$ is increasing and concave in $x$). The analytics of expected utility theory are robust indeed.

The developers of this model have shown how specific assumptions on the form of the regret/rejoice function will generate the common consequence effect, the common ratio effect, the preference reversal phenomenon, and other observed properties of choice over lotteries. The theoretical and empirical prospects for this approach accordingly seem quite impressive.

### Implications of the Psychological Worldview

On the other hand, how should economists respond if it turns out that the psychologists are right, and the preference reversal phenomenon really is generated by some form of response mode effect (or effects)? In that case, the first thing to do would be to try to determine if there were analogues of such effects in real-world economic situations.[22] Will individuals behave differently when determining their valuation of an object (e.g. reservation bid on a used car) than when reacting to a fixed and non-negotiable price for the same object? Since a proper test of this would require correcting for any possible strategic and/or information-theoretic (e.g. signalling) issues, it would not be a simple undertaking. However, in light of the experimental evidence, I feel it is crucial that we attempt it.

Say we found that response mode effects did not occur outside of the laboratory. In that case we could rest more easily, although we could not forget about such issues completely: experimenters testing other economic theories and models (e.g. auctions) would have to be forever mindful of the possible influence of the particular response mode used in their experimental design.

---

[22] It is important to note that neither the evidence of response mode effects (e.g. Slovic, 1975) nor their implications for economic analysis are confined to the case of choice under uncertainty.

On the other hand, what if we did find response mode effects out in the field? In that case we would want to determine, perhaps by going back to the laboratory, whether the rest of economic theory remained valid provided the response mode is held constant. If this were true, then with further evidence on exactly how the response mode mattered, we could presumably incorporate it as a new independent variable into existing theories. Since response modes tend to be constant within a given economic model, e.g. quantity responses to fixed prices in competitive markets, valuation announcements (truthful or otherwise) in auctions, etc., we should expect most of the testable implications of this approach to appear as cross-institutional predictions, such as systematic violations of the various equivalency results involving prices versus quantities or second price-sealed bid versus oral English auctions. In such a case, the new results and insights regarding our theories of institutions and mechanisms could be exciting indeed.[23]

## Framing Effects

### Evidence

In addition to response mode effects, psychologists have uncovered an even more disturbing phenomenon, namely that alternative means of representing or "framing" probabilistically equivalent choice problems will lead to systematic differences in choice. An early example of this phenomenon was reported by Slovic (1969), who found that offering a gain or loss contingent on the joint occurrence of four independent events with probability $p$ elicited different responses than offering it on the occurrence of a single event with probability $p^4$ (all probabilities were stated explicitly). In comparison with the single-event case, making a gain contingent on the joint occurrence of events was found to make it more attractive, and making a loss contingent on the joint occurrence of events made it more unattractive.

In another study, Payne and Braunstein (1971) used pairs of gambles of the type illustrated in Figure 10. Each of the gambles in the figure, known as a *duplex gamble*, involves spinning the pointers on both its "gain wheel" (on the left) and its "loss wheel" (on the right), with the individual receiving the sum of the resulting amounts. Thus an individual choosing Gamble A would win $.40 with probability .3 (i.e. if the pointer in the gain wheel landed up and the pointer in the loss wheel landed down), would lose $.40 with probability .2 (if the pointers landed in the opposite positions), and would break even with probability .5 (if the pointers landed either both up or both down). An examination of Gamble B reveals that it has an identical underlying distribution, so that subjects should be indifferent between the two gambles regardless

---

[23]A final "twist" on the preference reversal phenomenon: Holt (1986) and Karni and Safra (1987) have shown how the procedures used in most of these studies will only lead to truthful revelation of preferences under the added assumption that the individual satisfies the independence axiom, and has given examples of transitive non-expected utility preference rankings which lead to the typical "preference reversal" choices. How (and whether) experimenters will be able to address this issue remains to be seen.

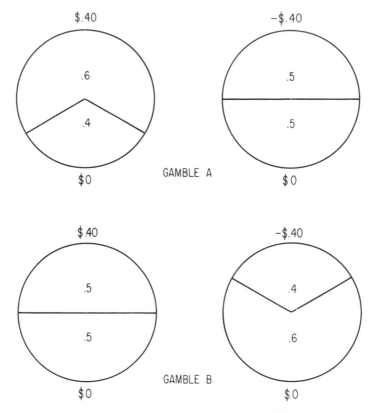

Fig. 10. Duplex gambles with identical underlying distributions

of their risk preferences. However, Payne and Braunstein found that individuals in fact chose between such gambles (and indicated nontrivial strengths of preference) in manners which were systematically affected by the attributes of the component wheels. When the probability of winning in the gain wheel was greater than the probability of losing in the loss wheel for each gamble (as in the figure), subjects tended to choose the gamble whose gain wheel yielded the greater probability of a gain (Gamble A). In cases where the probabilities of losing in the loss wheels were respectively greater than the probabilities of winning in the gain wheels, subjects tended toward the gamble with the lower probability of losing in the loss wheel.

Finally, although the gambles in Figure 10 possess identical underlying distributions, continuity suggests that a slight worsening of the terms of the preferred gamble could result in a pair of non-equivalent duplex gambles in which the individual will actually choose the one with the stochastically dominated underlying distribution. In an experiment where the subjects were allowed to construct their own duplex gambles by choosing one from a pair of prospects involving gains and one from a pair of prospects involving losses, stochastically dominated prospects were indeed chosen (Tversky and Kahneman, 1981).[24]

A second class of framing effects involves the phenomenon of a *reference point*. Theoretically, the variable which enters an individual's von Neumann-Morgenstern utility function should be total (i.e. final) wealth, and gambles phrased in terms of gains and losses should be combined with current wealth and re-expressed as distributions over final wealth levels before being evaluated. However, economists since Markowitz (1952) have observed that risk attitudes over gains and losses are more stable than can be explained by a fixed utility function over final wealth, and have suggested that the utility function might be best defined in terms of changes from the "reference point" of current wealth. This stability of risk attitudes in the face of wealth variations has also been observed in several experimental studies.[25]

Markowitz (p. 155) also suggested that certain circumstances may cause the individual's reference point to temporarily deviate from current wealth. If these circumstances include the manner in which a given problem is verbally described, then differing risk attitudes over gains and losses can lead to different choices depending upon the exact description. A simple example of this, from Kahneman and Tversky (1979), involves the following two questions:

In addition to whatever you own, you have been given 1,000 (Israeli pounds). You are now asked to choose between a $1/2 : 1/2$ chance of a gain of 1,000 or 0 or a sure gain of 500.

and

In addition to whatever you own, you have been given 2,000. You are now asked to choose between a $1/2 : 1/2$ chance of loss of 1,000 or 0 or a sure loss of 500.

These two problems involve identical distributions over final wealth. However, when put to two different groups of subjects, 84 percent chose the sure gain in the first problem but 69 percent chose the $1/2 : 1/2$ gamble in the second. A nonmonetary version of this type of example, from Tversky and Kahneman (1981, 1986), posits the following scenario:

Imagine that the U.S. is preparing for the outbreak of an unusual Asian disease, which is expected to kill 600 people. Two alternative programs to combat the disease have been proposed. Assume that the exact scientific estimate of the

---

[24]Subjects were asked to choose either (A) a sure gain of $240 or (B) a $1/4 : 3/4$ chance of $1,000 or $0, and to choose either (C) a sure loss of $750 or (D) a $3/4 : 1/4$ chance of $-$1,000 or 0. 84 percent chose A over B and 87 percent chose D over C, even though B + C dominates A + D, and choices over the combined distributions were unanimous when they were presented explicitly.

[25]See the discussion and references in Machina (1982, pp. 285–86).

consequences of the programs are as follows:

If program A is adopted, 200 people will be saved.

If Program B is adopted, there is 1/3 probability that 600 people will be saved, and 2/3 probability that no people will be saved.

Seventy-two percent of the subjects who were presented with this form of the question chose Program A. A second group was given the same initial information, but the descriptions of the programs were changed to read:

If Program C is adopted 400 people will die.

If Program D is adopted there is 1/3 probability that nobody will die, and 2/3 probability that 600 people will die.

Although this statement of the problem is once again identical to the former one, 78 percent of the respondents chose Program D.

In other studies, Schoemaker and Kunreuther (1979), Hershey and Schoemaker (1980), McNeil, Pauker, Sox and Tversky (1982) and Slovic, Fischhoff and Lichtenstein (1982) have found that subjects' choices in otherwise identical problems will depend upon whether they are phrased as decisions whether or not to gamble or whether or not to insure, whether the statistical information for different therapies is presented in terms of cumulative survival probabilities or cumulative mortality probabilities, etc. For similar examples of this phenomenon in non-stochastic situations, see Thaler (1980).

In a final class of examples, not based on reference point effects, Moskowitz (1974) and Keller (1982) found that the proportion of subjects choosing in conformance with or in violation of the independence axiom in examples like the Allais Paradox was significantly affected by whether the problems were described in the standard matrix form (e.g. Raiffa, 1968, p. 7), decision tree form, or as minimally structured written statements. Interestingly enough, the form which was judged the "clearest representation" by the majority of Moskowitz's subjects (the tree form) led to the lowest degree of consistency with the independence axiom, the highest proportion of fanning out choices, and the highest persistency rate of these choices (pp. 234, 237–38).

### Two Issues Regarding Framing

The replicability and pervasiveness of the above types of examples is indisputable. However, before being able to assess their implications for economic modelling we need to resolve two issues.

The first issue is whether these experimental observations possess any analogue outside of the laboratory. Since real-world decision problems do not present themselves as neatly packaged as the ones on experimental questionnaires, monitoring such effects would not be as straightforward. However this does not mean that they do not exist, or that they cannot be objectively observed or quantitatively measured. The real-world example which comes most quickly to mind, and is presumably of no small importance to the involved parties, is whether gasoline price differentials should be represented as "cash discounts" or "credit surcharges." Similarly, Russo, Krieser and Miyashita (1975) and Russo (1977) found that the practice, and even method, of displaying unit price information in supermarkets (information which consumers could calculate for themselves) affected both the level and distribution of consumer expenditures. The empirical marketing literature is no doubt replete with findings that we could legitimately interpret as real-world framing effects.

The second, more difficult issue is that of the independent observability of the particular frame that an individual will adopt in a given problem. In the duplex gamble and matrix/decision tree/written statement examples of the previous section, the different frames seem unambiguously determined by the form of presentation. However, in instances where framing involves the choice of a reference point, which presumably include the majority of real-world cases, this point might not be objectively determined by the form of presentation, and might be chosen differently, and what is worse, unobservably, by each individual.[26] In a particularly thorough and insightful study, Fischhoff (1983) presented subjects with a written decision problem which allowed for different choices of a reference point, and explored different ways of predicting which frame individuals would adopt, in order to be able to predict their actual choices. While the majority choice of subjects was consistent with what would appear to be the most appropriate frame, Fischhoff noted "the absence of any relation within those studies between [separately elicited] frame preference and option preference." Indeed to the extent that frame preferences varied across his experiments, they did so inversely to the incidence of the predicted choice.[27] If such problems can occur in predicting responses to specific written questions in the laboratory, imagine how they could plague the modelling of real world choice behavior.

### Framing Effects and Economic Analysis: Have We Already Solved this Problem?

How should we respond if it turns out that framing actually is a real-world phenomenon of economic relevance, and in particular, if individuals' frames cannot always be observed? I would argue that the means of responding to this issue can already be found in the "tool box" of existing economic analysis.

Consider first the case where the frame of a given economic decision problem, even though it should not matter from the point of view of standard theory, can at least be independently and objectively observed. I believe that economists have in fact already solved such a problem in their treatment of the phenomenon of "uninformative advertising." Although it is hard to give a formal definition of this term, it is widely felt that economic theory is hard put to explain a large proportion of current advertising in terms of traditional informational considerations.[28] However, this has

---

[26] This is not to say that well-defined reference points never exist. The reference points involved in credit surcharges vs. cash discounts, for example, seem unambiguous.

[27] Fischhoff (1983, pp. 115–16). Fischhoff notes that "If one can only infer frames from preferences after assuming the truth of the theory, one runs the risk of making the theory itself untestable."

[28] A wonderful example, offered by my colleague Joel Sobel, are milk ads which make no reference to either price or a specific dairy. What could be a more well-known commodity than milk?

hardly led economists to abandon classical consumer theory. Rather, models of uninformative advertising proceed by quantifying this variable (e.g. air time) and treating it as an additional independent variable in the utility and/or demand function. Standard results like the Slutsky equation need not be abandoned, but rather simply reinterpreted as properties of demand functions holding this new variable constant. The amount of advertising itself is determined as a maximizing variable on the part of the firm (given some cost curve), and can be subjected to standard comparative static analysis.

In the case when decision frames can be observed, framing effects can presumably be modelled in an analogous manner. To do so, we would begin by adopting a method of quantifying, or at least categorizing, frames. The second step, some of which has of course already been done, is to study both the effect of this new independent variable holding the standard economic variables constant, and conversely, to retest our standard economic theories in conditions where we carefully held the frame fixed. With any luck we would find that, holding the frame constant, the Slutsky equation still held.

The next step in any given modelling situation would be to ask "who determines the frame?" If (as with advertising) it is the firm, then the effect of the frame upon consumer demand, and hence upon firm profits, can be incorporated into the firm's maximization problem, and the choice of the frame as well as the other relevant variables (e.g. prices and quantities) can be simultaneously determined and subjected to comparative static analysis, just as in the case of uninformative advertising.

A seemingly more difficult case is when the individual chooses the frame (for example, a reference point) and this choice cannot be observed. Although we should not forget the findings of Fischhoff (1983), assume that this choice is at least systematic in the sense that the consumer will jointly choose the frame and make the subsequent decision in a manner which maximizes a "utility function" which depends both on the decision and the choice of frame. In other words, individuals make their choices as part of a joint maximization problem, the other component of which (the choice of frame or reference point) cannot be observed.

Such models are hardly new to economic analysis. Indeed, most economic models presume that the agent is simultaneously maximizing with respect to variables other than the ones being studied. When assumptions are made on the individual's joint preferences over the observed and unobserved variables, the well-developed *theory of induced preferences*[29] can be used to derive testable implications on choice behavior over the observables. With a little more knowledge on exactly how frames are chosen, such an approach could presumably be applied here as well.

The above remarks should not be taken as implying that we have already solved the problem of framing in economic analysis or that there is no need to adapt, and if necessary abandon, our standard models in light of this phenomenon. Rather, they

---

[29] E.g. Milne (1981). For an application of the theory of induced preferences to choice under uncertainty, see Machina (1984).

reflect the view that when psychologists are able to hand us enough systematic evidence on how these effects operate, economists will be able to respond accordingly.

## Other Issues: Is Probability Theory Relevant?

### The Manipulation of Subjective Probabilities

The evidence discussed so far has primarily consisted of cases where subjects have been presented with explicit (i.e. "objective") probabilities as part of their decision problems, and the models which have addressed these phenomena possess the corresponding property of being defined over objective probability distributions. However, there is extensive evidence that when individuals have to estimate or revise probabilities for themselves they will make systematic mistakes in doing so.

The psychological literature on the processing of probabilistic information is much too large even to summarize here. However, it is worth noting that experimenters have uncovered several "heuristics" used by subjects which can lead to predictable errors in the formation and manipulation of subjective probabilities. Kahneman and Tversky (1973), Bar-Hillel (1974) and Grether (1980), for example, have found that probability updating systematically departs from Bayes Law in the direction of underweighting prior information and overweighting the "representativeness" of the current sample. In a related phenomenon termed the "law of small numbers," Tversky and Kahneman (1971) found that individuals overestimated the probability of drawing a perfectly representative sample out of a heterogeneous population. Finally, Bar-Hillel (1973), Tversky and Kahneman (1983) and others have found systematic biases in the formation of the probabilities of conjunctions of both independent and non-independent events. For surveys, discussions and examples of the psychological literature on the formation and handling of probabilities see Edwards, Lindman and Savage (1963), Slovic and Lichtenstein (1971), Tversky and Kahneman (1974) and the collections in *Acta Psychologica* (December 1970), Kahneman, Slovic and Tversky (1982) and Arkes and Hammond (1986). For examples of how economists have responded to some of these issues see Arrow (1982), Viscusi (1985) and the references cited there.

### The Existence of Subjective Probabilities

The evidence referred to above indicates that when individuals are asked to formulate probabilities they do not do it correctly. However, these findings may be rendered moot by evidence which suggests that when individuals making decisions under uncertainty are not explicitly asked to form subjective probabilities, they might not do it (or even act as if doing it) at all.

In one of a class of examples due to Ellsberg (1961), subjects were presented with a pair of urns, the first containing 50 red balls and 50 black balls and the second also containing 100 red and black balls but in an unknown proportion. When faced with the choice of staking a prize on: ($R_1$) drawing a red ball from the first urn, ($R_2$)

drawing a red ball from the second urn, $(B_1)$ drawing a black ball from the first urn, or $(B_2)$ drawing a black ball from the second urn, a majority of subjects strictly preferred $(R_1)$ over $(R_2)$ and strictly preferred $(B_1)$ over $(B_2)$. It is clear that there can exist no subjectively assigned probabilities $p: (1 - p)$ of drawing a red vs. black ball from the second urn, even $1/2 : 1/2$, which can simultaneously generate both of these strict preferences. Similar behavior in this and related problems has been observed by Raiffa (1961), Becker and Brownson (1964), Slovic and Tversky (1974) and MacCrimmon and Larsson (1979).

### Life (and Economic Analysis) Without Probabilities

One response to this type of phenomenon has been to suppose that individuals "slant" whatever subjective probabilities they might otherwise form in a manner which reflects the amount of confidence/ambiguity associated with them (Fellner, 1961; Becker and Brownson, 1964; Fishburn, 1986; Hogarth and Kunreuther, 1986). In the case of the complete ignorance regarding probabilities, Arrow and Hurwicz (1972), Maskin (1979) and others have presented axioms which imply principles such as ranking options solely on the basis of their worst and/or best outcomes (e.g. maximin, maximax), the unweighted average of their outcomes ("principle of insufficient reason"), or similar criteria.[30] Finally, generalizations of expected utility theory which drop the standard additivity and/or compounding laws of probability theory have been developed by Schmeidler (1986) and Segal (1987).

Although the above models may well capture aspects of actual decision processes, the analytically most useful approach to choice in the presence of uncertainty but the absence of probabilities is the so-called *state-preference* model of Arrow (1953/1964), Debreu (1959) and Hirshleifer (1966). In this model uncertainty is represented by a set of mutually exclusive and exhaustive *states of nature* $S = \{ s_i \}$. This partition of all possible unfoldings of the future could be either very coarse, such as the pair of states {it rains here tomorrow, it doesn't rain here tomorrow} or else very fine, so that the definition of a state might read "it rains here tomorrow and the temperature at Gibraltar is 75° at noon and the price of gold in New York is below \$700.00/ounce." Note that it is neither feasible nor desirable to capture all conceivable sources of uncertainty when specifying the set of states for a given problem: it is not feasible since no matter how finely the states are defined there will always be some other random criterion on which to further divide them, and not desirable since such criteria may affect neither individuals' preferences nor their opportunities. Rather, the key requirements are that the states be mutually exclusive and exhaustive so that exactly one will be realized, and (for purposes of the present discussion) that the individual cannot influence which state will actually occur.

Given a fixed (and say finite) set of states, the objects of choice in this framework consist of alternative *state-payoff bundles*, each of which specifies the outcome the individual will receive in every possible state. When the outcomes are monetary payoffs, for example, state-payoff bundles take the form $(c_1, \ldots, c_n)$, where $c_i$ denotes

---

[30] For an excellent discussion of the history, nature and limitations of such approaches, see Arrow (1951).

the payoff the individual would receive should state $s_i$ occur. In the case of exactly two states of nature we could represent this set by the points in the $(c_1, c_2)$ plane. Since bundles of the form $(c, c)$ represent prospects which yield the same payoff in each state of nature, the $45°$ line in this plane is known as the *certainty line*.

Now if the individual did happen to assign probabilities $\{p_i\}$ to the states $\{s_i\}$, each bundle $(c_1, \ldots, c_n)$ would imply a specific probability distribution over wealth, and we could infer his or her preferences (i.e. indifference curves) over state-payoff bundles. However, since these bundles are defined directly over the respective states and without reference to any probabilities, it is also possible to speak of preferences over these bundles without making any assumptions regarding the coherency, or even existence, of such probabilistic beliefs. Researchers such as the ones cited above as well as Yaari (1969), Diamond and Yaari (1972) and Mishan (1976) have shown how this indifference curve-based approach can be used to derive results from individual demand behavior through general equilibrium in a context which requires neither the expected utility hypothesis nor the existence or commonality of subjective probabilities. In other words, life without probabilities does not imply life without economic analysis.

### Final Thoughts

*Welfare Implications.* Although the theme of this paper has been the descriptive theory of choice under uncertainty, another important issue is the implications of these developments for normative economics. Can welfare analysis be conducted in the type of world implied by the above models?

The answer to this question depends upon the model. Fanning-out behavior and the non-expected utility models used to characterize it, as well as the state-payoff approach of the previous section, are completely consistent with the assumption of well-defined, transitive individual preference orderings, and hence with traditional welfare analysis along the lines of Pareto, Bergson and Samuelson (e.g. Samuelson, 1947/1983, Ch. VIII). For example, the proof of Pareto-efficiency of a system of complete contingent-commodity markets (Arrow, 1953/1964; Debreu, 1959, Ch. 7) requires neither the expected utility hypothesis nor the assumption of well-defined probabilistic beliefs. On the other hand, it is clear that the preference reversal phenomenon and framing effects, and at least some of the non-transitive and/or non-economic models used to address them, will prove much more difficult to reconcile with welfare analysis, at least as currently practiced.

*A Unified Model?* Another issue is the lack of a unified model capable of simultaneously handling all of the phenomena described in this paper: fanning-out, the preference reversal phenomenon, framing effects, probability biases and the Ellsberg paradox. After all, it is presumably the same ("typical") individuals who are exhibiting each of these phenomena—shouldn't there be a single model out there capable of generating them all?

Although I am doubtful of our present ability to do this, I am also doubtful about the need to establish a unified model as a prerequisite for continued progress. The aspects of behavior considered in this paper are very diverse, and if (like the wave versus particle properties of light) they cannot be currently unified, this does not mean that we cannot continue to learn by studying and modelling them separately.

*An Essential Criterion.* The evidence and theories reported in this paper have taken us a long way from the classical expected utility approach presented at the outset. To what extent will these new models be incorporated into mainstream economic thought and practice? I believe the answer will depend upon a single factor: the extent to which they can address the important issues in the economics of uncertainty, such as search, investment, bargaining or auctions, to which the expected utility model has been so usefully applied.

■ *I am grateful to Brian Binger, John Conlisk, Jim Cox, Vincent Crawford, Gong Jin Dong, Elizabeth Hoffman, Michael Rothschild, Carl Shapiro, Vernon Smith, Joseph Stiglitz, Timothy Taylor and especially Joel Sobel for helpful discussions on this material, and the Alfred P. Sloan Foundation for financial support.*

# References

**Akerlof, George A.,** "The Market for 'Lemons': Quality Uncertainty and the Market Mechanism," *Quarterly Journal of Economics*, August 1970, *84*, 488–500.

**Allais, Maurice,** "Le Comportement de l'Homme Rationel devant le Risque, Critique des Postulates et Axiomes de l'École Americaine," *Econometrica*, October 1953, *21*, 503–46.

**Allais, Maurice,** "The Foundations of a Positive Theory of Choice Involving Risk and a Criticism of the Postulates and Axioms of the American School," in Allais and Hagen (1979).

**Allais, Maurice and Ole Hagen,** eds., *Expected Utility Hypotheses and the Allais Paradox*. Dordrecht, Holland: D. Reidel, 1979.

**Allen, Beth,** "Smooth Preferences and the Local Expected Utility Hypothesis," *Journal of Economic Theory*, 1987, forthcoming.

**Arkes, Hal R. and Kenneth R. Hammond,** eds., *Judgement and Decision Making: An Interdisciplinary Reader*. Cambridge: Cambridge University Press, 1986.

**Arrow, Kenneth J.,** "Alternative Approaches to the Theory of Choice in Risk-Taking Situations," *Econometrica*, October 1951, *19*, 404–37. Reprinted in Arrow (1965).

**Arrow, Kenneth J.,** "Le Role des Valeurs Boursières pour la Répartition le meilleure des risques," *Économetrie*, Colloques Internationaux du Centre National de la Recherche Scientifique, Paris, 1953, *40*, 41–47. English translation: *Review of Economic Studies*, April 1964, *31*, 91–96.

**Arrow, Kenneth J.,** *Aspects of the Theory of Risk-Bearing*, Helsinki: Yrjo Jahnsson Saatio, 1965.

**Arrow, Kenneth J.,** "Risk Perception in Psychology and Economics," *Economic Inquiry*, January 1982, *20*, 1–9.

**Arrow, Kenneth J. and Leonid Hurwicz,** "An Optimality Criterion for Decision-Making under Ignorance." In Carter, C. F. and J. L. Ford, eds., *Uncertainty and Expectations in Economics*. Oxford: Basil Blackwell, 1972.

**Bar-Hillel, Maya,** "On the Subjective Probability of Compound Events," *Organizational Behavior and Human Performance*, June 1973, *9*, 396–406.

**Bar-Hillel, Maya,** "Similarity and Probability," *Organizational Behavior and Human Performance*, April 1974, *11*, 277–82.

**Battalio, Raymond C., John H. Kagel and Don N. MacDonald,** "Animals' Choices over Uncertain Outcomes," *American Economic Review*, September 1985, *75*, 597–613.

**Becker, Selwyn W. and Fred O. Brownson,** "What Price Ambiguity? Or the Role of Ambiguity in Decision-Making," *Journal of Political Economy*, February 1964, *72*, 62–73.

Becker, Gordon M., Morris H. DeGroot and Jacob Marschak, "Measuring Utility by a Single-Response Sequential Method," *Behavioral Science*, July 1964, *9*, 226–32.

Bell, David E., "Regret in Decision Making Under Uncertainty," *Operations Research*, September–October 1982, *30*, 961–81.

Bell, David E., "Disappointment in Decision Making Under Uncertainty," *Operations Research*, January–February 1985, *33*, 1–27.

Berg, Joyce E., John W. Dickhaut and John R. O'Brien, "Preference Reversal and Arbitrage," manuscript, University of Minnesota, September 1983.

Bernoulli, Daniel, "Specimen Theoriae Novae de Mensura Sortis," *Commentarii Academiae Scientiarum Imperialis Petropolitanae*, 1738, *5*, 175–92. English translation: *Econometrica*, January 1954, *22*, 23–36.

Blyth, Colin R., "Some Probability Paradoxes in Choice from Among Random Alternatives," *Journal of the American Statistical Association*, June 1972, *67*, 366–73.

Chew Soo Hong, "A Generalization of the Quasilinear Mean With Applications to the Measurement of Income Inequality and Decision Theory Resolving The Allais Paradox," *Econometrica*, July 1983, *51*, 1065–92.

Chew Soo Hong, Edi Karni and Zvi Safra, "Risk Aversion in the Theory of Expected Utility with Rank Dependent Probabilities," *Journal of Economic Theory*, 1987, forthcoming.

Chew Soo Hong and William Waller, "Empirical Tests of Weighted Utility Theory," *Journal of Mathematical Psychology*, March 1986, *30*, 55–72.

Debreu, Gerard, *Theory of Value: An Axiomatic Analysis of General Equilibrium*. New Haven: Yale University Press, 1959.

Diamond, Peter A. and Menaham Yaari, "Implications of the Theory of Rationing for Consumer Choice Under Uncertainty," *American Economic Review*, June 1972, *62*, 333–43.

Edwards, Ward, "The Theory of Decision Making," *Psychological Bulletin*, July 1954, *51*, 380–417.

Edwards, Ward, "The Prediction of Decisions Among Bets," *Journal of Experimental Psychology*, September 1955, *50*, 201–14.

Edwards, Ward, Harold Lindman and Leonard J. Savage, "Bayesian Statistical Inference for Psychological Research," *Psychological Review*, May 1963, *70*, 193–242.

Ellsberg, Daniel, "Risk, Ambiguity and the Savage Axioms," *Quarterly Journal of Economics*, November 1961, *75*, 643–69.

Epstein, Larry, "Decreasing Risk Aversion and Mean-Variance Analysis," *Econometrica*, 1985, *53*, 945–61.

Fellner, William, "Distortion of Subjective Probabilities as a Reaction to Uncertainty," *Quarterly Journal of Economics*, November 1961, *75*, 670–89.

Fischhoff, Baruch, "Predicting Frames," *Journal of Experimental Psychology: Learning, Memory and Cognition*, January 1983, *9*, 103–16.

Fishburn, Peter C., "Nontransitive Measurable Utility," *Journal of Mathematical Psychology*, August 1982, *26*, 31–67.

Fishburn, Peter C., "Transitive Measurable Utility," *Journal of Economic Theory*, December 1983, *31*, 293–317.

Fishburn, Peter C., "SSB Utility Theory: An Economic Perspective," *Mathematical Social Sciences*, 1984, *8*, 63–94.

Fishburn, Peter C., "A New Model for Decisions Under Uncertainty," *Economics Letters*, 1986, *21*, 127–30.

Friedman, Milton and Leonard J. Savage, "The Utility Analysis of Choices Involving Risk," *Journal of Political Economy*, August 1948, *56*, 279–304.

Grether, David M., "Bayes Rule as a Descriptive Model: The Representativeness Heuristic," *Quarterly Journal of Economics*, November 1980, *95*, 537–57.

Grether, David M. and Charles R. Plott, "Economic Theory of Choice and the Preference Reversal Phenomenon," *American Economic Review*, September 1979, *69*, 623–38.

Hagen, Ole, "Towards a Positive Theory of Preferences Under Risk," in Allais and Hagen (1979).

Hershey, John C. and Paul J. H. Schoemaker, "Risk-Taking and Problem Context in the Domain of Losses—An Expected Utility Analysis," *Journal of Risk and Insurance*, March 1980 *47*, 111–32.

Hershey, John C. and Paul J. H. Schoemaker, "Probability Versus Certainty Equivalence Methods in Utility Measurement: Are They Equivalent?," *Management Science*, October 1985, *31*, 1213–31.

Hirshleifer, Jack, "Investment Decision Under Uncertainty: Applications of the State-Preference Approach," *Quarterly Journal of Economics*, May 1966, *80*, 252–77.

Hogarth, Robin, "Cognitive Processes and the Assessment of Subjective Probability Distributions," *Journal of the American Statistical Association*, June 1975, *70*, 271–89.

Hogarth, Robin and Howard Kunreuther, "Decision Making Under Ambiguity," *Journal of Business*, October 1986, Prt. 2, *4*, 225–50.

Holt, Charles A., "Preference Reversals and the Independence Axiom," *American Economic Review*, June 1986, *76*, 508–15.

Kahneman, Daniel, Paul Slovic and Amos Tversky, eds., *Judgement Under Uncertainty: Heuristics and Biases*, Cambridge: Cambridge University Press, 1982.

Kahneman, Daniel and Amos Tversky, "On the Psychology of Prediction," *Psychological Review*, July 1973, *80* 237–51.

Kahneman, Daniel and Amos Tversky, "Prospect Theory: An Analysis of Decision Under Risk," *Econometrica*, March 1979, *47*, 263–91.

Karmarkar, Uday S., "The Effect of Probabilities on the Subjective Evaluation of Lotteries," Massachusetts Institute of Technology Sloan School of Business Working Paper, 1974.

Karmarkar, Uday S., "Subjectively Weighted Utility: A Descriptive Extension of the Expected Utility Model," *Organizational Behavior and Human Performance*, February 1978, *21*, 61–72.

Karni, Edi and Zvi Safra, "'Preference Reversal' and the Observability of Preferences by Experimental Methods," *Econometrica*, 1987, forthcoming.

Keller, L. Robin, "The Effects of Decision Problem Representation on Utility Conformance," manuscript, University of California, Irvine, 1982.

Knetsch, Jack L. and J. A. Sinden. "Willingness to Pay and Compensation Demanded: Experimental Evidence of an Unexpected Disparity in Measures of Value," *Quarterly Journal of Economics*, August 1984, *99*, 507–21.

Knez, Marc and Vernon L. Smith, "Hypothetical Valuations and Preference Reversals in the Context of Asset Trading," manuscript, University of Arizona, 1986.

Lichtenstein, Sarah and Paul Slovic, "Reversals of Preferences Between Bids and Choices in Gambling Decisions," *Journal of Experimental Psychology*, July 1971, *89*, 46–55.

Lichtenstein, Sarah and Paul Slovic, "Response-Induced Reversals of Preference in Gambling: An Extended Replication in Las Vegas," *Journal of Experimental Psychology*, November 1973, *101*, 16–20.

Lindman, Harold, "Inconsistent Preferences Among Gambles," *Journal of Experimental Psychology*, May 1971, *89*, 390–97.

Loomes, Graham and Robert Sugden, "Regret Theory: An Alternative Theory of Rational Choice Under Uncertainty," *Economic Journal*, December 1982, *92*, 805–24.

MacCrimmon, Kenneth R., "Descriptive and Normative Implications of the Decision-Theory Postulates." In Borch Karl H., and Jan Mossin, eds., *Risk and Uncertainty: Proceedings of a Conference Held by the International Economic Association*. London: Macmillan, 1968.

MacCrimmon, Kenneth R. and Stig Larsson, "Utility Theory: Axioms Versus 'Paradoxes,'" in Allais and Hagen (1979).

MacCrimmon, Kenneth R. and Donald A. Wehrung, *Taking Risks: The Management of Uncertainty*, New York: The Free Press, 1986.

Machina, Mark J., "'Expected Utility' Analysis Without the Independence Axiom," *Econometrica*, March 1982, *50*, 277–323.

Machina, Mark J., "The Economic Theory of Individual Behavior Toward Risk: Theory, Evidence and New Directions," Stanford University Institute for Mathematical Studies in the Social Sciences Technical Report, 1983a.

Machina, Mark J., "Generalized Expected Utility Analysis and the Nature of Observed Violations of the Independence Axiom," 1983b, in Stigum and Wenstøp (1983).

Machina, Mark J., "Temporal Risk and the Nature of Induced Preferences," *Journal of Economic Theory*, August 1984, *33*, 199–231.

Markowitz, Harry "The Utility of Wealth," *Journal of Political Economy*, April 1952, *60*, 151–58.

Marschak, Jacob, "Rational Behavior, Uncertain Prospects, and Measurable Utility," *Econometrica*, April 1950, *18*, 111–41. "Errata," *Econometrica*, July 1950, *18*, 312.

Mas-Colell, Andreu, "An Equilibrium Existence Theorem Without Complete or Transitive Preferences," *Journal of Mathematical Economics*, December 1974, *3*, 237–46.

Maskin, Eric, "Decision Making Under Ignorance with Implications for Social Choice," *Theory and Decision*, September 1979, *11*, 319–37.

May, Kenneth O., "Intransitivity, Utility, and the Aggregation of Preference Patterns," *Econometrica*, January 1954, *22*, 1–13.

McCord, Marc and Richard de Neufville, "Empirical Demonstration that Expected Utility Analysis Is Not Operational." In Stigum and Wenstøp (1983).

McCord, Marc and Richard de Neufville, "Utility Dependence on Probability: An Empirical Demonstration," *Large Scale Systems*, February 1984, *6*, 91–103.

McNeil, Barbara J., Stephen G. Pauker, Harold C. Sox, Jr. and Amos Tversky, "On the Elicitation of Preferences for Alternative Therapies," *New England Journal of Medicine*, May 1982, *306*, 1259–62.

Milne, Frank, "Induced Preferences and the Theory of the Consumer," *Journal of Economic Theory*, April 1981, *24*, 205–17.

Mishan, E. J., "Choices Involving Risk: Simple Steps Toward an Ordinalist Analysis," *Economic Journal*, December 1976, *86*, 759–77.

Morrison, Donald G., "On the Consistency of Preferences in Allais' Paradox," *Behavioral Science*, September 1967, *12*, 373–83.

Moskowitz, Herbert, "Effects of Problem Representation and Feedback on Rational Behavior in Allais and Morlat-Type Problems," *Decision Sciences*, 1974, *5*, 225–42.

**Mowen, John C. and James W. Gentry**, "Investigation of the Preference-Reversal Phenomenon in a New Product Introduction Task," *Journal of Applied Psychology*, December 1980, *65*, 715–22.

**Payne, John W. and Myron L. Braunstein**, "Preferences Among Gambles with Equal Underlying Distributions," *Journal of Experimental Psychology*, January 1971, *87*, 13–18.

**Pommerehne, Werner W., Friedrich Schneider and Peter Zweifel**, "Economic Theory of Choice and the Preference Reversal Phenomenon: A Re-examinaton," *American Economic Review*, June 1982, *72*, 569–74.

**Pratt, John W.**, "Risk Aversion in the Small and in the Large," *Econometrica*, January/April 1964, *32*, 122–36.

**Quiggin, John**, "A Theory of Anticipated Utility," *Journal of Economic Behavior and Organization*, December 1982, *3*, 323–43.

**Raiffa, Howard**, "Risk, Ambiguity, and the Savage Axioms," *Quarterly Journal of Economics*, November 1961, *75*, 690–94.

**Raiffa, Howard**, *Decision Analysis: Introductory Lectures on Choice Under Uncertainty*. Reading, Mass.: Addison-Wesley, 1968.

**Reilly, Robert J.**, "Preference Reversal: Further Evidence and Some Suggested Modifications of Experimental Design," *American Economic Review*, June 1982, *72*, 576–84.

**Rothschild, Michael and Joseph E. Stiglitz**, "Increasing Risk: I. A Definition," *Journal of Economic Theory*, September 1970, *2*, 225–43.

**Russo, J. Edward**, "The Value of Unit Price Information," *Journal of Marketing Research*, May 1977, *14*, 193–201.

**Russo, J. Edward, Gene Krieser and Sally Miyashita**, "An Effective Display of Unit Price Information," *Journal of Marketing*, April 1975, *39*, 11–19.

**Samuelson, Paul A.**, *Foundations of Economic Analysis*, Cambridge, Mass.: Harvard University Press, 1947. Enlarged Edition, 1983.

**Samuelson, Paul A.**, *Foundations of Economic Analysis*, Cambridge, Mass.: Harvard University Press, 1947. Enlarged Edition, 1983.

**Savage, Leonard J.**, *The Foundations of Statistics*, New York: Wiley, 1954. Revised and Enlarged Edition, New York: Dover, 1972.

**Schmeidler, David**, "Subjective Probability and Expected Utility Without Additivity," manuscript, Tel-Aviv University, 1986.

**Schoemaker, Paul J. H. and Howard Kunreuther**, "An Experimental Study of Insurance Decisions," *Journal of Risk and Insurance*, December 1979, *46*, 603–18.

**Segal, Uzi**, "Nonlinear Decision Weights with the Independence Axiom," manuscript, University of California, Los Angeles, November 1984.

**Segal, Uzi**, "The Ellsberg Paradox and Risk Aversion: An Anticipated Utility Approach," *International Economic Review*, 1987, forthcoming.

**Shafer, Wayne J.**, "The Nontransitive Consumer," *Econometrica*, September 1974, *42*, 913–19.

**Slovic, Paul**, "Manipulating the Attractiveness of a Gamble Without Changing its Expected Value," *Journal of Experimental Psychology*, January 1969, *79*, 139–45.

**Slovic, Paul**, "Choice Between Equally Valued Alternatives," *Journal of Experimental Psychology: Human Perception and Performance*, August 1975, *1*, 280–87.

**Slovic, Paul, Baruch Fischhoff and Sarah Lichtenstein**, "Response Mode, Framing, and Information Processing Effects in Risk Assessment." In Hogarth, Robin ed., *New Directions for Methodology of Social and Behavioral Science: Question Framing and Response Consistency*. San Francisco: Jossey-Bass, 1982.

**Slovic, Paul, Baruch Fischhoff and Sarah Lichtenstein**, "Relative Importance of Probabilities and Payoffs in Risk Taking," *Journal of Experimental Psychology*, November 1968, Prt. 2, *78*, 1–18.

**Slovic, Paul, Baruch Fischhoff and Sarah Lichtenstein**, "Comparison of Bayesian and Regression Approaches to the Study of Information Processing in Judgment," *Organizational Behavior and Human Performance*, November 1971, *6*, 649–744.

**Slovic, Paul, Baruch Fischhoff and Sarah Lichtenstein**, "Preference Reversals: A Broader Perspective," *American Economic Review*, September 1983, *73*, 596–605.

**Slovic, Paul and Amos Tversky**, "Who Accepts Savage's Axiom?," *Behavioral Science*, November 1974, *19*, 368–73.

**Sonnenschein, Hugo F.**, "Demand Theory Without Transitive Preferences, With Applications to the Theory of Competitive Equilibrium," In Chipman, John S., Leonid Hurwicz, Marcel K. Richter, and Hugo F. Sonnenschein, eds., *Preferences, Utility and Demand*. New York: Harcourt Brace Jovanovich, 1971.

**Spence, A. Michael and Richard J. Zeckhauser**, "Insurance, Information and Individual Action," *American Economic Review Papers and Proceedings*, May 1971, *61*, 380–87.

**Stigum, Bernt and Fred Wenstøp**, *Foundations of Utility and Risk Theory with Applications*, Dordrecht, Holland: D. Reidel, 1983.

**Sugden, Robert**, "New Developments in the Theory of Choice Under Uncertainty," *Bulletin of*

82

*Economic Research*, January 1986, *38*, 1–24.

Thaler, Richard, "Toward a Positive Theory of Consumer Choice," *Journal of Economic Behavior and Organization*, March 1980, *1*, 39–60.

Tversky, Amos, "Intransitivity of Preferences," *Psychological Review*, January 1969, *76*, 31–48.

Tversky, Amos, "A Critique of Expected Utility Theory: Descriptive and Normative Considerations," *Erkenntnis*, 1975, *9*, 163–73.

Tversky, Amos and Daniel Kahneman, "Belief in the Law of Small Numbers," *Psychological Bulletin*, July 1971, *2*, 105–10.

Tversky, Amos and Daniel Kahneman, "Judgement under Uncertainty: Heuristics and Biases," *Science*, September 1974, *185*, 1124–31.

Tversky, Amos and Daniel Kahneman, "The Framing of Decisions and the Psychology of Choice," *Science*, January 1981, *211*, 453–58.

Tversky, Amos and Daniel Kahneman, "Extensional vs. Intuitive Reasoning: The Conjunction Fallacy in Probability Judgment," *Psychological Review*, October 1983, *90*, 293–315.

Tversky, Amos and Daniel Kahneman, "Rational Choice and the Framing of Decisions," *Journal of Business*, October 1986, Prt. 2, *4*, 251–78.

Viscusi, W. Kip, "Are Individuals Bayesian Decision Makers?" *American Economic Review Papers and Proceedings*, May 1985, *75*, 381–85.

von Neumann, John and Oskar Morgenstern, *Theory of Games and Economic Behavior*. Princeton: Princeton University Press, 1944. 2nd Ed., 1947. 3rd Ed., 1953.

Yaari, Menahem, "Some Remarks on Measures of Risk Aversion and On their Uses," *Journal of Economic Theory*, October 1969, *1*, 315–29.

Yaari, Menahem, "The Dual Theory of Choice Under Risk," *Econometrica*, January 1987, *55*, 95–115.

*Econometrica*, Vol. 32, No. 1–2 (January–April, 1964)

# RISK AVERSION IN THE SMALL AND IN THE LARGE[1]

## By John W. Pratt

This paper concerns utility functions for money. A measure of risk aversion in the small, the risk premium or insurance premium for an arbitrary risk, and a natural concept of decreasing risk aversion are discussed and related to one another. Risks are also considered as a proportion of total assets.

## 1. SUMMARY AND INTRODUCTION

LET $u(x)$ BE a utility function for money. The function $r(x) = -u''(x)/u'(x)$ will be interpreted in various ways as a measure of local risk aversion (risk aversion in the small); neither $u''(x)$ nor the curvature of the graph of $u$ is an appropriate measure. No simple measure of risk aversion in the large will be introduced. Global risks will, however, be considered, and it will be shown that one decision maker has greater local risk aversion $r(x)$ than another at all $x$ if and only if he is globally more risk-averse in the sense that, for every risk, his cash equivalent (the amount for which he would exchange the risk) is smaller than for the other decision maker. Equivalently, his risk premium (expected monetary value minus cash equivalent) is always larger, and he would be willing to pay more for insurance in any situation. From this it will be shown that a decision maker's local risk aversion $r(x)$ is a decreasing function of $x$ if and only if, for every risk, his cash equivalent is larger the larger his assets, and his risk premium and what he would be willing to pay for insurance are smaller. This condition, which many decision makers would subscribe to, involves the third derivative of $u$, as $r' \leq 0$ is equivalent to $u'''u' \geq u''^2$. It is not satisfied by quadratic utilities in any region. All this means that some natural ways of thinking casually about utility functions may be misleading. Except for one family, convenient utility functions for which $r(x)$ is decreasing are not so very easy to find. Help in this regard is given by some theorems showing that certain combinations of utility functions, in particular linear combinations with positive weights, have decreasing $r(x)$ if all the functions in the combination have decreasing $r(x)$.

The related function $r^*(x) = xr(x)$ will be interpreted as a local measure of aversion to risks measured as a proportion of assets, and monotonicity of $r^*(x)$ will be proved to be equivalent to monotonicity of every risk's cash equivalent measured as a proportion of assets, and similarly for the risk premium and insurance.

These results have both descriptive and normative implications. Utility functions for which $r(x)$ is decreasing are logical candidates to use when trying to describe the behavior of people who, one feels, might generally pay less for insurance against

[1] This research was supported by the National Science Foundation (grant NSF-G24035). Reproduction in whole or in part is permitted for any purpose of the United States Government.

a given risk the greater their assets. And consideration of the yield and riskiness per investment dollar of investors' portfolios may suggest, at least in some contexts, description by utility functions for which $r^*(x)$ is first decreasing and then increasing.

Normatively, it seems likely that many decision makers would feel they ought to pay less for insurance against a given risk the greater their assets. Such a decision maker will want to choose a utility function for which $r(x)$ is decreasing, adding this condition to the others he must already consider (consistency and probably concavity) in forging a satisfactory utility from more or less malleable preliminary preferences. He may wish to add a further condition on $r^*(x)$.

We do not assume or assert that utility may not change with time. Strictly speaking, we are concerned with utility at a specified time (when a decision must be made) for money at a (possibly later) specified time. Of course, our results pertain also to behavior at different times if utility does not change with time. For instance, a decision maker whose utility for total assets is unchanging and whose assets are increasing would be willing to pay less and less for insurance against a given risk as time progresses if his $r(x)$ is a decreasing function of $x$. Notice that his actual expenditure for insurance might nevertheless increase if his risks are increasing along with his assets.

The risk premium, cash equivalent, and insurance premium are defined and related to one another in Section 2. The local risk aversion function $r(x)$ is introduced and interpreted in Sections 3 and 4. In Section 5, inequalities concerning global risks are obtained from inequalities between local risk aversion functions. Section 6 deals with constant risk aversion, and Section 7 demonstrates the equivalence of local and global definitions of decreasing (and increasing) risk aversion. Section 8 shows that certain operations preserve the property of decreasing risk aversion. Some examples are given in Section 9. Aversion to proportional risk is discussed in Sections 10 to 12. Section 13 concerns some related work of Kenneth J. Arrow.[2]

Throughout this paper, the utility $u(x)$ is regarded as a function of total assets rather than of changes which may result from a certain decision, so that $x=0$ is equivalent to ruin, or perhaps to loss of all readily disposable assets. (This is essential only in connection with proportional risk aversion.) The symbol $\sim$ indicates that two functions are equivalent as utilities, that is, $u_1(x)\sim u_2(x)$ means there exist constants $a$ and $b$ (with $b>0$) such that $u_1(x)=a+bu_2(x)$ for all $x$. The utility functions discussed may, but need not, be bounded. It is assumed, however, that they are sufficiently regular to justify the proofs; generally it is enough that they be twice continuously differentiable with positive first derivative, which is already re-

[2] The importance of the function $r(x)$ was discovered independently by Kenneth J. Arrow and by Robert Schlaifer, in different contexts. The work presented here was, unfortunately, essentially completed before I learned of Arrow's related work. It is, however, a pleasure to acknowledge Schlaifer's stimulation and participation throughout, as well as that of John Bishop at certain points.

quired for $r(x)$ to be defined and continuous. A variable with a tilde over it, such as $\tilde{z}$, is a random variable. The risks $\tilde{z}$ considered may, but need not, have "objective" probability distributions. In formal statements, $\tilde{z}$ refers only to risks which are not degenerate, that is, not constant with probability one, and interval refers only to an interval with more than one point. Also, increasing and decreasing mean nondecreasing and nonincreasing respectively; if we mean strictly increasing or decreasing we will say so.

## 2. THE RISK PREMIUM

Consider a decision maker with assets $x$ and utility function $u$. We shall be interested in the *risk premium* $\pi$ such that he would be indifferent between receiving a risk $\tilde{z}$ and receiving the non-random amount $E(\tilde{z}) - \pi$, that is, $\pi$ less than the actuarial value $E(\tilde{z})$. If $u$ is concave, then $\pi \geq 0$, but we don't require this. The risk premium depends on $x$ and on the distribution of $\tilde{z}$, and will be denoted $\pi(x, \tilde{z})$. (It is not, as this notation might suggest, a function $\pi(x, z)$ evaluated at a randomly selected value of $z$, which would be random.) By the properties of utility,

$$(1) \qquad u(x + E(\tilde{z}) - \pi(x, \tilde{z})) = E\{u(x + \tilde{z})\} \ .$$

We shall consider only situations where $E\{u(x+\tilde{z})\}$ exists and is finite. Then $\pi(x, \tilde{z})$ exists and is uniquely defined by (1), since $u(x + E(\tilde{z}) - \pi)$ is a strictly decreasing, continuous function of $\pi$ ranging over all possible values of $u$. It follows immediately from (1) that, for any constant $\mu$,

$$(2) \qquad \pi(x, \tilde{z}) = \pi(x + \mu, \tilde{z} - \mu) \ .$$

By choosing $\mu = E(\tilde{z})$ (assuming it exists and is finite), we may thus reduce consideration to a risk $\tilde{z} - \mu$ which is actuarially neutral, that is, $E(\tilde{z} - \mu) = 0$.

Since the decision maker is indifferent between receiving the risk $\tilde{z}$ and receiving for sure the amount $\pi_a(x, \tilde{z}) = E(\tilde{z}) - \pi(x, \tilde{z})$, this amount is sometimes called the cash equivalent or value of $\tilde{z}$. It is also the asking price for $\tilde{z}$, the smallest amount for which the decision maker would willingly sell $\tilde{z}$ if he had it. It is given by

$$(3a) \qquad u(x + \pi_a(x, \tilde{z})) = E\{u(x + \tilde{z})\} \ .$$

It is to be distinguished from the bid price $\pi_b(x, \tilde{z})$, the largest amount the decision maker would willingly pay to obtain $\tilde{z}$, which is given by

$$(3b) \qquad u(x) = E\{u(x + \tilde{z} - \pi_b(x, \tilde{z}))\} \ .$$

For an unfavorable risk $\tilde{z}$, it is natural to consider the insurance premium $\pi_I(x, \tilde{z})$ such that the decision maker is indifferent between facing the risk $\tilde{z}$ and paying the non-random amount $\pi_I(x, \tilde{z})$. Since paying $\pi_I$ is equivalent to receiving $-\pi_I$, we have

$$(3c) \qquad \pi_I(x, \tilde{z}) = -\pi_a(x, \tilde{z}) = \pi(x, \tilde{z}) - E(\tilde{z}) \ .$$

If $\tilde{z}$ is actuarially neutral, the risk premium and insurance premium coincide.

The results of this paper will be stated in terms of the risk premium $\pi$, but could equally easily and meaningfully be stated in terms of the cash equivalent or insurance premium.

### 3. LOCAL RISK AVERSION

To measure a decision maker's local aversion to risk, it is natural to consider his risk premium for a small, actuarially neutral risk $\tilde{z}$. We therefore consider $\pi(x, \tilde{z})$ for a risk $\tilde{z}$ with $E(\tilde{z}) = 0$ and small variance $\sigma_z^2$; that is, we consider the behavior of $\pi(x, \tilde{z})$ as $\sigma_z^2 \to 0$. We assume the third absolute central moment of $\tilde{z}$ is of smaller order than $\sigma_z^2$. (Ordinarily it is of order $\sigma_z^3$.) Expanding $u$ around $x$ on both sides of (1), we obtain under suitable regularity conditions[3]

(4a) $\qquad u(x - \pi) = u(x) - \pi u'(x) + O(\pi^2)$,

(4b) $\qquad E\{u(x + \tilde{z})\} = E\{u(x) + \tilde{z}u'(x) + \tfrac{1}{2}\tilde{z}^2 u''(x) + O(\tilde{z}^3)\}$
$\qquad\qquad = u(x) + \tfrac{1}{2}\sigma_z^2 u''(x) + o(\sigma_z^2)$ .

Setting these expressions equal, as required by (1), then gives

(5) $\qquad \pi(x, \tilde{z}) = \tfrac{1}{2}\sigma_z^2 r(x) + o(\sigma_z^2)$ ,

where

(6) $\qquad r(x) = -\dfrac{u''(x)}{u'(x)} = -\dfrac{d}{dx} \log u'(x)$ .

Thus the decision maker's risk premium for a small, actuarially neutral risk $\tilde{z}$ is approximately $r(x)$ times half the variance of $\tilde{z}$; that is, $r(x)$ is twice the risk premium per unit of variance for infinitesimal risks. A sufficient regularity condition for (5) is that $u$ have a third derivative which is continuous and bounded over the range of all $\tilde{z}$ under discussion. The theorems to follow will not actually depend on (5), however.

If $\tilde{z}$ is not actuarially neutral, we have by (2), with $\mu = E(\tilde{z})$, and (5):

(7) $\qquad \pi(x, \tilde{z}) = \tfrac{1}{2}\sigma_z^2 r(x + E(\tilde{z})) + o(\sigma_z^2)$ .

Thus the risk premium for a risk $\tilde{z}$ with arbitrary mean $E(\tilde{z})$ but small variance is approximately $r(x + E(\tilde{z}))$ times half the variance of $\tilde{z}$. It follows also that the risk premium will just equal and hence offset the actuarial value $E(\tilde{z})$ of a small risk ($\tilde{z}$); that is, the decision maker will be indifferent between having $\tilde{z}$ and not having it when the actuarial value is approximately $r(x)$ times half the variance of $\tilde{z}$. Thus $r(x)$

---

[3] In expansions, $O(\ )$ means "terms of order at most" and $o(\ )$ means "terms of smaller order than."

may also be interpreted as twice the actuarial value the decision maker requires per unit of variance for infinitesimal risks.

Notice that it is the variance, not the standard deviation, that enters these formulas. To first order any (differentiable) utility is linear in small gambles. In this sense, these are second order formulas.

Still another interpretation of $r(x)$ arises in the special case $\tilde{z} = \pm h$, that is, where the risk is to gain or lose a fixed amount $h > 0$. Such a risk is actuarially neutral if $+h$ and $-h$ are equally probable, so $P(\tilde{z} = h) - P(\tilde{z} = -h)$ measures the *probability premium* of $\tilde{z}$. Let $p(x, h)$ be the probability premium such that the decision maker is indifferent between the status quo and a risk $\tilde{z} = \pm h$ with

(8)    $P(\tilde{z} = h) - P(\tilde{z} = -h) = p(x, h)$ .

Then $P(\tilde{z} = h) = \frac{1}{2}[1 + p(x, h)]$, $P(\tilde{z} = -h) = \frac{1}{2}[1 - p(x, h)]$, and $p(x, h)$ is defined by

(9)    $u(x) = E\{u(x + \tilde{z})\} = \frac{1}{2}[1 + p(x, h)]u(x + h) + \frac{1}{2}[1 - p(x, h)]u(x - h)$ .

When $u$ is expanded around $x$ as before, (9) becomes

(10)    $u(x) = u(x) + hp(x, h)u'(x) + \frac{1}{2}h^2 u''(x) + O(h^3)$ .

Solving for $p(x, h)$, we find

(11)    $p(x, h) = \frac{1}{2}hr(x) + O(h^2)$ .

Thus for small $h$ the decision maker is indifferent between the status quo and a risk of $\pm h$ with a probability premium of $r(x)$ times $\frac{1}{2}h$; that is, $r(x)$ is twice the probability premium he requires per unit risked for small risks.

In these ways we may interpret $r(x)$ as a measure of the *local risk aversion* or *local propensity to insure* at the point $x$ under the utility function $u$; $-r(x)$ would measure locally liking for risk or propensity to gamble. Notice that we have not introduced any measure of risk aversion in the large. Aversion to ordinary (as opposed to infinitesimal) risks might be considered measured by $\pi(x, \tilde{z})$, but $\pi$ is a much more complicated function than $r$. Despite the absence of any simple measure of risk aversion in the large, we shall see that comparisons of aversion to risk can be made simply in the large as well as in the small.

By (6), integrating $-r(x)$ gives $\log u'(x) + c$; exponentiating and integrating again then gives $e^c u(x) + d$. The constants of integration are immaterial because $e^c u(x) + d \sim u(x)$. (Note $e^c > 0$.) Thus we may write

(12)    $u \sim \int e^{-\int r}$ ,

and we observe that the local risk aversion function $r$ associated with any utility function $u$ contains all essential information about $u$ while eliminating everything arbitrary about $u$. However, decisions about ordinary (as opposed to "small") risks are determined by $r$ only through $u$ as given by (12), so it is not convenient entirely to eliminate $u$ from consideration in favor of $r$.

## 4. CONCAVITY

The aversion to risk implied by a utility function $u$ seems to be a form of concavity, and one might set out to measure concavity as representing aversion to risk. It is clear from the foregoing that for this purpose $r(x) = -u''(x)/u'(x)$ can be considered a measure of the concavity of $u$ at the point $x$. A case might perhaps be made for using instead some one-to-one function of $r(x)$, but it should be noted that $u''(x)$ or $-u''(x)$ is not in itself a meaningful measure of concavity in utility theory, nor is the curvature (reciprocal of the signed radius of the tangent circle) $u''(x)(1 + [u'(x)]^2)^{-3/2}$. Multiplying $u$ by a positive constant, for example, does not alter behavior but does alter $u''$ and the curvature.

A more striking and instructive example is provided by the function $u(x) = -e^{-x}$. As $x$ increases, this function approaches the asymptote $u = 0$ and looks graphically less and less concave and more and more like a horizontal straight line, in accordance with the fact that $u'(x) = e^{-x}$ and $u''(x) = -e^{-x}$ both approach 0. As a utility function, however, it does not change at all with the level of assets $x$, that is, the behavior implied by $u(x)$ is the same for all $x$, since $u(k+x) = -e^{-k-x} \sim u(x)$. In particular, the risk premium $\pi(x,\tilde{z})$ for any risk $\tilde{z}$ and the probability premium $p(x,h)$ for any $h$ remain absolutely constant as $x$ varies. Thus, regardless of the appearance of its graph, $u(x) = -e^{-x}$ is just as far from implying linear behavior at $x = \infty$ as at $x = 0$ or $x = -\infty$. All this is duly reflected in $r(x)$, which is constant: $r(x) = -u''(x)/u'(x) = 1$ for all $x$.

One feature of $u''(x)$ does have a meaning, namely its sign, which equals that of $-r(x)$. A negative (positive) sign at $x$ implies unwillingness (willingness) to accept small, actuarially neutral risks with assets $x$. Furthermore, a negative (positive) sign for all $x$ implies strict concavity (convexity) and hence unwillingness (willingness) to accept any actuarially neutral risk with any assets. The absolute magnitude of $u''(x)$ does not in itself have any meaning in utility theory, however.

## 5. COMPARATIVE RISK AVERSION

Let $u_1$ and $u_2$ be utility functions with local risk aversion functions $r_1$ and $r_2$, respectively. If, at a point $x$, $r_1(x) > r_2(x)$, then $u_1$ is locally more risk-averse than $u_2$ at the point $x$; that is, the corresponding risk premiums satisfy $\pi_1(x,\tilde{z}) > \pi_2(x,\tilde{z})$ for sufficiently small risks $\tilde{z}$, and the corresponding probability premiums satisfy $p_1(x,h) > p_2(x,h)$ for sufficiently small $h > 0$. The main point of the theorem we are about to prove is that the corresponding global properties also hold. For instance, if $r_1(x) > r_2(x)$ for all $x$, that is, $u_1$ has greater local risk aversion than $u_2$ everywhere, then $\pi_1(x,\tilde{z}) > \pi_2(x,\tilde{z})$ for every risk $\tilde{z}$, so that $u_1$ is also globally more risk-averse in a natural sense.

It is to be understood in this section that the probability distribution of $\tilde{z}$, which determines $\pi_1(x,\tilde{z})$ and $\pi_2(x,\tilde{z})$, is the same in each. We are comparing the risk premiums for the same probability distribution of risk but for two different utilities. This does not mean that when Theorem 1 is applied to two decision makers, they must have the same personal probability distributions, but only that the notation is imprecise. The theorem could be stated in terms of $\pi_1(x, \tilde{z}_1)$ and $\pi_2(x, \tilde{z}_2)$ where the distribution assigned to $\tilde{z}_1$ by the first decision maker is the same as that assigned to $\tilde{z}_2$ by the second decision maker. This would be less misleading, but also less convenient and less suggestive, especially for later use. More precise notation would be, for instance, $\pi_1(x, F)$ and $\pi_2(x, F)$, where $F$ is a cumulative distribution function.

THEOREM 1: *Let $r_i(x)$, $\pi_i(x, \tilde{z})$, and $p_i(x)$ be the local risk aversion, risk premium, and probability premium corresponding to the utility function $u_i$, $i = 1, 2$. Then the following conditions are equivalent, in either the strong form (indicated in brackets), or the weak form (with the bracketed material omitted).*

   (a)   $r_1(x) \geq r_2(x)$ *for all $x$* [*and $>$ for at least one $x$ in every interval*].

   (b)   $\pi_1(x, \tilde{z}) \geq [>] \pi_2(x, \tilde{z})$ *for all $x$ and $\tilde{z}$.*

   (c)   $p_1(x, h) \geq [>] p_2(x, h)$ *for all $x$ and all $h > 0$.*

   (d)   $u_1(u_2^{-1}(t))$ *is a* [*strictly*] *concave function of $t$.*

   (e)   $\dfrac{u_1(y) - u_1(x)}{u_1(w) - u_1(v)} \leq [<] \dfrac{u_2(y) - u_2(x)}{u_2(w) - u_2(v)}$ *for all $v$, $w$, $x$, $y$ with $v < w \leq x < y$.*

*The same equivalences hold if attention is restricted throughout to an interval, that is, if the requirement is added that $x, x + \tilde{z}, x + h, x - h, u_2^{-1}(t), v, w$, and $y$, all lie in a specified interval.*

PROOF: We shall prove things in an order indicating somewhat how one might discover that (a) implies (b) and (c).

To show that (b) follows from (d), solve (1) to obtain

(13)     $\pi_i(x, \tilde{z}) = x + E(\tilde{z}) - u_i^{-1}(E\{u_i(x + \tilde{z})\})$ .

Then

(14)     $\pi_1(x, \tilde{z}) - \pi_2(x, \tilde{z}) = u_2^{-1}(E\{u_2(x + \tilde{z})\}) - u_1^{-1}(E\{u_1(x + \tilde{z})\})$

                    $= u_2^{-1}(E\{\tilde{t}\}) - u_1^{-1}(E\{u_1(u_2^{-1}(\tilde{t}))\})$ ,

where $\tilde{t} = u_2(x + \tilde{z})$. If $u_1(u_2^{-1}(t))$ is [strictly] concave, then (by Jensen's inequality)

(15)     $E\{u_1(u_2^{-1}(\tilde{t}))\} \leq [<] u_1(u_2^{-1}(E\{\tilde{t}\}))$ .

Substituting (15) in (14), we obtain (b).

To show that (a) implies (d), note that

(16) $$\frac{d}{dt}u_1(u_2^{-1}(t)) = \frac{u_1'(u_2^{-1}(t))}{u_2'(u_2^{-1}(t))},$$

which is [strictly] decreasing if (and only if) $\log u_1'(x)/u_2'(x)$ is. The latter follows from (a) and

(17) $$\frac{d}{dx}\log\frac{u_1'(x)}{u_2'(x)} = r_2(x) - r_1(x).$$

That (c) is implied by (e) follows immediately upon writing (9) in the form

(18) $$\frac{1-p_i(x,h)}{1+p_i(x,h)} = \frac{u_i(x+h)-u_i(x)}{u_i(x)-u_i(x-h)}.$$

To show that (a) implies (e), integrate (a) from $w$ to $x$, obtaining

(19) $$-\log\frac{u_1'(x)}{u_1'(w)} \geq [>] -\log\frac{u_2'(x)}{u_2'(w)} \quad \text{for} \quad w<x,$$

which is equivalent to

(20) $$\frac{u_1'(x)}{u_1'(w)} \leq [<] \frac{u_2'(x)}{u_2'(w)} \quad \text{for} \quad w<x.$$

This implies

(21) $$\frac{u_1(y)-u_1(x)}{u_1'(w)} \leq [<] \frac{u_2(y)-u_2(x)}{u_2'(w)} \quad \text{for} \quad w\leq x<y,$$

as may be seen by applying the Mean Value Theorem of differential calculus to the difference of the two sides of (21) regarded as a function of $y$. Condition (e) follows from (21) upon application of the Mean Value Theorem to the difference of the reciprocals of the two sides of (e) regarded as a function of $w$.

We have now proved that (a) implies (d) implies (b), and (a) implies (e) implies (c). The equivalence of (a)–(e) will follow if we can prove that (b) implies (a), and (c) implies (a), or equivalently that not (a) implies not (b) and not (c). But this follows from what has already been proved, for if the weak [strong] form of (a) does not hold, then the strong [weak] form of (a) holds on some interval with $u_1$ and $u_2$ interchanged. Then the strong [weak] forms of (b) and (c) also hold on this interval with $u_1$ and $u_2$ interchanged, so the weak [strong] forms of (b) and (c) do not hold. This completes the proof.

We observe that (e) is equivalent to (20), (21), and

(22) $$\frac{u_1(w)-u_1(v)}{u_1'(x)} \geq [>] \frac{u_2(w)-u_2(v)}{u_2'(x)} \quad \text{for} \quad v<w\leq x.$$

### 6. CONSTANT RISK AVERSION

If the local risk aversion function is constant, say $r(x) = c$, then by (12):

(23) $\quad u(x) \sim x \qquad$ if $\quad r(x) = 0$ ;

(24) $\quad u(x) \sim -e^{-cx} \quad$ if $\quad r(x) = c > 0$ ;

(25) $\quad u(x) \sim e^{-cx} \qquad$ if $\quad r(x) = c < 0$ .

These utilities are, respectively, linear, strictly concave, and strictly convex.

If the risk aversion is constant locally, then it is also constant globally, that is, a change in assets makes no change in preference among risks. In fact, for any $k$, $u(k+x) \sim u(x)$ in each of the cases above, as is easily verified. Therefore it makes sense to speak of "constant risk aversion" without the qualification "local" or "global."

Similar remarks apply to constant risk aversion on an interval, except that global consideration must be restricted to assets $x$ and risks $\tilde{z}$ such that $x + \tilde{z}$ is certain to stay within the interval.

### 7. INCREASING AND DECREASING RISK AVERSION

Consider a decision maker who (i) attaches a positive risk premium to any risk, but (ii) attaches a smaller risk premium to any given risk the greater his assets $x$. Formally this means

(i) $\quad \pi(x, \tilde{z}) > 0$ for all $x$ and $\tilde{z}$;
(ii) $\quad \pi(x, \tilde{z})$ is a strictly decreasing function of $x$ for all $\tilde{z}$.

Restricting $\tilde{z}$ to be actuarially neutral would not affect (i) or (ii), by (2) with $\mu = E(\tilde{z})$.

We shall call a utility function (or a decision maker possessing it) *risk-averse* if the weak form of (i) holds, that is, if $\pi(x, \tilde{z}) \geq 0$ for all $x$ and $\tilde{z}$; it is well known that this is equivalent to concavity of $u$, and hence to $u'' \leq 0$ and to $r \geq 0$. A utility function is *strictly risk-averse* if (i) holds as stated; this is equivalent to strict concavity of $u$ and hence to the existence in every interval of at least one point where $u'' < 0, r > 0$.

We turn now to (ii). Notice that it amounts to a definition of strictly decreasing risk aversion in a global (as opposed to local) sense. On would hope that decreasing global risk aversion would be equivalent to decreasing local risk aversion $r(x)$. The following theorem asserts that this is indeed so. Therefore it makes sense to speak of "decreasing risk aversion" without the qualification "local" or "global." What is nontrivial is that $r(x)$ decreasing implies $\pi(x, \tilde{z})$ decreasing, inasmuch as $r(x)$ pertains directly only to infinitesimal gambles. Similar considerations apply to the probability premium $p(x, h)$.

THEOREM 2: *The following conditions are equivalent.*
(a') *The local risk aversion function $r(x)$ is [strictly] decreasing.*

(b') *The risk premium $\pi(x,\tilde{z})$ is a [strictly] decreasing function of x for all $\tilde{z}$.*

(c') *The probability premium $p(x,h)$ is a [strictly] decreasing function of x for all $h>0$.*

*The same equivalences hold if "increasing" is substituted for "decreasing" throughout and/or attention is restricted throughout to an interval, that is, the requirement is added that $x$, $x+\tilde{z}$, $x+h$, and $x-h$ all lie in a specified interval.*

PROOF: This theorem follows upon application of Theorem 1 to $u_1(x)=u(x)$ and $u_2(x)=u(x+k)$ for arbitrary $x$ and $k$.

It is easily verified that (a') and hence also (b') and (c') are equivalent to

(d') $u'(u^{-1}(t))$ is a [strictly] convex function of $t$.

This corresponds to (d) of Theorem 1. Corresponding to (e) of Theorem 1 and (20)–(22) is

(e') $u'(x)u'''(x) \geqq (u''(x))^2$ [and $>$ for at least one $x$ in every interval].

The equivalence of this to (a')–(c') follows from the fact that the sign of $r'(x)$ is the same as that of $(u''(x))^2 - u'(x)u'''(x)$. Theorem 2 can be and originally was proved by way of (d') and (e'), essentially as Theorem 1 is proved in the present paper.

## 8. OPERATIONS WHICH PRESERVE DECREASING RISK AVERSION

We have just seen that a utility function evinces decreasing risk aversion in a global sense if an only if its local risk aversion function $r(x)$ is decreasing. Such a utility function seems of interest mainly if it is also risk-averse (concave, $r \geqq 0$). Accordingly, we shall now formally define a utility function to be [*strictly*] *decreasingly risk-averse* if its local risk aversion function $r$ is [strictly] decreasing and nonnegative. Then by Theorem 2, conditions (i) and (ii) of Section 7 are equivalent to the utility's being strictly decreasingly risk-averse.

In this section we shall show that certain operations yield decreasingly risk-averse utility functions if applied to such functions. This facilitates proving that functions are decreasingly risk-averse and finding functions which have this property and also have reasonably simple formulas. In the proofs, $r(x)$, $r_1(x)$, etc., are the local risk aversion functions belonging to $u(x)$, $u_1(x)$, etc.

THEOREM 3: *Suppose $a>0$: $u_1(x)=u(ax+b)$ is [strictly] decreasingly risk-averse for $x_0 \leqq x \leqq x_1$ if and only if $u(x)$ is [strictly] decreasingly risk-averse for $ax_0+b \leqq x \leqq ax_1+b$.*

PROOF: This follows directly from the easily verified formula:

(26)     $r_1(x)=ar(ax+b)$ .

THEOREM 4: *If $u_1(x)$ is decreasingly risk-averse for $x_0 \leqq x \leqq x_1$, and $u_2(x)$ is decreasingly risk-averse for $u_1(x_0) \leqq x \leqq u_1(x_1)$, then $u(x)=u_2(u_1(x))$ is decreasingly* *risk-averse for $x_0 \leq x \leq x_1$, and strictly so unless one of $u_1$ and $u_2$ is linear from some x on and the other has constant risk aversion in some interval.*

PROOF: We have $\log u'(x) = \log u_2'(u_1(x)) + \log u_1'(x)$, and therefore

(27)  $\quad r(x) = r_2(u_1(x))u_1'(x) + r_1(x)$ .

The functions $r_2(u_1(x))$, $u_1'(x)$, and $r_1(x)$ are $\geq 0$ and decreasing, and therefore so is $r(x)$. Furthermore, $u_1'(x)$ is strictly decreasing as long as $r_1(x) > 0$, so $r(x)$ is strictly decreasing as long as $r_1(x)$ and $r_2(u_1(x))$ are both $> 0$. If one of them is 0 for some $x$, then it is 0 for all larger $x$, but if the other is strictly decreasing, then so is $r$.

THEOREM 5: *If $u_1, \ldots, u_n$ are decreasingly risk-averse on an interval $[x_0, x_1]$, and $c_1, \ldots, c_n$ are positive constants, then $u = \Sigma_1^n c_i u_i$ is decreasingly risk-averse on $[x_0, x_1]$, and strictly so except on subintervals (if any) where all $u_i$ have equal and constant risk aversion.*

PROOF: The general statement follows from the case $u = u_1 + u_2$. For this case

(28)  $\quad r = -\dfrac{u_1'' + u_2''}{u_1' + u_2'} = \dfrac{u_1'}{u_1' + u_2'} r_1 + \dfrac{u_2'}{u_1' + u_2'} r_2$ ;

(29)  $\quad r' = \dfrac{u_1'}{u_1' + u_2'} r_1' + \dfrac{u_2'}{u_1' + u_2'} r_2' + \dfrac{u_1'' u_2' - u_1' u_2''}{(u_1' + u_2')^2} (r_1 - r_2)$

$\quad\quad = \dfrac{u_1' r_1' + u_2' r_2'}{u_1' + u_2'} - \dfrac{u_1' u_2'}{(u_1' + u_2')^2} (r_1 - r_2)^2$ .

We have $u_1' > 0$, $u_2' > 0$, $r_1' \leq 0$, and $r_2' \leq 0$. Therefore $r' \leq 0$, and $r' < 0$ unless $r_1 = r_2$ and $r_1' = r_2' = 0$. The conclusion follows.

## 9. EXAMPLES

9.1. *Example 1.* The utility $u(x) = -(b-x)^c$ for $x \leq b$ and $c > 1$ is strictly increasing and strictly concave, but it also has strictly *increasing* risk aversion: $r(x) = (c-1)/(b-x)$. Notice that the most general concave quadratic utility $u(x) = \alpha + \beta x - \gamma x^2$, $\beta > 0$, $\gamma > 0$, is equivalent as a utility to $-(b-x)^c$ with $c = 2$ and $b = \frac{1}{2}\beta/\gamma$. Therefore a quadratic utility cannot be decreasingly risk-averse on any interval whatever. This severely limits the usefulness of quadratic utility, however nice it would be to have expected utility depend only on the mean and variance of the probability distribution. Arguing "in the small" is no help: decreasing risk aversion is a local property as well as a global one.

94

9.2. *Example 2.* If

(30)     $u'(x)=(x^a+b)^{-c}$   with   $a>0, c>0$,

then $u(x)$ is strictly decreasingly risk-averse in the region

(31)     $x>[\max\{0, -b, b(a-1)\}]^{1/a}$.

To prove this, note

(32)     $r(x)= -\dfrac{d}{dx} \log u'(x) = \dfrac{ac}{x+bx^{1-a}}$,

which is $\geq 0$ and strictly decreasing in the region where the denominator $x+bx^{1-a}$ is $\geq 0$ and strictly increasing, which is the region (30). (The condition $x\geq 0$ is included to insure that $x^a$ is defined; for $a\geq 1$ it follows from the other conditions.)

By Theorem 3, one can obtain a utility function that is strictly decreasingly risk-averse for $x>0$ by substituting $x+d$ for $x$ above, where $d$ is at least the right-hand side of (31). Multiplying $x$ by a positive factor, as in Theorem 3, is equivalent to multiplying $b$ by a positive factor.

Given below are all the strictly decreasingly risk-averse utility functions $u(x)$ on $x>0$ which can be obtained by applying Theorem 3 to (30) with the indicated choices of the parameters $a$ and $c$:

(33)     $a=1, 0<c<1$:     $u(x)\sim(x+d)^q$                     with   $d\geq 0, 0<q<1$ ;
(34)     $a=1, c=1$:        $u(x)\sim\log(x+d)$                  with   $d\geq 0$ ;
(35)     $a=1, c>1$:        $u(x)\sim -(x+d)^{-q}$               with   $d\geq 0, q>0$ ;
(36)     $a=2, c=.5$:       $u(x)\sim\log(x+d+[(x+d)^2+b])$   with   $d\geq|b|^{\frac{1}{2}}$ ;
(37)     $a=2, c=1$:        $u(x)\sim\arctan(\alpha x+\beta)$ or
                              $\log(1-(\alpha x+\beta)^{-1})$     with   $\alpha>0, \beta\geq 1$ ;

(38)     $a=2, c=1.5$:      $u(x)\sim[1+(\alpha x+\beta)^{-2}]^{-\frac{1}{2}}$ or
                              $-[1-(\alpha x+\beta)^{-2}]^{-\frac{1}{2}}$   with   $\alpha>0, \beta\geq 1$.

9.3. *Example 3.* Applying Theorems 4 and 5 to the utilities of Example 2 and Section 6 gives a very wide class of utilities which are strictly decreasingly risk-averse for $x>0$, such as

(39)     $u(x)\sim -c_1 e^{-cx}-c_2 e^{-dx}$   with   $c_1>0, c_2>0, c>0, d>0$.
(40)     $u(x)\sim\log(d_1+\log(x+d_2))$   with   $d_1\geq 0, d_2\geq 0, d_1+\log d_2\geq 0$.

## 10. PROPORTIONAL RISK AVERSION

So far we have been concerned with risks that remained fixed while assets varied. Let us now view everything as a proportion of assets. Specifically, let $\pi^*(x,\tilde z)$ be the *proportional risk premium* corresponding to a proportional risk $\tilde z$; that is, a decision maker with assets $x$ and utility function $u$ would be indifferent between receiving a risk $x\tilde{z}$ and receiving the non-random amount $E(x\tilde{z}) - x\pi^*(x,\tilde{z})$. Then $x\pi^*(x,\tilde{z})$ equals the risk premium $\pi(x, x\tilde{z})$, so

$$(41) \qquad \pi^*(x, \tilde{z}) = \frac{1}{x}\, \pi(x, x\tilde{z}) \,.$$

For a small, actuarially neutral, proportional risk $\tilde{z}$ we have, by (5),

$$(42) \qquad \pi^*(x,\tilde{z}) = \tfrac{1}{2}\sigma_z^2\, r^*(x) + o(\sigma_z^2) \,,$$

where

$$(43) \qquad r^*(x) = xr(x) \,.$$

If $\tilde{z}$ is not actuarially neutral, we have, by (7),

$$(44) \qquad \pi^*(x,\tilde{z}) = \tfrac{1}{2}\sigma_z^2 r^*(x + xE(\tilde{z})) + o(\sigma_z^2) \,.$$

We will call $r^*$ the *local proportional risk aversion* at the point $x$ under the utility function $u$. Its interpretation by (42) and (44) is like that of $r$ by (5) and (7).

Similarly, we may define the *proportional probability premium* $p^*(x,h)$, corresponding to a risk of gaining or losing a proportional amount $h$, namely

$$(45) \qquad p^*(x,h) = p(x,xh) \,.$$

Then another interpretation of $r^*(x)$ is provided by

$$(46) \qquad p^*(x,h) = \tfrac{1}{2}hr^*(x) + O(h^2) \,,$$

which follows from (45) and (11).

## 11. CONSTANT PROPORTIONAL RISK AVERSION

If the local proportional risk aversion function is constant, say $r^*(x) = c$, then $r(x) = c/x$, so the utility is strictly decreasingly risk-averse for $c > 0$ and has negative, strictly increasing risk aversion for $c < 0$. By (12), the possibilities are:

$$(47) \qquad u(x) \sim x^{1-c} \qquad \text{if} \quad r^*(x) = c < 1 \,,$$
$$(48) \qquad u(x) \sim \log x \qquad \text{if} \quad r^*(x) = 1 \,,$$
$$(49) \qquad u(x) \sim -x^{-(c-1)} \quad \text{if} \quad r^*(x) = c > 1 \,.$$

If the proportional risk aversion is constant locally, then it is constant globally, that is, a change in assets makes no change in preferences among proportional risks. This follows immediately from the fact that $u(kx) \sim u(x)$ in each of the cases above. Therefore it makes sense to speak of "constant proportional risk aversion" without the qualification "local" or "global." Similar remarks apply to constant proportional risk aversion on an interval.

## 12. INCREASING AND DECREASING PROPORTIONAL RISK AVERSION

We will call a utility function [strictly] increasingly or decreasingly proportionally risk-averse if it has a [strictly] increasing or decreasing local proportional risk aversion function. Again the corresponding local and global properties are equivalent, as the next theorem states.

THEOREM 6: *The following conditions are equivalent.*
(a'') *The local proportional risk aversion function* $r^*(x)$ *is [strictly] decreasing.*
(b'') *The proportional risk premium* $\pi^*(x,\tilde{z})$ *is a [strictly] decreasing function of* $x$ *for all* $\tilde{z}$.
(c'') *The proportional probability premium* $p^*(x,h)$ *is a [strictly] decreasing function of* $x$ *for all* $h>0$.

*The same equivalences hold if "increasing" is substituted for "decreasing" throughout and/or attention is restricted throughout to an interval, that is, if the requirement is added that* $x$, $x+x\tilde{z}$, $x+xh$, *and* $x-xh$ *all lie in a specified interval.*

PROOF: This theorem follows upon application of Theorem 1 to $u_1(x)=u(x)$ and $u_2(x)=u(kx)$ for arbitrary $x$ and $k$.

A decreasingly risk-averse utility function may be increasingly or decreasingly proportionally risk-averse or neither. For instance, $u(x)\sim-\exp[-q^{-1}(x+b)^q]$, with $b\geqq0$, $q<1$, $q\neq0$, is strictly decreasingly risk-averse for $x>0$ while its local proportional risk aversion function $r^*(x)=x(x+b)^{-1}[(x+b)^q+1-q]$ is strictly increasing if $0<q<1$, strictly decreasing if $q<0$ and $b=0$, and neither if $q<0$ and $b>0$.

## 13. RELATED WORK OF ARROW

Arrow[4] has discussed the optimum amount to invest when part of the assets $x$ are to be held as cash and the rest invested in a specified, actuarially favorable risk. If $\tilde{\imath}$ is the return per unit invested, then investing the amount $a$ will result in assets $x+a\tilde{\imath}$. Suppose $a(x,\tilde{\imath})$ is the optimum amount to invest, that is $a(x,\tilde{\imath})$ maximizes $E\{u(x+a\tilde{\imath})\}$. Arrow proves that if $r(x)$ is [strictly] decreasing, increasing, or constant for all $x$, then $a(x,\tilde{\imath})$ is [strictly] increasing, decreasing, or constant, respectively, except that $a(x,\tilde{\imath})=x$ for all $x$ below a certain value (depending on $\tilde{\imath}$). He also proves a theorem about the asset elasticity of the demand for cash which is equivalent to the statement that if $r^*(x)$ is [strictly] decreasing, increasing, or constant for all $x$, then the optimum proportional investment $a^*(x,\tilde{\imath})=a(x,\tilde{\imath})/x$ is [strictly] increasing, decreasing, or constant, respectively, except that $a^*(x,\tilde{\imath})=1$ for all $x$ below a certain value. In the present framework it is natural to deduce these re-

---

[4] Kenneth J. Arrow, "Liquidity Preference," Lecture VI in "Lecture Notes for Economics 285, The Economics of Uncertainty," pp. 33-53, undated, Stanford University.

sults from the following theorem, whose proof bears essentially the same relation to Arrow's proofs as the proof of Theorem 1 to direct proofs of Theorems 2 and 6. For convenience we assume that $a_1(x, \bar{\imath})$ and $a_2(x, \bar{\imath})$ are unique.

THEOREM 7: *Condition* (a) *of Theorem 1 is equivalent to*
   (f) $a_1(x, \bar{\imath}) \leq a_2(x, \bar{\imath})$ *for all* $x$ *and* $\bar{\imath}$ [*and* $<$ *if* $0 < a_1(x, \bar{\imath}) < x$].
*The same equivalence holds if attention is restricted throughout to an interval, that is, if the requirement is added that $x$ and $x + \bar{\imath}x$ lie in a specified interval.*

PROOF: To show that (a) implies (f), note that $a_j(x, \bar{\imath})$ maximizes

$$(50) \qquad v_j(a) = \frac{1}{u_j'(x)} E\{u_j(x + a\bar{\imath})\}, \qquad j = 1, 2 .$$

Therefore (f) follows from

$$(51) \qquad \frac{d}{da}\{v_1(a) - v_2(a)\} = E\left\{\bar{\imath}\left(\frac{u_1'(x + a\bar{\imath})}{u_1'(x)} - \frac{u_2'(x + a\bar{\imath})}{u_2'(x)}\right)\right\} \leq [<]0,$$

which follows from (a) by (20).

If, conversely, the weak [strong] form of (a) does not hold, then its strong [weak] form holds on some interval with $u_1$ and $u_2$ interchanged, in which case the weak [strong] form of (f) cannot hold, so (f) implies (a). (The fact must be used that the strong form of (f) is actually stronger than the weak form, even when $x$ and $x + \bar{\imath}x$ are restricted to a specified interval. This is easily shown.)

Assuming $u$ is bounded, Arrow proves that (i) it is impossible that $r^*(x) \leq 1$ for all $x > x_0$, and he implies that (ii) $r^*(0) \leq 1$. It follows, as he points out, that if $u$ is bounded and $r^*$ is monotonic, then $r^*$ is increasing. (i) and (ii) can be deduced naturally from the following theorem, which is an immediate consequence of Theorem 1 (a) and (e).

THEOREM 8: *If* $r_1(x) \geq r_2(x)$ *for all* $x > x_0$ *and* $u_1(\infty) = \infty$, *then* $u_2(\infty) = \infty$. *If* $r_1(x) \geq r_2(x)$ *for all* $x < \varepsilon$, $\varepsilon > 0$, *and* $u_2(0) = -\infty$, *then* $u_1(0) = -\infty$.
   This gives (i) when $r_1(x) = 1/x$, $r_2(x) = r(x)$, $u_1(x) = \log x$, $u_2(x) = u(x)$. It gives (ii) when $r_1(x) = r(x)$, $r_2(x) = c/x$, $c > 1$, $u_1(x) = u(x)$, $u_2(x) = -x^{1-c}$.
   This section is not intended to summarize Arrow's work,[4] but only to indicate its relation to the present paper. The main points of overlap are that Arrow introduces essentially the functions $r$ and $r^*$ (actually their negatives) and uses them in significant ways, in particular those mentioned already, and that he introduces essentially $p^*(x, h)$, proves an equation like (46) in order to interpret decreasing $r^*$, and mentions the possibility of a similar analysis for $r$.

*Harvard University*

## ERRATUM

In "Risk Aversion in the Small and in the Large," by John W. Pratt, the first term on the right side of equation ( 44 ) should be divided by $1 + E(\tilde{z})$. A discrepancy discovered by John V. Lintner, Jr. brought this error to light. Four lines after equation ( 7 ), the semicolon should be a comma and there should be a comma at the end of the line. Footnote 2 should have made clear that Robert Schlaifer's contribution included formulating originally the concept of decreasing risk aversion in terms of the probability premium and proving that it implies $r(x)$ is decreasing, i.e., that $(c')$ implies $(a')$ in Theorem 2.

Reprinted from JOURNAL OF ECONOMIC THEORY          Vol. 2, No. 3, September 1970

# Increasing Risk: I. A Definition*

## MICHAEL ROTHSCHILD

*Harvard University, Cambridge, Massachusetts 02138*

AND

## JOSEPH E. STIGLITZ

*Cowles Foundation, Yale University, New Haven, Connecticut 06520
and Gonville and Caius College, Cambridge, England*

## I. INTRODUCTION

This paper attempts to answer the question: When is a random variable $Y$ "more variable" than another random variable $X$?

Intuition and tradition suggest at least four plausible—and apparently different—answers to this question. These are:

### 1. *Y is Equal to X Plus Noise*

If we simply add some uncorrelated noise to a random variable, (r.v.), the new r.v. should be riskier[1] than the original. More formally, suppose $Y$ and $X$ are related as follows:

$$Y \underset{d}{=} X + Z, \qquad (1.i)$$

where "$\underset{d}{=}$" means "has the same distribution as" and $Z$ is a r.v. with the property that

$$E(Z \mid X) = 0 \qquad \text{for all } X.[2] \qquad (1.ii)$$

---

* The research described in this paper was carried out under grants from the National Science Foundation and the Ford Foundation.

[1] Throughout this paper we shall use the terms more variable, riskier, and more uncertain synonomously.

[2] David Wallace suggested that we investigate this concept of greater riskiness. Arthur Goldberger has pointed out to us that (1.ii) is stronger than lack of correlation as earlier versions of this paper stated.

That is, $Y$ is equal to $X$ plus a disturbance term (noise.) If $X$ and $Y$ are discrete r.v.'s, condition (1) has another natural interpretation. Suppose $X$ is a lottery ticket which pays off $a_i$ with probability $p_i$ ; $\Sigma p_i = 1$. Then, $Y$ is a lottery ticket which pays $b_i$ with probability $p_i$ where $b_i$ is either a payoff of $a_i$ or a lottery ticket whose expected value is $a_i$ . Note that condition (1) implies that $X$ and $Y$ have the same mean.

## 2. *Every Risk Averter Prefers X to Y*

In the theory of expected utility maximization, a risk averter is defined as a person with a concave utility function. If $X$ and $Y$ have the same mean, but every risk averter prefers $X$ to $Y$, i.e., if

$$EU(X) \geqslant EU(Y) \quad \text{for all concave } U \tag{2}$$

then surely it is reasonable to say that $X$ is less risky than $Y$.[3]

## 3. *Y Has More Weight in the Tails Than X*

If $X$ and $Y$ have density functions $f$ and $g$, and if $g$ was obtained from $f$ by taking some of the probability weight from the center of $f$ and adding it to each tail of $f$ in such a way as to leave the mean unchanged, then it seems reasonable to say that $Y$ is more uncertain than $X$.

## 4. *Y Has a Greater Variance Than X*

Comparisons of riskiness or uncertainty are commonly restricted to comparisons of variance, largely because of the long history of the use of the variance as a measure of dispersion in statistical theory.

The major result of this paper is that the first three approaches lead to a single definition of greater riskiness, different from that of the fourth approach. We shall demonstrate the equivalence as follows. In Section II, it is shown that the third approach leads to a characterization of increasing uncertainty in terms of the indefinite integrals of differences of cumulative distribution functions (c.d.f.'s). In Section III it is shown that this indefinite integral induces a partial ordering on the set of distribution functions which is equivalent to the partial ordering induced by the first two approaches.

In Section IV we show that this concept of increasing risk is not equivalent to that implied by equating the risk of $X$ with the variance of $X$. This suggests to us that our concepts lead to a better definition of increasing risk than the standard one.

It is of course impossible to prove that one definition is better than

---

[3] It might be argued that we should limit our discussion to increasing concave functions. Imposing this restriction would gain nothing and would destroy the symmetry of some of the results. For example, since $U(X) = X$ and $U(X) = -X$ are both concave functions, condition (2) implies that $X$ and $Y$ have the same mean.

another. This fact is not a license for agnosticism or the suspension of judgment. Although there seems to us no question but that our definition is more consistent with the natural meaning of increasing risk than the variance definition, definitions are chosen for their usefulness as well as their consistency. As Tobin has argued, critics of the mean variance approach "owe us more than demonstrations that it rests on restrictive assumptions. They need to show us how a more general and less vulnerable approach will yield the kind of comparative static results that economists are interested in [8]." In the sequel to this paper we show how our definition may be applied to economic and statistical problems.

Before we begin it will be well to establish certain notational conventions. Throughout this paper $X$ and $Y$ will be r.v.'s with c.d.f.'s, $F$ and $G$, respectively. When they exist, we shall write the density functions of $F$ and $G$ as $f$ and $g$. In general we shall adhere to the convention that $F$ is less risky than $G$.

At present our results apply only to c.d.f.'s whose points of increase lie in a bounded interval, and we shall for convenience take that interval to be [0, 1], that is $F(0) = G(0) = 0$ and $F(1) = G(1) = 1$. The extension (and modification) of the results to c.d.f.'s defined on the whole real line is an open question whose resolution requires the solution of a host of delicate convergence problems of little economic interest. $H(x, z)$ is the joint distribution function of the r.v.'s $X$ and $Z$ defined on [0, 1] $\times$ [−1, 1], the cartesian product of [0, 1] and [−1, 1]. We shall use $S$ to refer to the difference of $G$ and $F$ and let $T$ be its indefinite integral, that is, $S(x) = G(x) - F(x)$ and $T(y) = \int_0^y S(x)\, dx$.

## II. THE INTEGRAL CONDITIONS

In this section we give a geometrically motivated definition of what it means for one r.v. to have more weight in the tails than another (Subsections 1 and 2). A definition of "greater risk" should be transitive. An examination of the consequence of this requirement leads to a more general definition which, although less intuitive, is analytically more convenient (Subsections 3 and 4).

### 1. Mean Preserving Spreads: Densities

Let $s(x)$ be a step function defined by

$$s(x) = \begin{cases} x \geqslant 0 & \text{for} \quad a < x < a + t \\ -x \leqslant 0 & \text{for} \quad a + d < x < a + d + t \\ -\beta \leqslant 0 & \text{for} \quad b < x < b + t \\ \beta \geqslant 0 & \text{for} \quad b + e < x < b + e + t \\ 0 & \text{otherwise,} \end{cases} \tag{3.i}$$

where

$$0 \leqslant a \leqslant a + t \leqslant a + d \leqslant a + d + t$$
$$\leqslant b \leqslant b + t \leqslant b + e \leqslant b + e + t \leqslant 1 \qquad (3.ii)$$

and

$$\beta e = \alpha d. \qquad (3.iii)$$

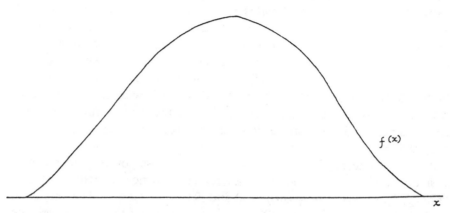

FIGURE 1

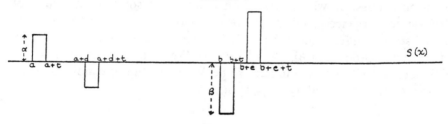

FIGURE 2

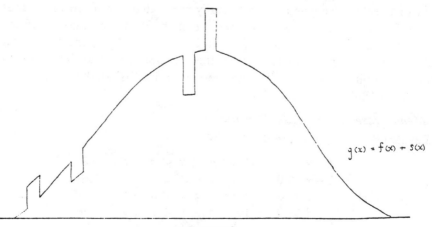

FIGURE 3

Such a function is pictured in Fig. 2. It is easy to verify that $\int_0^1 s(x)\,dx = \int_0^1 xs(x)\,dx = 0$. Thus if $f$ is a density function and if $g = f + s$, then $\int_0^1 g(x)\,dx = \int_0^1 f(x)\,dx + \int_0^1 s(x)\,dx = 1$ and $\int_0^1 xg(x)\,dx = \int_0^1 x(f(x) + s(x))\,dx = \int_0^1 xf(x)\,dx$. It follows then that if $g(x) \geqslant 0$ for all $x$, $g$ is a density function[4] with the same mean as $f$. Adding a function like $s$ to $f$ shifts probability weight from the center to the tails. See Figs. 1 and 3. We shall call a function which satisfies conditions (3) a mean preserving spread (MPS) and if $f$ and $g$ are densities and $g - f$ is a MPS we shall say that $g$ differs from $f$ by a single MPS.

## 2. Mean Preserving Spreads: Discrete Distributions

We may define a similar concept for the difference between discrete distributions. Let $F$ and $G$ be the c.d.f.'s of the discrete r.v.'s $X$ and $Y$. We can describe $X$ and $Y$ completely as follows:

$$\Pr(X = \hat{a}_i) = \hat{f}_i \quad \text{and} \quad \Pr(Y = \hat{a}_i) = \hat{g}_i,$$

where $\sum_i \hat{f}_i = \sum_i \hat{g}_i = 1$, and $\{\hat{a}_i\}$ is an increasing sequence of real numbers bounded by 0 and 1. Suppose $\hat{f}_i = \hat{g}_i$ for all but four $i$, say $i_1$, $i_2$, $i_3$, and $i_4$ where $i_k < i_{k+1}$. To avoid double subscripts let $a_k = \hat{a}_{i_k}$, $f_k = \hat{f}_{i_k}$, and $g_k = \hat{g}_{i_k}$, and define

$$\gamma_k = g_k - f_k$$

Then if

$$\gamma_1 = -\gamma_2 \geqslant 0 \quad \text{and} \quad \gamma_4 = -\gamma_3 \geqslant 0, \tag{4.i}$$

$Y$ has more weight in the tails than $X$ and if

$$\sum_{k=1}^4 a_k \gamma_k = 0, \tag{4.ii}$$

the means of $X$ and $Y$ will be the same. See Fig. 4. If two discrete r.v.'s $X$ and $Y$ attribute the same weight to all but four points and if their differences satisfy conditions (4) we shall say that $Y$ differs from $X$ by a single MPS.

## 3. The Integral Conditions

If two densities $g$ and $f$ differ by a single MPS, $s$, the difference of the corresponding c.d.f.'s $G$ and $F$ will be the indefinite integral of $s$. That is,

[4] That is, if $f(x) > \alpha$ for $a + d < x < a + d + t$ and $f(x) > \beta$ for $b < x < b + t$.

$s = g - f$ implies $S = G - F$ where $S(x) = \int_0^x s(u)\, du$. $S$, which is drawn in Fig. 5, has several interesting properties. The last two of these ((6) and (7) below) will play a crucial role in this paper, and we will refer to them as the integral conditions. First $S(0) = S(1) = 0$. Second, there is a $z$ such that

$$S(x) \geqslant 0 \quad \text{if} \quad x \leqslant z \quad \text{and} \quad S(x) \leqslant 0 \quad \text{if} \quad x > z. \qquad (5)$$

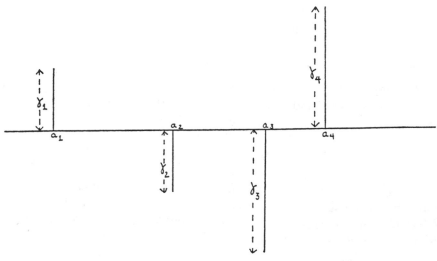

FIGURE 4

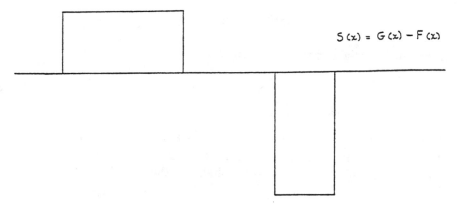

$$S(x) = G(x) - F(x)$$

FIGURE 5

Thirdly, if $T(y) = \int_0^y S(x)\, dx$ then

$$T(1) = 0 \qquad (6)$$

since $T(1) = \int_0^1 S(x)\, dx = xS(x)]_0^1 - \int_0^1 xs(x)\, dx = 0$.

Finally, conditions (5) and (6) together imply that

$$T(y) \geqslant 0, \qquad 0 \leqslant y < 1. \tag{7}$$

If $G$ and $F$ are discrete distributions differing by a single MPS and if $S = G - F$ then $S$ satisfies (5), (6), and (7). See Fig. 6.

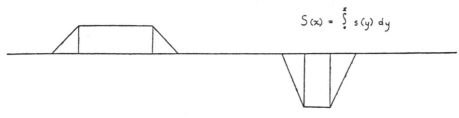

$$S(x) = \int_0^x s(y) \, dy$$

FIGURE 6

## 4. Implications of Transitivity

The concept of a MPS is the beginning, but only the beginning, of a definition of greater variability. To complete it we need to explore the implications of transitivity. That is, for our definition to be reasonable it should be the case that if $X_1$ is riskier than $X_2$ which is in turn riskier than $X_3$, then $X_1$ is riskier than $X_3$. Thus, if $X$ and $Y$ are the r.v.'s with c.d.f.'s $F$ and $G$, we need to find a criterion for deciding whether $G$ could have been obtained from $F$ by a sequence of MPS's. We demonstrate in this section that the criterion is contained in conditions (6) and (7) above.[5]

We will proceed by first stating precisely in Theorem 1(a) the obvious fact that if $G$ is obtained from $F$ by a sequence of MPS's, then $G - F$ satisfies the integral conditions ((6) and (7)). Theorem 1(b) is roughly the converse of that statement: That is, we show that if $G - F$ satisfies the integral conditions, $G$ could have been obtained from $F$ to any desired degree of approximation by a sequence of MPS's.

THEOREM 1(a). *If* (a) *there is a sequence of c.d.f.'s* $\{F_n\}$ *converging (weakly) to* $G$, (written $F_n \to G$)[6] *and* (b) $F_n$ *differs from* $F_{n-1}$ *by a single MPS,* (*which implies* $F_n = F_{n-1} + S_n = F_0 + \sum_{i=1}^{n} S_i$, *where* $F_0 \equiv F$, *and where each* $S_i$ *satisfies* (6) *and* (7)), *then* $G = F + \sum_{i=1}^{\infty} S_i = F + S$ *and* $S$ *satisfies* (6) *and* (7).

The proof, which is obvious, is omitted.

---

[5] Condition (5) could not be part of such a criterion for it is easy to construct examples of c.d.f.'s which differ by two MPS's such that their difference does not satisfy (5).

[6] Let $E(u) = \int_0^1 u(x) \, dG(x)$ and $E_n(u) = \int_0^1 u(x) \, dF_n(x)$. Then $F_n \to G$ if and only if $E_n(u) \to E(u)$ for all continuous $u$ on $[0, 1]$. See [3, p. 243].

THEOREM 1(b). *If $G - F$ satisfies the integral conditions (6) and (7), then there exist sequences $F_n$ and $G_n$, $F_n \to F$, $G_n \to G$, such that for each n, $G_n$ could have been obtained from $F_n$ by a finite number of MPS's.*

The proof is an immediate consequence of the following two lemmas: the first proves the theorem for step functions with a finite number of steps; and the second states that $F$ and $G$ may be approximated arbitrarily closely by step functions which satisfy the integral conditions.

LEMMA 1. *If X and Y are discrete r.v.'s whose c.d.f.'s F and G have a finite number of points of increase, and if $S = G - F$ satisfies (6) and (7), then there exist c.d.f.'s, $F_0$,..., $F_n$ such that $F_0 = F$, $F_n = G$, and $F_i$ differs from $F_{i-1}$ by a single MPS.*

*Proof.* $S$ is a step function with a finite number of steps. Let $I_1 = (a_1, a_2)$ be the first positive step of $S$. If $I_1$ does not exist, $S(x) \equiv 0$ implying that $F = G$ and the lemma is trivally true. Let $I_2 = (a_3, a_4)$ be the first negative step of $S(x)$. By (7), $a_2 < a_3$. Let $\gamma_1$ be the value of $S(x)$ on $I_1$ and $-\gamma_2$ be the value of $S(x)$ on $I_2$.
Either

$$\gamma_1(a_2 - a_1) \geqslant \gamma_2(a_4 - a_3) \tag{8}$$

or

$$\gamma_1(a_2 - a_1) < \gamma_2(a_4 - a_3). \tag{9}$$

If (8) holds, let $\hat{a}_4 = a_4$. There is an $\hat{a}_2$ satisfying $a_1 < \hat{a}_2 \leqslant a_2$ such that

$$\gamma_1(\hat{a}_2 - a_1) = \gamma_2(\hat{a}_4 - a_3). \tag{10}$$

If (9) holds, let $\hat{a}_2 = a_2$; then there is an $\hat{a}_4$ satisfying $a_3 < \hat{a}_4 < a_4$ such that (10) holds. Define $S_1(x)$ by

$$S_1(x) = \begin{cases} \gamma_1 & \text{for} \quad a_1 < x < \hat{a}_2 \\ -\gamma_2 & \text{for} \quad a_3 < x < \hat{a}_4 \\ 0 & \text{otherwise.} \end{cases}$$

Then if $F_1 = F_0 + S_1$, $F_1$ differs from $F$ by a single MPS and $S^{(1)} = G - F_1$ satisfies (6) and (7).

We use this technique to construct $S_2$ from $S^{(1)}$ and define $F_2$ by $F_2 = F_1 + S_2$. Because $S$ is a step function with a finite number of steps, the process terminates after a finite number of iterations.

LEMMA 2. *Let F and G be c.d.f.'s defined on [0, 1]. Let $T(y) = \int_0^y (G(x) - F(x))\, dx$. If*

$$T(y) \geqslant 0, \qquad 0 \leqslant y \leqslant 1, \tag{6}$$

*and*

$$T(1) = 0 \tag{7}$$

*then, for each n, there exists $F_n$ and $G_n$ , c.d.f.'s of discrete r.v.'s with a finite number of points of increase, such that if*

$$\| F_n - F \| = \int_0^1 | F_n(x) - F(x)| \, dx$$

*and*

$$\| G_n - G \| = \int_0^1 | G_n(x) - G(x)| \, dx,$$

*then*[7]

$$\| F_n - F \| + \| G_n - G \| \leqslant \frac{4}{n} \tag{11}$$

*and if $T_n(y) = \int_0^y (G_n(x) - F_n(x)) \, dx$ then*

$$T_n(y) \geqslant 0 \tag{12}$$

*and*

$$T_n(1) = 0. \tag{13}$$

*Proof.* We prove this by constructing $F_n$ and $G_n$ for fixed $n$. For $i = 1,..., n$ let $I_i = ((i - 1)/n, i/n)$. Let $\tilde{f}_i = F(i/n)$ and define $\bar{F}_n$ by $\bar{F}_n(x) = \tilde{f}_i$ for $x \in I_i$ (see Fig. 7). Since $F$ is monotonic $\bar{F}_n(x) \geqslant F(x)$. It follows also from monotonicity that $\| \bar{F}_n - F \| \leqslant 1/n$. If $\hat{F}_n(x)$ is any step function constant on each $I_i$ such that $\hat{F}_n(x) \in F(I_i)$ for $x \in I_i$ then $\| \hat{F}_n - \bar{F}_n \| \leqslant 1/n$ and

$$\| \hat{F}_n - F \| \leqslant \| \hat{F}_n - \bar{F}^n \| + \| \bar{F}_n - F \| \leqslant \frac{2}{n}.$$

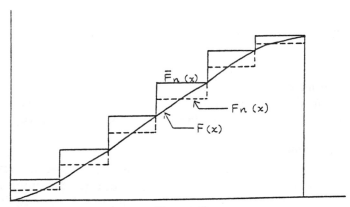

$\bar{F}_n (x)$

$F_n (x)$

$F (x)$

FIGURE 7

[7] Condition (11) implies weak convergence. See [3, p. 243].

Similarly if $\check{G}_n(x)$ is a step function such that $x \in I_i$ implies $\check{G}_n(x) \in G(I_i)$ then $\| \check{G}_n - G \| \leqslant 2/n$.

For every $i$ there exist $f_i \in F(I_i)$ and $g_i \in G(I_i)$ such that $(g_i - f_i)/n = \int_{I_i} (G(x) - F(x))\, dx$. Let $\hat{F}_n(x) = f_i$ and $\hat{G}_n(x) = g_i$, $x \in I_i$. We now show that $\hat{F}_n$ and $\hat{G}_n$ satisfy (11), (12), and (13). We have already shown that (11) is satisfied. Observe that

$$\hat{T}_n(1) = \int_0^1 (\hat{G}_n(x) - \hat{F}_n(x))\, dx$$

$$= \sum_{i=1}^n \int_{I_i} (\hat{G}_n(x) - \hat{F}_n(x))\, dx$$

$$= \sum_{i=1}^n \frac{g_i - f_i}{n} = \sum_{i=1}^n \int_{I_i} (G(x) - F(x))\, dx$$

$$= \int_0^1 (G(x) - F(x))\, dx = T(1) = 0,$$

so that (13) is satisfied. It remains to show that $\hat{T}_n(y) \geqslant 0$. If $y = j/n$ for $j = 0, 1, ..., n$, then $\hat{T}_n(y) = T(j/n) \geqslant 0$ so we need only examine the case where $y = j/n + \alpha$, $0 < \alpha < 1/n$. Then, $\hat{T}_n(x) = T(j/n) + \alpha(g_i - f_i)$. If $g_i > f_i$ both terms of the sum are positive. If $g_i < f_i$ then

$$T\left(\frac{j}{n}\right) + \alpha(g_i - f_i) > T\left(\frac{j}{n}\right) + \frac{1}{n}(g_i - f_i) = T\left(\frac{j+1}{n}\right) \geqslant 0.$$

This completes the proof except for a technical detail  Neither $\hat{F}_n$ nor $\hat{G}_n$ are necessarily c.d.f.'s. We remedy this by defining $F_n(x) = \hat{F}_n(x)$ for $x \in (0, 1)$ and $F_n(0) = 0$ and $F_n(1) = 1$. $G_n$ is defined similarly and if $\hat{F}_n$ and $\hat{G}_n$ satisfy (11), (12), and (13) so do $F_n$ and $G_n$.


### III. PARTIAL ORDERINGS OF DISTRIBUTION FUNCTIONS

A definition of greater uncertainty is, or should be, a definition of a partial ordering on a set of distribution functions. In this section we formally define the three partial orderings corresponding to the first three concepts of increasing risk set out in Section I and prove their equivalence.

### 1. Partial Orderings

A partial ordering $\leqslant_p$ on a set is a binary, transitive, reflexive and antisymmetric[8] relation. The set over which our partial orderings are defined is the set of distribution functions on $[0, 1]$. We shall use $F \leqslant_p G$

[8] A relation $\leqslant_p$ is antisymmetric if $A \leqslant_p B$ and $B \leqslant_p A$ implies $A = B$.

interchangeably with $X \leqslant_p Y$ where $F$ and $G$ are the c.d.f.'s of the r.v.'s $X$ and $Y$.

## 2. Definition of $\leqslant_I$

Following the discussion of the last section we define a partial ordering $\leqslant_I$ as follows: $F \leqslant_I G$ if and only if $G - F$ satisfies the integral conditions (6) and (7).

LEMMA 3. $\leqslant_I$ is a partial ordering.

*Proof.* It is immediate that $\leqslant_I$ is transitive and reflexive. We need only demonstrate antisymmetry. Assume $F \leqslant_I G$ and $G \leqslant_I F$. Define $S_1$ and $S_2$ as follows:

$$S_1 = G - F \quad \text{and} \quad S_2 = F - G.$$

Thus $S_1 + S_2 = 0$. Furthermore, if $T_i(y) = \int_0^y S_i(x) \, dx$, then $T_i(y) \geqslant 0$, since $F \leqslant_I G$ and $G \leqslant_I F$. Since $0 = \int_0^y (S_1(x) + S_2(x)) \, dx = T_1(y) + T_2(y) = 0$ and $T_i(y) \geqslant 0$, $T_i(y) = 0$. We shall prove this implies that $S_1(x) = 0$ a.e. (almost everywhere), or $F(x) = G(x)$ a.e. This will prove the lemma.[9]

Since $S_1(x)$ is of bounded variation (it is the difference of two monotonic functions) its discontinuities form a set of measure zero. Let us call this set $N$. Define

$$\hat{S}_1(x) = \begin{cases} 0 & \text{for } x \in N \\ S_1(x) & \text{otherwise.} \end{cases}$$

Then $\int_0^y S_1(x) \, dx = \int_0^y \hat{S}_1(x) \, dx = T_1(y)$. Suppose there is an $\hat{x}$ such that $\hat{S}_1(\hat{x}) \neq 0$, say $\hat{S}_1(\hat{x}) > 0$. Then $\hat{S}_1(x) > 0$ for $x \in (\hat{x} - \epsilon, \hat{x} + \epsilon)$ for some $\epsilon > 0$ (since $\hat{S}_1(x)$ is continuous at $\hat{x}$). Then, $T_1(x - \epsilon) < T_1(x + \epsilon)$. This contradiction completes the proof.

## 3. Definition of $\leqslant_u$

We define the partial ordering $\leqslant_u$ corresponding to the idea that $X$ is less risky than $Y$ if every risk averter prefers $X$ to $Y$ as follows. $F \leqslant_u G$ if and only if for every bounded concave function $U$, $\int_0^1 U(x) \, dF(x) \geqslant \int_0^1 U(x) \, dG(x)$. It is immediate that $\leqslant_u$ is transitive and reflexive. That $\leqslant_u$ is antisymmetric is an immediate consequence of Theorem 2 below.

## 4. Definition of $\leqslant_a$

Corresponding to the notion that $X$ is less risky than $Y$ if $Y$ has the same distribution as $X$ plus some noise is the partial ordering $\leqslant_a$ which

---

[9] We shall follow the convention of considering two distribution functions to be equal if they differ only on a set of measure zero.

we now define. $F \leqslant_a G$ if and only if there exists a joint distribution function $H(x, z)$ of the r.v.'s $X$ and $Z$ defined on $[0, 1] \times [-1, 1]$ such that if

$$J(y) = \Pr(X + Z \leqslant y),$$

then

$$F(x) = H(x, 1), \qquad 0 \leqslant x \leqslant 1,$$
$$G(y) = J(y), \qquad 0 \leqslant y \leqslant 1,$$

and

$$E(Z \mid X = x) = 0 \qquad \text{for all } x. \tag{14}$$

The equivalent definition in terms of r.v.'s follows: $X \leqslant_a Y$ if there exists an r.v. $Z$ satisfying (14) such that

$$Y \underset{d}{=} X + Z. \tag{15}$$

It is important to realize that (15) does *not* mean that $Y = X + Z$.

For the special case where $X$ and $Y$ are discrete distributions concentrated at a finite number of points, the relation $\leqslant_a$ can be given a useful and tractable characterization. Without loss of generality assume that $X$ and $Y$ are concentrated at the points $a_1, a_2, ..., a_n$. Then the c.d.f.'s of $X$ and $Y$ are determined by the numbers

$$f_i = \Pr(X = a_i)$$

and

$$g_i = \Pr(Y = a_i).$$

Then $X \leqslant_a Y$ if and only if there exist $n^2$ numbers $c_{ij} \geqslant 0$ such that

$$\sum_j c_{ij} = 1, \qquad i = 1, ..., n, \tag{16}$$

$$\sum_j c_{ij}(a_j - a_i) = 0, \qquad i = 1, ..., n, \tag{14'}$$

and

$$g_j = \sum_i f_i c_{ij}, \qquad j = 1, ..., n. \tag{15'}$$

To see that this is so, define an r.v. $Z$ conditional on $X$ as follows,

$$c_{ij} = \Pr(Z = a_j - a_i \mid X = a_i).$$

Then (16) states that this equation in fact defines a r.v. while (14') and (15') are the analoges of (14) and (15). These conditions can be written in matrix form:

$$Ca = a, \tag{14''}$$

$$g = fC, \tag{15''}$$

$$Ce = e, \tag{16''}$$

where $e = (1,..., 1)$ is the vector composed entirely of 1's. If $f^1, f^2$, and $f^3$ are vectors defining the c.d.f.'s of the discrete r.v.'s $X^1$, $X^2$, and $X^3$, ($f_i^k = \Pr(X^k = a_i)$), and if $X^1 \leqslant_a X^2$ and $X^2 \leqslant_a X^3$ then there exist matrices $C^1$ and $C^2$ such that $C^1a = C^2a = a$; $C^1e = C^2e = e$, while $f^2 = f^1C^1$ and $f^3 = f^2C^2$. Let $C^* = C^1C^2$. Then $f^3 = f^1C^*$ and $C^*a = C^1C^2a = C^1a = a$ and similarly $C^*e = e$. We have proved

LEMMA 4. *If $X^1$, $X^2$, and $X^3$ are concentrated at a finite number of points, then $X^1 \leqslant_a X^2 \leqslant_a X^3$ implies $X^1 \leqslant_a X^3$.*

5. *Equivalence of $\leqslant_I$, $\leqslant_a$, $\leqslant_u$*

We now state and prove the major result of this paper.

THEOREM 2. *The following statements are equivalent:*

(A) $F \leqslant_u G$;

(B) $F \leqslant_I G$;

(C) $F \leqslant_a G$.

*Proof.* The proof consists of demonstrating the chain of implications (C) $\Rightarrow$ (A) $\Rightarrow$ (B) $\Rightarrow$ (C). Throughout the proof we adhere to the notational conventions introduced at the end of Section I.

(a) $X \leqslant_a Y \Rightarrow X \leqslant_u Y$.

By hypothesis there is an r.v. $Z$ such that $Y \underset{a}{=} X + Z$ and $E(Z \mid X) = 0$. For every fixed $X$ and concave $U$ we have, upon taking expectations with respect to $Z$, by Jensen's inequality

$$E_xU(X + Z) \leqslant U(E(X + Z)) = U(X).$$

Taking expectations with respect to $X$,

$$EE_xU(X + Z) \leqslant EU(X)$$

or

$$EU(Y) \leqslant EU(X).$$

(b) $F \leqslant_u G \Rightarrow F \leqslant_I G$.[10]

If $S = G - F$ then $F \leqslant_u G$ implies $\int_0^1 U(x) \, dS(X) \leqslant 0$ for all concave $U$. Since the identity function and its negative are both concave we have that $\int_0^1 x \, dS(x) \leqslant 0$ and $\int_0^1 (-x) \, dS(x) \leqslant 0$ so that $\int_0^1 x \, dS(x) = 0$. Integrating by parts we find that $T(1) = 0$. It remains to show that $T(y) \geqslant 0$ for all $y \in [0, 1]$. For fixed $y$, let $b_y(x) = \text{Max}(y - x, 0)$. Then $-b_y(x)$ is concave and $0 \leqslant \int_0^1 b_y(x) \, dS(x) = \int_0^y (y - x) \, dS(x) = yS(y) - \int_0^y x \, dS(x)$. Integrating the last term by parts we find that

$$-\int_0^y x \, dS(x) = -xS(x) \Big]_0^y + \int_0^y S(x) \, dx$$
$$= -yS(y) + T(y).$$

Thus, $T(y) = \int_0^1 b_y(x) \, dS(x) \geqslant 0$.

(c) $F \leqslant_I G \Rightarrow F \leqslant_a G$.

We prove this implication first for the case where $F$ and $G$ are discrete r.v.'s which differ by a single MPS. Using the notation of Section II.2, let $F$ and $G$ attribute the same probability weight to all but four points $a_1 < a_2 < a_3 < a_4$. Let $\text{Pr}(X = a_k) = f_k$ and $\text{Pr}(Y = a_k) = g_k$. If $\gamma_k = g_k - f_k$, then

$$\gamma_1 = -\gamma_2 \geqslant 0, \qquad \gamma_4 = -\gamma_3 \geqslant 0 \tag{4.i}$$

and

$$\sum_{k=1}^{4} \gamma_k a_k = 0 \tag{4.ii}$$

are the conditions that $G$ differs from $F$ by a single MPS. To prove that $F \leqslant_a G$ we need only show the existence of $c_{ij} \geqslant 0$ $(i, j = 1, 2, 3, 4)$ satisfying (14'), (15'), and (16). Consider,

$$\{c_{ij}\} = \begin{pmatrix} 1 & 0 & 0 & 0 \\ \dfrac{\gamma_1(a_4 - a_2)}{f_2(a_4 - a_1)} & \dfrac{g_2}{f_2} & 0 & \dfrac{\gamma_1(a_2 - a_1)}{f_2(a_4 - a_1)} \\ \dfrac{\gamma_4(a_4 - a_3)}{f_3(a_4 - a_1)} & 0 & \dfrac{g_3}{f_3} & \dfrac{\gamma_4(a_3 - a_1)}{f_3(a_4 - a_1)} \\ 0 & 0 & 0 & 1 \end{pmatrix} \tag{17}$$

[10] We are indebted to David Wallace for the present simplified form of the proof. For continuously differentiable $U$, the reverse implication may be proved simply by integration by parts.

It is easy to verify that the $c_{ij}$ defined by (17) do satisfy (16) and (14'). Thus if we define $Z$, as before, by

$$c_{ij} = \Pr(Z = a_j - a_i \mid X = a_i)$$

then $Z$ is a random variable, conditional on $X$, satisfying $E(Z \mid X) = 0$. It remains to establish (15') or that $Y \underset{d}{=} X + Z$. Consider $Y^1 = X + Z$. $Y^1$ is a discrete r.v. which, since $E(Z) = 0$, has the same mean as $Y$. It can differ from $Y$ only if it attributes different probability weight to the points $a_1$, $a_2$, $a_3$, $a_4$. But,

$$\Pr(Y^1 = a_2) = \Pr(X = a_2) \cdot \Pr(Z = 0 \mid X = a_2)$$

$$= f_2 \cdot \frac{g_2}{f_2} = g_2 = \Pr(Y = a_2).$$

Similarly, $\Pr(Y^1 = a_3) = \Pr(Y = a_3)$. Then $Y$ and $Y^1$ can differ in the assignment of probability weight in at most two points. But $\Pr(Y = a_1) > \Pr(Y^1 = a_1)$ implies $\Pr(Y^1 = a_4) > \Pr(Y = a_4)$ which in turn implies that $E(Y^1) > E(Y)$, a contradiction. Thus, $Y \underset{d}{=} Y^1 \underset{d}{=} X + Z$.

Lemmas 1 and 4 allow us to extend this result to all discrete distributions with a finite number of points of increase. We use Theorem 1(b) to extend it to all c.d.f.'s. If $F \leqslant_I G$, there exists sequences $\{F_n\}$ and $\{G_n\}$ of discrete distributions with a finite number of points of increase such that $F_n \to F$ and $G_n \to G$ and $F_n \leqslant_I G_n$. We have just shown $F_n \leqslant_a G_n$. Let $X_n$ and $Y_n$ be the r.v.'s with distributions $F_n$ and $G_n$. There is for each $n$ an $H_n(x, z)$, the joint distribution function of the r.v.'s $X_n$ and $Z_n$, such that if $J_n(y) = \Pr(X_n + Z_n \leqslant y)$, then

$$J_n(y) = G_n(y), \tag{18}$$

$$F_n(x) = H_n(x, 1), \tag{19}$$

and

$$E(X_n \mid Z_n) = 0. \tag{20}$$

Since $H_n$ is a discrete distribution function Eq. (20) can be phrased as

$$\int_0^1 \int_{-1}^1 u(x)z \, dH_n(x, z) = 0 \tag{21}$$

for all continuous functions $u$ defined on $[0, 1]$. Since $H_n$ is stochastically bounded, the sequence $\{H_n\}$ has a subsequence $\{H_{n'}\}$ which converges to a distribution function[11] $H(x, z)$ of the r.v.'s $X$ and $Z$. Since $H_{n'}(x, 1) = F_{n'}(x) \to F$, $H_{n'}(x, 1) \to F$. Similarly, $J_{n'} \to G$. Let

$$M_{n'} = \int_0^1 \int_{-1}^1 u(x)z \, dH_{n'}(x, z).$$

[11] See [3, pp. 247, 261].

By the definition of weak convergence $M_{n'} \to \int_0^1 \int_{-1}^1 u(x)z \, dH(x, z)$. But $\{M_{n'}\}$ is a sequence all of whose terms are 0 and it must therefore converge to 0. Therefore $\int_0^1 \int_{-1}^1 u(x)z \, dH(x, z) = 0$, which implies $E(Z \mid X) = 0$. This completes the proof.

## 6. Further Remarks

We conclude this section with two remarks about these orderings.

A. *Partial versus Complete Orderings.* In the previous subsection, we established that $\geqslant_a$, $\geqslant_I$, and $\geqslant_u$ define equivalent partial orderings over distributions with the same mean. It should be emphasized that these orderings are only partial, that is, if $F$ and $G$ have the same mean but $\int_0^1 (F(x) - G(x)) \, dx = T(y)$ changes sign, $F$ and $G$ cannot be ordered. But this means in turn that there always exist two concave functions, $U_1$ and $U_2$, such that $\int_0^1 U_1 \, dF(x) > \int_0^1 dG(x)$ while $\int_0^1 U_2 \, dF(x) < \int_0^1 U_2 \, dG(x)$; that is, there is some risk averse individual who prefers $F$ to $G$ and another who prefers $G$ to $F$. On the other hand, the ordering $\geqslant_V$ associated with the mean-variance analysis ($X \leqslant_V Y$ if $EX = EY$ and $EX^2 \leqslant EY^2$) is a complete ordering, i.e., if $X$ and $Y$ have the same mean, either $X \leqslant_V Y$ or $X \geqslant_V X$.[12]

B. *Concavity.* We have already noted that if $U$ is concave, $X \leqslant_I Y$ implies $EU(X) \leqslant EU(Y)$. Similarly, given any differentiable function $U$ which over the interval $[0, 1]$ is neither concave nor convex, then there exist distribution functions $F$, $G$, and $H$, $F \geqslant_I G \geqslant_I H$, such that $\int_0^1 U(x) \, dF \leqslant \int_0^1 U(x) \, dG$, but $\int_0^1 U(x) \, dG \geqslant \int_0^1 U(x) \, dH$.

In short, $\geqslant_I$ defines the set of all concave functions: A function $U$ is concave if and only if $X \leqslant_I Y$ implies $EU(X) \leqslant EU(Y)$.

---

[12] Another way of making this point is to observe that $\geqslant_V$ is stronger than $\geqslant_I$ because many distributions which can be ordered with respect to $\geqslant_V$ cannot be ordered with respect to $\geqslant_I$. Clearly there exist weaker as well as stronger orderings than $\geqslant_I$. One such weaker ordering, to which we drew attention in earlier versions of this paper, is the following. A r.v. $X$ which is a mixture between a r.v. $Y$ and a sure thing with the same mean—a random variable concentrated at the point $E(Y)$—is surely less risky than $Y$ itself. We could use this notion to define a partial ordering $\geqslant_M$. It is obvious that $\geqslant_M$ implies $\geqslant_I$ since the difference between $X$ and $Y$ satisfies the integral conditions. It is also clear that $\geqslant_M$ is a very weak ordering in the sense that very few r.v.'s can be ordered by $\geqslant_M$. In fact if $\bar{Y}$ is the sure thing concentrated at $E(Y)$ than it can be shown that $Y \geqslant_M X$ iff $X \underset{d}{=} aY + (1 - a) \bar{Y}$ for $0 \leqslant a \leqslant 1$. This indicates that $\geqslant_M$ is not a particularly interesting partial ordering. We are indebted to an anonymous referee for pointing out the deficiencies of $\geqslant_M$.

## IV. Mean-Variance Analysis

The method most frequently used for comparing uncertain prospects has been mean-variance analysis. It is easy to show that such comparisons may lead to unjustified conclusions. For instance, if $X$ and $Y$ have the same mean, $X$ may have a lower variance and yet $Y$ will be preferred to $X$ by some risk averse individuals. To see this, all we need observe is that, although $F \leqslant_u G \Rightarrow F \geqslant_V G$ (since variance is a convex function), $F \geqslant_V G$ does not imply $F \geqslant_u G$. Indeed by arguments closely analogous to those used earlier, it can be shown that a function $U$ is quadratic if and only if $X \geqslant_V Y$ implies $EU(X) \geqslant EU(Y)$. An immediate consequence of this is that if $U(x)$ is any nonquadratic concave function, then there exists random variables $X_i$, $i = 1, 2, 3$, all with the same mean such that $EX_1^2 < EX_2^2$ but $EX_2^2 > EX_3^2$ while $EU(X_1) < EU(X_2) < EU(X_3)$, i.e., the ranking by variance and the ranking by expected utility are different.

Tobin has conjectured that mean-variance analysis may be appropriate if the class of distributions—and thus the class of changes in distributions—is restricted. This is true but the restrictions required are, as far as is presently known, very severe. Tobin's proof is—as he implicitly recognizes (in [7, pp. 20–21])—valid only for distributions which differ only by "location parameters." (See [3, p. 144] for a discussion of this classical concept.) That is, Tobin is only willing to consider changes in distributions from $F$ to $G$ if there exist $a$ and $b$ ($a > 0$) such that $F(x) = G(ax + b)$. Such changes amount only to a change in the centering of the distribution and a uniform shrinking or stretching of the distribution—equivalent to a change in units.

There has been some needless confusion along these lines about the concept of a two parameter family of distribution functions. It is undeniable that all distributions which differ only by location parameters form a two parameter family. In general, what is meant by a "two parameter family"? To us a two parameter family of distributions would seem to be any set of distributions such that one member of the set would be picked out be selecting two parameters. As Tobin has put it, it is "one such that it is necessary to know just two numbers in order to describe the whole distribution." Technically that is, a two parameter family is a mapping from $E^2$ into the space of distribution functions.[13] It is clear that for this broad definition of two parameter family, Tobin's conjecture cannot possibly hold, for nothing restricts the range of this mapping.

Other definitions of two parameter family are of course possible. They involve essentially restrictions to "nice" mappings from $E^2$ to the space of

---

[13] Or some subset of $E^2$; we might restrict one or both of our parameters to be nonnegative.

116

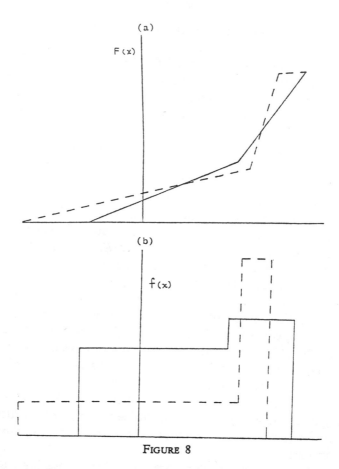

FIGURE 8

distribution functions, e.g., a family of distributions with an explicit algebraic form containing only two parameters which can vary. It is easy, however, to construct examples where if the variance, $\sigma^2$, changes with the mean, $\mu$, held constant, $\partial T(y)/\partial \sigma^2$ changes sign, where $T(y, \sigma^2, \mu) = \int_0^y F(x, \sigma^2, \mu)$; that is, there exist individuals with concave utility functions who are better off with an increase in variance.[14]

[14] Consider, for instance, the family of distributions defined as follows: $(a, c > 0)$. (In this example, for expositional clarity we have abandoned our usual convention of defining distributions over $[0, 1]$)

$$F(x; a, c) = \begin{cases} 0 & \text{for } x \leqslant 1 - 0.25/a \\ ax + 0.25 - a & \text{for } 1 - 0.25/a \leqslant x \leqslant 1 + (2c - 0.5)/c - a) \\ cx + 0.75 - 3c & \text{for } 1 + (2c - 0.5)/(c - a) \leqslant x \leqslant 3 + 0.25/c \\ 1 & \text{for } x > 3 + 0.25/c \end{cases}$$

Two members of the family with the same mean but different variances are depicted in Fig. 8(a). They clearly do not satisfy condition (7). The density functions are illustrated in Fig. 8(b).

ACKNOWLEDGMENTS

This is a revised version of papers presented at the Cowles Symposium on Capital Theory and Uncertainty (November, 1968), and at the Chicago Growth Symposium (November, 1967).

The authors are deeply indebted to the participants in the symposiums and to David Ragozin, Peter Diamond, David Wallace, and David Grether.

Our problem is not a new one, nor is our approach completely novel; our result is, we think, new. Our interest in this topic was whetted by Peter Diamond [2]. Robert Solow used a device similar to our Mean Preserving Spread (Section II, above) to compare lag structures in [6]. The problem of "stochastic dominance" is a standard one in the (statistics) operations research literature. For other approaches to the problem, see, for instance, [1]. [4, 5] have recently provided an alternative proof to our Theorem 2(b) and its converse (p. 238).

REFERENCES

1. S. A. Bessler and A. F. Veinott, Jr., Optimal policy for a dynamic multi-echelon inventory model, *Naval Research Logistics Quarterly* 13 (1966), 355–387.
2. P. A. Diamond, Savings decisions under uncertainty, Working paper no. 71, Institute of Business Economic Research, University of California, Berkeley, June 1965.
3. W. Feller, "An Introduction to Probability Theory and Its Applications," Vol. II, Wiley, New York, 1966.
4. J. Hader and W. Russell, Rules for ordering uncertain prospects, *Amer. Econ. Rev.* 59 (1969), 25–34.
5. G. Hanoch and C. Levy, Efficiency Analysis of Choices Involving risk, *Review of Economic Studies* 36 (1969).
6. R. M. Solow, A note on dynamic multipliers, *Econometrica* 19 (1951), 306–316.
7. J. Tobin, The theory of portfolio selection, *in* F. Hahn and F. Brechling, "The Theory of Interest Rates," MacMillan, London, 1965.
8. J. Tobin, Comment on Borch and Feldstein, *Rev. Econ. Studies* 36 (1969), 13–14.

# Aspects of Rational Insurance Purchasing

## Jan Mossin*

*Norwegian School of Economics and Business Administration*

## I. Introduction

Problems concerned with purchasing of insurance coverage appear to be a fascinating and potentially fruitful field for application and testing of theories of riskbearing. In this note we shall analyze a series of such problems from the point of view of an individual facing certain risks. Given his risk situation and his economic background (as measured by his initial wealth), his problem is to decide whether he should provide for insurance coverage and, if so, how much.

The analysis serves two purposes. On the one hand, the solution to problems of optimal insurance coverage in various situations is clearly of considerable practical interest in itself. From another point of view, however, the analysis can be regarded as a set of methodological exercises: They illustrate the power of the expected utility approach to problems of risk taking, and, in particular, they demonstrate the applicability and implications of hypotheses about the individual's *risk aversion function*.

Absolute risk aversion (in the Pratt-Arrow sense) is defined as

$$R_a(Y) = -U''(Y)/U'(Y),$$

where $U$ is a utility function representing preferences over alternative levels of wealth (or net worth) $Y$. The risk aversion function is clearly uniquely determined by this preference ordering and contains all essential information about the utility function. Pratt (1964) and Arrow (1965) illustrate how (local) values of the risk aversion function reflect behavior with regard to small risks. Arrow advances the hypothesis of $R_a$ as a decreasing function of wealth, and he uses this hypothesis in analyzing a portfolio selection problem to show it implies that investment in a risky asset

* An earlier version appeared as CORE Discussion Paper No. 6705. It was written during the author's stay as visitor to the Center for Operations Research and Econometrics, University of Louvain.

increases with the size of the portfolio. In analyzing a model incorporating both consumption and portfolio choices, Sandmo (1968) derives similar, plausible conclusions from the hypothesis of decreasing risk aversion. Mossin (1968a) has shown how the same hypothesis can be employed to derive implications of taxation for risk taking.

In itself, the hypothesis of decreasing risk aversion is just a formalization of a certain property of a preference ordering. As such it leaves a good deal to be desired in the way of meaningfulness. It is only when its implications for behavior in a wide variety of circumstances are explored that its usefulness is established.

Parts II and III of this article deal with problems of property insurance; Part IV analyzes a reinsurance decision by an insurance company (based on a model by Borch [1961]); while Part V considers the determination of an optimal deductible encountered in several types of insurance.

## II. Property Insurance: Maximum Acceptable Premium for Full Coverage

Consider an individual owning a piece of property the value of which is $L$. In addition, he owns other assets to a total amount of $A$. His total wealth in the initial situation is thus $A + L$. To keep things simple, we shall disregard here any yield that might be earned on this wealth. The property in question may be subject to damage of one sort or another, and, again for simplicity, it will be assumed that during any specified time interval the property will either be completely lost with probability $\pi$ or it will suffer no damage at all with probability $1 - \pi$.

The individual has the possibility of insuring his property. The premium he would have to pay (in absolute money terms) will be denoted by $p$. We are interested in the maximum premium he would be willing to pay for the insurance, that is, the premium where he would just be indifferent between having and not having the insurance. That such a premium exists is actually one of the axioms of the von Neumann-Morgenstern utility theory.

If he does not take insurance, his final wealth will be a stochastic variable $Y_1$:

$$Y_1 = \begin{cases} A & \text{with probability} \quad \pi \\ A + L & \text{with probability } 1 - \pi \end{cases}$$

Expected utility from this prospect is thus $\pi U(A) + (1 - \pi)U(A + L)$. If he does take insurance, however, his final wealth will with certainty amount to

$$Y_2 = A + L - p,$$

so that his utility from this alternative is $U(A + L - p)$.

The maximum premium he is willing to pay is therefore defined by the condition

$$\pi U(A) + (1 - \pi)U(A + L) = U(A + L - p). \tag{1}$$

This equation determines $p$ as a function of the parameters $\pi$, $L$, and $A$. When general risk aversion is assumed ($U'' < 0$), it is clear that the maximum premium exceeds the actuarial value of the loss ($p > \pi L$). This fact is easily seen from Figure 1, $a$, which gives a geometrical representation of the condition (1).

It is obvious that the maximum $p$ will increase with both $\pi$ and $L$. More interesting, and more important, is the dependence of $p$ on $A$, that is, the wealth effect on the individual's willingness to provide insurance coverage. We shall demonstrate the following: *If the individual has decreasing risk aversion, then the maximum acceptable premium is lower the larger his wealth.*

By differentiation of (1), we obtain

$$\frac{dp}{dA} = -\frac{\pi U'(A) + (1 - \pi)U'(A + L) - U'(A + L - p)}{U'(A + L - p)}. \qquad (2)$$

Thus, $dp/dA$ will be negative if and only if the numerator on the right-hand side (RHS) is positive, that is, if

$$N = \pi U'(A) + (1 - \pi)U'(A + L) - U'(A + L - p) > 0 \qquad (3)$$

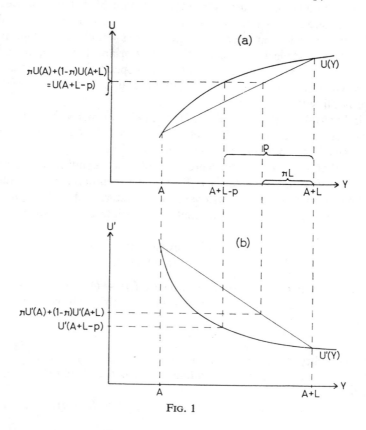

Fig. 1

for any $\pi$. (We assume $U$ to be twice continuously differentiable with $U' > 0$ and $U'' < 0$.) The relation between (2) and (3) is illustrated in Figure 1 for a given $\pi$.

We now substitute (1) into the expression for $N$ by eliminating $\pi$; then

$$N(p) = \frac{U(A + L) - U(A + L - p)}{U(A + L) - U(A)} U'(A)$$

$$+ \frac{U(A + L - p) - U(A)}{U(A + L) - U(A)} U'(A + L) - U'(A + L - p).$$

We now show that for any $0 < p < L$ (corresponding to any $0 < \pi < 1$), $N > 0$ when $R_a$ is monotonically decreasing on the interval $(A, A + L)$.

The derivative of $N(p)$ is

$$N'(p) = U''(A + L - p) + \frac{U'(A) - U'(A + L)}{U(A + L) - U(A)} U'(A + L - p)$$

$$= -U'(A + L - p) \left[ R_a(A + L - p) - \frac{U'(A) - U'(A + L)}{U(A + L) - U(A)} \right].$$

It is easy to see that $N(0) = N(L) = 0$. Then, by Rolle's theorem, $N(p)$ has at least one extreme point in the interval $(A, A + L)$, such a point being defined by

$$R_a(A + L - p) - \frac{U'(A) - U'(A + L)}{U(A + L) - U(A)} = 0,$$

where the second term on the left is a positive constant. Since $R_a$ is monotonically decreasing, there can be only one such extreme point, say $\bar{p}$. Further, for $p < \bar{p}$, $N'(p) > 0$, and conversely. Thus, $\bar{p}$ must be a maximum point. It therefore follows that $N(p)$ is uniformly positive, which in turn implies that $dp/dA < 0$.[1]

### III. Property Insurance: Optimal Coverage at Given Premium

This section describes an optimization problem. As above, total initial wealth of our individual is $A + L$, of which $L$ is the value of the risky property. We now assume, however, that if he buys insurance, he can specify the desired amount of coverage $C$ (expressed in absolute money terms). Regular insurance practice would require the condition $0 \leq C \leq L$, although the buyer of insurance might possibly be able to buy more than $L$ by gambling with another source, say a bookie or Lloyd's. We shall return to this possibility below.

With coverage $C$, the premium will be proportional to $C$, while, on the other hand, the compensation from the company in case of damage will also be in proportion to $C$. Thus, if $p$ is the premium *rate* (a percentage in

---

[1] I am grateful to W. Szwarc for providing the basis for this proof.

this case) that the company charges, the premium will be $pC$, while if a damage of size $X$ occurs, the compensation received from the company will be $(C/L)X$. Therefore the individual's final wealth will be the random variable

$$Y = A + L - X + \frac{C}{L}X - pC,$$
(4)

and the problem is to maximize $E[U(Y)]$ subject to the condition $0 \leq C \leq L$.

The first two derivatives of $E[U(Y)]$ with respect to $C$ are

$$\frac{dE[U(Y)]}{dC} = E\left[U'(Y)\left(\frac{X}{L} - p\right)\right],$$
(5)

and

$$\frac{d^2E[U(Y)]}{dC^2} = E\left[U''(Y)\left(\frac{X}{L} - p\right)^2\right] < 0.$$
(6)

Since risk aversion is assumed, the second derivative is negative, which insures a unique maximum point.

We may first examine conditions for taking full coverage, that is, choosing $C = L$. A necessary and sufficient condition is clearly that the first derivative at this point is non-negative, that is,

$$\frac{dE[U(Y)]}{dC}\bigg|_{C=L} = U'(A + L - pL)\left[\frac{E(X)}{L} - p\right] \geq 0.$$

But since $U' > 0$, this is the same as requiring $pL \leq E(X)$, that is, that *the premium should be actuarially favorable* (or at least fair) to the individual. This is the same as saying that *if the premium is actuarially unfavorable, then it will never be optimal to take full coverage.* Thus, under conditions of risk aversion, and with an unfavorable premium, the condition $C \leq L$ will not be binding. Overinsurance at unfavorable odds is pure gambling, which is ruled out by risk aversion.

The condition for not taking insurance at all, that is, choosing $C = 0$, does not seem to afford any clearcut interpretation,[2] and we shall therefore proceed on the assumption that the individual selects an interior maximum point, this point being defined by

$$E\left[U'(Y)\left(\frac{X}{L} - p\right)\right] = 0.$$
(7)

The condition (7) reflects the balancing of the loss in expected utility from an increased premium against the gain in expected utility from additional security against loss. Since $(X/L) - p$ is the (random) net receipt

[2] The condition is that the derivative at this point is negative, that is,

$$E[U'(A + L - X)(X/L - p)] \leq 0.$$

from the company from an additional unit of coverage, $U'(Y)[(X/L) - p]$ is the random utility increment from an additional unit of coverage, so that coverage is pushed to the point where the expected increment becomes zero. On this interpretation, the conclusion that full coverage is never optimal seems quite plausible, at least when considered as a normative guideline.

Casual empirical evidence seems to contradict the conclusion, however; some of our best friends take full coverage. Several explanations for such behavior can of course be offered, among them: (a) they simply behave irrationally, for example, by not bothering to determine optimal coverage; (b) there may be some uncertainty as to what will be the actual evaluation of the property in case of damage. We have not taken this kind of randomness into account in our theory, but it seems a perfectly reasonable hypothesis that it will lead to a number of observed cases of full (or over-) insurance; (c) they may uniformly overestimate the probability distribution for damage (although such overestimation must really lead them to believe the company to be so benevolent as to offer actuarially favorable premiums).

Apart from this it is clear that we have said nothing about the *magnitude* of the discrepancy between optimal and full coverage. To do so would require specifications of both the utility function and probability distribution for damage. We may give an illustration by assuming the binary distribution used in Part II and a utility function $U = \ln Y$. (Some theoretical support for utility functions of this form, at least as an approximation for intermediate values of wealth, is given in Arrow [1965].) It is easy to verify that the optimal coverage in this case is given by

$$C = \frac{\pi}{p} L - \left( \frac{1 - \pi}{1 - p} - \frac{\pi}{p} \right) A.$$

Thus, if $\pi = 0.01$ and $p = 0.01$ (a loading factor of 1), the coverage never exceeds 50 per cent of the property value and decreases with increasing wealth to become zero when the property represents less than 50/99 of total initial wealth $A + L$. For very small $\pi$, and with a moderate loading factor $\lambda = (p - \pi)/\pi$, the difference between full and optimal coverage becomes approximately

$$L - C = \frac{\lambda}{1 + \lambda} (A + L).$$

The example anticipates a proposition similar to the one in Part II, which we shall now prove generally: *If the individual has decreasing risk aversion, then the optimal coverage is lower the larger his wealth.*

Differentiation of (7) yields

$$\frac{dC}{dA} = -\frac{E\left[U''(Y)\left(\frac{X}{L} - p\right)\right]}{E\left[U''(Y)\left(\frac{X}{L} - p\right)^2\right]}. \tag{8}$$

The denominator being negative, the effect will be of the same sign as $E\{U''(Y)[(X/L) - p]\}$. We shall show that this is negative if $R_a(Y)$ is decreasing. Observe first that (4) can be written as

$$Y = (A + L - pL) - (L - C)\left(\frac{X}{L} - p\right).$$

Consider first the case where $(X/L) - p \geq 0$; then clearly $Y \leq A + L - pL$, and therefore

$$R_a(Y) \geq R_a(A + L - pL)$$

or

$$\frac{U''(Y)}{U'(Y)} \leq -R_a(A + L - pL). \tag{9}$$

Trivially,

$$U'(Y)\left(\frac{X}{L} - p\right) \geq 0, \tag{10}$$

so multiplying through in (9) by $U'(Y)[(X/L) - p]$ does not change the direction of the inequality. Thus,

$$U''(Y)\left(\frac{X}{L} - p\right) \leq -R_a(A + L - pL)U'(Y)\left(\frac{X}{L} - p\right). \tag{11}$$

Suppose now that $[(X/L) - p] < 0$. Then the inequalities (9) and (10) are both reversed, and so (11) must hold for any $X$. We now take expectations on both sides of (11); since $R_a(A + L - pL)$ is not a random variable this gives

$$E\left[U''(Y)\left(\frac{X}{L} - p\right)\right] \leq -R_a(A + L - pL)E\left[U'(Y)\left(\frac{X}{L} - p\right)\right]. \tag{12}$$

But in view of (7), the RHS is zero, proving our proposition.

## IV. Optimal Reinsurance Quota

An optimization problem closely akin to the preceding one has been presented by Borch (1961). He considers an insurance company holding total funds $A$ which it can draw upon to pay claims $X$ being made under the contracts of its portfolio. In this risk situation, the company wants to reinsure a quota $k$ of its portfolio. For this reinsurance cover it has to pay the net premium $kE(X)$, plus a loading $\lambda kE(X)$. With this arrangement the company pays $(1 - k)X$ of the claims itself, so that its net worth is the random variable

$$Y = A - (1 + \lambda)kE(X) - (1 - k)X. \tag{13}$$

The optimal value of $k$ is the one which maximizes $E[U(Y)]$, and it is easily verified that it can never be optimal to provide complete reinsurance cover, that is, to choose $k = 1$. This is completely analogous to the result obtained in Part III. If the optimum occurs at a value of $k > 0$, we have here

$$\frac{dE[U(Y)]}{dk} = E\{U'(Y)[X - (1 + \lambda)E(X)]\} = 0. \qquad (14)$$

This condition has again an immediate interpretation in terms of balancing profit loss against added security and also suggests the implausibility of $k = 0$ being optimal.

Assuming (14) to hold, it is also possible here to demonstrate that *if the company has decreasing risk aversion, then the optimal reinsurance quota is smaller the larger its funds.*

Differentiation of (14) gives

$$\frac{dk}{dA} = -\frac{E\{U''(Y)[X - (1 + \lambda)E(X)]\}}{E\{U''(Y)[X - (1 + \lambda)E(X)]^2\}}, \qquad (15)$$

so that $dk/dA$ is negative if the numerator is. The trick here is to rewrite (13) as

$$Y = A - (1 + \lambda)E(X) - (1 - k)[X - (1 + \lambda)E(X)],$$

and then proceed exactly as in Part III, thereby showing that the numerator in (15) is negative.

The derivative (15) is, of course, to be considered as a partial derivative for constant $E(X)$. Ordinarily, there will be a fairly close relationship between the funds of a company and the size of its contract portfolio, the funds consisting in large part of prepaid premiums on the contracts. If we were to study the relationship between funds and reinsurance quotas in companies, this relationship would have to be taken into account. Clearly, the effect of variations in $E(X)$ would offset the effect of variations in $A$ to a smaller or larger extent. To illustrate, we may consider the case of direct proportionality between $A$ and $E(X)$, as $A = (1 + \mu)E(X)$. Such a relationship, for example, would exist if the funds consisted entirely of prepaid premiums on the current portfolio, all having been charged with a loading factor $\mu$. The expression for the effect of changes in $S$ can in this case be written conveniently as

$$\left. \frac{dk}{dA} \right|_{A/(1+\mu)} = \left(1 - \frac{1 + \lambda}{1 + \mu} k\right) \left. \frac{dk}{dA} \right|_{E(X) = \text{constant}}. \qquad (16)$$

The factor $1 - [(1 + \lambda)/(1 + \mu)]k$ is clearly less than 1 but, unless $\lambda$ is quite large relative to $\mu$, also positive. Presumably, insurance companies charge other companies a smaller loading than they do ordinary people.

126

## V. Optimal Amount of Deductible

In the final model we shall consider an individual who may have to pay a claim in the random amount of $X$·and who wishes to provide insurance cover against this contingency. We shall assume that he may do so by signing an insurance contract fixing a certain amount $S$ (the amount deductible) such that he covers the first $S$ units or part thereof himself, while the company covers any excess. Such arrangements characterize, for example, automobile collision insurance and are also used in various forms of medical insurance. Certain aspects of this problem have been investigated by Pashigian, Schkade, and Menefee (1966).

The amount paid by the company under such an arrangement is the random variable

$$W = \begin{cases} 0 & \text{if } X \leq S \\ X - S & \text{otherwise} \end{cases}$$

We assume that the premium will depend upon the amount of deductible chosen; specifically such that

$$p(S) = (1 + \lambda)E(W),$$

where $E(W)$ is the net premium and $\lambda E(W)$ the loading.

If the individual has present wealth $A$, his final wealth under the contract is the random variable

$$Y = A - p(S) - X + W.$$

We shall assume that the variable $X$ is continuous with a density $f(x)$. In that case we have

$$E(W) = \int_S^\infty (x - S)f(x)dx,$$

and expected utility of final wealth is

$$E[U(Y)] = \int_0^S U(A - p - x)f(x)dx + U(A - p - S)\int_S^\infty f(x)dx. \quad (17)$$

The optimal $S$ is the one which maximizes this expression.[3]

The first two derivatives of (17) are

$$\frac{dE[U(Y)]}{dS} = \int_S^\infty f(x)dx\Big\{(1 + \lambda)\int_0^S U'(A - p - x)f(x)dx$$

$$- U'(A - p - S)\Big[1 - (1 + \lambda)\int_S^\infty f(x)dx\Big]\Big\},$$

---

[3] Clearly, it is assumed here that the individual and the company base their calculations on the same probability distribution, the main reason being mathematical simplicity. It may be satisfied rarely in practice, as the company presumably bases its premium schedule on some average individual's risk distribution. However, the reader can verify that some of our conclusions hold for an arbitrary (decreasing) $p(S)$.

and

$$\frac{d^2E[U(Y)]}{dS^2} = -f(S)\left\{(1 + \lambda) \int_0^S U'(A - p - x)f(x)dx\right.$$

$$- U'(A - p - S)\left[1 - (1 + \lambda) \int_S^\infty f(x)dx\right]\right\}$$

$$+ \int_S^\infty f(x)dx\left\{(1 + \lambda)^2 \int_S^\infty f(x)dx \int_0^S U''(A - p - x)f(x)dx\right.$$

$$+ U''(A - p - S)\left[1 - (1 + \lambda) \int_S^\infty f(x)dx\right]^2\right\}.$$

We can immediately conclude that some positive amount deductible will always be optimal, because at $S = 0$ the first derivative is

$$\frac{dE[U(Y)]}{dS}\bigg|_{S=0} = \lambda U'[A - (1 + \lambda)E(X)],$$

which is positive for any positive loading factor.

In this case, the second derivative is not necessarily negative everywhere. It is seen that whenever the first derivative is positive or zero the second derivative is negative. Two possibilities for the shape of $E[U(Y)]$ as a function of $S$ emerge: (a) $E[U(Y)]$ is monotonically increasing. If so, the second derivative is uniformly negative. The optimal solution is to let $S$ go to infinity, that is, not taking any insurance at all. (b) $E[U(Y)]$ has a maximum at a finite value of $S$, say $S^*$. At such a point we have

$$(1 + \lambda) \int_0^S U'(A - p - x)f(x)dx$$

$$= U'(A - p - S)\left[1 - (1 + \lambda) \int_S^\infty f(x)dx\right]. \quad (18)$$

It is clear that if $E[U(Y)]$ has an extremum at a finite value of $S$, it must be a maximum, and it must be unique.

On the assumption that the optimal value of $S$ is finite, we can proceed to prove a proposition on the wealth effect similar to the earlier ones: *If the individual has decreasing risk aversion, the optimal amount deductible is larger the larger his wealth.*

By differentiation of (18) we get

$$\frac{dS}{dA} = -\frac{1}{D}\left\{(1 + \lambda) \int_0^S U''(A - p - x)f(x)dx\right.$$

$$- U''(A - p - S)\left[1 - (1 + \lambda) \int_S^\infty f(x)dx\right]\right\},$$

where $D$ is the (negative) factor in braces in the second term of the expression for $d^2E/dS^2$. Let

$$B = 1 - (1 + \lambda) \int_S^\infty f(x)dx.$$

For $X < S$, we have $A - p - X > A - p - S$, and so by hypothesis $R_a(A - p - X) \leqq R_a(A - p - S)$, that is,

$$\frac{U''(A - p - X)}{U'(A - p - X)} \geqq -R_a(A - p - S),$$

and thus

$$(1 + \lambda)U''(A - p - X) \geqq -R_a(A - p - S)(1 + \lambda)U'(A - p - X).$$

Therefore

$$(1 + \lambda) \int_0^S U''(A - p - x)f(x)dx$$

$$\geqq -R_a(A - p - S)(1 + \lambda) \int_0^S U'(A - p - x)f(x)dx,$$

and also

$$(1 + \lambda) \int_0^S U''(A - p - x)f(x)dx - U''(A - p - S)B$$

$$\geqq -R_a(A - p - S)(1 + \lambda) \int_0^S U'(A - p - x)f(x)dx$$

$$- U''(A - p - S)B$$

$$= -R_a(A - p - S)\left[(1 + \lambda) \int_0^S U'(A - p - x)f(x)dx\right.$$

$$\left. - U'(A - p - S)B\right].$$

But the last expression is zero; hence $dS/dA$ is positive.

## VI. Concluding Remarks

We have analyzed four different problems, each concerned with rational behavior in buying insurance coverage against given risks. In particular, we have directed attention to the *wealth effect* on the propensity to take insurance coverage, and the common conclusion in all four cases was that this effect is negative if the individual's utility function shows risk aversion decreasing with wealth. In more general terms, the conclusion was that if the individual has decreasing risk aversion he will assume more risk the larger his wealth.

On the face of it, such a statement may look like a tautology: "If your risk aversion decreases with your wealth, then the amount of risk you assume increases with your wealth." It is not a tautology, however: The *assumption* is one concerning the individual's (unobservable) structure of preferences over probability distributions, while the *conclusion* concerns his (observable) behavior under various conditions. That is, the assumption of decreasing risk aversion serves as a tool for advancing meaningful hypotheses on actual behavior. If anything, the resemblance of a tautology merely reflects the fact that the name "absolute risk aversion" given to the function $-U''(Y)/U'(Y)$ is particularly well chosen in view of its behavioral implications.

Is it a reasonable conclusion that the wealth effect on the propensity to take insurance is negative? In principle, of course, this is a question of empirical testing. Most people would probably find the hypothesis quite plausible. Moreover, it is completely in line with the various studies cited in Part I. Therefore, if the conclusion were to be confirmed by data, then the present analysis could be taken as an additional piece of evidence of the usefulness of assumptions about the risk aversion function for economic theory.

In the formulation of our hypotheses, two critical elements appear: the slope of the risk aversion function, and the level of initial wealth. This immediately raises two important questions. First, on what basis are we entitled to make assumptions about the shape of the utility function? Second, how is initial wealth to be measured? Both of these problems are usually neglected in the literature on theories of risk taking based on the expected utility approach. To warn against too simpleminded interpretations of the theory (including that presented here), these problems should be briefly discussed (even if not resolved).

The problem of the specification of the utility function in terms of which alternative decisions are evaluated is principally of a theoretical nature. When a utility function $U$ of final wealth $Y$ is postulated, the assumption is implicit that $Y$ can be considered as representing future consumption opportunities. It is therefore clear that $U$ must somehow reflect preferences with respect to ultimate consumption variables.[4] This relationship may be clarified by considering the following extremely simple situation:

A person is to make a decision now which will bring his wealth to a (random) level $Y$. When a value $y$ of this variate materializes, he plans to spend it all on the consumption of two goods whose prices he knows will be 1 and $p$; after this, nothing else matters. To make his decision on the allocation of $y$ (which will take place under conditions of certainty) it is sufficient to specify an ordinal utility function over points $(x_1, x_2)$ in the commodity plane. Let us assume, however, that our person (by the standard procedure of comparing gambles among commodity bundles) has managed to express his preferences by a cardinal utility function $u(x_1, x_2)$,

---

[4] We shall limit attention to preferences of individual consumers. The specification of a utility function for an impersonal being such as an insurance company is a rather baffling problem. It is reasonably clear that in one way or another it must be derived on the basis of preferences involving future dividend payments and ruin probabilities. For a further discussion of this problem, see Borch (1966).

say $u(x_1, x_2) = ln\, x_1 x_2$ (this function being some positive transformation of the ordinal utility function). The optimal decision will therefore be $x_1 = y/2$, $x_2 = y/2p$, with the resulting maximum utility level

$$\varphi(y) = \max_{x_1,\, x_2} u(x_1, x_2) = ln(y^2/4p),$$

which is equivalent, as a utility function, to $ln\, y$. Thus, in this case, the relevant utility function for evaluation of the *immediate* decision is $U(Y) = ln\, Y$. This is referred to as the "derived" or "indirect" utility function (relative to the subsequent consumption opportunities).[5]

It is clear that if the immediate decision is the only one that will affect $Y$, then $E[U(Y)]$ is the appropriate evaluator of that decision. However, when the present decision constitutes but one in a sequence of decisions to be taken before the target date for wealth accumulation, it can be evaluated in terms of $U$ only on a second level of indirectness as part of a complete optimal strategy for subsequent decisions. In that case the function $\psi$ whose expectation is to be maximized by the immediate decision is the *maximum* of $E[U(Y)]$ with respect to all subsequent decisions. Without specifying details of the complete sequence of decision problems little can be said in general about the relationship between $U$ and $\psi$. This means that even if it were known that $U$ exhibits decreasing risk aversion it is not necessarily true that $\psi$ also does so. For a further discussion of some of these aspects (in a portfolio choice setting), see Mossin (1968b).

The situation is further complicated when there is not a single consumption target but a whole sequence of consumption decisions to be made. We cannot take up these problems in detail, but refer to the study by Drèze and Modigliani (1966).

The problems connected with the specification of the utility function arise partly because in most decision problems certain variables enter as *stocks* (assets) in an essential manner. For some types of decisions it may be possible to circumvent the problem by considering the argument $Y$ of the utility function as disposable income in the present period and disregarding the possibility of carryovers in the form of stocks. In determining a deductible for a medical insurance policy (as in Part V), we might not come out too badly by reinterpreting $A$ as the period's income before medical expences (premium plus amount deductible) and $Y$ as the amount available for "ordinary" consumption. In the other examples, such a procedure would be much less reasonable, because stock concepts (such as "property") are explicitly involved. However, in spite of all theoretical difficulties, it is of course possible (and meaningful) to test behavioral hypotheses like those we have advanced.

---

[5] Alternatively, it is possible to construct the cardinal utility function $u(x_1, x_2)$ on the basis of a specified $U(Y)$ and an ordinal preference ordering over $(x_1, x_2)$. See Drèze and Modigliani (1966).

The second problem mentioned above concerns the appropriate definition, or measure, of "initial wealth." This question is more immediately relevant for purposes of empirical testing, although it is closely related to the problem of specification of the utility function.

Again the issue may be clarified by reference to some simplified situations. In the case of a single subsequent consumption target examined above, $Y$ represented the (random) amount available for consumption and must therefore be identified with the value of the individual's *marketable assets* as of the time of consumption. Since $Y$ is simply $A$ plus the net outcome of the immediate decision, $A$ must correspondingly be taken as the current value of marketable assets; that is, $A$ is the amount that could be obtained by liquidating all assets in order to spend the proceeds on consumption.

Faced with a more complex future, the appropriate measure of $A$ may be different, however. Consider next the following situation: The immediate decision will bring the value of marketable assets to the random amount $Y$. When a value $y$ of this variate is realized, the individual will with certainty receive annual incomes $z_i$ for the rest of his life (the length $n$ of which is also taken as known), and he will decide upon annual amounts of consumption $c_i$ in order to maximize some preference ordering $f(c_1,\ldots,c_n)$. It is further assumed that a constant, known interest rate will prevail throughout his lifetime. Under these conditions we can meaningfully measure the present value of future incomes as $v = \Sigma\beta^i z_i$ (where $\beta$ is the discount factor) and therefore also the individual's *net worth*, $w$, as the sum of marketable assets and present value of future incomes: $w = y + v$. The budget restraint is of the form $\Sigma\beta^i c_i = w$, and it is clear that the maximum utility level is determined uniquely by $w$: $\max f(c_1,\ldots,c_n) = \varphi(w)$. Therefore, the appropriate measure of initial wealth in this case should include the present value of future incomes.

Consider now what happens if the assumption of certain future incomes and interest rate is dropped; these are now random variables described in terms of some joint probability distribution. Then it is only possible for the individual to adopt an optimal (contingent) consumption *strategy* and to calculate the corresponding expected maximum utility level (conditional upon the strategy being optimal). But this maximum of expected utility can evidently be expressed only in terms of $y$ and parameters $\theta$ of the probability distribution for incomes and interest rate, say as $\varphi(y; \theta)$, which as before is the relevant utility function for evaluating the immediate decision. There is no reason why it should be possible to construct an index of the parameters $\theta$ that could be compared to $v$ and added to $y$ as above. In this case we are led to consider $y$ as the argument of a derived utility function $\psi(y)$, with everything else about the future being absorbed in the *form* of this function. We are therefore back to marketable assets as the measure of initial wealth. To illustrate: It is to be expected that a man who has just completed his Ph.D. will behave differently from an unskilled laborer even if they each own identical amounts of marketable assets and have identical preference structures over future consumption possibilities. This, however, need not be interpreted as an indication that marketable assets is a poor measure of initial wealth; the difference is accounted for by the different *derived* utility functions $\psi$, because these depend upon the probability distributions that each man will encounter, and these will generally be quite different.

It is also trivial that even in the case of complete certainty it is possible to consider differences in future incomes as being absorbed in the form of the derived utility function, that is, to write $\varphi(y + v_1) = \psi_1(y); \varphi(y + v_2) = \psi_2(y)$, and so on, for different values of $v$.

It may seem like hairsplitting to try to establish whether a change in future incomes "should" be accounted for by the form of the derived utility function or by the value of its argument. It should be kept in mind, however, that the kind of hypotheses we have advanced are *not* concerned with future decision problems but with effects on *immediate* decisions, and for this problem it seems that the measure of $A$ most generally relevant as an argument of the utility function is the individual's marketable assets.

It should also be clear that even if this may be correct on the theoretical level it is not true that all problems connected with empirical testing are thus resolved. On the contrary. But this is due to the well-known incongruity between the nature of the hypothesis to be tested and the nature of the available data. The hypothesis concerns a single individual's decisions under alternative, hypothetical, levels of initial wealth, while the data typically consists of observations on different individuals' actual decisions. These individuals differ with respect to basic consumption preferences, with respect to marketable assets, and with respect to the kind of future they face. The first type of differences is unobservable and is evidently the type which we hope will cancel out in the sample of observations, so that in spite of these differences it may be possible to evaluate the effect of the other differences. Now suppose we choose to measure initial wealth by the value of marketable assets. Then, if marketable assets were uncorrelated with the kind of future individuals face we might even hope that these differences would cancel out in the sample. But they are not uncorrelated, and for that reason the relationship between risk bearing and marketable assets as evidenced by the sample observations may contain spurious correlations (the form of the derived utility functions and their arguments being systematically related to each other). It is easy to think of situations that may cause both of the classical error types: rejecting the hypothesis when it is in fact true, and accepting it when it is in fact false. We shall not pursue this, but would think, offhand, that the most important such errors might be accounted for by differences in *age* and *education* (compare example given earlier).

How this should be handled statistically is largely a technical question. One might just subdivide the sample by age and educational level and study each subgroup independently; or one might prefer to work directly with a model with three independent variables. A more tempting possibility would be to construct a single index of all three, and it would be difficult not to think of this as some measure of net worth. This may be a perfectly acceptable procedure as long as we realize that when institutional arrangements are such that certainty equivalents for future random patterns of income and interest rates are not traded in the market, then any such measure is in general only a proxy variable. When the future is uncertain, there is in principle no meaningful measure of expected present value of future incomes which can enter as an argument of a utility function. It is probably not generally meaningful to speak of present value of future incomes as a scalar stochastic variable; even if it were, and its expectation could be calculated, it would not be relevant as part of the argument of the utility function. This is seen by considering an individual who, after making an immediate decision which will bring his marketable assets to $Y$, will receive an additional random amount $V$ (independent of the immediate decision), and who then will make a single consumption decision. The relevant evaluator of the immediate decision is $E[U(Y + V)]$, which is (in general) quite a different thing from $E\{U[Y + E(V)]\}$.

As an approximation, however, some measure of net worth based on future income potential might perform excellently for predicting behavior both on the individual and the aggregate level. And, after all, the ultimate criterion of the usefulness of a specified measure of initial wealth is its ability to produce good predictions.

**References**

Arrow, K. J. *Aspects of the Theory of Risk-Bearing*. Helsinki: Yrjö Jahnsson Foundation, 1965.

Borch, K. H. "The Utility Concept Applied to the Theory of Insurance," *ASTIN Bull.* (1961), pp. 245–55.

———. "A Utility Function Derived From a Survival Game," *Management Sci.* (1966), pp. B287–95.

Drèze, J., and Modigliani, F. "Epargne et consommation en avenir aléatoire," *Cahiers du Séminaire d'Econometrie No. 9* (1966), pp. 7–33.

Mossin, J. "Taxation and Risk-taking: An Expected Utility Approach," *Economica* (1968), pp. 74–82. (*a*)

———. "Optimal Multiperiod Portfolio Policies," *J. Bus.*, XLI (April, 1968), 215–29. (*b*)

Pashigian, B. P., Schkade, L. L., and Menefee, G. H. "The Selection of an Optimal Deductible for a Given Insurance Policy," *J. Bus.*, XXXIX, No. 1, Pt. I (January, 1966), 35–44.

Pratt, John. "Risk Aversion in the Small and in the Large," *Econometrica* (1964), pp. 122–36.

Sandmo, A. "Portfolio Choice in a Theory of Saving," *Swedish J. Econ.*, Vol. LXX, No. 2 (1968).

# Incomplete Markets for Insurance: An Overview

Harris Schlesinger
Vanderbilt University


Neil A. Doherty
University of Illinois

## ABSTRACT

An area of much recent theoretical attention is the modeling of insurance decisions when markets are incomplete. Such incompleteness is said to exist when insurance contracts do not exist for all risks facing an individual or a firm. In such a market, insurance decisions cannot be made myopically and must recognize the presence of uninsurable background risk. This paper presents a nontechnical overview of the incomplete-market theory. The way in which market incompleteness may invalidate some long-standing theoretical results — and may indeed even cause seemingly perverse results — is examined. Possible causes of incomplete markets as well as some implications of the theory for reinsurance and for corporate purchases of insurance are also discussed.

## I. Introduction

In an uncertain world, a person could eliminate individual financial risk if it were possible to provide a perfect hedge against any possible event. Such a market is defined as complete, since contingent claims can be written on every state of nature without restriction. This is not to say that individuals would

Revised for publication in the *Journal of Risk and Insurance*

Harris Schlesinger is an Assistant Professor of Economics at Vanderbilt University. He earned his Ph.D. at the University of Illinois at Urbana-Champaign.

Neil A. Doherty is a Professor of Finance at the University of Illinois at Urbana-Champaign. He has a Ph.D. from the Cranfield Institute of Technology in England.

Both Dr. Schlesinger and Dr. Doherty have published articles previously in this Journal as well as other professional journals in economics, finance, and insurance. Both are members of the Risk Theory Seminar and the Euopean Group of Risk and Insurance Economists. Dr. Schlesinger is an associate editor for *Insurance: Mathematics and Economics*; Dr. Doherty is on *The Journal of Risk and Insurance* Editorial Board.

choose to eliminate all risk; only that this solution is found in the possible set. In reality, this outcome is rarely available and markets are rarely complete. Contingent claims are traded routinely against many states in the form of insurance policies, futures (in commodities, currencies, and stock indices), stock options, short sales, hedges, gambles, and the like. Yet the set of claims is inevitably smaller than the set of possible financial outcomes, leaving the unavoidable prospect of uncertain lifetime wealth. Hirshliefer and Riley [21] point out that because the total wealth of society will be lower following destructive losses such as fires and earthquakes, full insurance cannot be obtained on every potential loss. They term this type of risk ''social risk'' and discuss some of its implications for insurance markets.

In a world of such incomplete markets, it is not evident that individuals would choose a portfolio of contingent claims duplicating that available in a complete market save for omission of unavailable contracts. Portfolio effects are more pervasive. Risks that cannot be transferred between states interact with those than can in complex ways. These interactions depend upon the signs and magnitudes of the correlations. In spite of these portfolio effects, a literature has developed on insurance strategies that, by implication, treats markets as being complete. For example, it is well-known that if insurance is sold at actuarially fair prices, a risk-averse individual will purchase full coverage. However, this need not be the case in an incomplete-market context as was shown by Doherty [13], Doherty and Schlesinger [14, 15] and Mayers and Smith [32]. In fact, an individual might prefer no coverage to full coverage in an incomplete market.

The problem with modeling insurance decisions within the confines of a complete market is that it does not allow for any background risk. Background risk might arise due to any number of the following:

(i)     ''Social risks'' such as war, earthquakes, and nuclear hazards. These perils contain an substantial element of nondiversifiable risk, impeding the existence of insurance on them.

(ii)    General market risk. In a completely diversified market portfolio of capital assets, unsystematic risk may be substantially eliminated. However, the return on the market portfolio still follows a random process since macroeconomic, political, technological factors and the like commonly affect market performance.

(iii)   Informational asymmetries. Problems such as moral hazard and/or adverse selection might preclude the purchase of certain lines of insurance coverage to certain individuals. These individuals might find insurance to be too expensive on certain risks for their personal degree of exposure. For example, possessing all of the risk-classification characteristics of the most risky group of insureds (and hence facing the highest insurance premiums) might encourage self-insurance on the part of the least risky individuals within the group. Consequently, this adverse-selection problem might effectively price some individuals out of certain insurance markets.

(iv)  Transaction costs of insurance. These costs might render insurance too expensive on some risks for some individuals. The same holds true for informational costs. In some cases, the expenses envisioned might be too high to enable insurance to be sold at reasonable prices.

(v)  Search costs for insurance. Similar to (iv) above, if the envisioned cost of an individual seeking out potential insurers and obtaining information about coverage options outweighs the potential benefits of coverage, it may be worthwhile for the individual to self-insure in order to avoid the cost of search. This approach would seem to be particularly relevant for reasonably small surplus-line policies. (For example, would the authors find it worthwhile to seek coverage against possible rejection of this article?)

(vi)  Nonmarketable assets. Since insurance is only an indemnification for a loss, even with full coverage of monetary values, the world is a risky place. Insuring so-called "irreplaceable commodities" is an example. (See Cook and Graham [9].) In this case, full coverage in a monetary sense is not the same as full coverage in a sense of total well being. Another example might be insuring against the loss of one's own human capital.

(vii)  Risk vs. uncertainty. Frank Knight's [25] seminal contribution distinguished between risk and uncertainty, treating the latter as the complete unknown. The past half-century has seen that distinction disappear due to the use of subjective probabilities. However, insurance markets do not operate efficiently when objective probabilities cannot be estimated. The recent rise in the number of asbestosis claims is partly due to the unknown nature of exposure to asbestos during the past. Who is to say what loss exposures each of us unknowingly faces? While individuals might not be able to ascertain the nature of these exposures, they might allow for this extra risk when making insurance decisions.

Several recent papers — Buser and Smith [7], Doherty [13], Doherty and Schlesinger [14, 15], Turnbull [47], and Mayers and Smith [32] — have examined insurance-purchasing decisions within the context of an incomplete market. The purpose of this paper is to provide a nontechnical overview of this theory.

## II. Problems With The Complete Market Theory

The theoretical analysis of decision making under risk and uncertainty blossomed with the presentation of the Von Neumann-Morgenstern expected utility hypothesis. A subset of this literature has examined insurance-buying strategies. Typically, the assumption of risk aversion has been adopted and simple buying strategies have been derived, relating the quantity of insurance purchased to the insurance premium schedule; the latter being the relationshp between the dollar premium and the indemnities paid following a loss. But, observed buying strategies often differ from those predicted. Despite the intuitive appeal of the assumption of concave utility functions, the coexistence of gambling and insurance led Friedman and Savage [19] and Markowitz [30] to propose utility functions with inflections to show areas of risk preference. More recently, Kahneman and Tversky [24] have suggested that the "framing" of the insurance decision plays a major role in individual decision making and they note, among other things, that individuals might exhibit risk-averse behavior when seeking gains but risk-taking behavior when avoiding losses. This again gives an inflection point in the individual's value function.

Anderson [1] has found a strong reluctance to purchase flood insurance even though premiums were highly subsidized. Similar findings on earthquake insurance were pesented by Kunreuther et. al [27]. At the other end of this spectrum, we find high levels of insurance are purchased under rather adverse premium conditions. One example is the preference for low deductibles despite the clear expense (Pashigian, Schkade and Menefee [35]). Another is the sale of dread disease insurance at highly unfavorable rates (Illinois Department of Insurance). While these results are gleaned from studies of market behavior, experimental studies also have yielded challenging conclusions. A good example is the apparent preference for insuring small probable losses over large improbable losses reported by Slovic et. al. [45], and the consistent and apparent underestimation of high probabilities/overestimation of low probabilities (Shoemaker and Kunreuther [43].) Other examples are cited by Hershey and Shoemaker [20] and by Shoemaker [42].

Some explanations for these curious results can be accommodated within a complete market theory. The context of a decision may affect the outcome (Hershey and Shoemaker [20]). Utility functions may be state dependent, leading to different insurance strategies for replaceable and irreplaceable goods (Cook and Graham [9]). More drastically, the concavity of the utility function may be questioned, at least over part of its domain (Friedman and Savage [19]). Explanations of a different form include the mis-estimation of probabilities and simple irrational behavior, though explanations of this form do not facilitate the construction of alternative testable hypotheses. But these explanations fail to question the Achilles heel of this theory, the implicit assumption that markets are complete.

Even in cases where insurance markets may be complete, the interactions of different sources of risk are often ignored. Mayers and Smith [32], for example, suggest that substitution effects may exist among insurance policies purchased against different nonindependent loss events. Additionally, various institutional constraints may prove to be binding. Individuals might (ideally) demand contingent claims contracts that do not fall under the usual rubric of insurance such as desiring larger insurance indemnities for smaller losses than for larger losses, or desiring to pay premiums when a loss occurs in return for indemnity in the event that no loss occurs. Examples of these seemingly bizarre forms of behavior are discussed later in the paper.

Some headway has recently been made on the study of insurance decisions in incomplete markets. Mayers and Smith [32], and Doherty [13] use mean-variance analysis to show the conditions under which full coverage is optimal and examine a ''separation'' theorem for insurance. Buser and Smith [7] and Kahane and Kroll [23] use these results to model the insurance decision within an optimal-portfolio framework. Schulenburg [44] considers how compulsory coverage for one insurance line may affect purchases in other lines. Other extensions of the nonseparability of insurance decisions from other risks is an area of much current research. While results of these models are of interest, they apply only to the restricted class of distributions and/or utility functions for which mean-variance analysis is applicable. In particular, possible skewness of loss distributions presents serious problems and more general results are required. (Fieldstein [18].)

This paper focuses on more general results concerning incomplete markets. Although the literature in this area is still young, some important insights have already been unturned. Some of the key results are discussed and the underpinnings of the incomplete-market theory are examined.

### III. The Desirability of Insurance with Multiple Sources of Risk

A simple example of an incomplete market situation serves to illustrate how things can differ quite drastically from the complete markets case. Consider a risk averse individual with total wealth equal to

$$\tilde{Y} = \tilde{W} - \tilde{X}. \tag{1}$$

In the notation above, the symbol $\sim$ is used to denote random variables. The random variable $\tilde{X}$ can be thought of as representing an insurable loss expressed in positive terms. If W is nonstochastic, equation (1) represents a standard complete-markets model from which to study the purchase of insurance. The individual is typically ascribed a von Neumann-Morgenstern utility function that is assumed to be strictly concave due to the individual's risk averseness. The frequency distribution of $\tilde{X}$ and the level of nonstochastic wealth, W, are both important factors in determining the individual's choice of an insurance policy.

To illustrate the above case for a nonstochastic wealth, W, suppose that $E\tilde{X} = W-k$, where E denotes the expectation operator and k is some positive constant.[1] Actuarially fair insurance prices would lead the individual to purchase full coverage at a premium equalling $W-k$. Since the individual's wealth without insurance is random with an expected monetary value of $k$, a risk-averse individual would prefer full coverage that yields the same expected level of final wealth, but with no variability. This preference is seen in Figure 1. One can think of choosing a random point along the axis denoted by T, and then observing the realized values of $\tilde{X}$ and $\tilde{Y}$ for that particular T. In

---

[1] This analysis ignores discounting. If W can be invested to earn a risk-free rate of return, end-of-period wealth would need to be adjusted accordingly. Since this would not affect the results of the present model, the risk-free rate can be thought of as zero for the sake of simplicity.

Figure 1

Standard Complete–Markets Model

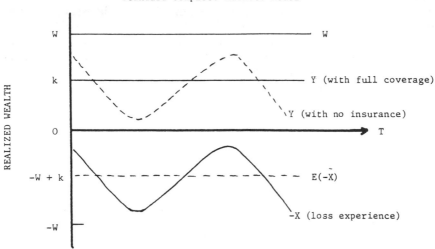

Figure 1, the realization of $W - X$ is shown as the dashed line varying about k. This is the prospect facing the individual if no insurance is purchased. By purchasing full insurance at an actuarially fair price, the individual eliminates the variation in total wealth. In fact, a risk-averse individual is willing to pay a premium exceeding $E\tilde{X}$ for full coverage as was shown by Pratt [1964]. The maximum excess over actuarial value is called the risk premium. Pratt showed that a more risk averse individual is willing to pay a higher risk premium.[2]

Now, consider the case where $\tilde{W}$ is random (and nondegenerate). This may be partly due to uninsurable assets that are included in the value of $\tilde{W}$. As an extreme case, consider $\tilde{X} = -\tilde{W}$. In this case,

$$\tilde{Y} = 2\tilde{W}. \tag{2}$$

However, by assumptions made above, only partial insurance is available on total wealth. In particular, total wealth remains uncertain, even after purchasing full coverage on $\tilde{X}$. The purchase of full coverage at actuarially fair prices yields

$$\tilde{Y}_I = \tilde{W} + E\tilde{W}. \tag{3}$$

---

[2] The measure of risk aversion is defined by Pratt [1964] and Arrow [1965] as $-U''(Y)/U'(Y)$ where U is the utility function. This is a type of measure of concavity; in particular it measures the rate of decay of marginal utility. A faster rate of decay (i.e., a strictly more concave utility) implies a higher degree of risk aversion. Also, note that this paper only considers the absolute measure of risk aversion, and not the relative measure.

Although the uninsured and fully insured total wealth prospects have the same expected value, $2E\tilde{W}$, the insured wealth prospect has a variance only one-fourth as large. Hence, the risk-averse individual will choose to insure the full amount.

The case where $\tilde{X} = \tilde{W} - k$ shows how insurance may be undesirable. In this case, note that final wealth is nonstochastic when no insurance is purchased. Large losses in $\tilde{X}$ are offset by large gains in $\tilde{W}$ and small losses in $\tilde{X}$ are counterbalanced by correspondingly low realizations of $\tilde{W}$. In other words, a natural hedge exists between the riskiness of $\tilde{X}$ and the riskiness of $\tilde{W}$. Any purchase of actuarially-fair insurance against $\tilde{X}$ will leave expected wealth unchanged, but will introduce risk where none existed before. Following the purchase of full insurance on $\tilde{X}$, for example, total wealth would be

$$\tilde{Y}_I = \tilde{W} - E\tilde{X} = \tilde{W} - E\tilde{W} + k. \qquad (4)$$

The variance of total wealth would be equal to the variance of $\tilde{W}$. This compares with a zero variance in the case where no insurance is purchased. This situation is demonstrated in Figure 2. In Figure 2, the realization of total wealth with insurance is shown as the dashed line varying about k. This situation is less preferred by a risk averter than the wealth prospect with no insurance, which equals k with no variation. In fact, with actuarially-fair prices, the purchase of no coverage (complete self-insurance) is the individual's best alternative as is shown by Doherty and Schlesinger [14].

Figure 2

Incomplete Market with Positive Correlation

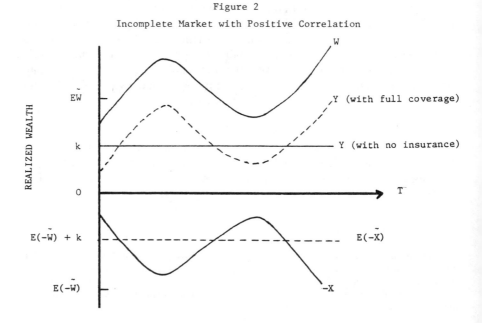

The latter result is not difficult to see. Since any amount of insurance at actuarially-fair prices introduces risk where none exists without insurance, no coverage is the optimal level of insurance. More formally, suppose insurance involves pure coinsurance and let $\alpha$ denote the level of coinsurance where $0 \leq \alpha \leq 1$. Thus, the individual retains $(1-\alpha)X$ of a loss X and pays a premium equalling $\alpha E\tilde{X}$. The purchase of coinsurance level $\alpha$ yields the total wealth prospect.

$$\tilde{Y}_\alpha = \tilde{W} - (1-\alpha)\tilde{X} - \alpha E\tilde{X}. \tag{5}$$

Since $\tilde{X} = \tilde{W}-k$ in the case considered here, (5) is equivalent to

$$\tilde{Y}_\alpha = \alpha[\tilde{W} - E\tilde{W}] + k. \tag{6}$$

It is evident that the expected value of total wealth is k for all values of $\alpha$. However, the variance of total wealth, $\text{Var}(\tilde{Y}_\alpha)$, depends on $\alpha$ as $\text{Var}(\tilde{Y}_\alpha) = \varphi^2 \hat{V}\text{ar}(\tilde{W})$. The most preferred coinsurance level for a risk averter is thus $\alpha = 0$, i.e., complete self-insurance.

Obviously the case where $\tilde{X} = \tilde{W}-k$ is quite extreme. However, it does indicate how the correlation between $\tilde{X}$ and $\tilde{W}$ might affect insurance decisions. Considering insurance purchases on $\tilde{X}$ alone, and treating $\tilde{W}$ as if it were constant, can yield incorrect results.

## IV. The Optimal Level of Coverage

As discussed in the preceding section, it is possible within the context of an incomplete market for no coverage to be the optimal (i.e., expected-utility-maximizing) choice of the individual. More generally, a positive correlation between $\tilde{X}$ and $\tilde{W}$ will lessen the attractiveness of any particular insurance policy written against $\tilde{X}$, since this positive correlation acts as a natural hedge against losses in $\tilde{X}$. If the composition of $\tilde{W}$ is at least partially chosen by the individual, positive correlation might be considered a type of "homemade insurance" (Mayers and Smith [32]). In this section, the optimal insurance against $\tilde{X}$ is examined for a specified distribution of $\tilde{W}$. No attempt is made here to discuss how the distribution of $\tilde{W}$ might be derived.

The coefficient of correlation between $\tilde{X}$ and $\tilde{W}$ is generally not a sufficient measure of the interrelationship between these variables, except for a limited set of distribution functions. It is sufficient, for example, if the joint distribution of $\tilde{X}$ and $\tilde{W}$ is bivariate normal (Doherty and Schlesinger [14]). A more general measure, presented in Doherty and Schlesinger [16], considers the stochastic relationship between $\tilde{W} - \tilde{X}$ and $\tilde{W} - \tilde{X}'$, where $\tilde{X}'$ has the same marginal distribution as $\tilde{X}$ but is assumed to be statistically independent of $\tilde{W}$. If either of these distributions stochastically dominates the other in the sense of second degree stochastic dominance, some strong conclusions can be derived. However, this development goes beyond the scope of the present paper and the interested reader is referred to the paper by Doherty and Schlesinger [16].

The insufficiency of the correlation coefficient is apparent if one observes that a zero correlation does not necessarily imply that $\tilde{X}$ and $\tilde{W}$ are statistically independent. Rather than use the less-familiar stochastic dominance approach, the analysis can be simplified by assuming that $\tilde{W}$ and $\tilde{X}$ each possess two-state marginal distributions (i.e., each of these random variables can take on only two possible values). In this case, the correlation coefficient is sufficient and the simplicity of the two-state model allows the reader to focus on the inherent differences between complete and incomplete markets.

To this end, let $W = w$ or $\bar{w}$ where $\bar{w} > w$, and let $X = 0$ or $L$. There are four mutually exclusive final states of wealth. If $\tilde{W}$ and $\tilde{X}$ are independently distributed, it can be shown that full coverage on $\tilde{X}$ will be optimal if insurance is sold at actuarially fair prices. Also, less than full coverage is optimal if the premium includes a positive proportional loading.[3] These results are identical to those existing in the literature for the complete markets case where W is nonstochastic. (See Mossin [33] and Smith [46].)

If $\alpha$ denotes a level of coinsurance on $\tilde{X}$, as in the preceding section, and $\alpha^*$ denotes the optimal level of $\alpha$, $\alpha^* = 1$ if insurance prices are actuarially fair and $\tilde{X}$ and $\tilde{W}$ are statistically independent. If the price of insurance includes a proportional loading, $\alpha^* < 1$. These results (full coverage at actuarially fair prices and partial coverage with proportionate premium loadings) apparently are the same as those prevailing in complete markets. But it should not be concluded that the optimal insurance decision is unaffected by the randomness of $\tilde{W}$, even though the correlation with $\tilde{X}$ is zero. In the case where partial coverage is optimal, the level of coverage, $\alpha^*$, is dependent on the distribution of $\tilde{W}$ if the risk averseness of the individual is not independent of the level of total wealth.[4] For example, an individual who is extremely risk averse at low levels of wealth might be especially fearful of the possibility that a high loss value for $\tilde{X}$ could accompany a simultaneously realized low level of noninsurable wealth, $\tilde{W}$. This individual would likely purchase a higher level of coverage than if W were nonrandom (with the same expected value). Surprisingly, it does not necessarily follow that a more risk-averse individual will purchase a higher level of insurance coverage. This relationship is discussed more fully in Section VI of the paper.

An effect of diversification should also be noted. With random $\tilde{W}$ that is independent of $\tilde{X}$, the individual's portfolio is already somewhat diversified. The incremental contribution of $\tilde{X}$ to the riskiness of total wealth (as measured by the standard deviation) is less than the riskiness of $\tilde{X}$ considered in

---

[3] Both of these results as well as those stated below for the case of nonindependence of X and W are proved in Doherty and Schlesinger [15]. The premium loading is assumed proportional to the actuarial value of a policy so that the total premium equals some fixed percentage (exceeding 100 percent) of the policy's actuarial value.

[4] Only linear and exponential utility functions result in risk averseness that is independent of the level of total wealth. Pratt [37].

isolation.[5] Other things being the same, this diversification effect might reduce the optimal level of coverage from that prevailing with a nonrandom W.

If $\tilde{W}$ and $\tilde{X}$ are negatively correlated, high losses are likely to be exacerbated by the simultaneous realization of low values of $\tilde{W}$. In the case of two-state marginal distributions, w is more likely to occur when $X = L$ than when $X = 0$. "When it rains, it pours," so to speak. Although it is also true that low values of $\tilde{X}$ most frequently occur with high values of $\tilde{W}$, the risk averter attaches more weight to the increased downside risk. If insurance on $\tilde{X}$ is available at actuarially fair prices, the individual would again purchase full coverage. However, this is a constrained optimum. If the individual is allowed to insure more than 100 percent of the loss, then $\alpha^* > 1$. Ideally, the individual will buy coverage in excess of 100 percent indemnity. Note that in the case where $\tilde{X}$ and $\tilde{W}$ are independent, the individual would not choose to overinsure, even if allowed to do so. While many insurance policies might not allow such overinsurance to be purchased, there are likely to be some policies that do allow for coverage in excess of 100 percent.

For example, consider an individual who for some reason does not (or cannot) obtain disability insurance but can obtain hospitalization insurance in excess of 100 percent coverage. Large hospitalization claims are likely to be accompanied by periods of temporary unemployment, and consequently by low wealth realizations. By overinsuring on the hospitalization coverage, this individual provides a partial hedge against the risk of temporary unemployment due to poor health.

If $\tilde{W}$ and $\tilde{X}$ are negatively correlated but insurance premiums include a proportional loading, it is not possible to determine whether $\alpha^* < 1$ without additional information. If the loading is very small, it is possible that $\alpha^* > 1$ or $\alpha^* = 1$. Two effects need to be considered. A correlation effect makes coverage in excess of 100 percent look attractive as is discussed above. However, a price effect generated by the premium loading makes positive retention levels (i.e., $\alpha^* < 1$) look attractive. The total effect must weight the relative strengths of these two effects.

Probably the best way to view the situation is as follows. With negative correlation between $\tilde{X}$ and $\tilde{W}$, any insurance contract on $\tilde{X}$ appears more attractive to a risk-averse individual than it would under independence of $\tilde{X}$ and $\tilde{W}$.

---

[5] Let $\sigma$ denote the standard deviation. Then,

$$\sigma(\tilde{W} - \tilde{X}) = [\text{Var}(\tilde{W}) + \text{Var}(\tilde{X})]^{\frac{1}{2}} < \sigma(\tilde{W}) + \sigma(\tilde{X})$$

or equivalently,

$$\sigma(\tilde{W} - \tilde{X}) - \sigma(\tilde{W}) < \sigma(\tilde{X}).$$

The left hand side of this last inequality represents the incremental contribution of $\tilde{X}$ to the riskiness of total wealth.

If $\bar{X}$ and $\bar{W}$ are positively correlated, of course, the reverse is true. Any insurance contract on $\bar{X}$ appears less attractive than it would if $\bar{X}$ and $\bar{W}$ were independent. This is due to the fact that positive correlation implies there already exists some "homemade insurance" inherent in $\bar{W}$ that partially offsets the riskiness of $\bar{X}$. Consequently, less than full coverage, $\alpha^* < 1$, is optimal regardless of whether or not there is a premium loading. The correlation effect and price effect will reinforce each other.

One example of positive correlation between $\bar{X}$ and $\bar{W}$ seems almost too obvious. If $\bar{W}$ already includes an insurance contract on $\bar{X}$, this contract would provide a partial degree of positive correlation (barring any other offsetting factors). Consequently, any additional insurance contract on $\bar{X}$ (if available) will seem less attractive than if the existing insurance was not already a part of $\bar{W}$. As another example, consider a rice farmer who is considering flood insurance on his or her home. Since rice harvests benefit from localized excessive rain, the farmer is likely to have high crop yields, and consequently high income, during periods with high levels of rainfall. Rice yields might benefit if flooding occurred. Thus, flood damage to the farmer's home might be partially offset by these higher yields. Of course, this assumes that erosion and/or other problems associated with flooding do not damage the crop.

## V. Some Illustrations

This section presents a few examples of the optimal levels of insurance coverage and uses the geometry of state-claims space to illustrate the effects of market incompleteness. Readers unfamiliar with the state-claims modelling will lose no continuity by skipping to the next section of the paper.

### a. All Risk is Insurable

This structure is defined by setting $w = \bar{w}$, the usual assumption made in the economic literature examining insurance purchases. The optimal insurance levels are illustrated in Figure 3. Point E in Figure 3 represents the individual's contingent wealth claims with no insurance. If the probability of a loss is known, the locus of actuarially fair insurance contracts can be represented by a line such as EF. A risk-averse individual will choose full insurance at these prices, which occurs at the intersection of EF with the 45° certainty line. This point is labeled A in Figure 3. The curve labeled $I_2$ is an indifference curve (iso-expected-utility curve) representing the highest attainable expected utility with actuarially fair pricing. (See Rothschild and Stiglitz [1976] for details.)

With a proportional premium loading, the locus of available contracts rotates counterclockwise through the no-insurance contingent-claims point E. This locus is represented by the line EG in Figure 3. The individual's highest expected utility occurs at point B on indifference curve $I_2$. At point B the individual's contingent claims lies below the 45° line, thereby indicating that partial coverage is optimal.

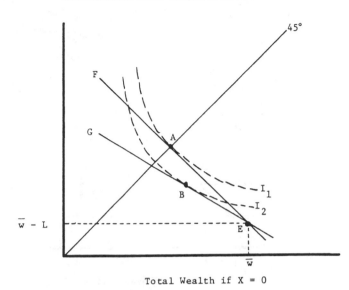

Figure 3

State Claims for a Complete Market

b. *Perfect Negative Correlation*

In this example, the extreme case of perfect negative correlation is examined. Suppose X = 0 if and only if W = w. Consequently, X = L if and only if W = w. Only two final states of nature can be realized:

(i)  Y = w    with probability (1-p)

or

(ii)  Y = w - L with probability p.

This case is identical to the one in which w represents initial wealth and the probability is p that a loss of size J will occur, where J = w − (w − L). In Figure 4, the actuarially-fair price line for insurance on X̃ is again denoted by the line EF, where E represents the individual's contingent claims with no insurance. If full coverage is purchased on X̃, the fair premium will be pL. This premium, once paid, leaves the individual with contingent claims represented by point C. At point C the individual has full-coverage insurance for X̃ and the expected utility level is that associated with indifference curve $I_2$.

If coverage in excess of 100 percent is not possible, this will be the individual's optimal insurance purchase. However, if coverage in excess of 100 percent is obtainable, the individual would ideally prefer to be at point A. This full-coverage insurance would yield a higher level of expected utility, namely that associated with indifference curve $I_1$. It should be noted that coverage in excess of 100 percent, at actuarially fair rates, still leaves the insurer with an expected profit of zero on this policy. Consequently, if the

146

Figure 4

State Claims with Negative Correlation

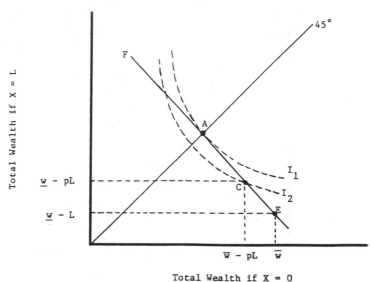

Total Wealth if X = 0

insurer is risk neutral, coverage in excess of 100 percent will be Pareto superior to full coverage.

A similar analysis is easily done for the case where the premium includes a proportional loading. The details of such an analysis, which are straightforward, are not presented here and are left to the reader.

c. *Perfect Positive Correlation*

In this example, let $L = \bar{w} - w$ and suppose that $X = 0$ if and only if $W = w$. Again there are two final states of nature:

(i)  $Y = \underline{w}$     with probability 1-p

or

(ii) $Y = \bar{w} - L$ with probability p.

However, by assumption these two final wealth values are equal. Thus, no risk is present in the individual's contingent claims when no insurance is purchased. In Figure 5, this absence of risk is shown by E being located on the 45° line. With insurance available at actuarially fair prices along line EF, the individual would choose to reamin at E and not purchase any insurance. That is, the indifference curve for no insurance, $I_2$, represents the highest level of expected utility for the individual.

For this extreme example, where a perfect hedge exists with no insurance, a rather strange result obtains when insurance premiums include a proportional loading. In this case, the optimal level of coverage on $\bar{X}$ turns out to be negative, $\alpha^* < 0$. Ideally, the individual would like a policy that pays a

Figure 5

State Claims with Positive Correlation

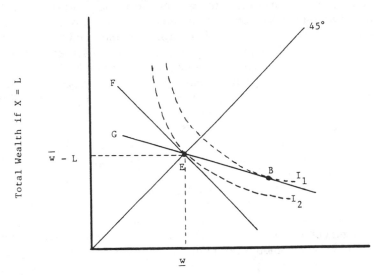

premium to the individual and contracts the individual to pay the insurer when a loss (on $\tilde{X}$) occurs. This type of ''reverse insurance'' is illustrated by point B in Figure 5. Point B represents the optimal contingent claims when the insurance price line is EG. Obviously, this type of contract is not a type of insurance; rather, the individual finds the price of insurance to be sufficiently favorable to warrant placing a bet that a loss will occur. Thus, the individual is induced into gambling on the outcome of $\tilde{X}$.

This result can be seen more formally by considering equations (5) and (6) of section 3 for the case where $\tilde{X} = \tilde{W} - k$. If these equations are modified to include a proportional loading, $\beta > 0$, in the price of insurance, equation (6) becomes

$$\tilde{Y}_\alpha = \alpha[\tilde{W} - (1+\beta)E\tilde{W}] + k. \tag{7}$$

Analysis of equation (7) reveals an expected final wealth and variance as follows.

$$\text{Expected Value of } \tilde{Y}_\alpha = \alpha[-\beta E\tilde{W}] + k. \tag{8}$$

$$\text{Var}(\tilde{Y}_\alpha) = \alpha^2 \text{Var}(\tilde{W}). \tag{9}$$

Note that the expected value of $\tilde{Y}_\alpha$ exceeds k if and only if $\alpha < 0$. It is also true that $\alpha < 0$ yields a higher variance (more risk) than $\alpha = 0$. However, for small $\alpha$, this variance will be low enough (of order $\alpha^2$) that the increased expected value of $\tilde{Y}_\alpha$ is worth the extra risk.

# VI. Effects of Risk Aversion

Recently, several papers have focused on the adequacy of the Pratt-Arrow measure of absolute risk aversion in predicting rational investment behavior under uncertainty. (Ross [39], Kihlstrom, Romer and Williams [26], Nachman [34] and Pratt [37].) The key result of this literature from an insurance standpoint, which was pointed out by Turnbull [47] and Doherty and Schlesinger [14], is that an increase in the risk averseness of the insured (*ceteris paribus*) does not guarantee the purchase of a higher level of insurance coverage if markets are not complete. This result holds even if $\tilde{W}$ and $\tilde{X}$ are independent. Some examples of cases where an increase in risk aversion might lead to a lower level of insurance are presented in Turnbull [47].

These results have canonical interpretations with regards to the willingness to pay for full coverage. The excess that the insured is willing to pay over and above the actuarial value of full coverage is called the risk premium, as was described in Section III of the present paper. For the case where W is nonstochastic, Pratt [37] showed that a more risk averse individual is willing to pay a higher risk premium, *ceteris paribus*, for any given insurance contract. If $\tilde{W}$ is random, this result might reverse itself. For example, if there is a positive correlation between $\tilde{X}$ and $\tilde{W}$, $\tilde{W} - \tilde{X}$ might be less risky than $\tilde{W}$ alone. In this case, the individual would not be willing to pay in excess of actuarial value to insure $\tilde{X}$ fully. In fact, it already has been demonstrated that it is possible for insurance on $\tilde{X}$ to be worth less than its actuarial value with these correlations. This situation would imply the existence of a negative risk premium. In other words, if the riskiness of $\tilde{X}$ can be eliminated by replacing it with its expected loss value, $E\tilde{X}$, the individual would require additional compensation to accept such an offer. A further discussion of this result can be found in Doherty and Schlesinger [16].

If W is random and $\tilde{W}$ and $\tilde{X}$ are independently distributed, the risk premium for $\tilde{X}$ is the maximum excess over actuarial value that the individual is willing to pay for full coverage on $\tilde{X}$ while maintaining the riskiness inherent in $\tilde{W}$. (See Kihlstrom, Romer, and Williams [26], Nachman [34] and Pratt [37].) Suppose that for every possible realized level of noninsurable wealth, W, individual A is more risk averse than individual B and, consequently, is willing to pay a higher risk premium to obtain full coverage on $\tilde{X}$. Does it necessarily follow that individual A also has a higher risk premium that individual B when $\tilde{W}$ is stochastic? The somewhat surprising answer to this query is no. Since individual A is more risk averse, relatively more weight (utility) is put on lower values of $\tilde{W}$ and less weight on higher values of $\tilde{W}$. If the risk premiums that would be paid by A and B for given realized levels of $\tilde{W}$ are increasing as W increases, i.e., if there are higher risk premiums for higher W values, the risk premiums when $\tilde{W}$ is random might reverse due to the relative utility weightings. Examples of this reversal can be found in Kihlstrom, Romer, and Williams [26]. This reversal is not possible if either of the individual's risk premiums for realized levels of $\tilde{W}$ is nonincreasing in W. For a fuller discussion, see Pratt [37] or Kihlstrom, Romer, and Williams [26].

## VII.  The Optimality of Deductibles

If the insurance premium depends only upon the actuarial value of an insurance policy, Arrow [2] showed that a risk averter would prefer a policy with a straight deductible over other actuarially equivalent types of coverage. Raviv [38], Buhlmann and Jewell [6], and Doherty [12] have extended these results to formulate Pareto-optimal policy designs and preference rankings among various risk-sharing devices. All of these results were obtained under the implicit assumption that markets are complete.

Doherty and Schlesinger [15] and Doherty [13] showed that these results do not necessarily hold when insurance markets are incomplete. In particular, they showed that Arrow's result does hold if $\tilde{W}$ and $\tilde{X}$ are statistically independent, but does not necessarily hold if $\tilde{W}$ and $\tilde{X}$ are not independent.

Consider the following example. Suppose the loss, X, can be either 0, sL, or L. Thus, the individual experiences either no loss, a full loss, or a partial loss. In this example, the partial loss is s of the total loss. Again assume that W can be either w or $\bar{w}$. Suppose correlations are such that the conditional probability of a loss equalling sL is higher when $\bar{w}$ is realized than it would be if $\tilde{W}$ and $\tilde{X}$ were independent. Also suppose that the conditional probability of a loss equalling sL is higher when w is realized than it would be if $\tilde{W}$ and $\tilde{X}$ were independent. Hence, compared to the case where $\tilde{W}$ and $\tilde{X}$ are independent, a large loss, L, is more likely to occur simultaneously with a high uninsurable wealth, $\bar{w}$; and, a smaller loss, sL, is more likely to occur simultaneously with a low uninsurable wealth, w. This correlation essentially lessens the severity of a large loss, L, since it is more likely to be partially offset by a high uninsurable wealth, $\bar{w}$. Similarly, the correlation increases the severity of a smaller loss, sL. These effects make a straight deductible policy look particularly unattractive, since a deductible policy would pay out little or nothing for a small insurable loss, sL. The insured would prefer a larger insurance payment following a smaller insurable loss, and a smaller insurance payment following a total insurable loss, L, than the deductible policy provides. The optimal policy design would require that the individual insure at least part of the small loss while retaining some of the excess over the deductible limit for a total loss. In extreme cases, it is even possible that the insured would desire an insurance policy paying a higher indemnity for a partial loss than for a total loss. (See Doherty and Schlesinger [15].)

Obviously, other correlations and other results are possible. The point is that the optimality of the deductible form depends on the independence of $\tilde{X}$ and $\tilde{W}$. Other results, such as those of Raviv [38], Buhlmann and Jewel [6], and Doherty [12] revert to special cases if insurable losses are not independent from other risks in the individual's total wealth portfolio.

## VIII.  Implications for Reinsurance and for Corporate Insurance

Thus far, this paper has addressed some formal results in the economic theory of insurance. It has also intimated that the results of their theory have some practical application. Indeed, motivation for this paper partly derives from the fact that the complete-markets theory is not always supported by observable behavior. This section examines some implications of the incomplete-markets approach.

Consider the formulation of a reinsurance-purchasing strategy for an insurer. Such reinsurance represents an insurance contract written on the insurer's direct underwriting portfolio. However, the context of this decision also includes the insurer's investment portfolio which also is risky. This nonseparability of investment and underwriting decisions is examined more fully by MacMinn and Witt [29]. If the insurer seeks to maintain an acceptable balance between the risk and the expected value of its overall profits, the reinsurance decision cannot be viewed independently from the insurer's investment activity. For example, if the underwriting results exhibit a negative correlation with the investment results, the respective portfolios already partially hedge each other. This hedge might not be sufficiently strong to eliminate the desire for reinsurance, but it will cause the optimal level of reinsurance for a risk-averse insurer to be lower than the amount that would be ceded if the reinsurance decision was made independently.

Conversely, if there is a positive correlation between underwriting and investment results, the demand for reinsurance will increase. This increased demand follows since the reinsurance will effectively provide partial protection against poor investment results. Even in the case of zero correlation, the optimal reinsurance-purchasing strategy is not unaffected. The combined risk of the two portfolios, as measured by the standard deviation, is somewhat less than the sum of the individual risks. (See footnote 3.) Less technically, the insurer has some degree of diversification for its overall risk by having two risky income sources. Consequently, the insurer's optimal level of reinsurance may be reduced.

Readers who are familiar with portfolio theory will realize that this reasoning can be taken further. The owners of most insurance companies, notably stock companies, are likely to hold equity of other companies in an investment portfolio of their own. Such investors are not especially concerned with the riskiness of the returns for each stock *per se*, but rather are concerned with the effects of such risk on their entire investment portfolio. Following the approach of this paper, the optimal reinsurance portfolio can be formulated with respect to the properties of the direct portfolio and its covariance with a well-diversified market portfolio. This reasoning is embodied in the well-known Capital Asset Pricing Model (CAPM) and its various derivatives. The relevant covariance is measured with a proxy for the well-diversified market portfolio such as the Standard and Poor's, New York Stock Exchange or Dow Jones indices. The covariance of the underwriting portfolio and the market portfolio is known as the "beta" coefficient (with some slight normalization). The effect of underwriting betas on the optimal reinsurance strategy might turn out to be significant, especially in the light of recent research by Cummins and Harrington [10] which shows that underwriting betas may differ significantly from zero (though their results also reveal some beta instability).

A somewhat extreme example of the effects of betas on the optimal reinsurance strategy was considered by Doherty and Tinic [17]. If underwriting profits of the (ceding) insurer exhibit zero correlation with the market portfolio, the riskiness of the underwriting portfolios can be diversified away by investors in the management of their own personal portfolios. Consequently, the purchase of reinsurance would be redundant. To explain why reinsurance exists one has to look beyond the simple risk-return tradeoff ascribed to the firm's owners. One explanation is that individuals who purchase insurance might be willing to pay higher premiums to an insurer that reduces its probability of ruin by careful reinsurance purchases.

Along lines similar to the reinsurance discussion above, consider another application of the incomplete-markets approach: the purchase of property-liability insurance by a noninsurance corporation on its insurable risks. The purchase of this insurance may duplicate the ''homemade insurance'' already existing either in the portfolio of income-generating assets of the firm that are not insurable, or in the individual investors' own investment portfolios. (See Main [28] and Mayers and Smith [31].) This duplication does not necessarily imply that corporate property-liability insurance is totally redundant, only that reasons for its prevalence, other than risk aversion of the owners, must be found. Mayers and Smith [31], for example, suggest that corporate insurance decisions may be motivated *inter alia* by the relative transactions costs of insurance and portfolio diversification, taxation, borrowing requirements, and price effects impounded in contracts between the company and risk-averse employees and customers.

Now consider the prospect that the insurable risks may be correlated with the market portfolios held by the individual investors, i.e., insurable risks have nonzero betas. Depending on the sign and magnitude of the betas, insurable risks might not be diversifiable for investors in their portfolio management. Consequently, risk-averse owners might desire the corporation to purchase insurance. However, the optimal level of coverage will depend upon the correlation between insurable risk and market risk, i.e., beta. Other things being the same, the optimal level of insurance coverage will be higher for lower values (including negative values) of beta. In other words, the optimal level of insurance is negatively related to the beta of the firm's loss exposure.

## IX. Concluding Remarks

In a recent paper, Cummins and Wiltbank [11] point out the benefits of estimating total loss claims using a multivariate approach when multiple loss processes are present. They favor this approach over the traditional approach which represents only the collective risk. Their approach seems even more attractive when viewed in the context of an incomplete market. ''Unlike the traditional approach, the multivariate technique allows explicit recognition of dependencies among the components of the overall process'' (Cummins and Wiltbank [11, p. 377]). Although the present paper focuses on the demand for insurance, the effects of market incompleteness should also be significant for suppliers of insurance and other risk services. For example, an insurer that does not supply certain lines of insurance coverage might wish to consider the correlation effects between these lines and its own.

The incomplete-markets literature is in its infancy, yet its power should not be ignored. Theorems developed in the context of complete markets are not robust when this assumption is relaxed. At the very least, authors of new results in the insurance literature should point out explicitly whether or not market completeness is necessary for their results to hold. It also should be apparent that many' of the recent experimental studies concerning rational risk-averse behavior, some of which are mentioned in section II of the paper, have ignored the possible interactions of the experimental risks with those in the wealth portfolios of their subjects. This observation is not meant to imply that many of the problems this literature attributes to expected-utility do not exist; but psychological inferences should take possible risk interdependencies into account.

The incomplete-markets literature to date has had relatively little to say on how individuals will behave when markets are incomplete, mostly describing how they will not behave. Part of the problem is due to the lack of very good measures of statistical dependencies between sources of risk. As mentioned previously, correlation is only of limited usefulness. Although measures based on stochastic dominance provide more robust results, stochastic dominance often fails to provide a clear ranking of available choices. An alternative to stochastic dominance is presented in Nachman [34], but this approach is also very restrictive, although somewhat less restrictive than stochastic dominance.[6]

Until a satisfactory measure of interdependencies between risks is established, normative aspects of the incomplete-markets theory will probably remain dormant. However, the inappropriateness of extending the complete-markets results to possibly incomplete-market situations should be apparent.

## REFERENCES

1. Anderson, D.R., "The National Flood Insurance Program — Problems and Potentials," *Journal of Risk and Insurance*, 41(1974), 579-599.
2. Arrow, K.J., "Uncertainty and the Welfare Economics of Medical Care," *American Economic Review*, 53(1963), 941-969.
3. Arrow, K.J., *Aspects of the Theory of Risk Bearing*, Helsinki: Yrjo Johnssonin Saatio (1965).
4. Borch, K., "Indifference Curves and Uncertainty," *Swedish Journal of Economics*, 70, 19-24.

---

[6] Nachman considers $\tilde{W} = f(\tilde{X}, \tilde{Z})$ for some function f and some random variable $\tilde{Z}$ that is independent of $\tilde{X}$.

5. Borch, K., "Static Equilibrium Under Uncertainty and Incomplete Markets," *The Geneva Papers on Risk and Insurance*, 8(1983), 307-315.

6. Buhlmann, M. and W.S. Jewell, "Optimal Risk Exchanges," *Astin Bulletin*, 10(1979), 242-262.

7. Buser, S.A. and M.L. Smith, "Life Insurance in a Portfolio Context," *Insurance: Mathematics and Economics*, 2(1983), 147-157.

8. Buser, S.A. and M.L. Smith, "Optimal Insurance in a Portfolio Context," unpublished manuscript, Ohio State University (1984).

9. Cook, P.J. and D.A. Graham, "The Demand for Insurance and Protection: The Case of Irreplaceable Commodities," *Quarterly Journal of Economics*, 91(1977), 143-156.

10. Cummins, J.D. and S. Harrington, "Property-Liability Insurance Rate Regulation: Estimation of Underwriting Betas Using Quarterly Profit Data," *Journal of Risk and Insurance* (forthcoming).

11. Cummins, J.D. and L.J. Wiltbank, "Estimating the Total Claims Distribution Using Multivariate Frequency and Severity Distributions," *Journal of Risk and Insurance*, 50(1983), 377-403.

12. Doherty, N.A., "Stochastic Ordering of Risk/Insurance Exchanges," *Scandinavian Actuarial Journal* (1980), 203-208.

13. Doherty, N.A. "Efficient Insurance Buying Strategies for Portfolios of Risky Assets," *Journal of Risk and Insurance*, 51(1984), 205-224.

14. Doherty, N.A. and H. Schlesinger, "The Optimal Deductible for Insurance Policy When Initial Wealth is Random," *Journal of Business*, 56(1983a), 555-565.

15. Doherty, N.A. and H. Schlesinger, "Optimal Insurance in Incomplete Markets," *Journal of Political Economy*, 91(1983b), 1045-1054.

16. Doherty, N.A. and H. Schlesinger, "Risk Premiums with Multiple Sources of Risk," unpublished manuscript, Vanderbilt University (1983c).

17. Doherty, N.A. and S. Tinic, "A Note on Reinsurance Under Conditions of Capital Market Equilibrium," *Journal of Finance*, 48(1981), 949-953.

18. Feldstein, M.S., "Mean Variance Analysis in the Theory of Liquidity Preference and Portfolio Selection," *Review of Economics Studies*, 36(1969), 5-12.

19. Friedman, M. and L.J. Savage, "The Utility Analysis of Choices Involving Risk," *Journal of Political Economy*, 56(1948), 279-304.

20. Hershey, J.C. and P.J.H. Shoemaker, "Risk Taking and Problem Context in the Domain of Losses: An Expected Utility Analysis," *Journal of Risk and Insurance*, 47(1980), 111-132.

21. Hirschliefer, J. and J.G. Riley, "The Analytics of Uncertainty and Information — An Expository Survey," *Journal of Economic Literature*, 17(1979), 1375-1421.

154

22. Illinois Department of Insurance, "Dread Disease Insurance," Study and Report, September 1980.

23. Kahane, Y. and Y. Kroll, "Optimal Insurance Coverage in Situations of Pure and Speculative Risks and the Risk-Free Asset, "unpublished manuscript, Tel-Aviv University (1983).

24. Kahneman, D. and A. Tversky, "Prospect Theory: An Analysis of Decision Under Risk," *Econometrica*, 47(1979), 263-291.

25. Knight, F.H., *Risk, Uncertainty and Profit*, Hart, Schraffner and Marks (1921).

26. Kihlstrom, R.E., D. Romer and S. Williams, "Risk Aversion With Random Initial Wealth," *Econometrica*, 49(1981), 911-920.

27. Kunreuther, H.C., R. Ginsberg, L. Miller, P. Sagi, P. Slovic, B. Bostein and N. Katz, *Disaster Insurance Protection: Public Policy Lessons*, New York: Wiley (1978).

28. Main, B.G.M., "Corporate Insurance Purchases and Taxes," *Journal of Risk and Insurance*, 50(1983), 197-223.

29. MacMinn, R.D. and R.C. Witt, "A Financial Theory of the Insurer Under Uncertainty," unpublished manuscript, University of Texas at Austin (1984).

30. Markowitz, H., "The Utility of Wealth," *Journal of Political Economy*,1 60(1952), 151-158.

31. Mayers, D. and C.W. Smith, "On the Corporate Demand for Insurance," *Journal of Business*, 55(1982), 281-296.

32. Mayers, D. and C.W. Smith, Jr., "The Interdependence of Individual Portfolio Decisions and the Demand for Insurance," *Journal of Political Economy*, 91(1983), 304-311.

33. Mossin, J., "Aspects of Rational Insurance Purchasing," *Journal of Political Economy*, 76(1968), 553-568.

34. Nachman, D., "Preservation of 'More Risk Averse' Under Expectations," *Journal of Economic Theory*, 28(1982), 361-368.

35. Pashigian, B.P., L. Schkade and G.H. Menefee, "The Selection of an Optimal Deductible for a Given Insurance Policy," *Journal of Business*, 39(1966), 35-44.

36. Pratt, J.W. "Risk Aversion in the Small and in the Large," *Econometrica*, 32(1964), 122-136.

37. Pratt, J.W. "Aversion to One Risk in the Presence of Others," unpublished manuscript, Harvard University (1982).

38. Raviv, A., "The Design of an Optimal Insurance Policy," *American Ecnomic Review*, 69(1979), 223-239.

39. Ross, S., "Some Stronger Measures of Risk Aversion in the Small and Large With Applications," *Econometrica*, 49(1981), 621-638.

40. Rothschild, M. and J. Stiglitz, "Equalibrium in Competitive Insurance Markets: An Essay on the Economics of Imperfect Information," *Quarterly Journal of Economics*, 90(1976), 629-650.

41. Schlesinger, H., "The Optimal Level of Deductibility in Insurance Contracts," *Journal of Risk and Insurance*, 48(1981), 465-481.

42. Shoemaker, P.J.H., "The Expected Utility Model: Its Variants, Purposes, Evidence and Limitations," *Journal of Economic Literature*, 20(1982), 529-563.

43. Shoemaker, P.J.H. and H.C. Kunreuther, "An Experimental Study in Insurance Decisions," *Journal of Risk and Insurance*, 46(1979), 603-618.

44. Schulenburg, J.-M. Graf v.d., "Deregulation of Statutory Health Insurance: The Effects of Increased Cost-Sharing Arrangements," unpublished manuscript, Wissenschaftszentrum Berlin (1984).

45. Slovic, P., B. Fischhoff, S. Lichenstein, B. Corrigan and B. Combs, "Preference for Insurance Against Probable Small Losses: Insurance Implications," *Journal of Risk and Insurance*, 44(1977), 237-258.

46. Smith, V., "Optimal Insurance Coverage," *Journal of Political Economy*, 68(1968), 68-77.

47. Turnbull, S.M., "Additional Aspects of Rational Insurance Purchasing," *Journal of Business*, 56(1983), 217-229.

# The Interdependence of Individual Portfolio Decisions and the Demand for Insurance

## David Mayers

*University of California, Los Angeles*

## Clifford W. Smith, Jr.

*University of Rochester*

We analyze the individual's demand for insurance as a special case of general portfolio hedging activity. The demand for insurance contracts is determined simultaneously with the demands for other assets in the portfolio. We demonstrate that when the payoffs of the policy are correlated with the payoffs to the individual's other assets, the demand for insurance contracts is generally not a separable portfolio decision. We argue that this separability condition is not generally met because of significant interdependence of claims across different insurance policies. Furthermore, our generalizations can reverse the standard prediction that wealthier individuals will demand less insurance.

## I. Introduction

Most analyses of the demand for insurance assume (1) that there is only one source of uncertainty in the individual's opportunity set and (2) that an insurance contract is the only available asset for hedging risk (see, e.g., Arrow 1963; Mossin 1968; Pauly 1968; Smith 1968; Gould 1969; Zeckhauser 1970; Ehrlich and Becker 1972; Razin 1976; Harris and Raviv 1978; Spence 1978; Holmström 1979; Shavell 1979). But insurance contracts are only a subset of the assets of an

This research was partially supported by the Managerial Economics Research Center, Graduate School of Management, University of Rochester.

[*Journal of Political Economy*, 1983, vol. 91, no. 2]

individual's portfolio. As Gould (1969, p. 151) notes in discussing potential generalizations of his analysis: "One important such generalization would be a model that considered all aspects of the consumer's portfolio decision instead of treating his collision insurance choice independently." Our analysis provides that generalization. We demonstrate that the demand for a specific insurance policy is generally not a separable portfolio decision (see Leontief 1947),[1] that there are potentially important interdependencies among the demands for insurance policies and other assets.

## II. A Characterization of the Individual's Demand for Insurance

In the perfect capital markets framework (e.g., Fama and Miller 1972) there is no demand for specific insurance contracts even though risk aversion and uncertain future consumption opportunities are explicitly assumed. Individuals can sell shares in any claim (including human capital claims) and effectively eliminate insurable risks through diversification. Thus, a necessary condition for a specific demand for insurance is that costs of eliminating risks through diversification exceed the costs of hedging them with insurance (see Benston and Smith 1976; Mayers and Smith 1982). Mayers (1972, 1973) has modified the traditional analysis by assuming that assets are either perfectly marketable (zero contracting costs) or completely nonmarketable such as human capital (infinite contracting costs). This framework is consistent with a specific demand for insurance because it assumes risk-averse individuals, uncertain consumption opportunities, and relevant contracting costs.

We assume that both nonmarketable and perfectly marketable assets exist and that there are two classes of insurable events, which for convenience we call health and liability events.[2] Thus we decompose the individual's end-of-period random dollar return on his nonmarketable assets into the gross return, $\tilde{Y}_i$; losses generated by liability events, $\tilde{l}_i$; and losses generated by health events, $\tilde{h}_i$. His net nonmarketable asset return is $\tilde{N}_i \equiv \tilde{Y}_i - \tilde{l}_i - \tilde{h}_i$.

Insurance policy payouts are assumed perfectly negatively correlated with the losses from each class of events. Let $\alpha_i$ and $\eta_i$ be the individual's insurance choice variables such that $\alpha_i \tilde{l}_i$ and $\eta_i \tilde{h}_i$ are the payouts actually received from the respective policies. Thus $\alpha_i$ or $\eta_i$ equal to one indicates a policy providing full coverage for that loss,

---

[1] Separability requires that the marginal rate of substitution between any pair of other assets be unaffected by the utilization of this insurance contract.

[2] Two events are sufficient to illustrate our point; generalizing to more events is straightforward.

while $\alpha_i$ and $\eta_i$ less than one indicates a policy providing fractional coverage.

To analyze the individual's demand for insurance, we define end-of-period wealth as

$$\tilde{R}_i \equiv \mathbf{X}_i'\tilde{\mathbf{R}} + \tilde{N}_i + \alpha_i\tilde{l}_i + \eta_i\tilde{h}_i - rd_i,^3 \tag{1}$$

where $\mathbf{X}_i$ is a column vector $(X_{i1}, X_{i2}, \ldots, X_{iN})'$, $X_{ij}$ is the fraction of firm $j$'s shares held by individual $i$, $\tilde{\mathbf{R}}$ is a column vector $(\tilde{R}_1, \tilde{R}_2, \ldots, \tilde{R}_N)'$, $\tilde{R}_j$ is the end-of-period total dollar value of firm $j$'s shares, $r$ is one plus the one-period riskless rate of return, and $d_i$ is the net debt of individual $i$. We also assume that the individual's preferences are a positive function of expected end-of-period wealth $\bar{R}_i$ and a negative function of the variance of end-of-period wealth $\sigma^2(\tilde{R}_i)$,

$$U^i = U^i[\bar{R}_i, \sigma^2(\tilde{R}_i)], \tag{2}$$

where

$$\frac{\partial U^i}{\partial \bar{R}_i} \equiv U_e^i > 0 \text{ and } \frac{\partial U^i}{\partial \sigma^2(\tilde{R}_i)} \equiv U_v^i < 0.$$

The individual's portfolio/insurance problem is to choose $\mathbf{X}_i$, $\alpha_i$, $\eta_i$, and $d_i$ to maximize his preference function (eq. [2]), subject to the budget constraint

$$W_i \equiv \mathbf{X}_i'\mathbf{P} + \alpha_i P_{li} + \eta_i P_{hi} - d_i, \tag{3}$$

where $\mathbf{P}$ is a column vector $(P_1, P_2, \ldots, P_N)'$, $P_j$ is the current total market value of firm $j$'s shares, and $P_{li}$ and $P_{hi}$ are the premiums for full coverage under the health and liability policies. The solution to this portfolio problem provides a demand equation for each type of insurance policy as well as the individual's demand functions for risky marketable assets.[4]

The demand equations for insurance are symmetric so we need only examine one. The optimal coverage under the liability insurance policy can be characterized as follows:[5]

---

[3] Thus, in our model the individual's end-of-period wealth is the sum of (1) the end-of-period equity values of his fractional ownerships of the firms in the market, (2) his net nonmarketable asset return, (3) the payoffs from his insurance policies, and (4) the repayment of any riskless loans.

[4] Additional assumptions are infinite divisibility, price-taking behavior, and no short sales constraints. We suppress the risky marketable asset demand functions in our analysis.

[5] This equation is really a characterization since we have not solved out the other choice variables. This form is more interpretable. For example, by defining the liability policy as asset $N + 1$ and the health policy as asset $N + 2$, the full solution, equivalent to eq. (4), is

$$\alpha_i = 1 + k_i \sum_{j=1}^{N+2} Q_{N+1,j}(\bar{R}_j - rP_j) + \sum_{j=1}^{N+2} Q_{N+1,j}\sigma_{ij},$$

$$\alpha_i^* = \frac{1}{\sigma^2(\tilde{l}_i)} [-\mathbf{X}_i'\boldsymbol{\gamma}_i - \text{cov}(\tilde{l}_i, \tilde{Y}_i) + (1 - \eta_i) \text{cov}(\tilde{l}_i, \tilde{h}_i)]$$

$$+ \frac{1}{\sigma^2(\tilde{l}_i)} [\sigma^2(\tilde{l}_i) + k_i(\tilde{l}_i - rP_{li})], \tag{4}$$

where $\boldsymbol{\gamma}_i$ is the column vector $(\sigma_{l1}, \sigma_{l2}, \dots, \sigma_{lN})'$, $\sigma_{lj}$ is the covariance between $\tilde{l}_i$ and $\tilde{R}_j$, cov is the covariance operator, and $k_i \equiv -(U_e^i/2U_v^i)$ $> 0$, given $U_e^i > 0$, $U_v^i < 0$. Thus, $k_i$ can be interpreted as a marginal rate of substitution between expected return and variance evaluated at the optimum.

The first bracketed term in equation (4) collects the factors that are added by considering the demand for insurance in a portfolio context. These factors all represent substitution alternatives for the insurance policy under consideration. The second bracketed term in equation (4) reflects those factors which would appear in an analysis done in isolation. If the insurance were priced at its actuarial/discounted-at-the-riskless-rate value (i.e., $P_{li} \equiv \tilde{l}_i/r$) and if the first term were zero, then the individual would demand full coverage: $\alpha_i^* = [\sigma^2(\tilde{l}_i)/\sigma^2(\tilde{l}_i)] \equiv$ 1. If the premium included a loading fee (i.e., $P_{li} > \tilde{l}_i/r$), the individual would demand less than full coverage. Moreover, the coverage demanded is affected by the consumer's degree of risk aversion, $k_i$ (e.g., if wealthier individuals are less risk averse, with positive loading fees, they will have a lower demand for insurance).

## III. Separability of the Demand for Insurance

A sufficient condition for the separability of the demand for insurance from other portfolio decisions is that the losses of a particular type are orthogonal to the payoffs to all marketable assets, the individual's gross human capital, and the losses associated with other insurable events. We examine each term in the first bracketed expression in (4) to see how restrictive this assumption might be.

The first term, $-\mathbf{X}_i'\boldsymbol{\gamma}_i$, could be described as "homemade" insurance. It represents the insurance protection provided by the marketable assets held in the consumer's optimal portfolio, that is, $-\mathbf{X}_i'\boldsymbol{\gamma}_i \equiv$ $-\text{cov}(\tilde{l}_i, \tilde{R}_{pi})$, where $R_{pi}$ is the individual's marketable asset portfolio return. Of course, how much protection the consumer obtains through homemade insurance depends both on the availability of marketable assets that can provide such a hedge and on the relative costs of a standard insurance policy versus homemade insurance (see Mayers and Smith 1981).[6] Hence risks which have a large market

---

where $\sigma_{ij} = \text{cov}(\tilde{Y}_i, \tilde{R}_j), j = 1, \dots, N + 2$, and $Q_{N+1,j}$ are elements from row $N + 1$ of the inverse of the $(N + 2) \times (N + 2)$ variance-covariance matrix.

[6] One dimension in which the cost should be reduced with homemade insurance is

component are likely to be hedged through homemade insurance. Moreover, since the dollar magnitude of the individual's risky marketable asset holdings enters in the term $\mathbf{X}_i' \boldsymbol{\gamma}_i$ for two individuals who face the same risk ($\tilde{l}_i$) and hold the same proportions of marketable securities, but one with twice the marketable assets as the other, assuming cov ($\tilde{l}, \tilde{R}_{pi}$) > 0, the individual with the greater marketable wealth will demand less insurance. Although there is some evidence that suggests there is a market component to health-related events, we doubt that the magnitude of the effect is empirically important in determining the demand for health insurance.[7]

The second term, $-$cov ($\tilde{l}_i, \tilde{Y}_i$), represents the individual's incentive to self-insure.[8] If liability losses are likely to be large in states of the world that are otherwise "bad," the consumer will demand more insurance. For example, a physician who suffers a successful malpractice suit would expect the demand for his services to fall. This would make the cov ($\tilde{l}_i, \tilde{Y}_i$) negative and his demand for liability insurance is correspondingly higher. Similarly, if claims under health insurance policies tend to be associated with reductions in productivity, the demand for health insurance is higher. Nonmarketable wealth also enters directly into the cov ($\tilde{l}_i, \tilde{Y}_i$) term. If one consumer has twice the return $\tilde{Y}_i$ as another in every state of nature and if they both face the same distribution of liability losses, the wealthier individual will tend to purchase more insurance assuming cov ($\tilde{l}_i, \tilde{Y}_i$) < 0. This will tend to reverse the usual implication that individuals with greater wealth will demand less insurance.

The final term, $(1 - \eta_i)$ cov ($\tilde{l}_i, \tilde{h}_i$), reflects the possibility of substitutions between insurance of different types where the risks are not orthogonal. We think that quantitatively the dependence of payoffs across different insurance policies is the most important of the factors isolated in our analysis. There are likely to be important correlations in claims across different insurance policies; for example, given a claim under an automobile insurance policy, the probability of a claim under health, life, or liability policies is likely to be increased. Thus

---

the elimination of incentive conflicts which must be reflected in the insurance premium. We abstract from these costs.

[7] Gerald Seib reports: "An expert calculates that over a six-year period, a one-percentage-point rise in unemployment causes about 37,000 deaths. 'Virtually all major illnesses, virtually all major causes of death are affected,' he says" (*Wall Street Journal* [August 25, 1980], p. 17, "Recessions Cause Death Rates to Rise as Pressures of Coping Take Hold").

[8] This incentive to self-insure does not derive from the insured's "willingness" to bear risk. Quite the contrary, it derives from his aversion to risk; he retains some of the risk for diversification purposes. Consider the problem of choosing $\alpha_i$ to minimize the variance of $\tilde{R}_i \equiv \tilde{Y}_i - \tilde{l}_i + \alpha_i \tilde{l}_i$. The solution is $\alpha_i = 1 -$ cov ($\tilde{l}_i, \tilde{Y}$)$/\sigma^2(\tilde{l}_i)$, not $\alpha_i = 1$.

with more than one type of risk, where the risks are correlated, and specialization exists across insurance policies there is an indeterminacy with regard to the demand for a particular insurance contract.[9]

## IV. Conclusions

Much of the analysis of the demand for insurance focuses on insurance in isolation. Yet insurance is a special case of hedging risk by risk-averse individuals. Capital markets provide a rich array of contractual forms convenient for risk reduction; insurance contracts are but a subset of this array of available alternatives. We examine the interrelationship between insurance holdings and other portfolio decisions. Sufficient conditions for insurance decisions to be independent of other portfolio decisions are: (1) There is no moral hazard or adverse selection; and (2) the payoffs to the insurance policy are orthogonal to those of all marketable securities, the consumer's gross human capital, and the payoffs to other insurance policies. Although the first restriction is well known, the second has been unrecognized. Moreover, we argue that this omission is not trivial. There are potentially important covariances in the payoffs with other insurance policies and with human capital which lead to different predictions about insurance demands than obtained under the assumption of separability.

Our analysis has abstracted from a number of important considerations which also affect the structure of observed insurance contracts. For example, we have ignored the general prohibition against insurance exceeding 100 percent of value. This prohibition obviously constrains the ability of individuals to purchase more than full coverage of one type of insurance as a partial hedge against another risk. However, we have also omitted consideration of moral hazard and loading fees which lead to an optimal choice of less than full coverage when demands are separable (see Mayers and Smith 1981). In general, incorporation of these considerations should not overturn the qualitative implications of the interdependencies on which we focus.

Some types of analyses will be more robust than others in ignoring portfolio considerations. For example, analyses concerned with the impact of administrative expenses on the structure of the deductible schedule of an insurance contract are likely to be little affected. On the other hand, analyses of the type done by Pashigian, Schkade, and

---

[9] The interdependencies in demand across insurance contracts could be internalized if insurance coverage were provided through a single blanket insurance policy. Observed contracts typically cover a collection of related hazards; we believe that the analysis of the covariance in payoffs across hazards will be important in explaining how coverage is bundled across contracts.

Menefee (1966), Gould (1969), and Drèze (1981), where the question concerns whether observed individual demand behavior conforms to the predictions of a model that does not consider alternatives for risk reduction, are less likely to be robust (a point admitted by Gould).

## References

Arrow, Kenneth J. "Uncertainty and the Welfare Economics of Medical Care." *A.E.R.* 53 (December 1963): 941–73.

Benston, George J., and Smith, Clifford W., Jr. "A Transactions Cost Approach to the Theory of Financial Intermediation." *J. Finance* 31 (May 1976): 215–31.

Drèze, Jacques H. "Inferring Risk Tolerance from Deductibles in Insurance Contracts." *Geneva Papers Risk and Insurance,* no. 20 (1981), pp. 48–52.

Ehrlich, Isaac, and Becker, Gary S. "Market Insurance, Self-Insurance, and Self-Protection." *J.P.E.* 80 (July/August 1972): 623–48.

Fama, Eugene F., and Miller, Merton H. *The Theory of Finance.* New York: Holt, Rinehart & Winston, 1972.

Gould, John P. "The Expected Utility Hypothesis and the Selection of Optimal Deductibles for a Given Insurance Policy." *J. Bus.* 42 (April 1969): 143–51.

Harris, Milton, and Raviv, Artur. "Some Results on Incentive Contracts with Applications to Education and Employment, Health Insurance and Law Enforcement." *A.E.R.* 68 (March 1978): 20–30.

Holmström, Bengt. "Moral Hazard and Observability." *Bell J. Econ.* 10 (Spring 1979): 74–91.

Leontief, Wassily W. "Introduction to a Theory of the Internal Structure of Functional Relationships." *Econometrica* 15 (October 1947): 361–73.

Mayers, David. "Nonmarketable Assets and Capital Market Equilibrium under Uncertainty." In *Studies in the Theory of Capital Markets,* edited by Michael C. Jensen. New York: Praeger, 1972.

———. "Nonmarketable Assets and the Determination of Capital Asset Prices in the Absence of a Riskless Asset." *J. Bus.* 46 (April 1973): 258–67.

Mayers, David, and Smith, Clifford W., Jr. "Contractual Provisions, Organizational Structure, and Conflict Control in Insurance Markets." *J. Bus.* 54 (July 1981): 407–34.

———. *Toward a Positive Theory of Insurance.* Monograph Series Econ. and Finance. New York: New York Univ. Graduate School Bus., Salomon Brothers Center Study Financial Inst., 1982.

Mossin, Jan. "Aspects of Rational Insurance Purchasing." *J.P.E.* 76, no. 4, pt. 1 (July/August 1968): 553–68.

Pashigian, B. Peter; Schkade, Lawrence L.; and Menefee, George H. "The Selection of an Optimal Deductible for a Given Insurance Policy." *J. Bus.* 39 (January 1966): 35–44.

Pauly, Mark V. "The Economics of Moral Hazard: Comment." *A.E.R.* 58 (June 1968): 531–37.

Razin, Assaf. "Rational Insurance Purchasing." *J. Finance* 31 (March 1976): 133–37.

Shavell, Steven. "Risk Sharing and Incentives in the Principal and Agent Relationship." *Bell J. Econ.* 10 (Spring 1979): 55–73.

Smith, Vernon L. "Optimal Insurance Coverage." *J.P.E.* 76 (January/ February 1968): 68–77.

Spence, Michael. "Product Differentiation and Performance in Insurance Markets." *J. Public Econ.* 10 (December 1978): 427–47.

Zeckhauser, Richard. "Medical Insurance: A Case Study of the Tradeoff between Risk Spreading and Appropriate Incentives." *J. Econ. Theory* 2 (March 1970): 10–26.

# Market Insurance, Self-Insurance, and Self-Protection

## Isaac Ehrlich

*University of Chicago and Tel-Aviv University*

## Gary S. Becker

*University of Chicago*

The article develops a theory of demand for insurance that emphasizes the interaction between market insurance, "self-insurance," and "self-protection." The effects of changes in "prices," income, and other variables on the demand for these alternative forms of insurance are analyzed using the "state preference" approach to behavior under uncertainty. Market insurance and self-insurance are shown to be substitutes, but market insurance and self-protection can be complements. The analysis challenges the notion that "moral hazard" is an inevitable consequence of market insurance, by showing that under certain conditions the latter may lead to a reduction in the probabilities of hazardous events.

The incentive to insure and its behavioral implications have usually been analyzed by applying the expected utility approach without reference to the indifference curve analysis ordinarily employed in consumption theory. In this paper insurance is discussed by combining expected utility and an indifference curve analysis within the context of the "state preference" approach to behavior under uncertainty (the preferences in question relating to states of the world).[1] We use this framework to restate

Becker's contribution was primarily an unpublished paper that sets out the approach developed here. Ehrlich greatly extended and applied that approach and was primarily responsible for writing this paper. We have had many helpful comments from Harold Demsetz, Jacques Drèze, Jack Hirshleifer, and members of the Labor Workshop at Columbia University and the Industrial Organization Workshop at the University of Chicago.

[1] An approach originally devised by Arrow (1963–64) and worked out in application to investment decisions under uncertainty by Hirshleifer (1970).

and reinterpret in a simpler and more intuitive way some familiar propositions concerning insurance behavior; more important, we derive a number of apparently new results, especially those concerned with self-insurance and self-protection. Our approach separates objective opportunities from "taste" and other environmental factors, which facilitates an independent investigation of each class of factors analytically as well as empirically. In addition, we consider not only the incentive to insure, but also how much insurance is purchased under varying "opportunities"[2] and in view of the existence of the alternatives of self-insurance and self-protection. We use the basic analytical tools employed throughout traditional consumption and production theory.

It has been argued that insurance is different from "ordinary" goods and services because it is not desired per se, but as a means of satisfying more basic needs.[3] Recent developments in consumption theory[4] suggest, however, that the distinction between goods and services purchased in the market and more basic needs they satisfy is not a unique characteristic of insurance, but applies to all goods and services. The demand for the latter is also derived from the needs they satisfy, just as the demand for factors of production in ordinary production theory is derived from their contribution to final products.

The basic needs underlying the purchase of insurance will be identified with consumption opportunities contingent upon the occurrence of various mutually exclusive and jointly exhaustive "states of the world."[5] Market insurance in this approach redistributes income and, consequently, consumption opportunities, toward the less well-endowed states. Self-insurance, however, redistributes income similarly, self-protection has a related effect, and either might be pursued when market insurance was not available. Moreover, optimal decisions about market insurance depend on the availability of these other activities and should be viewed within the context of a more comprehensive "insurance" decision.

[2] Theorems concerning optimal insurance decisions have been derived in two recent contributions by Smith (1968) and Mossin (1968). Our approach differs not only in form but also in substance; for example, in the analysis of the interaction between market insurance, self-insurance, and self-protection.

[3] For example, Arrow (1965) says, "Insurance is not a material good . . . its value to the buyer is clearly different in kind from the satisfaction of consumer's desires for medical treatment or transportation. Indeed, unlike goods and services, transactions involving insurance are an exchange of money for money, not money for something which directly meets needs" (p. 45).

[4] See, for example, Becker and Michael (1970).

[5] By consumption opportunities in each state of the world is meant command over commodities, $C_i$, produced by combining market goods, $X_i$, time spent in consumption, $t_i$, and the "state environment," $E_i$, via household production functions (for the latter concept see Becker and Michael 1970): $C_{ij} = f_{ij}(X_{ij}, t_{ij}, E_i)$ $j = 1, \ldots, m$ where $j$ refers to different commodities. If the production functions fully incorporate the effects of environment, the utility function of commodities would not depend on which state occurred. In particular, for an aggregate commodity $C$, $U(C_0) = U(C_1)$ if $C_0 = {}_1$, where 0, 1 denote different states.

The first part of this paper spells out a model of market insurance and discusses the effects of changes in terms of trade, "income," and other environmental factors on optimal insurance decisions. Self-insurance, self-protection, and a simultaneous determination of the full insurance decision are then discussed in the second and more original part.

## I.   Market Insurance

We assume for simplicity that an individual is faced with only two states of the world $(0, 1)$ with probabilities $p$ and $1 - p$, respectively, and that his real income endowment in each state is given with certainty by $I_0^e$ and $I_1^e$, where $I_1^e - I_0^e$ is the prospective loss if state 0 occurs. If income in state 1 can be exchanged for income in state 0 at the fixed rate

$$- \frac{dI_1}{dI_0} = \pi, \tag{1}$$

$\pi$ can be called the "price of insurance" measured in terms of income in state 1. The amount of insurance purchased in state 0 can be defined as the difference between the actual and endowed incomes:[6]

$$s = I_0 - I_0^e. \tag{2}$$

The expenditure on insurance measured in terms of state 1's income is

$$b = I_1^e - I_1 = s\pi. \tag{3}$$

Substituting (2) in (3) gives the opportunity boundary

$$I_1^e - I_1 = \pi(I_0 - I_0^e), \tag{4}$$

or the line $\overline{AB}$ in figure 1.[7] It is assumed that the individual chooses the optimal income in states 1 and 0 by maximizing the expected utility of the income prospect,

$$U^* = (1 - p) U(I_1) + p U(I_0),^{8} \tag{5}$$

subject to the constraint given by the opportunity boundary. The first-order optimality condition is

$$\pi = \frac{p U_0'}{(1 - p)U_1'}, \tag{6}$$

---

[6] Note that insurance is defined not in terms of the liability "coverage" of potential losses, as in Smith's (1968) and Mossin's (1968) papers, but in terms of "coverage minus premium," or the net addition to income in state 0.

[7] In figure 1, the opportunity boundary $\overline{AB}$ is drawn as a straight line. This assumes that the same terms of trade apply to both insurance and "gambling," that is, to movements to the right and to the left of $E$, the endowment position. In practice, the opportunity boundary may be kinked about the endowment point.

[8] For analytical simplicity we ignore the time and environment inputs and assume only a single aggregate commodity in each state. Then the output of commodities can be identified with the input of goods and services, or with income.

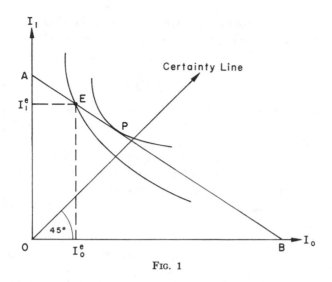

$$\text{FIG. 1}$$

where $(pU_0')/(1-p)U_1'$ is the slope of the indifference curve (defined along $dU^* = 0$), and $\pi$ is the slope of the budget line. In equilibrium, they must be the same (see point $P$).

One can more completely separate tastes from environmental factors by dividing $p/(1-p)$ through in (6) to obtain

$$\bar{\pi} = \frac{1-p}{p} \, \pi = \frac{U_0'}{U_1'}. \tag{7}$$

Further, $\bar{\pi}$, the price of insurance deflated by the actuarially "fair"[9] price, $p/(1-p)$, is a measure of the "real" price of insurance because a fair price is "costless" to the individual (see the second paragraph below). Equation (7) thus implies that, in equilibrium, the real price of insurance equals the ratio of the marginal utility of $I_0$ to that of $I_1$, the ordinary result in consumer demand theory.

The second-order condition requires that the indifference curve be convex to the origin at the equilibrium point, or

$$D = -\, p \, U_0'' - \pi^2 \, (1-p) \, U_1'' > 0. \tag{8}$$

A sufficient condition is that the marginal utility of income is strictly declining.[10]

An immediate implication of equation (7) is that insurance would be

---

[9] An actuarially fair exchange is an exchange of $p/(1-p)$ units of income in state 1 for an additional unit of income in state 0, where $p/(1-p)$ is the odds that state 0 would occur.

[10] Hirshleifer (1970, p. 233) points out that although diminishing marginal utility of income is not a necessary condition for equilibrum at any given point, it is a necessary condition for the indifference curve to be convex at all points.

demanded—some $I_1$ would be traded for $I_0$—if the slope of the indifference curve exceeded the price of insurance at the endowment point, $E$:

$$\bar{\pi} < \frac{U'(I_0^e)}{U'(I_1^e)}. \tag{9}$$

If the opposite were true, "gambling" would be demanded, provided similar terms of trade apply in redistributions of income toward state 1. Note that gambling can occur without increasing marginal utility of income if the opportunities available are sufficiently favorable. Therefore, inferences about attitudes toward risk cannot be made independently of existing market opportunities: a person may appear to be a "risk avoider" under one combination of prices and potential losses and a "risk taker" under another.[11]

If the price of insurance were actuarially fair, equation (7) would reduce to $1 = U_0'/U_1'$: incomes would be equalized in both states of the world if the marginal utility of income were always diminishing. This is "full insurance" in the sense that a person would be indifferent as to which state occurred.[12] In particular, for small changes around the equilibrium position, he would act as if he were indifferent toward risk and interested only in maximizing his expected income. Indeed, his income in each state would equal his expected income;[13] therefore, fair insurance can be regarded as costless to him.[14]

[11] Indeed, when faced with several independent hazards, a person might "gamble" and "insure" at the same time, provided the different hazards were associated with different opportunities. For example, given a fair price of theft insurance, he may fully insure his household against theft and at the same time engage in a risky activity if his expected earnings there were greater than his earnings in alternative "safe" activities (see Ehrlich 1970).

[12] Full insurance can be identified with full coverage of potential losses, since the equation $I_1 = I_0$ implies that $I_1^e - b = I_0^e + d - b$, where $d$ is the gross coverage and $b$ is the premium. Clearly, then, $d = I_1^e - I_0^e$. By the same reasoning, since an "unfair" price of insurance $\bar{\pi} > 1$ implies that $I_1 > I_0$, it also implies necessarily less than full coverage of potential losses.

[13] If $I_0 = I_1 = I$ that is, $I_1 = I_1^e - s\pi = I_0 = I_0^e + s$, where $\pi = p/(1-p)$, then $I = p I_0^e + (1-p) I_1^e$.

[14] Although the model has been developed for two states of the world, the analysis applies equally well to $n$ states. We define the state with the highest income—say, state $n$—as the state without hazard and define all the states with hazard ($h = 1, \ldots, n-1$) relative to that state. Denoting by $p_h$ the probability of state $h$, by

$$p = 1 - \sum_{h=1}^{n-1} p_h$$

the probability of state $n$, and by $\pi_h$ the implicit terms of trade between income in state $n$ and income in state $h$, it can easily be shown that if the terms of trade were fair ($\bar{\pi}_h = [p/p_h] \pi_h = 1$) $s_h$ would be chosen to equalize incomes in all states of the world and losses would be "fully covered." If the real terms of trade were unfair but

## A. *Substitution Effects*

The effect of an exogenous increase in the price of insurance on the demand for $I_0$, with the probability of loss and the initial endowment being the same, can be found by partially differentiating the first-order optimality condition with respect to $\pi$:

$$\frac{\partial I_0}{\partial \pi} = \frac{1}{D} \left[ -(1-p) U_1' + (I_0 - I_0^e) \pi (1-p) U_1'' \right]. \quad (10)$$

Since the denominator $D$ has already been shown to be positive, the sign of equation (10) is the same as the sign of the numerator, or negative if $I_0 > I_0^e$, since we are assuming $U_1'' < 0$. An increase in the relative cost of income in state 0 necessarily decreases the demand for income in this state. Moreover, it also reduces the amount of insurance purchased, since $I_0^e$ remains unchanged: $\partial s/\partial \pi = \partial I_0/\partial \pi - \partial I_0^e/\partial \pi = \partial I_0/\partial \pi$.

Similarly, the effect of an increase in $\pi$ on $I_1$, and thus on the amount spent on insurance, is

$$\frac{\partial I_1}{\partial \pi} = \frac{1}{D} \left[ (1-p) U_1' \pi + (I_0 - I_0^e) p U_0'' \right]. \quad (11)$$

Here the result is ambiguous since $U_1'$ is positive whereas

$$(I_0 - I_0^e) p U_0'' = s p U_0''$$

is negative if $U_0'' < 0$ and $s > 0$. The result is ambiguous because, although an increase in $\pi$ reduces the amount of insurance purchased, each unit purchased becomes more expensive. Consequently, the amount spent on insurance would decline only if the price elasticity of demand for insurance exceeded unity[15] (a proof is obvious).

Equations (10) and (11) do not isolate a "pure" substitution effect because an increase in $\pi$ lowers the opportunities available (if $s > 0$). If both $I_1$ and $I_0$ are superior goods, the income and substitution effects both reduce the demand for $I_0$, whereas they have opposite effects on the demand for $I_1$. Diagrammatically, as the opportunity boundary changes from $\overline{AB}$ to $\overline{CD}$ (see fig. 2), the equilibrium point shifts from $P$ to $Q$. If $I_0$ were a superior good, $Q$ must be to the left of $P'$. Even if $I_0$ were an inferior good, however, a "pure" (that is, expenditure-compensated) increase in the terms of trade must always reduce the demand for $I_0$ and increase $I_1$: the equilibrium must shift from $P$ to a point to its left, like $S$.

---

constant ($\bar{\pi}_h = \pi = 1 + \lambda > 1$ for all $h$), $s_h$ would be chosen to equalize incomes in states with hazard only, that is, we would achieve what has been called full insurance above a deductible (for a definition of this concept and an alternative proof see Arrow 1963).

[15] This analysis, therefore, also shows that the effect of a change in $\pi$ on the "fullness" of insurance (the difference $I_1 - I_0$) and thus on the degree of gross coverage is generally not unambiguous.

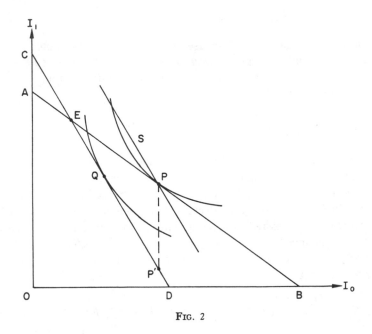

FIG. 2

### B. Income Effects

Equation (4) can be written as

$$I_1^e + \pi I_0^e = W = I_1 + \pi I_0, \tag{12}$$

where $W$ is a measure of the total opportunities available. (This is shown in fig. 1 by the intercept $\overline{OA}$ on the $I_1$ axis.) The effect of a change in the endowments on the income demanded in each state can be determined by differentiating the first-order condition:

$$\frac{\partial I_0}{\partial W} = \frac{\partial I_0}{\partial I_0^e} = \frac{\partial I_0}{\partial I_1^e} \frac{\partial I_0^e}{\partial W} = -\frac{D_{31}}{D}$$

$$\frac{\partial I_1}{\partial W} = \frac{\partial I_1}{\partial I_0^e} = \frac{\partial I_1}{\partial I_1^e} \frac{\partial I_0^e}{\partial W} = -\frac{D_{32}}{D} \tag{13}$$

where $D_{31} = \pi(1 - p)U_1''$, and $D_{32} = pU_0''$. The income demanded in each state necessarily increases with opportunities if the marginal utility of income is falling. Hence, an increase in each state's endowment increases the demand for income in other states as well. The effects on the demand for insurance are more complicated, however, since they depend on how different endowments change. For example, if $I_1^e$ alone increased,

$$\frac{\partial s}{\partial I_1^e} = \frac{\partial I_0}{\partial I_1^e} > 0, \tag{14}$$

and the demand for insurance would increase. Similarly, if $I_0^e$ alone increased,

$$\frac{\partial s}{\partial I_0^e} = \frac{\partial I_0}{\partial I_0^e} - 1 < 0,[16] \tag{15}$$

and the demand for insurance would decrease. Equations (14) and (15) imply that if the difference in endowed income—the endowed loss from the hazard—increased either because $I_0^e$ decreased or $I_1^e$ increased, the demand for insurance would increase. Put differently, a person would be more likely to insure large rather than small losses (see Lees and Rice 1965).[17] The effects of a change in total opportunities on the demand for insurance cannot be derived without knowledge of the way opportunities change essentially because insurance is a "residual" that bridges the gap between endowed and desired levels of income in different states of the world.[18]

For example, if both endowments (and hence the size of the loss) are changed by the same percentage, then

$$(\varepsilon_{sW} - 1) = \frac{I_0}{s}(\eta_0 - 1), \tag{16}$$

where $\varepsilon_{sW} = \partial s/\partial W \cdot W/s$ and $\eta_0 = \partial I_0/\partial W \cdot W/I_0$ are the opportunity elasticities of demand for $s$ and $I_0$, respectively.[19]

Equation (16) incorporates the rather obvious conclusion that the effect of a change in opportunities on the demand for insurance depends on the effects on the income demanded in each state. If the slopes of the indifference curves are constant along a given ray from the origin (the indifference curves are like $EPF$ and $GQ_1H$ in fig. 3)—there is constant

---

[16] According to equation (13), $\partial I_0/\partial I_0^e = [-\pi^2 (1-p) U_1'']/[-pU_0'' - \pi^2 (1-p) U_1''] = \delta$, where clearly $0 < \delta < 1$ if $U_1''$ and $U_0'' < 0$. But since $s = I_0 - I_0^e$, $\partial s/\partial I_0^e = \delta - 1 < 0$.

[17] Similarly, he would be less likely to take large gambles (see the discussion in Hirshleifer 1966). Of course, if insurance is fair he will fully insure all losses, large or small.

[18] Note the analogy between insurance and savings: the latter bridges the gap between "endowed" and desired levels of consumption at different points in time.

[19] Given $s = I_0 - I_0^e$ and $I_1^e = \gamma I_0^e$, then $(\partial s/\partial W)(W/s) = (ds/dI_0^e)(I_0^e/s) = \eta_0 (I_0/s) - (I_0^e/s)$; by collecting terms, we get equation (16). Since $I_0 \geqslant s$, $e_{sW} \geqslant 1$ if $\eta_0 \geqslant 1$.

If the loss is unaffected by an equal increase in endowments, that is, if $I_0^e = I_1^e - L$ where $L$ is a constant, then $\varepsilon_{se} = (ds/dI_1^e)(I_1^e/s) = (I_0/s)\eta_0 (d \log W)/(d \log I_1^e) - (I_1^e/s)$. This implies that

$$\varepsilon_{se} \begin{array}{c} > \\ = \\ < \end{array} 0 \quad \text{as} \quad \eta_0 \begin{array}{c} > \\ = \\ < \end{array} \frac{W}{I_0(1+\pi)} \geqslant 1 \quad (\text{if } I_1 \geqslant I_0). \tag{16a}$$

172

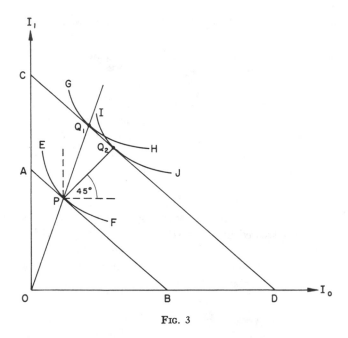

FIG. 3

relative risk aversion[20]—then all equilibrium positions lie on a given ray from the origin, as $P$ and $Q_1$ do in figure 3, and $\eta_0 = \eta_1 = 1$. An equal proportional increase in all endowments would then increase the demand for insurance by the same proportion. If the slopes of the indifference

[20] Note that

$$\frac{d \text{ slope}}{dI_0} = \frac{d}{dI_0} \left[ \frac{pU_0'}{(1-p)U_1'} \right]$$

subject to $I_1 = \gamma I_0$ is $\gtreqless 0$ as $-(U_1''/U_1') \;\; \gamma \gtreqless -(U_0''/U_0')$; the latter defines increasing, constant, or decreasing relative risk aversion. Similarly

$$\frac{d}{dI_0} \left[ \frac{pU_0'}{(1-p)U_1'} \right]$$

subject to $I_1 - I_0 = L$ is $\gtreqless 0$ as $-(U_1''/U_1') \gtreqless -(U_0''/U_0')$; the latter defines increasing, constant, or decreasing absolute risk aversion (see Pratt 1964, Arrow 1965). (Diagramatically, constant absolute risk aversion implies that the slopes of the indifference curves are constant along any 45° line joining two equilibrium positions— the indifference curves are like $EPF$ and $IQ_2J$ in fig. 3.) Equation (16a) in n.19 implies that increasing relative risk aversion, $\eta_0 > 1$, is compatible with decreasing absolute risk aversion, $\epsilon_{se} < 0$, only if $\eta_0 < W/I_0(1+\pi)$.

curves increase along a given ray from the origin, as shown by *EPF* and *IQ₂J* in figure 3, there is increasing relative risk aversion, and $\eta_0$ and thus $\varepsilon_{sw}$ would exceed unity. Increasing relative risk aversion implies that the elasticity of substitution between $I_0$ and $I_1$ tends to decline as opportunities increase.[21] Regardless of the shape of preferences elsewhere in the preference space, however, relative (and absolute) risk aversion remains constant along the certainty line. This constancy always characterizes choices when the price of insurance is actuarially fair (see fig. 4).

## C. *Rare Losses*

An inspection of the necessary conditions for insurance given in equation (9) shows that changes in $p$, the probability of loss, do not affect the incentive to insure as long as the real price of insurance is independent of $p$. If insurance were actuarially fair, the real price would always equal unity, and thus would be independent of $p$.

The deviation from a fair price, or the "loading" in insurance terminology, can be defined from the identity

$$\pi \equiv \frac{(1+\lambda)\,p}{1-p}, \tag{17}$$

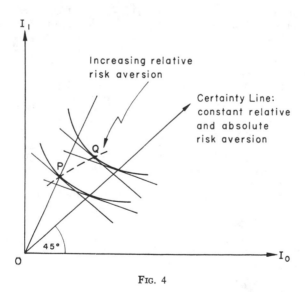

FIG. 4

[21] Since the slopes of the indifference curves necessarily are constant along the "certainty line" and by assumption become increasingly steep toward $I_0$ along other rays from the origin, a given percentage deviation of the price of insurance from the fair price results in smaller percentage changes in the ratio $I_1/I_0$ at higher indifference levels. That is, $\sigma = (d \log I_1/I_0)/d \log \pi$ decreases at higher indifference levels when $\pi$ equals the fair price.

where $\lambda$ is the "loading factor." If $\lambda$ were independent of $p$, so also would be the real price of insurance and $p$ would have no effect on the incentive to insure. In particular, there would *not* then be a greater incentive to insure "rare" losses of a given size.[22]

Since, apparently, rare losses are more frequently insured,[23] $\lambda$ is presumably positively related to $p$, perhaps because processing and investigating costs increase as $p$ increases.[24] (An alternative explanation is provided by the interaction between market and self-insurance analyzed in the next section.) Even if the *incentive* to insure were independent of $p$, the *amount* insured would decline and the expenditure on insurance would increase as $p$ increased.[25]

## II. Self-Insurance and Self-Protection

Two alternatives to market insurance that have not been systematically analyzed in the literature on insurance are self-insurance—a reduction in the size of a loss—and self-protection—a reduction in the probability of a loss.[26] For example, sprinkler systems reduce the loss from fires; burglar alarms reduce the probability of illegal entry; cash balances reduce fluctuations in consumption; medicines, certain foods, and medical

---

[22] This result appears to contradict one by Lees and Rice (1965) because they define the loading factor in terms of the gross rather than net amount paid in claim; that is by $\lambda'$ in $\pi = [(1 + \lambda') \, p]/[1 - (1 + \lambda') \, p]$. A reduction in $p$, $\lambda'$ held constant, would reduce $\lambda$—our definition of the loading factor—and thus would increase the incentive to insure.

[23] Some evidence is presented in Lees and Rice (1965).

[24] Let the amount $a$ that is spent processing and investigating each claim be the only administrative cost of providing insurance. In a zero profit equilibrium position, the unit price of insurance would equal the ratio of the total amount collected in premiums in state 1 (including administration costs) to the difference between the net amount paid in claims in state 0 and administration costs: $\pi = (p \, d + p \, a)/[d \, (1 - p) - p \, a]$, where $d$ is the amount covered by insurance. The degree of loading defined by $\lambda = [(1 - p)/p] \, \pi - 1 = (d + a)/[d - p \, a/(1 - p)] - 1 = a/[d - p \, (d + a)]$ would be larger the larger $p$ was if $d$ were fixed ($d$ would tend to decrease as $p$ increased, and this would increase $\lambda$ even further).

[25] Generally, the effect of an increase in $p$ on the optimal values of $I_0$ and $I_1$, assuming that $\pi = [(1 + \lambda) \, p]/(1 - p)$ and that $\lambda$, $I_0^e$, and $I_1^e$ are constant, is given by

$$\frac{\partial I_0}{\partial p} = \frac{1}{D} \left[ U_1'' \, s \, \pi \, \frac{1 + \lambda}{1 - p} \right] < 0$$

$$\frac{\partial I_1}{\partial p} = \frac{1}{D} \left[ U_0'' \, s \, \pi \, \frac{1}{1 - p} \right] < 0$$

provided $U'' < 0$. An increase in $p$ would then lower the optimal amount of insurance $s = I_0 - I_0^e$ and increase the optimal expenditure on insurance $b = I_1^e - I_1$.

[26] These have been called "loss protection" and "loss prevention," respectively (see Mehr and Commack 1966, pp. 28–29).

checkups reduce vulnerability to illness; and good lawyers reduce both the probability of conviction and the punishment for crime. As these examples indicate, it is somewhat artificial to distinguish behavior that reduces the probability of a loss from behavior that reduces the size of a loss, since many actions do both. Nevertheless, we do so for expository convenience and because self-insurance clearly illustrates the insurance principle of redistributing income toward less favorable states.

## A. Self-Insurance

Assume that market insurance is unavailable and write the loss to a person as $L = L(L^e, c)$, where $L^e = I_1^e - I_0^e$ is the endowed loss, $c$ is the expenditure on self-insurance, and $\dfrac{\partial L}{\partial c} = L'(c) \leqslant 0$. The expected utility can be written as

$$U^* = (1 - p)\, U(I_1^e - c) + p\, U(I_1^e - L(L^e, c) - c).^{27} \quad (18)$$

The value of $c$ that maximizes equation (18), $c^0$, satisfies the first-order condition

$$-\frac{1}{L'(c^0) + 1} = \frac{p\, U_0'}{(1 - p)\, U_1'}. \quad (19)$$

This maximizes expected utility if the marginal utility of income and the marginal productivity of self-insurance are decreasing, that is, if the indifference curves are convex and if the production transformation curve between income in states 1 and 0 ($TN$ in fig. 5) is concave to the origin.[28] A necessary condition for a positive amount of self-insurance obviously is $-L'(c^0) > 1$, or that there be a net addition to income in state 0. A sufficient condition, if the transformation and indifference curves do not have kinks, is that

$$-\frac{1}{L'(L^e, 0) + 1} < \frac{p\, U'(I_0^e)}{(1 - p)\, U'(I_1^e)}.^{29} \quad (20)$$

An increase in the unit cost of self-insurance, measured by the marginal

---

[27] For analytical convenience we assume that $I_0^e$ alone is affected by $c$, although, of course, both endowments may be affected. Moreover, the assumption that $\partial L/\partial c \leqslant 0$ is not always true: an individual could increase $I_1^e$ and reduce $I_0^e$ by deliberately exposing himself to hazards; for example, by committing a crime or engaging in a risky legal occupation (see Ehrlich 1970). The condition $\partial L/\partial c > 0$ can be said to define "negative self-insurance."

[28] See equation (A5). Note that the transformation curve may be kinked at the endowment point.

[29] If the opposite were true, there would be an incentive to increase the loss by increasing $I_1$ and reducing $I_0$ (see n. 27 above).

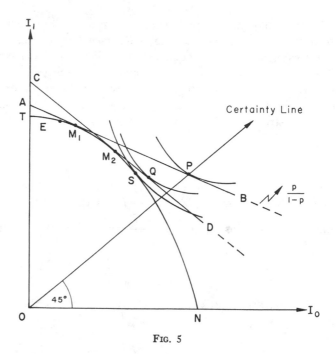

FIG. 5

productivity of self-insurance, would reduce the demand for self-insurance, measured by $c^0$:[30]

$$\frac{\partial c^0}{\partial \alpha} < 0,^{31} \tag{21}$$

where $\alpha$ is a parameter that reduces the absolute value of $L'$ for a given $c$. Similarly, a reduction in $I_0^e$ would increase the demand for self-insurance:

$$-\frac{\partial c^0}{\partial I_0^e} > 0.^{32} \tag{22}$$

Equation (20) shows clearly that the incentive to self-insure, unlike the incentive to use market insurance, is smaller for rare losses. The reason is that the loading factor of self-insurance is *larger* for rare losses because

[30] Although $c$ denotes the expenditure on self-insurance rather than the reduction in the size of the loss, there is a one-to-one relationship between expenditure and insurance because $-L'(c) > 1$.

[31] By differentiating equation (19) with respect to $\alpha$—$p$, $I_0^e$ and $I_1^e$ held constant—one obtains $\partial c^0/\partial \alpha = (pU_0'/U^*_{cc})(\partial L'/\partial \alpha) = (+)/(-) < 0$, where $U^*_{cc} = \partial^2 U^*/\partial c^2 < 0$ (see Appendix A), and by assumption $\partial L'/\partial \alpha > 0$.

[32] By differentiating equation (19) with respect to $I_0^e - I_1^e$, $p$ and $L'$ held constant, one obtains $-\partial c^0/\partial I_0^e = \partial c^0/\partial L^e = -\{pU_0''[L'(c) + 1]/U^*_{cc}\}\ \partial L/\partial L^e = (-)/(-) > 0$, where by assumption $\partial L/\partial L^e > 0$.

its price, unlike the price of market insurance, can be presumed to be independent of the probability of loss.[33]

An increase in endowed incomes that resulted from investment in human capital would probably be associated with an increase in the marginal productivity of self-insurance.[34] Therefore, the effect on self-insurance of a change in income has to be separated from the effect of the associated change in marginal productivity.

If market and self-insurance were both available, values of $c$ and $s$ would be chosen simultaneously to maximize the expected utility function,

$$U^* = (1 - p) \, U(I_1^e - c - s\,\pi) + p \, U(I_1^e - L(L^e, c) - c + s).$$

(23)

If the price of market insurance were independent of the amount of self-insurance, the first-order optimality conditions would be

$$- (1 - p) \, U_1' \, \pi + p \, U_0' = 0.$$

(24)

$$- (1 - p) \, U_1' - p \, U_0'[L'(c) + 1] = 0.$$

By combining these equations we get

$$\pi = - \frac{1}{L'(c) + 1}.$$

(25)

In equilibrium, therefore, the "shadow price" of self-insurance would equal the price of market insurance.

Clearly, market insurance and self-insurance are "substitutes" in the sense that an increase in $\pi$, the probability of loss being the same, would decrease the demand for market insurance and increase the demand for self-insurance.[35] For example, a change in the market insurance line from $\overline{AB}$ to $\overline{CD}$ in figure 5 would increase self-insurance by the horizontal distance between $M_1$ and $M_2$ and reduce market insurance by the horizontal distance between $Q$ and $P$. In particular, the purchase of market insurance would reduce the demand for self-insurance—compare points $S$ and, say, $M_1$.

When market insurance is available at a fair price, the equilibrium condition (25) becomes

$$- \frac{1}{L'(c) + 1} = \frac{p}{1 - p},$$

or

(26)

---

[33] The price of self-insurance is given by $\pi = - 1/[L'(c) + 1]$, where $L'(c)$ presumably does not depend on $p$. The loading factor is then given by $\lambda = - \{1/[L'(c) + 1]\} \, [(1 - p)/p] - 1$. Hence $\partial\lambda/\partial p < 0$.

[34] That is, not only would $\partial I_i^e/\partial E > 0 \; i = 0, 1$ where $E$ is the stock of human capital, but probably also $\partial^2 L/\partial c \partial E < 0$.

[35] A mathematical proof can be found in Appendix A.

$$- L'(c) = \frac{1}{p},$$

precisely the condition that maximizes expected income.[36] Even with diminishing marginal utility of income, a person would act as if he were risk neutral and choose the amount of self-insurance that maximized his expected income. Consequently, apparent attitudes toward risk are dependent on market opportunities, and real attitudes cannot easily be inferred from behavior.

More generally, even if the price of market insurance were not fair, the optimal amount of self-insurance would maximize the market value of income (given by $W$ in equation [12]), and would not depend on the shape of the indifference curves or even on the probability distribution of states.[37] Geometrically, optimal self-insurance is determined by moving along the transformation curve in figure 5 to the point of tangency between this curve and a market insurance line; since the market value of income is the intercept on the $y$-axis, that intercept would be maximized at such point of tangency.

The effects of specific parameters on the demand for market and self-insurance when both are available often are quite different from their effect when market insurance or self-insurance alone is available. For example, although an increase in the endowed loss increases the demand for self- or market insurance when either alone is available since an increase in market insurance itself reduces self-insurance, and vice versa, the indirect effects can offset the direct effects when both market and self-insurance are positive (see Appendix A for an example of this). Similarly, because a decrease in the probability of loss with no change in the market loading factor reduces the demand for self-insurance, it increases the demand for market insurance. Therefore, people may be more likely to use the market to insure rare losses not necessarily because of a positive relation between the probability of loss and the loading factor (see the discussion in Section IC), but because of a substitution between market and self-insurance.

### B. Self-Protection, Subjective Probabilities, and "Moral Hazard"

Self-insurance and market insurance both redistribute income toward hazardous states, whereas self-protection reduces the probabilities of these states. Unlike insurance, self-protection does not redistribute income, because the amount spent reducing the probability of a loss decreases income

[36] Equation (26) can be derived by maximizing $(1 - p)$ $(I_1^e - c)$ $+ p [I_1^e - L(L^e, c) - c]$ with respect to $c$.

[37] Equation (25) can be derived by maximizing $W = (I_1^e - c) + \pi [I_1^e - L(L^e, c) - c]$ with respect to $c$. We are indebted to Jacques Drèze for emphasizing this point.

in all states equally, leaving unchanged the absolute size of the loss (its relative size actually increases).

Studies using the states-of-the-world approach to analyze decision making under uncertainty have assumed that the probability of a state is entirely determined by "nature" and is independent of human actions. With this approach there is no such thing as self-protection; the activities we call by this name would be subsumed under self-insurance. It has been claimed that states can always be defined to guarantee the independence of their probabilities from human actions,[38] but we deny that this can be done in a meaningful way. Consider, for example, the probability that a given house will be damaged by lightning.[39] Since this probability can be reduced by the installation of lightning rods, independent state probabilities could be obtained only by using a more fundamental state description: the probability of a stroke of lightning itself. If control of the weather is ruled out, the probability of lightning can be assumed to be unaffected by human actions. We are concerned, however, about the probability of damage to the house—we do not care about the probability of lightning per se—and the probability of damage is affected by lightning rods.

In other words, although an appropriate definition of states would produce state probabilities that are independent of human actions, it would not produce a probability distribution of outcomes—the relevant probability distribution—that is independent of these actions. Since one of the main purposes of the state-of-the-world approach is to equate the probability distribution of outcomes with the probability distribution of states, a search for state probabilities that are independent of human actions would be self-defeating.

To look at the difference between self-protection and self-insurance from the viewpoint of outcomes, assume the probability distribution of endowed outcomes given by $AB$ in figure 6. Self-insurance, by contracting the distribution to, say, $CD$, lowers the probability of both high and low outcomes, thereby unambiguously reducing the dispersion of outcomes. Self-protection, on the other hand, by shifting the whole distribution to the left to, say, $EF$, reduces the probability of low outcomes and raises the probability of high ones and does not have an unambiguous effect on the dispersion.[40]

Since the preceding discussion shows that self-insurance is to be distinguished from self-protection, we develop a formal analysis of the latter. Let us assume that the probability of a hazardous state can be reduced by

---

[38] The only explicit discussion is by Hirshleifer (1970, p. 217).

[39] This example is discussed by Hirshleifer (1970).

[40] The effect of the introduction of self-protection on the variance of income, $p(1-p)$ $(I_1^e - I_0^e)^2$, can be found by differentiation $v'(r) \equiv \partial \operatorname{Var}(I^e)/\partial r = (1 -$

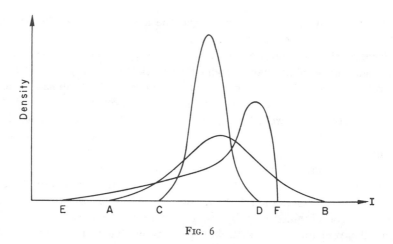

appropriate expenditure: $p = p(p^e, r)$, where $p^e$ is the endowed probability of hazard, $r$ is the expenditure on self-protection, and $\partial p / \partial r = \mathrm{p}'(\mathrm{r}) \leqslant 0$. If no market or self-insurance were available, the optimal expenditure on self-protection would maximize

$$U^* = [1 - p(p^e, r)] \, U(I_1{}^e - r) + p(p^e, r) \, U(I_0{}^e - r); \qquad (27)$$

the optimality condition is

$$- p'(r^0) \, (U_1 - U_0) = (1 - p) \, U_1' + p \, U_0'. \qquad (28)$$

The term on the left is the marginal gain from the reduction in $p$; that on the right, the decline in utility due to the decline in both incomes, is the marginal cost. In equilibrium, of course, they must be equal.

The second-order optimality condition requires that

$$U^*{}_{rr} = - p''(r^0) \, (U_1 - U_0) + 2p'(r^0)(U_1' - U_0')$$

$$+ (1 - p) \, U_1'' + p \, U_0'' < 0. \qquad (29)$$

Decreasing marginal utility of income is neither a necessary nor a sufficient condition. If $p''(r^0) > 0$, equation (29) is always satisfied if the marginal utility of income is constant and may or may not be satisfied if the marginal utility is decreasing or increasing. This shows that the incentive to self-protect, unlike the incentive to insure, is not so dependent

---

$2p) \ (I_1{}^e - I_0{}^e)^2 \, p'(0)$, where $r$ is the expenditure on self-protection. Clearly $v'(r) \gtreqless 0$

as $p \gtreqless 1/2$.

on attitudes toward risk, and could be as strong for risk preferrers as for risk avoiders.

As with market and self-insurance, the effect of a change in incomes on the demand for self-protection depends on the source of the change as well as on preferences.[41] A decline in $I_0^e$ alone might not increase the demand for self-protection, even if the marginal utility of income were falling, because a decline in $I_0^e$ would increase the marginal cost of self-protection.[42]

A decline in the marginal productivity of self-protection—an increase in the shadow price of protection—always decreases the demand for self-protection regardless of attitudes toward risk.[43] Therefore, if the endowed probabilities and incomes were the same, more efficient providers of self-protection would have lower equilibrium probabilities of hazard. Consequently, different persons use different probabilities in their decision-making process not only because of differences in "temperament," or optimism, but also because of differences in productivity at self-protection. As suggested in the last section, differences in productivity, in turn, may be attributed to differences in education and other forms of "human capital."

If market insurance and self-protection were jointly available, the function

$$U^* = [1 - p(p^e, r)] U(I_1^e - r - s\pi(r)) + p(p^e, r) U(I_0^e - r + s) \tag{30}$$

would be maximized with respect to $r$ and $s$; the first-order optimality conditions are

$$- (1 - p) U_1' \pi + p U_0' = 0 \tag{31}$$

$$- p'(r^*)(U_1 - U_0) - (1 - p) U_1'[1 + s^* \pi'(r^*)] - p U_0' = 0. \tag{32}$$

The term $\pi'(r^*)$ measures the effect of a change in self-protection on the price of market insurance through its effects on $p$ and the loading factor $\lambda$. From the definition of $\pi$ in equation (17) we obtain:

$$\frac{\partial \pi}{\partial r} = \pi'(r) = \pi'(p) \, p'(r) + \pi'(\lambda) \, \lambda'(r). \tag{33}$$

---

[41] An equal proportional increase in endowments ($I_1^e = \gamma I_0^e$) would increase the demand for self-protection if $(dr^0/dI_0^e) = (1/U^*_{rr})[p'(r^0)(U_1'\gamma - U_0') + (1 - p) U_1'' \gamma + p U_0''] > 0$. A sufficient condition if $U'' < 0$ is $(U_1'/U_0')(I_1^e/I_0^e) \geq 1$, or that the "average relative risk aversion" between $I_0^e$ and $I_1^e$ be sufficiently greater than one.

[42] That is, $-\partial r^0/\partial I_0^e = [p'(r^0) U_0' - pU_0'']/U^*_{rr} \gtreqless 0$ as $-[p'(r^0)]/p \gtreqless -U_0''/U_0'$.

[43] That is, $\partial r^0/\partial \beta = [(U_1 - U_0)/U^*_{rr}] (\partial p'/\partial \beta) = (+)/(-) > 0$, where by assumption $\partial p'/\partial \beta < 0$.

The effect of market insurance on the demand for self-protection has generally been called "moral hazard." In particular, moral hazard refers to an alleged deterrent effect of market insurance on self-protection[44] that increases the actual probabilities of hazardous events (Arrow 1962). Consequently, moral hazard is said to be "a relevant cost of producing insurance that is imposed by the insured on the insurance company" (Demsetz 1969, p. 7) and to provide a "limit to the possibilities of insurance" (Arrow 1962, p. 612). We showed in the last section that market insurance does reduce self-insurance, but no one has shown rigorously why, or under what conditions, market insurance reduces self-protection.

Market insurance has two opposite effects on self-protection. On the one hand, self-protection is discouraged because its marginal gain is reduced by the reduction of the difference between the incomes and thus the utilities in different states (see equation [28]); on the other hand, it is encouraged if the price of market insurance is negatively related to the amount spent on protection through the effect of these expenditures on the probabilities. Consider the relative importance of these opposite effects in two extreme cases:

If market insurance were always available at an actuarially fair price regardless of the amount spent on self-protection, then $\pi = p/(1 - p)$, and equation (31) implies that the optimal amount of market insurance $(s^*)$ equalizes income in both states of the world. There is still an incentive to spend on self-protection, however, because $\pi$ is negatively related to these expenditures $(r)$:

$$\pi'(r) = \frac{p'(r)}{(1 - p)^2}. \tag{33a}$$

Substituting $U_1 = U_0$ and $U_1' = U_0$ into equation (32), and using equation (33a) and the fact that $s^* = (1 - p)(I_1^e - I_0^e)$, we get

$$p'(r^*) = -\frac{1 - p}{s^*} = -\frac{1}{I_1^e - I_0^e}, \tag{34}$$

precisely the condition to maximize expected income. As with self-insurance, a fair price of market insurance encourages an expenditure on self-protection that maximizes expected income. Consequently, moral hazard would not then increase the real cost of insurance, reduce an economy's technical efficiency, or limit the development of market insurance since an

---

[44] See, for example, Arrow (1962, pp. 612, 613, 616; 1963, pp. 945, 961). Some writers have viewed moral hazard, in part, as a moral phenomenon related to fraud in the collection of benefits (see, for example, Mehr and Commack 1966, p. 174): a fire insurance policy, for example, may create an incentive for arson as well as for carelessness. Our analysis deals explicitly only with the effects of market insurance on self-protection, although implicitly it applies also to the effects on fraud.

amount of market insurance equalizing income in all states would be chosen.

Even more important is that, contrary to the moral hazard argument, the optimal expenditure on self-protection, $r^*$, can be *larger* than the amount spent in the absence of market insurance, $r^0$. By equations (34) and (28), and the condition $p'(r) < 0$, $r^*$ would be larger than $r^0$ if

$$\frac{U(I_1^e - r^0) - U(I_0^e - r^0)}{I_1^e - I_0^e}$$

$$= \overline{U}' < (1 - p)\, U'(I_1^e - r^0) + p\, U'(I_0^e - r^0), \qquad (35)$$

which is likely provided $p$ is not very small and $U$ is concave. Indeed, if utility were a quadratic function of income, $r^*$ would be larger than $r^0$ if $p$ were larger than one-half.[45] Not only are market insurance and self-protection complements in the sense that the availability of the former could increase the demand for the latter, but also in the sense that an increase in the productivity of self-protection or a decrease in the real cost of market insurance would increase the demand for both (see Appendix B).

Suppose, at the other extreme, that the price of market insurance was independent of expenditures on self-protection—the loading factor increased sufficiently to offset exactly the reduction in the probability of loss. Self-protection would then usually be discouraged by market insurance—moral hazard would exist—because the main effect of introducing market insurance would be to narrow the differences between incomes in different states.[46] Moreover, since the demand for market insurance is negatively related to the degree of loading, it would be negatively related to expenditures on self-protection. Consequently, for those kinds of market insurance with prices that are largely independent of expenditures on self-protection, one should observe either a large demand for insurance and a small demand for self-protection, or the converse. In our judgment, this

---

[45] If $U = a\,I + b\,I^2$, with $b < 0$, equation (35) becomes $[p - (1/2)]\,I_1^e - [p - (1/2)]\,I_0^e > 0$. Since $I_1^e > I_0^e$, this implies that $p > 1/2$.

[46] If $\pi'(r) = 0$, the optimality condition for $r$, given the value of $s$, is from equation (32): $-p'(r^*)\,[U(I_1^e - r^* - s\,\pi) - U(I_0^e - r^* + s)] - (1 - p)\,U'(I_1^e - r^* - s\,\pi) - p\,U'(I_0^e - r^* + s) = 0$. Self-protection would be discouraged by market insurance if an exogenous increase in the latter always reduced the optimal value of $r^*$; that is, if $dr^*/ds < 0$, or $dr^*/ds = \{p'(r^*)\,[U_1'(-\pi) - U_0'] + [(1 - p)\,U_1''(-\pi) + p U_0'']\}/U^*_{rr} < 0$, where $U^*_{rr} < 0$. The first term in the numerator is necessarily positive since $p'(r^*)$ is negative and $\pi$, $U_0'$ and $U_1'$ are all positive. Therefore, a sufficient condition for the inequality to hold is that the second term be nonnegative, or since $\pi = [(1 + \lambda)\,p]/(1 - p)$, that $U_0'' \geqslant (1 + \lambda)\,U_1''$. If $\lambda \geqslant 0$—no negative loading—this latter inequality necessarily holds provided $U''$ and $U''' \leqslant 0$; for example, if $U$ were the quadratic function $a\,I + b\,I^2$, with $b \leqslant 0$. Of course, it *might* hold even if $U''' > 0$.

is the major reason why certain kinds of hazards, like failure in business, are not considered insurable by the market.

Since the price of self-insurance is independent of the probability of hazard (see the discussion in Section IIA) and thus of expenditures on self-protection, our analysis of market insurance implies that self-insurance is likely to create a moral hazard. That is to say, the availability of self-insurance would discourage self-protection and vice versa. Moreover, technological progress in the provision of one would tend to discourage the other.

This analysis of moral hazard applies not only to the relation between self-protection and insurance as ordinarily conceived, but also to the relation between protection and insurance for all uncertain events that can be influenced by human actions. For example, do unemployment compensation, relief, or negative income tax rates increase the probability that someone becomes unemployed? Does the presence of underground shelters increase the probability that a country goes to war, the use of seat belts the probability of an automobile accident, or generous parental support the probability that children become "irresponsible"?

Since each of these, in effect, relates a form of insurance to a form of protection, our answers are not necessarily "yes," and depend on how responsive the cost of insurance is to the amount spent on protection. Shelters and seat belts are ways to self-insure, and have costs that are essentially unrelated to the probability of the hazards; therefore they would tend to reduce (perhaps only slightly) the incentive to avoid a war or an automobile accident. On the other hand, if the cost—in time, embarrassment, etc.—of applying for relief, unemployment compensation, or parental support were sufficiently positively related to its frequency, the answers might well be "no": the availability of insurance might encourage the insured to make his own efforts.

### Appendix A

#### Self-Insurance and Market Insurance

If both self-insurance and market insurance are available, the expected utility is

$$U^* = (1 - p)\, U(I_1^e - c - s\,\pi) + p\, U(I_1^e - L(L^e, c) - c + s). \quad \text{(A1)}$$

The values of $c$ and $s$ that maximize this function must satisfy the first-order optimality conditions

$$U^*_s = -(1 - p)\, U_1'\,\pi + p\, U_0' = 0 \qquad\qquad \text{(A2)}$$

$$U^*_c = -(1 - p)\, U_1' - p\, U_0'[L'(c^*) + 1] = 0. \qquad \text{(A3)}$$

Clearly, equation (A3) would be satisfied only if $\delta = [L'(c^*) + 1] < 0$: only if expenditures on self-insurance increased the net income in the hazardous state.

Second-order optimality conditions are

$$U^*_{ss} = (1-p)\, U_1'' \,\pi^2 + p\, U_0'' < 0 \qquad (A4)$$

$$U^*_{cc} = (1-p)\, U_1'' + p\, U_0'' \,\delta^2 - p\, U_0' \,L'' < 0 \qquad (A5)$$

$$\Delta = U^*_{ss}\, U^*_{cc} - (U^*_{sc})^2 > 0. \qquad (A6)$$

Equations (A4) and A5) are obviously satisfied if everywhere $U'' < 0$ and $L'' = \partial^2 L/\partial c^2 > 0$, that is, if the marginal utility of income and the marginal productivity of self-insurance are both decreasing. These assumptions are also sufficient to satisfy equation (A6) since

$$U^*_{sc} = (1-p)\, U_1'' \,\pi - p\, U_0'' \,\delta < 0. \qquad (A7)$$

Utilizing the first-order condition $\pi\,\delta = -1$, we can write

$$\Delta = -\,p(1-p)\, U_0'\, U_1''\, L''\, \pi^2 - p^2\, U_0'\, U_0''\, L'',$$

which is positive if $U'' < 0$ and $L'' > 0$.

## A. Terms of Trade Effects

The effect of an increase in $\pi$ on the optimal values of $s$ and $c$—$I_1^e$, $L^e$, and $p$ held constant—can be found by differentiating equations (A2) and (A3) with respect to $\pi$. By Cramer's rule,

$$\frac{ds^*}{d\pi} = \frac{A_1 U^*_{cc} - A_2 U^*_{sc}}{\Delta} = \frac{1}{\Delta}\big[(1-p)^2 U_1' U_1'' + p(1-p) U_1' U_0'' \delta^2$$

$$- p(1-p) U_0' U_1' L'' + p(1-p) U_0' U_1'' s^* \pi L''\big] = \frac{(-)}{(+)} < 0 \qquad (A8)$$

where $-A_1 = -(1-p) U_1' + (1-p) U_1'' s^* \pi$ and $-A_2 = (1-p) U_1'' s^*$ are the partial derivatives of (A2) and (A3) with respect to $\pi$. Similarly,

$$\frac{dc^*}{d\pi} = \frac{A_2 U^*_{ss} - A_1 U^*_{sc}}{\Delta} = \frac{1}{\Delta}\big[-(1-p)^2 U_1' U_1'' \pi$$

$$+ p(1-p) U_1' U_0'' \delta\big] = \frac{(+)}{(+)} > 0. \qquad (A9)$$

Hence, market insurance and self-insurance can be considered substitutes.

By similar reasoning, the effect of an increase in $p$ on the optimal values of $s$ and $c$, given that $\lambda$ in $\pi = [(1+\lambda)p]/(1-p)$, $I_1^e$ and $I_1^e$ are constant, is found to be

$$\frac{ds^*}{dp} = \frac{B_1 U^*_{cc} - B_2 U^*_{sc}}{\Delta} = \frac{1}{\Delta}\big[U_0' U_1'' L'' s^* \pi^2 + (1-p) U_1' U_1'' \pi$$

$$+ (1-p) U_0' U_1'' - p U_1' U_0'' \delta + p U_0' U_0'' \delta^2\big] = \frac{(-)}{(+)} < 0; \qquad (A10)$$

also

$$\frac{dc^*}{dp} = \frac{B_2 U^*_{cc} - B_1 U^*_{sc}}{\Delta} = \frac{1}{\Delta} [- (1-p) U_1' U_1'' \pi^2$$

$$- (1-p) U_0' U_1'' \pi - p U_1' U_0'' + p U_0' U_0'' \delta] = \frac{(+)}{(+)} > 0$$

$$(A11)$$

where $- B_1 = (1-p) U_1'' s^* \pi'(p) \pi$, $- B_2 = U_1' - U_0' \delta + (1-p) U_1'' s^* \pi'(p)$, and $\pi'(p) = \partial \pi / \partial p = \pi / [p(1-p)]$.

### B. An Endowment Effect

The effect of a decrease in $I_0^e = I_1^e - L^e$—$I_1^e$, $\pi$, $p$, and $L'$ held constant—can be shown to be

$$- \frac{ds^*}{dI_0^e} = \frac{-p^2 U_0' U_0'' L''}{\Delta} \frac{\partial L}{\partial L^e} = \frac{(+)}{(+)} > 0, \qquad (A12)$$

where, by assumption, $\partial L / \partial L^e > 0$; and

$$- \frac{dc^*}{dI_0^e} = \frac{-p U_0'' \delta U^*_{ss} - p U_0'' U^*_{sc}}{\Delta} \frac{\partial L}{\partial L^e} = 0, \qquad (A13)$$

since by equations (A7) and (A8) $U^*_{sc} = - \delta U^*_{ss}$. If the change in $I_0^e$ also changed $L'$, the results would be different.

## Appendix B

### Self-Protection and Market Insurance

If both market insurance and self-protection are available, the expected utility is

$$U^* = [1 - p(p^e, r)] U(I_1^e - r - s \pi(r)) + p(p^e, r) U(I_0^e - r + s).$$

$$(B1)$$

The first-order optimality conditions are

$$U^*_s = - (1-p) U_1' \pi + p U_0' = 0 \qquad (B2)$$

$$U^*_r = - p'(r^*)(U_1 - U_0) - (1-p) U_1' [1 + s^* \pi'(r)] - p U_0' = 0$$

$$(B3)$$

where $p'(r^*) < 0$ and $\pi'(r^*) \leqslant 0$.

Second-order conditions are that

$$U^*_{ss} = (1-p) U_1'' \pi^2 + p U_0'' < 0 \qquad (B4)$$

$$U^*_{rr} = - p''(r^*)(U_1 - U_0) + (1-p) U_1'' [1 + s^* \pi'(r^*)^2 + p U_0''$$

$$(B5)$$

$$+ 2p'(r^*) \{ U_1' [1 + s^* \pi'(r)] - U_0' \} - (1-p) U_1' s^* \pi''(r^*) < 0.$$

$$(B6)$$

$$\Sigma = U^*_{ss} U^*_{rr} - (U^*_{sr})^2 > 0.$$

Equations (B4) and (B5) would be satisfied if $U'' < 0$, if both $p''(r^*)$ and $\pi''(r^*) > 0$, and if $D = 2p'(r^*)\{U_1'[1 + s^*\pi'(r^*)] - U_0'\}$ (which is positive if $U'' < 0$)[47] were small in absolute value relative to the other terms in equation (B5). These conditions are also sufficient to satisfy equation (B6) if, in particular, $D < (1 - p)U_1' s^* \pi''(r^*) + p''(r^*)(U_1 - U_0)$.

Since $\pi = [(1 + \lambda)p]/(1 - p)$, the effect of an increase in $r$ on $\pi$ would be

$$\pi'(r) = \frac{(1 + \lambda)p'(r)}{(1 - p)^2} + \frac{p\lambda'(r)}{(1 - p)}, \qquad (B7)$$

where $\lambda'(r)$ gives the effect on the loading of an additional expenditure on self-protection and is generally assumed to be positive.[48]

If insurance were always available at an actuarially fair price, then $\lambda(p) = 0$ for all $p$; hence

$$\pi = \frac{p(r)}{1 - p(r)}, \pi'(r) = \frac{p'(r)}{(1 - p)^2}, \quad \text{and}$$

$$\pi''(r) = \frac{p''(r)}{(1 - p)^2} + \frac{2[p'(r)]^2}{(1 - p)^3} > 0.$$

Equation (B2) reduces to

$$U_1' = U_0', \qquad (B8)$$

and equation (B3) to

$$p'(r^*) = -\frac{(1 - p)}{s^*}. \qquad (B9)$$

Therefore, $\pi'(r^*) = -1/[s^* (1 - p)]$ and $1 + s^* \pi'(r^*) = -\pi$.

## A. Terms of Trade Effects

If an initially fair price $\pi = [p(r^*)]/[1 - p(r^*)]$ were increased by an increase in the loading with no change in $\pi'(r)$,[49] the change in the optimal values of $s$ and $r$ would be given by

$$\frac{ds^*}{d\pi} = \frac{C_1 U^*_{rr} - C_2 U^*_{sr}}{\Sigma} = \frac{C_1\left[\dfrac{2U_1'}{s^*} - (1 - p)U_1's^*\pi''(r)\right]}{\Sigma}$$

$$= \frac{(-)}{(+)} < 0,[50] \qquad (B10)$$

[47] According to equations (B2) and (B9) and the condition $U'' < 0$, $U_1'[1 + s^* \pi'(r^*)] < U_0'$ if $\pi \geq p/1 - p)$.

[48] One can write $\lambda'(r) = (\partial\lambda/\partial p)(\partial p/\partial r)$, where $\partial p/\partial r < 0$. Hence, $\lambda'(r) > 0$ only if $\partial\lambda/\partial p < 0$. (But see our discussion in Section IC.)

[49] According to equation (B7), an increase in $\lambda$ due to an exogenous factor $\theta$ would not change $\pi'(r)$ if, and only if, $[p'(r)/(1 - p)][\partial\lambda(r, \theta)/\partial\theta] = -p[\partial\lambda(r, \theta)/\partial\theta]$. This assumption is made to separate an autonomous change in the price of insurance from an autonomous change in the effect of self protection on the price of insurance.

[50] Using equations (B8) and (B9) and the second-order optimality conditions

$$\frac{dr^*}{d\pi} = \frac{C_2 U^*_{ss} - C_1 U^*_{sr}}{\Sigma} = \frac{-2(1-p)U_1'U^*_{sr}}{\Sigma} = \frac{(-)}{(+)} < 0,$$

where

$$\text{(B11)}$$

$$-C_1 = U^*_{s\pi}\bigg]_{\substack{s^*, r^*, p, \pi'(r^*) \\ \text{constant}}} = -(1-p)U_1' + (1-p)U_1''s^*\pi$$

and

$$-C_2 = U^*_{r\pi}\bigg]_{\substack{s^*, r^*, p, \pi'(r^*) \\ \text{constant}}}$$

$$= p'(r^*)U_1's^* + (1-p)U_1''s^*[1 + s^*\pi'(r^*)]$$

$$= -(1-p)U_1' - (1-p)U_1''s^*\pi$$

(from equation [B9]). Hence, if the price of insurance increased from an initially fair level, the demand for both self-protection and market insurance would decrease.

If the price of insurance were always actuarially fair, the effect of an exogenous increase in the productivity of self-protection on $s^*$ and $r^*$ with no change in the endowed probabilities and in the endowed incomes would be given by

$$\frac{ds^*}{d\beta} = \frac{D_2 U^*_{sr}}{\Sigma} = \frac{(+)}{(+)} > 0 \qquad \text{(B12)}$$

and

$$\frac{dc^*}{d\beta} = \frac{-D_2 U^*_{ss}}{\Sigma} = \frac{(+)}{(+)} > 0, \qquad \text{(B13)}$$

where $D_2 = -U_1'[s/(1-p)]\partial p'/\partial\beta$ and, by assumption $\partial p'/\partial\beta < 0$. Technological improvements in self-protection are thus seen to increase the demand for both market insurance and self-protection.

### B. The Effect of Exogenous Changes in p and L

If insurance were provided at an actuarially fair price, and if the endowed probability increased due to an exogenous factor $\gamma$ with no change in $p'(r)$, then

discussed above, it follows that $U^*_{rr} = (1-p)\ U_1''\pi^2 + pU_0'' + 2U_1'/s^* - (1-p)\ U_1's^*\pi''\ (r) < 0$; $U^*_{sr} = -(1-p)\ U_1''\pi^2 - pU_0'' > 0$; and

$$\Sigma = U^*_{ss}\left[\frac{2U_1'}{s^*} - (1-p)U_1'\ s^*\ \pi''(r)\right] > 0.$$

Since by equation (B4) $U^*_{ss} < 0$, $2U_1'/s^* - (1-p)\ U_1'\ s^*\ \pi''\ (r)$ must be negative in order for $\Sigma$ to be positive.

$$\frac{ds^*}{d\gamma} = \frac{\left[ -(1-p)U_1''s^*\pi\,\pi'(p) \right]\left[ \frac{2U_1'}{s} - (1-p)U_1's^*\pi''(r) \right]}{\Sigma}$$

$$\cdot \frac{\partial p}{\partial \gamma} = \frac{(-)}{(+)} < 0 \qquad \text{(B14)}$$

where, by assumption, $\partial p/\partial \gamma > 0$, and

$$\frac{dr^*}{d\gamma} = \frac{(1-p)U_1''s^*\pi\,\pi'(p)[U^*_{ss} + U^*_{sr}]}{\Sigma}\frac{\partial p}{\partial \gamma} = 0, \qquad \text{(B15)}$$

since $U^*_{ss} = -U^*_{s}$.[51] The last result is intuitively obvious since a fair price of insurance implies that $-p'(r^*) = 1/(I_1^e - I_0^e)$; therefore, $r^*$ is independent of $p$ provided that $p'(r)$ is unaffected by changes in $p\gamma$. By the same reasoning one can show that an increase in the size of the prospective loss increases the optimal values of both $s$ and $r$.

### References

Arrow, K. J. "Economic Welfare and the Allocation of Resources for Invention." In *The Rate and Direction of Inventive Activity: Economic and Social Factors*, edited by National Bureau Committee for Economic Research. Princeton, N.J.: Nat. Bur. Econ. Res., 1962.

———. "Uncertainty and the Welfare Economics of Medical Care." *AER* 53 (December 1963):941–73.

———. "The Role of Securities in the Optimal Allocation of Risk Bearing." *Rev. Econ. Studies* (April 1964):91–96.

———. *Aspects of the Theory of Risk Bearing*. Helsinki: Yrgö Jahnssonin Säätio, 1965.

Becker, G. S. "Uncertainty and Insurance, a Few Notes." Unpublished paper, 1968.

Becker, G. S., and Michael, R. T. "On the Theory of Consumer Demand." Unpublished paper, March 1970.

Demsetz, H. "Information and Efficiency: Another Viewpoint." *J. Law and Econ.* 12, no. 1 (April 1959): 1–22.

Ehrlich, I. "Participation in Illegitimate Activities: An Economic Analysis." Ph.D. dissertation, Columbia Univ., 1970.

Hirshleifer, J. "Investment Decision under Uncertainty: Applications of the State Preference Approach." *Q.J.E.* 80 (May 1966):252–77.

———. *Investment, Interest and Capital*. Englewood Cliffs, N.J.: Prentice-Hall, 1970.

Lees, D. S., and Rice, R. G. "Uncertainty and the Welfare Economics of Medical Care: Comment." *A.E.R.* 55 (March 1965):140–54.

Mehr, R. I., and Commack, E. *Principles of Insurance*. 4th ed. Homewood, Ill.: Irwin, 1966.

Mossin, J. "Aspects of Rational Insurance Purchasing." *J.P.E.* 76 (July/August): 1968):553–68.

Pratt, J. W. "Risk Aversion in the Small and in the Large." *Econometrica* 32, nos. 1–2 (January–April 1964):122–36.

Smith, V. L. "Optimal Insurance Coverage." *J.P.E.* 76 (January/February 1968): 68–77.

[51] See equation (B4) and the footnote following equation (B10).

**David Mayers**

*University of California, Los Angeles*

**Clifford W. Smith, Jr.**

*University of Rochester*

# On the Corporate Demand for Insurance*

## I. Introduction

Insurance contracts are regularly purchased by corporations. The Insurance Information Institute reports that "business insurance accounted for approximately 54.2 percent of the $79, 032,923,000 in direct property and liability insurance premiums written in the United States in 1978" (1979, p. 9). Yet even though annual premiums exceeded $42.8 billion,[1] the importance of these contracts has been largely ignored by the finance profession. For example, the topic of insurance is completely absent from the index of virtually all corporate finance textbooks.

The insurance literature is little better. The risk management area in the insurance literature examines corporate purchases of insurance, but the literature assumes the underlying source of corporate demand for insurance is risk aversion. Although risk aversion is unquestionably at the heart of the demand for insurance by individuals, it provides an unsatisfactory basis for analyzing the demand for insurance by corporations. The

We provide a positive analysis of the set of incentives for the purchase of insurance policies by corporations which is consistent with the modern theory of finance. We show how the corporation's insurance contracts can (1) allocate risk to those of the firms' claimholders who have a comparative advantage in risk bearing, (2) lower expected transactions costs of bankruptcy, (3) provide real service efficiencies in claims administration, (4) monitor the compliance of contractual provisions, (5) bond the firm's real investment decisions, (6) lower the corporation's expected tax liability, and (7) reduce regulatory costs.

*We thank our colleagues at UCLA and the University of Rochester and Gene Fama for their comments and criticisms. This research was partially supported by the Managerial Economics Research Center, Graduate School of Management, University of Rochester.

1. As a benchmark to assess the significance of these payments, Miller and Scholes (1978) report that total corporate dividends in 1976 were $31 billion.

(*Journal of Business*, 1982, vol. 55, no. 2)

corporate form provides an effective hedge since stockholders can eliminate insurable risk through diversification. Thus, the purchase of insurance by firms at actuarially unfair rates would represent a negative net present value project, reducing stockholder wealth.

Because risk reduction does not provide an obvious basis for a specific demand for insurance by corporations, we analyze the set of incentives for the corporate purchase of insurance which are consistent with the modern theory of finance.[2] Our analysis treats insurance purchases by corporations as just another part of the firm's financing decision. Modigliani and Miller (1958) show that given investment policy, with no contracting costs or taxes, corporate financing policy is irrelevant. Thus if the firm's financing policy is important it is so because of (1) taxes, (2) contracting costs, or (3) the impact of financing policy on the firm's investment decisions. We examine each as an explanation of observed insurance purchases by corporations.[3]

*Overview of the Paper*

In Section II, we examine the optimal allocation of risk among the firm's claimholders and suggest that those with divisible claims and access to capital markets have a comparative advantage in risk bearing over such claimholders as employees and managers.

In Section III, we discuss that set of real services which insurance firms have a comparative advantage in providing, such as processing and administering claims and loss-prevention project assessment. With a comparative advantage in these areas, resulting cost efficiencies favor the purchase of insurance. We also demonstrate how the inclusion of insurance among the corporation's set of contracts can control particular incentive conflicts. We suggest that insurance firms have a comparative advantage over outside stockholders, bondholders, customers, etc., in monitoring certain aspects of the firm's real activities, so that a firm which purchases insurance will engage in a different set of activities than a firm which does not.

In Section IV, we examine the implications of specific insurance-

---

2. We are specifically concerned with the purchase of insurance by corporations with diffuse ownership. Closely held corporations are more likely to purchase insurance (essentially for the same reasons individuals purchase insurance) than corporations with less concentrated ownership. Insurance contracts allow owners of closely held corporations to specialize in risk bearing only in specific dimensions in which they have specialized expertise and thus a comparative advantage (see also Arrow 1974, chap. 5).

3. The corporation is a set of contracts among various parties who have claim to a common object; these parties include stockholders, bondholders, managers, employees, suppliers, and customers. The bounds of the corporation are defined by the set of rights under the contracts. Our analysis demonstrates how the addition of insurance contracts can increase the firm's market value. Implicitly, Alchian and Demsetz (1972) view the corporation this way; Jensen and Meckling (1976) and, more recently, Fama (1980) are explicit. Although our grouping of parties is somewhat arbitrary, it is convenient for the distinctions we want to make.

related provisions within the tax code. We indicate the conditions under which these provisions can motivate the corporate purchase of insurance by reducing the corporation's expected tax liability. Finally, we examine the effects of regulation on the corporate demand for insurance. Rate regulation establishes incentives for firms to purchase insurance, and statutes like workmen's compensation laws effectively require some firms to purchase insurance.

We present our conclusions in Section V.


## II.  Corporate Insurance and Risk Shifting

Corporations regularly enter into explicit and implicit long-term contracts (e.g., bond contracts, labor contracts, product guarantees, and service contracts). The bondholders, employees, customers, and suppliers will make rational forecasts of the payoffs under their respective contracts, reflecting the forecasts in their reservation prices.

In a Coase (1960) or Fama and Miller (1972) world, the value of the firm is unaffected by the assignment of property rights through these contracts. With no contracting costs, the set of potential securities spans the state space; the packaging of securities is irrelevant because individuals can costlessly repackage them. For example, if the firm chooses to purchase liability insurance, thus reducing the probability of contract noncompliance, bondholders', customers', suppliers', and employees' demand prices change to reflect the different expected payoffs. With zero contracting costs, the loading fee for the insurance contract is zero; moreover with costless marketability of all assets, customers, suppliers, and employees would charge only the expected opportunity cost of contract noncompliance, discounted to reflect marginal risk. Consequently, the sum of the contract price changes must equal the insurance premium, and the value of the firm is not affected.


### Comparative Advantage in Risk Bearing

If the contracting process is expensive, incentives exist to allocate risk to those agents who have a comparative advantage in risk bearing. The equityholders and debtholders of the corporation have divisible claims which are traded in organized secondary markets. The resulting ability to diversify risk implies that these claimholders have a comparative advantage in risk bearing over such other classes of claimholders as employees, managers, customers, or suppliers. Since the ability to diversify claims on human capital is limited, risk-averse individuals for whom labor contracts represent an important component of their cash flows will use higher discount rates in setting their reservation prices, reflecting the level of uncertainty associated with the contract payments. Thus, shifting the risk bearing within the corporation to those claimholders who will bear the risk at lowest cost increases the value of the firm.

If the equity and debt claims of the corporation were large enough, the firm could simply shift risk to stockholders and bondholders providing the optimum level of risk for the firm's other contracts. But the amount of risk that can be allocated to the stockholders and bondholders is limited by the capital stock of the firm. Insurance contracts allow the firm to shift risk to the insurance company, achieving an efficient allocation of risk for the firm's other claimholders.[4] The reduction in the required compensating differential in contract prices can be sufficient to cover the loading fees of the policy. This is a risk-shifting incentive for the purchase of insurance by corporations.[5] Thus, our analysis suggests the higher the employees', customers', and suppliers' fraction of the claims to the firm's output, the higher the probability that the firm will purchase insurance.

*Transactions Costs of Bankruptcy*

The existence of transactions costs of bankruptcy can induce firms with widely dispersed ownership to purchase insurance against some risks. The probability of incurring the costs is lowered by shifting the risk associated with certain hazards to the insurance company (even if the insurance price is actuarially unfair). For example, if a large fraction of a firm's assets were represented by one plant, fire insurance might be optimal. Although Warner's (1977) evidence suggests that transactions costs associated with bankruptcy are a small fraction of a large firm's assets, even small transactions costs of bankruptcy will be sufficient to induce large firms to purchase insurance if the present value of the reduction in expected bankruptcy costs is greater than the present value of the contract's loading fees.

Warner's evidence also indicates that the transactions costs of bankruptcy are less than proportional to firm size. Therefore small corporations are more likely to purchase insurance to reduce the probability of incurring these costs than are large firms. For example, assume the density function of dollar losses for a particular risk is the same for

4. We must also assume that it is more expensive for the employees, suppliers, and customers to purchase this insurance than for the firm. This occurs both because of economies of scale in contracting and because employees, customers, and suppliers are unlikely to have an "insurable interest" in the firm (because of moral hazard, they are unlikely to be able to purchase insurance).

5. Although models of asset pricing with transactions costs imply that higher residual variability should imply lower stock prices, convincing empirical verification of this hypothesis has yet to be offered. However, if the present value of the loading fee were less than the present value of the expected reduction in trading costs imposed on security holders, the purchase of insurance would be value increasing. Again, what is fundamental is risk shifting to agents who have a comparative advantage in risk bearing, even if no agent will bear it at a zero price.

small and large corporations. This implies the probability of bankruptcy is greater for a small corporation than a large one. Assuming the present value of the contract's loading fees is the same for small and large firms, the present value of the reduction in expected bankruptcy costs from purchasing insurance will also be greater for the small corporation.[6]

### III. Real Production and Incentive Contracting Aspects of Corporate Insurance Contracts

*Real-Service Efficiencies*

Insurance firms develop a comparative advantage in processing claims because of economies of scale and gains from specialization. For claims resulting from property losses or liability suits, insurance companies provide a range of administrative services associated with claims management. Claims management is frequently accomplished through a nationwide network of independent adjusters who are employed to negotiate certain types of settlements. The decisions are then reviewed by the claims department of the insurance firm. Furthermore, in liability claims, the insurance firm typically provides legal representation.[7] The insurance firm usually retains a local lawyer who has expertise in the defense of liability suits. Thus, the corporate demand for insurance reflects the insurance company's comparative advantage in providing claims administration services. In fact, "claims only" contracts are negotiated wherein the insurance company provides only claims management services, the firm pays all the claims. Our analysis suggests that for a given premium efficiencies in claims administration motivate the corporate purchase of insurance the higher the frequency of insurance claims.

We believe that this comparative advantage in claims administration also provides an explanation for the observed purchase of retroactive liability coverage. For example, the *Wall Street Journal* reports that "when fire hit the MGM Grand Hotel in Las Vegas last November 21, killing 85 persons, the hotel's owners had $30 million in liability insur-

---

6. We arrive at the same result by assuming that the probability of bankruptcy with a particular risk is the same across firm size and that the transaction costs of bankruptcy are constant across firm size. This implies the present value of the reduction in expected bankruptcy costs from purchasing insurance will also be the same. However, holding the probability of bankruptcy constant implies the present value of the contract's loading fees should be less for the small corporation than the large. This assumes the loading fees are an increasing function of the size of the risk insured against. Thus, if (1) the density functions of dollar loss for a particular risk imply a probability of bankruptcy at least as great for the small corporation as the large, (2) the transactions costs of bankruptcy are constant across firm size, and (3) loading fees are positively related to the size of the risk, small corporations will more likely purchase insurance than large corporations.

7. See Mayers and Smith 1981.

ance. Since then the hotel company has increased its liability coverage to nearly $200 million. Significantly, the new insurance is backdated to November 1, or 20 days *before* the catastrophic blaze."[8] Without the additional coverage, the insurance company's adjusters' incentives to negotiate efficient settlements is limited because the total claims exceed the previous coverage limits.

## Insurance and Monitoring

Jensen and Meckling (1976) and Fama (1980) discuss the conflict of interest between the owners and the managers of a corporation. They assume that the contracting parties form rational expectations and innovatively seek to maximize their individual expected utilities within the effective constraints implied by their contracts. Thus conflicts of interest arise among the contracting parties whenever discretionary behavior is authorized. Jensen and Meckling demonstrate that incentives exist to write contracts which maximize the current market value of the firm.

Conflicts of interest between the owners and the managers can provide a basis for the corporate demand for insurance. For example, the manager's working life is limited while the corporate form gives the firm an indefinite life; this difference in time horizons produces an incentive conflict. The manager's claim on the firm has a life which is related to the life of his job. If his compensation package includes a bonus based on reported earnings, postponing selected expenditures until after retirement can increase his expected compensation. Specifically, he might elect against maintaining a sprinkler system. But predictable behavior by management will be anticipated by the owners of the corporation, and the manager's overall compensation will be adjusted to reflect his anticipated actions. Because the adjustment will include anticipated avoidable costs, managers have incentives to make believable promises not to engage in these activities by allowing monitoring and offering to bond their actions.[9]

If the insurance company has a comparative advantage in monitoring the sprinkler system's maintenance, an efficient mechanism to control management can be the purchase of insurance.[10] Therefore, our analysis suggests that firms whose managers have greater discretion over the choice of hazard-reducing projects will be more likely to purchase insurance.

8. Tim Metz, "Why Insurers and Insured Like the Idea of Covering Disasters after They Happen," *Wall Street Journal* (May 12, 1981).
9. This provides another interpretation of actions analyzed by Ehrlich and Becker (1972).
10. Note that this incentive to purchase insurance to control the manager/firm conflict is in addition to the risk-shifting incentive resulting from manager's risk aversion, discussed above.

*Insurance and Bonding*

Jensen and Meckling (1976), Myers (1977), and Smith and Warner (1979) indicate that actions available to the firm after bonds are sold can reduce the value of the bonds. For example, if the firm sells bonds for the stated purpose of engaging in low-risk projects and the bonds are valued at prices commensurate with that low risk, the aggregate value of the other claims on the firm rises and the value of the bonds falls if the firm substitutes projects which increase risk. Note that the mere exchange of low-risk assets for high-risk assets does not alter the value of the firm if both sets of assets have the same net present value; however, the purchase of negative net present value projects can increase the value of the nondebt claims if the increase in firm risk from accepting these projects is large enough. Even though such projects reduce the total value of the firm, ex post, the aggregate value of the other claims rises. Similarly, there are incentives to reject some risk-reducing positive net present value projects.

The purchase of insurance contracts can guarantee (or bond) a particular set of real investment decisions by the corporation. Prospective bondholders recognize the incentives to deviate from value maximization after the sale of the bonds. Consequently, bonds will be priced to reflect anticipated wealth transfers. Thus the existing claimholders of the firm are motivated to include provisions in the debt contract limiting the opportunities to transfer wealth from the bondholders. Bond indentures frequently contain covenants requiring the firm to maintain certain types of insurance coverage.[11] Our analysis suggests that these provisions reduce the incentive of the firm's other claimholders to accept certain risk-increasing negative net present value projects or to reject risk-reducing positive net present value projects after the sale of the bond issue.[12] Since potential wealth transfers from bondholders to the firm's other claimholders are increased the larger the fixed claims in the capital structure, we suggest that the probability of inclusion of insurance covenants will increase with the firm's debt/equity ratio.

Insurance covenants are regularly included in other corporate contracts. For example, subcontracting agreements between corporations regularly incorporate provisions requiring the subcontractor to main-

11. See American Bar Foundation 1971 or Smith and Warner 1979.
12. For example, if fire insurance has been purchased, the variance of corporate cash flows (including indemnity payments) does not fall if the firm invests in a safety project such as a sprinkler system, and thus there is no wealth transfer to the firm's fixed claimholders. Moreover, as long as the insurance firm quotes premiums associated with various levels of loss prevention (such schedules are common; see Bickelhaupt [1974]), competition among insurance companies will insure only a normal rate of return for the insurance firm. Thus, the premium equals the expected cost of the insurance. This induces the firm to accept loss-prevention projects for which the present value of the reduction in insurance premiums exceeds the present value of costs.

tain an acceptable level of insurance coverage.[13] If an independent subcontractor were sued for a liability claim, the subcontractor might renege on the contract, go bankrupt, impose costs on the firm from contract noncompletion, and increase the liability of the firm. This is a form of ex post opportunistic behavior discussed by Klein, Crawford, and Alchian (1978). Thus we suggest that the purchase of insurance by the subcontractor bonds the promise that the subcontractor makes not to default on performance of his job. Moreover if the insurance company has a comparative advantage in monitoring the firm, the insurance policy will induce a different set of real activities than would occur if no insurance had been purchased.

There are other corporate examples of ex post opportunistic behavior that can lead to a demand for insurance. Since contracting is expensive, actions to be taken in unusual circumstances generally will not be specified, so the occurrence of an unusual circumstance can alter incentives. Suppose a fire destroys a large part of a single plant of a multiplant corporation. The firm might have an incentive to reduce employment, violating the anticipated allocation of risk bearing. Business-interruption insurance covering ordinary payroll would control the incentive. In this case, by guaranteeing the contract the reduction in the workers' reservation prices can be sufficient to cover the loading fee for the insurance policy.[14] Similar arguments can be made regarding product guarantees and service contracts where insurance bonds an agreement that under usual circumstances would be carried out.

*Alternatives to Insurance*

There are alternative contractual arrangements that could be used. For example, the firm could hire an independent consultant to prescribe loss-prevention measures, report to bondholders, and monitor management. But we believe the insurance firm is better suited for these jobs. First, the insurer bonds his appraisal by agreeing to indemnify the firm for any losses which occur. Competition from other insurance firms restrains the insurer from over- or underprescribing loss prevention. Second, the claimholders recognize that there are incentives to bribe the consultant to allow the firm to engage in actions which would result in wealth transfers. Therefore prior to entering these contracts it is in the firm's interest to choose an agent who is expensive to bribe because the reservation prices of the claimholders will reflect the probability of enforcement. Bribing an insurance firm is

---

13. See *American Jurisprudence Legal Forms* 1973.

14. This appears similar to the risk-shifting incentive discussed earlier, but the rationale is different. In this case the firm can provide the optimum level of risk for the contract.

expensive; a large fraction of an insurance company's revenues is related to the sale of long-term financial contracts. These revenues will be reduced if the insurance company is discovered accepting bribes; further, the costs of accepting a bribe must be discounted over an infinite horizon.

## IV. Regulation, Taxes, and Corporate Insurance

Provisions in the tax code establish incentives for the corporate demand for insurance;[15] in certain cases the corporation's expected tax liability can be reduced by the purchase of insurance.

### Insurance-related Provisions of the Tax Code

Note the following provisions in the tax code:

1. A casualty loss (e.g., the loss of a building or machine in a fire) is a deductible business expense. The amount of the loss is the difference between the adjusted basis and its value after the casualty.
2. Insurance premiums are deductible business expenses.
3. Insurance indemnities reduce the deductible loss.
4. If the indemnity exceeds the adjusted basis of the property, the corporation has a gain. If the property is not replaced, taxes on the gain must be paid. If the indemnity does not exceed the original cost, the difference between the indemnity and the adjusted basis is taxed as ordinary income (recapture of depreciation). If the indemnity exceeds the original cost, the excess is subject to capital-gains tax.
5. If the property is replaced with a similar property on a timely basis, and the cost of the new property exceeds the indemnity payment, the firm can elect to not recognize a gain. However, the depreciable basis for the new property is cost adjusted for the difference between the indemnity received and the adjusted basis on the old property. (E.g., if the indemnity equals the replacement cost of the property, the adjusted basis of the new property equals that of the old property.)

The impact of these provisions is derived in the Appendix. As a benchmark with (1) zero loading fees, (2) a zero interest rate, and (3) a constant marginal tax rate, the sum of the expected depreciation charges plus the premium with insurance equals the sum of the expected depreciation charges and the expected casualty loss without

---

15. Although a firm can self-insure in the sense that it can establish reserves for anticipated losses, the tax code imparts no bias between self-insurance and remaining uninsured. Self-insurance reserves cannot be deducted as business expenses. This rule applies even if the corporation is unable to obtain insurance coverage and sets aside an amount equal to what might have been paid for insurance protection. Moreover, Financial Accounting Standards Board Statement No. 5 prohibits adjusting reported earnings for self-insurance reserves. Thus for both tax and reporting purposes, self-insurance and being uninsured are equivalent.

insurance. Thus from a tax standpoint the corporation would be indifferent between insurance and no insurance; the present value of the expected tax liabilities are equal. This indifference is broken by violations of any of the three conditions in the benchmark case. Since positive loading fees obviously favor self-insurance, we now concentrate on the implications of positive interest rates and nonconstant effective marginal tax rates.

*Interest Rates and Tax Liabilities*

Positive interest rates favor insurance for depreciable assets to be replaced. Although the undiscounted sum of the expected tax shields are the same whether insured or not, the required adjustment in the depreciable basis of the new property (for the difference between the indemnity and the basis on the old property) gives the expected tax shield sooner with insurance. Hence, the present value of the firm's expected tax liability is lower with insurance than without. Therefore, higher interest rates favor corporate casualty insurance purchases, and firms holding assets with long depreciable lives should be more likely to purchase insurance.

*Tax Rates and Tax Liabilities*

There are several provisions in the tax code which have the effect of changing the firm's effective marginal tax bracket so that the purchase of insurance is favored. First, there is a 3-year carry-back and a 7-year carry-forward provision in the tax code.[16] If an uninsured loss exceeds the sum of the most recent 4 years' earnings, the additional loss must be carried forward at a zero interest rate, and if the loss exceeds the earnings over the 11-year period, the excess casualty loss is lost.[17] Hence, if the magnitude of a potential loss is large compared with the firm's expected annual taxable earnings, the expected tax liability of a self-insured firm can be higher than for a firm with insurance.

Second, there is some progressivity in the corporate profits tax. If the loss reduces the corporation's taxable earnings so that the firm's marginal tax rate is reduced, the expected tax shield of self-insurance is reduced. Furthermore, when a firm employs the carry-back provisions the current year's tax must be totally offset before any of the previous year's taxes can be used. This further increases the firm's expected tax liability without insurance.

Third, the option of immediately recognizing the gain if the indem-

16. The carry-forward is 5 years for tax years before 1976. Regulated transportation companies are allowed a carry-forward of 9 years for tax years after 1975 (and 7 years before 1976).

17. If the uninsured loss forces the firm into bankruptcy which results in liquidation, any loss carry-forward will be lost.

nity received under the insurance policy exceeds the cost basis of the property further reduces the expected tax liability of the insured corporation. If the present value of the tax reduction from increasing the depreciation on the new property (from the adjusted basis to replacement cost) exceeds the taxes from immediately realizing the gain (recapturing depreciation plus paying capital gains tax on the difference between cost and original cost), then the firm's tax liability is reduced by realizing the gain on the property at the date of the casualty.

While the implications of our analysis are largely consistent with the notion that firms with large risks will insure while those with small risks will self-insure, the rationale is different; moreover, some distinction can be made. For example, consider two firms with equal expected net cash flow and equal expected casualty losses, but allow one firm to have lower expected taxable earnings because of an investment tax credit, perhaps. This firm would more likely purchase insurance while the other would more likely self-insure even though both have the same potential to "cover" their casualty losses. Large firms with spatially dispersed operations would be less likely to expect casualty losses that are large relative to their taxable earnings. For these firms positive loading fees outweigh the benefits derived from existing tax provisions and motivate self-insurance.

### Tax Incentives for Liability and Indirect-Loss Insurance

Since liability claims are tax-reducing expenses to the corporation and indemnity payments under business interruption insurance are generally taxed at ordinary tax rates, with constant tax rates the expected tax liability is the same with insurance or without. There is no interest rate effect because the impact of interest rates works only through the adjustment to the assets depreciation basis. Thus, of the above considerations only the carry-back/carry-forward provision and tax rate progressively provide incentives for the corporate purchase of liability insurance or business-interruption (indirect-loss) insurance. An implication of the analysis of tax-induced incentives is that firms would purchase more complete casualty insurance coverage than liability coverage (e.g., firm's casualty insurance policies should have lower deductibles than their liability insurance policies).

A final provision of the tax code can provide an incentive for the firm to purchase liability insurance. The tax code limits the deduction of fines and penalties as ordinary business expenses while the premium a corporation pays for liability insurance, indemnifying the firm for penalties and fines in addition to ordinary liability claims, is deductible. Thus, the present value of the corporation's expected tax liability is smaller with insurance than without. Note, however, that some states (e.g., California) limit insurance contracts covering fines and penalties.

*Insurance and Regulated Industries*

Myers (1972) provides a simple characterization of the regulatory process. In his model regulators set prices which are expected to generate revenues covering the sum of expected costs plus depreciation plus a normal rate of return on the rate base. If the firm does not insure against a particular hazard, the expected-cost figure used in establishing allowed revenues and prices must reflect the probability and magnitude of the loss to yield a normal rate of return to the firm's owners.[18] Thus, the regulator must obtain an assessment of the loss distribution.

Consider the incentives this regulatory process provides to purchase insurance. First, the insurance company, because of specialization, should be expected to have a comparative advantage in assessing the distribution of losses. If so, it would be efficient for the regulators to "subcontract" this assessment by having the insurance firm reflect their assessment of the loss distribution in the insurance premium. Second, the loading fees also reflected in the premium are costs which, through the regulatory process, are shifted from the firm's owners to the customers. Note that this typically is not the case with an unregulated firm. For unregulated competitive firms output price and revenues will be determined in the market, independent of whether the firm insures.[19] Thus, our analysis suggests that a regulated firm would buy significantly more insurance than an unregulated firm with similar characteristics.

*Compulsory Insurance Laws*

Workmen's compensation laws have been enacted in every state. These laws essentially impose on employers the responsibility of providing no-fault insurance to their workers for job-related accidents. Although self-insurance is allowed in all but five states, to qualify for self-insurance under the law the firm must demonstrate that it has sufficient size and diversification of risks. Thus regulation will effectively constrain some firms to purchase workmen's compensation insurance policies. Further, the benefits suggested above involving real-service efficiencies, taxes, risk shifting, and monitoring provide additional incentives for corporations to purchase insurance rather than self-insure. In 1968, only 14% of all workmen's compensation benefits were provided through self-insurance programs.

Also, in every state some form of automobile insurance law has been

---

18. Since uninsured casualty or liability losses are likely to be idiosyncratic rather than systematic, an allowed rate of return derived from some capital-asset pricing model would not be affected.

19. The exception is where the insurance in some sense bonds product quality to the consumer and thus can sustain a compensating differential in product prices.

passed to provide compensation for an innocent victim. These laws·
have taken several forms: (1) financial responsibility laws, (2) compulsory liability insurance laws, (3) unsatisfied judgment funds, (4) uninsured motorist endorsements, and (5) no-fault and compensation laws.
Financial responsibility laws require that for continued registration of
the vehicle after an accident the owner must provide evidence of
liability insurance coverage or provide proof of financial responsibility
for a stated period after the accident (usually 3 years). Some states
(Massachusetts, New York, and North Carolina) have adopted compulsory liability insurance statutes requiring proof of liability insurance coverage prior to registration of a vehicle. Illinois requires all
trucks registered in the state to be covered by liability insurance, with
some minor exceptions.

## V. Summary and Conclusions

Insurance contracts, regularly purchased by corporations, have received virtually no attention in the finance literature. Our purpose in
this paper has been to analyze the set of incentives, consistent with the
modern theory of finance, which motivate the purchase of insurance
policies by corporations.

For the closely held firm the task is fairly simple: These firms are
likely to purchase insurance for the same reasons individuals do. But
for corporations with diffuse ownership risk aversion by the owners
apparently provides no incentive for the purchase of insurance, since
stockholders and bondholders with their access to capital markets can
eliminate insurable risk through diversification. We argue that the
corporate demand derives from the ability of insurance contracts to (1)
allocate risk to those of the firm's claimholders who have a comparative advantage in risk bearing, (2) lower expected transactions costs of
bankruptcy, (3) provide real-service efficiencies in claims administration, (4) monitor the compliance of contractual provisions, (5) bond the
firm's real investment decisions, (6) lower the corporation's expected
tax liability, and (7) reduce regulatory constraints on firms.

We believe each of these incentives for insurance purchases by
corporations is relevant. For example, the existence of covenants in
bond contracts and subcontracting agreements requiring the firm to
maintain insurance coverage is important evidence favoring the
incentive-conflict control hypothesis. Similarly, the existence of
claims-only policies and retroactive liability insurance coverage are
important evidence favoring the real-service efficiency hypothesis.
Obviously the relative importance of the incentives will vary across
corporations. For example, our analysis suggests that for large firms
with spatially dispersed operations and short-lived assets the tax-
induced incentives will be of relatively minor importance, while for

corporations with large debt-equity ratios the acquisition of bonding services would provide an important incentive.

We believe our analysis also has important implications for the study of insurance purchases by individuals. Our focus on insurance purchases by large corporations with diffuse ownership largely eliminates risk aversion as the source of the demand for insurance and allows us to highlight other incentives, such as the real-service efficiencies provided by the insurance companies. These incentives generally apply to the purchase of insurance by individuals, yet have been overlooked.

## Appendix
### Tax Incentives for Corporate Insurance Purchases

In this Appendix, we provide a more formal discussion of the results presented in Section IV. We first consider the simple case of liability insurance. The present value of the expected cash flows for insurance and self-insurance can be represented as

| Period | 0 | 1 |
|---|---|---|
| Insurance | $-P(1 - \tau)$ | 0 |
| Self-insurance | 0 | $-\dfrac{\pi L(1 - \tau')}{1 + r}$ |

where $P$ is the insurance premium; $\pi$ is the probability of the loss; $L$ is the loss; $\tau$ is the effective marginal tax rate; $\tau'$ is the effective marginal tax rate conditional on the loss; and $r$ is the interest rate. For insurance with no loading fee, the premium will equal the present value of the expected loss, $P = \pi L/(1 + r)$. Thus with a constant tax rate there is no tax advantage to insurance. However, if conditional on the loss the effective marginal tax rate is lower, $\tau' < \tau$, then the present value of the expected tax advantage of insurance over self-insurance, $\Phi$, is $\Phi = [\pi L(\tau - \tau')]/(1 + r)$. Thus the tax advantage is greater (1) the larger the expected loss, (2) the greater the difference in effective tax rates.

We now examine casualty insurance. We assume that there are no partial losses and that the policy is for one period. The present values of the expected cash flows for insurance and self-insurance can be represented as

| Period | 0 | 1 |
|---|---|---|
| Insurance | $-P(1 - \tau)$ | $\dfrac{\pi\{(I - C') + \tau[C' - I + (C - \Sigma D)]\Delta\}}{1 + r}$ |
| Self-insurance | 0 | $\dfrac{\pi[\tau'(C - \Sigma D) - C' + \tau'C'\Delta]}{1 + r}$ |

where $I$ is the indemnity under the insurance policy; the book value of the asset is cost, $C$, minus accumulated depreciation, $\Sigma D$; $C'$ is the replacement cost of the asset; $\Delta$ is the factor that represents the present value of depreciation charges from \$1.00 of assets under whatever depreciation method is employed.[20] With actuarially fair insurance, $P = \pi I/(1+r)$, and constant tax rates, $\tau = \tau'$, the tax advantage of insurance over self-insurance is $\Phi = \{\pi\tau(1 - \Delta)[I - (C - \Sigma D)]\}/(1 + r)$. Thus the tax advantage of insurance is larger (1) the larger the difference between the indemnity and book value, (2) the slower the depreciation schedule, (3) the higher the interest rate, (4) the higher the probability of the loss. If the effective tax rate conditional on an uninsured loss is lower, $\tau' < \tau$, then the tax advantage of insurance is $\Phi = \{\pi[\tau(1 - \Delta)I - (C - \Sigma D)(\tau' - \tau\Delta) + C'\Delta(\tau - \tau')]\}/(1 + r)$. Thus the greater the difference in effective tax rates, the greater the tax advantage of insurance.

The insured has the option to recognize the gain from an indemnity, pay taxes on the gain, and make no adjustment in the depreciable basis of the property. We can compare the difference in the present values of the expected cash flows for deferral of the gain with the recognition of the gain. The expected cash flows can be represented as

| Period | 0 | 1 |
|---|---|---|
| Deferral option | $-P(1 - \tau)$ | $\dfrac{\pi\{(I - C') + \tau[C' - I + (C - \Sigma D)]\Delta\}}{1 + r}$ |
| Recognition option | $-P(1 - \tau)$ | $\dfrac{\pi[(I - C') + \tau C'\Delta - \tau\Sigma D - \tau_g(I - C)]}{1 + r}$ |

where $\tau_g$ is the capital-gains rate. The difference in cash flows between the recognition option and the deferral option in period 1, after the casualty, is

$$\Theta = \tau\Delta[I - (C - \Sigma D)] - \tau\Sigma D - \tau_g(I - C)$$

$$= (\tau\Delta - \tau_g)(I - C) - \tau(1 - \Delta)\Sigma D.$$

Thus, the option of recognizing the gain is more valuable (1) the greater the difference between ordinary tax rates and the capital-gains tax rates, (2) the lower interest rates, (3) the faster the rate of depreciation, (4) the greater the difference between the indemnity and original cost, and (5) the smaller accumulated depreciation.

## References

Alchian, A. A., and Demsetz, H. 1972. Production, information costs, and economic organization. *American Economic Review* 62 (December): 777–95.

American Bar Foundation. 1971. *Commentaries on Model Debenture Indenture Provisions*. Chicago: American Bar Foundation.

*American Jurisprudence Legal Forms*. 1973. 2d ed. Rochester, N.Y.: Lawyers Cooperative.

Arrow, K. J. 1974. *Essays in the Theory of Risk-Bearing*. Amsterdam: North-Holland.

Bickelhaupt, D. L. 1974. *General Insurance*. Homewood, Ill.: Irwin.

Coase, R. H. 1960. The problem of social cost. *Journal of Law and Economics* 3 (October): 1–44.

20. See Wakeman (1980) for an analysis of the present value of the tax shield from alternative depreciation methods.

Ehrlich, I., and Becker, G. S. 1972. Market insurance, self-insurance, and self-protection. *Journal of Political Economy* 80 (July–August): 623–48.

Fama, E. F. 1980. Agency problems and the theory of the firm. *Journal of Political Economy* 88 (April): 288–307.

Fama, E. F., and Miller, M. H. 1972. *The Theory of Finance.* New York: Holt, Rinehart & Winston.

Insurance Information Institute. 1979. *Insurance Facts.* New York: Insurance Information Institute.

Jensen, M. C., and Meckling, W. H. 1976. Theory of the firm: managerial behavior, agency costs and ownership structure. *Journal of Financial Economics* 3 (October): 305–60.

Klein, B.; Crawford, R. G.; and Alchian, A. A. 1978. Vertical integration appropriable rents and the competitive contracting process. *Journal of Law and Economics* 21, no. 2 (October): 297–326.

Mayers, D., and Smith, C. W. 1981. Contractual provisions, organizational structure, and conflict control in insurance markets. *Journal of Business* 54, no. 3 (July): 407–34.

Miller, M. H., and Scholes, M. S. 1978. Dividends and taxes. *Journal of Financial Economics* 6, no. 4 (December): 333–64.

Modigliani, F., and Miller, H. H. 1958. The cost of capital, corporation finance and the theory of investment. *American Economic Review* 48, no. 3 (June): 333–91.

Myers, S. C. 1972. The application of finance theory to public utility rate cases. *Bell Journal of Economics and Management Science* 3 (Spring): 58–97.

Myers, S. C. 1977. The determinants of corporate borrowing. *Journal of Financial Economics* 4 (November): 147–75.

Smith, C. W., and Warner, J. B. 1979. On financial contracting: an analysis of bond covenants. *Journal of Financial Economics* 5 (June): 117–61.

Wakeman, L. M. 1980. Optimal tax depreciation. *Journal of Accounting and Economics* 2 (December): 213–37.

Warner, J. B. 1977. Bankruptcy costs: some evidence. *Journal of Finance* 32, no. 2 (May): 337–47.

# THE DEMAND FOR INSURANCE AND PROTECTION: THE CASE OF IRREPLACEABLE COMMODITIES*

## PHILIP J. COOK
## DANIEL A. GRAHAM

Insurance and protection against various kinds of losses are both valuable activities provided to a large and perhaps increasing extent by the public sector.

If these activities are to be organized at an appropriate level of intensity, it is necessary to have a conceptual understanding of their value to the individual. While I. Ehrlich and G. Becker[1] have provided a theoretical development of individual demands for insurance and self-protection (and the interactions between these two activities) for the case of commodities that are valued appropriately in the market place, a similar theory is lacking for the large class of commodities that are essentially unique or irreplaceable (commodities for which there are no perfect market substitutes) such as family snapshots, the family pet, good health, the life of a beloved spouse or child, etc.

In this paper we present a new theoretical characterization of such commodities and develop some results concerning the demand for insurance and the value of increases in the level of protection for such commodities. Replaceable commodities are shown to be a special case of the more general theory.

Some of our more interesting results are as follows:

1. A rational individual, risk-averse with respect to lotteries on wealth, will typically not fully insure an irreplaceable commodity and may even choose to bet *against* losing it. The conventional explanation of such risk-taking behavior in the state-preference approach depends upon state preferences for wealth being asymmetrical. (See, for example, discussions in J. Hirshleifer[2] and R. Zeckhauser.[3]) For example, a dollar received contingent upon the state "individual lives" is to be viewed as a different commodity than a dollar contingent upon

*We have benefited from discussions with Martin Bronfenbrenner, Jack Hirshleifer, John M. Marshall, and Richard Zeckhauser.

1. "Market Insurance, Self-Insurance, and Self-Protection," *Journal of Political Economy*, LXXX (July/Aug. 1972), 623–48.

2. "Investment Decision Under Uncertainty: Choice-Theoretic Approaches," this *Journal*, LXXIX (Nov. 1965), 509–36.

3. "Coverage for Catastrophic Illness," *Public Policy*, XXI (Spring 1973), 149–72.

"individual dies." We provide a complementary interpretation by focusing upon the value that the individual places upon the commodity whose loss distinguishes the two states (e.g., the person's life) and the manner in which this value changes with his wealth. The rational insurance decision is shown to depend in a simple way on the wealth elasticity of the individual's personal valuation of the commodity.

2. In assessing the benefit of an increase in public protection activity, the correct value of a commodity is bracketed by the amount of money the owner would pay to avoid its loss and the amount of money required to fully compensate him for its loss, assuming that there is no bar to other forms of contingent payments being made. One application of this result is to clarify the appropriate benefit measure for public investments, which have the effect of changing the rates of serious injury or death.[4]

### IRREPLACEABLE COMMODITIES

The individual's demand for insurance coverage or protection of an asset depends upon his *personal* valuation of the asset; its *market* (sale) value is relevant only insofar as it influences his personal valuation. We expect market and personal valuations to coincide for assets that are usually perceived to have perfect substitutes readily available in the market (e.g., General Motors stock certificates), but these values may diverge widely for an asset that is perceived by the owner as having unique attributes. Indeed, there are no markets for some continuing sources of utility, such as good health, the life of a friend, or freedom of speech. Although the individual may be able to assess the monetary value of such "assets" (and may indeed be faced with decisions that in effect require such assessments), his personal valuation is not tied to any market price. Since in general the individual's personal valuation of unique or irreplaceable assets will change with changes in his wealth, this possibility should be incorporated into a general theory of behavior under risk.

Consider the value its owner places on a commodity $\theta$ in the context of calculating his demand for insurance or protection. This value is equivalently defined as the owner's minimum selling price;

4. See E. J. Mishan, "Evaluation of Life and Limb: A Theoretical Approach," *Journal of Political Economy*, LXXIX (July/Aug. 1971), 253–71; M. Jones-Lee, "The Value of Changes in the Probability of Death or Injury," *Journal of Political Economy*, LXXII (July/Aug. 1974), 835–49; and B. C. Conley, "The Value of Human Life in the Demand for Safety," *American Economic Review*, LXVI (March 1976), 45–55. Conley's model is closest in its basic approach to ours; see P. J. Cook, "The Earnings Approach to Life Valuation: A Reply to Conley," Duke University, March, 1976.

the rate at which he is willing to exchange $\theta$ for "all other goods;" or the minimum payment necessary to fully compensate him in the event that he loses $\theta$. We denote this value by $C$. $C$ is under some circumstances bounded by market prices: Assuming that there are no transactions costs, we see that $C$ is not less than the market price of commodities, which potential buyers view as equivalent to $\theta$, since otherwise it would pay the owner to sell $\theta$. Furthermore, $C$ is not greater than the market price of any commodity that the owner perceives as equivalent to $\theta$.[5] When these lower and upper bounds are equal, $C$ is precisely determined by market prices and invariant with respect to the owner's wealth—this is the conventional case in economic theory of "homogeneous" product and a "frictionless" market. More commonly, perhaps, transactions and information costs introduce a wedge between these lower and upper bounds; it is also possible (and most relevant to our analysis) that no market exists for $\theta$ or that the owner perceives no other commodity as equivalent to $\theta$. In any of these cases $C$ is determined by the owner's tastes and may in general change with changes in his wealth.

In the analysis that follows, we shall denote a commodity $\theta$ as "irreplaceable" if (in the owner's view) equivalent commodities are not available in the market or if $C$ is less than the price of an equivalent commodity for at least some levels of the owner's wealth.[6] Oth-

5. "Equivalence" is necessarily a matter of the individual's tastes and perceptions, since no commodity has an exact physical duplicate; each snowflake, sugar crystal, and Chevrolet is essentially unique. However, differences between commodities will not influence an individual's economic behavior if he perceives whatever differences that do exist as unimportant. Formally, we define two commodities as equivalent if the individual in question is indifferent between any two commodity bundles that differ only in which of the two commodities is included.

6. This definition would include the "irreplaceable assets" discussed in the "option value" literature. See most recently C. Henry, "Option Values in the Economics of Irreplaceable Assets," *Review of Economic Studies, Symposium,* (1974), 89–104.

When the market is not homogeneous and frictionless, the availability of an equivalent commodity does not guarantee that the individual will feel that replacement of $\theta$ with the equivalent commodity is the least-cost method of making himself "whole" following the loss of $\theta$. Some other commodity (or even some extensive change in his asset holdings) may accomplish this purpose at less cost. The cost of restoring himself following the loss of $\theta$ may then change with changes in his wealth simply because the least cost combination of commodities required to restore him to his pre-loss utility level may depend on his other asset holdings.

For example, consider a woman who inherits a diamond brooch that she could sell for $200, but that retails for $500 (i.e., she could buy another brooch she perceives as equivalent for that amount). Her personal valuation of the brooch will most likely lie somewhere strictly between these two numbers, implying that if the brooch were stolen she would not buy another one even if she received $500 compensation for the loss. Thus, although the brooch is replaceable in one sense, she would not actually choose to replace it. We have limited the definition of replaceability to those commodities that both *can and would* be replaced when their loss is fully compensated. Perhaps the most interesting applications of the theory, however, are to commodities for which it is highly unlikely that any equivalent commodities are available (e.g., commodities whose value depends largely on sentiment).

erwise, $\theta$ will be denoted "replaceable." Note that $C$ is necessarily fixed by a market price if $\theta$ is replaceable, but may vary with the owner's wealth if it is irreplaceable. The remainder of this section presents a somewhat more formal discussion of this wealth effect, as a prelude to next section's discussion of the demand for insurance.

Suppose that an individual faces two states of the world: in state $b$ the commodity in question is kept; in state $a$ it is lost. We assume that the individual's preferences can be represented by the von Neumann-Morgenstern utility function

$$U(W, \theta),$$

where $W$ represents a composite commodity involving all goods other than the commodity in question and is measured in dollars, and where $\theta$ (an indicator for the given commodity) equals zero in state $a$ and one in state $b$. For simplicity we define

$$U_a(W) \equiv U(W, 0)$$

$$U_b(W) \equiv U(W, 1)$$

and assume that for all $W \geq 0$

$$U_a(W) < U_b(W)$$

and

$$U_i''(W) < 0 < U_i'(W)\ i = a, b.$$

How much is the commodity worth to the individual? As previously discussed, one measure is the minimum compensation (selling price) that would induce the individual to accept a certainty of state $a$ in exchange for a certainty of state $b$. This compensation $C(W)$ is defined by

$$U_a(W + C(W)) = U_b(W),$$

provided that such a $C(W)$ exists and by $C(W) = \infty$ otherwise.[7]

Alternatively, the value of the commodity could be expressed as the maximum amount the individual would be willing to pay to exchange a certainty of state $a$ for a certainty of state $b$. This *ransom* $R(W)$ is defined by

$$U_a(W) = U_b(W - R(W)),$$

---

7. As Mishan, *op. cit.*, p. 693, footnote, points out, $C(W)$ may be finite for small values of $W$ and infinite for others where the loss of life is involved: "if a man and his family were so destitute and their prospects so hopeless that one or more members were likely to die of starvation, or at least suffer from acute deprivation, then the man might well be persuaded to sacrifice himself for the sake of his family. But without dependents or close and needy friends, the inducement to sacrifice himself for others is not strong."

210

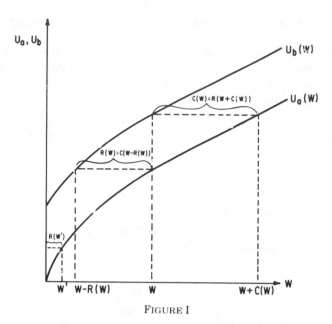

FIGURE I

provided that such an $R(W)$ exists and by $R(W) = W$ otherwise.[8]

Of course compensation and ransom differ by only a wealth effect, since

(1) $$C(W - R(W)) = R(W)$$

(2) $$C(W) = R(W + C(W))$$

for all $W$ such that the defining equalities hold. There is thus no loss of generality in focusing the analysis upon the ransom value of the commodity. These relationships are illustrated in Figure I.

Notice that the derivative of $R(W)$ is given by

(3) $$R'(W) = 1 - \frac{U'_a(W)}{U'_b[W - R(W)]}.$$

The irreplaceable commodity can be classified as normal or inferior, respectively, according to whether $R'(W)$ is positive or negative.[9] Thus,

(4) $$U'_a(W) < U'_b(W - R(W))$$

8. The fact that $U_b(W) > U_a(W)$ and $U'_a(W)$ and $U'_b(W) > 0$ implies that $R(W)$ is uniquely defined and positive for all $W > 0$.

9. This terminology conforms to conventional usage: if a commodity is normal in the sense that an increase in wealth, *ceteris paribus*, entails an increase in the consumption of the commodity, then it is also necessarily true that the maximum amount an individual would pay for a *given amount of the commodity* increases with wealth. It is our impression that most irreplaceable commodities are normal for most owners. In fact, we have not been able to think of clear examples of an inferior commodity.

if the irreplaceable commodity is normal, and

(5) $$U'_a(W) > U'_b(W - R(W))$$

if it is inferior. Moreover, given this ransom concept, a replaceable commodity can be viewed as a special case of an irreplaceable commodity in which the wealth effect $R'(W)$ is zero and thus for which

(6) $$U'_a(W) = U'_b(W - R(W)).$$

Last, notice that[10]

$$C(W) \gtrless R(W) \quad as \quad R'(W) \gtrless 0.$$

## INSURING IRREPLACEABLE COMMODITIES

In what way will the risk-averse individual's demand for insurance coverage of an irreplaceable commodity differ from his demand for insurance coverage of a replaceable commodity? A defining characteristic of a risk-averse individual is that he will insure fully against the loss of a replaceable commodity if he is able to buy any actuarially fair policy (i.e., he will exchange any risky portfolio of replaceable assets for a riskless portfolio of the same expected value if given the opportunity): surprisingly, he will buy less than full coverage for a normal irreplaceable commodity if he can buy insurance at actuarially fair rates.

With "fair" transfers of wealth between states available, the individual's budget constraint is

(7) $$W \equiv p\overline{W}_a + (1 - p)\overline{W}_b = pW_a + (1 - p)W_b,$$

where $p$ is the probability of state $a$, $\overline{W}_i$ is endowed wealth in state $i$, $i = a, b$, and $W_i$ is the financial claim contingent upon state $i$ to be purchased, $i = a, b$.[11] The utility maximization problem[12] is then

---

10. This follows from the fact, for example, that if $R'(W) > 0$, then $R(W) < R[W + C(W)] = C(W)$.

11. Note that endowed wealth is not assumed to be the same in both states. For example, if the commodity in question were the individual's right arm, $\overline{W}_b$ would be greater than $\overline{W}_a$ by an amount equal to the loss in earning potential associated with the loss of the arm.

12. A rigorous justification for an expected utility approach in a state-dependent utility framework is presented in P. Fishburn, "On the Foundations of Decision Making Under Uncertainty," in M. Balch, D. McFadden, and S. Wu, eds., *Essays on Economic Behavior Under Uncertainty* (Amsterdam: North Holland, 1974), pp. 25–44. We do not require that the loss of $\theta$ be the only risk faced by the individual. To see this, let $Y$ be a random variable representing fluctuations in wealth from sources other than the risk involved in the loss of $\theta$, where $E_Y Y$, the expectation over the distribution of the random variable $Y$, is zero. Then we may replace $U_a(W)$ with $\overline{U}_a(W) \equiv E_Y U_a(W + Y)$ and $U_b(W)$ with $\overline{U}_b(W) \equiv E_Y U_b(W + Y)$. These new expressions have the same concavity properties assumed for the original expressions. We are indebted to John Marshall for this observation.

$$\max_{W_a, W_b} pU_a(W_a) + (1 - p)U_b(W_b),$$

subject to equation (7). It is necessary and (given our assumptions) sufficient for $W_a^*$, $W_b^* > 0$ to be a solution that

(8) $$U_a'(W_a^*) = U_b'(W_b^*).$$

The solutions $W_a^*$ and $W_b^* = (W - pW_a^*)/(1 - p)$ are unique and have a close correspondence to the value of $R'(W)$. A number of possibilities exist. If $R'(W_a^*) = 0$, then equations (6) and (8) imply that $W_b^* = W_a^* - R(W_a^*)$ or that

(9) $$W_a^* - W_b^* = R(W_a^*).$$

The individual has insured himself fully ($U_a(W_a^*) = U_b(W_b^*)$) and is indifferent as to which state of the world occurs. This, of course, is the case corresponding to a replaceable commodity.

If the irreplaceable commodity is normal (if $R'(W_a^*)$ is positive), then equations (4) and (8) imply that $W_b^* > W_a^* - R(W_a^*)$ or that

(10) $$W_a^* - W_b^* < R(W_a^*).$$

In this case the individual stops short of full insurance ($U_a(W_a^*) < U_b(W_b^*)$) and prefers the occurrence of state $b$ to state $a$. If the wealth effect is sufficiently large, and in particular if

$$R'(W_a^*) = 1 - U_b'(W_a^*)/U_b'(W_a^* - R(W_a^*)),$$

then $U_a'(W_a^*) = U_b'(W_a^*)$, and the individual will purchase insurance against only the financial loss associated with the loss of the commodity ($W_a^* = W_b^*$).[13] Still larger values of $R'(W)$ would be associated with less than complete insurance against even the financial loss; he may buy no insurance whatever, or even bet on the occurrence of state $b$ (e.g., with the purchase of an annuity rather than the life insurance).[14] Examples illustrating these possibilities are examined in the Appendix.

Last, if the irreplaceable commodity is inferior, then equations (5) and (8) imply that $W_b^* < W_a^* - R(W_a^*)$ or that

13. For example, a household would demand life insurance on each household member equal to the net financial contribution of that person to the household (plus funeral expenses). The demand for insurance on a dependent child would be negative.

14. A fan's decision to bet for or against his favorite sports team may thus depend on how much the team's winning is worth to him and how his value changes with his wealth; his decision does not necessarily reflect his assessment of the odds. This possibility suggests that two risk-averse people who agree on the probability of an event may find it profitable to bet with each other as long as at least one of them cares about the outcome itself. Ordinarily, a fan would be expected to bet against his own team, but he will bet for his team if the wealth effect is large enough.

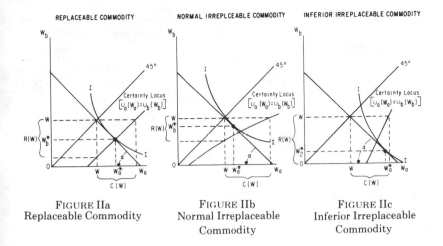

FIGURE IIa
Replaceable Commodity

FIGURE IIb
Normal Irreplaceable
Commodity

FIGURE IIc
Inferior Irreplaceable
Commodity

$$(11) \qquad W_a^* - W_b^* > R(W_a^*).$$

Here the individual overinsures ($U_a(W_a^*) > U_b(W_b^*)$) attaining a position in which state $a$ is the preferred outcome.

These possibilities are illustrated in Figures IIa through IIc. In all cases the slope of the budget line is given by

$$\tan \alpha = p/(1 - p),$$

and the indifference curve corresponding to the best insurance purchase is labeled $I$. The certainty locus represents arrangements of contingent claims under which the individual would be indifferent as to which state of the world occurs and which therefore may be regarded as riskless. Since the horizontal distance from the 45° line to the certainty locus corresponds to $R$, this distance will increase if $R'(W)$ is positive and fall if $R'(W)$ is negative. The tangency of an indifference curve to the fair bet budget line, which necessarily characterizes the optimal insurance purchase, must occur to the left of the certainty locus if the irreplaceable commodity is normal, and to the right if it is inferior.

Before making behavioral predictions from this theoretical analysis, it should be emphasized that it is directly applicable only to the individual's *demand* for insurance when the probability of loss $p$ is determined exogenously and can be costlessly monitored by all parties. Actual insurance transactions are of course influenced by the insurer's perception of the moral hazard created by certain contractual arrangements. For this reason, and because (contrary to our assumption of a "fair" price) insurance is usually available only with a positive "loading," the actual quantity of insurance purchased on the private market for an irreplaceable commodity will tend to be *less* than the quantity demanded under our assumptions.[15] A normative implication of our analysis follows from the reasonable assumption that life, good health, the absence of pain and suffering, etc. are "normal" irreplaceable commodities: the goal of full compensation to victims of violent crime or accidents that result in injury or death is not compatible with economic efficiency (since the settlements will be "too high"). This conclusion is strengthened by the fact that administering programs for criminal victim compensation, workmen's compensation, and other tort settlements is costly (i.e., there is a large positive loading on these types of "insurance").

## THE VALUE OF COLLECTIVE PROTECTION

The individual probability of loss in many cases is influenced by public activities such as law enforcement, highway design, and medical research. Investments in such areas produce a good (reductions in the probability of loss for each of a number of individuals) that, from an efficiency point of view, should be valued at an amount equal to the sum of the resulting benefits accruing to individuals.

E. Mishan points out that the appropriate individual benefit measure in such cases is the "compensating variation" in wealth: the reduction in the individual's wealth, which, when coupled with a reduction in the probability of loss, leaves him at the same (expected) utility level.[16]

Mishan does not mention what we are to assume about the existence and nature of contingency markets in calculating this benefit measure, although this issue is clearly salient; note Zeckhauser's example of the community that, because it lacks fire insurance, finds it worthwhile to rent a fire engine for $12,000 a year to prevent one $10,000 fire a year.[17] (If the community could organize an insurance pool, the benefit of the fire engine would be only $10,000.) We think it theoretically appropriate and useful to identify the *pure protection benefit* of a proposed public investment as its value when fair transfers of wealth between states are possible. An investment may have some

15. For example, if the premium for a payment of $I$ dollars contingent on state $a$ is $\beta I$, then it can be shown that the demand for insurance falls as $\beta$ increases. It should be noted that the presumption that $\beta$ is typically greater than $p/(1 - p)$ (the fair rate) is not necessarily correct, since $p$ is the individual's *perception* of the probability of loss and may be an exaggeration of the actuarial probability.

16. *Op. cit.*, pp. 691–95.

17. "Resource Allocation with Probabilistic Individual Preferences," *American Economic Review*, LIX (May 1969), 546–52.

additional benefit (as in Zeckhauser's example) if the project is undertaken in the context of imperfect contingency markets; this type of benefit results from changes with respect to the efficiency of the *distribution* of wealth among states of the world, and is conceptually distinct from changes in the expected value of wealth.[18] The pure protection benefit of a reduction in $p$ is then defined as the maximum expected payment made by the individual, which, when coupled with the reduction in $p$, leaves the individual's expected utility unchanged. This benefit measure is the same whether (1) the individual is viewed as contracting to make *identical* payments in states $a$ and $b$ and then adjusting his insurance coverage appropriately; or (2) the individual is viewed as contracting for payments in the two states that are chosen so as to leave him in equilibrium. (In the latter case the payments will in general be different, and one "payment" may even be negative.) We employ the latter definition in the analysis that follows.

Suppose that an individual is initially endowed with expected wealth $\overline{W}$ and a probability of loss $\overline{p}$. This endowment is one point on the indifference curve depicting the trade-off between expected wealth $W(p)$ and the probability of loss, where

$$(12) \qquad W(p) \equiv pW_a^*(p) + (1 - p)W_b^*(p),$$

such that

$$(13) \qquad U_a'(W_a^*(p)) = U_b'(W_b^*(p)),$$

and

$$(14) \quad pU_a(W_a^*(p)) + (1 - p)U_b(W_b^*(p))$$
$$= \text{expected utility of the endowment.}$$

Equation (12) defines expected cost of that bundle $(W_a^*(p), W_b^*(p))$, which would be purchased at fair odds (equation (13)) and which yields the same expected utility as the endowment bundle (equation (14)).

18. The value of any public investment in protection can be analyzed as the algebraic sum of (1) the value of moving from the initial wealth distribution to an efficient risk distribution of wealth; (2) the pure protection benefit of the investment; and (3) the cost of financing the investment inefficiently if the postinvestment distribution of wealth is inefficient. This trichotomy provides a useful framework in which to evaluate the financing scheme associated with the project, as distinct from the activity that produces greater protection. Such an analysis would perhaps facilitate a quest for more efficient financing mechanisms. It should be pointed out that this analysis implicitly assumes that the law of large numbers applies to the losses we are discussing—there is a large group of potential insurers whose aggregate wealth is invariant over states of the world. Some such assumptions are necessary to guarantee even the theoretical possibility of actuarially fair insurance. See J. M. Marshall, "Insurance Theory: Reserves Versus Mutuality," *Western Economic Journal*, XII (Dec. 1974), 476–92.

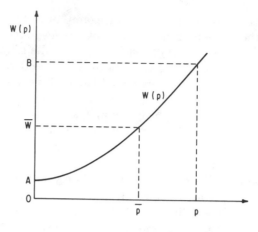

FIGURE III

The indifference curve $W(p)$ is illustrated in Figure III.[19] The shape of this curve is dictated by the conditions (derived below) that $0 \leq W'(p)$, $W''(p)$. The slope of the indifference curve at $(\bar{p}, \overline{W})$ can be regarded as the *value of the commodity* for purposes of calculating the value of small reductions in $p$. That is, if we define

$$V \equiv W'(\bar{p}),$$

then the value of a 0.01 reduction in the probability of loss is approximately 0.01 $V$.[20]

Differentiation of (12), (13), and (14) with respect to $p$ yields (after simplifying)

(15) $\qquad V = W_a^* - W_b^* + (U_b(W_b^*) - U_a(W_a^*))/U_b'(W_b^*).$

In the special (and conventional) case that the commodity is replaceable, $R'(W)$ equals zero, $U_a(W_a^*) = U_b(W_b^*)$, and

$$V = W_a^* - W_b^*.$$

---

19. Figure III can be related to the results of previous sections. If the endowment wealth were $OB$, for example, then $AB$ would be the ransom value of the commodity. Alternatively, if endowment wealth were $OA$, then $AB$ would give the compensation value of the commodity. For the case in which the endowment is given by $(\bar{p}, \overline{W})$, the fact that the indifference curve has a positive vertical intercept means that there is a positive certain prospect of wealth in state $b$ that the individual would consider equivalent to his uncertain endowment. Alternatively, the individual would not bankrupt himself to buy a certainty of state $b$. See the related result in Jones-Lee, *op. cit.* The case in which $C = \infty$ corresponds to the indifference curve being asymptotic to the vertical line at $p = 1$.

20. Conversely, $V$ can be approximated as one hundred times the amount the individual would be willing to pay for a 0.01 reduction in the probability of state $a$.

Here the price appropriate for calculating the value of probability reductions can be inferred directly from knowledge of the amount of insurance that the individual would buy at fair odds.[21] For the case in which the commodity is irreplaceable and normal, the amount of insurance that would be purchased at fair odds, $W_a^* - W_b^*$ understates the correct $V$, since $(U_b(W_b^*) - U_a(W_a^*))/U_b'(W_b^*)$ is positive in such circumstances.[22]

In general, $V$ is bounded above and below by two other measures of the value of the irreplaceable commodity—$R$ and $C$. This observation is demonstrated for the normal case $(U_a(W_a^*) < U_b(W_b^*))$ as follows: If $C(W_b^*)$ is finite,

$$U_b(W_b^*) = U_a(W_b^* + C(W_b^*))$$

$$< U_a(W_a^*) + (W_b^* + C(W_b^*) - W_a^*)U_a'(W_a^*)$$

from the definition of $C(W_b^*)$ and concavity of $U_a(W_a^*)$. Substituting in (15) and (13) yields

$$V < C(W_b^*),$$

which holds trivially for $C(W_b^*) = \infty$ as well. Similarly,

$$U_a(W_a^*) = U_b(W_a^* - R(W_a^*))$$

$$< U_b(W_b^*) + (W_a^* - R(W_a^*) - W_b^*)U_b'(W_b^*),$$

together with (15) and (13) gives

$$V > R(W_a^*).$$

21. Notice that $W_a^* - W$ represents the market value or price of a replaceable commodity that is subject to a probability loss $p$, provided that a fair insurance market exists. (I.e., $W_a^* - W$ equals the maximum amount an individual with wealth $W$ and a certainty of state $a$ would pay for a lottery involving a probability $p$ of state $a$, probability $(1 - p)$ of state $b$, and an ability to make fair bets.) This price is, of course, "discounted" by the probability of loss and is less than the ransom value of the same commodity $R(W) = W_a^* - W_b^*$, which represents the purchase price of a replaceable commodity that is subject to a zero probability of loss. It is this ransom value or undiscounted price *and not the market price* that is appropriate for valuing probability reductions.

22. Since $R$ and $C$ are nonnegative, this establishes the fact that $W'(p) = V > 0$. $W''(p) \geq 0$ is obtained by differentiation of (15) with respect to $p$ and simplification:

$$W''(p) = - [U_b(W_b^*) - U_a(W_a^*)]U_b''(W_b^*)W_b^{*'}(p)/U_b'(W_b^*)^2.$$

or

$$\text{sign } W''(p) = \text{sign } [U_b(W_b^*) - U_a(W_a^*)] \cdot \text{sign } [W_b^{*'}(p)].$$

But from (13) and (14) sign $[W_b^{*'}(p)] = \text{sign } [W_a^{*'}(p)] = \text{sign } [U_b(W_b^*) - U_a(W_a^*)]$.

Thus, sign $W''(p) = \text{sign } [U_b(W_b^*) - U_a(W_a^*)]^2 > 0$.

Combining results for the case of normal irreplaceable commodity, we have[23]

$$(16) \qquad W_a^* - W_b^* < R(W_a^*) < V < C(W_b^*).$$

Equation (10) suggests that in general it is necessary for calculating the value of collective protection that one have knowledge not only of the amount of insurance the individual would purchase at fair odds but also of the ransom function of the individual $R(W)$.[24]

While a complete analysis of the issue would require introducing considerations that are well beyond the scope of this paper, it is interesting to note that our conclusion that $V < C(W_b^*)$ adds a second dimension to our argument that full compensation is an inefficient policy for tort settlements that involve irreplaceable commodities. Tort law provides an incentive for private firms and individuals to invest in reducing the probability of becoming responsible for an injury; if courts typically award "full compensation" settlements, then this incentive is "too strong" in the sense that induced investments in safety will be larger than the efficient level.

## APPENDIX

We present here examples of utility functions for states $a$ and $b$ for which the irreplaceable commodity is normal. In all cases $b > a > 0$. Example 1 (linear utility functions) has the property that, given fair odds, the individual would bet everything on state $b$. In this case $R(W_a^*) = V = 0$; the value of the irreplaceable commodity for purposes of calculating the value of reductions in the probability of loss is zero despite the fact that the individual who has placed the appropriate fair bet still prefers the occurrence of state $b$ to that of state $a$. The less advantageous terms at which bets could be placed following a probability reduction has a cost to the individual equal to the benefit of the probability reduction.

In example 2 the individual purchases insurance against the loss of the irreplaceable commodity for values of $W > [1/(b - a)] \ln b/a$.

---

23. Should the utility functions be concave rather than strictly concave, i.e., $U_i'(W) \leq 0, i = a, b$, then the strict inequalities in this expression would be replaced with weak inequalities. For the case of a replaceable commodity, $U_a(W_a^*) = U_b(W_b^*)$, and $W_a^* - W_b^* = R(W_a^*) = V = C(W_b^*)$. The case of an inferior irreplaceable commodity is characterized by $U_a(W_a^*) > U_b(W_b^*)$ and $W_a^* - W_b^* > R(W_a^*) > V > C(W_b^*)$. As in the normal case these inequalities would be weakened if concavity rather than strict concavity were assumed.

24. From a knowledge of $R(W)$ one can obtain $Z(W) \equiv W - R(W)$ and thus $C(Z)$, since by equation (1), $C(W - R(W)) = R(W)$, provided that the defining equality holds. Moreover, since $Z'(W) > 0$ if $0 < R'(W) < 1$, one can solve $Z(\hat{W}) = W_b$ uniquely for $\hat{W}$ and thus obtain $C(W_b) = R(\hat{W})$. In this case knowledge of $R(W)$ is sufficient to bracket $V$.

APPENDIX

| Example | $U_a(W)$ | $U_b(W)$ | $R(W)$ | $C(W)$ | Fair bet solutions |
|---------|----------|----------|--------|--------|---------------------|
| 1 | $aW$ | $bW$ | $(b-a)W/b$ | $(b-a)W/a$ | $W_a^* = 0$ <br> $W_b^* = W/(1-p)$ |
| 2 | $-\exp(-aW)$ | $-\exp(-bW)$ | $(b-a)W/b$ | $(b-a)W/a$ | $W_b^* = a/b\ W_a^* +$ <br> $\ln\ b/a$ |
| 3 | $\ln\ aW$ | $\ln\ bW$ | $(b-a)W/b$ | $(b-a)W/a$ | $W_b^* = W_a^*$ |
| 4 | $a\ln W$ | $b\ln W$ | $W - W^{a/b}$ | $W^{a/b} - W$ | $W_b^* = b/a\ W_a^*$ |

In example 3 he purchases no insurance against the loss of the irreplaceable commodity, and in example 4 he bets on the occurrence of state $b$. In any of these cases, state $a$ may entail a pure financial loss in addition to the loss of the irreplaceable commodity; in this case we can view him as initially buying full insurance against the financial loss and then modifying his risk position according to the rules specified above.

Analytic solutions for $V$ can be calculated for examples 2–4, but they are complex and not particularly enlightening.

DUKE UNIVERSITY

# Insurance, Risk and Resource Allocation

## Kenneth J. Arrow

Insurance is an item of considerable importance in the economies of advanced nations, yet it is fair to say that economic theorists have had little to say about it, and insurance theory has developed with virtually no reference to the basic economic concepts of utility and productivity. Insurance is not a material good; although it is usually classified as a service, its value to the buyer is clearly different in kind from the satisfaction of consumers' desires for medical treatment or transportation. Indeed, unlike goods and services, transactions involving insurance are an exchange of money for money, not money for something which directly meets needs. The closest analog in ordinary economic theory to an insurance policy is a bond or note, an exchange of money now for money later. But an insurance is a more subtle kind of contract; it is an exchange of money now for money payable contingent on the occurrence of certain events.

I wish to explore, in a tentative way, the lessons that economic theory on the one hand and insurance theory and practice on the other can bring to each other. It will be seen that the shifting of risks, the very essence of insurance, occurs in many forms in the economic system, but always with some limits. The economic system is hobbled by these limits; it is desirable to extend the scope of risk-shifting, and indeed from time to time new economic institutions arise with precisely this aim in view. But an examination of insurance itself shows that there are strong reasons for its being limited to such a relatively narrow field. By understanding the restrictions on insurability of risks, we can understand better the reasons why the economic system in general is so limited in its risk-bearing ability and therefore will be in a better position to expand that ability.

Although our economics textbooks have remarkably little to say about the matter, nothing is more obvious than the universality of risks in the economic system. Machines break down from time to time; the coordination of complex production processes can never be perfect; despite the decreasing importance of agriculture, the uncertainties of the elements still play an important role; the search for mineral deposits is notoriously chancy; the demand for a product may change unpredictably in relatively short time spans, due to changing tastes or the development of substitutes; in a capitalist society, the success of new businesses and the movements of the stock market cannot be foreseen; and above all, technological progress and the development of new knowledge are by their very nature leaps into the unknown.

In any economic system, capitalist or socialist, there is a responsible agent on whom the burden of any given risk falls in the first instance. In a capitalist world, with which I shall be mostly concerned, the owner of a business typically is supposed to assume all the risks of uncertainty, paying out the unexpected losses and enjoying the unexpected gains. But society has long recognized the need for permitting him to shed some of the risks. A man's capacity for running a business will need not be accompanied by a desire or ability for bearing the accompanying risks, and a series of institutions for shifting risks has evolved.

Insurance itself is an early and important example of such an institution. The risks of business losses due to maritime disaster or fire were at an early stage shifted from the business firm to specialized insurance companies. But other institutions for risk-shifting have emerged. The most important is the market for common stocks. By this means, the owner of a business could divest himself of some of the risks, permitting others to share in the benefits and losses. Since each individual could now own a diversified portfolio of common stocks, each with a different set of risks attached, he could derive the benefits of a reduced aggregate risk through pooling; thus, the stock market permits a reduction in the social amount of risk-bearing.

To my knowledge, there are no other major institutions in which the shifting of risks through a market appears in such an explicit form as in insurance and common stocks. Nevertheless, the universal presence of risk is necessarily felt, even though only implicitly, in any contracts requiring performance in the future. A case in which the risk elements still show fairly clearly is contracting for military procurement. If the government were to purchase in accordance with the usual procedure of the market, it would settle, by bargaining or bidding, on a fixed price which would be paid to the producer for each unit delivered. Indeed, this procedure is followed for products of a routine nature, such as clothing or office supplies or even arms and ammunition of types that have been in production for a long time. But in purchasing very large and expensive items which have not been produced in large quantities previously, most especially airplanes, the contract used is of the so-called cost-plus variety. The government agrees beforehand to reimburse the producer for all his costs, whatever they may be, plus a fixed agreed profit.

The reason for this alternative mode of payment is, of course, that the producer finds himself very uncertain about costs and is unwilling to bear the risks. One can, for analytic purposes, regard a cost-plus contract as being made up of two contracts, one a fixed-price contract of the usual commercial type, and one an insurance contract by which the government agrees to reimburse the manufacturer for his unexpected costs. Thus the change from one contact to another can be regarded as a shifting of cost uncertainties from its normal locus in the producing firm to the purchaser, in this case, the government. We notice that private purchasers do not offer similar contracts to their suppliers, even in analogous cases; for example, airlines do not offer cost-plus contracts to aircraft manufacturing companies. The explanation for the range of use of cost-plus contracts is the same as that for the existence of insurance companies; it is profitable for all concerned that risks be shifted to the agency best able to bear them through its wealth and its ability to pool risks. The government, above all other economic agencies, fits this description.

Risks enter necessarily into all contracts into the future, but only as one element among others. Any bond has, after all, the risk of default, and the rate of interest is in fact greater on bonds judged risky by the market than for government bonds; the interest rate differential is in effect a premium paid by the borrower for insurance against default, the lender being at the same time the insurer. Futures contracts in commodities and in foreign exchange are well known to supply insurance against price movements among their other social functions.

At this point, it might be useful to ask more specifically what is the social usefulness of markets for shifting risks? Of course, there is always the simple justification for any contract freely arrived at between two individuals; if both of them choose to enter the contract, then both of them must be better off. Society after all is just a convenient label for the totality of individuals, and if the two contracting parties are better off, then so is society, unless other individuals are injured in some way. If I dislike an uncertainty and if I can find someone else or some organization to whom the cost of bearing the uncertainty is less than it is to me, then there will be some trade possible, by which the other party assumes the risk, I pay a fixed premium, and both of us are better off.

But the mere trading of risks, taken as given, is only part of the story and in many respects the less interesting part. The possibility of shifting risks, of insurance in the broadest sense, permits individuals to engage in risky activities which they would not otherwise undertake. I may well hesitate to erect a building out of my own resources, if I have to stand the risk of its burning down; but I would build if the building can be insured against fire. The shifting of risks through the stock market permits an adventurous industrialist to engage in productive activities, even though he is individually unable to bear the accompanying risks of failure. Of course, under these circumstances, some projects will be undertaken which will turn out to be mistakes; that is what is meant by risk. But at any moment society is faced with a set of possible new projects which are on the average profitable though one cannot know for sure which particular projects will succeed and which will fail. If risks cannot be shifted, then very possibly none of the projects will be undertaken; if they can be, then each individual investor, by diversification, can be fairly sure of a positive outcome, and society will be better off by the increased production.

A particularly important class of projects that society may consider are research activities. By definition, research is a venture into the unknown, such as geographical exploration was in the time of Columbus. The outcome of any research project is necessarily uncertain, and the most important results are likely to come from projects whose degree of uncertainty to begin with was greatest. The shifting of risk is thus most needed for what is very likely the most profitable of activities from society's point of view.

Suppose that we could introduce into the economic system any institutions we wish for shifting risks instead of being confined to those developed historically. In view of the preceding discussion, it is not hard to see what an ideal arrangement would consist of. We would want to find a market in which we can insure freely against any economically relevant event. That is, an individual should be able to bet, at fixed odds, any amount he wishes on the occurrence of any event which will affect his welfare in any way. The odds, or, in a different and more respectable language, the premium on the insurance, should be determined, as any other price, so that supply and demand are equal.

Under such a system, productive activity and risk-bearing can be divorced, each being carried out by the one or ones best qualified. It must be pointed out, though, that the range of insurance policies required by this ideal system is indeed very wide. An entrepreneur would wish to be insured against shifts in demand for his product as well as against unexpected difficulties in production. He or the investor in his enterprises might even wish to insure against his failure to make an appropriate judgment in some future situation.

The devices actually available for risk-shifting, common stocks and forward contracts, are far from meeting the ideal standards suggested above. The entrepreneur can shift his risks through floating common stocks but only in an undiscriminating way. Suppose he is quite certain about the production costs of a new product but uncertain about the market. He would like insurance only about sales, but the issue of common shares means that he has to share the fruits of his special knowledge of production methods, about which he is not uncertain, in order to be protected against selling risks. He may therefore be motivated not to enter into production at all.

Another example of the inadequacy of the stock market can be given. Suppose that all firms tend to be profitable or unprofitable together, due, for example, to shifts in foreign demand. The investors would like to find insurance against a generally unfavorable development, but they cannot find it by any amount of diversification. There may indeed be individuals or organizations who would be willing, at a price, to pay compensation for the occurrence of the unfavorable event, but the stock market does not provide for a mutually advantageous insurance transaction to occur.

It would prolong the analysis too much to go into other types of risk-shifting, such as forward contracts. In each case, one can see that not all the risks which it would be desirable to shift can be shifted through the market.

The incomplete shifting of risks gives rise to problems which have been recognized by society and solved in different ways. Let me start with one example different in character from those represented before. An individual who needs the services of a physician is uncertain of the quality of medical care he will get. He is further unable to buy insurance against poor quality of care. Society has met this problem by insisting on the licensing of physicians; the uncertainty is reduced by a special process of information gathering and, at the same time, restriction of entry. It is not left to the market to discriminate among different qualities of physicians.

A second solution to problems created by the inability to shift risks is represented by bankruptcy and limited liability laws. The law in effect requires creditors to assume some of the risks of the debtor; it does not leave him free to negotiate a risk-free investment, and it provides for an inalienable limitation of risks to the debtor. The law thus steps in and forces a risk-shifting not created in the market place.

A still further step in surmounting market limitations to the shifting of risks is expansion of the scope of direct authority. In all countries, we have seen the development of large integrated business organizations. Within these organizations, there are economic problems of allocation and distribution, and in particular there are risk elements, most especially in the production and delivery of component parts and semi-finished goods which go into assembly or other additional processing. But the price system, which the economist tends to regard as essential to the rational allocation of resources, is not used within a business organization at all. There are, of course, many reasons for the superior survival value of large organizations, but one of the most important, surely, is its ability to bear risks in individual parts of its total activity.

To illustrate, consider the activity of supplying engines to an automobile assembly line. The engines could in principle be produced by a company different from that assembling the automobiles; indeed, just such a separation does occur in aircraft manufacturing. However, relatively minor variations in the rate at which engines are delivered may cause very considerable losses to the automobile assembly plant, which might find the resulting risks too great to bear. An ideal market for risks, of the type sketched earlier, would create appropriate incentives to the supplier to regularize his delivery, for example by building up inventories. The way this works is that the assembly plant would be willing to pay large premiums for insurance against delivery delays; the supplier would find it profitable to sell such insurance and then take steps to minimize his payments of claims. In addition, it may be profitable for third parties to sell such insurance if they have a greater capability for pooling risks.

This ideal market could be approximated by an agreement between the two parties whereby the supplier pays penalties for poor timing of his deliveries. But such arrangements quickly become too complex for practical application. Instead, we have a tendency towards vertical integration. The supplier of engines and the assembly plant are placed under single management. The overall efficiency of the two units is now achieved by authoritarian rather than market relations; the engine supply is regularized, insofar as possible, by direct orders to do so, rather than by price incentives.

Thus, in one way or another, the failures of the market to achieve adequate risk-shifting lead to compensatory alterations in social institutions, licensing, bankruptcy and limited liability, and large business organizations. But all of these institutions are steps away from the free working of the price system, which, with the defects that we have noted, has also many virtues which do not need to be expanded on here. Especially, we expect all these institutions to decrease the flexibility and responsiveness of the system to change and innovation. What we observe is that the failure of the price system to handle risk-bearing adequately leads to a diminished use of prices even in contexts where they would be most useful in bringing about a careful and flexible confrontation of needs and resources.

Let us now ask why the economic system has not developed a more completely adequate set of markets for risk-bearing. To gain insight, we return to the workings of the insurance sector, where risk-bearing markets appear in their purest form. As suggested at the beginning of this paper, we start from the observation that the operations of insurance are limited in many ways; the reasons for these limitations are the primary reasons for the limited markets for risk-bearing in general.

In the first place, insurance is limited as to scope. Many (indeed, most) risks are classified as "uninsurable". (This concept is not absolute; the risks that are regarded as insurable vary somewhat from company to company, and there are special groups, such as Lloyd's of London, which will, for suitable prices, insure many risks that ordinary insurance companies will not.)

In the second place, insurance is frequently limited as to amount. Thus, an insurance against fire or similar property loss is invariably limited to the amount of actual loss. This seems so reasonable that one may be surprised at my bringing this up; but in fact the matter is not so simple. If the fire or other loss is a purely random affair, the company is engaging in a bet; if it finds the odds satisfactory, there is no reason why it should not take as much of the bet as the insured wants, provided any individual policy is still relatively small compared to the total resources of the company.

In the case of fire insurance, it might perhaps be held that a rational insurer would never want to insure for more than the value of the loss; but it is easy to find similar types of insurance, most especially private medical insurance, where the limitation on the total amount for which the company is liable is in fact very undesirable for the insurer. Indeed, it is precisely the rare case of extraordinarily high medical expenses that one would most want to be insured against.

A third limitation of insurance from the economic viewpoint is its resort to direct controls over the insured. He must submit to a medical examination, in the case of life insurance; his premises must be inspected and he must agree to certain precautions, in the case of fire insurance.

The reasons for these limits have been discussed of course in the standard insurance literature. There are more than one reason, and it would be tedious, though not unprofitable from our general point of view, to examine them in detail. But the factor known as the "moral hazard" is perhaps the most important. *The insurance policy might itself change incentives and therefore the probabilities upon which the insurance company has relied.* Thus, a fire insurance policy for more than the value of the premises might be an inducement to arson or at least to carelessness.

Once stated, it is clear that this principle explains the limitations of both insurance in particular and risk-shifting through the market in general. The problem is that the insurer, or more broadly, the risk-bearer cannot completely define his risks; in most circumstances he only observes a result which is a mixture of the unavoidable risk, against which he is willing to insure, and human decision. If the motives of the insured for decision are to reduce loss, then the insurance company has little problem. But the insurance policy may, as we have seen, lead to a motive for increased loss, and then the insurer or risk-bearer is bearing socially unnecessary costs. Either he will refrain from insuring or he will resort to direct inspection and control, to make as certain as he can that the insured is minimizing all losses under the latter's control.

The case of cost-plus contracts, discussed earlier as a risk-shifting device, has indeed attracted much attention. The supplier is relieved of all risks attached to costs; by the same token he has no incentive to keep costs to a minimum. If life is made more comfortable by not paying strict attention to economy, it is to be expected that costs will show a tendency to rise above the necessary level. Indeed, it is widely charged that this is precisely what does occur.

It is now easy to see why insurance against failure of business or of research projects has not arisen; the incentive to succeed may be too greatly reduced.

I have now first sketched an ideal method of shifting risks and then argued that the moral hazard, as well as other factors not discussed, will prevent the method from being realized in practice.

Can we say nothing further? I think we can go back to insurance practice once more for a general principle, that of "coinsurance". When told that two ideals are in conflict, the economist's typical reaction is, or should be, that some middle way can be found which will best compromise the two goals. If a complete absence of risk-shifting is bad because it inhibits the undertaking of risky enterprises and if total risk-shifting is bad because it reduces the incentives for their success, then it is reasonable to suggest that partial risk-shifting might be best. This is precisely what is meant by coinsurance; the insurer pays some stated proportion of the loss. Devices can undoubtedly be found whereby part but not all of the risks on new businesses or on research projects will be borne by others, reducing as far as possible the obstacles to risk-taking without diluting too greatly the necessary motivation for efficiency.

*Econometrica*, Vol. 30, No. 3 (July, 1962)

# EQUILIBRIUM IN A REINSURANCE MARKET

## By Karl Borch

This paper investigates the possibility of generalizing the classical theory of commodity markets to include uncertainty. It is shown that if uncertainty is considered as a commodity, it is possible to define a meaningful price concept, and to determine a price which makes supply equal to demand. However, if each participant seeks to maximize his utility, taking this price as given, the market will not in general reach a Pareto optimal state. If the market shall reach a Pareto optimal state, there must be negotiations between the participants, and it seems that the problem can best be analysed as an $n$-person cooperative game.

The paper is written in the terminology of reinsurance markets. The theoretical model studied should be applicable also to stock exchanges and other markets where the participants seek to reach an optimal distribution of risk.

## 1. INTRODUCTION

1.1. THE WALRAS-CASSEL system of equations which determines a static equilibrium in a competitive economy is certainly one of the most beautiful constructions in mathematical economics. The mathematical rigour which was lacking when the system was first presented has since been provided by Wald [10] and Arrow and Debreu [4]. For more than a generation one of the favourite occupations of economists has been to generalize the system to dynamic economies. The mere volume of the literature dealing with this subject gives ample evidence of its popularity.

1.2. The present paper investigates the possibilities of generalizing the Walras-Cassel model in another direction. The model as presented by its authors assumes complete certainty, in the sense that all consumers and producers know exactly what will be the outcome of their actions. It will obviously be of interest to extend the model to markets where decisions are made under uncertainty as to what the outcome will be. This problem seems to have been studied systematically only by Allais [1] and Arrow [3] and to some extent by Debreu [7] who includes uncertainty in the last chapter of his recent book. It is surprising that a problem of such obvious and fundamental importance to economic theory has not received more attention. Allais ascribes this neglect of the subject to *son extrême difficulté*.

1.3. The subject does not appear inherently difficult, however, at least not when presented in Allais' elegant manner. What seems to be forbiddingly difficult is to extend his relatively simple model to situations in the real world where uncertainty and attitude toward risk play a decisive part, for instance in the determination of interest rates, share prices, and supply and demand for risk capital. Debreu's abstract treatment also seems very remote from such familiar problems. There are further difficulties of which Allais, particularly, seems acutely aware, such as the psychological problems connected with the elusive concepts of "subjective probabilities" and "rational behaviour." In the present paper we shall put these latter difficulties aside. It then appears fairly simple to construct a model of a competitive market which seems reasonably close to the situations in real life where rational beings exchange risk and cash among themselves. The problem still remains difficult, but it seems that the difficulty is the familiar one of laying down assumptions which lead to a determinate solution of an $n$-person game.

1.4. The reason why neither Allais nor Arrow has followed up his preliminary study of the problem is probably that their relatively simple models appear too remote from any really interesting practical economic situation. However, the model they consider gives a fairly accurate description of a *reinsurance market*. The participants in this market are insurance companies, and the commodity they trade is risk. The purpose of the deals which the companies make in this market is to redistribute the risks which each company has accepted by its direct underwriting for the public. The companies which gain from this redistribution of risks are ready to pay compensation in cash to the other companies. This is a real life example of just the situation which Allais and Arrow have studied in rather artificial models.

It seems indeed that the reinsurance market offers promising possibilities of studying how attitudes toward risk influence decision making and the interaction between the decisions made by the various participants. This problem has so far been studied mainly in the theory of investment and capital markets where one must expect that a large number of "disturbing factors" are at play. It is really surprising that economists have overlooked the fact that the problem can be studied, almost under laboratory conditions, in the reinsurance market.

## 2. A MODEL OF THE REINSURANCE MARKET

2.1. Consider $n$ insurance companies, each holding a portfolio of insurance contracts.

The *risk situation* of company $i$ $(i = 1, 2, \ldots, n)$ is defined by the following two elements: (i) The *risk distribution*, $F_i(x_i)$, which is the probability that the total amount of claims to be paid under the contracts in the company's portfolio shall not exceed $x_1$. (ii) The *funds*, $S_i$, which the company has available to pay claims.

We shall assume that $x_1, \ldots, x_n$ are stochastically independent. To this risk situation the company attaches a utility $U_i(S_i, F_i(x_i))$. From the so-called "Bernoulli hypothesis" it follows that

$$U_i(S_i, F_i(x_i)) = \int_0^\infty u_i(S_i - x_i)\, dF_i(x_i) .$$

Here $u_i(S) = U_i(S, \varepsilon(x))$, where $\varepsilon(x)$ is the degenerate probability distribution defined by

$$\varepsilon(x) = 0 \qquad\qquad \text{for } x < 0 ,$$
$$\varepsilon(x) = 1 \qquad\qquad \text{for } 0 \leqslant x .$$

Hence $u_i(S)$ is the utility attached to a risk situation with funds $S$ and probability of 1 that claims shall be zero. In the following we shall refer to the function $u_i(S)$ as the "utility of money to company $i$." We shall assume that $u_i(S)$ is continuous and that its first derivative is positive and decreases with increasing $S$.

2.2. Von Neumann and Morgenstern [9] proved the Bernoulli hypothesis as a theorem, derived from a few simple axioms. Since then there has been considerable controversy over the plausibility of the various formulations which can be given to these axioms. There is no need to take up this question here, since it is almost trivial that the Bernoulli hypothesis must hold for a company in the insurance business.

2.3. In the initial situation company $i$ is committed to pay $x_i$, the total amount of claims which occur in its own portfolio. The commitments of company $i$ do not depend on the claims which occur in the portfolios of the other companies. In the reinsurance market the companies can conclude agreements, usually referred to as *treaties* which redistribute the commitments that the companies had in the initial situation.

In general these treaties can be represented by a set of functions:

$$y_i(x_1, x_2, \ldots, x_n) \qquad\qquad (i = 1, 2, \ldots, n)$$

where $y_i(x_1, x_2, \ldots, x_n)$ is the amount company $i$ has to pay if claims in the respective portfolios amount to $x_1, x_2, \ldots, x_n$. Since all claims have to be paid, we must obviously have

$$\sum_{i=1}^n y_i(x_1, \ldots, x_n) = \sum_{i=1}^n x_i .$$

These treaties will change the utility of company $i$ from

$$U_i(x) = \int_0^\infty u_i(S_i - x_i)\, dF_i(x_i)$$

to

$$U_i(y) = \int_R u_i(S_i - y_i(x))\, dF(x) ,$$

where $F(x)$ is the joint probability distribution of $x_1, \ldots, x_n$, and where $R$ stands for the positive orthant in the $n$-dimensional $x$-space.

For simplicity we have written $x$ and $y$ respectively for the vectors $\{x_1, \ldots, x_n\}$ and $\{y_1(x), \ldots, y_n(x)\}$

2.4. If the companies act rationally, they will not conclude a set of treaties represented by a vector $y$ if there exists another set of treaties with a corresponding vector $\bar{y}$, such that

$$U_i(y) \leqslant U_i(\bar{y}) \qquad \text{for all } i,$$

with at least one strict inequality. $y$ will in this case clearly be inferior to $\bar{y}$. If there exists no vector $\bar{y}$ satisfying the above condition, the set of treaties represented by $y$ will be referred to as *Pareto optimal*. If the companies act rationally, the treaties they conclude must obviously constitute a Pareto optimal set.

2.5. It has been proved in a previous paper [6] that a necessary and sufficient condition that a vector $y$ is Pareto optimal is that its elements, the functions $y_1(x), \ldots, y_n(x)$ satisfy the relations:

(1) $$u_i'(S_i - y_i(x)) = k_i u_1'(S_1 - y_1(x)),$$

(2) $$\sum_{i=1}^{n} y_i(x) = \sum_{i=1}^{n} x_i,$$

where $k_2, k_3, \ldots, k_n$ are positive constants which can be chosen arbitrarily.

The proof is elementary. It will not be repeated here since a rigorous statement is lengthy and rather tedious. Heuristically it is almost self-evident that if the condition is fulfilled, a change in $y$ cannot increase the utility of all the companies, i.e., that the condition is sufficient. The proof that it is necessary is slightly less transparent.

2.6. Differentiation of the equations in the preceding paragraph with respect to $x_j$ gives

$$u_i''(S_i - y_i(x)) \frac{\partial y_i}{\partial x_j} = k_i u_1''(S_1 - y_1(x)) \frac{\partial y_1}{\partial x_j}$$

and

$$\sum_{i=1}^{n} \frac{\partial y_i}{\partial x_j} = 1.$$

Dividing the first equation by $u_i''(S_i - y_i(x))$ and summing over all $i$, we obtain

$$u_1''(S_1 - y_1(x)) \frac{\partial y_1}{\partial x_j} \sum_{i=1}^{n} \frac{k_i}{u_i''(S_i - y_i(x))} = 1$$

where $k_1 = 1$.

It then follows that for any $i$ and $j$ we must have

$$\frac{\partial y_1}{\partial x_i} = \frac{\partial y_1}{\partial x_j}.$$

This implies that the vector function $y_1(x)$ is a scalar function of one single variable

$$z = \sum_{i=1}^{n} x_i.$$

It is easy to verify that in general we have

$$\frac{dy_i(z)}{dz} = \frac{\dfrac{k_i}{u_i''(S_i - y_i(z))}}{\displaystyle\sum_{j=1}^{n} \dfrac{k_j}{u_j''(S_j - y_j(z))}}.$$

This means that the amount $y_i(z)$ which company $i$ has to pay will depend only on $z = x_1 + \ldots + x_n$, i.e., on the total amount of claims made against the insurance industry. Hence any Pareto optimal set of treaties is equivalent to a pool arrangement, i.e., all companies hand their portfolios over to a pool, and agree on some rule as to how payment of claims against the pool shall be divided among the companies. In general there will be an infinity of such rules, since the $n - 1$ positive constants $k_2, k_3, \ldots, k_n$ can be chosen arbitrarily. In general the utility of company $i$ will decrease with increasing $k_i$ ($i \neq 1$). Since the company will not be party to a set of treaties unless $U_i(y) \geqslant U_i(x)$ there must be an upper limit to $k_i$. We shall return to this question in Section 4.

2.7. The results reached in the preceding paragraphs correspond very well to what one could expect on more intuitive grounds. If all companies are averse to risk, it was to be expected that the best arrangement would be to spread the risks as widely as possible. It was also to be expected that the solution should be indeterminate, since no assumptions were made as to how the companies should divide the gain resulting from the greater spread of risks.

In the Walras-Cassel model there is a determinate equilibrium, i.e., unique Pareto optimal distribution of the goods in the market. The basic assumption required to reach this result is that each participant considers the market price as given, and then buys or sells quantities of the various goods so that his utility is maximized. In the following section we shall investigate the possibility of finding some equally simple assumptions which will bring a reinsurance market into an equilibrium.

### 3. THE PRICE CONCEPT IN A REINSURANCE MARKET

3.1. In insurance circles it is generally assumed that there exists a well defined market price, at least for some particular forms of reinsurance. It is also generally believed that Lloyd's in London is willing to quote a price for any kind of reinsurance cover.

If a market price exists, it must mean that it is possible to associate a number $P(F)$ to any probability distribution $F(x)$, so that an insurance company can receive the amount $P(F)$ from the market by undertaking to pay the claims which occur in a portfolio with risk distribution $F(x)$. It must also be possible for the company to be relieved of the responsibility for paying such claims by paying the amount $P(F)$ to the market.

3.2. Assume now that a company accepts responsibility for two portfolios with risk distributions $F_1(x_1)$ and $F_2(x_2)$. Assume further that $x_1$ and $x_2$ are stochastically independent and that $x = x_1 + x_2$ has the probability distribution $F(x)$. It is natural to require that the company shall receive the same amount whether it accepts the two portfolios separately or in one single transaction. This means that we must have

$$P(F) = P(F_1) + P(F_2) .$$

This additivity condition is clearly a parallel to the assumption in the classical model that the price per unit is independent of the number of units included in a transaction.

3.3. The additivity condition is obviously satisfied by a number of functionals. It is for instance satisfied by the cumulant generating function

$$\psi(t) = \log \varphi(t)$$

where $\varphi(t)$ is the characteristic function

$$\varphi(t) = \int_0^\infty e^{itx} dF(x) .$$

As it is inconvenient to work with a complex valued function, we shall in the following use the corresponding real functions

$$\varphi(t) = \int_0^\infty e^{-tx} dF(x)$$

and

$$\psi(t) = \log \varphi(t)$$

which exist for any nonnegative value of $t$. The cumulants are then given by the expansion

$$\psi(t) = \sum_{n=1}^\infty (-1)^{n-1} \frac{K_n}{n!} t^n .$$

3.4. It follows that for any nonnegative value of $t$, $\psi(t)$ can be interpreted as a price which satisfies the additivity condition. The same will hold for any linear combination of the form:

$$c_1 \psi(t_1) + c_2 \psi(t_2) + \ldots$$

where $c_1, c_2, \ldots$ are constants. Similar expressions containing derivatives of $\psi(t)$ of any order will also satisfy the condition.

It is obvious that any expression of this kind can be written as a sum of cumulants. Hence we can write

$$P(F) = \sum_{n=1}^{\infty} p_n \kappa_n$$

where $p_1, \ldots, p_n$ are constants.

It follows from a theorem by Lukacs [8] that this is the most general expression which satisfies the additivity condition.

3.5. Let now $\varepsilon(x)$ be the degenerate probability distribution defined in paragraph 2.1.

$\varepsilon(x - m)$ can then be interpreted as a risk distribution according to which the amount $m$ will be claimed with probability 1. The price associated with this distribution will be

$$P(\varepsilon(x - m)) = p_1 m$$

since $\kappa_n = 0$ for $1 < n$. We shall therefore require as a continuity condition that $p_1 = 1$.

3.6. We now assume that a market price of this form is given, and we consider a company in the risk situation $(S, F(x))$. The utility of the company in this situation is

$$U(S, F(x)) = \int_0^{\infty} u(S - x)\, dF(x).$$

If the company undertakes to pay a claim $y$ with probability distribution $G(y)$, it will receive an amount $P(G)$. If $x$ and $y$ are stochastically independent this transaction will change the company's utility to

$$U(S + P(G), H(x)) = \int_0^{\infty} u(S + P(G) - x)\, d\left\{ \int_0^{\infty} F(x - y)\, dG(y)\right\}$$

$$= \int_0^{\infty} u(S + P(G) - x)\, dH(x)$$

where $H(x)$ is the convolution of $F(x)$ and $G(y)$.

If the company acts rationally, it will select among the portfolios available in the market one with a risk distribution $G_0(y)$ which maximizes $U(S + P(G), H(x))$. This function $G_0(y)$ can be considered as the amount of reinsurance cover which the company will *supply* at the given price.

3.7. The nature of the maximization problem appears more clearly if we introduce the cumulants explicitly in the formula of the preceding paragraph.

Let $f(t)$ and $g(t)$ be the characteristic functions of $F(x)$ and $G(y)$ respectively. The characteristic function of $H(x)$ is then $f(t) g(t)$, and if $H(x)$ has a derivative, we have

$$\frac{dH(x)}{dx} = \frac{1}{2\pi} \int_{-\infty}^{+\infty} e^{-itx} f(t) g(t)\, dt = \frac{1}{2\pi} \int_{-\infty}^{+\infty} e^{-itx} e^{\log f(t) + \log g(t)}\, dt$$

$$= \frac{1}{2\pi} \int_{-\infty}^{+\infty} \exp\left\{ -itx + \sum_{n=1}^{\infty} \frac{(it)^n}{n!} (k_n + \kappa_n) \right\}\, dt$$

where $k_n$ and $\kappa_n$ are the $n$th cumulants of $F(x)$ and $G(y)$, respectively. Hence the problem becomes that of determining the values of $\kappa_1, \kappa_2, \ldots, \kappa_n$ which maximize the expression

$$\int_0^{\infty} u\left(S - x + \sum_{n=1}^{\infty} p_n \kappa_n\right) \int_{-\infty}^{+\infty} \exp\left\{ -itx + \sum_{n=1}^{\infty} \frac{(it)^n}{n!} (k_n + \kappa_n) \right\}\, dt\, dx .$$

It is interesting to note that the cumulants of different order appear as different commodities, each with its particular price. The "quantities" $\kappa_1, \ldots, \kappa_n$, however, must satisfy certain restraints in order to be the cumulants of a probability distribution. These restraints will be of a complicated nature. A sufficient set of restraints can be derived from the Liapounoff inequalities

$$\frac{1}{n} \log m_n \leqslant \frac{1}{n+1} \log m_{n+1}$$

where $m_n$ is the $n$th absolute moment about an arbitrary point. Since $G(y) = 0$ for $y < 0$, the inequalities must hold for the moments about zero of $G(y)$. It is easy to see that the sign of equality will hold only in the degenerate case when $G(y) = \varepsilon(y - m)$.

The problem on the *supply* side of a reinsurance market thus appears to be similar to the problems of maximization under restraints which occur in some production models. It is clear that the problem will have a solution, at least under certain conditions.

3.8. The problems on the *demand* side are more complicated. Assume that with a given price a company demands reinsurance cover corresponding to a probability distribution $G(y)$. This means that in order to be relieved of an obligation to pay a claim with a probability distribution $G(y)$, the company is willing to pay an amount

$$P(G(y)) = \sum_{n=1}^{\infty} p_n \kappa_n$$

where $\kappa_1, \ldots, \kappa_n, \ldots$ are the cumulants of $G(y)$.

Assume now that the company can buy its reinsurance cover in two transactions, for instance by placing two portfolios with risk distribution $G(\tfrac{1}{2}y)$ with two different reinsurers. If the market price is applied to both transactions, the company will have to pay

$$2P(G(\tfrac{1}{2}y)) = \sum_{n=1}^{\infty} \frac{p_n}{2^{n-1}} \kappa_n$$

for the reinsurance cover. $2P(G(\tfrac{1}{2}y))$ will generally be different from $P(G(y))$. Hence the reinsurance arrangement which maximizes the company's utility will depend not only on the given price, but also on the number of reinsurers who are willing to deal at this price. This makes it doubtful if any meaning can be given to the term "market price" in a reinsurance market. We shall not at present discuss this problem in further detail. We shall, however, consider it again for a special case in Section 4.

## 4. EXISTENCE OF AN EQUILIBRIUM PRICE

4.1. In the preceding section we studied separately the demand and supply of reinsurance cover. It is fairly obvious, however, that if the companies shall reach the Pareto optimum which we found in Section 2.5, each company must act *both* as seller and buyer of reinsurance cover. In a previous paper [5] it was proved by a more direct approach that it will in general be to the advantage of a company to act in both capacities at the same time.

In this section we shall study whether a price mechanism can bring supply and demand into an equilibrium which also represents a Pareto optimal distribution of the risks.

4.2. Since the problem is rather complex, we shall analyse only a special case. We assume that the utility of money to all companies can be represented by a function of the form:

$$u_i(x) = -a_i x^2 + x, \qquad \text{for } i = 1, 2, \ldots, n.$$

We assume that $a_i$ is positive and so small that $u_i(x)$ is an increasing function over the whole range which enters into consideration.

$a_i$ can evidently be interpreted as a measure of the company's "risk aversion." If $a_i = 0$, the company will be indifferent to risk. Its sole objective will then be to maximize expected profits, ignoring all risk of deviations from the expected value. The greater $a_i$ is, the more concerned will the company be about the possibility of suffering great losses.

From the formulae in section 2.6 we find

$$\frac{dy_i(z)}{dz} = \frac{k_i/a_i}{\Sigma\, k_j/a_j} = q_i \,.$$

Hence the optimum arrangement is that company $i$ shall pay a fixed quota $q_i$ of the amount of claims $z$ made against the pool. It is easily verified that

$$y_i(z) = q_i z + q_i \sum_{j=1}^{n}\left(\frac{1}{2a_j} - S_j\right) - \left(\frac{1}{2a_i} - S_i\right) = q_i z + q_i \sum_{j=1}^{n} A_j - A_i \,.$$

For $z = 0$ we find

$$y_i(0) = q_i \sum_{j=1}^{n} A_j - A_i \,.$$

$y_i(0)$ is the amount (positive or negative) that company $i$ has to pay if there are no claims. Hence $y_i(0)$ must be the difference between the amount the company pays for the reinsurance cover it buys and the amount the company receives for the reinsurance cover it sells.

4.3. If $u(x) = -ax^2 + x$, the utility of the company in the initial situation is

$$U(0) = \int_0^\infty u(S - x)\, dF(x) = \int_0^\infty \{-a(S - x)^2 + (S - x)\}\, dF(x)$$
$$= -a(S - \kappa_1)^2 + (S - \kappa_1) - a\kappa_2$$

where $\kappa_1$ and $\kappa_2$ are the two first cumulants, i.e., the mean and the variance of $F(x)$. We see that in this case the utility which the company attaches to a risk situation will depend only on the two first cumulants of the risk distribution. If the utility function $u(x)$ is of the form $-ax^2 + x$ for all companies, the cumulants of higher order can have no effect of the optimal arrangement. They will appear as "free goods" in the market, i.e., with price zero. Hence, in the expression for price we must have $p_n = 0$ for all $n > 2$. The amount paid for reinsurance cover of a risk distribution $F(x)$ will then be

$$P(F) = \kappa_1 + p_2\kappa_2 = m + pV$$

if we drop the index of $p_2$, and write $m$ and $V$ for the mean and variance of $F(x)$, respectively.

4.4. We now consider two companies, $i$ and $j$, with risk distributions $F_i(x_i)$ and $F_j(x_j)$ where $x_i$ and $x_j$ are stochastically independent. In a Pareto optimal set of reinsurance treaties the two companies will have to pay fixed quotas, $q_i$ and $q_j$, of the claims made against the pool $z = \sum_{j=1}^{n} x_j$.

It is evident that a Pareto optimal arrangement will result if every pair of companies concludes a reciprocal treaty, according to which company $i$ undertakes to pay $q_i x_j$ if claims against company $j$ amount to $x_j$, and company $j$ in return pays $q_j x_i$ if claims $x_i$ are made against company $i$ (i.e., $q_i$ is the same for every $j$).

If $m_i$ and $V_i$ are the mean and variance of $F_i(x_i)$, company $i$ will receive an amount $q_i m_j + p q_i^2 V_j$ for the reinsurance cover it gives company $j$. Similarly company $i$ will have to pay out $q_j m_i + p q_j^2 V_i$ for the cover it receives from company $j$.

Hence the net payment from company $i$ to company $j$ will be

$$q_j m_i + p q_j^2 V_i - q_i m_j - p q_i^2 V_j .$$

Summing this for all $j \neq i$, we obtain

$$m_i \, \Sigma \, q_j - q_i \, \Sigma \, m_j + p \{ V_i \, \Sigma \, q_j^2 - q_i^2 \, \Sigma \, V_j \}$$

which is equal to

$$m_i - q_i \sum_{j=1}^{n} m_j + p \left\{ V_i \sum_{j=1}^{n} q_j^2 - q_i^2 \sum_{j=1}^{n} V_j \right\} .$$

This expression, however, must be equal to the total net payment of company $i$, which according to Section 4.2 is

$$y_i(0) = q_i \sum_{j=1}^{n} A_j - A_i .$$

Hence we must have

$$p \left\{ V_i \sum_{j=1}^{n} q_j^2 - q_i^2 \sum_{j=1}^{n} V_j \right\} - q_i \sum_{j=1}^{n} (A_j + m_j) + (A_i + m_i) = 0 .$$

This expression for $i = 1, 2, \ldots, n$, together with $\sum_{j=1}^{n} q_j = 1$ gives a system of $n + 1$ equations for the determination of the $n + 1$ unknowns $q_1, \ldots, q_n$ and $p$.

These equations are not independent, however, since the last one can be obtained by adding together the first $n$. Hence the system will give $q_1, \ldots, q_n$ as functions of $p$.

For $p = 0$ we find

$$q_i(0) = \frac{A_j + m_j}{\sum\limits_{j=1}^{n}(A_j + m_j)} .$$

Differentiating the equations with respect to $p$, we find

$$\left[ \frac{dq_i(p)}{dp} \right]_{p=0} \sum_{j=1}^{n} (A_j + m_j) = V_i \sum_{j=1}^{n} q_j^2 - q_i^2 \sum_{j=1}^{n} V_j .$$

Hence it follows from considerations of continuity that $q_i(p)$ will be real and positive when $p$ lies in some interval containing zero.

4.5. We shall now assume that a price $p$ is given, and study how company 1 can increase its utility by dealing in the market at this price.

(i) The company can *sell* reinsurance cover, i.e., it can accept responsibility for paying a claim with mean $m_0$ and variance $W_1$. For giving this cover the company will receive the amount $m_0 + pW_1$.

According to the formulae in Section 4.3, this transaction will change the utility of the company from

$$- a_1(S_1 - m_1)^2 + (S_1 - m_1) - a_1 V_1 = U_1(S_1 - m_1, V_1) = U_1(R_1, V_1)$$

to

$$- a_1(S_1 - m_1 + pW_1)^2 + (S_1 - m_1 + pW_1) - a_1(V_1 + W_1)$$
$$= U_1(R_1 + pW_1, V_1 + W_1) .$$

Here $R_1 = S_1 - m_1$, which in insurance terminology is called the "free reserves" of the company, i.e., funds in excess of expected amount of claims. We see that the utility does not depend on $m_0$, but only on free reserves and variance.

(ii) The company can *buy* reinsurance cover from the $n - 1$ other companies, i.e. by paying the amounts $pv_2, \ldots, pv_n$ of its free reserves to the other companies, it can "get rid of" variances $v_2, \ldots, v_n$.

These transactions will leave the company with a variance

$$v_1 = V_1 - \sum_{i=2}^{n} v_i - 2 \sum_{i \neq j} C_{ij}$$

where $C_{ij}$ is the covariance between claims in the portfolios taken by companies $i$ and $j$.

Since the utility of company 1 will increase with decreasing $v_1$, the company will seek to arrange its purchases so that $C_{ij}$ is as great as possible, i.e., so that

$$C_{ij} = (v_i v_j)^{\frac{1}{2}} .$$

This clearly means that there must be perfect positive correlation between claims in the part of the original portfolio which the company retains and the parts which are reinsured. Hence we must have $v_i = q_i^2 V_1$ and $\sum_{j=1}^{n} q_i = 1$. This is the same as the result which we in Section 4.2 derived from the general condition for Pareto optimality of Section 2.5.

4.6. If the company buys and sells reinsurance cover in this way, its utility will become

$$U_1\left(\left\{R_1 + p\left(W_1 - \sum_{i=2}^{n} v_i\right)\right\}, \left\{W_1 + \left(V_1^{\frac{1}{2}} - \sum_{i=2}^{n} v_i^{\frac{1}{2}}\right)^2 - V_1\right\}\right) .$$

The company will then seek to determine $W_1$, and $v_2, \ldots, v_n$ so that this expression is maximized.

The first order conditions for a maximum are

$$\frac{\partial U_1}{\partial W_1} = -p\left\{2a_1\left(R_1 + p(W_1 - \sum_{j=2}^{n} v_j)\right) - 1\right\} - a_1 = 0 \,,$$

$$\frac{\partial U_1}{\partial v_i} = p\left\{2a_1\left(R_1 + p(W_1 - \sum_{j=2}^{n} v_j)\right) - 1\right\} + a_1 \frac{V_1^{\frac{1}{2}} - \sum_{j=2}^{n} v_j^{\frac{1}{2}}}{v_{i}^{\frac{1}{2}}} = 0 \;\; (i = 2, 3 \ldots n) \,.$$

Adding the first of these equations to the one obtained by differentiating with respect to $v_i$, we obtain

$$V_1^{\frac{1}{2}} - \sum_{j=2}^{n} v_j^{\frac{1}{2}} = v_i^{\frac{1}{2}} \,.$$

Since this must hold for all $i$, we must have

$$v_i = \frac{1}{n^2} V_1 \qquad \text{for all } n.$$

This means that regardless of what the price is, the company will seek to divide its portfolio into $n$ identical parts, and reinsure $n - 1$ of these with the other companies.

Inserting the values of $v_i$ in the first equation, we find

$$W_1 = \frac{n-1}{n^2} V_1 + \frac{2p\left(\frac{1}{2a_1} - R_1\right) - 1}{2p^2} \,.$$

4.7. In general we find that for a given price $p$, company $i$ is willing to supply reinsurance cover for a variance

$$W_i = \frac{n-1}{n^2} V_i + \frac{2p\left(\frac{1}{2a_i} - R_i\right) - 1}{2p^2} \,.$$

The company will demand cover for a variance

$$W'_i = \frac{n-1}{n^2} V_i$$

regardless of what the price is, provided that this variance can be divided equally between the $n - 1$ other companies.

It is obvious that in this case we cannot determine $p$ by simply requiring that total supply shall be equal to total demand, i.e., from the "market equation"

$$\sum_{i=1}^{n} W_i = \sum_{i=1}^{n} W'_i \,.$$

Instead we have the conditions that supply from company $i$ must equal the sum of $1/(n-1)$ of the demand from the other $n-1$ companies, i.e.,

$$W_i = \frac{1}{n-1} \sum_{j \neq i} W'_i = \frac{1}{n^2} \sum_{j \neq i} V_j .$$

Hence $p$ must satisfy the $n$ equations

$$\frac{1}{n^2} \sum_{j=1}^{n} V_j - \frac{1}{n} V_i = \frac{2p\left(\frac{1}{2a_i} - R_i\right) - 1}{2p^2} \qquad (i = 1, 2, \ldots, n).$$

This is clearly impossible, except for special values of $a_i$, $R_i$ and $V_i$.

4.8. It is obvious from the preceding paragraph that unrestricted utility maximization with a given price has little meaning in our model. The procedure may, however, have some meaning if we introduce restrictions so that it necessarily leads to a Pareto optimal arrangement.

These restrictions can be formulated as follows. For all $i$ and $j$, $j \neq i$, company $i$ can satisfy its demand for reinsurance cover only by placing a part $q_j^2 V_i$ of its variance with company $j$.

Company $i$ will then be willing to supply reinsurance cover for a variance

$$W_i = V_i \sum_{j \neq i}^{n} q_j^2 + \frac{2p\left(\frac{1}{2a_i} - R_i\right) - 1}{2p^2} .$$

The $n$ market equations from Section 4.7 will then take the form

$$q_i^2 \sum_{j=1}^{n} V_j - V_i \sum_{j=1}^{n} q_j^2 = \frac{2p\left(\frac{1}{2a_i} - R_i\right) - 1}{2p^2} \qquad (i = 1, 2, \ldots, n).$$

It is easy to see that these $n$ equations, which are linear in $q_i^2$, have a determinant of rank $n-1$. Hence the equations have a solution only if the sum of the right hand sides is zero. This condition is satisfied: (i) if the right hand sides all vanish, i.e., if $p$ tends to infinity. The corresponding values of $q_i$ are then

$$q_i = \frac{V_i^{\frac{1}{2}}}{\sum_{j=1}^{n} V_j^{\frac{1}{2}}} ;$$

(ii) if

$$p = \frac{n}{2 \sum_{j=1}^{n} \left(\frac{1}{2a_j} - R_j\right)} .$$

This appears to be all that we can get, even from a diluted principle of utility maximization.

The result is not very satisfactory. The general assumptions which lead to these "equilibrium prices" are rather artificial, and it is easy to construct numerical examples where the result becomes meaningless.

From the formulae in Section 4.2 we see that the utility of company $i$ will decrease with increasing $q_i$. The price we have found may lead to values of $q_i$ which will give some companies a lower utility than they have in the initial situation. These companies will obviously refuse to trade at such a price.

The conditions which $q_i$ must satisfy in order to give a meaningful solution are discussed in the paper [6] already referred to, and we shall not pursue the point further in the present paper.

## 5. THE MODELS OF ALLAIS AND ARROW

5.1. Both Allais [1] and Arrow [3] have proved that in models very similar to ours, there exists a price such that utility maximization, when this price is considered as given, will lead to a Pareto optimal situation. To explain the apparent contradiction with our result, we shall examine their models in some detail.

5.2. Allais [1] studied a model which essentially is a market for lottery tickets. The prize of the tickets is a normally distributed random variable with mean equal to one unit of money, and a given standard deviation. Allais proves that in this model there exists a market price for lottery tickets which will lead to a uniquely determined, optimal distribution of the risks.

The crucial assumption which Allais makes in order to reach this result is that lottery tickets can be bought and sold only in integral numbers, i.e., one can buy one ticket, but not a 50 per cent interest in two tickets. It is obvious that when this assumption is given up, the Pareto optimum is no longer unique. The situation will be similar to the one we found in Section 2.7, which is an example of the familiar problem that an $n$-person game has an indeterminate solution. To make it determined, one will have to make some assumptions about how the participants form coalitions to buy packages of lottery tickets.

5.3. In the model of Allais there is only one kind of lottery ticket. If tickets are indivisible as Allais assumes, it is almost trivial that there must exist a price which leads to a Pareto optimal situation. The problem will change completely, however, if the model is generalized by the introduction of several kinds of tickets, i.e., tickets where the prize is drawn from different probability distributions. The problem can be handled as we did in the preceding sections if one accepts the Bernoulli hypothesis. Allais [2] has emphatically rejected this hypothesis, however, and thus barred the most obvious, and probably the only way to generalize his model.

5.4. The model studied by Arrow [3] is far more general. He considers $n$ different commodities, and he assumes that each participant in the market may have his own subjective probabilities. In this paper we shall disregard both these refinements. The generalization to $n$ commodities appears inessential when our main objective is to study the interplay of different attitudes toward risk and uncertainty. The subjective probabilities play a key part in Arrow's model, but it seems unnecessary to introduce them in a study of a reinsurance market. When a reinsurance treaty is concluded, both parties will survey all information relevant to the risks concerned. To hide information from the other party is plain fraud. Whether two rational persons on the basis of the same information can arrive at different evaluations of the probability of a specific event, is a question of semantics. That they may act differently on the same information is well known, but this can usually be explained assuming that the two persons attach different utilities to the event. In some situations, for instance in stock markets, it may be useful to resort *both* to subjective probabilities and different utility functions to explain observed behaviour. This seems, however, to be an unnecessary complication in a first study of reinsurance markets.

5.5. When simplified as indicated in the preceding paragraph, Arrow's model can be described as follows: (i) Company $i$ has a utility of money $u_i(x)$, $i = 1, 2, \ldots, I$.

(ii) As a result of its direct underwriting the company is committed to pay an amount $x_{is}$ if "state of the world" $s$ occurs, $s = 1, 2, \ldots, S$.

(iii) The company has funds amounting to $S_i$ available for meeting the commitments.

(iv) The probability that state of the world $s$ shall occur is $p_s$ ($\sum_{s=1}^{S} p_s = 1$). The utility of company $i$ in the initial situation is then

$$U_i(0) = \sum_{s=1}^{S} p_s u_i(S_i - x_{is})$$

where $x_{is}$ may be zero for some $s$.

5.6. It is then assumed that there exists a price vector $g_1, \ldots, g_s, \ldots, g_S$, so that the company can pay an amount $g_s y_{is}$, and then be assured of receiving the amount $y_{is}$ if state of the world $s$ occurs. This means that should this state occur, the company will have to make a net payment of $x_{is} - y_{is}$. If the company makes a series of such contracts, its utility will change to

$$U_1(y) = \sum_{s=1}^{S} p_s u_i\left(\left\{S_i - \sum_{s=1}^{S} g_s y_{is}\right\} - (x_{is} - y_{is})\right)$$

where $y_{is}$ may be positive or negative.

Differentiating with respect to $y_{it}$ we find:

$$\frac{\partial U_i(y)}{\partial y_{it}} = -g_t \sum_{s=1}^{S} p_s u_i'\left(\left\{S_i - \sum_{s=1}^{S} g_s y_{is}\right\} - x_{is} + y_{is}\right)$$

$$+ p_t u_i'\left(\left\{S_i - \sum_{s=1}^{S} g_s y_{is}\right\} - x_{it} + y_{it}\right).$$

Since we have placed no restrictions on $y_{it}$, the first order conditions for a maximum will be

$$g_t \sum_{s=1}^{S} p_s u_i'\left(S_i - \sum_{s=1}^{S} g_s y_{is} - x_{is} + y_{is}\right) = p_t u_i'\left(S_i - \sum_{s=1}^{S} g_s y_{is} - x_{it} + y_{it}\right)$$

$$(t = 1, 2, \ldots, S).$$

5.7. We now assume that the utility function is of the same simple form as in Section 4, i.e., that

$$u_i(x) = -a_i x^2 + x \qquad (i = 1, 2, \ldots, I).$$

The first order conditions for a maximum will then become

$$2a_i g_t \sum_{s=1}^{S} p_s\left(S_i - \sum_{s=1}^{S} g_s y_{is} - x_{is} + y_{is}\right) - g_t =$$

$$2a_i p_t\left(S_i - \sum_{s=1}^{S} g_s y_{is} - x_{it} + y_{it}\right) - p_t.$$

By some rearrangement this system of equations can be written

$$(g_t - p_t)\left(\frac{1}{2a_i} - S_i\right) + g_t \sum_{s=1}^{S} p_s x_{is} - p_t x_{it} =$$

$$g_t \sum_{s=1}^{S} p_s y_{is} - p_t y_{it} - (g_t - p_t) \sum_{s=1}^{S} g_s y_{is}$$

$$(t = 1, 2, \ldots, S \text{ and } i = 1, 2, \ldots, I).$$

$y_{is}$ is the amount (positive or negative) which company $i$ will receive if state of the world $s$ occurs. Since this amount necessarily must be paid out by the other companies, we must have

$$\sum_{i=1}^{I} y_{is} = 0 \qquad\qquad \text{for all } s.$$

Hence if we sum the equations over all $i$, the right hand side will disappear, so that we get the system

$$(g_t - p_t) \sum_{i=1}^{I} \left(\frac{1}{2a_i} - S_i\right) + g_t \sum_{s=1}^{S} p_s \sum_{i=1}^{I} x_{is} - p_t \sum_{i=1}^{I} x_{tt} = 0 \qquad (t = 1, 2, \ldots, S).$$

From this we obtain

$$g_t = p_t \frac{X_t + A}{X + A}$$

where

$$A = \sum_{i=1}^{I} A_i = \sum_{i=1}^{I} \left(\frac{1}{2a_i} - S_i\right),$$

$$X_s = \sum_{i=1}^{I} x_{is} \qquad \text{and} \qquad X = \sum_{s=1}^{S} p_s X_s.$$

The complete solution of the system is given by

$$x_{tt} - y_{tt} = q_i X_t$$

and

$$q_i = \frac{A_i + \sum_{s=1}^{S} g_s x_{is}}{A + \sum_{s=1}^{S} g_s X_s}$$

where

$$\sum_{i=1}^{I} q_i = 1.$$

5.8. This solution implies that company $i$ $(i = 1, 2, \ldots, I)$ shall pay a fixed quota $q_i$ of the total claim payment, regardless of which state of the world may occur. Hence the solution belongs to the set of Pareto optimal arrangements that we found in Section 4.2.
Since

$$\sum_{s=1}^{S} g_s x_{is} = \sum_{s=1}^{S} p_s \frac{X_s + A}{X + A} x_{is} = \frac{1}{X + A} \sum_{s=1}^{S} p_s (A x_{is} + X_s x_{is})$$

$$= \frac{1}{X + A} \left\{ A m_i + X m_i + \sum_{s=1}^{S} p_s (X_s - X)(x_{is} - m_i) \right\}$$

$$= m_i + \frac{\sum_{s=1}^{S} p_s (X_s - X)(x_{is} - m_i)}{X + A} = m_i + \frac{C_i}{X + A}$$

where $m_i = \sum_{s=1}^{S} p_s x_{is}$, and since $X = \sum_{i=1}^{I} m_i$, we have

$$q_i = \frac{A_i + m_i + \dfrac{C_i}{X + A}}{\sum\limits_{j=1}^{i} (A_j + m_j) + \dfrac{\operatorname{var} X_s}{X + A}} \, .$$

It is interesting to compare this with the expression which we found in Section 4.4 for the case $p = 0$.

5.9. The difference between Arrow's model and ours obviously lies in the price concept. In Arrow's model there is a price associated with every state of the world. The price will be the same for all states which lead to the same amount of total claim payment.

Our model is essentially a drastic simplification. Instead of the really infinite number of prices considered by Arrow, we have introduced one single price, a specific *price of risk*. We found that this price would have to be a vector with an infinite number of elements. If the utility function has the simple form studied in Section 4, the number of elements is reduced to two. However, in this case a competitive equilibrium cannot in general be a Pareto optimal distribution of risks.

5.10. The price in Arrow's model increases with the probability of a particular state of the world, and with the total amount to be paid if this state occurs. In insurance this means that a reinsurer who is asked to cover a modest amount if a certain person dies, will quote a price increasing with the total amount which is payable on the death of this person.

Such considerations are not unknown in insurance practice. It is well known that it can be difficult, i.e., expensive to arrange satisfactory reinsurance of particularly large risks. Practice seems here to be ahead of insurance theory, however, which still is firmly based on the *principle of equivalence*, i.e., that "net premiums" should be equal to the expected value of claim payments.

To apply Arrow's theory to stock market speculation we just have to reverse the signs of the formulae in this section.

We then find that the price of a certain share will depend not only on its "intrinsic value," but also on the number of such shares in the market. This may seem reasonable, although it implies that one pays more for a chance of getting rich alone, than for an identical chance of getting equally rich together with a lot of other speculators. The implication is that even in a model using essentially classical assumptions, there is a positive price attached to "getting ahead of the Joneses," and this may be a little unexpected.

## 6. THE PROBLEM SEEN AS AN $n$-PERSON GAME

6.1. We noted in Section 2.6 that a Pareto optimal set of reinsurance treaties was equivalent to a pool arrangement. Once the pool was established, the companies had to agree on some rule as to how each company should contribute to the payment of claims against the pool. In the special case which we considered in Section 4, this rule was that each company should pay a fixed proportion of these claims, regardless of its size. The quotas which each company should pay remained to be fixed, however.

When the problem is presented in this way, it seems natural to consider it as a problem of bargaining and negotiation which logically should be analysed in the terms of the theory of games. A priori it appears unlikely that there should exist some price mechanism which automatically will lead the companies to such a rather special arrangement as a Pareto optimal set of treaties.

6.2. In general an $n$-person game has an indeterminate solution. To get a determinate solution we must make *additional assumptions* about how the companies negotiate their way to an agreement.

The point is brought out clearly by the special case studied in Section 4. The usual assumptions of game theory leave the quotas $q_1,\ldots,q_n$ undetermined, except for the restriction $\Sigma q_i = 1$. The solution has, so to speak, $n-1$ "degrees of freedom." During the negotiations each company will try to get the smallest possible quota for itself.

We then lay down the additional rule that the same price must be applied to all the reciprocal treaties which constitute a Pareto optimal set. This amounts really to a ban on "price discrimination" or a partial ban on coalitions. The rule leaves only the price $p$ to be determined by negotiation, so that the number of degrees of freedom is reduced to one.

6.3. From the expressions in Section 4.4 we can conjecture that a given price $p$ will divide the companies in two groups or coalitions. One group will benefit from a higher price, the other from a lower one. The higher the price, the more companies will be in the latter group. The "equilibrium price" must then be determined so that it divides the companies in two groups, which in some unspecified manner are equal in strength. There are obviously a number of possible ways in which the concept "strength" can be defined, and hence a number of possible determinate solutions. We shall, however, not explore these possibilities in the present paper.

6.4. In real life reinsurance treaties are concluded after lengthy negotiations, often with brokers acting as intermediaries. The concept of prevailing market prices plays a part in the background of these negotiations, but the whole situation is more similar to an $n$-person game than to a classical market with utility maximization when the price is considered as given.

Little is known about the laws and customs ruling such negotiations in the reinsurance market. It seems, however, that further studies of this subject should be a promising, if not the most promising, way of gaining deeper knowledge of attitudes toward risk and the decisions which rational people make under uncertainty.

*The Norwegian School of Economics and Business Administration*

## REFERENCES

[1] ALLAIS, MAURICE: "L'Extension des Théories de l'Équilibre Économique Général et du Rendement Social au Cas du Risque," *Econometrica*, 1953, pp. 269–290.

[2] ————: "Le Comportement de l'Homme Rationnel devant le Risque: Critique des Postulates et Axiomes de l'École Américaine," *Econometrica*, 1953, pp. 503–546.

[3] ARROW, KENNETH J.: "Le Rôle de Valeurs boursières pour la Répartition la meilleure des Risques," *Colloques Internationaux du Centre National de la Recherche Scientifique*, XL, pp. 41–48, Paris, 1953.

[4] ARROW, KENNETH J., AND GERARD DEBREU: "Existence of an Equilibrium for a Competitive Economy," *Econometrica*, 1954, pp. 265–290.

[5] BORCH, KARL: "An Attempt to Determine the Optimum Amount of Stop Loss Reinsurance," *Transactions of the XVI International Congress of Actuaries*, Vol. II, pp. 597–610.

[6] ————: "The Safety Loading of Reinsurance Premiums," *Skandinavisk Aktuarie-tidskrift*, 1960, pp. 163–184.

[7] DEBREU, GERARD: *Theory of Value*, New York: John Wiley & Sons, 1959.

[8] LUKACS, E.: "An Essential Property of the Fourier Transforms of Distribution Functions," *Proceedings of the American Mathematical Society*, 1952, pp. 508–510.

[9] NEUMANN, J. VON, AND O. MORGENSTERN: *Theory of Games and Economic Behavior*, Princeton: Princeton Univ. Press, 1944.

[10] WALD, ABRAHAM: "Über einige Gleichungssysteme der mathematischen Ökonomie," *Zeitschrift für Nationalökonomie*, 1936, pp. 637–670. English translation, *Econometrica*, 1951, pp. 368–403.

# The Design of an Optimal Insurance Policy

Almost every phase of economic behavior is affected by uncertainty. The economic system has adapted to uncertainty by developing methods that facilitate the reallocation of risk among individuals and firms. The most apparent and familiar form for shifting risks is the ordinary insurance policy. Previous insurance decision analyses can be divided into those in which the insurance policy was exogenously specified (see John Gould, Jan Mossin, and Vernon Smith), and those in which it was not (see Karl Borch, 1960, and Kenneth Arrow, 1971, 1973). In this paper, the pioneering work of Borch and Arrow—the derivation of the optimal insurance contract form from the model—is synthesized and extended.

The incentive to insure and insurance decisions have been treated extensively by Gould, Mossin, and Smith. They analyzed the problem of rational insurance purchasing from the point of view of an individual facing a specific risk, given his wealth level and preference structure. In their analysis the individual is offered an insurance policy specifying the payment to be received from the insurance company if a particular loss occurs. The individual may choose the level of the deductible, the level of the maximum limit of coverage, or the fraction of the total risk which is to be insured. Since the premium paid by the individual is directly related to the features chosen, the optimal insurance coverage involves balancing the effects of additional premium against the effects of additional coverage. In this approach the terms of the policy are assumed to be exogenously specified and are imposed on the insurance purchaser.

Borch (1960) was the first to take the

more general approach of deriving the optimal insurance policy form endogenously. He sought to characterize a Pareto optimal risk-sharing arrangement in a situation where several risk averters were to bear a stochastic loss. This framework was then used by Arrow (1971) to obtain Pareto optimal policies in two distinct cases: 1) if the insurance seller is risk averse, the insured prefers a policy that involves some element of coinsurance; (i.e., the coverage will be some fraction (less than 1) of the loss); and 2) if the premium is based on the actuarial value of the policy plus a proportional loading (i.e., the insurer is risk neutral) and the insurance reimbursement is restricted to be nonnegative, the insurance policy will extend full coverage of losses above a deductible. Arrow (1973) extended this result to the case of state dependent utility functions. In this case, the optimality of a deductible which depends upon the state was proved. Robert Wilson also dealt with the endogenous determination of optimal risk-sharing arrangements, focusing on the incentive problem and the existence of surrogate functions. Consequently, constraints on the contract or costs associated with contracting were not included.

The purpose of this paper is to explain the prevalence of several different insurance contracts observable in the real world. The previous studies addressed this issue with a diversity of underlying assumptions and, therefore, the essential ingredients of the model that give rise to the insurance policy's various characteristics are not clear. For example, in Arrow's 1971 paper it is unclear whether an insurance policy with a deductible is the consequence of risk neutrality of the insurer, nonnegativity of the insurance coverage, or loading on the premium. Could a deductible be obtained when the insurer is risk averse? Could the loading be interpreted as risk premium? Could we explain the prevalence of deduct-

*Associate professor of economics, Carnegie-Mellon University and Tel-Aviv University. I would like to thank E. Green, M. Harris, R. Townsend, T. Romer, D. Epple, and G. Constantinides for several helpful discussions.

ibles and coinsurance in insurance policies? These and other questions can be answered only from a general formulation of the insurance problem, a formulation in which the previous models are imbedded.

In this paper I undertake the development of such a model. Using the same basic framework as Borch (1960), and Arrow (1971, 1973) the choice of contracts subject to various restrictions on the class of feasible contracts is considered. The analysis generalizes and extends the previous results in several directions: 1) The form of the Pareto optimal insurance contract is identified under general assumptions regarding the risk preferences of both the insurer and insured. The necessary and sufficient conditions leading to deductibles and coinsurance are investigated. 2) The cost of insurance is explicitly recognized and shown to be the driving force behind the deductible results. This clarifies the results obtained by Arrow (1971). 3) I show the conditions under which an insurance policy with an upper limit on coverage is adopted. 4) All results are extended to the case where more than one loss can occur during the period of insurance protection. A thorough understanding of the above issues not only contributes to our understanding of insurance policies, but provides a foundation for the analysis of optimal contracts in more general situations.

In this paper, the insurance policy is characterized by the premium paid by the insured and by a coverage function specifying the transfer from the insurer to the insured for each possible loss. The admissible coverage functions are restricted to be nonnegative and less than the size of the loss. Provision of the insurance is costly, with the cost consisting of fixed and variable (depending on the size of the insurance payment) components. The premium depends on the insurance policy and the insurance cost through a constraint on the insurer's expected utility of final wealth.

It is shown that the Pareto optimal insurance policy involves a deductible and coinsurance of losses above the deductible. The deductible is strictly positive if and only if the cost of insurance is a function of the insurance coverage. In other words, if the cost of providing insurance is independent of the insurance coverage then the Pareto optimal contract does not have a deductible. I conclude that the deductible clause in insurance policies exists due to two sources: the nonnegativity constraint on the transfer from the insurer to the insured and the variable insurance cost. The coinsurance arrangement is due to either the risk aversion of the insurer or the nonlinearity of the insurance costs. The exact functional relationship for the coinsurance is derived. These results are generalizations of Arrow's 1971 work and point out the crucial assumptions underlying his results. (Arrow's results are included as special cases.) Contrary to what might be inferred from Arrow it is shown that 1) insurer's risk neutrality is neither a necessary nor sufficient condition for a policy to have a deductible; 2) insurer's risk aversion is not a necessary condition for coinsurance; 3) an optimal policy may involve a deductible and a coinsurance. A policy with an upper limit on coverage, a feature common in major medical, liability, and disability insurance, is shown not to be Pareto optimal. To explain the prevalence of upper limits, a model is provided in which a risk-averse insurer is restricted (by regulation) in determining his premium by an actuarial constraint.

These results are initially derived under the assumption that at most one loss can occur during the period of insurance protection. When several losses are allowed to occur during the insurance period (from a single or several perils), the optimal insurance policy should be based on the aggregate loss and possess the same characteristics as previously discussed. If a policy with a deductible was optimal in the single loss case, then the policy should stipulate a deductible from the total claims when two or more losses occur. Similarly, in the case of insurance with upper limits, the upper limit should apply to the aggregate loss of the insured and not to each loss separately.

The assumptions and the model are specified in the next section, followed by a characterization of optimal insurance coverage when the premium is exogenously fixed. Section III completes the determination of Pareto optimal insurance policies. The behavior of a risk-averse insurer is investigated in Section IV while Section V extends all previous results to the multiple loss case. Conclusions and a critique are contained in the last section.

### I. Assumptions and the Model

The insurance buyer faces a risk of loss of $x$, where $x$ is a random variable with probability density function $f(x)$. Assume that $f(x) > 0$ for $0 \leq x \leq T$.[1]

The insurance policy is characterized by the payment, denoted by $I(x)$, transferred from the insurer to the insured if loss $x$ obtains. Let us refer to $I(x)$ as the *insurance policy* or as the *coverage function*. Any admissible coverage function satisfies

(1)     $0 \leq I(x) \leq x$     for all $x$

This constraint reflects the assumption that an insurance reimbursement is necessarily nonnegative and cannot exceed the size of the loss. The latter implies that the insured cannot gamble on his risk. This constraint also implies $I(0) = 0$; there is no reimbursement if there is no loss. The price paid by the insured, *the premium*, is denoted by $P$. Provision of insurance is costly due to administrative or other expenses and this cost is a deadweight loss relative to the insurer and the insured. It is assumed that the cost consists of fixed and variable (depending on the size of the insurance payment) components; $c(I)$ denotes the *cost* when the insurance payment is $I$ with

(2)     $c(0) = a \geq 0$,

$c'(\cdot) \geq 0$,     $c''(\cdot) \geq 0$

The insurer is assumed to maximize the expected value of his utility, which is a concave function of wealth; $V(W)$ denotes the utility function of the insurer with $V'(W) > 0$ and $V''(W) \leq 0$ for all $W$. Thus,

the insurer is assumed to be risk averse (but not necessarily strictly risk averse). The special case of risk-neutral insurer, $V''(W) = 0$, is of particular interest.

If $W_0$ denotes the initial wealth of the insurer, then after selling the insurance policy and receiving the premium $P$, his final wealth is $W_0 + P - I(x) - c(I(x))$ if the loss $x$ obtains. In other words, the insurer exchanges his initial certain utility $V(W_0)$ for the expected utility $E\{V[W_0 + P - I(x) - c(I(x))]\}$. A necessary condition for the insurer to offer such a policy is

(3)

$$E\{V[W_0 + P - I(x) - c(I(x))]\} \geq V(W_0)$$

In the special case of a risk-neutral insurer, the risk premium equals zero and equation (3) takes the form: $P \geq E[I(x) + c(I(x))]$. Here, the policy is evaluated by the insurer according to the actuarial value of the coverage and cost. Often, in the insurance literature, it is assumed that

(2')     $a = 0, c'(I) = l$     for all $I$

That is, the costs are proportional to the insurance payment (fixed percentage loading $l$). In this case, the constraint on the policies offered is:

(3')          $P \geq (1 + l)E[I(x)]$

On the insurance demand side, the insured is assumed to maximize the expected value of his utility of wealth. The insured's utility function of wealth is denoted by $U(w)$ with

(4)     $U'(w) > 0, U''(w) < 0$     for all $w$

If $w$ is the initial level of wealth, $x$ the loss (a random variable), $I(x)$ the payment received from the insurer when loss $x$ occurs, and $P$ the premium paid for the insurance coverage, then the insured's final wealth is $w - P - x + I(x)$. Without purchasing insurance, his final wealth is $w - x$ when the loss $x$ occurs. Thus, a necessary condition for purchasing the coverage $I(x)$ for a premium $P$ is

(5)

$$E\{U[w - P - x + I(w)]\} \geq E\{U[w - x]\}$$

---

[1]We could assume $f(x) \geq 0$. However, this would complicate the exposition without adding any content.

Necessary conditions for a *given* insurance contract to be acceptable to each party were given above. In order for a contract to be acceptable to both sides, both (3) and (5) have to be satisfied. In what follows, we will assume that the set of acceptable insurance contracts which satisfy these necessary conditions is nonempty. From this set, a Pareto optimal insurance policy will be chosen.

To find the form of the Pareto optimal insurance contract, we find the premium $P$ and the function $I(\cdot)$ that maximize the insured's expected utility of final wealth subject to the constraint that the insurer's expected utility is constant. The problem is stated as follows:

$$(6) \quad \max_{P, I(x)} \overline{U}(P, I) \equiv$$
$$\int_0^T U[w - P - x + I(x)] f(x)\, dx$$

subject to (1) and

$$(7) \quad \overline{V}(P, I) \equiv \int_0^T V[W_0 + P - I(x)$$
$$- c(I(x))] f(x)\, dx \geq k$$

where $k$ is a constant and $k \geq V(W_0)$.

The above problem is solved in two steps. First, in Section II, the premium $P$ is assumed fixed and the form of the optimal insurance coverage is found as a function of $P$. Second, in Section III, the optimal $P$ is chosen, thus completing the solution to our problem.

## II. Optimal Insurance Coverage for a Fixed Premium

The next theorem characterizes the solution to equation (6) subject to constraints (1) and (7) when $P$ is fixed. The theorem states that optimal insurance policies have one of two possible forms: there is either a deductible provision coupled with coinsurance of losses above the deductible, or there is full coverage of losses up to a limit and coinsurance of losses above that limit. Coverage functions satisfying (8) below are referred to as *policies with a deductible*. The deductible $\overline{x}_1$ is the largest loss not covered by the insurance policy. Policies satisfying (9) are referred to as policies with an upper

limit on full coverage or *policies with upper limit*. The *upper limit* $\overline{x}_2$ is the largest loss which is fully covered by insurance. Usually, the coinsurance level is the proportion of the loss covered by insurance. In our analysis this proportion varies with the size of the loss. Consequently, the *coinsurance* is defined as the marginal coverage, $I^{*\prime}(x)$. From (10) it is seen that the coinsurance depends on the risk preferences of the insurer and the insured as well as on the cost function $c(\cdot)$.[2]

THEOREM 1: *The solution* $I^*(x)$ *to equation* (6), *subject to constraints* (1) *and* (7) *when* $P$ *is fixed, takes one of the two forms* (8) *or* (9) *where*

$$(8) \quad I^*(x) = 0 \qquad \text{for } x \leq \overline{x}_1$$
$$0 < I^*(x) < x \qquad \text{for } x > \overline{x}_1$$
$$(9) \quad I^*(x) = x \qquad \text{for } x \leq \overline{x}_2$$
$$0 < I^*(x) < x \qquad \text{for } x > \overline{x}_2$$

In both cases, in the range where $0 < I^*(x) < x$, the marginal coverage satisfies

$$(10) \quad I^{*\prime}(x) =$$
$$\frac{R_U(A)}{R_U(A) + R_V(B)(1 + c') + c''/(1 + c')}$$

where

$$A = w - P - x + I^*(x)$$
$$B = W_0 + P - I^*(x) - c(I^*(x))$$

$R(\cdot)$ denotes the index of absolute risk aversion, and $c'$, $c''$ are evaluated at $I^*(x)$.

PROOF:

Constraint (7) is binding at the optimum. Since the specified problem is solved via optimal control theory we rewrite (7) as

$$(11) \quad \dot{z}(x) = V[W_0 + P - I(x)$$
$$- c(I(x))] f(x)$$
$$z(0) = 0$$
$$z(T) = k$$

Using $I(x)$ as the control variable and

---

[2]When we have no constraints on the insurance function and when $c(\cdot) \equiv 0$ then (10) is identical to the sharing rule given by Wilson.

$z(x)$ as the state variable, the Hamiltonian for this problem is

$$H = \{U[w - P - x + I(x)] + \lambda V[W_0 + P - I(x) - c(I(x))]\} f(x)$$

Since the Hamiltonian does not depend on the state variable it is clear that the auxilary function $\lambda$ is constant with respect to $x$.

The necessary conditions for the optimal coverage function to maximize the Hamiltonian subject to constraint (1) are

(12)  $I^*(x) = 0$  if $\mathbf{J} \equiv U'(w - P - x)$
$- \lambda V'(W_0 + P - a)(1 + c'(0)) \leq 0$

(13)  $I^*(x) = x$  if $\mathbf{K} \equiv U'(w - P)$
$- \lambda V'(W_0 + P - x - c(x))$
$(1 + c'(x)) \geq 0$

(14)  $U'[w - P - x + I^*(x)]$
$- \lambda V'[W_0 + P - I^*(x)$
$-c(I^*(x))][1 + c'(I^*(x))] = 0$
for $0 < I^*(x) < x$

First, note that either (12) or (13) has to occur for some $x$, although both cannot be satisfied simultaneously. This follows directly from the fact that $\mathbf{J}$ (as defined in (12)) is continuous and increasing in $x$ while $\mathbf{K}$ is continuous and decreasing in $x$. If

$\mathbf{L} \equiv U'(w - P) - \lambda V'(W_0 + P - a)$
$(1 + c'(0)) \geq 0$

then (12) cannot obtain for $x > 0$. If $\mathbf{L} \leq 0$ then (13) cannot obtain for $x > 0$. Hence the optimal solution satisfies either (12) and (14), or (13) and (14). Define $\bar{x}_i$, $i = 1, 2$ from

(12')  $U'(w - P - \bar{x}_1)$
$- \lambda V'(W_0 + P - a)(1 + c'(0)) = 0$

(13')  $U'(w - P)$
$- \lambda V'(W_0 + P - x_2 - c(\bar{x}_2))$
$(1 + c'(\bar{x}_2)) = 0$

Clearly, $\bar{x}_i$ is uniquely defined by (12') and (13'), respectively. (The special case $\bar{x}_1 = \bar{x}_2 = 0$ occurs if $U'(w - P) - \lambda V'(W_0 + P - a)(1 + c'(0)) = 0$.) As a result, the

optimal coverage function takes one of the two forms (8) or (9). In both cases, for $x > \bar{x}_i$ (14) is satisfied. Differentiating with respect to $x$ and using the earlier definitions of $A$ and $B$ we obtain for $x > \bar{x}_i$:

(15)  $U''(A)[I^*{}'(x) - 1]$
$+ \lambda V''(B)[1 + c'(I^*(x))]^2 I^*{}'(x)$
$- \lambda V'(B)c''(I^*(c))I^*{}'(x) = 0$

Substituting $\lambda$ from (14) and solving for $I^*{}'(x)$, (10) is obtained.

Notice also that, since the Hamiltonian does not depend on the state variable, the sufficiency theorem concavity requirement as shown by Morton Kamien and Nancy Schwartz is satisfied trivially. Hence, $I^*(x)$ satisfies the necessary and sufficient conditions of optimality.

Theorem 1 is easily interpreted. In the absence of constraint (1), risk aversion of both parties implies that Pareto optimal coverage involves sharing the risk according to the sharing rule (10). Equation (10) is a differential equation which, together with a boundary condition, results in a coverage function. Whether the optimal policy has a deductible or an upper limit depends on the appropriate boundary condition. For example, if the boundary condition is $I(\bar{x}_1) = 0$, then the policy has a deductible. The appropriate boundary condition depends on the fixed premium. When the premium is $P$, let $I_P(x)$ denote the function which solves the differential equation (10) with the boundary condition $I_P(0) = 0$. Since $0 < I'_P < 1$, this function also satisfies constraint (1). To verify whether this function is the solution to the problem the insurer's expected utility $\bar{V}(P, I_P)$ must be evaluated. Three cases could occur: 1) If $\bar{V}(P, I_P) = k$, then (7) is satisfied, $I_P(0) = 0$ is the appropriate boundary condition, and $I_P$ is the optimal coverage function. 2) If $\bar{V}(P, I_P) < k$, then $I_P$ is not the solution since (7) is violated. To increase the insurer's expected utility to the required level, the payment to the insured has to be reduced for some losses. This could be achieved by a boundary condition specifying that $I^*(0)$ is negative. However, the constraint $I^*(x) \geq 0$ becomes binding and the appropriate boundary condition is $I^*(x) = 0$ for $x \leq \bar{x}_1$. In this case, the optimality of the deductible policy is obtained. 3) If $\bar{V}(P, I_P) > k$, the coverage can be increased. This increases the insured's expected utility, while the constraint (7) on insured's utility is not violated. The appropriate boundary condition is $I^*(0) > 0$, which together with the constraint $I(x) \leq x$, results in $I^*(x) = x$ for $x \leq \bar{x}_2$. In this case, the policy with an upper limit is obtained.

Let $P_0$ be the fixed premium corresponding to the first case above and let $I_0(\cdot)$ be the function solving (10). Thus, $\bar{V}(P_0, I_0) = k$ and the coverage function has the property $\bar{x}_1 = \bar{x}_2 = 0$ (i.e., $(P_0, I_0)$ is the policy with no deductible or upper limit provision). Denote

(16)  $$S_1 = \{P \mid \bar{V}(P, I_P) \leq k\}$$

and  $$S_2 = \{P \mid \bar{V}(P, I_P) \geq k\}$$

By definition, $P_0 \, \epsilon \, S_i$ for $i = 1$ and 2. Lemma 1 summarizes the discussion above and states that the optimal coverage involves a nontrivial deductible if $P \, \epsilon \, S_1$ and a nontrivial upper limit if $P \, \epsilon \, S_2$.

LEMMA 1: *For $P \, \epsilon \, S_i$, $i = 1$ or 2 and $P \neq P_0$, $I^*(x)$ is specified by (8) and (10) or (9) and (10), respectively, with $\bar{x}_i > 0$, $i = 1$ or 2.*

Lemma 2 determines the effect of a change in $\bar{x}_i$ on $I^*(x)$ for $P \, \epsilon \, S_i$. It is stated that for policies with a deductible, the coverage function decreases with the deductible level. Similarly, for policies with upper limit, the coverage function increases with the upper limit. If the sharing proportion $I^{*\prime}$ was constant, then these results clearly follow from the changes in the initial conditions of the differential equation. The proof that it is correct in the present, more general, case is given in Appendix A.

LEMMA 2: *a) If $P \, \epsilon \, S_1$ then $\partial I^*/\partial \bar{x}_1 < 0$ for $x > \bar{x}_1$ and b) If $P \, \epsilon \, S_2$ then $\partial I^*/\partial \bar{x}_2 > 0$ for $x > \bar{x}_2$.*

## III. Pareto Optimal Insurance Policy

In the previous section the premium was assumed fixed. Therefore, in Theorem 1, $\bar{x}_1$, $\bar{x}_2$ and $I^*(x)$ are functions of $P$. We proceed to determine $P^*$, thus completing the determination of the Pareto optimal insurance policy. Theorem 2 proves that the search for the optimal premium can be restricted to the subset $S_1$ of premiums which generate policies with a deductible. Within this subset, Theorem 3 characterizes the necessary and sufficient conditions for the deductible to be nontrivial. These two results together complete the derivation of Pareto optimal policies and allow us to clearly distinguish the cases under which we would expect to observe deductibles and coinsurance clauses in insurance contracts. The results obtained by Arrow (1971) are treated as special cases thus allowing us to focus on the specific assumptions which generate these results.

The next theorem states that any insurance policy with an upper limit is dominated by the policy $(P_0, I_0)$ with zero upper limit. In other words, the pure sharing arrangment dominates any policy with an upper limit. Intuitively, starting with the $(P_0, I_0)$ policy, any increase in $\bar{x}_2$ (from $\bar{x}_2 = 0$) has the effect of increasing insurance coverage for all losses which, in turn, increases the dead-weight loss due to increased insurance costs and therefore is suboptimal.

THEOREM 2: $\bar{U}(P_0, I_0) \geq \bar{U}(P, I^*)$ *for all $P \, \epsilon \, S_2$.*

The proof consists of comparing the slopes of the indifference curves for the insured and the insurer in $P, \bar{x}_2$ space. It is shown that for an incremental increase in $\bar{x}_2$ the insured is willing to increase $P$ less than is required for the insurer to remain indifferent. Because of the limited space and since the proof is similar to the proof of Theorem 3 the details are omitted. The interested reader can receive the proof from the author upon request.

After showing that the Pareto optimal

insurance policy will not be of the upper-limit type, we now investigate the conditions under which the Pareto optimal policy will or will not include a deductible clause. The next theorem specifies that a (nontrivial) deductible is obtained if and only if the insurance cost depends on the insurance payment.

THEOREM 3: *A necessary and sufficient condition for the Pareto optimal deductible to be equal to zero is $c'(\cdot) \equiv 0$ (i.e., $c(I) = a$ for all $I$).*

The proof is given in Appendix B. We compare the insurer's and the insured's tradeoff between $x_1$ and $P$. If $c'(\cdot) = 0$, it is shown that for a marginal increase in the deductible the amount the insured is willing to pay in premium is less than that required by the insurer. On the other hand, if $c'(\cdot) > 0$, the insured is willing to pay more than what is required by the insurer and, therefore, the deductible is greater than zero.

Theorems 2 and 3 characterize the Pareto optimal insurance policy. What are the implications of these results regarding the contract form that we would expect to observe? The persistence of deductibles is explained by Theorem 3. If the cost of insurance depends on the coverage, then a nontrival deductible is obtained. This result does not depend on the risk preferences of the insured or the insurer. I stress this fact to point out that Arrow's (1971, Theorem 1) deductible result was not a consequence of the risk-neutrality assumption. Rather, it was obtained because of the assumption that insurance cost is proportional to coverage. For completeness Arrow's result is reproduced as a special case of my treatment.[3]

COROLLARY 1 (Arrow 1971): *If $c(I) = lI$ and the insurer is risk neutral, the Pareto*

*optimal policy is given by*

$$(17) \qquad I^*(x) = \begin{cases} 0 & \text{for } x \leq \bar{x}_1 \\ x - \bar{x}_1 & \text{for } x > \bar{x}_1 \end{cases}$$

*where $\bar{x}_1 > 0$ if and only if $l > 0$.*

PROOF:
By Theorem 3, the Pareto optimal policy involves $\bar{x}_1 > 0$ iff $c' = l > 0$. The form of the coverage function is specified by (10). Since $R_V \equiv 0$ and $c'' = 0$, we have $I^{*\prime} = 1$ for $x > \bar{x}_1$. Thus $I^*(x)$ is given by (17).

Even if risk neutrality is not assumed, we still obtain a nontrivial deductible. The coverage involves, however, a coinsurance arrangement for losses above the deductible. The coinsurance level is given by (10) and in this special case is

$$I^{*\prime}(x) = \frac{R_U(A)}{R_U(A) + R_V(B)(1 + l)} < 1$$

This is the generalization of Arrow's (1971, Theorem 1) result to the risk-averse insurer case. Risk aversion of the insurer causes the coinsurance of losses above the deductible. Because of the insurance costs, the deductible is strictly positive.

What are the conditions that lead to a coinsurance arrangement? As already pointed out, risk aversion on the part of the insurer could be the cause for coinsurance. With no insurance costs this was proved by Arrow (1971, Theorem 2). In this case, there is no deductible. Our results prove, however, that a Pareto optimal policy may include a deductible and coinsurance of losses above the deductible.

COROLLARY 2: *If the insurer is risk averse, then the Pareto optimal insurance policy involves coinsurance of losses above the deductible.*

PROOF:
From (10) it is clear that $I^{*\prime} < 1$ for $x > \bar{x}_1 \geq 0$.

---

[3]Strictly speaking, Arrow (1971) did not fully discuss the Pareto optimal policy. His theorem characterizes only the optimal coverage function for a given premium.

Risk aversion, however, is not the only explanation for coinsurance. Even if the insurer is risk neutral, coinsurance might be observed, provided the insurance costs are a strictly convex function of the coverage. The intuitive reason for this result is that the cost function nonlinearity substitutes for the utility function nonlinearity.

COROLLARY 3: *If the insurer is risk neutral and* $c'' > 0$, *the Pareto optimal policy involves a deductible,* $\bar{x}_1 > 0$, *and coinsurance of losses above the deductible.*

PROOF:

Since $c' > 0$, we know $\bar{x}_1 > 0$ by Theorem 3. From (10) we have that for $x > \bar{x}_1$,

$$I^{*\prime}(x) = \frac{R_U(A)}{R_U(A) + c''/(1 + c')} < 1$$

In this section, the Pareto optimal insurance policy which was shown to specify a deductible and coinsurance of losses above the deductible was characterized. The deductible was shown to be strictly positive if and only if the insurance cost depended on the insurance payment. Coinsurance results from either insurer risk aversion or the cost function nonlinearity.

### IV. Policies with Upper Limit on Coverage

The previous section explained deductibles and coinsurance arrangements in insurance contracts, as well as why Pareto optimal insurance policy does not involve an upper limit on coverage. In this section, I attempt to explain the prevalence of upper limits on coverage which are frequently incorporated in major medical, liability, and property insurance. The explanation rests on the fact that insurance companies are frequently regulated and therefore operate subject to a regulatory constraint. In what follows, it is argued that the upper limit on insurance coverage is desired by the insurance seller restricted in his policy offering by an actuarial constraint. Intuitively,

the insurer is required to sell a policy with a prescribed actuarial value, for any given premium. This actuarial value might be smaller than the expected monetary loss, and then the policy cannot fully cover all potential losses. Being risk averse, the insurer prefers to allocate this given policy actuarial value to full coverage of small losses and limited coverage of large losses, rather than any other feasible form of the coverage. Heavy losses above that limit will not be insured under this contract.

To make the above statements precise, the results of the previous section are specialized to characterize the insurance policy desired by the insurance seller. Assume that the insurer devises contracts so as to maximize his expected utility of final wealth:

$$(18) \quad \bar{V}(P, I) = \underset{P, I(x)}{\text{Max}}$$
$$\int_0^T V[W_0 + P - I(x) - c(I(x))] f(x) dx$$

The class of feasible insurance contracts is restricted by (1) and by the assumption that the premium received is required (by regulation) to be a function of the policy's actuarial value.[4] Denoting this function by $R$, assume

$$(19) \quad P = R\left\{ \int_0^T I(x) f(x) dx \right\}$$

Equation (19) specifies a general relationship between the premium charged and the actual value of the policy. This specification is consistent with the procedure used by regulatory agencies under the prior approval laws which are the predominant form of regulation of the property-liability insurance industry. (See Paul Joskow for the description of the pricing behavior in this industry.) In general, rates are established so as to yield a particular rate of return on sales (premiums). As Joskow states: "A standard rate of return on sales figure

---

[4]The result of this section would not change if we assume that the premium depends on the actuarial value of the coverage and insurance cost.

of 5 percent is employed in most states as a result of a recommendation by the National Association of Insurance Commissioners in 1921" (p. 394). Under this procedure, the pricing formula is

$$P(1 - .05) = \text{Expected Losses} + \text{Operating Expenses}$$

which is a special case of our formulation in (19).

Theorem 4 characterizes the solution to the insurer's problem specified above, stating that if a risk-averse insurer selects an insurance policy to maximize his expected utility, then the policy offered fully covers losses up to certain upper limit, and covers no losses above the limit.

THEOREM 4: *The solution to problem* (18) *subject to constraints* (1) *and* (19) *is* $P^*$ *and* $I^*(x)$ *such that*

$$(20) \qquad I^*(x) = \begin{cases} x \text{ for } x \leq \bar{x} \\ \bar{x} \text{ for } x > \bar{x} \\ 0 \leq \bar{x} \leq T \end{cases}$$

*and* $\bar{x} = \bar{r}(P^*)$.

PROOF:

Starting with a fixed $P$, the optimal solution is shown to have the form of equation (20). The determination of the optimal $P^*$ is then discussed.

The policies obtained in Theorem 1 can be viewed as the solution to the following problem: Maximize the insurer's expected utility of final wealth subject to constraint (1) and a restriction on the insured's expected utility of final wealth: $EU[w - P - x + I(x)] = c_1$, where $c_1$ is a constant. If the utility function $U$ is linear and $P$ is given, this restriction can be rewritten as $EI(x) = c_2$, which is equivalent to constraint (19). Thus, the solution to the present problem is obtained directly from Theorem 1 by specifying $R_U(\cdot) = 0$. This yields $I^{*\prime}(x) = 0$, for $x > \bar{x}_i$. In the first case, $I^*(x) = 0$ for $x \leq \bar{x}_1$, and, therefore, $I^*(x) = 0$ for all $x$. In the second case, $I^*(x) = x$ for $x \leq \bar{x}_2$, and, therefore, $I^*(x) = \bar{x}_2$ for $x > x_2$ thus proving that the optimal form of the con-

tract is given by (20). The constant $\bar{x}_2$ is determined by the optimal premium $P^*$, which depends on the function $R$ and the insurance cost. If loading is sufficiently high, full coverage of all losses could be obtained (i.e., $\bar{x}_2 = T$). On the other hand, loading could be low enough so that no insurance is offered (i.e., $\bar{x}_2 = 0$). In general, therefore, $0 \leq \bar{x}_2 \leq T$.

### V. Optimal Insurance Policies when Multiple Losses Can Occur

In the previous sections the insurance policy contracted between the insurance buyer and the insurance seller was analyzed. My model, however, incorporated the simplifying assumption that only a single loss can occur during the period of insurance protection. This assumption appears to be too restrictive; business firms and individuals may be faced with risks that could result in more than one loss during the period of insurance protection. Furthermore, the insurance buyer will typically purchase several different policies to cover different perils that he faces. The present analysis will extend the results of the previous sections to derive the properties of an optimal policy when several potential losses are faced by the insured. To facilitate notation, the proofs have been restricted to the case of two potential losses. The analysis carries over to more general cases.

The insurance buyer is assumed to face two potential losses during the period of insurance coverage. His total monetary loss is $x_1 + x_2$ where $x_i, i = 1, 2$, are assumed to be random variables defined on $[0, T_i]$ with a joint probability density function $f(x_1, x_2)$.

The insurance policy is characterized by the payment $I(x_1, x_2)$ transferred from the insurer to the insured if losses $x_1, x_2$ obtain. As before, $I(x_1, x_2)$ is referred to as the insurance policy or coverage function. Similar to condition (1) a restriction is imposed on the insurance function:

$$(21) \quad 0 \leq I(x_1, x_2) \leq x_1 + x_2$$

$$\text{for all } x_1, x_2$$

The Pareto optimal coverage function $I(x_1, x_2)$ is obtained by maximizing the insured's expected utility of final wealth subject to the constraint that the insurer's expected utility exceeds a given constant. The problem is then stated as follows:

$$(22) \quad \underset{P, I}{\text{Max}} \int_0^{T_2} \int_0^{T_1} U[w - P - x_1 - x_2$$
$$+ I(x_1, x_2)] f(x_1, x_2) dx_1 dx_2$$

subject to

$$(23) \quad \int_0^{T_2} \int_0^{T_1} V[W_o + P - I(x_1, x_2)$$
$$- c(I(x_1, x_2))] f(x_1, x_2) dx_1 dx_2 \geq k$$

and

$$(24) \quad 0 \leq I(x_1, x_2) \leq x_1 + x_2$$

The above problem has the form of an iso-parametric problem in the calculus of variations with the additional constraint (24). Since the unknown function $I(x_1, x_2)$ depends on two variables, the extension of the simple Euler equation can be used to include two dimensions and constraints in order to derive the optimal insurance policy. Rather than proceeding along those lines, we first prove that the optimal function depends only on the sum $(x_1 + x_2)$.[5] Thus, the coverage function depends on one variable, the aggregate loss, and all previous results apply to this aggregate loss.

THEOREM 5: *Let $I^*(x_1, x_2)$ be the solution to the problem* (22) *subject to constraints* (23) *and* (24). *Then, $I^*(x_1, x_2)$ depends on the sum* $(x_1 + x_2)$ *only, i.e., $I^*(x_1, x_2) = \bar{I}^*(x_1 + x_2)$.*

The proof consists of showing that for any function $I(x_1, x_2)$ which does not depend on the sum only, there exists another coverage function $I^*(x_1, x_2)$ which increases the objective (22), is feasible, and depends

[5] Borch (1962) proved that "any Pareto optimal set of treaties is equivalent to a pool arrangement" (p. 428). In his analysis, however, insurance was costless, and there were no constraints imposed on the feasible insurance policy. Therefore, he did not obtain the deductible or upper-limit results and could not generalize these results to the multiple loss case.

on the sum only. The detailed proof is tedious and can be obtained from the author upon request. In what follows I provide the intuition behind the result and its proof.[6]

For simplicity, suppose that with probability $p(p')$ the losses are $x_1$, $x_2(x_1', x_2')$. Thus, the total loss is $x_1 + x_2$ or $x_1' + x_2'$ with probabilities $p$ and $p'$, respectively. Assume that $x_1 + x_2 = x_1' + x_2' = y$. Consider a coverage function $I(\cdot, \cdot)$ which does not depend only on the sum; $I(x_1, x_2) \neq I(x_1', x_2')$. A risk averter prefers to exchange any uncertainty for a certain outcome. In particular, the insured's expected utility for these two states can be increased by providing a coverage function which depends on $y$ only:

$$p U[w - P - y + I(x_1, x_2)]$$
$$+ p' U[w - P - y + I(x_1', x_2')]$$
$$\leq U[w - P - y + I^*(y)]$$

where $I^*(y) = p I(x_1, x_2) + p' I(x_1', x_2')$. Thus, the function $I$ is dominated by the function $I^*$. $I^*$ is the "weighted average" or the expected value of the coverages of equal total losses. By a similar argument, it can be shown that the insurer also prefers the coverage $I^*$. The above intuitive argument can be generalized. The driving force for the proof is, as above, the concavity of the utility functions; the dominance of $I^*$ is established via Jensen's inequality.

Recall that our objective is to find optimal insurance policies when the insured is facing two potential losses. In Theorem 5 it was proved that any Pareto optimal coverage function depends only on the aggregate loss. The aggregate loss is denoted by $y = x_1 + x_2$ with probability density function $g(y)$. Using Theorem 5, we can rewrite problem (22)–(24) as: Find a coverage function $I(y)$ to maximize

$$\int_y U[w - P - y + I(y)] g(y) dy$$

subject to the constraints

[6] I am indebted to Arie Tamir for suggesting this intuitive approach.

$\int_y V[W_0 + P - I(y) - c(I(y))]g(y)dy \geq k$

$$0 \leq I(y) \leq y$$

The above problem has the same structure as the problem considered in Sections II–IV with $y$ replacing $x$. Thus, all the results regarding optimal insurance policies hold unchanged when the insured faces more than one risk, when the loss considered is the aggregate loss from all those risks. For example, if a risk-neutral insurer offers insurance policies and incurs linear cost, then it was proved that the Pareto optimal policy involves full coverage of losses beyond the deductible. Hence, we can now state:

**COROLLARY 1′:** *If $c(I) = lI$ and the insurer is risk neutral, the Pareto optimal policy is given by:*

$$I^*(x_1, x_2) = \begin{cases} 0 & \text{for } x_1 + x_2 \leq \overline{x} \\ x_1 + x_2 - \overline{x} & \text{for } x_1 + x_2 > \overline{x} \end{cases}$$

*where $\overline{x} > 0$ if and only if $l > 0$.*

Similarly, all the theorems of the previous sections can be now restated with the only difference being that the loss considered is interpreted as the aggregate loss during the period of insurance protection.

### VI. Conclusions

In this paper the prevalence of different insurance contracts was explained. It was shown that the Pareto optimal insurance contract involves a deductible and coinsurance of losses above the deductible. The deductible feature was shown to depend on the insurance costs. The coinsurance is due to either risk or cost sharing between the two parties. The upper limits on insurance were shown to be Pareto suboptimal. Their prevalence was shown to be in the interest of the regulated insurer. All results were obtained for single as well as multiple losses.

Two shortcomings of the above analysis should be noted. First, adverse selection problems were not analyzed; both the insurer and the insured were assumed to know the probability distribution function of the losses. Second, moral hazard problems were ignored; the monetary loss was assumed exogenous and not under the insured's control. A detailed analysis of the optimal contracts in these cases is much more difficult and was not attempted here.

### APPENDIX A

PROOF of Lemma 2:
a) If $P \epsilon S_1$, $I^*(x) = 0$ for $x \leq \overline{x}_1$. For $x > \overline{x}_1$, $I^*(x) = \int_{\overline{x}_1}^x I^{*\prime}(t)dt$, where $I^{*\prime}$ is given by (10). Differentiating with respect to $\overline{x}_1$,

$$\frac{\partial I^*(x)}{\partial \overline{x}_1} = -I^{*\prime}(\overline{x}_1) + \int_{\overline{x}_1}^x \frac{\partial I^{*\prime}(t)}{\partial I^*} \cdot \frac{\partial I^*(t)}{\partial \overline{x}_1} dt$$

Solving this equation yields

$$\frac{\partial I^*(x)}{\partial \overline{x}_1} = -I^*(\overline{x}_1) \exp \left\{ \int_{\overline{x}_1}^x \frac{\partial I^{*\prime}(t)}{\partial I^*} dt \right\} < 0$$

Part (b) is proved similarly.

### APPENDIX B

PROOF of Theorem 3:
From (7) we have that for all $P \epsilon S_1$

$$\overline{V}(P, I^*) = \int_0^{\overline{x}_1} V[W_0 + P - a] f(x)dx + \int_{\overline{x}_1}^T V(B) f(x)dx = k$$

By differentiating we obtain expressions for $d\overline{P}/d\overline{x}_1$ when $\overline{V}$ and $\overline{U}$ are held constant. These are shown on page 95. From (12′) and (14) we have that for $x \geq \overline{x}_1$

(A1) $\dfrac{U'(A)}{U'(w - P - \overline{x}_1)} =$

$\dfrac{V'(B)(1 + c')}{V'(W_0 + P - a)[1 + c'(0)]}$

Therefore,

(A2) $\dfrac{1}{U'(w - P - \overline{x}_1)}$

$\int_{x_1}^T U'(A) \dfrac{\partial I^*}{\partial \overline{x}_1} f(x)dx =$

$$\frac{dP}{d\bar{x}_1}\Big|_{V\text{-}const} = \frac{\int_{\bar{x}_1}^{T} V'(B)(1 + c')\frac{\partial I^*}{\partial \bar{x}_1} f(x)dx}{\int_{0}^{\bar{x}_1} V'[W_0 + P - a]f(x)dx + \int_{\bar{x}_1}^{T} V'(B)[1 - (1 + c')\frac{\partial I^*}{\partial P}]f(x)dx}$$

$$\frac{dP}{d\bar{x}_1}\Big|_{\bar{U}\text{-}const} = \frac{\int_{\bar{x}_1}^{T} U'(A)\frac{\partial I^*}{\partial \bar{x}_1} f(x)dx}{\int_{0}^{\bar{x}_1} U'(w - P - x)f(x)dx + \int_{\bar{x}_1}^{T} U'(A)\left(1 - \frac{\partial I^*}{\partial P}\right)f(x)dx}$$

---

$$\frac{1}{V'(W_0 + P - a)[1 + c'(0)]}$$
$$\int_{x_1}^{T} V'(B)(1 + c')\frac{\partial I^*}{\partial \bar{x}_1} f(x)dx$$

To prove sufficiency, assume $c'(\cdot) = 0$. From (A1) and since $x$ in the first integral is smaller than $\bar{x}_1$ we have

(A3) $\dfrac{1}{U'(w - P - \bar{x}_1)}$
$$\left\{\int_{0}^{\bar{x}_1} U'(w - P - x)f(x)dx + \int_{\bar{x}_1}^{T} U'(A)\left(1 - \frac{\partial I^*}{\partial P}\right)f(x)dx\right\}$$

$$\leq \frac{1}{V'(W_0 + P - a)}$$
$$\left\{\int_{0}^{\bar{x}_1} V'(W_0 + P - a)f(x)dx + \int_{\bar{x}_1}^{T} V'(B)\left(1 - \frac{\partial I^*}{\partial P}\right)f(x)dx\right\}$$

Dividing (A2) by (A3) and recalling that, by Lemma 2, $\partial I^*/\partial \bar{x}_1 < 0$

$$\frac{dP}{d\bar{x}_1}\Big|_{\bar{U}\text{-}const} \leq \frac{dP}{d\bar{x}_1}\Big|_{\bar{V}\text{-}const}$$

with the equality holding only if $\bar{x}_1 = 0$. Thus the optimal policy is $\bar{x}_1 = 0$ and the premium is $P_0$ as was claimed.

To prove necessity, assume $c'(0) > 0$. There exists $y > 0$ such that

$$\frac{U'(w - P)}{U'(w - P - y)} = \frac{1}{1 + c'(0)}$$

Using (A1) for $\bar{x}_1 > y$ we obtain

(A4) $\dfrac{1}{U'(w - P - \bar{x}_1)}$
$$\left\{\int_{0}^{\bar{x}_1} U'(w - P - x)f(x)dx + \int_{\bar{x}_1}^{T} U'(A)\left(1 - \frac{\partial I^*}{\partial P}\right)f(x)dx\right\}$$

$$\geq \frac{1}{V'(W_0 + P - a)[1 + c'(0)]}$$
$$\left\{\int_{0}^{\bar{x}_1} V'(W_0 + P - a)f(x)dx + \int_{\bar{x}_1}^{T} V'(B)(1 + c')\left(1 - \frac{\partial I^*}{\partial P}\right)f(x)dx\right\}$$

$$> \frac{1}{V'(W_0 + P - a)[1 + c'(0)]}$$
$$\left\{\int_{0}^{\bar{x}_1} V'(W_0 + P - a)f(x)dx + \int_{\bar{x}_1}^{T} V'(B)[1 - (1 + c')\frac{\partial I^*}{\partial P}]f(x)dx\right\}$$

The last inequality is obtained since $c' > 0$. Dividing (A2) by (A4) and since $\partial I^*/\partial \bar{x}_1 < 0$ we have that for $\bar{x}_1 < y$

$$\frac{dP}{d\bar{x}_1}\Big|_{\bar{U}\text{-}const} > \frac{dP}{d\bar{x}_1}\Big|_{\bar{V}\text{-}const}$$

Therefore, the optimal deductible level in this case is different from zero, as we argued.

## REFERENCES

**Kenneth J. Arrow,** *Essays in the Theory of Risk Bearing,* Chicago 1971.

———, "Optimal Insurance and Generalized Deductibles," Rand Corp., R-1108-OEO, Feb. 1973.

**K. Borch,** "The Safety Loading of Reinsurance Premiums," *Skand. Aktuarietidskrift,* 1960, 162–84.

———, "Equilibrium in a Reinsurance Market," *Econometrica*, July 1962, *30*, 424–44.

**J. P. Gould,** "The Expected Utility Hypothsis and the Selection of Optimal Deductibles for a Given Insurance Policy," *J. Bus., Univ. Chicago*, Apr. 1969, *42*, 143–51.

**P. L. Joskow,** "Cartels, Competition and Regulation in the Property-Liability Insurance Industry," *Bell J. Econ.*, Autumn 1973, *4*, 375–427.

**M. I. Kamien and N. L. Schwartz,** "Sufficient Conditions in Optimal Control Theory," *J. Econ. Theory*, June 1971, *3*, 207–14.

**J. Mossin,** "Aspects of Rational Insurance Purchasing," *J. Polit. Econ.*, July/Aug. 1968, *76*, 533–68.

**V. L. Smith,** "Optimal Insurance Coverage," *J. Polit. Econ.*, Jan./Feb. 1968, *76*, 68–77.

**R. B. Wilson,** "The Theory of Syndicates," *Econometrica*, Jan. 1968, *36*, 119–32.

# Risk Aversion and the Negotiation of Insurance Contracts

Richard E. Kihlstrom and Alvin E. Roth

## ABSTRACT

A game-theoretic model is used to study the effect of risk aversion on the outcome of bargaining over the terms of an insurance contract. When the insurer is risk netural, it prefers to bargain with the more risk averse of any two potential clients, since that client will agree to spend more, for less insurance, than will a less risk averse client. Bargaining over insurance contracts leads to results that differ from those obtained in a competitive insurance market. In a competitive market, clients seeking to insure against the same loss choose the same insurance contract, regardless of their risk posture.

## Introduction

This paper uses a game-theoretic model to study the insurance contracts reached through direct negotiation, in a non-competitive context. In this situation, a single insurer insures many risks similar to and approximately independent of that being analyzed. This permits the insurer to diversify these risks, to behave as though it were risk neutral, and to insure at essentially fair rates. The client, on the other hand, faces a relatively small number of these risks and therefore cannot self-insure at fair rates. The client therfore bargains as though he or she were risk averse. The fact that clients bargain rather than behaving competitively is justified if the client is a relatively large client who does repeat business and who faces large risks.[1] Industrial insurance of large companies or marine insurance of oil tankers are examples of situations to which this analysis might, at least as an approximation, be applied.

Richard E. Kihlstrom is Professor of Finance and Economics at the University of Pennsylvania. A Ph.D. in Economics from the University of Minnesota, he has also taught at Northwestern University, the University of Massachusetts, the State University of New York at Stony Brook, the University of Illinois, and the University of Iowa. He has co-edited a forthcoming book entitled *Bayesian Models in Economic Theory* and is a frequent contributor to professional journals. In 1979 he was elected a Fellow of the Econometric Society.

Alvin E. Roth is a Professor in the Department of Business Administration and the Department of Economics of the University of Illinois. A Ph.D. from Stanford University, he won the 1980 Founders' Award of the Texas Instruments Foundation. He also has published articles in several professional journals.

*The work of the two authors was supported by NSF Grants SOC 77-27403 and SOC 78-09928 to the University of Illinois.

[1] Competitive behavior is price taking. In other words, a client who behaves competitively takes prices as given.

In other interesting situations, the assumption of insurer risk neutraility cannot be justified by the above or other arguments. In these situations, the approach developed in this paper can be viewed as a first step toward a theory of negotiated insurance contracts. Subsequent steps would, of course, require an extension of the results presented below to the case of risk averse insurers.

This paper focuses on the effect of the clients' risk aversion on the outcome of bargaining about the terms of an insurance contract. In particular, consider a situation in which a risk averse individual, faced with a possible financial loss, bargains with a risk neutral insurance company. The two parties bargain about the amount of insurance to be provided as well as its price. In such a situation it seems reasonable to expect that the insurance company will be more successful in bargaining against a more risk averse client than against one who is less risk averse. The formal analysis of this situation that follows considers a game theoretic model of bargaining whose predictions are consistent with this expectation. This result is contrasted with results obtained when insurance contracts are determined through exchanges in competitive insurance markets. When insurance markets are competitive, risk aversion need be of no disadvantage to the insured. In fact, as is well known, in a competitive market equilibrium the price of insurance is actuarily fair regardless of the risk aversion of the insured, as long as the insurer is risk netural. Futhermore, at this price the risk averse insured always chooses to be fully covered.

The formal model used to obtain these results has the following features. Risk aversion of the insured is introduced by assuming that he or she maximizes the expected value of a concave von Neumann-Morganstern utility function. As usual, risk neutrality of the insurer is interpreted to mean that it maximizes expected income.[2] Associated with each possible insurance contract is an expected utility for the insured and an expected income for the insurer. The set of all expected utility-expected income pairs associated with all possible contracts describes a Nash bargaining game in which the "disagreement point" is the expected utility-expected income pair that results when no insurance is provided. This means that if bargaining breaks down and no agreement is achieved, no insurance is provided. The outcome of bargaining is assumed to be the insurance contract predicted by the Nash solution to this bargaining game.

In this situation, increases in the risk aversion of the insured are introduced using the Arrow-Pratt risk aversion measure. Using arguments similar to those in Kihlstrom, Roth and Schmeidler [1979], it is possible to describe the effect of an increase in the Arrow-Pratt risk averseness of the insured on the set of expected utility-expected income pairs that defines the Nash bargaining game and on the Nash solution to this game. In particular, it will be shown that the insurer obtains a higher expected income when it bargains against a more

---

[2] That is, the insurer maximizes the expected value of a linear von Neumann-Morganstern utility function, so that his or her utility for a given lottery is equal to the expected income received from that lottery.

risk averse client than when it bargains against a less risk averse client seeking to insure against the same potential loss. This is shown to imply that more risk averse clients who bargain against risk neutral insurers pay higher insurance premiums for less insurance than less risk averse clients in the same situation.

Before the insurance situation is described in Section 3, Section 2 discusses the bargaining game and Nash's solution. Section 4 begins with a derivation of the bargaining game implicit in the insurance situation. The manner in which the game depends on the risk aversion of the client is then characterized, and this characterization is used to determine the influence of an increase in the client's risk aversion on the insurance contract that yields the Nash solution to the bargaining game.

## A Model of Bargaining

Nash [1950] modeled any two-player bargaining game by a pair (S,d), where S is a compact and convex subset of the plane, representing the set of feasible expected utility payoffs to the players in the event of disagreement. He also assumed that S contains at least one point s such that s > d. This confines our attention to games in which it is possible for both players to gain from an agreement. The rules of the game are that any payoff vector in S will be the result of the game if it is agreed to by both players, and if no agreement is reached, each player receives his disagreement payoff. That is, if the players agree on a point $y = (y_1, y_2)$ in S, the resulting utility payoffs to the two players are $y_1$ and $y_2$, and in the event that no agreement is reached, the players receive $d_1$ and $d_2$, respectively. Thus the rules of the game give each player a veto over any outcome different from d, and it will be natural here to think of the disagreement outcome d as corresponding to the "status quo," which can only be altered by an agreement between the bargainers.

Nash modeled the bargaining process as a function called a *solution*, which selects, for any bargaining game, a unique feasible outcome. Letting B denote the class of all bargaining games, a solution f is a function f: $B \rightarrow R^2$ such that, for every game (S,d) in B, f(S,d) is a point contained in S. (So a solution f models the bargaining process by predicting the outcome that will result.)

Nash proposed that a solution intended to model bargaining among rational players should possess the following properties.

Property 1: Pareto optimality. If f(S,d) = z and $y \geq z$, either y = z or else y is not contained in S.

Property 2: Symmetry. If (S,d) is a symmetric game (i.e., if $d_1 = d_2$ and if $(x_1,x_2) \in$ S implies $(x_2,x_1) \in$ S), $f_1(S,d) = f_2(S,d)$.

Property 3: Independence of irrelevant alternatives.[3] If (S,d) and (T,d) are games such that T contains S and f(T,d) is an element of S, f(S,d) = f(T,d).

Property 4: Independence of equivalent utility representatives. If (S',d') is related to (S,d) by the transformations $d' = (a_1d_1 + b_1, a_2d_2 + b_2)$ and S' = $\{(a_1y_1 + b_1, a_2y_2 + b_2) \mid (y_1,y_2) \in$ S$\}$ where $a_1$, $a_2$, $b_1$ and $b_2$ are numbers such that $a_1, a_2 > 0$, f(S',d') is related to f(S,d) by the same transformations. That is, if f(S',d') = z' and f(S,d) =

---

[3] Perhaps a more descriptive name for this property is "independence of alternatives other than the disagreement point" (cf. Roth [1977b]).

$z, z' = (a_1 z_1 + b_1, a_2 z_2 + b_2)$.

Because these properties have been discussed elsewhere at great length (cf. Nash [1950], Luce and Raiffa [1957], Roth [1979]), this paper will not discuss them further, except to note that Property 4 is the only property that is directly motivated by the fact that the payoffs to the players are assumed to be expressed in terms of their expected utility functions. Since each player's utility function is uniquely defined only up to the arbitrary choice of its origin and scale, Property 4 requires that the utility payoff selected by the solution for a player should be defined with respect to the same origin and scale as are the other feasible payoffs for that player. Nash proved the following important theorem:

> Theorem 2.1: There is a unique solution which possesses Properties 1-4. It is the solution $f = F$ defined by $F(S,d) = z$ such that $z \geq d$ and $(z_1 - d_1)(z_2 - d_2) > (y_1 - d_1)(y_2 - d_2)$ for all y in S such that $y \geq d$ and $y \neq z$.

That is, Nash's solution F selects the (unique) outcome z in S that is individually rational (i.e., $z \geq d$) and that maximizes the geometric average (i.e., the product) of the gains that the players achieve by agreeing instead of disagreeing.

A well-known alternative characterization of Nash's solution F is that it selects the unique point $z = F(S,d)$ such that the line joining d to z has the negative slope of some tangent to S at z. That is, let $\phi$ be the function such that all Pareto optimal points $y = (y_1, y_2)$ of S can be represented as $y = (y_1, \phi(y_1))$. Then the tangent to S at z has slope $\phi'(z_1)$, and the following lemma results. (For simplicity, the result is stated for the case of $\phi$ differentiable at $z_1$.)

> Lemma 2.1: For any game $(S,d)$, $F(S,d) = z$ is the point such that $(\phi(z_1) - d_2)/(z_1 - d_1) = -\phi'(z_1)$.

Note that the individual rationality of Nash's solution is consistent with the assumption that each player's payoffs are expressed in terms of his or her expected utility function, which models the choice behavior. The disagreement outcome can be chosen by either player acting alone, and so if Player i is faced with a choice of agreeing on an outcome z or taking the disagreement payoff, he or she will choose z only if $z_i \geq d_i$. That is, because each player chooses between a potential agreement z and the disagreement payoff so as to maximize his or her utility, only if $z \geq d$ can it be agreed to by both players. Roth [1977a, 1979] has recently shown that when the individual rationality of the players is made explicit, it is not necessary to assume Pareto optimality in order to characterize Nash's solution. That is, the following theorem results.

Theorem 2.2: There are precisely two solutions f which are individually rational (i.e., $f(S,d) \geq d$) and which possess properties 2-4. One is Nash's solution $f = F$, and the other is the *disagreement solution* $f = D$, defined by $D(S,d) = d$ for every game $(S,d)$.

Consequently, there are only two individually rational modes of behavior consistent with Properties 2-4; one of which yields disagreement in every game, while the other yields Nash's solution. In other words, Nash's solution

F is the unique individually rational solution that is consistent with Properties 2-4 and that yields an outcome other than disagreement for at least one game.

Thus Nash's solution is intimately associated with the individual rationality of the players, which is an ordinal property of their utility functions. Although Nash made no explicit use of individual rationality, it can essentially replace the assumption of Pareto optimality, which can be viewed as an assumption of collective rationality.

Of course, the expected utility functions of the players convey more than just ordinal information about the players' preferences. In particular, each player's expected utility function also summarizes his or her preferences over risky alternatives. A recent paper by Kihlstrom, Roth and Schmeidler [1979] showed that, for bargaining games that arise from bargaining over riskless alternatives, Nash's solution is responsive in an intuitively plausible way to changes in the risk posture of the bargainers. It was further shown that this property of "risk sensitivity" could be used to replace Property 4 in the assumptions used in Theorem 2.1 to characterize the solution F on games that arise from bargaining over riskless alternatives.

This paper studies the responsiveness of Nash's solution to changes in the risk posture of the players in bargaining games that arise from bargaining over risky alternatives. In particular, the paper will examine bargaining games that arise from bargaining over possible insurance contracts. The paper will use the notion of risk posture first introduced by Arrow [1965,1971] and Pratt [1964]. For the case of utility functions a single variable (such as money), a utility function $\hat{w}$ will be said to be *at least as risk averse* as another utility function w if $\hat{w} = k(w)$, where k is an increasing concave function. The utility function $\hat{w}$ is said to be (strictly) *more risk averse* than w if the function k is strictly concave.

Note that for any model of bargaining that depends in a non-trivial way on the expected utility function of the bargainers, the underlying assumption is that the risk aversion of the bargainers influences the outcome of bargaining. That is, the risk aversion of the bargainers influences the decisions they make in the course of negotiations, which in turn influence the outcome of bargaining. (See Roth [1979], for an explicit treatment.) Consequently, when the paper considers the effect that risk aversion has on the outcome of bargaining, it does not assume that the bargainers need to know one another's risk posture.

### An Insurance Problem

Envision a sitution with two individuals, one of whom faces a possible financial loss. This individual will be referred to as the client, and his or her wealth (in dollars) will be $\omega_C > 0$ if the loss fails to occur. If, however, the loss occurs, it will amount to L dollars and his or her resulting after-loss wealth will be $\omega_C - L > 0$. The other individual will be referred to as the insurer. The insurer's wealth is $\omega_I$ dollars and he or she is not faced with the possibility of any exogenously determined losses. The insurer may however agree to bear some of the burden of the client's loss in the event it arises; i.e., he or she may agree to insure the client. Of course, the insurer must be induced to assume this risk. The inducement comes in the form of a premium payment made from the client to the insurer in the event that no loss is incurred. If the insurer assumes A dollars of the client's loss and receives a premium payment of P dollars in the event of no loss, his or her resulting wealth will be

$$x_{I\ell} = \omega_I - A \tag{1}$$

if the loss occurs and

$$x_{In} = \omega_I + P \tag{2}$$

if no loss occurs.[4] With this insurance contract in force, the client's wealth is

$$x_{C\ell} = \omega_C - L + A \tag{3}$$

if the loss is incurred and

$$x_{Cn} = \omega_C - P \tag{4}$$

when no loss is incurred.

Following Arrow [1963-4] and Debreu [1959], a claim to wealth that is contingent on the event that there is no loss can be considered to be a different good than a claim to wealth contingent on the event of a loss. If the event "no loss" is called "state n" and the event "loss" is called "state $\ell$," then $x_{is}$ is individual i's claims to wealth contingent on the occurence of state s. The variable i can equal I or C and s can equal $\ell$ or n.

The economy composed of these two individuals has $\omega_C + \omega_I$ contingent claims to wealth in state n and $x_C + \omega_I - L$ contingent claims to wealth in state $\ell$. Before an insurance contract is agreed to, $x_{I\ell} = \omega_I = x_{In}$ while $x_{Cn} = \omega_C$ and $x_{C\ell} = \omega_C - L$. If (A,P) is the agreed upon insurance contract, $x_{is}$ is given by (1)–(4) for i = I and C and s = $\ell$ and n.

The contingent claims allocations $(x_{In}, x_{I\ell}, x_{Cn}, x_{C\ell})$ which are feasible for this economy in the sense that

$x_{In} + x_{Cn} = \omega_C + \omega_I$
and

$x_{I\ell} + x_{C\ell} = \omega_C + \omega_I - L$
are described as points in the Edgeworth Box represented in Figure 1.

In Figure 1, the initial allocation of contingent claims is denoted by $\alpha$ and the allocation of these claims implied by some insurance contract (A, P) is shown as $\beta$. In fact, any allocation can be achieved from $\alpha$ by an insurance contract (A, P). However, only a small subset of these insurance contracts would be entered into voluntarily by both the client and the insurer. This subset is the shaded region in Figure 1, if $J_I(\alpha)$ is the indifference curve of the insurer through the initial allocation $\alpha$ and if $J_C(\alpha)$ is the indifference curve of the client through the initial allocation.

---

[4] A is, in fact, the net payment made by the insurer when a loss occurs. It equals the gross payment less the premium P which is paid at the outset when the insurance agreement is arranged.

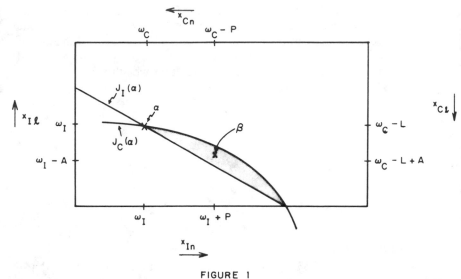

FIGURE 1

Since the insurer maximizes expected wealth, his or her indifference curve through $\alpha$ is

$$J_I(\alpha) = \{(x_{In}, x_{I\ell}) : \mu_\ell x_{I\ell} + \mu_n x_{In} = \omega_I\}$$

where $\mu_s$ is the *objective* probability of state s. That is, $J_I(\alpha)$ is the set of contingent claim vectors $(x_{In}, x_{I\ell})$ with expected value equal to $\omega_I$. Note that, at every point on the indifference curve $J_I(\alpha)$, the marginal rate of substitution for the insurer is

$$MRS_I(x_{In}, x_{I\ell}) = \mu_n/\mu_\ell \tag{5}$$

the ratio of the probabilities. In fact, similar comments can be made about any of the insurer's indifference curves. That is, along any insurer indifference curve, the expected wealth of all contingent claim vectors is constant and, as a result, the MRS is given by (5).

The situation is different for the client since $u_C$, his or her utility function of wealth, is strictly concave. A number of authors have shown that the function $U_C(x_{Cn}, x_{C\ell})$ defined by

$$U_C(x_{Cn}, x_{C\ell}) \equiv \mu_n u_C(x_{Cn}) + \mu_\ell u_C(x_{C\ell}) \tag{6}$$

is strictly concave if and only if the function $u_C$ is strictly concave. On this subject see, for example, Arrow [1963-4], Hirshleiffer [1965], Cox [1973], and Debreu and Koopmans [1978]. Because $U_C$ is strictly concave, all of his or her indifference curves have the same shape as $J_C(\alpha)$ in Figure 1. $J_C(\alpha)$ is the client's indifference curve through his or her initial allocation $(\omega_C, \omega_C - L)$. Also notice that since the client's utility function $U_C$ for contingent claims vectors $(x_{Cn}, x_{C\ell})$ is defined in (6), his or her marginal rate of substitution at $(x_{Cn}, x_{C\ell})$ is

$$\text{MRS}_C(x_{Cn}, x_{C\ell}) = \frac{\mu_n u'_C(x_{Cn})}{\mu_\ell u'_C(x_{C\ell})} , \qquad (7)$$

if, as assumed here, $u'_C$ exists.

Before deriving the bargaining game implicit in this situation, it is instructive to describe the Pareto optimal allocations of contingent claims and the core of this economy as well as the competitive equilibrium allocation that would result if there existed competitive markets for contingent claims to wealth in each state. Kihlstrom and Pauly [1971] have shown how the model of competitive contingent claims markets can be reinterpreted to yield a model of a competitive market for insurance contracts. Using this interpretation, the competitive equilibrium to be described below can be viewed as the equilibrium that would result if insurance contracts were competitively traded.

The derivation of the Pareto optimal allocations begins by noting that the concavity assumptions made about $u_C$ and the risk neutrality of the insurer imply that an interior Pareto optimal allocation $(x_{In}, x_{I\ell}, x_{Cn}, x_{C\ell})$ satisfies the familar condition

$$\text{MRS}_C(x_{Cn}, x_{C\ell}) = \text{MRS}_I(x_{In}, x_{I\ell}) \qquad (8)$$

Using (5) and (7), (8) simplifies to

$$\frac{\mu_n u'_C(x_{Cn})}{\mu_\ell u'_C(x_{C\ell})} = \mu_n/\mu_\ell . \qquad (9)$$

Because the insurer and the client have been assumed to agree about the probability of a loss, the ratio $\mu_n/\mu_l$ is the same on both sides of (9), which can therefore be reduced to

$$\frac{u'_C(x_{Cn})}{u'_C(x_{C\ell})} = 1 . \qquad (10)$$

Since $u_C$ is assumed to be strictly concave, equation (10) implies that in any interior Pareto optimal allocation the client must be completely insured in the sense that

$$x_{Cn} = x_{C\ell} ; \qquad (11)$$

i.e., his or her wealth is subject to no random fluctuation. Since all losses must be covered, (11) in turn implies that

$$x_{I\ell} = x_{In} - L ; \qquad (12)$$

i.e., the entire loss must be borne by the insurer. This result is not surprising in view of the fact that the insurer is risk neutral while the client is risk averse. Three interior Pareto optimal allocations $\gamma$, $\delta$ and $\epsilon$ are depicted in the Edgeworth Box of Figure 2. Clearly, the insurer prefers $\epsilon$ to $\delta$ and $\delta$ to $\gamma$, while the ranking is reversed for the client.

All of the interior optima lie on the line $x_{Cn} = x_{C\ell}$ shown in Figure 2. The noninterior Pareto optimal allocations are those that lie on the lower edge of the box between $\xi$ and $\zeta$. Notice that at a noninterior optimal allocation, say $\eta$, the client's losses are not completely covered; i.e., $x_{C\ell} < x_{Cn}$; and $x_{I\ell} = 0$. Uncovered losses can be optimal if the insurer does not have the financial

272

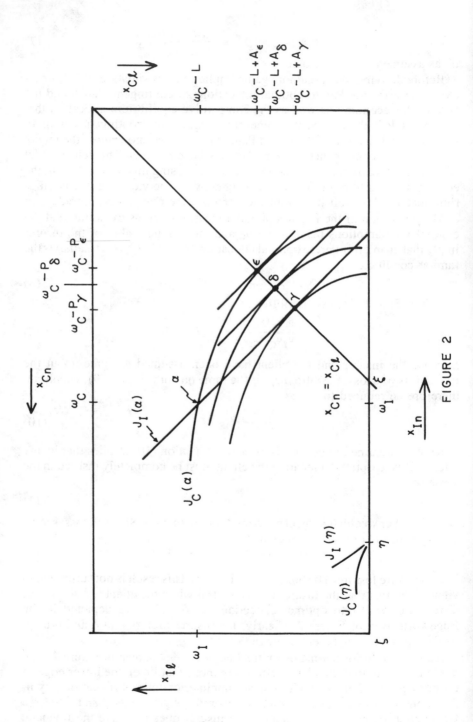

FIGURE 2

resources to provide complete coverage; i.e., if $x_{1\ell}$ becomes zero before $x_{C\ell}$ is raised to $x_{Cn}$.

The Pareto optimal allocations between $\gamma$ and $\epsilon$ are the only ones that both the insurer and the client would voluntarily choose in preference to $\alpha$ at which no insurance is provided. These are the core allocations for this economy. At $\epsilon$, all of the gains from insurance accrue to the insurer. The client is indifferent between $\alpha$ and $\epsilon$, and the wealth, $x_{Cn} = x_{C\ell}$, he or she receives in this allocation is the certainty equivalent of the gamble faced without insurance. At $\gamma$, on the other hand, the client receives all of the gains from insurance. The insurer is indifferent between $\alpha$ and $\gamma$ because he or she has the same expected wealth in both allocations.

Figure 2 assumes that all of the core allocations are interior. The remaining analysis will continue to assume that this property of Figure 2 holds; i.e., that all core allocations are interior allocations. This means that in any core allocation the insurer is financially able to provide complete coverage. Since

$$P_\gamma < P_\delta < P_\epsilon \tag{13}$$

and

$$A_\gamma > A_\delta > A_\epsilon \ , \tag{14}$$

the policy $(A_\gamma, P_\gamma)$ requires more finanical reserves from the insurer than any other core policy. Thus, if the insurer has sufficient wealth to provide policy $(A_\gamma, P_\gamma)$, he or she will indeed have the resources to provide complete coverage in all other core allocations.

Inequalities (13) and (14) assert that although $(P_\delta, A_\delta)$ is a more [less] expensive policy than $(P_\gamma, A_\gamma)$ [$(P_\epsilon, A_\epsilon)$], it provides less [more] insurance than $(P_\gamma, A_\gamma)$ [$(P_\epsilon, A_\epsilon)$]. In fact, it is in general true that as the Pareto optimal allocation is moved from $\gamma$ to $\epsilon$, the client does worse in two ways: the net coverage, A, is reduced and the premium, P, is increased.

The allocation $\gamma$ is the unique competitive equilibrium allocation in this economy and $\mu_n/\mu_\ell$ is the equilibrium relative price of contingent claims in state n in terms of claims to wealth in state $\ell$. Thus the competitive equilibrium insurance policy is $(P_\gamma, A_\gamma)$ at which point the client is receiving more coverage than at any other core policy and at which the price of this coverage is lower than at any other core policy.

Having described the Pareto optimal, core and competitive allocations, the paper now asks how an increase in risk aversion changes these allocations. These changes are described in Figure 3, in which the indifference curves of a client whose utility function is $u_C[\bar{u}_C]$ are denoted by $J_C[\bar{J}_C]$. The utility function $u_C$ is assumed to be less risk averse than $\bar{u}_C$ in the Arrow-Pratt sense. The indifference curves of the less [more] risk averse client are thus depicted as solid [dotted] curves. Observe that the increase in risk aversion from $u_C$ to $\bar{u}_C$ does not alter the set of Pareto optimal allocations. For a client with utility function $\bar{u}_C$, as for a client with utility function $u_C$, the interior optima continue to satisfy (11) and (12) and lie on the line $x_{Cn} = C_{C\ell}$ in Figure 3. Similarly for clients with either utility function, the noninterior optima are

274

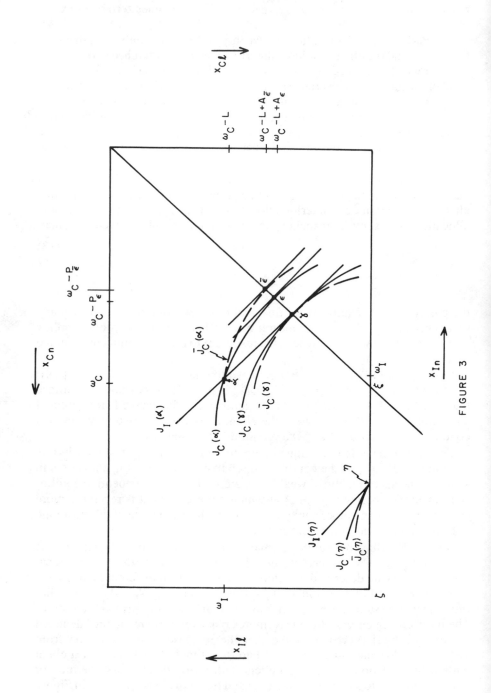

FIGURE 3

the allocations between $\xi$ and $\zeta$ on the lower edge of the Edgeworth Box in Figure 3.

Although the set of Pareto optimal allocations is unaffected when the client becomes more risk averse, the core is enlarged by this change. Specifically, when the utility function $u_c$ is replaced by $\bar{u}_C$, the certainty equivalent of the gamble faced by the uninsured client is reduced. Thus $\epsilon$ is replaced by $\bar{\epsilon}$. The Pareto optimal allocation that is indifferent to $\alpha$ for the insurer continues to be $\dot{\gamma}$ even after $\bar{u}_C$ replaces $u_C$. In Figure 3, the change in the utility function from $u_C$ to $\bar{u}_C$ changes the core from the points between $\gamma$ and $\epsilon$ to those between $\gamma$ and $\bar{\epsilon}$.

Finally, the competitive equilibrium allocation is unchanged by the increase in risk aversion. In Figure 3, $\gamma$ is the competitive allocation whether the client's utility function is $u_C$ or $\bar{u}_C$.

The following section considers insurance contracts arrived at through bargaining between the client and the insurer, using Nash's model of bargaining. It will show that, in contrast to the situation just described in which a change in the client's risk aversion has no impact on the competitive contract, the client's risk aversion does influence the contract arrived at as the Nash solution to the bargaining game played by the insurer and client.

## Bargaining Over the Insurance Contract

Let the insurer be Player 1 and the client Player 2, in a bargaining game (S,d) such that S is the set of expected utility payoffs to the players resulting from feasible insurance contracts and d is the pair of utility payoffs corresponding to the initial allocation $\alpha$. That is, $d_1 = U_I(\alpha) = u_I(\omega_I) = \omega_I$, $d_2 = U_C(\alpha) = U_C(\omega_C, \omega_C-L) = \mu_n u_C(\omega_C) + \mu_\ell u_C(\omega_C-L)$, and if $(y_1,y_2)$ is a point in S, there exists an insurance contract (A,P) such that

$$y_1 = \mu_n u_I(\omega_I+P) + \mu_\ell u_I(\omega_I-A) = \mu_n(\omega_I+P) + \mu_\ell(\omega_I-A)$$

$$y_2 = \mu_n u_C(\omega_C-P) + \mu_\ell u_C(\omega_C-L+A)$$

That is, each $(y_1,y_2)$ in S is the utility payoff vector to the players that corresponds to some feasible allocation of contingent claims $(x_{In}, x_{I\ell}, x_{Cn}, x_{C\ell})$; i.e., $y_1 = U_I(x_{In},x_{I\ell})$ and $y_2 = U_C(x_{Cn},x_{C\ell})$. Then S is a compact set, and the concavity of $U_C$ insures that S is convex.

The set of Pareto optimal utility payoffs in S corresponds to the set of contingent claims allocations that satisfy equations (11) and (12). So if $(z_1,z_2)$ is Pareto optimal in S, $z_1 = x_{In} - \mu_\ell L$ (since $x_{I\ell} = x_{In} -L$) and $z_2 = u_C(\omega_C+\omega_I-x_{In})$, since $x_{C\ell} = x_{Cn} = \omega_C+\omega_I-x_{In}$. So for any Pareto optimal point $(z_1,z_2)$, $z_2 = \phi(z_1)$ where $\phi$ is the decreasing concave function defined by $\phi(z_1)= u_C(\omega_C+\omega_I-(z_1+\mu_\ell L))$. The function $\phi$ can be thought of as determining the Pareto optimal subset P(S), since all Pareto optimal utility payoffs are of the form $(z_1, \phi(z_1))$.

Consider two potential insurance clients with utility functions for money w and $\hat{w}$, such that $\hat{w}$ is more risk averse than w. Then $\hat{w} = k(w)$, where k is an increasing concave function. Suppose that the game (S,d) is the bargaining game that results when client w bargains with the insurer over the set of feasible insurance contracts; i.e., (S,d) is the game in which $u_c = w$. Let $(\hat{S},\hat{d})$ be the game that results when, instead, client $\hat{w}$ bargains with the insurer; i.e., $(\hat{S},\hat{d})$ is the game in which $u_C = \hat{w} = k(w)$. Note that the set of insurance contracts corresponding to Pareto optimal utility payoffs is unaffected by the change from w to $\hat{w}$. So if $\phi$ and $\hat{\phi}$ are the functions that define the Pareto optimal subsets of S and $\hat{S}$ respectively, $\hat{\phi} = k(\phi)$. This observation will permit a proof of the following result.

> Theorem 4.1: Let $(\hat{S},\hat{d})$ be a bargaining game over insurance contracts, derived from (S,d) by replacing Player 2 (the client with utility function w) with a more risk averse client (whose utility function is $\hat{w} = k(w)$).
>
> 1) Then Nash's solution predicts that Player 1 will gain a higher utility when bargaining with the more risk averse client; i.e., $F_1(\hat{S},\hat{d}) > F_1(S,d)$.
>
> 2) If (A,P) and $(\hat{A},\hat{P})$ are the insurance contracts predicted by Nash's solution in the games (s,d) and $(\hat{S},\hat{d})$, respectively, $\hat{A} < A$ and $\hat{P} > P$. That is, a more risk averse client pays a higher premium and receives less coverage of his or her potential loss.

Roth [1978] has shown that Nash's solution can be interpreted as the utility function for bargaining in a given game for certain kinds of risk neutral players.[5] Interpreted in this way, Theorem 4.1 means that a risk neutral insurer prefers to bargain with a more risk averse client than with a less risk averse client.

Since bargaining over insurance contracts involves risky events, the results of Kihlstrom, Roth and Schmeidler [1979] cannot be directly applied to prove Theorem 4.1. Instead, the proof will proceed via the following lemma.

> Lemma 4.1: Let (S,d) be a bargaining game whose Pareto optimal points are of the form $(y_1, \phi(y_1))$, and let $(\hat{S},\hat{d})$ be a game whose Pareto optimal points are of the form $(y_1, \hat{\phi}(y_1))$, where $\phi$ and $\hat{\phi}$ are decreasing concave functions. Then, if $\hat{\phi} = k(\phi)$ where k is an increasing (strictly) concave function, it follows that $F_1(\hat{S},\hat{d}) > F_1(S,d)$.

Proof of the lemma: Since Nash's solution F is independent of equivalent utility representations, it will be sufficient to prove the lemma for the case when $d = \hat{d} = \overline{0}$, where $\overline{0}$ denotes the origin (i.e., $\overline{0} = (0,0)$). So let $z = F(S,\overline{0})$ and $\hat{z} = F(\hat{S},\overline{0})$; it is necessary to show that $\hat{z}_1 > z_1$. Since Nash's solution selects the point in S that maximizes the geometric average of the gains, it will be sufficient to show that the geometric average $A(y_1) = k(\phi(y_1))y_1$ as positive first derivative at $z_1$. But

$$A'(z_1) = k'(\phi(z_1))\phi'(z_1)z_1 + k(\phi(z_1)),$$

and by Lemma 2.1, $\phi'(z_1)z_1 = -\phi(z_1)$, so

$$A'(z_1) = -k'(\phi(z_1))\phi(z_1) + k(\phi(z_1))$$

$$= -k'(z_2)z_2 + k(z_2) = z_2[-k'(z_2) + (k(z_2)/z_2)] .$$

---

[5] Specifically, the Nash solution represents the utility of bargaining for a player who is neutral both to ordinary (probabilistic) risk and to strategic risk (cf. Roth [1978]).

Because the (strict) concavity of the function $k$ imples that $(k(z_2)/z_2) > k'(z_2)$, while the (strict) individual rationality of Nash's solution implies $z_2 > 0$, $A'(z_1) > 0$, as required.

Proof of Theorem 4.1: Part (1) of the theorem will follow from Lemma 4.1 once it can be shown that $\hat{\phi} = k(\phi)$, where $\hat{\phi}$ and $\phi$ are the functions defining the Pareto sets of $\hat{S}$ and $S$, respectively. But if $(y_1, \phi(y_1))$ is a Pareto optimal point in $S$, $y_1 = x_{In} - \mu_\ell L$ and $\phi(y_1) = w(\omega_c + \omega_I - x_{In})$, and the point $(y_1, k(\phi(y_1)))$ is Pareto optimal in $\hat{S}$, since $\hat{w}(\omega_c + \omega_I - x_{In}) = k(w(\omega_c + \omega_I - x_{In}))$. So $\hat{\phi} = k(\phi)$, and so $F_1(\hat{S}, \hat{d}) > F_1(S, d)$, as required.

To prove Part (2) of the theorem, note that if $x = (x_{In}, x_{I\ell}, x_{Cn}, x_{C\ell})$ and $\hat{x} = (x_{In}, x_{I\ell}, x_{Cn}, x_{C\ell})$ are the contingent claims allocations corresponding to the utility pairs $z = F(S, d)$ and $\hat{z} = \hat{F}(\hat{S}, \hat{d})$, $F_1(\hat{S}, \hat{d}) > F_1(S, d)$ implies that $\hat{x}_{In} > x_{In}$, (since x and $\hat{x}$ satisfy equations (11) and (12)). Consequently

$$x_{Cn} = x_{C\ell} = \omega_I + \omega_C - x_{In} < \omega_I + \omega_C - \hat{x}_{In} = \hat{x}_{Cn} = \hat{x}_{C\ell}.$$

By equation (2), $\hat{x}_{In} > x_{In}$ implies that $\hat{P} > P$, and by equation (3) $\hat{x}_{C\ell} < x_{C\ell}$ imples $\hat{A} < A$ where $(A, P)$ and $(\hat{A}, \hat{P})$ are the contracts that give rise to the contingent claims allocations x and $\hat{x}$, respectively. This completes the proof of the theorem.

The lemma can also be quickly demonstrated via the following informal, graphical representation. In figure 4 below, the solid curve $\phi$ represents the Pareto set of S. Then Lemma 2.1 states that the angles $\alpha$ and $\beta$ are equal, where $\alpha$ is the angle with the $x_1$ axis formed by the line joining d to $z = F(S, d)$, and $\beta$ is the angle with the $x_1$ axis formed by the tangent to $\phi$ at $F(S, d)$.

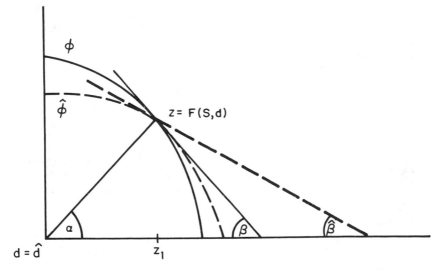

FIGURE 4

The dotted curve $\hat{\phi} = k(\phi)$ represents the Pareto set of $\hat{S}$. The angle $\hat{\beta}$ made by the tangent to $\hat{\phi}$ at $z$ is smaller than the angle $\beta$. Therefore $F(\hat{s}, \hat{d}) = \hat{z}$ must fall further to the right than $z_1$ so the angle $\hat{a}$ made by the line from $\hat{d}$ to $\hat{Z}$ will equal $\hat{\beta}$, as required by Lemma 2.1.

The results presented above can be generalized to bargaining solutions other than Nash's solution. In particular, Kihlstrom, Roth and Schmeidler [1981] showed that several solutions found in the literature possess essentially the same risk sensitivity property as does Nash's solution, and it is straightforward to generalize those results to the insurance problem considered here.

It is less clear how the results presented here can be generalized to insurance problems in which both the insurer and client are risk averse. Roth and Rothblum [1982] characterize how Nash's solution responds to changes in the risk aversion of the bargainers in a general setting where bargaining may involve lotteries, but where the disagreement point is riskless. Their results show that there are situations in which risk aversion can be advantageous, so that the results of Kihlstrom, Roth and Schmeidler [1981] do not generalize in a straightforward manner to all bargaining situations. The behavior of negotiated insurance contracts for more general insurance problems thus remains an open question.

## REFERENCES

1. Arrow, Kenneth J., *Aspects of the Theory of Risk-Bearing*, (Helsinki: Yrgo Foundation, 1965).

2. Arrow, Kenneth J., *Essays in the Theory of Risk-Bearing*, (New York: American Elsevier, 1971).

3. Arrow, Kenneth J., "The Role of Securities in the Optimal Allocation of Risk Bearing," *Review of Economic Studies*, Vol. XXXI (1963-1964), pp. 91-96; reprinted as Chapter 3 in Arrow, Kenneth J., *Essays in the Theory of Risk Bearing*, (New York: American Elsevier, 1971).

4. Cox, James, "A Theorem on Additively-Separable Quasi-Concave Functions," *Journal of Economic Theory*, Vol. VI (April 1973), pp. 210-213.

5. Debreu, Gerard, *Theory of Value*, (New York: Wiley, 1959).

6. Debreu, Gerard and Tjalling C. Koopmans, "Additively Decomposed Quasi-Convex Functions," unpublished paper presented at the 1978 Summer Meetings of the Econometric Society at Boulder, Colorado, June 1978.

7. Hirshleiffer, Jack, "Investment Decision Under Uncertainty: Choice Theoretic Approaches," *Quarterly Journal of Economics*, Vol. LXXIX (1965), pp. 509-536.

8. Kihlstrom, Richard E. and Mark Pauly, "The Role of Insurance in the Allocation of Risk," *The American Economic Review*, Vol. LXI, No. 2 (1971), pp. 371-379.

9. Kihlstrom, Richard E., Alvin E. Roth and David Schmeidler, "Risk Aversion and Solutions to Nash's Bargaining Problem," *Mathematical Economics,* O. Moeschlin and D. Pallasachke (eds.), (Amsterdam: North Holland, 1981).

10. Luce, R. Duncan and Howard Raiffa, *Games and Decisions: Introduction and Critical Survey,* (New York: John Wiley, 1957).

11. Nash, John F., "The Bargaining Problem," *Econometrica,* Vol. XXVIII (1950), pp.155-162.

12. Pratt, J.W, "Risk Aversion in the Small and in the Large," *Econometrica,* Vol. XXXII (1964), pp. 122-136.

13. Roth, Alvin E., "Individual Rationality and Nash's Solution to the Bargaining Problem," *Mathematics of Operations Research,* Vol. II, No. 1 (1977a), pp. 64-65.

14. Roth, Alvin E., "Independence of Irrelevant Alternatives and Solutions to Nash's Bargaining Problem," *Journal of Economic Theory,* Vol. XVI, No. 2 (1977b), pp. 247-251.

15. Roth, Alvin E., "The Nash Solution and the Utility of Bargaining," *Econometricia,* Vol. XLVI (1978), pp. 587-594, 983.

16. Roth, Alvin E., *Axiomatic Models of Bargaining,* (Berlin and New York: Springer, 1979).

17. Roth, Alvin E. and Uriel G. Rothblum, "Risk Aversion and Nash's Solution for Bargaining Games with Risky Outcomes," *Econometrica,* (forthcoming, 1982).

# ON MORAL HAZARD AND INSURANCE*

## STEVEN SHAVELL

## I. INTRODUCTION

Moral hazard refers here to the tendency of insurance protection to alter an individual's motive to prevent loss. This affects expenses for the insurer and therefore, ultimately, the cost of coverage for individuals. Beginning with Arrow [1963] and Pauly [1968], economists have discussed two partial solutions to the problem of moral hazard: (i) incomplete coverage against loss and (ii) "observation" by the insurer of the care taken to prevent loss. Incomplete coverage gives an individual a motive to prevent loss by exposing him to some financial risk; and observation of care also gives an individual a motive to prevent loss, as it allows the insurer to link to the perceived level of care either the insurance premium or the amount of coverage paid in the event of a claim.

In examining the partial solution to the problem of moral hazard afforded by incomplete coverage, it is convenient, and in some situations certainly realistic, to assume that observation of care is either impossible or too expensive to be worthwhile. Under that assumption, the degree to which it is desirable to reduce coverage and subject the insured to risk would depend on the incentive thereby created to exercise care, and such an incentive would in turn depend on the cost of taking care. This is the logic underlying the following results: as the cost of taking care falls from very high levels (at which full coverage is best), partial coverage becomes desirable; but at no point is the optimal level of coverage zero—moral hazard cannot entirely eliminate the possibilities for insurance; and as the cost of taking care approaches zero, the optimal coverage, although partial, approaches full coverage.

It is then assumed that observation of care is worthwhile. In this case attention is paid to the accuracy of the insurer's observations and to the timing of the observations, whether they are made ex ante—

* I wish to thank L. Weiss for helpful discussion; K. Arrow, P. Diamond, J. Green, L. Kotlikoff, M. Manove, J. Mirrlees, A. M. Polinsky, and A. Robson for comments; and the National Science Foundation (Grant #SOC76-20862) for financial support.

*The Quarterly Journal of Economics*, November 1979          0033-5533/79/0093-0541$01.00

whenever a policy is purchased—or ex post—only when a claim is presented.

If the insurer's observations are perfectly accurate, full coverage is desirable,[1] and the value of the information from the observations turns out to be the same whether they are made ex ante or ex post. Thus, if the total cost of ex post observation (which, recall, involves only those individuals presenting claims) is less than that of ex ante observation, it is best for the insurer to acquire information ex post.

If the insurer's observations are not precise, the problem arises that use of the perceived level of care imposes a new kind of risk on the insured. This is because the premium or level of coverage depends on the random factors influencing the insurer's observations. Nevertheless, if the observations convey information about changes in the level of care, it is possible to construct a policy for which the usefulness of the imperfect information as an incentive outweighs its negative effect through the imposition of risk. In contrast to the situation with perfectly accurate observations, partial coverage is generally desirable, and the value of information acquired ex ante exceeds that of information acquired ex post. This complicates the determination of the optimal timing of observations.

The present paper seems most closely related to Pauly [1974] on moral hazard when the insurer does not attempt to observe care; but the paper differs from this reference and most others[2] in that it (i) determines exactly when an insurance policy represents a compromise between no coverage and full coverage (in the case in which the insurer does not observe care), (ii) analyzes the choice concerning the timing of observation of care, and (iii) proves that imperfect information about care is valuable.

## II. THE MODEL

Individuals in the model are identical. Therefore, the analysis is relevant either when differences among individuals are unimportant or when these differences are in some way recognizable. In that case, different types of individuals may be treated in an independent manner by insurers.

---

1. This fact (at least for the case of ex ante observation) is well-known and is noted in most of the papers cited here.
2. See Ehrlich and Becker [1972], Helpman and Laffont [1975], Mirrlees [1975], Spence and Zeckhauser [1970], Stiglitz [1974], Townsend [1976], and Zeckhauser [1970]. See also Harris and Raviv [1978] and Shavell [1979] on the principal and agent relationship.

Each individual is assumed to act so as to maximize the expected utility of wealth, is averse to risk, faces the possibility of financial loss, and is able to affect the probability distribution of loss by taking care. Although care enters formally as an expenditure (for example, on the purchase of an anti-theft device), it may be interpreted also as "effort" (for example, remembering to lock up). Let

$U(\cdot)$      be a twice-differentiable, increasing, and strictly concave function giving utility of wealth;

$y > 0$      be initial wealth;

$x \geq 0$      be expenditure on care;

$l_i > 0$      $(i = 1, \ldots, n)$ be a possible loss;

$p_i(x) > 0$      $(i = 1, \ldots, n)$ be the probability of loss of $l_i$; and

$p_0(x) > 0$      be the probability of no loss.

Suppose that the expected value of losses falls with care; that is,

$$(1) \qquad \frac{d}{dx} \left[ \sum_{i=1}^{n} p_i(x) l_i \right] < 0.$$

However, to reduce the notational burden on the reader, the text considers only the case $i = 1$, in which there is a loss $l = l_1$ of fixed size occurring with probability $p(x) = p_1(x)$, where, by (1), $p'(x) < 0$. The Appendix discusses the general case; the three propositions of the text remain true in the general case.

The general case makes what appears to be the minimal assumption concerning the relation between care and the probability distribution of loss; that more care reduces loss on average. This allows for "self-insurance" (care that has the effect of reducing the magnitude of loss without affecting the probability of loss), for "self-protection" (care that has the effect of reducing the probability of loss without affecting the magnitude of loss), as well as for care that has more complicated effects.[3]

Insurance policies will be formally defined later. An insurance policy resulting in expected profits[4] of zero will be called a *break-even* policy. Ordinarily, different break-even policies would yield different levels of expected utility to an individual. *The problem investigated here is to determine a break-even policy that maximizes expected*

3. The terms self-insurance and self-protection are due to Ehrlich and Becker [1972]. Self-insurance is descriptive of the special case of the general model in which $\sum_{i=1}^{n} p_i(x)$ is a constant, but $p_i(x)$ falls for losses that are high and rises for losses that are low. Self-protection is descriptive of the case in which $p_i(x)$ is for each loss decreasing in $x$.

4. That insurers use the criterion of expected profits is based on the conventional assumptions that an insurer's risks are borne by many individuals (stockholders) and that the risks insured are numerous, small, and approximately independent.

*utility.* Such a break-even policy will be called the *optimal insurance policy under moral hazard.*

The optimal insurance policy under moral hazard may be interpreted in two ways: it may be regarded as the best policy that could be sold by a self-financing public insurer. Alternatively, it may be regarded as the policy that would be sold by firms in a competitive insurance industry with free entry, for then it is natural to assume that the only policies which could survive in the marketplace are those that yield expected profits of zero to insurers and, given that constraint, the highest possible expected utility to individuals.

The optimal insurance policy under moral hazard is to be distinguished from the *fully optimal insurance policy.* The latter is the policy that would be sold if an insurer could, in selecting the best break-even policy, choose *independently* an individual's care and the terms of the insurance policy. The problem of moral hazard is precisely that care is chosen by individuals and therefore *does* depend in general on the terms of the insurance policy.

### III. Moral Hazard When Care Is Not Observed by the Insurer

If it is either too expensive or impossible for the insurer to observe care, the terms under which insurance is sold obviously cannot depend on care. An insurance policy is therefore described simply by a premium $\pi \geq 0$ and level of coverage $q \geq 0$.[5] If an individual decides for some reason to buy a policy $(\pi, q)$, he then selects $x$ to maximize expected utility:

$$(2) \quad EU = (1 - p(x))U(y - \pi - x) + p(x)U(y - \pi - x - l + q).$$

It is assumed that the $x$ chosen (which will sometimes be written $x(\pi, q)$) is unique,[6] and therefore, if it is positive, it is identified by the first-order condition,

---

5. It is assumed here that $\pi$ and $q$ are not random. It is, however, possible (but, I would say, only a theoretical curiosity) that randomness might be desirable: Consider the function $e(r)$, where $e(r)$ is the highest expected utility that can be provided to individuals by insurers selling nonrandom policies and earning a return of $r$. Let $(\pi(r), q(r))$ be a policy that gives individuals expected utility $e(r)$ when the return to the insurer is $r$. There is no reason to suspect that $e(r)$ is not locally convex at 0. If it is locally convex at 0, choose $\epsilon$ small and let the insurer offer the policy $(\pi(-\epsilon), q(-\epsilon))$ with probability $\frac{1}{2}$ and $(\pi(\epsilon), q(\epsilon))$ with probability $\frac{1}{2}$. Then the insurer will break even, and individual expected utility will be $\frac{1}{2} e(-\epsilon) + \frac{1}{2} e(\epsilon) > e(0)$.

6. Expected utility may not be concave in $x$; there does not seem to be any simple condition on the function $p$ that would guarantee concavity. Mirrlees [1975] contains an interesting disscussion of this problem.

(3) $\quad p'(x)[U(y - \pi - x - l + q) - U(y - \pi - x)]$
$$= (1 - p(x))U'(y - \pi - x) + p(x)U'(y - \pi - x - l + q).$$

The left-hand side is the marginal benefit of taking care and the right-, the marginal cost. If (3) does not hold, then $x(\pi, q) = 0$ and

(4) $\quad p'(0)[U(y - \pi - l + q) - U(y - \pi)]$
$$< (1 - p(0))U'(y - \pi) + p(0)U'(y - \pi - l + q).$$

A break-even policy must satisfy

(5) $$\pi = p(x(\pi,q))q,$$

since expected profits of the insurer must be zero given that individuals choose care. It is assumed that given the coverage $q$, there is a unique premium $\pi(q)$ such that the insurer breaks even.[7] Writing $x(q)$ for $x(\pi(q),q)$, we may express expected utility as a function of $q$:

(6) $\quad EU(q) = (1 - p(x(q)))U(y - \pi(q) - x(q))$
$$+ p(x(q))U(y - \pi(q) - x(q) - l + q).$$

The optimal insurance policy under moral hazard is found by maximizing (6) over $q$; this policy will be denoted $(\bar{\pi}, \bar{q})$ and will be assumed unique. Differentiate (6) with respect to $q$ to obtain (noting that $\pi' = x'p'q + p$):

(7)
$$EU'(q) = x'p'[U(y - \pi - x - l + q) - U(y - \pi - x)]$$
$$-x'[(1 - p)U'(y - \pi - x) + pU'(y - \pi - x - l + q)]$$
$$-x'p'q[(1 - p)U'(y - \pi - x) + pU'(y - \pi - x - l + q)]$$
$$-p[(1 - p)U'(y - \pi - x) + pU'(y - \pi - x - l + q)]$$
$$+ pU'(y - \pi - x - l + q).$$

The five terms in this expression reflect, respectively, the following changes that would accompany a small increase in coverage, with the premium adjusting so as to allow the insurer to break even:

(a) a change in the probability of loss

(b) a change in the level of care

(c) a change in the premium due to a change in the premium *rate* per dollar of coverage

(d) a change in the premium due to an increased *level* of coverage

---

7. That there exists some such $\pi$ is clear: Assuming that $x(\pi,q)$ is continuous, we note that the function $f(\pi) = p(x(\pi,q))q$ is continuous and maps $[0,q] \rightarrow [0,q]$. Therefore $f(\cdot)$ has a fixed point, at which $\pi = p(x(\pi,q))q$.

(e) a change in the level of coverage.

The changes in expected utility due to (a) and (b) are offsetting (if $x(q) > 0$), since the individual adjusts the level of care to equate them. Thus, (7) reduces to the last three terms, and (c), (d), and (e) are all that one needs to think about. It is in fact only (c), the change in the premium attributable to a change in the rate per dollar of coverage, that reflects moral hazard; (d) and (e) correspond to the benefits and costs of purchasing additional coverage at an actuarially fair rate in the absence of moral hazard. This will help to motivate the following result.

PROPOSITION 1. When care is not observed by the insurer, the optimal insurance policy under moral hazard

(a) always offers positive coverage—moral hazard alone cannot eliminate possibilities for insurance,

(b) offers partial rather than full coverage if the cost of taking care is sufficiently low, but the level of coverage approaches full coverage as the cost of taking care tends to zero.

*Note.* Starting from a position of no coverage, the term corresponding to (c) must be zero, since no premium is being paid. This is the explanation for the first part of the proposition.

The interpretation of the cost of care, denoted by $r$, is as follows. If one is thinking of care as an actual expenditure on a good, then $r$ should be regarded as the price of the good. Thus, if $x$ is the level of expenditure, $x/r$ is the amount purchased, and $p(x/r)$ is the probability of loss. On the other hand, if one is thinking of care as effort, $1/r$ should be regarded as the efficiency of effort. Thus, if $x$ is the level of effort, $x/r$ is a measure in "efficiency units," and $p(x/r)$ is the probability of loss. We shall assume here that the probability of loss is bounded above zero.

The explanation for the second part of the proposition is straightforward:[8] If it is not very costly to take care, then the incentive effect due to partial coverage should be strong. Therefore, the advantage of the incentive effect should outweigh the disadvantage of partial coverage, namely, the imposition of risk. Accordingly, we would

8. With regard to the use of partial coverage in a competitive setting, Pauly [1974] brings up the problem that private insurers may not know an individual's purchase of coverage from all sources, so that nothing would prevent an individual from arranging for full coverage by getting partial coverage from different insurers. To the extent that this is a problem, it would be advantageous to have coverage sold by only a single source, such as a public insurer. On the other hand, private insurers often have specific provisions concerning collection from multiple policies. For this and a variety of other reasons, individuals frequently choose to deal with a single company for related lines of insurance.

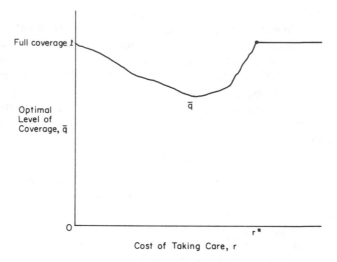

FIGURE I
Optimal Insurance Coverage Under Moral Hazard

expect partial coverage to be optimal if the cost of taking care is below some critical level. However, if it is very cheap to take care, little exposure to risk is needed to induce an individual to take care. Thus, we would expect nearly complete coverage to be optimal if the cost of taking care is close to zero. Figure I illustrates the second part of the proposition. Below a critical level $r^*$, optimal coverage $\bar{q}$ is partial, but $\bar{q}$ tends to $l$ as $r$ tends to 0. (As drawn, the graph falls and then rises between 0 and $r^*$, but it could look more complicated.)

*Proof.* To show that $\bar{q} > 0$, we want to verify that (7) is positive at $q = 0$. If at $q = 0$ the first-order condition (3) is satisfied, then (7) reduces to

$$(8) \quad - p[(1 - p)U'(y - \pi - x) + pU'(y - \pi - x - l)]$$
$$+ pU'(y - \pi - x - l)$$
$$= p(1 - p)[U'(y - \pi - x - l) - U'(y - \pi - x)] > 0.$$

On the other hand, if at $q = 0$ (3) is not satisfied, (4) holds, and $x(0) = 0$. In this case, it is easy to show that for all $q$ sufficiently small, $x(q) = 0.$[9] Therefore, $x'(0) = 0$, and (7) again reduces to (8).

---

9. Since $p'(0)[U(y - l) - U(y)] < (1 - p(0))U'(y) + p(0)U'(y - l)$, we must have for $q$ sufficiently small $p'(0)[U(y - qp(0) - l + q) - U(y - qp(0))] < (1 - p(0))U'(y - qp(0)) + p(0)U'(y - qp(0) - l + q)$.

Let $\bar{q}(r)$ be optimal coverage when the cost of taking care is $r$. To show that $\bar{q}(r) = l$ if $r$ is sufficiently high, note first that the first-order condition (3), which is appropriate only when $r = 1$, must be rewritten as

(3') $\quad (1/r)p'(x/r)[U(y - \pi - x - l + q) - U(y - \pi - x)]$
$\qquad = (1 - p(x/r))U'(y - \pi - x) + p(x/r)U'(y - \pi - x - l + q).$

Since this equation cannot hold if $r$ is sufficiently high (the maximum over $x$ and $q$ of the left-hand side tends to 0 as $r$ grows large, but the right-hand side is bounded above 0), we must have for such $r$ that $x(q) \equiv 0$. Hence $x'(q) = 0$, so that $EU'(q)$ reduces to $p(0)(1 - p(0))[U'(y - \pi - l + q) - U'(y - \pi)]$, which is positive for $q < l$. Thus, for such $r$, $\bar{q}(r) = l$.

To prove that $\bar{q}(r) < l$ if $r$ is sufficiently low, select $\hat{p} < p(0)$ (and in the range of the function $p(\cdot)$), $\hat{q} < l$, and $\hat{x} > 0$ such that[10]

(9) $\quad (1 - \hat{p})U(y - \hat{p}\hat{q} - \hat{x}) + \hat{p}U(y - \hat{p}\hat{q} - x - l + \hat{q})$
$\qquad\qquad\qquad\qquad > U(y - p(0)l).$

Note that the right-hand side is the utility of the policy giving complete coverage. If the cost of care $r$ is sufficiently low, the care, say $x^0$, chosen by an individual with the policy $(\hat{p}\hat{q}, \hat{q})$ is clearly such that $p(x^0/r) < \hat{p}$. Hence an insurer would make profits selling that policy. On the other hand, $r$ can also be chosen low enough so that if $\tilde{x}$ is such that $p(\tilde{x}/r) = \hat{p}$, then $\tilde{x} < \hat{x}$. Thus, as $x^0$ is the *optimal* choice of the individual with the policy $(\hat{p}\hat{q}, \hat{q})$,

(10)
$(1 - p(x^0/r))U(y - \hat{p}\hat{q} - x^0) + p(x^0/r)U(y - \hat{p}\hat{q} - x^0 - l + q)$
$\quad \geq (1 - p(\tilde{x}/r))U(y - \hat{p}\hat{q} - \tilde{x}) + p(\tilde{x}/r)U(y - \hat{p}\hat{q} - \tilde{x} - l + q)$
$\quad > (1 - \hat{p})U(y - \hat{p}\hat{q} - \tilde{x}) + \hat{p}U(y - \hat{p}\hat{q} - \hat{x} - l + q) > U(y - p(0)l).$

In other words, if $r$ is sufficiently small, the policy $(\hat{p}\hat{q}, \hat{q})$ affords greater expected utility than that giving complete coverage and, as constructed, makes profits. Therefore, the policy giving complete coverage cannot be optimal.[11]

To show that $\bar{q}(r) < l$ implies $\bar{q}(r') < l$ for $r' < r$, consider an in-

10. This is clearly possible. Given the choice of $\hat{p}$, choose a small $\hat{x}$ and a $\hat{q}$ close to $l$.

11. It is easy to rule out the possibility of greater than complete coverage: If $q > l$, then (since the optimal $x = 0$) expected utility is $(1 - p(0))U(y - p(0)q) + p(0)U(y - p(0)q - l + q))$, which (by concavity of $U$) is less than $U(y - p(0)l)$. In any event, if $q > l$, there would be a motive for fraud.

dividual who is offered $(\pi(\bar{q}(r)), \bar{q}(r))$—the optimal policy if the cost of taking care is $r$—but who in fact faces the cost $r'$. He would choose an $x$ leading to a lower probability of loss than his counterpart who faces the cost $r$ and who buys the policy. (This follows from (3').) Therefore, the insurer would make profits selling the policy. Also, the individual would clearly be better off than his counterpart. But his counterpart would, by assumption, be better off with the policy than if he had full coverage. Therefore, the individual who faces the cost $r'$ would be better off with the policy than with full coverage. Since an insurer selling the policy would make profits and since the individual would be better off with the policy than with full coverage, certainly the optimal policy $(\pi(\bar{q}(r')), \bar{q}(r'))$ cannot involve full coverage.

To show that $\bar{q}(r)$ tends to $l$ as $r$ tends to 0, fix $q < l$ and consider what happens under the policy $(\pi(q),q)$ as $r$ tends to 0. (Note that $\pi(q)$, the break-even premium, depends on $r$.) First, we claim that $x$ tends to 0 as $r$ tends to 0. This follows from the first-order condition (3').[12] Second, we assert that $p(x/r)$ tends to $p^*$ as $r$ tends to 0. (Let $p^* > 0$ be the limit of $p$ as its argument tends to infinity.) This is obvious, and the details of the argument are left to the reader. These two facts directly imply that $EU(q)$ tends to $(1 - p^*)U(y - p^*q) + p^*U(y - p^*q - l + q)$ as $r$ tends to 0. Thus, $\lim_{r \to 0} EU(q)$ is increasing in $q$ for $q < l$, and so $\bar{q}(r)$ must approach $l$ as $r$ tends to 0.

Q.E.D.

Of course, the fully optimal insurance policy always involves full coverage.[13] The level of care associated with the fully optimal policy could be either above or below that associated with the optimal policy

---

12. We only sketch the argument here. Suppose on the contrary that

$$\lim_{r \to 0} x = x^* > 0$$

and consider

$$l^* = \lim_{r \to 0} (1/r)p'(x/r) = \lim_{r \to 0} (1/r)p'(x^*/r)$$

(these limits are assumed to exist). If $l^* < 0$, then, using $x^* > 0$, it can be shown that

$$\lim_{t \to \infty} \int_0^t p'(\tau)d\tau = \lim_t p(t)$$

is unbounded from below, a contradiction, since $p(t)$ is a probability. On the other hand, if $l^* = 0$, then the left-hand side of (3') tends to zero. But the right-hand side of (3') is bounded away from zero, a contradiction.

13. This is well-known. To prove it, maximize expected utility given by (2) (and subject to $\pi = p(x)q$) with respect to $q$ and $x$ to determine that $q = l$ at the optimum.

under moral hazard. The latter situation may arise when the optimal policy under moral hazard involves relatively little coverage, in which case the insured is induced to take relatively much care. However, moral hazard does result in too little care in a restricted sense: given the level of coverage, a marginal increase in care (from the level $x(\pi(q)$, $q)$ raises expected utility.[14] This obviously helps to explain why insurers may find it profitable to exhort individuals to take more care even though the cost of such effort by the insurer must be reflected in premiums.

## IV. MORAL HAZARD WHEN CARE IS OBSERVED BY THE INSURER

Both the cost and the potential usefulness of observations of care may depend on when the observations are made.[15] As noted before, it is assumed that observations are made, if at all, either ex ante, when a policy is purchased, or ex post, when a claim is presented.[16] The total cost incurred by the insurer in making observations depends on their timing for two reasons: ex ante observation requires that all policyholders are investigated, while ex post observation requires only that those who make claims are investigated; and the costs of making an individual ex ante versus an individual ex post observation may differ. The potential usefulness of observations also depends on their timing: the quality of ex ante versus ex post observations may differ; and, the quality of ex ante and ex post observations held equal, ex ante observations turn out to be at least useful.

In thinking about the observation of care by insurers, it will be helpful to consider several examples.

(a) *Fire insurance*. Evidence of care (alarms and smoke detectors, absence of oily rags and other hazards) taken to prevent or reduce loss might itself be partially or completely destroyed in a fire, so that an ex ante observation might have an advantage over an ex post observation in quality or cost.

---

14. Expected utility is $(1 - p(x))U(y - p(x)q - x) + p(x)U(y - p(x)q - x - l + q)$, where $x = x(q)$. The derivative of this with respect to $x$ is $p'(x)[U(y - p(x)q - x - l + q) - U(y - p(x)q - x)] + (-1 - p'(x)q)[(1 - p(x))U'(y - p(x)q - x) + p(x)U'(y - p(x)q - x - l + q)]$, which is positive when evaluated at a point at which (3) holds.

15. The interest here is of course in the potential usefulness of observations as an incentive to take care, not as a means of separating high- from low-risk individuals (for individuals are assumed to be identical).

16. It is also assumed that observations are not made at both times and are not for only a random sample of individuals. Random sampling is discussed in Townsend [1976].

(b) *Theft insurance*. Unless a burglar destroyed or removed evidence of care (burglar alarms, locks), the quality or cost of an observation made after a theft might be equal to that of one made ex ante.

(c) *Automobile collision insurance*. It might be more difficult to evaluate an individual's driving behavior when a policy is purchased than it would be after a collision. An individual would typically be able to alter his driving behavior if evaluated (say, in a driving test) when buying a policy, but if evaluated (using testimony of witnesses or police) after a collision this might not be as much of a problem.

Indeed, for most examples that come to mind, the quality of an ex ante observation is at least as good as—or the cost at least as low as—that of an ex post observation when care is an expenditure on assets that are fixed over the period of insurability, whereas the opposite is true for risk-reducing activity that can be varied to some extent over the period.

Now let

$z$    be the observed level of care (a random variable, the distribution of which depends on the true care $x$);

$F(\ ;x)$    be the cumulative probability distribution function of $z$ given $x$; and

$c$    be the cost of making an observation.

The variables $z$ and $c$ and the function $F$ all depend on the timing of observations, but this dependence is not made explicit in the notation, since the timing will usually be clear from context or else it will not matter.

There are two slightly different ways of interpreting a discrepancy $z - x$. First, it may represent an error in observation. For example, an insurance company's inspector may forget to note how many burglar alarms are installed or may not be able to judge adequately their effectiveness. Second, a discrepancy may reflect a random element in the momentary level of care actually taken by an individual. This interpretation, made by Diamond [1974] in a different context, is illustrated by the example of an automobile owner with collision insurance. His true level of care may be thought of as his usual or average driving behavior. His behavior at a particular instant might be due to factors beyond his control (he may be temporarily blinded by the sun). Of course, if the actual driving behavior at the time of an accident is observed with error, both interpretations of a discrepancy might apply.

It is assumed that observations convey information about care in the sense that

$$(11) \qquad\qquad z = x + \eta,$$

here $\eta$ is "noise," a random variable (with a distribution that may depend on $x$) that has a mean of zero.[17] A special case is $\eta = 0$, observations are perfectly accurate.

An insurance policy is a pair $(\pi, q)$ where, obviously, the premium $\pi$ may be a function of the observation $z$ only if it is made ex ante, and where the level of coverage $q$ may be a function of the observation whether it is made ex ante or ex post.[18]

If observation of care is made ex ante, an insured individual maximizes over $x$[19]

$$(12) \quad (1 - p(x)) \int U(y - \pi(z) - x) dF(z; x)$$
$$+ p(x) \int U(y - \pi(z) - x - l + q(z)) dF(z; x).$$

Thus, the individual takes into account the effect of $x$ on the probability of an accident and on the probability distribution of $z$. The break-even constraint for the insurer is

$$(13) \qquad \int \pi(z) dF(z; x) = c + p(x) \int q(z) dF(z; x).$$

Similarly, if observation of care is made ex post, the individual's problem is to maximize over $x$

$$(14) \quad (1 - p(x)) U(y - \pi - x)$$
$$+ p(x) \int U(y - \pi - x - l + q(z)) dF(z; x),$$

and the break-even constraint is

$$(15) \qquad \pi = p(x)(c + \int q(z) dF(z; x)).$$

Two cases are now considered: one in which observations are perfectly accurate and one in which they are not.

17. However, it is clear from Shavell [1979] that Proposition 3 holds under the general assumption that the probability distribution of $z$ is different for different $x$.

18. There is, however, a constraint of sorts on the use of less than perfectly accurate ex ante observations: whereas it is assumed here that an individual decides whether to purchase a policy before an ex ante observation is made, in fact an individual would usually have the opportunity to refuse to buy a policy if its terms—determined after an ex ante observation—were to turn out to be sufficiently unfavorable. The results of this subsection would not be changed if account were taken of the constraint, but a study attempting a detailed characterization of insurance policies would have to recognize it.

19. In the case of a probability distribution with a density function $f(z;x)$, the notation $\int U(y - \pi(z) - x) dF(z;x)$ is a shorthand for $\int U(y - \pi(z) - x) f(z;x) dz$; in the case of a discrete probability distribution, it is a shorthand for $\sum_j U(y - \pi(z_j) - x) f(z_j;x)$, where $z_j$ is a possible value of $z$ and $f(z_j;x)$ is the probability of $z_j$ given $x$.

## A. Care Is Observed with Perfect Accuracy by the Insurer

In this simple case, by linking the terms of insurance to the level of care, the insured may be given an appropriate incentive to take care. In particular, there is no need to provide him with an incentive by use of partial coverage. Since this is true whether observations are made ex ante or ex post and since fewer ex post observations are made, ex post observation is superior to ex ante other things equal.

PROPOSITION 2. Suppose that the insurer observes care and that he does so with perfect accuracy. Then[20]
(a) an optimal insurance policy under moral hazard involves full coverage,
(b) care is observed ex post (and the amount of coverage depends on care) unless the relative cost of an ex ante observation is sufficiently small.

*Note.* The insurer will observe care if the cost of an observation is sufficiently low.

*Proof.* Let us first verify (a). Suppose that it is optimal to observe care ex ante and consider the policy $(c + p(x)l, l)$. This policy must be optimal given moral hazard and ex ante observation as it breaks even and results in the fully optimal expected utility given ex ante observation.[21] Therefore, any optimal policy given moral hazard and ex ante observation must result in the fully optimal expected utility. But, as shown in the previous footnote, this requires that coverage is full.

Similarly, suppose that it is optimal to observe care ex post and consider the policy $(\pi, \pi/p(x) - c)$, which, given $\pi$ and $x$, yields expected utility,

$$(16) \quad (1 - p(x))U(y - \pi - x)$$
$$+ p(x)U(y - \pi - x - l + \pi/p(x) - c).$$

Let $\bar{\pi}$ and $\bar{x}$ maximize (16). Then if the insurer offers the policy $(\bar{\pi}, \bar{\pi}/p(x) - c)$, the individual will select $\bar{x}$. On the other hand, maximizing (16) over $\pi$ and $x$ is equivalent to maximizing (17) over $q$ and $x$ (make the substitution $q = \pi(x) - c$):

---

20. Part (a) of this proposition is, as previously remarked, well-known, at least with regard to ex ante observation.
21. Under this policy, the individual selects $x$ to maximize $U(y - c - p(x)l - x)$. On the other hand, to find fully optimal expected utility given ex ante observation, it is necessary to maximize over $q$ and $x$ $(1 - p(x))U(y - c - p(x)q - x) + p(x)U(y - c - p(x)q - x - l + q)$. It is easy to check that the optimal $q = l$, so that the problem becomes maximize $U(y - c - p(x)l - x)$ over $x$.

$$(17) \quad (1 - p(x))U(y - p(x)(q + c) - x)$$
$$+ p(x)U(y - p(x)(q + c) - x - l + q).$$

But this is the problem of determining fully optimal expected utility given ex post observation. Therefore, this case is complete by the logic of the previous paragraph.

The claim of the note to Proposition 2 is true, since we have shown that an optimal insurance policy under moral hazard results in the fully optimal expected utility given that care is observed.

Part (b) is also clear. Let $c_a$ and $c_p$ be the costs of an ex ante and an ex post observation. If care is observed ex ante, expected utility is the maximum over $x$ of $U(y - c_a - p(x)l - x)$ and if care is observed ex post, it is the maximum of $U(y - p(x)(c_p + l)-x)$. Therefore, if $c_a = c_p$, ex ante observation cannot be optimal (since then $y - c_a - p(x)l - x > y - p(x)(c_p + l) - x$ for all $x$). Also it is easy to see that if it is optimal to observe care ex ante given $c_a$ and $c_p$, it must be optimal to observe care ex ante given $c_a'$ and $c_p$ for $c_a' < c_a$. Furthermore, if $c_a$ is low enough to make ex ante observation superior to no observation and if, in addition, $c_a < p(l)c_p$, ex ante observation must be optimal.[22] 

Q.E.D.

## B. Care is Observed with Less Than Perfect Accuracy by the Insurer

The motivation for the proof that it is possible to design an insurance policy for which the usefulness as an incentive of imperfect information about care outweighs any negative effect due to the imposition of risk is as follows (and is probably easiest to understand after a look at the general argument of the proof): First, suppose the contrary, that the premium and the amount of coverage are fixed. Now alter the policy by making the amount of coverage depend very slightly on observed care. There will be no first-order effect on the individual's expected utility that can be attributed to the imposition of risk because, initially, his coverage and thus his final wealth were fixed, *conditional* on there being a loss.[23] However, if the policy is

---

22. The optimal $x$ must certainly be bounded by the loss $l$ and if $x < l$ and $c_a < p(l)c_p$, then $y - c_a - p(x)l - x < y - p(x)(c_p + l) - x$.

23. To illustrate this idea, let us ignore the role of care and assume that the probability of loss is exogenous. Now suppose that a scalar multiple $t$ of a random variable $z$, which has zero mean, is added to coverage if there is a loss. Then expected utility as a function of $t$ is $EU(t) = (1 - p)U(y - \pi) + p \int U(y - \pi - l + q + tz)dG(z)$. Thus, $EU'(t) = p \int z U'(y - \pi - l + q + tz)dG(z)$ so that $EU'(0) = pU'(y - \pi - l + q) \int z dG(z) = 0$, since $z$ has mean zero. (Here $G$ is the cumulative distribution function of $z$.) In other words, the first-order effect of the imposition of risk is zero. This is as expected, since a differentiable function is by definition linear, and therefore displays risk neutrality, in the small.

altered in the appropriate way, there will be a positive first-order effect on the care taken by the individual, lowering the probability of loss and therefore allowing a reduction in the premium. The motivation for the proof that imperfect information is more valuable when acquired ex ante is analogous: Suppose that care is observed ex post; that is, suppose that only the amount of coverage can depend on information about care. In this case conditional on there *not* being a loss, final wealth is constant. But the previous logic then suggests that it would be advantageous to make the premium as well depend to some degree on observed care; this requires that care be observed ex ante.

PROPOSITION 3. Suppose that the insurer's observations are made without cost and convey only imperfect information about care (see (11)). Then

(a) either ex ante or ex post observations are of positive value—the terms of the insurance policy will depend to some extent on them;

(b) ex ante observations are more valuable than ex post, at least when the quality of the two types of observations is the same (more precisely, when the probability distribution of $z$ given $x$ is the same in the ex ante and ex post cases and is not degenerate).

*Note.* It follows from (a) that if the cost of either ex ante or ex post observation is sufficiently low, the insurer will observe care. Moreover, it follows from (b) that if the cost of ex ante observation is sufficiently low, the insurer will observe care ex ante no matter how low the cost of ex post observation (given that the quality of the two types of observation is the same and that the observations are not perfectly accurate).

It can also be shown that the optimal policy typically involves less than complete coverage.

*Proof.* Recall that $(\bar{\pi}, \bar{q})$ is the optimal policy under moral hazard when care is not observed and let $\bar{x}$ be the associated level of care. Define a new policy by

(18) $$(\pi, q(z)) = (\bar{\pi} - \alpha\epsilon, \bar{q} + \epsilon(z - \bar{x})),$$

where $\epsilon$ and $\alpha$ are greater than zero and will be determined below. This policy has a lower premium than $\bar{\pi}$. It also appears to give an additional incentive to take care, since if $x$ is raised above $\bar{x}$, $z$ will exceed $\bar{x}$ on average, increasing coverage on average. To prove (a), we shall show that if $\alpha$ and $\epsilon$ are properly chosen, expected utility will be higher under $(\pi, q(z))$ than under $(\bar{\pi}, \bar{q})$, and that the insurer will at least break even under $(\pi, q(z))$.

The individual now maximizes over $x$

(19)  $g(x, \epsilon) = (1 - p(x))U(y - \bar{\pi} + \alpha\epsilon - x) + p(x)$
$$\times \int U(y - \bar{\pi} + \alpha\epsilon - x - l + \bar{q} + \epsilon(z - \bar{x}))dF(z; x),$$

and it is assumed that

(20)  $$g_x(x, \epsilon) = 0$$

determines the optimal $x$. Let $G(\epsilon) = \max_x g(x, \epsilon)$. Using (20) and noting that at $\epsilon = 0$, $(\pi, q(z)) = (\bar{\pi}, \bar{q})$, we have

(21)  $$G'(0) = g_x(\bar{x}, 0) \frac{dx}{d\epsilon} + g_\epsilon(\bar{x}, 0) = g_\epsilon(\bar{x}, 0).$$

To prove (a), we need to show that $G'(0) > 0$ and that $\alpha$ can be chosen so that the premium covers the insurer's expected expenses. Now

(22)  $g_\epsilon(\bar{x}, 0) = (1 - p(\bar{x}))\alpha U'(y - \bar{\pi} - \bar{x})$
$$+ p(\bar{x}) \int (\alpha + z - \bar{x})U'(y - \bar{\pi} - \bar{x} - l + \bar{q})dF(z; \bar{x})$$
$$= \alpha[(1 - p(\bar{x}))U'(y - \bar{\pi} - \bar{x}) + p(\bar{x})U'(y - \bar{\pi} - \bar{x} - l + \bar{q})] > 0,$$

since $\int(z - \bar{x})dF(z; \bar{x}) = 0$. To show that the insurer remains solvent, write his net revenues $R$ as a function of $\epsilon$,

(23)  $$R(\epsilon) = \bar{\pi} - \alpha\epsilon - p(x)[\bar{q} + \epsilon\int(z - \bar{x})dF(z; x)],$$

where $x$ is understood to be a function of $\epsilon$, determined implicitly by (20). Differentiating (23) gives

(24)  $R'(\epsilon) = -\alpha - p'(x) \frac{dx}{d\epsilon} [\bar{q} + \epsilon\int(z - \bar{x})dF(z; x)]$
$$- p(x) \left[ \int (z - \bar{x})dF(z; x) + \epsilon \frac{dx}{d\epsilon} \int (z - \bar{x})dF_x(z; x) \right]$$

so that

(25)  $$R'(0) = -\alpha - p'(\bar{x}) \left( \frac{dx(0)}{d\epsilon} \right) \bar{q}.$$

We need to show that $R'(0) > 0$ if $\alpha$ is chosen appropriately. To do this, we shall show that $dx(0)/d\epsilon$ is greater than some $\delta > 0$ whenever

$\alpha$ is less than some $\gamma > 0$, for then we need only choose $\alpha$ less than min $(\gamma, -p'(\bar{x})\delta\bar{q})$. Let us write (20) in explicit form:

$$(26) \quad 0 = p'(x)[\int U(y - \bar{\pi} + \alpha\epsilon - x - l + \bar{q} + \epsilon(z - \bar{x}))dF(z; x)$$
$$- U(y - \bar{\pi} + \alpha\epsilon - x)] - [(1 - p(x))U'(y - \bar{\pi} + \alpha\epsilon - x)$$
$$+ p(x)\int U'(y - \bar{\pi} + \alpha\epsilon - x - l + \bar{q} + \epsilon(z' - \bar{x}))dF(z; x)]$$
$$+ p(x)\int U(y - \bar{\pi} + \alpha\epsilon - x - l + \bar{q} + \epsilon(z - \bar{x}))dF_x(z; x).$$

On the other hand, differentiating (20) and solving for $dx(0)/d\epsilon$, we get

$$(27) \qquad \frac{dx(0)}{d\epsilon} = \frac{-g_{x\epsilon}(\bar{x}; 0)}{g_{xx}(\bar{x}; 0)}.$$

As $g_{xx}(\bar{x}; 0) < 0$ (this is the second-order sufficiency condition for the optimal choice of $x$) and is independent of $\alpha$, it is enough to show that $g_{x\epsilon}(\bar{x}, 0) > \delta > 0$ whenever $\alpha$ is less than some $\gamma > 0$. Differentiating the right-hand side of (26) with respect to $\epsilon$ and evaluating at $(\bar{x}, 0)$, gives

$$(28)$$
$$g_{x\epsilon}(\bar{x}, 0) = \alpha\{p'(\bar{x})[U'(y - \bar{\pi} - \bar{x} - l + \bar{q}) - U'(y - \bar{\pi} - \bar{x})]$$
$$- [(1 - p(\bar{x}))U''(y - \bar{\pi} - \bar{x}) + p(\bar{x})U''(y - \bar{\pi} - \bar{x} - l + \bar{q})]\}$$
$$+ p(\bar{x})U'(y - \bar{\pi} - \bar{x} - l + \bar{q})\int z\,dF_x(z; \bar{x}).$$

Use was made here of $\int dF_x(z; \bar{x}) = 0$, which follows from the identity $\int dF(z; x) = 1$. Now $\int z\,dF_x(z; x) = d(\int z\,dF(z; x))/dx$. But by (11), $\int z\,dF(z; x) = x$. Thus, $\int z\,dF_x(z; x) = 1$, so that the right-hand side of (28) is of the form $\alpha K_1 + K_2$ with $K_2 > 0$. Therefore, if $\delta = K_2/2$ and $\gamma = K_2/(|K_1|2)$, then $g_{x\epsilon}(\bar{x}, 0) > \delta$ for all $\alpha < \gamma$, which completes the proof of (a).

We shall prove (b) by contradiction. Thus, suppose that $z$ is observed ex ante and that $(\pi, q(z))$ is the best policy under moral hazard. We shall construct a new policy $(\hat{\pi}(z), \hat{q}(z))$ under which expected utility is higher and the insurer at least breaks even. Let

$$(29) \qquad \hat{\pi}(z) = \pi - \alpha\epsilon - \epsilon\beta(z - x^*),$$

where $\alpha$, $\beta$, and $\epsilon$ are positive and $x^*$ is the optimal $x$ given $(\pi, q(z))$. Also, let

$$(30) \qquad \hat{q}(z) = q(z) - \epsilon\beta(z - x^*).$$

Note that $(\hat{\pi}(z), \hat{q}(z))$ is designed so that if there is a loss, the stochastic component of the premium in the new policy is exactly offset by the new stochastic component of coverage. Thus, additional risk in the new policy is imposed only when there is not loss. The individual maximizes over $x$

$$(31) \quad h(x, \epsilon) = (1 - p(x)) \int U(y - \pi + \alpha\epsilon$$
$$+ \epsilon\beta(z - x^*) - x) dF(z; x) + p(x) \int U(y - \pi$$
$$+ \alpha\epsilon - x - l + q(z)) dF(z; x),$$

and it is assumed that

$$(32) \qquad\qquad h_x(x, \epsilon) = 0$$

determines the optimal $x$. Let $H(\epsilon) = \max\limits_{x} h(x, \epsilon)$, so that

$$(33) \qquad\qquad H'(0) = h_\epsilon(x^*, 0).$$

To prove (b), we need to show that $H'(0) > 0$ and that $\alpha$ and $\beta$ can be chosen so that the premium covers the insurer's expected expenses. Now

$$(34) \quad h_\epsilon(x^*, 0) = \alpha[(1 - p(x^*)) U'(y - \pi - x^*)$$
$$+ p(x^*) \int U'(y - \pi - x^* - l + q(z)) dF(z; x^*)] > 0.$$

To show that the insurer remains solvent, write his net revenue $S$ as a function of $\epsilon$:

$$(35) \qquad S(\epsilon) = \pi - \alpha\epsilon - (1 - p(x)) \epsilon\beta \int (z - x^*) dF(z; x)$$
$$- p(x) \int q(z) dF(z; x),$$

where $x$ is understood to be a function of $\epsilon$ determined by (32). Differentiating (35), we see that

$$(36) \quad S'(\epsilon) = -\alpha - (1 - p(x))\beta \int (z - x^*) dF(z; x)$$

$$+ \frac{dx}{d\epsilon} p'(x) [\epsilon\beta \int (z - x^*) dF(z; x) - \int q(z) dF(z; x)]$$

$$- \frac{dx}{d\epsilon} [(1 - p(x)) \epsilon\beta \int (z - x^*) dF_x(z; x)$$

$$+ p(x) \int q(z) dF_x(z; x)].$$

Therefore,

$$(37) \quad S'(0) = -\alpha + \frac{dx(0)}{d\epsilon} [-p'(x^*) \int q(z) dF(z; x^*)$$
$$- p(x^*) \int q(z) dF_x(z, x^*)].$$

The two terms in brackets represent two effects of an increase in the level of care: a reduction in expected payments by the insurer due to a decline in the probability of an accident and a change in expected payments by the insurer due to a change in the distribution of $z$.

Suppose that the net effect of these terms is postive. Then, as in the proof of (a), $S'(0) > 0$ holds if $dx(0)/d\epsilon$ is greater than some positive $\delta$ whenever $\alpha$ is sufficiently small and $\beta$ is chosen appropriately. The latter is shown to hold by steps analogous to those used in the proof of (a): The first-order condition determining individual behavior is

$$
\begin{aligned}
(38) \quad h_x(x, \epsilon) = {} & p'(x)[- \int U(y - \pi + \alpha\epsilon + \epsilon\beta(z - x^*) - x) \\
& \times dF(z; x) + \int U(y - \pi + \alpha\epsilon - x - l \\
& + q(z))dF(z; x)] \\
& - \{(1 - p(x))\int U'(y - \pi + \alpha\epsilon \\
& + \epsilon\beta(z - x^*) - x)dF(z; x) \\
& + p(x)\int U'(y - \pi + \alpha\epsilon - x - l + q(z))dF(z; x)\} \\
& + (1 - p(x))\int U(y - \pi + \alpha\epsilon \\
& + \epsilon\beta(z - x^*) - x)dF_x(z; x) \\
& + p(x) \int U(y - \pi + \alpha\epsilon - x - l \\
& + q(z))dF_x(z; x) = 0.
\end{aligned}
$$

Differentiating $h_x(x, \epsilon) = 0$ with respect to $\epsilon$ and solving for $dx/d\epsilon$, we get

$$
(39) \qquad \frac{dx}{d\epsilon} = \frac{-h_{x\epsilon}(x, \epsilon)}{h_{xx}(x, \epsilon)}.
$$

As $h_{xx}(x^*, 0) < 0$ (the second-order sufficiency condition for a maximum) and is independent of $\alpha$ and $\beta$, it suffices to show that $h_{x\epsilon}(x^*, 0) > \delta > 0$ as long as $\alpha$ is sufficiently small. But

$$
\begin{aligned}
(40) \quad h_{x\epsilon}(x^*, 0) = {} & \alpha\{p'(x^*)[-U'(y - \pi - x^*) \\
& + \int U'(y - \pi - x^* - l + q(z))dF(z; x^*)] \\
& - [(1 - p(x^*))U''(y - \pi - x^*) \\
& + p(x^*)\int U''(y - \pi - x^* - l \\
& + q(z))dF(z; x^*)] \\
& + p(x^*)\int U'(y - \pi - x^* - l + q(z))dF_x(z; x^*)\} \\
& + (1 - p(x^*))U'(y - \pi - x^*)\beta \int z dF_x(z; x^*),
\end{aligned}
$$

which is of the form $\alpha K_1 + \beta K_2$ where $K_2 > 0$. Thus, if $\alpha$ is less than or equal to, say, $\omega$, (40) will be positive if $\beta$ is chosen to be a least $|K_1\omega|/K_2$.

On the other hand, suppose that the terms in brackets in (37) have a negative sum. Then redefine $(\hat{\pi}(z), \hat{q}(z))$ as follows:

(41) $$\hat{\pi}(z) = \pi - \alpha\epsilon + \epsilon\beta(z - x^*)$$

(42) $$\hat{q}(z) = q(z) + \epsilon\beta(z - x^*).$$

Then the proof that was just used for $(\hat{\pi}(z), \hat{q}(z))$ as initially defined may be carried out, the only change being that $dx(0)/d\epsilon$ is shown to be negative rather than positive.

The terms in brackets in (37) cannot sum to zero if $z$ is not a degenerate random variable: Otherwise, assume that

(43) $$-p'(x^*)\int q(z)dF(z; x^*) - p(x^*)\int q(z)dF_x(z; x^*) = 0.$$

We shall show that this allows us to construct a new policy that breaks even and improves expected utility, in contradiction to the supposed optimality of $(\pi, q(z))$. To do so, select $z_1$ and $z_2$ such that $q(z_1) > q(z_2)$. (This can be done by part (a) of the Proposition.) Hence

(44) $$U'(y - \pi - x - l + q(z_1)) < U'(y - \pi - x - l + q(z_2)).$$

Suppose that $z_1$ and $z_2$ occur with positive probabilities $p(z_1; x)$ and $p(z_2; x)$ (it will be clear that the argument can be easily modified if the distribution of $z$ is not discrete). Then define a new policy $(\tilde{\pi}, \tilde{q}(z); \lambda, \delta(\lambda))$ by

.(45) $$\tilde{\pi} = \pi + \delta(\lambda)$$

$$\tilde{q}(z_1) = q(z_1) - \lambda$$

$$\tilde{q}(z_2) = q(z_2) + \frac{p(z_1; x^*)}{p(z_2; x^*)}\lambda$$

$$\tilde{q}(z) = q(z) \qquad \text{otherwise,}$$

where $\lambda > 0$ and $\delta(\lambda)$ is chosen to satisfy the break-even constraint (13) given that $x$ is chosen optimally. Let expected utility as a function of $x$ be $f(x, \lambda, \delta(\lambda))$. Since the individual chooses $x$ optimally, his expected utility is $F(\lambda) = \max_x f(x; \lambda, \delta(\lambda))$. Thus, since $\delta(0) = 0$,

(46) $$\frac{dF(0)}{d\lambda} = f_\lambda(x^*; 0,0) + \delta'(0)f_\delta(x^*; 0,0).$$

But

(47) $$f_\lambda(x^*; 0,0) = (U'(y - \pi - x^* - l + q(z_2))$$
$$- U'(y - \pi - x^* - l + q(z_1)))$$
$$\times p(z_1; x^*)p(x^*) > 0.$$

Consequently, it suffices to show that $\delta'(0) = 0$, for then (46) must be positive. Now profits of the insurer as a function of $\lambda$ and $\delta$ are

(48). $$T(\lambda, \delta) = \pi + \delta - p(x)\int\tilde{q}(z)dF(z; x),$$

where $x$ is understood to have been chosen optimally. Since by definition of $\delta(\lambda)$, $T(\lambda, \delta(\lambda)) = 0$, we have $\delta'(\lambda) = -T_\lambda(\lambda, \delta)/T_\delta(\lambda, \delta)$. But if we use (43),

$$(49) \quad T_\lambda(0,0) = \frac{dx}{d\lambda}\left[-p'(x^*)\int q(z)dF(z; x^*)\right.$$

$$\left. - p(x)\int q(z)dF_x(z; x^*)\right] = 0$$

so that $\delta'(0) = 0$ as required. Q.E.D.

In summary of Propositions 2 and 3 and of the earlier discussion in this section, three factors may be identified as influencing the optimal timing of observations: (1) The number of individuals that have to be checked. Consideration of this factor works in favor of ex post observation. (2) The value of imperfect information. Consideration of this factor works in favor of ex ante observation. And (3) the cost and quality of the two types of observation. Consideration of this factor usually works in favor of ex ante observation when care is an expenditure on a good that is fixed over the period of insurability, whereas it may favor ex post observation for risk-reducing activity that can be varied over the period.

## APPENDIX

In the general case the proofs to the propositions are virtually identical to what was given in the text. All that we shall write here are the analogs of several equations of the text. The analog of (2) is

$$(2') \quad EU = p_0(x)U(y - \pi - x) + \sum_{i=1}^{n} p_i(x)U(y - \pi - x - l_i + q_i);$$

that of (7),

$$(7') \quad \frac{\partial}{\partial q_j} EU(q_1, \ldots, q_n)$$

$$= \frac{\partial x}{\partial q_j} \sum_{i=1}^{n} p_i'(U(y - \pi - x - l_i + q_i) - U(y - \pi - x))$$

$$- \frac{\partial x}{\partial q_j}\left[p_0 U'(y - \pi - x) + \sum_{i=1}^{n} p_i U'(y - \pi - x - l_i + q_i)\right]$$

$$- \frac{\partial x}{\partial q_j} \sum_{i=1}^{n} p_i' q_i\left[p_0 U'(y - \pi - x)\right.$$

$$\left. + \sum_{i=1}^{n} p_i U'(y - \pi - x - l_i + q_i)\right]$$

$$- p_j\left[p_0 U'(y - \pi - x) + \sum_{i=1}^{n} p_i U'(y - \pi - x - l_i + q_i)\right]$$

$$+ p_j U'(y - \pi - x - l_j + q_j);$$

that of (12),

$$(12') \quad p_0(x)\int U(y - \pi(z) - x)dF(z; x)$$
$$+ \sum_{i=1}^{n} p_i(x)\int U(y - \pi(z) - x - l_i + q_i(z))dF(z; x);$$

that of (18),

$$(18') \qquad \qquad \pi = \bar{\pi} - \alpha\epsilon$$
$$q_i(z) = \bar{q}_i + \epsilon(z - \bar{x}),$$

and so forth. The only difference in the general case is with regard to the first proposition: in the general case "positive coverage" means that $q_i \geq 0$ with strict inequality for some $i$ and "partial coverage" means that $q_i \leq l_i$ with strict inequality for some $i$.

HARVARD UNIVERSITY

## REFERENCES

Arrow, Kenneth J., "Insurance, Risk and Resource Allocation," in *Essays in the Theory of Risk-Bearing* (Chicago: Markham, 1971).
Diamond, P., "Single Activity Accidents," *Journal of Legal Studies,* III (Jan. 1974), 107–64.
Ehrlich, I., and G. Becker, "Market Insurance, Self-insurance, and Self-protection," *Journal of Political Economy,* LXXX (1972), 623–48.
Harris, M., and A. Raviv, "Optimal Incentive Contracts with Imperfect Information," Carnegie-Mellon University, mimeo, 1978.
Helpman, E., and J. Laffont, "On Moral Hazard in General Equilibrium Theory," *Journal of Economic Theory,* X (Feb. 1975), 8–23.
Mirrlees, J., "On Moral Hazard and the Theory of Unobservable Behavior," Oxford, mimeo, 1975.
Pauly, M., "The Economics of Moral Hazard: Comment," *American Economic Review,* LVIII (June 1968), 531–36.
——, "Overinsurance and Public Provision of Insurance," this *Journal,* LXXXVII (1974), 44–62.
Shavell, S., "Risk Sharing and Incentives in the Principal and Agent Relationship," *Bell Journal of Economics,* X (1979), 55–73.
Spence, A. M., and R. Zeckhauser, "Insurance, Information, and Individual Action," *American Economic Review,* LXI (1971), 380–87.
Stiglitz, J. E., "Incentives and Risk Sharing in Sharecropping," *Review of Economic Studies,* LXI (1974), 219–56.
Townsend, R., "Optimal Contracts and Competitive Markets with Costly State Verification," Carnegie-Mellon University, mimeo, 1976.
Zeckhauser, R., "Medical Insurance: A Case Study of the Trade-off Between Risk-Spreading and Appropriate Incentives," *Journal of Economic Theory,* II (March 1970), 10–26.

*Econometrica*, Vol. 51, No. 1 (January, 1983)

# AN ANALYSIS OF THE PRINCIPAL-AGENT PROBLEM

## By Sanford J. Grossman and Oliver D. Hart[1]

Most analyses of the principal-agent problem assume that the principal chooses an incentive scheme to maximize expected utility subject to the agent's utility being at a stationary point. An important paper of Mirrlees has shown that this approach is generally invalid. We present an alternative procedure. If the agent's preferences over income lotteries are independent of action, we show that the optimal way of implementing an action by the agent can be found by solving a convex programming problem. We use this to characterize the optimal incentive scheme and to analyze the determinants of the seriousness of an incentive problem.

## 1. INTRODUCTION

IT HAS BEEN RECOGNIZED for some time that, in the presence of moral hazard, market allocations under uncertainty will not be unconstrained Pareto optimal (see Arrow [1], Pauly [13]). It is only relatively recently, however, that economists have begun to undertake a systematic analysis of the properties of the second-best allocations which will arise under these conditions. Much of this analysis has been concerned with what has become known as the principal-agent problem. Consider two individuals who operate in an uncertain environment and for whom risk sharing is desirable. Suppose that one of the individuals (known as the agent) is to take an action which the other individual (known as the principal) cannot observe. Assume that this action affects the total amount of consumption or money which is available to be divided between the two individuals. In general, the action which is optimal for the agent will depend on the extent of risk sharing between the principal and the agent. The question is: What is the optimal degree of risk sharing, given this dependence?

Particular applications of the principal-agent problem have been made to the case of an insurer who cannot observe the level of care taken by the person being insured; to the case of a landlord who cannot observe the input decision of a tenant farmer (sharecropping); and to the case of an owner of a firm who cannot observe the effort level of a manager or worker.[2]

Although considerable progress has been made in the recent literature towards understanding and solving the principal-agent problem (see, in particular, Harris and Raviv [6], Holmstrom [7], Mirrlees [10, 11, 12], Shavell [19, 20], as well as the other references in footnote 2), the mathematical approach which has been adopted in most of this literature is unsatisfactory. The procedure usually followed is to suppose that the principal chooses the risk-sharing contract, or incentive scheme, to maximize his expected utility subject to the constraints that

[1] Support from the U.K. Social Science Research Council and NSF Grant No. SOC70-13429 is gratefully acknowledged. We would like to thank Bengt Holmstrom, Mark Machina, Andreu Mas-Colell, and Jim Mirrlees for helpful comments.
[2] These and other applications are discussed in a number of recent papers. See, for example, Harris and Raviv [6], Holmstrom [7], Mirrlees [10, 11, 12], Radner [15], Ross [17], Rubinstein and Yaari [18], Shavell [19, 20], Spence and Zeckhauser [21], Stiglitz [22], and Zeckhauser [24].

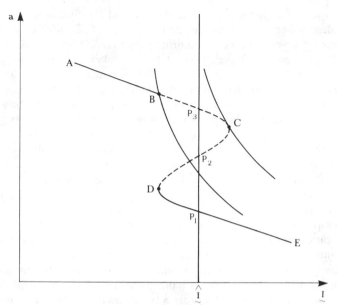

For a given $\underset{\sim}{I}$ the agent strictly prefers lower actions

FIGURE 1.

(a) the agent's expected utility is no lower than some pre-specified level; (b) the agent's utility is at a stationary point, i.e., the agent satisfies his first-order conditions with respect to the choice of action. That is, the agent's second-order conditions (and the condition that the agent should be at a global rather than a local maximum) are ignored. Mirrlees [10], however, in an important paper, has shown that this procedure is generally invalid unless, at the optimum, the solution to the agent's maximum problem is unique. In the absence of uniqueness (and it is difficult to guarantee uniqueness in advance), the first-order conditions derived by the above procedure are not even necessary conditions for the optimality of the risk-sharing contract.[3]

---

[3] The reason for this can be seen quite easily in Figure 1 (we are grateful to Andreu Mas-Colell for suggesting the use of this figure). On the horizontal axis, $I$ represents the agent's incentive scheme and on the vertical axis $a$ represents the agent's action. The curve $ABCDE$ is the locus of pairs of actions and incentive schemes which satisfy the agent's first order conditions, i.e., given $I$ the agent's utility is at a stationary point. Of these points, only those lying on the segments $AB$ and $DE$ represent global maxima for the agent, e.g. given the incentive scheme $I$ the agent's optimal action is at $p_1$, not at $p_2$ or $p_3$. Indifference curves—in terms of $a$ and $I$—are drawn for the principal ($C$ is on a higher curve than $B$). The true feasible set for the principal are the segments $AB$ and $DE$ and the optimal outcome for the principal is therefore $B$. However, $B$ does not satisfy the first order conditions of the problem: maximize the principal's utility subject to $(a, I)$ lying on $ABCDE$, i.e., subject to $(a, I)$ satisfying the agent's first order conditions (the solution to this problem is at $C$). In other words, $B$ does not satisfy the necessary conditions for optimality of the problem which has been studied in much of the literature. Note finally that perturbing Figure 1 slightly does not alter this conclusion.

The purpose of this paper is to develop a method for analyzing the principal-agent problem which avoids the difficulties of the "first-order condition" approach.[4] Our approach is to break the principal's problem up into a computation of the costs and benefits of the different actions taken by the agent. For each action, we consider the incentive scheme which minimizes the (expected) cost of getting the agent to choose that action. We show that, under the assumption that the agent's preferences over income lotteries are independent of the action he takes, this cost minimization problem is a fairly straightforward convex programming problem. An analysis of these convex problems as the agent's action varies yields a number of results about the form of the optimal incentive scheme. We will also be able to analyze what factors determine how serious a particular incentive problem is; i.e., how great the loss is to the principal from having to operate in a second-best situation where the agent's action cannot be observed relative to a first-best situation where it can be observed.

The assumption that the agent's preferences over income lotteries are independent of action is a strong one. Yet it seems a natural starting point for an analysis of the principal-agent problem. Special cases of this assumption occur when the agent's utility function is additively or multiplicatively separable in action and reward. One or other of these cases is typically assumed in most of the literature. In Section 6 we discuss briefly the prospects for the non-independence case.

In addition to providing greater rigor, the costs versus benefits approach also provides a clear separation of the two distinct roles the agent's output plays in the principal-agent problem. On the one hand, the agent's output contributes positively to the principal's consumption, so the principal desires a high output. On the other hand, the agent's output is a signal to the principal about the agent's level of effort. This informational role may be in conflict with the consumption role. For example, there may be a moderate output level which is achieved when the agent takes low effort levels and never occurs at other effort levels. If the agent is penalized whenever this moderate output occurs, then he is discouraged from taking these low effort actions. However, there may be lower output levels which have some chance of occurring regardless of the agent's action. To encourage the agent to take high effort levels, it is then optimal to pay the agent more in low output states than in moderate output states, even though the principal prefers moderate output levels to low output levels.

The dual role of output makes it difficult to obtain conditions which ensure even elementary properties of the incentive scheme, such as monotonicity. In Section 3, sufficient conditions for monotonicity are given. It is also shown in this section that a monotone likelihood ratio condition, which the "first-order condition" approach suggests is a guarantee of monotonicity, must be strengthened once we take into account the possibility that the agent's action is not unique at the optimal incentive scheme.

The paper is organized as follows. In Section 2, we show how the principal's optimization problem can be decomposed into a costs versus benefits problem.

---

[4] Mirrlees [12] has identified a class of cases where the "first-order condition" approach *is* valid. We will consider this class in Section 3.

In Section 3, we use our approach to analyze the monotonicity and progressivity of the optimal incentive scheme. In Section 4, we give a simple algorithm for computing an optimal incentive scheme when there are only two outcomes associated with the agent's actions. In Section 5, we analyze the effects of risk aversion and information quality on the incentive problem. Finally, in Section 6 we consider some extensions of the analysis.

## 2. STATEMENT OF THE PROBLEM

The application of the principal-agent problem that we will consider is to the case of the owner of a firm who delegates the running of the firm to a manager. The owner is the principal and the manager the agent. The owner is assumed not to be able to monitor the manager's actions. The owner does, however, observe the outcome of these actions, which we will take to be the firm's profit. It is assumed that the firm's profit depends on the manager's actions, but also on other factors which are outside the manager's control—we model these as a random component. Thus, in particular, if the firm does well, it will not generally be clear to the owner whether this is because the manager has worked well or whether it is because he has been lucky.[5]

We will simplify matters by assuming that there are only finitely many possible gross profit levels for the firm, denoted $q_1, \ldots, q_n$, where $q_1 < q_2 < \cdots < q_n$. We will assume that the principal is interested only in the firm's net profit, i.e. gross profit minus the payment to the manager. We will also assume that the principal is risk neutral—our methods of analysis can, however, be applied to the case where the principal is risk averse (see Remark 3 and Section 6).

Let $A$ be the set of actions available to the manager. We will assume that $A$ is a non-empty, compact subset of a finite dimensional Euclidean space. Let $S = \{x \in R^n \mid x \geq 0, \sum_{i=1}^n x_i = 1\}$. We assume that there is a continuous function $\pi : A \to S$, where $\pi(a) = (\pi_1(a), \ldots, \pi_n(a))$ gives the probabilities of the $n$ outcomes $q_1, \ldots, q_n$ if action $a$ is selected. It is assumed that, when the agent chooses $a \in A$, he knows the probability function $\pi$ but not the outcome which will result from his action. We assume that the agent has a von Neumann–Morgenstern utility function $U(a, I)$ which depends both on his action $a$ and his remuneration $I$ from the principal. We include $a$ as an argument in order to capture the idea that the agent dislikes working hard, taking care, etc.

The crucial assumption that we will make about the form of $U(a, I)$ is:

ASSUMPTION A1: $U(a, I)$ can be written as $G(a) + K(a)V(I)$, where (1) $V$ is a real-valued, continuous, strictly increasing, concave function defined on some open interval $\mathcal{I} = (\underline{I}, \infty)$ of the real line; (2) $\lim_{I \to \underline{I}} V(I) = -\infty$; (3) $G, K$ are

---

[5] The assumption that the principal cannot monitor the agent's actions at all may in some cases be rather extreme. For a discussion of the implications of the existence of imperfect monitoring opportunities, see Harris and Raviv [6], Holmstrom [7] and Shavell [19, 20]. See also Remark 4 in Section 2.

real-valued, continuous functions defined on $A$ and $K$ is strictly positive; (4) for all $a_1, a_2 \in A$ and $I, \hat{I} \in \mathcal{I}$, $G(a_1) + K(a_1)V(I) \geq G(a_2) + K(a_2)V(I) \Rightarrow G(a_1) + K(a_1)V(\hat{I}) \geq G(a_2) + K(a_2)V(\hat{I})$.

In the above, we allow for the case $\underline{I} = -\infty$.

The main part of Assumption A1 has a simple ordinal interpretation. Assumption A1 implies that the agent's preferences over income lotteries are independent of his action (Assumption A1(1) tells us also that these preferences exhibit risk aversion). The converse can also be shown to be true: if the agent's preferences over income lotteries are independent of $a$, then $U$ can be written as $G(a) + K(a)V(I)$ for some functions $G, K, V$ (for a proof, see Keeney [8]). Note that Assumption A1 does not imply that the agent's preferences for *action* lotteries are independent of income. We will insist, however, that the agent's ranking over *perfectly certain* actions is independent of income—this is condition (4) of Assumption A1.

Note that if $K(a)$ is not constant then (2) and (4) imply that $V(I)$ must be bounded from above. Further if it is also the case that $G(a) \equiv 0$, then $V(I)$ must be non-positive everywhere.

Two special cases of Assumption A1 occur when $K(a) = $ constant, i.e. $U$ is additively separable in $a$ and $I$, and when $G(a) = 0$, i.e. $U$ is multiplicatively separable in $a$ and $I$. In these cases the agent's preferences over action lotteries *are* independent of income, as well as preferences over income lotteries being independent of action.[6]

An interesting special case of multiplicative separability is when $V(I) = -e^{-kI}$, $K(a) = e^{ka}$ and $A$ is a subset of the real line. Then $U(a, I) = -e^{-k(I-a)}$; i.e., effort appears just as negative income.

In the "first-best" situation where the principal can observe $a$, it is optimal for him to pay the agent according to the action he chooses. Let $\bar{U}$ be the agent's reservation price, i.e. the expected level of utility he can achieve by working elsewhere, and let $\mathcal{U} = V(\mathcal{I}) = \{v \mid v = V(I) \text{ for some } I \in \mathcal{I}\}$. We make the following assumption.

ASSUMPTION A2: $[\bar{U} - G(a)]/K(a) \in \mathcal{U}$ for all $a \in A$.

DEFINITION: Let $C_{FB} : A \to R$ be defined by $C_{FB}(a) = h([\bar{U} - G(a)]/K(a))$, where $h \equiv V^{-1}$.

Here $C_{FB}$ stands for first-best cost. $C_{FB}(a)$ is simply the agent's reservation price for picking action $a$. To get the agent to pick $a \in A$ in the first-best

---

[6]The converse is also true: if preferences over action lotteries are independent of income as well as preferences over income lotteries being independent of action, then $U$ is additively or multiplicatively separable (see Keeney [8] or Pollak [14]).

situation, the principal will offer him the following contract: I will pay you $C_{FB}(a)$ if you choose $a$ and $\tilde{I}$ otherwise, where $\tilde{I}$ is very close to $\underline{I}$.

DEFINITION: Let $B : A \to R$ be defined by $B(a) = \sum_{i=1}^{n} \pi_i(a)q_i$. $B(a)$ is the expected benefit to the principal from getting the agent to pick $a$.

DEFINITION: A first-best optimal action is one which maximizes $B(a) - C_{FB}(a)$ on $A$.

The function $C_{FB}$ induces a complete ordering on $A : a \gtrsim a'$ if and only if $C_{FB}(a) \geq C_{FB}(a')$. For obvious reasons we will refer to actions with higher $C_{FB}(a)$'s as costlier actions. It is easy to show, in view of Assumption A1(4), that $C_{FB}(a) \geq C_{FB}(a') \Leftrightarrow G(a) + K(a)v \leq G(a') + K(a')v$ for all $v \in \mathfrak{A} \Leftrightarrow G(a) + K(a)v \leq G(a') + K(a')v$ for some $v \in \mathfrak{A}$. This in turn implies that the ordering $\gtrsim$ is independent of $\bar{U}$. In the second-best situation where $a$ is not observed by the principal, it is not possible to make the agent's remuneration depend on $a$. Instead, the principal will pay the agent according to the *outcome* of his action, i.e. according to the firm's profit. An incentive scheme is therefore an $n$-dimensional vector $I = (I_1, I_2, \ldots, I_n) \in \mathcal{I}^n$, where $I_i$ is the agent's remuneration in the event that the firm's profit is $q_i$. Given the incentive scheme $I$, the agent will choose $a \in A$ to maximize $\sum_{i=1}^{n} \pi_i(a)U(a, I_i)$.

We will assume that the principal knows the agent's utility function $U(a, I)$, the set $A$ and the function $\pi : A \to S$. In other words, the principal is fully informed about the agent and about the firm's production possibilities. The incentive problem which we will study therefore arises entirely because the principal cannot monitor the agent's actions.[7]

The principal's problem can be described as follows. Let $F$ be the set of pairs of incentive schemes $I^*$ and actions $a^*$ such that, under $I^*$, the agent will be willing to work for the principal and will find it optimal to choose $a^*$, i.e. $\max_{a \in A} \sum_{i=1}^{n} \pi_i(a)U(a, I_i^*) = \sum_{i=1}^{n} \pi_i(a^*)U(a^*, I_i^*) \geq \bar{U}$. Then the principal chooses $(I, a) \in F$ to maximize $\sum_{i=1}^{n} \pi_i(a)(q_i - I_i)$. It simplifies matter considerably if we break this problem up into two parts. We consider first, given that the principal wishes to implement $a^*$, the least cost way of achieving this. We then consider which $a^*$ should be implemented. Thus, to begin, suppose that the principal wishes the agent to pick a particular action $a^* \in A$. To find the least (expected) cost way of achieving this, the principal must solve the following

---

[7]This distinguishes our study from the literature on incentive compatibility; see, e.g., the recent *Review of Economic Studies* symposium [16]. The incentive compatibility literature has been concerned with incentive problems arising from differences in information between individuals rather than with those arising from monitoring problems. In cases of differential information, there is a role for an exchange of information through messages, whereas in the model we study messages would serve no purpose.

problem:

(2.1)    Choose $I_1, \ldots, I_n$ to minimize $\sum_{i=1}^{n} \pi_i(a^*)I_i$

subject to  $\sum_{i=1}^{n} \pi_i(a^*)U(a^*, I_i) \geq \bar{U},$

$$\sum_{i=1}^{n} \pi_i(a^*)U(a^*, I_i) \geq \sum_{i=1}^{n} \pi_i(a)U(a, I_i) \qquad \text{for all} \quad a \in A,$$

$I_i \in \mathcal{I} \qquad \text{for all } i.$

This problem can be simplified considerably in view of Assumption A1. It will be convenient to regard $v_1 = V(I_1), \ldots, v_n = V(I_n)$ as the principal's control variables. Recall that $\mathcal{U} = V(\mathcal{I}) = \{v \,|\, v = V(I) \text{ for some } I \in \mathcal{I}\}$. By Assumption A1, $\mathcal{U}$ is an interval of the real line $(-\infty, \bar{v})$. Thus we may rewrite (2.1) as follows:

(2.2)    Choose $v_1, \ldots, v_n$ to minimize $\sum_{i=1}^{n} \pi_i(a^*)h(v_i)$

subject to  $G(a^*) + K(a^*)\left( \sum_{i=1}^{n} \pi_i(a^*)v_i \right) \geq G(a) + K(a)\left( \sum_{i=1}^{n} \pi_i(a)v_i \right)$

for all  $a \in A,$

$$G(a^*) + K(a^*)\left( \sum_{k=1}^{n} \pi_i(a^*)v_i \right) \geq \bar{U},$$

$v_i \in \mathcal{U} \qquad \text{for all } i,$

where $h \equiv V^{-1}$.

The important point to realize is that the constraints in (2.2) are linear in the $v_i$'s. Furthermore, $V$ concave implies $h$ convex, and so the objective function is convex in the $v_i$'s. Thus (2.2) is a rather simple optimization problem: minimize a convex function subject to (a possibly infinite number of) linear constraints. In particular, when $A$ is a finite set, the Kuhn–Tucker theorem yields necessary and sufficient conditions for optimality. These will be analyzed later.

It is important to realize that, in the absence of Assumption A1, it is not generally possible to convert (2.1) into a convex problem in this way.

DEFINITION: If $I = (I_1, \ldots, I_n)$ satisfies the constraints in (2.1) or $v = (v_1, \ldots, v_n)$ satisfies the constraints in (2.2), we will say that $I$ or $v$ *implements* action $a^*$. (We are assuming here that if the agent is indifferent between two actions, he will choose the one preferred by the principal.)

Consider the set of $v$'s which implement $a^*$. For some $a^*$, this set may be empty, in which case action $a^*$ cannot be implemented by the principal at any cost. If the set is non-empty, then, since $h$ is convex,

$$\sum_{i=1}^{n} \pi_i(a^*)h(v_i) \geq h\left(\sum_{i=1}^{n} \pi_i(a^*)v_i\right) \geq h\left(\frac{\bar{U} - G(a^*)}{K(a^*)}\right)$$

by (2.2), and so the principal's objective function is bounded below on this set. Let $C(a^*)$ be the greatest lower bound of $\sum_{i=1}^{n} \pi_i(a^*)h(v_i)$ on this set.

DEFINITION: Let $C(a^*) = \inf\{\sum_{i=1}^{n} \pi_i(a^*)h(v_i) \mid v = (v_1, \ldots, v_n) \text{ implements } a^*\}$ if the constraint set in (2.2) is non-empty. In the case where the constraint set of (2.2) is empty, write $C(a^*) = \infty$. This defines the second-best cost function $C : A \rightarrow Ru\{\infty\}$.

The above constitutes the first step(s) of the principal's optimization problem: for each $a \in A$, compute $C(a)$. The second step is to choose which action to implement, i.e. to choose $a \in A$ to maximize $B(a) - C(a)$. This second problem will not generally be a convex problem. This is because even if $B(a)$ is concave in $a$, $C(a)$ will not generally be convex. Fortunately, a significant amount of information about the form of the optimal incentive scheme can be obtained by studying the first step alone.

DEFINITION: A second-best optimal action $\hat{a}$ is one which maximizes $B(a) - C(a)$ on $A$. A second-best optimal incentive scheme $\hat{I}$ is one that implements a second-best optimal action $\hat{a}$ at least expected cost, i.e. $\sum_{i=1}^{n} \pi_i(\hat{a})\hat{I}_i = C(\hat{a})$.

Note that for a second-best optimal incentive scheme to exist, the greatest lower bound in the definition of $C(a)$ must actually be achieved. In order to establish the existence of a second-best optimal action and a second-best optimal incentive scheme, we need a further assumption.

ASSUMPTION A3: For all $a \in A$ and $i = 1, \ldots, n$, $\pi_i(a) > 0$.

Since there are only finitely many possible profit levels, Assumption A3 implies that $\pi_i(a)$ is bounded away from zero. Hence Assumption A3 rules out cases studied by Mirrlees [12] in which an optimum can be approached but not achieved by imposing higher and higher penalties on the agent which occur with smaller and smaller probability if the agent chooses the right action.

PROPOSITION 1: *Assume A1–A3. Then there exists a second-best optimal action $\hat{a}$ and a second-best optimal incentive scheme $\hat{I}$.*

PROOF: It is helpful to split the proof up into two parts. Consider first the case where $V$ is linear. Then it is easy to see that the principal can do as well in the second-best as in the first-best where the agent can be monitored. For let $a^*$ maximize $B(a) - C_{FB}(a)$ on $A$. Let the principal offer the agent the incentive scheme $I_i = q_i - t$, where $t = B(a^*) - C_{FB}(a^*)$. Then the principal's profit will be $B(a^*) - C_{FB}(a^*)$ whatever the agent does. On the other hand, by picking $a = a^*$, the agent can obtain expected utility $\bar{U}$. Hence Proposition 1 certainly holds when $V$ is linear.

On the other hand, suppose $V$ is not linear. We show first, that, if the constraint set is nonempty for an action $a^* \in A$, then problem (2.2) has a solution, i.e. $\sum_{i=1}^{n} \pi_i(a^*)h(v_i)$ achieves its greatest lower bound $C(a^*)$. Note that $\sum_{i=1}^{n} \pi_i(a^*)v_i$ is bounded below on the constraint set of (2.2). It therefore follows from a result of Bertsekas [2] that unbounded sequences in the constraint set make $\sum_{i=1}^{n} \pi_i(a^*)h(v_i)$ tend to infinity (roughly because the variance of the $v_i \to \infty$ while their mean is bounded below, and $h$ is convex and nonlinear—Assumption A3 is important here). Hence, we can artificially bound the constraint set. Since the constraint set is closed, the existence of a minimum therefore follows from Weierstrass' theorem.

We show next that $C(a)$ is a lower semicontinuous function of $a$. If $A$ is finite, then any function defined on $A$ is continuous and hence lower semicontinuous. Assume therefore that $A$ is not finite. Let $(a_r)$ be a sequence of points in $A$ converging to $a$. Assume without loss of generality (w.l.o.g.) that $C(a_r) \to k$. Then, if $k = \infty$, we certainly have $C(a) \leq \lim_{r \to \infty} C(a_r)$. Suppose therefore that $k < \infty$. Let $(I_1^r, \dots, I_n^r)$ be the solution to (2.1) when $a^* = a_r$. Then Bertsekas' result together with Assumption A3 shows that the sequence $((I_1^r, \dots, I_n^r))$ is bounded (otherwise $C(a_r) \to \infty$). Let $(I_1, \dots, I_n)$ be a limit point. Then clearly $(I_1, \dots, I_n)$ implements $a$ and so $C(a) \leq \sum_{i=1}^{n} \pi_i(a)I_i = \lim_{r \to \infty} C(a_r)$. This proves lower semicontinuity.

Given that $C(a)$ is lower semicontinuous and $A$ is compact, it follows from Weierstrass' theorem that $\max_{a \in A}[B(a) - C(a)]$ has a solution, as long as $C(a)$ is finite for some $a \in A$. To prove this last part, we show that $C(a^*) = C_{FB}(a^*)$ if $a^*$ minimizes $C_{FB}(a)$ on $A$. To see this, note that the $a^*$ which minimizes $C_{FB}(a)$ can be implemented by setting $I_i = C_{FB}(a^*)$ for all $i$.

We have thus established the existence of a second-best optimal action, $\hat{a}$, when $V$ is nonlinear. Since we have also shown that (2.2) has a solution as long as the constraint set is non-empty and $V$ is nonlinear, this establishes the existence of a second-best optimal incentive scheme. $\qquad\qquad$ Q.E.D.

It is interesting to ask whether the constraint that the agent's expected utility be greater than or equal to $\bar{U}$ is binding at a second-best optimum. The answer is no in general, i.e. for incentive reasons it may pay the principal to choose an incentive scheme which gives the agent an expected utility in excess of $\bar{U}$. One case where this will not happen is when the agent's utility function is additively or multiplicatively separable in action and reward:

PROPOSITION 2: *Assume* A1, A2, *and either* $K(a)$ *is a constant function on* $A$ *or* $G(a) = 0$ *for all* $a \in A$. *Let* $\hat{a}$ *be a second-best optimal action and* $\hat{I}$ *a second-best optimal incentive scheme which implements* $\hat{a}$. *Then* $\sum_{i=1}^{n} \pi_i(\hat{a}) U(\hat{a}, \hat{I}_i) = \overline{U}$.

PROOF: Suppose not. Write $\hat{v}_i = V(\hat{I}_i)$. Then $G(\hat{a}) + K(\hat{a})(\sum_{i=1} \pi_i(\hat{a})\hat{v}_i) > \overline{U}$ in (2.2). But it is clear that the principal's costs can be reduced and all the constraints of (2.2) will still be satisfied if we replace $\hat{v}_i$ by $(\hat{v}_i - \epsilon)$ for all $i$ in the additively separable case and by $v_i(1 + \epsilon)$ for all $i$ in the multiplicatively separable case where $\epsilon > 0$ is small (note that in the multiplicatively separable case, it follows from (2)–(4) of Assumption A1 that $V(I) < 0$ for all $I \in \mathcal{I}$, and so $\hat{v}_i < 0$). In other words, $\hat{a}$ can be implemented at lower expected cost, which contradicts the fact that we are at a second-best optimum. *Q.E.D.*

REMARK 1: The proof of Proposition 1 establishes that $C(a^*) = C_{FB}(a^*)$ if $a^*$ minimizes $C_{FB}(a)$ on $A$. This is a reflection of the fact that there is no trade-off between risk sharing and incentives when the action to be implemented is a cost-minimizing one (i.e. involves the agent in minimum "effort").

REMARK 2: In general, there may be more than one second-best optimal action and more than one second-best optimal incentive scheme. It is clear from (2.2), however, that, if $V$ is strictly concave, there is a unique second-best optimal incentive scheme which implements any particular second-best optimal action.

DEFINITION: Let $L = \max_{a \in A}(B(a) - C_{FB}(a)) - \sup_{a \in A}(B(a) - C(a))$ be the difference between the principal's expected profit in the first-best and second-best situations.

$L$ represents the loss which the principal incurs as a result of being unable to observe the agent's action (we write $\sup(B(a) - C(a))$ rather than $\max(B(a) - C(a))$ to cover cases where the assumptions of Proposition 1 do not hold). Proposition 3 shows that, while there are some special cases in which $L = 0$, in general $L > 0$.

PROPOSITION 3: *Assume* A1 *and* A2. *Then*: (1) $C(a) \geq C_{FB}(a)$ *for all* $a \in A$, *which implies that* $L \geq 0$. (2) *If* $V$ *is linear*, $L = 0$. (3) *If there exists a first-best optimal action* $a^* \in A$ *satisfying: for each* $i$, $\pi_i(a^*) > 0 \Rightarrow \pi_i(a) = 0$ *for all* $a \in A$, $a \neq a^*$, *then* $L = 0$. (4) *If* $A$ *is a finite set and there is a first-best optimal action* $a^*$ *which satisfies: for some* $i$, $\pi_i(a^*) = 0$ *and* $\pi_i(a) > 0$ *for all* $a \in A$, $a \neq a^*$, *then* $L = 0$. (5) *If there is a first-best optimal action* $a^* \in A$ *which minimizes* $C_{FB}(a)$ *on* $A$, $L = 0$. (6) *If Assumption* A3 *holds, every maximizer* $\tilde{a}$ *of* $B(a) - C_{FB}(a)$ *on* $A$ *satisfies* $C_{FB}(\tilde{a}) > \min_{a \in A} C_{FB}(a)$, *and* $V$ *is strictly concave, then* $L > 0$.

PROOF: (1) is obvious since anything which is second-best feasible is also first-best feasible. (2) follows from the first part of the proof of Proposition 1. (5) follows from the proof of Proposition 1 (see also Remark 1). (3) and (4) follow from the fact that $a^*$ can be implemented by offering the agent $I_i = C_{FB}(a^*)$ for those $i$ such that $\pi_i(a^*) > 0$ and $I$ close to $\underline{I}$ otherwise.

To prove (6), note that, if $V$ is strictly concave,

$$G(a^*) + K(a^*) \sum_{i=1}^{n} \pi_i(a^*)V(I_i) \geq \overline{U}$$

implies

$$C(a^*) = \sum_{i=1}^{n} \pi_i(a^*)h(V(I_i))$$

$$> h\left(\sum_{i=1}^{n} \pi_i(a^*)V(I_i)\right) \geq h\left((\overline{U} - G(a^*))/K(a^*)\right)$$

$$= C_{FB}(a^*)$$

unless $I_i = $ constant with probability 1. But, since $\pi_i(a^*) > 0$ for all $i$, $I_i = $ constant with probability $1 \Rightarrow I_i$ is independent of $i$. However, in this case, the constraints of problem (2.2) imply that $C_{FB}(a)$ is minimized at $a^*$.          *Q.E.D.*

Most of Proposition 3 is well known. Proposition 3(2) and (6) can be understood as follows. In the first-best situation, if the agent is strictly risk averse, the principal bears all the risk and the agent bears none. In the second best situation, this is generally undesirable. For if the agent is completely protected from risk, then he has no incentive to work hard; i.e., he will choose $a \in A$ to minimize $C_{FB}(a)$. Hence the second-best situation is strictly worse from a welfare point of view than the first-best situation. The exception is when the agent is risk neutral, in which case it is optimal both from a risk sharing and an incentive point of view for him to bear all the risk, or when the first-best optimal action is cost minimizing.

In the case of Proposition 3(3) and 3(4), a scheme in which the agent is penalized very heavily if certain outcomes occur can be used to achieve the first best. This relates to results obtained in Mirrlees [12].

REMARK 3: We have assumed that the principal is risk neutral. Our analysis generalizes to the case where the principal is risk averse, however. In this case, instead of choosing $v$ to minimize $\sum \pi_i(a^*)h(v_i)$ in problem (2.2), we choose $v$ to maximize $\sum \pi_i(a^*)U_p(q_i - h(v_i))$, where $U_p$ is the principal's utility function. Note that (2.2) is still a convex problem. Although we can no longer analyze costs and benefits separately, we can, for each $a^* \in A$, define a net benefit function $\max_v \sum \pi_i(a^*)U_p(q_i - h(v_i))$. An optimal action for the principal is now one that maximizes net benefits. See also Section 6 on this.

REMARK 4: We have taken the outcomes observed by the principal to be profit levels. Our analysis generalizes, however, to the case where the outcomes are more complicated objects, such as vectors of profits, sales, etc., or to the case where profits are not observed at all but something else is (see, e.g., Mirrlees [11]). The important point to realize is that profit does not appear in the cost minimization problem (2.1) or (2.2). Thus, if the principal observes the realizations of a signal $\tilde{\theta}$, then $I_i$ refers to the payment to the agent when $\tilde{\theta} = \theta_i$. Let $\hat{C}(a, \tilde{\theta})$ be the cost of implementing $a$ when the information structure is $\tilde{\theta}$ (e.g. if $\tilde{\theta}$ reveals $a$ exactly, then $\hat{C}(a, \tilde{\theta}) = C_{FB}(a)$). Note that if the distribution of output is generated by a production function $f(a, \tilde{w})$, such that the marginal distribution of $\tilde{w}$ is independent of the information structure, then $B(a) = Ef(a, \tilde{w}) = E[E[f(a, \tilde{w})|\theta]]$ is independent of the information structure, given $a$. It follows that the effect of changes in the information structure is summarized by the way that $C(a, \tilde{\theta})$ changes when the information structure changes. As will be seen in Section 5, this is quite easy to analyze.

### 3. SOME CHARACTERISTICS OF OPTIMAL INCENTIVE SCHEMES

It is of interest to know whether the optimal incentive scheme is monotone increasing (i.e., whether the agent is paid more when a higher output is observed) and whether the scheme is progressive (i.e., whether the marginal benefit to the agent of increased output is decreasing in output). These questions are quite difficult to answer because of the informational role of output. As we noted in the introduction, the agent may be given a low income at intermediate levels of output in order to discourage particular effort levels. Nevertheless, some general results about the shape of optimal schemes can be established. We begin with the following lemma.

LEMMA 1: *Assume* A1–A3. *Let* $(I_i)_{i=1}^n, (I_i')_{i=1}^n$ *be incentive schemes which cause* $a$ *and* $a'$ *to be optimal choices for the agent, respectively, and minimize the respective costs (i.e. (2.1) or (2.2) is solved). Let* $v_i = V(I_i)$ *and* $v_i' = V(I_i')$. *Then, if* $G(a) + K(a)(\sum_{i=1}^n \pi_i(a)v_i) = G(a') + K(a')(\sum_{i=1}^n \pi_i(a')v_i')$, *i.e. the agent's expected utility is the same under both schemes, we must have*

$$(3.1) \qquad \sum_i [\pi_i(a') - \pi_i(a)](v_i' - v_i) \geq 0.$$

PROOF: From (2.2) and the assumption that the agent's expected utility is the same, we have

$$G(a') + K(a')\left(\sum_{i=1}^n \pi_i(a')v_i\right) \leq G(a) + K(a)\left(\sum_{i=1}^n \pi_i(a)v_i\right)$$

$$= G(a') + K(a')\left(\sum_{i=1}^n \pi_i(a')v_i'\right),$$

$$G(a) + K(a)\left(\sum_{i=1}^n \pi_i(a)v_i'\right) \leq G(a') + K(a')\left(\sum_{i=1}^n \pi_i(a')v_i'\right)$$

$$= G(a) + K(a)\left(\sum_{i=1}^n \pi_i(a)v_i\right).$$

It follows from the first of these that $\sum_{i=1}^{n} \pi_i(a')(v_i' - v_i) \geq 0$ and from the second that $\sum_{i=1}^{n} \pi_i(a)(v_i - v_i') \geq 0$ (since $K(a) > 0$ by Assumption A1(3)). Adding yields (3.1).                                                                                 Q.E.D.

We now use Lemma 1 to show that an optimal incentive scheme will have the property that the principal's and agent's returns are positive related over some range of output levels; i.e., it is not optimal to have, for all output levels $q_i$, $q_j : I_i > I_j \Rightarrow q_i - I_i < q_j - I_j$. The proof proceeds by showing that, if the principal's and agent's payments are negatively related, then a twist in the incentive schedule which raises the agent's payment in high return states for the principal and lowers it in low return states for the principal can make the principal better off. The reason is that such a twist will be good for incentives since it gets the agent to put more probability weight on states yielding the principal a high return, and it is also good for risk-sharing since it raises the agent's return in low return states for the agent and lowers the agent's return in high return states for the agent. Since the incentive and risk-sharing effects reinforce each other, the principal is made better off.

In order to bring about both the incentive and risk-sharing effects, the twist in the incentive scheme must be chosen carefully. It is for this reason that the proof of the next proposition may seem rather complicated at first sight.

PROPOSITION 4: *Assume A1–A3 and V strictly concave. Let $(I_1, \ldots, I_n)$ be a second-best optimal incentive scheme. Then the following cannot be true: $I_i > I_j \Rightarrow q_i - I_i \leq q_j - I_j$ for all $1 \leq i, j \leq n$ and for some $i, j$, $I_i > I_j$ and $q_i - I_i < q_j - I_j$.*

PROOF: Suppose that

$$(3.2) \qquad I_i > I_j \Rightarrow q_i - I_i \leq q_j - I_j$$

for all $1 \leq i, j \leq n$ and for some $i, j$, $I_i > I_j$ and $q_i - I_i < q_j - I_j$.

Let $(I_1', \ldots, I_n')$ be a new incentive scheme satisfying

$$(3.3) \qquad v_i' + \lambda h(v_i') = v_i + \lambda q_i - \mu \qquad \text{for all } i$$

where $v_i = V(I_i)$, $v_i' = V(I_i')$, $\lambda > 0$, and $\mu$ is such that

$$(3.4) \qquad \lambda \max_i (q_i - h(v_i)) \geq \mu \geq \lambda \min_i (q_i - h(v_i)).$$

If $\lambda = \mu = 0$, then $v_i' = v_i$ solves (3.3). The implicit function theorem therefore implies that (3.3) has a solution as long as $\lambda$, $\mu$ are small. (Even if $h$ is not differentiable it has left and right hand derivatives.)

It follows from (3.2) and (3.4) that the change to the new incentive scheme has the effect of increasing the lowest $I_i$'s and decreasing the highest ones. For each $\lambda$ pick $\mu$ so that $G(a') + K(a')(\sum_{i=1}^{n} \pi_i(a')v_i') = \max_{a \in A}[G(a) + K(a)(\sum_{i=1}^{n} \pi_i(a) v_i')] = \max_{a \in A}[G(a) + K(a)(\sum_{i=1}^{n} \pi_i(a)v_i)]$. This ensures that the agent's expected utility remains the same. We now show that the principal's expected profit is higher under the new incentive scheme than under the old, which contradicts the optimality of $(I_1, \ldots, I_n)$.

Substituting (3.1) of Lemma 1 into (3.3) yields:

$$\sum_i \pi_i(a')(q_i - h(v_i')) \geq \sum_i \pi_i(a)(q_i - h(v_i')).$$

If we can show that $\sum \pi_i(a)h(v_i') < \sum \pi_i(a)h(v_i)$, it will follow that

$$\sum \pi_i(a')(q_i - h(v_i')) > \sum \pi_i(a)(q_i - h(v_i)),$$

i.e., the principal is better off.

To see that $\sum \pi_i(a)h(v_i') < \sum \pi_i(a)h(v_i)$, note that

$$\sum \pi_i(a)(h(v_i) - h(v_i')) \geq \sum \pi_i(a)h'(v_i')(v_i - v_i')$$

by the convexity of $h$ (here $h'$ is the right-hand derivative if $h$ is not differentiable). It suffices therefore to show that the latter expression is positive. By (3.3),

$$\sum \pi_i(a)h'(v_i')(v_i - v_i') = \sum \pi_i(a)h'(v_i')(\lambda h(v_i') - \lambda q_i + \mu).$$

Suppose that this is nonpositive for small $\lambda$. Divide by $\lambda$ and let $\lambda \to 0$. Assuming without loss of generality $\mu/\lambda$ converges to $\hat{\mu}$ (we allow $\hat{\mu}$ infinite) and that $h'(v_i')$ converges to $\hat{h}_i'$, and using the fact that $v_i' \to v_i$, we get

$$(3.5) \qquad \sum \pi_i(a)\hat{h}_i'(h(v_i) - q_i + \hat{\mu}) \leq 0.$$

However, from the fact that $h'(v_i')$ is nondecreasing in $v_i'$ and $v_i' \to v_i$, $h'(v_i') \to \hat{h}_i'$, it follows that $v_i > v_j \Rightarrow \hat{h}_i' \geq \hat{h}_j'$. Hence by (3.2) $\hat{h}_i'$ and $(h(v_i) - q_i)$ are similarly ordered in the sense of Hardy, Littlewood, and Polya [5]; i.e., as one moves up so does the other. Therefore, by Hardy, Littlewood, and Polya [5, p. 43], $\hat{h}_i'$ and $(h(v_i) - q_i)$ are positively correlated, i.e.,

$$(3.6) \qquad \sum \pi_i(a)\hat{h}_i'(h(v_i) - q_i + \hat{\mu}) > \left( \sum \pi_i(a)\hat{h}_i' \right)\left( \sum \pi_i(a)(h(v_i) - q_i + \hat{\mu}) \right)$$

$$\geq 0,$$

where the last inequality follows from the fact that (1) $h' \geq 0$; (2) $G(a) + K(a)$ $(\sum \pi_i(a)v_i') \leq G(a') + K(a')(\sum \pi_i(a')v_i') = G(a) + K(a)(\sum \pi_i(a)v_i)$ (since the agent's expected utility stays constant), which implies that

$$\lim_{\lambda \to 0} (1/\lambda) \sum \pi_i(a)(v_i - v_i') \geq 0.$$

(3.6) contradicts (3.5).

This proves that $\sum \pi_i(a)h(v_i') < \sum \pi_i(a)h(v_i)$, which establishes that the principal's expected profit is higher under $(I_1', \ldots, I_n')$. Contradiction.          Q.E.D.

REMARK 5: Another way of expressing Proposition 4 is that there is no permutation $i_1, \ldots, i_n$ of the integers $1, \ldots, n$ such that $I_{i_k}$ is nondecreasing in $k$, and $(q_{i_k} - I_{i_k})$ is nonincreasing in $k$, with $I_{i_k} < I_{i_{k+1}}$, $(q_{i_k} - I_{i_k}) > (q_{i_{k+1}} - I_{i_{k+1}})$ for some $k$. Note that there is an interesting contrast between Proposition 4 and results found in the literature on optimal risk sharing in the absence of moral hazard. In this literature (see Borch [4]), it is shown that (if the individuals are risk averse) it is optimal for the individuals' returns to be positively related over the *whole* range of outcomes, whereas here we are only able to show that this is true over some range of outcomes.

Proposition 4 may be used to establish the following result about the monotonicity of the optimal incentive scheme.

PROPOSITION 5: *Assume A1–A3 and V strictly concave. Let $(I_1, \ldots, I_n)$ be a second-best optimal incentive scheme. Then (1) there exists $1 \leq i \leq n - 1$ such that $I_i \leq I_{i+1}$, with strict inequality unless $I_1 = I_2 = \cdots = I_n$; (2) there exists $1 \leq j \leq n - 1$ such that $q_j - I_j < q_{j+1} - I_{j+1}$.*

PROOF: (1) follows directly from Proposition 4. So does (2) once we rule out the case $q_1 - I_1 = q_2 - I_2 = \cdots = q_n - I_n$. We do this by a similar argument to that used in Proposition 4. Suppose that $I$ is an optimal incentive scheme satisfying

(3.7) $\qquad q_1 - I_1 = q_2 - I_2 = \cdots = q_n - I_n = k.$

Then $I_1 < I_2 < \cdots < I_n$. Consider the new incentive scheme $I' = (I_1 + \epsilon, I_2 + \epsilon, \ldots, I_{n-1} + \epsilon, I_n - \mu\epsilon)$ where $\epsilon > 0$ and $\mu$ is chosen so that $\max_{a \in A}[G(a) + K(a)(\sum \pi_i(a) V(I_i'))] = \max_{A \in A}[G(a) + K(a)(\sum \pi_i(a) V(I_i))]$, i.e. the agent's expected utility is kept constant. We show that the principal's expected profit is higher under $I'$ than under $I$ for small $\epsilon$. Suppose not. Then

$$\sum \pi_i(a')(q_i - I_i') \leq \sum \pi_i(a)(q_i - I_i) = k,$$

where $a'$ (resp. $a$) is optimal for the agent under $I'$ (resp. $I$). Substituting for $I'$ yields

$$-(1 - \pi_n(a'))\epsilon + \pi_n(a')\mu\epsilon \leq 0.$$

Take limits as $\epsilon \to 0$. Without loss of generality $a' \to \hat{a}$. Hence we have

(3.8) $\qquad -(1 - \pi_n(\hat{a})) + \pi_n(\hat{a})\mu \leq 0.$

Now since $a'$ is an optimal action for the agent under $I'$, it follows by uppersemicontinuity that $\hat{a}$ is optimal under $I$. Hence we have

$$G(\hat{a}) + K(\hat{a})\left(\sum \pi_i(\hat{a}) V(I_i')\right) \leq G(a') + K(a')\left(\sum \pi_i(a') V(I_i')\right)$$

$$= G(\hat{a}) + K(\hat{a})\left(\sum \pi_i(\hat{a}) V(I_i)\right).$$

Hence $\sum \pi_i(\hat{a})(V(I_i) - V(I_i')) \geq 0$. Using the concavity of $V$ and taking limits as

$\epsilon \to 0$, we get

$$\sum_{i=1}^{n-1} \pi_i(\hat{a})V'(I_i) - \pi_n(\hat{a})V'(I_n)\mu \le 0.$$

But since $V'(I_i)$ is decreasing in $i$, this contradicts (3.8). (If $V$ is not differentiable, $V'$ denotes the right-hand derivative.)

This proves that the principal does better under $I'$ than under $I$. Hence we have ruled out the case $q_1 - I_1 = \cdots = q_n - I_n$. This establishes Proposition 5.

*Q.E.D.*

Proposition 5 says that it is not optimal for the agent's marginal reward as a function of income to be negative everywhere or to be greater than or equal to one everywhere.[8] However, the proposition does allow for the possibility that either of these conditions can hold over some interval. To see when this may occur, it is useful to consider in more detail the case where $A$ is a finite set. When $A$ is finite, we can use the Kuhn–Tucker conditions for problem (2.2) to characterize the optimum. If Assumption A3 holds and $h$ is differentiable, these yield:

$$(3.9) \qquad h'(v_i) = \left[\lambda + \sum_{\substack{a_j \in A \\ a_j \ne a^*}} \mu_j\right] K(a^*) - \sum_{\substack{a_j \in A \\ a_j \ne a^*}} \mu_j K(a_j)\left(\frac{\pi_i(a_j)}{\pi_i(a^*)}\right) \qquad \text{for all } i,$$

where $\lambda, (\mu_j)$ are nonnegative Lagrange multipliers and $\mu_j > 0$ only if the agent is indifferent between $a^*$ and $a_j$ at the optimum. The following proposition states that $\mu_j > 0$ for at least one action which is less costly than $a^*$. This implies that at an optimum the agent must be indifferent between at least two actions (unless $a^*$ is the least costly action, i.e. where there is no incentive problem).

PROPOSITION 6: *Assume A1–A3 and A finite. Suppose that (2.2) has a solution for $a^* \in A$. Then if $C_{FB}(a^*) > \min_{a \in A} C_{FB}(a)$, this solution will have the property that $G(a^*) + K(a^*)(\sum_{i=1}^{n}\pi_i(a^*)v_i) = G(a_j) + K(a_j)(\sum_{i=1}^{n}\pi_i(a_j)v_i)$ for some $a_j \in A$ with $C_{FB}(a_j) < C_{FB}(a^*)$. Furthermore, if $V$ is strictly concave and differentiable, the Lagrange multiplier $\mu_j$ will be strictly positive for some $a_j$ with $C_{FB}(a_j) < C_{FB}(a^*)$.*

PROOF: Suppose that the agent strictly prefers $a^*$ to all actions less costly than $a^*$ at the solution. Then, since (2.2) is a convex problem, we can drop all the constraints in (2.2) which refer to less costly actions without affecting the

---

[8] Among other things, Proposition 5 shows that it is not optimal to have $q_1 - I_1 = q_2 - I_2 = \cdots = q_n - I_n$. This result has also been established by Shavell [20] under stronger assumptions.

solution. In other words, we can substitute $A' = \{a \in A \mid a$ is at least as costly as $a*\}$ for $A$ in (2.2) and the solution will not change. But since $a*$ is now the least costly action, we know from the proof of Proposition 1 that it is optimal to set $I_i = I_j$ for all $i, j$. However, $I_i = I_j$ is not optimal for the original problem since, under these conditions, the agent will pick an $a$ which minimizes $C_{FB}(a)$, and by assumption $C_{FB}(a*) > \min_{a \in A} C_{FB}(a)$. Contradiction.

That $\mu_j > 0$ follows from the fact that if all the $\mu_j = 0$, then $h'(v_i)$ is the same for all $i$, which implies that $I_1 = \cdots = I_n$; however, this means that the agent will choose a cost-minimizing action, contradicting $C_{FB}(a*) > \min_{a \in A} C_{FB}(a)$.

$$Q.E.D.$$

It should be noted that Proposition 6 depends strongly on the assumption that $A$ is finite.

The simplest case occurs when $\mu_j > 0$ for just one $a_j$ with $C_{FB}(a_j) < C_{FB}(a*)$ (this will be true in particular if $A$ contains only two actions). In this case, we can rewrite (3.9) as

$$(3.10) \quad h'(v_i) = (\lambda + \mu_j)K(a*) - \mu_j K(a_j) \frac{\pi_i(a_j)}{\pi_i(a*)} .$$

We see that what determines $v_i$, and hence $I_i$, in this case is the relative likelihood that the outcome $q = q_i$ results from $a_j$ rather than from $a*$. In particular, since $h$ convex $\Rightarrow h'$ nondecreasing in $v_i$, a sufficient condition for the optimal incentive scheme to be nondecreasing everywhere, i.e. $I_1 \leq I_2 \leq \cdots \leq I_n$, is that $\pi_i(a_j)/\pi_i(a*)$ is nonincreasing in $i$, i.e. the relative likelihood that $a = a_j$ rather than $a = a*$ produces the outcome $q = q_i$ is lower the better is the outcome $i$.

This observation has led some to suggest that the following is a sufficient conditon for the incentive scheme to be nondecreasing.

MONOTONE LIKELIHOOD RATIO CONDITION (MLRC): Assume A3. Then MLRC holds if, given $a, a' \in A$, $C_{FB}(a') \leq C_{FB}(a)$ implies that $\pi_i(a')/\pi_i(a)$ is nonincreasing in $i$.

It should be noted that the "first-order condition" approach described in the introduction, which is based on the assumption that the agent is indifferent between $a$ and $a + da$ at an optimum, does yield MLRC as a sufficient condition for monotonicity.[9] We now show, however, that, once we take into account the possibility that the agent may be indifferent between several actions at an

---

[9] See Mirrlees [11] or Holmstrom [7]. Milgrom [9] has shown that MLRC, as stated here, implies the differential version of the monotone likelihood condition which is to be found in Mirrlees [11] or Holmstrom [7].

optimum, i.e. $\mu_j > 0$ for more than one $a_j$, MLRC does not guarantee monotonicity.

EXAMPLE 1: $A = \{a_1, a_2, a_3\}$, $n = 3$. $\pi(a_1) = (\frac{2}{3}, \frac{1}{4}, \frac{1}{12})$, $\pi(a_2) = (\frac{1}{3}, \frac{1}{3}, \frac{1}{3})$, $\pi(a_3) = (\frac{1}{12}, \frac{1}{4}, \frac{2}{3})$. Assume additive separability with $G(a_1) = 0$, $G(a_2) = -(\frac{1}{12}\sqrt{2} + \frac{1}{4}\sqrt{7/4})$, $G(a_3) = -\frac{7}{12}\sqrt{7/4}$, $V(I) = (3I)^{1/3}$ (i.e. $h(v) = \frac{1}{3}v^3$), $K(a) \equiv 1$ and $\overline{U} = \frac{1}{4}\sqrt{2} + \frac{1}{12}\sqrt{7/4}$. Note that MLRC is satisfied here.[10]

We compute $C(a_1), C(a_2), C(a_3)$. Obviously, $C(a_1) = C_{FB}(a_1) = \frac{1}{3}(\overline{U} - G(a_1))^3 = 0.033$. To compute $C(a_2)$, we use the first-order conditions (3.9). These are

$$v_1^2 = \lambda - \mu_1 + \tfrac{3}{4}\mu_2,$$

$$v_2^2 = \lambda + \tfrac{1}{4}\mu_1 + \tfrac{1}{4}\mu_2,$$

$$v_3^2 = \lambda + \tfrac{3}{4}\mu_1 - \mu_2,$$

plus the complementary slackness conditions. These equations are solved by setting $\lambda = \frac{5}{4}$, $\mu_1 = 2$, $\mu_2 = 1$. This yields $v_1 = 0$, $v_2 = \sqrt{2}$, $v_3 = \sqrt{7/4}$, and the agent is then indifferent between $a_1$, $a_2$, and $a_3$:

$$\tfrac{2}{3}v_1 + \tfrac{1}{4}v_2 + \tfrac{1}{12}v_3 + G(a_1) = \tfrac{1}{3}v_1 + \tfrac{1}{3}v_2 + \tfrac{1}{3}v_3 + G(a_2)$$

$$= \tfrac{1}{12}v_1 + \tfrac{1}{4}v_2 + \tfrac{2}{3}v_3 + G(a_3) = \overline{U}.$$

Since the first-order conditions are necessary and sufficient, we may conclude that $C(a_2) = \frac{1}{3}(\frac{1}{3}v_1^3 + \frac{1}{3}v_2^3 + \frac{1}{3}v_3^3) = 0.571$.

Note that the incentive scheme which implements $a_2$, $I_1 = 0$, $I_2 = \frac{1}{3}2^{3/2}$, $I_3 = \frac{1}{3}(\frac{7}{4})^{3/2}$, is not nondecreasing.

Observe that $C(a_3) \geq C_{FB}(a_3) = \frac{1}{3}(\overline{U} - G(a_3))^3 = 0.635 > C(a_2)$. Since $C(a_3) > C(a_2) > C(a_1)$, it is easy to show that we can find $q_1 < q_2 < q_3$ such that $B(a_2) - C(a_2) > \max[B(a_3) - C(a_3), B(a_1) - C(a_1)]$. But this means that it is optimal for the principal to get the agent to pick $a_2$. Hence the optimal incentive scheme is as described above. It is not nondecreasing despite the satisfaction of MLRC.

The reason that monotonicity breaks down in Example 1 is because, at the optimum, the agent is indifferent between $a_2$, the action to be implemented, $a_1$ a less costly action, and $a_3$ a more costly action. By MLRC $\pi_i(a_1)/\pi_i(a_2), \pi_i(a_2)/\pi_i(a_3)$ are decreasing in $i$. However, $\mu_1(\pi_i(a_1)/\pi_i(a_2)) + \mu_2(\pi_i(a_3)/\pi_i(a_2))$ need not be monotonic.

This observation suggests that one way to get monotonicity is to strengthen MLRC so that it holds for weighted combinations of actions as well as for the

---

[10] The function $V$ violates (2) of Assumption A1, but this is unimportant for the example.

basic actions themselves. In particular, suppose that

(3.11)     given any finite subset $\{a_1, \ldots, a_m\}$ of $A$, $a \in A$,

and nonnegative weights $w_1, \ldots, w_m$ summing to 1,

it is the case that $\left( \sum_{j=1}^{m} w_j \pi_i(a_j) / \pi_i(a) \right)$

is either nondecreasing in $i$ or nonincreasing in $i$.

Then, by the first-order conditions (3.9),

$$(3.12) \quad h'(v_i) = \left[ \lambda + \sum_{\substack{a_j \in A \\ a_j \neq a^*}} \mu_j \right] K(a^*) - \left[ \sum_{\substack{a_j \in A \\ a_j \neq a^*}} \mu_j K(a_j) \right] \left[ \sum_{\substack{a_j \in A \\ a_j \neq a^*}} w_j \left( \frac{\pi_i(a_j)}{\pi_i(a^*)} \right) \right],$$

where

$$w_j = \mu_j K(a_j) \Bigg/ \sum_{\substack{a_h \in A \\ a_h \neq a^*}} \mu_h K(a_h).$$

But, by (3.11), the right-hand side (RHS) of (3.12) is monotonic. Hence, the $v_i$'s are either monotonically nondecreasing or nonincreasing. By Proposition 5, however, they cannot be nonincreasing; hence they are nondecreasing.

Unfortunately, (3.11) turns out to be a very strong condition. In fact, it is equivalent to the following spanning condition.

SPANNING CONDITION (SC): There exists $\hat{\pi}, \hat{\pi}' \in S$ such that (1) for each $a \in A$, $\pi(a) = \lambda(a)\hat{\pi} + (1 - \lambda(a))\hat{\pi}'$ for some $0 \leq \lambda(a) \leq 1$; (2) $\hat{\pi}_i / \hat{\pi}_i'$ is nonincreasing in $i$.

That SC implies (3.11) is easy to see. We are grateful to Jim Mirrlees for pointing out and proving the converse.[11]

PROPOSITION 7: *Assume A1–A3, V strictly concave and differentiable. Suppose that SC holds. Then a second-best optimal incentive scheme satisfies* $I_1 \leq I_2 \leq \cdots \leq I_n$.

PROOF: If $A$ is finite, the argument following (3.12) establishes the result. To establish the result for the case $A$ infinite, let $\hat{a} \in A$ be a second-best optimal

---

[11] To prove the converse, define $a \lesssim a'$ if $\pi_i(a') / \pi_i(a)$ is nondecreasing in $i$. (3.11) implies that $\lesssim$ is a complete pre-ordering on $A$. Furthermore, $\lesssim$ is continuous. Since $A$ is compact, there exist $\underline{a}, \bar{a} \in A$ such that $\underline{a} \lesssim a \lesssim \bar{a}$ for all $a \in A$. Given $a \in A$, consider $\lambda(\pi_i(\bar{a}) / \pi_i(a)) + (1 - \lambda)(\pi_i(\underline{a}) / \pi_i(a))$. When $\lambda = 1$, this is nondecreasing in $i$, and when $\lambda = 0$, it is nonincreasing in $i$. Furthermore, (3.11) implies that it is monotonic in $i$ for all $0 < \lambda < 1$. It follows by continuity that it is independent of $i$ for some $0 < \lambda < 1$.

action and let $I$ be the second-best optimal incentive scheme which implements it. By Remark 2 of Section 2, $I$ is unique. Let $A_r$ be a finite subset of $A$ containing $\hat{a}$ such that the Euclidean distance between $A_r$ and $A$ is less than $(1/r)$. Let $I_r$ be the second-best optimal incentive scheme which implements $\hat{a}$ when the agent is restricted to choosing from $A_r$. From Proposition 7 for the finite $A$ case, we know that $I_r$ is nondecreasing. Take limits as $r \to \infty$. It is straightforward to show that $I_r \to I$. It follows that $I$ is nondecreasing.     *Q.E.D.*

An alternative sufficient condition for monotonicity may be found in the work of Mirrlees [12], who establishes a similar result to Proposition 8 below. For each $a \in A$, let $F(a) = (\pi_1(a), \pi_1(a) + \pi_2(a), \ldots, \pi_1(a) + \cdots + \pi_n(a))$. In the following proposition, the notation $F(a) \geq F'(a)$ is used to mean $F_i(a) \geq F_i'(a)$ for all $i = 1, \ldots, n$.

CONCAVITY OF DISTRIBUTION FUNCTION CONDITION (CDFC): CDFC holds if $a, a', a'' \in A$, and

$$\left( \frac{\overline{U} - G(a)}{K(a)} \right) = \lambda \left( \frac{\overline{U} - G(a')}{K(a')} \right) + (1 - \lambda) \left( \frac{\overline{U} - G(a'')}{K(a'')} \right),$$

$$0 \leq \lambda \leq 1,$$

imply that $F(a) \leq \lambda F(a') + (1 - \lambda) F(a'')$.

PROPOSITION 8: *Assume A1–A3, $V$ strictly concave and differentiable. Assume also that $U$ is additively or multiplicatively separable, i.e., either $G(a) \equiv 0$ or $K(a) \equiv$ constant. Suppose that MLRC and CDFC hold. Then a second-best optimal incentive scheme $(I_1, \ldots, I_n)$ satisfies $I_1 \leq I_2 \leq \cdots \leq I_n$.*

PROOF: Assume first that $A$ is finite. Let $a^*$ maximize $B(a) - C(a)$. Let $A' = \{a \in A \mid C_{FB}(a) \leq C_{FB}(a^*)\}$. Consider the cost minimizing way of getting the agent to pick $a^*$ given that he can choose only from $A'$. It is clear from (3.9) that, since $\pi_i(a_j)/\pi_i(a^*)$ is nonincreasing in $i$ by MLRC, the incentive scheme $(I_1, \ldots, I_n)$ is nondecreasing. We will be home if we can show that $(I_1, \ldots, I_n)$ is optimal when $A'$ is replaced by $A$. Since adding actions cannot reduce the cost of implementing $a^*$, all we have to do is to show that $(I_1, \ldots, I_n)$ continues to implement $a^*$, i.e. there does not exist $a''$, $C_{FB}(a'') > C_{FB}(a^*)$, such that

$$(3.13) \quad G(a'') + K(a'')\left( \sum \pi_i(a'') v_i \right) > G(a^*) + K(a^*)\left( \sum \pi_i(a^*) v_i \right).$$

However, we know from Propositions 2 and 6 that

$$(3.14) \quad G(a^*) + K(a^*)\left( \sum \pi_i(a^*) v_i \right) = G(a')+ K(a')\left( \sum \pi_i(a') v_i \right) = \overline{U}$$

for some $a'$ with $C_{FB}(a') < C_{FB}(a^*)$. Writing

$$\frac{\overline{U} - G(a^*)}{K(a^*)} = \lambda \left( \frac{\overline{U} - G(a'')}{K(a'')} \right) + (1 - \lambda) \left( \frac{\overline{U} - G(a')}{K(a')} \right)$$

and using CDFC and the fact that $v_1 \leq v_2 \leq \cdots \leq v_n$, we get

$$\sum \pi_i(a^*)v_i - \left( \frac{\overline{U} - G(a^*)}{K(a^*)} \right)$$

$$\geq \lambda \sum \pi_i(a'')v_i + (1 - \lambda)\left( \sum \pi_i(a')v_i \right) - \left( \frac{\overline{U} - G(a^*)}{K(a^*)} \right)$$

$$= \lambda \left[ \sum \pi_i(a'')v_i - \left( \frac{\overline{U} - G(a'')}{K(a'')} \right) \right]$$

$$+ (1 - \lambda)\left[ \sum \pi_i(a')v_i - \left( \frac{\overline{U} - G(a')}{K(a')} \right) \right].$$

But this contradicts (3.13) and (3.14).

To prove the result for $A$ finite, one again proceeds by way of finite approximation.                                                                 Q.E.D.

To understand CDFC, consider, for each $a \in A$, $V(C_{FB}(a)) = ((\overline{U} - G(a)) / K(a))$. In utility terms $V(C_{FB}(a))$ is a measure of the first-best cost of getting the agent to pick $a$. CDFC says that if $a$ is a convex combination of $a'$ and $a''$ in terms of this measure of cost then the distribution function of outcomes corresponding to $a$ dominates in the sense of first degree stochastic dominance the corresponding convex combination of the distribution functions corresponding to $a'$ and $a''$. It is worth noting that under the assumption of additive or multiplicative separability in Proposition 8, the $\lambda$ in the CDFC definition is independent of $\overline{U}$.

So far we have considered only the monotonicity of the optimal incentive scheme. One would also like to know when the optimal incentive scheme is *progressive*, i.e. $(I_{i+1} - I_i)/(q_{i+1} - q_i)$ is nonincreasing in $i$, or *regressive*, i.e. $(I_{i+1} - I_i)/(q_{i+1} - q_i)$ is nondecreasing in $i$. To get results about this, one needs considerably stronger assumptions, as the following proposition indicates.

PROPOSITION 9: *Assume A1–A3, $V$ strictly concave and differentiable. Assume also that $U$ is additively or multiplicatively separable, i.e., either $G(a) \equiv 0$ or $K(a) \equiv$ constant. Suppose that MLRC and CDFC hold and that $(q_{i+1} - q_i)$ is independent of $i$, $1 \leq i \leq n - 1$. Then a second-best optimal incentive scheme will be regressive (resp. progressive) if*

(3.15)    *$(1/V'(I))$ is concave (resp. convex) in $I$ and $a, a' \in A$,*

$$C_{FB}(a') < C_{FB}(a), \text{ implies that } (\pi_{i+1}(a')/\pi_{i+1}(a)) - (\pi_i(a')/\pi_i(a))$$

*is nonincreasing (resp. nondecreasing) in $i$.*

PROOF: Assume first that $A$ is finite. Let $a^*$ be a second-best optimal action. Let $a'$ maximize $C_{FB}(a)$ subject to $C_{FB}(a) < C_{FB}(a^*)$, i.e. $a'$ is the next most costly action after $a^*$. Consider the cost minimizing way of implementing $a^*$ given that $a'$ is the only other action that the agent can choose. Using the same concavity argument as in the proof of Proposition 8, we can show that the resulting incentive scheme $(I_1, \ldots, I_n)$ also implements $a^*$ when the agent can choose from all of $A$. Hence $(I_1, \ldots, I_n)$ is an optimal incentive scheme.

By (3.10),

$$\frac{1}{V'(I_i)} = h'(v_i) = (\lambda + \mu)K(a^*) - \mu K(a') \frac{\pi_i(a')}{\pi_i(a^*)}$$

and so

$$\frac{1}{V'(I_{i+1})} - \frac{1}{V'(I_i)} = -\mu K(a') \left( \frac{\pi_{i+1}(a')}{\pi_{i+1}(a^*)} - \frac{\pi_i(a')}{\pi_i(a^*)} \right).$$

(3.15) now follows immediately. To prove the result for the $A$ infinite case, one again proceeds by way of a finite approximation. $\qquad$ *Q.E.D.*

Note that $1/V'$ is linear if $V = \log I$; is concave if $V = -e^{-\alpha I}$, $\alpha > 0$, or $V = I^\alpha$, $0 < \alpha < 1$; is convex if $V = -I^{-\alpha}$, $\alpha > 1$.

It should also be noted that Mirrlees [12] has shown that if CDFC holds, the "first-order condition" approach referred to in the introduction is valid. Thus Propositions 8 and 9 can also be proved by appealing to the characterization of an optimal incentive scheme to be found in much of the literature (see, e.g., Holmstrom [7] and Mirrlees [11]).

Let us summarize the results of this section. We have shown that an optimal incentive scheme will not be declining everywhere, but that only under quite strong assumptions (SC or MLRC plus concavity) will it be nondecreasing everywhere. We have also shown that it is not optimal for the agent's marginal remuneration for an extra pound of profit to exceed one everywhere, although it may exceed one sometimes. Finally, we have obtained sufficient conditions for the incentive scheme to be progressive or regressive.

The conclusion that only under strong assumptions will the optimal incentive scheme be monotonic may seem disappointing at first sight. One feels that monotonicity is a minimal requirement. This may not be the right reaction, however. There are many interesting situations where it is clear that the optimal scheme will not be monotonic. We have described one example in the introduction. Another example is the following. Suppose that actions are two dimensional, with one dimension referring to how hard the agent works and the other dimension to how cautious he is—greater caution might lead to a lower variance of profit but also to a lower mean. The optimal action for the principal might involve the agent working fairly hard and also not being too cautious. The best way to implement this may be to pay the agent high amounts for both very good outcomes (to encourage high effort) and very bad outcomes (to discourage excessive caution). This example seems far from pathological. In fact, one might argue that a number of real world incentive schemes operate in this way. In view of examples like this, the difficulty of finding general conditions guaranteeing monotonicity may become less surprising.[12]

In the next section, we show that considerably stronger results than those of this section can be proved for the case $n = 2$. We also provide a simple algorithm for computing optimal incentive schemes when $n = 2$.

### 4. THE CASE OF TWO OUTCOMES

When $n = 2$, we will refer to $q_1$ as the "bad" outcome and $q_2 > q_1$ as the "good" outcome. In this case, the agent's incentive scheme can be represented simply by a fixed payment $w$ and a share of profits, $s$, where $w + sq_1 = I_1$, $w + sq_2 = I_2$, i.e., $s = (I_2 - I_1)/(q_2 - q_1)$. Proposition 5 of the last section shows that it is not optimal for $I_i$ to be everywhere declining in $q_i$. When $n = 2$, this means that $s \geq 0$.[13] Similarly the proposition implies that $s < 1$ when $n = 2$. This has a number of interesting implications.

DEFINITION: Let $n = 2$. We say that $a \in A$ is *efficient* if there does not exist $a' \in A$ satisfying $C_{FB}(a') \leq C_{FB}(a)$ and $\pi_2(a') \geq \pi_2(a)$, with at least one strict inequality.

In other words, an action is efficient if the probability of a good outcome can only be increased by incurring greater cost.

PROPOSITION 10: *Assume A1–A3 and V strictly concave. Let $n = 2$. Then every second-best optimal action is efficient.*

PROOF: Let $a$ be a second-best optimal action. Then $a$ maximizes $G(a) + K(a)$ $[\pi_1(a)v_1 + \pi_1(a)v_2]$. Suppose $C_{FB}(a') \leq C_{FB}(a)$ and $\pi_2(a') \geq \pi_2(a)$, with at least one strict inequality. Then, by the definition of $C_{FB}$,

$$G(a) + K(a)V(C_{FB}(a)) = \overline{U} = G(a') + K(a')V(C_{FB}(a'))$$

$$\leq G(a') + K(a')V(C_{FB}(a)),$$

---

[12] There are some cases where monotonicity may be a *constraint* on the optimal incentive scheme. An example is where the agent can always make a better outcome look like a worse outcome by reducing the firm's profits after the outcome has occurred. This case can be analyzed by adding the (linear) constraints $v_1 \leq v_2 \leq \cdots \leq v_n$ to the problem (2.2).

[13] Shavell [19] also proves that $s \geq 0$ when $n = 2$, but under stronger assumptions.

since $C_{FB}(a') \leq C_{FB}(a)$. Hence, by Assumption A1(4), $G(a) + K(a)v \leq G(a') + K(a')v$ for all $v \in \mathfrak{U}$. Therefore using the fact that $v_1 \leq v_2$ since $s \geq 0$, and the fact that $\pi_2(a') \geq \pi_2(a)$, we have

$$G(a) + K(a)\left[\pi_1(a)v_1 + \pi_2(a)v_2\right]$$

$$\leq G(a') + K(a')\left[\pi_1(a)v_1 + \pi_2(a)v_2\right]$$

$$\leq G(a') + K(a')\left[\pi_1(a')v_1 + \pi_2(a')v_2\right]$$

with at least one strict inequality unless $C_{FB}(a) = C_{FB}(a')$ and $v_1 = v_2$. This contradicts the optimality of $a$ unless $C_{FB}(a) = C_{FB}(a')$ and $v_1 = v_2$. However, in this case, the agent is indifferent between $a$ and $a'$, while the principal prefers $a'$, again contradicting the optimality of $a$.                    *Q.E.D.*

We may use Proposition 10 to prove that when $n = 2$ it will never pay the principal to offer the agent an expected utility in excess of $\overline{U}$ (recall that when $n > 2$ this is only generally true when $U(a, I)$ is additively or multiplicatively separable—see Proposition 2).

PROPOSITION 11: *Assume A1–A3 and $V$ strictly concave. Let $n = 2$. Let $\hat{a}$ be a second-best optimal action and $\hat{I}$ a second-best optimal incentive scheme which implements $\hat{a}$. Then $\sum_{i=1}^{n} \pi_i(\hat{a}) U(\hat{a}, \hat{I}_i) = \overline{U}$.*

PROOF: Suppose not, i.e., $\sum_{i=1}^{n} \pi_i(\hat{a}) U(\hat{a}, \hat{I}_i) > \overline{U}$. Consider a new incentive scheme $(I_1, I_2) = (\hat{I}_1 - \epsilon, \hat{I}_2)$ where $\epsilon > 0$ is small. Let $a$ be an optimal action for the agent under the new scheme, i.e., $a$ maximizes $G(a) + K(a)[\pi_1(a)V(\hat{I}_1 - \epsilon) + \pi_2(a)V(\hat{I}_2)]$. Then,

$$\pi_1(a)(q_1 - I_1 + \epsilon) + \pi_2(a)(q_2 - I_2) > \pi_1(a)(q_1 - I_1) + \pi_2(a)(q_2 - I_2)$$

$$\geq \pi_1(\hat{a})(q_1 - \hat{I}_1) + \pi_2(\hat{a})(q_2 - \hat{I}_2)$$

as long as $\pi_2(\hat{a}) \leq \pi_2(a)$ (since $0 \leq s < 1$). Thus, if we can show that $\pi_2(\hat{a}) \leq \pi_2(a)$, we will have contradicted the optimality of $(\hat{I}_1, \hat{I}_2)$, since the principal's profits will be higher under $(I_1, I_2)$ than under $(\hat{I}_1, \hat{I}_2)$.

Suppose $\pi_2(\hat{a}) > \pi_2(a)$. Now the same argument as in Proposition 10 shows that $a$ is efficient. Thus we must have $C_{FB}(\hat{a}) > C_{FB}(a)$. Hence $G(a) + K(a) V(C_{FB}(a)) = \overline{U} = G(\hat{a}) + K(\hat{a})V(C_{FB}(\hat{a})) > G(\hat{a}) + K(\hat{a})V(C_{FB}(a))$, and so, by Assumption A1(4),

(4.1)      $G(a) + K(a)v > G(\hat{a}) + K(\hat{a})v$

for all $v \in \mathfrak{U} \equiv \{V(I) | I \in \mathfrak{I}\}$. Since $\mathfrak{U}$ contains arbitrarily large negative numbers, we may conclude from (4.1) that $K(a) \leq K(\hat{a})$. Now by revealed preference,

(4.2) $\qquad G(a) + K(a)\left[\pi_1(a)V(\hat{I}_1) + \pi_2(a)V(\hat{I}_2)\right]$

$\qquad\qquad \leq G(\hat{a}) + K(\hat{a})\left[\pi_1(\hat{a})V(\hat{I}_1) + \pi_2(\hat{a})V(\hat{I}_2)\right],$

(4.3) $\qquad G(a) + K(a)\left[\pi_1(a)V(\hat{I}_1 - \epsilon) + \pi_2(a)V(\hat{I}_2)\right]$

$\qquad\qquad \geq G(\hat{a}) + K(\hat{a})\left[\pi_1(\hat{a})V(\hat{I}_1 - \epsilon) + \pi_2(\hat{a})V(\hat{I}_2)\right].$

Subtracting (4.3) from (4.2) yields $K(a)\pi_1(a) \leq K(\hat{a})\pi_1(a)$. Hence, since $\pi_2(\hat{a}) > \pi_2(a)$ by assumption, $K(a) < K(\hat{a})$. However, rewriting (4.2), we obtain

$$G(a) + K(a)\bar{v} + K(a)\left[\pi_1(a)(V(\hat{I}_1) - \bar{v}) + \pi_2(a)(V(\hat{I}_2) - \bar{v})\right]$$

$$\leq G(\hat{a}) + K(\hat{a})\bar{v} + K(\hat{a})\left[\pi_1(\hat{a})(V(\hat{I}_1) - \bar{v}) + \pi_2(\hat{a})(V(\hat{I}_2) - \bar{v})\right]$$

where $\bar{v} = \sup \mathcal{U}$. (Note that $\bar{v} < \infty$, for $\bar{v} = \infty$ and $K(a) < K(\hat{a})$ violate (4.1).) Setting $v = \bar{v}$ in (4.1), we may conclude that

$$K(a)\pi_1(a)(V(\hat{I}_1) - \bar{v}) + K(a)\pi_2(a)(V(\hat{I}_2) - \bar{v})$$

$$\leq K(\hat{a})\pi_1(\hat{a})(V(\hat{I}_1) - \bar{v}) + K(\hat{a})\pi_2(\hat{a})(V(\hat{I}_2) - \bar{v}).$$

But this is impossible since $K(a)\pi_1(a) \leq K(\hat{a})\pi_1(\hat{a})$, $K(a) < K(\hat{a})$, $\pi_2(a) < \pi_2(\hat{a})$, $V(\hat{I}_1) - \bar{v} < 0$, $V(\hat{I}_2) - \bar{v} < 0$. We have thus shown that $\pi_2(a) \geq \pi_2(\hat{a})$, which contradicts the optimality of $(\hat{I}_1, \hat{I}_2)$. $\qquad\qquad Q.E.D.$

Proposition 11 tells us that the agent's fixed payment $w$ is determined once $s$ is. In particular, $w$ will be the unique solution of

$$\max_{a \in A}\left[G(a) + K(a)(\pi_1(a)V(w + sq_1) + \pi_2(a)V(w + sq_2))\right] = \overline{U}.$$

We have shown that one implication of Proposition 5 for the case $n = 2$ is that every second-best optimal action is efficient. We consider now a second implication. Suppose that we start off in the situation where the agent has access to a set of actions $A$, and now some additional actions become available, so that the new action set is $A' \supset A$. Then, if the new actions are all higher cost actions for the agent than those in $A$—in the sense that their $C_{FB}$'s are higher—the principal cannot be made worse off by such a change.

PROPOSITION 12: *Assume A1 and A2. Let $n = 2$. Suppose that $A' \supset A$ and that $a \in A$, $a' \in A' \backslash A \Rightarrow C_{FB}(a') \geq C_{FB}(a)$. Assume that A3 holds for both $A$ and $A'$. Then $\max_{a \in A}[B(a) - C'(a)] \geq \max_{a \in A}[B(a) - C(a)]$, where $C'$ is the second-best cost function under $A'$.*

PROOF: Suppose $(I_1, I_2)$ is an optimal second-best incentive scheme when the action set is $A$. Let the principal keep this incentive scheme when the new actions

$A' \backslash A$ are added. The only way that the principal can be made worse off is if the agent now switches from $a \in A$ to $a' \in A' \backslash A$. But $a'$ must then provide higher utility for the agent, i.e., $G(a') + K(a')[\pi_1(a')v_1 + \pi_2(a')v_2] > G(a) + K(a)[\pi_1(a) v_1 + \pi_2(a)v_2]$. Since $C_{FB}(a') \geq C_{FB}(a)$, however, $G(a') + K(a')v \leq G(a) + K(a)v$ for all $v \in \mathfrak{A}$ (by Assumption A1(4)). Hence $\pi_1(a')v_1 + \pi_2(a')v_2 > \pi(a)v_1 + \pi_2(a)v_2$, which implies, since $v_2 \geq v_1$ by Proposition 5, that $\pi_2(a') > \pi_2(a)$. But it follows that the principal's expected profits $\pi_1(q_1 - I_1) + \pi_2(q_2 - I_2)$ rise when the agent moves from $a$ to $a'$ since, again by Proposition 5, $s < 1$, i.e. $q_2 - I_2 > q_1 - I_1$. $\hspace{2cm} Q.E.D.$

As a final implication of Proposition 5, when $n = 2$, consider a manager-entrepreneur who initially owns 100 per cent of a firm, i.e. $\tilde{w} = 0$, $\tilde{s} = 1$. In the absence of any risk-sharing possibilities the manager will choose $a$ to maximize $\pi_1(a)U(a, q_1) + \pi_2(a)U(a, q_2)$. Let $\tilde{a}$ be a solution to this. Clearly $\tilde{a}$ is efficient. Now suppose a risk neutral principal appears with whom the manager can share risks. We know from Proposition 5 that at the new optimum $s < 1 = \tilde{s}$. Therefore, by Lemma 1 and Proposition 11, $\pi_2(a^*) \leq \pi_2(\tilde{a})$. In addition, $C_{FB}(a^*) \leq C_{FB}(\tilde{a})$ by Proposition 10. Thus, the existence of risk-sharing possibilities leads the agent to choose a less costly action with a lower probability of a good outcome.

We may use Propositions 10–12 to develop a method for computing a second-best optimal incentive scheme when $n = 2$. Consider the case where $A$ is finite. Recall that Proposition 6 states that, in this case, the agent will be indifferent between $a^*$ and some less costly action. This fact makes the computation of an optimal incentive scheme fairly straightforward. We know from Proposition 10 that it is never optimal to get the agent to choose an inefficient action. Hence we can assume without loss of generality that $C_{FB}(a_1) < C_{FB}(a_2) < \cdots < C_{FB}(a_m)$ and $\pi_2(a_1) < \pi_2(a_2) < \cdots < \pi_2(a_m)$. The computation of $C(a_1)$ is easy: by Remark 1 of Section 2 it is just $C_{FB}(a_1)$. To compute $C(a_k)$, $k > 1$, we use Propositions 6 and 11. For each action $a_j, j < k$, find $I_1, I_2$ so that the agent is indifferent between $a_k$ and $a_j$ and the agent's expected utility is $\bar{U}$. This means solving

$$(4.4) \quad \begin{aligned} G(a_k) + K(a_k)(\pi_1(a_k)v_1 + \pi_2(a_k)v_2) &= \bar{U}, \\ G(a_j) + K(a_j)(\pi_1(a_j)v_1 + \pi_2(a_j)v_2) &= \bar{U}, \end{aligned}$$

which yields

$$(4.5) \quad \begin{aligned} v_1 &= \frac{\pi_2(a_j)\Big(\big(\bar{U} - G(a_k)\big)/K(a_k)\Big) - \pi_2(a_k)\Big(\big(\bar{U} - G(a_j)\big)/K(a_j)\Big)}{\pi_1(a_k) - \pi_1(a_j)}, \\ v_2 &= \frac{\pi_1(a_j)\Big(\big(\bar{U} - G(a_k)\big)/K(a_k)\Big) - \pi_1(a_k)\Big(\big(\bar{U} - G(a_j)\big)/K(a_j)\Big)}{\pi_2(a_k) - \pi_2(a_j)}. \end{aligned}$$

We then set $I_1 = h(v_1)$, $I_2 = h(v_2)$. Note that $v_1 < v_2$ in (4.5) so that $I_1 < I_2$.

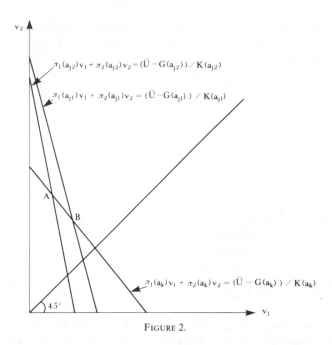

FIGURE 2.

Doing this for each $j = 1, \dots, k - 1$ yields $(k - 1)$ different $(v_1, v_2)$ (and $(I_1, I_2)$) pairs, each with $v_1 < v_2$. This is illustrated in Figure 2 for the case $k = 3$, where the $(v_1, v_2)$ pairs are at $A, B$. We know from Proposition 6 that one of these pairs is the solution to (2.2). In fact, the solution must occur at the $(v_1, v_2)$ pair with the *smallest* $v_1$ (and hence, by (4.4), with the largest $v_2$)—denote this pair by $(\hat{v}_1, \hat{v}_2)$. To see this, suppose that the agent is indifferent between $a_k$ and $a_j$ under $(\hat{v}_1, \hat{v}_2)$. Consider the expression

$$(4.6) \qquad \pi_1(a_k)v_1 + \pi_2(a_k)v_2 - \pi_1(a_j)v_1 - \pi_2(a_j)v_2$$

$$= (\pi_1(a_k) - \pi_1(a_j))v_1 + (\pi_2(a_k) - \pi_2(a_j))v_2.$$

When $v_1 = \hat{v}_1$, $v_2 = \hat{v}_2$, this expression equals $[(\overline{U} - G(a_k))/K(a_k)] - [(\overline{U} - G(a_j))/K(a_j)]$. Suppose now that $v_1 > \hat{v}_1$, $v_2 < \hat{v}_2$. Then (4.6) falls since $\pi_1(a_k) < \pi_1(a_j)$). Hence the agent now prefers $a_j$ to $a_k$ and so $a_k$ is not implemented.

In Figure 2, the solution is at $A$. (The solution could not be at $B$ since it is clear from the diagram that, at $B$, $a_{j2}$ gives the agent an expected utility greater than $\overline{U}$, i.e. $a_k$ is not implemented at $B$.) Note that it is possible that the $(\hat{v}_1, \hat{v}_2)$ picked in this way does not lie in $\mathfrak{U} \times \mathfrak{U}$; i.e., $h(\hat{v}_1)$ or $h(\hat{v}_2)$ may be undefined. In this case, the constraint set of (2.2) is empty and so $C(a_k) = \infty$. If $(\hat{v}_1, \hat{v}_2) \in \mathfrak{U} \times \mathfrak{U}$, then the principal's minimum expected cost of getting the agent to pick $a_k$ is $C(a_k) = \pi_1(a_k)h(\hat{v}_1) + \pi_1(a_k)h(\hat{v}_2)$. The expected net benefits of implementing $a_k$ are $B(a_k) - C(a_k)$. This procedure must be undergone for each $a_k$,

$k = 1, \ldots, m$. Finally, the overall optimum is determined by selecting the $a$ which maximizes $B(a_k) - C(a_k)$.

REMARK 6: In computing the cost of implementing $a_k$, we have ignored actions which are more costly for the agent than $a_k$. This means that the cost function which we have computed is not the true cost function $C(a)$ but a modified cost function $\tilde{C}(a)$. Clearly, $\tilde{C}(a) \le C(a)$ for each $a$ since more actions can only make implementation more difficult. On the other hand, Proposition 12 tells us that $\max_{a \in A}[B(a) - \tilde{C}(a)] \le \max_{a \in A}[B(a) - C(a)]$. Combining these yields $\max_{a \in A}[B(a) - C(a)] = \max_{a \in A}[B(a) - \tilde{C}(a)]$, which means that we are justified in working with $\tilde{C}(a)$ instead of $C(a)$.

Another case where computation is quite simple is when $A$ is infinite and $\{C_{FB}(a) | a \in A\}$ is an interval $[\underline{c}, \bar{c}]$ of the real line. For reasons of space, we do not cover this case.

Unfortunately, the computational techniques presented above do not appear to generalize in a useful way to the case $n > 2$. In order to compute an optimum when $n > 2$, in the finite action case, it seems that we must, for each $a \in A$, solve the convex problem in (2.2) and then, by inspection, find the $a \in A$ which maximizes $B(a) - C(a)$. If $A$ is infinite, one takes a finite approximation. These steps can be carried out on a computer, although the amount of computer time involved when the number of elements of $A$ is large may be considerable.

One case where a considerable simplification can be achieved when $n > 2$ is where MLRC and CDFC hold. Then the solution to (2.2) has the property that (1) if $A$ is finite, the agent is indifferent only between $a^*$, the action the principal wants to implement, and $a'$, where $a'$ maximizes $C_{FB}(a)$ subject to $C_{FB}(a) < C_{FB}(a^*)$, i.e. $a'$ is the next most costly action after $a^*$ (see the proof of Proposition 8); (2) if $A$ is convex, then $a^*$ is the unique maximizer of $G(a) + K(a)(\sum \pi_i(a)V(I_1))$, and $[d(G(a^*) + K(a^*)(\sum \pi_i(a^*)V(I_i)))/da] = 0$ is a necessary and sufficient condition for the agent to pick $a^*$. In the latter case, Mirrlees [12] has shown that the first-order condition approach referred to in the introduction is valid.

One may ask also whether Propositions 10 and 12 hold in the case $n > 2$. The answer is no (but see Remark 7 below). Second-best optimal actions may be inefficient; i.e., there may exist lower cost actions which dominate the optimal action in the sense of first degree stochastic dominance.[14] Also the addition of actions costlier than the second-best optimal action may make the principal worse off (in Example 1, the principal's expected profits increase if action $a_3$

---

[14] Let $A = \{a_1, a_2, a_3\}$, $n = 3$. Assume $C_{FB}(a_1) < C_{FB}(a_2) < C_{FB}(a_3)$, and that $\pi(a_1) = (3/4, 1/8, 1/8)$, $\pi(a_2) = (1/3, 1/3, 1/3)$, $\pi(a_3) = (1/2, 1/2, 0)$ (Assumption A3 is violated, but this is unimportant.) Then $C(a_1) = C_{FB}(a_1)$ since $a_1$ is the least cost action, and $C(a_3) = C_{FB}(a_3)$ since $a_3$ can be implemented by setting $I_1 = I_2$, $I_3 = -\infty$. However, $C(a_2) > C_{FB}(a_2)$ and, in fact, if the agent is very risk averse, $C(a_2)$ will be so big that it is profitable for the principal to implement $a_3$ rather than $a_2$ (the effect of risk aversion on $C(a)$ is discussed in Section 5). This is in spite of the fact that $a_3$ is inefficient relative to $a_2$.

becomes unavailable to the agent). Finally, as Shavell [19] has noted the agent may choose a higher cost action when there are opportunities to share risks with a principal than in the absence of these opportunities.

REMARK 7: It is interesting to note that it is possible to extend all the results of the $n = 2$ case to the $n > 2$ case when the spanning condition (SC) holds. This is because when SC holds, both the principal and the agent are essentially choosing between lotteries of the probability vectors $\hat{\pi}$ and $\hat{\pi}'$.

In particular, let $I_1(v_1) = \min_{\{I_i\}} \sum_{i=1}^{n} \hat{\pi}_i I_i$ subject to $\sum_{i=1}^{n} \hat{\pi}_i V(I_i) \geq v_1$; $I_2(v_2) = \min_{\{I_i\}} \sum_{i=1}^{n} \hat{\pi}_i' I_i$ subject to $\sum_{i=1}^{n} \hat{\pi}_i' V(I_i) \geq v_2$. Now consider the principal's minimum cost problem as: for each $a^*$, choose $v_1$ and $v_2$ to minimize $\lambda(a^*) I_1(v_1) + (1 - \lambda(a^*))I_2(v_2)$ subject to (1) $G(a^*) + [\lambda(a^*)v_1 + (1 - \lambda(a^*))v_2]K(a^*) \geq G(a) + [\lambda(a)v_1 + (1 - \lambda(a))v_2]K(a)$ for all $a \in A$; (2) $G(a^*) + [\lambda(a^*)v_1 + (1 - \lambda(a^*))v_2]K(a^*) \geq \overline{U}$. Then the principal's problem looks exactly the same as in the $n = 2$ case. Note that from stochastic dominance (i.e. part (2) of the SC condition) $\sum_{i=1}^{n} \pi_i q_i \leq \sum_{i=1}^{n} \pi_i' q_i$, so "state 2" is the good state. We are grateful to Bengt Holmstrom for alerting us to the fact that all of the results for the $n = 2$ case hold when $n > 2$ and the Spanning Condition is satisfied.

## 5. WHAT DETERMINES HOW SERIOUS THE INCENTIVE PROBLEM IS?

In previous sections, we have studied the properties of an optimal incentive scheme. We turn now to a consideration of the factors which determine the magnitude of $L$, the loss to the principal from being unable to observe the agent's action.

One feels intuitively that the worse is the quality of the information about the agent's action that the principal obtains from observing any outcome, the more serious will be the incentive problem. This idea can be formalized as follows. Suppose that we start with an incentive problem in which the agent's action set is $A$, his utility function is $U$, his reservation utility is $\overline{U}$, the probability function is $\pi$, and the vector of outputs is $q = (q_1, \ldots, q_n)$. We denote this incentive problem by $(A, U, \overline{U}, \pi, q)$. Consider the new incentive problem $(A, U, \overline{U}, \pi', q')$ where $\pi'(a) = R\pi(a)$ for all $a \in A$ and $R$ is an $(n \times n)$ stochastic matrix (here $\pi(a)$, $\pi'(a)$ are $n$ dimensional column vectors and the columns of $R$ sum to one). Below we show that $C'(a) \geq C(a)$ for all $a \in A$, where unprimed variables refer to the original incentive problem and primed variables to the new incentive problem.

The transformation from $\pi(a)$ to $R\pi(a)$ corresponds to a decrease in informativeness in the sense of Blackwell (see, e.g., Blackwell and Girshick [3]).[15] That is, if we think of the actions $a \in A$ as being parameters with respect to which we

---

[15] The possibility of using Blackwell's notion of informativeness to characterize the seriousness of an incentive problem was suggested by Holmstrom [7].

have a prior probability distribution, then an experimenter who makes deductions about $a$ from observing $q_1, \ldots, q_n$ would prefer to face the function $\pi$ than the function $R\pi$.

PROPOSITION 13: *Consider the two incentive problems* $(A, U, \overline{U}, \pi, q)$, $(A, U, \overline{U}, \pi', q')$ *and assume that Assumptions* A1–A3 *hold for both. Suppose that* $\pi'(a)$ $= R\pi(a)$ *for all* $a \in A$, *where* $R$ *is an* $(n \times n)$ *stochastic matrix. Then* $C'(a)$ $\geq C(a)$ *for all* $a \in A$. *Furthermore, if* $V$ *is strictly concave and* $R \gg 0$,[16] *then* $C_{FB}(a^*) > \min_{a \in A} C_{FB}(a)$ *and* $C(a^*) < \infty \Rightarrow C'(a^*) > C(a^*)$.

PROOF: Let $(I'_1, \ldots, I'_n)$ be the cost minimizing way of implementing $a$ in the primed problem. Suppose that in the unprimed problem, the principal offers the agent the following *random* incentive scheme: for each $i$, if $q_i$ is the outcome, an $n$-sided die will be thrown where the probability of side $j$ coming up is $r_{ji}$, the $(j, i)$th element of $R$ $(j = 1, \ldots, n)$. If side $j$ then comes up, you get $I'_j$. With this random incentive scheme, the probability of the agent getting $I'_j$ if he chooses a particular action is the same as in the primed problem. Therefore the agent's optimal action will be $a$. Furthermore, the principal's expected costs are the same as in the primed problem. This shows that the principal can implement $a$ at least as cheaply in the unprimed problem as in the primed problem by using a random incentive scheme. The final part of the proof is to note that the principal can reduce his expected cost further and continue to implement $a$ by offering the agent the perfectly certain utility level $v_i = \sum_{j=1}^{n} r_{ji} V(I'_j)$ if the outcome is $q_i$ rather than the above lottery. That is, there is a deterministic incentive scheme which is better for the principal than the above random incentive scheme.
$$Q.E.D.$$

REMARK 8: The last part of the proof of Proposition 13 shows that it is never desirable under our assumptions for the principal to offer the agent an incentive scheme which makes his payment conditional on a particular outcome a lottery rather than a perfectly certain income.[17] This result may also be found in Holmstrom [7].

Note that if $\pi' = R\pi$ and $q'R = q$, the random variable $q'$ will have the same mean as $q$. In this case the following is true:

COROLLARY 1: *Make the hypotheses of Proposition 13. If, in addition,* $q'$ *is such that* $q'R = q$, *we have* $L' \geq L$.

PROOF: Obvious since $B'(a) = q'\pi'(a) = q'R\pi(a) = q\pi(a) = B(a)$.

---

[16] We use this notation to mean that every element of $R$ is strictly positive.

[17] This result depends strongly on our Assumption A1 that attitudes to income risk are independent of action. In the absence of this assumption, random incentive schemes may be desirable.

In the case $n = 2$, the transformation $\pi \to \pi' = R\pi$ is easy to interpret. Take any two actions $a_1, a_2 \in A$, and consider the likelihood ratio vector $(\pi_1(a_1)$ $/\pi_1(a_2), \pi_2(a_1)/\pi_2(a_2))$. Assume without loss of generality that $\pi_1(a_1)/\pi_1(a_2)$ $\leq \pi_2(a_1)/\pi_2(a_2)$. Then it is easy to show that

$$(5.1) \qquad \left[ \frac{\pi_1'(a_1)}{\pi_1'(a_2)}, \frac{\pi_2'(a_1)}{\pi_2'(a_2)} \right] \subset \left[ \frac{\pi_1(a_1)}{\pi_1(a_2)}, \frac{\pi_2(a_1)}{\pi_2(a_2)} \right],$$

where $[x, y]$ is the interval between $x$ and $y$. In other words, the likelihood ratio vector becomes less variable in some sense when the stochastic transform $R$ is applied. In fact the converse to this is also true: if (5.1) holds, then there exists a stochastic matrix $R$ such that $\pi' = R\pi$ (see Blackwell and Girshick [3]). When $n > 2$, a simple characterization of this sort does not seem to exist, however.

One might ask whether a converse to Proposition 13 holds. That is, suppose $C'(a) \geq C(a)$ for all $a \in A$ and all concave utility functions $V$. Does it follow that $\pi'(a) = R\pi(a)$ for all $a \in A$, for some stochastic $R$? A converse along these lines can in fact be established when $n = 2$. Whether it holds for $n > 2$, we do not know.

Corollary 1 gives us a simple way of generating worse and worse incentive problems: repeatedly apply stochastic transforms to $\pi$. Suppose that we do this using always the same stochastic transform $R$, when $R \gg 0$ and is invertible. That is, we consider a sequence of incentive problems $1, 2, \ldots$, where in the $m$th problem $\pi_m(a) = R^{m-1}\pi(a)$ for all $a \in A$, and the gross profit vector $q_m$ satisfies $q_m R^{m-1} = q$ (this has a solution since $R$ is invertible). We know from Corollary 1 that $L_m$ will be increasing in $m$. The next proposition says that in the limit the loss from not being able to observe the agent reaches its maximal level.

DEFINITION: Let $L^* = \max_{a \in A}(B(a) - C_{FB}(a)) - \max\{B(a') - C_{FB}(a') \,|\, a'$ minimizes $C_{FB}(a)$ on $A\}$.

Since $C(a') = C_{FB}(a')$ if $a'$ minimizes $C_{FB}(a)$, $L^*$ is an upper limit on the loss to the principal from being unable to observe the agent. The next proposition shows that as the information $q$ reveals about $a$ gets smaller and smaller, the principal loses control over the agent, i.e., the agent chooses the least-cost action.

PROPOSITION 14: *Consider the sequence of incentive problems $(A, U, \overline{U}, \pi_m, q_m)$, $m = 1, 2, \ldots$, where $\pi_m(a) = R^{m-1}\pi_1(a)$ for all $a \in A$, $q_m R^{m-1} = q_1$ for some invertible stochastic matrix $R \gg 0$. Assume A1, A2, and $\pi_{1i}(a) > 0$ for all $i = 1, \ldots, n$, and $a \in A$. Then if $V$ is not a linear function, $\lim_{m \to \infty} L_m = L^*$.*

PROOF: It suffices to show that $\lim_{m \to \infty} C(a^*) = \infty$ for all $a^*$ with $C_{FB}(a^*) > \min_{a \in A} C_{FB}(a)$. Suppose not for some such $a^*$. Let $(I_{m1}, \ldots, I_{mn})$ be the cost minimizing way of implementing $a^*$ in problem $m$. Then $\sum_i \pi_{mi}(a^*)I_{mi}$ and $\sum_i \pi_{mi}(a^*)V(I_{mi})$ are both bounded in $m$. It follows from Bertsekas [2] that the $(I_{mi})$ are bounded. Hence without loss of generality we may assume $I_{mi} \to I_i$ for each $i$. It is easy to show that, since $R$ is a strictly positive stochastic matrix, $\lim_{m \to \infty} R^{m-1} = R^*$ where $R^*$ has the property that all of its columns are the same. Therefore $\lim_{m \to \infty} \pi_m(a) = R^* \pi_1(a) = \bar{\pi}$ is independent of $a$. But this means $\lim_{m \to \infty} \sum_i \pi_{mi}(a^*) V(I_{mi}) = \sum_i \bar{\pi}_i V(I_i) = \lim_{m \to \infty} \sum_i \pi_{mi}(a) V(I_{mi})$ for all $a \in A$. Hence the agent will prefer actions $a$ with $C_{FB}(a) < C_{FB}(a^*)$ to $a^*$. This contradicts the assumption that the incentive scheme implements $a^*$.  *Q.E.D.*

We turn now to a consideration of another factor which influences $L$: the agent's degree of risk aversion. Since no incentive problem arises when the agent is risk netural, but an incentive problem does arise when the agent is risk averse, one is led to ask whether $L$ increases as the agent becomes more risk averse. One difficulty in answering this question in general is the following. The way one makes the agent more risk averse is to replace his utility function $U(I, a)$ by $H(U(I, a))$ where $H$ is a real-valued, increasing, concave function. However, if $U$ satisfies Assumption A1, then $H(U)$ will generally not. To get around this difficulty, we will confine our attention to the case where $A$ is a subset of the real line, $V(I) = -e^{-kI}$, $G(a) = 0$, and $K(a) = e^{ka}$, i.e., the agent's utility function is $U(a, I) = -e^{-k(I-a)}$, where $k > 0$. Assume also that $\bar{U} = -e^{-ka}$, i.e., the agent's outside opportunity is represented by the perfectly certain income $\alpha$. An increase in risk aversion can then be represented simply by an increase in $k$.

Note that if the agent's utility function is $-e^{-k(I-a)}$ and $\bar{U} = -e^{-ka}$, then $C_{FB}(a) = a + \alpha$, which is independent of $k$. Hence first best profits are independent of $k$.

PROPOSITION 15: *Consider the incentive problem $(A, U, \bar{U}, \pi, q)$ where $A$ is a subset of the real line, $U(a, I) = -e^{-k(I-a)}$, $\bar{U} = -e^{-ka}$, and $k > 0$. Assume A3. Write the loss from being unable to observe the agent as $L(k)$. Then $\lim_{k \to 0} L(k) = 0$, $\lim_{k \to \infty} L(k) = L^*$.*

PROOF: To show that $\lim_{k \to \infty} L(k) = L^*$, it suffices to show that $\lim_{k \to \infty} C(a^*, k) = \infty$ for all $a^*$ with $C_{FB}(a^*) > \min_{a \in A} C_{FB}(a)$. Suppose not for some such $a^*$, and let $C_{FB}(a) < C_{FB}(a^*)$. Then if $(I_1, \dots, I_n)$ implements $a^*$, we must have

$$-\left( \sum_i \pi_i(a^*) e^{-kI_i} \right) e^{ka^*} \geq -\left( \sum_i \pi_i(a) e^{-kI_i} \right) e^{ka}$$

$(I_1, \dots, I_n$ of course depend on $k$). Therefore,

(5.2)  $$e^{k(a^* - a)} \leq \sum_i \pi_i(a) e^{-kI_i} \Big/ \sum_i \pi_i(a^*) e^{-kI_i}.$$

Now let $k \to \infty$. The LHS of (5.2) $\to \infty$. Therefore so must the RHS. We may assume w.l.o.g., however, that $I_1 = \min_i I_i$. Then

$$\frac{\sum_i \pi_i(a) e^{-kI_i}}{\sum_i \pi_i(a^*) e^{-kI_i}} = \frac{\sum_i \pi_i(a) e^{k(I_1 - I_i)}}{\sum_i \pi_i(a^*) e^{k(I_1 - I_i)}},$$

which is bounded since the denominator $\geq \pi_1(a^*)$. Contradiction.

We show now that $\lim_{k\to 0} L(k) = 0$. Let $I_i = q_i - F$. Then the agent maximizes

(5.3) $\quad E(-e^{-k(I-a)}) = -E\left(1 - k(I-a) + \frac{k^2}{2}(I-a)^2 + \cdots\right)$

$$= -1 + k\left(\sum \pi_i(a)q_i - F - a\right) - \frac{k^2}{2}E(I-a)^2 + \cdots.$$

It follows that the agent maximizes

$$\left(\sum \pi_i(a)q_i - F - a\right) - \frac{k}{2}E(I-a)^2 + \cdots,$$

which means that in the limit $k\to 0$ the agent maximizes $B(a) - C_{FB}(a)$, i.e. chooses a first-best action. Furthermore, setting (5.3) equal to $-e^{-ka} = -1 + ka + \cdots$, we see that in the limit $k\to 0$,

$$\max_{a\in A}\left(\sum_i \pi_i(a)q_i - a\right) - F = \alpha,$$

so that the principal's expected profit equals $F = \max_{a\in A}(\sum_i \pi_i q_i - a) - \alpha = \max_{a\in A}(B(a) - C_{FB}(a)) = $ first-best profit. $\hspace{1cm} Q.E.D.$

Proposition 15 tells us about the behavior of $L(k)$ for extreme values of $k$. It would be interesting to know whether $L(k)$ is increasing in $k$. We do not know the answer to that question except for the case $n = 2$, $A$ finite.

PROPOSITION 16: *Make the same hypotheses as in Proposition 14. Assume in addition that $n = 2$ and $A$ is finite. Then $L(k)$ is increasing in $k$.*

PROOF: See Appendix.

REMARK 9: Propositions 15 and 16 tell us how the principal's welfare varies with $k$. It is also interesting to ask how the shape of the optimal incentive scheme depends on $k$. Unfortunately, even in the case $n = 2$, very little can be said. In this case, the incentive scheme is characterized by the agent's share $s$. It is not difficult to construct examples showing that an increase in the agent's risk aversion may increase the optimal value of $s$, or may decrease it.

We conclude this section by considering how $L$ depends on the agent's incremental costs. Consider the case of additive separability, i.e., $K(a) \equiv$ constant. Suppose that we write the agent's utility function as $U_\lambda(a, I) = G_\lambda(a) + V(I)$, where $G_\lambda(a) = \alpha + \lambda F(a)$, $\lambda > 0$. (Without loss of generality, we take $K = 1$.) Then, when $\lambda$ is small, one feels that $L$ will be small since the agent does not require much of a reward to work hard. The fact that $\lim_{\lambda\to 0} L(\lambda) = 0$ has in fact been established by Shavell [20]. We prove a somewhat stronger result.

PROPOSITION 17: *Consider the incentive problem $(A, U_\lambda, \bar{U}, \pi, q)$, where $U_\lambda(a, I) = \alpha + \lambda F(a) + V(I)$ for all $a \in A$, $\lambda > 0$. Assume that A1–A3 hold for this* *problem. Assume also that* (1) *A is an interval of the real line;* (2) *B(a) and F(a) are twice differentiable in the interior of A;* (3) *V is twice differentiable on $\mathcal{G}$ and V' > 0;* (4) *There is a unique maximizer a\* of B(a) lying in the interior of A and B''(a\*) < 0. Then* $\lim_{\lambda \to 0}(L(\lambda)/\lambda) = 0$.

PROOF: Consider the incentive problem with $\lambda = 1$. Then there are $a$'s arbitrarily close to $a^*$ for which $C(a)$ is finite. For let the principal set $v_i = rq_i - k$ where $k$ is chosen so that $v_i \in \mathcal{U}$ for all $i$. Then the agent will maximize $\sum \pi_i(a) U_\lambda(a, I_i)$, i.e. $\sum \pi_i(a) q_i + F(a)/r$. By letting $r \to \infty$, we can get the agent to choose an action arbitrarily close to $a^*$. For such an action, $C(a)$ will be finite.

Consider now an $a$ arbitrarily close to $a^*$. Let $(v_1, \ldots, v_n)$ be the cost minimizing way of implementing $a$ when $\lambda = 1$. Then it is clear from (2.2) that $(\lambda v_1 + \beta, \ldots, \lambda v_n + \beta)$ will implement $a$ for $\lambda \neq 1$, where

$$\lambda \left( \sum \pi_i(a) v_i + F(a) \right) + \alpha + \beta = \overline{U}.$$

It follows that

$$L(\lambda) \leq \sum \pi_i(\hat{a}) q_i - h\left( \overline{U} - \alpha - \lambda F(\hat{a}) \right)$$
$$- \left( \sum \pi_i(a) q_i - \sum \pi_i(a) h(\lambda v_i + \beta) \right),$$

where $\hat{a}$ maximizes $\sum \pi_i(a) q_i - h(\overline{U} - \alpha - \lambda F(a))$, i.e. $\hat{a}$ is the first-best action in problem $\lambda$.

Therefore,

$$\frac{L(\lambda)}{\lambda} \leq \left[ \frac{1}{\lambda} \left\{ \sum \pi_i(a^*) q_i - h\left( \overline{U} - \alpha - \lambda F(a^*) \right) \right. \right.$$
$$\left. - \left( \sum \pi_i(a) q_i - \sum \pi_i(a) h(\lambda v_i + \beta) \right) \right\} \Big]$$
$$+ \left[ \frac{1}{\lambda} \left\{ \sum \pi_i(\hat{a}) q_i - h\left( \overline{U} - \alpha - \lambda F(\hat{a}) \right) \right. \right.$$
$$\left. - \sum \pi_i(a^*) q_i + h\left( \overline{U} - \alpha - \lambda F(a^*) \right) \right\} \Big].$$

Now $\hat{a} \to a^*$ as $\lambda \to 0$. Furthermore, by differentiating the first-order conditions $(d/da)(\sum \pi_i(\hat{a}) q_i - h(\overline{U} - \alpha - \lambda F(\hat{a})) = 0$, one can show that $d\hat{a}/d\lambda$ exists at $\lambda = 0$. It follows from the mean-value theorem and the fact that $B'(a^*) = 0$ that the second square bracket $\to 0$ as $\lambda \to 0$. To see that the first square bracket $\to 0$, note that, since $a$ is arbitrary, we can make $a$ converge to $a^*$ as fast as we like. Therefore we need only show that

(5.4) $\quad \lim_{\lambda \to 0} \frac{1}{\lambda} \left( \sum \pi_i(a) h(\lambda v_i + \beta) - h(\overline{U} - \alpha - \lambda F(a^*)) \right) = 0.$

336

But

$$\sum \pi_i(a)\Big[ h(\lambda v_i + \beta) - h\big(\overline{U} - \alpha - \lambda F(a^*)\big)\Big]$$

$$= \sum \pi_i(a)\Big[ h\big(\lambda v_i + \overline{U} - \alpha - \lambda \sum \pi_j(a)v_j - \lambda F(a)\big)$$

$$\qquad - h\big(\overline{U} - \alpha - \lambda F(a^*)\big)\Big]$$

$$= \sum \pi_i(a)\Big[ h(\overline{U} - \alpha) + h'(\overline{U} - \alpha)\big(\lambda v_i - \lambda \sum \pi_j(a)v_j - \lambda F(a)\big)$$

$$\qquad + \cdots - h(\overline{U} - \alpha) + h'(\overline{U} - \alpha)(\lambda F(a^*)) + \cdots \Big]$$

$$= h'(\overline{U} + \alpha)(-\lambda F(a) + \lambda F(a^*)) + \cdots$$

from which (5.4) follows. $\qquad\qquad Q.E.D.$

The proof of Proposition 17 is based on an envelope argument. It appears that a similar result can be established for the more general case where $U$ is not additively separable, but Assumption A1 holds. Since the proof is more complicated, however, we will not pursue this result here. The assumption that $a^*$ lies in the interior of $A$ may seem quite strong. Note, however, that if $a^*$ is a boundary point and $B'(a^*) \neq 0$, then the second-best optimal action equals $a^*$ for small enough $\lambda$. It is straightforward to apply the proof of Proposition 17 to show that $\lim_{\lambda \to 0}(L(\lambda)/\lambda) = 0$ in this case too.

Since the marginal product of labor of the agent—that is, the increase in expected profit resulting from an extra pound of expenditure by the agent—is proportional to $1/\lambda$, Proposition 17 can be interpreted as saying that the welfare loss $L$ is of a smaller order of magnitude than the reciprocal of the agent's marginal product of labor.

## 6. EXTENSIONS

We have assumed throughout the paper that the principal is risk-neutral and that the agent's attitudes to risk over income lotteries are independent of action—Assumption A1. We now briefly consider what happens if we relax these assumptions.

As we have noted in Section 2, Remark 3, our method of analysis generalizes without any difficulty to the case where the principal is risk-averse. Specific results change, however, The main difference is that now, even in the first-best situation, the principal will not bear all the risk. One implication of this is that even if there is no disutility of action for the agent, i.e. $a$ does not enter the agent's utility function, the first-best will not generally be reached. The reason is that there may be a conflict between the principal and agent over what income lottery should be selected (for a study of this conflict, see Ross [17] and Wilson [23]).

As a result of this, Proposition 3, part (5), is no longer true when the principal is risk-averse. Nor is Proposition 17 since $L(0) \neq 0$. Propositions 1 and 2 and Proposition 3, parts 1–4, continue to hold, however. So do Propositions 4 and 5 on the characterization of an optimal incentive scheme. Propositions 7, 8 generalize, as do Propositions 10, 11, and 12 (note that the function $C_{FB}$ is still well defined although it no longer refers to first-best cost). Proposition 3(6) does not hold and neither does Proposition 6 nor Proposition 9 (at least in its present form). Finally Corollary 1 of Proposition 13 and Propositions 14–16 do not generalize in an obvious way, since changing the risk aversion of the agent or the probability distribution of outcomes affects the first-best as well as the second-best.

The computational procedure presented in Section 4 for the two outcome case can be extended to the case where the principal is risk-averse. In the finite action case, it is still true that the agent will be indifferent between two actions at the optimum, except in the case where the first-best can be achieved. Thus it is necessary to check whether the first-best can be achieved. Otherwise the procedure is unaltered.

We turn now to the consequences of relaxing Assumption A1. These are much more serious since most of our analysis has depended crucially on being able to choose the control variables $V(I_1), \ldots, V(I_n)$ independently of $a$. Some results do generalize, however. In particular one can show that Propositions 1, 3, 10, and 12 generalize. It seems unlikely that the characterization of an optimal incentive scheme in Proposition 4 and Proposition 5, part 1, holds, but we do not have a counterexample. Surprisingly, perhaps, Proposition 5, part 2 does hold. Proposition 6 does not hold and it seems unlikely that Propositions 7–9 do.

In the two outcome case, one can still show that it is optimal for the agent's share $s$ to satisfy $0 \leq s < 1$. As a consequence Propositions 10 and 12 generalize. Proposition 11 does not generalize, however, and nor does our computational procedure for the two outcome case. Propositions 13 and 14 and Corollary 1 of Proposition 14 do not hold as they stand, although they do if one enlarges the set of feasible incentive schemes to include random schemes. (As we have noted in footnote 17, once Assumption A1 is dropped, random incentive schemes may be superior to deterministic schemes.) Finally, it seems likely that Proposition 17 could be generalized to the nonseparable case.

## 7. SUMMARY

The purpose of this paper has been to develop a method for analyzing the principal-agent problem in the case where the agent's attitudes to income risk are independent of action. Our method consists of breaking up the principal's problem into a computation of the costs and benefits accruing to the principal when the agent takes a particular action. We have used this method to establish a number of results about the structure of the optimal incentive scheme and about the determinants of the welfare loss resulting from the principal's inability to observe the agent's action. We have shown that it is never optimal for the incentive scheme to be such that the principal's and agent's payoff are negatively related over the whole outcome range, although such a relationship may be optimal over part of the range. We have found sufficient conditions for the incentive scheme to be monotonic, progressive, and regressive. We have shown that a decrease in the quality of the principal's information in the sense of Blackwell increases welfare loss. When there are only two outcomes, welfare loss also increases when the agent becomes more risk averse. Finally, we have discussed how our techniques can be used to compute optimal incentive schemes in particular cases.

While we have talked throughout about "the" principal-agent problem, we have in fact been considering the simplest of a number of such problems. More complicated principal-agent problems arise when not only is the principal unable to monitor the agent, but also the agent possesses information about his environment, i.e. about $A$, $\pi$, or $U(a, I)$, which the principal does not. Such problems possess a number of features of the preference revelation problems studied in the recent incentive compatibility literature; see, for example, the *Review of Economic Studies* Symposium [16]. A start has been made in the analysis of such problems by Harris and Raviv [6], Holmstrom [7], and Mirrlees [12]. It will be interesting to see whether the techniques presented here will also be useful in the solution of these more complicated principal-agent problems.

*University of Chicago*
*and*
*London School of Economics*

*Manuscript received September, 1980; revisions received September, 1981.*

## APPENDIX

PROOF OF PROPOSITION 16: It suffices to show that $C(a, k)$ is increasing locally in $k$ for each $a \in A$ whenever $C(a, k)$ is finite. Let $\tilde{k} = \lambda k$ $\lambda \geq 1$. Assume that $(I_1, I_2)$ is the cost minimizing way of implementing $a$, given $\tilde{k}$. Then, by the results of Section 4, e.g. equation (4.4),

(A1)
$$\pi_1 w_1 + \pi_2 w_2 = \frac{1}{e^{\tilde{k}(a + \alpha)}},$$

$$\pi_1' w_1 + \pi_2' w_2 = \frac{1}{e^{\tilde{k}(a' + \alpha)}},$$

where $w_1 = e^{-\tilde{k} I_1}$, $w_2 = e^{-\tilde{k} I_2}$, $\pi_1 = \pi_1(a)$, $\pi_2 = \pi_2(a)$, $\pi_1' = \pi_1(a')$, $\pi_2' = \pi_2(a')$, $a' \in A$, $a' < a$. Furthermore we can pick $a'$ so that $a'$ is independent of $k$ for $\lambda$ close to 1.

Equations (A1) determine $w_1$ and $w_2$ for each value of $\tilde{k}$. The cost of implementing $a$, $C(a, \tilde{k})$, is then given by

(A2)
$$C(a, \tilde{k}) = \pi_1 I_1 + \pi_2 I_2 = -\frac{1}{\tilde{k}} (\pi_1 \log w_1 + \pi_2 \log w_2).$$

Differentiating (A2) with respect to $\lambda$ we get

(A3)
$$\left. \frac{\partial C(a, \lambda k)}{\partial \lambda} \right|_{\lambda = 1} = \frac{1}{k} \left( \pi_1 \log w_1 + \pi_2 \log w_2 - \frac{\pi_1}{w_1} \frac{dw_1}{d\lambda} - \frac{\pi_2}{w_2} \frac{dw_2}{d\lambda} \right).$$

Set $x = e^{-k(a+\alpha)}$, $y = e^{-k(a'+\alpha)}$ in (A1). Then $e^{-\tilde{k}(a+\alpha)} = x^\lambda$, $e^{-\tilde{k}(a'+\alpha)} = y^\lambda$. Hence

(A4)

$$\pi_1 \frac{dw_1}{d\lambda} + \pi_2 \frac{dw_2}{d\lambda} = x \log x,$$

$$\pi_1' \frac{dw_1}{d\lambda} + \pi_2' \frac{dw_2}{d\lambda} = y \log y,$$

where derivatives are evaluated at $\lambda = 1$. Solving (A1), (A4) yields

$$w_1 = \frac{\pi_2' x - \pi_2 y}{\pi_1 \pi_2' - \pi_1' \pi_2} = \frac{\pi_2' x - \pi_2 y}{\pi_2' - \pi_2},$$

$$\frac{dw_1}{d\lambda} = \frac{\pi_2' x \log x - \pi_2 y \log y}{\pi_2' - \pi_2}.$$

It follows that $\log w_1 \geq (1/w_1)(dw_1/d\lambda)$. For

(A5)
$$w_1 \log w_1 - \frac{dw_1}{d\lambda} = \frac{\pi_2' x - \pi_2 y}{\pi_2' - \pi_2} \log \frac{\pi_2' x - \pi_2 y}{\pi_2' - \pi_2} - \left( \frac{\pi_2' x \log x - \pi_2 y \log y}{\pi_2' - \pi_2} \right)$$

$$= \frac{1}{\pi_2' - \pi_2} \left[ (\alpha x - \beta y) \log \frac{\alpha x - \beta y}{\alpha - \beta} - \alpha x \log x - \beta y \log y \right],$$

where $\alpha = \pi_2'$, $\beta = \pi_2$. However, the RHS of (A5) $\geq 0$ by Lemma 3 below. The same argument shows that $\log w_2 \geq (1/w_2)(dw_2/d\lambda)$. It follows from (A3) that $(\partial C/\partial \lambda) \geq 0$, i.e., $C$ is increasing locally in $k$.

LEMMA 3: *Assume* $\alpha, \beta, x, y > 0$. *Then if* $\alpha > \beta$ *and* $\alpha x > \beta y$, $\alpha x \log x - \beta y \log < (\alpha x - \beta y)$ $\log((\alpha x - \beta y)/(\alpha - \beta))$. *On the other hand, if* $\alpha < \beta$ *and* $\alpha x < \beta y$, $\alpha x \log x - \beta y \log y > (\alpha x - \beta y)$ $\log((\alpha x - \beta y)/(\alpha - \beta))$.

PROOF: Since $z \log z$ is a convex function,

$$\frac{\beta}{\alpha} (y \log y) + \left( \frac{\alpha - \beta}{\alpha} \right) \left( \frac{\alpha x - \beta y}{\alpha - \beta} \log \frac{\alpha x - \beta y}{\alpha - \beta} \right) \geq x \log x.$$

This proves the first part. The second part follows similarly.                    *Q.E.D.*

REFERENCES

[1] ARROW, K. J.: "Insurance, Risk and Resource Allocation," *Essays in the Theory of Risk Bearing.* Chicago: Markham, 1971.
[2] BERTSEKAS, D.: "Necessary and Sufficient Conditions for Existence of an Optimal Portfolio," *Journal of Economic Theory*, 8(1974), 235–247.
[3] BLACKWELL, D., AND M. A. GIRSHICK: *Theory of Games and Statistical Decisions.* New York: John Wiley and Sons, Inc., 1954.
[4] BORCH, K.: *The Economics of Uncertainty.* Princeton: Princeton University Press, 1968.
[5] HARDY, G. H., J. E. LITTLEWOOD, AND G. POLYA: *Inequalities.* Cambridge: Cambridge University Press, 1952.
[6] HARRIS, M., AND A. RAVIV: "Optimal Incentive Contracts with Imperfect Information," *Journal of Economic Theory*, 20(1979), 231–259.
[7] HOLMSTROM, B.: "Moral Hazard and Observability," *Bell Journal of Economics*, 10(1979), 74–91.
[8] KEENEY, R.: "Risk Independence and Multiattributed Utility Functions," *Econometrica*, 41(1973), 27–34.
[9] MILGROM, P. R.: "Good News and Bad News: Representation Theorems and Applications," Discussion Paper No. 407, Northwestern University, Illinois, Mimeo, 1979.

[10] MIRRLEES, J. A.: "The Theory of Moral Hazard and Unobservable Behavior—Part I," Nuffield College, Oxford, Mimeo, 1975.

[11] ————: "The Optimal Structure of Incentives and Authority Within an Organization," *Bell Journal of Economics*, 7(1976), 105–131.

[12] ————: "The Implications of Moral Hazard for Optimal Insurance," Seminar given at Conference held in honour of Karl Borch, Bergen, Norway, Mimeo, 1979.

[13] PAULY, M.: "The Economics of Moral Hazard: Comment," *American Economic Review*, 58(1968), 531–536.

[14] POLLAK, R.: "The Risk Independence Axiom," *Econometrica*, 41(1973), 35–39.

[15] RADNER, R.: "Monitoring Cooperative Agreements in a Repeated Principal-Agent Relationship," Mimeo, Bell Laboratories, 1980.

[16] *Review of Economic Studies* Symposium on Incentive Compatibility, April, 1979.

[17] ROSS, S.: "The Economic Theory of Agency: The Principal's Problem," *American Economic Review*, 63(1973), 134–139.

[18] RUBINSTEIN, A. AND M. YAARI: Seminar given at Conference held in honour of Karl Borch, Bergen, Norway, 1979.

[19] SHAVELL, S.: "On Moral Hazard and Insurance," *Quarterly Journal of Economics*, 93(1979), 541–562.

[20] ————: "Risk Sharing and Incentives in the Principal and Agent Relationship," *Bell Journal of Economics*, 10(1979), 55–73.

[21] SPENCE, M., AND R. ZECKHAUSER: "Insurance, Information, and Individual Action," *American Economic Review*, 61(1971), 380–387.

[22] STIGLITZ, J. E.: "Incentives and Risk Sharing in Sharecropping," *Review of Economic Studies*, 61(1974), 219–256.

[23] WILSON, R.: "The Theory of Syndicates," *Econometrica*, 36(1968), 119–132.

[24] ZECKHAUSER, R.: "Medical Insurance: A Case Study of the Trade-Off Between Risk Spreading and Appropriate Incentives," *Journal of Economic Theory*, 2(1970), 10–26.

*International Review of Law and Economics* (1986), 6 (45–58)

# THE JUDGMENT PROOF PROBLEM

S. SHAVELL*

*Harvard Law School, Cambridge, MA 02138, USA*

## I. INTRODUCTION

Parties who cause harm to others may sometimes turn out to be 'judgment proof,' that is, unable to pay fully the amount for which they have been found legally liable.[1] This possibility is an important and realistic one. Certainly individuals may readily be imagined to cause personal injury or property damage resulting in judgments that exceed their assets plus any liability insurance coverage; and the same is true of firms.[2]

To understand the nature of this problem, a theoretical model of the occurrence of accidents is studied here. Using the model and assuming that potential injurers' assets are less than the harm they might cause, questions about the effects of liability on their behavior and on their purchase of liability insurance are considered.[3] The conclusions reached may be summarized as follows.

(a) *Liability does not furnish adequate incentives to alleviate risk.* (See Propositions 1 and 2.) An injurer will treat liability that exceeds his assets as imposing an effective financial penalty only equal to his assets; an injurer with assets of $30 000, for example, will treat an accident resulting in liability of $100 000 identically with an accident resulting in liability of only $30 000. Hence, injurers' expected penalties may be less than the expected losses for which they are liable. This has two implications. First, *injurers may engage in risky activities to a socially excessive extent.*[4] (An electric utility company may decide to build a nuclear power plant that could cause losses in the billions of dollars just because its expected financial penalty is limited by its assets of only a hundred million dollars.) Second, *injurers may have too little incentive to take care* to reduce risks given their level of activity. (The utility may invest too little in safety given that it builds the nuclear facility.) This problem, however, is less pronounced under the negligence rule than under strict liability, owing to the sharpness of incentives under the former rule;[5] namely, taking proper care allows injurers to escape liability entirely under the negligence rule, whereas it merely lowers the likelihood of liability under strict liability.

(b) *The motive to purchase liability insurance is diminished.* (See Remark 2 and Proposition 2.) Because their assets are less than the harm they might cause, part of the premium injurers would pay for liability insurance would be to cover losses that they would not otherwise have to bear. If the injurer with assets of $30 000 bought full

*This is a revision of a 1983 version with the same title; it is expanded upon in parts of Chapters 7 and 10 of a book tentatively entitled *An Economic Analysis of Accident Law* to be published by Harvard University Press. I wish to thank L. Bebchuk and R. Mrofka for comments and the National Science Foundation (grant nos. SES-8014208 and SES-8420226) for financial support.

liability coverage of $100000, seven-tenths of his premium would pay for the $70000 amount of liability that he would not bear if he did not own liability insurance. It follows that risk averse injurers may rationally decide against buying liability insurance, or at least may buy less coverage than the harm they might cause.[6]

(c) *To the extent that liability insurance is purchased, the problem of excessive engagement in risky activities is mitigated; but the problem of inadequate levels of care could be exacerbated if insurers' ability to monitor care is imperfect.* (See Proposition 2.) The purchase of liability insurance by injurers will result in their bearing more of the expected losses that their engaging in an activity would create, making it less likely that they will choose to engage in an activity when they ought not. (If the utility were to buy full coverage against losses, then in principle it would not build the nuclear facility unless that were appropriate.) On the other hand, whether injurers' incentives to take care would be altered for the better or the worse by their purchase of liability coverage depends on the ability of insurers to link premiums or the conditions under which they will honor claims to injurers' precautions. Where insurers can establish this connection fairly easily (where, for instance, installation of safety devices could be verified at low cost), they will tend to do so, and injurers will therefore be induced to act in a way that properly reduces risk. But where insurers find it too difficult to make the connection (especially where what is of concern is injurers' *behavior* rather than their acquisition of some physical entity), injurers' incentives will be dulled by their ownership of coverage, and risks may be higher than otherwise. (If insurers cannot tell how well the utility trains the operators of its nuclear facility, then the utility's motive to do this will be reduced by its ownership of liability insurance.)

After these points are developed in the model, a brief concluding section will discuss informally the use of various social policies to remedy the judgment proof problem.[7]

## II. ANALYSIS OF THE MODEL

The model is concerned primarily with *injurers*, parties who might cause accident losses for *victims*, but who can lower the probability of this by taking care.[8] (Victims cannot affect the probability of accident losses, so they play no role in the analysis.) Let

$x$ = level of care of injurers; $x \geq 0$;
$p(x)$ = probability of an accident; $0 < p(x) < 1$; $p'(x) < 0$; $p''(x) > 0$;
$\ell$ = magnitude of losses if an accident occurs; $\ell > 0$;
$y$ = initial assets of injurers; $0 \leq y \leq \ell$; and
$U(\cdot)$ = von Neumann–Morgenstern utility function of wealth of injurers, who are either risk neutral or risk averse.

It is assumed that the variable care is non-monetary but has a monetary equivalent cost of $x$;[9] hence, if injurers exercise care of $x$, their utility will be $U(y - x)$ other things equal. It is also assumed that if losses occur, they will be of fixed magnitude. In addition, it is assumed (without loss of generality) that if injurers are risk neutral, the utility of wealth $y$ equals $y$; and that if injurers are risk averse, $U(0) = 0$, $U'(y) > 0$, and $U''(y) < 0$.

Define $x^*$ as the level of care that minimizes

$$x + p(x)\ell, \tag{1}$$

so that $x^*$ satisfies

$$1 + p'(\mathrm{x})\ell = 0. \tag{2}$$

Call $x^*$ the *efficient* level of care.

Before proceeding, it is of interest to state what a benevolent dictator would do to solve the accident problem. The dictator would choose the level of injurers' care and levels of wealth contingent on accident involvement for injurers and victims so that no alternative choice would raise the expected utility of both injurers and victims. It is easy to show the following about this first-best Pareto efficient solution to the problem.[10]

*Remark 1.* The first-best Pareto efficient solution to the accident problem is such that (a) risk averse parties are left with the same level of wealth regardless of whether accidents actually occur; and (b) the level of care is the efficient level $x^*$, that which minimizes expected accident losses plus the cost of care.

*Notes.* (i) The explanation for the Remark is that the dictator can fully insure risk averse parties and thus that it is Pareto efficient for him simply to minimize expected accident losses plus the cost of care.

(ii) Suppose that the model was extended to allow injurers to choose whether to engage in their activity, that the benefit they obtain from it is $b$, and that if they do not engage in it the enjoy no benefit but cause no accidents. Then the first-best solution would be such that injurers would engage in their activity if and only if $b > p(x^*)\ell$.

A. *Injurers' behavior under liability rules in the absence of liability insurance*

Let us now consider injurers' behavior under the two major forms of liability: *strict liability*, under which injurers are liable for $\ell$ whenever they cause an accident; and the *negligence rule*, under which they are liable for the accident losses $\ell$ only if their level of care was less than the level of *due care*, which is assumed to be $x^*$. If an injurer is liable under a liability rule, his actual payment is of course limited to his wealth $y$.[11] For this reason, an injurer's behavior will depend on his wealth; hence let

$x_s(y)$ = care taken by injurers under strict liability if their wealth is $y$;
$x_n(y)$ = care taken by injurers under the negligence rule if their wealth is $y$.

We have
*Proposition 1.* (a) Under strict liability, injurers will take no care if their assets are sufficiently low; they will then take a positive and increasing level of care as a function of their assets. (b) Under the negligence rule, injurers will act negligently—and thus will take the level of care they do under strict liability—if their assets are sufficiently small; they will then act non-negligently, taking the efficient level of care. Moreover, they will begin to take the efficient level of care when their assets are less than the losses they might cause, and when under strict liability their level of care would be lower.

*Notes.* (i) The Proposition is illustrated in Figure 1. The reason that $x_n(y) = x^*$ when $x_s(y)$ is lower than $x^*$ is, as explained in the Introduction, that the incentive to take care is sharper under the negligence rule, for injurers will avoid liability entirely by choosing $x^*$ rather than only reducing its probability. It should also be observed that although as drawn, $x_s(\ell)$ equals $x^*$, this is the case only if injurers are risk neutral; if they are risk averse, $x_s(\ell)$ would presumably exceed $x^*$.

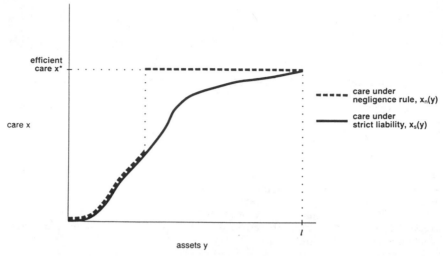

FIG. 1. Exercise of care under the liability rules (in the absence of liability insurance).

(ii) If the model were extended to allow injurers to choose whether to engage in their activity, then under strict liability injurers might engage in their activity when they ought not if their assets are less than $\ell$.[12] As noted earlier, however, this is true under the negligence rule even if their assets are not less than $\ell$, for under that rule injurers do not pay for the losses they cause if they take due care.

*Proof.* (a) Under strict liability, an injurer's expected utility will be

$$EU^s(x,y) = (1 - p(x))U(y - x) + p(x)U(-x). \tag{3}$$

The partial derivative of (3) with respect to $x$ is

$$\begin{aligned} EU_x^s(x,y) = &-p'(x)[U(y - x) - U(-x)] \\ &-[(1 - p(x))U'(y - x) + p(x)U'(-x)]. \end{aligned} \tag{4}$$

Since $EU_x^s(0,0) = -U'(0) < 0$, it follows that for all $y$ sufficiently small, $x_s(y) = 0$. Otherwise, $x_s(y)$ is determined by the first-order condition $EU_x^s(x,y) = 0$; and as the partial derivative of $EU_x^s(x,y)$ with respect to $y$ is $-p'(x)U'(y - x) - (1 - p(x)) U''(y - x)$ and is positive, $x_s(y)$ increases with $y$.[13]

(b) An injurer's expected utility under the negligence rule will be

$$EU^n(x,y) \begin{aligned} &= EU^s(x,y) &&\text{if } x < x^* \\ &= U(y - x) &&\text{otherwise;} \end{aligned} \tag{5}$$

thus, if $x$ is not less than $x^*$, $x^*$ will be chosen. The claims now follow from a series of steps:

(i) If $x_n(y) < x^*$, then $x_n(y) = x_s(y)$: From (5), we know that $x_n(y)$ maximizes $EU^s$ over $x < x^*$. We also know that $EU^s(x_n(y),y) > U(y - x^*)$; and since $U(y - x^*) >$

$EU^s(x,y)$ for $x \geq x^*$, we conclude that $x_n(y)$ in fact maximizes $EU^s$ over all $x$, so that it must equal $x_s(y)$.

(ii) If $y$ is sufficiently low, then $x_n(y) < x^*$: If $y < x^*$, then choosing $x = 0$ would be superior to choosing $x^*$. Hence, certainly for such $y$, $x_n(y) < x^*$.

(iii) If $x_n(y_1) = x^*$ and $y_2 > y_1$, then $x_n(y_2) = x^*$: If $x_s(y) \geq x^*$ anywhere in $[y_1, y_2]$, then since by (a) $x_s$ is increasing in $y$, $x_s(y_2) \geq x^*$. This, however, implies that $x_n(y_2) = x^*$; for if not, $x_n(y_2) < x^*$, in which case by (i), $x_n(y_2) = x_s(y_2)$; but as $x_s(y_2) \geq x^*$, this means $x_n(y_2) \geq x^*$, which is a contradiction. Hence, suppose that $x_s(y) < x^*$ throughout $[y_1, y_2]$ and consider any $y$ in that interval. Now by the envelope theorem the derivative of $EU^s(x_s(y), y)$ with respect to $y$ equals the partial derivative of $EU^s$ with respect to $y$, or $(1 - p(x_s(y))) U'(y - x_s(y))$; but this is less than $U'(y - x^*)$ since $x_s(y) < x^*$. Hence $U(y - x^*)$ grows faster with $y$ than $EU^s(x_s(y), y)$ in the interval. This fact and the fact that $U(y_1 - x^*) > EU(x_s(y_1), y_1)$ imply that the same inequality holds at $y_2$, which implies the required result.

(iv) The set of $y$ such that $x_n(y) = x^*$ strictly includes that where $x_s(y) \geq x^*$: If $x_s(y) \geq x^*$, then $x_n(y) = x^*$; for otherwise, $x_n(y) < x^*$, but from (i), this means that $x_n(y) = x_s(y)$, contradicting the assumption that $x_s(y) \geq x^*$. Hence, we have shown that the first set weakly includes the second. Now let $y_0$ be the least $y$ such that $x_s(y) = x^*$,[14] and observe that $U(y_0 - x^*) > (1 - p(x^*)) U(y_0 - x^*) + p(x^*) U(-x^*) = EU^s(x^*, y_0)$. Hence, by continuity, $U(y - x^*) > EU^s(x(y), y)$ in a neighborhood to the left of $y_0$; it follows that in this neighborhood $x_n(y) = x^*$ whereas $x_s(y) < x^*$.

(v) $x_n(y)$ first equals $x^*$ for $y < \ell$: By Jensen's inequality,[15] $(1 - p(x_s(\ell)) U(\ell - x_s(\ell)) + p(x_s(\ell)) U(-x_s(\ell)) < U(\ell - x_s(\ell) - p(x_s(\ell))\ell)$. But the latter is less than or equal to $U(\ell - x^* - p(x^*)\ell)$, which is less than $U(\ell - x^*)$. Hence, at $\ell$, choosing $x^*$ and being non-negligent is strictly preferred to choosing $x_s(\ell)$ and being subject to liability. Thus, by continuity, the assertion follows.

## B. *Injurers' behavior under liability rules given the availability of liability insurance*[17]

Assume now that liability insurance is sold at an actuarially fair rate and that the policy purchased by injurers maximizes their expected utility, where $q =$ level of coverage; and $\pi =$ premium for coverage. In order to analyze the expected utility-maximizing policy, it is convenient first to consider the decision to purchase insurance of a party who faces a *fixed* probability $0 < p < 1$ of liability for losses $\ell$ that would exceed his assets. If this party purchases coverage $q$ and losses do not occur, his wealth will be $y - \pi$; and if losses do occur, his wealth will be $\max(0, y - \pi + q - \ell)$. In addition, $\pi = pq$, as the premium is fair, and therefore the maximum $q$ the party can purchase is $y/p$. Hence, the party's insurance purchase problem is

$$\max_{0 \leq q < y/p} (1 - p) U(y - pq) + p U(\max(0, y - pq + q - \ell)), \tag{6}$$

the solution to which is as follows.

*Remark 2.* Suppose that the probability of a party's being liable for losses is fixed. Then (a) assuming that the party is risk averse, there is a critical level of his assets below which he will not purchase any insurance coverage and above which he will purchase full coverage. (b) If, however, the party is risk neutral, he will not purchase any insurance coverage regardless of his level of assets.

*Notes.* (i) What is to be proved in (a) is that there is a $y'$ where $p\ell < y' < \ell$, such that $q = 0$ for $y$ in $[0, y')$ and $q = \ell$ for $y \geq y'$. The explanation is, as mentioned in the Introduction, that to buy coverage is to pay for losses that one would otherwise not bear, and since this factor is more important the smaller one's assets, at some sufficiently low level of assets, one will no longer wish to buy coverage despite aversion to risk. If, however, one wishes to buy positive coverage, it must then be optimal to buy full coverage, since there is always a marginal advantage to increasing coverage if it is not full.[18]

(ii) What is to be proved in (b) is that if $y < \ell$, then $q = 0$ is strictly preferred. This is true because a risk neutral party, not being averse to risk, will clearly not wish to pay for any losses which he would not otherwise bear.[19]

*Proof.* (a) If a risk averse party chooses $q > 0$, then it must be that $y - pq + q - \ell > 0$—his net wealth if he causes losses is positive—for otherwise the coverage will not have done him any good. Hence, if $q > 0$, the party's expected utility will be

$$(1 - p)U(y - pq) + pU(y - pq + q - \ell). \tag{7}$$

Therefore (since $q = y/p$ is obviously not optimal), $q$ will be determined by the first-order condition

$$(1 - p)(-p)U'(y - pq) + p(1 - p)U'(y - pq + q - \ell) = 0. \tag{8}$$

This implies that $U'(y - pq) = U'(y - pq + q - \ell)$, which in turn means that $q = \ell$ (since $U'' < 0$), so that the party's utility will be $U(y - p\ell)$.

On the other hand, if $q = 0$, the party's utility will be $(1 - p)U(y)$.

Hence, the party will not buy coverage when

$$(1 - p)U(y) > U(y - p\ell); \tag{9}$$

otherwise he will buy full coverage. Now at $y = p\ell$, (9) holds strictly, for $(1 - p)U(p\ell) > U(p\ell - p\ell) = 0$. And at $y = \ell$, the inequality in (9) is reversed, for $(1 - p)U(\ell) = (1 - p)U(\ell) + pU(0) < U(\ell - p\ell)$ since $U$ is strictly concave. Also, clearly, $(1 - p)U'(y) < U'(y - p\ell)$. It therefore follows that the claimed $y'$ exists.

(b) If a risk neutral party does not buy coverage and $y < \ell$, his expected wealth will be $(1 - p)y$. If he does buy coverage, his expected wealth will be, from (6), $(1 - p)(y - pq) + p\max(0, y - pq + q - \ell)$. Thus, if $q > 0$ and the second term zero, expected wealth will equal $(1 - p)(y - pq) < (1 - p)y$, so the party will be worse off; and similarly, if the second term is positive, expected wealth will be $y - p\ell < (1 - p)y$ (since $y < \ell$), so the party will be worse off. This completes the proof.

Let us now return to our model, where injurers can affect the probability of losses, and let us assume initially that liability is strict. An injurer's expected utility will therefore be

$$EU^s(x, q, \pi) = (1 - p(x))U(y - \pi - x) + p(x)U(\max(0, y - \pi + q - \ell) - x). \tag{10}$$

There are two situations to consider regarding insurers. In the first, insurers can observe $x$ and link the premium charged to it. In this situation, the premium will be $p(x)q$ and the injurer's problem will thus be to maximize $EU^s(x, q, p(x)q)$ over $x$ and $q$. In the other situation, insurers cannot observe $x$ and link the premium to it. Here the injurer's problem will be to maximize $EU^s(x, q, \pi)$ over $q$ subject to the constraint that $EU^s$ is maximized over $x$ alone (as the injurer will choose $x$ knowing that that will not affect his premium) and also to the constraint $\pi = p(x)q$.[20] (In both situations $\pi \leq y$ is an additional constraint but it will be assumed not to be binding.)

Under the negligence rule, the formal statement of the injurer's problem in the two situations is the same, with $EU^n$ (the expression for which we omit) replacing $EU^s$. We have

*Proposition 2.* Suppose that liability is strict. Then (a) if insurers can observe levels of care, risk averse injurers will buy no coverage if their assets are less than a critical level; otherwise they will buy full coverage and take efficient care. (b) If insurers cannot observe levels of care, risk averse injurers will again buy no coverage if their assets are less than a critical level, where this level will be higher than in (a); otherwise, they will purchase positive, but less than complete coverage and generally not take efficient care. (c) In either situation, risk neutral injurers will not buy coverage.

(d) Under the negligence rule (risk averse or risk neutral) injurers will not buy coverage.

*Notes.* (i) The claim in (a) is that there is a $y'$, where $p(x^*)\ell + x^* < y' < \ell$ such that $q = 0$ and $x = x_s(y)$ for $y < y'$; and $q = \ell$ and $x = x^*$ for $y \geq y'$. The explanation for the existence of the critical level $y'$ is that given for Remark 2(a). Also, because if an injurer purchases coverage, it will be full and the premium will depend on $x$ and equal $p(x)\ell$, the injurer will choose $x$ to minimize $x + p(x)\ell$; thus he will choose $x^*$.

(ii) The claim in (b) is there is a $y''$, where $y' < y'' < \ell$, such that $q = 0$ and $x = x_s(y)$ for $y < y''$; and $q > 0$ and $x$ is generally unequal to $x^*$ (where $q$ and $x$ depend on $y$) for $y \geq y''$. The reason that $y''$ exists is essentially that given for Remark 2(a). If injurers purchase positive coverage, their levels of care would be expected to be less than efficient because their incentives to avoid losses will be reduced. Injurers will not, however, purchase full coverage; for were they to do this, they would not be exposed to risk, not have any incentive to take care, and therefore have to pay a high premium. Finally, $y''$ will exceed $y'$ because insurance, being incomplete, will be less valuable to own in the present situation.

Figure 2 illustrates (a) and (b) in the typical case.

(iii) The claim in (c) is that $q = 0$ is strictly preferred for $y < \ell$. This is true for the reason given for Remark 2(b).

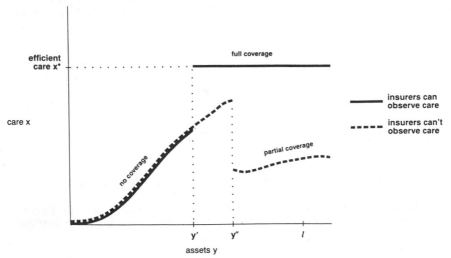

FIG. 2. Exercise of care and purchase of liability insurance under strict liability.

(iv) The claim in (d) is that $q=0$ is strictly preferred. This is true because only if an injurer chooses $x<x^*$ would he possibly wish to buy insurance coverage; for otherwise he will not be liable if he causes a loss. Now if $x<x^*$ and an injurer buys coverage, it must be high enough to leave him with positive assets if he causes a loss (else the coverage is of no value). But this turns out to imply that the premium plus expected liability directly borne equals $pt$, and this implies that the injurer would have been better off choosing $x^*$ and escaping liability. Hence, injurers will not wish to buy coverage (and will behave as described in Proposition 1).

(v) If the model were extended to allow injurers to choose whether to engage in their activity, then under strict liability, injurers would engage in it exactly when they ought if insurers can observe their levels of care and they buy full coverage. Otherwise, as noted after Proposition 1, they will engage in their activity too often.

(vi) If the model were extended to allow for uncertainty over the negligence determination, then risk averse injurers might buy liability insurance under the negligence rule.

*Proof.* (a) By the argument in the proof of Remark 2(a), we know that if an injurer chooses $q>0$, then he will in fact choose $q=t$ (for given any $x$, the argument may be applied). And because when $q=t$, an injurer's utility will be $U(y-x-p(x)t)$, he will choose $x$ to minimize $x+p(x)t$; but this is $x^*$. Hence, if $q>0$, then $q=t$, $x=x^*$, and the injurer's utility will be $U(y-x^*-p(x^*)2t)$.

If an injurer chooses $q=0$, then he will select $x$ to maximize $(1-p(x))U(y-x) + p(x)U(-x)$, so he will choose $x_s(y)$. Thus, he will buy no coverage when

$$(1-p(x_s(y)))U(y-x_s(y))+p(x_s(y))U(-x_s(y))>U(y-x^*-p(x^*)t); \qquad (11)$$

otherwise he will buy full coverage. By the envelope theorem, the derivative with respect to $y$ of the left-hand side of (11) is $(1-p(x_s(y)))U'(y-x_s(y))$ and that of the right-hand side is $U'(y-x^*-p(x^*)t)$; and the latter is greater than the former whenever the two sides of (11) are equal, since then $x_s(y)<x^*+p(x^*)t$.[21] From this it follows (we omit details) that if it becomes optimal to buy insurance for some $y'$, it must remain optimal to do so. Hence, as (11) holds at $y=p(x^*)t+x^*$ and is reversed at $y=t$,[22] the claimed $y'$ exists.

(b) This is clear from note (ii).

(c) Suppose that a risk neutral injurer were to buy positive coverage. Then by the proof of Remark 2(b), the injurer would be worse off than if he did not buy coverage and chose the same $x$. Hence, certainly, the injurer would be worse off than if he did not purchase coverage and chose $x$ optimally.

(d) Suppose that an injurer strictly prefers to buy $q>0$. Then $x<x^*$ must be true (for if $x\geq x^*$, the injurer bears no risk under the negligence rule). Also, as observed before, if $q>0$, for the insurance to benefit the injurer, $y-\pi+q-t\geq 0$ must hold. Using this fact, $\pi=p(x)q$, and concavity of $U$, we have that the injurer's expected utility must be

$$(1-p(x))U(y-x-p(x)q) + p(x)U(y-x-p(x)q+q-t) \leq U(y-x-p(x)t). \quad (12)$$

But the latter is less than $U(y-x^*-p(x^*)t)$, which is less than $U(y-x^*)$. Thus the injurer must be worse off than if he chose $x^*$ and did not purchase insurance coverage.

C. *Requirements to purchase liability insurance and prohibitions against its purchase*

From the above results we can determine the effect of the policy of making purchase of full liability insurance coverage mandatory and of the policy of prohibiting its purchase.

*Proposition 3.* Suppose that injurers are required to purchase full liability insurance coverage. Then (a) if insurers can observe their levels of care, injurers will be led to take efficient care, whereas they might not have done so otherwise. But (b) if insurers cannot observe their levels of care, injurers will take no care, whereas they would usually have taken positive care otherwise.

*Notes.* (i) It is of course assumed here that injurers' assets are sufficient to pay the premium for full coverage.

(ii) The claim of (a) is clear: Since injurers must purchase full coverage and their premiums will depend on $x$, they will choose $x^*$; whereas if otherwise they would not have purchased coverage, they might not have chosen $x^*$ under the negligence rule and, generally, would not have done so under strict liability.

(iii) With regard to the claim of (b), observe that since injurers are fully covered and their premiums will not depend on $x$, they will choose $x = 0$; whereas otherwise they would have purchased no coverage or only partial coverage, so that $x > 0$ would have been expected (unless $y$ were extremely low).

(iv) Suppose that the model were extended to allow injurers to choose whether to engage in their activity. Then requiring injurers to purchase full coverage if they engage in their activity would mean that under strict liability, they would engage in it if and only if that were socially worthwhile (given their possibly suboptimal level of care).

*Proof.* (a) If liability is strict and injurers must purchase full coverage, then as in the proof to Proposition 2(a), they will choose $x^*$. But if injurers are either risk averse and $y < y'$ of Proposition 2, or if they are risk neutral, they would not have purchased liability coverage and would have taken $x_s(y)$, which is generally unequal to $x^*$.

If the negligence rule determines liability and injurers must purchase full coverage, then their wealth will be constant and equal to $y - [x + p(x)\ell]$ if $x < x^*$ (as their premium will be $p(x)\ell$) and to $y - x$ if $x \geq x^*$ (as their premium will be 0). Thus, injurers will be best off choosing $x^*$. In the absence of the requirement to purchase coverage, on the other hand, by Proposition 2, if $y$ were sufficiently low, injurers would have chosen $x_s(y)$.

(b) This is clear from note (iii) above.

*Proposition 4.* Suppose that injurers are prohibited from purchasing liability insurance. Then (a) if insurers could have observed their levels of care and injurers had wished to purchase coverage, they would have taken efficient care; whereas under the prohibition they generally will not take efficient care. But (b) if insurers could not have observed their levels of care and injurers had wished to purchase coverage, they would have taken different (and presumably lower) levels of care than they will under the prohibition.

*Notes.* (i) The explanation and proof of this is immediate from a comparison of Propositions 1 and 2, for if injurers are prohibited from purchasing liability insurance, they will behave as described in Proposition 1.

(ii) If the model were extended to allow injurers to choose whether to engage in their activity, then the effect of a prohibition against purchase of liability insurance could only be to lead risk averse injurers not to engage in their activity. This might or might not be socially beneficial, as injurers might or might not have made the socially appropriate choice whether to engage in their activity in the absence of a prohibition against liability insurance.

## III. CONCLUDING REMARKS ON SOCIAL POLICY

In closing let us comment briefly on the use of social policy to alleviate the three problems created by injurers' lack of assets, that is, the tendency of injurers to engage excessively in risky activities and to fail to exercise adequate care when so doing; the bearing of risk by injurers due to their propensity not to purchase liability insurance; and the possibility that victims would not be completely compensated for their losses.

(a) *The problem of injurers' excessive engagement in risky activities and the dulling of their incentives to take care.* This problem may be meliorated in a variety of ways.[23] Consider first a requirement to purchase liability insurance.[24] (See Proposition 3.) This will have essentially the effect that the voluntary purchase of liability insurance was noted to have in the Introduction.[25] Specifically, because injurers who engage in risky activities will have to pay premiums equal to the expected losses that they would impose on victims,[26] injurers will be led to make socially correct decisions whether to engage in activities.[27] Injurers will also be induced to take the appropriate level of care if insurers can assess their level of care and link terms of insurance policies to it. But if insurers cannot do this, a requirement to purchase liability insurance may have a perverse effect on injurers' exercise of care, and injurers might take less care than if they did not have to buy coverage and were exposed at least to the risk of losing their assets.[28]

Consider next an opposite possibility: prohibiting purchase of liability insurance.[29] (See Proposition 4.) This would tend to discourage injurers from engaging in risky activities where they would otherwise voluntarily have purchased liability coverage. Hence, this effect could be beneficial, helping to cure the problem of excessive engagement in activities; but it could also turn out to have a disadvantageous chilling influence on behavior.[30] Similarly, prohibiting purchase of liability insurance would be expected to increase the level of care exercised by injurers who would otherwise have insured; and one can imagine that this increase in the level of care might either be desirable or too great.

Another policy to consider is a requirement that injurers have some minimum level of assets to be allowed to engage in an activity.[31] While by definition this requirement will eliminate problems due to injurers' having assets less than the minimum level, it is undiscriminating in whom it excludes from engaging in an activity. In particular, it excludes those injurers who would be able and willing to pay for the *expected* losses that engaging in an activity would cause even though they might be unable to pay for the *actual* losses they could cause.[32]

A further policy of use is the extension of liability from actual injurers to other parties who have some sort of relationship with injurers; this extension of liability can take the form of vicarious liability[33] or of piercing the corporate veil.[34] To the degree that the other parties on whom liability is also imposed have assets of their own at stake and can control injurers' actions, extension of liability will lead indirectly to reduction in risk.

An additional policy of interest is the direct regulation of safety. This will help in an immediate way to solve the problem of dilution of injurers' incentives, assuming that they would have to take called-for steps to reduce risk as a precondition for engaging in an activity. But the value of safety regulation is of course limited by the regulatory authority's ability to devise appropriate regulation. Moreover, safety regulation does not solve the problem that injurers have too great an incentive to engage in a risky activity; for it does not impose on injurers the expected losses caused by an activity (injurers need merely adhere to regulations).

A final policy to consider is resort to criminal liability. Clearly, parties who would not take good care (or who would engage in a risky activity when they ought not) if only their assets were at stake might be induced to act otherwise for fear of criminal sanctions, notably imprisonment. The fact that criminal sanctions are socially costly to impose, however, diminishes their utility.

(b) *The problem of risk-bearing by injurers.* The tendency of potentially judgment proof injurers not to purchase liability insurance means that they are exposed to risk, which is a problem to the extent that they are risk averse. Of the policies we have mentioned, the only one that addresses this problem is a requirement that injurers purchase liability insurance coverage.[35]

(c) *The problem of inadequate compensation of victims.* This problem will in principle automatically be solved where victims are well-informed purchasers of insurance. For in that situation, victims would be expected to obtain insurance policies protecting them against the possibility that injurers would be unable to compensate them fully for their losses.[36]

But where victims do not voluntarily purchase such insurance coverage, two types of social policy may be employed to guarantee that they will nevertheless have adequate coverage.[37] First, victims may simply be made to obtain coverage[38] or a publicly-financed insurance fund may be established.[39] Second, injurers may be required to purchase a minimum level of liability insurance or to have a minimum level of assets, or vicarious liability may be imposed on third parties with ample assets. In assessing the appeal of these latter policies, it is necessary to take into account their effects on injurers' behavior, which, as discussed above, may or may not be desirable. For example, if the use of a requirement to purchase liability insurance coverage adversely affected injurers' incentives to take care, then a requirement that victims purchase greater coverage might be the best way to assure them adequate compensation.

## REFERENCES AND NOTES

1. The term judgment proof is sometimes meant to apply only where an injuring party has no assets whatever and is thus unable to pay any of the losses for which he is liable. But here, as stated, the term is interpreted more generally and is meant to apply whenever a party is unable to pay some portion of the losses for which he is liable.
2. Fires at nightclubs or hotels could well create losses greater than the worth of their owners; the harm caused by mass consumption of spoiled foods or by drugs with adverse side effects could exhaust the holdings of even large enterprises, and similarly with losses resulting from explosions, oil spills, or the release of toxic agents or radioactive substances.
3. A number of writers have considered these or closely related questions from an economic perspective; *see* notes 5 and 6 below. The analysis here adds to theirs in that it studies formally the judgment proof problem in a more general model that (a) takes into joint account liability and liability insurance, and (b) draws distinctions between problems concerning injurers' engagement in activities and those concerning their exercise of care when so doing. In addition, (c) solutions to the judgment proof problem are discussed.
4. Of course, injurers may engage in activities to an excessive extent even in the absence of the judgment proof problem if the form of liability is the negligence rule (rather than strict liability); for under that rule injurers do not have to pay for the losses that their activity causes if they act with due care. *See* S. Shavell, 'Strict Liability versus Negligence', (1980) 9 J. Legal Stud. 1–25. But this tendency will be worsened by the judgment proof problem.

5. This particular point has been analyzed in J. S. Summers, 'The Case of the Disappearing Defendant: An Economic Analysis', (1983) 132 Univ. Pennsylvania Law Rev. 145–185 (which had not been published when I wrote the previous version of this paper) in a model in which injurers are risk neutral and liability insurance is not sold.

6. This point was first emphasized to my knowledge by G. Calabresi, *The Costs of Accidents: A Legal and Economic Analysis*, Yale University Press (1970), p. 58. It was studied formally in W. Keeton and E. Kwerel, 'Externalities in Automobile Insurance and the Underinsured Driver Problem', (1984) 27 J. Law and Econ. 149–181, and in G. Huberman, D. Mayers and C. Smith, 'Optimal Insurance Policy Indemnity Schedules', (1983) 14 Bell. J. Econ. 415–426, in models assuming a fixed risk of liability; it is studied here in a model where the risk of liability is affected by injurers' exercise of care.

7. However, two of these policies (requirements to purchase liability insurance, and prohibitions against its purchase) are also studied in the model.

8. It will be easy to see how the conclusions we will reach would be altered if the model were extended to allow injurers to choose not only their level of care but also whether to engage in their activity; we will comment on this below.

9. The assumption that $x$ is non-monetary is largely an analytical convenience; see note 11 below.

10. Formally, the problem may of course be put as maximizing the expected utility of injurers subject to the constraint that victims' expected utility is held constant and to a resource constraint. *See* S. Shavell, 'On Liability and Insurance', (1982) 13 Bell J. Econ. 120–132, which proves the Remark for virtually the same model as is studied here.

11. Note that were care monetary, an injurer's payment would be limited to $y - x$, for the injurer's expenditures on care itself would lower his available wealth (a point that is overlooked in Summers, *supra*, note 5). Care is assumed to be non-monetary here to avoid considering the effect of care on available wealth; although the effect is not important, considering it would introduce complications into the analysis. (The 1983 version of this paper assumed that care is monetary and dealt with the complications.)

12. An injurer's expected liability will be $p(x)y < p(x)\ell$ if he engages in the activity (where $x = x_s(y)$). Hence, if, for instance, the injurer is risk neutral, he will decide to engage in the activity whenever $b > x + p(x)y$ rather than only when $b > x + p(x)\ell$.

13. Differentiating $EU_x{}^s(x(y), y) = 0$ with respect to $y$ and solving for $x'(y)$, we obtain $x'(y) = -EU_{xy}{}^s(x,y)/EU_{xx}{}^s(x,y)$. The denominator is negative (the second-order regularity condition for a maximum), so that the sign of $x'(y)$ is that of $EU_{xy}{}^s(x,y)$.

14. If no such $y$ exists, then $x_s(y)$ is always less than $x^*$, so that the claim is clearly true given that the set of $y$ where $x_n(y) = x^*$ is non-empty, a fact we shall show in the next step of the proof.

15. *See* M. DeGroot, *Optimal Statistical Decisions*, McGraw Hill (1970), p. 97.

16. This result is proved in Keeton and Kwerel, *supra*, note 6, pp. 155–156 and 174–175.

17. For an analysis of liability and insurance in the absence of the judgment proof problem, see Shavell, *supra*, note 10.

18. However, in a model with a variable level of loss, this would not generally be true; in such a model, it might well be optimal to purchase positive but less than full coverage.

19. Note, by contrast, that if a risk neutral party's assets exceed $\ell$—so that he would have to bear $\ell$ if he did not insure—the party would merely be indifferent between buying coverage and not.

20. *See* S. Shavell, 'On Moral Hazard and Insurance', (1979) 92 Quart. J. Econ. 541–562, for details.

21. By Jensen's inequality, the left-hand side of (11) is less than $U((1 - p(x_s(y)))y - x_s(y))$. Hence if the two sides of (11) are equal, then $(1 - p(x_s(y)))y - x_s(y) > y - x^* - p(x^*)\ell$, which implies that $x_s(y) < x^* + p(x^*)\ell$.

22. At $y = \ell$, the left-hand side of (11) is, by Jensen's inequality, less than $U(\ell - x_s(\ell) - p(x_s(\ell)\ell)$, which is clearly less than or equal to $U(\ell - x^* - p(x^*)\ell)$.

23. The imperfect nature of each of the social policies we are about to review suggests that a combined approach would be best; but discussion of this issue is beyond our scope.

Another issue that will not be discussed here is the administrative costs associated with use of the different policies.

24. Requirements to purchase liability insurance are common. For instance, purchase of liability insurance is compulsory for owners of automobiles in most states (*see*, for example, N. Y. Veh. & Traf. Law § 312; Cal. Veh. Code § 16020); and purchase of worker's compensation insurance must be made by employers according to many states' statutes (*see*, for example, 34 N.J. Stat. Ann. 15–71).

25. But as the reader will recall, injurers' lack of assets reduces their motive to purchase liability insurance voluntarily.

26. More exactly, injurers would have to pay such premiums under strict liability; under the negligence rule, their premiums would be lower.

27. Think again of the electric utility company. If it is made to buy liability coverage, it will decide to build a nuclear-powered facility instead of a coal-powered facility if and only if the savings in production costs exceed the increase in expected accident losses as reflected in higher liability insurance premiums. Or think of the decision of a parent whether to allow a teenaged child to drive. If the parent would have to purchase additional liability coverage if the child drives, the parent might, beneficially, choose to defer the time when the child begins driving if the child's immediate reasons for doing so are not strong. Such arguments have led some to suggest the desirability of a requirement to purchase liability insurance; *see*, for instance, O. Williamson, D. Olson and A. Ralston, 'Externalities, Insurance, and Disability Analysis', (1967) 34 Economica 235–253, at 247–249, W. Vickrey, 'Automobile Accidents, Tort Law, Externalities, and Insurance: An Economist's Critique', (1968) 33 Law and Contemporary Problems, 464–487, at 485, and Keeton and Kwerel, *supra*, note 6, p. 161.

28. Suppose the electric utility has net worth of $200 million and is required to purchase a $1 billion liability insurance policy for its nuclear-powered facility. (Let us say that $1 billion approximates the harm that a serious accident could cause.) Thus, being well insured, the utility might decide not to bear the expense of, for instance, more frequent safety inspections or (as noted earlier) better training of its workers where this would not affect its premium or its coverage in the event of a claim. But if the utility is not required to carry the $1 billion liability coverage, perhaps it would choose not to purchase any coverage or only a small amount. (Indeed, if the utility were risk neutral, it definitely would decide against obtaining coverage; see Proposition 4.) In this case, then, its $200 million would be at risk, and it might therefore choose to invest desirably in the additional inspections and training of workers.

29. The possibility of prohibiting the purchase of liability insurance should not be thought unreal. Liability insurance is barred in the Soviet Union, apparently because of a fear that its ownership would dilute the deterrent effect of liability; *see* B. Rudden, *Soviet Insurance Law*, Monograph No. 12, *Law in Eastern Europe*, Sijthoff, Leyden (1966). Moreover, in the past, fears about this prospect were voiced in Western countries, and its sale was prevented for a time; *see* Section 90 of A. Tunc, *Torts*, Introduction to Volume XI, *International Encyclopedia of Comparative Law*, Mouton, The Hague (1974). In addition, even today insurance contracts may be void if they indemnify conduct in contravention of public policy; *see*, for the United States, 44 C.J.S. *Insurance* § 241(a).

30. Consider a situation where most parties' assets are very low compared to the harm they might do and where it would be best for most parties not to engage in the activity. Here prohibiting purchase of liability coverage might be desirable. In other types of situation, however, the suspicion is that it would reduce engagement in activities too much. (Perhaps too few teenagers would drive if liability insurance for them was disallowed.)

31. This type of policy is not usual; modern state statutes typically do not require a minimum initial level of capital to incorporate. For example, in Delaware the incorporators have the discretion to specify in the certificate of incorporation the amount of authorized shares and par value, if any, and are not bound by a minimum capitalization requirement. *See* General Corp. Law of Delaware § 102(a)(4). Some statutes that formerly required a nominal level of paid in capital (ranging from $200–$1000) have been amended to delete

the minimum capitalization requirement. *See*, for example, Ky. Rev. Stat. § 271A.270 eliminated $1000 minimum capitalization requirement in Ky. Rev. Stat. § 271.095.

32. Suppose that engaging in an activity, say operation of a chemical plant, could cause losses ranging up to several million dollars, but that *expected* losses would be in the neighborhood of only $100 000, as the probability of an accident is low. Parties therefore ought to be able to engage in the activity whenever they would be willing to pay about $100 000 to do so. To insist that parties have assets of a much higher amount, such as $2 million, would exclude from the activity some parties that would have been willing to pay $100 000 (and that might have been induced to take tolerably good care despite having assets considerably less than $2 million).

33. Masters, for instance, may be liable for the torts of their servants, parents for the torts of their children, and firms for the torts of their employees. For economic analyses of vicarious liability, *see* A. Sykes, 'An Efficiency Analysis of Vicarious Liability Under the Law of Agency', (1981) 91 Yale Law J. 168–206; 'The Economics of Vicarious Liability', (1984) 93 Yale Law J. 1231–1282; L. Kornhauser, 'An Economic Analysis of the Choice Between Enterprise and Personal Liability for Accidents', (1982) 70 California Law Rev. 1345–1392.

34. Piercing the corporate veil refers of course to holding a shareholder (which might be a parent corporation) of a corporation liable for the torts of the corporation. For economic analysis of this practice, *see* R. Posner, *Economic Analysis of Law*, Little Brown, Boston (2nd ed.—1977), p. 296; P. Halpern, M. Trebilcock and S. Turnbull, 'An Economic Analysis of Limited Liability in Corporation Law', (1980) 30 Univ. Toronto Law J. 117–150; F. Easterbrook and D. Fischel, 'Limited Liability and the Corporation', (1985) 52 Univ. Chicago Law Rev. 89–117.

35. Calabresi, *supra*, note 6, p. 59 points out that such a requirement is desirable for precisely the presently discussed reason, as do Keeton and Kwerel, *supra*, note 6, p. 161.

36. Thus drivers might voluntarily purchase policies providing coverage against losses caused by other uninsured drivers (so-called uninsured motorists).

37. A reason that victims might not purchase insurance coverage when it would be in their interests to do so—and thus why social policy may be called for—is that they do not appreciate the value of insurance (perhaps because they do not understand the magnitude of the risk they face, perhaps because of some psychological quirk).

38. The most common form of compulsory victims' insurance is uninsured motorist coverage; *see*, for example, Mass. Ann. Laws ch. 175 § 113L; N.Y. Ins. Law § 167(2–a); N.J. Stat. Ann. § 17:28–1.1.

39. Public unsatisfied judgment funds are used in compulsory third-party liability insurance jurisdictions for victims injured in automobile accidents. *See*, for example, N.J. Stat. Ann. § 39:6–61 (third party automobile liability insurers contribute to the fund); N.Y. Ins. Law § 5201. The public fund acts as a gap-filler to ensure full compensation when the injury is caused by an underinsured party, a hit-and-run driver that escapes detection, or a judgment proof out of state resident that is not required to carry liability insurance. Also, the Federal Government has recently established insurance funds to cover certain types of losses (due, for example, to miners' black lung disease).

# EQUILIBRIUM IN COMPETITIVE INSURANCE MARKETS: AN ESSAY ON THE ECONOMICS OF IMPERFECT INFORMATION*

## MICHAEL ROTHSCHILD AND JOSEPH STIGLITZ

## INTRODUCTION

Economic theorists traditionally banish discussions of information to footnotes. Serious consideration of costs of communication, imperfect knowledge, and the like would, it is believed, complicate without informing. This paper, which analyzes competitive markets in which the characteristics of the commodities exchanged are not fully known to at least one of the parties to the transaction, suggests that this comforting myth is false. Some of the most important conclusions of economic theory are not robust to considerations of imperfect information.

We are able to show that not only may a competitive equilibrium not exist, but when equilibria do exist, they may have strange properties. In the insurance market, upon which we focus much of our discussion, sales offers, at least those that survive the competitive process, do not specify a price at which customers can buy all the insurance. they want, but instead consist of both a price and a quantity—a particular amount of insurance that the individual can buy at that price. Furthermore, if individuals were willing or able to reveal their information, everybody could be made better off. By their very being, high-risk individuals cause an externality: the low-risk individuals are worse off than they would be in the absence of the high-risk individuals. However, the high-risk individuals are no better off than they would be in the absence of the low-risk individuals.

These points are made in the next section by analysis of a simple model of a competitive insurance market. We believe that the lessons gleaned from our highly stylized model are of general interest, and attempt to establish this by showing in Section II that our model is robust and by hinting (space constraints prevent more) in the conclusion that our analysis applies to many other situations.

* This work was supported by National Science Foundation Grants SOC 74-22182 at the Institute for Mathematical Studies in the Social Sciences, Stanford University and SOC 73-05510 at Princeton University. The authors are indebted to Steve Salop, Frank Hahn, and Charles Wilson for helpful comments, and to the participants in the seminars at the several universities at which these ideas were presented.

## I. THE BASIC MODEL

Most of our argument can be made by analysis of a very simple example. Consider an individual who will have an income of size $W$ if he is lucky enough to avoid accident. In the event an accident occurs, his income will be only $W - d$. The individual can insure himself against this accident by paying to an insurance company a premium $\alpha_1$, in return for which he will be paid $\hat{\alpha}_2$ if an accident occurs. Without insurance his income in the two states, "accident," "no accident," was $(W, W - d)$; with insurance it is now $(W - \alpha_1, W - d + \alpha_2)$, where $\alpha_2 = \hat{\alpha}_2 - \alpha_1$. The vector $\alpha = (\alpha_1, \alpha_2)$ completely describes the insurance contract.[1]

### I.1 Demand for Insurance Contracts

On an insurance market, insurance contracts (the $\alpha$'s) are traded. To describe how the market works, it is necessary to describe the supply and demand functions of the participants in the market. There are only two kinds of participants, individuals who buy insurance and companies that sell it. Determining individual demand for insurance contracts is straightforward. An individual purchases an insurance contract so as to alter his pattern of income across states of nature. Let $W_1$ denote his income if there is no accident and $W_2$ his income if an accident occurs; the expected utility theorem states that under relatively mild assumptions his preferences for income in these two states of nature are described by a function of the form,

$$(1) \qquad \hat{V}(p, W_1, W_2) = (1 - p)U(W_1) + pU(W_2),$$

where $U(\ )$ represents the utility of money income[2] and $p$ the probability of an accident. Individual demands may be derived from (1). A contract $\alpha$ is worth $V(p, \alpha) = \hat{V}(p, W - \alpha_1, W - d + \alpha_2)$. From

1. Actual insurance contracts are more complicated because a single contract will offer coverage against many potential losses. A formal generalization of the scheme above to cover this case is straightforward. Suppose that an individual will, in the absence of insurance, have an income of $W_i$ if state $i$ occurs. An insurance contract is simply an $n$-tuple $(\alpha_1, \ldots, \alpha_n)$ whose $i$-th coordinate describes the net payment of the individual to the insurance company if state $i$ occurs. We confine our discussion to the simple case mentioned in the text, although it could be trivially extended to this more complicated case.

Many insurance contracts are not as complicated as the $n$-tuples described above—Blue Cross schedules listing maximum payments for specific illnesses and operations are an isolated example—but are instead resolvable into a fixed premium and a payment schedule that is in general a simple function of the size of the loss such as $F(L) = \text{Max}\,[0, c(L-D)]$, where c × 100% is the co-insurance rate and $D$ is the deductible. With such a contract when a loss occurs, determining its size is often a serious problem. In other words, finding out exactly what state of the world has occurred is not always easy. We ignore these problems. A large literature analyzes optimal insurance contracts. See, for example, Arrow (1971) and Borch (1968).

2. We assume that preferences are not state-dependent.

all the contracts the individual is offered, he chooses the one that maximizes $V(p, \alpha)$. Since he always has the option of buying no insurance, an individual will purchase a contract $\alpha$ only if $V(p, \alpha) \geq V(p, 0) = \hat{V}(p, W, W - d)$. We assume that persons are identical in all respects save their probability of having an accident and that they are risk-averse ($U'' < 0$); thus $V(p, \alpha)$ is quasi-concave.

## I.2 Supply of Insurance Contracts

It is less straightforward to describe how insurance companies decide which contracts they should offer for sale and to which people. The return from an insurance contract is a random variable. We assume that companies are risk-neutral, that they are concerned only with expected profits, so that contract $\alpha$ when sold to an individual who has a probability of incurring an accident of $p$, is worth

$$(2) \qquad \pi(p, \alpha) = (1 - p)\alpha_1 - p\alpha_2 = \alpha_1 - p(\alpha_1 + \alpha_2).$$

Even if firms are not expected profit maximizers, on a well-organized competitive market they are likely to behave as if they maximized (2).[3]

Insurance companies have financial resources such that they are willing and able to sell any number of contracts that they think will make an expected profit.[4] The market is competitive in that there is free entry. Together these assumptions guarantee that any contract that is demanded and that is expected to be profitable will be supplied.

3. Since the theory of the firm behavior under uncertainty is one of the more unsettled areas of economic theory, we cannot look to it for the sort of support of any assumption we might make, which the large body of literature devoted to the expected utility theorem provides for equation (1) above. Nonetheless, two arguments (and the absence of a remotely as attractive distinguishable alternative) justify (2): the first is the rather vaguely supported but widely held proposition that companies owned by stockholders who themselves hold diversified portfolios ought to maximize their expected profits; management that does not follow this policy will be displaced. The second supposes that insurance companies are held by a large number of small shareholders each of whom receives a small share of the firm's profits. If the risks insured against are independent or otherwise diversifiable, then the law of large numbers guarantees that each shareholder's return will be approximately constant and any individual insurance contract contributes to his profits only through its expected value. In this case stockholders' interests will be well served if, and only if, management maximizes expected profits.

A variant of the second argument is obtained by considering the case in which shareholders and policyholders are the same people, or in more familiar terms, when the insurance company is a mutual company. In this case the insurance company is just a mechanism for risk pooling. Under conditions where diversification is possible, each contract's contribution to the company's dividend (or loss) is proportional to its expected value.

4. The same kinds of arguments used to justify (2)—in particular the appeal to the law of large numbers—can be used to justify this assumption. Weaker conditions than independence will suffice. See Revesz (1960), p. 190, for a theorem that states roughly that, if insurance contracts can be arranged in space so that even though con-

### I.3 Information about Accident Probabilities

We have not so far discussed how customers and companies come to know or estimate the parameter $p$, which plays such a crucial role in the valuation formulae (1) and (2). We make the bald assumption that individuals know their accident probabilities, while companies do not. Since insurance purchasers are identical in all respects save their propensity to have accidents, the force of this assumption is that companies cannot discriminate among their potential customers on the basis of their characteristics. This assumption is defended and modified in subsection II.1.

A firm may use its customers' market behavior to make inferences about their accident probabilities. Other things equal, those with high accident probabilities will demand more insurance than those who are less accident-prone. Although possibly accurate, this is not a profitable way of finding out about customer characteristics. Insurance companies want to know their customers' characteristics in order to decide on what terms they should offer to let them buy insurance. Information that accrues after purchase may be used only to lock the barn after the horse has been stolen.

It is often possible to force customers to make market choices in such a way that they both reveal their characteristics and make the choices the firm would have wanted them to make had their characteristics been publicly known. In their contribution to this symposium, Salop and Salop call a market device with these characteristics a *self-selection mechanism*. Analysis of the functioning of self-selection mechanisms on competitive markets is a major focus of this paper.

### I.4 Definition of Equilibrium

We assume that customers can buy only one insurance contract. This is an objectionable assumption. It implies, in effect, that the seller of insurance specifies both the prices and quantities of insurance purchased. In most competitive markets, sellers determine only price and have no control over the amount their customers buy. Nonetheless, we believe that what we call price and quantity competition is more appropriate for our model of the insurance market than tradi-

---

tracts that are close to one another are not independent, those that are far apart are approximately independent, then the average return from all contracts is equal to its expected value with probability one. Thus, an insurance company that holds a large number of health policies should be risk-neutral, even though the fact that propinquity carries illness implies that not all insured risks are independent. Some risks that cannot be diversified; i.e., the risk of nuclear war (or of a flood or a plague) cannot be spread by appeal to the law of large numbers. Our model applies to diversifiable risks. This class of risks is considerably larger than the independent ones.

tional price competition. We defend this proposition at length in subsection II.2 below.

Equilibrium in a competitive insurance market is a set of contracts such that, when customers choose contracts to maximize expected utility, (i) no contract in the equilibrium set makes negative expected profits; and (ii) there is no contract outside the equilibrium set that, if offered, will make a nonnegative profit. This notion of equilibrium is of the Cournot-Nash type; each firm assumes that the contracts its competitors offer are independent of its own actions.

### I.5 Equilibrium with Identical Customers

Only when customers have different accident probabilities, will insurance companies have imperfect information. We examine this case below. To illustrate our, mainly graphical, procedure, we first analyze the equilibrium of a competitive insurance market with identical customers.[5]

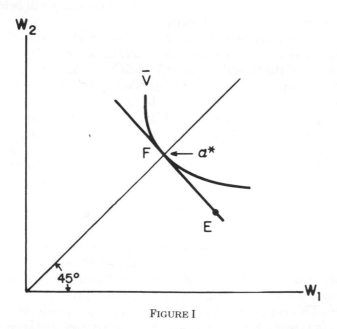

FIGURE I

In Figure I the horizontal and vertical axes represent income in

5. The analysis is identical if individuals have different $p$'s, but companies know the accident probabilities of their customers. The market splits into several submarkets—one for each different $p$ represented. Each submarket has the equilibrium described here.

the states: no accident, accident, respectively. The point $E$ with coordinates $(\hat{W}_1, \hat{W}_2)$ is the typical customer's uninsured state. Indifference curves are level sets of the function of equation (1). Purchasing the insurance policy $\alpha = (\alpha_1, \alpha_2)$ moves the individual from $E$ to the point $(\hat{W}_1 - \alpha_1, \hat{W}_2 + \alpha_2)$.

Free entry and perfect competition will ensure that policies bought in competitive equilibrium make zero expected profits, so that if $\alpha$ is purchased,

$$(3) \qquad\qquad \alpha_1(1 - p) - \alpha_2 p = 0.$$

The set of all policies that break even is given analytically by (3) and diagrammatically by the line $EF$ in Figure I, which is sometimes referred to as the fair-odds line. The equilibrium policy $\alpha^*$ maximizes the individual's (expected) utility and just breaks even. Purchasing $\alpha^*$ locates the customer at the tangency of the indifference curve with the fair-odds line. $\alpha^*$ satisfies the two conditions of equilibrium: (i) it breaks even; (ii) selling any contract preferred to it will bring insurance companies expected losses.

Since customers are risk-averse, the point $\alpha^*$ is located at the intersection of the 45°-line (representing equal income in both states of nature) and the fair-odds line. In equilibrium each customer buys complete insurance at actuarial odds. To see this, observe that the slope of the fair-odds line is equal to the ratio of the probability of not having an accident to the probability of having an accident $((1 - p)/p)$, while the slope of the indifference curve (the marginal rate of substitution between income in the state no accident to income in the state accident) is $[U'(W_1)\,(1 - p)]/[U'(W_2)p]$, which, when income in the two states is equal, is $(1 - p)/p$, independent of $U$.

### I.6 Imperfect Information: Equilibrium with Two Classes of Customers

Suppose that the market consists of two kinds of customers: low-risk individuals with accident probability $p^L$, and high-risk individuals with accident probability $p^H > p^L$. The fraction of high-risk customers is $\lambda$, so the average accident probability is $\bar{p} = \lambda p^H + (1 - \lambda)p^L$. This market can have only two kinds of equilibria: *pooling equilibria* in which both groups buy the same contract, and *separating equilibria* in which different types purchase different contracts.

A simple argument establishes that *there cannot be a pooling equilibrium*. The point $E$ in Figure II is again the initial endowment of all customers. Suppose that $\alpha$ is a pooling equilibrium and consider $\pi(\bar{p}, \alpha)$. If $\pi(\bar{p}, \alpha) < 0$, then firms offering $\alpha$ lose money, contradicting

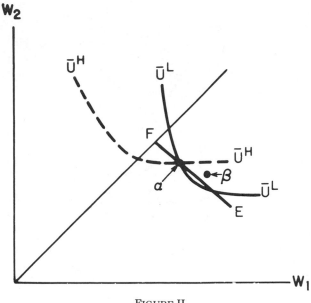

FIGURE II

the definition of equilibrium. If $\pi(\bar{p}, \alpha) > 0$, then there is a contract that offers slightly more consumption in each state of nature, which still will make a profit when all individuals buy it. All will prefer this contract to $\alpha$, so $\alpha$ cannot be an equilibrium. Thus, $\pi(\bar{p}, \alpha) = 0$, and $\alpha$ lies on the market odds line $EF$ (with slope $(1 - \bar{p})/\bar{p}$).

It follows from (1) that at $\alpha$ the slope of the high-risk indifference curve through $\alpha$, $\bar{U}^H$, is $(p^L/1 - p^L)(1 - p^H/p^H)$ times the slope of $\bar{U}^L$, the low-risk indifference curve through $\alpha$. In this figure $\bar{U}^H$ is a broken line, and $\bar{U}^L$ a solid line. The curves intersect at $\alpha$; thus there is a contract, $\beta$ in Figure II, near $\alpha$, which low-risk types prefer to $\alpha$. The high risk prefer $\alpha$ to $\beta$. Since $\beta$ is near $\alpha$, it makes a profit when the less risky buy it, $(\pi(p^L, \beta) \simeq \pi(p^L, \alpha) > \pi(\bar{p}, \alpha) = 0)$. The existence of $\beta$ contradicts the second part of the definition of equilibrium; $\alpha$ cannot be an equilibrium.

If there is an equilibrium, each type must purchase a separate contract. Arguments, which are, we hope, by now familiar, demonstrate that each contract in the equilibrium set makes zero profits. In Figure III the low-risk contract lies on line $EL$ (with slope $(1 - p^L)/p^L$), and the high-risk contract on line $EH$ (with slope $(1 - p^H)/p^H$). As was shown in the previous subsection, the contract on $EH$ most preferred by high-risk customers gives complete insurance.

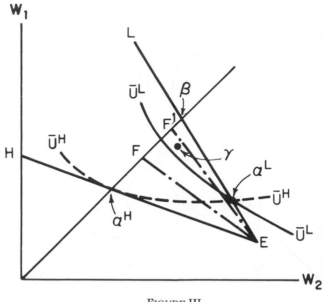

FIGURE III

This is $\alpha^H$ in Figure III; it must be part of any equilibrium. Low-risk customers would, of all contracts on $EL$, most prefer contract $\beta$ which, like $\alpha^H$, provides complete insurance. However, $\beta$ offers more consumption in each state than $\alpha^H$, and high-risk types will prefer it to $\alpha^H$. If $\beta$ and $\alpha^H$ are marketed, both high- and low-risk types will purchase $\beta$. The nature of imperfect information in this model is that insurance companies are unable to distinguish among their customers. All who demand $\beta$ must be sold $\beta$. Profits will be negative; $(\alpha^H, \beta)$ is not an equilibrium set of contracts.

An equilibrium contract for low-risk types must not be more attractive to high-risk types than $\alpha^H$; it must lie on the southeast side of $U^H$, the high-risk indifference curve through $\alpha^H$. We leave it to the reader to demonstrate that of all such contracts, the one that low-risk types most prefer is $\alpha^L$, the contract at the intersection of $EL$ and $U^H$ in Figure III. This establishes that *the set $(\alpha^H, \alpha^L)$ is the only possible equilibrium for a market with low- and high-risk customers.*[6] However, $(\alpha^H, \alpha^L)$ may not be an equilibrium. Consider the contract $\gamma$ in Figure III. It lies above $U^L$, the low-risk indifference curve through $\alpha^L$ and also above $U^H$. If $\gamma$ is offered, both low- and high-risk types

6. This largely heuristic argument can be made completely rigorous. See Wilson (1976).

will purchase it in preference to either $\alpha^H$ or $\alpha^L$. If it makes a profit when both groups buy it, $\gamma$ will upset the potential equilibrium of ($\alpha^H$, $\alpha^L$). $\gamma$'s profitability depends on the composition of the market. If there are sufficiently many high-risk people that $EF$ represents market odds, then $\gamma$ will lose money. If market odds are given by $EF'$ (as they will be if there are relatively few high-risk insurance customers), then $\gamma$ will make a profit. Since ($\alpha^H$, $\alpha^L$) is the only possible equilibrium, in this case the competitive insurance market will have no equilibrium.

This establishes that *a competitive insurance market may have no equilibrium.*

We have not found a simple intuitive explanation for this nonexistence; but the following observations, prompted by Frank Hahn's note (1974), may be suggestive. The information that is revealed by an individual's choice of an insurance contract depends on all the other insurance policies offered; there is thus a fundamental informational externality that each company, when deciding on which contract it will offer, fails to take into account. Given any set of contracts that breaks even, a firm may enter the market using the informational structure implicit in the availability of that set of contracts to make a profit; at the same time it forces the original contracts to make a loss. But as in any Nash equilibrium, the firm fails to take account of the consequences of its actions, and in particular, the fact that when those policies are no longer offered, the informational structure will have changed and it can no longer make a profit.

We can characterize the conditions under which an equilibrium does not exist. An equilibrium will not exist if the costs to the low-risk individual of pooling are low (because there are relatively few of the high-risk individuals who have to be subsidized, or because the subsidy per individual is low, i.e., when the probabilities of the two groups are not too different), or if their costs of separating are high. The costs of separating arise from the individual's inability to obtain complete insurance. Thus, the costs of separating are related to the individuals' attitudes toward risk. Certain polar cases make these propositions clear. If $p^L = 0$, it never pays the low-risk individuals to pool, and by continuity, for sufficiently small $p^L$ it does not pay to pool. Similarly, if individuals are risk-neutral, it never pays to pool; if they are infinitely risk averse with utility functions

$$(1') \qquad \bar{V}(p, W_1, W_2) = \mathrm{Min}\ (W_1, W_2),$$

it always pays to pool.

*I.7 Welfare Economics of Equilibrium*

One of the interesting properties of the equilibrium is that the presence of the high-risk individuals exerts a negative externality on the low-risk individuals. The externality is completely dissipative; there are losses to the low-risk individuals, but the high-risk individuals are no better off than they would be in isolation.

If only the high-risk individuals would admit to their having high accident probabilities, all individuals would be made better off without anyone being worse off.

The separating equilibrium we have described may not be Pareto optimal even relative to the information that is available. As we show in subsection II.3 below, there may exist a pair of policies that break even together and that make both groups better off.

## II. ROBUSTNESS

The analysis of Section I had three principal conclusions: First, competition on markets with imperfect information is more complex than in standard models. Perfect competitors may limit the quantities their customers can buy, not from any desire to exploit monopoly power, but simply in order to improve their information. Second, equilibrium may not exist. Finally, competitive equilibria are not Pareto optimal. It is natural to ask whether these conclusions (particularly the first, which was an assumption rather than a result of the analysis) can be laid to the special and possibly strained assumptions of our model. We think not. Our conclusions (or ones very like) must follow from a serious attempt to comprehend the workings of competition with imperfect and asymmetric information. We have analyzed the effect of changing our model in many ways. The results were always essentially the same.

Our attempts to establish robustness took two tacks. First, we showed that our results did not depend on the simple technical specifications of the model. This was tedious, and we have excised most of the details from the present version. The reader interested in analysis of the effects (distinctly minor) of changing our assumptions that individuals are alike in all respects save their accident probabilities, that there are only two kinds of customers, and that the insurance market lasts but a single period, is referred to earlier versions of this paper.[7] An assessment of the importance of the as-

---

7. See Rothschild and Stiglitz (1975). One curious result of these investigations should be mentioned. In other areas of economic theory where existence of equilibrium has been a problem, smoothing things by introducing a continuum of individuals of

sumption that individuals know their accident probabilities, while insurance companies do not (which raises more interesting issues), is given in subsection II.1 below.

Another approach to the question of robustness is the subject of the next three subsections. In them we question the behavioral assumptions and the equilibrium concepts used in Section I.

## II.1 Information Assumptions

Suppose that there are two groups of customers and that not all individuals within each group have the same accident probability. The average accident probability of one group is greater than that of the other; individuals within each group know the mean accident probability for members of their group, but do not know their own accident probabilities. As before, the insurance company cannot tell directly the accident probability of any particular individual, or even the group to which he belongs. For example, suppose that some persons occasionally drink too much, while the others almost never drink. Insurance firms cannot discover who drinks and who does not. Individuals know that drinking affects accident probabilities, but it affects different people differently. Each individual does not know how it will affect him.

In such a situation the expected utility theorem states that individuals make (and behave according to) estimates of their accident probabilities; if these estimates are unbiased in the sense that the average accident probability of those who estimate their accident probability to be $p$ actually is $p$, then the analysis goes through as before.

Unbiasedness seems a reasonable assumption (what is a more attractive alternative?). However, not even this low level of correctness of beliefs is required for our conclusions. Suppose, for example, that individuals differ both with respect to their accident probabilities and to their risk aversion, but they all assume that their own accident probabilities are $\bar{p}$. If low-risk individuals are less risk-averse on average, then there will not exist a pooling equilibrium; there may exist no equilibrium at all; and if there does exist an equilibrium, it will entail partial insurance for both groups. Figure IV shows that there

---

different types can insure existence. Not so here. If there is a continuous distribution of accident probabilities (but customers are otherwise identical), then equilibrium never exists. There is an intuitive explanation for this striking result. We argued above that, if accident probabilities were close together, then equilibrium would not exist. When there is a continuum of probabilities, there always are individuals with close probabilities with whom it pays to "pool." For a proof of this result, which is not elementary, see Riley (1976).

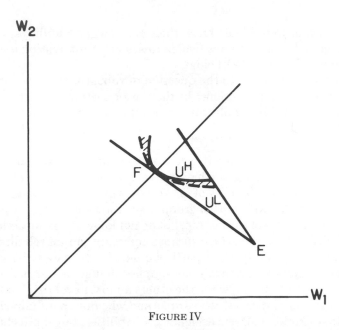

FIGURE IV

will not exist a pooling equilibrium. If there were a pooling equilibrium, it would clearly be with complete insurance at the market odds, since both groups' indifference curves have the slope of the market odds line there. If the low-risk individuals are less risk-averse, then the two indifference curves are tangent at $F$, but elsewhere the high-risk individuals' indifference curve lies above the low-risk individuals' indifference curve. Thus, any policy in the shaded area between the two curves will be purchased by the low-risk individuals in preference to the pooling contract at $F$.

Other such cases can be analyzed, but we trust that the general principle is clear. Our pathological conclusions do not require that people have particularly good information about their accident probabilities. They will occur under a wide variety of circumstances, including the appealing case of unbiasedness. Neither insurance firms nor their customers have to be perfectly informed about the differences in risk properties that exist among individuals: What is required is that individuals with different risk properties differ in some characteristic that can be linked with the purchase of insurance and that, somehow, insurance firms discover this link.

## II.2 Price Competition Versus Quantity Competition

One can imagine our model of the insurance market operating in two distinct modes. The first, price competition, is familiar to all students of competitive markets. Associated with any insurance contract $\alpha$ is a number $q(\alpha) = \alpha_1/\alpha_2$, which, since it is the cost per unit coverage, is called the price of insurance. Under price competition, insurance firms establish a price of insurance and allow their customers to buy as much or as little insurance as they want at that price. Thus, if contract $\alpha$ is available from a company, so are the contracts $2\alpha$ and $(\frac{1}{2})\alpha$; the former pays twice as much benefits (and costs twice as much in premiums) as $\alpha$; the latter is half as expensive and provides half as much coverage.

Opposed to price competition is what we call price and quantity competition. In this regime companies may offer a number of different contracts, say $\alpha^1, \alpha^2, \ldots, \alpha^n$. Individuals may buy at most one contract. They are not allowed to buy arbitrary multiples of contracts offered, but must instead settle for one of the contracts explicitly put up for sale. A particular contract specifies both a price and a quantity of insurance. Under price and quantity competition it is conceivable that insurance contracts with different prices of insurance will exist in equilibrium; people who want more insurance may be willing to pay a higher price for it (accept less favorable odds) than those who make do with shallower coverage. Under price competition customers will buy insurance only at the lowest price quoted in the market.

The argument of Section I depends heavily on our assumption that price and quantity competition, and not simply price competition, characterizes the competitive insurance market. This assumption is defended here. The argument is basically quite simple. Price competition is a special case of price and quantity competition. Nothing in the definition of price and quantity competition prevents firms from offering for sale a set of contracts with the same price of insurance. Since the argument above characterized all equilibria under price and quantity competition, it also characterized all equilibria when some firms set prices and others set prices and quantities. Thus, it must be that price competition cannot compete with price and quantity competition.[8]

This argument hinges on one crucial assumption: regardless of the form of competition, customers purchase but a single insurance contract or equivalently that the total amount of insurance purchased

8. We leave to the reader a detailed proof. A sketch follows. Suppose that there are two groups in the population. If the price of insurance is $q$, high- and low-risk customers will buy $\alpha^H(q)$ and $\alpha^L(q)$, respectively. It is easy to figure out what total insurance company profits, $P(q)$, are. The equilibrium price $q^*$ is the smallest $q$ such that $P(q) = 0$. Since $P(q)$ is continuous in $q$ and it is easy to find $q$ such that $P(q) > 0$ and $P(q) < 0$, such a $q^*$ exists. To show that price competition will not survive, it is only necessary to show that $(\alpha^H(q^*), \alpha^L(q^*))$ is not an equilibrium set of contracts as defined in subsection I.4 above.

by any one customer is known to all companies that sell to him. We think that this is an accurate description of procedures on at least some insurance markets. Many insurance policies specify either that they are not in force if there is another policy or that they insure against only the first, say, $1,000 of losses suffered. That is, instead of being a simple bet for or against the occurrence of a particular event, an insurance policy is a commitment on the part of the company to restore at least partially the losses brought about by the occurrence of that event. The person who buys two $1,000 accident insurance policies does not have $2,000 worth of protection. If an accident occurs, all he gets from his second policy is the privilege of watching his companies squabble over the division of the $1,000 payment. There is no point in buying more than one policy.

Why should insurance markets operate in this way? One simple and obvious explanation is moral hazard. Because the insured can often bring about, or at least make more likely, the event being insured against, insurance companies want to limit the amount of insurance their customers buy. Companies want to see that their customers do not purchase so much insurance that they have an interest in an accident occurring. Thus, companies will want to monitor the purchases of their customers. Issuing contracts of the sort described above is the obvious way to do so.

A subtler explanation for this practice is provided by our argument that price and quantity competition can dominate price competition. If the market is in equilibrium under price competition, a firm can offer a contract, specifying price and quantity, that will attract the low-risk customers away from the companies offering contracts specifying price alone. Left with only high-risk customers, these firms will lose money. This competitive gambit will successfully upset the price competition equilibria if the entering firm can be assured that those who buy its contracts hold no other insurance. Offering insurance that pays off only for losses not otherwise insured is a way to guarantee this.

It is sometimes suggested that the term "competitive" can be applied only to markets where there is a single price of a commodity and each firm is a price taker. This seems an unnecessarily restrictive use of the term competitive. The basic idea underlying competitive markets involves free entry and noncollusive behavior among the participants in the market. In some economic environments price taking without quantity restrictions is a natural result of such markets. In the situations described in this paper, this is not so.

*II.3 Restrictions on Firm Behavior and Optimal Subsidies*

An important simplification of the analysis of Section I was the assumption that each insurance company issued but a single contract. We once thought this constraint would not affect the nature of equilibrium. We argued that in equilibrium firms must make nonnegative profits. Suppose that a firm offers two contracts, one of which makes an expected profit of say, $S, per contract sold, the other an expected loss of $L per contract. The firm can make nonnegative expected profits if the ratio of the profitable to the unprofitable contracts sold is at least $\mu$, where $\mu = L/S$. However, the firm can clearly make more profits if it sells only the contracts on which it makes a profit. It and its competitors have no reason to offer the losing contracts, and in competitive equilibrium, they will not be offered. Since only contracts that make nonnegative profits will be offered, it does not matter, given our assumptions about entry, that firms are assumed to issue only a single contract. If there is a contract that could make a profit, a firm will offer it.

This argument is not correct. The possibility of offering more than one contract is important to firms, and to the nature and existence of equilibrium. Firms that offer several contracts are not dependent on the policies offered by other firms for the information generated by the choices of individuals. By offering a menu of policies, insurance firms may be able to obtain information about the accident probabilities of particular individuals. Furthermore, although there may not be an equilibrium in which the profits from one contract subsidize the losses of another contract, it does not follow that such a pair of contracts cannot break what would otherwise be an equilibrium.

Such a case is illustrated in Figure V. *EF* is again the market odds line. A separating equilibrium exists ($\bar{\alpha}^H$, $\bar{\alpha}^L$). Suppose that a firm offered the two contracts, $\alpha^{H\prime}$ and $\alpha^{L\prime}$; $\alpha^{H\prime}$ makes a loss, $\alpha^{L\prime}$ makes a profit. High-risk types prefer $\alpha^{H\prime}$ to $\bar{\alpha}^H$, and low-risk types prefer $\alpha^{L\prime}$ to $\bar{\alpha}^L$. These two contracts, if offered by a single firm together, do not make losses. The profits from $\alpha^{L\prime}$ subsidize the losses of $\alpha^{H\prime}$. Thus, ($\alpha^{H\prime}$, $\alpha^{L\prime}$) upsets the equilibrium ($\bar{\alpha}^H$, $\bar{\alpha}^L$).

This example points up another possible inefficiency of separating equilibria. Consider the problem of choosing two contracts ($\alpha^H$, $\alpha^L$) such that $\alpha^L$ maximizes the utility of the low-risk individual subject to the constraints that (a) the high-risk individual prefers $\alpha^H$ to $\alpha^L$ and (b) the pair of contracts $\alpha^H$ and $\alpha^L$ break even when bought by high- and low-risk types, respectively, in the ratio $\lambda$ to $(1 - \lambda)$. This

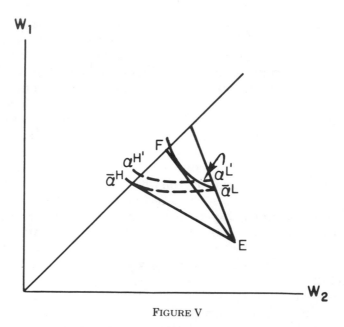

FIGURE V

is a kind of optimal subsidy problem. If the separating equilibrium, when it exists, does not solve this problem, it is inefficient. Figure V shows that the separating equilibrium can be inefficient in this sense. We now show that if there are enough high-risk people, then the separating equilibrium can be efficient.

The optimal subsidy problem always has a solution $(\alpha^{H*}, \alpha^{L*})$. The optimal high-risk contract $\alpha^{H*}$ will always entail complete insurance so that $V(p^H, \alpha^{H*}) = U(W - p^H d + a)$, where $a$ is the per capita subsidy of the high risk by the low risk. This subsidy decreases income for each low-risk person by $\gamma a$ (where $\gamma = \lambda/(1 - \lambda)$) in each state. Net of this charge $\alpha^{L*}$ breaks even when low-risk individuals buy it. Thus, $\alpha^{L*} = (\alpha_1 + \gamma a, \alpha_2 - \gamma a)$, where $\alpha_1 = \alpha_2 p^L/(1 - p^L)$.

To find the optimal contract, one solves the following problem: Choose $a$ and $\alpha_2$ to maximize

$$U(X)(1 - p^L) + U(Z)p^L,$$

subject to

$$U(Y) \geq U(X)(1 - p^H) + U(Z)p^H$$

$$a \geq 0,$$

where

$$X = W_0 - \gamma a - \alpha_2 p^L/(1 - p^L),$$
$$Y = W_0 - p^H d + a,$$

and

$$Z = W_0 - d - \gamma a + \alpha_2.$$

The solution to this problem can be analyzed by standard Kuhn-Tucker techniques. If the constraint $a \geq 0$ is binding at the optimum, then the solution involves no subsidy to the high-risk persons; $(\alpha^{H*}, \alpha^{L*})$ is the separating equilibrium. It is straightforward but tedious to show that a sufficient condition for this is that

(4)
$$\frac{(p^H - p^L)\,\gamma}{p^L(1 - p)^L)} > \frac{U'(Y)[U'(Z) - U'(X)]}{U'(X)U'(Z)}$$

where $X$, $Y$, and $Z$ are determined by the optimal $a^*$, $\alpha_2^*$. The right-hand side of (4) is always less than

$$\frac{U'(W_0 - d)[U'(W_0 - d) - U'(W_0)]}{U'(W_0)^2}$$

so that there exist values of $\gamma$ (and thus of $\lambda$) large enough to satisfy (4).

## II.4 Alternative Equilibrium Concepts

There are a number of other concepts of equilibrium that we might have employed. These concepts differ with respect to assumptions concerning the behavior of the firms in the market. In our model the firm assumes that its actions do not affect the market—the set of policies offered by other firms was independent of its own offering.

In this subsection we consider several other equilibrium concepts, implying either less or more rationality in the market. We could, for instance, call any set of policies that just break even given the set of individuals who purchase them an *informationally consistent equilibrium*. This assumes that the forces for the creation of new contracts are relatively weak (in the absence of profits). Thus, in Figure III, $\alpha^H$ and any contract along the line $EL$ below $\alpha^L$ is a set of informationally consistent separating equilibrium contracts; any single contract along the line $EF$ is an informationally consistent pooling equilibrium contract. This is the notion of equilibrium that Spence (1973) has employed in most of his work. The longer the lags in the system, the greater the difficulty of competing by offering different contracts, the more stable is an informationally consistent equilibrium. Thus, while this seems to us a reasonable equilibrium concept for the models of educational signaling on which Spence focused, it is less compelling when applied to insurance or credit markets (see Jaffee and Russell's contribution to this symposium).

A *local* equilibrium is a set of contracts such that there do not exist any contracts in the vicinity of the equilibrium contracts that will be chosen and make a positive profit. If we rule out the subsidies of the last subsection, then the set of separating contracts, which maximizes the welfare of low-risk individuals, is a local equilibrium.

The notion that firms experiment with contracts similar to those already on the market motivates the idea of a local equilibrium. Even if firms have little knowledge about the shape of utility functions, and about the proportions of population in different accident probabilities, one would expect that competition would lead to small perturbations around the equilibrium. A stable equilibrium requires that such perturbations not lead to firms making large profits, as would be the case with some perturbations around a pooling point.

These two concepts of equilibrium imply that firms act less rationally than we assumed they did in Section I. It is possible that firms exhibit a greater degree of rationality; that is, firms ought not to take the set of contracts offered by other firms as given, but ought to assume that other firms will act as they do, or at least will respond in some way to the new contract offered by the firm. Hence, in those cases where in our definition there was no equilibrium, because for any set of contracts there is a contract that will break even and be chosen by a subset of the population, given that the contracts offered by the other firms remain unchanged, those contracts that break the equilibrium may not break even if the other firms also change their contracts. The peculiar provision of many insurance contracts, that the effective premium is not determined until the *end* of the period (when the individual obtains what is called a dividend), is perhaps a reflection of the uncertainty associated with who will purchase the policy, which in turn is associated with the uncertainty about what contracts other insurance firms will offer.

Wilson (1976) introduced and analyzed one such nonmyopic equilibrium concept. A Wilson equilibrium is a set of contracts such that, when customers choose among them so as to maximize profits, (a) all contracts make nonnegative profits and (b) there does not exist a new contract (or set of contracts), which, if offered, makes positive profits even when all contracts that lose money as a result of this entry are withdrawn. In the simple model of Section I, such equilibria always exist. Comparing this definition with the one of subsection I.4 above makes it clear that, when it exists, our separating equilibrium is also a Wilson equilibrium. When this does not exist, the Wilson equilibrium is the pooling contract that maximizes the utility of the low-risk customers. This is $\beta$ in Figure VI. $\beta$ dominates the separating pair ($\alpha^L$, $\alpha^H$). Consider a contract like $\gamma$, which the low risk prefer to $\beta$. Under our definition of equilibrium it upsets $\beta$. Under Wilson's it does not. When the low risk desert $\beta$ for $\gamma$, it loses money and is withdrawn. Then the high risk also buy $\gamma$. When both groups buy $\gamma$, it loses money. Thus, $\gamma$ does not successfully compete against $\beta$.

Although this equilibrium concept is appealing, it is not without its difficulties. It seems a peculiar halfway house; firms respond to competitive entry by dropping policies, but not by adding new policies. Furthermore, although counterexamples are very complicated to construct, it appears that a Wilson equilibrium may not exist if groups differ in their attitudes towards risk. Finally, in the absence of collusion or regulation, in a competitive insurance market, it is hard to see how or why any single firm should take into account the consequences of its offering a new policy. On balance, it seems to us that nonmyopic equilibrium concepts are more appropriate for models of monopoly (or oligopoly) than for models of competition.

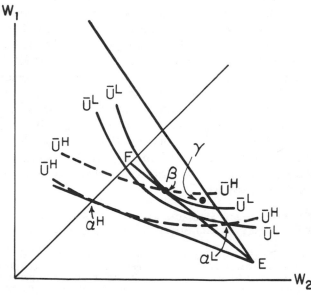

FIGURE VI

### III. Conclusion

We began this research with the hope of showing that even a small amount of imperfect information could have a significant effect on competitive markets. Our results were more striking than we had hoped: the single price equilibrium of conventional competitive analysis was shown to be no longer viable; market equilibrium, when it existed, consisted of contracts which specified both prices and quantities; the high-risk (low ability, etc.) individuals exerted a dissipative externality on the low-risk (high ability) individuals; the structure of the equilibrium as well as its existence depended on a number of assumptions that, with perfect information, were inconsequential; and finally, and in some ways most disturbing, under quite plausible conditions equilibrium did not exist.

Our analysis, and our conclusions, extend beyond the simple insurance market described above. The models of educational screening and signaling studied by, among others, Arrow (1973), Riley (1975), Spence (1973, 1974), and Stiglitz (1971, 1972, 1974a, 1975b), are obvious examples. The other papers in this symposium describe models that can be profitably studied using our techniques and our concepts. Models in which communities choose the level of public goods and individuals choose among communities on the basis of the menu of public goods and taxes that the different communities offer, provide a less obvious but, we think, important case.[9]

Do these theoretical speculations tell us anything about the real world? In the absence of empirical work it is hard to say. The market on which we focused most of our analysis, that for insurance, is probably not competitive; whether our model may partially explain this fact is almost impossible to say. But there are other markets, particularly financial and labor markets, which appear to be competitive and in which imperfect and asymmetric information play an important role. We suspect that many of the peculiar institutions of these labor markets arise as responses to the difficulties that they, or any competitive market, have in handling problems of information. Establishing (or refuting) this conjecture seems to provide a rich agenda for future research.

University of Wisconsin, Madison
Stanford University and All Souls College, Oxford

9. See F. Westhoff's dissertation (1974), and Stiglitz (1974b). A more complete discussion of these is in our earlier working paper referred to in footnote 7 above. Salop and Salop (1972) demonstrated, in an early draft of their symposium paper, that contingent loan plans for repayment of tuition, and their possible defects, can be analyzed along these lines.

## References

Arrow, K. J., *Essays in the Theory of Risk Bearing* (Chicago: Markham, 1971).

———, "Higher Education as a Filter," *Journal of Public Economics, II* (July 1973), 193–216.

Borch, K., *The Economics of Uncertainty* (Princeton, N.J.: Princeton University Press, 1968).

Hahn, F. H., "Notes on R-S Models of Insurance Markets," mimeo, Cambridge University, 1974.

Riley, J., "Competitive Signaling," *Journal of Economic Theory,* X (April 1975), 174–86.

———, "Informational Equilibrium," mimeo, Rand Corporation, 1976.

Revesz, P., *Laws of Large Numbers* (New York: Academic Press, 1960).

Rothschild, M., and J. E. Stiglitz, "Equilibrium in Competitive Insurance Markets," Technical Report No. 170, IMSSS Stanford University, 1975.

Spence, M., "Job Market Signaling," this *Journal,* LXXXVII (Aug. 1973), 355–79.

———, *Market Signaling* (Cambridge: Harvard University Press, 1974).

Stiglitz, J. E., "Perfect and Imperfect Capital Markets," paper presented to Econometric Society Meeting, New Orleans, 1971.

———, "Education as a Screening Device and the Distribution of Income," mimeo, Yale University, 1972.

———, "Demand for Education in Public and Private School Systems," *Journal of Public Economics,* III (Nov. 1974a), 349–86.

———, "Pure Theory of Local Public Goods," in M. Feldstein ed. IEA Conference Volume (Turin, 1974b.).

———, "The Theory of Screening, Education, and Distribution of Income," *American Economic Review,* LXV (June 1975), 283–300.

Westhoff, Frank H., "The Theory of Local Public Goods," Ph.D. thesis, Yale University, 1974.

Wilson, Charles A., "Equilibrium in a Class of Self-Selection Models," Ph.D. thesis, University of Rochester, 1976.

Journal of Public Economics 20 (1983) 121–130. North-Holland Publishing Company

# ADVERSE SELECTION AND STATISTICAL DISCRIMINATION

## An analysis of Canadian automobile insurance

### B.G. DAHLBY*

*University of Alberta, Edmonton, Alberta T6G 2H4, Canada*

Received February 1980, revised version received October 1981

Statistical discrimination occurs when a characteristic, such as sex, is used as an indicator of the risk group of an individual. The theory of adverse selection is used to explain the occurrence of statistical discrimination. A model of the market for collision insurance, which is based on the theory of adverse selection, is estimated on Canadian data. The results suggest that adverse selection occurs in this market. Simulations of the effect of prohibiting sexual discrimination in the 21–24 age group indicate that the premiums for single females would increase substantially and that a significant proportion would no longer purchase collision insurance.

## 1. Introduction

In 1978, a Board of Industry in Alberta ruled that insurance premiums based on the sex of the insured contravene The Individual's Rights Protection Act (Statutes of Alberta, 1972). This act prohibits discrimination in the provision of '...any accomodation, services or facilities customarily available to the public, because of the race, religious beliefs, colour, sex, ancestry or place of origin of that person...'. The Board of Inquiry was established because a number of males complained that automobile insurance companies charge females, with similar characteristics, lower premiums. This practice by the insurance industry is based on statistical evidence that the accident rate for young females is lower than that for young males. However, the Board of Inquiry ruled that 'if a discrimination prohibited by law exists it is no less a prohibited discrimination because it is supported by statistics'.[1] A policy of eliminating, in stages, age, sex, marital status, and geographic location as factors in setting auto insurance premiums has been initiated by the publicly-owned Insurance Corporation of British Columbia under its Fundamental Auto Insurance Rating (FAIR) program.

*I would like to thank A. Buse, N. Doherty, D. Gillen and two anonymous referees for their comments and suggestions, A. Cooper and J. Lyndon of the Insurance Bureau of Canada for supplying the data, and Y.K. Lee for his research assistance. The financial support of the Faculty of Graduate Studies and Research at the University of Alberta in the form of a research grant is gratefully acknowledged.

[1] Alberta Human Rights Commission (1978, p. 18).

Whether insurance companies should be able to levy premiums based on the average risk of individuals in different sex, marital status, or age groups is a political or ethical question, but the prohibition of statistical discrimination has economic implications because it will alter the premiums that are levied in insurance markets. The objective of this paper is to analyze statistical discrimination in insurance markets using the theory of adverse selection. In section 2 the theory of adverse selection is reviewed and the nature of the equilibrium in a competitive insurance market in which statistical discrimination occurs is briefly described. In section 3 some statistics from the private automobile insurance industry are presented which suggest that there is an adverse selection problem in this market. A simple model of the market for collision insurance, which is based on the theory of adverse selection, is estimated and the results are consistent with the theory. In the final section the model is used to simulate the effect of prohibiting sexual discrimination in collision insurance in the 21–24 age group. The model suggests that the premiums for single females would increase substantially and that there would be a significant decline in the proportion of single females purchasing collision insurance.

## 2. Adverse selection and statistical discrimination

The problem of adverse selection arises in insurance markets when the purchaser of insurance has more information about the probability of a loss than the insurance company and it has been analyzed by Akerlof (1970), Rothschild and Stiglitz (1976), Wilson (1977), Miyazaki (1977), and Spence (1977). In this literature it is usually assumed that there are two states of the world, and in one state there is an accident which costs $C$ dollars. The cost and the probability of an accident are exogenous variables, and thus there is no problem of moral hazard. There are only two risk groups, high-risk individuals and low-risk individuals, with accident probabilities of $\pi_H$ and $\pi_L$, respectively. All individuals have the same wealth in the absence of an accident and utility function which displays risk aversion. An insurance company cannot observe the risk group of an individual when he purchases an insurance policy, but the individual knows his risk group. Assuming that there are no costs in writing insurance policies and that firms are risk neutral, Rothschild and Stiglitz (1976) have shown that with a Nash equilibrium high-risk individuals purchase full coverage at an actuarially fair premium, low-risk individuals purchase partial coverage at an actuarially fair premium, and high-risk individuals are indifferent between the two types of policies. Wilson (1977) has introduced an alternative concept of equilibrium in which each firm correctly anticipates which policies will be dropped by other firms when it changes its menu of policies and his analysis has been extended by Miyazaki (1977) and Spence (1977) to allow for cross-subsidization of contracts purchased by high-risk and low-risk individuals.

The theory of adverse selection can explain the existence of statistical discrimination in a competitive insurance market. [See Dahlby (1980) and Hoy (1982) for a detailed analysis of statistical discrimination based on adverse selection.] Suppose that an insurance company can observe, at no cost, the sex of the policy-holder and that the probability of an accident for a female is less than that for a male because the proportion of females who are high risk is lower than the proportion of males who are high-risk. Then a firm may find it profitable to offer policies with lower premiums to females. The insurance market will then be segmented with a Wilson equilibrium in each segment. High-risk individuals will purchase full coverage, low-risk individuals will purchase partial coverage and the policies purchased by low-risk individuals will subsidize the policies purchased by high-risk individuals of the same sex.

This theory of discrimination in insurance markets based on adverse selection is empirically testable and it may shed some light on the nature of the equilibrium in insurance markets. The model predicts that the proportion of individuals purchasing full coverage in each segment of the market will vary directly with the average probability of an accident in that segment. Cross-subsidization will occur within each segment with low-coverage policies subsidizing high-coverage policies. Cross-subsidization between different segments of the market will not occur. The model predicts that discrimination can occur under competitive conditions, but non-myopic behaviour on the part of firms is required. The Nash equilibrium concept, which assumes myopic behaviour, does not explain the existence of discrimination in insurance markets in the presence of an adverse selection problem. Thus, although Rothschild and Stiglitz (1976) have argued that the Wilson equilibrium concept is not relevant for competitive markets, it does explain discrimination in competitive insurance markets while the Nash equilibrium does not. Of course this is not conclusive evidence in favour of the Wilson concept because discrimination in insurance markets may be due to a non-competitive market structure.

In the following section we have attempted to test for the presence of adverse selection in the Canadian automobile insurance market. Unfortunately, the available data do not indicate the premiums levied and the number of cars insured at different levels of coverage. Therefore, we have been unable to perform a direct test of the model of adverse selection described above which emphasizes differences in the levels of coverage purchased by high-risk and low-risk drivers and the cross-subsidization of high- and low-coverage policies within each segment of the market. Instead, we have used Akerlof's hypothesis that low-risk individuals are more prone to drop out of an insurance market than are high-risk individuals in developing a simple model of adverse selection which is empirically testable.

## 3. Adverse selection in Canadian automobile insurance: An empirical analysis

The characteristics which are mainly used in setting premiums by the private automobile insurance industry in Canada are the age, sex, marital status, and claim history of the principal driver of the automobile. Discrimination on the basis of sex and marital status is primarily used in the under 25 age group. Table 1 shows some statistics for the 21–24 age group in urban areas in Canada for the policy years 1975–78. There are two major types of automobile insurance, namely bodily injury and property damage (BIPD) insurance (which is also known as third party liability insurance), and collision insurance. BIPD insurance was compulsory in all of the provinces from which these data were compiled (except Ontario where most drivers took out BIPD insurance in any case because they were required to have $100,000 minimum coverage) and collision insurance was optional. The first row of the table shows that the average claim frequency for BIPD insurance was substantially higher for single males than for married males or females.

Table 1

Canadian automobile insurance statistics for the 21–24 age group, 1975–78.

| Driver class | | | | |
|---|---|---|---|---|
| Age | 21–22 | 23–24 | 21–24 | 21–24 |
| Sex | Male | Male | Male | Female |
| Marital status | Single | Single | Married | Single or married |
| *BIPD insurance* | | | | |
| Claim frequency —entire class ($\pi^b$) | 0.124 | 0.104 | 0.0980 | 0.0821 |
| —at least 5 years claim-free ($\pi_L$) | 0.0917 | 0.0783 | 0.0741 | 0.0659 |
| Proportion of drivers with at least 5 years of claim-free driving | 0.175 | 0.311 | 0.312 | 0.289 |
| *Collision insurance* ($100 and $250 deductible) | | | | |
| Claim frequency —entire class ($\pi^c$) | 0.142 | 0.123 | 0.109 | 0.0998 |
| Average premium in 1978 (P) | $264 | $192 | $162 | $147 |
| Expected loss cost in 1978 ($\pi^c \cdot C$) | $162 | $137 | $96 | $87 |
| Proportion of drivers purchasing collision insurance (Z) | 0.497 | 0.588 | 0.694 | 0.747 |

*Source*: The Insurance Bureau of Canada, *1977 Automobile Insurance Experience* and *1978 Automobile Insurance Experience*.

The second row shows that the average claim frequency for drivers with at least five years of claim-free driving was about 25 percent lower than the average claim frequency for all individuals in that driver class. These figures indicate that each class of drivers is not homogeneous with respect to the risk of an accident, but can be viewed as containing different proportions of high-risk and low-risk drivers, as was assumed in the theoretical model described in section 2. If there are members of the two risk groups in each class of drivers, then the average probability of an accident among individuals with zero accidents for $n$ years approaches $\pi_L$ as $n$ approaches infinity. In the empirical analysis which follows, we have used the claim frequency for BIPD insurance among individuals with at least five years of claim-free driving as a proxy for the probability of an accident for a low-risk individual in that driver class. The third row of the table shows that the proportion of drivers with at least five years of claim-free driving is about the same for single males 23–24 years of age, married males, and females in spite of the differences among these classes in the average claim frequencies and the claim frequencies of individuals with five years of claim-free driving. This suggests that there may be differences in $\pi_L$ between driver classes.

The average claim frequency for individuals purchasing $100 or $250 deductible collision insurance is shown in the fourth row of the table. The average claim frequency for collision insurance is higher than that for BIPD insurance in each driver class. One possible explanation of higher claim frequencies for collision insurance is that it may cover accidents where there are no claims for third party damages, i.e. single car accidents where there is no damage to the persons or property of others. However, these statistics may also indicate the presence of adverse selection in the market for collision insurance. The theory of adverse selection predicts that low-risk individuals will purchase less than full coverage for collision damages if insurance companies cannot distinguish low-risk and high-risk individuals. If some low-risk individuals do not purchase $100 or $250 deductible collision insurance, then the average accident rate among those purchasing collision insurance will exceed the average accident rate for the entire population, which in this case may be approximated by the claim frequency for BIPD insurance. Thus, the higher claim frequency for collision insurance may be explained by the decisions of some low-risk individuals not to purchase collision insurance because it is not attractive at the high premiums that must be charged because of the presence of high-risk individuals in the market.

Table 1 also shows the average premium per car insured and the expected loss per car insured in 1978, where the latter variable is the product of the average claim frequency for collision insurance and the average loss cost per claim to the insurance industry. Finally, the table shows that proportion of drivers purchasing collision insurance was highest among females and lowest among single males 21–22 years of age.

In attempting to test for adverse selection in the market for collision insurance, we have utilized data from the Insurance Bureau of Canada for nine classes of drivers over the age of 20 for the years 1975–78. The figures do not include Manitoba, Saskatchewan, and British Columbia which have public insurance programs. The proportion of drivers purchasing collision insurance in each driver class was obtained by dividing the number of cars insured for collision by the numbers of cars insured for bodily injury and property damage. The data include all drivers in a given driver class and not just those drivers with the same history of claims. We have treated the average loss cost per claim in each driver class, $C$, as an exogenous variable which proxies the average payout by the insurance industry. However, there may be systematic differences in $C$ between driver classes because of variations in coverage, and $C$ does not equal the average payout because it includes adjustment costs. A more detailed description of the data is given in an appendix which is available from the author upon request.

In testing for adverse selection in the market for collision insurance, we have postulated the following simple model which focuses on the decision to purchase collision insurance:

$$\ln Z = \alpha_1 + \alpha_2 \ln (P/(\pi_L \cdot C)) + \alpha_3 \ln h + \sum_{j=1}^{8} \delta_j D_j;$$

$$\alpha_2 < 0, \quad \alpha_3 > 0, \tag{1a}$$

$$\ln P = \beta_1 + \beta_2 \ln (\pi^c \cdot C) + \beta_3 \ln R + \beta_4 t;$$

$$0 < \beta_2 < 1, \quad \beta_3 > 0, \quad \beta_4 < 0, \tag{2a}$$

$$\ln \pi^c = \gamma_1 + \gamma_2 \ln h + \gamma_3 \ln \pi_L + \gamma_4 \ln Z;$$

$$\gamma_2 > 0, \quad \gamma_3 > 0, \quad \gamma_4 < 0. \tag{3a}$$

Eq. (1a) is based on the hypothesis that the proportion of individuals in a given driver class that purchase collision insurance, $Z$, is inversely related to the relative price of insurance for a low-risk individual and is directly related to the proportion of high-risk individuals in that class. The relative price of insurance is the ratio of the average premium, $P$, to the expected payout for a low-risk individual where the latter variable is the product of $\pi_L$, the BIPD claim frequency for drivers with five or more years of claim-free driving, and $C$, the average loss cost per claim. A proxy for the proportion of high-risk drivers, $h$, is given by $((\pi^b - \pi_L)/\pi_L)$, where $\pi^b$ is the average claim frequency for BIPD insurance.[2] A dummy variable for driver class $j$, $D_j$, is also

[2] With two risk groups, $\pi^b$ is equal to $(h\pi_H + (1-h)\pi_L)$, and $\ln ((\pi^b - \pi_L)/\pi_L)$ equals $(\ln h + \ln ((\pi_H/\pi_L) - 1))$.

included in the equation to reflect the effects of other variables, such as average net worth and attitudes toward risk, which may influence the decision to purchase collision insurance.

In eq. (2a) the premium for collision insurance is determined by the expected loss cost per car insured, $\pi^c \cdot C$, where $\pi^c$ is the average claim frequency for collision insurance in that driver class, a measure of the insurance risk for that driver class, $R$, and a time trend $t$. The elasticity of the premium with respect to the expected loss cost per car should be positive but less than one because the other costs associated with providing insurance, such as administration costs, probably do not vary with the expected loss cost. A measure of insurance risk has been included in eq. (2a) because the segmentation of the insurance market may limit the extent of risk-pooling and because there may be unexpected changes in the cost of automobile repairs. The measure of insurance risk that we have used is the ratio of the variance in the loss cost per car insured to the average loss cost per car insured for the period 1975–78 in each driver class. That is, $R$ is equal to $(\text{var}(\pi^c \cdot C)/\overline{\pi^c \cdot C})$, where $\overline{\pi^c \cdot C}$ is the average loss cost per car insured for the period 1975–78. The data indicate that this measure of insurance risk is generally lower in the driver classes where the number of cars insured is relatively large. It should be noted that this measure of insurance risk is based on the variability of the loss cost per car insured for the entire industry and thus it is probably an underestimate of the insurance risk for an individual firm. Finally, a time trend was included because a study of the Canadian insurance industry by Quirin et al. (1974) indicated a significant decline in operating costs over time.

In eq. (3a), $\pi^c$ is hypothesized to vary directly with $h$ and $\pi_L$ and inversely with $Z$. The latter relation arises because low-risk individuals have a greater tendency to drop out of the insurance market than do high-risk individuals. Thus, the lower the proportion of individuals in a given driver class purchasing collision insurance, the higher the ratio of high-risk individuals to all individuals purchasing collision insurance and hence the higher the average claim frequency for collision insurance. Therefore, in this simple model of adverse selection, $Z$, $P$, and $\pi^c$ are endogenous variables, and $h$, $\pi_L$, $C$, $R$, $t$, and the $D_j$'s are exogenous variables.

This system of equations was estimated using two-stage least-squares on pooled cross-section data for nine driver classes for the policy years 1975–78.[3] The results are shown below with the absolute values of the $t$-statistics

[3]The observation for driver class 06 (occasional male driver under 25) in 1978 was not included in the regressions because the value for $((\pi^b - \pi_L)/\pi_L)$ in that year was about three times as large as it was in other years.

in parentheses:

$$\ln Z = 0.3160 - 0.2893 \ln (P/(\pi_L \cdot C)) + 0.2441 \ln h;$$
$$\phantom{\ln Z =} (1.83) \quad (2.64) \phantom{\ln (P/(\pi_L \cdot C)) +} (4.29)$$

$$R^2 = 0.8475, \tag{1b}$$

$$\ln P = 1.3376 + 0.8793 \ln (\pi^c \cdot C) + 0.02193 \ln R - 0.07772t;$$
$$\phantom{\ln P =} (5.54) \quad (16.67) \phantom{\ln (\pi^c \cdot C) +} (2.05) \phantom{\ln R} (5.32)$$

$$R^2 = 0.9482, \tag{2b}$$

$$\ln \pi^c = 0.6051 + 0.2175 \ln h + 0.9916 \ln \pi_L - 0.07639 \ln Z;$$
$$\phantom{\ln \pi^c =} (6.41) \quad (10.52) \phantom{\ln h +} (40.29) \phantom{\ln \pi_L} (1.22)$$

$$R^2 = 0.9826. \tag{3b}$$

All of the coefficients in the demand relation in eq. (1b) have the predicted signs and are significant by the $t$-test. (The estimated coefficients of the dummy variables are not reported here, but are shown in an appendix which is available from the author upon request.) One problem with the log-linear specification of eq. (1b) is that $Z$ is not restricted to be less than one. A logit specification of the demand relation was also estimated and is shown below:

$$\ln \left( \frac{Z}{1-Z} \right) = 4.568 - 2.609 \ln (P/(\pi_L \cdot C)) + 0.8792 \ln h,$$
$$\phantom{\ln \left( \frac{Z}{1-Z} \right) =} (7.93) \quad (6.42) \phantom{\ln (P/(\pi_L \cdot C)) +} (5.57)$$

$$R^2 = 0.9205. \tag{4}$$

The logit specification also indicates that the proportion of individuals purchasing collision insurance in a given driver class varies inversely with the relative price of insurance for a low-risk individual and directly with the proportion of high-risk individuals in that driver class. Eq. (2b) indicates that the elasticity of the premium with respect to the expected loss cost per car insured is positive, as expected, and the null hypothesis that $\beta_2$ equals one is rejected by the $t$-test at the 95 percent confidence level. The measure of insurance risk has a significant positive effect on premiums and the coefficient of the time trend indicates that, in the absence of increases in expected loss costs, the average premium would have declined at an average annual rate of 8 percent, which is somewhat higher than anticipated. Eq. (3b) indicates that $h$ and $\pi_L$ have significant positive effects on $\pi^c$ and that $Z$ has a negative effect, but the null hypothesis that $\gamma_4$ is zero cannot be rejected at the 95 percent confidence level.

The within sample predictions of $Z$, $P$, and $\pi^c$, based on reduced form equations using the estimates of the structural parameters in eqs. (1b)–(3b), were calculated and the statistics in table 2 provide some measures of the predictive power of the model. The correlations between the actual and predicted values of the variables are high and the mean absolute prediction error is less than 5 percent of the mean value of $Z$ and $\pi^c$ and 8 percent of the mean value of $P$. Therefore we conclude that the simple model estimated in eqs. (1b)–(3b) is consistent with the observed behaviour of the market for collision insurance, and it supports the view that there is an adverse selection problem in this market.

Table 2

Measures of the within sample predictive power of the model.

| | $Z$ | $P$ | $\pi^c$ |
|---|---|---|---|
| Correlation coefficient between the actual and predicted values | 0.901 | 0.970 | 0.988 |
| Regression coefficient of actual on predicted | 1.028 | 1.044 | 0.995 |
| Root-mean-squared error | 0.0409 | 15.60 | 0.00438 |
| Mean absolute error | 0.031 | 12.85 | 0.00368 |
| Ratio of the mean absolute error to the mean values | 0.047 | 0.080 | 0.0381 |

## 4. Simulating the effect of prohibiting discrimination on the basis of sex in collision insurance

The model has been used to simulate the effect of prohibiting discrimination on the basis of sex in collision insurance in the 21–24 age group in 1977. This year was chosen for the simulation because the average absolute prediction error of the premiums with discrimination was smallest in this year. If discrimination on the basis of sex had been prohibited in 1977, it is assumed that uniform premiums would have been charged in three classes of drivers, namely single individuals 21–22 years, single individuals 23–24 years, and married individuals 21–24 years. The first row in table 3 shows the predicted premiums in 1977 with discrimination.[4] The predicted premiums in 1977 without discrimination are $221 for a single individual 21–22 years, $187 for a single individual 23–24 years, and $153 for a married individual 21–24 years. As anticipated, the premiums paid by males decline

[4] The differences between the actual premiums and the predicted premiums are $21 for single males 21–22 years, −$6 for single males 23–24 years, $7 for married males 21–24 years, and $16 for females 21–24 years.

Table 3

A simulation of the effect of prohibiting discrimination on the basis of sex in collision insurance in 1977.

| Age | 21–22 | | 23–24 | | 21–24 | |
|---|---|---|---|---|---|---|
| Marital status | Single | | Single | | Married | |
| Sex | Male | Female | Male | Female | Male | Female |
| *Predicted premium* | | | | | | |
| With discrimination | $250 | $137 | $205 | $137 | $160 | $137 |
| Without discrimination | $221 | $221 | $187 | $187 | $153 | $153 |
| Change | −$29 | $84 | −$18 | $50 | −$7 | $16 |
| Percentage change | −11.6 | 61.3 | −8.8 | 36.5 | −4.4 | 11.8 |
| *Predicted proportion of drivers purchasing collision insurance* | | | | | | |
| With discrimination | 0.47 | 0.73 | 0.56 | 0.73 | 0.69 | 0.73 |
| Without discrimination | 0.49 | 0.63 | 0.57 | 0.67 | 0.70 | 0.71 |
| Change | 0.02 | −0.10 | 0.01 | −0.06 | 0.01 | −0.02 |

and the premiums paid by females increase when discrimination on the basis of sex is prohibited. The increases in the premiums paid by single females are 62.3 and 36.5 percent in the 21–22 and 23–24 age groups, respectively. Table 3 also shows that the percentage of males purchasing collision insurance would increase slightly and that the percentage of females purchasing collision insurance would decline by 10 percentage points among single females 21–22 years, six percentage points among single females 23–24 years, and two percentage points among married females 21–24 years. Thus, the model predicts that the prohibition of sexual discrimination in collision insurance would lead to substantial increases in the premiums paid by single females and a significant decline in the proportion purchasing collision insurance.

## References

Akerlof, G., 1970, The market for lemons: Qualitative uncertainty and the market mechanism, Quarterly Journal of Economics 84, 488–500.

Alberta Human Rights Commission, 1978, Report of a board of inquiry (Edmonton).

Dahlby, B.G., 1980, The welfare effects of prohibiting statistical discrimination in insurance markets, Research paper 80-5, Department of Economics, University of Alberta.

Hoy, M., 1982, Categorizing risks in the insurance industry, Quarterly Journal of Economics 97, 321–336.

Insurance Bureau of Canada, 1977 and 1978, Automobile insurance experience (Toronto).

Miyazaki, H., 1977, The rat race and internal labour markets, Bell Journal of Economics 8, 394–418.

Quirin, G., et al., Competition, economic efficiency and profitability in the Canadian property and casualty insurance industry (Insurance Bureau of Canada, Toronto).

Rothschild, M. and J. Stiglitz, 1976, Equilibrium in competitive insurance markets, Quarterly Journal of Economics 90, 629–649.

Spence, M., 1977, Product differentiation and performance in insurance markets, Journal of Public Economics 10, 427–447.

Wilson, C., 1977, A model of insurance markets with incomplete information, Journal of Economic Theory 16, 167–207.

International Journal of Industrial Organization 5 (1987) 211–231. North-Holland

# MULTI-PERIOD INSURANCE CONTRACTS

## Russell COOPER*

*University of Iowa, Iowa City, IA 52242, USA*

## Beth HAYES*

*Northwestern University, Evanston, IL 60201, USA*

Final version received September 1986

This paper examines the form of insurance contracts in the presence of asymmetric information about consumers' accident probabilities. Our goal is to understand the adjustment in contract terms as a function of accident histories in a finite horizon model. We also compare these adjustments between alternative market structures. Our principal findings indicate that history dependent insurance contracts serve a useful sorting role. Individuals who declare themselves 'low risks' to insurance companies face adverse contractural terms if they subsequently have many accidents. These adjustments are strongest in the case of a single insurance seller but are present in the competitive model as well.

## 1. Introduction[1]

Insurance contracts typically provide less than perfect insurance and insurance rates are generally adjusted to reflect previous accidents. For example, automobile insurance includes deductibles and frequent automobile mishaps lead to costlier insurance. The usual explanation of deductibles and coinsurance is the necessity to overcome problems of moral hazard and self-selection. In single-period models, Arrow (1965), Pauly (1968, 1974) and Shavell (1979b) have shown that incomplete insurance provides an incentive for agents to take actions which reduce accident probabilities. In fact, the entire agency literature [see, for example, Ross (1973), Shavell (1979a) or Harris–Raviv (1979)] rests on this tradeoff between risk sharing and incentives. Rothschild–Stiglitz (1976) and Stiglitz (1977) show that imperfect

*We wish to thank Costas Azariadis, John Bigelow, Marcel Boyer, V.V. Chari, George Dionne, Larry Jones, P. Lasserre, Paul Milgrom, Joseph Stiglitz, Colette Waternaux - and seminar participants at the University of Chicago, Northwestern University, the University of Montreal, participants at the 1984 Summer Econometric Society meetings and the anonymous referees for comments.

[1]Beth Hayes was killed tragically on June 3, 1984. This revision of our February 1984 and November 1984 manuscripts reflects comments of anonymous referees and is intended to clarify our earlier exposition while retaining its original spirit. Her contributions to this line of research will certainly be missed.

0167-7187/87/$3.50 © 1987, Elsevier Science Publishers B.V. (North-Holland)

insurance also induces the sorting of agents with different accident probabilities.

While the issues of self-selection and moral hazard have received considerable attention, the dynamic behavior of insurance rates is not as well understood. Recent papers by Radner (1981), Rogerson (1985) and Rubinstein–Yaari (1983), have shown that multi-period contracts help overcome moral hazard problems within insurance arrangements. Dionne (1983), Dionne–Lassere (1985), Malueg (1981) and Townsend (1982) have investigated the role of multi-period insurance agreements in the presence of information asymmetries. In some cases, infinite length contracts can support a Pareto optimal allocation of risks.[2] The key to these results is the use of information about past experience in the formulation of insurance terms. Faced with a threat of adverse adjustments to insurance terms, agents are induced to take 'appropriate' measures to reduce risks or to disclose their true accident probabilities. In either case, the outcome obtained under complete information is again implementable.

In this paper we consider experience rating in a multi-period self-selection model. Experience rating of insurance contracts is done in two ways. The contract can depend upon the outcome of previous insurance contracts, or, in the case of retrospective experience rating, it depends on the insured's experience during the policy period. In both cases, premia and indemnities change as a function of experience. A variety of insurance contracts offer experience rating. These include automobile insurance, group health insurance, group life insurance, and workmen's compensation. For group health and group life insurance, moral hazard seems unimportant and adverse selection is important in all of these insurance contracts.

To provide an explanation for the existence of both imperfect insurance and the conditioning of insurance terms on past experience we investigate a model of finite duration in which an agent's accident probabilities are private information. Firms do not observe risk types and hence insurance contracts must satisfy certain self-selection constraints. By offering multi-period contracts, insurance companies can adjust the terms of agreements over time. This adjustment allows for a more efficient sorting of agents relative to the single-period contract. However, we are unable to support first-best allocations because of the finite lives of the agents. Accident probabilities will be exogenously determined so there will not be any moral hazard problems.

We first investigate the optimal multi-period insurance contract when there is a single firm. In an example with two periods and two risk classes, our results indicate that the contract for low-risk agents will reflect experience while that offered to the high-risk agents will not. Low-risk agents who have accidents are faced with an increased premium and a lower indemnity while

<hr />

[2]The result that the first-best allocation of risk is obtainable requires that agents do not discount the future. Section 2 provides more detail on this issue.

low-risk agents who do not have accidents will receive more favorable terms. We also discuss extensions of this example to more risk classes and an arbitrary number of periods. With a finite time horizon, contract terms are monotone functions of low-risk agents' accident records.

We also consider the use of multi-period contracts in a competitive market in two cases. First, we determine the optimal contract when consumers are legally bound to a single firm for a number of periods. This yields contracts where high-risk consumers' rates do not depend on past history, while low-risk consumers are punished or rewarded based on their accident records. This contract is qualitatively similar to the monopoly contract in terms of experience rating.

The alternative situation is where consumers cannot be legally bound to a multi-period contract. Thus, in a two period model consumers who have accidents (or don't) cannot be 'punished' in a way that would result in second period expected utility that is lower than that which an entering firm could afford to offer (which, in our model, will be the standard one period separating contract). This additional constraint changes the optimal contract. The low risk consumers receive a contract which has first period utility that is lower than utility in the standard one period contract, but expected utility in the second period is greater than the standard one period contract if the consumer didn't have an accident and is exactly equal to the standard one period contract if he did have an accident. Firm profits from the first period contract will be positive. These results are analogous to those in Harris–Holmstrom (1982) in that a form of 'bonding' occurs. This analysis is also an example in which competition in the second period of a non-binding contract actually *reduces* social welfare. One other issue we comment on is the existence of a competitive equilibrium in a multi-period model.

Section 2 of the paper outlines the basic model and investigates the optimal contract for a single firm. Section 3 discusses the competitive multi-period contract and section 4 contains our conclusions.

## 2. Monopoly

We begin with a rather simple model to illustrate the role of multi-period insurance contracting. Consumers are identical except for their accident probabilities. They possess von Neumann–Morgenstern utility functions, $U(\cdot)$, which are strictly increasing and strictly concave. Their wealth is $W$ if no accident occurs and $W - D$ if an accident takes place where $W > D$. We denote by $\pi_H$ and $\tau_L$ the probability of an accident for *high-risk* and *low-risk* agents, respectively, and assume $\pi_H > \pi_L$. These probabilities are out of the agent's control so that no moral hazard problem arises. There are $N_H$ high-risk and $N_L$ low-risk agents in the economy.

If agents do not purchase insurance, they obtain expected utility, $\bar{U}_i$. For $i = H, L$,

$$\bar{U}_i = \pi_i U(W - D) + (1 - \pi_i)U(W).$$

In this section of the paper we assume there is a single, risk neutral, insurance company. We begin by reviewing the analysis by Stiglitz (1977) on single-period insurance contracts. The monopoly offers to the agents an insurance contract which specifies for each date a premium $P$ to be paid to the firm if no accident occurs and an indemmity $I$ paid to the consumer if an accident takes place. We use the notation $\delta_i = \{P_i, I_i\}$ to denote the single-period contract offered to type $i = H, L$ agents.

First we analyze the optimal contract when agents' accident probabilities are known by the firm. We then investigate the case of asymmetric information.

### 2.1. Full-information solution

In the full-information solution, agents' accident probabilities are publicly known. Therefore the monopolist chooses $\delta_H$ and $\delta_L$ to

$$\text{Maximize} \quad \sum_{i = H, L} N_i((1 - \pi_i)P_i - \pi_i I_i), \tag{1}$$

$$\text{subject to} \quad V(\delta_i | \pi_i) \geq \bar{U}_i \quad \text{for} \quad i = H, L. \tag{2}$$

The objective function is simply the sum of the expected profits from the contracts offered to each of the risk types. Constraint (2) is an individual rationality constraint where

$$V(\delta_i | \pi_i) \equiv \pi_i U(W - D + I_i) + (1 - \pi_i)U(W - P_i) \tag{3}$$

is the expected utility of contract $\delta_i$ for agents with accident probability $\pi_i$.

The solution to (1) has full insurance offered to *both* risk classes and (2) is binding for $i = H, L$. That is, the agents shed all their risk to the insurance company at the expense of the consumers' surplus. Hence the full-information solution $(\delta_H^*, \delta_L^*)$ satisfies

$$U(W - D + I_i^*) = U(W - P_i^*) = \bar{U}_i \quad \text{for} \quad i = H, L. \tag{4}$$

This solution is shown in fig. 1, where the horizontal axis is wealth in the 'no accident' state. Point $E$ is the initial endowment and points H* and L* are the wealth levels for the agents under $\delta_H^*$ and $\delta_L^*$, respectively. These

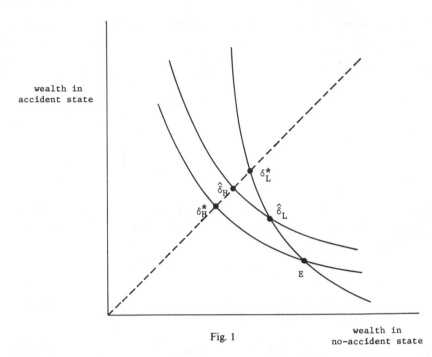

wealth in
accident state

Fig. 1

wealth in
no-accident state

indifference curves are convex due to the concavity of $U(\cdot)$. As discussed by Townsend (1982), with full information there are no gains to multi-period contracting.

## 2.2. Imperfect information solution

Once we relax the assumption that accident probabilities are public information, we need to constrain (1) further to ensure that agents have an incentive to reveal their types. These *self-selection constraints*, following the notation in (3), are

$$V(\delta_H|\pi_H) \geqq V(\delta_L|\pi_H) \tag{5}$$

and

$$V(\delta_L|\pi_L) \geqq V(\delta_H|\pi_L). \tag{6}$$

Expression (5) guarantees that high-risk agents prefer $\delta_H$ to $\delta_L$. Expression (6) does the same for low-risk agents.

From fig. 1, it is easy to see that the full-information solution will violate (5) since $\delta_L^*$ is preferred to $\delta_H^*$ by high-risk agents. Solving (1) subject to (2), (5) and (6) yields a solution in which

(i)   High-risk agents obtain full insurance,

(ii)  Low-risk agents bear some risks, i.e., $I_L < D - P_L$,

(iii) $V(\delta_H|\pi_H) = V(\delta_L|\pi_H), \quad V(\delta_L|\pi_L) > V(\delta_H|\pi_L)$

and

(iv)  $V(\delta_H|\pi_H) > \bar{U}_H, \quad V(\delta_L|\pi_L) = \bar{U}_L.$

These results are shown formally in Stiglitz (1977).

This solution is depicted in fig. 1 as points $\hat{\delta}_L$ and $\hat{\delta}_H$. Essentially, the monopolist extracts all surplus subject to the self-selection constraints. The high-risk agents strictly prefer $\hat{\delta}_H$ to $E$ and hence receive some consumers' surplus which the monopolist chooses not to extract. Due to the imperfect information, risks are *not* shared efficiently.

### 2.3. Multi-period contracts

Relative to the full-information solution, the monopolist's profits are lower in the imperfect information case due to the self-selection constraints. In order to increase profits, the monopolist must relax the binding constraints. One means of doing so in a multi-period setting is to tie the terms of the insurance contract to past experience. This can increase profits by providing an alternative means for the sorting of agents.

The contracts now offered by the insurance company are somewhat more complicated since they reflect past experience. For the present, we consider a two-period extension of the basic model. An insurance contract will now include premia and indemnities for each of the periods contingent on past experience. We denote by $P_i(A)$ [$P_i(N)$] the second period premium of a type $i$ agent experiencing an accident (no accident) in period 1. A similar definition holds for $I_i(A)$ and $I_i(N)$. With this notation,

$$\delta_H^2 = \{P_H, I_H, P_H(A), I_H(A), P_H(N), I_H(N)\}$$

and

$$\delta_L^2 = \{P_L, I_L, P_L(A), I_L(A), P_L(N), I_L(N)\}.$$

The firm chooses $\delta_H^2$ and $\delta_L^2$ to

Maximize   $N_H\{[(1-\pi_H)P_H - \pi_H I_H] + \pi_H[(1-\pi_H)P_H(A) - \pi_H I_H(A)]$

$\qquad + (1-\pi_H)[(1-\pi_H)P_H(N) - \pi_H I_H(N)]\}$

$\qquad + N_L\{[(1-\pi_L)P_L - \pi_L I_L] + \pi_L[(1-\pi_L)P_L(A) - \pi_L I_L(A)]$

$\qquad + (1-\pi_L)[(1-\pi_L)P_L(N) - \pi_L I_L(N)]\},$ \hfill (7) subject to

$$V(\delta_i^2|\pi_i) \geqq 2\bar{U}_i \quad \text{for} \quad i = H, L, \tag{8}$$

$$V(\delta_H^2|\pi_H) \geqq V(\delta_L^2|\pi_H) \tag{9}$$

and

$$V(\delta_L^2|\pi_L) \geqq V(\delta_H^2|\pi_L). \tag{10}$$

In this problem, the objective function is the sum of expected profits from the two risk types. Consider the $N_H$ high-risk agents. They have a premium and an indemnity of $\{P_H, I_H\}$ in the first period. In the second period, those who had an accident in the first period face $\{P_H(A), I_H(A)\}$. Those who did not have an accident receive terms of $\{P_H(N), I_H(N)\}$. Expression (8) is simply a two-period individual rationality constraint since the agents agree to *binding* two periods contracts. Constraints (9) and (10) ensure the self-selection of agents. Following (3),

$$V(\delta_i^2|\pi_j) = \pi_j U(W - D + I_i) + (1 - \pi_j)U(W - P_i)$$

$$+ \pi_j[\pi_j U(W - D + I_i(A)) + (1 - \pi_j)U(W - P_i(A))]$$

$$+ (1 - \pi_j)[\pi_j U(W - D + I_i(N)) + (1 - \pi_j)U(W - P_i(N))]. \tag{11}$$

From this expression, it is clear that we are *not* permitting borrowing and lending by consumers. Furthermore, we have assumed that neither the firm nor customers discount future utility. Hence, in the absence of the incentive constraints, the optimal insurance arrangement would generate constant consumption for customers across both time and states of nature. As in the one-period problem this full-information solution will not be implementable when accident probabilities are not observable to the monopolist. This will affect the variability of income both over time and states of nature. Our interest, indicated in Proposition 1, is mainly in the differences in contract terms across agents with different accident histories at a given point in time. Coupled with these differences across histories are, undoubtedly, variations in expected income across time since the insurance company is also acting as a 'banker'. These adjustments are not highlighted in our analysis and have been investigated, in a related setting, by Rogerson (1985).

*Proposition 1. In the solution to* (7), $V(\delta_L^2|\pi_L) = 2\bar{U}_L$ *and* $V(\delta_H^2|\pi_H) = V(\delta_L^2|\pi_H)$. *Furthermore, in the optimal contract,* (i) *the high-risk agents obtain perfect insurance and*

$$P_H(A) = P_H(N) = P_H, \quad I_H(A) = I_H(N) = I_H,$$

*(ii)* *the low-risk agents do not obtain perfect insurance and*

$$P_L(A) > P_L > P_L(N), \quad I_L(A) < I_L < I_L(N).$$

*Proof.* See appendix A.

From this proposition we see that the monopolist uses insurance contracts contingent on past experience to increase expected profits. As in the single-period case, high-risk agents continue to receive full insurance and the elements of $\delta_H^2$ are not contingent on experience. However, the premia paid by a low-risk agent increase if an accident occurs in the first period and decrease if no accident occurs. Indemnities, on the other hand, adjust in the opposite direction.

This adjustment of terms across histories in the second period helps in the sorting of agents. High-risk agents who purchase $\delta_L^2$ have a greater chance of facing *costlier* insurance in the second period than do low-risk agents. That is, $\delta_L^2$ stipulates a lottery over period 2 contracts which high-and low-risk agents evaluate differently. With $\pi_H > \pi_L$, $P_L(A) > P_L(N)$ and $I_L(A) < I_L(N)$, high-risk agents assign a higher probability to the bad outcome of the lottery than do low-risk agents. By exploiting this difference, the monopolist can relax the single-period self-selection constraint and increase expected profits. As in the single-period case, low-risk agents have zero surplus.

It is possible to extend this analysis in a number of directions: adding more risk classes and increasing the number of time periods. We conjecture that adding more risk classes would yield a solution in which all agents, except the high-risk class, face premia and indemnities which are adjusted over time.

A more interesting extension concerns the addition of more time periods. To see the impact of this, we first require some additional notation. Let $h_{i,j}^t$ be the history at time $t$ of agent $j$ in risk class $i = H, L$. The relevant history is simply whether or not an agent had an accident in each of the $t-1$ periods. In terms of the optimal contract, the insurance company cares only about the number of accidents in the past $t-1$ periods.[3] Hence, $h_{i,j}^t$ is simply the number of accidents reported in the $t-1$ periods. We also define $\alpha_{i,j}^t$ as the probability that an agent in risk class $i = H, L$ will have $j$ accidents through $t-1$ periods. Hence agents are identified by their risk class and number of accidents. These probabilities are given by the simple binomial

---

[3]To see this formally, one must write down the $T$-period version of (7). Since the probabilities associated with the history enter multiplicatively, their order does not matter. Hence, the contract terms will depend on the relative numbers of accident and no-accident probabilities preceding the firm's profits for that history. We leave the details to the interested reader.

distribution since we are concerned with repeated trials which are independent over time. Therefore,

$$\alpha_{i,j}^t = (\pi_i)^j (1-\pi_i)^{t-1-j} \binom{t-1}{j}. \tag{12}$$

Finally, as in the two-period case, $\delta_H^T$ and $\delta_L^T$ will refer to $T$-period contracts for high- and low-risk agents, respectively. These contracts will specify both premia and indemnities as functions of agents' histories. Using the obvious generalization of (11) for $V(\delta_i^T|\pi_j)$, the monopolist chooses $\delta_H^T$ and $\delta_L^T$ to

$$\text{Maximize} \quad N_H \left\{ \sum_{t=1}^{T} \sum_{j=0}^{t-1} \alpha_{H,j}^t \left[ (1-\pi_H)P_H(h_{H,j}^t) - \pi_H I_H(h_{H,j}^t) \right] \right\}$$

$$+ N_L \left\{ \sum_{t=1}^{T} \sum_{j=0}^{t-1} \alpha_{L,j}^t [(1-\pi_L)P_L(h_{L,j}^t) - \pi_L I_L(h_{L,j}^t)] \right\}, \tag{13}$$

subject to

$$\frac{1}{T} V(\delta_i^T|\pi_i) \geq \bar{U}_i \quad \text{for} \quad i = H, L, \tag{14}$$

$$V(\delta_H^T|\pi_H) \geq V(\delta_L^T|\pi_H) \tag{15}$$

and

$$V(\delta_L^T|\pi_L) \geq V(\delta_H^T|\pi_L). \tag{16}$$

As in the two-period solution described in Proposition 1, high-risk agents will continue to receive full insurance, (14) is binding for $i = L$ and (15) is binding in the optimal $T$-period contract. Denoting the multiplier for the binding constraint in (14) by $\phi$ and the multiplier for (15) by $\lambda$,

$$N_L = \left[ \phi - \lambda \left( \frac{\alpha_{H,j}^t}{\alpha_{L,j}^t} \right) \left( \frac{1-\pi_H}{1-\pi_L} \right) \right] U'(W - P_L(h_{L,j}^t)) \tag{17}$$

and

$$N_L = \left[ \phi - \lambda \left( \frac{\alpha_{H,j}^t}{\alpha_{L,j}^t} \right) \left( \frac{\pi_H}{\pi_L} \right) \right] U'(W - D + I_L(h_{L,j}^t)) \quad \forall j, t. \tag{18}$$

These are the first-order conditions to (13)–(16) for an agent who had $j$ accidents over $t-1$ periods and announced he was a low-risk consumer. So, in period $t$, given this history *and* his announcement, the agent will be charged a premium of $P_L(h^t_{L,j})$ and receive an indemnity of $I_L(h^t_{L,j})$.

We can use (17) and (18) to investigate the adjustments in the contract terms over histories and time. First, keeping $t$ fixed, the adjustments in $P_L$ and $I_L$ will depend on the ratio of probabilities of agents having a given history. From (12),

$$\frac{\alpha^t_{H,j}}{\alpha^t_{L,j}} = \frac{(\pi_H)^j(1-\pi_H)^{t-1-j}}{(\pi_L)^j(1-\pi_L)^{t-1-j}}. \tag{19}$$

Therefore, as $j$, the number of accidents in the $t-1$ previous periods increases, from (19) we see that the ratio of probabilities will increase as well since $\pi_H > \pi_L$. From (17) this implies that $P_L(h^t_{L,j})$ will increase with $j$ while $I_L(h^t_{L,j})$ falls with $j$ as seen from (18).

The monotonicity of these contract terms with respect to the histories should not be surprising. From (19), we see that the ratio of probabilities will satisfy the monotone likelihood ratio condition [see Milgrom (1981) or Grossman–Hart (1983)].

We also see from (17) and (18) that agents whose records strongly indicate that they are in the low-risk class will receive closer to full insurance. That is, if you have an accident record for which $\alpha^t_{H,j}$ is close to zero, then your wealth will be almost completely stabilized. Alternatively, if your history is more likely to be held by a high-risk agent, your wealth becomes more variable. Again, these adjustments are made to profitably sort the agents.

As $T \to \infty$, the first-best allocation of risks is obtainable as long as agents do not discount the future (as in our model). A formal proof of this is contained in Dionne–Lasserre (1985) which uses simple review strategies to support the full information level of payoffs. The seller offers full insurance to buyers unless their average loss exceeds a bound for their risk class. If average losses become too high, coverage is then offered at a higher price only. Of course, this contract is not optimal for finite horizons.

One other interesting issue concerns the reporting of accidents if their occurrence is not public information, e.g., a fender-bender. If adjustments in the terms of the contract are adverse enough following an accident, then agents may not inform the companies about bad realizations. This obviously can occur only in a multi-period insurance setting. Once insurance companies realize that agents may not report accidents, they will take that information into account when formulating the optimal contract. This issue merits further investigation.

## 3. Competitive contracts

The model in this section differs from the model presented in section 2 because firms will be constrained to earn zero expected profits because of competition. The equilibrium concept will be a Nash equilibrium, as opposed to the reactive equilibrium proposed by Wilson. In the one period competitive model presented in Rothschild–Stiglitz (1976) it is shown that the equilibrium must be a separating equilibrium where different risk-type consumers receive different insurance. A pure strategy equilibrium may not exist because contracts that pool all risk classes could yield higher utility for all consumers. However, a pooling contract cannot be an equilibrium. This section will mainly consider the contracts supporting a separating equilibrium. We comment at the end of the section on the question of existence and pooling contracts.

### 3.1. Full information solution

With full information, the firm knows the risk type of each consumer. For each type the insurance contract would solve

$$\text{Maximize} \quad \pi_i U(W - D + I_i) + (1 - \pi_i)U(W - P_i),$$

$$\text{subject to} \quad (1 - \pi_i)P_i - \pi_i I_i = 0. \tag{20}$$

This maximizes the expected utility of the type $i$ consumer along the zero profit locus of the firm. The solution yields full insurance for each type of consumer. No firm could offer a contract that two or more types of consumers would prefer (pooling two types) to the contract that solves (20) for his own type and that yields zero profits for the firm. The reason is that all risk types prefer their own contract to any contract for a higher-risk class. A multi-period competitive contract where the risk classes of consumers are observable consists of the one period contract repeated in each period for each risk class. The contracts are $\delta_L^*$ and $\delta_H^*$ in fig. 2. (Note that these contracts differ from the full-information monopoly solution despite the duplication of the notation.)

### 3.2. Incomplete information solution

If consumer accident probabilities are not an observable characteristic, insurance contracts must be designed with the knowledge that consumers will misrepresent their risk class if this will increase expected utility. The full information solution cannot be implemented because high-risk types have an incentive to claim that they are the lowest-risk class as was the case in the monopoly section. If all consumers choose that contract, the firm will earn negative profits. Thus the solution to offer full insurance to all types cannot be a competitive equilibrium.

For a discussion of the one period information constrained competitive

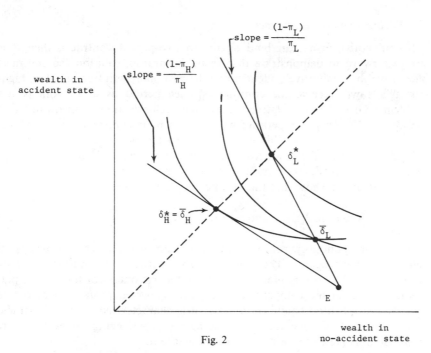

Fig. 2

wealth in
accident state

wealth in
no-accident state

solution, see Rothschild–Stiglitz (1976). The equilibrium contracts are $\bar{\delta}_H$, $\bar{\delta}_L$ pictured in fig. 2. To summarize their results:

(i)   The high-risk types receive full insurance.
(ii)  Low-risk types receive less than full insurance.
(iii) The high-risk type is indifferent between his contract and that for the low-risk class.
(iv)  Profits are zero on all contracts.
(v)   If an equilibrium exists it will be a separating solution. No equilibrium may exist because of pooling possibilities.

Thus in a one period model where consumers know their accident probabilities and firms do not, if a competitive equilibrium exists, consumer types are revealed. In a model with multi-period contracts, a consumer's accident record may affect his insurance contract. We will first consider an example with two periods and solve for the contract when consumers can sign an agreement that (legally) binds them to the agreement for the two periods. Then we consider the two-period contracts where the consumer can leave the contract after the first period. These two solutions are very different. We assume that the firm is always bound by any multi-period agreement.

### 3.3. Binding two-period contracts

If competitive firms can bind agents to two-period contracts, then it is straightforward to demonstrate that in the separating solution the contracts offered will be qualitatively identical to the monopoly solution. That is, high-risk agents will receive the contract $\delta_H^*$ *each* period as in the one-period problem. Given this contract and the self-selection constraint that $2V(\delta_H^*|\pi_H) \geqq V(\delta_L^2|\pi_H)$, competitors will offer $\delta_L^2$ to maximize $V(\delta_L^2|\pi_L)$ subject to zero expected profits. This is analogous to the problem specified in (7)–(10) except that in the competitive case we maximize $V(\delta_L^2|\pi_L)$ subject to a zero expected profits constraint on the firm. With this in mind, it is straightforward to show that the optimal contract satisfies

$$P_L(A) > P_L > P_L(N) \quad \text{and} \quad I_L(A) < I_L < I_L(N). \tag{21}$$

As in the monopoly solution, these adjustments represent a means of efficiently sorting agents. The main difference between the market structure is, of course, that the monopolist extracts the maximal consumers' surplus possible while, in the competitive case, firm's expected profits are driven to zero. Hence, when an equilibrium exists, it is characterized by an adjustment of the terms of $\delta_L^2$ such that low-risk agents experiencing an accident are 'punished' relative to those not having an accident.

### 3.4. Non-binding two-period contracts

We now relax our assumption that consumers sign a two-period binding contract and instead allow them to costlessly switch to another firm in the second period if they so desire. While we term this other firm an 'entrant', it could also be a firm from period 1 re-entering the market. These second-period entrants are most likely to attract the low-risk agents who are being 'punished' for having an accident. Hence, we ask whether we can have adjustments in contract terms as a sorting mechanism in the absence of commitment to a two-period contract.

To answer this, we first need to carefully specify the game played by the entrants in the second period. Then, taking entrants' decision rules as given, we can determine the optimal two-period contract for low-risk agents. In general, entrants know the two-period contracts being offered $(\delta_H^2, \delta_L^2)$ and may also have some information about individual agents such as their histories (in this case their first period realizations) and the type of contract they chose in period 1. Obviously, the optimal strategies of the entrants will critically depend on their knowledge about individual agents. In this paper we make the extreme assumption that entrants do *not* know either agents' accident histories or their choice of contract in the first period. While they do know that a customer has left a previous contract, this does not imply that the buyer is low-risk since high-risk agents can leave their contracts as well.

With this assumption, the second-period behaviour for entrants is really no different from that of firms in the one-period model. As we indicate below, high-risk agents will continue to receive $\delta_H^*$. Hence competition will force entrants to offer either the separating contract to attract low-risk agents or the pooling contract from the one-period solution. Given our focus on separating solutions as a means of circumventing the existence problem, second-period competition implies that entrants will offer $\bar{\delta}_L$, the optimal separating contract in the single-period model.

Given that entrants will provide $\bar{\delta}_L$, we can determine the optimal two-period contract. For notational purposes, define $\delta_L^2 = \{\delta_L^1, \delta_L^A, \delta_L^N\}$ where $\delta_L^1 = (P_L, I_L)$, $\delta_L^A = (P_L(A), I_L(A))$ and $\delta_L^N = (P_L(N), I_L(N))$. Competition ensures that $\delta_L^2$

$$\text{maximizes} \quad V(\delta_L^2 | \pi_L), \tag{22}$$

$$\text{subject to} \quad 2V(\delta_H^* | \pi_H) \geq V(\delta_L^1 | \pi_H) + \pi_H \max \{V(\delta_L^A | \pi_H), V(\bar{\delta}_L | \pi_H)\}$$

$$+ (1 - \pi_H) \max \{V(\delta_L^N | \pi_H), V(\bar{\delta}_L | \pi_H)\}, \tag{23}$$

$$V(\delta_L^2 | \pi_L) \geq 2V(\delta_H^* | \pi_L), \tag{24}$$

$$V(\delta_L^A | \pi_L) \geq V(\bar{\delta}_L | \pi_L), \tag{25}$$

$$V(\delta_L^N | \pi_L) \geq V(\bar{\delta}_L | \pi_L), \tag{26}$$

$$(1 - \pi_L)P_L - \pi_L I_L + \pi_L[(1 - \pi_L)P_L(A) - \pi_L I_L(A)]$$

$$+ (1 - \pi_L)[(1 - \pi_L)P_L(N) - \pi_L I_L(N)] = 0. \tag{27}$$

Constraints (23) and (24) are similar to the two-period self-selection constraints that arose in the binding contracts problem. However, in this problem, high-risk agents who declare themselves low-risk agents have the option of taking the entrants' contract ($\bar{\delta}_L$) in the second period as well. Constraint (23) explicitly allows this option. Since entrants can attract low-risk agents as well, we have added (25) and (26). Because of (25) and (26) we do not have to include the options of leaving the low-risk contract in the sorting constraint for low-risk agents. Finally, (27) is the expected zero profits constraint.

Before solving this problem, it is insightful to determine whether the *optimal* binding two-period contract is feasible. It is not surprising that the punishments described by (21) for low-risk agents having an accident in period 1 will be too severe – i.e., (25) will be violated. To see this assume that, to the contrary, $V(\delta_L^A|\pi_L) \geqq V(\delta_L|\pi_L)$ in the solution to the binding contracts problem. From (21), we know that $V(\delta_L^A|\pi_L) < V(\delta_L^1|\pi_L) < V(\delta_L^N|\pi_L)$. The two possible configurations of contracts that satisfy the conditions specified in (21) and (25) are shown in fig. 3. The $\delta'$ contracts are ruled out as they are not incentive compatible – i.e., (23) is violated since $V(\delta_L^A|\pi_H) > V(\delta_H^*|\pi_H)$. The $\underline{\delta}$ contracts are also ruled out as expected profits are negative. Hence the two-period binding contract is not implementable in the presence of second period competition.

Therefore, in the solution to (22), one or both of (25) and (26) must be binding and the welfare of low-risk consumers (in terms of two-period expected utility) is *lower* due to the absence of ability to commit to a two-period contract. Since all other agents (including firms) have the same expected utility as in the case of binding contracts, the possibility of second-period competition combined with agents' inability to enforce multi-period contracts clearly *reduces* social welfare.

The qualitative characteristics of the solution are summarized below.

*Proposition 2. In the solution to (22), constraints (23), (25) and (27) are binding. The relevant maxima in constraint (23) are $V(\delta_L^A|\pi_H)$ and $V(\delta_L^N|\pi_H)$.*

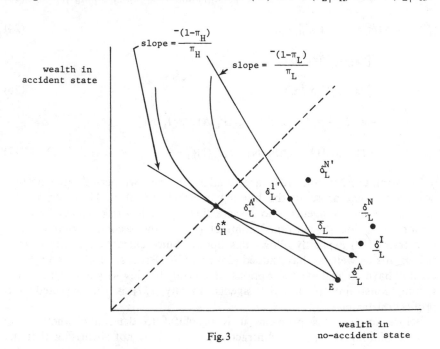

Fig. 3

*Furthermore,*

(i)   $I_L(N) > I_L$   *and*   $P_L(N) < P_L$,

(ii)   $V(\delta_L^N | \pi_L) > V(\delta_L^A | \pi_L) > V(\delta_L^1 | \pi_L)$,   *and*

(iii)' $\delta_L^1$ *and* $\delta_L^A$ *earn positive expected profits for the firm while* $\delta_L^N$ *earns negative expected profits.*

*Proof.*   See appendix B.

The key aspect of this proposition is that the presence of second-period competition for consumers will limit but not destroy the use of experience rating as a sorting device. From (i), we see that agents who avoid an accident in period 1 receive favorable insurance terms in period 2. From (ii), we see that agents experiencing an accident in the first period are punished relative to agents avoiding an accident, i.e., $V(\delta_L^N | \pi_L) > V(\delta_L^A | \pi_L)$. The difference between this contract and that arising when consumers can be bound to firms, is that here the punishment for period 1 accidents is tempered by the presence of other firms offering $\bar{\delta}_L$ in the second period. That is, $V(\delta_L^A | \pi_L)$ cannot be less than $V(\bar{\delta}_L | \pi_L)$. Nonetheless, the differential between $V(\delta_L^N | \pi_L)$ and $V(\delta_L^A | \pi_L)$ serves as a useful sorting device. Note that the firm makes positive expected profits from both the first-period contract and $\delta_L^A$ as a means of financing $\delta_L^N$. This is a form of 'bonding' similar to that found in the paper by Harris–Holmstrom (1982) and elsewhere. In these models, the inability of agents to sign intertemporal binding arrangements is overcome by tilting payoffs towards the future to provide an incentive for consumers (or workers) to remain with the firm.

Denote the solution to (22) by $\hat{\delta}_L^2$. It remains to be shown that the contracts $(\hat{\delta}_L^2, \delta_H^*, \bar{\delta}_L)$ constitute a separating equilibrium. Clearly $\delta_H^*$ is a best response to $\hat{\delta}_L^2$ and $\bar{\delta}_L$ is the best entrants can offer low-risk agents. As constructed $\hat{\delta}_L^2$ is a utility maximizing contract $(\delta_H^*, \hat{\delta}_L)$. Therefore *if* a separating equilibrium exists, for this economy it is characterized by the two-period contracts $(\hat{\delta}_L^2, \delta_H^*)$.

Finally, as is well understood from the initial work by Rothschild–Stiglitz, there may not be a pure strategy equilibrium in insurance models of this type. In the one-period model a pooling contract (i.e., one which does not separate agents) may dominate the separating contract for all agents. Since this pooling contract can also be dominated, no equilibrium may exist.

Our results in this paper provide a characterization of a separating equilibrium *if* it exists. We leave for further research the much more difficult question of providing a full characterization of equilibria in multi-period competitive insurance markets with imperfect information on accident probabilities.

## 4. Conclusions

This paper provides a theoretical explanation for the common observation of both incomplete insurance and experience rating. Due to asymmetric information about accident probabilities, insurance contracts must provide incentives for consumers to reveal their true types to the firm. In a multi-period setting, experience rating is a means of improving the sorting of consumers. The monopolist links the terms of future contracts to past experience in a manner which thwarts the incentive of high-risk agents to claim that they are in the low-risk class. In a competitive environment, experience rating can serve the same purpose though its effectiveness is tempered by the possible entry of other insurance companies once punishments for a bad accident record are imposed. This model should be contrasted with the recent work of Harris–Holmstrom. In that model, information was imperfect and symmetric. In our framework, this would mean that neither the insurance company nor the consumer knew true accident probabilities.[4] Harris–Holmstrom show that in this setting the evolving terms of the contract would reflect the public information on consumer characteristics contained in past experience. In our model, consumers do know their true accident probabilities. Experience rating is still used as a means of extracting this information.

Our analysis is still incomplete in a number of important ways. We have restricted attention in the competitive case to separating solutions. We need to relax this assumption which may require the use of either a Wilson equilibrium or a consideration of mixed strategies. Also, we have assumed that the choice of contract in the first period and histories are not public information. We plan to consider the optimal contract under these alternative information structures. Finally, the nature of multi-period pooling contracts and the existence of competitive equilibrium with multi-period contracts remains to be examined.

### Appendix A: Proof of Proposition 1

Using $\phi_H$ and $\phi_L$ as the Lagrange multipliers for constraint (8), $\lambda_H$ for (9) and $\lambda_L$ for (10), it is necessary to first show that $\lambda_H > 0$ and $\lambda_L = 0$ in the solution to (7). This pattern of binding constraints is common in self-selection problems although this problem is more complicated due to the number of choice variables exceeding two.

First, one can demonstrate that *both* $\lambda_H$ and $\lambda_L$ cannot be positive. If the high-risk agents are indifferent between $\delta_L^2$ and $\delta_H^2$ then the low-risk agents will strictly prefer $\delta_L^2$. Next, $\lambda_L > 0$ and $\lambda_H = 0$ leads to a violation of the individual rationality constraint for the low-risk agents.

---

[4] A similar situation of experience rating with imperfect and asymmetric information is considered by Bigelow (1983).

Given that $\lambda_H > 0$, it is obvious from the first-order conditions that $\phi_L > 0$. Whether or not $\phi_H$ is positive remains an (unimportant) open question. The first-order conditions below assume $\phi_H = 0$ (which we conjecture is correct). Our main results reported in Proposition 1 do *not* depend on the sign of $\phi_H$. It is straightforward to generalize these arguments to characterize the $T$-period contract as in (17) and (18).

With $\phi_L$ and $\lambda_H$ positive, we can write the first-order conditions to (7) as

$$(P_L) \qquad N_L = \left( \phi_L - \lambda_H \frac{(1 - \pi_H)}{(1 - \pi_L)} \right) U'(W - P_L), \tag{A.1}$$

$$(I_L) \qquad N_L = \left( \phi_L - \lambda_H \frac{\pi_H}{\pi_L} \right) U'(W - D + I_L), \tag{A.2}$$

$$(P_H) \qquad N_H = \lambda_H U'(W - P_H), \tag{A.3}$$

$$(I_H) \qquad N_H = \lambda_H U'(W - D + I_H), \tag{A.4}$$

$$(P_L(A)) \quad N_L = \left( \phi_L - \lambda_H \frac{\pi_H(1 - \pi_H)}{\pi_L(1 - \pi_L)} \right) U'(W - P_L(A)), \tag{A.5}$$

$$(I_L(A)) \quad N_L = \left( \phi_L - \lambda_H \frac{\pi_H \pi_H}{\pi_L \pi_L} \right) U'(W - D + I_L(A)), \tag{A.6}$$

$$(P_L(N)) \quad N_L = \left( \phi_L - \lambda_H \frac{(1 - \pi_H)(1 - \pi_H)}{(1 - \pi_L)(1 - \pi_L)} \right) U'(W - P_L(N)), \tag{A.7}$$

$$(I_L(N)) \quad N_L = \left( \phi_L - \lambda_H \frac{\pi_H(1 - \pi_H)}{\pi_L(1 - \pi_L)} \right) U'(W - D + I_L(N)). \tag{A.8}$$

Note that these do not include the conditions for the choice of $P_H(A)$, $P_H(N)$, $I_H(A)$ and $I_H(N)$. It is easy to show that (A.3) and (A.4) will characterize the choice of these variables. Hence, high-risk agents obtain perfect insurance.

Conditions (A.5) through (A.8) characterize the adjustments in the insurance of low-risk agents. Since $\pi_H > \pi_L$, the remainder of Proposition 1 is easy to show.

## Appendix B: Proof of Proposition 2

The proof proceeds in two steps. First, we need to determine which of the constraints, (23)–(27), are binding. Second, we need to determine which are the relevant maxima in (23).

Because of competition, (27) must be binding. Furthermore, (23) must be binding. Otherwise, the solution to (22) is to offer full insurance to low-risk types and this is not incentive compatible. From our earlier demonstration that the optimal two-period binding contract violated (25), we conjecture (and show later) that this constraint must be binding too. Finally, we ignore (24) and (26) and argue below that these constraints are met in the solution.

Given this configuration of constraints, we first demonstrate that the relevant maxima in (23) are $V(\delta_L^A|\pi_H)$ and $V(\delta_L^N|\pi_H)$. To see that this must be the case, consider the three alternatives.

*Case 1.* $V(\bar{\delta}_L|\pi_H) \leqq V(\delta_L^N|\pi_H)$ and $V(\bar{\delta}_L|\pi_H) > V(\delta_L^A|\pi_H)$.

Suppose we use this configuration of maxima and solve (22) using $\lambda$ as a multiplier for (23), $\gamma$ for (25) and $\mu$ for (27). The first-order conditions for $(P_L(A), I_L(A))$ are

$$U'(W - P_L(A))(1 + \gamma/\pi_L) = \mu,$$

$$U'(W - D + I_L(A))(1 + \gamma/\pi_L) = \mu.$$

Together these conditions imply that low-risk agents receive full insurance in period 2 if they had an accident in period 1. This occurs because $\delta_L^A$ does not enter into (23). If $V(\delta_2^A|\pi_L) \geqq V(\bar{\delta}_L|\pi_L)$ and $\delta_L^A$ delivers full insurance, then $V(\delta_L^A|\pi_H) > V(\bar{\delta}_L|\pi_H)$ as well. This contradicts the hypothesis of this case. Note that this result is independent of whether or not (24) and (26) bind.

*Case 2.* $V(\delta_L^N|\pi_H) < V(\bar{\delta}_L|\pi_H)$ and $V(\delta_L^A|\pi_H) \geqq V(\bar{\delta}_L|\pi_H)$. This is analogous to Case 1 in that the solution to (22) implies that $\delta_L^N$ will provide full insurance to low-risk agents. Again, this occurs because $\delta_L^N$ does not enter (23). This leads to a contradiction as before since $V(\delta_L^N|\pi_L) \geqq V(\bar{\delta}_L|\pi_L)$, from (26) and $V(\delta_L^N|\pi_H) < V(\bar{\delta}_L|\pi_H)$ are inconsistent if $\delta_L^N$ provides full insurance.

*Case 3.* $V(\bar{\delta}_L|\pi_H) > V(\delta_L^i|\pi_H)$ for $i = N, A$.

As in the first two cases, the absence of $\delta_L^i$ for $i = N, A$ from (23) implies that both $\delta_L^A$ and $\delta_L^N$ are full insurance contracts. Hence, $V(\delta_i|\pi_L) \geqq V(\bar{\delta}_L|\pi_L)$ for $i = N, A$ implies that $V(\delta_L^i|\pi_H) > V(\bar{\delta}_L|\pi_H)$ which contradicts our hypothesis.

So the relevant maxima in (23) must be $\delta_L^A$ and $\delta_L^N$. Solving (22) using the multipliers described in Case 1 yields the following first-order conditions:

$$U'(W - P_L)\left(1 - \lambda\frac{(1 - \pi_H)}{(1 - \pi_L)}\right) = \mu, \tag{B.1}$$

$$U'(W - D + I_L)\left(1 - \lambda\frac{\pi_H}{\pi_L}\right) = \mu, \tag{B.2}$$

$$U'(W - P_L(A))\left(1 - \lambda\frac{(1-\pi_H)\pi_H}{(1-\pi_L)\pi_L} + \gamma/\pi_L\right) = \mu, \tag{B.3}$$

$$U'(W - D + I_L(A))\left(1 - \lambda\frac{\pi_H^2}{\pi_L^2} + \gamma/\pi_L\right) = \mu, \tag{B.4}$$

$$U'(W - P_L(N))\left(1 - \lambda\frac{(1-\pi_H)^2}{(1-\pi_L)^2}\right) = \mu, \tag{B.5}$$

$$U'(W - D + I_L(N))\left(1 - \lambda\frac{\pi_H(1-\pi_H)}{\pi_L(1-\pi_L)}\right) = \mu. \tag{B.6}$$

To see (i) of the Proposition, note that comparing (B.6) with (B.2) implies that $I_L(N) > I_L$ since $(1-\pi_H) < (1-\pi_L)$. Similarly, (B.5) and (B.1) imply that $P_L(N) < P_L$.

To see (ii), we know from (25) and (26) that $V(\delta_L^N|\pi_L) \geqq V(\delta_L^A|\pi_L) = V(\bar\delta_L|\pi_L)$. In fact $V(\delta_L^N|\pi_L) > V(\delta_L^A|\pi_L)$. If not, offering $\bar\delta_L$ each period to all types would be a preferred, feasible contract. This contradicts (i). To see that $V(\delta_L^1|\pi_L) < V(\delta_L^A|\pi_L) = V(\bar\delta_L|\pi_L)$, suppose to the contrary that $V(\delta_L^1|\pi_L) \geqq V(\delta_L^A|\pi_L)$. From (23), the argument about the maxima in (23) and (25) we know that $\delta_L^1$ must therefore make positive profit for the firm as shown in fig. B1. If $V(\delta_L^1|\pi_L) \geqq V(\delta_L^A|\pi_L)$, then $\delta_L^1$ should make negative profits as indicated in the figure and must lie in the shaded region. This configuration requires that $P_L(A) \geqq P_L$. From the first-order conditions, $P_L(A) \geqq P_L$ implies

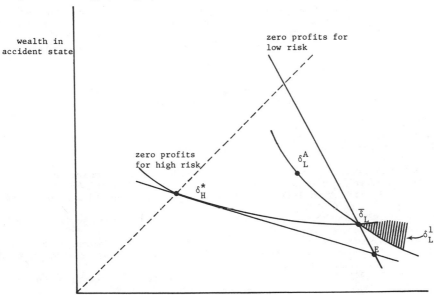

Fig. B1

that $I_L(A) < I_L$. This is inconsistent with either the zero profit constraint or the self-selection constraint for high-risk agents. Hence $V(\delta_L^1|\pi_L) < V(\delta_L^A|\pi_L)$.

By the same argument, we see that $\delta_L^1$ must make positive profits. From (25) and the fact that $V(\delta_L^A|\pi_H) > V(\bar{\delta}_L|\pi_H)$, we know that $\delta_L^A$ makes positive profits too. Hence $\delta_L^N$ must earn negative profits for (27) to hold. This proves (iii).

As a final note, we need to check whether the solution to the problem satisfies (24) and (26). Since the solution to (22) dominates offering $\bar{\delta}_L$ each period (and this is feasible) and $V(\bar{\delta}_L|\pi_L) > V(\delta_H^*|\pi_L)$, (24) must be met. As shown earlier, $V(\delta_L^N|\pi_L) > V(\delta_L^A|\pi_L)$ so that (26) is met.

## References

Arrow, K., 1965, Aspects of the theory of risk bearing (Yrjö Jahnsson Säätio, Helsinki).

Bigelow, J., 1983, Learning, experience rating and adverse selection, ISPS working paper no. 1001 (Yale University, New Haven, CT).

Dionne, G., 1983, Adverse selection and repeated insurance contracts, Geneva Papers on Risk and Insurance 8, 316–333.

Dionne, G. and P. Lasserre, 1985, Adverse selection, repeated insurance contracts and announcement strategy, Review of Economic Studies 52, 719–723.

Grossman, S. and O. Hart, 1983, An analysis of the principal–agent problem, Econometrica 51, 7–47.

Harris, M. and B. Holmstrom, 1982, A theory of wage dynamics, Review of Economic Studies 49, 315–355.

Harris, M. and A. Raviv, 1979, Optimal incentive contracts with imperfect information, Journal of Economic Theory 20, 231–259.

Harris, M. and R. Townsend, 1981, Resource allocation under asymmetric information, Econometrica 49, 33–64.

Holmstrom, B., 1979, Moral hazard and observability, Bell Journal of Economics, Spring, 74–91.

Malueg, D., 1981, Pareto optimality of repeated insurance contracts when there are problems of moral hazard and adverse selection, Mimeo. (Northwestern University, Evanston, IL).

Milgrom, P., 1981, Good news and bad news: Representation theorems and applications, Bell Journal of Economics 12, 380–392.

Pauly, M.V., 1968, The economics of moral hazard; Comment, American Economic Review 58, 531–536.

Pauly, M.V., 1974, Overinsurance and the public provision of insurance: The roles of moral hazard and adverse selection, Quarterly Journal of Economics 88, 44–62.

Radner, R., 1981, Monitoring cooperative agreements in a repeated principal–agent relationship, Econometrica 49, 1127–1148.

Rogerson, W., 1985, Repeated moral hazard, Econometrica 53, 69–76.

Ross, S., 1973, The economic theory of agency: The principal's problem, American Economic Review 63, 134–139.

Rothschild, M. and J. Stiglitz, 1976, Equilibrium in competitive insurance markets: An essay on the economics of imperfect information, Quarterly Journal of Economics 90, 629–650.

Rubinstein, A. and M. Yaari, 1983, Repeated insurance contract and moral hazard, Journal of Economic Theory 30, 74–97.

Shavell, S., 1979a, Risk sharing and incentives in the principal and agent relationship, Bell Journal of Economics, Spring, 55–73.

Shavell, S., 1979b, On moral hazard and insurance, Quarterly Journal of Economics 93, 541–563.

Stiglitz, J., 1977, Monopoly, nonlinear pricing, and imperfect information: The insurance market, Review of Economic Studies 44, 407–430.

Townsend, R., 1982, Optimal multiperiod contracts and the gain from enduring relationships under private information, Journal of Political Economy 90, 1166–1185.

Wilson, C., 1977, A model of insurance markets with incomplete information, Journal of Economic Theory 16, 167–207.

*The Geneva Papers on Risk and Insurance*, 8 (No 29, October 1983), 316-332

# Adverse Selection and Repeated Insurance Contracts *

by Georges Dionne **

## 1. Introduction

Adverse selection in insurance markets is defined as a problem of misallocation of resources explained by a situation of asymetrical information between the insured and the insurer. The insured has no incentive to reveal his true risk and it is costly for the insurer to observe the individual risk. In order to reduce this problem of resource allocation, insurers have developed imperfect mechanisms such as 1) the use of risk classes, 2) partial insurance coverage and 3) experience rating to establish the appropriate premium.

In this paper we shall concentrate more specifically on the third mechanism but in a different perspective than the one mentioned above. In the model presented here, the insurer uses the information related to past experience of the insured in order to motivate him to reveal, ex-ante, his true risk, instead of using this information to adjust his insurance premium.

This approach is similar to that proposed by Rubinstein and Yaari [1980] to eliminate inefficiency associated with the problem of moral hazard, but differs from the approaches put forth in the economic literature concerning adverse selection since the pioneering paper of Akerloff [1970]: the "self-selection mechanism" [Rothschild and Stiglitz, 1976; Wilson, 1977; Miyazaki 1977; Spence 1978] and the "categorization of risks" [Hoy 1982]. Both are private markets mechanisms. In the first case, insurers offer policies with different prices and quantity levels so that different risks choose insurance policies and, under certain conditions, it is possible to obtain Pareto improvement for resource allocation with respect to the single contract solution with an average premium. In the second case, insurers used imperfect information to differentiate risks via risk categorization and, again, under certain conditions, it is also possible to obtain Pareto

* This paper was written partly during a visit to the Université des Sciences Sociales de Toulouse. I would like to thank M. Boyer, M. Blanchard, J. P. Cresta, S. Harrington, M. Hoy, J. J. Laffont, R. Lafrance, P. Lasserre, M. Moreaux, F. Vaillancourt and the participants of the meetings of the Canadian Economic Association, the Econometric Society and the Association of Property and Casualty Insurance Economists for their stimulating discussions on this paper. The author remains responsible for any errors or shortcomings in the text. The Université de Montréal, the Société Saint-Jean-Baptiste (Prêt d'Honneur) and the Geneva Association gave financial support for this study.

** Department of Economics, Université de Montreal.

improvement for resource allocation. However these solutions are second best i.e. constrained solutions, since there still exists inefficiency due to asymetrical information.

Without asymetrical information and under the standard assumptions of insurance models (same attitude toward risk and risk aversion on the demand side, risk neutrality on the supply side, no transaction cost, and no moral hazard), a fully optimal solution is characterized by full insurance coverage for all individuals in each class of risk. In the model presented in this paper, it is possible to obtain such a solution under asymetrical information using multi-period contracts. These contracts are in the following form : the insurer and the insured agree to negociate their insurance contracts at the beginning of each period using the information of the insured's past experience. Both use long-term strategies taking into account factual past information and anticipated future information. In the first period, the insurer offers a continuum of premiums corresponding to all classes of risk. The consumer, if he decides to insure, may choose to pay any insurance premium. But, as mentioned above, the contract is negociated at the beginning of each future period and if the insured hasn't chosen to pay the insurance premium corresponding to his true class of risk, he will be penalized in the following periods in such a way that his long run average utility will be less than the long run average utility corresponding to the strategy of always saying the truth.

Under asymetrical information, the insurer cannot observe easily if the insured has announced his true class of risk since the average loss is a function of both the action of the insured (the announcement of the class of risk) and the environment. Therefore he must use time. Moreover he must identify those who don't say the truth rapidly enough without penalizing too often those who say the truth. The law of the Iterated Logarithm permits the insurer to apply the above strategy and to motivate the potential insured to say the truth. In section II, it is demonstrated that the optimal strategy of the consumer consists of always telling the truth and that this strategy yields a first best solution for the allocation of risks under asymetrical information.

In its presentation, this paper is similar to that of Rubinstein and Yaari [1980] but it differs largely in its content since it presents a different problem and therefore uses different information vectors, suggests different strategies and presents an adapted proof of Theorem I to the problem of adverse selection. The optimal choice of insurance in a single period is presented in Section 1, followed by the multi period problem. Section 3 presents a discussion based on the results. The concluding section of this paper summarizes the main results and proposes a new avenue of research on competitive markets and multi period contracts.

## 2. Optimal choice of insurance coverage : the one-period case

### 2.1. Perfect information

There are two possible states of the world ($x \in \{1, 2\}$) in this model : State (1) " no accident ", having the probability $(1 - p_i)$ and State (2), " accident ", having the probability $0 < p_i < 1$. Consumers are identical in all respect except for their probability of having an accident. There exists a continuous distribution of accident probabilities ($F(p_i)$) and each consumer belongs to one class of risk $i \in I$. Furthermore $p_i \in [\underline{p}, \overline{p}]$ and

$0 < \underline{p} < \overline{p} < 1$. $D(x)$ is the value of the asset owned by each consumer and $D(x)$ is assumed to be null in State (2), ($D(2) = 0$), and assumed to be equal to $D$ in State (1), ($D(1) = D$). Therefore the expected average loss ($\overline{D}(i)$) from an individual of the class of risk $i$ in a given period, is equal to the product of $p_i$ and $D$. That is :

(1) $$\overline{D}(i) = p_i D$$

It is also assumed that the individuals know the class of risk to which they belong. Moreover, the amount of loss and the probability of loss are not a function of the actions of the consumers to avoid the problem of moral hazard.

Insurance coverage is offered by a risk neutral monopoly. The provision of insurance is costless and under information, the insurer may observe the characteristics of each individual without cost. The insurance contract is simple : the insurer offers to cover all losses against an insurance premium ($P_i(z) \in [0, D]$) for each individual in each class of risk $i$ :

(2) $$P_i(z) = \overline{D}(i) + z$$

where $z \geqslant 0$ is a monetary value representing the profit associated to each premium. This unit-profit is assumed independent of $i$.

The use of coinsurance rates and/or deductibles is not permitted in this model. In view of this offer, a consumer from a class of risk $i$ may decide whether or not to insure himself. $c_i$ is a variable representing his choice ; $c_i \in \{0, 1\}$. The individual will accept to insure ($c_i = 1$) if and only if $U(S - P_i(z)) \geqslant \overline{V}_i$ where :

$U(S - P_i(z))$ is the certain utility associated to full insurance. $U(\cdot)$ is a twice differentiable, increasing and strictly concave utility function of wealth. $U'(\cdot) > 0$, $U''(\cdot) < 0$.

$S$ is the initial wealth of the consumer. The value of the asset is included in $S$, and $S$ is assumed to be greater than $D$ to avoid the problem of bankruptcy.

$\overline{V}_i$ is the expected utility associated to no insurance.
$$\overline{V}_i = (1 - p_i)U(S) + p_i U(S - D).$$

We may summarize the payoff of each agent in the following way :

A) The payoff of the insurer given the choices of $c_i$ and $z$ is :
$$\begin{cases} = 0 \text{ if } c_i = 0 \\ = P_i(z) - \overline{D}(i) \text{ if } c_i = 1 \end{cases}$$

B) The payoff of a consumer in the class of risk $i$ given the choices of $c_i$ and $z$ is :
$$\begin{cases} = \overline{V}_i \text{ if } c_i = 0 \\ = U(S - P_i(z)) \text{ if } c_i = 1 \end{cases}$$

Under perfect information and actuarial insurance premium, it may be shown that $U(S - P_i(0)) > \overline{V}_i$ for all individuals in each class of risk. This result corresponds to the fully optimal solution under perfect information. Moreover $U(S - P_i(z)) \geqslant \overline{V}_i$ is also possible for some $z > 0$.

## 2.2. *Asymmetrical information between insurer and insureds*

In this case it is assumed that the insurer cannot observe without cost the individual risks. However his experience in the market, permits him to evaluate precisely the distribution of the classes of risks among the individuals. It is important to remember here that, in this model, only full insurance contracts are possible. Since the insurer cannot discriminate among his potential customers on the basis of their probabilities, he must use another strategy. One possible strategy is to offer an average premium to each individual regardless of his true risk. This average premium is assumed to be equal to:

(3) $\qquad \bar{P}(z) = \int_p^{\bar{p}} P_i(z) f(p_i) \, dp_i$

where $f(p_i)$ is the PDF of the $p_i$

$\qquad P_i(z) = p_i D + z$

Under this strategy, the payoffs of the agents become:

A) The payoff of the insurer given the choices of $c_i$ and $z$ is:
$$\begin{cases} = 0 \text{ if } c_i = 0 \\ = \bar{P}(z) - \bar{D}(i) \text{ if } c_i = 1 \end{cases}$$

B) The payoff of a consumer in the class of risk $i$ given the choices of $c_i$ and $z$ is:
$$\begin{cases} = \bar{V}_i \text{ if } c_i = 0 \\ = U(S - \bar{P}(z)) \text{ if } c_i = 1 \end{cases}$$

The individuals from the class of risk $i$ will choose to insure if and only if $U(S - \bar{P}(z)) \geqslant \bar{V}_i$. Assume for a moment, that $z$ is null. With actuarial insurance premium, the individuals from the lowest class of risk characterized by the probability of accident $\underline{p}$, will choose to insure solely if, for a given distribution of the classes of risks, the gap between $\bar{p}$ and $\underline{p}$ is small enough to verify that $U(S - \bar{P}(0)) \geqslant \bar{V}_p$ where $\bar{V}_p$ corresponds to their expected utility associated to no insurance. The same reasoning applies for all classes of risks characterized by a probability of accident $(p_i)$ less than $\mu$ where $\mu$ is the average accident probability:

(4) $\qquad \mu = \int_p^{\bar{p}} p_i f(p_i) \, dp_i$

Otherwise there is inefficiency due to adverse selection. However, those from the classes of risks having a probability of accident above $\mu$, will always take insurance at this price since $U(S - \bar{P}(0)) \geqslant U(S - P_i(0))$ for them. The same reasoning applies for $z > 0$ with the exception that the possibility of being insured is less for all classes of risk since $U(S - \bar{P}(z)) < U(S - \bar{P}(0))$ for all $z > 0$.

From this analysis, we may now define inefficiency due to adverse selection as a reduction of the possibilities of taking insurance for the lower classes of risk. At the extreme, adverse selection drives out of the market the good risks [Akerloff, 1970]. As mentioned in a previous section, many other insurance strategies may be used to reduce the inefficiency associated to adverse selection. Those solutions will not be presented here. Instead, we will focus on the possibility of using past experience of the insured in order to motivate him to reveal his true risk.

The insurer may use the following strategy. Before selling insurance coverage to a new potential customer, he announces the terms of the agreement: " I don't know in what class of risk you belong to but I know that you have this information. Therefore I will insure you using your risk announcement but if, at the end of the period, your average loss is greater than the expected average loss associated to the class of risk you announced at the beginning of the period, you will be penalized ". It is well known from statistical theory that this strategy cannot be applied on one period contract since the average loss is function of both the environment and the risk of the individuals. Those who tell the truth may be penalized without reason under that strategy. Therefore the insurer, in order to be able to use such a strategy requires many observations or many periods.

## 3. Optimal choice of insurance coverage : the multi period case

In this case the insurer and the potential insured agree on the following rules. An initial insurance contract is negociated in the first period and, if there is an agreement, both parties will meet at the beginning of each subsequent period in order to negociate again the insurance contract using information on the past experience of the insured in the preceding periods. At the first meeting, the insurer offers insurance contracts characterized by their premium and the consumer decides both if he will take insurance or not and which insurance premium he will pay. In the following periods, the insurer using the new information, will offer one insurance premium to each consumer and the consumer will decide to maintain insurance or not.

Each agent knows that the actions of the other are consequent to his long term strategy and not from a myopic (one period) strategy. Moreover, the information on past experience is not used to adjust the premium but to motivate the insured to notice the true class of risk to which he belongs. In other words, the expectations of the agents concerning this information are elements of their strategy. The assets to be insured has the same monetary value ($D > 0$) at the beginning of each period whatever the state of the world in the preceding period. If there is an accident, the asset is restored to its initial value at the end of the period. Only full insurance contracts are possible. Finally, as in the model of Rubinstein and Yaari [1980], the Stackelberg's behavior assumption is used in this multi-period model.

### 3.1. The information available to each agent

The insurer cannot observe directly the individual risks at the beginning of the first period, but at the end of the first period he knows :

1) if the asset belonging to a particular customer was insured or not in that period ; this information may be measured using $\Theta_c \in \{0, 1\}$ where 0 means not insured ;

2) if the consumer took insurance, what insurance premium he paid and therefore what declaration about his risk he did in buying insurance ; $\Theta_{P_i} \in [0, D]$ ;

3) what was the amount of loss if the asset was insured ; $\Theta_D \in \{0, D\}$ where 0 means no loss.

This information is summarized in the following vector $\Theta_1 \in I_1$ (the insurer's one-period information set) :

$$\Theta_1 = (\Theta_c, \Theta_{P_i}, \Theta_D)$$

where 1 means insurer.

Under the assumption of perfect memory, at the end of the period $t$, the information vector becomes:

$$\Theta_1^t = (\Theta_c^t, \Theta_P^t, \Theta_D^t)$$

where $\Theta_c^t = (\Theta_c^{t1}, ..., \Theta_c^{tt})$

$$\Theta_P^t = (\Theta_P^{t1}, ..., \Theta_P^{tt})$$

$$\Theta_D^t = (\Theta_D^{t1}, ..., \Theta_D^{tt})$$

$\Theta_1^t, \in I_1^t$, the insurer's information set at the end of the period $t$ and therefore in the period $t + 1$.

On the other hand, at the end of each period, a consumer from the class of risk $i$ knows the insurance premium(s) offered to him by the insurer in that period. He also knows what was the loss during that period. But we don't need this last information in order to compute the strategies of the insured since, in this model, the consumers cannot affect the amounts of loss. Therefore only the first kind of information will be considered. At the end of the first period, the information of a consumer in the class of risk $i$ is measured by:

$$\Theta_{2i} = \Theta_{Pi}$$

where 2 means consumer,

$$\Theta_{Pi} \in [0, D]$$

$\Theta_{2i} \in I_{2i}$, the consumer's one-period information set.

At the end of the period $t$ we have:

$$\Theta_{2i}^t = \Theta_P^t$$

where $\Theta_P^t \in I_{2i}^t$ the consumer's information set in period $t + 1$.

$$\Theta_P^t = (\Theta_P^{t1}, ..., \Theta_P^{tt})$$

### 3.2. The possible actions of the agents

The set $P = [0, D]$ represents all the insurer's possible actions in a given period. Those actions are limited to offer insurance premiums to the consumer at the beginning of each period. The consumer from the class of risk $i$ has to decide:

1) whether or not he will insure; $C_i = \{0, 1\}$;

2) if he has decided to insure, what announcement of risk he will do in choosing an insurance premium; $\hat{P}_i = [0, D]$.

Therefore the set of all possible actions is equal to the product $C_i \times \hat{P}_i$.

### 3.3. The possible strategies of the agents

The vector of possible strategies for the insurer is represented by $F = (F^1, F^2, ...)$ such that $F^1 \in P$ and $F^{t+1}$, $t = 1, 2, ...$, is a function defined on the information set $I_1^t$ and having values in $P$.

On the other hand, the vector of possible strategies of a consumer from the class of risk $i$, is represented by $G_i = (G_i^1, G_i^2, ...)$ such that $G_i^1 \in C_i \times \hat{P}_i$ and $G_i^{t+1}$, $t = 1, 2, ...$, is a function defined on $I_{2i}^t$ and having values in $C_i \times \hat{P}_i$.

### 3.4 The anticipated states of information of the agents

Knowing the sets of strategies of the agents, it is now possible to compute their anticipated states of information at the end of each period. The values of those states of information are random variables since the events are function of the states of the world. Defining $(F, G_i)$ as a given pair of strategies in the set of all pairs of strategies $(Z)$, $((F, G_i) \in Z)$, the value of the state of anticipated information for the insurer at the end of the first period is equal to:

$$\Theta_1^1(F, G_i) = (\Theta_c^1(F, G_i), \Theta_{P_i}(F, G_i), \Theta_D^1(F, G_i))$$

where $\Theta_c^1(F, G_i) = G_{ci}^1$ and $G_{ci}^1 \in C_i$

$\quad \Theta_P^1(F, G_i) = G_{ci}^1 \times G_{P_i}^1$ and $G_{P_i}^1 \in \hat{P}_i$

$\quad \Theta_D^1(F, G_i) = G_{ci}^1 \times D(x)$ and $D(x) \in \{0, D\}$.

Moreover, for a consumer from the class of risk $i$ we have:

$$\Theta_{2i}^1(F, G_i) = \Theta_{P_i}^1(F, G_i)$$

where $\Theta_{P_i}^1(F, G_i) = F_P^1$ and $F_P^1 \in P$

Then for $t = 2, 3, ...$, we obtain:

$$\Theta_1^t(F, G_i) = (\Theta_1^{t-1}(F, G_i), \Theta_c^t(F, G_i), \Theta_P^t(F, G_i), \Theta_D^t(F, G_i))$$

where $\Theta_c^t(F, G_i) = G_{ci}^t(\Theta_{2i}^{t-1}(F, G_i))$

$\quad \Theta_P^t(F, G_i) = G_{ci}^t(\Theta_{2i}^{t-1}(F, G_i)) \times G_{P_i}^t(\Theta_{2i}^{t-1}(F, G_i))$

$\quad \Theta_D^t(F, G_i) = G_{ci}^t(\Theta_{2i}^{t-1}(F, G_i)) \times D(x')$

and

$$\Theta_{2i}^t(F, G_i) = (\Theta_{2i}^{t-1}(F, G_i), \Theta_P^t(F, G_i))$$

where $\Theta_P^t(F, G_i) = F_P^t(\Theta_1^{t-1}(F, G_i))$

### 3.5. The anticipated actions of the agents

The anticipated actions of the agents are a function of their anticipated states of information in the previous periods for $t = 2, 3, ...$ . Therefore we have $F^t(\Theta_1^{t-1}(F, G_i))$ and $G_i^t(\Theta_{2i}^{t-1}(F, G_i))$ for $t = 2, 3, ...$ and $F^1, G_i^1$ for the first period. Since the states of anticipated information are random variables, the anticipated actions are also random variables. Moreover, they have their values respectively in $P$ and in $C_i \times \hat{P}_i$. Therefore it is now possible to obtain the single-period payoffs of the agents for $t = 2, 3, ...$:

$$h_1^t(F, G_i) \begin{cases} = 0 & \text{if } G_{ci}^t(\Theta_{2i}^{t-1}(F, G_i)) = 0 \\ = F^t(\Theta_1^{t-1}(F, G_i)) - D(x') & \text{if } G_{ci}^t(\Theta_{2i}^{t-1}(F, G_i)) = 1 \end{cases}$$

$$h_{2i}^t(F, G_i) \begin{cases} = U(S - D(x')) & \text{if } G_{ci}^t(\Theta_{2i}^{t-1}(F, G_i)) = 0 \\ = U(S - F^t(\Theta_1^{t-1}(F, G_i))) & \text{if } G_{ci}^t(\Theta_{2i}^{t-1}(F, G_i)) = 1 \end{cases}$$

where $h_1^t(F, G_i)$, $h_{2i}^t(F, G_i)$ are written for the agents' anticipated random payoffs in period $t$.

In the long run, we shall assume, as Rubinstein and Yaari [1980] did, that both groups of agents are interested in evaluating the infinite streams of anticipated random payoffs. If we still consider the pair of strategies $(F, G_i)$, we may calculate the long-run average value of the payoffs in the following way : denote $H_1(F, G_i)$ and $H_2(F, G_i)$ as two real numbers such that as $T \to \infty$ we obtain :

$$\frac{1}{T} \sum_{t=1}^{T} h_1^t(F, G_i) \to H_1(F, G_i) \text{ almost surely}$$

$$\frac{1}{T} \sum_{t=1}^{T} h_{2t}^t(F, G_i) \to H_2(F, G_i) \text{ almost surely.}$$

Moreover we shall assume that all pairs of strategies in the subset $\tilde{Z}$ of $Z$ are averageable pairs of strategies.

### 3.6. The strategies of the agents

Now, the important question is : " What will be the insurer's strategy to eliminate inefficiency due to adverse selection ? " In other words, what strategy will he use to make incentives in such a way that the insured will reveal the truth concerning his risk ? We propose the following strategy : he will say to a potential insured " I don't know what kind of risk you represent but I know that you have this information. Therefore I propose the following long term contract of insurance. In the first period I will offer a continuum of insurance premiums in which each premium corresponds to one and only one class of risk. You choose the one you prefer and I insure you based on your choice. But, the insurance contract will be negotiated at the beginning of each subsequent period. If over time, you have a reasonable average loss related to the risk you announced in choosing your insurance premium in the first period, I will insure you again at the same price (without bonus). But if your average loss is greater than the reasonable average loss corresponding to your declaration, you will be penalized in such a way that the insurance premium offered $(P_K)$ will give you a certain utility level $(U(S - P_K))$ less than $\overline{V}_i$, the expected utility associated to no insurance. "

This strategy corresponds to the " no-claims discount strategy " proposed by Rubinstein and Yaari [1980] for the problem of moral hazard. By choosing a continuum of insurance premiums $[\underline{P}, \overline{P}]$ and two numbers $P_* \in [0, D]$ and $P_K \in [0, D]$ with $0 \leqslant P_* \leqslant P_K \leqslant D$, this strategy may be written formally as :

$$F^1 = [\underline{P}, \overline{P}]$$

and for $t = 1, 2, \ldots$

$$F^{t+1}(\Theta_1^t) \begin{cases} = P_* \text{ if } \sum_{s=1}^{t} \frac{\Theta_D^{ts}}{N(t)} < \overline{D}(*) + \alpha^{N(t)} \\ = P_K \text{ otherwise} \end{cases}$$

where $(\alpha^t)$ is a statistical margin of error to be defined and

$$N(t) = \sum_{s=1}^{t} \Theta_c^{ts}.$$

From the construction of the model, we know that $\Theta_c^{ts} \in \{0, 1\}$ and that $\Theta_D^{ts} \in \{0, D\}$. Therefore $\sum_{s=1}^{t} \frac{\Theta_D^{ts}}{N(t)}$ is the average loss claimed by the insured in the first $t$ periods.

$\overline{D}(*)$ is the true average loss corresponding to the declaration of risk done in the first period in choosing the insurance premium. $P_*$ is the insurance premium corresponding to $\overline{D}(*)$ and $P_K$ is an insurance premium that has to be considered as a penalty by any insured in any class of risk. If the observed average loss obtained is strictly less than the true average loss corresponding to the declaration of risk plus some margin of error, the insurer will offer $P_*$. This margin of error is used in order not to penalise too often those who tell the truth. But it has to be small enough to detect those who try to increase their utility in announcing a risk class inferior to their true risk. We shall return to this statistical tool later.

But is this kind of strategy enforceable? By definition, a pair of strategies $(\tilde{F}, \tilde{G}_i)$ is enforceable if $\tilde{G}_i$ is a best response to $\tilde{F}$. In other words, a $G_i$ doesn't exist in all possible strategies of the consumer such that the event,

$$\frac{1}{T} \sum_{t=1}^{T} h_{2i}^{t}(\tilde{F}, G_i) \geqslant H_2(\tilde{F}, \tilde{G}_i) + \varepsilon,$$

has positive probability for infinitely many values of $T$ and for some $\varepsilon > 0$.

In the present model, we have to verify if the insurer, in using the " no-claims discount strategy ", may eliminate the inefficiency associated with adverse selection. In other words, we have to verify if the insurer can enforce the potential insured to tell the truth about his risk in the first period and to take full insurance coverage in all subsequent periods, as in the case of perfect information described in the first part of this paper.

We may summarize the preceding discussion with the following theorem :

*Theorem I* : (Rubinstein and Yaari's Theorem I, adapted to the problem of adverse selection).

Let $P_o \in [0, D]$ be such that :

(1) $\qquad P_o - \overline{D}(o) \geqslant 0 \text{ and } U(S - P_o) \geqslant \overline{V}_o$

Therefore there exists a pair $(\tilde{F}, \tilde{G}_o) \in \tilde{Z}$ having the following properties :

(2) $\qquad \tilde{F}$ is a " no-claims discount strategy "

(3) $\qquad H_1(\tilde{F}, \tilde{G}_o) = P_o - \overline{D}(o), H_2(\tilde{F}, \tilde{G}_o) = U(S - P_o)$

(4) $\qquad (\tilde{F}, \tilde{G}_o)$ is enforceable.

The proof used here is similar to the proof of Rubinstein and Yaari [1980], but has some important differences that have to be emphasized. In this part of the paper, only the main differences will be presented. The whole proof including similar and different parts is presented as reference in Appendix I.

The main differences concern No (4) of the Theorem. In this section it must be proven that $\tilde{G}_o$ is a best response to $\tilde{F}$. In doing their proof, Rubinstein and Yaari [1980] constructed a convex hull using two real valued functions of the expected damages for given insurance premiums and used this convex hull to complete their proof. They were interested in the variation of the expected damage since they studied the problem of moral hazard. Here we are concerned with adverse selection and therefore our focus is on the variation of the expected insurance premiums for given expected damages. Therefore the convex hull that we shall construct comes from the graphs of $P_o^+(v)$ and $P_o^-(v)$ where :

$$P_o^+(v) = P(S - D - U^{-1}(v))$$
$$P_o^-(v) = P(S - \overline{D}(o) - U^{-1}(v))$$

$P_o^+(v)$ and $P_o^-(v)$ are the levels of premiums corresponding to a utility level $v$ for an insured of the class of risk $o$ when the average losses are $D$ and $\overline{D}(o)$ respectively. $P_o^+(v)$ and $P_o^-(v) \in [0, D]$. From the assumptions of the model, those functions are strictly decreasing concave functions and may be represented as follows :

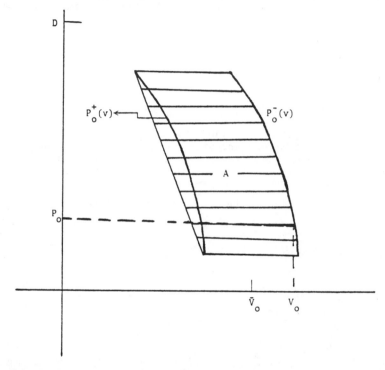

The graph of $P_o^-(v)$ is on the right of the graph $P_o^+(v)$ and the choice of $D$ implies that $\overline{V}_o$ is at the right of $P_o^+(v)$, that is : " no insurance " gives more utility than insurance with premiums in the range of $P_o^+(v)$. Finally the convex hull $A$ is constructed using the graphs and is used to complete the proof of Theorem I (See Appendix I).

Now let's return to the sequence $\alpha'$ which is assumed to be equal to :

$$\sqrt{\frac{2\lambda \sigma^2 \log \log t}{t}} \quad , \quad \lambda > 1, \sigma^2 = \text{var } D(x') ;$$

This statistical tool prevents the insurer from penalising too often, without reason, those who tell the truth and permits him to find rapidly enough those who cheat. Its value converges to 0 over time but sufficiently slowly and sufficiently fast to obtain the desired results: if an insured tells the truth he will be penalized only finitely many times with probability one; on the other hand, an insured cannot increase his utility in announcing a class of risk inferior to his true class of risk. Therefore from Theorem I (under the no claims discount strategy) we obtain full efficiency allocation of risks that is the insurer is now able both to enforce the consumer to announce the true class of risk he belongs and to sell full insurance coverage to all individuals regardless of their class of risk. (For other applications of this statistical method, see Rubinstein [1979] and Radner [1981]).

Finally, in their paper, Rubinstein and Yaari [1980] also showed that the converse of Theorem I is true, that is, the pair $(H_1(\bar{F}, \tilde{G}_o), H_2(\bar{F}, \tilde{G}_o))$ is an individual rational income for a single contract. This result may be obtained too for the case of adverse selection.

## 4. Discussion

In section 1 of this paper (one-period case) we have shown that, under perfect information, a fully optimal solution can be obtained with one-period insurance contract: the risk-neutral insurer absorbs all risk. The consumer can then use certain $(S - P_i(Z))$ in order to set his optimal consumption level. In Section 2 we have shown that a fully optimal solution can also be obtained under asymmetrical information when the length of the insurance contract is infinite. Now two questions remain: 1) Under perfect information, is a multi period insurance contract superior to a sequence of one-period contracts?, 2) Does a consumer need insurance when borrowing and lending is possible in a multi period environment?

The answer to the first question is negative. A multi period insurance contract does not increase the welfare of the agents under perfect information. This proposition can easily be proved using the model presented in the preceding section without the assumption of asymmetrical information. Therefore there is no need for optimal strategies in order to motivate the consumer to notice the true class of risk to which he belongs.

The optimal solution corresponds to the long-run average value of the payoffs: $P_i - \bar{D}(i)$ for the insurer and $U(S - P_i(Z))$ for the insured as $T \to \infty$ almost surely. This solution is the same as in the one-period case which implies that there is no gain using a multi period contract.

The answer to the second question is also negative when the number of periods is infinite. To see this, we will use the model presented by Yaari [1976]. (See also Bewley [1977] and Schechtman [1976] on the same subject). Yaari showed that if a consumer

maximizes $E \sum_{t=1}^{T} U(C_t(S_t))$

subject to $S_1$ given

$$S_{t+1} = S_t + y_t - C_t(S_t) \qquad t = 1 \ldots\ldots T-1$$
$$C_T(S_T) = S_T$$

where $S_t$ = asset at the beginning of period $t$

$C_t$ = consumption at period $t$

$y_t$ = earning at period $t$

$E$ = expectation operator,

then, the optimal consumption level will tend to $\mu$ the average earning, as $T \to \infty$, if the consumer could borrow and lend at the bank at a zero rate of interest and if events are independent and identically distributed over time. In our notation, the average " earning " is $S - p_i D$, and both solutions coincide when $Z \equiv 0$ since $P_i(0) = p_i D$ for all $i$. The risk averse consumer can either buy insurance or lend and borrow at the bank. This result is true under both perfect information and asymmetrical information when the number of periods is infinite. However, it is important to notice that the risk averse consumer needs to exchange his risk with a risk neutral agent (either a bank or an insurer) in order to consume his average earning in each period. In other words self-insurance is not sufficient to obtain such a solution.

The correspondance between the insurance and the borrowing-lending solution seems no longer true when the number of periods is finite. In the one period case, it is straightforward to see that insurance dominates borrowing-lending possibilities under perfect information. Under asymetrical information, the comparison of both approaches is not easily obtained and one interesting avenue of research is to compare the two approaches and to show which one dominates the other. R. Townsend [1982] has made such a comparison for another type of contract other than insurance contract.

## 5. Conclusion

This paper is an extension of the model of Rubinstein and Yaari [1980] on the problem of adverse selection. It is shown that their concept of " no-claims discount strategy " may be used in order to eliminate inefficiency due to adverse selection. Under this strategy it is now possible to obtain a full efficiency solution under asymetrical information. By full efficiency solution, we mean full insurance coverage in each period for all consumers regardless of the class of risk to which they belong. A further step of analysis would be to show that under this strategy, it would be possible to solve both problems of asymetrical information in insurance markets, i.e. adverse selection and moral hazard, at the same time.

However these solutions are restricted to a monopoly and one important contribution would be to figure out how we may obtain first best solution in a competitive market under asymetrical information. In the remainder of this paper, I shall present a short discussion on this last issue which will be limited to the problem of adverse selection but can be applied directly to the moral hazard problem.

The main issue concerns the credibility of imposing a penalty premium when there are more than one insurer or equivalently when there are potential competitors in the market. It should be repeated that, in the model presented in this paper, the insurer (monopoly) has information from a consumer only when the latter is insured. In a competitive market the same situation applies and an insurer (under competition) would obtain information concerning a consumer only when the latter takes his insurance policy. Therefore it would be easy for a consumer in a competitive economy, to increase his utility by moving to another company if a former company detected that he hadn't said the truth about his risk.

In order to reduce the possibility of an insured person moving among insurance company to insurance company and declaring false class of risk many times, one way would be to permit individual insurers to have access to the same set of information as the monopoly. The information would circulate among all insurers as in the case of a monopoly but competition for clients would remain. In this case each individual firm will be able to prevent the possibility of an individual making the same false declaration many times.

But there still remains the problem of how to enforce the penalty in a competitive market, since even if an insurer knows that an insured has made a false declaration, and even if he is determined not to permit him to make false declarations many times, he would accept to insure him as a bad risk and make money with him. Therefore there still remains the possibility of the insured persons giving false information thereby increasing their utility instead of always saying the truth.

Coalitions between insurers may in two ways reduce the movements among insurance companies. But as in all coalitions, there always exists an insurer who is willing to break the agreement. The first way consists of asking each insurer to apply the penalty rule as in the case of a monopoly even if the consumer hasn't made any false declaration to him. This would eliminate the possibility of false declaration but, for the reasons mentioned above, there will always be an insurer willing to insure bad risks as bad risks and to make money from them.

The other possibility consists of asking each consumer to pay a high amount of money when approaching an insurance for a first insurance contract. This amount of money will be paid back at the end of the contract only if the insured told the truth. Moreover, this amount has to be high enough to prevent individuals who don't say the truth to increase their utility in moving from one company to another. But under competition, individual insurers would have incentive to reduce this amount of money in order to attract new customers.

As mentioned above, there is no straightforward solution to this problem and more research is needed to find fully efficient allocation of risks under both asymetrical information and competition.

### Appendix I : Proof of Theorem I

This Appendix reproduces the adapted proof of Theorem I to the problem of adverse selection. The Assertions used for the proof are presented in Appendix II.

Let us write $U(S - P_o) \equiv V_o$. In order to specify the no claims discount strategy, $\tilde{F}$, select $[\underline{P}, \overline{P}]$, $P_*$, $P_K$ and $\{\alpha^t\}_{t=1}^{\infty}$ as follows :

$$[\underline{P}, \overline{P}] = [0, D], P_* = P_o, P_K = D$$

and
$$\alpha^t = \sqrt{\frac{2\lambda\sigma^2 \log \log t}{t}}$$

where $\lambda > 1$ and $\sigma^2 = \operatorname{var} D(x^t)$.

By definition of insurance premium, $P_o = \overline{D}(o) + z$ and $Z \geqslant 0$. Now assume that $\hat{G}_o \equiv (1, P_o)$ for all $t$, that is the consumer always insures the asset and announces his true class of risk in the first period and maintains his announcement in all periods.

To see that (3) in Theorem I is satisfied, note that $D(x^t)$ is a sequence of independent, identically distributed random variables. Therefore, by Assertion A, we have almost surely for all but finitely many $T$,

$$\frac{1}{T} \sum_{t=1}^{T} D(x^t) - \bar{D}(o) < \alpha^T \text{ for an individual of the class of risk } o.$$

Moreover, since $\Theta_c^{Tt} \equiv 1$, we have $\sum_{t=1}^{T} \Theta_c^{Tt} \equiv T$ and so, almost surely, it is true for all but finitely many values of $T$ that:

$$\frac{\sum_{t=1}^{T} \Theta_D^{Tt}}{\sum_{t=1}^{T} \Theta_c^{Tt}} < \bar{D}(o) + \alpha^t$$

Then, almost surely, $\tilde{F}^T = P_*$ except for the first period and for finitely many values of $T$. Now using Assertion C, we have:

$$\frac{1}{T} \sum_{t=1}^{T} h_1^t(\tilde{F}, \tilde{G}_o) \to P_* - \bar{D}(*) = P_o - \bar{D}(o) \text{ a.s.}$$

and

$$\frac{1}{T} \sum_{t=1}^{T} h_{2o}^t(\tilde{F}, \tilde{G}_o) \to U(S - P_*) = U(S - P_o) \equiv V_o \text{ a.s.}$$

which satisfies (3) in Theorem I.

Now we have to show that (4) in Theorem I is satisfied, that is $\tilde{G}_o$ is a best response to $\tilde{F}$. To do that, we assume, contrary to (4), that there exists a $G_o$ in all possible strategies of the consumer from the class of risk $o$ such that

$$Pr(\bar{V}_o^T > V_o + \varepsilon_o, \text{ for infinitely many values of } T) > \varepsilon_o,$$

where $\bar{V}_o^T = \frac{1}{T} \sum_{t=1}^{T} h_{2o}(\tilde{F}, G_o).$

By assertion G, it is possible to assume that $G_{co}^t \equiv 1$ for all $t$. Now let $\bar{P}_o^T$ be the average premium paid by a consumer from a class of risk $o$ in the first $T$ periods, when the consumer plays $G_o$.

That is,

$$\bar{P}_o^T = \frac{1}{T} \sum_{t=1}^{T} \Theta_{P_o}^{Tt}(\tilde{F}, G_o)$$

Define two real valued functions, $P_o^+(v)$ and $P_o^-(v)$ as follows:

$$P_o^+(v) = P(S - D - U^{-1}(v))$$
$$P_o^-(v) = P(S - D(o) - U^{-1}(v))$$

$P_o^+(v)$ and $P_o^-(v)$ are the levels of premium corresponding to a utility level $v$ for a consumer from the class of risk $o$ and when the average losses are $D$ and $D(o)$ respectively. From the assumptions of this model, the functions are strictly decreasing concave functions and may be represented as in the figure I.

$A$ is the convex hull of the graphs of $P_o^+(v)$ and $P_o^-(v)$. It follows from Assertion F that $\rho[(\overline{V}_o^T, \overline{P}_o^T), A] \to 0$ a.s., where $\rho$ denotes Euclidian distance. From Assertion E, we now obtain that for every $\hat{\varepsilon} > 0$, there exists an event $\hat{E}$ with $Pr(\hat{E}) > 1 - \hat{\varepsilon}$ and there exists $T$, such that for every $t \geqslant T$, $\rho[\overline{V}_o^T, \overline{P}_o^T), A]$ is arbitrarily small. Since $P_o^-(o)$ is a concave function, we may have this distance to be small enough to assume that the inequality

$$\overline{V}_o^T - (P_o^-(v))^{-1}(\overline{P}_o^T) < \frac{\varepsilon_o}{2}$$

is satisfied for $t > T$.

Now let's consider the random vectors $(V_o^t, P_o^t)$ and the conditional random vectors $[(V_o^t, P_o^t)| V_o^1...V_o^{t-1}, P_o^1...P_o^{t-1}]$. The expectations of any such random vector, by construction, must lie either on the graph $P_o^+(v)$ or on the graph $P_o^-(v)$. Moreover those vectors are uniformly bounded. From Assertion D, it follows that we can select $\hat{\varepsilon}$, $0 < \hat{\varepsilon} < \hat{\varepsilon}_o$, to be so small that $E[(V_o^t, P_o^t)| V_o^1...V_o^{t-1}, P_o^1...P_o^{t-1}, \hat{E}]$ will be contained in a band exceeding the graphs $p_o^+(v)$ and $P_o^-(v)$ horizontally by at most $\frac{\varepsilon_o}{4}$.

To obtain the desired result, we have to show that

$$\limsup \overline{V}_o^T \leqslant V_o + \varepsilon, \text{ a.s. on } \hat{E}.$$

We know that $\alpha^t \to 0$ and therefore we can have a $T_0$ such that, for $t \geqslant T_0$, we obtain

$$P_o + \alpha_t < P_o^-(v_o + \frac{\varepsilon_o}{4}) \quad \text{where } P_o = P_o^-(V_o)$$

Now let's define the set $B$ using the Assertion B:

$$B = \{(x, y)| 0 \leq y \leq D, x \leqslant \min[(P_o^-(v))^{-1}(y) + \frac{\varepsilon_o}{2}, P_o + \frac{3\varepsilon_o}{4}]\}$$

Let's assume that $(\overline{V}_o^t, \overline{P}_o^t) \notin B$ for some $t > t_0$. Then $\overline{V}_o^t > U_o + \frac{3\varepsilon_o}{4}$ by the construction of $B$. Consider $z_1 = (V_o + \frac{3\varepsilon_o}{4}, \overline{P}_o^t)$ be closest to $(\overline{V}_o^t, \overline{P}_o^t)$ in $B$. The line $x \equiv V_o + \frac{3\varepsilon_o}{4}$ is orthogonal to the segment $[(\overline{V}_o^t, \overline{P}_o^t), z_1]$ and it separates $(\overline{V}_o^t, \overline{P}_o^t)$ from $E[(V_o^{t+1}, P_o^{t+1})|(\overline{V}_o^t, \overline{P}_o^t), \hat{E}]$ since $t > T_o$ and $\overline{P}_o^t > P_o + \alpha^t$. Under strategy $\tilde{F}$, $P_K = D$ is being charged so that $E[(V_o^{t+1}, P_o^{t+1})|(\overline{V}_o^t, \overline{P}_o^t)]$ lies on the graph of $P_o^+(v)$, which is entirely to the left of $\overline{V}_o$ with $\overline{V}_o \leqslant V_o$. Therefore $E[(V_o^{t+1})|(\overline{V}_o^t, \overline{P}_o^t), \hat{E}] < V_o + \frac{\varepsilon_o}{4}$ which means that in $\tilde{E}$, whose probability exceeds $1 - \hat{\varepsilon}$, the distance $\rho[(\overline{V}_o^t, \overline{P}_o^t), B] \to 0$ a.s. Therefore $\limsup \overline{V}_o^t < V_o + \frac{3\varepsilon_o}{4}$, contradicting the original assumption about the strategy $G_o$.

## Appendix II

This appendix reproduces the Assertions needed to proof Theorem I as they are presented in the paper of Rubinstein and Yaari [1980].

*Assertion A* (Law of the Iterated Logarithm). Let $\{X^t\}$ be as sequence of independent, identically distributed random variables, with finite means $\mu$ and finite variances $\sigma^2$. Then, for every $\lambda > 1$, almost surely,

$$\limsup_{T} \frac{|\mu - \frac{1}{T} \sum_{t=1}^{T} X^t|}{(2\lambda\sigma^2 \log\log T / T)^{\frac{1}{2}}} < 1.$$

*Assertion B* (Blackwell). Let $C$ be a closed subset of $R^n$ and let $\{x^t\}$ be a sequence of random vectors with values in $R^n$. Finally, let $\underline{x}^t$ denote a value of $\underline{X}^T$ and, for every $\underline{x}^1, ..., \underline{x}^T$, let $\frac{1}{T} \sum_{t=1}^{T} \underline{x}^t$ be denoted $\overline{\underline{x}}^T$. Suppose $\overline{\underline{x}}^T \notin C$ and consider $\underline{z} \in C$, with $\underline{z}$ being closest to $\overline{\underline{x}}^T$ in $C$, in the sense of Euclidean norm. If $\{\underline{X}^t\}$ has the property that, for every $\underline{x}^1, ..., \underline{x}^T$, the hyperplane which is orthogonal to the segment $[\overline{\underline{x}}^T, \underline{z}]$ separates $\overline{\underline{x}}^T$ *from* $E(\underline{X}^{T+1}|\underline{x}^1, ..., \underline{x}^T)$, then, almost surely, $\rho(\overline{\underline{x}}^T, C) \to 0$ where $\rho$ is Euclidean distance.

*Assertion C* (Strong Law of Large Numbers). Let $\{X^t\}$ be a uniformly bounded sequence of random variables. Then, almost surely,

$$\frac{1}{T} \sum_{t=1}^{T} [X^t - E(X^t|X^1, ..., X^{t-1})] \to 0.$$

*Assertion D.* Let $X$ be a random variable, bounded by some real number $B$. Let $A$ be an event with $Pr(A) = 1 - \varepsilon$. Then

$$|E(X) - E(X|a)| \leqq \frac{2B\varepsilon}{1 - \varepsilon}$$

*Assertion E* (Consequence of Egoroff's Theorem). Let $\{\underline{X}^t\}$ be a sequence of random vectors with values in $R^n$. Let $A \subset R^n$ be a closed set with the property that $\rho(\underline{X}^t, A) \to 0$ a.s., where $\rho$ denotes Euclidean distance. Then, for every $\delta > 0$, there exists an event $E$ with $Pr(E) \geqq 1 - \delta$ such that $\rho(\underline{X}^t, A) \to 0$ uniformly on $E$.

*Assertion F.* Let $A \subset R^n$ be a convex compact set, and let $\{\underline{X}^t\}$ be a sequence of random vectors, with values in $R^n$, such that $E(\underline{X}^1, ..., \underline{X}^{t-1}) \in A$ for all $t$. Let $\frac{1}{T} \sum_{t=1}^{T} \underline{X}^t$ be denoted $\overline{\underline{X}}^T$. Then $\rho(\overline{\underline{X}}^T, A) \to 0$ a.s., where $\rho$ is the Euclidean distance.

*Assertion G.* Let $\{X^t\}$ be a sequence of bounded random variables such that, for all $t$ and for all values $x^1, ..., x^{t-1}$ taken on by $X^1, ..., X^{t-1}$, $E(X^t|x^1, ..., x^{t-1}) \leqq \overline{U}$. Let $\{\delta^t\}$ be a sequence of random variables such that $\delta^t = 0$ or $1$ and $\delta^t$ is measurable in the sigma-field generated by $X^1, ..., X^{t-1}$. Then

$$\text{Prob } \{\limsup (\sum_{t=1}^{T} \delta^t X^t) / (\sum_{t=1}^{T} \delta^t) \leqq \overline{U} \text{ or } \sum_{t=1}^{\infty} \delta^t < \infty\} = 1.$$

## REFERENCES

AKERLOFF, G. A. [1970]: "The market for "Lemons": quality, uncertainty and the market mechanism ", *Quarterly Journal of Economics*, 84 (August 1970), 488-500.

BEWLEY, T. [1977]: " The permanent income hypothesis: A theoretical formulation ", *Journal of Economic Theory*, 16, 252-292.

HOY, M. [1982]: " Categorizing risks in the insurance industry ", *Quarterly Journal of Economics*, 97 (May 1982), 321-337.

MIYAZAKI, H. [1977]: " The rate race and internal labor markets ", *Bell Journal of Economics*, 8 (Autumn 1977), 394-418.

RADNER, R. [1981]: "Monitoring cooperative agreements in a repeated principal-agent relationship ", *Econometrica*, 49 (September 1981), 1127-1148.

ROTHSCHILD, M., and STIGLITZ, J. [1976]: " Equilibrium in competitive insurance markets: An essay on the economics of imperfect information ", *Quarterly Journal of Economics*, (November 1976), 629-649.

RUBINSTEIN, A. [1979]: " An optimal conviction policy for offences that may have been committed by accident ", in *Applied Game Theory*, S. J. Brams, A. Schotter and G. Schwödianer (Ed.), Physica-Verlag, Wurzburg, 406-413.

RUBINSTEIN, A., and YAARI, M. E. [1980]: " Repeated insurance contracts and moral hazard ", Research Memorandum No. 37, Center for Research in Mathematical Economics and Game Theory, The Hebrew University.

SCHECHTMAN, J. [1976]: " An income fluctuation problem ", *Journal of Economic Theory*, 12, 218-241.

SPENCE, M. [1978]: " Product differentiation and performance in insurance markets ", *Journal of Public Economics*, 10, 427-447.

TOWNSEND, R. M. [1982]: "Optimal multiperiod contracts and the gain from enduring relationships under private information ", *Journal of Political Economy*, 90 (December 1982), 1166-1187.

WILSON, C. [1977]: " A model of insurance markets with incomplete information ", *Journal of Economic Theory*, 16, 167-207.

Journal of Public Economics 26 (1985) 269–288. North-Holland

# MARKET EQUILIBRIUM WITH PRIVATE KNOWLEDGE

## An insurance example

### Howard KUNREUTHER and Mark PAULY*

*The Wharton School, University of Pennsylvania, Philadelphia, PA 19104, USA*

Received August 1983, revised version received September 1984

## 1. Introduction

The effect of asymmetric information between buyers and sellers on product quality was first explored by Akerlof (1970) in his pathbreaking paper on the market for 'lemons'. He showed that if all purchasers have imperfect information on quality, then a market for the product may not exist, or if it does function it may not be efficient. These results have led to a number of papers concerning insurance and labor markets under different assumptions regarding how agents discriminate between 'products' of varying quality [see Pauly (1974), Rothschild and Stiglitz (1976), Wilson (1977), Miyasaki (1977), and Spence (1978)].

These treatments assume that all of the imperfectly informed agents have identical levels of knowledge of product quality. In contrast, this paper will consider situations where some agents learn over time about the quality of a particular good. However, this knowledge is private or agent-specific and may be costly for others to obtain. For example, firms may learn about the differential skills of their labor force by observing their productivity; other firms do not have easy access to this information. Insurance firms learn about the risk characteristics of their customers by observing claims records; they will not share these data costlessly with their competition.

We are interested in characterizing the nature of the market equilibrium when agents have such private knowledge on the endowed qualities of a good. Our analysis is undertaken in the context of insurance markets,

*The research in this paper is partially supported by the Bundesministerium für Forschung und Technologie, F.R.G., contract no. 321/7591/RGD 8001 and NSF grant 5-22669. While support for this work is gratefully acknowledged, the views expressed are the authors' own and are not necessarily shared by the sponsor. We are grateful to Zenan Fortuna and Serge Medow for computational assistance and to David Cummins, Michael Riordan and Peyton Young and the participants in the Conference on Regulation of the International Institute of Management, Berlin, July 1981, especially Jorg Finsinger and Paul Kleindorfer, for helpful comments and suggestions. An earlier version of this paper is included in the conference proceedings.

0047-2727/85/$3.30 © 1985, Elsevier Science Publishers B.V. (North-Holland)

although it is applicable to those situations where sellers cannot easily communicate their products' special qualities to prospective buyers even though the current purchasers have at least partially observed these features. In this sense the paper differs from the models developed by Jovanovich (1979), Harris and Townsend (1981) or Bigelow (1983), where information learned by one seller immediately becomes known to all others in the market.

The following problem is first analyzed in detail. Suppose that a set of cutomers has been with a specific insurance firm for $t$ years, during which time the firm has collected information on their claims experience. The insurer naturally will not make these data available to other firms, and customers are unable to furnish verified histories. Not having direct knowledge of each customer's risk class, the insurance firm utilizes claims data to set premiums. What is the schedule of profit-maximizing rates at which no customer will have an incentive to purchase insurance elsewhere in period $t+1$, given that the initial firm does not reveal its specialized information to other insurance firms?

In an insurance context, the assumption that agents keep information to themselves when it is advantageous to do so means that one insurer will not communicate to other firms any data that would help them identify good risks. Specifically, it will not communicate observed loss experience, the premium charges, or the quantity of insurance purchased by each customer. If firms keep this information private, then separating price–quantity policies proposed by Rothschild and Stiglitz (1976) are infeasible because other firms cannot know the quantity of insurance purchased by an individual either in the present period or in previous periods. In addition, the insurer himself will have difficulty determining the total quantity of insurance an individual has purchased because of the costs of monitoring these amounts.

For these reasons, we make Pauly's (1974) assumption that insurers sell 'price policies' rather than Rothschild–Stiglitz 'price–quantity policies'.[1] The models thus differ from those of Cooper and Hayes (1983) who assume that a 'new' insurer knows the total amount of coverage an individual currently has purchased, even though this firm is not aware of the quantity bought in the previous period.

We consider two polar cases with regard to the assumption made about firm behavior. In one case, we assume that the firm has *no foresight*, so that it sets prices to make non-negative expected profits in every period. In the other, we assume that the firm has *perfect foresight*, in the sense that it maximizes the present discounted value of the expected profit stream over the planning horizon.

We assume that consumers choose the firm making the most attractive offer in the current period. This assumption of myopic behavior on the part

[1] Hellwig (1983) also defends price policies for similar reasons.

of individuals is in the spirit of Strotz (1955) and is consistent with recent empirical evidence from controlled laboratory experiments and field surveys [Schoemaker (1982)]. In the context of insurance decisions, an analysis of field survey data by Kunreuther et al. (1978) revealed that insured individuals have limited knowledge of their premiums and coverage and tend to make purchase decisions by focusing on recent experiences rather than analyzing past history. These findings suggest that buyers examine insurance options by collecting information on next period's premium rather than considering the stream of premiums charged in the current and all future periods. It is thus not surprising that insurance firms normally quote a premium for next year without any commitment as to specific contingent rates in future years.

This assumption of myopic consumer behavior represents one polar case, with perfect consumer foresight models such as those of Dionne (1981), Radner (1981), and Rubinstein and Yaari (1980) at the other extreme. We refer to situations in which neither firm nor customers have foresight as *single-period equilibria*, since firms can change their price from one period to the next and consumers are free to stay or leave as they see fit. We refer to the situation in which firms maximize discounted expected profits but consumers choose only on the basis of current period premiums as *myopic multi-period equilibrium*.[2]

The paper is organized as follows. We first begin at the end, so to speak, by considering in section 2 a static model in which the firm currently selling insurance to individuals has perfect private knowledge about each person's risk class. We show how the premiums charged are nevertheless constrained by other insurance firms. Section 3 develops a model in which firms use information from the claims experience of the insured in a Bayesian fashion to adjust individual premiums to experience. We show that in the single-period equilibrium model, the resulting premium schedule yields positive expected profits and monopoly distortions even if entry by new firms into the market is completely free. Profit or rate regulation would be a natural remedy if reality approximated this equilibrium. We further consider briefly the impact on the single period equilibrium of permitting customers to buy verified information on their experience. This would include purchase of data on premium classification or claim records.

Section 4 shows that in a myopic multi-period equilibrium, expected profits are zero with free entry, but price distortions remain. Premiums are generally below expected costs in the early periods, but eventually rise to exceed expected costs. The concluding section suggests applications and extensions of the analysis.

---

[2]One of the purposes of experience rating is to cope with problems of moral hazard. This paper does not answer the question as to whether a premium adjustment process can eliminate or substantially reduce moral hazard. The paper also does not consider the possibility of requiring individuals to state their probability of loss and using experience to 'punish' those who misstate [cf. Radner (1981), Rubinstein and Yaari (1980)].

## 2. Market equilibrium with one fully informed firm

Our world consists of two types of consumers. Every consumer faces the possibility of an identical single loss $(X)$ which is correctly estimated and which is independently distributed across individuals. Each consumer of type $i$ has a probability of a loss $\Phi_i$, $i = H, L$ for the high- and low-risk group, respectively $(\Phi_H > \Phi_L)$. The consumers correctly perceive these values of $\Phi_i$. The proportion of high- and low-risk consumers in the population is given by $N_H$ and $N_L$, respectively. Type $i$'s preferences are represented by a von Neumann–Morgenstern utility function, $U_i$, and each consumer determines the optimal amount of insurance to purchase by maximizing expected utility $E(U_i)$. The insurance industry consists of $n$ firms, all of whom correctly estimate $X$ and the average probability of loss.

We initially assume that each consumer has been insured by the same firm for a sufficiently long period of time that the insurer has collected enough information through claim payments and other data to specify $\Phi_i$ exactly. The remaining $n-1$ firms in the industry *cannot* determine whether individuals insured by others are high- or low-risk people; an insured's past history does not become common knowledge.

If firms have information on the risk class of their clients they can charge differential premiums to high- and low-risk individuals; other firms in the industry are forced to charge the same premium to both groups because they cannot distinguish high risks from low risks. However, each firm does know how many periods the individual has been in the market, including whether he is a new customer.

### 2.1. Insurers' potential strategies

We now characterize the strategies available to insurers and consider the possibility of equilibrium. With regard to a particular client, it is useful to think of firms as either being 'informed', i.e. having sold a policy to an individual in the previous period, or 'uninformed', i.e. treating the client as a customer new to that firm. Of course, every firm who has been in business for more than one period will be 'informed' for some customers and 'uniformed' for others. Each informed insurer offers a per-unit premium, $P_i$, to all individuals in risk group $i$, without specifying the amount of coverage, $Q_i$, which an individual may purchase, except that $0 \le Q_i \le X$. Insurers who are not informed about a set of individuals charge the same price to all of them.

Consider first the situation of a representative uninformed firm. It knows that each consumer has the insurance demand curve:

$$Q_i^D = f(\Phi_i, P_i), \quad i = H, L, \tag{1}$$

which is derived from constrained utility maximization. Since there is only one event being insured against, the quantity of insurance is simply interpreted as the number of dollars the insured received when a loss occurs. The difference, if any, between the loss and the amount of coverage can therefore either be interpreted as coinsurance or as a deductible. More elaborate aspects of real-world insurance policies which cover many different loss states simultaneously would add complexities not associated with the informational asymmetries on which we wish to focus.

The simple form of the contract we examine is one which is conventional in the insurance equilibrium literature. Since the uninformed firm cannot distinguish among risks, it will have to set $P_H = P_L = P$. In a free-entry world with firms that maximize expected profit $E(\Pi)$, the breakeven premium $P^*$ for such uninformed firms would be given by the lowest value of $P$ such that

$$E(\Pi) = (P^* - \Phi_L)Q_L N_L + (P^* - \Phi_H)Q_H N_H = 0 \qquad (2)$$

where $Q_L$ is the total amount purchased by each L and $Q_H$ is the total amount purchased by each H at the uniform premium $P^*$. If equilibrium exists, the low-risk group will subsidize the high risk group and purchase partial coverage $Q_L < X$, while high-risk individuals will purchase full coverage, $Q_H = X$, at subsidized rates.[3]

The informed insurer can use his exact knowledge of each present customer's $\Phi_i$, $i = H, L$, to set rates tailored to each customer's experience. For high-risk individuals, the informed firm will never charge less than $\Phi_H$. For low-risk individuals, the rate it will charge will depend on the premium charged by uninformed firms. We assume that if each firm sets the same price, customers stay with their existing informed firm, given the transaction costs of switching insurers. Then the informed firm maximizes expected profits by charging low-risk individuals a price $P_L^l$ that is the same as the uniform price offered by the uninformed firm to all purchasers of insurance. The informed firm then attracts all low risks, sells each of them $Q_L$ units and makes profits of $(P_L^l - \Phi_L)Q_L^l$ per type L person.

If, for example, uninformed firms are charging $P^* + \delta$, the informed firm will want to charge its low-risk customers the lower of one of two rates. It will either charge $P^*$, or it will charge $\hat{P}_L$, the premium which would maximize profits on low-risk insureds if the firm were a monopolist. At the other extreme, if uninformed firms are charging $\Phi_H$ to everyone, then the informed firm will charge $\Phi_H$ or $\hat{P}_L$, whichever is less, thereby keeping its customers while maximizing expected profits.

But just as the informed firm's profit maximizing strategy depends on the strategies selected by uninformed firms, so does an uninformed firm's profit

[3]When the only value of $P$ which satisfies (2) is $P^* = \Phi_H$, then $Q_L = 0$, and the market will only provide coverage to high-risk individuals. This is a case of market failure due to adverse selection, since low-risk individuals cannot purchase insurance due to imperfect information by firms.

maximizing strategy with regard to a particular set of customers depend on what the informed firm is doing. The strategic combinations and payoffs are shown as the payoff matrix in fig. 1, with the upper expression in each labeled cell 1...4 being the payoff (profits) to the informed firm (I), and the lower expression the payoffs to the uninformed firm (U). When one type of firm obtains no business from this set of customers, a profit level of zero is entered. Here we are assuming that both $P^*$ and $\Phi_H$ are less than $\hat{P}_L$.[4]

| Uninformed Firm (U) <br><br> Informed Firm (I) | $P^U = P^* + \delta < \Phi_H$ | $P^U = \Phi_H$ |
|---|---|---|
| $P^I_L = P^*, P^I_H = \Phi_H$ | **1** $\quad N_L Q_L (P^* - \Phi_L) > 0$ <br><br> $N_H Q_H (P^* + \delta - \Phi_H) < 0$ | **2** $\quad N_L Q_L (P^* - \Phi_L) > 0$ <br><br> $0$ |
| $P^I_L = \Phi_H, P^I_H = \Phi_H$ | **3** $\quad 0$ <br><br> $(N_L Q_L + N_H Q_H)(P^* + \delta) - N_L Q_L \Phi_L -$ <br> $N_H Q_H \Phi_H > 0$ | **4** $\quad N_L Q_L (\Phi_H - \Phi_L) > 0$ <br><br> $0$ |

Fig. 1. Payoff matrix for informed and uninformed firms.

## 2.2. Existence of equilibrium

We will now show that there are no Nash equilibrium prices with both informed and uninformed firms. The argument is straightforward. If U (uninformed) firms choose $P^U = \Phi_H$, then I (informed) should choose $P^I_L = \Phi_H$ to maxmize profits (cell 4). But if I chooses $\Phi_H$, there exists some smaller $P^* + \delta$ at which U can make positive profits, while I gets no business and makes zero profit (cell 3). But if U charges some $P^* + \delta$, I should charge a little less (e.g. $P^*$). Then I makes positive profits, but U suffers a loss (cell 1). To prevent this loss, U must charge at least $\Phi_H$ (cell 2). But then I should charge $\Phi_H$, etc. If there are many players, the absence of a Nash equilibrium makes stability unlikely.[5]

What other concepts of equilibrium might apply here? If both parties followed maximin strategies, the outcome would be in cell 2, with the

---

[4]If $\hat{P}_L$ is less than $P^*$, then the informed firm will always charge $P^I_H = \Phi_H$ and $P^I_L = \hat{P}_L$ making positive profits. Uninformed firms will not obtain any business from this set of customers no matter what they do.

[5]Note that, from the viewpoint of a single uninformed firm, the maximum value that $\delta$ can take in cell 3 in fig. 1 depends on what the firm assumes that the other uninformed firms will do. If they continue playing strategy, $\Phi_H$, then the single uninformed firm can charge anything less than $\Phi_H$ and capture all the business with a large profit. If each uninformed firm assumes the other uninformed firms will match its prices, then profits will be lower.

strategy $\{P_L^I = P^*, P_H^I = \Phi_H\}$ for the informed firm, and $\{P^U = \Phi_H\}$ for the uninformed firm. In this cell, the uninformed firm is sure that it will not lose money (although it will not make profits either). The informed firm guarantees itself positive profits. Thus, in a single-play context, or with a small number of players, we might expect the outcome to be in cell 2.

Another possibility, already used in the literature on insurance markets and imperfect labor markets, is the concept of Wilson equilibrium.[6] A given set of actions is a Wilson equilibrium if no firm can alter its behavior (i.e. propose a different premium) that will (a) earn larger positive profits immediately, and (b) continue to be more profitable after other firms have dropped all policies rendered unprofitable by the initial firm's new behavior. Is the pair $\{P_L^I = P^*, \ P_H^I = \Phi_H\}$ and $\{P^U = \Phi_H\}$ a Wilson equilibrium? The alternative strategy for the informed firm is to set $\{P_L^I = \Phi_H, \ P_H^I = \Phi_H\}$. This earns it larger profits and does *not* cause the uninformed firms to lose money if they maintain their same policy as before. However, an informed firm's charging $\{P_L^I = \Phi_H, P_H^I = \Phi_H\}$ would permit uninformed firms to make positive profits by switching to $P^U = P^* + \delta$; this change reduces the informed firm's profit to zero. Thus, if we substitute the notion 'rendered less profitable' for 'rendered unprofitable' in part (b) of the above definition, then cell 2 does qualify as a Wilson equilibrium.

An alternative equilibrium concept which leads to the same conclusion is based on a Stackelberg leader–follower model. It seems reasonable to suppose that the (single) informed firm will play the leadership role. We will assume that the informed firm always sets $P_H^I = \Phi_H$. The reaction function for the uninformed firm is $P^U = f(P_L^I)$, and the informed firm therefore maximizes its expected profit $(\Pi^I)$:

$$\Pi^I = g(P_L^I, f(P_L^I)). \tag{3}$$

If the informed firm sets $P_L^I = P^*$, then $P^U = f(P_L^I) = \Phi_H$, and the informed firm makes positive profits of $Q_L(P^* - \Phi_L)$ on each type-L person. If the informed firm sets $P_L^I = \Phi_H$, then $P^U = f(P_L^I) = P^* + \delta$, and $\Pi^I$ is zero. Hence, maximization of (3) requires $P_L^I$ to be $P^*$, and the Stackelberg equilibrium is given by cell 2.

To summarize, there are two conclusions based on the above discussion:[7]
(1) no single-period equilibrium exists, or
(2) a single-period equilibrium is represented by $\{P_L^I = P^*, P_H^I = \Phi_H\}$ for informed firms, $\{P^U = \Phi_H\}$ for uninformed firms, with all business going to informed firms.

In what follows, we adopt the second conclusion by assuming that the

---

[6]It was proposed by Wilson (1977) and has been utilized by, among others, Miyasaki (1977), and Spence (1978), to characterize equilibrium.
[7]We have not considered the possibility of mixed strategies.

informed and uninformed firms behave in a Stackelberg fashion, with the informed firm as the leader and the uninformed firms as the followers. This equilibrium is also achieved if one assumes that either firm follows a policy that maximizes the minimum profit they could attain no matter what uninformed firms did, or that the modified definition of a Wilson equilibrium is appropriate.

### 2.3. Welfare effects

In the no-information case, the equilibrium premium is $P^*$ for both high and low risks. Compared to the no-information case, perfect private knowledge for just one firm leads generally to no gain in welfare for any insured person. All of the gains from information go to informed insurance firms as positive long-run profits. In the special case where low-risk individuals are charged the monopoly price (i.e. $P_L^* = \hat{P}_L$), the low-risk class benefits by the amount that the premium is below $P^*$. Even then, the higher risk consumers are made unequivocally worse off with perfect private knowledge, since the price they pay increases from $P^*$ to $\Phi_H$. Moreover, the positive profits being earned by informed firms are not eroded by entry, since new firms are by definition uninformed ones.

## 3. Informed firms: learning over time

### 3.1. Nature of equilibrium

We now turn to the more general case where firms learn over time about the characteristics of their customers through loss data. Initially each firm only knows from statistical records that the proportion of high- and low-risk individuals in the insured population is given by $N_H$ and $N_L$, respectively. It does not know whether an individual is in the H or L class but does know how many periods each potential customer has been in the market (e.g. all 20-year-old males are assumed to have been driving legally since age 18).[8] Any new customer would be offered a premium $P^*$, which is defined, as before, so that

$$E(\pi) = N_L(P^* - \Phi_L)Q_L + N_H(P^* - \Phi_H)Q_H = 0. \tag{4}$$

That is, the insurer prices so as to yield expected profits of zero on all new business.[9]

[8] In this sense, a firm can distinguish between new arrivals to the market and customers formerly insured by other firms.

[9] This seems to be the rule that actuaries are instructed to follow in an experience rating context. For example, the premium in any one year is supposed to be the previous year's

During each time period, we assume that an individual can suffer *at most* one loss, which will cause $X$ dollars damage. Any time a claims payment is made, this information is recorded on the insured's record and a new premium, which reflects his overall loss experience, is set for the next period. As before, we are assuming that informed firms do not disclose their records to other firms. Individuals who are dissatisfied with their new premium can seek insurance elsewhere. Other firms will not have access to the insured's record and hence cannot verify whether an applicant has had few or many losses under previous insurance contracts.

The informed firm uses a Bayesian updating process in readjusting its premium structure on the basis of its loss experience. Consider all customers who have been with the same insurance company for exactly $t$ periods. They can have anywhere from 0 to $t$ losses during this interval. The premium charged for period $t+1$ to individuals with $j$ losses during a $t$ period interval is $P^*_{jt}$, $j=0,\ldots,t$.[10] Firms with loss experience data will set each premium $P^*_{jt}$ so that they maximize expected profits, subject to the constraint that customers remain with them. Let $w^L_{00}$ and $w^H_{00}$ be the respective probabilities that an individual is in the low- and high-risk class when the firm initially insures him. We can update these probabilities by using Bayes' procedure. If a customer has suffered exactly $j$ losses in a $t$-period interval, then we define $w^i_{jt}$, $i=L,H$, as the probability that he is in the $i$th risk class, where $w^H_{jt} + w^L_{jt} = 1$.[11] The premium set for each loss classification will also be determined in part by the relative values of $w^i_{jt}$, $i=L,H$. As $j$ increases so does the probability that the individual is in the high-risk class. Hence, $w^H_{jt} > w^H_{j-1,t}$, $j=1,\ldots,t$.

Suppose, for example, an informed firm offers a set of premiums $\{P'_{jt}\}$, with $P'_{jt}$ increasing as $j$ increases.[12] An uninformed firm which charged a lower premium than $P'_{jt}$ in any period would attract all customers with $j$ or

---

premium plus a 'bonus' $G$, where $G$ is defined as:

$$G = k[(1+l)P - \xi], \quad G \geq 0,$$

and $P$ is the expected value of losses, $\xi$ is the actual amount of loss in the previous period, $l$ is the 'safety loading' (including normal profit) and $k$ is a fraction less than one. In the initial period when $G=0$, actuaries will recommend that the premium equal $(1+l)P$ [see Beard, Pentikainen and Pesonen (1979)].

[10] We are assuming that losses for an individual are independent of previous experience so the premium at the end of $t$ is determined only by the number of claims.

[11] We determine $w^i_{jt}$ as follows. Let $\lambda^i_{jt}$ = the probability that an individual experiences $j$ losses in $t$ periods, if he is in risk class $i$. Specifically,

$$\lambda^i_{jt} = \frac{t!}{(t-j)!j!}(\Phi_i)^j(1-\Phi_i)^{t-j}.$$

Using Bayes' formula:

$$w^i_{jt} = \frac{\lambda^i_{jt}N_i}{\sum_i \lambda^i_{jt}N_i}.$$

[12] We will show below that $P_{jt}$ increases as $j$ increases.

more losses.[13] The proportion of high and low customers in its portfolio would be given by

$$W^i_{jt} = \frac{\sum_{k=j}^{t} w^i_{kt} s_{kt}}{\sum_{k=j}^{t} s_{kt}},$$

where $s_{kt} = $ the probability of a person suffering exactly $k$ losses in a $t$-period interval. In other words, $W^i_{jt}$ is a weighted average over the loss range $j, \ldots, t$. Since $w^i_{jt}$ increases with $j$ we know that $W^H_{jt} > w^H_{jt}$ for all $j = 1, \ldots, t-1$ and $W^H_{tt} = w^H_{tt}$.

The minimum premium ($P''_{jt}$) at which expected profit equals zero for uninformed firms is given by

$$W^H_{jt}(P''_{jt} - \Phi_H)Q^H_{jt} + W^L_{jt}(P''_{jt} - \Phi_L)Q^L_{jt} = 0, \tag{5}$$

where $Q^i_{jt}$ is demand for group $i$ given a premium $P''_{ji}$. We know that $P''_{ji}$ increases with the number of losses $j$ since $Q^i_{jt}$ varies inversely with $P''_{jt}$ and $W^H_{jt}$ increases with $j$. Hence, any new firm which sets $P = P''_{jt}$ attracts only customers with $j$ or more losses and makes zero expected profits. So (5) correctly describes the minimum level of premiums that uninformed firms can charge.

If the informed firm sets $P_{jt} = P''_{jt}$ for *only* those customers who have suffered exactly $j$ losses, then these individuals will still prefer the informed firm. Its expected profits are given by

$$E(\Pi_{jt}) = w^H_{jt}(P''_{jt} - \Phi_H)Q_H + w^L_{jt}(P''_{jt} - \Phi_L)Q_L \geq 0. \tag{6}$$

Expected profits in (6) are thus positive for $j = 1, \ldots, t-1$ since $w^H_{jt}$ is less than $W^H_{jt}$. For $j = t$, expected profits by definition are zero since $w^i_{tt} = W^i_{tt}$.

To determine the premium structure, an informed firm will also have to find the monopoly premiums $\{\hat{P}_{jt}\}$ for each $j = 0, \ldots, t$, which maximize $E(\Pi_{jt})$. It will maximize expected profits for each loss category if it then sets premiums ($P^*_{jt}$) as follows:

$$P^*_{jt} = \min\{P''_{jt}, \hat{P}_{jt}\}, \quad j = 0, \ldots, t.$$

The structure of the premiums is thus similar to that in the case of perfect private knowledge outlined above; profits will be lower because firms must now use claims information to categorize their customers and hence will

---

[13]We are assuming no transaction costs for insured individuals to switch firms.

misclassify some of them. Aggregate expected profits for each period $t$ are given by

$$E(\Pi_t) = \sum_{j=0}^{t} s_{jt} E(\Pi_{jt}). \tag{7}$$

### 3.2. An illustrative example

A two-period example using a specific utility function will help to illustrate the meaning of learning from loss experience. The appendix describes the basic form of this problem for the exponential utility function $U(y) = -e^{-cy}$. Consider the specific case where $\Phi_H = 0.3$, $\Phi_L = 0.1$, $X = 40$, $c = 0.04$, and $N_L = N_H = 0.5$. Then the equilibrium premium in the first period, obtained by solving eq. (4), would be $P^* = 0.254$. Table 1 illustrates how one calculates the weights for determining the optimal premium structure at the end of period 1 when $j = 0$ $or$ 1, and fig. 2 details the optimal rate structure at the end of period 1.

Table 1
Calculation of weights $w_{j1}^i$ and $W_{j1}^i$, $i = L, H$, for two-period model.

| $\Phi_L = 0.1$ | $\Phi_H = 0.3$ | $X = 40$ | $c = 0.04$ | $N_H = N_L = 0.5$ | |
|---|---|---|---|---|---|
| $j$ | $s_{ji}$ | $w_{j1}^H$ | $w_{j1}^L$ | $W_{j1}^H$ | $W_{j1}^L$ |
| 0 | 0.5 | 0.4375 | 0.5625 | 0.5 | 0.5 |
| 1 | 0.2 | 0.75 | 0.25 | 0.75 | 0.25 |

$$s_{01} = (1 - \Phi_H)N_H + (1 - \Phi_L)N_L$$

$$s_{11} = \Phi_H N_H + \Phi_L N_L$$

$$i = L, H \begin{cases} w_{01}^i = \dfrac{(1 - \Phi_i)N_i}{s_{01}} \\[2ex] w_{11}^i = \dfrac{\Phi_i N_i}{s_{11}} \\[2ex] W_{01}^i = \dfrac{\sum_{k=0}^{1} w_{k1}^i s_{k1}}{\sum_{k=0}^{1} s_{k1}} \\[2ex] W_{11}^i = w_{11}^i \end{cases}$$

The optimal premiums are $P_{01}^* = 0.254$ and $P_{11}^* = 0.288$ since $\hat{P}_{01} = \hat{P}_{11} = 0.495$. The premium charged to the group suffering one loss ($P_{11}^*$), yields $E(\Pi_{11}) = 0$ since $P_{11}^* = P_{11}''$, and $w_{11}^H = W_{11}^H$. Expected profits for the 'zero

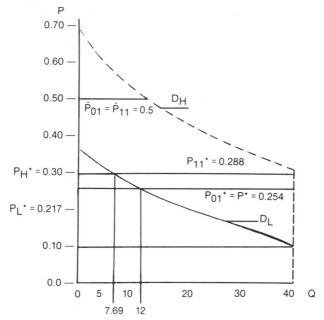

Fig. 2. A two-period example based on loss experience.

loss' class is given by (6) and is

$$E(\Pi_{01}) = 0.5625(0.254 - 0.10)12 + 0.4375(0.254 - 0.30)40 = 0.23.$$

Aggregate expected profits for period 1 are given by (7) and in this case are $E(\Pi_1) = 0.8(0.23) = 0.18$.

What effect does experience rating have on consumer well-being in this example? In the absence of any information, both high and low risks would have been charged 0.254 in each of the two periods. When information is obtained through experience, those individuals with no losses are charged the same rate as initially, 0.254. Since uninformed firms will never charge a premium less than this rate, those with one loss are charged 0.288. Thus, both high- and low-risk customers are made either no better off or worse off if firms can generate information. All gains go to the firm in the form of higher profits. In contrast, if the firm would have charged breakeven prices, its premium would have been 0.237 to individuals with zero losses.

As a customer's life with the company increases, then he faces a larger number of rate classes reflecting possible outcomes. Firms make the largest profit on those insured individuals who experience the fewest losses. In the limit as $t \to \infty$, all customers will be accurately classified and we have the case of perfect private knowledge. Fig. 3 graphically depicts how aggregate expected profit changes over time as a function of the proportion of low-risk customers in the population. As $N_L$ decreases, then the informed firm's profit potential decreases since a larger proportion of individuals will suffer losses.

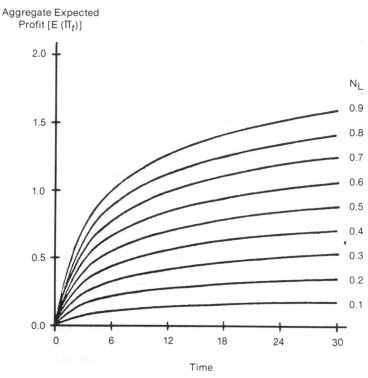

Fig. 3. Aggregate expected profits $[E(\Pi_t)]$ as a function of proportion of low-risk customers $(N_L)$ and time $(t)$.

### 3.3. Obtaining verified information

The problem in achieving optimality arises, of course, because informed firms — the ones from which the consumer is currently purchasing — price so as to obtain positive long-run expected profits. A natural response of low-risk consumers facing such a situation is to seek some way of providing reliable information on their status to other insurance firms. There are three ways in which such data might be disseminated: (1) consumers might provide verified information on their actual number of losses (claims); (2) consumers might provide verified information on the size of their premium bill for a given level of insurance, since this is a perfect indicator of the risk class into which they are being placed by their current insurer; and/or (3) consumers might provide information on the total amount of insurance bought, since a higher quantity would indicate a lower price was charged.

We would expect that consumers will find it difficult and costly to undertake any of these actions. For one thing, the current insurer has an incentive to conceal its claims and premium data. For another thing, purchasers of insurance who have had unfavorable loss experiences may also try to represent themselves as being a better risk by using techniques such as bogus invoices, or applying for insurance right after an accident but before a new bill is issued. Note that the informed firm will not discourage these actions, because such behavior makes it more difficult for customers with good experience to communicate their status reliably.

The cost of providing reliable information by insured individuals will still permit the original insurer to earn some positive profits and the above models would still be relevant in determining what rate structure could be set by informed firms. One could formally incorporate the costs of communicating verified information into a more general model of the choice processes of insurers and insured. Profits would then be limited by the alternatives available to consumers for purchasing verified information.

## 4. A myopic multi-period model

We now investigate the consequences of changing the assumption that there is no insurer foresight. We consider a model in which firms look beyond current period losses to potential future profits. Firms are therefore assumed to be concerned with the present discounted value of the profit stream they expect to earn. But purchasers are still assumed to be myopic, in the sense that they choose which insurer to patronize by looking only at current period prices and selecting the firm with the lowest current premium. If the firm is willing to tolerate negative expected profits for a while in order to attract customers and observe their claims experiences, it can then use this information to make positive expected profits in the future to offset (in present value terms) the initial losses.

It is easy to see that the 'single-period' premium schedule $\{P_{jt}^*\}$ may then not be an equilibrium. On the one hand, a firm that charged less than $P_{00}^*$ in the initial period would have an expected loss in that period; on the other hand, it would have the opportunity to observe which individuals did and did not have losses during that period. If it used that information to charge the schedule $P_{jt}^*$ in subsequent periods, the present discounted value of the profit stream associated with this pricing policy could be sufficient to offset the initial expected losses. Hence, a new schedule, with the lower $P_{00}$, would dominate the single-period equilibrium schedule.

What new set of premiums would represent an equilibrium schedule? It would be one where, for all $t$ and $j$, there would be no opportunity for a

438

previously uninformed firm to enter and earn positive expected profits. Below we provide an example of one type of premium schedule which satisfied those conditions, although the existence and uniqueness of such an equilibrium remain to be proved.

To simplify the explanation of how such a schedule is derived, assume an interest rate of zero, so as not to be concerned with discounting. Suppose the firm which has attracted a customer in period $k$ wants to set its premiums for all future periods up to the end of the planning horizon $T$ so that no firm entering the market in later periods can attract any set of its customers and make a stream of profits whose sum is positive. That is, it wants to set $P''_{jt}$ so that

$$E(\pi^{**}_{jt}) = \sum_{k=t}^{T} [w^L_{jk}(P^{**}_{jk} - \Phi_L)Q^L_{jk} + w^H_{jk}(P^{**}_{jk} - \Phi_H)Q^H_{jk}] = 0,$$

for all $j$. Here $P^{**}_{jt}$ is also the price that the new entrant would charge.[14]

The procedure in constructing such a set of premiums $\{P^{**}_{jt}\}$ requires one to start at period $T$ and work backwards. Any uninformed firm who enters the market at the beginning of period $T$ must break even, because there is by definition no future period in which losses can be recouped. Hence, $P^{**}_{jT} = P^*_{jT}$ for all $j$. Now consider period $T-1$. If a firm entered in this period it could observe the experience of its customers for one period and make profits on all those individuals who did not have a loss during this period.

The expected profits in period $T$ are derived using the same type of Bayesian updating procedure described in section 3. In order to prevent new entrants from coming into the market in period $T-1$, the informed firm must set its premium in period $T-1$ sufficiently low so that a potential new entrant would suffer a loss just a little larger than the profit he would earn in period $T$. As in the single-period equilibrium model, there will be a different premium for each value of $j$. This set of policies $\{P^{**}_{j,T-1}\}$ would then be the equilibrium schedule for the fully informed firm.

The same type of reasoning is utilized to compute the equilibrium set of premiums for period $T-2$. In this case a potential entrant who attracts customers can make profits in period $T-1$ and $T$ by utilizing claims information on their insured population. The informed firm will then have to set $\{P^{**}_{t,T-2}\}$ at levels which erase all these potential profits of a new firm. The same process is repeated sequentially for all periods through $t=0$.

To illustrate the differences between resulting premiums in the single-period equilibrium and myopic multi-period equilibrium cases we consider an example with $T=5$. Table 2 compares the set of premiums and expected

---

[14]We will assume that purchasers buy all of their insurance from a single firm. Alternatively, we could have assumed that each firm receives a constant share of an insured's business in every period, and that all firms are aware of this fact.

Table 2

Comparison between premiums and expected profits for single-period equilibrium and myopic multi-period equilibrium schedule for five-period problem.

(a) Single-period equilibrium

| Number of losses $j$ | | Period $t$ | | | | | |
|---|---|---|---|---|---|---|---|
| | | 0 | 1 | 2 | 3 | 4 | 5 |
| 0 | $P^*_{0t}$ | 0.254 | 0.254 | 0.254 | 0.254 | 0.254 | 0.254 |
| | $E(\pi^*_{0t})$ | 0 | 0.18 | 0.30 | 0.36 | 0.39 | 0.39 |
| 1 | $P^*_{1t}$ | | 0.288 | 0.286 | 0.285 | 0.283 | 0.281 |
| | $E(\pi^*_{1t})$ | | 0 | 0.02 | 0.04 | 0.08 | 0.12 |
| 2 | $P^*_{2t}$ | | | 0.296 | 0.296 | 0.295 | 0.294 |
| | $E(\pi^*_{2t})$ | | | 0 | 0.00 | 0.01 | 0.01 |
| 3 | $P^*_{3t}$ | | | | 0.299 | 0.299 | 0.298 |
| | $E(\pi^*_{3t})$ | | | | 0 | 0.00 | 0.00 |
| 4 | $P^*_{4t}$ | | | | | 0.30 | 0.30 |
| | $E(\pi^*_{4t})$ | | | | | 0.00 | 0.00 |
| 5 | $P^*_{5t}$ | | | | | | 0.30 |
| | $E(\pi^*_{5t})$ | | | | | | 0 |
| $E(\pi^*_t)$ | | 0 | 0.18 | 0.32 | 0.40 | 0.48 | 0.52 |

(b) Myopic multi-period equilibrium

| Number of losses $j$ | | Period $t$ | | | | | |
|---|---|---|---|---|---|---|---|
| | | 0 | 1 | 2 | 3 | 4 | 5 |
| 0 | $P^{**}_{0t}$ | 0.191 | 0.225 | 0.245 | 0.252 | 0.254 | 0.254 |
| | $E(\pi^{**}_{0t})$ | $-1.21$ | $-0.15$ | 0.24 | 0.35 | 0.38 | 0.39 |
| 1 | $P^{**}_{1t}$ | | 0.250 | 0.280 | 0.284 | 0.283 | 0.281 |
| | $E(\pi^{**}_{1t})$ | | $-0.21$ | $-0.03$ | 0.04 | 0.08 | 0.12 |
| 2 | $P^{**}_{2t}$ | | | 0.286 | 0.295 | 0.295 | 0.294 |
| | $E(\pi^{**}_{2t})$ | | | $-0.02$ | $-0.00$ | 0.01 | 0.01 |
| 3 | $P^{**}_{3t}$ | | | | 0.299 | 0.299 | 0.298 |
| | $E(\pi^{**}_{3t})$ | | | | 0.00 | 0.00 | 0.00 |
| 4 | $P^{**}_{4t}$ | | | | | 0.30 | 0.30 |
| | $E(\pi^{**}_{4t})$ | | | | | 0.00 | 0.00 |
| 5 | $P^{**}_{5t}$ | | | | | | 0.30 |
| | $E(\pi^{**}_{5t})$ | | | | | | 0 |
| $E(\pi^{**}_t)$ | | $-1.21$ | $-0.36$ | 0.19 | 0.39 | 0.47 | 0.52 |

profits for the two models. In the single-period equilibrium model the informed firm's premium ($P^*_{00}$) starts off equal to the average actuarial value ($P^* = 0.254$) and increases above this level for customers who experience losses. In the myopic case, the initial premium, $P^{**}_{00}$, is less than $P^*$, and increases over time whether or not the person suffers a loss.[15] As $t$ approaches $T$, the premiums for the two types of equilibria converge, as expected. In the single-period case the stream of profits is positive, in all periods; in the multi-period myopic case the firm suffers losses in the early periods recouping them in later periods so that the expected stream of profits is zero.

Note that there are striking contrasts between this result and that from the Cooper–Hayes (1983) model. In that model, firms earn profits in the initial period, which are then offset in the second period. In our model, firms suffer losses in the first period in exchange for private knowledge about risk levels. These losses are then offset with profits generated by the income in subsequent periods. We conjecture that this premium stream will be a stable equilibrium because myopic consumers are attracted by lower prices in any given period. Given the zero long-run expected profit constraint, the process has to begin with a set of below-cost premiums. These differential predictions about the time paths of profits might furnish an empirical test for distinguishing between the two classes of models for different types of problems.

Table 2 reveals that there can be a perversity and allocative inefficiency in the multi-period myopic case. Consumers are undercharged in the early periods but will find that their premiums are raised even if they are accident free. Persons nearing the end of their risk horizons (e.g. the aged who will only be driving for a few more years) will tend to be overcharged for insurance, whereas the young will tend to be undercharged. Hence, consumers will tend to overpurchase insurance in the early periods, and underpurchase insurance in the later periods. If regulation could be used to bring premiums closer to the actuarial values, there would be a welfare gain.

## 5. Conclusions and extensions

Our results have some important implications for the notion that development of 'reputations' for quality can over time alleviate the problem of agent ignorance [Akerlof (1970)]. In both of our models there is an incentive to keep information about quality private, even if the explicit cost of communicating it to others is low. In our first model, the agent with private knowledge loses monopoly rents by communicating this information to

---

[15]It is theoretically possible for consumers initially to be charged a negative premium to attract them to the insurance company so that they could be charged higher premiums as $t$ increases. In this case, individuals could be given a free gift for taking out insurance, in an analogous fashion to the approach used by savings banks to attract new accounts.

others. In the second model he earns no rents in the long run; however, he would impose losses on himself if he initially followed the loss-leader strategy but then communicated the information he had gained from claims experience before he had time to recoup his losses. Conversely, even if he 'promised' in the initial period to communicate the truth, he would always gain from concealing or corrupting information which identifies the good (high quality) risks. These disincentives to communicate reliable information are greater if the item being transacted is bought in lumpy amounts, as in the case of a worker's services; the employer who learns which of his employees are of higher productivity will be downright reluctant to communicate that knowledge to other potential employers.

While 'friends and neighbors' do sometimes communicate infomation about product quality (good restaurants, good doctors) and while employers do write letters of reference for good employees, our models suggest that such behavior is not likely to occur in all circumstances. Even where concealing private information ends up benefiting none and harming all, it will still be difficult for the market to break away from such an equilibrium.

The most obvious extensions of these models is to permit consumers to be less myopic. If consumers do have foresight, then they may want the insurer to agree in the initial (purchase) time period to provide accurate information on future loss experience.

Guaranteeing that such information is provided is not easy, of course, since the low risk must not only ensure that accurate information of his own experience is provided but also that accurate (unfavorable) information is provided on the experience of those high risks who are thinking of switching to another firm. That is, he must monitor the accuracy of all information provided. For example, in a labor market application of our theory, a high productivity worker must not only verify that his employer will provide him with a good and true recommendation; he must also verify that poorer quality workers are being furnished bad recommendations or references.

If the worker has foresight, it is easy to see that he will be concerned, in the initial period, with the *schedule* by which his future premiums will be adjusted as a result of his future experience. Different risk types might be expected to select different schedules and Dionne's work (1981) shows that it is possible in a monopoly context to find schedules which separate these groups ex ante when each risk type chooses the schedule which maximizes its utility. But as Dionne remarks, it is not obvious that these schedules will be sustainable if persons with unfavorable experience can switch from firm to firm without being compelled to provide a valid history of their experience. That is to say, if a high risk's history does not necessarily 'follow' him from firm to firm, optimal equilibrium may not be sustainable. These concerns suggest that even if the consumer had perfect foresight, there may not be any

442

legitimate way for firms to make credible long-run commitments. In this case, the model developed in this paper may be appropriate even if the consumer is not myopic.

There needs to be further development of the theory for such consumer-foresight models. At the same time, there needs to be further empirical verification of the degree of foresight individuals actually display. Do purchasers of automobile insurance know and fully take account of the way their premiums will vary with their claims history? Do workers know and take into account the way their future wages will vary with observed productivity? If consumers display only limited foresight, the models of market equilibrium developed in this paper will be appropriate.

### Appendix[16]

Risk-averse consumers of each type $i$ with wealth $A_i$ want to choose a value of $Q_i$ given $\Phi_i$ and $P_i$ which maximizes:

$$\mathrm{E}[U_i(Q_i)] = \Phi_i U_i[A_i - X + (1 - P_i)Q_i] + (1 - \Phi_i)U_i(A_i - P_iQ_i) \quad \text{(A.1)}$$

subject to

$$0 \leq Q_i \leq X.$$

Let $R_i$ be the contingency price ratio

$$R_i = \frac{P_i(1 - \Phi_i)}{(1 - P_i)\Phi_i},$$

and define $R_i^{\max}$ and $R_i^{\min}$ as the values of $R_i$ where $Q_i = 0$ and $Q_i = X$, respectively, when one maximizes $\mathrm{E}[U_i(Q_i)]$ without any constraint on $Q_i$.

Then if

$$U_i' = \frac{\mathrm{d}U_i}{\mathrm{d}Q_i} > 0 \quad \text{and} \quad U_i'' = \frac{\mathrm{d}^2 U_i}{\mathrm{d}Q_i^2} < 0,$$

the optimal solution to (A.1) is given by:

$$Q_i = 0 \qquad\qquad\qquad \text{if } R_i \geq R_i^{\max},$$

$$R_i = \frac{U_i'(A_i - P_iQ_i)}{U_i'(A_i - X + (1 - P_i)Q_i)} \quad \text{if } R_i^{\min} < R_i < R_i^{\max},$$

$$Q_i = X \qquad\qquad\qquad \text{if } R_i \leq R_i^{\min}.$$

[16]A more detailed discussion of this model appears in Kunreuther (1976).

Whenever $P_i \leqq \Phi_i$, then $Q_i = X$, since in this range the premium is either actuarially fair or subsidized. Suppose both consumer types have identical utility functions given by the exponential $U_H(Y) = U_L(Y) = -e^{-cY}$, where $c$ is the risk aversion coefficient. Then $Q_i$ is determined by

$$Q_i = 0 \qquad \text{if } (\ln R_i) \geqq cX,$$

$$Q_i = X - (\ln R_i)/c \quad \text{if } e^{cX} > R_i > 1,$$

$$Q_i = X \qquad \text{if } R_i \leqq 1.$$

## References

Akerlof, G., 1970, The market for lemons: Quality uncertainty and the market mechanisms, Quarterly Journal of Economics 84, 488–500.

Beard, R., T. Pentikainen and E. Pesonsen, 1979, Risk theory, 2nd edn. (Chapman and Hall, London) section 5.8.

Bigelow, J., 1983, Learning, experience rating and adverse selection, ISPS Working Paper No. 1001, Yale University.

Cooper, R. and B. Hayes, 1983, Multiperiod insurance contracts, Presented at the Econometric Society Winter Meetings.

Dionne, G., 1981, Adverse selection and repeated insurance contracts, Cahier 8/39, Departement de Science Economique, Universite de Montreal, July.

Harris, M. and R. Townsend, 1981, Resource allocation under asymmetric information, Econometrica 49, 33–64.

Hellwig, M., 1983, On moral hazard and non-price equilibrium in competitive insurance markets, Discussion Paper 109, Institut fur Gesellschafts und Wirtschaftswissenschaften, University of Bonn, May.

Jovanovich, B., 1979, Job matching and the theory of turnover, Journal of Political Economy 87, 972–990.

Kunreuther, H., 1976, Limited knowledge and insurance protection, Public Policy 24, 227–261.

Kunreuther, H. et al., 1978, Disaster Insurance Protection (Wiley, New York).

Miyasaki, H., 1977, The rat race and internal labor markets, The Bell Journal of Economics 8, 394–418.

Pauly, M., 1974, Over insurance and public provision of insurance: The roles of moral hazard and adverse selection, Quarterly Journal of Economics 88, 44–62.

Radner, R., 1981, Monitoring cooperative agreements in a repeated principal–agent relationship, Econometrica 49, 1127–1149.

Rothschild, M. and J. Stiglitz, 1976, Equilibrium in competitive insurance markets: An essay in the economics of imperfect information, Quarterly Journal of Economics 90, 629–649.

Rubinstein, A. and M.E. Yaari, 1980, Repeated insurance contracts and moral hazard, Research Memorandum no. 37, Center for Research in Mathematical Economics and Game Theory, The Hebrew University, Jerusalem.

Schoemaker, P., 1982, The expected utility model: Its variants, purposes, evidence and limitations, Journal of Economic Literature 20, 529–563.

Spence, M., 1978, Product differentiation and consumer choice in insurance markets, Journal of Public Economics 10, 427–447.

Strotz, R., 1955, Myopia and inconsistency in dynamic utility maximization, The Review of Economic Studies 23, 165–180.

Wilson, C., 1977, A model of insurance markets with incomplete information, Journal of Economic Theory 16, 167–207.

# The Efficiency Effects of Categorical Discrimination in the Insurance Industry

Keith J. Crocker

*University of Virginia*

Arthur Snow

*Georgetown University*

Recent public policy debate has focused concern on the equity dimensions of categorical discrimination based on sex, age, or race in insurance and similar markets. We consider the efficiency effects of such discrimination and establish that costless imperfect categorization always enhances efficiency. When categorization entails a nonnegligible resource cost, however, no unambiguous efficiency ranking of informational regimes is possible. When categorization is costless, we demonstrate that government, having no better information than market participants, can effect redistribution without assuming dictatorial control of the market, implying that a market equilibrium with costless categorization is potentially Pareto superior to one without it. When categorization is costly, however, the market may categorize when Pareto improvements are not possible.

## I. Introduction

Although many economists have examined risk categorization by insurance firms, the efficiency effects of such categorical discrimination remain unclear. Schmalensee (1984, p. 442) has observed that there is "no general theorem establishing that making information *better* [costlessly] always enhances efficiency in [the insurance market] con-

We gratefully acknowledge the helpful comments and suggestions of an anonymous referee of this *Journal*.

[*Journal of Political Economy*, 1986, vol. 94, no. 2]

text."[1] This paper provides such a theorem. We show that the utilities possibilities frontier for a regime with costless but imperfect categorization lies partly outside and nowhere inside the frontier without categorization. With respect to the introduction of costly information, our conclusions are mixed. When information entails a resource cost, the utilities possibilities frontiers necessarily "cross" so that no unambiguous efficiency ranking of the information regimes is possible.

To demonstrate these results, we use hypothetical compensation tests to compare the informational regimes and to determine whether the gainers from categorization are potentially able to compensate the losers. Our approach contrasts with Schmalensee's assertion that an informational asymmetry "rules out [such] compensation even in principle" (1984, p. 442), rendering inapplicable this standard tool of normative economic analysis. The conjecture is false. We show that risk-discriminating wealth transfers and, hence, hypothetical compensation are possible and could be implemented by a government having no better information about agents' risk than the market participants. Thus a rigorous efficiency-based evaluation of risk categorization is possible.

Our results have implications for the regulation of insurance and similar markets. Concern for equity has led to the suggestion that certain types of costless categorization, such as that based on sex, age, or race, should not be allowed in insurance and pension funds.[2] Our analysis indicates that, if these attributes are (at least imperfectly) correlated with risk and are observable at little or no resource cost, then a ban on such categorization would be unambiguously inefficient. Alternatively, if the resource cost of categorization is nontrivial, as in the case where accident or health records are available but only at finite cost, competitive pressures may force firms to categorize even when the gainers from categorization would be unable in principle to compensate the losers. In this sense a ban on certain types of costly categorization may be efficient.

The paper proceeds as follows. Section II sets out the basic model and characterizes the utilities possibilities frontier in an information-

---

[1] Other authors such as Dahlby (1980) and Hoy (1982) have found the welfare effects of introducing costless categorization to be ambiguous: there could be winners as well as losers.

[2] See, e.g., the Supreme Court rulings in Arizona Governing Committee for Tax Deferred Annuity and Deferred Compensation Plans, etc., et al., Petitioners v. Nathalie Norris, etc., 459 U.S. 904, and City of Los Angeles Department of Water and Power et al. v. Manhart et al., 435 U.S. 702, which disallowed categorization on the basis of sex in pension funds. For a discussion of the legal issues, see Brilmayer et al. (1980). Also, Dahlby (1983) notes that some Canadian provinces have moved to eliminate statistical discrimination in auto insurance based on sex, age, marital status, or geographic location.

ally constrained environment when insurance firms are not allowed to categorize.[3] Section III introduces costless and costly categorization and compares the resulting utilities possibilities frontiers with those of the no-categorization regime. Although any utility position on the utilities possibilities frontier can be attained by dictatorial fiat, no inferences can be made about the efficiency of *market equilibria* in the different informational regimes since there is no general analogue to the First Optimality Theorem for informationally constrained environments.[4] In Section IV we demonstrate that, when categorization is costless, there exists a balanced budget tax system, implementable by a government having no better information than market participants, that allows a categorization equilibrium to be attained that is Pareto superior to equilibrium in the no-categorization regime. Since this result holds for any of the received definitions of market equilibrium, we conclude that any market equilibrium with costless categorization is potentially Pareto superior to the corresponding equilibrium when categorization is disallowed. Finally, we demonstrate by a counterexample that, when categorization entails a significant resource cost, the market may categorize even when the categorization equilibrium is *not* a potential Pareto improvement over the equilibrium without categorization. We conclude that, when information is costly, the market can be an inefficient mechanism for allocating resources to the acquisition of information.

## II. Efficient Allocations without Risk Categorization

The insurance market is represented in the manner first introduced by Rothschild and Stiglitz (1976). There is assumed to be a continuum of risk-averse consumers each of whom has the von Neumann–Morgenstern utility function $U(W_i)$, where $W_i$ is the consumer's wealth in the loss ($i = 2$) or no-loss ($i = 1$) state. A consumer's expected utility, given the contingent wealth $W = (W_1, W_2)$ and probability of loss $p$, is

$$V(p, W) = (1 - p)U(W_1) + pU(W_2). \tag{1}$$

---

[3] The utility possibilities frontier consists of the utility positions associated with allocations that are second-best efficient given the constraints on exchange imposed by the informational asymmetry. The concept of efficiency we use was first developed by Harris and Townsend (1981) and is termed "interim incentive efficiency" by Holmström and Myerson (1983).

[4] That market equilibria are not generally efficient is shown in Crocker and Snow (1985a). Thus knowledge that the efficiency frontier shifts outward provides no information about the relative efficiency of market equilibria.

Consumers are identical except that some risk the loss with high probability $p^H < 1$ whereas others have a lower, but positive, probability of loss $p^L$ $(< p^H)$. Each consumer knows only his own probability of loss, although everyone knows the proportion of high risks in the population, which is denoted by $\lambda \in (0, 1)$.

The economy is endowed with the per capita wealth $\overline{W}$. Since, by assumption, consumers' risks are independent and all consumers are subject to the same loss $d$, the economy's per capita real wealth endowment is $\overline{W} - \overline{p}d$, where $\overline{p} = \lambda p^H + (1 - \lambda)p^L$ is the average probability of loss. The resource cost of allocating the contingent wealth $W$ to a consumer with loss probability $p$ is

$$\rho(p, W) = (1 - p)W_1 + p(W_2 + d) \tag{2}$$

since the loss $d$ must be covered if the consumer is to receive $W_2$ net of loss.

An allocation $(W^H, W^L)$ is a specification of a contingent wealth position for the members of each risk class. The per capita resource cost associated with an allocation is given by[5]

$$R(W^H, W^L; \lambda) = \lambda\rho(p^H, W^H) + (1 - \lambda)\rho(p^L, W^L).$$

To be attainable, an allocation must meet the resource constraint

$$R(W^H, W^L; \lambda) - \overline{W} = 0 \tag{3}$$

and, because of the informational asymmetry, must also satisfy the self-selection conditions[6]

$$V(p^i, W^i) \geq V(p^i, W^j) \quad \text{for } i, j \in \{H, L\}. \tag{4}$$

The latter require that each consumer prefer (at least weakly) the contingent wealth assigned to his risk class. The class of efficient allocations can be characterized by solving the following welfare problem:

$$\max_{(W^H, W^L)} V(p^L, W^L) \tag{PE}$$

[5] In specifying a nonstochastic resource constraint we are assuming that a law of large numbers holds so that there is no aggregate risk. Feldman and Gilles (1985) and Judd (1985) discuss the technical difficulties that must be dealt with and alternative assumptions that are sufficient to ensure the applicability of a law of large numbers in models with a continuum of agents.

[6] This constraint on exchange necessitated by the informational asymmetry was introduced by Myerson (1979) and Harris and Townsend (1981). Although Holmström and Myerson (1983) have suggested several alternative efficiency concepts for informationally constrained environments, the nature of the insurance market indicates the appropriate concept in this environment to be that of interim incentive efficiency. This follows since insurance is purchased by agents who know their own risk, which is inherently unobservable to all other agents in the economy. For a more complete discussion, see Holmström and Myerson (1983, p. 1807).

subject to (3), (4), and a constraint on the welfare of $H$-risk consumers:

$$V(p^H, W^H) \geq \overline{V}^H. \tag{5}$$

The following theorem, which is proved in the Appendix, gives the necessary conditions for a solution to problem PE.[7] Since we introduce categorization in the next section, we shall refer to allocations satisfying the conditions set out in theorem 1 as being efficient relative to the no-categorization (NC) regime.

THEOREM 1. A solution to PE satisfies the following conditions:

$$W_1^H = W_2^H; \tag{a}$$

$$V(p^H, W^H) = V(p^H, W^L); \tag{b}$$

$$\frac{(1 - p^L)U'(W_1^L)}{p^L U'(W_2^L)} \tag{c}$$

$$= \frac{\lambda(1 - p^H)U'(W_1^L) + (1 - \lambda)(1 - p^L)U'(W_2^H)[1 + (\delta/\mu_H)]}{\lambda p^H U'(W_2^L) + (1 - \lambda)p^L U'(W_2^H)[1 + (\delta/\mu_H)]},$$

where $\mu_H$ and $\delta$ are the Lagrange multipliers associated with constraints (4) for $i = H$ and (5), respectively, and $V(p^H, W^H) = \overline{V}^H$ if $\delta \neq 0$; and

$$R(W^H, W^L; \lambda) = \overline{W}. \tag{d}$$

The conditions given in the theorem are illustrated in figure 1. Condition $a$ states that $W^H$ provides full insurance, so $W^H$ is located on the 45-degree line, and condition $b$ states that $H$-risks are indifferent between $W^H$ and $W^L$. The point $F = (\overline{W} - \overline{p}d, \overline{W} - \overline{p}d)$ represents the equal per capita full insurance wealth allocation in which each consumer receives $\overline{W} - \overline{p}d$ regardless of state or risk class. The locus $FL$ depicts the $L$-risk wealth allocations, which, when coupled with an $H$-risk allocation satisfying $a$ and $b$, meet the resource constraint $d$. The marginal condition $c$ fixes a particular position along this locus. It can be shown that the right-hand side of $c$, when evaluated at $\delta = 0$, is the slope of the $FL$ locus and that this slope decreases as the 45-degree

---

[7] For brevity, we consider only solutions to problem PE for $\overline{V}^H \leq V(p^H, F)$, where $F$ is defined later. Efficient allocations for $\overline{V}^H > V(p^H, F)$ can be characterized by interchanging the roles of $H$ and $L$ in problem PE, resulting in solution conditions identical to those of the theorem with $H$ and $L$ interchanged. Such efficient allocations result in *overinsurance* for $H$-risks, but otherwise all of the arguments presented in the comparison of informational regimes go through.

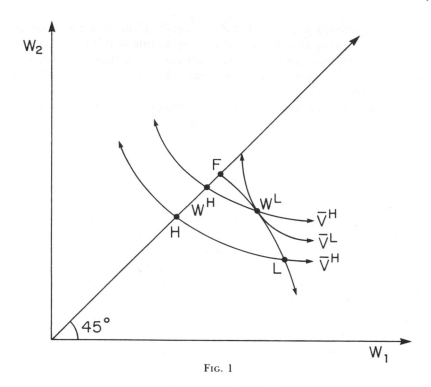

FIG. 1

line is approached. For a sufficiently low value of $\overline{V}^H$, the utility constraint (5) is not binding at a solution to PE. In that case, $\delta = 0$ and a solution is located at the tangency of the $FL$ locus and an $L$-risk indifference curve. Such a case is depicted in figure 1, with $(W^H, W^L)$ solving PE when $\overline{V}^H = V(p^H, H)$. There is a critical value $\overline{V}_0^H$, equal to $V(p^H, W^H)$ in figure 1, at which the utility constraint (5) becomes binding. For $\overline{V}^H > \overline{V}_0^H$, $\delta > 0$ and $W^L$ ($W^H$) lies closer to $F$ along $FL$ (the 45-degree line).

## III. The Efficiency of Categorical Discrimination

We now suppose that consumers differ by an observable trait that is correlated with, and hence informative about, the unobservable risk of loss. We call this the categorization (C) regime. The question we investigate is whether or not the information available through categorical discrimination enhances the possibilities for efficiency. To answer the question we compare the utilities possibilities frontier for the C regime with the frontier for the NC regime.

Throughout this section we assume that each consumer belongs either to group $A$ or to group $B$ and that he is more likely to be low-risk if he belongs to group $A$ rather than $B$. Thus, using $\lambda_i$ to denote the proportion of $H$-risks in group $i$, we assume that $0 < \lambda_A < \lambda < \lambda_B < 1$, implying that categorization is informative, although imperfectly so. The proportion $\theta$ of the population belongs to group $A$ so that $\theta\lambda_A + (1 - \theta)\lambda_B = \lambda$.

We consider first the case in which categorical discrimination entails no resource cost. This same framework of analysis is then applied to costly categorization.

### A.    Costless Categorization Enhances Efficiency

We prove that costless categorization enhances efficiency by showing that the efficiency frontier for the C regime lies "outside" the frontier for the NC regime. Specifically, the C regime's frontier contains allocations Pareto superior to some of the NC regime's frontier and contains no allocations Pareto inferior to any of the NC regime's frontier.

In the C regime an allocation is specified by two pairs of contingent wealth positions, one for consumers in group $A$, denoted $(A^H, A^L)$, and one for those in $B$, denoted $(B^H, B^L)$. The resource constraint can be expressed as

$$\theta R(A^H, A^L; \lambda_A) + (1 - \theta)R(B^H, B^L; \lambda_B) - \overline{W} = 0. \qquad (6)$$

The relevant efficiency problem is

$$\max V(p^L, B^L) \qquad \text{(PS)}$$

by choice of an allocation subject to the resource constraint (6), the self-selection condition (4) for those in group $A$ and for $H$-risks in group $B$, and a set of utility constraints

$$V(p^i, A^i) \geq V(p^i, W^i) \quad \text{for } i \in \{H, L\}, \qquad (7)$$

$$V(p^H, B^H) \geq V(p^H, W^H). \qquad (8)$$

By letting $(W^H, W^L)$ be an efficient allocation for the NC regime, we are assured that no efficient allocation in the C regime is Pareto inferior to any allocation attainable in the NC regime.

To demonstrate that efficiency is enhanced, that portions of the C regime's frontier lie outside the NC regime's frontier, we examine the necessary conditions for a solution to PS in the following theorem, the proof of which is contained in the Appendix.

THEOREM 2. A solution to PS satisfies the following conditions: For group $A$,

$$A_1^H = A_2^H; \qquad (aA)$$

$$V(p^H, A^H) = V(p^H, A^L); \qquad (bA)$$

$$\frac{(1 - p^L)U'(A_1^L)}{p^L U'(A_2^L)} \quad\quad (cA)$$

$$= \frac{\lambda_A(1 - p^H)U'(A_1^L) + (1 - \lambda_A)(1 - p^L)U'(A_2^H)[1 + (\delta_{AH}/\mu_{AH})]}{\lambda_A p^H U'(A_2^L) + (1 - \lambda_A)p^L U'(A_2^H)[1 + (\delta_{AH}/\mu_{AH})]},$$

where $\mu_{AH}$ and $\delta_{AH}$ are the Lagrange multipliers associated with constraints (4) and (7), respectively, for group $A$ when $i = H$; $V(p^H, A^H)$ $= V(p^H, W^H)$ if $\delta_{AH} \neq 0$; and $V(p^L, A^L) = V(p^L, W^L)$. For group $B$,

$$B_1^H = B_2^H; \quad\quad (aB)$$

$$V(p^H, B^H) = V(p^H, B^L); \quad\quad (bB)$$

$$\frac{(1 - p^L)U'(B_1^L)}{p^L U'(B_2^L)} \quad\quad (cB)$$

$$= \frac{\lambda_B(1 - p^H)U'(B_1^L) + (1 - \lambda_B)(1 - p^L)U'(B_2^H)[1 + (\delta_B/\mu_B)]}{\lambda_B p^H U'(B_2^L) + (1 - \lambda_B)p^L U'(B_2^H)[1 + (\delta_B/\mu_B)]},$$

where $\mu_B$ and $\delta_B$ are the Lagrange multipliers associated with constraints (4) for group $B$ when $i = H$ and (8), respectively; and $V(p^H, B^H) = V(p^H, W^H)$ if $\delta_B \neq 0$. For the economy as a whole,

$$\theta R(A^H, A^L; \lambda_A) + (1 - \theta)R(B^H, B^L; \lambda_B) - \overline{W} = 0. \quad\quad (d')$$

The solution to PS depends on the particular efficient allocation $(W^H, W^L)$ from the NC regime chosen as the constraint allocation in (7) and (8). At a solution, the resource cost for group $A$ is minimized subject to the self-selection and utility constraints on that group. Any resources saved by allocating $(A^H, A^L)$ to group $A$ instead of $(W^H, W^L)$ are transferred to group $B$ through condition $d'$. If the utility constraint on the $H$-risks is high enough, then categorization does not permit a reduction in the resource cost of serving group $A$ without violating a constraint. In this event, $\delta_{AH} > 0$ and conditions $aA$, $bA$, $aB$, and $bB$, along with the resource constraint $d'$, imply that a solution to PS is the constraint allocation from the NC regime. In these cases the utility frontiers for the two regimes are coincident.

For lower utility constraints on $H$-risk consumers, categorization allows those in group $A$ to be served at a lower resource cost than in the NC regime while preserving both self-selection and the utility constraints (7) and (8). In this event, $\delta_{AH} = 0$ and the resource savings are transferred to group $B$ through condition $d'$. If the transfer is large enough, then $\delta_B = 0$ and both $H$- and $L$-risk consumers in group $B$ are better off than in the NC regime. For smaller, but positive, transfers, $\delta_B > 0$ and in group $B$ only the $L$-risks are better off as a result of categorization.

To establish that the utilities possibilities frontier for the C regime in some cases lies strictly outside the frontier of the NC regime, we must demonstrate the existence of efficient NC allocations that, when used to constrain PS, admit a solution where the resource cost associated with group $A$ is less than $R(W^H, W^L; \lambda_A)$. To do so we suppose the contrary, that $(A^H, A^L) = (W^H, W^L)$. The $H$-risks in group $A$ could be made better off with the change

$$dA_1^H = dA_2^H > 0 \tag{9}$$

while leaving $L$-risks in group $A$ no worse off and preserving self-selection if

$$-dA_2^L = \frac{(1 - p^L)U'(A_1^L)}{p^L U'(A_2^L)} dA_1^L, \tag{10}$$

$$(1 - p^H)U'(A_1^H)dA_1^H + p^H U'(A_2^H)dA_2^H$$
$$= (1 - p^H)U'(A_1^L)dA_1^L + p^H U'(A_2^L)dA_2^L. \tag{11}$$

By recalling that $A^H = W^H$ provides full insurance, substitution of (9) and (10) into (11) yields

$$U'(A_2^H)dA_2^H = -\left(\frac{p^H - p^L}{p^L}\right)U'(A_1^L)dA_1^L. \tag{12}$$

The change in resource cost for group $A$ is

$$dR(A^H, A^L; \lambda_A) = \lambda_A dA_2^H + (1 - \lambda_A)[(1 - p^L)dA_1^L + p^L dA_2^L], \tag{13}$$

and substitution from (10) and (12) yields

$$dR(A^H, A^L; \lambda_A)$$
$$= \left\{\lambda_A - (1 - \lambda_A)(1 - p^L)\left[1 - \frac{U'(A_1^L)}{U'(A_2^L)}\right]\frac{p^L U'(A_2^H)}{(p^H - p^L)U'(A_1^L)}\right\}dA_2^H, \tag{14}$$

which is negative, as desired, when the term in braces is negative. Since $(A^H, A^L) = (W^H, W^L)$, the marginal condition $c$ from problem PE holds and can be solved for $U'(A_2^H)$.[8] On substitution into (14) one finds that the term in braces is negative if and only if

$$\frac{\delta}{\mu_H} < \frac{\lambda - \lambda_A}{\lambda_A(1 - \lambda)}. \tag{15}$$

---

[8] The marginal condition applies only when $A_1^L \neq A_2^L$, i.e., at constraint allocations where $L$-risks do not receive full insurance. The case when the constraint allocation gives full insurance to $L$-risks is addressed immediately following the corollary.

For the inequality to hold it is sufficient that $\delta = 0$, which obtains when the utility constraint in problem PE is $\overline{V}^H \leq \overline{V}_0^H$. It follows that a critical value $\overline{V}_{00}^H (> \overline{V}_0^H)$ exists such that, when the utility constraint in PE is set below $\overline{V}_{00}^H$, the solution to the corresponding PS problem is Pareto superior to the solution of PE. Moreover, the more informative is categorization, the smaller is $\lambda_A$ and the larger is the right-hand side of (15). For example, if categorization were uninformative ($\lambda = \lambda_A$), then (15) could never hold. If categorization were perfectly informative ($\lambda_A = 0$), then (15) would always hold. The preceding remarks establish the following result.

COROLLARY. In the case where informative categorization is costless, a portion of the C regime's utilities possibilities frontier lies outside, and no portion lies inside, the NC regime's frontier. In addition, as categorization becomes increasingly informative, more of the NC regime's efficiency frontier is Pareto dominated by the frontier of the C regime.

Finally, note that if $A_1^L = A_2^L$, (14) reduces to

$$dR(A^H, A^L; \lambda_A) = \lambda_A dA_2^H \qquad (16)$$

and any change that made the $H$-risks in group $A$ better off would result in an increased resource cost of serving group $A$. In this event (when $A_1^L = A_2^L$), conditions $a$, $b$, and $d$ of theorem 1 imply that the constraint allocation is the equal per capita full insurance wealth allocation $F = (\overline{W} - \overline{p}d, \overline{W} - \overline{p}d)$. Thus the allocation $F$ can never be improved on by the introduction of categorization; the utilities possibilities frontiers for the C and NC regimes always coincide at $F$ regardless of the degree of informativeness of the categorization.

## B. The Ambiguous Efficiency Effects of Costly Categorization

We can use the framework established above to consider the case in which categorization entails a nontrivial resource cost, as when consumers' health or safety records can be obtained but only at finite cost. Specifically, we assume that a firm can learn with certainty whether an individual belongs to group $A$ or $B$, but only at a fixed (per capita) cost $x$. In this case, the resource constraint for the C regime becomes

$$\theta R(A^H, A^L; \lambda_A) + (1 - \theta)R(B^H, B^L; \lambda_B) + x - \overline{W} = 0. \qquad (17)$$

Let $(W_0^H, W_0^L)$ be the solution to PE for some $\overline{V}^H \leq \overline{V}_{00}^H$ and let $(A_0^H, A_0^L)$ be the $A$ group solution to PS when $(W_0^H, W_0^L)$ is the constraint allocation in (7) and (8). In this case, $R(W_0^H, W_0^L; \lambda_A) > R(A_0^H, A_0^L; \lambda_A)$ as established earlier. Also, define $x_0$ to be the per capita reduction in resource cost of serving group $A$ when categorization is introduced, so that

$$x_0 = \theta[R(W_0^H, W_0^L; \lambda_A) - R(A_0^H, A_0^L; \lambda_A)]. \tag{18}$$

If $x > x_0$, then the information in categorization does not permit a sufficient resource saving to improve on the allocation $(W_0^H, W_0^L)$. When $x < x_0$, categorization permits a Pareto improvement over the constraint allocation $(W_0^H, W_0^L)$.

The magnitude of $x_0$ depends on the particular efficient allocation from the NC regime used as the constraint allocation. Specifically, $x_0$ declines as constraint allocations closer to $F$ are selected and equals zero for constraint allocations sufficiently close to the equal per capita ful insurance allocation $F$. Thus, for constraint allocations close enough to $F$, the cost of categorization overwhelms any resource saving it permits in serving group $A$.

It follows that, for costly categorization, the efficiency frontiers of the two regimes cross, each containing allocations Pareto superior to a portion of the other frontier. As a result, costly categorization is never unambiguously efficiency enhancing. Only when the cost of categorization is so large that the frontier of the C regime lies everywhere inside the NC frontier is an unambiguous efficiency ranking of the two regimes possible, in which case categorization is inefficient.

## IV. Market Equilibria and Efficiency

In the efficiency comparison of alternative informational regimes we have made no explicit reference to a mechanism for implementing the various solutions to problems PE and PS. In each case the allocations can be attained if government assumes dictatorial control of the insurance market. Although government cannot correctly assign contingent wealth positions to individuals given the informational asymmetry, it can dictate the contracts available to consumers in the insurance market. Because efficient allocations satisfy self-selection, individuals would voluntarily choose their assigned wealth positions.

Thus the preceding analysis demonstrates the feasibility of applying hypothetical compensation tests to compare the efficiency of alternative informationally constrained regimes. As yet unanswered is the question of the relative efficiency of market equilibria in the NC and C regimes. This is of particular importance since there is, as a general proposition, no version of the First Optimality Theorem showing that market equilibria in informationally constrained environments are necessarily efficient. Since market equilibria may not be efficient, the fact that categorization shifts the efficiency frontier provides no direct implications regarding the efficiency of the market's use of categorical discrimination.[9]

## A. Market Equilibrium with Costless Categorization

Hoy (1982) has shown that the market generally uses costless categorization but the welfare effects are ambiguous since there are losers as well as winners. In this section we demonstrate the existence of a balanced-budget tax-subsidy policy that provides firms the incentive to use costless categorization (even when they would not do so without the tax) and, regardless of the type of equilibrium attained by the market, can ensure that no one loses as a result of categorization.

To ease the exposition we confine attention to the case in which each consumer is endowed with the same contingent wealth $E = (\overline{W}, \overline{W} - d)$. An insurance contract $\alpha = (-\alpha_1, \alpha_2)$, where $\alpha_1$ is the premium and $\alpha_2$ is coverage net of premium. The purchase of $\alpha$ results in the contingent wealth $(E + \alpha) = (\overline{W} - \alpha_1, \overline{W} - d + \alpha_2)$. The expected profit earned when $\alpha$ is purchased by a $p$-risk consumer is

$$\pi(p, \alpha) = (1 - p)\alpha_1 - p\alpha_2. \tag{19}$$

Initially we consider the Miyazaki-type Wilson (MW) equilibrium[10] and later extend our results to other equilibrium concepts. As a point of reference we first consider the NC regime. Free entry requires zero expected profits in equilibrium; hence

$$\lambda\pi(p^H, \alpha^H) + (1 - \lambda)\pi(p^L, \alpha^L) = 0, \tag{20}$$

which is equivalent to the resource constraint (3). When we apply the results of Miyazaki (1977) and Spence (1978), the MW equilibrium is given by a solution to PE with the utility constraint $\overline{V}^H = V(p^H, H^*)$, where $H^*$ is the full insurance position earning zero profit when bought by $H$-risk consumers. Thus the MW equilibrium in the NC regime is efficient.

There are "interior" and "corner"-type MW equilibria. When $\lambda$ is less than a critical value $\lambda^*$, $V(p^H, H^*) < \overline{V}_0^H$ and the equilibrium contracts are $\alpha^i = W_0^i - E$ for $i = H, L$, resulting in interior-type

---

[9] Indeed, Hoy (1982) demonstrates in his "knife's edge" example that, when the market attains a Wilson equilibrium, costless categorization may actually result in a market equilibrium that is *less efficient* than that of the NC regime. Also, if the market attains a "reactive" equilibrium of the type examined by Riley (1979), the market would never use the information provided by the type of categorization examined in this paper (since a reactive equilibrium does not depend on $\lambda$). In each of these situations, the introduction of costless categorization shifts out the utility possibilities frontier, but the benefits from categorization are not realized by the market.

[10] This equilibrium is formally defined in Miyazaki (1977) and extends the "anticipatory" concept of equilibrium introduced by Wilson (1977) to admit cross-subsidization.

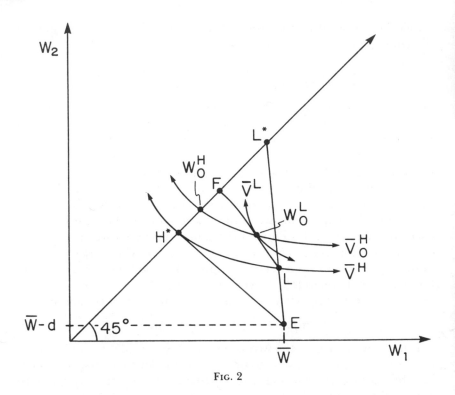

FIG. 2

allocations depicted as $(W_0^L, W_0^H)$ in figure 2. For this case $\delta = 0$ in condition $c$ of theorem 1 and the $L$-risk allocation $W_0^L$ is located at the tangency of an $L$-risk indifference curve and the locus $FL$. In this equilibrium profits earned on the $L$-risk contract subsidize losses made from $H$-risk contracts. As $\lambda$ increases, the $FL$ locus becomes flatter until $W_0^L$ and $L$ coincide when $\lambda = \lambda^*$. For $\lambda > \lambda^*$ the utility constraint $\overline{V}^H = V(p^H, H^*)$ binds ($\delta > 0$) and the allocations $(H^*, L)$ are sustained as a corner-type MW equilibrium in which both contracts break even individually.

We now show that any solution $(A^H, A^L)$ and $(B^H, B^L)$ to PS can be sustained as a corner-type MW equilibrium. Since categorization is based on an observable trait, consumers can be segregated into groups $A$ and $B$ and, therefore, can be treated differently by firms offering insurance contracts in the market. We consider group $A$ first.

The contingent allocation $(A^H, A^L)$ can be reached if the market offers the contracts $\alpha^i = A^i - E$ for $i \in \{H, L\}$ to group $A$ in equilibrium. Let

$$\pi_A^i =: \pi(p^i, \alpha^i) \quad \text{for } i \in \{H, L\} \tag{21}$$

represent the profit (or loss) earned by the contract $\alpha^i$. Since MW equilibrium is necessarily a separating equilibrium (in which consumers of different risks purchase different contracts), each consumer reveals his risk type ex post by his choice of contract. Government can exploit this signaling property of equilibrium ex ante by taxing firms $\pi_A^H$ on each $H$-type contract and $\pi_A^L$ on each $L$-type contract sold to group $A$. Inclusive of tax, the contracts $\alpha^i$ each earn zero profit and together constitute a corner-type MW equilibrium for group $A$ since the allocations resulting from $\alpha^i$ satisfy conditions $a$ and $b$ of theorem 1 and, after tax, earn zero profit.[11] The average per capita tax collected from group $A$ is ·

$$T_A = \theta[\lambda_A \pi_A^H + (1 - \lambda_A)\pi_A^L]. \tag{22}$$

In a similar fashion, the allocation $(B^H, B^L)$ for group $B$ can be supported as a corner-type MW equilibrium by subsidizing $p^i$-risks an amount $\pi_B^i = \pi(p^i, \beta^i)$, where $\beta^i = B^i - E$ for $i \in \{H, L\}$. After tax, each contract $\beta^i$ earns zero profit, and the allocations supported by the contracts satisfy conditions $a$ and $b$ of theorem 1. The average per capita amount of subsidy to group $B$ is

$$T_B = (1 - \theta)[\lambda_B \pi_B^H + (1 - \lambda_B)\pi_B^L]. \tag{23}$$

Substituting for $\alpha^i$ and $\beta^i$ in $T_A$ and $T_B$, using (21), (19), and the definition of $R$, yields

$$T_A + T_B = -\theta R(A^H, A^L; \lambda_A) - (1 - \theta)R(B^H, B^L; \lambda_B) + \overline{W}, \tag{24}$$

which equals zero by condition $d'$ of theorem 2. Thus the budget is balanced and a solution to PS is sustained as an MW equilibrium after tax.

Notice that $\pi_i^H \neq \pi_j^L$ for $i, j \in \{A, B\}$, so the tax discriminates by risk as well as by group. Risk-discriminating taxation is accomplished by assigning taxes to contracts, not to individuals. The separation property of equilibrium associates different contracts with different individuals depending on risk. In equilibrium, the taxes are passed forward to consumers in contracts that incorporate the risk-specific taxes or subsidies. Put differently, the tax system provides firms the incentive to offer a menu of optimal contracts to consumers.

When costless categorization is possible the market uses the information by treating the two groups $A$ and $B$ differently. In essence, two MW equilibria are attained, one for each of the two groups. For

---

[11] Intuitively, after the tax is levied, the allocations $A^H$ and $A^L$ coincide with positions analogous to $H^*$ and $L$. Moreover, any feasible allocation preferred by $L$-risks would make $H$-risks worse off than at $A^H$, which is always attainable since it earns zero profit after tax.

each group the equilibrium is a solution to a group-specific efficiency problem PE in which $\lambda_i$, $i \in \{A, B\}$, replaces $\lambda$. Thus, if the market attains MW equilibrium, the equilibrium is efficient in both the NC and C regimes. Imposing the tax system described above moves the MW equilibrium along the C regime efficiency frontier and ensures that no one loses from categorization. As a result, the MW equilibrium for the C regime is a potential Pareto improvement over the MW equilibrium for the NC regime.

We have shown elsewhere (Crocker and Snow 1985$b$) that the same type of tax system can be used to sustain any efficient allocation as a Nash equilibrium in the market.[12] Moreover, it is easy to show that such a tax could be used to support any efficient allocation as a Wilson (1977) "anticipatory" equilibrium or as a Riley (1979) "reactive" equilibrium. Thus, regardless of the type of equilibrium attained by the market, and whether it is efficient or not, the tax system allows any solution to PS always to be sustained as an equilibrium in the market. In this sense any of the received market equilibria in the C regime are potentially Pareto superior to the corresponding equilibrium in the NC regime.

## B. Equilibrium with Costly Categorization

Although market equilibria are always potentially more efficient when costless categorization is possible and is allowed, the same conclusion does not follow when categorization is costly. In that case the market may categorize even when the winners from categorization are unable in principle to compensate the losers. We demonstrate this by means of a counterexample that uses the MW equilibrium introduced above. Although the MW equilibrium is efficient in both informational regimes, the equilibrium in the C regime may not be potentially Pareto superior to the equilibrium in the NC regime.

Consider as a point of reference the case of costless categorization. In figure 3 we depict the allocations supported by the MW equilibrium in the NC regime as $(W_0^H, W_0^L)$ and then those of the MW equilibria in the C regime as $(\hat{A}^H, \hat{A}^L)$ and $(\hat{B}^H, \hat{B}^L)$ for groups $A$ and $B$, respectively.[13]

---

[12] It is well known (Rothschild and Stiglitz 1976) that a Nash equilibrium may not exist and that, if one does, it may not be efficient. However, the type of tax system set out above changes the market environment and effectively constrains firms, if they are to break even, to offer optimal contracts. In this way, any desired efficient allocation is sustainable as a Nash equilibrium.

[13] Note that there are four possibilities for postcategorization equilibria that have different distributional implications. If $\lambda^* < \lambda_A < \lambda < \lambda_B$, then categorization does not change the MW equilibrium because all the pre- and postcategorization equilibria are

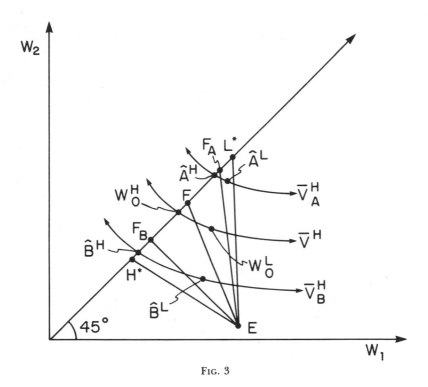

FIG. 3

The introduction of a positive cost to categorization amounts to levying a state-independent wealth tax $x$ on each consumer. Thus costly categorization has two effects: it allows resource savings to be realized when serving group $A$, to the potential benefit of all consumers, but it also imposes an additional resource cost $x$ on all consumers. Both of these effects are depicted in figure 4 for those in group $A$. The effect of the categorization cost $x$ is to reduce the endowed contingent wealth from $E = (\overline{W}, \overline{W} - d)$ to $E' = (\overline{W} - x, \overline{W} - d - x)$. The allocation resulting from the MW equilibrium for group $A$ is depicted in figure 4 as $(A^H, A^L)$ and is characterized by the conditions of theorem 1 with $\lambda$ replaced by $\lambda_A$ and condition $d$ modified to account for the cost of categorization as follows:

$$R(A^H, A^L; \lambda_A) - x - \overline{W} = 0. \tag{25}$$

---

of the "corner" variety. Also, if $\lambda_A < \lambda^* < \lambda < \lambda_B$, then the postcategorization MW equilibrium leaves members of group $A$ better off but does not affect group $B$ because its pre- and postcategorization equilibria are the "corner" solution. When $\lambda_A < \lambda < \lambda^* < \lambda_B$ or $\lambda_A < \lambda < \lambda_B < \lambda^*$, group $A$ is better off and group $B$ worse off than in the no-categorization case. Although this counterexample applies to both of the cases when categorization makes group $B$ worse off, the figures illustrate only the latter case in which the MW equilibrium for each group is of the interior variety.

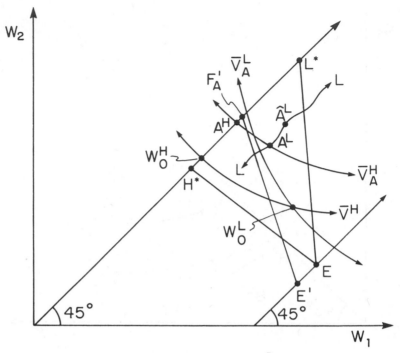

FIG. 4

The locus $LL$ identifies the $L$-risk allocations that satisfy the marginal condition $c$ for an MW equilibrium (i.e., that satisfy $c$ with $\delta = 0$ and $\lambda_A$ replacing $\lambda$). In the case depicted in figure 4, the resource saving from categorization dominates the resource cost, and the MW equilibrium of the costly C regime results in the allocation $(A^H, A^L)$, which is preferred by all members of group $A$ to the equilibrium allocations $(W_0^H, W_0^L)$ of the NC regime.

For any cost $x$, as long as $L$-risks in group $A$ prefer $A^L$ to $W_0^L$, competitive pressures will force firms to categorize, since any firm offering contracts resulting in allocations $(W_0^H, W_0^L)$ would lose all members of group $A$ to firms offering $(A^H, A^L)$. As a result, non-categorizing firms would attract only members of group $B$, from whom contracts offering the allocation $(W_0^H, W_0^L)$ earn negative profit.[14]

Let $\hat{x}$ be the categorization cost for which $V(p^L, W_0^L) = V(p^L, A^L)$ so that $L$-risks in group $A$ are indifferent regarding categorization. For a lower cost $(x \leq \hat{x})$, both risk types in group $A$ gain weakly (at least)

[14] Note that members of group $B$ are always made worse off from categorization whenever $\lambda_B > \lambda^*$. Moreover, with costly categorization, members of group $B$ are also forced to pay, in addition, the resource cost $x$ of categorization.

from categorization, so the market categorizes. For a higher cost ($x >$ $\hat{x}$), $L$-risks in group $A$ prefer $W_0^L$ to $A^L$ and could not be attracted by categorizing firms. In this event, a categorizing firm would either attract only $H$-risks in group $A$ if $V(p^H, A^H) > V(p^H, W_0^H)$ and earn negative profit or attract no one if $V(p^H, A^H) < V(p^H, W_0^H)$. Thus when the cost exceeds $\hat{x}$ the market would not categorize.

Observe that when the cost just equals $\hat{x}$ there is no possibility for the gainers from categorization (group $A$) to compensate the losers (group $B$). Any tax levied on $L$-risks in group $A$ would make them worse off than at $W_0^L$ and would upset categorization; any tax levied solely on $H$-risks in group $A$ would upset self-selection because $H$-risks would then prefer $A^L$. Thus there is no possibility of extracting resources from group $A$ to compensate the members of group $B$, who are made worse off by both the effects of categorization and the categorization cost $x$. We know from the previous section that, in the case of costless categorization, the gainers from categorization can compensate the losers. Hence there exists a categorization cost such that group $A$ can just compensate group $B$ for a movement from an MW equilibrium in the NC regime to an MW equilibrium in the C regime.

Thus if the cost of categorization is large enough the market does not categorize, which is efficient. If the cost is small enough the market does categorize, which is again efficient since the winners from categorization could compensate the losers. However, for intermediate levels of cost the market still categorizes even though the winners from categorization could not compensate the losers. We conclude that the market can be an inefficient mechanism for allocating resources to the acquisition of information.

Unfortunately, it does not follow that, in such cases, imposing a ban on costly categorization would enhance efficiency. The members of group $B$ would gain at the expense of those in $A$, and in order for government to transfer wealth from the gainers to the losers the categorization cost would have to be incurred without realizing any of its benefits given the prohibition on using categorization to allocate insurance contracts. As a result, a ban on costly categorization fails the compensation test even though the use of costly categorization also fails the test. In these cases an efficiency comparison of equilibria in the two regimes yields ambiguous conclusions.

## V. Conclusions

Recent public policy debate has focused attention on the equity dimensions of permitting categorical discrimination in insurance and similar markets. Sex, race, and age discrimination have been of special concern as instances in which prohibitions on discrimination appeal to widely held norms. However, in these instances categorization has a negligible resource cost. Our analysis shows that prohibiting discrimination on equity grounds in these cases necessarily imposes efficiency costs in addition to the costs of enforcement. While there are as yet no estimates of these costs, choice of policy should not proceed as if the equity objective could be achieved without loss in efficiency.

In other cases where observing the categorizing signal entails a significant resource cost, the trade-off between equity and efficiency is less clear-cut. The efficiency of a prohibition on discrimination in these cases cannot be determined without the income distributional equity judgments made explicit in a social welfare function of the Bergson-Samuelson type. Thus whether there is conflict between efficiency and the equity norm of nondiscrimination in cases of costly categorization depends on the distributional weighting adopted for evaluating the efficiency of alternative risk allocations.

## Appendix

This Appendix provides proofs of theorems 1 and 2.

*Proof of Theorem 1*

The Lagrangean expression for problem PE is

$$\mathcal{L} = V(p^L, W^L) + \mu_L[V(p^L, W^L) - V(p^L, W^H)] + \mu_H[V(p^H, W^H)$$
$$- V(p^H, W^L)] + \gamma[\overline{W} - R(W^H, W^L; \lambda)] + \delta[V(p^H, W^H) - \overline{V}^H],$$

where $\mu_L$, $\mu_H$, $\gamma$, and $\delta$ are Lagrange multipliers. The first-order conditions for an interior solution are

$$\frac{\partial \mathcal{L}}{\partial W_i^L} = (1 + \mu_L) \frac{\partial V(p^L, W^L)}{\partial W_i^L} - \mu_H \frac{\partial V(p^H, W^L)}{\partial W_i^L} - \gamma(1 - \lambda) \frac{\partial \rho(p^L, W^L)}{\partial W_i^L} = 0,$$
$$\text{(A1)}$$

$$\frac{\partial \mathcal{L}}{\partial W_i^H} = (\mu_H + \delta) \frac{\partial V(p^H, W^H)}{\partial W_i^H} - \mu_L \frac{\partial V(p^L, W^H)}{\partial W_i^H} - \gamma\lambda \frac{\partial \rho(p^H, W^H)}{\partial W_i^H} = 0, \quad \text{(A2)}$$

for $i = 1, 2$, where we have used the definition of $R$.

Since there is no satiation, $\gamma > 0$ and condition $d$ holds. By totally differentiating the objective and constraint functions we can show that both self-selection constraints cannot hold with strict inequality at solution, for then both risk types' welfare can be increased without violating any constraint. Also, if both self-selection constraints hold with equality, it is easy to see that both risk types receive the equal per capita full insurance wealth allocation $F$. For this solution to obtain, the utility constraint must be set at $\overline{V}^H = V(p^H, F)$. In addition, solving (A1) for the first term, dividing (A1) for $i = 1$ by (1) for $i = 2$, and doing the same for (A2) shows that $\mu_L = 0 = \mu_H$ at this solution since both risk types are fully insured. At this solution we therefore have conditions $a$ and $b$ holding. Condition $c$ does not hold as stated since the right-hand side is undefined when $\mu_H = 0$. However, multiplying the right side of $c$ by $\mu_H/\mu_H$ and then using $\mu_H = 0$ confirms the equality. Hence, as stated $c$ applies to solutions other than $F$.

When the utility constraint is set at $\overline{V}^H < V(p^H, F)$, it can be shown, again by totally differentiating the objective and constraint functions, that a solution fully insures $H$-risks (condition $a$), leaves them indifferent to the $L$-risk alloca-tion (condition $b$), and leaves $L$-risks underinsured. Solving (A2) as before for the marginal rate of substitution for $H$-risks shows that we must have $\mu_L = 0$ since $H$-risks are fully insured. Solving (A1) for the marginal rate of substitu-tion and substituting for $\gamma$ from (A2) yields $c$.

When the utility constraint is set at $\overline{V}^H > V(p^H, F)$ a different type of solution obtains. In this case a solution is most easily characterized by revers-ing the roles of $H$ and $L$ in problem PE and maximizing $H$-risk welfare with a constraint on $L$-risk welfare set at $\overline{V}^L < V(p^L, F)$. One obtains conditions $a$, $b$, and $c$ with $H$ and $L$ exchanging roles. This class of solutions entails full insurance for $L$-risks and overinsurance for $H$-risks. For brevity we have omitted these conditions in stating theorem 1.

To complete the proof, we show that a constraint qualification holds so that the first-order conditions are necessary for a solution. The constraint qualification (Luenberger 1973, p. 233) requires that the gradient of the ac-tive constraints be independent vectors at a solution. We confine attention to solutions for $\overline{V}^H < V(p^H, F)$. A parallel argument applies to the other cases. The active constraints are conditions $b$ and $d$ and, perhaps, equation (5). We will consider the case when all three are active.

Thus we have the constraint equations

$$H_1 = V(p^H, W^H) - V(p^H, W^L) = 0,$$
$$H_2 = \lambda\rho(p^H, W^H) + (1 - \lambda)\rho(p^L, W^L) - \overline{W} = 0,$$
$$H_3 = V(p^H, W^H) - \overline{V}^H = 0.$$

The gradients are

$$\nabla H_1 = \left\{ \frac{\partial V(p^H, W^H)}{\partial W_1^H}, \frac{\partial V(p^H, W^H)}{\partial W_2^H}, -\frac{\partial V(p^H, W^L)}{\partial W_1^L}, -\frac{\partial V(p^H, W^L)}{\partial W_2^L} \right\},$$

$$\nabla H_2 = \left\{ \lambda \frac{\partial\rho(p^H, W^H)}{\partial W_1^H}, \lambda \frac{\partial\rho(p^H, W^H)}{\partial W_2^H}, (1 - \lambda) \frac{\partial\rho(p^L, W^L)}{\partial W_1^L}, \right.$$
$$\left. (1 - \lambda) \frac{\partial\rho(p^L, W^L)}{\partial W_2^L} \right\},$$

$$\nabla H_3 = \left\{ \frac{\partial V(p^H, W^H)}{\partial W_1^H}, \frac{\partial V(p^H, W^H)}{\partial W_2^H}, 0, 0 \right\}.$$

Clearly, $\nabla H_3$ is independent of either $\nabla H_1$ or $\nabla H_2$ since $\partial V/\partial W_i \neq 0$ and $\partial\rho/\partial W_i \neq 0$.

We shall prove by contradiction that $\nabla H_1$ and $\nabla H_2$ are linearly indepen-dent. Supposing $\nabla H_1$ and $\nabla H_2$ to be linearly dependent, there exists a con-stant $\xi$ such that $\xi\nabla H_1 = \nabla H_2$, implying

$$\xi \frac{\partial V(p^H, W^H)}{\partial W_i^H} = \lambda \frac{\partial\rho(p^H, W^H)}{\partial W_i^H}, \tag{A3}$$

$$-\xi \frac{\partial V(p^H, W^L)}{\partial W_i^L} = (1 - \lambda) \frac{\partial\rho(p^L, W^L)}{\partial W_i^L}, \tag{A4}$$

for $i = 1, 2$. Dividing (A3) for $i = 1$ by (A3) for $i = 2$ shows that $W^H$ results in full insurance. Similarly, dividing (A4) for $i = 1$ by (A4) for $i = 2$ shows that $W^L$ is located at the tangency of an $H$-risk indifference curve and an $L$-risk isoprofit locus. Since $H$-risk indifference curves are flatter than $L$-risk indifference curves, $W^L$ must entail overinsurance and be located above the 45-degree line in figure 1. These results, in conjunction with the active constraint $H_1$, imply that solution is a pair of allocations that violate self-selection for the $L$-risks. Hence linear dependence of $\nabla H_1$ and $\nabla H_2$ can occur only at unattainable allocations. It follows that the constraint qualification holds for every attainable allocation, implying the necessity of the Kuhn-Tucker conditions for a maximum. Q.E.D.

### Proof of Theorem 2

For brevity we have confined the statement of theorem 2 to constraint allocations from the NC regime in which $H$-risks are fully insured and $L$-risks are underinsured. When the constraint allocation is $F$, it follows immediately that $F$ is the solution to PS. For the remaining cases, in which $H$-risks are overinsured in the NC regime, $H$ and $L$ exchange roles in the statement of PS and the conditions of the theorem. Hence, in the proof we consider explicitly only cases in which $V(p^H, W^H) < V(p^H, F)$.

The Lagrangean associated with problem PS is

$$
\begin{aligned}
\mathscr{L} = {} & V(p^L, B^L) + \mu_{AH}[V(p^H, A^H) - V(p^H, A^L)] + \mu_{AL}[V(p^L, A^L) \\
& - V(p^L, A^H)] + \mu_B[V(p^H, B^H) - V(p^H, B^L)] + \delta_{AH}[V(p^H, A^H) \\
& - V(p^H, W^H)] + \delta_{AL}[V(p^L, A^L) - V(p^L, W^L)] + \delta_B[V(p^H, B^H) \\
& - V(p^H, W^H)] + \gamma[\overline{W} - \theta R(A^H, A^L; \lambda_A) - (1 - \theta)R(B^H, B^L; \lambda_B)].
\end{aligned}
$$

The first-order conditions are

$$
\begin{aligned}
\frac{\partial \mathscr{L}}{\partial A_i^L} = {} & -\mu_{AH} \frac{\partial V(p^H, A^L)}{\partial A_i^L} + (\mu_{AL} + \delta_{AL}) \frac{\partial V(p^L, A^L)}{\partial A_i^L} \\
& - \gamma\theta(1 - \lambda_A) \frac{\partial \rho(p^L, A^L)}{\partial A_i^L} = 0,
\end{aligned} \tag{A5}
$$

$$
\frac{\partial \mathscr{L}}{\partial A_i^H} = (\mu_{AH} + \delta_{AH}) \frac{\partial V(p^H, A^H)}{\partial A_i^H} - \mu_{AL} \frac{\partial V(p^L, A^H)}{\partial A_i^H} - \gamma\theta\lambda_A \frac{\partial \rho(p^H, A^H)}{\partial A_i^H} = 0, \tag{A6}
$$

$$
\frac{\partial \mathscr{L}}{\partial B_i^L} = \frac{\partial V(p^L, B^L)}{\partial B_i^L} - \mu_B \frac{\partial V(p^H, B^L)}{\partial B_i^L} - \gamma(1 - \theta)(1 - \lambda_B) \frac{\partial \rho(p^L, B^L)}{\partial B_i^L} = 0, \tag{A7}
$$

$$
\frac{\partial \mathscr{L}}{\partial B_i^H} = (\mu_B + \delta_B) \frac{\partial V(p^H, B^H)}{\partial B_i^H} - \gamma(1 - \theta)\lambda_B \frac{\partial \rho(p^H, B^H)}{\partial B_i^H} = 0 \tag{A8}
$$

for $i = 1, 2$.

Nonsatiation implies that $\gamma > 0$ and condition $d'$ holds or that

$$
\theta R_A = \overline{W} - (1 - \theta)R_B, \tag{A9}
$$

where $R_A$ ($R_B$) is the average per capita resource cost of serving group $A$ ($B$). Notice that $V(p^L, B^L)$ can increase as long as $R_A$ can decrease so that any contractual pair that does not minimize the cost of serving group $A$ subject to the constraints of group $A$ cannot be a solution to PS. This fact is exploited in the proof. Also, since $\gamma > 0$ and $\partial V/\partial B_i^H$ and $\partial \rho/\partial B_i^H$ are of the same sign, equations (A8) imply that $\mu_B + \delta > 0$, while (A5) and (A6) imply that $\mu_{AL} + \delta_{AL} > 0$ and $\mu_{AH} + \delta_{AH} > 0$.

$\mu_{AH} > 0$

Equations (A5) can be used to show that $\mu_{AH} > 0$. To do so, we show that if $\mu_{AH} = 0$, then $R_A$ can be decreased. Expand equations (A5) to find

$$(\mu_{AL} + \delta_{AL})(1 - p^L)U'(A_1^L) = \mu_{AH}(1 - p^H)U'(A_1^L) + \gamma\theta(1 - \lambda_A)(1 - p^L),$$
(A5a)

$$(\mu_{AL} + \delta_{AL})p^L U'(A_2^L) = \mu_{AH}p^H U'(A_2^L) + \gamma\theta(1 - \lambda_A)p^L. \qquad (A5b)$$

If $\mu_{AH} = 0$, then dividing (A5a) by (A5b) shows that $U'(A_1^L)/U'(A_2^L) = 1$, which implies that $A^L$ provides full insurance. With reference to figure A1, since $V(p^L, A^L) \geq V(p^L, W^L)$ the allocation $A^L$ must lie on the 45-degree line above point $k$. The self-selection constraints for group $A$ imply that, given an $L$-risk position such as $\overline{A}^L$, the $H$-risk contract must lie in the shaded region. Hence $H$-risks are fully or overinsured, that is,

$$\frac{U'(A_1^H)}{U'(A_2^H)} \geq 1. \qquad (A10)$$

Also, since $\overline{A}^L$ cannot lie below $k$, we must have $V(p^H, A^H) > V(p^H, W^H)$. It follows that $A^H$ can be changed to decrease $R_A$ by making $H$-risks in group $A$ worse off without violating any constraint. In particular, with $dA_1^H > 0$, $dA_1^L = 0 = dA_2^L$, and

$$dA_2^H = \frac{(1 - p^L)U'(A_1^H)}{p^L U'(A_2^H)} dA_1^H,$$

to ensure that self-selection constraint (4) for $H$-risks continues to hold, one finds

$$dR_A = \lambda_A \left[ 1 - p^H - p^H \frac{(1 - p^L)U'(A_1^H)}{p^L U'(A_2^H)} \right] dA_2^H,$$

which is negative since $dA_2^H$ is positive, and the term in brackets is negative once (A10) is taken into account. It follows that $\mu_{AH} > 0$, which implies condition $bA$.

$\mu_B > 0$

Similar reasoning shows that $\mu_B > 0$. By supposing $\mu_B = 0$ one can show that within group $B$ the $H$ types can be made worse off and the $L$ types better off without affecting those in group $A$ or violating any constraint. Hence, $\mu_B > 0$ and condition $bB$ holds.

$\mu_{AL} = 0$

One can also show that $\mu_{AL} = 0$. Since $\mu_{AH} > 0$, if $\mu_{AL} > 0$ then both self-selection constraints for group $A$ are binding and $A^H = A^L$. However, a solution must entail separating contracts. It is easy to show that for any attainable pooling contract for group $A$ that meets the utility constraints (7), recalling that $V(p^H, W^H) < V(p^H, F)$, there is an attainable separating contract pair for group $A$ that meets the constraints for group $A$ and entails a lower resource cost $R_A$.

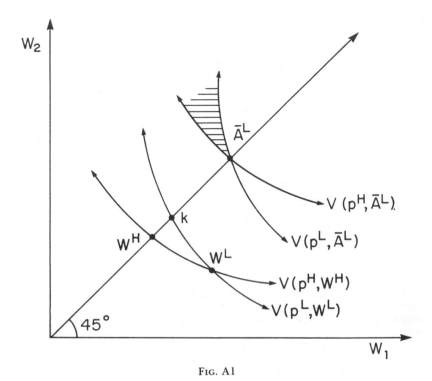

FIG. A1

Using $\mu_{AL} = 0$ and solving equations (A6) for the marginal rate of substitution shows that $A^H$ provides full insurance, establishing condition $aA$. In the same way equations (A8) imply condition $aB$.

Solving (A5) for the marginal rate of substitution and substituting $\mu_{AL} = 0$ and an expression for $\gamma$ derived from (A6) yields the marginal condition $cA$. Also $\mu_{AL} = 0$ and $\mu_{AL} + \delta_{AL} > 0$ implies $V(p^L, A^L) = V(p^L, W^L)$ as stated in $cA$. Solving (A7) for the marginal rate of substitution and substituting an expression for $\gamma$ derived from (A8) yields condition $cB$.

Finally, an argument parallel to that used in the proof of theorem 1 establishes that the constraint qualification holds, so the first-order conditions (A5)–(A8) are necessary for an interior solution to PS. Q.E.D.

### References

Brilmayer, Lea; Hekeler, Richard W.; Laycock, Douglas; and Sullivan, Teresa A. "Sex Discrimination in Employer-sponsored Insurance Plans: A Legal and Demographic Analysis." *Univ. Chicago Law Rev.* 47 (Spring 1980): 505–60.

Crocker, Keith J., and Snow, Arthur. "The Efficiency of Competitive Equilibria in Insurance Markets with Asymmetric Information." *J. Public Econ.* 26 (March 1985): 207–19. (a)

———. "A Simple Tax Structure for Competitive Equilibrium and Redistribution in Insurance Markets with Asymmetric Information." *Southern Econ. J.* 51 (April 1985): 1142–50. (*b*)

Dahlby, Beverly G. "The Welfare Effects of Prohibiting Statistical Discrimination in Insurance Markets." Mimeographed. Edmonton: Univ. Alberta, 1980.

———. "Adverse Selection and Statistical Discrimination: An Analysis of Canadian Automobile Insurance." *J. Public Econ.* 20 (February 1983): 121–30.

Feldman, Mark, and Gilles, Christian. "An Expository Note on Individual Risk without Aggregate Uncertainty." *J. Econ. Theory* 35 (February 1985): 26–32.

Harris, Milton, and Townsend, Robert M. "Resource Allocation under Asymmetric Information." *Econometrica* 49 (January 1981): 33–64.

Holmström, Bengt, and Myerson, Roger B. "Efficient and Durable Decision Rules with Incomplete Information." *Econometrica* 51 (November 1983): 1799–1819.

Hoy, Michael. "Categorizing Risks in the Insurance Industry." *Q.J.E.* 97 (May 1982): 321–36.

Judd, Kenneth L. "The Law of Large Numbers with a Continuum of IID Random Variables." *J. Econ. Theory* 35 (February 1985): 19–25.

Luenberger, David G. *Introduction to Linear and Nonlinear Programming.* Reading, Mass.: Addison-Wesley, 1973.

Miyazaki, Hajime. "The Rat Race and Internal Labor Markets." *Bell J. Econ.* 8 (Autumn 1977): 394–418.

Myerson, Roger B. "Incentive Compatibility and the Bargaining Problem." *Econometrica* 47 (January 1979): 61–73.

Riley, John G. "Informational Equilibrium." *Econometrica* 47 (March 1979): 331–59.

Rothschild, Michael, and Stiglitz, Joseph E. "Equilibrium in Competitive Insurance Markets: An Essay on the Economics of Imperfect Information." *Q.J.E.* 90 (November 1976): 630–49.

Schmalensee, Richard. "Imperfect Information and the Equitability of Competitive Prices." *Q.J.E.* 99 (August 1984): 441–60.

Spence, Michael. "Product Differentiation and Performance in Insurance Markets." *J. Public Econ.* 10 (December 1978): 427–47.

Wilson, Charles A. "A Model of Insurance Markets with Incomplete Information." *J. Econ. Theory* 16 (December 1977): 167–207.

# Cartels, competition and regulation in the property-liability insurance industry

Paul L. Joskow

Assistant Professor of Economics
Massachusetts Institute of Technology

*This paper provides a detailed study of the structure, behavior, and performance of the property and liability insurance industry in the United States. The property insurance industry is shown to possess all of the structural characteristics normally associated with competitive markets. Despite a competitive market structure, however, the property-liability insurance industry has traditionally set prices through cartel-like rating bureaus and has been subjected to pervasive state rate regulation. The study concludes that the combination of state regulation, cartel pricing, and other legal peculiarities has resulted in the use of an inefficient sales technique, supply shortages, and over-capitalization. Free entry, however, tends to drive profits toward the cost of capital. Based on recent experience in states where the competitive market is used to determine insurance rates, the study suggests a movement away from rate regulation and cartel pricing to open competition, as a means of eliminating prevailing performance problems.*

■ The property and liability insurance industry had assets of $68 billion and premiums of $35 billion in 1971. The products sold by this industry, in the form of contingent claims against accidental property loss and liability judgments, are purchased in one form or another by virtually all economic agents in the U. S. economy. Despite the size and importance of the property insurance industry in the U. S. economy, the literature in the area of industrial organization has all but ignored it. A leading text in the area mentions the

**1. Introduction**

Paul L. Joskow received the B.A. in economics from Cornell University (1968) and the M.Phil. and Ph.D. in economics from Yale University (1970 and 1972, respectively). At M.I.T. the current research of this Assistant Professor of Economics includes work in government regulation, energy demand modeling, and consumer protection.

The author became interested in the property insurance industry while working on the fire protection and prevention project of the New York City-Rand Institute during the summer of 1972. He has benefitted from discussions with members of the staff of the New York State Insurance Department, the Insurance Services Office, the New York Property Insurance Underwriting Association, Peter Diamond, Paul MacAvoy, Irving Plotkin, Peter Temin, and many others. He is grateful to the College of Insurance in New York City and the Insurance Library Association of Boston for making their library facilities available to him.

This research has been partially supported by the Ford Foundation Urban Grant to M.I.T. The views expressed here are the author's sole responsibility and do not reflect those of M.I.T. or the Ford Foundation. This paper was presented at the Dartmouth Seminar on Regulation and Public Utilities in August, 1973. Supplementary appendices to the paper are available from the author.

insurance industry in passing, but only to note that it will not be a subject of discussion in the book.[1] Scherer's relegation of the industry to the "money and banking" field may be justified in the context of past research work available, but it seems somewhat unfortunate that such an important private sector of the U. S. economy has not undergone more intensive study and analysis in the context of the structure-behavior-performance rubrick of industrial organization.

The property insurance industry is also a regulated industry. Virtually every state has an insurance commission charged with supervising the rates, financial organization, and quality of service provided by the insurance companies operating within the state. The way insurance rates are set in most states, as well as the basic structure of the regulatory process, appears to be quite different from that which has evolved in the regulated industries which are traditionally studied. A recent text dealing with the economics of regulation does little more than note the Supreme Court opinion which affirmed the power of the states to regulate insurance rates.[2] How the insurance industry is regulated, why it is regulated, and what the effects of regulation might be are not discussed.

For a number of reasons the time appears right for an analysis of the structure, behavior, and performance of the property and liability insurance industry operating within prevailing regulatory institutions. The recent performance of the industry has come under increasing criticism. Among other things, observers point to the shortages of fire and theft insurance in many of the nation's cities, a situation which required intervention by the federal government. Similarly there has been dissatisfaction with the availability of automobile insurance at desired coverage levels and reasonable rates through the voluntary insurance market. In addition, people have been concerned that the structure of insurance rates in many lines of insurance leads to levels of self-protection and self-insurance which are far from optimal. Finally, proposals for the implementation of no-fault auto insurance are intimately related to the structure and regulation of the insurance industry.

While unsatisfactory performance inevitably leads us to ask questions about industry structure and behavior, the presence of pervasive regulation necessitates an analysis of the regulatory environment in which this industry operates and of the possible effects of regulation on industry performance (as well as on industry structure and behavior). This appears to be a propitious time for an analysis of this regulatory process because after nearly 20 years of stability, many states are in the process of changing the way in which regulation of this industry proceeds. While some states are moving toward open competition and deregulation (New York for example), other states are moving toward adopting more traditional forms of rate-of-return regulation for the property insurance industry (New Jersey). Useful insights into the effects of regulation may be of help in aiding public policy makers in deciding which direction to move in.

This study pursues a basically traditional methodology familiar in studies of industrial organization and public utility regulation. The general lack of analyses of the property insurance industry

---

[1] Scherer [27], p. 2.
[2] Kahn [12], pp. 3 and 6.

justifies an initial attempt to lay out certain structural and institutional realities. The study therefore begins with an analysis of the structure of the property insurance industry. This section deals with such questions as market concentration, entry, economies of scale, as well as production and sales organization.

The second section examines the pricing behavior of the property insurance industry in the context of the institutional arrangements which affect pricing and the provision of property insurance. The effects of antitrust law, government regulation, and formal and informal cartel arrangements on the pricing behavior of property insurance firms are presented. Section 3 examines the performance of the property insurance industry in the context of a number of performance criteria, including supply shortages, profitability, and the efficiency of the product distribution system.

The major conclusions of the first three sections are that: (1) the property insurance industry has all of the structural characteristics of a competitive market; (2) the prior approval regulatory process employs a meaningless profitability criterion which does not necessarily "protect" consumers; (3) the insurance regulatory process has been the primary cause of supply shortages; (4) supply shortages exist at the same time that there is excess capacity; (5) the prevalent form of sales distribution system—the American Agency System— is extremely inefficient, costing consumers hundreds of millions of dollars per year; (6) available profitability studies indicate that rates of return for the industry as a whole are not excessive. While the presence of easy entry of agency firms does not make this result either surprising or particularly interesting, basic methodological flaws in these studies necessitate further research into insurance firm profitability. In addition there is evidence indicating that direct writers earn substantially higher rates of return than the industry as a whole; the underwriting behavior of direct writers is shown to be consistent with profit-maximizing oligopoly behavior of a small group of low cost firms, insulated from entry, and operating in a market where prices are kept above competitive levels by the combined actions of rating bureaus and insurance regulators.

In the final section, open competition as an alternative to all forms of direct government price regulation is suggested as a public policy goal. The property insurance industry provides a unique opportunity to do more than guess at what might happen under a regime of open competition (as opposed to regulation) because of the presence of a few instances of open or near-open competition in rates, which have actually been in operation during the period of general state regulation.

**2. The structure of the property and liability insurance industry**

■ **Basic structural characteristics.** Insurance is a method of spreading the risk of property loss among a group of individuals. The insured trades an uncertain state of the world in which he has a small probability of a large property loss and a high probability of no loss for a certain state in which he pays a small premium for insurance against loss. By purchasing insurance, the insured is able to move from a state of uncertainty to one of certainty. Insurance is generally a "bad bet." That is to say, the premium is generally greater than the expected property loss without insurance. The difference between premiums and losses over time is made up of underwriting and other transactions costs and the profits of insurance firms.

The insurance market is normally separated into two broad industry groups: the life insurance industry and the property and liability insurance industry. The property and liability insurance industry, which is the focus of this study, includes fire and marine insurance, extended coverage, automobile insurance, homeowners' and commercial multiperil insurance, some types of accident and health insurance, and various other types of property and liability insurance.

Automobile insurance accounted for nearly half of the total premiums written by the property-liability insurance industry in 1971.[3] This was not always the case. The dominance of automobile insurance is a post-World War II phenomenon, coinciding with increased automobile usage and the advent of compulsory auto liability insurance in many states. Historically, the structure, behavior, and regulation of this industry has its roots in fire insurance, which accounted for almost 30 percent of total property-liability premiums as late as 1943. This historical evolution is critical to an understanding of the property-liability insurance industry today, with regard to price determination and government regulation, and will be discussed extensively below.

Firms selling property and liability insurance in the U. S. are of four basic organizational forms. By far the most important type of firm is the *stock company*, owned by stockholders who have invested equity capital in the enterprise. Stock companies possessed $43 billion in assets in 1970 or 73 percent of the total assets of the property and liability industry and wrote over $22 billion in premiums or 68 percent of total industry premiums. *Mutual companies* are corporations which are owned by their policy holders. Instead of paying stock dividends out of profits, dividend payments are often made directly to policy holders, effectively lowering their insurance rates. In 1970 mutual companies had assets of $14 billion or 24 percent of

---

[3]

PREMIUM DISTRIBUTION BY LINE OF INSURANCE—1971

| Type of Insurance | Percent of Total |
|---|---|
| Fire | 6.3 |
| Allied Lines | 2.6 |
| Homeowners | 8.6 |
| Commercial Multiperil | 5.1 |
| Ocean Marine | 1.3 |
| Inland Marine | 2.6 |
| Group Accident and Health | 2.6 |
| All Other Accident and Health | 1.6 |
| Workmen's Compensation | 10.8 |
| Miscellaneous Liability | 6.9 |
| Auto Liability | 30.9 |
| Auto Physical Damage | 16.8 |
| Aircraft | 0.6 |
| Fidelity | 0.5 |
| Surety | 1.2 |
| Glass | 0.1 |
| Burglary | 0.4 |
| Boiler and Machinery | 0.4 |
| Credit | 0.1 |
| Miscellaneous | 0.6 |

Source: *Best's Review* [6], July 1972.

total industry assets and had premiums of almost $9 billion or 27 percent of total industry premiums. *A reciprocal exchange* is a co-operative organization formed to share specified risks of the members of the exchange. Reciprocal exchanges had assets of almost $2 billion in 1970 or 3 percent of total industry assets and wrote about $1.5 billion in premiums or 4 percent of total industry premiums. About 80 percent of the premiums of reciprocal exchanges are derived from auto insurance, and the reciprocals accounted for 7.6 percent of auto premiums in 1969. Finally, *Lloyd's Organizations* are made up of groups of underwriters, each taking on a portion of the insured's risks. Lloyd's Organizations accounted for only 0.1 percent of total industry assets and 0.1 percent of total industry premiums in 1970.[4]

Property insurance is marketed in two basic ways in the United States. The method employed by most stock companies is the American Agency System. Under the American Agency System independent retailers or agents represent a number of insurers and sell insurance for these companies to the public. For their efforts, the agents receive a commission, usually a fixed percentage of the premiums written. The system of "direct writing" arose in competition with the agency system, primarily (apparently) because of the high sales costs that had resulted. Insurance companies that became direct writers sold insurance directly, either through their own salesman or through the mail. Direct writing is a very important part of automobile insurance sales, accounting for nearly 50 percent of total auto premiums in 1971, but much less important in other insurance lines. Although the importance of direct writing has been growing over time, it has not grown so fast as one might expect.[5] An analysis of why this apparently superior marketing system has not completely taken over, and estimates of the economic losses attributable to the American Agency System, are presented in a section on industry performance below.

□ **Number of firms, concentration and entry.** *Best's* lists 840 stock companies, 311 mutual companies, 44 reciprocal exchanges, and 11 Lloyd's Organizations for a total of 1206 property-liability insurance companies operating in the United States in 1971. Most of these companies operate in more than one state and a substantial number of these companies operate nationwide. In 1971 about 80 percent of property-liability premiums were written by national agency companies or direct writers. Of 829 auto insurers analyzed for 1967, 650 of them were regional, multiregional or national and only 179 licensed to operate in only one state.[6]

---

[4] The previous data on market shares of the various types of "producers" comes from *Best's Aggregates and Averages* [4], 1971.

[5]

PERCENTAGE OF TOTAL PREMIUMS WRITTEN BY
AGENCY AND DIRECT WRITING COMPANIES

|  | 1967 | 1968 | 1969 | 1970 | 1971 |
|---|---|---|---|---|---|
| National and Regional Agency Companies | 71.5 | 70.5 | 69.5 | 69.0 | 68.5 |
| Direct Writers | 28.5 | 29.5 | 30.5 | 31.0 | 31.5 |

Source: *Best's Review* [6], July 1972.

[6] Federal Trade Commission Report [32], p. 13.

Any insurance company must be licensed in each of the states in which it operates. The various states have different laws governing the requirements for both incorporation in the state and for an out-of-state corporation operating within the state. In general, the state laws will specify a minimum amount of paid-in-capital necessary to commence operations. In addition, the laws will indicate what types of securities the minimum capital is to be kept in, as well as specify eligible investments for other financial reserves. In New York State, for example, the insurance law requires that a stock company have a minimum of $250,000 of paid-in-capital and an additional $250,000 of initial surplus to be organized as a fire insurance company in the state. In addition to selling fire insurance, such a company may also sell miscellaneous property insurance (essentially extended coverage), water damage insurance, collision insurance, motor vehicle and aircraft insurance (except liability for personal injuries), and certain types of marine insurance.[7] Out-of-state companies must maintain the same minimum capital requirements to be licensed in the state, while alien companies require 200 percent of the minimum capital requirements of domestic corporations. Companies wishing to sell various casualty lines not included under this classification must put up similar amounts of capital and surplus to be licensed to write such lines. In most states mutual companies have surplus requirements which are similar or identical to the total capital and surplus requirements of stock companies.

The presence of a large number of firms selling essentially identical products does not itself assure a competitive market structure in the industry. If a small number of firms control most of the market, the presence of many firms may only give the illusion of competition. As a result, we would like to examine the level of concentration in the property-liability insurance industry as a whole as well as within some individual lines of insurance. The concentration ratios presented below indicate the share of total property-liability insurance premiums written by the largest firm, the four largest firms, the eight largest firms, and the twenty largest firms for the nation as a whole. The definition of firm chosen here is that of the insurance *group*. Often individual insurance companies are part of the same jointly owned management group. Although individual companies within a group have considerable autonomy, joint directorships and ownership make it appropriate to consider an insurance group as one firm when examining questions of market control. Independent companies are considered as if they were groups composed of only one company.

A sales measure of concentration has been chosen—premiums written—instead of an asset measure so that national aggregate concentration ratios for the industry as a whole can be compared with concentration ratios for particular lines of insurance. Since asset accounts are not segregated by line, sales concentration measures are the only ones feasible. In addition, since group figures are being used, asset concentration ratios would probably be biased upward, reflecting the assets of particular companies in some groups which do very little actual property-liability insurance business.

The use of national concentration figures must also be defended.

---

[7] New York State Insurance Law, Article XI-A, Section 341.

In general, purchasers of insurance are limited to obtaining coverage from companies licensed within a particular state. However, since entry into any particular state by an established insurance company is very easy, sellers can easily move into any state if profitability conditions warrant it. In addition, the large national agency firms and the direct writers account for 81 percent of property-liability premiums written nationwide and operate in almost every state. Although there will be some local variation, the property-liability insurance firms are essentially operating in a national market.

The concentration ratios presented in Table 1 [8] indicate that although there were over 1200 firms selling property and liability

TABLE 1

CONCENTRATION IN THE PROPERTY AND LIABILITY INSURANCE INDUSTRY FOR SELECTED YEARS, % OF TOTAL NET PREMIUMS WRITTEN

| YEAR | TOP GROUP | TOP 4 GROUPS | TOP 8 GROUPS | TOP 20 GROUPS |
|------|-----------|--------------|--------------|---------------|
| 1962 | 4.4 | 16.5 | 29.0 | 48.1 |
| 1971 | 6.2 | 19.8 | 32.8 | 54.2 |

insurance in 1971, the top 20 groups controlled over half of the market. Comparisons with concentration ratios for other industries indicate that those for the property and liability insurance industry are relatively quite low.[9]

Table 1 does indicate, however, that the levels of concentration have been increasing over time. The rate of growth is relatively small, and even if the current growth rate in concentration continued, it would take many years before the four largest firms attained as much

[8] Calculated from data obtained from *Best's Aggregates and Averages* [4]. Comparable group data only available since 1962.

[9]

### 1963 CONCENTRATION RATIOS FOR REPRESENTATIVE INDUSTRIES
#### (4-Digit Industries)

| Industry | 4-Firm Ratio | 8-Firm Ratio |
|----------|--------------|--------------|
| Passenger Cars (5-digit) | 99 | 100 |
| Primary Aluminum | 96 | 100 |
| Cigarettes | 80 | 100 |
| Tires and Tubes | 70 | 89 |
| Motors and Generators | 50 | 59 |
| Beer and Malt Liquors | 34 | 52 |
| Cement | 29 | 49 |
| Fluid Milk | 23 | 30 |
| Men's and Boys' Suits | 14 | 23 |
| Bottled and Canned Soft Drinks | 12 | 17 |

Source: U. S. Senate, Committee on the Judiciary, Subcommittee on Antitrust and Monopoly, Report, *Concentration Ratios in American Manufacturing Industry:* 1963, Part I, 1966.

The comparison of sales concentration ratios for insurance firms with those for manufacturing enterprises probably overstates the relative degree of control of the firms in the insurance industry. Insurance firms can easily expand output in the short run with little or no increase in "capacity" and both output and capacity in the long run by obtaining more equity capital if such expansion is desirable to compete with a particular company which gets out of line in terms of price. Particular firms can vary output and "capacity" much more quickly and with less cost than could a steel or automobile firm.

as 50 percent of the market. More importantly, it will be argued below that the increasing levels of concentration are indicative of a secular movement of business away from high cost firms employing an inefficient marketing technique toward lower cost, more efficient firms. Increasing concentration in this case is the result of increasingly effective competition in a market constrained by a peculiar array of regulatory and other legal constraints. As shall be argued below, the slowly increasing level of concentration is indicative of an improvement, and not an erosion of consumer welfare.

Although these aggregate concentration ratios give us some indication of overall market control by leading firms in a national market, it is worthwhile to examine market concentration for individual lines of insurance. Automobile insurance appears to have concentration ratios somewhat higher than the industry as a whole, but these are still relatively low[10] and have been increasing at about the same rate as the industry as a whole. It will be argued below that these increased concentration ratios are indicative of movements of customers away from high cost firms operating under the American Agency System toward lower cost direct writers. Fire insurance possesses concentration levels almost identical to the property-liability industry as a whole (in 1971), and these concentration levels have been almost constant over time. This is indicative of the fact that fire insurance has been of declining importance to many property-liability firms and has been of only minor interest to direct writers using mass marketing techniques.[11] All things considered, the property-liability industry nationally and by line appears to possess an atomistic market structure.

☐ **Selling costs and scale economies.** Besides paying out money for losses and loss adjustment expenses, property-liability insurance companies also incur substantial sales or underwriting expenses. In 1970, selling expenses amounted to 36.0 percent of premiums written for stock companies, with commissions alone accounting for 21.4 percent of premiums written. Underwriting expenses were as high as 44.7 percent of premiums written in 1960. These figures may have important implications for theoretical work regarding economic

[10]

CONCENTRATION RATIOS FOR AUTOMOBILE INSURANCE
(% of Earned Premiums by Top Groups)

| Year | Top Group | Top 4 Groups | Top 8 Groups | Top 20 Groups |
|------|-----------|--------------|--------------|---------------|
| 1954 | 4.8 | 17.7 | 27.9 | 45.3 |
| 1962 | 7.5 | 21.0 | 31.1 | 46.6 |
| 1971 | 11.3 | 27.3 | 38.8 | 56.6 |

Calculated from data obtained from *The National Underwriter*, May 5, 1972, June 7, 1963, and May 19, 1955.

[11]

CONCENTRATION RATIOS FOR FIRE INSURANCE
(% of Net Premiums Written by Top Groups)

| Year | Top Group | Top 4 Groups | Top 8 Groups | Top 20 Groups |
|------|-----------|--------------|--------------|---------------|
| 1954 | 6.40 | 17.87 | 29.42 | 49.04 |
| 1962 | 5.28 | 19.42 | 31.64 | 53.88 |
| 1971 | 5.06 | 19.37 | 32.98 | 56.73 |

Calculated from data reported in *Best's Aggregates and Averages* [4].

decision making under uncertainty. The assumption of perfect "no-load" insurance markets is extremely questionable. With transactions costs for property-liability insurance ranging between 35 and 50 percent of premiums written, there may be many risks which are completely uninsurable under present market conditions. Assuming that selling costs plus a risk adjusted rate of return on investment are equal to 50 percent of the premiums, risks with probabilities of loss greater than $\frac{1}{2}$ may be uninsurable. Assuming that in a competitive market the premium for a risk is equal to the expected loss plus selling expenses plus a risk adjusted profit (profits will be discussed further below), with selling expenses equal to 50 percent of premiums, risks with a loss probability greater than $\frac{1}{2}$ will only be insured at a premium greater than the value of the property. Such a property is essentially uninsurable.

The property-liability insurance industry has traditionally been criticized for having excessive underwriting costs. Innovations or improved efficiency which could lower these costs would both increase the availability of property insurance and decrease the rates on those properties which are currently insured. Stock companies have traditionally borne the brunt of the criticism regarding selling costs, because their costs have traditionally been so much higher than those of mutual companies. This difference was especially pronounced ten years ago, but the difference between stock and mutual company expense ratios has declined secularly over the past ten years.[12]

The reduction of the proportion of the premiums going to selling and other underwriting expenses for stock companies appears to be in response to a fairly clear set of market stimuli. Relatively poor profit performance after the mid 1950s (the initial years of prior approval state regulation), resulting from rapid entry into the industry of all types of firms (especially the dramatic growth of direct writers selling at reduced prices in the profitable auto lines), led many stock companies operating under the American Agency System to cut costs by increasing internal efficiency and to force lower commission rates on the independent agents. Mutual companies have been able to keep their expenses low by paying lower commissions, concentrating on a few classes of business, and having exclusive agents who sell insurance for only one company. Even in 1970, brokerage and commission expenses for stock companies were substantially higher than similar expenses for mutual companies.

[12]

STOCK AND MUTUAL COMPANY EXPENSE RATIOS 1960–1970
(Expenses/Premiums Written)

| Year | Stock | Mutual |
|------|-------|--------|
| 1970 | 36.0 | 33.7 |
| 1969 | 37.6 | 34.4 |
| 1968 | 38.9 | 35.1 |
| 1967 | 39.7 | 34.3 |
| 1966 | 40.8 | 34.5 |
| 1965 | 42.1 | 35.2 |
| 1964 | 43.6 | 35.4 |
| 1963 | 44.3 | 36.2 |
| 1962 | 44.5 | 34.0 |
| 1961 | 45.0 | 34.9 |
| 1960 | 44.7 | 35.2 |

Source: *Best's Aggregates and Averages* [4], 1971.

It is argued below that the American Agency System is an extremely inefficient sales technique compared to the alternatives of direct writing and the use of exclusive agents. It has led to substantially higher insurance costs than would be yielded by the least cost marketing technique. It has been preserved as a combined result of price regulation by state commissions, price making in concert, and a quirk in the insurance law. The law vests property rights to policyholders in the independent agent who writes the insurance. It bars the company from independently writing insurance for a customer who was originally obtained through a particular agent. This issue is more conveniently analyzed after a discussion of economies of scale in the marketing of insurance is presented. We turn to this question now.

There is a tremendous range in the sizes (in terms of premiums written as well as assets) of property and liability insurance firms in the United States. There is a substantial number of firms with total annual premiums of less than $1 million and a few with total annual premiums of over $1 billion. Given this large variation in firm sizes, it is of interest to ask whether or not the larger firms have a cost advantage over the smaller firms. Such information will have important implications for a discussion of barriers to entry into the property-liability insurance industry, and the evaluation of the performance of the industry, especially with regard to the impact of state price regulation and cartel-like rating organizations. Substantial cost advantages for very large scale operations could indicate substantial barriers to entry and the possibility that large firms could set prices substantially above marginal cost without provoking competitive entry. At the same time the presence of a large number of small, high cost fringe firms may indicate that the large companies, acting through the cartel-like rating organizations, have succeeded in keeping prices above the competitive level, thus protecting inefficient producers. This latter phenomenon will most likely occur only if entry at optimum size is difficult.

A rather crude analysis of possible scale economies in the "production" of property-liability insurance has been performed by Hensley.[13] The study lacks any statistical tests, lumps American Agency companies together with direct writers, and does not correct for the "mix" of insurance lines in particular companies. His conclusion that there are moderate economies of scale may be especially sensitive to the nondifferentiation between direct writers and agency companies. Casual observation indicates that direct writers employ a more efficient sales technique and have a disproportionately high representation among large insurers. The study presented here should be an improvement on all of these counts. It offers a framework for answering the question of whether direct writing is the lower cost production technique. In addition, it provides useful empirical information for estimating the resource loss associated with the American Agency System.

The economies of scale analysis performed here relates expense ratios to measures of firm size, business character, and marketing technique for three different samples of companies: stock companies which are primarily auto insurance producers; mutual companies

[13] Hensley [11], p. 29.

which are primarily auto insurance producers; and stock companies which are primarily fire insurance producers. Each company sample is analyzed separately (the stock auto and stock fire samples for two different years), and then as a pooled regression.[14] The basic form of the model used in the economies of scale analysis is the following:

$$E = F(S, M, \epsilon),$$

where

    $E$ = Expense ratio,

    $S$ = Variables measuring size of the company,

    $M$ = Variables measuring marketing characteristics, and

    $\epsilon$ = Random disturbance term.

If there are economies of scale present, we would expect the expense ratio to decline with firm size. Since Hensley's analysis considered only the relationship between expense ratios and firm size, ignoring other characteristics of the firms, an initial set of regressions was run to see whether there is any "evidence" of scale economies when other company characteristics are omitted. Simple linear regressions relating the expense ratio to premium volume for three sets of data were calculated. The results for the regression equations in which premium volume enters linearly are reported below.[15]

*Fire and Allied Lines (1971)*

    $E = 34.28 - 0.5\ DPREM$     Observations: 25
       (21.22)    (−0.28)
    $R^2 = 0.003$

*Mutual Auto Insurers (1971)*

    $E = 26.41 - 0.60\ DPREM$     Observations: 34
       (23.30)    (−1.85)
    $R^2 = 0.09$

---

[14] All of the data employed in the expense analysis came from *Best's Aggregates and Averages* [4], 1972 and 1971 editions. The fire insurance company sample consists of 26 stock companies chosen from those listed in *Best's* as predominantly fire insurance writers in 1971. Additional data were collected for the 23 of these companies for which data were also available for 1970. The mutual company sample consists of 32 companies from those listed in *Best's* as predominantly auto (participating and deviating) for the year 1971 plus three additional companies listed under different headings but writing a substantial portion of their business in auto insurance. Finally the auto stock company sample originally consisted of 39 stock companies from those listed by *Best's* as predominantly auto (participating and deviating) for 1971—data inconsistencies and omissions reduced this sample to 36 companies for 1971. Additional data were collected for 37 of the original 39 companies for 1970.

    Determining which companies are direct writers was not an easy task. No generally available guide provides a concise listing. Attempts to get a listing of direct writers from *Best's*, etc., were only partially successful. As a result, it was necessary to supplement readily available information by going through corporate underwriting descriptions in *Best's Property and Liability Insurance Reports* [5], 1972 edition, company by company for each sample. Where there was some ambiguity the author's best judgment was used in making the allocations.

[15] These relationships were also estimated allowing premium volume to enter quadratically.

*Stock Auto Insurers (1971)*

$$E = 25.58 - 0.35 \ DPREM \qquad \text{Observations: 35}$$
$$(19.66) \quad (-0.92)$$
$$R^2 = 0.03$$

*Stock Auto Insurers (1970)*

$$E = 25.92 - 0.48 \ DPREM \qquad \text{Observations: 37}$$
$$(22.55) \quad (-1.13)$$
$$R^2 = 0.04,$$

where

$$E = \text{Expense ratio}$$
$$DPREM = \text{Direct premiums written.}$$

Even this naive formulation of the relationship between expenses and firm characteristics yields only weak evidence of scale economies. Although the coefficient of the premium volume variable was negative in all cases examined, it was only close to being significant at the 5-percent level in the mutual auto insurance sample. Allowing premium volume to enter quadratically did not yield any better results, nor did the use of net premiums instead of direct premiums. Even if no important explanatory relationships had been left out of these equations, the notion that there are economies of scale in the "production" of insurance is given only weak to moderate support by these results.

In addition to premium volume there are at least two prospective characteristics of the insurance firm which can be reasonably expected to affect expenses. One involves the firm's reinsurance activities. When a firm takes on insurance from other firms (reinsurance) it must make additional commission payments. When it cedes reinsurance to other firms, it receives commission income.[16] Therefore we would expect, *ceteris paribus*, that firms whose net premiums (after all reinsurance activity) are large relative to their direct premium writings will have higher expenses as a proportion of premiums written than firms whose net premiums are low relative to their direct premiums written.

A second important consideration is the method of sales. Some of the companies in these samples are direct writers and are in essence employing a different production activity than the agency firms. Although we would expect the least cost technique to be adopted in a competitive market in the long run, and would therefore expect the existence of two different techniques in competitive equilibrium to imply trivial cost differences, the behavior of this industry in this regard may be far from competitive. In particular, it is expected that direct writers will exhibit significant cost advantages, and that the agency firms have been able to survive because of a number of market imperfections. Finally, it is possible that direct writers or agency companies, but not both, exhibit economies of scale.

As a result, a far more reasonable production cost model is the following:

$$E = a + b \ DPREM + c \ INTER + d \ RATIO + e \ DWRITE,$$

---

[16] As the management of Equity Funding understood well.

where

$E =$ Expenses as a percentage of premiums written or earned,

$DPREM =$ Direct premium volume,

$INTER =$ Direct premium volume of direct writers and zero for agency companies,

$RATIO =$ Net premiums/direct premiums, and

$DWRITE =$ Dummy variable $= 1$ direct writers

$\qquad\qquad\qquad = 0$ otherwise.

The *a priori* expectations for the coefficients are the following.

$b$: This coefficient will be zero if economies of scale are absent and less than zero if economies of scale are present for agency companies.

$c$: This coefficient will be negative if direct writers have "more" scale economies than agency firms and positive if they have less.

$d$: This coefficient should be positive, indicating the premiums net "reinsurers" must pay.

$e$: This coefficient should be negative, indicating the cost savings associated with direct writing.

*Stock Auto (1970)*[17]

$$E = 21.41 - 0.28\ DPREM + 0.34\ INTER$$
$$\quad (7.35) \quad\ (-0.11) \qquad (0.14)$$
$$+ 8.10\ RATIO - 11.51\ DWRITE$$
$$\qquad (2.69) \qquad\qquad (-6.33)$$
$$R^2 = 0.61$$

*Stock Auto (1971)*

$$E = 20.70 + 0.86\ DPREM - 0.78\ INTER$$
$$\quad (6.66) \quad\ (0.34) \qquad (-0.30)$$
$$+ 7.49\ RATIO - 10.68\ DWRITE$$
$$\qquad (2.72) \qquad\qquad (-4.85)$$
$$R^2 = 0.54$$

*Stock Auto (1970 + 1971)*

$$E = 21.38 + 0.33\ DPREM - 0.24\ INTER$$
$$\quad (10.60) \quad\ (0.19) \qquad (-0.14)$$
$$+ 7.46\ RATIO - 11.08\ DWRITE$$
$$\qquad (3.88) \qquad\qquad (-8.07)$$
$$R^2 = 0.57$$

*Mutual Auto (1971)*

$$E = 14.63 - 0.62\ DPREM + 0.62\ INTER$$
$$\quad (2.45) \quad\ (-1.99) \qquad (1.99)$$
$$+ 16.36\ RATIO - 14.08\ DWRITE$$
$$\qquad (2.49) \qquad\qquad (-5.46)$$
$$R^2 = 0.55$$

---

[17] *T*-statistics appear in parentheses under the estimated coefficients.

*Stock Fire* (*1971*) (no Direct Writers in sample)
$$E = 33.74 - 0.45\ DPREM + 0.38\ RATIO$$
$$\quad\ (16.70)\qquad (-0.25)\qquad (0.45)$$

$R^2 = 0.01.$

The results of these regression estimates are of great interest. Evidence of economies of scale among stock companies and among direct writers is completely absent. There is evidence that mutual auto insurers exhibit scale economies,[18] although the direct writers in that sample do not. The conclusion must be that stock property and liability insurance companies and all types of direct writers, the types of companies which sell the vast majority of property and liability insurance, exhibit no significant scale economies. In addition, the *RATIO* variable and the dummy variable denoting direct writers always have the expected signs and are significant at the 5-percent level for each sample except that for the stock fire insurance companies.

This analysis leads to the conclusion that the production of property insurance is characterized by constant returns to scale. Large companies do not appear to be able to produce insurance less expensively than small companies. We observe higher costs for firms which assume reinsurance from other firms, but this can be viewed as a secondary production activity of insurance firms. Finally, direct writers appear to exhibit significant and substantial cost savings over agency companies.[19] This phenomenon will be discussed more fully in a section below.

☐ **Entry**. The difficulty of entry into an industry has important implications for the ability of the market to operate close to the competitive norm, especially in industries with high concentration ratios.[20] If a group of insurance companies act in concert through a cartel, attempting to hold prices well above competitive levels in the presence of only modest entry barriers, such efforts will ultimately be defeated by the entry of new firms. If existing firms wish to deter new entry, they must hold the margin between price and cost to a level less than the cost advantage existing firms have over potential entrants. Large deviations of price above the competitive level will tend to result only if the industry has a small enough number of firms to fix prices covertly or legal mechanisms which can enforce cooperative pricing *and* high barriers to the entry of new firms. Since concentration ratios are low in the property-liability industry, cartel-like pricing which might exist would have to rely on legal mechanisms supporting such pricing behavior. We will turn to the question of cooperative pricing

---

[18] This result may have emerged because the larger companies in the mutual company sample are all direct writers.

[19] This evidence should not be construed as implying that small companies are not *riskier* than large companies. The nature of insurance makes it essential that companies be large enough to exploit the law of large numbers. The opportunities for reinsurance facilitate this convergence greatly. An analysis of the loss experience of insurance firms and how it relates to company characteristics like size is now under way. In the context of the discussion presented here, the question of whether existing small firms exhibit significantly more loss variability than large firms will be analyzed.

[20] Bain [3].

in the next section, but it is shown below that even if regulation and rating bureaus can facilitate cooperative pricing, entry has been extensive and entry barriers are low to moderate, making it extremely unlikely that a substantial margin between prices and costs, resulting in excess profits, could persist.

The record for the past twelve years indicates that there has been continuous and substantial entry of corporations into the property-liability insurance industry. For the period 1960 to 1971 a total of 336 new companies are reported as entrants into the property-liability industry. The rate of entry has varied from a low of 14 companies in 1966 to a high of 51 companies in 1961.[21] This substantial amount of entry appears to be the result of rapid growth in the demand for property and liability insurance (especially auto insurance), a regulatory system which effectively pegs prices at a level that is on average above marginal cost,[22] and very low entry barriers. We examine entry barriers next and turn to the regulatory process in the next section.

Economies of scale have been examined in the previous section. Since they are nonexistent (at least for agency companies), they do not appear to be an important barrier to entry. In many American industries, even where substantial economies of scale in production do not exist, potential entrants face the problem of getting their products recognized by consumers in a market characterized by heavy product differentiation and entrenched brand loyalty. This has not been too much of a problem for potential entrants into insurance in the past for a number of reasons. The insurance product itself—the policy—is essentially identical from company to company within a state since most policy forms (except for special risks) are mandated by state law. Under the American Agency System consumers do not shop around for a company they recognize or like, but rather seek an agent who will try to get the customer insurance coverage from one of the companies that he represents, often at a price fixed by a rating bureau and adhered to by a large proportion of the companies in the market. Under the American Agency System the consumer must rely on his agent to find a company and secure the best price if there happens to be some price variation among com-

---

[21]

ENTRY INTO THE PROPERTY AND LIABILITY INSURANCE
INDUSTRY IN THE U. S. 1960–1971

| Year | Number of New Companies |
|------|------------------------|
| 1960 | 27 |
| 1961 | 52 |
| 1962 | 41 |
| 1963 | 35 |
| 1964 | 23 |
| 1965 | 18 |
| 1966 | 14 |
| 1967 | 24 |
| 1968 | 21 |
| 1969 | 15 |
| 1970 | 32 |
| 1971 | 34 |
| Total | 336 |

Source: *Best's Insurance News*, 1961–1971.

[22] See pp. 394–395, below.

panies. The company writing insurance under the American Agency System is therefore faced with minimal "product recognition" costs and instead must contact independent agents who will be willing to market the company's policies. The costs of "plugging in" to this existing marketing network should be very low.

Company identification is probably much more important for companies wishing to enter the market as direct writers. New companies must make expenditures to make consumers aware of their products. Mass advertising and direct mail campaigns are favorite devices for the establishment of product identification and for contacting potential customers. It is difficult to say whether this is an important barrier or not. The available information is quite ambiguous. For example, GEICO was able to enter the market at a relatively small size, has had extremely good earnings performance, and has become one of the largest automobile insurers in the country. However, the high levels of concentration among direct writers, as well as apparently consistent profit performance above the industry average, indicate that barriers to entry for direct writers may be quite high.[23] Substantial initial funding may be necessary to get a direct writer set up in the market.[24]

Artificial constraints on entry are also quite small. Rating bureaus must now be open to all to subscribe to or join. State licensing appears to be easily available to any company that can meet the minimum capital requirements and other statutory restrictions. Some states, however, still impose special taxes on companies domiciled in other states which would raise the costs of a foreign corporation. This is an effort by some states to protect domestic corporations and may deter entry by foreign or alien firms.

Entrants seeking to enter markets at deviated or bureau rates may experience opposition from rating bureaus which have often been recognized as aggrieved parties.[25] In addition, associations of insurance agents may attempt to restrict the entry of mutual companies, participating stock companies, and direct writers.[26]

All things considered, most of the traditional barriers to entry discussed so far appear to be quite low. The one remaining barrier is the capital requirement for entering the insurance market. We turn to this question now.

The capital requirements of a company seeking to become incorporated or to enter a state where it has not been licensed previously are not very high. State insurance laws normally set minimum amounts of paid-in-capital and surplus as a requirement for obtaining a license to sell insurance. The capital requirement varies

---

[23] These issues are discussed more fully below. The suggestion that there are moderate to high barriers to entry does not necessarily contradict the earlier finding that there are not economies of scale exhibited by direct writers. Those firms successfully operating in the market and included in our samples have probably been operating long enough to have achieved minimum efficient size. The entry barriers themselves are more of the nature of "threshold" barriers requiring substantial expenditures to gain even minimal market recognition.

[24] Allstate was able to use the existing Sears sales network, State Farm was able to use farm bureau contacts, and GEICO concentrated on a restricted group of customers at first.

[25] U. S. Senate, Subcommittee on Antitrust and Monopoly [31], Part 2, pp. 925, 930–931, 940.

[26] *Ibid.*, pp. 920–922.

from state to state and depends on the number of lines of insurance the company wishes to write. In New York State a stock company must have paid-in-capital and surplus of over $3,000,000 to write all nonlife lines. To write auto insurance it would require paid-in-capital and surplus of $500,000, but this would also entitle the company to write several other lines. Similar rules apply to mutuals.

All things considered, barriers to entry, at least for agency companies, appear to be low. Direct writers apparently are faced with higher barriers to entry, attributable primarily to advertising and other "product recognition" expenditures and the recruitment of a core of sales personnel. We would therefore expect that as long as the rating bureaus can keep insurance rates above the costs of agency companies, free entry will drive rates of return on capital toward the competitive level. However, we shall see below that such a "normal" profit equilibrium is characterized by prices above the competitive level, excess capacity in the industry as a whole, and selective underwriting (and above normal profits) by the low cost direct writers.

☐ **Market structure: conclusions.** The property-liability insurance industry possesses the structural characteristics normally associated with the idealized competitive market: a large number of firms, operating in a market with low concentration levels, selling essentially identical products, provided at constant unit costs and with ease of entry of new and potential competitors. The only deviation from the ideal is presented by the possibility that direct writers may face high entry barriers. It is indeed difficult to find too many other industries which conform more closely to the economist's idealized competitive market structure.

When we turn from market structure considerations to the behavior of the property-liability insurance industry, we do not find a continuation of the competitive ideal, however. Insurance rates have traditionally been set in concert through rating bureaus, with the rates subject to some form of state regulation in most cases. To understand the pricing behavior of the property-liability industry today, and to evaluate proposed changes in state regulation, the fault system and other public policy issues, we must first examine the development of rate making in concert, antitrust, and regulatory policy as it pertains to this industry.

■ **The development of government policy toward the insurance industry.** Although a majority of the property and liability insurance sold in the United States today consists of auto and homeowners' multiperil insurance, industry price setting behavior and government regulatory policy have their origins in fire insurance. Since fire and allied lines insurance was a very important component of the property insurance industry as recently as World War II, this is not too surprising. To understand how current pricing behavior and regulatory control evolved, we must take an excursion back into history.[27]

The history of fire insurance rating and regulation is a direct con-

**3. Pricing behavior in the property and liability insurance industry**

---

[27] A more detailed discussion of the history of government policy toward the insurance industry is contained in my paper, "Regulation and Deregulation in the Property Insurance Industry, 1870–1973," unpublished.

sequence of the essentially noncompetitive fire insurance market, dominated by cartels and essentially exempt from the federal antitrust laws, that existed through most of the first half of this century.

The development of cooperative fire rate making goes back to the beginning of the 19th century:

It began with local boards, one of which was organized in New York in 1819. In 1866, the National Board of Fire Underwriters was organized to establish and maintain uniform premium rates and to control agents' commissions . . . . During profitable periods in the fire insurance business, however, companies violated their membership agreements by ratecutting.[28]

The National Board was discontinued in 1877 as a countrywide rating organization and replaced with local and regional rating organizations. The National Board was essentially a cartel meant to fix rates, to overcome the "bad effects" of competition—namely insolvencies—and generally to "stabilize" the market. It had difficulty succeeding as a cartel because membership was voluntary and it was difficult to force a large number of firms to adhere to the bureau rates.

The development of the "compact system" succeeded the demise of the National Board.[29] Under this system local insurance agents agreed to respect uniform rates set by compact managers. The "compact system," however, was evolving at the peak of antitrust fever in the United States. From 1885 to 1907 about 20 states enacted anticompact laws to combat price fixing in fire insurance. The compact laws do not appear to have been very successful in stemming the *de facto* fixing of rates in concert.[30]

By the late 19th Century proposals for regulation of insurance rates were made in several states. A Joint Legislature Committee, known as the Merritt Committee, was formed in New York in 1910 to study problems of fire insurance rate making. Based primarily on the findings of the Merritt Committee, an insurance law was passed in New York State in 1911 which permitted "action in concert in the fixing of fire insurance rates, but required rating associations or bureaus to file such rates with the Superintendent of Insurance."[31] The legislation required that rates set not be unfairly discriminatory. Although the Superintendent of Insurance could evaluate rates after they were filed, prior approval was not required at this time.

There are two interesting features of government policy toward the insurance industry at this time. The primary concern of both the insurance companies and their regulators was to guard against rates that were *too low*. Competition was viewed by industry and its regulators as leading to instability and insolvencies among fire insurance firms. The regulatory agencies apparently did not view their jobs as guarding against monopolistic pricing resulting from rate making in concert, but rather as making sure that firms did not charge

---

[28] New York State Insurance Department [21], p. 69.

[29] The National Board continued to exist, but not as a formal rating bureau.

[30] Merritt Committee Report [22], reprinted in [31], p. 2791.

[31] New York State Insurance Department [21], p. 69. The *raison d'etre* of the Merritt Committee report seems to have been to convince state legislators that unregulated competition in insurance would be "destructive" with regard to the financial viability of insurance companies as well as incentives to provide rate structures which encourage fire prevention.

off-bureau rates that were too low. Competition in fire insurance rate making was viewed as being destructive and rating bureaus and regulatory agencies made sure that price competition became virtually nonexistent. No study seems to exist which shows that competition in fire insurance is any more "destructive" than in any other industry, and it appears that the evolution of regulation of the fire insurance industry stems more from an effort to protect existing firms than the interests of consumers.

The second interesting feature of public policy toward the insurance industry involves the federal antitrust statutes enacted between 1890 and 1914. The coordinated rate-setting activities engaged in by insurance firms through the rating organizations would appear to be in clear violation of the federal antitrust laws. However, the decision of the Supreme Court in *Paul v. Virginia*,[32] upholding a state law subjecting an out-of-state insurance company and its local agents to a licensing requirement, contained language which was interpreted for the next 75 years as meaning that insurance could not be classified as interstate commerce.[33] As a result, the insurance industry was considered to be exempt from the federal antitrust laws.

Before 1944 the position of the fire insurance industry vis-à-vis government control was characterized by a general exemption from federal antitrust laws and direct state regulation of fire insurance rates in about 35 states. On June 5, 1944, a dramatic shift occurred in the court's interpretation of the commerce clause and implicitly of the applicability of the antitrust laws to the insurance industry tool. The court's opinion in *United States v. South-Eastern Underwriters Association*[34] ruled that insurance was commerce and by implication that combinations of insurance companies designed to fix rates would be in violation of the Sherman Act:[35]

Overnight, the entire legal basis for the immunity of combinations in rate-making, the cornerstone of the fire insurance business—and hence, at that time, of the dominant segment of the property-liability insurance business—was eliminated. Moreover, doubt was cast on the system of state regulation and taxation of the insurance business. The decision precipitated widespread controversy and dismay. Chaos was freely predicted.[36]

Undoubtedly under tremendous pressure from the insurance industry, the U. S. Congress stepped into the picture. The McCarran-Ferguson Act,[37] signed by President Roosevelt on March 9, 1945, declared the continued regulation and taxation of the insurance industry to be in the public interest and that the federal antitrust laws

---

[32] 8 Wall 168 (1869).

[33] Among those cases that relied on this interpretation were Hooper v. California (155 U. S. 648), Liverpool Insurance Company v. Massachusetts (10 Wall 566), Philadelphia Fire Insurance Association v. New York (119 U. S. 110), Nutting v. Massachusetts (183 U. S. 533) and National Union Fire Insurance Co. v. Wanberg (260 U. S. 71).

[34] 322 U. S. 533 (1944).

[35] It is interesting to note that the state regulatory authorities were opposed to the majority opinion. Thirty-five state insurance departments joined in an *amicus curiae* brief opposing the classification of insurance as commerce. The dissenting opinions of Mr. Justice Jackson and Mr. Justice Stone indicated that the court's action might not only allow federal antitrust statutes to be applied to the insurance industry, but actually nullify the authority of individual states to regulate and tax the insurance industry.

[36] New York State Insurance Department [21], p. 69.

[37] Public Law 15, 79th Congress; 59 Stat. 33–34 (1945).

to be applied to the insurance industry only to the extent that the insurance business was not regulated by the states.

Exactly what was meant by regulation by the states was not made clear by the act nor by its legislative history.[38] The National Association of Insurance Commissioners, acting together with industry representatives, drafted two model bills which would establish state regulation of the business of insurance and preclude the application of the antitrust statutes against the insurance industry:

The overriding concern of the framers of these All-Industry model bills was to preserve the business and regulatory *status quo* and to demonstrate that rate-making, in particular, bureau rate-making, would be quite explicitly 'regulated' by the states. This approach was designed to provide a state regulatory umbrella under which cooperative rate-making by bureaus would be exempt from the Federal antitrust laws.[39]

Eventually 44 states enacted new laws or amended existing laws to conform to the NAIC-All Industry model bills. These laws, known as prior approval laws, were the predominant form of regulation of the property-liability insurance industry from 1940 to 1970.[40]

□ **Setting insurance rates under the prior approval regulatory system.** Setting rates for property and liability insurance is a relatively complex procedure. This section describes the general technique and rate-making formulas which regulatory agencies have been applying in the "prior approval" states since 1944.

Under the prior approval laws fire insurance rate making involved the use of a fairly standard formula for the production and evaluation of bureau rates, rate revisions and rate deviations. Prior approval regulation does not involve the traditional public utility concept of fair rate of return on capital. Instead rates are established so as to yield a particular rate of return on sales (premiums). A standard rate of return on sales figure of 5 percent is employed in most states as a result of a recommendation by the National Association of Insurance Commissioners in 1921.[41] This figure appears to have been picked out of thin air. It does not relate profitability to return on capital nor even to competitive profit margins on sales in other industries having the same capital base per unit of output or sales. In addition, investment income is not included as revenue. The technique appears to be *a priori* nonsensical. Although usually faced with many companies selling fire insurance in a particular state, adherence to bureau rates was so great that most regulatory agencies had to approve only bureau rate filings and a moderate number of rate

---

[38] Brainard and Dirlam [7], pp. 248–253.

[39] New York State Insurance Department [21], p. 72.

[40] Various other schemes were adopted in other states. California adopted a "No-Filing" system in 1947, essentially leaving rate determination to the market. Texas instituted state-made rates for many lines of insurance to which all insurers were required by law to adhere. North Carolina required bureau membership of all insurers. Other systems involved minor procedural differences from the prior approval laws.

[41] It is interesting to notice that the NAIC 1921 profit formula bears a strange resemblance to a report written by Wilfred Kurth of the Home Insurance Company in 1919 and entitled "What Constitutes a Reasonable Underwriting Profit and the Method of Determining Same." The profit formula recommended by the insurance commissioners in 1921 appears in fact to be almost identical to that recommended by Kurth.

deviations based on the rating bureau filings themselves. In New York, for example, the rating formula was applied to the rate applications of the New York Fire Insurance Rating Organization in determining fire insurance rates.

In general, we can summarize the pricing formula for rates of a particular line of property insurance as one which sets insurance rates to cover losses, expenses and a profit factor (5 percent of premiums) based on aggregate experience for the industry as a whole in a particular state. While individual class by class rates are set in a similar way, aggregate profitability is the binding constraint. Rates set below the "formula" figure for some class will be compensated for by rates set above the "formula" figure for one or more other classes:

$$E + \frac{L_i}{P_i} + 0.05 = 1$$

$$P_i = \frac{L_i}{(1 - 0.05 - E)}$$

$P_i$ = Total premiums for a particular territory and class,
$E$ = Measure of historical operating and production expense ratio, and
$L_i$ = Measure of historical losses (estimate of expected losses) for this territory and class.

If there are $X_i$ identical risks in a particular territory and class (let us say they are automobiles), we would expect the average basic premium for this class and territory to be $P_i/X_i$ per car. Letting $\Sigma P_i = P =$ total premiums indicated by the formula rating for all classes and territories in the state, we have:

$$P_i = \frac{L_i}{(0.95 - E)} \tag{1}$$

$$P = \frac{\Sigma L_i}{(0.95 - E)}. \tag{2}$$

Note that if for some reason the insurance regulators feel that some particular class $j$ yields an average premium $\frac{P_j}{K_j}$ which is in some sense "too high" (even though appropriate, given historical losses), the rating formula works in such a way that (2) is always met, whether or not (1) is met in all particular classes. This means that forced reductions in some classes' rates are automatically loaded on to the rates for the remaining classes of customers. We will return to this point when we discuss assigned risk pools, FAIR plans, and implicit attempts by regulatory agencies to redistribute income.

□ **Price competition under the prior approval regulatory system.** Although the property-liability insurance industry possesses a market structure that is characteristic of a competitive market, the industry is notable for the limited amount of price competition which actually exists. Fire insurance companies only rarely tend to deviate from fixed bureau rates which have been approved by the regulatory authority. The automobile lines have tended to have a greater amount of price competition, primarily because of the direct writers who often deviate below fixed bureau rates. But even by the end of the 1960s, a large proportion of automobile insurance was written at rates copied right out of the IRS guide. Most prior approval insurance laws authorized rating bureaus to make and file rates, rate changes, rating schedules, etc., for their member and subscriber companies. Companies not wishing to use the bureau rates had two options open to them: they could file deviated rates for one or more classes of insurance or they could submit an independent filing.

A company wishing to deviate from the bureau rates would simply have to file an application with the Superintendent of Insurance requesting to write one or more lines of insurance at some amount (say 15 percent) less than the rates then in effect for the members and subscribers of the rating bureau. The deviating company had to justify its rate deviation application by showing that its reduced rates were justified by lower costs than for the industry as a whole. Since its costs were lower, such a company could reduce its rates and still earn an "adequate" profit. Regulatory scrutiny of rate deviations appears to have been most concerned with keeping firms from filing deviations which would result in rates which were "too low" and might result in "destructive" competition.

Independent filings represent the submission of a complete set of rates, rating schedules, etc., which a particular company plans to follow, as opposed to the much simpler across-the-board reduction in bureau rates. For reasons which will become obvious presently, true independent filings have been rare in the insurance industry.

Observers have often criticized the administration of deviation procedures as tending to discourage companies from filing rate deviations. In many states rate deviations had to be renewed annually and rating organizations were often recognized as aggrieved parties. This allowed them to challenge rate deviations and independent filings. Groups of companies, acting through the rating bureaus, could thus challenge deviations and independent filings leading to protracted and often costly proceedings.[42] The possibility of opposition to deviations and independent filings has been pointed to as being especially discouraging to new entrants and small firms wishing to sell at off-bureau rates.[43] Some of the more restrictive deviation procedures were gradually liberalized. The right of bureaus to act as aggrieved parties was banned in many states and the requirement that deviation filings be renewed each year was eliminated. In addition, many insurance departments continued to support companies which could justify lower rates whether they were independent filings or deviations from bureau rates.[44]

Although it has been argued that price competition gradually increased over time under the prior approval laws,[45] it is extremely difficult to obtain adequate data necessary to quantify this trend in prior approval states. Some suggestive data for New York for the late 1960s are available, however.

---

[42] U. S. Senate, Subcommittee on Antitrust and Monopoly [31], Part 2, pp. 924–940, and Part 3, pp. 1794–1845.

[43] *Ibid.*, pp. 938–939, 1129, 1179.

[44] Cullen v. Bohlinger 350 U. S. 803 (1955), and Cullen v. Holtz and Allstate Insurance Co. 6 N. Y. 2nd 1971 (1959).

[45] Brainard and Dirlam [7], pp. 243–244.

Table 2 indicates the overall price competition for the property-liability insurance in New York State.[46] Given the large number of companies in New York and the encouragement that the insurance department gave to price competition under the strictures of prior approval, the New York experience should indicate the maximum tendencies to price at other than bureau rates under the prior approval system. Fire insurance had only 8.9 percent of its premiums written at off-bureau rates while auto physical damage had 24.7 percent of the premiums written at off-bureau rates. Even in 1967, after many of the initial blockages to deviations and independent filings had been removed, the vast majority of the insurance policies were sold at the agreed upon cartel rate.

Table 3 indicates the results for the 30 largest insurers in New York State for three years and for three different lines of insurance. These figures differ from those of the first table because if a company filed a substantial number of deviations, all insurance it wrote was counted as being written at deviated rates, even if some of the rates were the same as the bureau rates. These calculations therefore count as a "competitive" price those rates or classes for which deviating and independent companies felt the bureau rate was justified by expense

TABLE 2

PERCENTAGE OF DIRECT PREMIUMS WRITTEN IN NEW YORK AT OFF-BUREAU RATES – 1967

| | |
|---|---|
| FIRE AND ALLIED LINES, AND EXTENDED COVERAGE | 8.9% |
| HOMEOWNERS | 22.5% |
| COMMERCIAL MULTIPERIL | 14.4% |
| AUTOMOBILE LIABILITY | 22.6% |
| AUTOMOBILE PHYSICAL DAMAGE | 24.7% |
| LIABILITY OTHER THAN AUTO | 23.1% |

SOURCE: NEW YORK STATE INSURANCE DEPARTMENT [21], p.93.

TABLE 3

PRICE COMPETITION IN NEW YORK STATE AMONG THE TOP 30 INSURANCE COMPANIES AND ASSIGNED RISK PLAN (UNDER PRIOR APPROVAL)

| TYPE OF INSURANCE | | % AT BUREAU RATES | % OFF BUREAU RATES | NO. OF COMPANIES OFF BUREAU RATES |
|---|---|---|---|---|
| AUTO LIABILITY | 1967 | 61.8 | 38.2 | 8 |
| | 1968 | 61.3 | 38.7 | 8 |
| | 1969 | 61.7 | 38.3 | 7 |
| AUTO PHYSICAL DAMAGE | 1967 | 53.1 | 46.9 | 8 |
| | 1968 | 54.1 | 45.9 | 8 |
| | 1969 | 53.0 | 47.0 | 7 |
| HOMEOWNERS INSURANCE | 1967 | 77.2 | 22.8 | 6 |
| | 1968 | 77.9 | 22.1 | 6 |
| | 1969 | 75.3 | 24.7 | 6 |

SOURCE: NEW YORK STATE INSURANCE DEPARTMENT [18], pp. 21-25.
NEW YORK STATE INSURANCE DEPARTMENT [19], p. 63

and loss experience. As a result, these figures indicate substantially more competition in these lines than the latter. Even so, less than a third of the companies were filing deviating or independent rates, and both the number of companies and proportions of premiums written at off-bureau rates remained approximately constant for the three years.

Of course there is the chance that the rating bureaus are setting prices at or near competitive levels, and this is why there have been so little price diversity and differences from bureau rates. Preliminary evidence indicates that this is not the case and that bureau rate making under prior approval rate regulation leads to substantially

---

[46] Under prior approval rate regulation.

TABLE 4

PERCENTAGE OF DIRECT
PREMIUMS WRITTEN AT OFF
BUREAU RATES IN CALIFORNIA

| TYPE OF INSURANCE | |
|---|---|
| FIRE AND EXTENDED COVERAGE | 32.0% (1967) |
| HOMEOWNERS | 67.7% (1967) |
| AUTOMOBILE LIABILITY | 49.9% (1966) |
| AUTOMOBILE PROPERTY DAMAGE | 45.9% (1966) |

SOURCE: NEW YORK STATE
INSURANCE DEPARTMENT
[21], p. 93.

less competition. The evidence takes two forms. One is the experience in California where regulation was not based on the all-industry prior approval system, but has been instead much closer to open competition in rate setting. The second source is New York State experience since January 1, 1970, when an experimental law went into effect, which essentially eliminated the prior approval system and substituted a California-type open competition ("no filing") rating system. Tables 4 and 5 should be compared with Tables 2 and 3.

Table 4 shows that at the same period of time, California, operating under an open competition law, had a substantially larger proportion of premiums written at off-bureau rates than had New York, which was operating under the prior approval regulatory statutes. However, Table 5 indicates that when the prior approval restrictions were eliminated, the power of rating bureaus reduced, and price competition encouraged in New York in 1970, the percentage of premiums written (implicitly the number of companies writing at off-bureau rates) at off-bureau rates increased substantially.

TABLE 5

COMPANIES WRITING PREMIUMS AT OFF BUREAU RATES
AMONG 30 TOP INSURERS AND THE ASSIGNED RISK PLAN
(NEW YORK 1970-1972)

| TYPE OF INSURANCE | | % OF PREMIUMS AT BUREAU RATES | % OF PREMIUMS AT OFF BUREAU RATES | NO. OF COMPANIES OFF BUREAU RATES |
|---|---|---|---|---|
| AUTO LIABILITY | 1970 | 66.8 | 33.2 | 7 |
| | 1971 | 66.7 | 33.3 | 6 |
| | 1972 | 49.4 | 50.6 | 12 |
| AUTO PHYSICAL DAMAGE | 1970 | 56.0 | 44.0 | 9 |
| | 1971 | 40.5 | 59.5 | 15 |
| | 1972 | 14.6 | 85.4 | 26 |
| HOMEOWNERS | 1970 | 69.1 | 30.9 | 7 |
| | 1971 | 42.8 | 57.2 | 10 |
| | 1972 | 21.1 | 78.9 | 17 |

SOURCE: NEW YORK STATE INSURANCE DEPARTMENT [18], pp. 21-25.
NEW YORK STATE INSURANCE DEPARTMENT [19], p. 63.

The evidence supports the hypothesis that rate making in concert, combined with prior approval rate regulation, tended to discourage price competition. The rating bureaus with the knowing or unknowing help of the regulators had managed to maintain at least moderate cartel control of insurance prices in almost all of the property-liability insurance lines.

## 4. The performance of the property and liability insurance industry

■ The notion of industry performance is of course quite ambiguous, primarily because of its multidimensional nature. This section will analyze the following three aspects of the performance of the property-liability insurance industry:

(1) the efficiency of the prevailing production and distribution system;

(2) supply shortages; and

(3) profitability and capacity utilization.

The analysis is based on the notion that ideally we would like an insurance industry which provided insurance as cheaply as possible, confronting consumers with prices equal to the marginal (expected) costs of coverage and equilibrating supply and demand at the prevailing market price.

It is argued here that the combination of cartel rate making and other collusive behavior with state regulation of rates, rating classes, territories and other insurance practices has resulted in:

(1) the use of a grossly inefficient sales and distribution technique (the American Agency System);

(2) severe supply shortages; and

(3) unnecessarily high prices, excess capacity, but probably only normal profits for the industry as a whole.

☐ **Sales distribution technique: the American agency system.** Historically, fire and property insurance was sold through independent agents and brokers to the public. Insurance companies themselves did not possess their own retail sales personnel. For this service agents were paid on a fixed commission basis, with the commission set at some percentage of the customer's premium. Agents' organizations and rating bureaus often worked together to keep rates high by refusing to allow agents to sell the insurance of nonbureau firms. In return the agents sought high commission rates from the companies that they represented. Casual empiricism indicates that the selling costs through the American Agency System were higher than necessary to provide effective service. Mutual companies, writing through their own groups of agents or directly to consumers, often sold insurance at lower prices than the agency stock companies and still managed to have better underwriting results than the stock companies. The growth of direct writers in auto insurance after World War II, their ability to charge lower rates, and their financial success and fantastic growth rates reinforced the idea that the middlemen agents could be either eliminated or their numbers greatly reduced, resulting in substantial cost savings.

The analysis presented below indicates that the cost savings from full use of the direct writing or exclusive agency technique would result in substantial cost savings in the provision of insurance. It is argued that stock companies using the American Agency System have the highest costs and the highest prices and are employing an inefficient production technique, costing consumers hundreds of millions of dollars annually.

To explain company expense ratios we use the basic model employed in the returns to scale section. For the analysis presented in this section two relationships were estimated. In the first, observations on stock fire insurance companies, mutual auto insurance companies, and stock auto insurance companies were grouped together and the following relationship estimated:

$$E = \alpha + \beta \; DPREM + \lambda \; INTER + \gamma \; RATIO$$
$$+ \; \delta \; DWRITE + \phi \; D_1 + \psi \; D_2,$$

where

$$D_1 = 1 \quad \text{auto stock companies}$$
$$= 0 \quad \text{otherwise}$$
$$D_2 = 1 \quad \text{mutual auto companies}$$
$$= 0 \quad \text{otherwise.}$$

The estimate of $\delta$ is then used to measure potential efficiency gains from direct writing for the entire property-liability insurance industry. In the second, only observations on auto companies are used, and the following relationship is estimated:

$$E = \alpha_a + \beta_a \, DPREM + \lambda_a \, INTER$$
$$+ \gamma_a \, RATIO + \delta_a \, DWRITE + \phi_a \, D_1.$$

The estimate of $\delta_a$ is used to estimate potential efficiency gains from the use of direct writing in auto insurance only. For the first relationship with observations on stock fire, mutual auto, and stock auto insurance companies, we obtain:

$$E = 33.85 - 0.65 \, DPREM + 0.73 \, INTER + 0.70 \, RATIO$$
$$(31.42) \quad (-0.73) \quad (0.80) \quad (1.67)$$

$$- 10.82 \, DWRITE - 5.79 \, D_1 - 6.23 \, D_2$$
$$(-7.88) \quad (5.05) \quad (-3.70)$$

$$R^2 = 0.51 \quad 157 \text{ observations.}$$

For the second relationship with observations only on auto companies we obtain:[47]

$$E = 21.00 - 0.99 \, DPREM + 1.05 \, INTER + 7.90 \, RATIO$$
$$(10.84) \quad (-0.67) \quad (0.70) \quad (4.31)$$

$$- 11.48 \, DWRITE - 0.32 \, D_1$$
$$(-9.65) \quad (0.32)$$

$$R^2 = 0.54 \quad 108 \text{ observations.}$$

The results indicate that overall, the expense ratios of direct writers average 10.82 percentage points less than the agency companies *ceteris paribus*. For the auto companies themselves the figure is 11.48. In addition, the expense ratios for auto insurers average about 6 percentage points less than those for fire insurance companies. This latter result may have emerged because there has been much more competition in auto insurance lines than in fire lines. As a result, in order to stay competitive with direct writers who could justify rate deviations by their lower costs, agency companies may have been forced to cut commissions to agents selling auto policies. Finally (from $\phi_\alpha$) the cost structures for stock and mutual auto insurers are not significantly different from one another.

Let us assume that the technology for producing insurance business contains only two activities: direct writing and agency writing. Let us assume further that in a well-functioning competitive market the choice among these two activities would be based strictly on which was the least cost activity (the outputs are the same), first

---

[47] The results for the sample without the fire insurance companies and without $D_1$ and $D_2$ were the following:

$$E = 21.20 - 0.99 \, DPREM + 1.05 \, INTER + 7.92 \, RATIO - 11.44 \, DWRITE$$
$$(11.53) \quad (-0.67) \quad (0.70) \quad (4.34) \quad (-9.71)$$

$$R^2 = 0.54 \quad 108 \text{ observations.}$$

for the auto insurance industry only and then for the property-liability insurance as a whole. At current output and price levels we may calculate the efficiency gain from use of the direct writing system as follows:

$$EG = A \times B \times C,$$

where

    $EG$ = Efficiency gain per year

    $A$ = Expense saving (expressed as a percentage of premiums)

    $B$ = Total premiums

    $C$ = Proportion of premiums written by other than direct writers.

Factor ($A$) can be obtained from the regression results reported above and factor ($B$) is available from *Best's*. I was able to find a value for $C$ for the $P - L$ industry as a whole (direct writers = 31.5 percent) but was not able to find a precise figure for the auto lines. I have estimated it as 50 percent direct writing:[48]

$$EG \ (\text{Auto}) = \$830.0 \ \text{million}$$

$$EG \ (\text{Total} \ P - L) = \$2.64 \ \text{billion}$$

The measure can also be represented as the shaded area in Figure 1. Here $r^*$ is the prevailing price per unit of coverage, and $AC_1$ and $AC_2$ represent the average costs per unit of coverage under the agency system and direct writing, respectively (including the "regulated" profit factor).[49]

Now, this calculation assumes that the price remains at $r^* = AC_1$. However, even under regulation we would expect the price to fall to at least $AC_2$, yielding an additional increase in consumer surplus equal to the small triangle labelled *abl*. If prices remain at $r^*$, the entire efficiency gain has been absorbed as higher profits to the insurance industry. The additional gain in efficiency from a price reduction will

FIGURE 1

SUPPLY AND DEMAND FOR INSURANCE COVERAGE

PRICE PER UNIT OF COVERAGE

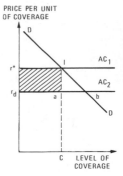

LEVEL OF COVERAGE

---

[48] This estimate is probably on the high side. I was able to obtain detailed evidence concerning the percentage of premiums written by direct writers in the State of New Jersey in 1971.

| Line | % of Premiums Written by Direct Writers |
| --- | --- |
| Fire | 8.24% |
| Homeowners | 24.20% |
| Auto Liability | 45.09% |
| Auto Physical Damage | 49.69% |
| Total for 9 Property Insurance Lines | 35.79% |

[49] Let $r^*$ = Price per dollar of coverage under the present system,

    $l_a$ = Expenses per dollar of coverage under present system,

    $L$ = Expected losses per dollar of coverage,

    $\pi$ = Profit per dollar of coverage,

    $l_d$ = Expenses per dollar of coverage under direct writing system,

    $C$ = Insured value,

    $r^* = l_a + L + \pi = AC_1,$

    $r^*C = P,$

    $P$ = Total premiums,

    $r_d = l_d + L + \pi = AC_2,$

$(r^* - r_d)C = EG = (l_a - l_d)C,$ and

    $r = \dfrac{r^* + r_d}{2}$

depend on the elasticity of demand and the difference between $r^*$ and $r_d$.

Assuming a linear demand function[50] and $\Delta r$ and $\Delta C$ small, we may approximate the dead weight loss resulting from setting price at $AC_1$ as

$$w = \tfrac{1}{2}\text{ (Premium Volume) (Elasticity of Demand)}$$
$$\text{(\% Change in Expense Ratio)}^2.[51]$$

TABLE 6

DEAD WEIGHT LOSSES FOR SELECTED ASSUMPTIONS ABOUT DIRECT
WRITING POSSIBILITIES AND THE ELASTICITY OF DEMAND FOR INSURANCE

(\$ MILLIONS)

| ELASTICITY | UNDERWRITING POSSIBILITIES | | | |
|---|---|---|---|---|
| | (1) | (2) | (3) | (4) |
| 0.5 | 46.9 | 23.5 | 104.1 | 71.3 |
| 1.0 | 93.8 | 46.9 | 208.3 | 142.7 |
| 1.5 | 140.8 | 70.4 | 312.4 | 214.0 |
| PRIMARY* EFFICIENCY GAIN | 830.0 | 830.0 | 2,640.0 | 2,640.0 |
| *AS CALCULATED PREVIOUSLY | | | | |

The dead-weight welfare gain from direct writing as shown in Table 6 is calculated for three different elasticity measures—$\eta = 0.5$, $1.0$, and $1.5$—based on different assumptions:

(1) Only auto insurance can be successfully sold using direct writing and *all* companies charge $r^*$ under the current system;

(2) Only auto insurance can be successfully sold using direct writing and direct writers charge $r_d$ under the current system;

(3) All property-liability insurance can be successfully sold using direct writing and direct writers charge $r^*$ under the current system;

(4) All property-liability insurance can be successfully sold using direct writing and direct writers charge $r_d$ under the current system.

---

[50] This ignores income effects.

[51] Under these assumptions the dead-weight welfare loss may be approximated as

$$w = \tfrac{1}{2}(r^*C)\eta \, \frac{\Delta r^2}{r},$$

where

$r^*C$ = total premiums $(P)$,
$\eta$ = elasticity of demand, and
$\Delta r$ = change in the price per unit of coverage $(r^* - r_d)$.

But what is the relationship between the percentage change in the price per unit of coverage and the expense ratio reduction which we have already calculated? We know that

$$r^*C = P$$

and

$$r^* - r_d = l - l_d$$

so that

$$C(r^* - r_d) = C(l_a - l_d) = \text{total expenses}$$

and

$$\frac{C(l_a - l_d)}{P} = \Delta E \ (\Delta E = \text{difference in expense ratios}).$$

These calculations give us some feeling for the range of values for the welfare gains which society might achieve by moving from a system of independent agents to one of direct writing. The minimum efficiency gain is $830 million dollars per year under the assumption that the auto insurance market is the only one congenial to direct writing and that the elasticity of demand for coverage is zero. The maximum gain is $2.64 billion under the assumption that the entire property-liability industry is susceptible to direct writing and that the elasticity of demand for coverage is 1.5. For argument's sake we shall say that the efficiency loss is $1.5 billion per year because of the prevalence of the American Agency System.

The natural question which arises here is why the American Agency System continues to exist at all. If direct writing is cheaper, and if direct writers can justify lower rates through deviation procedures before state regulatory commissions, why does the direct writing sales technique not drive the American Agency System out of the game? We turn to this question now.

A possible answer to this question is that the system of small independent agents dealing with the public is in some sense "better." The argument goes that the agent can service the specific problems and needs of each of his individual customers. For some lines of insurance and for certain types of properties with special insurance problems there certainly is need for individual insurance counseling. However, the Senate Judiciary Subcommittee hearings are full of testimony that this is just the kind of thing which the small independent agent does poorly. He has neither the training nor the day-to-day experience to handle tricky insurance problems. The customer in need of special advice will either have to deal directly with a service representative of a company or through a large agency or independent consultant with personnel capable of handling special problems. The kinds of things which the small independent agents handle well are the standard recurring day-to-day insurance coverage applications. Most auto insurance is of this form; standardized policies, printed application forms, and a book with rates printed in it. The customer need only appear, specify his age, sex, driving record, type of car, and desired coverage, and his policy application is complete. The agent will then "try" to get the customer coverage. This is also just the type of thing which direct writers do very well. For many types of homeowners policies and straight fire policies (especially for small dwellings and commercial properties) as well as auto insurance, the agent often does little more than fill out a pre-printed form and act as a go-between for the customer and the insurance company. In many urban areas the assigned risk plans (auto) and the FAIR plans (fire, extended coverage) are really no more than direct writing organizations for the insurance industry as a whole, serving those persons who cannot get insurance in the voluntary market. While the agent continues to be a middleman in this situation, he is certainly redundant. Much of this business could easily be handled by direct mail to customers, with service personnel available for questions or through large area sales outlets.

The advantages of independent agent contact for many types of insurance customers appear to be small or even perverse. Since an insurance company which integrates forward into sales can both sell insurance by mail and maintain regional offices to handle claims and deal with special problems, the need for the independent agent *per se* appears to be nonexistent.[52] Why then, in the face of large cost savings, have many companies not integrated forward into sales to eliminate the inefficient agency system as a sales technique?

As a matter of fact, no major company has ever switched over from the agency system to the direct writing system. Direct writers in existence appear to have begun as direct writers. While it would seem reasonable for companies to switch from an agency operation to a direct writing operation, there are substantial blockages to this. One of the primary barriers is legal. Since the National Fire Insurance case (1904), the "property rights" to an insurance customer belong to the agent who brought the customer to the company. A company is legally prohibited from going out and soliciting the business of one of its customers itself. It must deal with the customer through the agent who generated the business. Therefore, a company which wished to switch from a system of generating business through independent agents to direct writing would essentially have to give up all his existing customers. A large company might attempt to make this transition region by region or state by state, funding the change-over costs through remaining agency business; however, the strong national agents' trade associations would certainly frown on this. A company trying to shift gradually to direct writing might find itself informally blacklisted by the trade associations and lose its agents everywhere. In addition, evidence cited above indicates that there are moderate to high entry barriers facing potential entrants into the direct writing market. As a result, although the property-liability insurance industry taken as a whole possesses concentration ratios indicating a competitive market structure, the direct writing segment appears to be much more oligopolistic.

The problem of consumer information has also probably been a contributing factor. Undoubtedly, there is no other product for which consumer ignorance is so prevalent. Many consumers are unaware that there are price differences among insurance companies and that it is not necessary to go through an independent agent to obtain insurance. Comparative price shopping is very difficult since price differences for comparable coverages are not readily available in printed form and because it is difficult to obtain information from friends and neighbors. I can get good information on price differences and price levels for all kinds of products from the fellow in the next office if he has purchased these products and/or shopped around for them. Asking him about his insurance is of little value since he is in a different risk class, lives in a different community, and drives a different kind of car. In many states deviations from bureau rates were so rare that many consumers simply believed that all rates were the same and just left it to their agent to find them a company. The agent himself had little incentive to obtain cut-rate insurance since his commission usually varied directly with the size of the premium.[53] In the presence

[52] By independent agent we mean the agent whose incomes from commissions on policies he can actually sell. There is no reason to believe that truly independent insurance consultants, charging fees directly to customers with insurance problems, would not thrive with the elimination of the agency system. If services are in fact needed beyond those provided by the insurance firm, we would expect such consultants to be developed. The choice would then be left to consumers, and fees charged would not necessarily be tied to premium volume generated.

[53] This is less of a problem for large customers since there is some competition

of such large information problems it is not surprising that it has taken so long for the direct writers charging lower rates to capture a sizable portion of the property insurance markets, even given their relatively strict underwriting policies.

Regulatory commissions have given only limited recognition to this consumer information problem. Under the prior approval system, regulation seems more concerned with making sure that rates were "adequate" than with encouraging consumers to take advantage of lower rates where available. Only recently have the Pennsylvania and New York insurance departments published guides which give consumers more information on price differences among companies, for different classes of insurance, and in different areas of the state. It was recognized in New York that such information was essential if the new open competition rating system was to work in a way which would promote "adequate" and not excessive insurance prices through competitive market forces.

Even with these barriers, however, it would not be unreasonable to suppose that the large cost advantage direct writers possess would allow them to reduce prices so much that they could increase their market shares very quickly. Although direct writers have been increasing their share of the market, the movement has been gradual. Almost nonexistent before the Second World War, the four largest direct writers possessed 15.5 percent of the total auto insurance market in 1954 and 25.5 percent of the auto insurance market by 1971.[54]

By and large it does not seem as if the direct writers have tried to take over the market rapidly. Although the direct writers and many mutual companies tend to file across the board 10–20 percent deviations on all lines of insurance, they also tend to have very strict underwriting policies. They attempt to take the "cream" of each of the risk classes. Since the risk classes are not really homogeneous in terms of type of person or neighborhood character, the direct writers tend to look to additional characteristics which will differentiate out the best risks in the class. Driving record, accident record, home address, occupation, etc., are the kinds of things direct writers and some mutual companies look to in obtaining the "quality" risks in each class. The sales situation appears to be one in which the low expense direct writers charge reduced rates for quality risks, leaving the rest of the market to be serviced by agency companies and assigned risk plans.

While this behavior may appear to be paradoxical, we shall see below that it is not. On the contrary it appears to be consistent with profit-maximizing behavior of low cost oligopoly firms (the direct writers) insulated from entry and faced with short-run "capacity" constraints.

☐ **Supply shortages.** The problem of supply shortages in property and liability insurance has resulted in a great deal of criticism of the industry. By supply shortages we mean that customers who desire

---

among agents for customers' business. Even here severe information imperfections probably keep the market from working very effectively.

[54] It should not be assumed that direct writing is only suitable for auto insurance. The top 4 direct writers wrote 16.4 percent of homeowners' premiums in New York State in 1971 up from 12.4 percent in 1967.

insurance at prevailing market rates simply cannot obtain it through standard channels or cannot get so much insurance as they would like at posted rates. Fire, extended coverage, and theft insurance became very difficult to obtain in the ghetto core areas of many cities in the United States in the 1960s.[55] The exact extent of the shortage is difficult to measure, but some estimates run as high as 80 percent nonavailability in particular ghetto areas. Fire insurance pools, known as FAIR plans, have been set up in many states to provide insurance to those who could not get it in the open market (often at open market rates). Similar types of shortage problems have arisen in automobile insurance as well. These problems became especially evident when many states initiated mandatory financial responsibility laws, resulting in a situation in which those who could not get insurance in the voluntary market could no longer obtain car registrations.

Assigned risk plans were established in all states to provide at least the basic minimum insurance coverage to everyone (again often at bureau rates). The exact operations of the FAIR plans and the assigned risk plans will not be discussed here. However, FAIR plans in many states have been forced to write substantial volumes of fire, extended coverage, and burglary insurance. The New York FAIR plan was, by 1972, the largest fire insurance underwriter in New York state. The supply shortage situation in automobiles was not so severe, however. An examination of the activities of New York State's Assigned Risk Plan is revealing.[56]

Except for the years following the introduction of compulsory automobile liability insurance, the proportion of vehicles unable to obtain insurance in the voluntary market hovered near 10 percent and was 12.7 percent in 1971.[57] The situation in ghetto areas was

---

[55] *Meeting the Insurance Crises of Our Cities* [26].

[56]

PERCENTAGE OF TOTAL CAR-YEARS INSURED THROUGH
THE ASSIGNED RISK PLAN IN NEW YORK

| Year | Percentage |
|------|-----------|
| 1957 | 3.1 |
| 1958 | 6.7 |
| 1959 | 9.2 |
| 1960 | 10.4 |
| 1961 | 10.0 |
| 1962 | 9.3 |
| 1963 | 8.1 |
| 1964 | 7.8 |
| 1965 | 7.4 |
| 1966 | 7.7 |
| 1967 | 8.2 |
| 1968 | 8.4 |
| 1969 | 8.8 |
| 1970 | 9.9 |
| 1971 | 12.7 |

Source: New York State Insurance Department [17], p. 16.

[57] There may be an element of perverse behavior here which is putting some people into the assigned risk plan who might be able to find insurance in the voluntary market. This seems to be related to the American Agency System. Before 1969, agents in New York received only a 5-percent commission on business written through the assigned risk plan, based only on the basic premium charge which at that time was identical to the bureau rates in the voluntary

considerably worse than the yearly averages. In Bronx County South fully 34 percent of the automobiles were insured through the assigned risk plan in 1971.[58] Youthful owners or principal operators also found it difficult to obtain automobile insurance in the voluntary market, with 29 percent of the vehicles registered to this class of operators insured through the assigned risk plan in New York State. The proportion ran as high as 48 percent in one particular rating territory.[59]

In addition, until recently most states only provided minimum coverage through the assigned risk plans so that many of those in the plan may not have been obtaining the quantity of coverage which they desired at prevailing prices. In fire and extended coverage as well as in the auto insurance lines a far from insignificant proportion of the population is not being serviced adequately by the voluntary market.

Clearly an understanding of why supply shortages exist is crucial to the evaluation of the performance of the insurance industry under regulation. The contention here is that supply shortages exist because regulatory authorities have refused to allow the creation of enough truly homogeneous risk classes. Rates determined on the basis of average historical losses for a particular class may be profitable for a "typical" risk. However, as long as risk classes are not homogeneous from the viewpoint of insurers, and insurance underwriters can differentiate between "good" risks and "bad" risks within a particular class, no risk will be treated as "typical." On the contrary most insurance companies will attempt to insure the "good" risks first and may or may not insure the bad risks.

*Proposition 1:* The existence of supply shortages within a particular heterogeneous class will depend on the expected profits associated with its identifiable subclasses and the ability of insurers to differentiate successfully between good and bad risks within the class.

*Proposition 2:* Supply shortages within a particular heterogeneous rating class will vary inversely with the underwriting profit for the "typical" risk in the rating class.

---

market. Since commission rates on business written through the voluntary market were substantially higher, agents had an incentive to write their business through the voluntary market if they could. In 1969 the insurance law was amended to allow agents to charge 5 percent not only on the basic premium, but on the basic premium plus surcharges made due to accident and driving records. These surcharges could increase premiums as much as 100 percent, and although surcharge provisions were available to companies in the voluntary market, they were rarely used (especially for minor traffic violations). As a result, agents could now make more money by getting insurance for their clients at a surcharged rate through the assigned risk plan than they could by getting insurance at standard rates in the voluntary market. This incentive was strengthened when rates in the assigned risk plan were allowed to go above the standard bureau rates in 1971 and when the actual rates charged by many companies under the new open competition fell below bureau rates. Many agents were faced with a situation in which 5 percent of a large premium looked much better than 10 percent of a much smaller premium. They had an incentive to feed business into the assigned risk plan which had no real way of verifying whether a risk was really uninsurable in the voluntary market. This is probably why the number of risks in the assigned risk plan increased so dramatically between 1970 and 1971.

[58] New York State Insurance Department [17], p. 19.

[59] *Ibid.*, p. 22.

Arguments in favor of these two propositions are presented in the context of a simple model of the *short-run* underwriting behavior of a profit-maximizing property insurance company.

Consider a typical insurance company with some fixed capital base $(K)$ "backing" its insurance operations. The company earns income *from its insurance operations* in two ways:

(1) Direct underwriting profits; and

(2) Investment income from prepaid premiums, often called "unearned premium reserves."

Let us assume for simplicity that the typical firm sells one type of insurance to only one class of customers.

Let $\pi^* =$ profit per premium dollar for the "average" or typical customer in the class. $\pi^*$ is determined by the regulatory authority and defines a price per unit of coverage for *all* customers in the class:

$$\pi^* = 1 - l - e,$$

where

$l =$ Expected losses per premium dollar for the class as a whole

$e =$ Expenses per premium dollar.

Let us assume further that there are two types of risks in this class—"good" risks and "bad" risks—defined by some indicator variable not used for determining the rating class itself. Let us say that this variable is dichotomous and indicates "good" neighborhoods and "bad" neighborhoods within the territory used for establishing the prevailing price for all risks.

Let

$\pi_B =$ Expected profit per premium dollar for the "bad" risks in the group;

$\pi_G =$ Expected profit per premium dollar for the "good" risks in the class;

$\pi_B < \pi^* < \pi_G,$ and

$y_i = \pi_i + r^{**},$

where

$y_i =$ Expected net income from writing a risk with characteristic $i$, and

$r^{**} =$ Investment return per premium dollar from the "unearned" premium reserve.

Short-run expected profit-maximizing behavior of insurance firms, given $\pi_G$, $\pi_B$, and $r^{**}$, implies that an insurance company will write all subclasses of the heterogeneous rating class for which

$$y_i \geq 0$$

and will not write subclasses for which

$$y_i < 0.$$

In general the higher is $\pi^*$ (*ceteris paribus*), the more subclasses (with progressively poorer loss expectations) will be written. In the two-subclass case, the higher is $\pi^*$, the more likely the bad risk group will be taken on. If $\pi_B + r^{**} \geq 0$, both subclasses will be written. We therefore expect that a class will still be written for some values of $\pi_i < 0$.

This simple model includes only two types of risks and implies a simple dichotomous decision index which specifies good neighborhoods and bad neighborhoods, which in turn determines "good" risks and "bad" risks (and the expected profitability of each). Especially for automobile insurance, we might expect to find a decision index which takes on many values and is a function of such things as neighborhood residence, driving record, accident record, age, etc., which have not been used in defining the rating class itself. We define the index so that it varies inversely with the quality of the risk.

Let

$$\pi_I = F(I) \quad \text{(where } I \text{ is the value of the decision index and } \pi_I \text{ are expected profits),}$$

$$F'(I) < 0.$$

In the short run we would expect firms to write all customers for which $F(I) \geq -r^{**}$ which is essentially the result for the more simple case. Quite simply firms just will not write risks for which they expect to lose money. If risk classes are in fact really heterogeneous, all risks will be insured only if $\pi_i$ for the "worst" identifiable group in the class is equal to or greater than $-r^{**}$. This means, however, that persons in the intramarginal classes will be paying too much for insurance. In the short run firms would be earning profits in excess of what would induce them to write each subclass if each were priced according to its own expected losses in a competitive market with truly homogeneous risk classes. Note finally that $\pi^*$ may be so low that nobody within a particular class will be insured.

There is substantial evidence to indicate that rating classifications have been too large in many states. In New York City, for example, although there are 115 building hazard classifications, rates for each are based on data from a very large territory—the entire City of New York. Companies often believed that within any hazard class, some neighborhoods have higher expected losses than others. A system of "redlining," where some areas of the city were designated as not insurable, developed. The number of areas designated seems to have increased during the late 1960s as underwriting profits ($\pi^*$) declined and expectations of losses increased. The large supply shortages which resulted in many major cities appear to have been caused because companies felt that the premium rates did not justify the expected returns from writing in these areas. Attempts by insurance companies to put surcharges on particular neighborhoods have generally been resisted by regulatory authorities as being discriminatory. This was at least partially the fault of the industry, which did not collect industrywide loss data by neighborhood. Even if it had, changing expectations based on things other than historical loss experience might still have resulted in "regulated" prices which were too low for some risk classes.

Similar behavior appears to exist for auto insurance. While the number of territory classifications for auto insurance in New York City is much larger than for fire insurance, there is evidence that insurers tend to avoid people with poor driving records or poor traffic records, people in certain occupations, aliens, etc.[60] In particular, new inexperienced drivers tend to be avoided by insurance companies. For some of these characteristics surcharges are available, for others they simply are not.

The behavior of insurance companies in "risk selection" certainly appears to have been justified, when we look at the loss experience for auto risks insured through the voluntary market and those insured through the assigned risk plan. The losses and loss adjustment figures for assigned risk drivers are much higher than those for drivers insured through the voluntary market.[61] In 1970 the ratio of losses to premiums for risks insured through the voluntary market was 0.68, while it was almost twice as high as 1.28 for assigned risk drivers. Similar results were obtained during the previous 10 years.

Given excess demand and the contention by underwriters that the excess demand exists because particular subgroups of existing rate classifications are identifiably "unprofitable" at bureau rates, why does the regulatory authority not allow more rate classifications? In many cases *they have* allowed more rate classifications and special surcharges. Convincing regulatory authorities that additional risk classifications are justified is not easy, however. Data must be collected justifying new classifications, and often must be of at least five years' duration to be used for making rates. Chicago was recently broken up into four rating areas for auto insurance and New York City will soon be rated by borough for fire insurance. The burden of proof for justifying new classifications is up to the companies in the industry and must be supported by extensive loss data.

In addition, regulatory authorities have resisted attempts at certain types of classification schemes on equity and distributional grounds. The fact that the poor, the nonwhite, and the young would tend to pay more for all types of insurance, if risk classes were truly homogeneous, has certainly had a lot to do with the policies of the regulatory authorities. Insurance regulators seem to have felt that charging higher rates in slum areas, to black people, to persons with particular occupations, etc., for what to the layman appears to be an identical product, could present severe political difficulties.[62] The true price of

---

[60] See New York State Insurance Department [17], p. 36.

[61]

NEW YORK STATE AUTOMOBILE LIABILITY INSURANCE
PRIVATE PASSENGER CARS
(All Companies 1960 to 1970)

| Accident Year | Loss and Loss Adjustment Ratio | |
|---|---|---|
| | voluntary market | assigned risk plan |
| 1960 | 0.58 | 1.15 |
| 1961 | 0.55 | 1.07 |
| 1962 | 0.57 | 1.12 |
| 1963 | 0.60 | 1.14 |
| 1964 | 0.64 | 1.23 |
| 1965 | 0.66 | 1.30 |
| 1966 | 0.64 | 1.27 |
| 1967 | 0.67 | 1.28 |
| 1968 | 0.73 | 1.39 |
| 1969 | 0.72 | 1.39 |
| 1970 | 0.68 | 1.28 |

Source: New York State Insurance Department [17], p. 29.

[62] Attempts to separate out high risk areas have often been met with stiff

insuring some bad risks profitably would be so high that they appear to be "unconscionable" to many concerned. By lumping good risks together with bad risks in identical rating classifications, regulators could approve posted rates which appeared to be fair for all rating classifications. However, true cross-subsidization would be impossible because insurance companies are not forced to provide service to all customers who demand it.[63]

A cross-subsidy scheme which probably would have worked in the traditional public utility setting could not work here so long as companies could easily identify the poor risks in each class which would not be profitable to underwrite. The result would not be cross-subsidization, but a lack of supply availability at posted prices for many groups of consumers.

The introduction of assigned risk plans and FAIR plans was an ideal solution for the regulatory authorities. Companies were now being forced, indirectly, to provide all customers with at least some service. Since this service was often provided at bureau rates established on the basis of loss experience for customers insured both inside and outside of assigned risk plans, good risks ended up subsidizing bad risks. It has been estimated that this subsidy amounts to an increase of $9 per car per year on the rates of auto liability risks insured through the voluntary market, and a reduction of $76 per car per year on the rates of assigned risk participants below what would be required to cover losses, expenses, and a 5-percent profit factor.[64] The insurance industry appears to have been satisfied with this arrangement as long as overall rates were high enough to keep the number of customers in special insurance pools small and overall profitability acceptable. Recent experience with poor industry profits appears to be making the insurance industry as a whole far less satisfied with the current arrangement than it has been in the past. The question of profitability is one to which we turn now.

☐ **Profitability.** Profitability, in the context of a "fair rate of return" on capital, is an important aspect of the pricing process in most regulated industries. Overall allowed rates of return are normally determined by regulatory agencies in rate hearings on a company by company basis and price structures yielding the allowed rate of return approved.[65] The question of excess profits and of profit measurement methodology was not very much of an issue in insurance rate regulation until recently. A standard formula, yielding "fair" profits to the industry as a whole, was agreed to by the National Association of Insurance Commissioners in 1921. It has been in effect in most regulatory jurisdictions ever since. Recent criticism of rising insurance rates, coupled with a reconsideration of the effectiveness of regulation, has led to an examination of both the industry's profit performance

---

resistance by the persons who live in those areas. Attempts to get surcharges put on the fire insurance rates in the Lower East Side area of New York City by the insurance raters were met with great resistance. The insurance department indicated that such surcharges would be "discriminatory" unless backed up by substantial loss data for the area in question.

[63] See Posner [25].

[64] U. S. Senate, Subcommittee on Antitrust and Monopoly [31], Part 18A, p. 12677.

[65] A notable exception to company by company rate determination was the FPC's area rate method of determining the wellhead price of natural gas.

and the profitability measures to be used in approving and "surveying" property-liability premium rates.

☐ **Traditional measures of profitability.** The traditional measure of profitability used for property-liability insurance rate making is based on the "1921 Profit Formula" adopted by the National Association of Insurance Commissioners in 1921. While the rationale for this formula was based on the situation in fire insurance rate making, the basic profit allowance and its calculation have been applied to all major property-liability lines. This formula contains the following provisions:[66]

(1) Underwriting profit (or loss) is arrived at by deducting all incurred losses and incurred expenses from earned premiums;

(2) No items of profit or loss connected with the so-called banking end of the business should be taken into consideration; and

(3) A reasonable underwriting profit is 5 percent plus a 1-percent conflagration hazard (as modified by the NAIC in 1948) for fire insurance rate making.

In most regulatory jurisdictions the profit formula has been applied to the performance of the industry as a whole and not on a company by company basis. Individual companies wishing to reduce rates below approved bureau rates normally had to show that their operating expenses (but not their losses) were sufficiently below those for the industry as a whole, so that the rate reduction would still yield them the statutory profit figure. To evaluate this profitability measure and the actual profit performance of the insurance industry, the following simple model of the behavior of the insurance firm in the long run will be useful.

☐ **A simple model of the behavior of a property insurance firm in the long run.** The insurance firm is conveniently conceptualized as a levered investment trust. It obtains capital from an initial sale of stock and invests most of this capital in securities (both stocks and bonds). This is the strict "investment trust" aspect of the firm. The firm's portfolio is then used as backing for its insurance operations. The insurance operations yield two sources of net income: direct income from underwriting (premiums less losses and expenses) plus investable capital (unearned premium reserves) made up of prepaid premiums, with which the firm purchases more securities for its portfolio. For U. S. stock companies the value of capital attributable to unearned premium reserves is equal to about 80 percent of the equity capital (including retained earnings or surplus). By engaging in insurance operations, the "investment trust" gains additional investable capital and additional income, but must also assume the additional risk of engaging in the insurance business.

Let

$r^*$ = Expected rate of return on equity portfolio;

$I$ = Expected underwriting profit after losses and expenses per premium dollar (as determined by regulatory authority and rating bureau);

[66] *Proceedings of the National Association of Insurance Commissioners*, 1922, pp. 19–29.

$P_i$ = Total premiums written by firm $i$;
$r^{**}$ = Expected rate of return on "insurance capital" portfolio;[67]
$K_i$ = Equity investment in firm $i$
$U_i$ = Unearned premium reserve possessed by firm $i$.

Total expected net income of the insurance firm in a given period is

$$\pi_i = r^* K_i + IP_i + r^{**} U_i, \tag{3}$$

and the rate of return on the operations of the firm as a whole is given by

$$r_I = \pi_i / K_i. \tag{4}$$

Assuming $U_i/P_i$ remains constant at a value of approximately 0.8 we may rewrite (2) as

$$r_I = r^* + \frac{P_i}{K_i} [I + 0.8r^{**}].$$

With $r^*$, $I$, and $r^{**}$ constants given by the market, the expected rate of return for the insurance firm varies directly with the ratio of premium volume to equity capital, *ceteris paribus*.

Let us assume that premium rates have been fixed at some level by the rating bureau and/or regulatory agency so as to yield $I$ and that all firms adhere to these "cartel" rates. This premium rate level defines a level of total insurance coverage demanded, and in turn a level of total premium volume $P$ $(P = \Sigma P_i)$. If all firms are identical and there is free entry we would expect the long-run equilibrium positions of all firms to be characterized by:

$$r_I^c = r_I = r^* + I \frac{P_i}{K_i} + 0.8r^{**} \frac{P_i}{K_i}, \tag{5}$$

where $r_I^c$ is the competitive opportunity cost of capital.

Then $r_I^c$ is defined as follows:

$$r_I^c = r_c + g \left( \frac{P_i}{K_i} \right),$$

$$g' \left( \frac{P_i}{K_i} \right) > 0,$$

$$g'' \left( \frac{P_i}{K_i} \right) \geq 0, \quad r_c > r^{*},[68]$$

where $r_c$ is the expected return from operating a pure investment trust, and where the opportunity cost of capital rises as the investment portfolio "backs" more and more insurance claims (since prices are fixed here, this is represented by premium volume):

$$r_c + g \left( \frac{P_i}{K_i} \right) = r^* + I \left( \frac{P_i}{K_i} \right) + 0.8r^{**} \left( \frac{P_i}{K_i} \right), \quad (r_c > r^*). \tag{5'}$$

---

[67] We differentiate between $r^*$ and $r^{**}$, since certain regulatory restrictions may limit the ways in which certain sources of investable funds may be invested.

[68] Here $r_c > r^*$ because transformation of an investment trust into an insurance company, even if no insurance is actually written, requires some expenditures of funds for licensing and auditing (which would not otherwise be incurred) and also restricts somewhat the kinds of securities that may be purchased.

FIGURE 2

OPPORTUNITY COST OF CAPITAL
VERSUS EARNED RATE OF RETURN

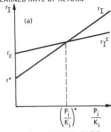

OPPORTUNITY COST OF CAPITAL,
EARNED RATE OF RETURN

PREMIUM CAPITAL RATIO

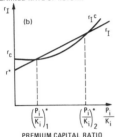

OPPORTUNITY COST OF CAPITAL,
EARNED RATE OF RETURN

PREMIUM CAPITAL RATIO

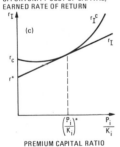

OPPORTUNITY COST OF CAPITAL,
EARNED RATE OF RETURN

PREMIUM CAPITAL RATIO

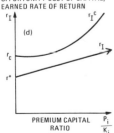

OPPORTUNITY COST OF CAPITAL,
EARNED RATE OF RETURN

PREMIUM CAPITAL
RATIO

Equation $(5')$ may be solved for an equilibrium value of $\frac{P_i}{K_i}$. Single and multiple equilibria are possible, depending upon the shape of $g(\cdot)$ and the level of $I$. The four possible situations are depicted in Figure 2 (a)–(d).

The force driving firms to an equilibrium point is the entry and exit of equity capital into and out of the industry. Since $\Sigma P_i$ is fixed (since prices are fixed), adjustment takes place in terms of $K$:

> if $r_I > r_I^c$, capital will enter the industry;
>
> if $r_I < r_I^c$, capital will leave the industry; and
>
> if $r_I = r_I^c$, equilibrium is reached.

We may think of this entry in terms of additional identical firms ($P_i$ for each firm then declines with entry, $K_i$ remaining constant), as existing firms expanding their capital base ($P_i$ constant and $K_i$ increasing), or as a combination of both.

Case (a) where $r_I^c$ is a linear function of $\left(\frac{P_i}{K_i}\right)$ leads to a unique and stable equilibrium position. Case (b) where $r_I^c$ increases more than proportionately with $\left(\frac{P_i}{K_i}\right)$ yields two equilibrium positions, however only $\left(\frac{P_i}{K_i}\right)^*$, is stable. Firms can avoid moving beyond $\left(\frac{P_i}{K_i}\right)^*_2$ by refusing to supply all insurance demanded, so that the system is not explosive. Case (c) is a polar case of (b) and is stable as long as firms can refuse to write some insurance demanded or recognize that entry will drive down the opportunity cost of capital. Finally (d) is a situation in which income from insurance operations is just not worth the risk.

Let us concentrate on the equilibrium positions in (a) and (b) $\left[\left(\frac{P_i}{K_i}\right)^*_1\right]$. The equilibrium premium-capital ratio for individual firms will vary inversely with $I$ (*ceteris paribus*). In (a) any $\left(\frac{P_i}{K_i}\right)^*$ value can be supported at some value for $I$ (and this is probably an unrealistic characterization of the cost of capital for this reason).[69] In (b) only a limited range of stable values for $\left(\frac{P_i}{K_i}\right)^*_1$ can be supported by varying $I$. In both cases there is some lower bound on $I$ below which firms will simply withdraw from the industry. Call this floor value on the underwriting profit level $I^*$.

In this world then, by defining a particular value for $I \geq I^*$, the regulatory authority and the rating bureau are implicitly defining an equilibrium level of $\left(\frac{P_i}{K_i}\right)$ at which firms will sell insurance. The higher $I$ is, the smaller the value of $\frac{P_i}{K_i}$ will tend to be. Since there is easy entry, we would expect that the earned rate of return for individual firms and for the industry as a whole should be equal to the

---

[69] Or of actual consumer preferences, which will be discussed presently.

opportunity cost of capital for all $I \geq I^*$. As long as the regulatory authority sets $I \geq I^*$, insurance will be provided in the long run. However, if the regulatory authority should also undertake to prescribe a maximum $\left(\dfrac{P_i}{K_i}\right)$ ratio at which firms must write insurance, it will either be applying an ineffective constraint—if it is greater than $\left(\dfrac{P_i}{K_i}\right)_1^*$—or will force firms out of the market—if it is less than $\left(\dfrac{P_i}{K_i}\right)_1^*$. Proposals to have regulators set both $I$ and $\left(\dfrac{P_i}{K_i}\right)^*$ may create considerable problems.

In a truly competitive market we would expect insurance premium rates to be driven down to the point where they were just high enough to clear the market. The competitive underwriting profit would therefore be $I^*$ (which *could* be negative because of the earnings from the increased premium reserves) which would be just high enough to coax firms into the industry, providing insurance to all who demand it with each firm operating at some premium-equity capital ratio which we may call $\left(\dfrac{P_i}{K_i}\right)^{**}$. If cartel prices are set above $I^*$, market equilibrium will result in a $\left(\dfrac{P_i}{K_i}\right)^*$ value smaller than $\left(\dfrac{P_i}{K_i}\right)^{**}$. The cartel pricing situation will result in less real insurance coverage's being offered (assuming demand is not perfectly inelastic), more capital (capacity) per premium dollar and per unit of real insurance coverage, and a lower rate of return (although still equal to the opportunity cost of capital) than would be achieved in a competitive market. To the extent that consumers are indifferent among the $\left(\dfrac{P_i}{K_i}\right)$ values $\leq \left(\dfrac{P_i}{K_i}\right)^*$, they will be better off with a competitive market.

A possible rationale for the cartel arrangement thus presents itself. If the demand for insurance coverage has a price elasticity less than or equal to unity and if demand itself is growing only slowly, the introduction of competitive pricing necessarily means that some existing firms will be forced to exit from the industry. Even for some values of the price elasticity greater than unity, exit would be necessary. Therefore, from the viewpoint of existing firms in the industry, the elimination of cartel pricing may indeed have resulted in excess capacity and competition destructive to some existing firms. The fact that a cartel with free entry could not achieve excess profits in the long run for the constituent firms is not a deterrent to the establishment or maintenance of a cartel. With the cartel all existing firms would stay in the ball game. The elimination of the cartel would probably have meant that some of the existing firms would have been forced out of the market. Once a cartel-type equilibrium has been attained (or if there is excess capacity for some other reason), existing firms have an interest in maintaining (or creating) the cartel to keep themselves in the market.

We may conclude that one of the reasons many insurance companies (especially the larger ones) have not resisted the movement to open competition in insurance pricing is that the cartel arrangement was falling apart with the direct writers and the eased deviation procedures. Effective prices were being driven toward the competitive level, and no doubt many of the larger companies felt that they could do much better, at least in the short run, with open competition, at the expense of many of the smaller companies.

Before moving on, certain consumer protection arguments in favor of regulated prices should be made. It is often argued that because of consumer ignorance, consumers appear to be indifferent between companies selling insurance with different $\left(\dfrac{P_i}{K_i}\right)$ values, but really would not be if they were apprised of the significance of the $\left(\dfrac{P_i}{K_i}\right)$ ratios to them. In some sense, the higher the value of the $\left(\dfrac{P_i}{K_i}\right)$ ratio of the firm from which one purchases an insurance policy *ceteris paribus*, the lower is the quality of the "product."[70] The quality of the product is reduced because the higher is $\left(\dfrac{P_i}{K_i}\right)$, the higher is the probability that the insurance firm will go bankrupt and that losses incurred will not be paid off. This argument implies that with perfect information, consumer demand would depend not only on price but also on the $\left(\dfrac{P_i}{K_i}\right)$ ratio maintained by firms selling contingent claims. The perfect competition equilibrium without proper consumer information will therefore yield a $\left(\dfrac{P_i}{K_i}\right)^*$ ratio higher than would result with perfect information about the risk of nonpayment due to bankruptcy.[71]

There is certainly some validity to this argument. However, it would seem that capital markets themselves recognize the chance of bankruptcy very well. Where $\left(\dfrac{P_i}{K_i}\right)$ ratios become high enough to raise the probability of bankruptcy to more than *de minimis* proportions, the opportunity cost of capital probably begins to rise rather quickly, thus probably restricting the value of $\left(\dfrac{P_i}{K_i}\right)^*$ in a competitive market to some fairly reasonable level. There certainly does remain room for fraud and manipulation which should probably be a source of some public policy concern. This is especially true if management is not particularly sensitive to stockholder pressures and in mutual companies where the policyholders themselves are the source of the capital base. Therefore, the cartel pricing scheme certainly does tend to yield a $\left(\dfrac{P_i}{K_i}\right)^*$ ratio less than what would be achieved in a competitive market, but it is not at all clear that this increase in product

---

[70] An appendix discussing bankruptcy and consumer protection may be obtained upon request from the author.

[71] And the efficient $\left(\dfrac{P_i}{K_i}\right)^*$ ratio in Figure 2(a) would then probably be finite without the necessity of having capital costs increase at an increasing rate with $\left(\dfrac{P_i}{K_i}\right)$.

quality is worth the price. A proposal is presented in the final section which should ensure that the risks associated with various $\left(\dfrac{P_i}{K_i}\right)$ ratios are properly taken into consideration by management and that consumers are protected from bankruptcy.

☐ **Profit results for the property-liability insurance industry.** There has been a great deal of recent controversy over the profitability of the property-liability insurance industry.[72] The analysis in the previous section indicated that since entry is easy we would expect the overall rate of return for the industry to be equal to the opportunity cost of capital. Although the Merritt Report (1911)[73] cast the question of profitability in terms of the ability to attract sufficient equity capital to provide service, this sensible notion of firm profitability, including all sources of income, was essentially lost from the regulatory process for over 50 years. The 1921 profit formula calling for a 5-percent return on premium volume gained acceptance as a just standard, even though no attempt had ever been made to show that this figure bore any relationship with rate of profit which would be sufficient to generate a rate of return just high enough to encourage entry and service. If profits fell below 5 percent of premiums, companies felt justified in asking that their rates be increased. Companies seeking to file deviated rates under prior approval laws were compelled to show that they would earn *at least* the 5 percent statutory profit figure.

It was not until the late 1960s that the profitability question again received detailed economic analysis. Under increasing pressures to return "high profits" to consumers (especially from some Senate Committees), the insurance industry commissioned a series of profitability studies by Arthur D. Little, Inc. (ADL).[74]

The ADL studies reject the traditional profitability concept adopted by insurance regulators, at least for comparing profitability among industries. Instead, ADL conclude that it is the rate of return on capital that should be used in making such profitability comparisons. Included in return were all sources of income—underwriting profits, interest, dividends, and capital gains. The initial ADL study examined the profitability of the insurance industry for the period 1955 to 1965. In this study ADL chose to examine rates of return on total capitalization as the relevant measure of comparable profitability. For an industrial firm total capitalization includes stockholder's equity and surplus plus debt. For an insurance company the "equivalent" of total capitalization was taken to be total investable funds, which include equity capital and surplus *plus* unearned premium reserves. ADL argued that rate of return on total capital was the relevant rate of return figure for comparing different industries because this would give a measure of the relative "efficiencies" of capital employment among industries. The ADL studies also contain figures on rates of return on equity capital, but ADL

---

[72] See National Association of Insurance Commissioners [16] for a discussion of the controversy and analysis of various measurement methodologies.

[73] Reported in U. S. Senate, Subcommittee on Antitrust and Monopoly [31], Part 5, p. 2791.

[74] Arthur D. Little, Inc. [1,2] and Irving Plotkin [24].

has continued to argue that those figures are not so relevant as are the rates of return on total capital.

The ADL studies use these figures in two ways. First ADL regressed the rates of return on total capitalization against the average intercompany temporal rate of return variance (a measure of risk) for a group of U. S. industries including the property-liability insurance industry (a sample of 43 stock companies). ADL found that the insurance industry point fell far below the regression line with an average rate of return on total investable funds of 4.4 percent and a risk measure of 10.89 (percent squared).[75] The study concludes that this indicates that the property-liability insurance industry is not earning a rate of return commensurate with that being earned in other industries with similar risks.

While the attempt to "adjust" rates of return by "risk" has great intuitive and theoretical appeal, the ADL reports, especially those following the initial report, have relied primarily on the straight comparison of rates of return between industries, using aggregate data from *Best's* to measure property-liability industry performance. For the period 1955 to 1967 ADL found that stock insurance companies earned an average rate of return on investable funds of 3.8 percent,[76] while the rate of return on total capital for all industrial companies was 9.8 percent during the same period.[77] ADL finds, in addition, that the property and liability insurance industry had an average rate of return lower than all 119 Standard and Poor's industrials.[78]

ADL also presents calculations for rates of return on equity (net worth) for the property and liability insurance industry. After making what appear to be reasonable adjustments for peculiarities in insurance industry accounting practices, ADL concludes that the rate of return on net worth was 7.3 percent[79] for stock insurance companies for the period 1955 to 1968. (It was about 9 percent without the adjustments.) This compared with an average rate of return on new worth of 11.8 percent for Standard and Poor's industrials (1955 to 1967) and 9.1 percent for 102 gas and electric public utilities. ADL concludes that even if one chooses rate of return on net worth as a measure for comparison, the property and liability insurance industry does very poorly.

There have been a number of criticisms of the ADL study. Most have pointed to minor accounting problems and some have been quite ridiculous.[80] There appear to be two serious flaws in the ADL profitability studies, however. First, although a comparison of long-run rates of return on total capital (adjusted for risk) may indicate the relative efficiences of capital usage in various industries, there is absolutely no reason to expect that the property and liability industry uses its total capital resources efficiently. On the contrary,

---

[75] Plotkin [24], p. 187.

[76] Arthur D. Little [2], p. 34.

[77] *Ibid.*, p. 37.

[78] *Ibid.*, p. 40.

[79] *Ibid.*, p. 45.

[80] Some of the criticisms have bordered on the ridiculous. See Norgaard and Schick [23]. They include as profits any increase in assets, whether or not such assets had attendant liabilities. With their measure a company could become very "profitable" by going deeply into debt.

the analysis in the previous section indicates that, although free entry will drive returns on equity capital to the competitive level, price regulation will result in an equilibrium position in which the ratio of premiums to equity capital is too small. Since increased premium reserves are directly related to premium volume, total investable funds (equity plus unearned premium reserves) will be *too large* relative to premium volume. We would expect *a priori* that the rate of return on total capital would be *lower* in the property and liability insurance industry than in an industry of equivalent risk characteristics, but which used its available capital efficiently. The results of the risk-return analysis of ADL are consistent, therefore, with the conclusion that there is excess capital in the property and liability insurance industry, and do not give us a good measure for answering the question of whether the industry earns "normal" profits or not. Other things being equal, the rate of return on net worth would be the relevant profitability measure to use if one were concerned with the industry's ability to attract capital. (There is no real debt financing.)

Is the solution to this problem then to recalculate the ADL risk-return results using the rate of return on net worth? The answer, I believe, is no. The measure of risk employed by the ADL study (temporal intercompany variance in rates of return) is simply not a good measure of the relative riskiness of a financial institution, whose assets are primarily liquid, and industrial corporations, whose assets are primarily fixed capital. An investor should certainly be willing to tolerate more variation in expected profits of an insurance firm which can easily liquidate its assets, than in a steel company which cannot. The comparison of the profitability of financial institutions with industrial corporations requires a much more sophisticated definition of risk.

One proper approach toward answering the profitability question properly might be to compare insurance firms with comparable financial institutions. It was suggested above that the insurance firm is best viewed as a levered investment trust. Table 7 presents First

TABLE 7

RATES OF RETURN ON NET WORTH FOR FIRE AND CASUALTY COMPANIES AND INVESTMENT TRUSTS

| YEAR | FIRE AND CASUALTY* | INVESTMENT TRUSTS** |
|---|---|---|
| 1965 | 2.9 | 2.9 |
| 1964 | 4.8 | 2.9 |
| 1963 | 4.4 | 3.1 |
| 1962 | 3.9 | 2.7 |
| 1961 | 6.0 | 3.2 |
| 1960 | 5.8 | 3.7 |
| 1959 | 7.4 | 4.0 |
| 1958 | 5.6 | 4.9 |
| 1957 | 2.0 | 4.7 |
| 1956 | 2.2 | 4.7 |
| 1955 | 5.5 | 5.2 |
| AVERAGE | 4.5 | 3.4 |

*NET WORTH = POLICYHOLDERS' EQUITY (PRIMARILY AT MARKET VALUE)
NET INCOME = UNDERWRITING PROFITS, INTEREST AND DIVIDENDS, AND
  REALIZED CAPITAL GAINS

**NET WORTH = NET ASSETS AT MARKET VALUE
NET INCOME = OPERATING PROFIT, INTEREST AND DIVIDENDS, NOT
  INCLUDING CAPITAL GAINS

National City Bank figures on rates of return on net worth for fire and casualty companies (property and liability) and for investment trust companies.[81] These figures are illustrative and do not represent a rigorous "comparable" earnings study. The comparability of these figures suffers from one serious problem. The investment trust figures do not include realized capital gains, while the insurance figures do. A crude adjustment is possible using some of ADL's own figures. ADL calculates the ratio of operating income to policyholders' surplus to be 4.2 percent for the period 1955 to 1965 and the ratio of operating income plus *all* realized gains (including interest and dividends) at 5.4 percent.[82] The elimination of all realized gains reduces the rate of return on policyholders' surplus by 22 percent. Let us assume that realized *capital* gains are about half of total realized gains, so that the elimination of realized capital gains would reduce the rate of return on net worth of insurance companies by 10 percent. Applying this figure to the First National City Bank figures, we get an "adjusted" rate of return on net worth of 4.1 percent for the insurance industry. This is somewhat higher than the 3.4 percent figure for investment trusts, which is exactly what we would expect.

The conclusion of this little exercise should be that, at least superficially, the returns earned by the property and liability insurance industry are not out of line with what we would expect when we compare industries which are realistically comparable. Most importantly, this discussion suggests that the issue of the profitability of the insurance industry is still an open question. Although the discussion above suggests that the rates of return observed for the property and liability insurance industry should approximate the competitive cost of capital, sound empirical verification is still an open area of research which should be pursued. Of special interest would be the more direct approach of estimating the cost of capital itself instead of relying on comparisons with other industries. A discussion of exactly how one might use the various approaches to the estimation of the cost of capital for insurance firms is outside the scope of this paper. However, it is an exercise that is certainly well worth pursuing.

But as the discussion in the previous section indicates, a rate of return analysis proves nothing about whether premium rates are too high or too low. Regulation and bureau rate making may still lead to prices which are higher than necessary and to excess industry capacity. Since entry into the industry continues to be vigorous, it appears that the rate of profit which bureaus and regulators have been able to achieve is sufficient to guarantee that overall industry capacity will be large enough to cover the demand for remunerative lines of insurance.

□ **The behavior of direct writers.** Finally an explanation of the behavior of direct writers must be attempted. Recall the following stylized facts regarding direct writers:

(1) Substantially lower underwriting costs than the industry as a whole;

---

[81] First National City Bank of New York, as reprinted in Plotkin [24].
[82] Plotkin [24], p. 192.

(2) Deviations below bureau rates for many lines of insurance and for many classes of customers;

(3) Moderate to high entry barriers into the "direct writers'" market;

(4) Gradually increasing market share in most lines of insurance; and

(5) Stricter underwriting policies than the industry as a whole.

The surprising elements of this picture are (4) and (5). Since direct writers have much lower costs than agency companies, even after small deviations below bureau rates (to attract customers), it would seem that any risk class which is profitable for an agency company to write ($y_i \geq 0$) would be at least as profitable for the direct writers. They should therefore be willing to accept all risks that agency companies accept (perhaps even more) and rather *quickly* take over the entire market as the word that direct writers have lower rates gets around. The problem of lack of consumer information limiting the speed with which "the word gets around" has already been mentioned. But why do direct writers consciously refuse to write risks which agency firms in the voluntary market are quite willing to write?

Recall the model of long-run behavior of the firm discussed above. In particular let us concentrate on case (b) [Figure 2(b)]. Since the direct writers' market is characterized by a small number of firms and moderate to high barriers to entry, oligopolistic pricing behavior is possible. If successful oligopoly behavior is achieved there is no reason to expect that $\left(\dfrac{P_i}{K_i}\right)^*$ will result as an equilibrium position for them. On the contrary, direct writers will seek a $\left(\dfrac{P_i}{K_i}\right)$ ratio where the difference between the earned rate of return and the cost of capital is maximized. (See Figure 3.) But the existing direct writers are certainly limited with regard to how quickly they can *individually* accumulate equity capital. As a result, in achieving the desired $\left(\dfrac{P_i}{K_i}\right)$ ratio they are limited with regard to the total premiums they can write in any period by the total equity capital which they have available. Adding premiums beyond this point increases their rate of return less than it increases the opportunity cost of capital.[83] Direct writers can achieve the profit-maximizing $\left(\dfrac{P_i}{K_i}\right)^d$ ratio in any period only by selling insurance to a portion of the profitable ($y_i \geq 0$) risks who demand it. Since they have to limit supply, they do best by choosing the best available risks in each class. Therefore, the strict underwriting policy is chosen. As equity capital is accumulated over time the direct writers would thus be expected to relax their underwriting policies, gaining a larger and larger share of the market.

In summary, the strategy of the direct writers in this scenario should be to lower their prices below bureau rates just enough to "differentiate" their products, and then fill up their premium "quota" with the best risks available. Even if entry barriers to direct writing

FIGURE 3

MAXIMIZATION OF DIFFERENCE BETWEEN EARNED RATE OF RETURN AND COST OF CAPITAL.

OPPORTUNITY COST OF CAPITAL, EARNED RATE OF RETURN

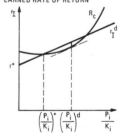

PREMIUM CAPITAL RATIO

---

[83] It is really stronger than this, since expected underwriting profits ($I$) will also decline as the poorer risks in each heterogeneous class are taken on.

are extremely high, they can exploit this "monopoly" power to only a limited extent, in a deregulated insurance market, because the competitive price for insurance written by agency firms will continue to provide a strong price ceiling.

There are two operating characteristics of insurance firms which should be consistent with the explanation of the behavior of direct writers. First, we would expect that direct writers will exhibit higher rates of return on net worth than the industry as a whole. Second, we should find that direct writers operate with a higher premium-equity capital ratio than the industry as a whole. A detailed analysis of these two indicators is still under way, but the following evidence is available at this time. Table 8 presents data on the average return on net worth after taxes and policyholder dividends of the five largest direct writers and the average rate of return for 1200 property-liability companies for the period 1959 to 1968. Four of the five direct writers exhibited rates of return substantially above the industry average, which is exactly what we expect from the hypothesis.

An examination of the relevant operating ratios for 1971 (a very good year for the insurance industry) is very revealing. Table 9

TABLE 8

RETURN ON NET WORTH AFTER TAXES AND POLICYHOLDER DIVIDENDS OF 5 LARGEST DIRECT WRITERS (1959-1968)

| COMPANY | RATE OF RETURN |
|---|---|
| STATE FARM | 13.1 |
| ALLSTATE | 20.9 |
| LIBERTY MUTUAL | 11.8 |
| NATIONWIDE | 7.4 |
| GEICO | 20.5 |
| 1200 PROPERTY–LIABILITY COMPANIES | 8.8 |

SOURCE: U.S. SENATE, SUBCOMMITTEE ON ANTITRUST AND MONOPOLY [31], PART 17, p. 10201.

TABLE 9

PREMIUM–NET WORTH RATIOS AND RATES OF RETURN FOR FIVE DIRECT WRITERS AND THE TOTAL PROPERTY AND LIABILITY INDUSTRY, 1971

| COMPANY | NET PREMIUMS NET WORTH | EARNED PREMIUMS NET WORTH | OPERATING INCOME NET WORTH | TOTAL RETURNS NET WORTH |
|---|---|---|---|---|
| ALLSTATE | 2.02 | 1.87 | 12.8 | 21.8 |
| STATE FARM | 2.19 | 2.11 | 25.1 | 29.4 |
| LIBERTY MUTUAL | 3.52 | 3.51 | 19.8 | 25.0 |
| GEICO | 3.45 | 3.04 | 19.1 | 22.7 |
| NATIONWIDE | 2.09 | 2.06 | 17.7 | 27.8 |
| TOTAL INDUSTRY | 1.79 | 1.73 | 13.1 | 19.5 |

SOURCE: CALCULATED FROM NEW YORK STATE INSURANCE DEPARTMENT, STATISTICAL TABLES AND ANNUAL STATEMENT 1972.

presents values for two measures of profitability—operating (insurance) income divided by net worth and total income (including interest, dividends, and capital gains) divided by net worth.

The model of the long-run behavior of direct writers indicates that direct writers should earn higher operating returns on net worth *and* operate at higher $\left(\frac{P}{K}\right)_i$ ratios than the industry as a whole. Table 9 presents additional evidence indicating that both predictions appear to be correct. All five direct writers operated at $\left(\frac{P}{K}\right)$ $\left(\text{where } \frac{P}{K} \text{ is calculated based on all of the companies' insurance operations}\right)$ ratios larger than the average for the industry. Liberty Mutual and GEICO operated with $\left(\frac{P}{K}\right)$ almost twice the industry average. In addition, four of the five direct writers had substantially higher ratios of operating income to net worth than the average for the industry. The one company (Allstate) which had an operating return slightly below the industry average also operated at a $\left(\dfrac{P}{K}\right)$ ratio closest to the industry average.

While the data presented in Tables 8 and 9 do not provide conclusive "proof" of the validity of the behavioral models presented here, the data are so consistent with the implications of these models that further consideration and attempts at empirical verification are certainly justified.

☐ **Conclusions: why regulate insurance rates?** In light of the foregoing analysis we may conclude that the property-liability insurance industry under prior approval rate regulation has the following features:

(1) A competitive market structure with a large number of firms and low levels of concentration;

(2) Constant returns to scale in production;

(3) Low to moderate barriers to entry for agency companies; moderate to high barriers to entry for direct writers;

(4) A combination of rate making in concert and regulation which makes true price competition difficult;

(5) An inefficient sales technique, probably costing consumers hundreds of millions of dollars per year, which is being eroded, but only slowly;

(6) Supply shortages induced by the inability or the resistance of regulatory authorities to establish truly homogeneous risk classifications; and

(7) Insurance premiums which are probably too high and effective capacity which is probably too large.

Faced with this picture, one wonders why insurance rates and rating classifications should be regulated at all. There are no natural monopoly characteristics which would indicate that open competition would be unstable and eventually lead to monopoly. Rather, the argument has been that rate making in concert through rating bureaus is a necessity to insure the public and the industry against "destructive" competition and large numbers of bankruptcies. There does not seem to be any reason why this industry should be more unstable than others as long as fraudulent practices are guarded against and proper consumer information is provided for. In many instances recommendations for deregulation of particular industries have rested on conclusions about performance after deregulation which are largely speculative. In the case of the property-liability insurance industry we do not have to rely on such speculation entirely, however. California has been operating under a "no-filing" regulatory statute since 1947. Rates and to some extent rating classes have essentially been regulated by the forces of free competition. While the insurance commissioner continues to have general supervisory power to guard against unfair prices or practices, his main job is to see that the free market works effectively as the regulator of prices.

The experience in California has been excellent; there have been neither mass bankruptcies nor price wars. While supply shortages continue to exist in some cases, this is primarily because of time lags inherent in adjusting rating classifications and collecting data to justify classification changes. The shortage problem appears to have been less severe than in other states, however. Rating bureaus continue to exist, but their powers are strictly advisory. Insurance companies find that they have much more freedom to adjust quickly rates to changing loss situations. This has become very important as inflation has been rapidly increasing the cost of accident repairs. As pointed out before, there tends to be more pricing at off-bureau rates in California than in prior approval states.

The success of the California system has not gone unnoticed. A number of states have recently enacted California-type rating laws.[84] The impetus and research backing the move was provided by the staff of the New York Commission. Along with the NAIC, the New York Insurance Department has strongly encouraged the move to more price competition in states where the market is competitive. In addition, a new emphasis on providing consumers with price information for premium rates charged by different companies has been instituted in New York.[85] The Department realized that such information is an important component of any open competition system, especially in the context of the American Agency System, where price comparisons have historically been difficult.

On the basis of this analysis, the experience in California, and the experience in New York since the no-filing statute was enacted in 1970, the following general public policy recommendations are made with regard to the property-liability insurance industry.

(1) Prior approval rate regulation should be eliminated and replaced with a no-filing system allowing insurance prices to be determined competitively. State Insurance Departments should be retained to perform certain consumer protection functions to be outlined below. Insurance companies should file rate schedules with the insurance department as a source of general information. Companies should be free, however, to set any level of rates which they please.

(2) All anticompetitive aspects of rating bureaus should be eliminated. The rating bureaus should become strictly service organizations, collecting and processing loss and expense data for their customers. Any information provided to one company should be provided to all at appropriate fees.

(3) Flexibility in establishing truly homogeneous rating classifications should be encouraged. While a great deal of uniformity among companies is probably desirable with regard to the establishment of risk classifications so as to facilitate the collection of consistent loss data, no company should be forced to adhere to any established structure if it believes rate variability is justified. Given the availability of automatic data processing equipment, wise coding of all policyholder characteristics should make it possible for a rating bureau to provide loss experience to a customer insurance company for almost any conceivable category. Competition among rating bureaus may even be desirable.

(4) The Insurance Department should play a consumer information and consumer protection role. The greatest possible amount of price information should be put into the hands of consumers. Handbooks listing representative rates for all major underwriters should

---

[84] Among them are New York, Illinois, Florida, Ohio, Connecticut, and Indiana.

[85] See New York State Insurance Department [17, 18, 19].

518

be provided. Possible additional savings available from mutual companies paying dividends and participating stock companies should be brought to the attention of consumers. The insurance department should continue to audit company books and enforce the minimum capital requirement provisions of the state insurance laws. They should assist consumers by mediating complaints against insurance companies and by publicizing the names of companies which have consistently poor payoff policies.[86]

(5) All insurance companies should be required to carry complete insurance against bankruptcy. Insurance rates should not be uniform for each company nor should a state insurance fund be made available to pay off for bankrupt companies. Neither of these schemes would give companies additional incentives to evaluate the premium-capital ratio they are carrying in terms of the true risk adjusted opportunity cost of capital. Rather, bankruptcy insurance rates should be geared to the insolvency risk of the companies themselves as determined by semiannual audits of their operations. Companies operating with very high $\left(\dfrac{P_i}{K_i}\right)$ ratios should pay higher insolvency insurance rates than those operating with lower $\left(\dfrac{P_i}{K_i}\right)$ ratios. Companies which do not have to go to the capital markets for new funds will thus continue to face the risk consequences of their underwriting policies. It will help avoid attempts by risk-loving managers to run companies at very high $\left(\dfrac{P_i}{K_i}\right)$ ratios in the face of consumer ignorance and temporary impotence of capital market forces.

(6) Attempts should be made to speed up the transition from agency production of customers to direct writing wherever possible. The social costs of current laws forbidding agency companies from writing existing customers should be more thoroughly studied and an equitable scheme for phasing out independent agents devised. Trade associations of insurance agents should be strictly enjoined from taking any concerted action against a company which attemps to switch to direct writing region by region. Other barriers to entry of direct writers should be isolated and efforts made to lower them.

(7) Assigned risk pools will, by necessity, have to be continued as long as supply shortages continue to exist. Hopefully competition in rates and rating classification and extended consumer information will eventually cause the shortage problem to disappear. The practice of subsidizing high risk drivers in the assigned risk plans should be carefully reevaluated.

(8) Attempts by some states to go toward more price regulation rather than less should be vigorously discouraged. New Jersey has recently attempted to introduce public utility type rate-of-return rate

---

[86] The consumer protection function should also extend beyond rates to include standardization of basic policy forms and contract provisions. A wide array of policy provisions for basic types of customers would probably result in more confusion than expected benefits from "innovation" are worth. Companies or groups of companies actually creating "innovations" in types of coverage should be encouraged to institute them after scrutiny of the policy provisions by the regulatory authority.

regulation for insurance.[87] While the rate of return on equity capital is certainly a much more meaningful profit figure than the traditional rate of return on premiums, the attempt to determine a fair rate of return for the entire insurance industry is fraught with difficulties. How should the rate of return be calculated? What is a fair rate of return? Should we not calculate a fair rate of return for each company? Regulators attempting to apply public utility ratemaking procedures to individual insurance firms or for the industry as a whole will be applying these techniques to an industry which has every single characteristic of historical regulatory disasters. Since there is no apparent reason to go this route, this can of worms should remain closed.

There are very few examples of deregulation in the history of rate regulation in the United States. Here is an example, however, of a situation in which regulation has worked to the benefit of almost no one (except perhaps the direct writers) in the last 15 years. A system designed to promote the orderly sale of fire insurance through cartels protected by state regulation finally broke down as the nature of the product changed, the sales technology changed, income redistribution attempts of regulators led to supply shortages, and falling short-run profitability for existing firms made almost everyone unhappy with the existing system. The availability of a real world model of a competitive market which really worked will no doubt make the transition politically more appealing. Those states which have eliminated formal rate regulation should be congratulated and other states encouraged to follow their example.

### References

1. ARTHUR D. LITTLE, INC. *Prices and Profits in the Property and Liability Insurance Industry: Summary Report.* November 1967.
2. ———. *Studies of the Profitability, Industrial Structure, Finance and Solving of the Property and Liability Insurance Industry.* June 15, 1970.
3. BAIN, J. S. *Barriers to New Competition.* Cambridge: Harvard Univ. Press, 1956.
4. *Best's Aggregates and Averages*—Property and Liability Insurance Edition. New York: Alfred M. Best, Inc., published annually.
5. *Best's Insurance Reports*—Property and Liability Insurance Edition. New York: Alfred M. Best, Inc., published annually.
6. *Best's Review.* New York: Alfred M. Best, Inc., published monthly.
7. BRAINARD, C. H. AND DIRLAM, J. B. "Antitrust, Regulation, and the Insurance Industry: A Study in Polarity." *The Antitrust Bulletin* (1966).
8. CRANE, F. G. *Automobile Insurance Rate Regulation: The Public Control of Competition.* Ohio State University, Bureau of Business Research, 1962.
9. DIRLAM, J. AND STELZER, I. M. "The Insurance Industry: A Case Study in the Workability of Regulated Competition." *U.P.L. Review* (December 1958).
10. HAMMOND, J. D. AND SCHILLING, N. "A Review Article—The Little Report on Prices and Profits in the Property and Liability Insurance Industry." *The Journal of Risk and Insurance* (March 1969).
11. HENSLEY, R. J. *Competition, Regulation and the Public Interest in Nonlife Insurance.* Berkeley: Univ. of California Press, 1962.
12. KAHN, A. E. *The Economics of Regulation: Principles and Institutions*, Volume I. New York: John Wiley, 1970.
13. LONG, J. "Comments on the Plotkin Paper." *The Journal of Risk and Insurance* (June 1969).

---

[87] See National Association of Insurance Commissioners [15].

520

14. LONG, J. D. AND GREGG, D. W., eds. *Property and Liability Insurance Handbook.* Homewood, Ill.: Richard D. Irwin, Inc., 1965.
15. NATIONAL ASSOCIATION OF INSURANCE COMMISSIONERS. "An Early Look at the Decision in the New Jersey Remand Case." May 8, 1972.
16. ———. "Measurement of Profitability and Treatment of Investment Income in Property and Liability Insurance." June 1970.
17. NEW YORK STATE INSURANCE DEPARTMENT. "The Automobile Assigned Risk Plan in New York State," Preliminary Report, 1973.
18. ———. "Competition among Auto Insurers in New York State." Preliminary Report, 1972 (as corrected by correspondence with Insurance Department).
19. ———. "Competition in Homeowners Insurance in New York State," Preliminary Report, 1973.
20. ———. "McCullough Report on Underwriting Profit." September 16, 1947.
21. ———. "The Public Interest Now in Property and Liability Insurance." January 7, 1969.
22. NEW YORK STATE LEGISLATURE. "Report of the Joint Committee of the Senate and Assembly of the State of New York, Appointed to Investigate Corrupt Practices in Connection with Legislation and the Affairs of Insurance Companies, Other Than Those Doing Life Insurance Business." February 1, 1911.
23. NORGAARD, R. AND SCHICK, G. "Profitability in the Property and Liability Insurance Industry." *The Journal of Risk and Insurance* (June 1968).
24. PLOTKIN, I. H. "Rates of Return in the Property and Liability Insurance Industry: A Comparative Analysis." *The Journal of Risk and Insurance* (June 1969).
25. POSNER, R. A. "Taxation by Regulation." *The Bell Journal of Economics and Management Science,* Vol. 2, No. 1 (Spring 1971), pp. 22–50.
26. PRESIDENT'S NATIONAL ADVISORY PANEL ON INSURANCE IN RIOT-AFFECTED AREAS. *Meeting the Insurance Crises of Our Cities.* Washington, D.C.: U.S. Government Printing Office, 1968.
27. SCHERER, F. M. *Industrial Market Structure and Economic Performance.* New York: Rand McNally, 1970.
28. SHAPIRO, H. "Fire Insurance and the Inner City." The New York City-Rand Institute, R–703-NSF, February 1971.
29. SMALLWOOD, D. "Competition, Regulation and Product Quality in the Automobile Insurance Industry." Mimeo, April 28, 1972.
30. STELZER, I. M. "The Insurance Industry and the Antitrust Laws: A Decade of Experience." *The Insurance Law Journal* (March 1955).
31. UNITED STATES SENATE. Hearings Before the Subcommittee on Antitrust and Monopoly—The Insurance Industry—Parts 1–19. Washington, D.C.: U.S. Government Printing Office, 1959–1971.
32. UNITED STATES DEPARTMENT OF TRANSPORTATION. "Structural Trends and Conditions in the Automobile Insurance Industry." A Report of the Federal Trade Commission to the Department of Transportation, Washington, D.C.: U.S. Government Printing Office, April 1970.

Reprinted from THE BELL JOURNAL OF ECONOMICS
Vol. 10, No. 2, Autumn 1979

# A note on the relative efficiency of property-liability insurance distribution systems

J. David Cummins*

and

Jack VanDerhei**

*Property-liability insurance is distributed through two major marketing channels—the independent and the exclusive agency systems. Independent agents place business with several companies, while exclusive agents write insurance for only one company. We find that the independent agency system is less efficient than the exclusive agency system. The efficiency differential did not change significantly during the period 1968 through 1976. When we used the total rather than the underwriting costs to measure expenses, we found that the relative but not the absolute expense differential was reduced. This suggests that the inefficiencies of the independent agency companies stem from marketing and administrative rather than loss adjustment procedures. The findings imply that regulators should play a more active role in the dissemination of information on property-liability insurance prices.*

## 1. Introduction

■ Property-liability insurance in the United States is distributed through two major channels—the independent (American) agency system and the exclusive agency system.[1] Independent agents maintain contracts with several insurance companies and are not obligated to place business with any one of them. Most exclusive agents, on the other hand, are contractually bound to place their business with a single company. The independent agency system is the traditional method for distributing property-liability insurance and for many years was dominant in all types of coverage. During the past 25 years, exclusive agency companies, led by State Farm and Allstate, have captured a substantial share of the market for automobile and homeowners' insurance and have begun to challenge the independent agency firms for the business of commercial clients.

---

* Associate Professor of Insurance, The Wharton School, University of Pennsylvania.

** Ph.D. candidate, Department of Insurance, The Wharton School, University of Pennsylvania.

[1] Property-liability insurance also is distributed by mail. In spite of the success of several of the direct mail companies, only a relatively small proportion of total premium volume is written in this way.

In his classic study of property-liability insurance markets, Joskow (1973) presented evidence that the exclusive agency system is substantially more efficient than the independent agency system. Based on regression results, Joskow (1973, p. 400) found that "the expense ratios of [exclusive agency companies] average 10.82 percentage points less than the agency companies *ceteris paribus*. For the auto companies themselves the figure is 11.48."[2] He recommended that attempts be made "to speed up the transition from agency production of customers to direct writing wherever possible" (p. 425).

Joskow's findings have received widespread attention both from the insurance industry and from regulators (MacAvoy, 1977). The defenders of the independent agency system have relied on three major arguments: (1) independent agents provide better, more personalized service than exclusive agents; (2) independent agency companies recently have introduced several cost-cutting innovations which may have narrowed the gap between their expense ratios and those of the exclusive agency firms;[3] and (3) Joskow's results were biased because they focused only on underwriting costs.[4] According to this argument, independent agency companies rely heavily on their agents to settle losses, while exclusive agency companies perform this service primarily through company personnel. Hence, if one considers total costs (for underwriting and loss adjustment services), the efficiency difference between the two systems should be less pronounced.

Recent evidence presented by Etgar (1976) and by Cummins and Weisbart (1977) indicates that the first argument is not valid, i.e., there is no systematic difference in quality of service between independent and exclusive agents. The purpose of this note is to investigate the latter two points to determine whether Joskow's conclusion should be modified in any way.

## 2. Hypotheses and methodology

■ Stated more formally, the hypotheses to be tested in this article are as follows:

*Hypothesis 1*: Exclusive agency companies are more efficient than independent agency companies, but the discrepancy has been declining.

*Hypothesis 2*: Exclusive agency companies are more efficient than independent agency companies, but the difference is smaller when one considers total costs rather than underwriting costs.

The hypotheses were tested by estimating several different regression equations utilizing pooled cross section and time series data. Before presenting the equations, we discuss the sample selection procedure.

The source of information on the distribution systems of insurance com-

---

[2] The expense ratio is the ratio of expenses to premiums written. It is usually expressed as a percentage.

[3] Among the innovations are automated accounting systems and direct billing, whereby the policyholder is billed by the company rather than by the agent (Florida Association of Insurance Agents, 1973). Because some agents have been reluctant to adopt direct billing and other innovations, it is doubtful that these techniques have been fully effective in reducing agency costs.

[4] Insurance company underwriting costs are defined as any expenses (including marketing, overhead, etc.) not associated with the loss settlement process.

panies was a list that appears in *Best's Executive Data Service*.[5] From this list, we focused on companies and groups that also appear in the automobile insurance sections of *Best's Aggregates and Averages*, thereby eliminating companies that are not active in the automobile insurance market.[6] We used the automobile insurance criterion because of the importance of this insurance line in terms of overall premium volume and because expense ratios differ significantly among lines of insurance. As explained below, we designed the equation specifications to control for other differences among companies in business mix.

The sample consists of 34 companies and groups—9 exclusive and 25 independent agency firms. We collected annual data on the sample for the period 1968 through 1976.[7] The firms vary widely in size (total premiums written in 1976 ranged from \$71 million to \$4.3 billion) and include both regional and national firms. In 1976 the companies and groups in the sample accounted for approximately 40 percent of the total net premiums written by property-liability insurance companies in the United States. A list of the companies and groups in the sample is presented in the Appendix.

We conducted the initial tests of the hypotheses by estimating the following equation, which is based on Joskow's specification:

$$E_{ijt} = \alpha_0 + \alpha_{1t}DPW_{jt} + \alpha_{2t}\frac{NPW_{jt}}{DPW_{jt}}$$
$$+ \alpha_{3t}DPW_{jt}D1_t + \alpha_{4t}D1_t + \alpha_{5t}D2_t + \alpha_{6t}S_{jt} + \epsilon_{ijt}, \quad (1)$$

where

$$j = 1, 2, \ldots, 34; \quad t = 1, \ldots, 9;$$

$E_{ijt}$ = the $i$th expense ratio of company $j$ in year $t$; the subscript $i = 1$ denotes the underwriting expense ratio, while $i = 2$ denotes the underwriting and loss adjustment expense ratio;

$DPW_{jt}$ = total direct premiums written by company $j$ in year $t$;

$NPW_{jt}$ = total net premiums written by company $j$ in year $t$, where net premiums written = direct premiums written + reinsurance assumed − reinsurance ceded;

$D1_t$ = 1 in year $t$ if company $j$ is an exclusive agency company, 0 in other years and for independent agency companies;

$D2_t$ = 1 in year $t$ if company $j$ is a stock company, 0 in other years and for mutual companies; and

$S_{jt}$ = a specialization variable, e.g., $WCPW_{jt}/DPW_{jt}$, where $WCPW_{jt}$ = workers' compensation direct premiums written by company $j$ in year $t$.

---

[5] This list is compiled by *Best's* on the basis of a survey of the largest 100 to 150 groups (depending on the year) in the United States. Slightly fewer than 100 groups usually respond to the survey.

[6] In Joskow's study, companies were selected which were classified as predominantly auto and predominantly fire by *Best's*. Joskow categorized these firms by type of marketing system by using information provided in *Best's Insurance Reports—Property/Liability Edition* (Joskow, 1973, p. 385n). Because the marketing information in *Best's Insurance Reports—Property/Liability Edition* is sketchy, the authors' procedure should reduce the likelihood of misclassification.

[7] The data were obtained from *Best's Aggregates and Averages* and from *Best's Insurance Reports—Property/Liability Edition*. Several companies which otherwise met the sample criteria were eliminated because they sell insurance primarily through the mail, because they specialize in reinsurance, or because of the unavailability of continuous data for the nine-year sample period.

Estimation of equation (1) yielded a separate coefficient for each independent variable in each year. To obtain more precise parameter estimates, constraints were then imposed sequentially on various sets of coefficients and the equation was reestimated. The null hypothesis that each restriction was valid was tested by using an $F$-statistic.[8]

We tested the effect of the distribution system on the dependent variable by using the dummy variables $D1_t$, $t = 1, 2, \ldots, 9$, separately and in interaction terms. If independent agency firms are less efficient than exclusive agency companies, the coefficients of the intercept dummies should be negative and significantly different from zero. If the efficiency differential has declined over time, a downward trend should be present in the coefficients.

The hypothesis that the efficiency differential in total costs is less than that in underwriting costs (Hypothesis 2) was tested by estimating the equation for each of two dependent variables. $E_{1jt}$ is the underwriting expense ratio, while $E_{2jt}$ is the total (underwriting plus loss adjustment) expense ratio.[9] If Hypothesis 2 is correct, the coefficients of the $D1_t$ terms should be smaller in absolute value when $E_{2jt}$ is the dependent variable.

In accordance with the usual procedure in insurance cost function research, premiums written are used as a proxy for output.[10] The interaction terms $DPW_{jt}D1_t$, are designed to determine whether economies of scale are more or less pronounced for exclusive agency companies. An alternative output measure, losses incurred, also was tested, on the basis of the rationale that the ultimate goal of insurance is loss redistribution and hence that the economic contribution of the industry can be measured in terms of loss disbursements. The equations in which losses appear as the output measure are reported where they provide a better fit to the data.

The variables constructed as the ratios of net to direct premiums are designed to control for the effects of reinsurance. Net premiums are defined as direct premiums plus reinsurance assumed less reinsurance ceded. Companies that accept reinsurance generally pay ceding commissions to the reinsuring companies to recognize the direct acquisition and administrative costs incurred by the latter. Thus, the ratio of net to direct premiums should be positively related to the expense ratio.

The dummy variables $D2_t$ are designed to test for expense ratio differences between stock and mutual companies. There is no clear *a priori* rationale for expecting a positive or negative sign on these terms. The specialization terms $S_{jt}$ are intended to control for differences in business mix among companies. Tests were run in the pooled cross section/time series models by using specialization variables for auto and workers' compensation insurance. The hypothesis is that these lines have different expense characteristics and hence that a concentration in one of them would affect the company's overall expense ratio.

Equation (1) may not be the best specification for testing efficiency differences among insurance companies. Cost function specifications incorporate

---

[8] All hypothesis tests reported in this article are at the 5-percent level of significance.

[9] The total expense ratio is defined as (underwriting expenses/premiums written) plus (loss adjustment expenses incurred/premiums earned). Different denominators are used to recognize the fact that property-liability insurance company underwriting expenses are reported on a cash basis, while loss adjustment expenses are on an accrual basis (Strain, 1976, p. 295).

[10] See, for example, Houston and Simon (1970) and Allen (1974). The theoretically correct output measure would be the companies' physical production, that is, the number of policies issued, the number of claims paid, and so on. Data of this type are not readily available.

implicit assumptions about the underlying production processes, and an accurate representation of these processes requires that the cost function be "consistent with the organization of production at the firm."[11] The recent tendency in insurance cost function research has been to hypothesize a Cobb-Douglas type production function and to estimate the cost equation in log-linear form (Houston and Simon, 1970; Allen, 1974; Cummins, 1977). Thus, we also tested the relative efficiency of the two distribution systems by estimating the following equation:

$$\ln C_{ijt} = \alpha_0 + \alpha_{1t}\ln DPW_{jt} + \alpha_{2t}\ln\left(\frac{NPW_{jt}}{DPW_{jt}}\right) + \alpha_{3t}D1_t\ln DPW_{jt}$$

$$+ \alpha_{4t}D1_t + \alpha_{5t}D2_t + \alpha_{6t}\ln(1 - S_{jt}) + \ldots + \epsilon_{ijt}, \quad (2)$$

where

$j = 1, 2, \ldots, 34; t = 1, \ldots, 9;$ and

$C_{ijt}$ = the expenses of the $j$th firm in year $t$. The subscript $i = 1$ denotes underwriting expenses, while $i = 2$ denotes underwriting and loss adjustment expenses.

The major difference between Joskow's regressions and equation (1) is the necessity for specialization variables in the latter due to the method of sample selection. To control for the possibility that the specialization variables may not be fully effective, we also estimated an equation for auto physical damage insurance costs.[12] This equation utilized a log-linear specification similar to equation (2).

## 3. Empirical findings

■ The regression results for equation (1) appear in Table 1.[13] For each dependent variable—the underwriting expense ratio and the underwriting plus loss adjustment expense ratio—two equations are shown. One of them includes a separate distribution system dummy variable for each year of the sample period, while the other includes a single distribution system dummy applicable to all years. The equations with the underwriting expense ratio as the dependent variable are labelled (1a) and (1b), and the equations in which the underwriting plus loss adjustment expense ratio is the dependent variable are denoted (1c) and (1d).

The annual coefficients for direct premiums written are negative and most are significant (equations (1a) and (1c)). The pooled estimates of this variable in equations (1b) and (1d) also are negative and significant. These results provide evidence of economies of scale, a finding at variance with Joskow (1973), whose equations showed no consistent evidence of scale economies. The interaction variables were eliminated from the final versions of the equations

---

[11] Schweitzer (1972, p. 159). The relationship between production and cost functions also is discussed in Shephard (1970).

[12] We chose automobile insurance because it is the line in which the exclusive agency companies have been most successful. We used automobile physical damage rather than liability insurance because the time to settlement is longer in the latter line, so that reported expense figures depend heavily on estimates.

[13] We estimated the equations by using the AVETRAN program, developed by Robert B. Avery of Carnegie-Mellon University.

TABLE 1

REGRESSION RESULTS FOR PROPERTY–LIABILITY INSURANCE COMPANY EXPENSE RATIOS: LINEAR
SPECIFICATION

| INDEPENDENT VARIABLE | UNDERWRITING EXPENSE RATIO | | UNDERWRITING AND LOSS ADJ. EXPENSE RATIO | |
|---|---|---|---|---|
| | EQUATION (1a)* | EQUATION (1b) | EQUATION (1c)* | EQUATION (1d) |
| DPW68 | $-1.353 \times 10^{-6}$ <br> $(-1.176)$ | | $-.853 \times 10^{-6}$ <br> $(-.687)$ | |
| DPW69 | $-2.327 \times 10^{-6}$ <br> $(-2.249)$ | | $-1.574 \times 10^{-6}$ <br> $(-1.409)$ | |
| DPW70 | $-3.062 \times 10^{-6}$ <br> $(-3.347)$ | | $-1.964 \times 10^{-6}$ <br> $(-1.988)$ | |
| DPW71 | $-2.838 \times 10^{-6}$ <br> $(-3.439)$ | | $-1.973 \times 10^{-6}$ <br> $(-2.213)$ | |
| DPW72 | $-2.246 \times 10^{-6}$ <br> $(-2.974)$ | | $-1.595 \times 10^{-6}$ <br> $(-1.956)$ | |
| DPW73 | $-2.040 \times 10^{-6}$ <br> $(-2.902)$ | | $-1.415 \times 10^{-6}$ <br> $(-1.864)$ | |
| DPW74 | $-1.542 \times 10^{-6}$ <br> $(-2.328)$ | | $-.553 \times 10^{-6}$ <br> $(-.773)$ | |
| DPW75 | $-2.233 \times 10^{-6}$ <br> $(-3.671)$ | | $-1.343 \times 10^{-6}$ <br> $(-2.045)$ | |
| DPW76 | $-2.282 \times 10^{-6}$ <br> $(-4.672)$ | | $-1.450 \times 10^{-6}$ <br> $(-2.750)$ | |
| DPW | | $-2.075 \times 10^{-6}$ <br> $(-7.041)$ | | $-1.373 \times 10^{-6}$ <br> $(-4.370)$ |
| NPW/DPW | 6.781 <br> (3.948) | 6.598 <br> (3.882) | 7.117 <br> (3.837) | 7.157 <br> (3.949) |
| S | $-15.876$ <br> $(-10.750)$ | $-15.603$ <br> $(-10.622)$ | $-13.715$ <br> $(-8.599)$ | $-13.580$ <br> $(-8.668)$ |
| D2 | 1.868 <br> (4.305) | 1.791 <br> (4.203) | 1.132 <br> (2.416) | 1.116 <br> (2.456) |
| D1 | | $-6.725$ <br> $(-13.937)$ | | $-6.550$ <br> $(-12.728)$ |
| D1-68 | $-8.069$ <br> $(-7.189)$ | | $-6.451$ <br> $(-5.323)$ | |

because their coefficients were not significantly different from zero. This suggests that scale economies are no more pronounced for exclusive than for independent agency firms.

The reinsurance variables, denoted $NPW/DPW$, are significant and have the expected positive signs in all four equations. The stock-mutual dummy variables also are positive and significant, providing evidence that stock companies have higher expense ratios than mutuals.[14] The specialization term for workers' compensation proved to be significant and negative as expected, while the automobile insurance specialization terms were not significant and were eliminated from the final versions of the equation.[15]

---

[14] This finding does not necessarily indicate that mutual companies are more efficient, however, because they traditionally have been more likely to pay dividends than stock companies. Since the relevant variables cannot easily be measured net of dividends, the denominators of the mutual company expense ratios may be artificially inflated. The impact of dividends is ambiguous because stock companies also pay dividends, especially to large commercial clients.

[15] Specialization variables for fire, allied lines, commercial multiple peril, and homeowners insurance were tested in annual equations for 1976. Only the commercial multiple peril variable was close to significance, with a $t$-ratio of 1.55. Although we did not deem this variable sufficiently important to be included in the pooled regressions, it is worth noting that the absolute value of the coefficient of the distribution system dummy was reduced somewhat when the commercial multiple peril term was present in the equation.

TABLE 1 (CONTINUED)

| INDEPENDENT VARIABLE | UNDERWRITING EXPENSE RATIO | | UNDERWRITING AND LOSS ADJ. EXPENSE RATIO | |
|---|---|---|---|---|
| | EQUATION (1a)* | EQUATION (1b) | EQUATION (1c)* | EQUATION (1d) |
| D1–69 | −7.411 (−6.538) | | −6.716 (−5.487) | |
| D1–70 | −7.321 (−6.421) | | −6.661 (−5.410) | |
| D1–71 | −6.992 (−6.134) | | −6.936 (−5.634) | |
| D1–72 | −6.960 (−6.122) | | −6.693 (−5.452) | |
| D1–73 | −6.012 (−5.300) | | −6.336 (−5.172) | |
| D1–74 | −5.408 (−4.763) | | −5.978 (−4.875) | |
| D1–75 | −5.233 (−4.576) | | −5.692 (−4.610) | |
| D1–76 | −6.299 (−5.489) | | −7.285 (−5.879) | |
| CONSTANT | 25.863 (15.411) | 26.004 (15.656) | 34.608 (19.096) | 34.552 (19.505) |
| $\bar{R}^2$ | .693 | .695 | .597 | .609 |
| S.E. | 2.837 | 2.828 | 3.064 | 3.016 |

*AN F−TEST INDICATES THAT THE COEFFICIENTS OF D1−68 THROUGH D1−76 ARE NOT SIGNIFICANTLY DIFFERENT FROM ONE ANOTHER AT THE 5−PERCENT LEVEL OF SIGNIFICANCE. A SIMILAR RESULT WAS OBTAINED FOR THE COEFFICIENTS OF DPW68 THROUGH DPW76.

NOTE: THE EQUATIONS WERE ESTIMATED BY USING ANNUAL DATA ON 34 INSURANCE COMPANIES AND GROUPS OVER THE PERIOD 1968 TO 1976, INCLUSIVE. THE ESTIMATES WERE OBTAINED THROUGH ORDINARY LEAST SQUARES. THE FIGURES IN PARENTHESES ARE t−STATISTICS.

KEY: DPW = DIRECT PREMIUMS WRITTEN; DPWxx = DIRECT PREMIUMS WRITTEN FOR YEAR xx IN YEAR xx, 0 IN OTHER YEARS, WHERE xx RANGES FROM 68 = 1968 THROUGH 76 = 1976; NPW = NET PREMIUMS WRITTEN; D1 = 1 IF THE COMPANY UTILIZES THE EXCLUSIVE AGENCY SYSTEM, 0 OTHERWISE; D2 = 1 IF THE COMPANY IS A STOCK COMPANY, 0 OTHERWISE; S = (WORKERS' COMPENSATION DIRECT PREMIUMS WRITTEN)/(TOTAL DIRECT PREMIUMS WRITTEN); D1−xx = 1 IN YEAR xx IF THE COMPANY UTILIZES THE EXCLUSIVE AGENCY SYSTEM, 0 OTHERWISE, WHERE xx RANGES FROM 68 = 1968 THROUGH 76 = 1976.

The intercept dummies for the type of distribution system have the expected signs and are always significant. While a slight downward trend in the coefficients of the annual intercept dummies appears to be present in equation (1a), an F-test indicates that these coefficients are not significantly different from one another. We obtained a similar result for equation (1c). The difference between the pooled estimates of the distributional system coefficients in equations (1b) and (1d) is not statistically significant.

The results reported in Table 1 suggest the following conclusions:

(1) Exclusive agency companies are significantly more efficient than independent agency companies, and this efficiency advantage did not decline appreciably from 1968 through 1976. The point estimate of the expense ratio differential is 6.72 percentage points for underwriting expenses and 6.55 percentage points for total expenses.[16] If the premiums written in 1976 by the independent agency companies in the sample had been written at the expense

---

[16] The differences are less than those reported by Joskow (1973, p. 400), who found an efficiency differential of approximately 11 percentage points. This discrepancy probably stems from differences in sampling procedures.

ratio of the exclusive agency companies, the savings would have been approximately $1 billion, *ceteris paribus*.

(2) The relative but not the absolute value of the efficiency differential is reduced when the total expense ratio rather than the underwriting expense ratio is the dependent variable. At average values for the entire sample period, the underwriting expense ratios of exclusive agency companies are approximately 23 percent lower than those of the independent agency companies, while the differential for the underwriting plus loss adjustment expense ratios is about 17 percent.

The regression results for the log-linear specifications appear in Table 2. Again, there are two equations for each dependent variable, one with annual

TABLE 2

TOTAL COST FUNCTIONS FOR PROPERTY—LIABILITY INSURANCE COMPANIES: LOG—LINEAR SPECIFICATION

| INDEPENDENT VARIABLES | ln (UNDERWRITING EXPENSES) | | ln (UNDERWRITING + LOSS ADJUSTMENT EXPENSES) | |
|---|---|---|---|---|
| | EQUATION 2(a)* | EQUATION 2(b) | EQUATION 2(c)* | EQUATION 2(d) |
| ln (DPW) | .957 (92.647) | .964 (85.062) | .970 (120.693) | .967 (109.422) |
| ln (NPW/DPW) | 1.039 (27.543) | 1.009 (26.065) | .918 (25.524) | .916 (25.333) |
| D2 | .094 (2.215) | .085 (1.963) | .058 (1.945) | .061 (1.978) |
| ln (1−S) | .264 (3.595) | .250 (3.287) | .127 (2.106) | .144 (2.331) |
| D1 | | −.257 (−5.456) | | −.164 (−4.984) |
| D1−68 | −.290 (−6.073) | | −.162 (−4.770) | |
| D1−69 | −.270 (−5.654) | | −.168 (−4.937) | |
| D1−70 | −.280 (−5.844) | | −.172 (−5.021) | |
| D1−71 | −.266 (−5.540) | | −.178 (−5.186) | |
| D1−72 | −.258 (−5.376) | | −.163 (−4.739) | |
| D1−73 | −.228 (−4.730) | | −.155 (−4.493) | |
| D1−74 | −.202 (−4.188) | | −.140 (−4.053) | |
| D1−75 | −.208 (−4.316) | | −.158 (−4.566) | |
| D1−76 | −.253 (−5.213) | | −.212 (−6.051) | |
| CONSTANT | −.680 (−5.492) | −0.760 (−5.621) | −.578 (−6.091) | −.548 (−5.260) |
| $\bar{R}^2$ | .990 | .990 | .994 | .994 |
| S.E. | .1161 | .1164 | .0929 | .0925 |

*AN F—TEST INDICATES THAT THE COEFFICIENTS OF D1−68 THROUGH D1−76 ARE NOT SIGNIFICANTLY DIFFERENT FROM ONE ANOTHER AT THE 5—PERCENT LEVEL OF SIGNIFICANCE.

NOTE: THE EQUATIONS WERE ESTIMATED BY USING ANNUAL DATA ON 34 INSURANCE COMPANIES AND GROUPS OVER THE PERIOD 1968 TO 1976, INCLUSIVE. AN ERROR COMPONENTS MODEL WAS EMPLOYED WITH BOTH TIME AND UNIT COMPONENTS. THE FIGURES IN PARENTHESES ARE t—STATISTICS.

KEY: DPW = DIRECT PREMIUMS WRITTEN; NPW = NET PREMIUMS WRITTEN; D1 = 1 IF THE COMPANY UTILIZES THE EXCLUSIVE AGENCY SYSTEM, 0 OTHERWISE; D2 = 1 IF THE COMPANY IS A STOCK COMPANY, 0 OTHERWISE; S = (WORKERS' COMPENSATION DIRECT PREMIUMS WRITTEN)/(TOTAL DIRECT PREMIUMS WRITTEN); D1−xx = 1 IN YEAR xx IF THE COMPANY UTILIZES THE EXCLUSIVE AGENCY SYSTEM, 0 OTHERWISE, WHERE xx RANGES FROM 68 = 1968 THROUGH 76 = 1976.

estimates of the coefficients of the distribution system intercept dummies and the other with a pooled estimate of this effect. In all four equations, the coefficient in $\ln(DPW)$ is significantly different from 1.0, which provides additional evidence that moderate scale economies are present in the sample group. We eliminated the interaction terms from the equations because they were insignificant. The findings with respect to the reinsurance, the stock-mutual, and the specialization variables are consistent with those reported for the linear specification.

The coefficients of the annual distribution system dummy variables in equation (2a) are negative and significant. However, neither these coefficients nor their counterparts in equation (2c) are significantly different from one another. Hence, there is no evidence of a downward trend in the efficiency advantage. As in the linear specification, the relative efficiency advantage is smaller when loss adjustment expenses are included in the dependent variable (15 percent rather than 23 percent). In the log-linear equations, the absolute differential also is smaller, but this difference is not statistically significant.

The cost functions for auto physical damage insurance, which are presented in Table 3, are noteworthy in several respects. First, a better fit resulted when losses rather than premiums were used as the output proxy. Second, all but one of the coefficients of the output variables are significantly different from 1.0, suggesting the existence of scale economies in automobile physical damage insurance.[17] Third, the hypothesis that the coefficients of the independent-exclusive agency dummy variables declined during the sample period is again rejected both for underwriting and for underwriting plus loss adjustment expenses. For this reason, we show only the equations with pooled estimates of this effect in Table 3. Finally, the estimated expense advantage of the exclusive agency companies is less in both absolute and relative terms when loss adjustment expenses are included in the dependent variable. Other things equal, underwriting expenses are estimated to be 21.5 percent less for exclusive than for independent agency companies. For total expenses, the figure is 15.2 percent. This difference, however, is not statistically significant.

## 4. Summary and conclusions

■ The results reported in this article clearly indicate that Joskow was correct in concluding that exclusive agency companies are more efficient than independent agency companies. *Ceteris paribus*, the expenses of exclusive agency companies are estimated to be from 15 to 23 percent less than those of independent agency companies, depending on the specification and the dependent variable. Significance tests indicate that Hypothesis 1 should be rejected, i.e., the efficiency advantage of the exclusive agency companies did not decline during the period 1968 through 1976.

Tests of Hypothesis 2 reveal that the relative but not the absolute efficiency differential is reduced when loss adjustment expenses are included in the dependent variable. This suggests that the inefficiencies of the independent agency companies stem from administrative and marketing rather than from loss adjustment procedures. Additional research would be needed to determine the regulatory implications of the findings. At a minimum, however, the results

---

[17] The coefficients of the annual $\ln(ALOSS)$ variables also differ significantly from one another, thereby accounting for their presence in the final version of the automobile insurance equations.

TABLE 3

COST FUNCTIONS FOR AUTO PHYSICAL DAMAGE INSURANCE: LOG–LINEAR SPECIFICATION

| INDEPENDENT VARIABLES | ln (AUTO UNDERWRITING EXPENSES)* | ln (AUTO UNDERWRITING AND LOSS ADJUSTMENT EXPENSES)* |
|---|---|---|
| ln (ALOSS68) | .977 (76.110) | .979 (103.426) |
| ln (ALOSS69) | .973 (76.709) | .974 (104.182) |
| ln (ALOSS70) | .972 (77.239) | .974 (104.991) |
| ln (ALOSS71) | .979 (77.438) | .983 (105.416) |
| ln (ALOSS72) | .983 (78.414) | .984 (106.397) |
| ln (ALOSS73) | .978 (78.769) | .979 (106.909) |
| ln (ALOSS74) | .973 (79.146) | .975 (107.529) |
| ln (ALOSS75) | .961 (79.366) | .965 (107.977) |
| ln (ALOSS76) | .967 (80.142) | .970 (108.980) |
| D1 | −.242 (−6.280) | −.165 (−5.820) |
| D2 | .194 (5.927) | .142 (5.865) |
| CONSTANT | −.466 (−2.775) | −.240 (−1.942) |
| $\bar{R}^2$ | .966 | .981 |
| S.E. | .220 | .162 |

*THE VARIABLES, D1–68 THROUGH D1–76 WERE ELIMINATED FROM THE FINAL VERSION OF THE EQUATIONS BECAUSE F–TESTS INDICATED THAT THEIR COEFFICIENTS WERE NOT SIGNIFICANTLY DIFFERENT FROM ONE ANOTHER. HOWEVER, THE HYPOTHESIS THAT THE COEFFICIENTS OF ln (ALOSS68) THROUGH ln (ALOSS76) ARE EQUAL WAS REJECTED WITH AN F–TEST AT THE 5–PERCENT LEVEL OF SIGNIFICANCE.

NOTE: THE EQUATIONS WERE ESTIMATED BY USING ANNUAL DATA ON 34 INSURANCE COMPANIES AND GROUPS OVER THE PERIOD 1968 TO 1976, INCLUSIVE. THE ESTIMATES WERE OBTAINED THROUGH ORDINARY LEAST SQUARES. THE FIGURES IN PARENTHESES ARE t–STATISTICS.

KEY: ALOSSxx = LOSSES INCURRED FOR AUTO PHYSICAL DAMAGE INSURANCE FOR YEAR xx IN YEAR xx, 0 IN OTHER YEARS, WHERE xx RANGES FROM 68 = 1968 THROUGH 76 = 1976; D1 = 1 IF THE COMPANY UTILIZES THE EXCLUSIVE AGENCY SYSTEM, 0 OTHERWISE; AND D2 = 1 IF THE COMPANY IS A STOCK COMPANY, 0 OTHERWISE.

imply that regulators should take a more active role in disseminating information on the prices of property-liability insurance policies issued by different companies.

### Appendix

## Companies and groups included in the sample

■ The nine exclusive agency companies and the 25 independent agency companies are as follows:

*Exclusive Agency Companies*:

Allstate Insurance Company
American Family Mutual
American Mutual Liability Group
Country Mutual Insurance

Federated Mutual Insurance
Liberty Mutual Group
MFA Mutual Insurance Company
Nationwide Mutual Insurance Group
State Farm Group

*Independent Agency Companies*:

American General Group
Atlantic Mutual Insurance Group
Auto-Owners Insurance Company
Central Mutual Insurance Company
Chubb Corporation
Cincinnati Insurance Company
CNA Insurance Group
Crum & Forster Group
Fireman's Fund American Group
General Accident Group
Home Insurance Group
Indiana Insurance Company
Insurance Company of North America

Merchants Mutual Insurance Group
Michigan Mutual Insurance Company
National Grange Mutual
NN Corporation
Ohio Casualty Insurance Group
Royal Globe Insurance Group
St. Paul Companies
Security Corporation
Transamerica Insurance Company
Travelers Indemnity/Phoenix Group
Unigard Mutual Insurance Group
United States Fidelity & Guarantee
Insurance Group

## References

ALLEN, R.F. "Cross Sectional Estimates of Cost Economies in Stock Property-Liability Companies." *Review of Economics and Statistics*, Vol. 56 (1974), pp. 100–103.

A.M. BEST COMPANY. *Best's Aggregates and Averages*. Oldwick, N.J.: annually.

———. *Best's Executive Data Service*. Oldwick, N.J.: annually.

———. *Best's Insurance Reports—Property/Liability Edition*. Oldwick, N.J.: annually.

CUMMINS, J.D. "Economies of Scale in Independent Insurance Agencies." *Journal of Risk and Insurance*, Vol. 44, No. 4 (December 1977), pp. 539–553.

——— AND WEISBART, S.N. *The Impact of Consumer Services on Independent Insurance Agency Performance*. Glenmont, N.Y.: IMA Education & Research Foundation, 1977.

ETGAR, M. "Service Performance of Insurance Distributors." *Journal of Risk and Insurance*, Vol. 43, No. 3 (September 1976), pp. 487–499.

FLORIDA ASSOCIATION OF INSURANCE AGENTS. *The Florida Agents' Manifesto—Objective: Survival*. Tallahassee: 1973.

HILL, R.D. "Capital Market Equilibrium and the Regulation of Property/Liability Insurance." Ph.D. dissertation, Massachusetts Institute of Technology, 1978.

HOUSTON, D.B. AND SIMON, R.M. "Economies of Scale in Financial Institutions: A Study in Life Insurance." *Econometrica*, Vol. 38 (1970), pp. 856–864.

JOSKOW, P.L. "Cartels, Competition, and Regulation in the Property-Liability Insurance Industry." *The Bell Journal of Economics and Management Science*, Vol. 4, No. 2 (Autumn 1973), pp. 375–427.

MACAVOY, P.W., ED. *Federal-State Regulation of the Pricing and Marketing of Insurance*. Washington, D.C.: American Enterprise Institute for Public Policy Research, 1977.

SCHWEITZER, S.A. "Economies of Scale and Holding Company Affiliations in Banking." *Southern Economic Journal*, Vol. 38 (1972), pp. 258–266.

SHEPHARD, R.W. *Theory of Cost and Production Functions*. Princeton: Princeton University Press, 1970.

STRAIN, R.W. *Property-Liability Insurance Accounting*. Santa Monica: The Merritt Company, 1976.

# OWNERSHIP STRUCTURE ACROSS LINES OF PROPERTY-CASUALTY INSURANCE*

DAVID MAYERS          and          CLIFFORD W. SMITH, JR.
Ohio State University                University of Rochester

## I. INTRODUCTION

THE range of ownership structures within the insurance industry is perhaps the broadest of any major industry. Included are Lloyds associations, where insurance contracts are offered by individual underwriters, stock companies that employ the standard corporate form, and mutuals and reciprocals that are more like cooperatives where customer and ownership functions are merged.

Coase's[1] analysis indicates that with no contracting costs the ownership structure of the insurance supplier (the assignment of property rights within the firm) will have no effect on real activity choices. Jensen and Meckling[2] develop a framework for analysis where contracting is costly. They presume that conflicting incentives among the parties to a contract generate costs. These costs, referred to as agency costs, include all of the costs incurred in attempting to control incentive conflicts (for example, negotiation, administration, information, and litigation costs) as well as the opportunity cost (the residual loss) that remains after control steps are taken since it generally will not be optimal to exercise complete control.

Recent analysis focuses on the effect that firms' ownership structures have on the costs of producing products. For example, Mayers and

---

* We would like to thank Gene Fama, Mike Hanssens, David Hirshleifer, Jay Shanken, Mike Smith, and members of the Risk Theory Seminar for comments and suggestions. This research was partially supported by the Managerial Economics Research Center, Graduate School of Management, University of Rochester.

[1] Ronald Coase, The Problem of Social Cost, 3 J. Law & Econ. 1 (1960).

[2] Michael C. Jensen & William H. Meckling, Theory of the Firm: Managerial Behavior Agency Costs and Ownership Structure, 3 J. Fin. Econ. 305 (1976).

[*Journal of Law and Economics*, vol. XXXI (October 1988)]

Smith[3] and Fama and Jensen[4] argue that alternative structures convey benefits in specific dimensions and that the operations of firms with different organizational structures should also differ.[5] To date, these hypotheses have received little empirical verification. In this article, we analyze the incentives to individuals performing the three major functions within the insurance firm: the management function, the ownership/risk-bearing function, and the customer/policyholder function. We suggest that differing costs of controlling incentive conflicts among the parties of the insurance firm lead to the efficiency of alternative ownership structures across lines of insurance. We examine evidence from the property-casualty insurance industry to determine if there are significant differences in activity choices associated with the alternative ownership structures.

Others have examined related issues. Several previous empirical analyses have examined the relative efficiency of stock versus mutual or reciprocal ownership structures. These studies generally conclude that mutuals and reciprocals are less efficient than stock companies, in spite of the fact that the former continue to survive within the industry. For example, Spiller[6] argues that management exploits its position in a mutual to gain personally at the expense of the firm's other claim holders. Frech[7] concludes that "[e]xamination of the actual property rights structure of mutual insurers indicates that their . . . owners do not have full property rights. Thus they are expected to perform less efficiently than stock insurers, and that expectation is borne out." Fletcher,[8] however, argues that there are no important differences between the stock and mutual forms of

---

[3] David Mayers & Clifford W. Smith, Jr., Contractual Provisions, Organizational Structure, and Conflict Control in Insurance Markets, 54 J. Bus. 407 (1981); and David Mayers & Clifford W. Smith, Jr., Ownership Structure and Control: The Mutualization of Stock Life Insurance Companies, 16 J. Fin. Econ. 73 (1986).

[4] Eugene F. Fama & Michael C. Jensen, Agency Problems and Residual Claims, 26 J. Law & Econ. 327 (1983).

[5] See also Eugene F. Fama & Michael C. Jensen, Separation of Ownership and Control, 26 J. Law & Econ. 301 (1983); Oliver E. Williamson, Organizational Form, Residual Claimants, and Corporate Control, 26 J. Law & Econ. 351 (1983); Benjamin Klein, Contracting Costs and Residual Claims: The Separation of Ownership and Control, 26 J. Law & Econ. 367 (1983); and Harold Demsetz, The Structure of Ownership and the Theory of the Firm, 26 J. Law & Econ. 375 (1983).

[6] R. Spiller, Ownership and Performance: Stock and Mutual Life Insurance Companies, 34 J. Risk & Ins. 17 (1972).

[7] H. E. Frech III, Health Insurance: Private, Mutuals or Government, Econ. Nonproprietary Organizations Res. L. & Econ. 61 (Suppl. 1980).

[8] Linda P. Fletcher, Mutualization of Stock Life Insurance Companies (unpublished Ph.D. dissertation, University of Pennsylvania 1964); and Linda P. Fletcher, Motivations Underlying the Mutualization of Stock Life Insurance Companies, 33 J. Risk & Ins. 19 (1966).

organization. Reinmuth,[9] in a study analyzing reciprocals, determines that they also are inefficient.

These past studies attempt to assess the relative efficiency of alternative ownership structures on a common scale (a disequilibrium approach). Our analysis differs in that we take the efficiency of alternative ownership structures as given and seek to explain why different structures are most efficient in different lines of business (an equilibrium approach). Past studies compare accounting estimates of costs or profitability. We examine geographical and line-of-business concentration, controlling for firm size, to assess the existence of differences in activity choice for alternative ownership structures.

## II.  Alternative Ownership Structures

This section analyzes the major ownership structures of the property/casualty insurance industry. There are three important functions in each ownership structure. The first is the managerial function. Managers are the decision makers—the administrators who quote rates, market the policies, and administer claims. The second function is the ownership/risk-bearing function. The owner/risk bearers provide capital and their own claims to the (risky) residual income stream of the organization. The third function is that of customer/policyholder. The customer/policyholders pay premiums in return for a promise that they will receive a stipulated amount from the insurance firm in the event that they incur specified losses.

Alternative ownership structures combine these functions in different ways, and different combinations produce different cost functions. We argue that variation in these costs is related to variables such as the degree of managerial discretion required in setting rates in a given line of insurance. Generally, the more discretion an agent is authorized to have, the larger is the potential for that agent to operate in his own self-interest at the expense of the other parties to the contract. Thus, alternative ownership structures provide control mechanisms that limit to varying degrees the ability of particular agents to operate in an opportunistic manner. In the analysis that follows, we focus on the costs and benefits of the alternative ownership structures in order to better understand the nature of their respective comparative advantages.

### A.  Lloyds Associations

The basic distinguishing characteristic of a Lloyds association is that the insurers are individual underwriters. Thus Lloyds associations merge

[9] Dennis F. Reinmuth, The Regulation of Reciprocal Insurance Exchanges (1967).

the managerial function and the ownership/risk-bearing function. Each member of the association is responsible for only that portion of a risk personally underwritten.

Merging the managerial function and the ownership/risk-bearing function controls any incentive problem that might exist were those functions performed by separate parties. Because the managers bear the wealth effects of their decisions, the Lloyds association underwriters have great discretion in providing insurance where flexibility in rate setting is important. However, this discretion does not come without cost. The restriction that ownership claims can be held only by managers precludes the owner/managers from taking advantage of risk-reducing opportunities afforded through unrestricted ownership claims. For example, unrestricted claims allow specialization in risk bearing. Risk-bearing specialists can diversify by holding ownership claims in many organizations and thereby provide risk-bearing services at lower cost.[10]

In a Lloyds association, membership in the association is subject to a number of restrictions. There are usually net worth requirements as well as other restrictions concerning audits and the size of commitments in relation to the capital individual members may undertake.[11] Moreover, mutual monitoring by members of the association helps to control incentive problems between the individual underwriters and the customer/policyholders.[12] Thus there are costs and benefits of the Lloyds association ownership structure. Because the benefits largely stem from managerial discretion, Lloyds associations should have a comparative advantage in writing insurance where discretion in rate setting is important—for example, in insuring against unusual or unique types of hazards.[13]

While the thrust of our analysis is on variation in private costs and benefits of alternative ownership structures, variation in regulation or

[10] The Lloyds association member can limit his risk exposure by diversifying his underwriting across many risks rather than just taking a few large positions. Any individual underwriter's ability to do this is limited by the membership of the association and the size of the risks being underwritten. Thus, bearing the risk of the residual income stream is probably an important function of Lloyds' underwriters.

[11] See D. Bickelhaupt, General Insurance 775–77 (1967) for further discussion on membership requirements for Lloyds associations.

[12] This mutual monitoring includes the enforcement of standards for membership and the central guarantee fund. Differences in the effectiveness of such monitoring devices help explain the variation in reputation of Lloyd's of London and American Lloyds.

[13] A good example of a case where risks were changing frequently and managerial discretion was important is marine insurance in the early nineteenth century. C. Wright & C. E. Fayle, A History of Lloyd's (1928) report the adjustment of rates by an underwriter at Lloyd's of London. "Take, for example, the year of Trafalgar, and the routes specially

taxes can have a significant impact on market participation. This appears to be an especially important concern in the case of Lloyds associations. For example, in many states, Lloyd's of London is restricted to the surplus line market. This market consists of risks that domestic insurers have rejected for one reason or another. Additionally, states have frequently restricted American Lloyds to only certain lines of insurance, such as fire, ocean marine, inland transportation, and automobile insurance. Furthermore, the largest of the American Lloyds, that in New York, enjoys a regulatory prohibition against formation of another Lloyds in the state. Obviously, such regulation, if binding, restricts the amount of business for reasons other than those on which we focus.

## B.  Common Stock Insurance Companies

The distinguishing characteristic of the common stock insurance company is the potentially complete separation of the managerial, ownership/risk-bearing, and customer/policyholder functions. Separation allows specialization in these functions, and that lowers costs. The unrestricted common stock of the insurance company allows efficiencies in risk bearing that are complemented by the benefits of managerial specialization.[14] For example, managerial talent can be chosen in the common stock insurance company without giving strong consideration to the manager's wealth or willingness to bear risk. In contrast, these are important considerations for a Lloyds association underwriter.

Nevertheless, the separation of the managerial and ownership/risk-bearing functions in the common stock insurance company means that the manager of such a company does not bear the full wealth effects of his actions. This leads to an important agency or incentive conflict control problem. The manager will generally not have interests that are perfectly aligned with those of the owner/risk bearers.[15] Several control mechanisms can help assure that actions taken by management will not harm the owners. For example, the board of directors is appointed by the stock-

---

affected by movements of hostile fleets. For homeward voyages from the West Indies, the average rate on 76 risks accepted by Mr. Janson during the first quarter of the year was 8½ per cent. The arrival of Villeneuve's fleet in the West Indies, sent it up to 13½ per cent, and thence to 15 per cent and over. It touched 16 per cent when he was making for the Channel, but fell to 11 per cent after his indecisive actions with Calder and his return to Cadiz.''

[14] These points are made by Fama & Jensen, *supra* note 4, as some of the advantages of common stock residual claims. They also mention the purchase of organization-specific assets and the market value rule for investment decisions as advantages.

[15] The general problem of the separation of ownership and control is discussed in Fama & Jensen, *supra* note 5.

holders. The board has the authority and responsibility to monitor the manager (where monitoring includes correcting as well as detecting managerial behavior inconsistent with owner welfare). Moreover, most firms complement the external managerial labor market with an internal managerial labor market through which potential executives compete. These control devices, as well as the charter of the firm itself, control the discretion allowed the manager. If these internal control devices fail, the threat of an outside takeover can be a significant factor in reducing the costs managers can impose on the other claim holders of the firm.

Separation of the customer/policyholder and ownership/risk-bearing functions also creates incentive conflicts. Policyholders face incentive-contracting problems in insurance markets that are analogous to those of lenders in credit markets. Stockholders have incentives to increase the value of their claims at the expense of policyholders after policies are sold. For example, if a firm sold insurance policies and the policies were priced with the assumption that the firm would maintain its dividend policy, the value of the policies would fall (the value of the shareholders' equity would rise) if the firm raised dividends and financed them by liquidating assets. At the limit, if the firm sells all its assets and pays a liquidating dividend, any subsequent policyholder's claims would be worthless.[16] Of course, policyholders recognize the incentives of stockholders. Rationally priced insurance contracts reflect unbiased estimates of these forecasted costs. Thus, by limiting their opportunities for expropriation from policyholders, the stockholders can sell insurance for higher prices.

### C. Mutual Insurance Companies

In a mutual insurance company, the customer/policyholder and ownership/risk-bearing functions are merged. The rights of the policyholders of a mutual are not equivalent to the sum of the rights of the policyholders and stockholders of a stock insurance company, however. For example, their ownership rights are limited through the company charter, policy provisions, and regulation in ways that are not imposed on stockholders of common stock firms. There has been a serious debate over the implica-

---

[16] Similarly, if a firm sold insurance policies asserting that the proceeds would be used to purchase low-risk assets and the policies were purchased at prices commensurate with that low risk, the value of the stockholders' equity would rise at the expense of the policyholders if the firm substituted assets of high risk. For further elaboration, see the discussion in Clifford W. Smith, Jr., & Jerold B. Warner, On Financial Contracting: An Analysis of Bond Covenants, 7 J. Fin. Econ. 117 (1979), or Jensen & Meckling, *supra* note 2, at 333–37, of the agency costs of debt in the context of a firm's capital structure.

tions of these limitations on ownership rights and the degree to which policyholders effectively control mutuals.[17] Yet even if policyholders of a mutual do not have all the rights of both policyholders and stockholders of a stock insurance firm, mutual ownership still eliminates the stockholder group with its separate and sometimes disparate interests. This reduces potential costs imposed on policyholders from the choice of dividend, financing, and investment decisions over the lives of their policies. We believe that this is the major benefit of the mutual form of organization.

The potential advantage mutuals have in controlling the incentive problem between policyholders and stockholders is offset by a worsened incentive problem between the owners and managers of the firm as compared with the stock insurance company. As previously stated, a potentially significant factor in reducing the costs management can impose on the owners of a stock firm is the threat of a takeover. If management imposes too many costs, someone can assemble a controlling block of shares and change management, thus realizing the capitalized value of the cost reduction.[18] In a mutual, the incentives are weaker since the owners would have to remove existing management through a proxy fight and, hence, fail to capture the gains.[19,20] Therefore, if the cost of controlling management in mutual insurance companies is higher than in stock firms, mutual firms should be more prevalent in lines of insurance where man-

---

[17] For example, see J. A. C. Hetherington, Fact v. Fiction: Who Owns Mutual Insurance Companies, 4 Wisc. Law Rev. 1068 (1969); and Gary Kreider, Who Owns the Mutuals? Proposals for Reform of Membership Rights in Mutual Insurance and Banking Companies, 41 Cincinnati L. Rev. 275 (1972), who argue that mutuals are controlled by incumbent management. Buist M. Anderson, Policyholder Control of a Mutual Life Insurance Company, 22 Cleveland St. L. Rev. 439 (1973), disagrees.

[18] This motivation for takeovers was originally suggested by Henry G. Manne, Mergers and the Market for Corporate Control, 73 J. Pol. Econ. 110 (1965). See Michael Bradley, Interfirm Tender Offers and the Market for Corporate Control, 53 J. Bus. 345 (1980), for a discussion of some specific problems with the mechanism Manne suggests for capturing the gains.

[19] Furthermore, proxy fights are expensive. For a colorful (almost funny) description of the costs of waging a proxy fight for control of mutual insurance firms, see the report of the Temporary National Economic Committee, Study of Legal Reserve Life Insurance Companies 14 (1940).

[20] Another control mechanism available to policyholders of a mutual is to withdraw patronage. Fama & Jensen, *supra* note 4, at 338, state, "[T]he unique characteristic of the residual claims of mutuals, which is important in understanding their survival value, is that the residual claims are redeemable on demand." The insurance policies of stock insurance companies are also redeemable on demand, but, in addition, stock insurance companies have a more effectively operating market for corporate control because of the potential for takeovers. Additionally, when a mutual policyholder withdraws patronage he does not receive his "share" of the firm's reserves (as would be the case for a shareholder in a mutual fund, for example).

agement exercises little discretion in setting rates (for example, in lines of insurance for which there are "good" actuarial tables) as compared with stock insurance companies.

The incentive conflict between policyholders and stockholders should be more severe with long-term than with short-term policies. Thus in lines of insurance where long-term policies are more important (or where explicit or implicit renewal options are more valuable) there are more opportunities to change dividend, investment, or financing policy to the detriment of the policyholders. While the stockholders' actions are partially controlled by the policyholders' option to cancel the policy, these are less effective disciplining mechanisms the greater the ex ante advantages of long-term policies. In such cases, the costs of this conflict between policyholders and stockholders can be reduced with mutual ownership, and thus mutuals should have a comparative advantage in longer-term policies.

## D. Reciprocal Insurance Associations

Although reciprocal insurance associations appear on the surface most similar to mutuals, there are potentially important differences between the two. A reciprocal is unincorporated with no capital as such, while mutuals are incorporated with a stated amount of capital and surplus. In a reciprocal, the owner/policyholders appoint an individual or a corporation as an attorney-in-fact to operate the company, while, in a mutual, policyholders elect a board of directors to manage the company. The reciprocal provides cooperative insurance, whereby individual subscribers assume their liability as individuals.[21] A separate account is often established for each subscriber, and subscribers can be required to accumulate reserves, typically equal to between two and five annual premiums, before being eligible to receive underwriting earnings.[22] Where reserves are fully allocated, the sum of the individual reserve accounts plus the current premiums represent the funds held by the reciprocal.[23] Beyond the reserve requirement, the reciprocal sometimes retains the option to levy a (limited) assessment.

The manager of a reciprocal, the attorney-in-fact, is usually thought of

---

[21] Reinmuth, *supra* note 9, at 20, notes, "[T]hat it is not entirely clear that the liability of a subscriber . . . is always separate and not joint." There have been legal outcomes imposing joint liability.

[22] Not all reciprocals operate on a separate accounts basis. The subscribers agreement may simply provide for dividends at the discretion of the attorney-in-fact (the manager). See Reinmuth, *supra* note 9, at 31.

[23] R. L. Norgaard, What Is a Reciprocal? 31 J. Risk & Ins. 51 (1964) indicates that unallocated surplus existed in thirty-nine out of forty-four reciprocals in his sample.

as being appointed by the policyholders, with an advisory committee representing the members of the association that presumably have some responsibility for his control.[24] Some reciprocals, however, have been organized and initially financed by corporate attorneys-in-fact.[25] In these cases, the ownership structure of the reciprocal is similar to that of a common stock insurance company, with the managerial and ownership/risk-bearing functions residing with the corporate attorney-in-fact.[26] Thus, depending on the structure of the reciprocal, the manager/owner control problem can be more similar to that of either a mutual insurance company or a common stock insurance company. Moreover, the owner/manager control problem could be more severe with the reciprocal than with either of the other cases because of the bond (reserve) the individual subscriber may be required to leave at risk. Of course, the policyholder's option to withdraw this capital is also a disciplining mechanism. As noted earlier, policyholders of stock or mutual insurance companies can also withdraw patronage as a disciplining device, but this mechanism is potentially more effective for reciprocal subscribers if their subscriber's agreement allows the withdrawal of surplus.[27]

Another control device reciprocal policyholders have is the potential to discipline management by forced dissolution of the association through the courts.[28] This is apparently more easily accomplished for reciprocals than for mutuals, due to the courts' interpretation of the nature

---

[24] This is really an oversimplification. The management of a reciprocal is appointed by each policyholder through the subscriber's agreement or power of attorney. Thus, whether a subscriber has voting rights depends on the terms of the subscriber's agreement. The job of management can in fact be proprietary. If it is, the subscriber usually has the right to vote for an advisory committee, which may or may not have the right to replace the manager. For further discussion see Reinmuth, *supra* note 9, at 15–16.

[25] The corporate attorney-in-fact advances a surplus in the form of a "guaranty surplus," which is an interest-bearing note. See Reinmuth, *supra* note 9, at 141.

[26] Even though the management function can be quite similar to a common stock insurance company, the insurance policies tend to differ. Reciprocals more frequently issue what amount to participating, assessable policies.

[27] Reinmuth, *supra* note 9, at 32, states, "Those reciprocals operating on a separate account basis usually provide in the subscriber's agreement for the accumulation of a 'contingency surplus' by withholding a stated percentage of each subscriber's deposit premium or 'savings' which will not be available on withdrawal."

[28] As reported by Reinmuth, *supra* note 9, at 36: "[I]t would appear that the subscribers of a reciprocal have the power to request a court of equity to dissolve the exchange. In McAlexander v. Waldscriber it was held that a court of equity, at the suit of a subscriber, had the power to appoint a receiver for a reciprocal insurance 'fund,' upon allegations that the fund was being mismanaged and dissipated by the attorney-in-fact. The receiver was directed to manage, disburse and liquidate the 'fund' so as to do justice to all parties in interest under their contracts. In Irwin v. Missouri Valley Bridge and Iron Company, a case involving a similar set of facts, the court reached a similar conclusion."

of an association as opposed to a mutual corporation. In this regard, Reinmuth[29] suggests that the reciprocal can be considered a "trust for a purpose."

In sum, it is difficult to classify the managerial control problem of reciprocals. The managerial control problem can vary from reciprocal to reciprocal and can be similar to that of a mutual insurance company or that of a stock insurance company. Only the rather weak statement that managerial discretion in a reciprocal should be somewhere in between that of these two alternative ownership structures seems appropriate.

### E.   Empirical Implications

*Line-of-Business Specialization.* Competition between insurance firms with different ownership structures suggests that for common lines of insurance there should be little difference in the types of insurance coverage offered or in the net premiums. Thus we do not think that significant differences should exist in contracts within a given line of insurance. Rather, we focus on comparative advantage of ownership structures and examine lines of insurance where particular ownership structures dominate. Our analysis suggests that if the cost of controlling management in mutual insurance companies is higher than in stock firms, then mutuals should be more prevalent in lines of insurance where management exercises little discretion in setting rates (for example, in lines of insurance for which there are "good" actuarial tables and where claims can be adjudicated within a relatively stable legal environment). Similarly, because of the solution to the managerial control problem, Lloyds associations should be more frequently observed where discretion in adjusting rates to changing risks is most important. Thus Lloyds associations and mutuals provide upper and lower bounds on managerial discretion with stock insurance companies falling in between and reciprocals falling in between stock insurance companies and mutual insurance companies. We should be able to distinguish between the various ownership structures based on the lines of insurance in which they do business.

*Line-of-Business Concentration.* Thus far, we have focused on insurance line choices of Lloyds, stocks, mutuals, and reciprocals based on required managerial discretion. The choice of ownership structure also provides incentives for a firm to concentrate in one line rather than to offer insurance across many lines. Three factors are important in our analysis of firm concentration across lines of business: (1) control of managerial discretion, (2) wealth and decision-making skills that are line-of-business specific, and (3) economies of scale. First, an insurance firm

---

[29] Reinmuth, *supra* note 9.

can limit managerial discretion by concentrating its business in a few lines rather than in many. Thus mutuals and reciprocals should be more concentrated than stock insurance companies; they should offer insurance across fewer different lines. While this argument suggests that Lloyds associations should be less concentrated than stock insurance companies, the resources of the Lloyds association are limited to the resources of the members. Necessary resources for expanding into multiple lines of insurance include wealth and specialized decision-making skills that relate to different lines of insurance.[30] Mutual and reciprocal associations are also limited in the resources available, but for the Lloyds association the problem is more severe because the managerial and ownership/risk-bearing functions are merged. Thus, Lloyds associations could be more or less concentrated than stock insurance companies depending upon which effect is dominant. Finally, for a given ownership structure, larger firms generally should be able to better exploit any gains from specialization. Hence, in our tests we control for resources available by examining ownership structure effects conditional on the size (total admitted assets) of the firm.

*Geographic Concentration.* Lines of insurance can have geographic complexities, and expanding a line of insurance into a new geographic area or selling insurance in many areas requires managerial discretion in setting rates. Moreover, monitoring by other members of the management team, by the board of directors, or by policyholders is more expensive the greater the geographical dispersion. Thus mutual insurance companies and reciprocal associations should have more geographically concentrated operations than stock insurance companies. Lloyds associations should be more or less geographically concentrated depending on whether the managerial discretion or limited resource effect is dominant.[31] Again, in these tests we control for the size of the insurance firm.

### III. Tests of Hypotheses

In this section we discuss our data and present the evidence on geographic concentration, line-of-business concentration, and specialization for the alternative ownership structures.

---

[30] The discussion in Fama & Jensen, *supra* note 4, at 332–33, concerning the advantages of restricted residual claims of proprietorships, partnerships, and closed corporations applies directly here. These forms (as compared with the stock company) are "more likely to dominate when technology does not involve important economies of scale that lead to large demands for specialized decision skills, specialized risk bearing, and wealth from the residual claimants."

[31] However, specific regulation also has a limiting effect on the geographic dispersion of Lloyds associations.

## A. Data Description

The data is from the A. M. Best Company (Oldwick, New Jersey). The A. M. Best line-of-business file contains 1981 data on premiums, losses, and expenses for a large sample of insurance firms by line of insurance. Line-of-business data is given for twenty-six lines of insurance. The file also identifies each firm as to type of ownership structure and provides total admitted assets and the number of states where licensed.

Our sample consists of 1,058 common stock insurance companies, 319 mutual insurance companies, sixty reciprocal associations, and forty-two Lloyds associations. The sample of common stock insurance companies is, according to A. M. Best, close to exhaustive: "We endeavor to report upon all U.S. domestic (non-captive) stock insurance companies which actively operate in the fifty United States, the District of Columbia and Puerto Rico."[32] The sample of mutuals, on the other hand, appears far from exhaustive and consists of the larger mutual insurance companies. Included are "practically all mutual property and casualty insurance companies, which possess $3,000,000 of admitted assets and $3,000,000 of income from premiums, . . . and in general are licensed in two or more states.[33] A. M. Best does not indicate their sampling criteria for Lloyds and reciprocal associations. They do indicate that the number of Lloyds in existence in the United States is small. Table 1 contains summary statistics on the sizes (total admitted assets) of the sample insurance firms of each ownership structure. As expected, the Lloyds associations are, on average, the smallest insurance firms. The next smallest (based on the mean) are the mutuals—the average mutual has about sixty-three times the total admitted assets of the average Lloyds. Stock, mutual, and reciprocal firms are fairly close in size. The reciprocals have the largest average assets while in our (admittedly biased) sample mutuals have the largest median assets. The largest stock company has over $14 billion of admitted assets, the largest mutual over $11 billion, the largest reciprocal over $2 billion, and the largest Lloyds association has approximately $17 million in admitted assets.

## B. Geographic Concentration

We first examine the association between size and geographic concentration using regression analysis. For stocks, mutuals, and reciprocals there is a strong inverse relation between size and geographic concentra-

---

[32] A. M. Best Company, Best's Insurance Reports Property-Casualty, at ix.
[33] Best, *supra* note 32.

TABLE 1

TOTAL ADMITTED ASSETS:*
SUMMARY STATISTICS BY TYPE OF OWNERSHIP STRUCTURE

| | OWNERSHIP STRUCTURE | | | |
|---|---|---|---|---|
| STATISTIC | Lloyds | Stock | Mutual | Reciprocal |
| Mean | 2.472 | 163.138 | 155.029 | 172.535 |
| Quantiles (%): | | | | |
| 100 (max) | 16.944 | 14,803.168 | 11,537.227 | 2,599.579 |
| 75 (Q3) | 3.438 | 67.939 | 71.905 | 90.398 |
| 50 (med) | .745 | 19.707 | 19.975 | 13.571 |
| 25 (Q1) | .447 | 5.735 | 6.668 | 4.854 |
| 0 (min) | .198 | .328 | .048 | .703 |
| Number of firms | 42 | 1,058 | 319 | 60 |

* Amounts shown are in millions of dollars.

tion; however, for Lloyds associations the relation is negative but not significant. Table 2 contains summary statistics by type of ownership structure on the number of states licensed. These data indicate that geographic concentration is consistent with the managerial-discretion hypothesis for mutuals and reciprocals. For Lloyds associations the limited resource effect appears to dominate. Lloyds associations, mutual insurance companies, and reciprocal associations are all more concentrated geographically than stock insurance companies.

We also test the observed differences and normalize for size using analysis of variance models. We form ten size groupings based on total admitted assets and control for possible interaction effects between size and ownership structure. We use the general linear model procedure of

TABLE 2

NUMBER OF STATES LICENSED:*
SUMMARY STATISTICS BY TYPE OF OWNERSHIP STRUCTURE

| | OWNERSHIP STRUCTURE | | | |
|---|---|---|---|---|
| STATISTIC | Lloyds | Stock | Mutual | Reciprocal |
| Mean | 1.48 | 18.19 | 10.88 | 10.3 |
| Quantiles (%): | | | | |
| 100 (max) | 17 | 52 | 52 | 52 |
| 75 (Q3) | 1 | 39 | 12 | 12 |
| 50 (med) | 1 | 7 | 3 | 2 |
| 25 (Q1) | 1 | 1 | 1 | 1 |
| 0 (min) | 1 | 1 | 1 | 1 |
| SD | 2.47 | 19.85 | 15.59 | 14.75 |
| Number of firms | 42 | 1,058 | 319 | 60 |

* Includes District of Columbia and Puerto Rico.

TABLE 3

NUMBER OF STATES LICENSED:
ANALYSIS OF VARIANCE RESULTS TESTING FOR SIZE
AND OWNERSHIP STRUCTURE EFFECTS FOR VARIOUS COMPARISONS

| Comparison | F Value | Pr > F | | LS Mean* |
|---|---|---|---|---|
| Lloyds/stock:† | | | | |
| Size | 1.65 | .1591 | Lloyds | 2.80 |
| Cotype | 2.30 | .1302 | Stock | 7.47 |
| Cotype and size | .84 | .4995 | | |
| Stock/mutual: | | | | |
| Size | 68.90 | .0001 | Stock | 17.97 |
| Cotype | 62.83 | .0001 | Mutual | 10.48 |
| Cotype and size | 2.35 | .0127 | | |
| Stock/reciprocal: | | | | |
| Size | 10.63 | .0001 | Stock | 17.97 |
| Cotype | 10.80 | .0010 | Reciprocal | 10.77 |
| Cotype and size | 2.97 | .0018 | | |
| Mutuals/reciprocals: | | | | |
| Size | 11.03 | .0001 | Mutual | 10.48 |
| Cotype | .02 | .8771 | Reciprocal | 10.77 |
| Cotype and size | 2.66 | .0054 | | |

NOTE.—Size = size category effect; Cotype = ownership structure effect; Cotype and size = interaction effect.

* LS Mean = Least-squared estimate of the marginal mean—an estimate of the class marginal mean that would be expected had the design been balanced.

† All comparisons except this one use ten size categories. Since the Lloyds associations only spanned the five smallest size categories, only those categories were used.

Statistical Analysis System (SAS) that allows for unbalanced experimental designs.[34]

Table 3 contains a summary of these tests. As can be seen, mutual insurance companies and reciprocal associations are significantly more geographically concentrated than stock insurance companies, even when we control for firm size. The geographic concentrations of mutuals and reciprocals appear to be indistinguishable. (Note that these tests could be influenced by the omission of the smallest and probably most geographically concentrated mutuals.) The ownership structure effect in the Lloyds association and stock insurance company comparison is not significant at usual levels of significance ($p$ value = .13). However, the level of insignificance is marginal and consideration should be given to the small sample size and probable low power of the test. Note also that the estimate of

[34] SAS software is obtained from SAS Institute, Inc., of Cary, North Carolina. Unbalanced experimental design simply means that the number of observations per cell are allowed to differ.

TABLE 4

HERFINDAHL CONCENTRATION INDEX:*
SUMMARY STATISTICS BY TYPE OF OWNERSHIP STRUCTURE

| STATISTIC | OWNERSHIP STRUCTURE | | | |
|---|---|---|---|---|
| | Lloyds | Stock | Mutual | Reciprocal |
| Mean | .520 | .459 | .429 | .626 |
| Quantiles (%): | | | | |
| 100 (max) | .999 | 1.000 | 1.000 | 1.000 |
| 75 (Q3) | .699 | .603 | .565 | .989 |
| 50 (med) | .495 | .372 | .342 | .534 |
| 25 (Q1) | .292 | .247 | .231 | .439 |
| 0 (min) | .169 | .094 | .125 | .158 |
| SD | .249 | .275 | .254 | .278 |
| Number of firms | 42 | 1,058 | 319 | 60 |

* The Herfindahl Index is calculated for each company as $H = \Sigma_{L=1}^{26} S_L^2$, where $L$ stands for line of insurance, and $S_L = PI_L/TPI$. $PI_L$ is the dollar amount of direct business written in a particular line of insurance, and TPI is the dollar amount of direct business totaled across all twenty-six lines of insurance.

the marginal mean for stock insurance companies is over twice that of the Lloyds associations (7.47 vs. 2.80).[35]

In summary, size is important: for each ownership structure, large firms are less concentrated geographically than small firms. Moreover, the relative geographic concentration of the various ownership structures appears consistent with the managerial-discretion hypothesis for mutuals and reciprocals: controlling for size, they are more geographically concentrated than stock insurance companies. The limited resource hypothesis with respect to Lloyds associations is only weakly supported as being dominant. Controlling for size, Lloyds associations are geographically more concentrated than stock insurance companies, but the difference appears insignificant.

## C.  Line-of-Business Concentration

Table 4 contains summary statistics by type of ownership structure for the Herfindahl concentration index.[36] The index is calculated using the percentages of direct business written in each of the twenty-six lines of insurance for each insurance company. If all business were concentrated

[35] The estimated marginal mean for the stock insurance companies is only 7.47 for this comparison (as compared to 17.97 for the other comparisons) because the Lloyds association/stock insurance company comparison is based only on the five smallest size categories—Lloyds associations only spanned the five smallest size categories.

[36] The Herfindahl index is described in the note to Table 4.

TABLE 5

HERFINDAHL CONCENTRATION INDEX:
ANALYSIS OF VARIANCE RESULTS TESTING FOR SIZE AND
OWNERSHIP STRUCTURE EFFECTS FOR VARIOUS COMPARISONS

| Comparison | F Value | Pr > F | | LS Mean* |
|---|---|---|---|---|
| Lloyds/stock:† | | | | |
| Size | 2.63 | .0336 | Lloyds | .395 |
| Cotype | 3.11 | .0782 | Stock | .535 |
| Cotype and size | .33 | .8567 | | |
| Stock/mutual: | | | | |
| Size | 8.00 | .0001 | Stock | .462 |
| Cotype | 2.14 | .1439 | Mutual | .436 |
| Cotype and size | 1.10 | .3594 | | |
| Stock/reciprocal: | | | | |
| Size | 3.15 | .0010 | Stock | .462 |
| Cotype | 16.00 | .0001 | Reciprocal | .613 |
| Cotype and size | .98 | .4527 | | |
| Mutuals/reciprocals: | | | | |
| Size | 1.87 | .0552 | Mutual | .436 |
| Cotype | 20.42 | .0001 | Reciprocal | .613 |
| Cotype and size | .84 | .5787 | | |

NOTE.—Size = size category effect; Cotype = ownership structure effect; Cotype and size = interaction effect.

* LS Mean = Least-squared estimate of the marginal mean—an estimate of the class marginal mean that would be expected had the design been balanced.

† All comparisons except this one use ten size categories. Since the Lloyds associations only spanned the five smallest size categories, only those categories were used.

in one line, the value of the Herfindahl index would be one. Smaller values of the index indicate less concentration and larger values more concentration. Direct business written is defined as gross premiums (less return premiums) including policy and membership fees written and renewed during the year. Direct business is chosen because it represents the level of business for particular lines of insurance.[37]

The data of Table 4 indicate that the business of Lloyds and reciprocal associations is more concentrated than the business of stock insurance companies. Mutual insurance companies appear slightly less concentrated than stock insurance companies.

Table 5 contains analysis of variance results where we control for size associations with line of business concentration. There is a pronounced size effect in all of the comparisons except for the mutual insurance

[37] The other choice available is net premiums written. Net premiums written equal direct business plus reinsurance assumed less reinsurance ceded. Thus, net premiums written could indicate little business in what is actually a major line of insurance.

company/reciprocal association comparison, where the effect is marginally insignificant (5 percent level). The ownership structure effect is significant at usual levels only for the stock insurance company/reciprocal association comparison. Thus reciprocals are more concentrated in their line of business activity than stock insurance companies. When we control for size, the inference concerning the relative concentration of Lloyds associations and stock insurance companies is reversed. Small stock insurance companies appear to be more line-of-business concentrated than Lloyds associations. The significance of the ownership-structure effect for this comparison, however, is marginal ($p$ value $= .08$).

In summary, the evidence on line-of-business concentration is mixed. The managerial-discretion hypothesis predicts that mutuals and reciprocal associations should be more concentrated than stock insurance companies. Reciprocals appear to be more concentrated than stock insurance companies, but mutuals and stock insurance companies appear indistinguishable based on the line-of-business concentration measure. For the Lloyds associations the limited-resource hypothesis appears not to be dominant. If anything, stock insurance companies of similar size are more concentrated than are the Lloyds associations. This result, however, is consistent with the managerial-discretion hypothesis, which predicts more concentration for stock companies than for Lloyds.

### D. Line-of-Business Specialization

The managerial-discretion hypothesis predicts that different ownership structures should dominate in particular lines of insurance, that is, these structures should operate where they have a comparative advantage. Table 6 contains direct business premiums by line of insurance and type of ownership structure. The percentage columns headed by L% indicate the percentage of the total direct business premiums of a given line attributed to a particular ownership structure, and the percentage columns headed by O% indicate the percentage of business done by a given ownership structure attributable to a given line. Thus the L% percentages in the rows add up to 100, and the O% percentages in the columns add up to 100. Stock insurance companies appear to dominate in all lines of insurance but one—farm owners multiple peril—where the mutual insurance companies dominate. One problem is, of course, that our sample is less than exhaustive. It is possible that a more complete sample would show additional lines of insurance dominated by mutuals. Given the classifications, however, Best's data base would have to omit a significant fraction of business by Lloyds associations for the Lloyds ever to dominate a line.

One problem of concern is that of aggregation. The line of insurance

## TABLE 6

DIRECT BUSINESS PREMIUMS FOR 1981 BY LINE OF INSURANCE AND TYPE OF OWNERSHIP STRUCTURE FOR SAMPLE OF 42 LLOYD'S ASSOCIATIONS, 1,058 STOCK COMPANIES, 319 MUTUAL COMPANIES, AND 60 RECIPROCAL ASSOCIATIONS

| LINE OF INSURANCE | LLOYDS | | | STOCK | | | MUTUAL | | | RECIPROCAL | | | TOTAL BY LINE | |
|---|---|---|---|---|---|---|---|---|---|---|---|---|---|---|
| | $M* | L%† | 0%‡ | $M | L% | 0% | $M | L% | 0% | $M | L% | 0% | $M | N§ |
| Fire | 28.22 | .84 | 10.71 | 2,387.55 | 71.23 | 3.24 | 832.80 | 24.85 | 3.42 | 103.29 | 3.08 | 2.19 | 3,351.88 | 1,047 |
| Allied lines | 26.55 | 1.46 | 10.07 | 1,346.03 | 73.87 | 1.83 | 393.29 | 21.58 | 1.62 | 56.36 | 3.09 | 1.19 | 1,822.24 | 1,003 |
| Farm owners multiple peril | .35 | .06 | .13 | 266.88 | 41.32 | .36 | 360.68 | 55.84 | 1.48 | 17.96 | 2.78 | .38 | 645.88 | 339 |
| Home owners multiple peril | 33.59 | .30 | 12.74 | 8,219.13 | 74.61 | 11.16 | 2,233.48 | 20.27 | 9.18 | 530.45 | 4.82 | 11.23 | 11,016.66 | 887 |
| Commercial multiple peril | 111.17 | 1.41 | 42.16 | 6,641.15 | 84.46 | 9.01 | 1,041.30 | 13.24 | 4.28 | 69.89 | .89 | 1.48 | 7,863.52 | 814 |
| Ocean marine | .00 | .00 | .00 | 1,288.50 | 88.49 | 1.75 | 160.63 | 11.03 | .66 | 6.95 | .48 | .15 | 1,456.09 | 267 |
| Inland marine | 21.48 | .67 | 8.15 | 2,800.01 | 87.27 | 3.80 | 316.95 | 9.88 | 1.30 | 70.14 | 2.19 | 1.48 | 3,208.60 | 1,006 |
| Miscellaneous | 4.94 | 2.18 | 1.88 | 187.63 | 82.53 | .25 | 32.50 | 14.30 | .13 | 2.25 | .99 | .05 | 227.34 | 484 |
| Medical malpractice | .13 | .01 | .05 | 868.08 | 54.21 | 1.18 | 383.08 | 23.92 | 1.57 | 350.03 | 21.86 | 7.41 | 1,601.33 | 265 |
| Earthquake | .00 | .00 | .00 | 73.58 | 82.74 | .10 | 2.74 | 3.09 | .01 | 12.60 | 14.17 | .27 | 88.93 | 393 |
| Group accident and health | .77 | .04 | .29 | 1,240.98 | 63.25 | 1.68 | 717.39 | 36.56 | 2.95 | 2.91 | .15 | .06 | 1,962.06 | 169 |

| Line of insurance | $M | L% | 0% | $M | L% | 0% | $M | L% | 0% | $M | L% | 0% | $M | N |
|---|---|---|---|---|---|---|---|---|---|---|---|---|---|---|
| Credit accident and health | .00 | .00 | .00 | 30.58 | 84.96 | .04 | 5.41 | 15.04 | .02 | .00 | .00 | .00 | 36.00 | 14 |
| Other accident and health | .35 | .04 | .13 | 495.93 | 60.27 | .67 | 324.96 | 39.49 | 1.34 | 1.61 | .20 | .03 | 822.86 | 195 |
| Workmen's compensation | 4.01 | .02 | 1.52 | 12,720.50 | 78.26 | 17.27 | 3,338.93 | 20.54 | 13.72 | 190.85 | 1.17 | 4.04 | 16,254.31 | 641 |
| Other liability | 4.30 | .05 | 1.63 | 6,960.01 | 86.99 | 9.45 | 952.18 | 11.90 | 3.91 | 84.35 | 1.05 | 1.79 | 8,000.85 | 1,032 |
| Auto liability | 11.23 | .05 | 4.26 | 15,452.75 | 62.07 | 20.97 | 7,629.62 | 30.65 | 31.36 | 1,802.09 | 7.24 | 38.14 | 24,895.71 | 973 |
| Auto physical damage | 15.51 | .09 | 5.88 | 10,069.92 | 59.78 | 13.67 | 5,355.64 | 31.80 | 22.01 | 1,403.05 | 8.33 | 29.70 | 16,844.14 | 1,023 |
| Aircraft | .00 | .00 | .00 | 457.96 | 92.53 | .62 | 18.76 | 3.79 | .08 | 18.21 | 3.68 | .39 | 494.95 | 97 |
| Fidelity | .06 | .01 | .02 | 416.68 | 96.64 | .57 | 23.37 | 5.31 | .10 | .15 | .04 | .00 | 440.27 | 344 |
| Surety | .08 | .01 | .03 | 1,069.86 | 95.37 | 1.45 | 51.54 | 4.59 | .21 | .30 | .03 | .01 | 1,121.80 | 437 |
| Glass | .02 | .08 | .01 | 26.71 | 85.17 | .04 | 4.30 | 13.71 | .02 | .02 | .08 | .01 | 31.36 | 562 |
| Burglary and theft | .12 | .10 | .05 | 119.76 | 88.54 | .16 | 14.51 | 10.73 | .06 | .84 | .63 | .02 | 135.25 | 577 |
| Boiler and machinery | .03 | .01 | .01 | 261.38 | 66.83 | .35 | 129.59 | 33.14 | .53 | .09 | .02 | .00 | 391.11 | 176 |
| Credit | .68 | .78 | .26 | 85.16 | 96.27 | .12 | 2.61 | 2.96 | .01 | .00 | .00 | .00 | 88.47 | 55 |
| International | .00 | .00 | .00 | 159.81 | 96.76 | .22 | 5.35 | 3.24 | .02 | .00 | .00 | .00 | 165.16 | 17 |
| Reinsurance | .00 | .00 | .00 | 28.29 | 99.75 | .04 | .07 | .25 | .00 | .00 | .00 | .00 | 28.36 | 6 |
| Total by ownership structure | 263.69 | | | 73,674.94 | | | 24,331.81 | | | 4,724.82 | | | | |

* $M indicates the numbers are in millions of dollars.

† L% indicates the percentage of the total direct business premiums of a given line (totaled across all firms in the sample) accounted for by firms with the indicated ownership structure.

‡ 0% indicates the percentage of the total direct business premiums of a given ownership structure accounted for by a particular line of insurance.

§ N is the number of firms that indicate any direct business premiums in the line of insurance.

data reported by *Best's* treats all fire insurance policies, for example, as identical. Thus, it is difficult to differentiate between insurance business where actuarial tables are well defined and where they are not or, more to the point, where more or less managerial discretion is required in the underwriting activity within one of Best's lines.

There are commonalities in the data that appear to be ownership-structure specific. Specific lines of insurance appear to be complementary for alternative ownership structures. These complementarities could provide indications of the types of risks being insured. For example, a firm that does the majority of its business in home owners multiple peril and fire insurance could be insuring risks that require relatively little managerial discretion, whereas a firm that has the majority of its business in commercial multiple peril and fire could be insuring risks that require a great deal of managerial discretion.

What we want to do is take advantage of the commonalities in the data to rebundle the lines of insurance. A methodology available for rebundling is factor analysis. Factor analysis can be used to exploit the covariance structure of the lines of business in the cross section of insurance firms that make up our sample.[38]

*Procedure.* Our procedure is to do a factor analysis, obtain the factor loadings, calculate factor scores for each insurance firm, and then regress the factor scores on dummy variables representing the alternative ownership structures. The factor loadings can be thought of as the weights applied to the traditional lines of insurance to obtain the new rebundled lines. Factor scores are obtained for each insurance firm for each rebundled line of insurance or factor. Each factor score is a weighted average of the direct business the insurance firm has in the original lines of insurance. The weights represent the importance of a particular line of insurance in the rebundled line. Thus, the scores can be thought of as the insurance firms' direct business in the rebundled lines of insurance. The regression analysis will tell us whether alternative ownership structures can be differentiated by their direct business in the rebundled lines of insurance.

We do the factor analysis using all 1,479 firms in the file. Direct business dollars are converted to percentages of total direct business in a particular line for each insurance firm. To avoid singularity in the input matrix for the factor analysis we omit one line of insurance (the line of business percentages sum to one for each firm). The line of insurance entitled "miscellaneous" seems a likely candidate, so we omit it.

[38] A brief intuitive description of factor analysis is presented in the Appendix. For more mathematical treatments, see D. F. Morrison, Multivariate Statistical Methods (1976) or H. H. Harman, Modern Factor Analysis (1976).

*Results*.   Table 7 contains the factor loadings or weights for nine factors, or rebundled lines of insurance.[39] Weights that have an absolute value greater than .20 are indicated in parentheses. It is not our intention to provide an interpretation of the relative weights or importance assigned to the original lines of insurance in the rebundled lines, but the weighting scheme devised by the factor analysis does not appear entirely nonsensical, either. For example, auto liability and auto physical damage appear to have similar weightings in several of the rebundled lines. Whether these rebundled lines really represent pseudolines of insurance that vary according to the level of managerial discretion required is a question that we would like to be able to answer, but one on which we could only speculate. Thus, the result that the alternative ownership structures can be differentiated on the basis of the rebundled lines would be consistent with our managerial-discretion hypothesis but would not prove it.

Table 8 contains the results of our cross-sectional regressions of factor scores on dummy variables representing the alternative ownership structures. The dummy variables represent mutuals, Lloyds, and reciprocals, while the intercept term represents the stock insurance companies. Thus the intercepts are the mean scores for stock companies on the rebundled lines of insurance (factors). The mean scores for the other ownership structure types are obtained by adding the appropriate dummy variable coefficients to the intercepts.

The regressions appear to have explanatory power; eleven of the dummy variable coefficients (out of twenty-seven) are significant. But most of the explanatory power is in the ability of the regressions to distinguish between mutual and stock insurance companies. Seven of the regressions indicate significant coefficients for the mutual insurance companies. Moreover, in every regression the coefficients indicate that the mean score for mutuals is opposite in sign to the mean score for the stock companies. This indicates that mutual and stock insurance companies tend to concentrate their business in different (rebundled) lines of insurance. Those lines that tend to be important for mutuals tend not to be important for stock insurance companies. Thus the line-of-business data discriminates between mutual and stock insurance companies, and this is consistent with the managerial-discretion hypothesis.

Interpretation of the results for reciprocals and Lloyds associations is

---

[39] There is some question about the criteria for determining the exact number of factor patterns for a set of data. We use the default criterion for our software package (SAS, principal factors method) called the proportion criterion. This criterion accepts all factors (ordered by eigenvalue) to the point where the factor eigenvalues sum to the total eigenvalue of the reduced correlation matrix.

TABLE 7

Factor Loadings (Weights) for Nine Factors (Rebundled Lines of Insurance)*

| | Factors (Rebundled Lines of Insurance)† | | | | | | | | |
|---|---|---|---|---|---|---|---|---|---|
| | (1) | (2) | (3) | (4) | (5) | (6) | (7) | (8) | (9) |
| FIRE | (.52550) | .17232 | .05434 | -.03420 | -.04235 | .03856 | -.03179 | -.04818 | .00734 |
| ALLLINES | (.45950) | (.21255) | -.06208 | -.03900 | -.00835 | .02347 | -.05867 | -.03867 | -.02769 |
| FARMMP | .02527 | (.34643) | -.08048 | -.01589 | -.01113 | -.02993 | -.02774 | -.02727 | -.03173 |
| HOMEMP | .02313 | (.48252) | .13655 | -.03091 | -.07893 | -.14736 | -.02432 | -.02975 | -.07421 |
| COMMMP | .02327 | -.02866 | (.048025) | -.04822 | .04306 | .04537 | -.04303 | -.01584 | -.03742 |
| OCEANMAR | -.01094 | -.04578 | .07070 | -.00578 | .00353 | -.00865 | .05999 | .00805 | (.24018) |
| INLANMAR | .05741 | -.02606 | .16232 | .03727 | -.008381 | .14973 | -.07475 | -.04336 | (.31557) |
| MEDMALPR | -.02705 | -.04968 | -.03039 | -.00990 | -.02507 | .03174 | (-.46809) | -.03101 | -.00387 |
| EARTHQKE | .12183 | -.03961 | -.00093 | .00272 | -.02195 | -.00386 | -.01431 | .00998 | -.02104 |
| GROUPAH | -.01890 | -.02531 | -.01185 | (.45736) | .02738 | -.00831 | .01440 | -.00266 | .03557 |
| CREDITAH | -.00681 | .00226 | -.05007 | -.01542 | .01043 | -.02837 | -.00425 | -.00321 | .19796 |
| OTHERAH | -.01392 | -.00837 | -.01657 | (.45812) | -.02005 | -.01281 | .02396 | .001007 | -.00969 |
| WORKCOMP | -.10492 | -.08827 | .04700 | -.00252 | (.51610) | .00127 | .02186 | -.01905 | -.02208 |
| OTHLIAB | -.00755 | -.10621 | -.02030 | -.02518 | .08337 | (.48061) | .05894 | -.02805 | -.00848 |
| AUTOLIAB | (-.29390) | (-.25097) | (-.31971) | -.12105 | (-.21155) | (-.22078) | (-.27384) | .11114 | (-.21991) |
| AUTOPD | (-.22687) | (-.25749) | (-.33197) | -.10360 | (-.30727) | (-.22930) | (-.26825) | -.10070 | .14544 |
| AIRCRAFT | -.01437 | -.00389 | -.04224 | -.00412 | .03653 | -.03195 | .01234 | -.00119 | (.22286) |
| FIDELITY | -.00903 | -.02099 | -.00058 | -.01189 | -.00806 | .03255 | -.00159 | (.37153) | -.01376 |
| SURETY | .01001 | .01792 | -.00752 | .01829 | .00527 | .00253 | .07605 | (.41390) | .02690 |
| GLASS | -.01462 | -.00857 | .04184 | -.00382 | -.00889 | .08081 | -.00258 | -.00714 | -.03011 |
| THEFT | .01248 | -.00110 | .00461 | .00212 | .02131 | .15440 | -.07031 | .07514 | .00723 |
| BOILER | .17161 | -.10208 | .05740 | -.00168 | -.00869 | -.07052 | .02742 | -.00014 | .00996 |
| CREDIT | -.00595 | -.00118 | .00088 | .01699 | -.01485 | .00148 | .03425 | .00873 | .09150 |
| INTERNAT | -.00356 | -.00420 | .00307 | .00609 | .00078 | -.00660 | .03086 | .01800 | .02547 |
| REINS | -.00502 | .00046 | -.00150 | .00445 | .00994 | -.01059 | .04011 | .01124 | .01720 |

* Loadings with an absolute value of greater than .20 are shown in parentheses.
† Factors are orthogonally rotated using the varimax rotation.

TABLE 8

CROSS-SECTIONAL REGRESSIONS OF FACTOR SCORES ON DUMMY VARIABLES
REPRESENTING ALTERNATIVE OWNERSHIP STRUCTURES
($t$-Statistics in Parentheses)

| | VARIABLE | | | | | |
|---|---|---|---|---|---|---|
| FACTOR | Intercept | Mutual | Lloyds | Reciprocal | ADJUSTED $R^2$ | $F$-STATISTIC |
| 1 | −.077** | .260** | .557** | .125 | .04 | 21.3 |
| | (−3.87) | (6.29) | (5.47) | (1.45) | | |
| 2 | −.144** | .667** | .138 | −.081 | .19 | 115.96 |
| | (−8.27) | (18.38) | (1.54) | (−1.08) | | |
| 3 | −.038* | .058 | 1.012** | −.087 | .08 | 41.42 |
| | (−2.104) | (1.56) | (11.01) | (−1.12) | | |
| 4 | .016 | −.046 | −.093 | −.091 | .00 | 1.05 |
| | (.88) | (−1.20) | (−.98) | (−1.14) | | |
| 5 | .033 | −.107** | −.155 | −.133 | .01 | 4.08 |
| | (1.84) | (−2.89) | (−1.70) | (−1.72) | | |
| 6 | .041* | −.180** | .023 | −.062 | .02 | 8.66 |
| | (2.36) | (−5.04) | (.26) | (−.83) | | |
| 7 | −.032 | .096** | −.142 | .374** | .02 | 10.97 |
| | (−1.82) | (2.64) | (−1.58) | (4.95) | | |
| 8 | .036* | −1.116** | −.114 | −.185* | .01 | 5.79 |
| | (2.17) | (−3.38) | (−1.35) | (−2.60) | | |
| 9 | .029 | −.131** | −.012 | −.000 | .01 | 5.18 |
| | (1.78) | (−3.91) | (−.14) | (−.01) | | |

* Indicates significance at .05 level.
** Indicates significance at .01 level.

more difficult. Part of the difficulty with respect to the reciprocals is that we have no clear picture of the ownership structure for our sample of firms. As we stated earlier, the managerial control problem for a reciprocal can be similar to that of a mutual insurance company or that of a stock insurance company. The results for seven of the regressions indicate that there is no difference between reciprocal associations and stock companies, and the results of two regressions indicate that reciprocals are similar to mutual companies. These results are consistent with the managerial-discretion hypothesis if reciprocals, on average, are between stock and mutual insurance companies with respect to managerial discretion.

The Lloyds association results are similar to the reciprocal results in that seven regressions indicate similarity with stock companies and two do not. The problem of interpretation here is that, for one of the two regressions where the mean scores are significantly different from those of stock companies, the direction of difference is the same direction as that found in the relation of mutuals to stock companies. For example, if the interpretation of the stock and mutual results for factor 1 is that mutuals do relatively more business in lines of insurance requiring little managerial discretion, then why are the Lloyds associations concentrating even more in those lines? One possible answer is that the Lloyds associations results are less reliable because of the small number of observations for that structure.

In summary, the lines of business results from comparing stock insurance companies and mutual insurance companies are consistent with the managerial-discretion hypothesis. The results for reciprocal associations are consistent with the managerial-discretion hypothesis if reciprocals are, on average, somewhere between mutual and stock insurance companies with respect to managerial discretion. The results for Lloyds associations are less clear. The data indicate some differences between stock companies and Lloyds associations, but it is not clear that all of the differences can be explained by the managerial-discretion hypothesis.

## IV. SUMMARY AND CONCLUSIONS

We have examined the impact of ownership structure on cross-sectional differences in the insurance industry across lines of insurance while controlling for size. We document differences in geographic concentration and concentration by line of business. (1) Stocks are less concentrated geographically than Lloyds, mutuals, or reciprocals. (2) Without controlling for size, Lloyds and reciprocals are more concentrated by line-of-business than stocks, and mutuals appear least concentrated of all. (3) When size is controlled, reciprocals are significantly more concentrated than stocks; stocks and mutuals appear indistinguishable; and (surprisingly) stocks appear more concentrated than Lloyds of similar size. (4) When we examine the covariance structure across lines, stocks and mutuals are significantly different; however, interpretation of observed differences between Lloyds and reciprocals is more difficult.

Our initial analysis of these cross-sectional differences is encouraging. There are, however, limitations in our analysis that we would like to overcome in subsequent work. (1) This analysis has limited the cross-sectional variation in the characteristics of insurance policies by restricting the analysis to property/casualty lines. By expanding the analysis to include health and life business, for example, the power of the tests would be increased. (2) We focus on the control-related comparative advantage of alternative ownership structures. Regulation and taxes are also potentially important determinants of variation for which we would like to control explicitly. We suspect that regulation is likely to be important in the case of Lloyds associations (but we have had difficulty deciding to what extent the regulation imposes binding constraints). Although we know that the tax treatment varies across ownership structure, it is not clear that the nature of the differences imposes a bias with respect to the dimensions on which we focus. (3) Our hypotheses about concentration in Lloyds associations seem more related to specialization by an individual underwriter or by an underwriting syndicate than to specialization within an association. We believe that additional work needs to be done to relate concentration by underwriters to concentration by an association of underwriters. This link is likely to require more careful consideration of the mutual monitoring technology for similar versus dissimilar insurance business. (4) We recognize that our data has been aggregated into lines. While our factor analysis addresses the problem of disaggregation of similar business, we cannot directly adjust for aggregation of dissimilar business into a specified line. (For example, the business written by mutuals under commercial multiple peril might differ in important ways from that written by stocks or Lloyds.) (5) Our analysis of reciprocals suggests that there may be an important distinction between firms with corporate, as opposed to individual, attorneys-in-fact. These perhaps should be examined separately. Additional analysis might suggest other ways to segregate the firms that would further increase power.

## APPENDIX

### FACTOR ANALYSIS DESCRIPTION

Factor analysis is a statistical technique that can take a large number of observations on a set of original variables, measure the degree of commonality among the original variables, and construct a smaller set of new, composite, independent indices. In our case, we take the data on the twenty-six original lines of business and derive nine rebundled insurance lines. A better understanding of the intuition behind factor analysis can be obtained by considering the geometry of the process. Each firm in the sample can be thought of as defining a coordinate axis of a geometric space. For example, three firms define a three-dimensional space as in Figure 1. (Although we are constrained pictorially to three dimensions, the space can be extended analytically to 1,479 dimensions, thereby representing each firm in the sample.) Now, in this space the fraction of business in a line of insurance can be plotted as a point. A plot of two points representing two lines of business is illustrated in Figure 1. Similarly, the twenty-five independent fractions of business for lines of insurance can be plotted as vectors in the space of 1,479 dimensions.

If for each point in Figure 1 we draw a line from the origin to the point, then we have a vector representation of the data. The angle between the two vectors represents the relation between the two lines of business for the firms. Geometrically, the closer to ninety degrees the angle is, the weaker the relation; and the closer to zero, the stronger the relation. If we plot the twenty-five lines of insurance in the firm space, the configuration of vectors reflects the data interrelations. Lines of business that are highly positively related will cluster together, while lines that are unrelated will be at right angles. By inspecting the configuration we

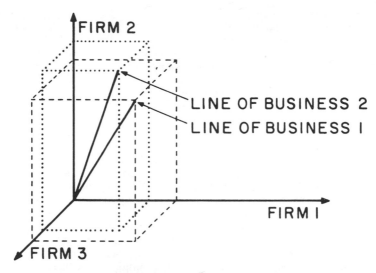

FIGURE 1.—A geometric representation of factor analysis with three firms and two lines of insurance. The fraction of business in each line of insurance plots as a point in this three-dimensional space. Lines connecting the points with the origin produce a vector representation of the data.

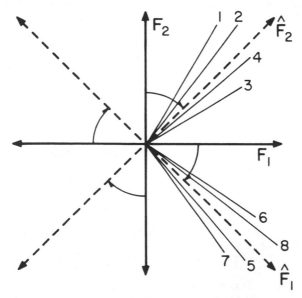

FIGURE 2.—An example of a representation of eight original insurance lines plotted for 1,479 insurance companies. The eight lines fall into two clusters, 1–4 and 5–8. The first factor, $F_1$, falls between the two clusters; the second factor, $F_2$, is added orthogonally to the first. A simple structure rotation redefines $\hat{F}_1$ and $\hat{F}_2$ as the new rotated factors, each associated primarily with one of the clusters.

558

can discern the distinct clusters of vectors; for example, in Figure 2, we identify two clusters, observations (lines of business) 1–4 and 5–8. Factor analysis identifies such commonality in the data.

There are many mathematically equivalent ways of expressing the underlying structure in the data, but some are easier to interpret than others. We employ a varimax rotation to identify the simplest factor structure of the interrelated variables. (This criterion maximizes the variance of the square of the factor loadings in each column of Table 7.) Orthogonality is a restriction placed on the search for clusters of independent variables; the total set of factors is rotated on a rigid frame, with each factor at a right angle to every other factor. Thus, in Figure 2, rather than describing the data in terms of the unrotated factors, $F_1$ and $F_2$, they can be associated with the rotated factors, $\hat{F}_1$ and $\hat{F}_2$. With a structure rotation, each cluster is identified with one factor or a small number of factors. Also, the number of original lines loading highly on a factor is minimized. These properties aid our interpretation of the factors as rebundled lines of insurance.

Factor analysis is in some ways similar to multiple regression analysis. In multiple regression one variable is considered the dependent variable and the others are independent variables. In factor analysis, each variable can be regarded as a dependent variable that is regressed on a set of unobserved independent factors, each of which is a function of all original variables. In this case the "regression coefficients" are the factor loadings that identify the nature of the unobserved factors.

Table 7 presents these estimated factor loadings. The factor scores are then derived by weighting each variable (insurance line) proportionally to its involvement in a rebundled line—the more involved an original insurance line in the rebundled line, the higher the weight. To determine the score for a firm on a rebundled line, a firm's fraction of business on each original line is multiplied by the weight for that factor. The sum of these weight-times-data products for all the original lines yields the factor score. Thus, firms will have high or low factor scores as their values are high or low on the values entering the rebundled line. In further statistical analysis, these factor scores are used instead of the original variables.

### BIBLIOGRAPHY

Anderson, Buist M. "Policyholder Control of a Mutual Life Insurance Company." *Cleveland State Law Review* 22 (1973): 439–49.

A. M. Best Company. *Best's Insurance Reports Property-Casualty*. Oldwick, N.J., 1981.

Bickelhaupt, D. L. *General Insurance*. Homewood, Ill.: Richard D. Irwin, Inc., 1983.

Bradley, Michael. "Interfirm Tender Offers and the Market for Corporate Control." *Journal of Business* 53 (1980): 345–76.

Coase, Ronald. "The Problem of Social Cost." *Journal of Law and Economics* 3 (1960): 1–44.

Demsetz, Harold. "The Structure of Ownership and the Theory of the Firm." *Journal of Law and Economics* 26 (1983): 375–90.

Fama, Eugene F., and Jensen, Michael C. "Agency Problems and Residual Claims." *Journal of Law and Economics* 26 (1983): 327–49.

Fama, Eugene F., and Jensen, Michael C. "Separation of Ownership and Control." *Journal of Law and Economics* 26 (1983): 301–25.

Fletcher, Linda P. "Mutualization of Stock Life Insurance Companies." Unpublished Ph.D. dissertation, University of Pennsylvania, 1964.

Fletcher, Linda P. "Motivations Underlying the Mutualization of Stock Life Insurance Companies." *Journal of Risk and Insurance* 33 (1966): 19–32.

Frech, H. E., III. "Health Insurance: Private, Mutuals or Government." *Economics of Nonproprietary Organizations Research in Law and Economics*, Suppl. 1. Greenwich, Conn.: JAI Press, Inc. (1980): 61–73.

Harman, H. H. *Modern Factor Analysis*. Chicago: University of Chicago Press, 1976.

Hetherington, J. A. C. "Fact v. Fiction: Who Owns Mutual Insurance Companies?" *Wisconsin Law Review* 4 (1969): 1068–1103.

Jensen, Michael C., and Meckling, William H. "Theory of the Firm: Managerial Behavior Agency Costs and Ownership Structure." *Journal of Financial Economics* 3 (1976): 305–60.

Klein, Benjamin. "Contracting Costs and Residual Claims: The Separation of Ownership and Control." *Journal of Law and Economics* 26 (1983): 367–74.

Kreider, Gary P. "Who Owns the Mutuals? Proposals for Reform of Membership Rights in Mutual Insurance and Banking Companies." *Cincinnati Law Review* 41 (1972): 275–311.

Manne, Henry G. "Mergers and the Market for Corporate Control." *Journal of Political Economy* 73 (1965): 110–20.

Mayers, David, and Smith, Clifford W., Jr. "Contractual Provisions, Organizational Structure, and Conflict Control in Insurance Markets." *Journal of Business* 54 (1981): 407–34.

Mayers, David, and Smith, Clifford W., Jr. "Ownership Structure and Control: The Mutualization of Stock Life Insurance Companies." *Journal of Financial Economics* 16 (1986): 73–98.

Morrison, D. F. *Multivariate Statistical Methods*. New York: McGraw-Hill, 1976.

Norgaard, R. L. "What Is a Reciprocal?" *Journal of Risk and Insurance* 31 (1964): 51.

Reinmuth, Dennis F. *The Regulation of Reciprocal Insurance Exchanges*. Homewood, Ill.: Richard D. Irwin, Inc., 1967.

Smith, Clifford W., Jr., and Warner, Jerold B. "On Financial Contracting: An Analysis of Bond Covenants." *Journal of Financial Economics* 7 (1979): 117–61.

Spiller, R. "Ownership and Performance: Stock and Mutual Life Insurance Companies." *Journal of Risk and Insurance* 34 (1972): 17–25.

Temporary National Economic Committee. *Study of Legal Reserve Life Insurance Companies*. Washington, D.C.: U.S. Government Printing Office, 1940.

Williamson, Oliver E. "Organizational Form, Residual Claimants, and Corporate Control." *Journal of Law and Economics* 26 (1983): 351–66.

Wright, C., and Fayle, C. E. *A History of Lloyd's*. London: Macmillan, 1928.

# Risk Considerations in Insurance Ratemaking

NAHUM BIGER AND YEHUDA KAHANE

## ABSTRACT

This paper examines insurance pricing and its regulation in the context of efficient capital markets. Starting with an aggregated model and generalizing results reported recently in the literature about "proper" underwriting profit, the paper turns to disaggregation of the model with m insurance lines. The main result is that no unique set of rates exists that regulators may impose to avoid disturbing market equilibrium. Preliminary empirical evidence presented shows that the "systematic risk" of underwriting profits approaches zero in most lines. Thus an intuitive solution for underwriting profit rates in these lines equal to minus the riskless interest rate, is reasonable.

*Key-words:*

Insurance Ratemaking, Financial Intermediaries, Insurance Regulation, Capital Assets Pricing, Portfolio Theory, Profitability of Insurance Companies, U.S. Property-Liability Insurance.

The delayed nature of claim payments enables insurers to raise funds from customers. The terms by which these funds are raised are often determined by regulatory authorities, through interference in the determination of insurance premiums; the actuarial formula which has been used in rate-setting in many North American jurisdictions reserved 2.5 (and sometimes 5.0) percent profit on the premiums.[1] Viewing the insurance reserves as an analogue to corporate debt capital leads to the observation that "To the extent that insurers earn positive underwriting profits, they in fact charge the customer for using his [or her] funds."[2]

Current literature focuses on various aspects of insurance ratemaking. Several articles examine the necessity of regulations.[3] Others deal with

---

Nahum Biger is an Associate Professor of Finance at the Faculty of Administrative Studies, York University, Toronto, Canada. He is visiting at the Faculty of Management, Tel-Aviv University, Israel.

Yehuda Kahane is the Director of the M. W. Erhard Center for Higher Studies and Research in Insurance, Faculty of Management, Tel-Aviv University, Israel and is a Senior Lecturer in the University.

The authors are grateful to Professors Robert Mehr and David Cummins, and to several anonymous referees for many helpful comments and suggestions.

[1] Some reservations seem to be in order: Massachusetts has just announced a negative rate for auto insurance. Also, many jurisdictions make various unofficial allowances for investment earnings by adjusting the target figure.

[2] This statement was offered by Quirin and Waters [19, p. 427].

[3] For a comprehensive discussion of this issue see, for example, Joskow [12].

empirical questions concerning performance under regulation, given the theoretical possibility of borrowing at a negative interest rate.[4] Specific rate-making formulae and the theoretical justification for the inclusion of investment income in the process of rate determination were also studied.[5]

This issue leads to the normative question of the appropriate rate of underwriting profit that should be included in the premiums when the risky nature of this type of "debt" instrument is considered. Several studies were addressed to this topic.[6] These studies examined a simplified model in which all insurance activities are aggregated, and there are one or two investable assets (risky and risk-free assets). Assuming independency between return on investments and aggregated underwriting profit, these studies concluded that the premium should be set so as to generate much lower and possibly negative underwriting profits.

This paper offers a re-examination of the single-line case and examines the more general case of multiple-line insurers. It assumes efficient capital markets and evaluates rate-making regulation under such conditions. The analysis is followed by a discussion of estimation problems and an indirect method to estimate market betas for underwriting is proposed. Some preliminary empirical evidence as to the correlation between underwriting profits of insurers and the return on a market portfolio also is presented.

## The Single-Line Case

The Capital Asset Pricing Model (CAPM) implies that in a number of important cases,[7] expected one-period return on each security j, $E(\tilde{r}_j)$, less return on a risk-free asset, $r_f$, is proportional to the security's systematic risk,

$\beta_j$, by: $\qquad$ (1) $\quad E(\tilde{r}_j)-r_f = \beta_j [E(r_m)-r_f]$

where $E(\tilde{r}_m)$ is the expected one-period return on the market portfolio. Stocks of a non-life insurer, being traded in the market, are assumed to be priced according to the equilibrium equation (1). This equilibrium equation is now used to examine implications for underwriting risk and return.

With uncertain cost of debt capital for the insurer, the one-period rate of return on equity, $\tilde{r}_y$, also can be written as: $\qquad$ (2) $\quad \tilde{r}_y = (1+L)\tilde{r}_p - L\tilde{r}_u$

where: $\quad$ L = the premium/equity ratio of the insurance company,

$\qquad \tilde{r}_u$ = the one-period rate of underwriting loss (profit) as a percentage of total premium,

$\qquad \tilde{r}_p$ = the one-period return on investment.

---

[4] This issue has been controversial in the insurance community, following the study by Plotkin [17].

[5] The rate-making formulae have been of major concern to the National Association of Insurance Commissioners. For a discussion of some of the problems associated with rate-making see Curry [5], Flanigan [8], Hedges [10] and the reports of NAIC [15] and NAII [16].

[6] See, for example, Ferrari [7], Pyle [18] and Quirin and Waters [19].

[7] For a summary of the assumptions underlying the model see Jensen [11].

The quantity $\tilde{r}_p$ is multiplied by $(1+L)$, reflecting that total investment in assets equals equity capital plus funds generated by the collection of premiums.[8, 9] The expected return on equity, $E(\tilde{r}_y)$ can now be obtained from (2) as:

$$(3) \quad E(\tilde{r}_y) = (1+L)E(\tilde{r}_p) - L E(\tilde{r}_u)$$

The systematic risk of the return on equity for the insurer, $\beta_y$, can be obtained using equation (2)[10]:

$$
\begin{aligned}
(4) \quad \beta_y &= \mathrm{Cov}(\tilde{r}_y, \tilde{r}_m)/\mathrm{Var}(\tilde{r}_m) \\
&= (1/\mathrm{Var}(\tilde{r}_m))\mathrm{Cov}\{[(1+L)\tilde{r}_p - L\tilde{r}_u], \tilde{r}_m\} \\
&= (1+L)\mathrm{Cov}(\tilde{r}_p, \tilde{r}_m)/\mathrm{Var}(\tilde{r}_m) - L \, \mathrm{Cov}(\tilde{r}_u, \tilde{r}_m)/\mathrm{Var}(\tilde{r}_m) \\
&= (1+L)\beta_p - L\beta_u
\end{aligned}
$$

where $\beta_u$ is the systematic risk of the insurance portfolio and $\beta_p$ the systematic risk of the asset portfolio.

Under efficient market conditions it can be stated that regulating authorities should determine the expected rate of underwriting profit, $E(\tilde{r}_u)$, which they seek to regulate, such that market equilibrium is undisturbed. Substituting (4) into the equilibrium relationship for the stock of the insurance company,

$$(5) \quad E(\tilde{r}_y) = [(1+L)\beta_p - L\beta_u][E(\tilde{r}_m)-r_f] + r_f \quad ,$$

and with definition (2),

$$(6) \quad (1+L)E(\tilde{r}_p) - L \, E(\tilde{r}_u) = [(1+L)\beta_p - L\beta_u][E(\tilde{r}_m)-r_f]+ r_f$$

Assuming that the parameters $\beta_u$, $\beta_p$, $r_f$, the leverage ratio $L$ as well as $E(\tilde{r}_p)$ and $E(\tilde{r}_m)$ are given,[11] $E(\tilde{r}_u)$ is to be determined. The asset portfolio P also satisfies the equilibrium risk-return relationship:

$$(7) \quad E(\tilde{r}_p) = \beta_p[E(\tilde{r}_m)-r_f] + r_f$$

---

[8] It is assumed that all premium funds are invested for one period. This assumption is a reasonable approximation of observed practices of insurance companies: Aggregate premiums usually are close to aggregate insurance reserves. (See Haugen and Kroncke [9] and Krouse [13]. Allocation of funds to selling and administration expenses is accounted for through $\tilde{r}_u$.

[9] A strong assumption is made that assets offsetting equity and reserve capital can be invested in the same instruments. Regulations usually restrict the types of investment of assets attributable to reserve capital.

[10] The risk coefficient, $\beta_y$, is the weighted average of the systematic risk of the firm's activities; see Fama and Miller [6, p. 304-307].

[11] The parameter $\beta_u$ is not directly observable, nor can it be estimated directly from market data. For a discussion of the estimation problem see a later section.

and substituting (7) into (6),

$$(8) \quad (1+L)\{\beta_p[E(\tilde{r}_m)-r_f]+r_f\}-L\ E(\tilde{r}_u) = [(1+L)\beta_p-L\beta_u][E(\tilde{r}_m)-r_f]+r_f$$

Rearranging and factoring L out, (8) reduces to:

$$(9) \quad E(\tilde{r}_u) = \beta_u[E(\tilde{r}_m)-r_f]+r_f$$

Equation (9) can be thought of as the regulators' yardstick. It states that when there is one line of insurance and when the investment portfolio is considered in aggregate, the expected rate of underwriting loss in equilibrium is independent of the size of the premium/equity ratio (or the insurance leverage) of the insurer. In addition, equation (9) corresponds to what intuition may have suggested: in equilibrium the expected rate of underwriting loss should be equal to the expected rate of profit on an investment portfolio with the same $\beta$. Finally, if underwriting profits are uncorrelated with the rate of return on the market portfolio (i.e., if underwriting portfolio is a zero-zeta portfolio[12]), their expected value in equilibrium equals to the negative of the risk-free rate.

The efficient market assumption amplifies the significance of the systematic, rather than total risk in rate-making;[13] the result: $E(\tilde{r}_u) = r_f$ is only valid when $\beta_u = 0$, not when underwriting profits are uncorrelated with returns on the insurers' portfolio.[14]

## The Multi-Line Case

The model is now extended for the more general case where the insurer underwrites contracts in m different insurance lines and the asset portfolio consists of n-m assets.

The one-period rate of return on equity is:

$$(10) \quad \tilde{r}_y = \sum_{i=m+1}^{n} x_i\tilde{r}_i - \sum_{i=1}^{m} x_i\tilde{r}_i$$

Where:

$r_i =$
(rate of loss on insurance line i
( (percent of premium) for $i = 1,\ldots,m$
(
(rate of return on investment i,
(for $i = m+1,\ldots,n$

$x_i =$
(ratio of premium to equity in line i
(for $i = 1,\ldots,m$
(
(ratio of investment in asset i to equity
(for $i = m+1,\ldots,n$

---

[12] This concept was introduced by Black [3] and incorporated into the CAPM by Black, Jensen and Scholes [4].

[13] Ferrari [7], Lange [14] and Pyle [18] employ the total risk concept ($\sigma_u$) in their analysis.

[14] This assumption is employed by Quirin and Waters [19]. Admittedly their assumption is equivalent to $\beta_u = 0$ if insurers' investment portfolio is well diversified, Sharpe-efficient, and perfectly correlated with the market portfolio.

Note that definition (10) still maintains the assumption that assets off-setting insurance reserves in all lines are invested for one period.[15] The systematic risk of the insurers' stock, $\beta_y$, again is a linear combination of the systematic risk coefficients, $\beta_i$, of the activities:

$$(11) \quad \beta_y = \sum_{i=m+1}^{n} x_i \beta_i - \sum_{i=1}^{m} x_i \beta_i$$

Capital market equilibrium implies:

$$(12) \quad E(\tilde{r}_y) = \beta_y [E(\tilde{r}_m) - r_f] + r_f$$

Taking expected value of equation (10) and substituting into (12),

$$(13) \quad \sum_{i=m+1}^{n} x_i E(\tilde{r}_i) - \sum_{i=1}^{m} x_i E(\tilde{r}_i) = [\sum_{i=m+1}^{n} x_i \beta_i - \sum_{i=1}^{m} x_i \beta_i][E(\tilde{r}_m) - r_f] + r_f$$

Expected return on the investment portfolio also must satisfy the risk-return relationship similar to (12), and every investment i $(i = m + 1, \ldots, n)$

satisfies: $\quad (14) \quad E(\tilde{r}_i) = \beta_i [E(\tilde{r}_m) - r_f] + r_f$

and as the expression $\sum_{i=m+1}^{n} x_i$ exceeds 1, the summation of (14) over the investment portfolio is:

$$(15) \quad \sum_{i=m+1}^{n} x_i E(\tilde{r}_i) = \sum_{i=m+1}^{n} x_i \{\beta_i [E(\tilde{r}_m) - r_f]\} + r_f$$

$$= \sum_{i=m+1}^{n} x_i \beta_i [E(\tilde{r}_m) - r_f] + r_f \sum_{i=m+1}^{n} x_i$$

Substituting (15) into (13), the expected loss on the insurance portfolio

can be expressed as: $(16) \quad \sum_{i=1}^{m} x_i E(\tilde{r}_i) = \sum_{i=1}^{m} x_i \beta_i [E(\tilde{r}_m) - r_f] + r_f \sum_{i=1}^{m} x_i$

Equation (16) is a general statement of the equilibrium expected under-writing returns. A few aspects are worth emphasizing. First, expected return on the aggregate insurance portfolio is again independent of the size of the financial leverage of the insurance company per se.

Second, the multi-line case does not necessarily lead to a clear-cut statement about the expected rate of profit on individual insurance lines. Given all $\beta_i$, $E(\tilde{r}_m)$ and $r_f$, even if the values of $x_i$'s are known, equation (16)

---

[15] One can define fund-generating coefficients, $g_i$, which can be treated as bounded decision variables of the insurer. Each insurance line may be associated with a different coefficient. Insurers can control this variable by delaying claim settlements or by collecting premiums on an installment basis.

is insufficient to determine a single set of $E(\tilde{r}_i)$s as there may be an infinite number of vectors satisfying the equation. One possible solution, analogous to the single-line case, is:

$$(17) \quad E(\tilde{r}_i) = \beta_i [E(\tilde{r}_m) - r_f] + r_f \quad (i=1,\ldots,m)$$

but this solution is only a private one. Any other set of numbers which satisfies (16) may have the same features of not disturbing equilibrium in the market. It follows that if, for one reason or another, rate regulation is deemed desirable, its imposition will not destruct efficient capital markets, as long as rates are determined in such a way as to preserve equation (16).

Notice that if it is assumed that $\beta_i = 0$ for all insurance lines, then the solution: $E(\tilde{r}_i) = r_f$ for $i = 1,\ldots m$ is the intuitive equivalent to the solution suggested in the literature for the single-line case. This solution, however, is not unique.

The solution suggested in (17) probably is the most convenient format regulators can adopt, as it does not require information concerning the specific composition of the insurance portfolio of each insurer (the set of $x_i$'s for each company j). At any rate, a flat profit rate suggested by regulators has extremely low probability of being consistent with the equilibrium equation (16).

## Some Estimation Problems

The application of the foregoing model necessitates the use of a series of beta coefficients for the underwriting profits in different insurance lines. Estimation of the beta coefficients for underwriting is rather complex and therefore deserves discussion.

Clearly, procedures similar to those developed for estimating the beta coefficients of securities may not be satisfactory for the task at hand. For security betas the estimation procedure is based on a time series regression of the returns of an asset on the returns of the market portfolio. Returns on assets and on the market portfolio are holding period (market) returns. They reflect changes in the values of the assets, as they are assessed by participants in the capital markets. The estimates of the systematic risk coefficients are thus market betas.

In analogy to the risk coefficients of securities, the underwriting betas presented in the preceding section have to reflect the systematic risk of the underwriting activities. The systematic risk also should reflect the risk as it is assessed by market participants. Unfortunately, market returns on underwriting activities are not observable. At the same time, underwriting profits reported by insurers are not necessarily equal to the way market participants assess those profits, their variability, and the systematic portion of the risk. It follows that evaluation of the systematic risk of underwriting, which is not based on market returns but on reported profits, may result in biased estimates of the coefficients. Straight-forward application of time series regression of underwriting profits against the rate of return on the market portfolio leaves something to be desired.

In essence, the problem is similar to the well-known problem of whether or not accounting betas are consistent substitutes for market betas.[16] In the case of accounting betas of securities the estimates are based on time series regressions of earnings per share against a composite of the earnings per share of all companies, or against the returns on the market portfolio. These betas can be compared to market betas of the same companies in order to determine whether they are reasonable substitutes. The issue is especially important in the case where no market returns are available for a certain firm, as would be the case in the valuation of private corporations.

In the context of insurance or underwriting portfolios, it is difficult even to assess the validity of the accounting beta estimates of underwriting profits in different lines, because no direct market betas are available for comparisons. At any rate, it is conceivable that the accounting rates of profit in the insurance case are less accurate than the earnings per share figures used for the standard accounting beta calculations. Several accounting procedures, unique to the insurance business, make the concept of profit or loss on any particular line of insurance less meaningful than the earnings per share figures for other business firms. In particular, the somewhat arbitrary allocation of overhead to individual lines makes the profit estimates even more questionable, as what is required are specific betas for specific lines. If one adds the empirical inconsistency between accounting betas and market betas for securities, reported in several studies to these reservations,[17] one must conclude that regulators should be cautious when accounting betas are used for the insurance lines in ratemaking.

One possible procedure to circumvent the problem is to derive market betas for underwriting in an indirect way. This method may indeed serve as a practical solution if one is ready to adopt two major assumptions:

1. The book values of the liabilities of insurance companies for each insurance line, $x_i$ $(i = 1, \ldots m)$, are reasonably similar to the market values of these liabilities.[18]

---

[16] The problem of the consistency between accounting betas of securities, based on earnings per share figures and market betas was noted in several studies in the Accounting and Finance literature. See Beaver, Kettler and Scholes [1], Beaver and Manegold [2] for a discussion of the problem.

[17] It should be pointed out that consistency between accounting betas and market betas was found to be satisfactory for portfolios, but weak for individual securities (See [3]). The betas here are individual betas and the above noted consistency on a portfolio level is no comfort for the case at hand.

[18] This assumption is somewhat heroic. The amount of liabilities in every insurance line, as it appears in the insurers' balance sheet, is affected by specific accounting procedures, and it contains estimated loss reserves. Obviously, the size of $x_i$ $(i = 1, \ldots, m)$, or its true market value is not observable. Thus, one may indeed be facing the problem of errors in the variables, common to most econometric studies. Large sample size in a cross section analysis however may reduce the significance of the (unobservable) errors.

2. The insurance lines are classified and defined in such a way so that the market-determined systematic risk of any particular line i ($i = 1,...m$) is the same for all insurers.

The estimation procedure consists of three stages. First, the market beta for the stock of every insurance company is estimated using time series regression. As the companies are public, holding period returns to the shareholders are available. Thus, one estimates the $\beta_{yj}$ coefficient for every company j.

Second, the market beta of every asset held by every insurer is estimated. Once again, the assets are traded in the market and so their holding period returns are available. Time series regression is applied to the holding period returns of every asset and the returns on the market porfolio.

As a result, one obtains market beta estimates for the coefficient $\beta_i$ ($i = m+1,...,n$) for every asset held in the portfolio by any insurance company.[19]

The third stage is based upon the following notion:

Equation (11) above sets out the balance of systematic risk for insurance companies. For every company j, the equation states:

$$(11) \quad \beta_{y,j} = \sum_{i=m+1}^{n} x_{ij}\, \beta_i - \sum_{i=1}^{m} x_{ij}\beta_i$$

The equation can also be written as:

$$(11') \quad \sum_{i=m+1}^{n} x_{ij}\beta_i - \beta_{yj} = x_{1j}\beta_1 + x_{2j}\beta_2 + \ldots + x_{mj}\beta_m$$

The estimates obtained in Stages 1 and 2 are now inserted in the left hand side of equation (11'). The $x_{ij}$ values are market values of the assets in the portfolio of company j, and they are observable in the market. Thus, after completion of stages 1 and 2, estimates of the left hand side of the equation (11') are available for a given moment in time. Furthermore, assumption 1 implies that the elements $x_{ij}(i = 1,...,m)$ on the right hand side also are available for the same point in time for every company j.

By making use of assumption 2, it is now possible to apply a cross section regression on equation (11') using the figures from all non-life stock companies, and to obtain ordinary least square estimates of the coefficients $\beta_1 \beta_2,...,\beta m$:

$$\text{Define} \quad \sum_{i=m+1}^{n} x_{ij}\beta_i - \beta_{yj} \equiv z_j.$$

The regression equation takes the form
$$z_j = \sum_{i=1}^{m} x_{ij}\beta_i + v_j \quad,$$

---

[19] Some assets, such as real estate, held by insurance companies, are not traded frequently and holding period returns in these assets are not easily available. Thus some problems are introduced in estimating the market betas of these assets. Changes in price indexes of groups of such assets (property values etc.) perhaps may be used as substitutes for market values of the assets.

where $v_j$ is a random disturbance term which has a mean zero; it is un-correlated with the $x_i$'s and it has no cross section correlation with the $v_j$'s terms of other companies.

The estimates $\beta_i (i = 1, \ldots m)$ derived from stage 3 can be considered as market betas for underwriting. They are market betas in the sense that the estimation procedure uses mostly market-determined values, except for the figures $x_{ij} (i = 1, \ldots, m)$, for which market values do not exist and cannot be obtained.[20]

These $\beta_i$ $(i = 1, \ldots, m)$ are to be used in the application of equation (16) for rate regulation. Clearly, the indirect process just described is quite laborious, for it involves a fairly heavy task of data collection. Furthermore, even if one would estimate the underwriting betas in this fashion, there is no benchmark for comparisons. Statistical tests on the regression equation would give some indication as to the validity of the model, but it is quite possible that noise in the data will cause the results to be obscure. For that reason, no actual application of the indirect method was performed. Instead, the following section presents some rough estimates of accounting betas of underwriting. These estimates are reported for the sole purpose of indicating the differences in the accounting betas when the regressors are different series of rates of return on two market portfolios.

## Some Empirical Evidence

Following Quirin and Waters [19], some estimates of the correlation between insurance lines' profit rates and the rate of return on the market portfolio are reported. Before turning to the presentation of the results, it should be stressed that estimation of the slope coefficients of an ex-post version of equation (17) is by no means the equivalent of the ex-post version of the Capital Asset Pricing Model.[21] This reservation is the direct result of the equilibrium equation (16) which not necessarily implies (17) ex-ante. Thus, the statistical summary below is presented only to indicate orders of magnitude of the correlation coefficients.

Annual underwriting profits, aggregated for all U.S. non-life stock insurance companies for the period 1956-1973, formed the data base for the estimates.[22] Underwriting profits as a percentage of unearned premiums in 18 lines (before Federal taxes) were regressed against two indexes representing well diversified market portfolios: Moody's stock index, including dividend yield, was used to represent the first market portfolio (stocks). Annual bond yield index, with proper adjustment for the average coupon

---

[20] The adoption of balance sheet figures as the $x_{ij}$'s does indeed reduce the confidence in the estimates. Therefore, regulators should be cautious when they apply the betas for underwriting rate-making. See also footnote 18.

[21] For a summary of the statistical assumptions and the return-generating process usually assumed to derive the ex-post regression equation, see Black, Jensen and Scholes, op. cit. [4].

[22] Insurance data were obtained from Best's *Property-Casualty Aggregates and Averages (1974)*, A. M. Best Co., New York. The estimates do not include hidden equity in the unearned premium reserve.

rate on long term U.S. Federal bonds,[23] was then added to the stock index with various proportions to represent a more comprehensive market portfolio. Table 1 summarizes the regression equations.

TABLE 1

SUMMARY STATISTICS OF CORRELATION BETWEEN UNDERWRITING RETURNS
AND THE RETURNS ON THE MARKET PORTFOLIO*
1956-1973

| Insurance Line | 1. Moody's Portfolio | | | 2. 70% Bonds 30% Stocks | | |
|---|---|---|---|---|---|---|
| | $\beta_i$ | $t(\beta_i)$ | $R^2$ | $\beta_i$ | $t(\beta_i)$ | $R^2$ |
| 1 Fire | .002 | .02 | .00 | .205 | .89 | .05 |
| 2 Allied Lines | .084 | .35 | .01 | .317 | .72 | .03 |
| 3 Homeowners | .056 | .19 | .00 | .258 | .47 | .01 |
| 4 Commercial | .013 | .40 | .01 | .363 | .62 | .02 |
| 5 Marine - Ocean | .061 | .39 | .01 | .339 | 1.20 | .08 |
| 6 Marine - Inland | .053 | .39 | .01 | .371 | 1.59 | .14 |
| 7 Group Health | -.013 | .24 | .00 | -.131 | 1.32 | .10 |
| 8 Health (other) | -.016 | .84 | .04 | -.203 | 1.58 | .13 |
| 9 Workmens Comp. | -.109 | 1.88 | .18 | -.230 | 2.19 | .23** |
| 10 Liability | .076 | .42 | .01 | .058 | .17 | .00 |
| 11 Auto - Liability | .059 | 1.07 | .07 | .207 | 2.23 | .24** |
| 12 Auto - Property | .119 | 1.31 | .10 | .352 | 2.26 | .24** |
| 13 Fidelity | .075 | .49 | .02 | .170 | .61 | .02 |
| 14 Surety | .024 | .17 | .00 | -.184 | .70 | .03 |
| 15 Glass | .000 | .00 | .00 | .120 | .62 | .02 |
| 16 Burglary | .009 | .04 | .00 | .288 | .70 | .03 |
| 17 Boiler | -.067 | .44 | .01 | .016 | .06 | .00 |
| 18 Credit | .199 | .32 | .01 | -.136 | .12 | .00 |

* $\tilde{r}_{it} = \alpha_i + \beta_i \tilde{r}_{mt} + \tilde{u}_{it}$

** significant at 95 percent

The results reported in Table 1 validate the assumption that $\beta_i$ for all insurance lines may indeed be zero, at least when the market portfolio contains only stocks. When Federal bonds are added to the market portfolio, ex-post correlations for some lines are non-zero. It follows that if regulatory authorities do indeed view the market portfolio as one which includes only stocks, regulating the prices of insurance contracts in all lines to be the equivalent of paying interest comparable to the return on risk-free debt instruments is consistent with market equilibrium, though this practice is not the only consistent one. Conversely, if regulators' assessment of the systematic risk of some insurance activities implies non-zero values, their task is more complicated.

## Conclusions

This paper examined pricing of insurance contracts and their regulation in the context of efficient capital markets. The aggregated model suggests

[23] Rates of return on bonds (annual holding period returns) were computed from price indexes of long term government bonds published monthly in the *Federal Reserve Bulletin*. An estimate of the annual coupon yield was added to annual capital gain or loss.

a single solution pointed out earlier in the literature, with a generalization to the case where uncertain underwriting profits are correlated with returns on the market asset portfolio. An extension to the multiple-line case has indicated that there may be numerous solutions to the insurance pricing regulation problem. It was found that in spite of the interest shared by rate-regulators and insurers concerning the proper leverage, this important decision variable does not affect ratemaking. Some estimation problems were discussed and a method of indirectly estimating market betas for underwriting was presented. Crude acounting betas for underwriting, based on aggregation of all insurance were presented. Some indication as to the ex-post correlation between underwriting profit rates and the return on two market portfolios also was reported. These findings do not contrast the assumption of zero-correlation with the market for most insurance lines. They give some initial indication as to the appropriateness of negative profit rates in the vicinity of the risk-free rate. It follows that recently adopted practices by insurance regulators and commissioners, whereby the pricing of insurance contracts reflects negative profit rates or incorporates allowances for investment earnings by adjusting the target margin figure, are proper.

## REFERENCES

1. Beaver, W. H., Kettler, P. and Scholes, M. "The Association Between Market Determined and Accounting Determined Risk Measures", *The Accounting Review*, 45, October 1970.

2. Beaver, W. and Manegold, J. "The Association Between Market Determined and Accounting Determined Measures of Risk: Some Further Evidence", *Journal of Financial and Quantitative Analysis*, 10 (June 1975).

3. Black, F. "Capital Market Equilibrium with Restricted Borrowing", *Journal of Business*, Vol. 45, No. 3 (July 1972).

4. Black, F., Jensen, M. C., and Scholes, M. "The Capital Asset Pricing Model: Some Empirical Tests", in M. C. Jensen, ed., *Studies in the Theory of Capital Markets*, New York, Praeger Publishers (1972).

5. Curry, H. E. "Investment Income in Fire and Casualty Rate Making", *The Journal of Risk and Insurance*, 36(4) (September 1969).

6. Fama, E. F. and Miller, M. H. *The Theory of Finance*, New York, Holt, Rinehart and Winston, Inc. (1972).

7. Ferrari, J. R. "The Relationship of Underwriting, Investment, Leverage and Exposure to Total Return on Owners' Equity", *Proceedings of the Casualty Actuarial Society*, 55 (1968).

8. Flanigan, G. B. "Investment Income in Rate-Making and Managerial Investment Attitude", *The Journal of Risk and Insurance* (June 1974).

9. Haugen, R. A. and Kroncke, C. O. "Rate Regulation and the Cost of Capital in the Insurance Industry", *Journal of Financial and Quantitative Analysis*, 6 (December 1971).

10. Hedges, R. "Insurance Rates and Investment Earnings Considered Together", *The Journal of Risk and Insurance*, 36(4) (September 1969).

11. Jensen, M. C. "Capital Markets, Theory and Evidence", *The Bell Journal of Economics and Management Science*, Vol. 3, No. 2 (Autumn 1972).

12. Joskow, P. L. "Cartels, Competition and Regulation in the Property Liability Insurance Industry", *The Bell Journal of Economics and Management Science*, Vol. 4, No. 2 (Autumn 1973).

13. Krouse, C. G. "Portfolio Balancing Corporate Assets and Liabilities with Specific Application to Insurance Management", *Journal of Financial and Quantitative Analysis*, 5 (March 1970).

14. Lange, J. T. "Application of a Mathematical Concept of Risk to Property-Liability Insurance Rate-making", *The Journal of Risk and Insurance*, 36(4) (September 1969).

15. National Association of Insurance Commissioners. Subcommittee A-4 on the Profitability and Investment Income in Property and Liability Insurance— Report of the Special Task Force, June 1973 and September 1973.

16. National Assoication of Independent Insurers, Comment on Report of Specific Task Force to the NAIC (A-4) Subcommittee on Profitability and Investment Income in Property and Liability Insurance, September 1973.

17. Plotkin, I. "Prices and Profits in the Property and Liability Insurance Industry", *American Insurance Association*, New York, 1967.

18. Pyle, D. H. "On the Theory of Financial Intermediation", *The Journal of Finance*, 26(3) (June 1971).

19. Quirin, D. G., and Waters, W. R. "Market Efficiency and the Cost of Capital: The Strange Case of Fire and Casualty Insurance Companies", *The Journal of Finance*, Vol. XXX, No. 2 (May 1975).

# Price Regulation in Property-Liability Insurance: A Contingent-Claims Approach

NEIL A. DOHERTY and JAMES R. GARVEN*

## ABSTRACT

A discrete-time option-pricing model is used to derive the "fair" rate of return for the property-liability insurance firm. The rationale for the use of this model is that the financial claims of shareholders, policyholders, and tax authorities can be modeled as European options written on the income generated by the insurer's asset portfolio. This portfolio consists mostly of traded financial assets and is therefore relatively easy to value. By setting the value of the shareholders' option equal to the initial surplus, an implicit solution for the fair insurance price may be derived. Unlike previous insurance regulatory models, this approach addresses the ruin probability of the insurer, as well as nonlinear tax effects.

IN RECENT YEARS, THE "fair"-rate-of-return-on-equity criterion has been used in the regulation of property-liability insurance premiums. As with utility regulation, the "fair" rate of return usually is interpreted as that which would prevail under competitive conditions, and in some cases the Sharpe [28]-Lintner [18]-Mossin [21] capital asset pricing model (CAPM) has been used to derive the equilibrium relationship (cf. Hill [15], Fairley [9]). But discontent with this model has led to questioning of its use. In addition to doubt over testability of the CAPM (cf. Roll [23]), this model leaves unexplained some significant pricing anomalies such as the earnings yield and size effects (cf. Reinganum [22]). Applications of the CAPM to insurance regulation have encountered three major problems. First, there are peculiar difficulties in estimating underwriting betas either through the use of market or accounting data (cf. Fairley [9], Hill [15], Cummins and Harrington [5]). Second, the models do not address the effect of insolvency on the return to shareholders despite the attention given to this prospect by regulators and actuaries. Third, the applications either ignore corporate taxation or assume it is proportional over the entire range of corporate income. Tax shields, which are especially important to insurance firms, are known to result in significant nonlinearities in the tax schedule.

In connection with utility regulation, Bower, Bower, and Logue [3] have recently noted the irony that, at the time the CAPM is gaining acceptance by regulators, its preeminent role in the explanation of security returns is being challenged by the arbitrage pricing theory (APT). This paradox obviously applies

* Professor, The Wharton School, University of Pennsylvania, and Assistant Professor, College of Business Administration, The Pennsylvania State University, respectively. We are grateful for useful comments from an anonymous referee and the participants of seminars at the University of Illinois, The Pennsylvania State University, and the Massachusetts Rating Bureaus. Of course, we are solely responsible for any remaining errors.

to insurance regulation as well. Does, then, the APT offer a more attractive alternative for insurance regulation? The answer is that it is too early to say. An analytic solution for the fair rate of return on underwriting has been derived by Kraus and Ross [17] in an APT framework, and attempts at the empirical application of the APT to insurance regulation have already been made by Urritia [30]. But, as in the case of the CAPM, doubts have also been raised in the finance literature over the testability of the APT (cf. Shanken [27]; Dhrymes, Friend, and Gultekin [7]; Dybvig and Ross [8]). Furthermore, it is not yet clear that the APT explains the well-known pricing anomalies left unanswered by the CAPM. In applying the APT to insurance regulation, the estimation problems associated with calculating underwriting betas (or factor loadings) remain, due to the inadequacy of market data and the unknown sampling errors that are sure to arise from using accounting data. Moreover, Kraus and Ross's insightful analysis does not address the possibilities of insolvency or tax shield redundancy, nor is it clear how such effects might be encompassed by their model.

We offer an alternative approach to insurance price regulation. The liabilities of the insurer to policyholders, shareholders, and the tax authorities are viewed as contingent claims written on the income generated by the insurer's asset portfolio. If the market value of the asset portfolio is observable, implicit values for these claims may be derived by means of risk-neutral valuation relationships (cf. Brennan [4], Rubinstein [25], Stapleton and Subrahmanyam [29]). Thus, option-pricing techniques may be used to derive the competitive price of the insurance contract as well as the "fair" rates of return on underwriting and on shareholders' equity. The advantages of this approach are that it addresses the possibility of insolvency and the nonlinear tax effects that may arise from the redundancy of tax shields. Although some estimation of risk premiums is required, the menu of possible option-pricing models that can be used permits some choice in the selection of an underlying process for pricing capital assets. In fact, we will limit our presentation to discrete-time models, noting that the advantages of such an approach to valuation are particularly useful in valuing discrete insurance contracts and tax liabilities.

The remainder of the paper is organized in the following manner: In Section I, we provide a generalized single-period valuation model of the claims held by the property-liability insurer's policyholders and shareholders and the tax authorities. In Section II, we offer two special cases of the first section's more general formulation that require restrictions on investor preferences and on the probability distributions that underlie insurance company investment returns and claims costs. In Section III, we present numerical simulations of our model. Section IV concludes.

## I. Basic Valuation Relationships for a Property-Liability Insurer

Consider a single-period model of the insurance firm in which investors contribute paid-in equity of $S_0$ and policyholders pay premiums of $P_0$. For convenience, premiums will be defined as net of production and marketing expenses. Therefore, the opening cash flow is given as

$$Y_0 = S_0 + P_0. \tag{1}$$

The claims of policyholders and the government are discharged at the end of the period, leaving a residual claim for shareholders. Allowing for investment income at a rate $\tilde{r}_i$, we obtain an expression for terminal cash flow $\tilde{Y}_1$:

$$\tilde{Y}_1 = S_0 + P_0 + (S_0 + kP_0)\tilde{r}_i. \tag{2}$$

The term $k$ is the funds-generating coefficient. This represents an adjustment to compensate for the difference between the period of our model (say one year) and the average delay between receipt of premiums and payment of policyholder claims.[1]

The value $\tilde{Y}_1$ is allocated to various claimholders in a set of payoffs having the characteristics of call options.[2] The payoffs to policyholders, $\tilde{H}_1$, and government, $\tilde{T}_1$, are given in the next two equations:[3]

$$\tilde{H}_1 = \max(\min[\tilde{L}, \tilde{Y}_1], 0) \tag{3}$$

$$\tilde{T}_1 = \max[\tau(\theta(\tilde{Y}_1 - Y_0) + P_0 - \tilde{L}), 0], \tag{4}$$

where the variable $\tilde{L}$ represents the insurer's end-of-period claims costs and $\tau$ is the corporate tax rate. The effective tax rate on the insurer's investment income is considerably less than $\tau$ in view of the insurer's holding of tax-exempt securities, the somewhat lower capital-gains rate, and the 85-percent shield of dividend income for corporations. The effective tax rate on investment income, therefore, is denoted $\theta\tau$.[4] Since these claims either directly or indirectly involve the valuation of call options, the appropriate expressions for the values of these

---

[1] Depending upon the type of risk being insured, the time lag between the receipt of the premium and payment of the claim can vary considerably. For example, most casualty insurance lines are characterized by claim delays of less than one year, whereas most liability lines have claim delays of more than one year. Consequently, for every dollar of premiums written, lines of insurance with longer claim delays generate more investable funds than insurance lines with shorter claim delays. Therefore, the "funds-generating coefficient" can be interpreted as the average amount of investable funds per dollar of annual premiums. This type of adjustment is also used in the papers by Hill [15], Fairley [9], Biger and Kahane [1], and Hill and Modigliani [16].

[2] We view shareholders as holding a long position in a call option on the pretax terminal value of the insurer's asset portfolio and a short position in a call option on the taxable income derived from that portfolio. Consequently, policyholders hold a long position in the pretax terminal value of the insurer's asset portfolio and a short position in the call option written on that portfolio, while the government holds a long position in the call option written against the insurer's taxable income. Similar characterizations have been used for modeling nonfinancial firms (e.g., cf. Black and Scholes [2], Galai and Masulis [13], Galai [12], Majd and Myers [19]).

[3] Since our purpose in this section of the paper is to provide as general a formulation of the problem as possible, we initially place explicit lower bounds of zero on both $\tilde{H}_1$ and $\tilde{T}_1$, so as to allow for limited liability. In other words, should a poorly endowed state of nature be revealed at the end of the contracting period, the worst possible outcome for policyholders is one in which they receive no settlement on their claims. Similarly, our restriction on the cash flow associated with the government's tax claim ensures that it does not provide tax rebates to unprofitable firms; viz., at worst, the government does not receive any tax revenues. Subsequently, when we build a model in which we assume that both $\tilde{r}_i$ and $\tilde{L}$ are normally distributed random variables, this lower bound will still need to be observed. However, in the lognormal formulation, this bound will obviously be redundant.

[4] $\theta$ is a factor of proportionality defined over the interval [0, 1]. This parameter is functionally related to the composition of the insurer's investment portfolio. For example, if the investment portfolio is comprised of strictly tax-exempt securities, then $\theta = 0$. Conversely, if only fully taxable claims such as corporate bonds and U.S. Treasury securities are chosen, then $\theta = 1$.

claims are given as follows:

$$H_0 = V(\tilde{Y}_1) - C(\tilde{Y}_1; \tilde{L}) \tag{5}$$

$$T_0 = \tau C[\theta(\tilde{Y}_1 - Y_0) + P_0; \tilde{L}], \tag{6}$$

where

$V(\cdot)$ = the valuation operator;

$R_f = 1 + r_f$, where $r_f$ is the riskless interest rate;[5]

$C[A; B]$ = the current market value of a European call option written on an asset with a terminal value of $A$ and exercise price of $B$.

The market value of the residual claim of the shareholders, $V_e$, is simply the difference between the market value of the asset portfolio, $V(\tilde{Y}_1)$, and the sum of the values of the policyholders' and government's claims, viz.,

$$\begin{aligned} V_e &= V(\tilde{Y}_1) - [H_0 + T_0] \\ &= C[\tilde{Y}_1; \tilde{L}] - \tau C[\theta(\tilde{Y}_1 - Y_0) + P_0; \tilde{L}] \\ &= C_1 - \tau C_2. \end{aligned} \tag{7}$$

The regulatory problem may now be couched in straightforward terms. Insurance prices must be set such that a "fair" return is delivered to shareholders. This will be achieved if the current market value of the equity claim $V_e$ is equal to the initial equity investment $S_0$. Noting that $\tilde{Y}_1$ and $Y_0$ are functions of $P_0$, we can state the fair rate of return as that implied by a value of $P_0^*$ that satisfies the following equation:

$$\begin{aligned} V_e &= C[\tilde{Y}_1(P_0^*); \tilde{L}] - \tau C[\theta(\tilde{Y}_1(P_0^*) - Y_0(P_0^*)) + P_0^*; \tilde{L}] \\ &= C_1^* - \tau C_2^* \\ &= S_0. \end{aligned} \tag{8}$$

The solution of equation (8) for $P_0^*$ requires the use of an appropriate option-pricing framework, which we present next. Since the payoffs on these call options depend upon the outcomes of the two random variables $\tilde{r}_i$ and $\tilde{L}$, our analysis requires the valuation of options with stochastic exercise prices.

## II. Implicit Solutions for the Fair Rate of Return

In this section of the paper, we present two special cases of the previous section's more general formulation. Specifically, we derive pricing relationships based

[5] Since we only consider corporate income taxation, the riskless rate of interest is simply the before-tax rate of interest on riskless bonds (e.g., T-bills). However, in the presence of personal and corporate taxes, it is not entirely clear whether the riskless rate of interest is the before-tax rate of interest on riskless bonds or the certainty-equivalent municipal bond rate. If investors are able to "launder" all of their personal taxes *a la* Miller and Scholes [20], then $r_f$ will continue to be defined as the before-tax rate of interest on riskless bonds. However, if investors are not able to launder taxes on investment income, then the certainty-equivalent municipal bond rate is the appropriate rate. For a lucid discussion of these points, see Hamada and Scholes [14].

upon the discrete-time, risk-neutral-valuation framework pioneered by Rubin-stein [25]. In both cases, we make use of Rubinstein's [24] representative investor device; viz., we assume that the conditions for aggregation are met so that securities are priced *as if* all investors have the same characteristics as a representative investor. In addition to the aggregation assumption, we shall assume for the first model that a) the wealth of the representative investor, the rate of return on the insurer's asset portfolio, and the aggregate value of the insurer's claims costs are jointly normally distributed and b) the utility function of the representative investor exhibits constant absolute risk aversion (CARA). The derivation of the second model similarly requires the use of the representative investor device but replaces the distributional and preference assumptions with joint lognormality and constant relative risk aversion (CRRA). Brennan [4] has shown that CARA (CRRA) is a necessary and sufficient condition for pricing *bivariate* contingent claims in discrete time when the price of the underlying asset is normally (lognormally) distributed, while Stapleton and Subrahmanyam [29] have shown that the Brennan results can also be extended to the pricing of *multivariate* contingent claims such as are being considered here.

Although we could have chosen alternative sets of distributional assumptions, we find it convenient to work with joint-normal and lognormal variates for two reasons. The primary advantage of assuming joint normality is that we are able to derive models of insurance pricing that are directly comparable to the existing set of CAPM's and APT-based models. Thus, when we perform our simulation experiments, we are able to determine the relative importance of default risk and tax-shield redundancy in the determination of "fair" insurance prices. As we stated earlier, such effects typically have not been addressed in the CAPM's and APT-based models. Unfortunately, the assumption that investors' utility functions exhibit constant absolute risk aversion is rather restrictive.[6] Furthermore, actual claims-cost distributions are probably better described by skewed proba-bility distributions such as the lognormal than by symmetric probability distri-butions such as the normal. In view of these considerations, we also offer a model of insurance pricing based upon joint lognormality and constant relative risk aversion.

## A. Case 1: Joint Normality and Constant Absolute Risk Aversion

Before we value the two call options described in the previous section, we will first determine the level of premium income $P_0$ and rate of return on underwriting $E(\tilde{r}_u)$ that would obtain in a competitive, default-free setting in which all tax shields are fully utilized. Under our joint normal and CARA assumptions, we can express the value of equity as the discounted value of the certainty-equivalent

---

[6] In a study of Federal Reserve data on consumer financial characteristics, Friend and Blume [10] discovered that the percentage of wealth typically invested in risky assets remains virtually unchanged over very different wealth levels. This finding implies that consumers' utility functions exhibit constant relative risk aversion and, consequently, decreasing absolute risk aversion. The same authors [11] also used IRS data to replicate portfolios with power utility functions. As in the study using Fed data, the empirics in the IRS study suggest that the typical investor's utility function exhibits decreasing absolute risk aversion and constant relative risk aversion.

terminal cash flow, viz.,

$$V_e = R_f^{-1} \int_{-\infty}^{\infty} \tilde{Y}_e \hat{f}(\tilde{Y}_e)\, d\tilde{Y}_e$$

$$= R_f^{-1} \hat{E}(\tilde{Y}_e), \tag{9}$$

where

$\tilde{Y}_e$ = random cash flow accruing to shareholders at the end of the period;
$\hat{f}(\tilde{Y}_e)$ = "risk-neutral" normal density function;[7]
$\hat{E}(\tilde{Y}_e)$ = the certainty-equivalent expectation of $\tilde{Y}_e$
$\quad = E(\tilde{Y}_e) - \lambda \operatorname{cov}(\tilde{Y}_e, \tilde{r}_m)$;
$\lambda$ = the market price of risk
$\quad = [E(\tilde{r}_m) - r_f]/\sigma_m^2$;
$\operatorname{cov}(\cdot)$ = the covariance operator.

The certainty-equivalent expectation of terminal cash flow accruing to shareholders, $\hat{E}(\tilde{Y}_e)$, is given by equation (10):

$$\hat{E}(\tilde{Y}_e) = S_0 + (1 - \theta\tau)\hat{E}(\tilde{r}_i)(S_0 + kP_0) + (1 - \tau)(P_0 - \hat{E}(\tilde{L})), \tag{10}$$

where

$\hat{E}(\tilde{r}_i)$ = the certainty-equivalent expectation of rate of return on the insurer's investment portfolio
$\quad = E(\tilde{r}_i) - \lambda \operatorname{cov}(\tilde{r}_i, \tilde{r}_m) = r_f$;
$\hat{E}(\tilde{L})$ = certainty-equivalent expectation of total claims costs
$\quad = E(\tilde{L}) - \lambda \operatorname{cov}(\tilde{L}, \tilde{r}_m).$[8]

By substituting the right-hand side of equation (10) into equation (9), setting $S_0$ equal to $V_e$, and simplifying, we derive the following analytic expressions for

---

[7] As shown by Brennan [4] and Stapleton and Subrahmanyam [29], a "risk-neutral" density function is a density function with the location parameter chosen so that the mean of the distribution is its certainty equivalent. In the case of a multivariate risk-neutral density function, the same result holds for the location parameters of the marginal distributions.

[8] In view of the problems associated with accurately estimating $\operatorname{cov}(\tilde{L}, \tilde{r}_m)$, an alternative expression for $\hat{E}(\tilde{L})$ can be derived by assuming that the relationship between $\tilde{L}$ and $\tilde{r}_m$ can be adequately accounted for by the common relationship $\tilde{L}$ has with $\tilde{r}_m$ via its relationship to $\tilde{r}_i$, viz.,

$$\operatorname{cov}(\tilde{L}, \tilde{r}_m) = \frac{\operatorname{cov}(\tilde{L}, \tilde{r}_i)\sigma_m^2}{\operatorname{cov}(\tilde{r}_i, \tilde{r}_m)}$$

$$= \frac{1}{\beta_i} \operatorname{cov}(\tilde{L}, \tilde{r}_i).$$

Substituting the right-hand side of the above expression into our expression for $\hat{E}(\tilde{L})$ yields

$$\hat{E}(\tilde{L}) = E(\tilde{L}) - \frac{\lambda}{\beta_i} \operatorname{cov}(\tilde{L}, \tilde{r}_i).$$

We make use of these results later in Section III of the paper when we perform numerical simulations of our models.

premium income and the rate of return on underwriting:

$$P_0 = \frac{E(\tilde{L})}{(1 - E(\tilde{r}_u))},$$ (11)

where

$$E(\tilde{r}_u) = [P_0 - E(\tilde{L})]/P_0$$

$$= -\frac{(1 - \theta\tau)}{(1 - \tau)} kr_f + (V_e/P_0) \frac{\theta\tau}{(1 - \tau)} r_f + \lambda \operatorname{cov}(\tilde{r}_u, \tilde{r}_m).$$ (11a)

Hill and Modigliani derive a comparable expression for $E(\tilde{r}_u)$ using the Sharpe-Lintner-Mossin CAPM, and a similar relationship is derived by Fairley.

Next, we value the call options described in equation (7). The value of the first call option, $C_1$, may be written as the discounted certainty-equivalent expectation of the terminal before-tax value of equity, viz.,

$$C_1 = C[\tilde{Y}_1; \tilde{L}]$$

$$= R_f^{-1} \int_{-\infty}^{\infty} \int_{-\infty}^{\infty} \max[(\tilde{Y}_1 - \tilde{L}), 0] \hat{f}(\tilde{Y}_1, \tilde{L}) \, d\tilde{Y}_1 \, d\tilde{L},$$ (12)

where $\hat{f}(\tilde{Y}_1, \tilde{L})$ is the bivariate risk-neutral density function governing the realization of the normal variates $\tilde{Y}_1$ and $\tilde{L}$. Examining equation (12), it is obvious that, if the terminal before-tax value of equity is positive, shareholders will own a valuable claim. However, if equity assumes a negative value, shareholders will exercise their "limited-liability option" by declaring bankruptcy.

Next, we simplify equation (12) by defining a normal variate $\tilde{X} = \tilde{Y}_1 - \tilde{L}$, with certainty-equivalent expectation $\hat{E}(\tilde{X}) = \hat{E}(\tilde{Y}_1) - \hat{E}(\tilde{L}) = S_0 + (S_0 + kP_0)r_f + P_0 - \hat{E}(\tilde{L})$, and variance $\sigma_x^2 = (S_0 + kP_0)^2\sigma_i^2 + \sigma_L^2 - 2(S_0 + kP_0)\operatorname{cov}(\tilde{L}, \tilde{r}_i)$. This transformation allows us to rewrite our option value as the solution to

$$C_1 = R_f^{-1} \int_0^{\infty} \tilde{X}\hat{f}(\tilde{X}) \, d\tilde{X}.$$ (13)

Since $\tilde{X}$ is normally distributed, equation (13) may be rewritten in terms of the standard normal variate $\tilde{z} = (\tilde{X} - \hat{E}(\tilde{X}))/\sigma_x$; hence,

$$C_1 = R_f^{-1}(2\pi)^{-1/2} \int_{-\hat{E}(\tilde{X})/\sigma_x}^{\infty} [\hat{E}(\tilde{X}) + \sigma_x\tilde{z}]e^{-\tilde{z}^2/2} \, d\tilde{z}.$$ (14)

Using the properties of the truncated normal distribution and of the standard normal variate, together with the expressions for $\hat{E}(\tilde{X})$ and $\sigma_x$, the value of the call can be written in the following form:

$$C_1 = R_f^{-1}(\hat{E}(\tilde{X})N[\hat{E}(\tilde{X})/\sigma_x] + \sigma_x n[\hat{E}(\tilde{X})/\sigma_x]),$$ (15)

where

$N[\hat{E}(\tilde{X})/\sigma_x]$ = the standard normal distribution evaluated at $\hat{E}(\tilde{X})/\sigma_x$;[9]
$n[\hat{E}(\tilde{X})/\sigma_x]$ = the standard normal density evaluated at $\hat{E}(\tilde{X})/\sigma_x$.

The value of the second call option, $C_2$, may be written as the discounted certainty-equivalent expectation of the insurer's terminal taxable income, viz.,

$$C_2 = C[\theta(\tilde{Y}_1 - Y_0) + P_0; \tilde{L}]$$

$$= R_f^{-1} \int_{-\infty}^{\infty} \int_{-\infty}^{\infty} \max[\theta(\tilde{Y}_1 - Y_0) + P_0 - \tilde{L}, 0] \hat{f}(\tilde{Y}_1, \tilde{L}) \, d\tilde{Y}_1 \, d\tilde{L}. \quad (16)$$

Examining equation (16), it is obvious that, if the terminal value of taxable income is positive, the government will own a valuable claim. However, if taxable income assumes a negative value, shareholders will exercise their "tax-exemption option." Thus, our model allows certain states of nature to arise in which shareholders' claims are less valuable due to the redundancy of tax shields related to the realization of investment losses, underwriting losses, or both.

Next, we simplify equation (16) by defining a normal variate $W = \theta(Y_1 - Y_0) + P_0 - \tilde{L}$, with certainty-equivalent expectation $\hat{E}(\tilde{W}) = \theta(S_0 + kP_0)r_f + P_0 - \hat{E}(\tilde{L})$, and variance $\sigma_w^2 = (S_0 + kP_0)^2\theta^2\sigma_i^2 + \sigma_L^2 - 2(S_0 + kP_0)\theta \, \text{cov}(\tilde{L}, \tilde{r}_i)$. This transformation allows us to rewrite our option value as the solution to

$$C_2 = R_f^{-1} \int_0^{\infty} \tilde{W}\hat{f}(\tilde{W}) \, d\tilde{W}. \quad (17)$$

Using identical analysis to that shown above, the value of the second call option is derived as

$$C_2 = R_f^{-1}(\hat{E}(\tilde{W})N[\hat{E}(\tilde{W})/\sigma_w] + \sigma_w n[\hat{E}(\tilde{W})/\sigma_w]), \quad (18)$$

where

$N[\hat{E}(\tilde{W})/\sigma_w]$ = the standard normal distribution evaluated at $\hat{E}(\tilde{W})/\sigma_w$;[10]
$n[\hat{E}(\tilde{W})/\sigma_w]$ = the standard normal density evaluated at $\hat{E}(\tilde{W})/\sigma_w$.

Substituting the right-hand sides of equations (15) and (18) into equation (7), we obtain an analytic expression for the market value of equity:

$$V_e = R_f^{-1}(\hat{E}(\tilde{X})N[\hat{E}(\tilde{X})/\sigma_x] - \tau\hat{E}(\tilde{W})N[\hat{E}(\tilde{W})/\sigma_w]$$

$$+ \sigma_x n[\hat{E}(\tilde{X})/\sigma_x] - \tau\sigma_w n[\hat{E}(\tilde{W})/\sigma_w]). \quad (19)$$

[9] The term $N[\hat{E}(\tilde{X})/\sigma_x]$ may be interpreted as the pretax certainty-equivalent terminal value of one dollar invested in the firm, provided the firm remains solvent. Because $N[\hat{E}(\tilde{X})/\sigma_x]$ is in effect a "risk-neutral" cumulative distribution function, it understates the solvency probability by the amount of risk-bearing costs borne per dollar of income generated in solvent states of nature, viz., by the difference $N[E(\tilde{X})/\sigma_x] - N[\hat{E}(\tilde{X})/\sigma_x]$.

[10] The term $N[\hat{E}(\tilde{W})/\sigma_w]$ may be interpreted as the certainty-equivalent terminal value of one dollar of taxable income, provided that tax shields are fully utilized. Because $N[\hat{E}(\tilde{W})/\sigma_w]$ is in effect a "risk-neutral" cumulative distribution function, it understates the probability of taxation by the amount of risk-bearing costs borne per dollar of taxable income generated in taxable states of nature, viz., by the difference $N[E(\tilde{W})/\sigma_w] - N[\hat{E}(\tilde{W})/\sigma_w]$.

An implicit solution for the value of $P_0^*$ that satisfies the fair-return criterion implied by equation (8) may be obtained by employing an appropriate algorithm.

### B. Case 2: Joint Lognormality and Constant Relative Risk Aversion

Next, we consider the valuation of the options described in equation (7) under the joint lognormal and CRRA assumptions. As in the joint-normal-with-CARA case, we will first determine the level of premium income and rate of return on underwriting that would obtain in a competitive, default-free setting in which all tax shields are fully utilized. As shown by Rubinstein [25], the equilibrium price of the $j$th risky security that trades in a discrete-time lognormal securities market, $V_0^j$, must obey the following pricing relationship:

$$V_0^j = R_f^{-1}\hat{E}(\tilde{Y}_1^j)$$

$$= R_f^{-1}E(\tilde{Y}_1^j)\exp\{-\psi \; \text{cov}[\ln \tilde{R}_j, \ln \tilde{R}_m]\}, \tag{20}$$

where

$\tilde{Y}_1^j$ = end-of-period cash flow paid to the holder of security $j$;
$\psi$ = the representative investor's relative risk aversion parameter
$= \dfrac{E(\ln \tilde{R}_m) - \ln R_f}{\text{var}(\ln \tilde{R}_m)} + \dfrac{1}{2}$;
$\tilde{R}_j = 1 + \tilde{r}_j$;
$\tilde{R}_m = 1 + \tilde{r}_m$.

Equation (20) allows us to specify the relationship between the certainty-equivalent expectation of the insurance firm's claims costs, $\hat{E}(\tilde{L})$, and the expected value of claims costs, $E(\tilde{L})$, as follows:

$$\hat{E}(\tilde{L}) = E(\tilde{L})\exp\{-\psi \; \text{cov}[\ln \tilde{L}, \ln \tilde{R}_m]\}. \tag{21}$$

Next, we incorporate equation (21) into our derivation of an analytic expression for premium income and the competitive rate of return on underwriting in a default-free setting in which all tax shields are fully utilized. By substituting the right-hand side of equation (10) into equation (9), setting $S_0$ equal to $V_e$, and simplifying, we derive the following expressions:

$$P_0 = \frac{E(\tilde{L})}{(1 - E(\tilde{r}_u))}, \tag{22}$$

where

$$E(\tilde{r}_u) = 1 - \left(1 + \frac{(1 - \theta\tau)}{(1 - \tau)} kr_f - (V_e/P_0) \frac{\theta\tau}{(1 - \tau)} r_f\right)\exp\{\psi \; \text{cov}[\ln \tilde{L}, \ln \tilde{R}_m]\}. \tag{22a}$$

Next, we value the call options described in equation (7). The value of the first call option, $C_1$, may be written as

$$C_1 = C[\tilde{Y}_1; \tilde{L}]$$

$$= R_f^{-1} \int_0^\infty \int_0^\infty \max[(\tilde{Y}_1 - \tilde{L}), 0]\hat{g}(\tilde{Y}_1, \tilde{L}) \; d\tilde{Y}_1 \; d\tilde{L}, \tag{23}$$

where $\hat{g}(\tilde{Y}_1, \tilde{L})$ is defined as the bivariate risk-neutral density function governing the realization of the *lognormal* variates $\tilde{Y}_1$ and $\tilde{L}$. By defining a new random variable $\tilde{U} = \tilde{Y}_1 - \tilde{L} + P_0$, we can rewrite equation (23) as

$$C_1 = R_f^{-1} \int_{P_0}^{\infty} (\tilde{U} - P_0)\hat{g}(\tilde{U}) \, d\tilde{U}, \tag{24}$$

where $\tilde{U}$ is a lognormal variate with risk-neutral density $\hat{g}(\tilde{U})$.[11]

Changing the random variable $\tilde{U}$ to the standardized normal variate $\tilde{z}$ and simplifying yield

$$C_1 = V_0^U \int_{-d_2}^{\infty} (\sqrt{2\pi})^{-1} \exp\left(-\sigma_u^2 + \tilde{z}\sigma_u - \frac{1}{2}\,\tilde{z}^2\right) d\tilde{z}$$

$$- R_f^{-1} P_0 \int_{-d_2}^{\infty} (\sqrt{2\pi})^{-1} \exp\left(-\frac{1}{2}\,\tilde{z}^2\right) d\tilde{z}, \tag{25}$$

where

$V_0^U$ = the contemporaneous value of the claim $\tilde{U}$
$\quad = V_0^Y - V_0^L + R_f^{-1} P_0 = S_0 + R_f^{-1} P_0 (2 + kr_f) - V_0^L;$
$V_0^L = R_f^{-1} \hat{E}(L)$
$\quad = R_f^{-1} E(\tilde{L}) \exp\{-\psi \operatorname{cov}[\ln \tilde{L}, \ln \tilde{R}_m]\};$
$d_1^U = \dfrac{\ln(V_0^U/P_0) + \ln R_f + \sigma_u^2/2}{\sigma_u};$
$d_2^U = d_1^U - \sigma_u;$
$\sigma_u$ = the standard deviation of the natural logarithm of $\tilde{U}$
$\quad = [\sigma_y^2 + \sigma_1^2 - 2 \operatorname{cov}(\ln \tilde{Y}, \ln \tilde{L})]^{1/2};$
$\sigma_y$ = the standard deviation of the natural logarithm of $\tilde{Y}_1;$
$\sigma_1$ = the standard deviation of the natural logarithm of $\tilde{L}$.

Rewriting equation (25) in terms of cumulative standard normal distribution functions yields an expression that is analogous to the familiar Black-Scholes call-option formula:

$$C_1 = V_0^U N(d_1^U) - R_f^{-1} P_0 N(d_2^U), \tag{26}$$

where $N(d_i^U)$ is the standard normal distribution function evaluated at $d_i^U$.[12]

Next, we consider the valuation of the tax claim, $C_2$. The value of this option may be written as the discounted certainty-equivalent expectation of the insurer's

---

[11] The solution procedure used here follows that of Stapleton and Subrahmanyam [29, pp. 223–24]. The caveat that these authors suggest in footnote 19, p. 223, of their article applies here as well; viz., strictly speaking, lognormal variates do not sum to a lognormal variate in a discrete-time setting. However, as these authors have suggested and Samuelson [26, p. 556] has rigorously proven, this would be an entirely valid operation in a continuous-time Black-Scholes-type model. If the reader regards this approximation as inappropriate, the integration can be carried out over the joint distribution of $\tilde{Y}_1$ and $\tilde{L}$ via numerical techniques.

[12] The term $N(d_2^U)$ may be given the same interpretation as the $N[\hat{E}(\tilde{X})/\sigma_x]$ term from equation (15); viz., this term represents the pretax certainty-equivalent terminal value of one dollar invested in the firm, provided the firm remains solvent.

**Table I**

Model Parameterization: The Base Case

| | |
|---|---|
| Initial Equity ($S_0$) | 100.00 |
| Funds-Generating Coefficient (k) | 1.00 |
| Standard Deviation of Investment Returns ($\sigma_i$) | 0.20 |
| Expected Claims Costs ($E(\tilde{L})$) | 200.00 |
| Standard Deviation of Claims Costs ($\sigma_L$) | 50.00 |
| Correlation Between Investment Returns/Claims Costs ($\rho_{iL}$) | 0.00 |
| Riskless Rate of Interest ($r_f$) | 0.07 |
| Statutory Tax Rate ($\tau$) | 0.46 |
| Tax-Adjustment Parameter ($\theta$) | 0.50 |
| Beta of Investment Portfolio ($\beta_i$) | 0.338 |
| Expected Return on the Market ($E(\tilde{r}_m)$) | 0.15 |
| Standard Deviation of Market Return ($\sigma_m$) | 0.224 |

terminal taxable income, viz.,

$$C_2 = C[\theta(\tilde{Y}_1 - Y_0) + P_0; \tilde{L}]$$

$$= R_f^{-1} \int_0^\infty \int_0^\infty \max[\theta(\tilde{Y}_1 - Y_0) + P_0 - \tilde{L}, 0]\hat{g}(\tilde{Y}_1, \tilde{L})\, d\tilde{Y}_1\, d\tilde{L}. \quad (27)$$

By defining a new random variable $\tilde{T} = \theta(\tilde{Y}_1 - Y_0) + 2P_0 - \tilde{L}$, we can rewrite equation (27) as

$$C_2 = R_f^{-1} \int_{P_0}^\infty (\tilde{T} - P_0)\hat{g}(\tilde{T})\, d\tilde{T}. \quad (28)$$

Using analysis identical to that shown above, the value of the second call option is derived as[13]

$$C_2 = V_0^T N(d_1^T) - R_f^{-1} P_0 N(d_2^T), \quad (29)$$

where

$V_0^T =$ the contemporaneous value of the claim $\tilde{T}$
$= R_f^{-1}[\theta(S_0 + kP_0)r_f + 2P_0)] - V_0^L$;
$d_1^T = \dfrac{\ln(V_0^T/P_0) + \ln R_f + \sigma_t^2/2}{\sigma_t}$;

$d_2^T = d_1^T - \sigma_t$;
$\sigma_t =$ the standard deviation of the natural logarithm of $\tilde{T}$
$= [\sigma_{\theta\Delta y}^2 + \sigma_1^2 - 2\,\text{cov}(\ln[\theta(\tilde{Y}_1 - Y_0)], \ln \tilde{L})]^{1/2}$;
$\sigma_{\theta\Delta y} =$ the standard deviation of the natural logarithm of $\theta(\tilde{Y}_1 - Y_0)$.

Substituting the right-hand sides of equations (26) and (29) into equation (7), we obtain an analytic expression for the market value of equity:

$$V_e = V_0^U N(d_1^U) - \tau V_0^T N(d_1^T) - R_f^{-1} P_0(N(d_2^U) - \tau N(d_2^T)). \quad (30)$$

---

[13] The term $N(d_2^T)$ that appears in equation (29) may be given the same interpretation as the $N[\hat{E}(\tilde{W})/\sigma_w]$ term from equation (18); viz., this term represents the certainty-equivalent terminal value of one dollar of taxable income, provided that tax shields are fully utilized.

## Table II

### Effects of Variations in Model Parameters upon the Equilibrium Rate of Return on Underwriting

#### Panel A: Effects of Variations in Initial Equity ($S_0$)

| $S_0$ | CAPM | OPM (Normal) | | | OPM (Lognormal) | | |
|---|---|---|---|---|---|---|---|
| | $E(\tilde{r}_u)$ | $E(\tilde{r}_u)$ | P(default) | P(no tax) | $E(\tilde{r}_u)$ | P(default) | P(no tax) |
| 25.00 | −0.0957 | −0.1444 | 0.3824 | 0.6135 | −0.1249 | 0.4088 | 0.6438 |
| 50.00 | −0.0917 | −0.0659 | 0.1895 | 0.5060 | −0.0636 | 0.2213 | 0.5452 |
| 75.00 | −0.0877 | −0.0347 | 0.0992 | 0.4558 | −0.0355 | 0.1254 | 0.4998 |
| 100.00 | −0.0837 | −0.0188 | 0.0534 | 0.4271 | −0.0199 | 0.0718 | 0.4744 |
| 150.00 | −0.0758 | −0.0028 | 0.0164 | 0.3941 | −0.0034 | 0.0236 | 0.4473 |
| 200.00 | −0.0680 | 0.0065 | 0.0055 | 0.3730 | 0.0061 | 0.0077 | 0.4318 |

#### Panel B: Effects of Variations in the Funds Generating Coefficient (k)

| k | CAPM | OPM (Normal) | | | OPM (Lognormal) | | |
|---|---|---|---|---|---|---|---|
| | $E(\tilde{r}_u)$ | $E(\tilde{r}_u)$ | P(default) | P(no tax) | $E(\tilde{r}_u)$ | P(default) | P(no tax) |
| 0.50 | −0.0345 | 0.0240 | 0.0264 | 0.3922 | −0.0216 | 0.0532 | 0.4310 |
| 1.00 | −0.0837 | −0.0188 | 0.0534 | 0.4271 | −0.0199 | 0.0718 | 0.4744 |
| 2.00 | −0.1820 | −0.1205 | 0.1192 | 0.4961 | −0.1037 | 0.1161 | 0.5526 |
| 3.00 | −0.2804 | −0.2401 | 0.1766 | 0.5538 | −0.1883 | 0.1571 | 0.6154 |
| 4.00 | −0.3787 | −0.3710 | 0.2204 | 0.5977 | −0.2726 | 0.1905 | 0.6653 |
| 5.00 | −0.4771 | −0.5086 | 0.2534 | 0.6306 | −0.3561 | 0.2164 | 0.7060 |
| 6.00 | −0.5754 | −0.6504 | 0.2786 | 0.6555 | −0.4387 | 0.2365 | 0.7403 |

#### Panel C: Effects of Variations in the Standard Deviation of Investment Returns ($\sigma_i$)

| $\sigma_i$ | CAPM | OPM (Normal) | | | OPM (Lognormal) | | |
|---|---|---|---|---|---|---|---|
| | $E(\tilde{r}_u)$ | $E(\tilde{r}_u)$ | P(default) | P(no tax) | $E(\tilde{r}_u)$ | P(default) | P(no tax) |
| 0.00 | −0.0837 | −0.0150 | 0.0059 | 0.4094 | −0.0196 | 0.0300 | 0.4543 |
| 0.20 | −0.0837 | −0.0188 | 0.0534 | 0.4271 | −0.0199 | 0.0718 | 0.4744 |
| 0.40 | −0.0837 | −0.0730 | 0.1805 | 0.4985 | −0.0364 | 0.1789 | 0.5283 |
| 0.60 | −0.0837 | −0.1867 | 0.2875 | 0.5771 | −0.0718 | 0.2882 | 0.5884 |

Panel D: Effects of Variations in the Standard Deviation of Claims Cost ($\sigma_L$)

| | CAPM | OPM (Normal) | | | OPM (Lognormal) | | |
|---|---|---|---|---|---|---|---|
| $\sigma_L$ | $E(\tilde{r}_u)$ | $E(\tilde{r}_u)$ | P(default) | P(no tax) | $E(\tilde{r}_u)$ | P(default) | P(no tax) |
| 25.00 | −0.0837 | −0.0336 | 0.0280 | 0.4205 | −0.0319 | 0.0169 | 0.4382 |
| 50.00 | −0.0837 | −0.0188 | 0.0534 | 0.4271 | −0.0199 | 0.0718 | 0.4744 |
| 75.00 | −0.0837 | −0.0099 | 0.0925 | 0.4384 | −0.0219 | 0.1555 | 0.5197 |
| 100.00 | −0.0837 | −0.0103 | 0.1379 | 0.4526 | −0.0372 | 0.2381 | 0.5643 |
| 150.00 | −0.0837 | −0.0411 | 0.2272 | 0.4836 | −0.0875 | 0.3677 | 0.6382 |
| 200.00 | −0.0837 | −0.1140 | 0.3038 | 0.5136 | −0.1435 | 0.4563 | 0.6920 |

Panel E: Effects of Variations in the Riskless Rate of Interest ($r_f$)

| | CAPM | OPM (Normal) | | | OPM (Lognormal) | | |
|---|---|---|---|---|---|---|---|
| $r_f$ | $E(\tilde{r}_u)$ | $E(\tilde{r}_u)$ | P(default) | P(no tax) | $E(\tilde{r}_u)$ | P(default) | P(no tax) |
| 0.05 | −0.0600 | 0.0005 | 0.0490 | 0.4007 | 0.0004 | 0.0692 | 0.4410 |
| 0.07 | −0.0837 | −0.0188 | 0.0534 | 0.4271 | −0.0199 | 0.0718 | 0.4744 |
| 0.09 | −0.1071 | −0.0381 | 0.0579 | 0.4529 | −0.0402 | 0.0743 | 0.5071 |
| 0.11 | −0.1304 | −0.0574 | 0.0626 | 0.4781 | −0.0605 | 0.0767 | 0.5390 |
| 0.13 | −0.1534 | −0.0767 | 0.0675 | 0.5026 | −0.0808 | 0.0789 | 0.5698 |

Panel F: Effects of Variations in the Tax Parameter Theta ($\theta$)

| | CAPM | OPM (Normal) | | | OPM (Lognormal) | | |
|---|---|---|---|---|---|---|---|
| $\theta$ | $E(\tilde{r}_u)$ | $E(\tilde{r}_u)$ | P(default) | P(no tax) | $E(\tilde{r}_u)$ | P(default) | P(no tax) |
| 0.00 | −0.1130 | −0.0446 | 0.0595 | 0.5678 | −0.0470 | 0.0755 | 0.5847 |
| 0.20 | −0.1013 | −0.0372 | 0.0577 | 0.5115 | −0.0389 | 0.0744 | 0.5377 |
| 0.40 | −0.0895 | −0.0258 | 0.0550 | 0.4538 | −0.0270 | 0.0728 | 0.4936 |
| 0.50 | −0.0837 | −0.0188 | 0.0534 | 0.4271 | −0.0199 | 0.0718 | 0.4744 |
| 0.60 | −0.0778 | −0.0110 | 0.0516 | 0.4026 | −0.0122 | 0.0708 | 0.4574 |
| 0.80 | −0.0660 | 0.0063 | 0.0478 | 0.3612 | 0.0044 | 0.0687 | 0.4296 |
| 1.00 | −0.0543 | 0.0255 | 0.0437 | 0.3294 | 0.0222 | 0.0665 | 0.4088 |

## PANEL A: VARY LEVEL OF INITIAL EQUITY

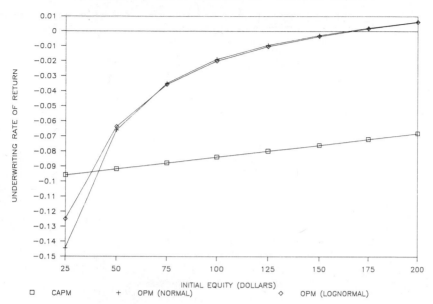

## PANEL B: VARY FUNDS GENERATING COEFF

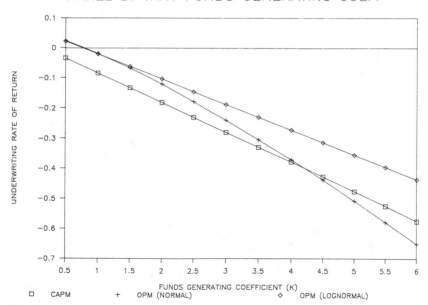

**Figure 1.** Plots of the Effects of Changes in Model Parameters upon the Equilibrium Rate of Return on Underwriting for a Property-Liability Insurer

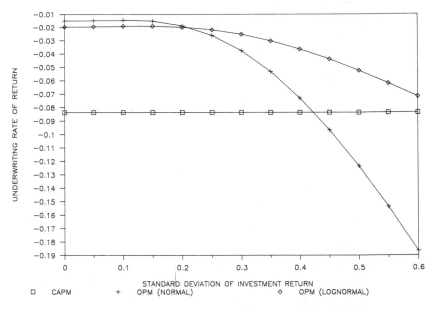

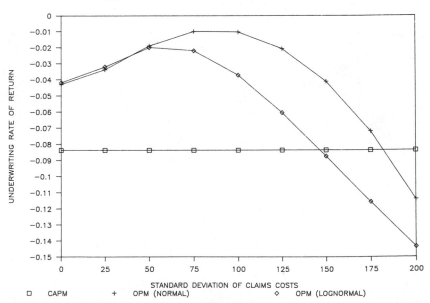

**Figure 1 (cont.).** Plots of the Effects of Changes in Model Parameters upon the Equilibrium Rate of Return on Underwriting for a Property-Liability Insurer.

## PANEL E: VARY RISKLESS RATE OF INTEREST

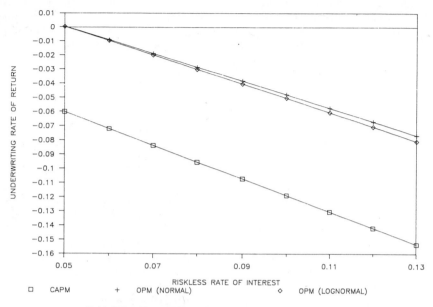

## PANEL F: VARY TAX PARAMETER THETA

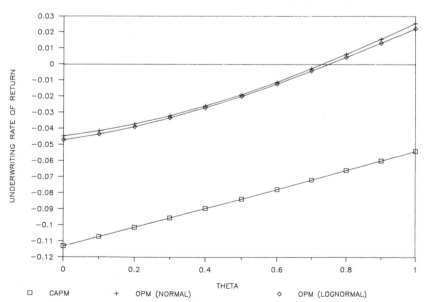

**Figure 1 (cont.).** Plots of the Effects of Changes in Model Parameters upon the Equilibrium Rate of Return on Underwriting for a Property-Liability Insurer.

An implicit solution for the value of $P_0^*$ that satisfies the fair-return criterion implied by equation (8) may be obtained by employing an appropriate algorithm. Furthermore, the implicit solution $P_0^*$ obtained from equations (19) and (30) may be translated into fair underwriting profit rates $E(\tilde{r}_u^*)$ by the routine solution of

$$E(\tilde{r}_u^*) = \frac{P_0^* - E(\tilde{L})}{P_0^*}. \tag{31}$$

### III. A Numerical Illustration

In this section we provide a numerical illustration that provides points of comparison between the alternative option-based models developed here and the regulatory CAPM. The option-based models were solved iteratively from equations (19) and (30), whereas the normal and lognormal CAPM's were solved from equations (11a) and (22a) after substituting for $P_0$ from equations (11) and (22).[14] The solutions were derived from a set of parameters presented in Table I that are intended as a crude representation of a short-tail (i.e., short settlement period for losses) line of property-liability business. Table II and Figure 1 show the rates of underwriting profit required to deliver a competitive rate of return on equity over different ranges of values for the model parameters. Furthermore, we also show the implied probabilities of insolvency and tax-shield redundancy for the option-based models in Table II.

The points of interest include the following. In general, the option-based models provide higher rates of underwriting profit than the CAPM. The most useful comparison is between the normal CAPM results and those produced under the joint-normal-with-CARA option-pricing model. Since the distributional assumptions are comparable, the differences in fair underwriting profit are explained by the attention paid in our option-pricing model to the probabilities of insolvency and redundant tax shields. Another point of interest is between the insolvency and tax shield redundancy probabilities produced by the two option models. It is well known in the actuarial literature that estimates of the probability mass in the extreme tail of a fitted distribution are highly sensitive to the function form used, a fact borne out by our simulation results. Both normal and lognormal density functions have been used to describe the insurer's aggregate loss distribution (cf. Cummins and Nye [6]), as well as other distributions. Since the probabilities of insolvency and tax-shield redundancy are at issue, some prudent curve fitting should influence the choice of regulatory model.

### IV. Conclusion

We have developed a contingent-claim model for estimating the fair rate of return for the property-liability insurance firm. This model offers an alternative regulatory device to the CAPM's and APT-based models. Such an alternative is

---

[14] Since the results obtained with the lognormal CAPM do not differ materially from the results obtained with the normal CAPM, only the latter model's results are presented here.

considered to be useful in light of the unsettled academic score regarding the appropriate asset-pricing paradigm. Moreover, the proposed option model addresses the ruin probability of the insurer as well as the nonlinear effects of corporate taxation.

Our model specifically applies to the property-liability insurance firm. The features of this particular institution that lend it to an option-pricing application are that its output is a contingent financial claim and that this claim is written on an underlying asset for which a reasonable market value can be provided. With the possible exception of deposit banking, such conditions do not necessarily prevail in other regulated industries.

We will conclude with some qualifying comments on the use of option-based models for insurance price regulation. The first concerns tax nonlinearities. Previous models either ignore taxes (e.g., Kraus and Ross) or assume that the corporate income tax is strictly proportional to corporate income. In effect, the proportional-tax assumption implies that unused tax shields can be sold or carried back and forward at their face value. In contrast, our model makes the opposite assumption that unused tax shields expire worthless. Perhaps a more accurate assumption would be that unused tax shields can be sold or carried back and forward at somewhat less than their face value. Thus, the tax function would still be nonlinear but not as concave as supposed here. While we have not addressed the intermediate approach, it clearly lends itself to the option-modeling techniques developed here.[15] Another problem is that it is not clear from current regulatory practices just how unused tax shields should be treated. This uncertainty gives some advantage to the present model since it is possible to generate a proportional tax as a special case by simply assuming that the probability of tax-shield redundancy is negligible.

A second qualification concerns the application of the regulatory model to individual lines of business. Like most other regulatory models, it is designed to solve the fair return for the firm as though it offered a single line of insurance. The problem in providing simultaneous solutions for multiple lines is that insurers hold common equity and assets and incur common expenses over several lines of business. Thus, the firm, and not the line of business, is valued by the market. In practice, some arbitrary allocations can be made across lines to produce answers, and this indeed is what is usually done. However, the current use of option-pricing models hints at some problems of additivity; e.g., it is well known that an option on a portfolio does not have the same value as a portfolio of options. These issues are not addressed here. Therefore, like previous models, our approach strictly applies only for a single-line insurer.

---

[15] By using a single-period model, we have implicitly assumed away the possibility of the insurer making use of tax-loss carrybacks and carryforwards (CB-CF), which could be introduced in a multiperiod framework. Although we cannot provide a formal demonstration of the effects of CB-CF provisions on insurance pricing, the effects can nevertheless be inferred from our model. Since tax-shield redundancy effectively increases the burden of the corporate tax on the insurer, this burden will be passed on to policyholders via higher insurance prices and underwriting rates of return, *ceteris paribus*. However, since the effect of CB-CF provisions is to reduce this tax burden, their existence implies lower insurance prices and underwriting rates of return, *ceteris paribus*. The interested reader is referred to the recent paper by Majd and Myers [19], which numerically simulates the valuation effects of CB-CF provisions in a contingent-claims setting.

590

## REFERENCES

1. N. Biger and Y. Kahane. "Risk Considerations in Insurance Ratemaking." *Journal of Risk and Insurance* 45 (March 1978), 121–32.
2. F. Black and M. Scholes. "The Pricing of Options and Corporate Liabilities." *Journal of Political Economy* 81 (May–June 1973), 637–59.
3. D. H. Bower, R. S. Bower, and D. E. Logue. "Arbitrage Pricing Theory and Utility Stock Returns." *Journal of Finance* 39 (September 1984), 1041–54.
4. M. J. Brennan. "The Pricing of Contingent Claims in Discrete Time Models." *Journal of Finance* 34 (March 1979), 53–68.
5. J. D. Cummins and S. Harrington. "Property-Liability Insurance Rate Regulation: Estimation of Underwriting Betas Using Quarterly Profit Data." *Journal of Risk and Insurance* 52 (March 1985), 16–43.
6. J. D. Cummins and D. J. Nye. "The Stochastic Characteristics of Property-Liability Insurance Underwriting Profits." *Journal of Risk and Insurance* 48 (March 1980), 61–77.
7. P. J. Dhrymes, I. Friend, and N. B. Gultekin. "A Critical Reexamination of the Empirical Evidence on the Arbitrage Pricing Theory." *Journal of Finance* 39 (June 1984), 323–46.
8. P. H. Dybvig and S. A. Ross. "Yes, the APT is Testable." *Journal of Finance* 40 (September 1985), 1173–88.
9. W. Fairley. "Investment Income and Profit Margins in Property-Liability Insurance: Theory and Empirical Results." *Bell Journal of Economics* 10 (Spring 1979), 192–210.
10. I. Friend and M. Blume. "The Asset Structure of Invidual Portfolios and Some Implications for Utility Functions." *Journal of Finance* 30 (May 1975), 585–603.
11. I. Friend and M. Blume. "The Demand for Risky Assets." *American Economic Review* 65 (December 1975), 900–22.
12. D. Galai. "Corporate Income Taxes and the Valuation of Claims on the Corporation." Working Paper No. 9-83, Graduate School of Management, University of California, Los Angeles, 1983.
13. —— and R. W. Masulis. "The Option Pricing Model and the Risk Factor of Stock." *Journal of Financial Economics* 3 (January/March 1976), 53–81.
14. R. S. Hamada and M. S. Scholes. "Taxes and Corporate Financial Management." In Altman and Subrahmanyam (eds.), *Recent Advances in Corporate Finance.* Homewood, IL: Richard D. Irwin, 1985, 189–226.
15. R. Hill. "Profit Regulation in Property-Liability Insurance." *Bell Journal of Economics* 10 (Spring 1979), 172–91.
16. —— and F. Modigliani. "The Massachusetts Model of Profit Regulation in Non-Life Insurance: An Appraisal and Extensions." Presented at Massachusetts Automobile Insurance Rate Hearing, Boston, Massachusetts, 1981.
17. A. Kraus and S. A. Ross. "The Determination of Fair Profits for the Property-Liability Insurance Firm." *Journal of Finance* 37 (September 1982), 1015–28.
18. J. Lintner. "The Valuation of Risk Assets and the Selection of Risk Investments in Stock Portfolios and Capital Budgets." *Review of Economics and Statistics* 47 (February 1965), 13–37.
19. S. Majd and S. C. Myers. "Valuing the Government's Tax Claim on Risky Corporate Assets." NBER Working Paper Series, National Bureau of Economic Research, 1984.
20. M. Miller and M. Scholes. "Dividends and Taxes: Some Empirical Evidence." *Journal of Political Economy* 90 (December 1982), 1118–41.
21. J. Mossin. "Equilibrium in a Capital Asset Market." *Econometrica* 34 (October 1966), 768–83.
22. M. Reinganum. "Misspecification of Asset Pricing: Empirical Anomalies Based on Earnings Yields and Market Values." *Journal of Financial Economics* 9 (March 1981), 19–46.
23. R. Roll. "A Critique of the Asset Pricing Theory's Tests; Part I: On Past and Potential Testability of the Theory." *Journal of Financial Economics* 4 (March 1977), 129–76.
24. M. Rubinstein. "An Aggregation Theorem for Securities Markets." *Journal of Financial Economics* 1 (September 1974), 225–44.
25. ——. "The Valuation of Uncertain Income Streams and the Pricing of Options." *Bell Journal of Economics* 7 (Autumn 1976), 407–25.
26. P. Samuelson. *Foundations of Economic Analysis*, enlarged ed. Cambridge, MA: Harvard University Press, 1983.

27. J. Shanken. "The Arbitrage Pricing Theory: Is It Testable?" *Journal of Finance* 37 (December 1982), 1129–40.
28. W. F. Sharpe. "Capital Asset Prices: A Theory of Market Equilibrium Under Conditions of Risk." *Journal of Finance* 19 (September 1964), 425–42.
29. R. C. Stapleton and M. G. Subrahmanyam. "The Valuation of Multivariate Contingent Claims in Discrete Time Models." *Journal of Finance* 39 (March 1984), 207–28.
30. J. Urritia. "An Arbitrage Pricing Theory Model for Pricing Property-Liability Insurance." Presented at the 1984 Conference of the American Risk and Insurance Association, 1984.

# Risk-Based Premiums for Insurance Guaranty Funds

J. DAVID CUMMINS*

## ABSTRACT

Insurance guaranty funds have been adopted in all states to compensate policyholders for losses resulting from insurance company insolvencies. The guaranty funds charge flat premium rates, usually a percentage of premiums. Flat premiums can induce insurers to adopt high-risk strategies, a problem that can be avoided through the use of risk-based premiums. This article develops risk-based premium formulas for three cases: a) an ongoing insurer with stochastic assets and liabilities, b) an ongoing insurer also subject to jumps in liabilities (catastrophes), and c) a policy cohort, where claims eventually run off to zero. Premium estimates are provided and compared with actual guaranty fund assessment rates.

PROPERTY-LIABILITY INSURANCE COMPANIES are levered firms in which debt capital is supplied by policyholders in the form of premiums paid at contract inception (Quirin and Waters [30]). In return, the insurer promises to pay claims, contingent upon the occurrence of specified events during a coverage period. Premiums are invested in marketable securities between the premium-payment and loss-payment dates. In many lines of insurance, claim payments cover a lengthy period of time extending far beyond the coverage period.

Incentive conflicts arise because insurers can gain by increasing asset risk following the policy issue date. This increases the value of the owners' call option on the residual value of the firm at the expense of commitments to policyholders. To some extent, policyholders foresee this and avoid companies that are likely to assume unstable risk-taking postures. A network of insurance brokers and financial rating firms has arisen to supply monitoring services, and a significant share of insurance costs is devoted to this function. Information generated by this system coupled with repeat buying (periodic negotiation of contracts) serves to protect policyholder interests. Reinsurance companies exist to monitor the behavior of managers and limit the risk of ruin, thus helping to prevent dilution of the value of policyholder claims.

In spite of the substantial resources devoted to private monitoring, government also engages in extensive solvency regulation. One rationale for government regulation is that private monitoring is less effective for individual buyers and small businesses than for large corporate buyers due to economies of scale in information acquisition. In addition, the consequences of insolvencies are more severe for individuals and small firms than for large firms since the latter are traded in capital markets, which provide an efficient mechanism for pooling

* Wharton School, University of Pennsylvania. The author benefited from valuable comments by Richard Derrig, Andrew Lo, A. S. Paulson, and George Pennacchi on earlier versions of this paper.

diversifiable risk. Thus, like banks, insurers have both risk-averse and risk-neutral customers with different needs and resources. (See Kanatas [17] for a discussion of the banking case.)

Another rationale for solvency regulation is the existence of incentive conflicts between buyers of insurance and third-party claimants. Many important types of insurance (e.g., liability insurance) are purchased to satisfy legal obligations toward potential claimants who have no role in the contracting process. To the extent that buyers are "judgment-proof" or have limited liability, an incentive exists to purchase the least expensive (i.e., highest risk) insurance permitted by law. This is obviously detrimental to the interests of third-party claimants, who will be unable to collect if the insurer becomes insolvent. Thus, solvency regulation also is motivated by the contention that private markets fail to incorporate the full social costs of insurer insolvencies.[1]

State regulators monitor the financial condition of insurance companies through an extensive auditing system. Insurer financial statements are subjected to computerized audits each year by the National Association of Insurance Commissioners (NAIC). Companies failing four or more of eleven audit ratio tests are singled out for special regulatory scrutiny. Site audits are carried out by a team of state examiners every three to five years (Troxel and Breslin [33]). Other solvency regulations include investment portfolio restrictions, minimum capitalization requirements, and (in many states) rate regulation.[2]

A recent addition to the regulatory arsenal is the insurance guaranty fund, which reimburses policyholders and third-party claimants of insolvent insurers. Property-liability insolvency funds exist in all United States jurisdictions. Nearly all funds operate on a post-assessment basis: solvent companies are assessed an amount equal to the shortfall in assets of the insolvent firm. Assessments are a flat percentage of premium volume for all solvent companies (Duncan [12]).

The guaranty fund system differs from bank deposit insurance in that the ultimate guarantor is the private insurance industry rather than the government. This is possible because property-liability insurers, unlike banks, do not have "instantaneously putable" debt and hence are not susceptible to runs. The establishment of guaranty funds reflects a political judgment that the costs of insurer insolvencies should be spread throughout the insurance system rather than borne by specific policyholders and claimants. It also reflects the view that the private market has proven inadequate as a risk-sharing mechanism for certain types of policyholders, as mentioned above.

Questions have been raised about the efficiency of governmental solvency regulation. For example, Munch and Smallwood [26] found that minimum capital and surplus requirements reduce the number of insolvencies by restricting entry into insurance markets but do not reduce the insolvency rate. Other regulatory

[1] It should be noted that reinsurance does not solve this problem. Insurers adopting high-risk strategies either will purchase no reinsurance or will buy from high-risk reinsurance companies to satisfy regulatory requirements. Since high-risk strategies often will benefit stockholders, this problem is unlikely to be alleviated by resolving manager-owner incentive conflicts.

[2] Rate regulatory laws usually incorporate the requirement that rates not be "excessive, inadequate, or unfairly discriminatory". In most recent periods, rate regulation has tended to set maximum rather than minimum rates. See Harrington [14].

measures were found to have little or no effect on the number of insolvencies. It is argued below that guaranty funds in their present form have done little to improve this situation.

In adopting guaranty funds, little attention was paid to the impact the funds might have on firm incentives, regulatory costs, or the risk-return characteristics of insurance markets.[3] Inadequate consideration has been given to the use of private alternatives or less intrusive regulatory approaches to protect risk-averse policyholders. For example, the results of regulatory solvency tests would assist smaller policyholders in overcoming their information disadvantage and avoiding insurers with a high probability of failure. However, the release of this information has been ruled out by the NAIC. The incentive conflict between insurance buyers and third-party claimants would be more difficult to handle in a private market context. Properly designed guaranty funds would seem to be advantageous in dealing with this problem in that they provide the broadest possible sharing of risk and low transactions costs.

This article is motivated by a defect in the design of guaranty funds—the use of flat rather than risk-based premiums. The objective is to point out the consequences of using flat premiums and to develop techniques for calculating risk-based premiums. The premium formulas should also be useful in providing information on insurer financial stability and in pricing private-market insurance contracts.

Guaranty funds with flat premiums create adverse incentives in insurance markets. In a competitive market with perfect information and no regulation, the cost of an insurer's debt capital (the underwriting loss (profit)) would vary directly with the risk of the firm (i.e., the uncertainty regarding the firm's ability to pay policyholder claims). Hence, more risky firms would have to charge lower premiums in order to attract policyholders.[4]

In a regime with guaranty funds, the market penalty is replaced by the guaranty fund premium.[5] If the premium does not reflect insurer risk, the introduction of guaranty funds will lead to a gain in the market value of equity for more risky firms, and an incentive is created for firms to adopt more risky strategies. Regulatory costs may arise as more intensive government monitoring is required to verify risk levels. The number of insolvencies also may increase. The higher regulatory costs and any deadweight losses arising from insurer insolvencies will be spread throughout the insurance system, raising the average cost of insurance.

---

[3] For an analysis of some of these issues in banking, see Buser, Chen, and Kane [6] and Chan and Mak [8].

[4] It is assumed here that private monitoring provides buyers with accurate information on firm risk and eliminates any problems of adverse firm behavior following policy issue. The important point is that buyers will be indifferent between high- and low-risk insurers following the introduction of the guaranty fund. Hence, even if some high-risk insurers were exploiting information imperfections prior to the adoption of the fund, the "lemons" problem would still exist after the fund were established. It is implicitly assumed here that rate and investment regulation are not binding.

[5] Insolvency funds may not totally eliminate the costs of insolvencies from the policyholders' perspective. For example, the payment of claims may be delayed if the insurer becomes insolvent and the liabilities are transferred to the guarantor. In addition, guaranty funds usually impose a maximum payment per claim. See Duncan [12].

Risk-based premiums thus have several advantages. They reduce the potential for distortions in insurance company asset and liability portfolios that raise the probability of insolvency. They provide a potentially more effective and less expensive means of monitoring solvency, monitoring competition (determining fair rate of return), and providing information to policyholders in both regulated and unregulated insurance markets. Finally, the premium formulas have potential intrinsic value in pricing insurance and reinsurance contracts (e.g., loss portfolio transfers among insurers).

The methodology developed in this paper is an extension of work on deposit insurance premiums by Merton [24 and 25], Pennacchi [29], and Ronn and Verma [31]. The approach is to model the assets and liabilities of the firm as diffusion processes.[6] Premium equations are developed for three cases: a) an insurer with stochastic assets and liabilities but no additional sources of risk, b) an insurer with stochastic assets, stochastic liabilities, and randomly occurring jumps in liabilities (catastrophes), and c) a policy cohort, where liabilities are gradually reduced as claims are paid.

The first two models provide risk-based guaranty fund premiums for ongoing insurers, while the third provides the fair market value of the guarantor's promise to discharge the obligations of a bankrupt insurer. The first model extends the work of Merton [24 and 25] and Pennacchi [29] by respecifying the drift terms and boundary conditions of the relevant diffusions to apply to insurers rather than banks. The second model breaks new ground by allowing for discrete jumps in liabilities (catastrophes), a major problem faced by insurers. It differs from previous jump-diffusion models (e.g., Merton [23]) in that both assets and liabilities are stochastic and that the jumps are in liabilities (i.e., the denominator of the asset/liability ratio). The cohort model is totally new and has significant potential for pricing insurance contracts, loss portfolio transfers, and guaranty fund premiums.

Related work in insurance pricing includes Kraus and Ross [19] and Doherty and Garven [11].[7] The former utilize arbitrage pricing theory to develop equilibrium premiums for property-liability insurers, while the latter present a more conventional Black-Scholes model of the property-liability firm. The present model is a useful alternative to the Kraus-Ross model since it requires fewer parameter estimates and allows for catastrophes. It is superior to the Doherty-Garven approach since it explicitly allows for multiple-period operations, catastrophes, and the pricing of policy cohorts. The present model also makes allowance for the long payout tail that characterizes many important lines of insurance (e.g., liability insurance).

---

[6] An alterntive approach based on stable processes rather than diffusion processes is suggested by McCulloch [21]. Another potential methodology is actuarial-ruin theory (Beard, Pentikainen, and Pesonen [3]). Ruin theory, though mathematically sophisticated, does not take into account the operation of market forces.

[7] A recent work that applies modern financial theory to the pricing of *individual* insurance contracts is Sabol [32]. Earlier papers on the financial theory of insurance pricing include Fairley [13] and Hill and Modigliani [15].

The final contribution of the article is to provide numerical illustrations of risk-based premiums. These are not inténded as a hypothesis test but rather to provide examples of potential estimation techniques and to indicate the order of magnitude of premiums generated by the models. The illustrative premiums are compared with actual guaranty fund assessment rates for the period 1970 to 1984.

# I. Premiums for Ongoing Insurers

## A. Stochastic Assets and Liabilities

Assume that the insurer enters into a contractual arrangement with the guaranty fund at the beginning of a specified contract period. The contract period is of fixed length (e.g., one year). The guaranty fund premium is determined and a premium charge made at the beginning of the period. At the end of the period, an audit occurs. If assets ($A$) exceed liabilities ($L$) at the audit date, the company is permitted to continue operating. A new premium is calculated, applying to the next contract period. If liabilities exceed assets, the guaranty fund takes over the assets of the company and discharges its liabilities at a cost to the fund of $L - A$. The fund is assumed to be certain to pay its obligations.

Except for the pre-payment of the guaranty fund premium, these assumptions are consistent with the current regulatory practices in insurance. Audits are nonrandom and conducted annually, with more extensive audits conducted at three- to five-year intervals. Audit costs are charged to insurers and can be considered proportional to the guaranty fund premium.

The following additional assumptions are made:

(A1) Trading in securities takes place continuously in time. Borrowing and lending take place at a known rate of interest $r$, which is assumed to be constant over time. The Fisher effect is assumed to prevail, i.e., $r = r_I + r^*$, where $r_I$ is the economy-wide inflation rate and $r^*$ is the real rate.

(A2) Security prices are assumed to satisfy the security market line equation in the continuous-time version of the capital asset pricing model (ICAPM).

(A3) Insurer assets consist of marketable securities. The value of these assets is determined according to the following diffusion process:

$$dA = (\mu_A A + \delta N - \theta L)dt + A\sigma_A dz_A, \qquad (1)$$

where $A$ = assets, $L$ = liabilities, $N$ = the number of policies, $\mu_A$ = the instantaneous expected rate of return on assets per unit of time, $\delta$ = the instantaneous rate of premium inflow per policy insured, $\theta$ = the instantaneous rate of claims payment per dollar of liabilities, $\sigma_A^2$ = the instantaneous variance of return on assets, and $z_A(t)$ = a standard Brownian motion process for assets. Assets thus are assumed to grow due to investment income and premium payments and to be reduced as claims are paid. Note that the model applies to the entire company rather than to any given entry-year class of policies.

(A4) Premiums are collected in advance and held until claims are paid. Liabilities are determined according to the following diffusion process:[8]

$$dL = (\mu_L L + \eta N - \theta L)dt + L\sigma_L dz_L, \tag{2}$$

where $\mu_L$ = the instantaneous growth rate of liabilities, $\eta$ = the instantaneous (dollar) rate of occurrence of new claims, $\sigma_L^2$ = the instantaneous variance of liabilities per unit of time, and $z_L(t)$ = a standard Brownian motion process for liabilities. Liabilities are assumed to grow due to inflation and the occurrence of new claims and to be drawn down due to the payment of claims.[9]

(A5) The asset and liability processes are related as follows:

$$dz_A dz_L = \rho_{AL} dt, \tag{3}$$

where $\rho_{AL}$ can be interpreted as an instantaneous correlation coefficient.[10]

The model assumes that both general inflation and liability inflation are constant over time. However, liability inflation will not necessarily equal general inflation. If liabilities have systematic risk, under assumption (A2) insurance prices will reflect a CAPM-type market risk premium.[11] Hence,

$$\mu_L = r_L + \pi, \tag{4}$$

where $r_L$ = the inflation rate in liabilities, which may be $\gtreqless r_I$, and $\pi$ = the market risk premium for bearing insurance risk, where $\pi$ may be $\gtreqless 0$. This equation implies that insurers promise to pay losses at the price level in effect at the loss-settlement date. However, deducted from outstanding liabilities is a risk charge, which constitutes the insurer's return for bearing insurance risk. This is similar in concept to the risk-adjusted discount rate used by Myers and Cohn [27] in a discrete-time context.

The value of guaranty fund insurance can be written as $P(A, L, \tau)$, where $\tau$ = the time remaining until the next audit. The guaranty is similar to a put option since its value at the audit date is $\max(0, L - A)$. Assets and liabilities both drift stochastically, and the guaranty fund assumes the insurer's obligations if liabilities have drifted above assets by the audit date.

Utilizing procedures analogous to those employed in Merton [25], a differential

---

[8] If $N$ can be expressed as a constant proportion of liabilities, equation (2) asserts that insurer liabilities follow a lognormal diffusion process. Cummins and Nye [10] have provided evidence that the lognormal distribution is a reasonable model for insurer liabilities.

[9] Conceptually, $\eta$ is designed as a diffusion-type approximation of the total claims process. The latter process is explained in Beard, Pentikainen, and Pesonen [3]. It involves the compounding of frequency (claims occurrence) and severity (claim amount) processes. Thus, $\eta$ is dollar valued and represents the infinitesimal growth in liabilities due to new claims.

[10] Much empirical work suggests that asset and liability processes of insurers have very low or no correlation (e.g., Hill and Modigliani [15] and Cummins and Harrington [9]). However, for completeness, the models are developed under the assumption that nonzero corrrelations may be present.

[11] Discrete-time insurance-pricing models with this type of risk premium have been developed by Fairley [13] and Hill and Modigliani [15].

equation for the guaranty fund premium is obtained:[12]

$$rP = (rA + \delta N - \theta L)P_A + (r_L L + \eta N - \theta L)P_L - P_\tau$$
$$+ \tfrac{1}{2}(A^2\sigma_A^2 P_{AA} + L^2\sigma_L^2 P_{LL} + 2AL\sigma_A\sigma_L\rho_{AL}P_{AL}). \tag{5}$$

This equation can be solved numerically to obtain the guaranty fund premium.

To facilitate the discussion and elucidate the key relationships, equation (5) is simplified by making an additional assumption: $\delta N = \theta L = \eta N$. That is, the insurer is assumed to have attained a *steady-state* position where premium inflow, claims outflow, and the (dollar) incidence of new claims are equal. These assumptions are merely an expositional convenience and are not necessary to obtain premium rates.

Making the change of variables $x = A/L$ and $p(x) = p = P(A, L, \tau)/L$ in equation (5), the following equation is obtained:

$$(r - r_L)p = (r - r_L)xp_x - p_\tau + (\tfrac{1}{2})x^2 p_{xx}(\sigma_A^2 + \sigma_L^2 - 2\sigma_A\sigma_L\rho_{AL}). \tag{6}$$

The boundary conditions for equation (6) are the following:

$$p(0, \tau) = \exp[-(r - r_L)\tau], \tag{7a}$$

$$p(x, 0) = \max(0, 1 - x). \tag{7b}$$

The guaranty fund premium thus is the value of a put option with interest rate $(r - r_L)$. If claims inflation is the same as general inflation, this is equivalent to valuing the option at the real rate of interest, $r^*$. The diffusion parameter is $(\sigma_A^2 + \sigma_L^2 - 2\sigma_A\sigma_L\rho_{AL})$. Thus, positive correlation between the asset and liability processes reduces the risk of the insurer.

The model can be used to analyze the impact of guaranty fund insurance on firm value.[13] Insurance liabilities can be considered analogous to risky corporate debt; i.e., the value of liabilities will be

$$V(L) = L[\exp(-r^*\tau) - p(x, \tau)], \tag{8}$$

where $V(L) =$ value of liabilities. Liabilities will be worth less than their discounted present value due to the probability that the insurer will default. The value of insurer assets is

$$A = E + L[\exp(-r^*\tau) - p(x, \tau)], \tag{9}$$

where $E =$ insurance company equity. Recalling that insurer assets are marketable securities, it is clear from equation (9) that the assets are obtained from two sources: stockholder funds ($E$) and premiums (discounted claims less the value of the put).

There is, of course, an interaction between the funds initially put up by

---

[12] The present model differs from Merton's [25] model in that both assets and liabilities are stochastic. The derivation utilizes Itô's Lemma and assumes that the deposit insurance premium is priced according to the continuous-time version of the CAPM. The details of the derivation are available from the author.

[13] This discussion assumes for simplicity that insurer liabilities have no systematic risk.

stockholders and the value of the put; i.e., the put value is affected by firm capital structure. It is assumed that insurance market equilibrium results in insurers being arrayed along a continuum of capital structures to serve policyholders with different levels of risk aversion. Policyholders are assumed to have complete information about the default risk of competing insurers and to choose a company with a premium/default risk combination consistent with their tastes.

Suppose that guaranty fund insurance is introduced with a flat premium $k$ expressed as a proportion of liabilities. Suppose that all existing policies are cancelled and replaced by new policies reflecting the existence of the guaranty fund. All insurers will now receive a premium of $\exp(-r^*\tau)$ per dollar of liabilities from policyholders and pay the guaranty fund a premium of $kL$. The value of the firm's assets becomes

$$A' = E + L[\exp(-r^*\tau) - k].$$ (10)

The change in the asset value of any given insurer due to the introduction of the guaranty fund will be

$$A' - A = L[p(x, \tau) - k].$$ (11)

The flat premium charge $k$ will be a pooled value based upon the insolvency costs of all insurers in the market. Thus, $k$ will be higher than $p(x, \tau)$ for some insurers and lower for others. The introduction of the guaranty fund will penalize the equityholders of better-than-average firms and reward equityholders of worse-than-average firms.

Viewing equity as the value of a call option, it is apparent that the firm has an incentive to assume greater risk.[14] This is the case because the value of the call option increases with the risk parameter ($\sigma_A^2 + \sigma_L^2 - 2\sigma_A\sigma_L\rho_{AL}$). Insurers are no longer penalized by the product market for assuming greater risk and are penalized by the guaranty fund only as a group (through increases in $k$ as risk increases). Hence, the introduction of guaranty funds may actually increase the rate of insolvency in insurance markets. Charging a risk-based premium reinstates equation (9), with insurers paying a premium of $Lp(x, \tau)$ to the guaranty fund.[15]

## B. Liability Jumps (Catastrophes)

The lognormal diffusion process hypothesized above implies a continuous sample path for liabilities. However, many types of insurance subject the insurer to large jumps in liabilities (catastrophes). Examples include chemical catastrophes, airline disasters, hurricanes, and changing judicial interpretations of contract provisions. Although reinsurance is used to cushion the impact of such events, it is impossible to perfectly insulate insurers from this type of claim. This

---

[14] The value of insurance company equity will be equal to the value of a call option, valued according to a differential equation exactly analogous to equation (6), with boundary conditions: $c(0, \tau) = 0$, $c(x, 0) = \max(0, x - 1)$.

[15] However, policyholders will pay higher premiums, reflecting the reduction in default probabilities. This may reduce overall consumer welfare because policyholders who prefer to take some default risk will not have this option available in insurance markets.

section develops a pricing model for guaranty fund insurance when insurers are subject to discontinuous changes in liabilities.

Assets are assumed to be governed by equation (1), while liabilities now develop according to the following equation:

$$dL = (\mu_L L + \eta N - \theta L - \lambda k L)dt + \sigma_L L dz_L + dq, \tag{12}$$

where $q(t) = $ a Poisson process with parameter $\lambda$, $k = E(Y - 1)$, and $Y = $ the random variable representing the jump magnitude, where $Y > 0$. Jumps occur according to a Poisson process; i.e., the intervals between jumps are exponentially distributed.[16] When a jump occurs, liabilities change from $Y$ to $LY$. Successive values of $Y$ are assumed to be independent and identically distributed. The expected impact of the jump process in any small interval is $\lambda k dt$. A similar model has been applied to stock prices by Merton [23] and other authors. The difference between the present model and Merton's [23] model is that both assets and liabilities are stochastic here and the jump applies to liabilities rather than assets (i.e., it is in the denominator of the asset/liability ratio).

Representing the guaranty fund premium by $P(A, L, \tau)$ and applying the Itô transformation formula and a corresponding formula for Poisson processes (see Merton [22, pp. 395–396]), a differential equation for the premium $P(A, L, \tau)$ can be obtained.[17] Two assumptions are invoked in order to eliminate the Brownian motion terms from the differential equation: a) the guaranty fund premium is priced according to the continuous-time version of the CAPM, and b) jump risk is nonsystematic. The first assumption is retained from the preceding case, while the second is needed because no hedge portfolio can be constructed that will eliminate the jump risk. (See Merton [23, p. 131].)

Assuming that the jump risk is nonsystematic is probably more reasonable for insurance liabilities than for stock prices. While certain "catastrophes" (e.g., liberalization of tort rules) undoubtedly have a systematic effect, most such events are unsystematic by definition. Nevertheless, to the extent that jump risk has a systematic component, the guaranty fund premium may be understated.

Introducing the above assumptions and taking expectations yield a differential equation for the guaranty fund premium. After making the change of variables $x = A/L$ and $p(x, \tau) = P/L$, the equation becomes

$$pr^{**} = xp_x r^{**} - p_\tau + \lambda E_Y[p(x/Y, \tau) - p(x, \tau)]$$
$$+ (\tfrac{1}{2})x^2 p_{xx}(\sigma_A^2 + \sigma_L^2 - 2\sigma_A\sigma_L\rho_{AL}), \tag{13}$$

where $r^{**} = r - r_L + \lambda k$. The solution to equation (13) is given below:

$$p(x, \tau) = \sum_{N=0}^{\infty} p(N)E_N[W(x/X_N, \tau; 1, r^{**}, \sigma^2)], \tag{14}$$

where $X_N = $ the product of $N$ independent random variables, each distributed identically to $Y$, $E_N = $ the expectation operator over the distribution of $X_N$,

---

[16] The Poisson model is the premier model of insurance claim arrivals. See Beard, Pentikainen, and Pesonen [3].

[17] The derivation is somewhat analogous to that presented in Merton [23]. However, since both assets and liabilities are stochastic and the jumps apply to liabilities, the analogy is not direct. Details of the derivation are presented in an Appendix available from the author.

$W(x/X_N, \tau; 1, r^{**}, \sigma^2)$ = the value of a put option on an asset with value $x/X_N$, time to expiration $\tau$, exercise price one, interest rate $r - r_L + \lambda k$, and risk parameter $\sigma^2$, and $\sigma^2 = \sigma_A^2 + \sigma_L^2 - 2\sigma_A\sigma_L\rho_{AL}$. Equation (14) is the weighted average of guaranty fund premiums with asset/liability ratios $x/X_N$ and exercise price one. In effect, the occurrence of catastrophes leads to multiplicative increases in liabilities and hence to decreases in the asset/liability ratio.

No distributional assumption has been made with regard to the random variable $Y$. However, if $Y$ is lognormal, then a closed-form expression can be derived for the value of the guaranty fund premium. This is equation (14) with the following substituted for $E_N[W(\cdot)]$:

$$E_N[W(\cdot)] = e^{-r^{**}\tau}\Phi[(-\ln x - \mu^*\tau)/\sigma^*\sqrt{\tau}]$$
$$- xe^{N\gamma}\Phi[(-\ln x - \mu^*\tau - \sigma^{*2}\tau)/\sigma^*\sqrt{\tau}], \qquad (15)$$

where $\mu^* = r - r_L + \lambda k - \sigma^2/2 - N\alpha/\tau$, $\sigma^{*2} = \sigma^2 + (N\zeta^2/\tau)$, $\Phi(\cdot)$ = the standard normal distribution function, $\alpha$, $\zeta^2$ = the mean and variance parameters of $\ln(Y)$, and $\gamma = -\alpha + \zeta^2/2$. The derivation of this equation utilizes the property that the product of lognormally distributed random variables is lognormally distributed.[18] The expected value of the jump, $E(Y)$ is $\exp(\alpha + \zeta^2/2)$. The expected impact of the jump on the asset/liability ratio is $E(1/Y) = \exp(-\alpha + \zeta^2/2)$.

If the Poisson intensity parameter and the liability-jump parameters are equal to zero, the jump model reverts to the no-jump case. However, if the expected value of the jump is zero (i.e., $\alpha = -\zeta^2/2$) but jumps can occur ($\lambda \neq 0$), the premium implied by equations (14) and (15) tends to be higher than in the no-jump case when $x > 1$. This occurs primarily because of the effect of the jump-variance parameter on $\sigma^{*2}$. When $x$ is sufficiently less than one, the premium implied by the jump model when $E(Y) = 1$ tends to be less than the premium in the no-jump case. The reason is that the expected impact of the jump on $x$, i.e., $E(1/Y)$, is positive when $\alpha = -\zeta^2/2$.

## II. Premiums for a Policy Cohort

In many cases of insurance company financial distress, the liabilities of the distressed firm are not actually discharged by the guaranty fund. Rather, the liabilities and assets are assumed by a solvent insurer that agrees to pay the remaining claims. This type of arrangement is rational if insurers have either cost or information advantages over the guaranty fund in claims settlement. In such situations, it is important to determine the fair market value of the business transferred to the solvent company. This section develops a pricing model for this type of transaction. The model also is appropriate for pricing the transfer of blocks of business between solvent firms, so-called "loss-portfolio transfers." A

---

[18] Equations (14) and (15) do not simplify into a weighted sum of Black-Scholes option values with Poisson parameter $\lambda' = \lambda(1 + k)$ as in Merton [23, p. 135]. This is due to the fact that $\ln(1 + k) = \alpha + \zeta^2/2$, while $\ln E(1/X_N) = -N\alpha + N\zeta^2/2$. The difference is that the jump affects the denominator rather than the numerator, as in Merton's jump model for stocks.

602

noteworthy feature of the model is that it prices a contingent claim with no expiration date and thus explicitly allows for a lengthy payout tail.

More specifically, consider a situation in which the insurer agrees to pay all claims arising from a group of policies in return for a fixed premium, $G$, to be paid at the inception of the contract. Assume that all claim events under the block of policies have already occurred and that the present market value of these claims ($L$) is known. The funds represented by $G$ are invested in marketable securities. $G$ and $L$ are governed by the following differential equations:

$$dG = (\mu_A G - \theta L)dt + G\sigma_A dz_A,$$ (16a)

$$dL = (\mu_L L - \theta L)dt + L\sigma_L dz_L,$$ (16b)

where the parameters of the diffusions are defined above.

The loss account, represented by $L$, increases due to claims inflation and is drawn down as claims are paid. The premium account grows due to investment income and is depleted by claims payments. If the premium account eventually is exhausted, the insurer is still liable for any claims remaining unpaid. It is assumed that the insurer is certain to fulfill this obligation. The value of the insurer's obligation is denoted by $\Pi(G, L)$.

The value of $\Pi(G, L)$ is derived conditional on the initial values of $G$ and $L$ being known. For example, if the guaranty fund or a solvent insurer were to assume control of an insolvent insurer, both assets and liabilities would have known or estimable market values at the time of the takeover and would be subject to stochastic variation thereafter. This is precisely the situation modeled in this section.

Differentiating $\Pi(G, L)$, one obtains

$$d\Pi = \Pi_G dG + \Pi_L dL + \tfrac{1}{2}[\Pi_{GG}(dG)^2 + \Pi_{LL}(dL)^2 + 2\Pi_{GL}dGdL].$$ (17)

As before, subscripts on $\Pi$ indicate partial derivatives. To obtain a differential equation for $\pi$, the guaranty premium per dollar of liabilities, the following procedure is followed: a) equations (16a) and (16b) are substituted into (17), b) the expected value of the resulting expression is obtained under the assumption that the guaranty value reflects only systematic risk, and c) the change of variables $x = G/L$ and $\pi = \Pi/L$ is carried out. The result is the following equation:

$$(r - r_L + \theta)\pi = \pi_x[(r - r_L + \theta)x - \theta]$$
$$+ \tfrac{1}{2}x^2\pi_{xx}(\sigma_G^2 + \sigma_L^2 - 2\sigma_G\sigma_L\rho_{GL}).$$ (18)

The boundary conditions are

$$\lim_{x\to 0}\pi(x) = 1,$$ (19a)

$$\lim_{x\to\infty}\pi(x) = 0.$$ (19b)

The conditions imply that the value of the guaranty approaches zero as the asset/liability ratio ($x$) becomes large and approaches the value of liabilities as $x$ goes to zero. Thus, if the premium account is exhausted, the value of the guarantor's promise is equal to the value of the remaining liabilities.

The solution of equation (18) subject to the boundary conditions is[19]

$$\pi(x) = \frac{\Gamma(2)}{\Gamma(2+a)} \, b^a x^{-a} e^{-b/x} M(2, 2+a, b/x), \qquad (20)$$

where $a = 2(r^* + \theta)/Q$, $b = 2\theta/Q$, $Q = \sigma_G^2 + \sigma_L^2 - 2\sigma_G\sigma_L\rho_{GL}$, and $M(\cdot, \cdot, \cdot) =$ Kummer's function. (See Abramowitz and Stegun [1].) The derivative of $\pi(x)$ with respect to $x$ is unambiguously negative; i.e., the value of the guaranty is less when the premium account is larger relative to the loss account. For reasonable parameter values (see below), $\pi(x)$ varies inversely with the risk-free rate and directly with the risk parameter $Q$.

The effect of the payout parameter $\theta$ on the value of the guaranty is ambiguous. For large values of $x$ (e.g., $x$ sufficiently greater than one), $\pi(x)$ tends to be inversely related to $\theta$. Intuitively, this occurs because a faster payout reduces the risk that adverse loss fluctuations will exhaust the premium fund. For sufficiently small values of $x$, on the other hand, the value of the guaranty tends to be directly related to the payout parameter. In this case, a proportion of the liabilities is very likely to be paid out of the guarantor's funds (rather than the premium account). Thus, it is best to delay payment as long as possible. Numerical examples are utilized in the next section to illustrate these and other effects.

### III. Numerical Examples

This section provides numerical examples of guaranty fund premia. The examples are purely illustrative and do not constitute a test of hypotheses regarding the models developed above. The goal is to provide an illustration of possible estimation techniques and of the orders of magnitude of the premiums implied by the models. The premium estimates are compared with actual guaranty fund assessment rates for the period 1970 to 1984.

The most basic guaranty fund model for an ongoing firm depends upon only five parameters: the risk-free rate ($r$), the liability inflation rate ($r_L$), the variance parameters for assets and liabilities ($\sigma_A^2$ and $\sigma_L^2$), and the correlation parameter of the asset and liability random shock terms ($\rho_{AL}$).

Two estimates of the "real" rate of return $r^* = r - r_L$ are used, 0.005 and 0.025. The former is approximately the same order of magnitude as the realized difference between ninety-day U.S. Treasury bill rates and inflation over the period 1926 to 1984, while the latter is more in accord with realized rates over more recent holding periods (Ibbotson Associates [16]).

It is assumed that insurers invest twenty-five percent of their assets in corporate equities and seventy-five percent in long-term bonds—a reasonable approximation of insurer asset portfolios over the past ten years. This assumes that noninvested assets (about fifteen percent of insurer assets) have the same risk characteristics as long-term bonds. (See Hill and Modigliani [15].)

To estimate the diffusion parameters of corporate equities and long-term bonds, annual data presented in Ibbotson Associates [16] are used. Parameters

---

[19] The derivation of equations (18) through (20) is presented in an Appendix available from the author.

were estimated for stocks, long-term corporate bonds, and long-term government bonds for the period 1926 to 1984.[20] The average of the long-term corporate and long-term government bond parameters (0.00465) was used as the diffusion parameter for bonds. For equities, the estimated parameter was 0.0415. The correlation parameter between stocks and bonds is the average of the stock/ government and stock/corporate bond parameters (0.115).

The risk parameter for insurance industry liabilities was estimated to be 0.0045, based on the variance of the log of $(L/L_{-1})$, where $L$ = total industry liabilities. The correlation coefficient between liabilities and assets was assumed to be zero.[21]

To estimate premiums using the jump-diffusion (catastrophe) model, three additional parameters are needed: the Poisson arrival rate and the parameters of the lognormal distribution of catastrophe magnitudes. Annual arrival rates of 0.33, 0.2, and 0.1 were arbitrarily selected, corresponding to the average arrival of catastrophes every three, five, and ten years, respectively. For catastrophe severity, the location parameter was assumed to be −0.005 and the dispersion parameter 0.01. This implies that the expected impact of a catastrophe is zero; i.e., "catastrophes" can either increase or decrease insurer liabilities.[22] The assumed-dispersion parameter implies that the standard deviation of catastrophe severity is ten percent of insurer liabilities.

The final parameter estimate needed to test the premium models is the claims-settlement parameter $(\theta)$. The setup of the model implies that the claims runoff follows an exponential distribution.[23] Analysis of automobile bodily injury liability insurance claims from Massachusetts revealed that the exponential distribution provides a good fit to the tail of the claims runoff, with a parameter $(\theta)$ of 0.4. This estimate is less than the runoff parameter for the industry as a whole because insurers write both short-tail (e.g., fire) and long-tail (e.g., auto liability) lines.

The premium estimates for the basic and catastrophe models are shown in Table I. Premiums were estimated using asset/liability ratios ranging from 1.2 to 1.4.[24] The premium estimates for the basic model with a real rate of 0.005 range from 0.13 to 0.001 of one percent of liabilities for asset/liability $(A/L)$ ratios of 1.2 and 1.4, respectively. For a real rate of 0.025, the premium is reduced

---

[20] The lognormal-diffusion assumption implies that the logs of value relatives are normally distributed. Hence, an approximate estimate of the diffusion parameter is the variance of the log of the value relative.

[21] The estimate of the liability variance is almost identical to the variance of $\ln(L/L-1)$ about its least-squares trend line. The estimated correlation parameters between $\ln(L/L_{-1})$ and the log asset relatives were very low (the largest was −0.16). Risk parameters for individual firms probably would be larger because a pooling effect occurs when aggregating across companies.

[22] The jump-severity parameters were chosen arbitrarily because data on catastrophe magnitudes are not readily available. The model can easily be modified to test the sensitivity of the estimated premiums to the jump-severity assumption and to reflect only non-negative jumps.

[23] Thus, the average claim-payoff date occurs $(1/\theta)$ periods after the starting date (time zero). The exponential-runoff assumption also was used by Kraus and Ross [19].

[24] The asset/liability ratio for the insurance industry over the past ten years has been about 1.4 (A. M. Best Company, *Best's Aggregates and Averages* (Oldwick, NJ)). However, this is probably overstated since bonds are reported at book rather than market values.

**Table I**

Guaranty Fund Premiums[a]

| A/L Ratio | Jump Model ($r^* = 0.005$) | | | No Jumps | |
|---|---|---|---|---|---|
| | $\lambda = 0.33$ | $\lambda = 0.2$ | $\lambda = 0.1$ | $r^* = 0.005$ | $r^* = 0.025$ |
| 1.2 | 0.002789 | 0.002194 | 0.001741 | 0.001293 | 0.000753 |
| 1.3 | 0.000645 | 0.000430 | 0.000275 | 0.000131 | 0.000067 |
| 1.4 | 0.000159 | 0.000091 | 0.000047 | 0.000010 | 0.000004 |

[a] Constant parameters: $\alpha = -0.005$; $\zeta^2 = 0.01$. Key: $\alpha$ = location parameter for jumps; $\zeta^2$ = dispersion parameter for jumps; $r^*$ = the real rate (the nominal risk-free rate minus the liability inflation rate); $\lambda$ = Poisson arrival rate for jumps; $A$ = assets; $L$ = liabilities.

**Table II**

Policy Cohort Premiums[a]

| $Q =$ | 0.01 | 0.02 | 0.01 | 0.01 | 0.02 |
|---|---|---|---|---|---|
| $r^* =$ | 0.005 | 0.005 | 0.025 | 0.005 | 0.005 |
| $\theta =$ | 0.4 | 0.4 | 0.4 | 0.2 | 0.2 |
| $x$ | Premiums = $\pi(x)$ | | | | |
| 1.4 | 0.000059 | 0.001272 | 0.000011 | 0.001011 | 0.007341 |
| 1.2 | 0.002317 | 0.009964 | 0.000708 | 0.008433 | 0.024921 |
| 1.0 | 0.038678 | 0.057026 | 0.020500 | 0.051495 | 0.077266 |
| 0.8 | 0.190896 | 0.195087 | 0.152593 | 0.186007 | 0.198244 |
| min $x$ | 0.772 | 0.698 | 0.792 | 0.718 | 0.634 |
| min $x + \pi$ | 0.991 | 0.992 | 0.953 | 0.983 | 0.985 |

[a] Key: $Q$ = sum of asset and liability risk parameters; $r^*$ = the real rate; $\theta$ = liability payout parameter; $x$ = asset/liability ratio.

by about forty percent for $A/L$ of 1.2 and by about sixty percent for $A/L$ of 1.4. The risk parameter also has a major impact. For the no-jump case with $r^* = 0.005$ and $A/L = 1.2$, raising the variance parameter ($\sigma^2$) from 0.01 to 0.02 leads to a premium increase of more than five hundred percent. The premiums with catastrophes are uniformly higher.

To gauge the realism of the results, the actual guaranty fund assessment rate over the period 1970 to 1984 was computed.[25] The assessments for this period amounted to about 0.025 of one percent of industry liabilities. This is the same order of magnitude as many of the premium estimates in Table I. For example, it is about the same as the estimate for the no-jump model with $r^* = 0.005$ and $A/L = 1.275$.

The premium estimates for the policy-cohort model are shown in Table II. As expected, the premiums vary inversely with the asset/liability ratio and the real rate and directly with the variance parameter. As explained above, the effect of the runoff parameter ($\theta$) depends upon the initial asset/liability ratio. For example, consider the second and fifth columns in Table II. For an asset/liability

[25] The first full year of operation of insurance guaranty funds was 1970. The assessment data (see National Committee on Insurance Guaranty Funds [28]) slightly understate the actual premium rate since the data base omits the pre-assessment funds operating in New York and in New Jersey prior to 1975.

ratio of 1.4, decreasing the runoff parameter (i.e., increasing the length of the payout period) increases the value of the guaranty. For $A/L$ of 0.8, on the other hand, a longer payout period tail leads to a lower premium.

If $r^* > 0$, the sum of $A/L = x$ and the premium $\pi$ has a unique minimum for any given set of parameter values.[26] The minima are shown in Table II for each parameter set tested. The accompanying minimum values of $x$ also are shown. Increasing the risk parameter $\sigma^2$ reduces the value of $x$ at which the minimum is attained but increases the sum of $x$ and the guaranty premium. Lengthening the payout tail reduces the minima of both $x$ and $x + \pi$.

Even though the present value of liabilities (per dollar of liabilities) is one, the minimum of $(x + \pi)$ is less than one. This result obtains as long as $r^* > 0$. If $r^* = 0$, $x + \pi$ approaches one from above.

## IV. Summary and Conclusions

This paper develops premium calculation models for insurance guaranty funds. Three models are developed: a) a basic model for a one-year guaranty applicable to an ongoing company, b) a one-year premium model with catastrophes, again for an ongoing company, and c) a policy cohort model for a block of policies with no fixed expiration date.

The models are based on the assumption that the paths of assets and liabilities over time can be described by diffusion processes. They also assume that the value of the guaranty fund itself reflects only systematic risk. The guaranty fund is assumed to be certain to pay its obligations.

The premium models account for asset risk, liability risk, and the risk of catastrophes. Unlike most previous pricing models for insurance risk (e.g., Fairley [13]), the models developed in this paper recognize the value of the guarantor's promise to pay losses even if the premium account has been exhausted. Thus, they provide a link between financial-theory and traditional actuarial-ruin models.

Additional research is needed to provide parameter estimates that take into account the asset and liability portfolio characteristics of individual companies. Further analysis of the liability-runoff and claims-inflation processes also would be helpful. Potential theoretical extensions include the effects of stochastic interest and jump processes other than the Poisson. If this research can be conducted successfully, the models developed in this paper have the potential to yield significant improvements in the pricing techniques utilized in insurance.

Finally, further research should be undertaken on the overall impact of solvency regulation on insurance markets. The objectives of regulation should be specified more clearly, and the assumption that the regulator's goal is the continued solvency of all presently existing insurers (see, for example, Mayerson [20, p. 150]) should be critically examined. This research should consider the joint effects of regulations such as minimum capitalization requirements, price regulation, asset portfolio restrictions, and guaranty funds. The goal should be to

---

[26] The proof is available from the author.

define economically viable regulatory objectives and to specify the combinations of policy variables that can achieve these objectives most effectively. The advantages and disadvantages of using private market mechanisms to accomplish regulatory goals should be thoroughly explored. By providing market prices for risks traded in insurance markets, the models presented in this article should play a central role in future research on the general effects of solvency regulation.

## REFERENCES

1. Milton Abramowitz and Irene Stegun. *Handbook of Mathematical Functions.* New York: Dover Publications, 1970.
2. James E. Bachman. *Capitalization Requirements for Multiple-Line Property-Liability Insurance Companies.* Philadelphia: Huebner Foundation, University of Pennsylvania, 1978.
3. R. E. Beard, T. Pentikainen, and E. Pesonen. *Risk Theory,* 3rd ed. New York: Chapman and Hall, 1984.
4. Fischer Black, Merton Miller, and Richard A. Posner. "An Approach to the Regulation of Bank Holding Companies." *Journal of Business* 51 (July 1978), 379–411.
5. Herbert Buchholz. *The Confluent Hypergeometric Function.* New York: Springer-Verlag, 1969.
6. Stephen A. Buser, Andrew H. Chen, and Edward J. Kane. "Federal Deposit Insurance, Regulatory Policy, and Optimal Bank Capital." *Journal of Finance* 36 (March 1981), 51–60.
7. Tim S. Campbell and David Glenn. "Deposit Insurance in a Deregulated Environment." *Journal of Finance* 39 (July 1984), 775–85.
8. Yuk-Shee Chan and King-Tim Mak. "Depositors' Welfare, Deposit Insurance, and Deregulation." *Journal of Finance* 40 (July 1985), 959–74.
9. J. David Cummins and Scott E. Harrington. "Property-Liability Insurance Rate Regulation: Estimation of Underwriting Betas Using Quarterly Profit Data." *Journal of Risk and Insurance* 52 (March 1985), 16–43.
10. J. David Cummins and David J. Nye. "The Stochastic Characteristics of Property-Liability Insurance Profits." *Journal of Risk and Insurance* 47 (March 1980), 61–80.
11. Neil A. Doherty and James R. Garven. "Price Regulation in Property-Liability Insurance: A Contingent-Claims Approach." *Journal of Finance* 41 (December 1986), 1031–50.
12. M. Duncan. "An Appraisal of Property and Casualty Post-Assessment Guaranty Funds." *Journal of Insurance Regulation* 2 (June 1984), 289–303.
13. William B. Fairley. "Investment Income and Profit Margins in Property-Liability Insurance: Theory and Empirical Tests." *Bell Journal* 10 (Spring 1979), 192–210.
14. Scott E. Harrington. "Impact of Rate Regulation on Prices and Underwriting Results in the Property-Liability Insurance Industry." *Journal of Risk and Insurance* 41 (December 1984), 577–623.
15. Raymond D. Hill and Franco Modigliani. "The Massachusetts Model of Profit Regulation in Non-Life Insurance: An Appraisal and Extensions." In J. David Cummins and Scott Harrington (eds.), *Fair Rate of Return in Property-Liability Insurance.* Norwell, MA: Kluwer Academic Publishers, 1987, 27–53.
16. Ibbotson Associates. *Stocks, Bonds, Bills, and Inflation: 1986 Yearbook.* Chicago: 1986.
17. George Kanatas. "Deposit Insurance and the Discount Window: Pricing under Asymmetric Information." *Journal of Finance* 41 (June 1986), 437–50.
18. Samuel Karlin and Howard Taylor. *A Second Course in Stochastic Processes.* New York: Academic Press, 1981.
19. Alan Kraus and Stephen A. Ross. "The Determination of Fair Profits for the Property-Liability Insurance Firm." *Journal of Finance* 37 (September 1982), 1015–28.
20. Allen L. Mayerson. "Ensuring the Solvency of Property and Liability Insurance Companies." In S. L. Kimball and H. S. Denenberg (eds.), *Insurance, Government, and Social Policy.* Homewood, IL: Richard D. Irwin, 1969, 146–90.
21. J. Houston McCulloch. "Interest-Risk Sensitive Deposit Insurance Premia: Stable ACH Estimates." *Journal of Banking and Finance* 9 (March 1985), 137–56.

22. Robert C. Merton. "Optimum Consumption and Portfolio Rules in a Continuous-Time Model." *Journal of Economic Theory* 3 (December 1971), 373–413.

23. ———. "Option Prices When Underlying Stock Returns Are Discontinuous." *Journal of Financial Economics* 3 (January–March 1976), 125–44.

24. ———. "An Analytic Derivation of the Cost of Deposit Insurance and Loan Guarantees: An Application of Modern Option Pricing Theory." *Journal of Banking and Finance* 1 (June 1977), 3–11.

25. ———. "On the Cost of Deposit Insurance When There Are Surveillance Costs." *Journal of Business* 51 (July 1978), 439–52.

26. Patricia Munch and Dennis Smallwood. "Solvency Regulation in the Property-Liability Insurance Industry: Empirical Evidence." *Bell Journal* 11 (Spring 1980), 261–79.

27. Stewart Myers and Richard Cohn. "Insurance Rate Regulation and the Capital Asset Pricing Model." In J. David Cummins and Scott Harrington (eds.), *Fair Rate of Return in Property-Liability Insurance*. Norwell, MA: Kluwer Academic Publishers, 1987, 55–78.

28. National Committee on Insurance Guaranty Funds. "State Insurance Guaranty Funds and Insurance Company Insolvency Assessment Information: 1969–1984." Schaumburg, IL: 1986.

29. George G. Pennacchi. "Valuing Alternative Forms of Deposit Insurance for Intermediaries Subject to Interest Rate Risk." Working paper, Wharton School, University of Pennsylvania, Philadelphia, 1984.

30. David G. Quirin and William R. Waters. "Market Efficiency and the Cost of Capital: The Strange Case of Fire and Casualty Insurance Companies." *Journal of Finance* 30 (May 1975), 427–50.

31. Ehud I. Ronn and Avinash K. Verma. "Pricing Risk-Adjusted Deposit Insurance: An Option-Based Model." *Journal of Finance* 41 (September 1986), 871–95.

32. Jaime Sabol. "Two Continent Claims Models of Insurance-Type Financial Instruments." Ph.D. dissertation, University of Pennsylvania, Philadelphia, 1986.

33. Terrie E. Troxel and Cormick Breslin. *Property-Liability Insurance Accounting and Finance*, 2nd. ed. Malvern, PA: The American Institute, 1983.

# An International Analysis of Underwriting Cycles in Property-Liability Insurance

J. David Cummins

J. François Outreville

## ABSTRACT

Most prior analyses of underwriting cycles have explained cycles as a supply-side phenomenon involving irrational behavior on the part of insurers. This paper proposes instead that insurance prices are set according to *rational* expectations. Although rational expectations per se would be inconsistent with an underwriting cycle, the authors hypothesize that cycles are "created" in an otherwise rational market through the intervention of institutional, regulatory, and accounting factors. Empirical evidence is presented indicating that underwriting profits in several industrialized nations are consistent with the hypothesis.

## Introduction

The underwriting cycle has been the subject of much recent discussion in the insurance literature (Conning & Co. [3]; Ferguson [11]). The consensus seems to be that the underwriting cycle in the United States is about six years

J. David Cummins is the Harry J. Loman Professor of Insurance at The University of Pennsylvania Wharton School. Professor Cummins earned his Ph.D. at the Wharton School where he is currently the Director of the Center for Research on Risk and Insurance and the Associate Director of the S.S. Huebner Foundation. The 1986-87 President of the American Risk and Insurance Association, Dr. Cummins is also a past chairman of its Risk Theory Seminar. Dr. Cummins is the author, co-author, or editor of many articles in professional journals and the following books: *Fair Rate of Return in Property-Liability Insurance, Strategic Planning and Modeling in Property-Liability Insurance,* and *Risk Classification in Life Insurance.*

J. François Outreville is presently an Economic Officer with UNCTAD in Geneva. The views in this article, however, should not be attributed to UNCTAD. Before his UNCTAD position Dr. Outreville was first an Associate Professor of Finance and Insurance at the Laval University and later a visiting Professor at the University of Texas at Austin.

The results of this research were presented at the 1984 Seminar of the European Group of Risk and Insurance Economists.

The authors are grateful to Abba Krieger for helpful comments on an earlier version of this article.

610

in length (Smith and Gahin [25]; Venezian [28]).[1] Experience during 1984–1985 may suggest that the cycle is lengthening, although it is too early to draw any conclusions. In any event, the same market forces seem to be at work; and institutional descriptions of the current cycle trough and upturn do not differ in any really significant way from prior discussions.

Although variations in profits suggest that a market mechanism may be operating, industry observers usually interpret the cycle as a supply-side phenomenon. The typical explanation is that the insurance industry causes the cycle more or less on its own, through periods of destructive competition followed by cutbacks in supply (Wilson [29]). More sophisticated versions usually relate the recurring phases of the cycle to key operating ratios such as the premiums-to-surplus ratio, which is said to represent capacity (Stewart [26]).

Advocates of the supply-side hypothesis typically do not provide an explanation of the causal mechanism through which market reversals take place. The assumption is that insurers "decide" at some point to constrict supply and raise prices. The motive for beginning to restrict supply at one point rather than another is not clearly specified, although some writers argue that it is related to the premiums-to-surplus ratio (Smith [23]) or, as Stewart suggests, to total income.

A supply-side analysis with a slightly different focus has been provided by Venezian [28]. He too implicitly assumes that prices are determined more or less unilaterally by the insurance industry, but he suggests a different connection between insurance industry behavior and the existence of cycles. Specifically, Venezian points out that ratemaking, at least as practiced in the United States, relies on extrapolations of past claim costs as predictors of future claim costs. These extrapolations typically involve an estimation period (for the extrapolation equation) of approximately three years, and an extrapolation period of about two years. (See Cummins and Griepentrog [5].)

Venezian presents a theoretical analysis demonstrating that this type of extrapolation procedure can generate a profit cycle. He conducts empirical tests on U.S. underwriting profit data and concludes that they follow a second order autoregressive process with a cycle length of about six years. In his view, the industry is responsible for creating the cycle through the use of naive forecasting procedures. Outreville [20] also points out problems related to the use of naive models.

Although not specifically concerned with cycles, Smith [24] provides results consistent with Venezian's findings. Specifically, Smith finds that underwriting profits follow a second-order autoregressive process. This type of process is the one hypothesized by Venezian, and it can generate a cyclical series.

Another empirical analysis of cycles is provided by Smith and Gahin [25]. They use spectral analysis to study several industry operating-variables for the period 1950–1978. The results indicate that statutory underwriting profits

---

[1] Doty [10] argues that, in addition to the short-term six-year underwriting cycle, both a 20-year insurance cycle and a 50 to 60 year general business cycle exist.

have a cycle period of 5.56 to 6.25 years, which is consistent with Venezian's findings and with the conventional wisdom.

A general equilibrium model of insurance pricing with the capability for explaining cycles has been developed by Doherty and Kang [9]. Their model considers both supply and demand, and the resulting prices and profits arise from the interaction of these two market forces. Relying on capital-asset pricing theory, supply is considered to be a function of interest rates and expected profits. The sign of the interest rate term is expected to be positive, i.e., insurers increase supply when interest rates rise in order to obtain funds to invest (known as cash-flow underwriting).

The demand for insurance in the Doherty-Kang model is hypothesized to be a function of price (the inverse of the loss ratio)[2] and aggregate economic activity (income), with the latter representing an index of the amount of insurable goods and services. The equilibrium price is determined in the model by equating the quantity demanded with the quantity supplied. Although clearly not the final word on the subject, the Doherty-Kang analysis represents the type of approach that must be used in order to develop a viable explanation of insurance prices and underwriting cycles.

As the foregoing discussion suggests, nearly all of the existing studies of underwriting cycles have focused almost exclusively on the United States.[3] If insurance markets have similar economic and institutional characteristics in other countries, one would expect to observe cyclical profit patterns on an international scale. These patterns would be reinforced through the operation of the international reinsurance market.

The purpose of this paper is to propose a new explanation for the existence of underwriting cycles. The explanation is consistent both with modern theories of financial markets and with the institutional realities of insurance markets. Specifically, the authors hypothesize that market equilibrium insurance premiums are set in competitive markets and reflect rational expectations.[4] I.e., the subjective expected values of future losses and other relevant variables reflected in market prices are hypothesized to be equal to the objective expectations, conditional on information available at the time rates are established. In the absence of other effects, rational expectations would be inconsistent with the existence of any type of profit cycle. The authors' contention is that institutional and regulatory factors intervene in insurance markets, leading to an "apparent" cycle.

The cycle hypothesized here is apparent in the sense that it has nothing to do with the underlying economic and statistical characteristics of insurance markets but rather is attributable to institutional and regulatory rigidities. Among the intervening factors are data collection lags, regulatory lags, policy

---

[2] The inverse of the loss ratio indicates the cost per dollar of losses required to administer the insurance mechanism. See for example Frech and Samprone [12].

[3] With the exception of De Witt [8], Helten [14], and Mormino [18].

[4] Like the Doherty-Kang model, the model postulated here is an equilibrium model. However, the authors explicitly specify only the equilibrium relationship and not the underlying supply and demand relationships.

renewal lags, and statutory accounting rules. Premiums need not be set irrationally in order to generate a cycle.

If this hypothesis proves to be correct, it would provide an explanation for the existence of cycles in countries other than the U.S., where extrapolative forecasting may not be so firmly entrenched. To provide preliminary evidence on this point, the authors test for the presence of cycles in several industrialized nations. Statistically significant cycles in all lines underwriting profits are present in eight of the thirteen countries tested. The cycles are between six and eight years in length in six of the eight countries where cycles exist. Automobile insurance cycles are present in all six of the countries for which auto data were available.

As suggested above, the existence of cycles (second-order autoregressive processes in reported profits) could be consistent both with the authors' hypothesis and with a Venezian-type hypothesis (which might be termed "irrational" expectations). Present data and institutional information on international ratemaking practices are insufficient to make a conclusive distinction between the two hypotheses. To conclude the article, the authors suggest the types of information that might be collected on a country-by-country basis in order to narrow further the range of possible explanations for cycles.

### Underwriting Cycles and Rational Decision Making

If cycles exist in insurance markets, institutional and regulatory factors may be responsible. One such institutional factor, the use of extrapolative forecasting techniques, has been investigated by Venezian [28]. Venezian's hypothesis implies a degree of irrationality on the part of insurers, i.e., past loss trends are extrapolated into the future in a rather mechanical way and other potentially relevant information is de-emphasized or disregarded.

In this section, the authors develop an alternative model that also is consistent with observed profit cycles in insurance. Specifically, they show that cycles in reported underwriting profits are consistent with a simple *rational expectations* model of insurance price determination, provided that institutional lags and reporting practices are taken into account. The rational expectations hypothesis implies that economic agents forecast economic variables without systematic error, i.e., that their *subjective* expected values of these variables are the same as the actual or objective expected values, *conditional on all information available at the time the forecasts are made.* The hypothesis is explained in more detail below.

The rational expectations model is intuitively appealing because it is consistent with recent economic theory developed for other types of financial markets. It also would help to explain the existence of underwriting cycles in countries other than the U.S., where mechanical trending procedures may not be employed.

The authors begin with the hypothesis that both demand and supply play a role in the determination of insurance prices. They also assume that insurance markets are competitive so that no monopoly rents exist. They hypothesize that the market's evaluation of the relevant economic variables is rational, but that observed prices (profit margins) are not consistent with rational expectations for the following reasons:

1. Contracting and informational features of the insurance transaction prevent prices from adjusting promptly to changing economic conditions.

2. Reporting practices average together prices from different periods and exacerbate any autocorrelation that may be present in the actual price relationships.

Among the contracting and informational features are (a) data collection lags, (b) regulatory lags, and (c) policy renewal lags. These features, any or all of which may be present in any given national insurance market, are discussed in more detail in Cummins and Nye [6]. A brief explanation of each type of lag is given below.

Ratemaking usually is based on annual data, which are not sufficiently mature for use, even in short-tail lines until several months after the close of the "experience period." This immaturity is due to delays in reporting and settling claims and delays in tabulating and analyzing the data. Projections are made from the experience period to the mid-point of the period for which the rates will apply, but these projections are necessarily based (at best) on information available prior to the projection date.

Insurance rates are regulated in many countries (Lemaire [16]). Insurers must have their rates approved by regulatory authorities prior to use (as in the U.S.) or conform to a uniform national tariff (as in Switzerland). Regulation almost always creates additional delays between the experience period and the effective date of the revised rates. In addition, rates may be revised less frequently than under a competitive system. (See, for example, MacAvoy [17].)

Renewal lags are present in most countries in virtually every line of property-liability insurance. Unlike prices for commodities and shares of stock, the prices of insurance policies cannot be changed simultaneously to reflect new information. Most insurance policies have terms of either six months or a year. Thus, for example, if policy terms are annual, rates are revised once a year, and new rates go into effect on January 1, the price for the average policy will change on about July 1 and the new rates will not be in effect for all policies until December 31.

The second major reason that insurance profits are inconsistent with rational expectations has to do with insurance company financial reporting. Most of the data used to demonstrate the existence of underwriting cycles are calendar year data. These data reflect loss estimates on an incurred basis, i.e., losses are matched to coverage provided during the calendar year. In a rational expectations world, loss estimates for any given year would reflect all information available at the end of that year, when the statutory statements are compiled.

The premium figures for the years also are based on accrual accounting, i.e., the premiums are those that were earned by the insurers by providing coverage during the year. However, the premiums earned during the year include premiums for policies issued during a period ranging from the first day of the preceding year to the last day of the reporting year. At best, these premiums reflect only information available at the time the corresponding policies were issued. Due to the lags discussed above, their information content is unlikely to be this current. Thus, a mismatch is very likely to exist between the information content of reported premiums and the information content of reported losses. As shown below, these factors can lead to seemingly irrational profit patterns.

### The Rational Expectations Hypothesis

Suppose that an economic variable $X_t$ is generated by the following linear model (see Abel and Mishkin [1]):

$$X_t = Z_{t-1} A + \mu_t \tag{1}$$

where $Z_{t-1}$ = a vector of variables known at the end of $t - 1$,

$\quad\quad A$ = a vector of coefficients, and

$\quad\quad \mu_t$ = a random error term.

Assume that $E(\mu_t | \phi_{t-1}) = 0$, where $\phi_{t-1}$ is the set of information available at the end of period $t - 1$. Then,

$$E(X_t | \phi_{t-1}) = Z_{t-1} A \tag{2}$$

Now consider a forecast of $X_t$, denoted $X_t^f$. Rationality requires that the subjective expectation of $X_t$, $X_t^f$, equals the objective expectation. A weak form of the hypothesis can be expressed as follows:

$$E(X_t - X_t^f | \phi_{t-1}) = 0 \tag{3}$$

where $\Xi_t = X_t - X_t^f$.

Since equation (3) is merely the regression of $\Xi_t$ on $\phi_{t-1}$, the implication is that $\Xi_t$ is serially uncorrelated and uncorrelated with any information in $\phi_{t-1}$. As explained below, a specific pattern of autocorrelation is necessary to develop an underwriting cycle. Thus, if the standard rational expectations model were applicable in insurance, no underwriting cycle would exist.

### A Simple Insurance Model With Rational Expectations

In this section, the authors develop a simple, stylized model of an insurance market. The model is based upon simplifying assumptions about ratemaking lags and reporting practices. Although the real world is clearly much more complex, it is remarkable that the model developed below predicts cyclical patterns in underwriting profits very similar to those observed in many industrialized nations.

Consider a second-order autoregressive model for underwriting profits:

$$\Pi_t = a_0 + a_1 \Pi_{t-1} + a_2 \Pi_{t-2} + \omega_t \qquad (4)$$

where $\Pi_t$ = underwriting profits in period t, and

$\omega_t$ = a random error term.

As Venezian [28] points out, a cycle will be present if $a_1 > 0$, $a_2 < 0$, and $a_1^2 + 4a_2 < 0$ (see below). Under reasonable assumptions, the model developed below predicts coefficients ($a_1$ and $a_2$) with the correct signs and magnitudes to generate a cycle in reported profits.

To provide a standard of comparison, the model is first developed assuming rational expectations with no institutional or reporting complications. Consider the following time line:

and assume that rates for all policies can be changed simultaneously at the end of any period on the basis of the information at that time. I.e., premiums are determined as follows:

$$P_t = f(Y_{t-1}) \qquad (5)$$

where $Y_{t-1}$ is some set of variables contained in $\phi_{t-1}$. $P_t$ is the premium net of expenses and underwriting profit loadings, which are assumed to be a constant proportion of the net premium over time.[5] Y could include past claims experience, interest rates, inflation rates, etc. Rational expectations requires that the following condition hold (Abel and Mishkin [1]):

$$E[L_t - f(Y_{t-1})|\phi_{t-1}] = 0 \qquad (6)$$

where $\Pi_t = L_t - f(Y_{t-1})$ is the unanticipated underwriting loss (profit).

To simplify the algebra, assume that all relevant information about insurance losses at the end of any year (say $t-1$) is contained in the loss experience for that year ($L_{t-1}$). This variable can be written as follows:

$$L_{t-1} = E(L_{t-1}) + \varepsilon_{t-1} + \mu_{t-1} \qquad (7)$$

where $E(L_{t-1})$ = the objective expected value of losses as of the beginning of period $t-1$,

---

[5] The profit loading assumption could be consistent with variance or systematic risk-based relationships, provided that the relationship between the loadings and expected losses remains relatively stable over time.

$\varepsilon_{t-1}$ = the permanent or systematic component of the difference between actual and expected losses, and

$\mu_{t-1}$ = the transitory or unsystematic component of the difference between actual and expected losses.

The error terms ($\mu$ and $\varepsilon$) have zero means, are not autocorrelated, and are uncorrelated with each other. The systematic error ($\varepsilon$) represents a permanent change in loss levels and thus becomes part of the expected value of losses in subsequent periods. The unsystematic error ($\mu$) applies only to the period under consideration.

Rational expectations would imply:

$$E(L_t - E^f(L_t|\phi_{t-1})|\phi_{t-1}) = 0 \tag{8}$$

where $E^f(L_t|\phi_{t-1})$ = the subjective (market assessed) expectation of $L_t$ conditional on information available at the end of $t-1$.

Considering equation (7), (8) implies

$$E(L_t|\phi_{t-1}) = E^f(L_t|\phi_{t-1}) = E(L_{t-1}) + \varepsilon_{t-1} \tag{9}$$

Thus, the premium generating model would be:

$$P_t = E(L_{t-1}) + \varepsilon_{t-1} \tag{10}$$

Underwriting losses (profits) would be:

$$\Pi_t = L_t - E(L_t) = \varepsilon_t + \mu_t \tag{11}$$

Equation (11) implies that profits would not be autocorrelated and no cycle would be observed.

Retaining the assumption that insurance markets take into account all information available at the time premiums are set, now introduce data collection and regulatory lags. Specifically, assume that these lags result in a delay of one year between the experience period and the effective date of the new rates. This assumption implies the following pricing model:

$$P_t = E(L_t|\phi_{t-2}) = E(L_{t-2}) + \varepsilon_{t-2} \tag{12}$$

The model is appropriate because no information from period $t-1$ is available at the time rates are set and because the expected values of $\varepsilon$ and $\mu$ are zero. Note that it is rational in the sense that the market distinguishes between systematic and unsystematic errors.

Underwriting losses under this rate structure would be:

$$\Pi_t = L_t - P_t = \varepsilon_t + \mu_t + \varepsilon_{t-1} \tag{13}$$

Thus, first-order autocorrelation would be present. Although the second and higher order autocorrelations of $\Pi_t$ would be zero, the least squares regression coefficient of $\Pi_t$ on $\Pi_{t-2}$ in the regression of $\Pi_t$ on $\Pi_{t-1}$ and $\Pi_{t-2}$ generally will not be zero. Thus, profits may appear to follow a second-order autoregressive process. The magnitude of the regression coefficient of $\Pi_{t-2}$ when profits are generated by equation (13) is less than that usually observed in practice (see appendix), implying that additional complications must be accounted for.

A second-order process can be created by combining informational and regulatory lags with renewal lags and calendar-year reporting practices. Recall that rates are assumed to change at the beginning of each year and to remain in effect for one year. Also assume that policy terms are one year in length and that policies are renewed evenly throughout the year. Under these assumptions, *reported* profits in any given year will be a weighted average of the *actual* profits implied by the two most recent pricing decisions, i.e.,

$$\Pi_t^R = \alpha \Pi_t + (1-\alpha) \Pi_{t-1}$$

$$= \alpha(\varepsilon_t + \mu_t + \varepsilon_{t-1}) + (1-\alpha)(\varepsilon_{t-1} + \mu_{t-1} + \varepsilon_{t-2}) \tag{14}$$

If the $\varepsilon$ and $\mu$ processes are stationary and neither autocorrelated nor cross-correlated, the regression coefficients of $\Pi_t^R$ on $\Pi_{t-1}^R$ and $\Pi_{t-2}^R$ will be of the correct signs and magnitudes to give rise to an apparent cycle similar to that observed in practice (see appendix). The cycle is apparent in the sense that it has nothing to do with the underlying economic and statistical characteristics of insurance profits but rather reflects institutional factors and accounting practices.

*Empirical Measurement of Cycle Periods*

A necessary but not sufficient condition for the above hypothesis to be valid is the existence of autoregressive profit patterns in insurance underwriting profits. Specifically, equation (4) should hold with $a_1^2 + 4 a_2 < 0$. In this case, the characteristic equation of the second order difference equation in underwriting profits will have complex roots, implying that profits follow a cyclical pattern.[6] The period of the cycle is obtained from the following formula:

---

[6] See for example Nelson and Plosser [19]. Slutsky [22] notes that the second-order case is simple and unambiguous but that there is no reason why we should not fit higher order difference equations if this adds to the explanatory power. A discussion on the measures of cyclic variation can be found in Harvey [13].

$$\text{Period (P)} = 2\,\pi/\cos^{-1}\,(a_1/2\sqrt{-a_2}\,) \qquad\qquad (15)$$

The cycle will be damped (i.e., have a tendency to die down over time) if $\sqrt{-a_2} < 1$. If $\sqrt{-a_2} > 1$, the cycle will be explosive. Even a damped cycle will be maintained over time if random shocks occur.

To test for the existence of international underwriting cycles, equation (4) was estimated using data from several industrialized nations. Two principal data sets were available: Outreville [21] and Szpiro [27]. The former included all lines and automobile insurance results for six countries, while the latter reported all lines results for thirteen countries.[7] A decision was made to utilize the largest possible data set for each variable. Hence, the Szpiro data were analyzed for overall results and the Outreville data for auto.[8]

The data period in all of the regressions is 1957–1979. A few additional years of data (either before or after the 1957–1979 data period) were available for a minority of the countries. Outside of the U.S., the earliest available data for any of the countries begain in 1950 and the most recent data were for 1981. The years of the early 1950s were not included in the analysis because they are unlikely to be comparable with more recent experience. The 1980 and 1981 data were eliminated because it was considered desirable to utilize a uniform sample period. Estimation including 1980 and 1981 where data for these years were available yielded results very similar to those for the period 1957–1979.

The dependent variable in most of the regressions is the ratio of premiums to losses. This ratio reflects the proportionate loading or transactions costs of insurance and is a measure of the aggregate economic value of insurance (Frech and Samprone [12]). Profit ratios were not used because expense data are unavailable for most of the countries analyzed. The authors do not consider this use of premiums-to-surplus ratios to be a serious limitation because profit ratios are highly correlated with premium-to-claim ratios in countries for which both types of data are available (see Cummins and Nye [6] and Outreville [21]) and because a trend variable was included in all equations to account for the downward trend in expenses which is present in many countries (see Outreville [21]).

The results for all lines profit ratios are shown in table 1. The equations in the table were estimated utilizing ordinary least squares. The coefficient of at least one of the lagged profits terms was statistically significant (at the 5 percent level) in 12 of the 13 countries, indicating some degree of autocorrelation in insurance profits in nearly all of the markets tested. The

---

[7] Data for Israel were included in Szpiro's data base but were omitted from the study because of the high rate of inflation and prevalence of indexation in the Israeli economy.

[8] Although the data available in Outreville [21] and Szpiro [27] represent a significant improvement over that in prior sources, a number of limitations are present. Loss and expense ratios are available for all lines combined in most of the countries, but in some European countries, the data reported are not consistent with North American countries' data. Comparative data by line are available only for automobile insurance, and in many cases only the loss ratio is available.

second-order lagged profits term was statistically significant and negative in eight countries and was close to significance for Italy. Thus, evidence of cyclicality was present in a majority of the countries tested. The cycle length was between six and eight years in six of the countries tested and slightly above eight years for a seventh (France). The cycle period for Italy also fell in this range when the observations for 1957–1959, apparent outliers for this country, were eliminated. As noted above (and in the appendix) a six to eight year cycle length is consistent with the rational expectations/institutional intervention hypothesis.

The automobile insurance profit ratio regressions are presented in table 2. A significant underwriting cycle is present in all six countries tested. The cycle length ranges from 5.17 to 9.92 with a mean of 7.09.

**Table 1**

ALL-LINES UNDERWRITING PROFIT RATIO REGRESSIONS
FOR THIRTEEN MAJOR NATIONS

| | a(0) | a(1) | a(2) | Time | R-SQ | Cycle Period |
|---|---|---|---|---|---|---|
| Australia | 1.911 | 0.294 | −0.411 | −0.016 | 0.63 | 4.69 |
| | | 1.407 | 1.939 | 3.402 | | |
| Canada | 1.193 | 0.959 | −0.670 | −0.008 | 0.76 | 6.65 |
| | | 6.031 | 4.161 | 3.545 | | |
| Denmark | 0.667 | 0.477 | 0.109 | −0.008 | 0.16 | NC |
| | | 2.074 | 0.476 | 1.556 | | |
| Finland | 0.932 | 0.490 | −0.029 | −0.004 | 0.29 | NC |
| | | 2.159 | 0.136 | 0.920 | | |
| France | 1.770 | 0.904 | −0.392 | −0.395 | 0.90 | 8.23 |
| | | 4.476 | 2.365 | 3.048 | | |
| Germany | 1.191 | 0.879 | −0.406 | −0.021 | 0.88 | 7.76 |
| | | 4.246 | 1.943 | 2.951 | | |
| Italy: 1957–1979 | 0.676 | 0.865 | −0.253 | < .001 | 0.65 | 11.71 |
| | | 4.779 | 1.398 | 0.011 | | |
| 1960–1979 | 1.036 | 0.775 | −0.346 | −0.003 | 0.46 | 7.38 |
| | | 3.475 | 1.680 | 0.674 | | |
| Japan | 1.268 | 0.812 | −0.349 | −0.005 | 0.65 | 7.72 |
| | | 4.588 | 2.017 | 1.029 | | |
| New Zealand | 1.305 | 0.694 | −0.397 | −0.010 | 0.73 | 6.36 |
| | | 3.337 | 1.995 | 2.635 | | |
| Norway | 0.377 | 0.515 | 0.233 | < .001 | 0.57 | NC |
| | | 2.320 | 1.074 | 0.338 | | |
| Sweden | 1.103 | 0.714 | −0.434 | 0.004 | 0.46 | 6.29 |
| | | 3.379 | 1.895 | 1.084 | | |
| Switzerland | 1.826 | 0.355 | −0.210 | −0.015 | 0.78 | 5.35 |
| | | 1.614 | 0.933 | 3.048 | | |
| United States | 1.379 | 0.904 | −0.767 | −0.010 | 0.90 | 6.11 |
| | | 6.848 | 5.946 | 5.694 | | |

NOTE: The estimation period is 1957–1979, unless otherwise indicated. The estimation equation is: $CR(t) = a(0) + a(1)CR(t-1) + a(2)CR(t-2) + u(t)$ where $CR(t)$ = the premiums to claims ratio in year t and $u(t)$ = a random error term. All equations were estimated by ordinary least squares. Absolute values of t-statistics appear below coefficients.

As suggested above, an examination of the institutional and regulatory characteristics of insurance markets in each of the countries tested would be needed to link the empirical findings with the rational expectations/ institutional intervention hypothesis. Little published information is available on the relevant institutional features of international insurance markets.

In order to judge the consistency of the results with the hypothesis, information would be needed on: (1) the automobile insurance ratemaking process, including any trending procedures, (2) the length of time between policy renewal dates, (3) regulatory practices and competitiveness of markets, and (4) profit and loss accounting practices. This listing can serve as a preliminary research agenda for future investigations of international underwriting cycles.

### Table 2

AUTOMOBILE INSURANCE LOSS RATIO REGRESSIONS
FOR SIX MAJOR NATIONS

|  | a(0) | a(1) | a(2) | Time | R-SQ | Cycle Period |
|---|---|---|---|---|---|---|
| Canada* | 1.297 | 0.851 | −0.635 | −0.014 | 0.78 | 6.24 |
|  |  | 5.012 | 3.764 | 3.985 |  |  |
| France | 0.696 | 0.946 | −0.431 | −0.007 | 0.90 | 8.20 |
|  |  | 4.802 | 2.612 | 2.955 |  |  |
| Italy | 0.741 | 1.261 | −0.612 | −0.014 | 0.87 | 9.92 |
|  |  | 7.619 | 4.016 | 1.320 |  |  |
| Sweden | 0.802 | 0.816 | −0.397 | −0.001 | 0.43 | 7.26 |
|  |  | 3.781 | 2.087 | 0.150 |  |  |
| Switzerland | 1.758 | 0.445 | −0.409 | −0.010 | 0.46 | 5.17 |
|  |  | 2.219 | 2.242 | 2.522 |  |  |
| United States | 1.347 | 0.735 | −0.653 | −0.007 | 0.73 | 5.72 |
|  |  | 4.816 | 4.657 | 3.896 |  |  |

NOTE: The estimation period is 1957–1979, unless otherwise indicated. The estimation equation is: $CR(t) = a(0) + a(1)CR(t-1) + a(2)CR(t-2) + u(t)$ where $CR(t)$ = the premiums to claims ratio in year t and $u(t)$ = a random error term. All equations were estimated by ordinary least squares. Absolute values of t-statistics appear below coefficients.

*Estimation period for Canada is 1958–1979.

### Summary and Conclusions

This paper proposes a new explanation for the cyclical profit patterns that appear to exist in property-liability insurance. Unlike most prior studies, which have assumed that insurance profits were determined primarily by supply- side considerations, the authors hypothesize that prices and profits are established in a rational, competitive market. Prices are rational in the sense that they accurately reflect the expected value of losses, conditional upon all information available at the time rates are set.

In the absence of intervening factors, the rational expectations hypothesis would be inconsistent with the existence of cycles. The authors hypothesize that institutional and regulatory lags, combined with insurer accounting practices, are responsible for the cyclical behavior of reported underwriting profits. A simple model is specified in the paper which generates apparent profit cycles.

A necessary but not sufficient condition for the hypothesis to be valid is the existence of cyclicality in observed underwriting profits. Tests of all lines underwriting profits in thirteen countries reveal that a cycle is present in a majority of the countries tested. In six of the countries, the cycle is between six and eight years in length. Cycles are present in automobile insurance profits in all six countries tested. The average cycle length for auto is 7.1 years.

While the empirical findings are consistent with the rational expectations/institutional intervention hypothesis, they also may be consistent with other hypotheses such as Venezian's extrapolative expectations hypothesis. In order to narrow the field of competing hypotheses, additional information is needed on the institutional and regulatory characteristics of insurance markets in the countries tested. Information on ratemaking procedures, regulatory constraints, lengths of policy terms, and accounting procedures would be helpful and should be the subject of future international insurance research. More precise and detailed information on actual rather than reported profits also would be useful.

If institutional features such as renewal lags are partially responsible for the existence of underwriting cycles, it is interesting to speculate on why these practices continue to be used. Market stability would seem to be enhanced if insurers were able to change premiums more easily to reflect newly emerging information. This change would imply shorter policy terms and less cumbersome rate calculation procedures.

Adverse selection and the accompanying underwriting costs may play a role in explaining why insurance prices do not change more rapidly. In the stock market, for example, relatively little investigation or "underwriting" of market participants is necessary; the price of a share is the same for all buyers. In insurance, on the other hand, the price is buyer-specific; and the transactions costs of underwriting and classifying risks are high. However, the underwriting process is necessary in order to prevent market failure due to misclassification (Cummins, et al. [7]). Perhaps profit cyclicality is the price that must be paid to keep underwriting costs within manageable limits. Future research into these and other aspects of insurance transactions would help to clarify further the causes of and possible solutions to the underwriting cycle.

### Appendix

The equation to be estimated is the following:

$$\Pi_t^R = a_1 \Pi_{t-1}^R + a_2 \Pi_{t-2}^R + \omega_t \tag{A1}$$

where $\Pi_t^R = \rho \, \Pi_t + (1 - \rho) \, \Pi_{t-1}$

$$= \rho(\varepsilon_t + \mu_t + \varepsilon_{t-1}) + (1-\rho)(\varepsilon_{t-1} + \mu_{t-1} + \varepsilon_{t-2}) \tag{A2}$$

The latter expression is equation (14) from the text.

The assumptions on the regressors and regression error terms are as follows:

$$E(\varepsilon_t) = E(\mu_t) = E(\omega_t) = 0 \tag{A3}$$

$$\mathrm{Var}(\varepsilon_t) = \sigma_\varepsilon^2 \, ; \, \mathrm{Var}(\mu_t) = \sigma_\mu^2 \, ; \, \mathrm{Var}(\omega_t) = \sigma_\omega^2 \tag{A4}$$

$$E(\varepsilon_t \varepsilon_{t-i}) = E(\mu_t \mu_{t-i}) = E(\omega_t \omega_{t-i}) = 0, \text{ all } i \geqslant 1 \tag{A5}$$

and $E(\varepsilon_{t-i} \mu_{t-j}) = E(\varepsilon_{t-i} \omega_{t-j}) = E(\mu_{t-i} \omega_{t-j}) = 0,$ all i,j $\qquad$ (A6)

Using a notational simplification that is correct in the limit, the regression coefficients in (A1) can be written as indicated below (in the following, the R superscripts on the $\Pi$s are dropped to simplify the notation; all $\Pi$s after this point are understood to refer to *reported* profits):

$$\hat{a}_1 = E(\Pi_t \Pi_{t-1}) \, [E(\Pi_t^2) - E(\Pi_t \Pi_{t-2})]/D \tag{A7}$$

$$\hat{a}_2 = [E(\Pi_t \Pi_{t-2}) \, E(\Pi_t^2) - E(\Pi_t \Pi_{t-1})^2]/D \tag{A8}$$

where $D = E(\Pi_t^2)^2 - E(\Pi_t \Pi_{t-1})^2$ $\qquad$ (A9)

Also:

$$E(\Pi_t^2) = (1/(T-2)) \sum_{t=3}^{T} \{ [\varepsilon_{t-1}^2 + \varepsilon_t^2 + \mu_t^2] \, \rho^2 +$$

$$[\varepsilon_{t-2}^2 + \varepsilon_{t-1}^2 + \mu_{t-1}^2] \, (1-\rho)^2 + 2\rho(1-\rho) \, \varepsilon_{t-1}^2 \} \tag{A10}$$

$$E(\Pi_t \Pi_{t-1}) = (1/(T-2)) \sum_{t=3}^{T} \{ [\varepsilon_{t-2}^2 + \varepsilon_{t-1}^2 + \mu_{t-1}^2] \, \rho \, (1-\rho)$$

$$+ (1-\rho)^2 \, \varepsilon_{t-2}^2 + \rho^2 \, \varepsilon_{t-1}^2 \} \tag{A11}$$

$$E(\Pi_t \Pi_{t-2}) = (1/(T-2)) \sum_{t=3}^{T} [\rho \, (1-\rho) \, \varepsilon_{t-2}^2] \tag{A12}$$

where $T$ = the number of periods for which data are available and the superscript R on the $\Pi$s has been dropped to simplify the notation.

Recalling that $\varepsilon$ and $\mu$ are stationary (i.e., their variances are constant through time) and taking probability limits in (A7) and (A8) yields:

$$\plim_{T\to\infty} \hat{a}_1 = \{\rho\,(1-\rho)\,[2\,\sigma_\varepsilon^2 + \sigma_\mu^2] + (1-\rho)^2\,\sigma_\varepsilon^2 + \rho^2\sigma_\varepsilon^2\}$$

$$\{[\rho^2\,(2\sigma_\varepsilon^2+\sigma_\mu^2) + (1-\rho)^2\,(2\sigma_\varepsilon^2+\sigma_\mu^2)$$

$$+2\,\rho\,(1-\rho)\,\sigma_\varepsilon^2] - \rho\,(1-\rho)\,\sigma_\varepsilon^2\}/D \tag{A13}$$

$$\plim_{T\to\infty} \hat{a}_2 = \{\rho\,(1-\rho)\,\sigma_\varepsilon^2\,[\rho^2\,(2\sigma_\varepsilon^2 + \sigma_\mu^2) + (1-\rho)^2\,(2\,\sigma_\varepsilon^2 +$$

$$\sigma_\mu^2) + 2\,\rho\,(1-\rho)\,\sigma_\varepsilon^2] - [\rho(1-\rho)\,(2\,\sigma_\varepsilon^2+\sigma_\mu^2)$$

$$+(1-\rho)^2\,\sigma_\varepsilon^2+\rho^2\,\sigma_\varepsilon^2]^2\}/D \tag{A14}$$

$$\plim_{T\to\infty} D = [\rho^2\,(2\,\sigma_\varepsilon^2+\sigma_\mu^2) + (1-\rho)^2\,(2\,\sigma_\varepsilon^2+\sigma_\mu^2) +$$

$$2\,\rho\,(1-\rho)\,\sigma_\varepsilon^2]^2 - [\rho\,(1-\rho)\,(2\,\sigma_\varepsilon^2+\sigma_\mu^2)$$

$$+(1-\rho)^2\,\sigma_\varepsilon^2+\rho^2\,\sigma_\varepsilon^2]^2 \tag{A15}$$

These expressions simplify considerably if $\rho = .5$. In this case:

$$\plim\,\hat{a}_1 = [(4\,\sigma_\varepsilon^2+\sigma_\mu^2)\,(6\sigma_\varepsilon^2+2\,\sigma_\mu^2-\sigma_\varepsilon^2)]/(16\,\plim\,D) \tag{A16}$$

$$\plim\,\hat{a}_2 = [\sigma_\varepsilon^2\,(6\sigma_\varepsilon^2+2\,\sigma_\mu^2) - (4\,\sigma_\varepsilon^2+\sigma_\mu^2)^2]/(16\,\plim\,D) \tag{A17}$$

$$\plim\,D = \{[6\,\sigma_\varepsilon^2+2\,\sigma_\mu^2]^2 - [4\,\sigma_\varepsilon^2+\sigma_\mu^2]^2\}/16 \tag{A18}$$

Further insight into the problem can be gained by considering three special cases:

Case 1: Assume that $\sigma_\varepsilon^2 = \sigma_\mu^2$

In this case, $\plim\,\hat{a}_1 = 35/39 = .897$
$\plim\,\hat{a}_2 = 17/39 = -.436$
The implied cycle length would be 7.63 periods.

Case 2: Assume that $\sigma_\varepsilon^2 = 0$

This assumption yields $\plim\,\hat{a}_1 = .667$; $\plim\,\hat{a}_2 = -.333$
This cycle length would be 6.57 periods.

Case 3: Assume that $\sigma_\mu^2 = 0$

This assumption yields $\plim\,\hat{a}_1 = 1$; $\plim\,\hat{a}_2 = -.5$
The cycle length would be 8.0 periods.

Of course, in practice, the coefficients would be more complicated functions of the $\varepsilon_t$ and $\sigma_t$ because policy renewals and rate changes would not occur in the predictable patterns assumed in developing the model. Nevertheless, it is quite revealing that a simple institutional lag hypothesis can generate

624

regression coefficients and cycle lengths very similar to those observed in practice.

Finally, assume that equation (13) applies, so that

$$\Pi_t = \varepsilon_t + \mu_t + \varepsilon_{t-1} \tag{A19}$$

In this case,

$$\text{plim } \hat{a}_1 = .375 \text{ and plim } \hat{a}_2 = -.125$$

The coefficients are smaller than those observed in most countries.

## REFERENCES

1. Abel, Andrew A. and Frederic S. Mishkin [1983]. "An Integrated View of Tests of Rationality, Market Efficiency and the Short-Run Neutrality of Monetary Policy." *Journal of Monetary Economics* 11: 3–24.
2. Chiang, Alpha C. [1974]. *Fundamental Methods of Mathematical Economics.* New York: McGraw-Hill Book Co.
3. Conning & Company. [1979]. A Study of Why Underwriting Cycles Occur. Hartforld, CT.
4. Conning & Company. [1981]. Investment Income in Ratemaking, A Risk and Return Analysis. Hartford, CT.
5. Cummins, J. David and Gary L. Griepentrog [1985]. "Forecasting Automobile Insurance Paid Claim Costs Using Econometric and ARIMA Models." *International Journal of Forecasting* 1: 203–215.
6. Cummins, J. David and David J. Nye [1984]. "Insurance and Inflation: Causes, Consequences, and Solutions." In John D. Long, ed., *Issues in Insurance.* 2nd ed. Malvern, PA: American Institute for Property-Liability Underwriters.
7. Cummins, J. David, et al. [1984]. *Risk Classification In Life Insurance.* Hingham, MA: Kluwer-Nijhoff.
8. De Witt, G.W. [1979]. "Cycles in Insurance: A Review of Past Researches and Proposals of Further Studies." *Etudes et Dossiers* 33: 6–30. Geneva: Association International pour l'Etude de l'Economie de l'Assurance.
9. Doherty, Neil and Han B. Kang [1984]. "Interest Rates and Cyclical Underwriting Profits in the Property-Liability Insurance Industry: An Equilibrium Approach." Working paper, Department of Finance, University of Illinois at Urbana-Champaign.
10. Doty, G.E. [1982]. "Cash Flow Underwriting: A Broader View." *Best's Review: Property and Casualty Edition* (December).
11. Ferguson, R.E. [1983]. "Will the Underwriting Cycle Turn at 10:55 A.M. on April 22, 1983?" *Best's Review: Property and Casualty Edition* (March).
12. Frech, H.E. and J.C. Samprone [1980]. "The Welfare Loss of Excess Nonprice Competition: The Case of Property-Liability Insurance Regulations." *Journal of Law and Economics* 13 (October): 429–440.
13. Harvey, A.D. [1985]. "Trends and Cycles in Macroeconomic Time Series." *Journal of Business and Economic Statistics* 3 (July): 216–227.

14. Helten, E. [1979]. "Elements of Loss Development: Trends, Business Cycles and Fortuitous Events." *Etudes et Dossiers* 33: 86–104. Geneva: Association Internationale pour l'Etude de l'Economie de l'Assurance.
15. Judge, George G., et al. [1982]. *Introduction to the Theory and Practice of Econometrics.* New York: John Wiley & Sons.
16. Lemaire, Jean [1985]. *Automobile Insurance: Actuarial Models.* Hingham, MA: Kluwer-Nijhoff.
17. MacAvoy, Paul W. [1977]. *Federal-State Regulation of the Pricing and Marketing of Insurance.* Washington, DC: American Enterprise Institute for Public Policy Research.
18. Mormino, C.A. [1979]. "Insurance Cycles: An Italian Experience." *Etudes et Dossiers* 33: 37–85. Geneva: Association Internationale pour l'Etude de l'Economie de l'Assurance.
19. Nelson, C.R. and C.I. Plosser [1982]. "Trends and Random Walks in Macroeconomic Time Series." *Journal of Monetary Economics* 10: 139–162.
20. Outreville, J. François [1981]. "Les operations des compagnies d'assurances IARD: Identification de modeles et simulation d'hypotheses de conjuncture economique." *Geneva Papers on Risk and Insurance* 6 (October).
21. Outreville, J. François [1984]. "Les Resultats techniques de l'assurance Incendie, Accidents et Risques Divers en Amerique du Nord et en Europe: 1955–1979." *Etudes et Dossiers* 82. Geneve: Association Internationale pour l'Etude de l'Economie de l'Assurance.
22. Slutsky, E. [1932]. "The Summation of Random Causes as the Source of Cyclical Processes." *Econometrica* 5 (April): 105–146.
23. Smith, B.D. [1982]. "The Property and Liability Underwriting Cycle: What Lies Ahead?" *CPCU Journal* (September): 138–142.
24. Smith, Michael L. [1984]. "Property-Liability Insurance Markets, Taxation, and Interest Rates: Preliminary Findings." *Proceedings.* International Insurance Seminar, New Orleans, LA.
25. Smith, Milton E. and Fikry S. Gahin [1983]. "The Underwriting Cycle in Property and Liability Insurance (1950–1978)." Paper presented at the 1983 Risk Theory Seminar, Helsinki, Finland.
26. Stewart, Barbara [1981]. "Profit Cycles in Property-Liability Insurance." In John D. Long, ed., *Issues In Insurance.* Malvern, PA: American Institute for Property-Liability Underwriters.
27. Szpiro, George G. [1984]. "Risk Aversion and Insurance: International Comparisons and Applications." Ph.D. diss., Hebrew University, Jerusalem, Israel.
28. Venezian, Emilio [1985]. "Ratemaking Methods and Profit Cycles in Property and Liability Insurance." *Journal of Risk and Insurance* 52 (September): 477–500.
29. Wilson, W.C. [1981]. "The Underwriting Cycle and Investment Income." *CPCU Journal* 34 (December): 225–232.

# Prices and Profits in the
# Liability Insurance Market

## Scott E. Harrington

COMMERCIAL liability insurance premiums increased dramatically in 1985 and 1986. The growth for general liability insurance was especially pronounced: net premiums written increased from $6.5 billion in 1984 to $20 billion in 1986. During this time, limits of coverage were shrinking for many of those insured, and cancellations and denials of renewal were widespread for some types of business in some states. Premium growth had moderated substantially by the end of 1986, but the large increases in the previous two years undoubtedly imposed high costs on many businesses and professionals. Insurers reported large accounting losses on operations in 1984 and 1985. The causes of the premium increases— whether rapidly escalating and unpredictable claim costs, severe underpricing of business written before 1985 because of cyclical influences in the industry, or both—have been vigorously debated, as has the extent to which industry operations actually were unprofitable. While widespread deregulation of commercial insurance rates occurred during the 1970s, a few states have enacted new forms of rate regulation in response to recent experience.

This chapter provides an overview of prices and profitability in the commercial liability insurance market to examine the nature and causes of recent experience. It describes the structure of the market and possible causes of underwriting cycles and reviews financial and operating results for recent years. Detailed information is provided about growth rates in losses for general liability and other major liability lines. A model of breakeven (that is, zero-profit) insurance prices is used to provide evidence of whether increases in general liability premiums were commensurate with increases in the discounted value of losses and expenses. The chapter does not deal directly with tort reform, nor with allegations of collusion recently raised in several lawsuits against major liability insurers, but the anaiysis sheds light on some of the key issues.

The findings suggest that overall financial results for the property and liability insurance industry deteriorated substantially in 1984 and 1985, regardless of the accounting conventions used to measure income. Losses for commercial liability coverage, especially general liability insurance, were largely responsible for this decline. Growth in several measures of insured losses for general liability coverage increased significantly relative to GNP. The results also suggest that the total increase in premiums since 1981 can largely be explained by increases in the discounted value of reported losses. However, premium increases appear to have been much smaller than cost increases through 1984, with the result that substantial increases were needed to catch up with the growth in the discounted value of losses. While questions remain concerning why premiums failed to keep pace with losses through 1984, the analysis suggests that, based on what we know, significant changes in regulatory policy for the industry are not warranted.

## Overview of the Market

Table 3-1 presents national market shares for the largest property and liability insurer group, the four largest groups, and the twenty largest groups by line of business. The low concentration levels indicate that the commercial liability insurance market is competitively structured.[1] The

1. See Paul L. Joskow, "Cartels, Competition and Regulation in the Property-Liability Insurance Industry," *Bell Journal of Economics and Mangement Science,* vol. 4 (Autumn 1973), pp. 375–427, for an early analysis of market structure in the property-liability industry. The competitive structure of the industry also has been emphasized by the Department of Justice, *The Pricing and Marketing of Insurance: A Report of the U.S. Department of Justice to the Task Group on Antitrust Immunities* (Washington, D.C., 1977). Also see the discusion in Tort Policy Working Group, *Report of the Tort Policy Working Group on the Causes, Extent and Policy Implications of the Current Crisis in Insurance Availability and Affordability* (Washington, D.C.: Department of Justice, 1986); and the Herfindahl-Herschmann indices reported by the Department of Justice, Antitrust Division, "The Crisis in Property-Casualty Insurance," in Tort Policy Working Group, *An Update on the Liability Crisis* (Washington, D.C.: Department of Justice, 1987), appendix. For some coverages, a more appropriate definition of the market might be the state. Average statewide concentration levels probably would not be much higher than those shown in table 3-1. Based on data reported on *Best's Insurance Management Reports: Property-Casualty Edition* (weekly), the mean market share of the largest firm across states for general liability was 12 percent in 1985; the maximum was 27 percent (these figures

Table 3-1. *Shares of National Net Premiums Written for Leading Property and Liability Groups, 1985*
Percent unless otherwise specified

| | Estimated | Market share (1985) | | |
|---|---|---|---|---|
| | *1986 net premiums* | *Largest* | *Largest* | *Largest* |
| *Line of business* | *written (billions of dollars)* | *group* | *4 groups* | *20 groups* |
| General liability | 20.0 | 9.0 | 22.4 | 66.1 |
| Medical malpractice | 3.6 | 19.9 | 38.6 | 73.7 |
| Commercial multiperil | 16.0 | 7.7 | 23.4 | 68.8 |
| Commercial auto liability | 9.5 | 5.1 | 18.5 | 59.9 |
| Private passenger auto liability | 34.3 | 18.8 | 39.8 | 62.5 |
| Workers' compensation | 19.6 | 10.0 | 24.8 | 65.4 |
| All property and liability | 176.4 | 9.8 | 22.1 | 55.1 |

Sources: Market shares calculated from data in *Best's Aggregates and Averages: Property-Casualty,* 1986 (Oldwick, N.J.: A. M. Best, 1986). Net premiums written are from estimates in Paul E. Wish, "Review and Preview: Up from the Ashes," *Best's Review: Property/Casualty Insurance Edition,* vol. 87 (January 1987), p. 12. Separate estimates for commercial and private passenger auto liability were not provided; the figures for these two lines are based on 1985 proportions.

data suggest that the minimum efficient scale of operations is small relative to the size of the market.[2] Most premiums are written through independent agents and brokers. There would appear to be no major barriers to companies entering this distribution channel, although some modest barriers exist because of such regulations as minimum capital and surplus requirements and other licensing requirements.[3]

---

exclude Michigan, in which a subsidiary of General Motors had a 41 percent market share because it provided insurance for its parent). For commercial multiperil insurers, who sell property and liability coverage as a package to small and medium-sized businesses, the mean market share was 12 percent and the maximum was 21 percent. The single-firm shares reported by *Best's* were much higher for medical malpractice, but they often do not reflect experience of provider-owned mutual companies.

2. Some studies have suggested that average costs of production in the property-liability insurance industry decrease as the size of the firm decreases. See, for example, Joseph E. Johnson, George B. Flanigan, and Steven N. Weisbart, "Returns to Scale in the Property and Liability Insurance Industry," *Journal of Risk and Insurance,* vol. 48 (March 1981), pp. 18–45. These studies have, however, been plagued by the lack of information about average account size and other factors that could produce a bias toward finding decreasing costs.

3. Patricia Munch and Dennis E. Smallwood, "Solvency Regulation in the Property-Liability Insurance Industry: Empirical Evidence," *Bell Journal of Economics,* vol. 11 (Spring 1980), pp. 261–79. Joskow, "Cartels, Competition and Regulation," suggested the possibility of entry or growth barriers for direct-writing distribution methods. Whether this is likely has been disputed; see, for example, Mark Pauly, Howard Kunreuther, and Paul Kleindorfer, "Regulation and Quality Competition in the U.S. Insurance Industry,"

The insurance industry is largely exempt from federal antitrust legislation as a result of the McCarran-Ferguson Act of 1945. The exemptions allow insurers to pool loss data through various rating organizations or bureaus. In most states, rating bureaus promulgate premium rates for most lines of business, and subscribers may use the rates. The available data for at least private passenger auto insurance nevertheless suggest that despite these pooling arrangements insurers display considerable pricing independence. The key exceptions are small companies that tend to use bureau rates to economize on costs.[4] The evidence and concern about underwriting cycles also suggest vigorous price competition in commercial liability lines, regardless of the existence of rating bureaus.[5]

Price information is likely to be readily available to consumers through agents and brokers, and there is considerable standardization of coverage as a result of both the influence of rating bureaus and state regulation of policy forms, especially for small to medium-sized buyers. Little information is available, however, for consumers to assess differences in claim settlement practices. To the extent that consumer preferences for quality of claim service differ, independent agents may play some role in placing coverage with appropriate insurers. Most states also have laws dealing with unfair claim practices, and consumers may seek tort recoveries in the event of arbitrary treatment.

Many consumers may not be aware of differences in financial strength among insurers, and both consumers and agents may find it difficult to assess whether an insurer will be able to pay claims. This problem has generally been used to justify state regulation designed to reduce the number of insurance company failures and to protect consumers from the consequences of defaults that do occur.[6] Before 1970, regulations

in Jörg Finsinger and Mark V. Pauly, eds., *The Economics of Insurance Regulation: A Cross-National Study* (St. Martin's Press, 1986), pp. 75–78.

4. See Department of Justice, *Pricing and Marketing of Insurance;* Patricia M. Danzon, "Rating Bureaus in U.S. Property-Liability Insurance Markets: Anti- or Pro-Competitive?" *Geneva Papers on Risk and Insurance,* vol. 8 (October 1983), pp. 371–402; and Scott Harrington, "The Impact of Rate Regulation on Prices and Underwriting Results in the Property-Liability Insurance Industry: A Survey," *Journal of Risk and Insurance,* vol. 51 (December 1984), pp. 578–623.

5. As is discussed later, at one time rating bureaus and the antitrust exemption may have facilitated cartel behavior. See also Joskow, "Cartels, Competition and Regulation."

6. Jörg Finsinger and Mark Pauly, "Reserve Levels and Reserve Requirements for Profit-Maximizing Insurance Firms," in Günter Bamberg and Klaus Spremann, eds., *Risk and Capital* (Berlin: Springer-Verlag, 1984,) pp. 160–80, consider whether consumer failure to base purchasing decisions on the probability of default leads to excessive risk

emphasized direct controls of pricing, product mix, and investment policy. Since then they have emphasized monitoring, primarily through the National Association of Insurance Commissioners (NAIC) Insurance Regulatory Information System, and paying the claims of insolvent insurers through state guaranty funds.[7] The extent to which state guaranty funds have increased insurer risk taking by reducing the incentives of buyers to purchase coverage from financially sound companies is not known.

Information problems facing insurers are also substantial. First, for a given average expected loss per unit of coverage in a given line of business, considerable heterogeneity exists among consumers. For liability insurance, rates generally vary by industry and state. Rating plans also commonly allow underwriters to apply credits and debits on the basis of firm-specific characteristics and judgment. While such experience rating commonly is used for medium and large corporate risks, the low frequency of liability claims for most businesses and professionals and the resulting lack of statistical credibility of a risk's own loss experience often seriously limits the extent to which experience rating can reduce problems of adverse selection and moral hazard.[8]

Adverse selection is the tendency for high risks to buy more coverage than low risks at any given rate. Because insurers cannot identify differences in risk with perfect accuracy and those insured often will have more knowledge about their risk than insurers, some adverse selection

---

taking by insurers; see also Patricia Munch and Dennis Smallwood, "Theory of Solvency Regulation in the Property and Casualty Insurance Industry," in Gary Fromm, ed., *Studies in Public Regulation* (MIT Press, 1981), pp. 119–67. Compulsory coverage requirements might also lead buyers of third-party coverage with few assets at risk to seek coverage from insurers with low premiums but a high probability of default. For detailed discussion of the insolvency problem and associated regulation, see Scott E. Harrington and Patricia M. Danzon, "An Evaluation of Solvency Regulation in the Property-Liability Insurance Industry," report to the Alliance of American Insurers, American Insurance Association, and National Association of Independent Insurers (University of Pennsylvania, Wharton School, June 1986).

7. All states have guaranty funds for property and liability insurance. New York prefunds its plan through assessments on insurers. The remaining states assess surviving companies following a default. The maximum claim payable through the funds for liability coverage commonly is no more than $500,000. A recent amendment to the NAIC model legislation allows guaranty funds to seek recovery from corporations with net worth greater than $50 million for liability claims paid on their behalf.

8. General liability insurance rating procedures are described in Michael F. McManus, "General Liability Ratemaking: An Update," *Proceedings of the Casualty Actuarial Society*, vol. 67 (November 1981), pp. 144–80.

will exist and will tend to become more pronounced as heterogeneity among buyers in a rate class increases.

The theory of competitive insurance markets with adverse selection has emphasized the existence and characteristics of market equilibrium when insurers can identify the total amount of coverage owned by each buyer and compete by offering different combinations of price and coverage.[9] But it is not clear that this theory describes reality in liability insurance markets. Adverse selection could cause the market for particular types of coverage to disappear.[10] For a given rate, low risks might be unwilling to buy coverage. As they drop out of the pool, the rate must go up, causing more risks with low expected loss relative to the group average to drop out, and so on. Given expense loadings in premiums, the highest risks may not be willing to insure unless subsidized by low risks. If so, no market would exist.[11] Whether this is true is not known, but adverse selection may help explain instances in recent years in which coverage has been alleged to be unavailable at any price.

Moral hazard is the tendency for the presence and characteristics of insurance coverage to produce inefficient changes in buyers' loss prevention activities, including carelessness and fraud, which are often emphasized in the insurance literature. If insurance prices were to reflect perfectly the influence of loss prevention activities on expected losses, moral hazard would not exist. But while experience rating, deductibles, and other forms of copayment by buyers may mitigate moral hazard, the inability of insurers to monitor loss prevention activities accurately leads to too little prevention and too many losses.

Prices are also determined by the average expected loss per unit of exposure in a given rating class and for all classes combined, which may vary considerably over time. Liability insurance contracts sold on an occurrence basis promise to pay all claims that arise out of actions during the policy period, regardless of when the claim is made. The long time that can elapse before all claims are paid for such coverage requires companies to predict payments that often will not be made for

9. Michael Rothschild and Joseph Stiglitz, "Equilibrium in Competitive Insurance Markets: An Essay on the Economics of Imperfect Information," *Quarterly Journal of Economics,* vol. 90 (November 1976), pp. 629–49.

10. George A. Akerlof, "The Market for 'Lemons': Quality Uncertainty and the Market Mechanism," *Quarterly Journal of Economics,* vol. 84 (August 1970), pp. 488–500. Also see George L. Priest, "The Current Insurance Crisis and Modern Tort Law," *Yale Law Journal,* vol. 96 (June 1987), pp. 1521–90.

11. For liability coverage, high-risk buyers with few assets to protect also could be unwilling to buy coverage unless subsidized by low risks.

many years.[12] As is discussed later, difficulty in accurately estimating future claims may cause coverage to be priced below expected costs. This difficulty may be a principal cause of underwriting cycles in the liability insurance market.

The possibility of destructive competition has been closely associated with regulation of property-liability insurance prices. Before the McCarran-Ferguson Act was passed in 1945, allegations of destructive competition were used to justify cartel behavior. Rating bureaus were effective in controlling prices and commissions, at least in property insurance where deviations from bureau rating schemes could be detected. Following the enactment of McCarran-Ferguson, most states passed laws that required prior approval of rates by regulators for all property-liability lines. These laws often encouraged insurers to use bureau rates by making it difficult or costly to obtain approval of independent rate filings. A period of rate deregulation began in the late 1960s. With the exception of workers' compensation rates, which remain heavily regulated in most states, property-liability insurance rates are now subject to some form of prior approval in just under half of the states. Regulation in these states, however, probably has not had much impact on rates for commercial lines in recent years because of passive administration of the laws, pricing flexibility provided to underwriters by rating plans, and other influences.[13] In contrast, there is considerable evidence that rate regulation has lowered average prices for private passenger auto liability insurance in recent years.[14] Evidence also suggests that restrictive rate regulation is more likely in states with high losses per insured driver.[15]

12. This so-called tail reflects lags between the time that rates are made and their effective date for all policies, between the accident date and the date the claim is made, and between the date the claim is made and the date it is paid.

13. For a review of the impact of rate regulation, see Harrington, "Impact of Rate Regulation." Also see Richard E. Stewart, *Remembering a Stable Future: Why Flex Rating Cannot Work* (New York: Insurance Services Office and Insurance Information Institute, 1987).

14. See Henry Grabowski, W. Kip Viscusi, and William N. Evans, "The Effects of Regulation on the Price and Availability of Automobile Insurance," paper presented at the Nineteenth Atlantic International Economic Conference in Rome, 1985; Pauly and others, "Regulation and Quality Competition"; and Scott E. Harrington, "A Note on the Impact of Auto Insurance Rate Regulation," *Review of Economics and Statistics,* vol. 69 (February 1987), pp. 166–70.

15. Scott E. Harrington, "Cross-Subsidization and the Economics of Regulation: Theory and Evidence from Automobile Insurance," working paper 87-12 (University of Pennsylvania, Center for Research on Risk and Insurance, August 1987), develops a model that suggests consumer pressure for lower prices is likely to increase with costs if

As a result of recent experience in the liability insurance market, a few states have reregulated rates for commercial lines. These so-called flex-rating laws require prior approval only for rate changes in excess of a given statutory benchmark. Whether rate regulation is likely to be an appropriate response to the problems of the liability insurance market is discussed later in this chapter and again in the concluding chapter of this volume.

## Overview of Financial Results

Table 3-2 shows reported income, capital structure, and insolvencies for the property-liability insurance industry from 1972 to 1986. Ratios of several alternative measures of income to both earned premiums and statutory surplus adjusted for prepaid acquisition expenses are shown in table 3-3.[16] All the income measures shown in tables 3-2 and 3-3 reflect calendar year losses, which equal losses paid plus the change in the loss reserve during the given year. As a result, the income measures for each year reflect revisions in the loss reserve for claims from previous years as well as loss experience for new claims during the year.[17]

The time period shown in tables 3-2 and 3-3 allows recent experience to be compared with that of the insurance crisis of 1974–75. Operating losses have been the major cause of problems in 1984–85; unrealized capital losses were the principle factor leading to the sharp declines in surplus in 1973–74. While unrealized capital gains contributed to rapid

---

demand is inelastic. The model provides a possible explanation of regulatory emphasis on affordability of coverage.

16. An introduction to insurance accounting and profit measurement using both statutory accounting principles (SAP) and generally accepted accounting principles (GAAP) is provided in appendix A. The underwriting income measures in table 3-3 are calculated with the combined ratio, which is defined as the sum of the ratio of incurred losses and policyholder dividends to earned premiums and the ratio of underwriting expenses to written premiums. As discussed in appendix A, 1 minus the combined ratio approximately equals the pretax GAAP underwriting profit margin relative to earned premiums. The income measures shown are divided by the average of the beginning and end-of-year values of adjusted surplus. Adjusted surplus is defined as SAP surplus plus the average underwriting expense ratio for the current and preceding year times the unearned premium reserve. GAAP surplus, which would also reflect items such as deferred taxes, generally is not reported for the aggregate industry.

17. Throughout the chapter *loss* refers to the sum of insurer loss-adjustment expenses and losses payable to claimants.

Table 3-2. *Selected Financial Results for the Property-Liability Industry, 1972–86*
Millions of dollars unless otherwise specified

| Item | 1972 | 1973 | 1974 | 1975 | 1976 | 1977 | 1978 | 1979 | 1980 | 1981 | 1982 | 1983 | 1984 | 1985 | 1986[a] |
|---|---|---|---|---|---|---|---|---|---|---|---|---|---|---|---|
| Combined ratio (percent) | 96.2 | 99.2 | 105.4 | 107.9 | 102.4 | 97.1 | 97.4 | 100.6 | 103.1 | 106.0 | 109.6 | 112.0 | 118.0 | 116.3 | 108.6 |
| Ratio of net investment income/earned premiums | 7.1 | 7.6 | 8.3 | 8.2 | 8.1 | 8.5 | 9.3 | 10.7 | 11.8 | 13.6 | 14.6 | 14.9 | 15.4 | 14.6 | 13.0 |
| Before-tax operating income[b] | 3,724 | 3,100 | 959 | −322 | 2,405 | 6,928 | 8,586 | 7,978 | 7,729 | 6,960 | 4,617 | 2,651 | −3,609 | −5,780 | 4,500 |
| After-tax operating income[b] | 2,895 | 2,631 | 1,284 | 232 | 2,256 | 5,913 | 7,197 | 7,083 | 7,137 | 6,906 | 5,333 | 3,869 | −1,942 | −3,822 | 6,000 |
| Realized capital gains | 301 | 412 | −154 | 139 | 286 | 329 | 57 | 300 | 533 | 276 | 572 | 2,110 | 3,063 | 5,483 | 5,500 |
| Unrealized capital gains | 2,836 | −4,915 | −6,999 | 4,035 | 3,803 | −1,083 | 41 | 2,030 | 4,274 | −2,666 | 2,908 | 1,358 | −2,848 | 5,227 | 4,500 |
| Net capital and surplus paid in[c] | −458 | −1,084 | −185 | 17 | −78 | −72 | −736 | −1,199 | −1,495 | −1,775 | −1,248 | −1,945 | 233 | 5,561 | 1,300 |
| Surplus at yearend[b] | 23,812 | 21,389 | 16,270 | 19,712 | 24,631 | 29,300 | 35,379 | 42,395 | 52,174 | 53,805 | 60,395 | 65,606 | 63,809 | 75,511 | 91,000 |
| Percent change in surplus | 24.9 | −10.2 | −23.9 | 21.2 | 24.9 | 18.9 | 20.7 | 19.8 | 23.1 | 3.1 | 12.2 | 8.6 | −2.7 | 18.3 | 20.5 |
| Percent change in net premiums written | 10.1 | 8.1 | 6.2 | 11.0 | 21.8 | 19.8 | 12.8 | 10.3 | 6.0 | 3.9 | 4.7 | 4.8 | 8.4 | 22.0 | 22.3 |
| Ratio of net premiums written/surplus | 1.63 | 1.97 | 2.75 | 2.52 | 2.45 | 2.47 | 2.31 | 2.13 | 1.83 | 1.85 | 1.72 | 1.67 | 1.86 | 1.92 | 1.94 |
| Ratio of liabilities/surplus | 2.12 | 2.64 | 3.70 | 3.47 | 3.29 | 3.32 | 3.21 | 3.10 | 2.79 | 2.95 | 2.84 | 2.80 | 3.15 | 3.12 | n.a. |
| Ratio of loss reserves/surplus | 1.12 | 1.42 | 2.13 | 2.00 | 1.91 | 1.94 | 1.94 | 1.91 | 1.77 | 1.90 | 1.85 | 1.87 | 2.11 | 2.05 | n.a. |
| Number of insolvencies | 2 | 2 | 5 | 20 | 4 | 6 | 6 | 3 | 4 | 6 | 9 | 4 | 20 | 20 | n.a. |

Sources: *Best's Aggregates and Averages: Property-Casualty*, 1986; and earlier years; and Wish, "Review and Preview." Number of insolvencies provided by National Committee on Insurance Guaranty Funds.

n.a. Not available.

a. Estimated.

b. Income and surplus calculated according to statutory accounting principles.

c. Net capital and surplus paid in equals new capital and surplus paid in less dividends to stockholders.

Table 3-3. *Adjusted Income Measures as a Percentage of Earned Premiums and Adjusted Surplus, 1972–86*

| Income measure[a] | 1972 | 1973 | 1974 | 1975 | 1976 | 1977 | 1978 | 1979 | 1980 | 1981 | 1982 | 1983 | 1984 | 1985 | 1986[b] |
|---|---|---|---|---|---|---|---|---|---|---|---|---|---|---|---|
| *Earned premiums* | | | | | | | | | | | | | | | |
| Pretax underwriting income | 3.8 | 0.8 | -5.4 | -7.9 | -2.4 | 2.9 | 2.6 | -0.6 | -3.1 | -0.6 | -9.6 | -12.0 | -18.0 | -16.3 | -8.6 |
| Pretax operating income | 10.9 | 8.4 | 2.8 | 0.3 | 5.6 | 11.4 | 11.9 | 10.1 | 8.7 | 7.6 | 5.0 | 2.9 | -2.6 | -1.7 | 4.4 |
| After-tax operating income | 8.7 | 7.2 | 3.6 | 1.4 | 5.4 | 9.9 | 10.1 | 9.0 | 8.1 | 7.5 | 5.7 | 4.0 | -1.2 | -0.2 | 5.3 |
| After-tax operating income plus realized capital gains | 9.5 | 8.2 | 3.2 | 1.7 | 5.9 | 10.4 | 10.2 | 9.4 | 8.6 | 7.8 | 6.3 | 6.0 | 1.5 | 3.9 | 8.7 |
| After-tax operating income plus realized and unrealized capital gains | 17.0 | -3.8 | -12.8 | 10.2 | 12.5 | 8.8 | 10.2 | 11.7 | 13.2 | 5.1 | 9.1 | 7.3 | -1.0 | 7.8 | 11.4 |
| *Adjusted surplus* | | | | | | | | | | | | | | | |
| Pretax underwriting income | 5.5 | 1.2 | -9.7 | -15.9 | -4.8 | 5.9 | 5.1 | -1.1 | -5.1 | -9.3 | -14.5 | -17.3 | -26.8 | -25.9 | n.a. |
| Pretax operating income | 15.6 | 12.4 | 5.1 | 0.5 | 11.3 | 23.0 | 23.4 | 18.5 | 14.4 | 11.8 | 7.5 | 4.2 | -3.9 | -2.7 | n.a. |
| After-tax operating income | 12.5 | 10.7 | 6.5 | 2.9 | 10.8 | 20.0 | 19.9 | 16.6 | 13.4 | 11.7 | 8.6 | 5.8 | -1.8 | -0.3 | n.a. |
| After-tax operating income plus realized capital gains | 13.6 | 12.2 | 5.8 | 3.5 | 11.8 | 21.0 | 20.0 | 17.2 | 14.3 | 12.1 | 9.4 | 8.6 | 2.2 | 6.2 | n.a. |
| After-tax operating income plus realized and unrealized capital gains | 24.5 | -5.6 | -23.0 | 20.5 | 25.2 | 17.8 | 20.1 | 21.5 | 21.9 | 7.9 | 13.7 | 10.5 | -1.5 | 12.5 | n.a. |

Sources: *Best's Aggregates and Averages: Property-Casualty,* 1986 and earlier years; and Wish, "Review and Preview."
n.a. Not available.
a. Underwriting income, operating income, and surplus are adjusted for prepaid acquisition expenses. Taxes do not include deferred income taxes.
b. Estimated.

surplus growth in both 1975–76 and 1985–86, realized capital gains also had a major impact in the latter period. New inflows of capital accounted for over 40 percent of the growth in surplus in 1985. Increases in premiums written in 1985 and 1986 were larger relative to the preceding few years than those in 1975 and 1976. However, the absolute increases in 1985 and 1986 are only slightly greater than those that occurred in 1976 and 1977. The percentage increases in surplus following the decline in 1984 have been smaller than those following the steeper declines in 1973 and 1974, but the data indicate that large unrealized capital gains played a relatively greater role in rebuilding surplus during the earlier period.

If unrealized capital gains are not included, 1984 ranks as the worst year for all of the income measures in table 3-3. When unrealized capital gains are included, results were worse in 1973 and 1974. If all capital gains are excluded, 1985 ranks second to 1984 as the worst year during the period. In fact, 1984 and 1985 are the only two years with negative income exclusive of capital gains. As will be discussed later, whether capital gains should be included in income has been a major issue in the debate about whether operations actually were unprofitable in recent years.

The three measures of financial leverage shown in table 3-2 indicate that the highest values occurred in 1974. The ratios of premiums to surplus and total liabilities to surplus are substantially higher for 1974 and 1975 than for 1984 and 1985. Part of this difference reflects higher premium levels in the earlier period, which have a direct impact on both ratios.[18] The ratio of loss reserves to surplus is about the same during both periods. A major problem in comparing results for the two periods is that small differences in reserve adequacy over time can have a large impact on reported income and measures of leverage.[19] In both periods a historically large number of insolvencies occurred, with the total number in 1984 and 1985 much larger than in 1974 and 1975. While detailed data are not yet available, the number of insolvencies most likely remained high in 1986. Premium increases also were much larger

18. Premium levels influence the magnitude of the unearned premium reserve as well as net premiums written.

19. George M. Gottheimer, Jr., "Crisis of Confidence," in Numan A. Williams, ed., *Crisis Avoidance: Insurance Responsibilities* (Malvern, Pa.: Society of Chartered Property and Casualty Underwriters, 1986), pp. 67–84, provides an illustration of the potential impact of underreserving on the premium-to-surplus ratio in 1985.

for commercial liability lines during 1985 and 1986 than in 1976 and 1977.

Table 3-4 presents calendar year combined ratios and operating ratios for each insurance line from 1977 to 1986.[20] Since more net investment income and realized capital gains are allocated to the longer-tailed lines, the difference between the combined ratio and the operating ratio is greater for general liability and medical malpractice than for commercial multiperil and auto business.[21] With the exception of workers' compensation, the data show gradually increasing ratios through 1984. For general liability, medical malpractice, and private passenger auto liability, the ratios increased through 1985. The operating ratios generally began to exceed 100 percent in 1981 and 1982. These results indicate substantial accounting losses for commercial liability lines after investment income, including realized capital gains, was allocated to operations during 1984 and 1985. While operating ratios were not available for 1986, the data suggest that they will be about 100 percent for general liability and will exceed 100 percent for medical malpractice. Since these are calendar year results, the high ratios in recent years reflect increases in reserves for losses experienced in earlier years.

## Errors in Estimating Reserves

As noted, previous errors in estimating loss reserves will affect calendar year financial results in the year in which reserves are restated to reflect the errors. Accident year results, which include losses only for accidents during a given calendar year, provide a better measure of experience during the period in which premiums were earned. However, errors in the reserve estimates as of any given statement date may be substantial, so that calendar year and accident year results and reported surplus may

20. A combined ratio greater than 100 percent indicates a pretax GAAP underwriting loss (exclusive of investment income). As discussed in appendix A, the operating ratio equals the combined ratio minus the ratio of net investment income and realized capital gains to earned premiums. An operating ratio greater than 100 percent indicates a pretax GAAP operating loss exclusive of both unrealized capital gains and the amount of net investment income and realized capital gains that are allocated to surplus.

21. General liability, which is denoted "other" or "miscellaneous" liability on annual statements and in many publications, includes all commercial liability coverage other than auto, workers' compensation and employers' liability, liability coverage provided in commercial multiperil contracts, and medical malpractice.

Table 3-4. *Combined Ratios and Operating Ratios, by Insurance Line, 1977–86*[a]
Percent

| Insurance line | 1977 | 1978 | 1979 | 1980 | 1981 | 1982 | 1983 | 1984 | 1985 | 1986 |
|---|---|---|---|---|---|---|---|---|---|---|
| General liability | | | | | | | | | | |
| Combined ratio | 100.0 | 97.3 | 98.2 | 107.2 | 116.0 | 129.4 | 138.1 | 151.8 | 145.8 | 120.3 |
| Operating ratio | 90.4 | 87.5 | 86.0 | 92.7 | 96.5 | 106.4 | 113.8 | 125.1 | 125.8 | n.a. |
| Medical malpractice | | | | | | | | | | |
| Combined ratio | 93.7 | 104.9 | 113.9 | 129.2 | 137.6 | 150.9 | 151.2 | 162.2 | 166.9 | 144.4 |
| Operating ratio | 79.6 | 87.3 | 92.0 | 99.8 | 101.4 | 109.8 | 108.9 | 118.3 | 129.5 | n.a. |
| Commerical multiperil | | | | | | | | | | |
| Combined ratio | 87.2 | 84.9 | 93.3 | 98.8 | 107.1 | 116.4 | 123.2 | 134.9 | 121.3 | 97.2 |
| Operating ratio | 82.8 | 80.7 | 88.6 | 93.4 | 100.5 | 109.1 | 114.8 | 125.1 | 112.2 | n.a. |
| Commercial auto liability | | | | | | | | | | |
| Combined ratio | 98.8 | 99.9 | 105.0 | 109.5 | 118.3 | 126.4 | 132.9 | 143.1 | 127.1 | 112.8 |
| Operating ratio | 92.7 | 93.7 | 97.6 | 101.1 | 108.4 | 115.3 | 121.3 | 130.8 | 116.4 | n.a. |
| Private passenger auto liability | | | | | | | | | | |
| Combined ratio | 99.5 | 99.8 | 101.6 | 103.3 | 109.6 | 110.9 | 112.1 | 113.6 | 119.6 | 119.0 |
| Operating ratio | 93.7 | 93.8 | 94.8 | 96.1 | 101.4 | 102.1 | 102.9 | 103.9 | 109.5 | n.a. |
| Workers' compensation | | | | | | | | | | |
| Combined ratio | 108.6 | 105.0 | 103.0 | 101.4 | 102.8 | 103.9 | 112.5 | 121.9 | 118.8 | 120.5 |
| Operating ratio | 101.2 | 97.2 | 93.7 | 90.7 | 89.8 | 88.9 | 96.3 | 105.2 | 103.8 | n.a. |
| All property-liability | | | | | | | | | | |
| Combined ratio | 97.1 | 97.4 | 100.6 | 103.1 | 106.0 | 109.6 | 112.0 | 118.0 | 116.3 | 108.6 |
| Operating ratio | 91.8 | 91.8 | 94.1 | 95.9 | 97.6 | 100.5 | 102.3 | 107.4 | 106.3 | n.a. |

Sources: *Best's Aggregates and Averages: Property-Casualty, 1986;* and Wish, "Review and Preview."
n.a. Not available.
a. All ratios are computed after payment of policyholder dividends.

differ greatly from the values that would be reported if future claims were known with certainty.

The problem of errors in estimating reserves always makes interpretation of insurance company financial results tenuous. Large errors in forecasting claims are often highly correlated among firms because of changes in factors that influence losses, such as inflation and the level of economic activity. Reserves also can be deliberately misstated to manage earnings and taxes. Consistent overstatement defers income taxes (or costs associated with tax avoidance, such as lower yields on tax-exempt securities). If shareholders are concerned about net cash flow and if tax deferral reduces costs and hence premiums, neither they nor policyholders would object to overstatement, provided they are aware that reported income and surplus are understated.[22] But deliberate understatement of reserves allows an insurer to show higher income and surplus. Whether shareholders, policyholders interested in security, or regulators would systematically be misled by such a strategy is uncertain.[23]

Errors in estimating reserves eventually can be measured by comparing total claim payments (or total payments plus any remaining reserve) with values initially reported. A number of studies have analyzed errors using historical data from the 1940s through the early 1970s on reserves and claims paid that are reported for third-party lines of business in schedule P of insurance company statutory statements. Almost all empirical studies have analyzed reserve errors for auto liability. Several have analyzed data for general liability and workers' compensation as well. The results, which often differ considerably among companies, indicate overreserving in the 1940s and 1950s for large auto liability insurers and in the 1950s for general liability.[24] The results for the

22. The Internal Revenue Service would object, but it could be difficult to prove deliberate misstatements in reserves, given the possibility of large random errors.

23. Companies that default are almost always grossly underreserved. A number of analysts have considered whether insurers are likely to use reserves to smooth reported income and have provided some evidence to this effect. See, for instance, Barry D. Smith, "An Analysis of Auto Liability Loss Reserves and Underwriting Results," *Journal of Risk and Insurance,* vol. 47 (June 1980), pp. 305–20; and Mary Weiss, "A Multivariate Analysis of Loss Reserving Estimates in Property-Liability Insurers," *Journal of Risk and Insurance,* vol. 52 (June 1985), pp. 199–221.

24. See Stephen Forbes, "Loss Reserving Performance within the Regulatory Framework," *Journal of Risk and Insurance,* vol. 37 (December 1970), pp. 527–38; Dan Robert Anderson, "Effects of Under and Overevaluations in Loss Reserves," *Journal of Risk and Insurance,* vol. 38 (December 1971), pp. 585–600; R. J. Balcarek, "Loss Reserve Deficiencies and Underwriting Results," *Best's Review: Property/Liability Insurance Edition,* vol. 76 (July 1975), pp. 20–23; Craig F. Ansley, "Automobile Liability Insurance Reserve

1960s and early 1970s indicate underreserving both for auto liability and for general liability.[25]

Table 3-5 presents accident year results and evidence on errors in reserve estimates in recent years for schedule P lines of business. The table shows the accident year loss ratios (incurred losses divided by earned premiums) originally reported and accident year loss ratios developed (that is, reflecting all payments and the remaining reserve) through 1985.[26] Results are shown for the industry for accident years 1980–85 using the consolidated schedule P information reported in *Best's Aggregates and Averages: Property-Casualty, 1986,* and for 1976–85 using aggregate information for forty-five large companies supplied by Aetna Life and Casualty.[27]

The data indicate substantial upward development in the loss ratios for malpractice and, especially, general liability in 1981–84. Loss ratios for general liability increased substantially during this time.[28] Substantial upward development occurred for accident years 1976 and 1977 for general liability in the sample data, but developments for malpractice were large and negative. In general, the results for multiperil (aggregated in schedule P and including first-party property losses for homeowners, farmowners, and commercial multiperil business), auto liability (aggregated for private passenger and commercial business), and workers' compensation generally indicate a smaller increase in loss ratios and smaller

---

Adequacy and the Effect on Inflation," *CPCU Journal,* vol. 31 (June 1978), pp. 105–12; Stephen W. Forbes, "The Credibility of the Earnings per Share of Nonlife Insurance Companies," *CPCU Journal,* vol. 31 (March 1978), pp. 30–36; and Smith, "Analysis of Auto Liability Loss Reserves."

25. For auto liability, see Anderson, "Effects of Under and Overevaluations"; Balcarek, "Loss Reserve Deficiencies"; Ansley, "Automobile Liability Insurance Reserve Adequacy"; Forbes, "Credibility of Earnings per Share"; and Smith, "Analysis of Auto Liability Loss Reserves." For general liability, see Anderson, "Effects of Under and Overevaluations"; and Balcarek, "Loss Reserve Deficiencies." See also Forbes, "Credibility of Earnings per Share."

26. Accident year incurred losses include only paid losses and the loss reserve for claims that have occurred (including those incurred but not reported) during the given year. Accident year incurred losses are divided by calendar year earned premiums to obtain the accident year loss ratios.

27. In 1985 these companies represented 69, 34, 76, and 69 percent of net premiums written for general liability, medical malpractice, commercial multiperil, and all property-liability lines, respectively.

28. Developed incurred losses for these years and initial reserves for 1985 still included a sizable reserve for unpaid losses.

Table 3-5. *Accident Year Loss Ratios by Insurance Line: Originally Reported (R) and Developed through 1985 (D), 1976–85*

| Sample | General liability | | Medical malpractice | | Multiperil [a] | | Auto liability [b] | | Workers' compensation | | Schedule P [c] | |
|---|---|---|---|---|---|---|---|---|---|---|---|---|
| | R | D | R | D | R | D | R | D | R | D | R | D |
| *Industry* | | | | | | | | | | | | |
| 1980 | 0.69 | 0.73 | 1.05 | 1.34 | 0.69 | 0.71 | 0.79 | 0.78 | 0.74 | 0.68 | 0.74 | 0.74 |
| 1981 | 0.79 | 0.86 | 1.13 | 1.48 | 0.69 | 0.69 | 0.85 | 0.85 | 0.77 | 0.72 | 0.78 | 0.79 |
| 1982 | 0.87 | 1.02 | 1.18 | 1.58 | 0.75 | 0.77 | 0.87 | 0.88 | 0.79 | 0.78 | 0.82 | 0.85 |
| 1983 | 0.94 | 1.09 | 1.19 | 1.51 | 0.75 | 0.80 | 0.89 | 0.91 | 0.84 | 0.86 | 0.85 | 0.90 |
| 1984 | 0.99 | 1.10 | 1.09 | 1.33 | 0.77 | 0.79 | 0.92 | 0.96 | 0.90 | 0.93 | 0.88 | 0.92 |
| 1985 | 0.95 | 0.95 | 1.20 | 1.20 | 0.77 | 0.77 | 0.92 | 0.92 | 0.89 | 0.89 | 0.88 | 0.88 |
| *45 companies* | | | | | | | | | | | | |
| 1976 | 0.69 | 0.86 | 0.75 | 0.66 | 0.63 | 0.62 | 0.79 | 0.78 | 0.77 | 0.89 | 0.73 | 0.76 |
| 1977 | 0.63 | 0.66 | 0.76 | 0.58 | 0.59 | 0.58 | 0.75 | 0.73 | 0.77 | 0.78 | 0.69 | 0.69 |
| 1978 | 0.62 | 0.59 | 0.77 | 0.73 | 0.58 | 0.57 | 0.75 | 0.75 | 0.77 | 0.73 | 0.69 | 0.68 |
| 1979 | 0.65 | 0.64 | 0.95 | 0.91 | 0.65 | 0.66 | 0.77 | 0.78 | 0.78 | 0.72 | 0.73 | 0.72 |
| 1980 | 0.69 | 0.71 | 1.15 | 1.10 | 0.69 | 0.70 | 0.79 | 0.79 | 0.76 | 0.69 | 0.75 | 0.74 |
| 1981 | 0.81 | 0.85 | 1.39 | 1.45 | 0.70 | 0.70 | 0.86 | 0.86 | 0.79 | 0.73 | 0.80 | 0.79 |
| 1982 | 0.90 | 1.05 | 1.40 | 1.65 | 0.75 | 0.77 | 0.88 | 0.87 | 0.80 | 0.78 | 0.83 | 0.85 |
| 1983 | 0.97 | 1.08 | 1.37 | 1.66 | 0.76 | 0.81 | 0.89 | 0.91 | 0.86 | 0.87 | 0.86 | 0.89 |
| 1984 | 1.03 | 1.12 | 1.09 | 1.24 | 0.78 | 0.79 | 0.92 | 0.95 | 0.92 | 0.94 | 0.89 | 0.92 |
| 1985 | 0.99 | ... | 1.19 | ... | 0.78 | ... | 0.93 | ... | 0.90 | ... | 0.89 | ... |

Sources: Industry data are from Best's *Aggregates and Averages: Property-Casualty*, 1986. Data for forty-five companies from Aetna Life and Casualty Co.
a. Includes commercial and homeowner's insurance.
b. Includes commercial and private passenger vehicle insurance.
c. Denotes aggregate for schedule P lines—general liability, medical malpractice, multiperil, auto liability, and workers' compensation.

Table 3-6.  *Estimated Reserve Inadequacy for General Liability Lines,*
*Based on Paid-Loss Development Methods, as of 1985*[a]
Percent

| Accident year | Industry | | | | 45 companies | | | |
| | Method A | | Method B | | Method A | | Method B | |
| | (1) | (2) | (1) | (2) | (1) | (2) | (1) | (2) |
|---|---|---|---|---|---|---|---|---|
| 1980 | −19 | 0 | −17 | 0 | −16 | 0 | −15 | 0 |
| 1981 | −28 | −14 | −26 | −12 | −22 | −10 | −21 | −10 |
| 1982 | −39 | −27 | −34 | −23 | −23 | −14 | −20 | −12 |
| 1983 | −36 | −27 | −34 | −25 | −26 | −18 | −26 | −20 |
| 1984 | −38 | −31 | −38 | −31 | −22 | −16 | −24 | −18 |
| 1985 | −12 | −6 | −15 | −10 | 9 | 13 | 3 | 7 |
| 1980–85 | −27 | −18 | −26 | −18 | −11 | −4 | −13 | −7 |

Sources: Industry data are from *Best's Aggregates and Averages: Property-Casualty, 1986*. Data for forty-five companies are from Aetna Life and Casualty Co.

a. Values shown are 1985 statement reserve minus projected reserve as a percentage of 1985 statement reserve. Method A uses sum-of-the-year digits to weight loss development factors. Method B uses the most recent factor. Values shown under (2) assume that the ratio of incurred losses to losses paid as of 1985 for accident year 1980 is accurate and applicable to future years. Values shown under (1) are based on paid loss development factors back through 1976. Development factors are shown in appendix B.

absolute development than for general liability. Thus the results generally suggest greater reserve inaccuracy for the longer-tailed liability lines.[29]

Another look at reserve adequacy for general liability is provided by table 3-6, which includes estimates of reserve inadequacy as of 1985 as a percentage of 1985 reported reserves for general liability business. The estimates were calculated using a basic reserve forecasting methodology involving historical data on paid losses. Negative values indicate estimated reserve inadequacy; positive ones indicate estimated redundancy.[30] Results are shown both for the industry and the forty-five-company sample and for two methods of weighting development factors (see appendix B, table 3-16) and two methods of projecting development of claims paid for years six and beyond.[31]

29. Data on cumulative development of statement reserves from 1976 through 1984 for the forty-five-company sample supplied by Aetna Life and Casualty generally had similar implications. The results for general liability and medical malpractice combined indicated especially large underreserving as of 1976 and 1977.

30. For a description of the paid loss development method, see Timothy M. Peterson, *Loss Reserving: Property/Casualty Insurance* (New York: Ernst and Whinney, 1981).

31. With regard to the latter issue, method (1) uses historical paid loss development factors for years six through ten to project future losses, and assumes that development beyond ten years will total 3 percent. Industry data were not available to calculate development factors for all payment years. Factors for the sample were used for method (1) in these instances (see appendix table 3-16). To allow for the possibility that the historical development factors for these years might overstate future development, method (2) uses the ratio of incurred losses to total payments for accident year 1980, as developed

In general, the projections imply that calendar year financial results reported during 1980–85 for the industry as a whole are likely to have overstated surplus and income from operations.[32] With the exception of 1985, reserves reported as of 1985 for the accident years shown in table 3-6 and for years 1980–85 combined were substantially lower than reserves projected using these methods. For 1985 the estimated inadequacy is considerably less for the industry, and projections for accident year 1985 losses for the forty-five-company sample were lower than the reported reserve. Since the sample includes the largest insurers in the industry, the results suggest that small companies may be underreserved to a greater extent than large companies. But the large potential error in projections using paid claims for long-tailed lines should be kept in mind when evaluating the results. In particular, any slowdown (or acceleration) in the rate of claim payment for 1985 accidents could cause projections for 1985 to be far too small (or large).

## Disputes about Profitability

The magnitude of profits in the property-liability insurance industry has been debated for at least two decades. In the late 1960s the dispute concerned whether profitability was inadequate compared with that of other industries based on comparisons of accounting returns for assets or net worth. In the 1980s the adequacy of profits was still being questioned based on similar analyses.[33] Recently profitability has been debated by the Insurance Services Office (ISO) and the National Insurance Consumer Organization (NICO).[34] ISO has argued that the indus-

---

through 1985, as the development factor beyond year five for each accident year. This procedure assumes that, as of 1985, reserves for accident year 1980 are accurate and that no development is expected after the sixth year for 1980 and subsequent accident years. This assumption might be considered optimistic, given recent experience and the possibility of continued growth in claims in such areas as liability for environmental hazards (see chapter 5). But changes in tort law might have some downward impact on future development compared with recent years.

32. A firm statement in this regard would require analysis of the impact of errors for each accident year on results in each calendar year.

33. See Emilio C. Venezian, "Are Insurers Under-Earning?" *Journal of Risk and Insurance,* vol. 51 (March 1984), pp. 150–56; and Insurance Services Office, *Insurer Profitability: A Long-Term Perspective* (New York, 1987).

34. See Insurance Services Office, *Insurer Profitability: The Facts* (New York, 1986); ISO, *Insurer Profitability: A Long-Term Perspective;* and National Insurance Consumer

try experienced large losses on operations in 1984 and 1985 and that it is inappropriate to consider capital gains, especially unrealized capital gains, when assessing income from insurance operations. NICO has argued that the industry's emphasis on operating income is deficient in that it fails to consider capital gains, fails to deduct GAAP expenses, inappropriately deducts policyholder dividends, and fails to discount future losses.[35] NICO concluded that the industry's measure of operating income seriously understates profitability and that the robust performance of stock prices for the industry in 1985 illustrates that operations were profitable despite large reported operating losses.

### Accounting Results

As table 3-3 shows, the inclusion of either realized or unrealized capital gains substantially improves income relative to premiums and net worth in 1985 and 1986. In contrast to NICO, ISO argued in 1986 that it is inappropriate to include capital gains because they are highly variable and nonrecurring. The variability of unrealized capital gains is pronounced, as can be seen in tables 3-2 and 3-3. In 1987 ISO has shown that unrealized capital gains had little impact on average return on equity for the industry during 1970–86, but that they substantially increased the variability of return on equity. This study also argued that the average return on equity (as defined by ISO) for the property-liability industry was below the average for other industries during 1970–86, regardless of whether unrealized capital gains were included in income.

The theory of competitive insurance prices provides some insight into the appropriate treatment of capital gains.[36] The theory has been developed under the assumption of zero default risk on insurance contracts.

Organization, "And Now the Real Facts: A Response to the Insurance Services Office's 'Insurer Profitability: The Facts'" (Alexandria, Va., undated).

35. NICO frequently cites a General Accounting Office study that argued SAP income was inappropriate for tax purposes; see Natwar M. Gandhi, group director, tax policy, of the General Government Division, U.S. General Accounting Office, speech before the 1985 meeting of the American Risk and Insurance Association, Vancouver.

36. See William B. Fairley, "Investment Income and Profit Margins in Property-Liability Insurance: Theory and Empirical Results," *Bell Journal of Economics,* vol. 10 (Spring 1979), pp. 182–210; also in J. David Cummins and Scott E. Harrington, eds., *Fair Rate of Return in Property-Liability Insurance* (Boston: Kluwer Nijhoff, 1987), pp. 1–26; and Stewart C. Myers and Richard A. Cohn, "A Discounted Cash Flow Approach to Property-Liability Insurance Rate Regulation," in Cummins and Harrington, *Fair Rate of Return,* pp. 55–78.

Since the risk from investing in risky assets is borne completely by shareholders (policyholders are assumed to be unaffected by investment risk), the higher expected return on such investments does not affect the break-even price of insurance paid by policyholders. Instead, the theory suggests that break-even prices will reflect only the risk-free rate of interest on funds supplied by policyholders.[37]

While there is not an exact relationship, most net investment income (interest, dividends, and rents) has a relatively low risk, whereas most realized capital gains and all unrealized capital gains may constitute returns to shareholders for holding risky investments.[38] As a result, the industry's emphasis on a definition of operating income that includes net investment income but excludes capital gains may be reasonable. If so, the magnitude of capital gains may be largely irrelevant to assessing whether income from insurance operations has been inadequate or subject to large increases or decreases.[39]

As noted in appendix A, the failure of SAP income to match revenues and expenses generally produces an income measure that is lower than GAAP income. However, as is shown in tables 3-2 and 3-3, the magnitude of this difference is unlikely to be significant when assessing profitability in recent years.[40] Moreover, common profit measures, such as the combined ratio and the operating ratio, measure income on a GAAP basis by implicitly adjusting for prepaid expenses.

The appropriate treatment of policy dividends depends on how they

37. This result is obtained by solving for the premium level or underwriting profit margin that leaves shareholder wealth unchanged when policies are sold. With default risk, policyholders would be affected by investment risk in the absence of guaranty funds. The theory of break-even prices is not well developed under these conditions, but the existence of guaranty funds suggests that the assumption of zero default risk may be reasonable in this context.

38. Most of the realized capital gains for 1985, the latest year for which data are available, were for stocks rather than bonds.

39. The lack of information concerning unrealized capital gains on bonds may complicate this issue. Depending on insurer investment strategy, changes in the value of the bond portfolio could be anticipated as a source of funds to pay losses. For example, if insurers held immunized portfolios of assets and liabilities, part of a reduction in net investment income due to declining interest rates would be expected to be offset by realized or unrealized capital gains on bonds. Under these conditions, it might be argued that a portion of capital gains on bonds would need to be included in any ex post analysis of profitability.

40. While pretax statutory income generally will be less than GAAP income, statutory surplus generally will be less than GAAP surplus. It is thus not clear that income relative to equity will be understated on a statutory basis relative to GAAP. Data reported in *Insurance Facts* (New York: Insurance Information Institute, annual) suggest that SAP returns on equity or surplus will often exceed similar measures based on GAAP.

affect ex ante prices. If dividends are not anticipated when policies are issued in a given line but instead arise only from favorable deviations of overall losses from those expected, then NICO's suggestion that dividends should not be deducted from income when assessing industry performance and price adequacy may have merit.[41] However, the only line in which dividends accounted for a substantial portion of premiums in 1984–86 was workers' compensation.[42] In this line, regulated premiums often are set well above expected costs so that dividends are anticipated when policies are issued, and it is reasonable to treat dividends as premium refunds. For general liability, medical malpractice, commercial multiperil, and commercial auto liability, the treatment of dividends does not materially affect measures of income relative to premiums or surplus. The fact that aggregate income is higher if a large amount of workers' compensation dividends is added to reported income is irrelevant to the issue of whether income was inadequate on any of these lines.

The failure of reported income to discount future claims payments tends to understate both income and surplus if undiscounted reserves are accurate. As a result, it is not clear that accounting returns to equity are either higher or lower than would be the case if reserves were to be discounted. Moreover, the impact on income and surplus of discounting reserves would depend on reserve adequacy with or without discounting. The evidence that undiscounted reserves probably were inadequate in recent years suggests that the use of discounted but accurate reserves would have much less impact than simply discounting statement reserves.[43] In any case, it is unlikely that discounting reserves would have

41. Claims of inadequate prices and profits in conjunction with large dividends would be incongruous. The GAO has suggested that dividends should not be deducted for tax purposes (Gandhi, address before American Risk and Insurance Association). Also see the statement by Johnny C. Finch, which argues that dividends should not be deducted from income because they are discretionary; statement of Johnny C. Finch, senior associate director, General Government Division, U.S. General Accounting Office, before the Subcommittee on Oversight, House Committee on Ways and Means, on profitability of the property/casualty insurance industry, Washington, D.C., April 28, 1986.

42. For example, according to data reported in *Best's Aggregates and Averages: Property-Casualty, 1986* (Oldwick, N.J.: A. M. Best, 1986), policyholder dividends in 1985 equaled 9.3 percent of earned premiums for workers' compensation but only 0.5, 1.0, 0.7, and 0.1 percent of earned premiums for general liability, medical malpractice, commercial auto liability, and commercial multiperil, respectively.

43. A study in *Best's Insurance Management Reports: Property-Casualty Edition,* June 7, 1986, of loss reserves for the one-hundred largest property-liability groups estimated that reported reserves in 1984 exceeded discounted (at 9 percent) estimates of future claims for ninety of the groups. The results were not disaggregated by line of business.

changed the evidence that operating income *fell* substantially in 1984 and 1985. The level of income would be higher, but the relative reduction in income would probably be similar.

In short, there is some merit to both the industry's position and the views of NICO. It also is not surprising that the magnitude of insurance accounting profits would be vigorously debated given the large premium increases that have occurred since 1984. What is clear is that reported income from operations, whether SAP or GAAP, declined abruptly in 1984, remained relatively low in 1985 and began to increase in 1986. Discounting of reserves, if done consistently over time, would be unlikely to change this picture very much. Omniscient elimination of errors in estimating reserves might well accentuate it. Capital gains contributed substantially to surplus growth in 1985 and 1986, but theory suggests that this may not be relevant to making statements about whether products sold in 1984–86 were priced above or below expected costs.

The debate over profitability has suffered from lack of attention to accident year results and to market values of bonds, the possibility of large errors in estimating reserves, and the lack of a clear standard based on theory against which to judge profitability, however defined. The detailed discussions of calendar year accounting results, especially total dollar income measures, have shed little light on the crucial questions of whether and how much policies in any given year were underpriced or overpriced relative to expected costs. The focus on aggregate results, as opposed to results for commercial liability or general liability alone, involves the implicit assumption that favorable experience in some lines makes unfavorable experience in general liability or other commercial liability lines acceptable. But multiproduct insurance companies cannot be expected to commit capital to a line that does not leave them just as well off as investing the capital in financial assets and not selling coverage in that line, regardless of the experience of other lines. The almost exclusive focus on calendar year results fails to clarify the relationship between premiums and losses for policies in force in a given period. Poor results for earlier years that influence current calendar year results need not imply anything about the adequacy of prices on current business. When evaluating recent performance, greater attention should be given to accident year results for each line, as is done for general liability later in this chapter.

The form of the insurance company annual statement, which is determined by regulators, has probably contributed to the focus on calendar year results. Accident year results are buried in schedule P and are

Table 3-7. *Annual Percentage Changes in A. M. Best and Standard and Poor's Common Stock Indexes, 1981–86*

| | A. M. Best stock indexes[a] | | | Standard and Poor's 500 | Standard and Poor's over-the- counter 250 |
|---|---|---|---|---|---|
| Year | Property- liability | Life- health | Multiple line | | |
| 1981 | 37.8 | 15.4 | 25.9 | −2.2 | 12.9 |
| 1982 | 18.3 | 23.2 | −3.6 | 13.0 | 50.8 |
| 1983 | 14.7 | 30.8 | 13.1 | 15.2 | 29.9 |
| 1984 | 0.2 | 19.2 | 3.9 | −0.4 | −5.0 |
| 1985 | 59.4 | 31.0 | 48.4 | 26.9 | 32.2 |
| 1986 | 14.7 | 11.8 | 3.4 | 19.9 | 15.4 |
| 1981–83[b] | 22.4 | 22.1 | 10.0 | 8.4 | 30.3 |
| 1984–86[b] | 22.4 | 20.4 | 16.8 | 14.8 | 13.2 |
| 1981–86[b] | 22.4 | 21.3 | 13.4 | 11.6 | 21.4 |

Sources: Annual percentage changes for the A. M. Best indexes calculated using index values as of the second week of December as reported in the January issues of *Best's Review: Property/Casualty Insurance Edition*. Standard and Poor index values as of the second week of December are from *Standard and Poor's Security Price Index Service*.

a. Indexes reflect returns for about thirty property-liability, twenty life-health, and five multiple-line companies. All returns exclude dividend yield. Stocks of most insurers in the property-liability and life-health indexes are traded on the over-the-counter market.

b. Values are calculated as of December the preceding year. Values for multiyear periods are geometric mean returns.

highly aggregated for such lines as multiperil. Considerable calculation is needed to determine the impact of developments in losses for earlier years on results for the current calendar year. In addition to providing greater detail and emphasis on accident year results in the annual statement, estimates of the market value of bonds should be reported. While many bonds held by insurers are not publicly traded, it still should be possible to develop reasonably accurate estimates for users of financial statements. Accident year and calendar year losses also should be discounted to facilitate comparison of results across lines and to allow more accurate assessment of changes in income over time.

### Stock Prices

Table 3-7 shows stock price performance for property and liability, life and health, and multiple-line insurers for 1981–86. Returns on the Standard and Poor's 500 and over-the-counter 250 indexes are also shown. The annual returns illustrate the source of controversy about recent insurance industry performance. Best's property-liability index appreciated by 59 percent in 1985, a year in which large operating losses were reported for the industry. Since the average beta for property-liability stocks during this period probably was less than 1, this performance probably cannot be attributed simply to factors influencing the 32 percent return on the Standard and Poor over-the-counter 250 index during this time.[44]

Rough comparison does not provide strong evidence of unusual performance for the property-liability index. Its average annual return for 1981–83, 1984–86, and 1981–86 was 22 percent in each period, about the same as those for the life-health index. The average return for the property-liability stocks during 1981–86 also is about equal to that for the Standard and Poor over-the-counter 250, although it was much less than that for the Standard and Poor over-the-counter 250 during 1981–83 and much greater during 1984–86. The same general pattern holds for the life-health index.

Stock returns are the ultimate measure of financial performance. In principle it is possible to determine whether returns are abnormally low or high in any given period conditional on some assumed asset-pricing model. However, even if such an analysis could be successfully undertaken for the property-liability insurance industry, the implications for whether business was underpriced or overpriced would be uncertain. Stock prices may reflect all information affecting security returns, but it may be impossible to sort out the impact of various factors that affect prices in a given period. The performance of the property-liability index in 1985 could be consistent with break-even premiums on business written in both 1985 and 1986. It also could be consistent with premiums above expected costs.

To illustrate, let the market value of a firm's equity at time $t$ (the value of its common stock) be

$$(1) \qquad E_t = A_t - L_t + \Pi_t,$$

where $A_t$ is the market value of assets for business written before time $t$; $L_t$ is the market value of liabilities (that is, the market's assessment of the true value of liabilities) for business written before time $t$; and $\Pi_t$ is the market's assessment of the excess of assets over liabilities for busi-

44. J. David Cummins and Scott Harrington, "The Relationship between Risk and Return: Evidence for Property-Liability Insurance Stocks," *Journal of Risk and Insurance* (forthcoming). Beta is defined as the covariance of the returns on a security with the returns on a broad portfolio of common stocks. Finance theory suggests that beta is a more appropriate measure of risk than return variance for investors with diversified portfolios. Nelson J. Lacey analyzed returns for life and property-liability insurance stocks for 1982–85. His results suggested that the stocks did less well than the market, but his sample included stocks for only five property-liability insurers. See "Recent Evidence on the Liability Crisis," unpublished manuscript (University of Massachusetts, Department of General Business and Finance, December 1986).

ness written at and after time $t$ (the market value of net cash flows on current and future business). After some manipulation, it can be shown (for $\Pi_{t-1}$ not equal to zero) that if no new equity is issued, the return on equity in period $t$ ($r_{et} = E_t/E_{t-1} - 1$) is given by

$$(2) \qquad r_{et} = \frac{[r_{At} + (r_{At} - r_{Lt})k_{t-1} + r_{\Pi t}\pi_{t-1}]}{(1 + \pi_{t-1})},$$

where $r_{At} = A_t/A_{t-1} - 1$ (growth in assets), $r_{Lt} = L_t/L_{t-1} - 1$ (growth in liabilities), $r_{\Pi t} = \Pi_t/\Pi_{t-1} - 1$ (growth in $\Pi$), $k_t = L_t/(A_t - L_t)$ (market value of liabilities on old business relative to the market value of equity for old business), and $\pi_t$ equals $\Pi_t/(A_t - L_t)$ (market value of net cash flows on current and future business relative to market value of equity for old business).

If investors believed that business were to be priced to break even, so that $\Pi = 0$ for all $t$, and if assets and liabilities were immunized against changes in interest rate risk, and forecasts of future claims were accurate, the percentage change in equity during a given period would be approximately equal to the percentage change in the value of assets. In general, property-liability assets have longer duration than liabilities, so that increases (or decreases) in interest rates will tend to produce negative (or positive) growth in the market value of equity for old business.[45] Changes in the value of equity in a given period will also reflect revisions in expectations about future claims on old business as well as changes in the profitability of current and future business. Positive or negative abnormal returns in a period could reflect any of these influences. Total returns in any period could be large and positive even if premiums on current and future business were expected to equal the discounted value of all costs.

As an example, consider a period such as 1985 in which returns on insurance company assets were large because of increasing stock prices and the favorable impact of declining interest rates on bond values. Assume that $r_{At} = 0.20$. Given the longer duration of assets than liabilities, assume that $r_{Lt} = 0.10$ and that there is no revision in expectations about claims on old business. Let $k_{t-1} = 2$. Finally, assume that $\pi_t = 0$ but that $\pi_{t-1} = -0.10$, that is, current and future business are expected to break even, but business written in period $t-1$ was priced below

---

45. Richard A. Derrig, "The Effect of Federal Taxes on Investment Income in Property-Liability Ratemaking," paper presented at the 1985 meeting of the American Risk and Insurance Association, Vancouver.

expected costs. Based on these assumptions, the value of $r_{Et}$ from equation 2 is 56 percent. While the assumptions are ad hoc, they nonetheless indicate the possibility that stock returns could be expected to be quite large in 1985 without positive profits on business written in 1985 or 1986, especially if business written in 1984 had been underpriced. The market reaction would simply reflect the return to break-even rates and favorable investment performance. The growth in premiums also could be very large, given declining interest rates, rapid growth in expected losses on new business, and a return to break-even pricing.

## Growth in Premiums and Losses

Table 3-8 presents annual growth rates in written premiums, earned premiums, and calendar year incurred losses for the major third-party lines and all lines for 1977–86. The growth rates in premiums generally were large in 1977 and 1978, low and even negative during 1979–83, and very large in 1985 and 1986. This pattern is most pronounced for general liability.[46] Calendar year incurred losses, which reflect revisions in reserves on previous years' claims, show a similar pattern, although the growth in losses generally is well above zero even for 1979–83. The 78 percent growth rate in written premiums in 1985 and the estimated 73 percent growth rate in 1986 for general liability, along with smaller but still large growth rates for medical malpractice, commercial multiperil, and commercial auto liability, clearly indicate what the debate is about, especially since the amount of coverage provided for general liability and perhaps other lines may have been declining during these years.[47]

Casual observation suggests the cyclical pattern of large but declining increases in premiums written following the adverse financial experience of 1974 and 1975 and dramatic increases following the adverse results of 1984. Without cyclical influences, growth rates would primarily re-

46. J. David Cummins and David J. Nye note that general liability (including medical malpractice) had the highest annual growth rate in net premiums written for all major property-liability lines from 1952 to 1980; see "Inflation and Property-Liability Insurance," in John D. Long and Everett D. Randall, eds., *Issues in Insurance,* 3d ed., vol. 1 (Malvern, Pa.: American Institute for Property and Liability Underwriters, 1984), p. 200.

47. Since there is no standard unit of exposure for most property-liability lines, and coverage levels are not reported, statements about reductions in coverage are anecdotal. It should also be noted that the growth figures for medical malpractice could be influenced by changes in the proportion of business written by insurers that report to A. M. Best Co.

Table 8

Table 3-8. *Growth Rates for Net Premiums Written, Net Premiums Earned, and Incurred Losses, by Line of Insurance, 1977–86*
Percent

| Item | General liability | Medical malpractice | Commercial multiperil | Commercial auto liability | Private passenger auto liability | Workers' compensation | All property-liability |
|---|---|---|---|---|---|---|---|
| Net premiums written | | | | | | | |
| 1976–77 | 37.5 | 10.2 | 22.7 | 23.5 | 20.3 | 24.2 | 19.8 |
| 1977–78 | 11.0 | –2.6 | 17.3 | 11.4 | 9.7 | 20.8 | 12.8 |
| 1978–79 | 1.9 | –0.9 | 14.4 | 8.8 | 13.0 | 16.5 | 10.3 |
| 1979–80 | –3.0 | 5.9 | 3.3 | 0.3 | 9.9 | 8.2 | 6.0 |
| 1980–81 | –5.7 | 4.9 | –0.2 | 0.3 | 7.2 | 2.7 | 3.9 |
| 1981–82 | –6.2 | 11.4 | 2.0 | –0.1 | 9.4 | –4.6 | 4.7 |
| 1982–83 | 0.2 | 5.2 | 4.0 | –0.1 | 8.6 | 0.4 | 4.8 |
| 1983–84 | 14.1 | 13.2 | 13.6 | 14.2 | 6.3 | 7.9 | 8.4 |
| 1984–85 | 78.2 | 56.0 | 46.0 | 45.0 | 13.8 | 12.8 | 22.0 |
| 1985–86 | 73.1 | 29.3 | 32.5 | n.a. | n.a. | 14.7 | 22.3 |
| Net premiums earned | | | | | | | |
| 1976–77 | 36.7 | 8.2 | 22.9 | 23.6 | 22.2 | 24.7 | 20.5 |
| 1977–78 | 15.2 | –0.4 | 17.3 | 13.2 | 12.9 | 18.7 | 14.3 |

|  | | | | | | | |
|---|---|---|---|---|---|---|---|
| 1978–79 | 5.8 | −1.3 | 15.7 | 11.1 | 11.1 | 17.5 | 10.4 |
| 1979–80 | 0.8 | 1.6 | 6.7 | 1.6 | 11.4 | 9.8 | 7.8 |
| 1980–81 | −7.5 | 5.6 | −0.2 | 1.9 | 7.3 | 3.7 | 4.0 |
| 1981–82 | −6.3 | 7.3 | 3.0 | −0.8 | 8.5 | −3.4 | 4.7 |
| 1982–83 | 0.2 | 11.1 | 4.0 | 0.1 | 9.2 | 1.3 | 4.9 |
| 1983–84 | 9.1 | 13.2 | 9.4 | 9.5 | 7.3 | 7.5 | 7.2 |
| 1984–85 | 49.1 | 41.6 | 30.9 | 33.1 | 10.2 | 11.3 | 15.7 |
| 1985–86 | 77.2 | 35.7 | 38.8 | n.a. | n.a. | 13.9 | 24.0 |
| Incurred losses (calendar year) | | | | | | | |
| 1976–77 | 27.4 | −9.4 | 9.6 | 17.0 | 3.6 | 25.1 | 13.0 |
| 1977–78 | 9.1 | 9.7 | 10.7 | 13.6 | 18.1 | 13.4 | 13.4 |
| 1978–79 | 5.1 | 10.9 | 33.0 | 16.7 | 18.1 | 12.7 | 15.1 |
| 1979–80 | 11.5 | 17.2 | 13.2 | 5.8 | 6.0 | 5.0 | 10.5 |
| 1980–81 | 1.0 | 11.7 | 10.8 | 10.9 | 9.5 | 2.3 | 6.6 |
| 1981–82 | 7.6 | 18.8 | 14.2 | 6.5 | 9.5 | −5.6 | 8.7 |
| 1982–83 | 8.6 | 11.2 | 12.6 | 6.3 | 10.4 | 10.3 | 7.1 |
| 1983–84 | 25.4 | 22.6 | 26.3 | 22.2 | 9.7 | 22.2 | 16.0 |
| 1984–85 | 49.9 | 49.3 | 20.5 | 18.9 | 18.7 | 10.9 | 16.4 |
| 1985–86 | 44.0 | 16.6 | 3.6 | n.a. | n.a. | 18.8 | 15.4 |

Sources: Data for 1976–85 are from *Best's Aggregates and Averages: Property-Casualty, 1986*. For 1986, estimated net premiums written are from Wish, "Review and Preview." Estimated net premiums earned and incurred losses for 1986 were calculated using data reported in Wish.
n.a. Not available.

flect growth in demand, expected losses, expenses, and changes in interest rates. As interest rates increase (or decrease), break-even premiums decline (or increase), other things being equal, since the discount rate for future losses increases (or decreases). The low and even negative growth rates in general liability premiums for 1979–82 were influenced by the sharp increases in interest rates through 1981 and their continued high level in 1982 (see appendix B, table 3-15). Whether the declines in premiums also reflected excessive competition is discussed later, as is whether decreases in interest rates after 1982 and growth in losses can explain the large growth in premiums in 1985 and 1986.

Table 3-9 shows geometric mean annual growth rates for premiums and incurred losses relative to growth in nominal GNP in 1976–86.[48] Both premiums and losses grew more slowly than GNP from 1976 to 1981, when interest rates were rising and the 11.4 percent growth rate in nominal GNP reflected a CPI growth rate of almost 10 percent. Since 1981, when interest rates were falling and the growth in GNP was slower, largely because of lower inflation, the growth of both premiums and losses significantly exceeded that for GNP. These rates contributed to substantial growth relative to GNP for the entire 1976–86 period. This pattern is most pronounced for general liability and for medical malpractice.

Growth rates for calendar year losses reflect revisions in reserves on losses incurred in earlier periods. An alternative measure of growth is provided by accident year data, which give losses incurred only for accidents (including claims not reported) during a given year. Nominal growth rates for accident year losses and rates relative to GNP growth are shown for the entire industry and for the forty-five company sample in table 3-10. Two sets of growth rates were calculated: accident year

48. The geometric mean growth rate for GNP was 11.4 percent for 1976–81, 6.6 percent for 1981–86, and 9.0 percent for 1976–86. Comparisons of real growth rates per capita would show values in all periods larger than those based on GNP, and the difference would be greatest for subperiods in the 1980s. Some of the increase in growth rates for losses relative to GNP after 1981 that are shown in table 3-9 and subsequent tables could be due to inflation in medical care costs. Norton E. Masterson has periodically reported claim cost indexes for various property-liability lines that are weighted averages of wage and price indexes that should be highly correlated with factors associated with loss costs for each line; see "Economic Factors in Liability and Property Insurance Claims Costs," *Best's Review: Property/Casualty Edition,* vol. 81 (June 1980), p. 74. Comparison of his index for "other bodily injury liability" through 1980 with the GNP implicit price deflator (Cummins and Nye, "Inflation and Property-Liability Insurance," pp. 211–15) provided little motivation for construction of a more elaborate index to analyze growth in premiums and losses in this study.

Table 3-9. *Growth Rates for Net Premiums Written, Net Premiums Earned, and Incurred Losses Relative to GNP, by Line of Insurance, Selected Periods, 1976–86*

Percent

| Item | General liability | Medical malpractice | Commercial multiperil | Commercial auto liability | Private passenger auto liability | Workers' compensation | All property-liability |
|---|---|---|---|---|---|---|---|
| **Net premiums written** | | | | | | | |
| 1976–81 | -3.6 | -7.2 | -0.2 | -2.5 | 0.5 | 2.5 | -0.8 |
| 1981–85 | 9.9 | 12.1 | 7.7 | 6.0 | 3.6 | -2.9 | 2.6 |
| 1976–85 | 2.1 | 1.0 | 3.2 | 1.2 | 1.9 | 0.1 | 0.7 |
| 1981–86[a] | 19.1 | 14.2 | 11.1 | n.a. | n.a. | -0.6 | 5.2 |
| 1976–86[a] | 7.1 | 3.0 | 5.3 | n.a. | n.a. | 1.0 | 2.1 |
| **Net premiums earned** | | | | | | | |
| 1976–81 | -1.9 | -7.8 | 0.7 | -1.2 | 1.4 | 3.0 | -0.1 |
| 1981–85 | 3.9 | 9.9 | 4.0 | 2.5 | 2.9 | -2.8 | 1.0 |
| 1976–85 | 0.6 | -0.3 | 2.2 | 0.4 | 2.0 | 0.4 | 0.4 |
| 1981–86[a] | 14.4 | 13.4 | 9.1 | n.a. | n.a. | -0.7 | 4.1 |
| 1976–86[a] | 5.9 | 2.3 | 4.8 | n.a. | n.a. | 1.1 | 2.0 |
| **Incurred losses (calendar year)** | | | | | | | |
| 1976–81 | -0.8 | -3.4 | 3.4 | 1.2 | -0.4 | 0.1 | 0.3 |
| 1981–85 | 13.8 | 16.5 | 10.5 | 5.8 | 3.2 | 1.9 | 4.7 |
| 1976–85 | 5.4 | 5.0 | 6.5 | 3.3 | 1.2 | 0.9 | 2.2 |
| 1981–86[a] | 18.1 | 15.4 | 8.0 | n.a. | n.a. | 4.0 | 5.6 |
| 1976–86[a] | 8.2 | 5.6 | 5.7 | n.a. | n.a. | 2.0 | 2.9 |

Sources: Premium and loss data are from Best's *Aggregates and Averages: Property-Casualty, 1986*; and Wish, "Review and Preview." Growth rates are annual geometric means. GNP data are from the *Economic Report of the President, January 1987*.

n.a. Not available.

a. Estimated.

Table 3-10. Growth Rates for Accident Year Incurred Losses, by Line of Insurance, Selected Periods, 1976–85

Percent

| Sample | Period | General liability | Medical malpractice | General liability and medical malpractice | Multiperil | Auto liability | Workers' compensation | Schedule P[a] | Schedule O[a] |
|---|---|---|---|---|---|---|---|---|---|
| *Initially reported* | | | | | | | | | |
| Industry | 1981–85 | 17.3 | 19.2 | 17.7 | 11.6 | 11.5 | 8.2 | 11.7 | n.a. |
| 45 companies | 1976–81 | 11.5 | 3.1 | 10.0 | 14.9 | 11.8 | 14.4 | 12.9 | 10.9 |
| | 1981–85 | 16.8 | 12.2 | 16.2 | 11.1 | 10.9 | 8.2 | 11.0 | 8.2 |
| | 1976–85 | 13.9 | 7.0 | 12.7 | 13.2 | 11.4 | 11.6 | 12.0 | 9.7 |
| *Ratio of initially reported/GNP* | | | | | | | | | |
| Industry | 1981–85 | 9.6 | 11.4 | 10.1 | 4.3 | 4.3 | 1.2 | 4.4 | n.a. |
| 45 companies | 1976–81 | 0.1 | −7.4 | −1.3 | 3.2 | 0.4 | 2.7 | 1.4 | −0.4 |
| | 1981–85 | 9.2 | 4.9 | 8.6 | 3.9 | 3.7 | 1.1 | 3.7 | 1.2 |
| | 1976–85 | 4.1 | −2.1 | 3.0 | 3.5 | 1.8 | 2.0 | 2.4 | 0.3 |
| *Developed through 1985* | | | | | | | | | |
| Industry | 1976–81 | 10.9 | 17.1 | 12.4 | 15.2 | 11.9 | 10.7 | 12.5 | 12.3 |
| | 1981–85 | 14.7 | 11.4 | 13.8 | 11.5 | 11.5 | 10.3 | 11.6 | 8.5 |
| | 1976–85 | 12.6 | 14.5 | 13.0 | 13.5 | 11.8 | 10.5 | 12.1 | 10.6 |
| 45 companies | 1976–81 | 7.9 | 6.8 | 7.7 | 15.1 | 11.8 | 9.3 | 11.5 | 10.7 |
| | 1981–85 | 15.4 | 11.0 | 14.8 | 11.1 | 11.0 | 10.6 | 11.4 | 9.3 |
| | 1976–85 | 11.2 | 8.7 | 10.8 | 13.3 | 11.5 | 9.8 | 11.5 | 10.1 |
| *Ratio of developed through 1985/GNP* | | | | | | | | | |
| Industry | 1976–81 | −0.4 | 5.2 | 0.9 | 3.4 | 0.5 | −0.6 | 1.1 | 0.8 |
| | 1981–85 | 7.2 | 4.2 | 6.4 | 4.2 | 4.2 | 3.1 | 4.3 | 1.4 |
| | 1976–85 | 2.9 | 4.7 | 3.3 | 3.8 | 2.2 | 1.0 | 2.5 | 1.1 |
| 45 companies | 1976–81 | −3.1 | −4.1 | −3.3 | 3.3 | 0.4 | −1.9 | 0.1 | −0.5 |
| | 1981–85 | 7.9 | 3.8 | 7.3 | 3.9 | 3.8 | 3.4 | 4.1 | 2.2 |
| | 1976–85 | 1.6 | −0.7 | 1.3 | 3.6 | 1.9 | 0.4 | 1.9 | 0.7 |

Sources: Industry data are from *Best's Aggregates and Averages: Property-Casualty,* 1986; data for forty-five companies provided by Aetna Life and Casualty Company. Growth rates are annual geometric means.

n.a. Not available.

a. Schedule P includes aggregate experience for the groupings of third-party lines. Schedule O includes aggregate experience for first-party coverages.

losses initially reported and losses for the accident year developed through 1985.[49]

The results have much the same pattern as those for the calendar year losses shown in table 3-9. For general liability and the forty-five company sample, losses grew at about the same rate as GNP during 1976–81, but grew 9.2 percent faster than GNP during 1981–85, which is much faster than the rates for the other lines shown. The results using developed losses provide some evidence of errors in estimated reserves but have the same general implication as those based on initially reported losses and calendar year losses. The results for medical malpractice are a possible exception, since they indicate a decline in the growth relative to GNP in 1981–85 compared with 1976–81. However, the possibility exists that changes in the market share of malpractice insurers that do not report data to A. M. Best could distort these rates.

Table 3-11 shows growth rates for total losses paid for the forty-five company sample and for accident year losses paid through three years for the industry and for the sample.[50] While the rates for total paid losses are shown separately for general liability and for medical malpractice, these results could be distorted by changes in reporting methods following 1975. Calculation of total paid losses uses the change in the total loss reserve during a given year. Before 1975, separate reserves were not reported for medical malpractice and general liability. After separate results began to be reported, some companies segregated reserves for the two lines for accidents before the change, others did not. Since the separate results for total losses paid may be distorted by these differences, it is better to focus on the combined results for the two lines.[51]

49. It is not clear which procedure is better. If loss development is similar over time, use of initially reported losses would provide a more accurate measure of the underlying growth in losses. If reserve accuracy improved, the use of developed losses as of 1985 would tend to be more accurate. The source for the industry data, *Best's Aggregates and Averages,* provided initially reported losses beginning with the 1979 accident year, so that growth rates for 1976–81 could not be calculated for the industry.

50. Total paid losses for a given year were calculated as calendar year incurred losses less the change in the loss reserve for the year. Since the loss reserve data began in 1976, the paid loss figures begin in 1977. Total paid losses could not be calculated for the industry using information provided in *Best's Aggregates and Averages.* Using other A. M. Best data, both Insurance Services Office and Carole Banfield provide graphs showing large growth in paid losses relative to GNP for general liability and medical malpractice since the late 1970s. See ISO, *Insurer Profitability: The Facts;* and Banfield, "P/C Insurer Profitability: ISO Paid Claims Data," *Journal of Insurance Regulation,* vol. 5 (December 1986), pp. 268–76.

51. The much higher rates shown for medical malpractice than for general liability probably are due to this effect.

Table 3-11. Growth Rates for Paid Losses, by Line of Insurance, Selected Periods, 1976–85
Percent

| Sample | Period | General liability[a] | Medical malpractice[a] | General liability and medical malpractice | Multiperil | Auto liability | Workers' compensation | Schedule P[b] | Schedule O[b] |
|---|---|---|---|---|---|---|---|---|---|
| **Total paid** | | | | | | | | | |
| 45 companies | 1981–82 | 12.8 | 24.6 | 14.2 | 13.9 | 11.9 | 9.8 | 12.3 | 3.5 |
| | 1982–83 | 10.0 | 43.2 | 14.2 | 5.3 | 8.1 | 6.5 | 7.6 | −11.7 |
| | 1983–84 | 17.6 | −11.9 | 12.9 | 17.9 | 12.4 | 13.6 | 14.2 | 29.3 |
| | 1984–85 | −2.9 | 30.6 | 13.8 | 7.7 | 12.6 | 13.0 | 11.4 | 12.4 |
| | 1977–81 | 11.9 | 33.0 | 13.6 | 17.6 | 12.1 | 12.5 | 13.8 | 11.7 |
| | 1981–85 | 9.1 | 38.0 | 13.8 | 11.1 | 11.2 | 10.7 | 11.4 | 9.9 |
| | 1977–85 | 10.5 | 35.5 | 13.7 | 14.3 | 11.7 | 11.6 | 12.6 | 10.8 |
| **Ratio of total paid/GNP** | | | | | | | | | |
| 45 companies | 1977–81 | 0.6 | 19.5 | 2.1 | 5.7 | 0.7 | 1.1 | 2.2 | 0.4 |
| | 1981–85 | 2.0 | 29.0 | 6.4 | 3.8 | 4.0 | 3.5 | 4.1 | 2.7 |
| | 1977–85 | 1.3 | 24.2 | 4.2 | 4.7 | 2.3 | 2.3 | 3.2 | 1.5 |
| **Accident year losses paid through three years** | | | | | | | | | |
| Industry | 1979–83 | 15.3 | 29.6 | 17.3 | 12.4 | 11.0 | 9.1 | 11.5 | n.a. |
| 45 companies | 1976–79 | 11.1 | 14.6 | 11.4 | 18.4 | 13.0 | 12.7 | 14.4 | 11.9 |
| | 1979–83 | 13.8 | 30.9 | 15.6 | 12.5 | 10.5 | 8.1 | 10.9 | 8.5 |
| | 1976–83 | 12.6 | 23.6 | 13.8 | 15.0 | 11.6 | 10.0 | 12.4 | 10.0 |
| **Ratio of accident year losses paid through three years/GNP** | | | | | | | | | |
| Industry | 1979–83 | 6.8 | 20.0 | 8.6 | 4.1 | 2.8 | 1.0 | 3.3 | n.a. |
| 45 companies | 1976–79 | −0.9 | 2.3 | −0.6 | 5.7 | 0.9 | 0.6 | 2.1 | −0.1 |
| | 1979–83 | 5.4 | 21.2 | 7.1 | 4.2 | 2.4 | 0.1 | 2.8 | 0.5 |
| | 1976–83 | 2.7 | 12.7 | 3.7 | 4.8 | 1.7 | 0.3 | 2.5 | 0.2 |

Sources: Industry data are from Best's Aggregates and Averages: Property-Casualty, 1986; data for forty-five companies provided by Aetna Life and Casualty Company. Growth rates are annual geometric means.

n.a. Not available.

a. Separate rates for general liability and medical malpractice distorted because of reserve reporting practices.

b. Schedule P includes aggregate experience for the groupings of third-party lines. Schedule O includes aggregate experience for first-party coverages.

Apart from this problem, the value of looking at growth rates for losses paid is that they will not be distorted by reserve errors. They will, however, be affected by changes in the speed at which claims are paid. A slowdown in the rate at which claims are settled will tend to reduce the growth rate in paid losses; more rapid payment will tend to increase it. For general liability, the paid loss development factors shown in appendix B, table 3-16, suggest some slowdown in claims payment during 1976–84, especially during 1976–80. Thus growth rates for this line would tend to be depressed.[52]

The nominal growth rates in total paid losses for general liability and medical malpractice combined were just under 14 percent for 1977–81, 1981–85, and 1977–85. As a result, the growth rate relative to GNP was 4.3 percent higher during 1981–85 than during 1977–81. The results for auto liability and workers' compensation are comparable. The results for multiperil show a decline relative to GNP during the two periods, although growth in total paid losses still exceeded the GNP growth rate by 3.8 percent during 1981–85. The decline in this line could reflect an increase in the proportion of third-party business with slower claims payment. The results for accident year paid losses through three years have implications similar to those for total paid losses.

Table 3-12 gives per capita growth rates in real written premiums and paid losses on direct business during 1976–84 for the ten most populous states in the 1980 census.[53] Based on the ten-state average for medical malpractice and general liability combined, the mean annual growth rate for real written premiums per capita was −0.6, 1.7, and 0.2 percent for 1976–81, 1981–84, and 1976–84, respectively. These periods precede the large premium increases in 1985 and 1986. The corresponding rates for real paid losses per capita were 6.6, 15.7 and 9.8 percent. While not directly comparable with the results for total paid claims net of reinsurance shown in table 3-11, these rates suggest that the growth of losses may have been considerably higher in large states than in the remainder of the country.

The overall results in tables 3-9 through 3-12 suggest that commercial

52. Comparable analysis was not conducted for the remaining lines.

53. GNP data are not available by state. These premium and loss data were reported by National Insurance Consumer Organization, "Property/Casualty Insurance Industry Income and Payouts" (Alexandria, Va., 1986); data were from *Best's Executive Data Service*. While NICO reported data for 1975–84, 1975 was excluded to make the first subperiod comparable to that used in the previous tables. The essence of the report was that insurers took in far more in written premiums than they paid in losses during the period.

Table 3-12. *Growth Rates for Direct Premiums Written and Losses Paid per Capita, by Line of Insurance, for Ten Largest States, Selected Periods, 1976–84*
Percent

| Line | Period | California | New York | Texas | Pennsylvania | Illinois | Ohio | Florida | Michigan | New Jersey | North Carolina | Average |
|---|---|---|---|---|---|---|---|---|---|---|---|---|
| *Real premiums written* | | | | | | | | | | | | |
| General liability | 1976–81 | -3.0 | 2.4 | 1.0 | -0.5 | -2.6 | 0.3 | -2.3 | 1.2 | 1.0 | 1.4 | -0.1 |
| | 1981–84 | -1.8 | 0.1 | -2.0 | -0.9 | -2.0 | -4.9 | 0.2 | 9.0 | -0.3 | 2.4 | 0.0 |
| | 1976–84 | -2.6 | 1.6 | -0.1 | -0.6 | -2.4 | -1.7 | -1.4 | 4.0 | 0.5 | 1.8 | -0.1 |
| Medical malpractice | 1976–81 | -11.8 | 4.9 | -5.9 | -6.2 | -3.8 | -5.3 | 10.8 | -3.0 | -2.9 | 0.6 | -2.3 |
| | 1981–84 | 4.9 | -3.7 | 0.7 | 10.6 | 9.3 | 4.7 | 14.1 | 7.6 | 28.6 | 15.7 | 9.3 |
| | 1976–84 | -5.8 | 1.6 | -3.5 | -0.2 | 0.9 | -1.7 | 12.0 | 0.8 | 7.9 | 6.0 | 1.8 |
| General liability and medical malpractice | 1976–81 | -5.3 | 3.0 | 0.2 | -1.5 | -2.8 | -1.0 | -0.6 | 0.5 | 0.4 | 1.2 | -0.6 |
| | 1981–84 | -0.3 | -0.8 | -1.7 | 1.1 | 0.1 | -2.9 | 2.9 | 8.8 | 4.5 | 5.1 | 1.7 |
| | 1976–84 | -3.5 | 1.6 | -0.5 | -0.5 | -1.7 | -1.7 | 0.7 | 3.5 | 1.9 | 2.7 | 0.2 |
| *Real losses paid* | | | | | | | | | | | | |
| General liability | 1976–81 | 5.0 | 8.4 | 9.4 | 12.7 | 1.3 | 6.6 | 0.3 | 13.1 | 3.5 | -7.4 | 5.3 |
| | 1981–84 | 11.1 | 16.0 | 14.3 | 9.0 | 16.7 | 24.1 | 13.2 | 14.6 | 14.1 | 19.8 | 15.3 |
| | 1976–84 | 7.3 | 11.2 | 11.2 | 11.3 | 6.8 | 12.8 | 5.0 | 13.7 | 7.4 | 2.0 | 8.9 |
| Medical malpractice | 1976–81 | 8.1 | 19.3 | 5.1 | 17.0 | 8.8 | 11.6 | 9.5 | 24.1 | 19.1 | 18.7 | 14.1 |
| | 1981–84 | 13.4 | 16.4 | 20.2 | 6.2 | 12.9 | 35.1 | -6.0 | 15.5 | 16.4 | 44.2 | 17.4 |
| | 1976–84 | 10.1 | 18.2 | 10.5 | 12.8 | 10.3 | 19.9 | 3.4 | 20.8 | 18.1 | 27.7 | 15.2 |
| General liability and medical malpractice | 1976–81 | 5.5 | 10.6 | 9.1 | 13.3 | 2.4 | 7.2 | 1.7 | 14.7 | 6.2 | -0.5 | 6.6 |
| | 1981–84 | 11.5 | 16.1 | 14.7 | 8.6 | 16.0 | 25.9 | 10.0 | 14.7 | 14.6 | 24.6 | 15.7 |
| | 1976–84 | 7.7 | 12.6 | 11.2 | 11.5 | 7.3 | 13.9 | 4.8 | 14.7 | 9.3 | 5.2 | 9.8 |

Sources: Loss and premium data are from A. M. Best's Executive Data Service: Experience by State, report A2, as reproduced in National Insurance Consumer Organization, "Property/Casualty Insurance Industry Income and Payouts" (Alexandria, Va., 1986). Growth rates are annual geometric means. State rankings are based on the 1980 census, and real values are calculated using CPI; see U.S. Bureau of the Census, *Statistical Abstract of the United States*, various years.

liability losses have grown rapidly relative to GNP in recent years. While the 1981 cutoff was largely arbitrary, the results indicate that when inflation slowed in the early 1980s, the growth rate in losses did not.

## Causes of Underwriting Cycles

Most observers believe that the property-liability market is characterized by underwriting cycles: soft markets with readily available coverage at falling prices followed by hard markets with difficulty in obtaining coverage and rapidly rising prices. Insurer profits (both accounting and economic), premiums written, and surplus vary accordingly. Theoretical work does not, however, provide a clear explanation for underwriting cycles. Empirical work also leaves something to be desired, perhaps because of the difficulty of using time series data for several decades to estimate structural relationships that are likely to alter because of changes in types of coverage, regulation, and other factors. Until the most recent cycle, the accepted wisdom was that the underwriting cycle had a period of about six years.[54] A number of authors have tried to explain why the most recent hard market began almost a decade after the hard market of 1975 and 1976.[55]

The traditional explanation of underwriting cycles is that competition

54. See, for example, Barbara D. Stewart, "Profit Cycles in Property-Liability Insurance," in John D. Long, ed., *Issues in Insurance*, 2d ed., vol. 2 (Malvern, Pa.: American Institute for Property and Liability Underwriters, 1981), pp. 79–140; and Milton E. Smith and Fikry S. Gahin, "The Underwriting Cycle in Property and Liability Insurance," unpublished manuscript (Brigham Young University, 1983). Some of this work has looked at combined ratios without considering the likely impact of changes in interest rates. Nonetheless, a casual look at premiums, accounting profits including investment income, and return on equity suggests cyclical patterns. The results of several studies indicate that such underwriting profit measures as the combined ratio follow a second-order autoregressive process that is consistent with a cycle; see Emilio C. Venezian, "Ratemaking Methods and Profit Cycles in Property and Liability Insurance," *Journal of Risk and Insurance*, vol. 52 (September 1985), pp. 477–500; and J. David Cummins and J. François Outreville, "An International Analysis of Underwriting Cycles in Property-Liability Insurance," *Journal of Risk and Insurance*, vol. 54 (June 1987), pp. 246–62. See also David Oakden, "Discussion," of Kaye D. James, "Underwriting Cycles in the Property-Casualty Insurance Industry," in Casualty Actuarial Society, *Inflation Implications for Property-Casualty Insurance* (New York, 1981). Some studies have suggested that the timing, amplitude, and frequency of cycles may vary by insurance line; see Stewart, "Profit Cycles in Property-Liability Insurance"; and Venezian, "Ratemaking Methods and Profit Cycles."

55. See, for example, Barry D. Smith, "The Property and Liability Underwriting Cycle: What Lies Ahead?" *CPCU Journal*, vol. 35 (September 1982), pp. 138–42; and

leads to excessive price cutting and that the resultant underwriting losses and reductions in surplus lead to a substantial reduction in aggregate supply so that prices, profits, and surplus increase until price cutting begins once again.[56] Two interesting questions arise in view of this explanation. Do prices on new business rise above costs? And why would rational, profit-maximizing firms have a persistent tendency in the first place to price business below cost so that retrenchment en masse is eventually needed to avoid financial collapse?

Empirical work has been silent about the extent to which prices exceed costs on a cycle's upswing. With free entry and perfectly informed buyers, existing insurers would not be able to raise prices above expected costs for new business to recoup past losses. Based on the current state of theory, it is unclear why existing insurers would not have incentives to issue new equity and to expand supply to prevent overpricing. This may have happened. The data in table 3-2 indicate an infusion of new capital into the industry in 1985 and 1986, which, along with the favorable capital gains experience, may have been expected to increase supply. Moreover, anecdotal evidence suggests that many specialty insurers entered the market in 1985 and 1986, often as association captives. Nonetheless, entry could have been slow enough to allow prices to exceed costs in the short run, provided that the previous deterioration in insurers' financial condition actually caused a substantial upward shift in supply.[57] Moreover, if competition periodically caused inadequate prices, recoupment of the attendant losses through subsequent price increases would be necessary for individual insurers to break even over the long run.

What about the pervasive tendency to price below cost? In a comprehensive review of regulation in other industries, Stephen Breyer has referred to the scenario of destructive competition as an "empty box."[58] Such competition has often been alleged to justify price and entry regulation, but there is little evidence it has existed in any industry. The

---

Robert T. McGee, "The Cycle in Property/Casualty Insurance," *Federal Reserve Bank of New York Quarterly Review* (Autumn 1986), pp. 22–30. Reasons discussed include increased capacity in the late 1970s and early 1980s because of entry by captives and numerous foreign reinsurers.

56. Stewart, "Profit Cycles in Property-Liability Insurance"; and Smith and Gahin, "Underwriting Cycle in Property and Liability Insurance."

57. The traditional view and theory currently do not provide a rigorous or concise explanation of why losses would actually lead to such a shift.

58. Stephen Breyer, *Regulation and Its Reform* (Harvard University Press, 1982).

possibility remains that prices may tend to go below expected costs in insurance because of difficulty in forecasting future claims. However, if forecasts were unbiased over the long run, errors would contribute to variability in cash flows and accounting profits, but they would not be expected to produce cycles, as opposed to random, although perhaps large, variation.

Cash-flow underwriting has been alleged to have aggravated the recent downturn in profits because high interest rates led insurers to sell coverage at inadequate prices to obtain funds for investment.[59] Since break-even premiums equal the discounted value of losses and other costs, premiums will tend to decline as interest rates increase.[60] But these suppositions shed little light on why this relationship should allow prices to fall too low. For example, if future claims were known with certainty, increases in interest rates would not be expected to cause insurers to sell coverage below cost in order to invest money at rates insufficient to pay future claims.

Emilio Venezian has argued that forecasting methods used by insurance rating bureaus may lead to profit cycles. While he presents some evidence consistent with his conjecture, it raises the difficult question of why forecasting techniques would be both widely used and relied on if they produced large fluctuations in premiums. In an alternative view Robert McGee has suggested that companies with optimistic expectations about the magnitude of future claims may cause prices to decline below average expectations of future costs. If so, companies that believe prices to be temporarily inadequate may maximize profits (minimize losses) by maintaining coverage to avoid substantial losses in volume in the presence of fixed costs.[61] In a world in which all economic agents are making accurate forecasts on the basis of all available information, expectations would be homogeneous. Since such a world does not exist, further development of this heterogeneous expectations argument that considers expectations of buyers as well as sellers might help explain cycles. As it is, this view would imply that insurers with unfavorable expectations about future claims would start to show large losses before those with favorable expectations, provided that loss reserves reflected

59. This view has often been expressed in the trade press and by NICO.

60. Michael L. Smith, "Investment Yields and Insurance Underwriting," unpublished manuscript (Ohio State University, February 26, 1987), provides evidence that premiums are negatively related to interest rates.

61. Venezian, "Ratemaking Methods and Profit Cycles"; and McGee, "Cycle in Property/Casualty Insurance."

expectations. However, incentives could exist for sellers with unfavorable expectations to underreserve, perhaps to avoid reaction by regulators, shareholders, or buyers that might be sensitive to the probability of default. Further work is needed to explore these issues.

The theory of insurance company capital structure raises the possibility that the supply functions of individual firms could differ, with the result that prices could fall below costs even with homogeneous expectations. If customer demand is inelastic with respect to default probability, the theory suggests that insurers with little to lose in the event of default would be willing to sell more coverage relative to capital at a given premium rate than insurers with a lot to lose.[62] The possibility exists under these conditions that high-risk insurers could cause prices to fall below costs. Again, other insurers might find it best to maintain volume at below-cost prices.

Both the hypotheses of heterogeneous expectations and of excessive risk taking could be consistent with a tendency toward large losses and increases in the number of insurance company failures. In contrast to these hypotheses and the traditional view, others suggest that cycles in reported prices and profits may arise even if decisions of all companies are based on unbiased estimates of expected future claims.[63] J. David Cummins and J. François Outreville argue that cycles in reported profits may arise despite rational expectations because of the reporting procedures and adjustment lags associated with data collection, regulation, and periodic renewal of contracts. Neil Doherty and Han Bin Kang argue that any apparent cyclicality in prices or profits could be caused by lagged adjustment of demand and supply to optimal levels based on break-even prices. It is unclear whether either approach is capable of explaining the large price increases that have occurred since 1984.

Another possibility consistent with unbiased forecasts of future claims is that insurers periodically make large errors. Future losses for long-tailed occurrence contracts are very difficult to predict, given possible changes in accident risk, legal rules and standards, medical care costs, and other factors. For a line in which many claims may be unpaid ten

---

62. See Munch and Smallwood, "Theory of Solvency Regulation"; and Finsinger and Pauly, "Reserve Levels and Reserve Requirements." The papers focus on fixed and sunk costs that may be borne by shareholders in the event of default.

63. Cummins and Outreville, "International Analysis of Underwriting Cycles"; and Neil A. Doherty and Han Bin Kang, "Price Instability for a Financial Intermediary: Interest Rates and Insurance Price Cycles," working paper 87–1 (University of Pennsylvania, Center for Research on Risk and Insurance, January 1987).

years after policies were sold, the rate-making process may use data on how much was paid the previous year for losses arising out of policies issued ten or more years before to forecast how much may be paid ten or more years after new policies are issued.[64] If substantial forecast errors arise, they may become apparent only slowly, and revisions in expectations and ultimate changes in supply might occur only after it is too late to avoid large losses and large premium increases to catch up with expected costs.

For the sake of argument, consider the following. Data indicate that percentage increases in paid and incurred losses were commensurate with increases in GNP during 1978–81. If this relationship were expected to persist, much of the apparently large increase in paid claims and incurred losses relative to GNP since 1981 may not have been anticipated. Evidence may have begun to become available in 1982 that claim costs were not declining with inflation, but it might have taken two years of additional information before expectations were substantially modified. If so, this lag would appear capable of explaining the deteriorating financial position of the industry through 1984 and into 1985 and the evident underreserving on business written between 1982 and 1984—without relying on any pervasive tendency to underprice.

A number of observers have also pointed to changes in reinsurance capacity as major factors that have affected recent financial results for the primary market.[65] Many new reinsurers entered the U.S. market in the 1970s and early 1980s, and a significant number withdrew from the market in 1984 and 1985. Financial results for the reinsurance market deteriorated in 1984 and 1985, a decline that may have been worse than for the primary market. As was the case for the primary market, a significant amount of new capital entered the reinsurance market in 1985 and 1986. Such expansions and contractions undoubtedly affect the primary market, especially the sale of excess coverage. However, the similarity in the performance of reinsurance and primary markets suggests that reinsurance problems are unlikely to be a major cause of primary-market problems. In periods of unanticipated growth in losses,

---

64. The difficulty in forecasting claims on long-tailed third-party lines may be reduced in the future if claims-made coverage that provides for claims presented to the insurer only during the policy period becomes more common.

65. See, for example, Smith, "Property and Liability Underwriting Cycle"; and McGee, "Cycle in Property/Casualty Insurance." For a detailed discussion of recent experience in the U.S. reinsurance market, see Gottheimer, "Crisis of Confidence."

reinsurers can be expected to experience worse results than primary insurers because of the nature of excess-of-loss contracts.[66] Subsequent price adjustments also could be expected to be greater than for primary limits of coverage considering that growth in losses would have greater effects on costs for excess coverage. Price fluctuations in the reinsurance market are probably subject to the same underlying causes as those in the primary market, although the effects could be greater, given the greater difficulty of forecasting claims for excess layers of coverage than for primary layers. Questions thus remain concerning the extent to which entry into the reinsurance market was associated with underpricing and, if so, whether this reflected excessive risk taking or heterogeneous expectations. These questions are essentially the same as those that remain unanswered for the primary market.

All of the factors discussed—heterogeneous expectations, excessive risk taking, lags in adjustment, and random but large forecast errors—could have contributed to the most recent round of deteriorating financial results and subsequent rate increases in both the primary and reinsurance markets. Little is known about the magnitude of each influence, which makes it difficult to evaluate appropriate public policy responses.

## Premium Increases for General Liability Insurance

Have premium increases for general liability, the line with the largest increases, been commensurate with changes in discounted expected costs during recent years? According to financial theory, break-even insurance premiums equal the total of the present value of expected future claims, taxes, and other costs using discount rates that reflect the risk of future cash flows.[67] While in principle the theory is simple, a number of difficult problems arise when applying it to estimate break-even premiums, especially with regard to the choice of discount rates and the treatment of taxes. Moreover, applying the model requires estimates of the timing of future claim payments, and any comparison of estimated break-even premiums with actual premiums in a given period must use estimates of incurred losses for the period, which may be subject to significant errors.

66. Excess-of-loss contracts require the reinsurer to pay losses in excess of a specified retention limit for the primary company. Unanticipated growth in losses increases the reinsurer's obligation for losses that would have exceeded the retention limit without such growth, and it causes more claims to exceed the limit.

67. See Myers and Cohn, "Discounted Cash Flow Approach."

As a result, any analysis that attempts to assess the relationship between premiums and expected costs cannot support firm conclusions.

These caveats notwithstanding, two methods are employed to compare premium increases for general liability insurance with growth in the discounted value of expected losses. The first projects earned premium increases that would have occurred in 1982–86 had the ratio of earned premiums to the estimated present value of expected accident year incurred losses in 1981 continued during 1982–86.[68] This method uses 1981 as a benchmark. As can be seen in table 3-4, the operating ratio for general liability was greater in 1981 than it had been in the preceding few years, but it was still less than 100. A sharp jump in both the combined ratio and operating ratio occurred in 1982. As table 3-5 shows, the accident year loss ratio initially reported for general liability in 1981 was 0.1 greater than the value for 1980 but much lower than the values for 1982–85.

The second method applies a variant of the Myers-Cohn model to derive estimates of break-even prices for 1981–86, which are then compared with actual prices. This method is used to try to control for changes in costs other than losses (underwriting expenses and taxes) that could cause changes in the relationship between premiums and the discounted value of expected losses. Since the calculations must be based on assumptions for which theory provides only rough guidance, the discussion focuses on the relationship between actual prices and predicted prices over time, again using 1981 as a benchmark, as opposed to absolute differences in a given year.

Consider first the simple case in which break-even premiums in time $t$ are a constant multiple of the present value of expected future losses:

$$(3) \qquad P_t = \lambda \gamma_t L_t,$$

where $\lambda$ is a constant loading factor, $L_t$ is the undiscounted value of expected future claims, and $\gamma_t$ is the present value of $1.00 of expected future claims, which will depend on the discount rate and the proportion of claims expected to be paid in each future year on business sold in year $t$.[69] If $\lambda$ were constant over time, equation 3 could be used to project break-even premiums using $\lambda$ and estimates of $L_t$ and $\gamma_t$.

68. Finch's statement before the House Ways and Means Committee contains some crude calculations to illustrate premium increases that would have been needed for insurers to break even on calendar year operating results for general liability and medical malpractice in 1984.

69. Factors influencing the choice of a discount rate are discussed briefly in appendix B.

Based on equation 3, the first method uses an estimate of $\gamma$ and reported accident year incurred losses for 1981 to calculate $\lambda$. The estimate of $\lambda$ is then used with estimates of $\gamma_t$ and reported losses for 1982–85 to project premiums for 1982–85. For 1986, in which accident year losses were not available, projections were made assuming two ratios of accident year losses to earned premiums: 70 and 80 percent. A loss ratio of 70 percent would have occurred if 1985 accident year losses were to increase by 10 percent during 1986 (which is commensurate with the one-year development in reported losses for 1984 and the two-year development for 1983) and if the growth rate for developed incurred losses for 1981–85 (17 percent a year) had continued for 1986. The estimated calendar year loss ratio reported by Paul Wish for general liability in 1986 was 99 percent.[70] The assumed loss ratios are substantially lower in view of the likelihood that increases in reserves on losses before 1986 contributed significantly to the 99 percent calendar year result.

The payout pattern for future losses was estimated using the average loss development factors shown for the industry in appendix B through year ten and assuming development factors of 1.02 and 1.01 in years eleven and twelve, at which time all claims are assumed to be paid.[71] Specifically, the proportion of losses assumed to be paid in years one through twelve is 0.083, 0.114, 0.130, 0.138, 0.134, 0.114, 0.095, 0.067, 0.054, 0.042, 0.019, and 0.010. It was assumed that each year's increment of losses would be paid at midyear. For 1981–85, average yields on five-year U.S. government bonds for years $t$ and $t-1$ were used along with this payout schedule to calculate $\gamma_t$.[72] For 1986 the average yield on January issues was employed since data for later months were not yet available in the source used.[73]

Table 3-13 shows the results of the projections, along with the inter-

---

70. Paul E. Wish, "Review and Preview: Up from the Ashes," *Best's Review: Property/Casualty Insurance Edition*, vol. 87 (January 1987), p. 91. Editor's note: The 1986 accident year loss ratio for general liability, which became available after this book was in press, was 80.8 percent. See *Best's Aggregates and Averages: Property-Casualty, 1987.*

71. Development factors for years seven through ten were based on data for the forty-five company sample.

72. The two-year average was used because earned premiums in year $t$ primarily will reflect business written in years $t$ and $t-1$.

73. See Salomon Brothers, *An Analytical Record of Yields and Yield Spreads* (New York: Salomon Brothers, 1986). Similar results would have been obtained with one- and ten-year yields. See appendix B.

Table 3-13. *Actual and Projected Earned Premiums for General Liability Using 1981 Ratio of Earned Premiums to Discounted Accident Year Losses, 1981–86*
Millions of dollars unless otherwise specified

| Item | 1981 | 1982 | 1983 | 1984 | 1985 | 1986[a] | 1986[b] |
|---|---|---|---|---|---|---|---|
| Actual net premiums earned | 6,023 | 5,638 | 5,688 | 6,291 | 9,472 | 16,506 | 16,506 |
| Initial loss ratio (percent) | 79 | 87 | 94 | 99 | 95 | 70 | 80 |
| Initial incurred losses | 4,733 | 4,919 | 5,364 | 6,238 | 8,985 | 11,554 | 13,205 |
| Projected net premiums earned | 6,023 | 6,063 | 6,969 | 8,247 | 11,936 | 16,935 | 19,355 |
| Actual/projected (percent) | 100 | 93 | 82 | 76 | 79 | 97 | 85 |
| Developed loss ratio (percent)[c] | 86 | 102 | 109 | 110 | n.a. | n.a. | n.a. |
| Developed incurred losses[c] | 5,180 | 5,762 | 6,222 | 6,901 | n.a. | n.a. | n.a. |
| Projected net premiums earned | 6,023 | 6,522 | 7,423 | 8,381 | n.a. | n.a. | n.a. |
| Actual/projected (percent) | 100 | 86 | 77 | 75 | n.a. | n.a. | n.a. |
| Interest rate[d] | 12.8 | 13.6 | 12.0 | 11.5 | 11.3 | 8.6 | 8.6 |
| Present value of $1.00 of incurred loss (dollars) | 0.608 | 0.592 | 0.624 | 0.635 | 0.640 | 0.704 | 0.704 |

Sources: Net premiums earned and losses incurred for 1981–85 are from schedule P, *Best's Aggregates and Averages: Property-Liability, 1986.* Earned premiums for 1986 calculated using estimates in Wish, "Review and Preview."
n.a. Not available.
a. Assumes accident year loss ratio of 70 percent.
b. Assumes accident year loss ratio of 80 percent.
c. Losses developed through 1985.
d. Rate for 1981–85 is two-year average of rate on five-year U.S. government bonds. Rate for 1986 is rate for January issues. See appendix B.

est rate used for discounting and the present value of $1.00 of estimated incurred loss for each year. Results are shown using both initially reported losses and losses developed through 1985. As can be seen, actual premiums earned for 1982–86 are less than projected premiums. The shortfall is greatest for 1984, when the ratio of actual to projected premiums is 76 percent for the initial loss comparison and 75 percent using developed losses. For a 1986 loss ratio of 70 percent, actual premiums are 3 percentage points lower than projected premiums; for a loss ratio of 80 percent, the shortfall is 15 percentage points. The present value factors indicate that projected premiums for 1986 would have been 16 percent (0.704/0.608 − 1) higher than 1981 premiums because of the decline in interest rates if the value of claims had not grown during the period.

The Myers and Cohn model of break-even prices provided some control for the possibility that changes in non-loss costs such as underwriting expenses or taxes could have led to the deterioration in the ratios shown above. The original model was modified to allow for underwriting expenses, and different assumptions were used to obtain the present value of costs resulting from income taxes. Myers and Cohn developed the model under the assumption that underwriting losses would be deductible from taxable income as paid, and their model did not consider the impact of investments in tax-exempt securities on the implicit tax rate for returns on the investment of premiums and surplus.[74] The formulation used here assumes that insurers would pay no income tax in any year (which would appear to be consistent with long-run experience before tax reform) and that the only impact of taxes on costs would be the return foregone from investing in tax-exempt securities. Yields on five-year U.S. government bonds and five-year prime municipal bonds (see appendix B) were used to calculate the implicit tax with the assumption that tax-exempt bonds represent half the investment portfolio.

The five-year U.S. government yields were used to discount the future implicit tax liability. The appropriate rate for discounting future losses is a risk-adjusted rate that compensates shareholders for bearing the risk of underwriting. To date, adjustments based on the capital asset pricing model have been used.[75] Betas for uncertain losses are very difficult to estimate and may be unstable. A downward adjustment (denoted $u$) in the risk-free rate of 2 percent would correspond to a beta of 0.2 if the expected excess return on the market portfolio were 10 percent. Previous analysis of the break-even pricing issue commonly has assumed a beta of 0.2.[76] Comparisons are shown under the assumption that the

74. Derrig, "Effect of Federal Taxes on Investment Income," discusses modification of the tax rate to reflect investment in tax-exempt securities.

75. For example, in Myers and Cohn, "Discounted Cash Flow Approach."

76. See Raymond D. Hill and Franco Modigliani, "The Massachusetts Model of Profit Regulation in Nonlife Insurance: An Appraisal and Extensions," in Cummins and Harrington, *Fair Rate of Return*, pp. 27–54; and Fairley, "Investment Income and Profit Margins." Evidence of considerable instability in underwriting betas and that beta estimates may have been negative in the late 1970s is provided in J. David Cummins and Scott Harrington, "Property-Liability Insurance Rate Regulation: Estimation of Underwriting Betas Using Quarterly Profit Data," *Journal of Risk and Insurance*, vol. 52 (March 1985), pp. 16–43. To date, beta estimates have been for all lines combined. The appropriate beta to use in the calculations for general liability is very uncertain.

Table 3-14. *Actual and Predicted Prices for General Liability, 1981–86$^a$*
Percent

| Category | $u^b$ | 1981 | 1982 | 1983 | 1984 | 1985 | 1986$^c$ | 1986$^d$ |
|---|---|---|---|---|---|---|---|---|
| Initial losses | | | | | | | | |
|   Actual price | ... | 208 | 194 | 170 | 159 | 165 | 203 | 178 |
|   Actual/predicted | 0 | 114 | 109 | 100 | 96 | 104 | 132 | 120 |
| | 2 | 109 | 104 | 96 | 92 | 99 | 126 | 114 |
| | 4 | 104 | 99 | 91 | 87 | 93 | 119 | 108 |
| Developed losses$^e$ | | | | | | | | |
|   Actual price | ... | 191 | 166 | 147 | 143 | n.a. | n.a. | n.a. |
|   Actual/predicted | 0 | 108 | 98 | 91 | 90 | n.a. | n.a. | n.a. |
| | 2 | 103 | 93 | 86 | 85 | n.a. | n.a. | n.a. |
| | 4 | 98 | 89 | 82 | 81 | n.a. | n.a. | n.a. |

Source: Author's calculations.
n.a. Not available.
a. Actual price is the ratio of earned premiums to discounted accident year losses. Predicted price is calculated using a variant of the Myers-Cohn model.
b. Variable denotes assumed risk-adjustment factor (percent).
c. Assumes loss ratio of 70 percent.
d. Assumes loss ratio of 80 percent.
e. Losses developed through 1985.

adjustment in the risk-free discount rate equals 0 percent (no underwriting risk), 2 percent, and 4 percent. Further details concerning application of the model and the assumptions used are provided in appendix B.

Table 3-14 presents actual prices for general liability and the ratios of actual to predicted prices. Prices are defined as the ratio of premiums to the discounted value of expected future losses using the assumed payout schedule and previously employed U.S. government bond rates.[77] The decline in actual prices during the period corresponds to the excess of projected over actual premiums in table 3-13. The ratios of actual to predicted prices decline through 1984, and while they increase in 1985, they are still 10 percentage points below the 1981 levels. The differences are smaller than those for actual prices and the premium projections because of declining underwriting expense ratios (whether relative to premiums, undiscounted losses, or discounted losses) and declining implicit tax rates on investment income during the period.

The ratios of actual to predicted prices for 1986 are larger than those for 1981 for both the 70 and 80 percent assumed-loss ratios. For the 70 percent loss ratio, the results imply that the ratio of premiums to the present value of expected costs for initial reported losses was about 15 percent higher in 1986 than in 1981 (132/114 − 1, and so forth).

77. The actual prices shown equal $\lambda_r$. See equation 3.

While this result may provide evidence that premiums rose above the present value of expected costs in 1986, the use of assumed-loss ratios and at least four other factors could have contributed to the increase in the ratios of actual to predicted prices for 1986.[78]

First, the accounting data on underwriting expenses used to calculate prices may include outlays for product and distribution network development that from an economic perspective constitute investment expenditures. If a decline in such expenditures occurred during 1981–86, which may not be unlikely given changes in market conditions, then the ratios of actual to predicted prices for 1986 could be overstated relative to those for 1981. Second, the assumed implicit tax on investment income, which equals one-half of the difference between the yield on five-year U.S. government bonds and that on prime municipal bonds, declined from 2.65 percent in 1981 to 2.00 percent in 1985 and to just 1.05 percent in 1986. If some of this decline actually reflects greater risk in the prime municipal bond market caused by, say, uncertainty about the treatment of tax-exempt interest under tax reform, the ratios for 1986 would again be overstated relative to those for 1981. Third, the predicted price calculations make no allowance for the possible increase in tax costs (because of tax reform) on business written late in 1986. Finally, if the risk of writing general liability increased from 1981 to 1986 so that greater capital per dollar of premiums was needed in 1986, the assumption of a constant premium-to-surplus ratio could cause the predicted price for 1986 to be understated relative to 1981.[79]

To illustrate the potential magnitude of the first two effects, assume that the expense ratio for 1986 would need to be 0.255 rather than the value used of 0.225 to be comparable with the 0.300 value used for 1981. Also assume that the implicit tax rate for 1986 would need to be 2 percent (the 1985 value). If $u$ equals 0 percent, the ratio of actual to predicted price would decline to 121 percent for a loss ratio of 70 percent and to 111 percent for a loss ratio of 80 percent.[80]

The comparisons of actual and projected premiums using both projection methods thus suggest that most of the recent increase in pre-

78. If the accident year loss ratio for 1986 were available (see note 70), the possibility of large reserve errors would still prevent solid conclusions. The possibility also exists that rates were too low in 1981 relative to the initially reported losses.

79. See Department of Justice, Antitrust Division, "Crisis in Property-Casualty Insurance," and the sources cited there for further discussion of the possible impact on prices of increases in risk.

80. Similar changes would occur if $u$ equals 2 or 4 percent. The changes in the expense ratio and implicit tax rate contribute about equally to the declines.

miums reflécted increases in reported losses. Without further developments in the theory of break-even prices and without waiting a number of years for reasonably accurate estimates of developed losses for 1985 and 1986 business, a stronger statement cannot be made. If, for example, it turns out that the fully developed accident year loss ratio for 1986 is much less than 70 percent, then this conclusion could be wrong. But given the competitive structure of the industry, the favorable impact of realized capital gains on surplus, and the inflow of new funds in 1985 and 1986, a reasonable expectation is that short-run prices would be unlikely to rise far above expected future costs.

## Policy Implications

Because of theoretical and empirical problems in measuring present value of expected future costs for liability insurance contracts, it is difficult to assess the extent to which prices may have deviated from costs in a cyclical manner. If there is a systematic tendency for prices to fall below costs, then a certain degree of recoupment would be expected so that individual insurers could break even over the long run. Otherwise the supply of capital to the industry would be likely to contract to the point at which a competitive structure would no longer exist.

Based on what is known, the case for relying on regulations requiring prior approval of rates to dampen price variability, whether in the form of flexible rating or more traditional modes, is very weak. If market problems are largely the result of unanticipated changes in claim costs as opposed to a systematic tendency to underprice, there is no case for rate regulation. If an unpredictable cycle of inadequate prices followed by recoupment of past losses does exist, it is far from clear that rate regulation would provide benefits in excess of its costs.[81] Risk-averse insurance buyers conceivably could benefit if regulation reduced the variance of prices. However, if inadequate prices were largely due to excessive risk taking by some insurers, other methods of regulation, such as improved monitoring of insurers' financial conditions, might be preferable to rate regulation.[82] Moreover, if inadequate prices were

81. If the cycle were predictable and capital markets were perfect, there could be no advantage to using regulation to smooth prices, since consumers could borrow and lend to achieve their optimal consumption pattern despite fluctuations in insurance prices.

82. Rate regulation also could reduce the attention paid to insolvency problems, given limited budgets for state insurance departments.

caused largely by heterogeneous expectations, limiting rate reductions for insurers with favorable expectations about future costs might not be of much use. Given the uncertainty about future costs that may result in heterogeneous expectations, regulators would probably not be able to identify firms seeking approval of inadequate prices.

Regulators could also have difficulty enforcing rate limits effectively.[83] And political pressure could lead to asymmetry in rate regulation, in that price reductions would be much easier to obtain than price increases.[84] Would regulators really be likely to keep prices above market levels for several years following the most recent round of price increases and availability problems? If rate regulation were used mostly to limit rate increases following periods of potentially large losses, the scope and duration of availability problems would likely become much worse. If so, the increased use of mandated markets involving cross-subsidization, such as reinsurance plans and joint underwriting associations, could be expected. The net result could be higher injury rates and a large efficiency loss. For all of these reasons, increased regulation of commercial liability insurance rates is unwarranted.

Two other issues have received considerable attention in conjunction with recent experience: whether it would be desirable to repeal the McCarran-Ferguson Act and whether some form of federal regulation should replace or augment state regulation. Both issues are complex and have been subject to extensive debate for many years, but a few observations can be made about their relationship to recent market problems. First, there is no evidence that the limited antitrust exemption under the McCarran-Ferguson Act has contributed to or aggravated these problems. Furthermore, if repeal of the act increased the difficulty in forecasting losses by making it either more costly or illegal for firms to pool data for analysis of expected losses, any tendency for firms to underprice could be made worse. Second, while the defects of state regulation have been subject to almost continuous study, there is little evidence that they have led to recent market problems or that some form of federal regulation would have prevented these problems. Again, not nearly enough

83. Stewart, *Remembering a Stable Future.*

84. The evidence of the depressing impact of rate regulation on auto insurance prices in the past decade is suggestive in this regard. Stewart, *Remembering a Stable Future,* shows that from 1972 to 1985 commercial liability insurance combined ratios were roughly equal in states with and without prior approval regulation, suggesting little impact of regulation on rates. However, given the recent interest of regulators in the affordability of commercial liability coverage, the possibility exists that any impact of regulation in the future would be in the direction of reducing rates.

is known about the causes of the problems to justify fundamental changes in the type or form of regulation. Moreover, the uncertainty associated with significant changes in regulations suggests extreme caution unless traditional mechanisms and institutions are clearly inadequate to prevent large welfare losses and a new system could be expected to reduce such losses significantly. While pressure exists for changing insurance regulation, deficiencies in state regulation do not clearly justify replacing all or part of a system that has survived for more than a century.

What does the future hold concerning the possible recurrence of deteriorating financial results followed by large price increases and availability problems? Will another crisis occur in five or ten years? The traditional view of underwriting cycles suggests the answer is yes, although the crisis might not be as severe. Other views that involve systematic underpricing also suggest that problems will eventually recur. If recent problems were largely caused by unexpected growth in losses, the possible recurrence of a crisis would be tied to factors that may lead to large unanticipated growth in claims, such as new sources of injury, changes in legal rules, and increased demand by the public for broader and greater compensation for injury. Increased regulation of the market may not be able to prevent a recurrence and could make things worse.

We need a greater understanding of the causes of market problems. Theoretical and empirical work on the possible impact of excessive risk taking and heterogeneous expectations on prices should be undertaken. Research also is needed using available data that focuses on the extent to which the growth in expected claims in recent years could have been anticipated. Although it is unlikely to be conclusive, work in these areas should provide greater insight into whether prior approval of rate changes or other forms of regulation would be likely to have a beneficial impact on prices and availability.

## Appendix A: Profit Measurement

Some knowledge of insurance accounting rules and alternative income measures is needed to interpret financial results and to understand the dispute about insurance industry profitability. If a few simplifying assumptions are used and arcane factors such as deferred income taxes are ignored, the major measures of profitability can be made fairly clear.

Insurance company annual statements that must be filed with regulators are prepared using statutory accounting principles (SAP). These principles tend to be more conservative than generally accepted accounting principles (GAAP) in that income and net worth (surplus) tend to be less than income and net worth calculated using GAAP. A major difference between SAP and GAAP is the treatment of acquisition expenses, those incurred in selling and issuing insurance contracts. SAP requires that acquisition expenses be charged against income and surplus when incurred. GAAP requires that revenues and expenses be matched, which means expenses generally are deferred compared with SAP.

Two important concepts in both SAP and GAAP accounting are earned premiums, $EP$, and incurred losses, $IL$. Premiums are said to be written when the policy is issued and the premium becomes payable. Premiums are earned evenly over the duration of the policy period. A principal liability of property and liability insurers is their unearned premium reserve, $UPR$, which reflects the amount of written premiums, $WP$, that have yet to be earned as of the statement date. The relationship between these items in a given year is given by $EP = WP - \Delta UPR$. If earned and written premiums are equal during a year, $UPR$ does not change.

Incurred losses are defined as losses paid, $LP$, plus the change in the insurer's second major liability, the loss reserve, $LR$: $IL = LP + \Delta LR$. The loss reserve is the estimated liability for all unpaid claims that have occurred as of the statement date. Since future claim payments traditionally have not been discounted, the book value of the liability, if accurately estimated, overstates its market value. Moreover, incurred losses for a given calendar year will be affected by revisions in reserves for previous years' claims to reflect new information about expected total claims. That is, increases in the loss reserve in year $t$ for claims that occurred in year $t - n$ will affect reported incurred losses in year $t$.

SAP surplus, $S$, is given by the basic accounting identity

$$(\text{A-1}) \qquad\qquad S = A - LR - UPR,$$

where $A$ is the SAP value of assets, which reflects bonds at amortized (book) value and common stocks at market value.[85] The change in surplus during a given period can be written

$$(\text{A-2}) \qquad\qquad \Delta S = \Delta A - \Delta LR - \Delta UPR.$$

The change in SAP assets equals premiums written less losses paid,

85. For simplicity the presentation assumes only two types of assets and two liabilities.

underwriting expenses, $E$, policyholder dividends, $D$, and income taxes, $T$, plus total investment gains, $IG$.[86] Substituting for $\Delta A$ in equation A-2 and using $\Delta UPR = WP - EP$ and $\Delta LR = IL - LP$ gives

(A-3) $$\Delta S = (EP - IL - E - D) - T + IG.$$

The first four terms total SAP underwriting income. $IG$ has three components: net investment income, $I$, which consists of interest (including changes in the book value of bonds due to amortization), dividends, and rents, less investment expenses; realized capital gains or losses on stocks and bonds, $RCG$; and unrealized capital gains or losses on common stocks, $URCG$. A popular measure of income in industry publications and the trade press is pretax operating income, which is defined as SAP underwriting income plus $I$; after-tax operating income deducts $T$.

The principal modification of SAP surplus to obtain GAAP surplus involves creating an asset account to reflect prepaid acquisition expenses. Assuming that all underwriting expenses are acquisition expenses gives the following definition of surplus adjusted for prepaid expenses ($S_A$):

(A-4) $$S_A = A + (E/WP)UPR - LR - UPR,$$

where $E/WP$, the underwriting expense ratio, is assumed to be constant from year to year. This treatment essentially adds to SAP surplus the amount of the unearned premium reserve being held for acquisition expenses associated with the remainder of the policy period that have already been paid. Using the definitions of $\Delta A$, $\Delta LR$, and $\Delta UPR$ gives the following expression for the change in adjusted surplus:

(A-5) $$\Delta S_A = [EP - IL - (E/WP)EP - D] - T + IG.$$

Pretax GAAP underwriting income is given by the first four terms of this expression. As noted, the difference between GAAP and SAP underwriting income is that GAAP automatically matches expenses with revenues as premiums are earned.[87]

The most common summary measure of underwriting profit (excluding investment income) is the combined ratio, $CR$, either before or after

86. Again for simplicity, stockholder dividends, new capital, nonadmitted assets, and other minor items are ignored.

87. In the absence of such matching, differences in premium growth rates may have a significant effect on reported income. When written premiums exceed earned premiums, SAP income is lower than GAAP income, which reduced taxable income before the tax reform in 1986.

policyholder dividends. If after dividends it is defined as the sum of the ratio of incurred losses and dividends to earned premiums plus the ratio of underwriting expenses to written premiums:

$$(A\text{-}6) \qquad CR = (IL + D)/EP + E/WP.$$

One minus the combined ratio gives the pretax GAAP underwriting margin relative to earned premiums: $(1 - CR)EP = [EP - IL - (E/WP)EP - D]$.[88] The pretax GAAP operating margin including net investment income is given by $(1 - CR) + I/EP$.

Another measure of income that analysts have looked to in recent years is the operating ratio, which is defined as

$$(A\text{-}7) \qquad OR = CR - \alpha(I + RCG)/EP,$$

where $\alpha$ is the amount of net investment income plus realized capital gains that is allocated to insurance operations (or, for results by line, to a given line of business) as opposed to surplus. Thus the operating ratio equals the combined ratio minus the ratio of investment income allocated to a line to earned premiums for the line.[89] The operating ratio differs from the pretax GAAP operating margin in that it reflects realized capital gains, and only net investment income and realized capital gains allocated to operations are included. If the operating ratio for all lines of business were equal to 1, the pretax increase in adjusted surplus would equal all unrealized capital gains plus the share of net investment income and realized capital gains allocated to surplus. A ratio greater than 1 indicates that the increase in adjusted surplus would be less than this amount.

The operating ratio essentially measures profit from insurance operations under the assumption that net investment income and realized capital gains on surplus plus all unrealized capital gains should be credited to owners. Critics have, however, argued that all capital gains should be included when assessing the profitability of insurance operations. Does the operating ratio provide a good measure of whether insurance operations were profitable in any year or over time even if

88. In practice, $1 - CR$ only approximates the GAAP margin, since some underwriting expenses are not acquisition expenses and should be deducted when incurred under GAAP, and since the acquisition expense ratio is not constant over time.

89. Insurers are required to allocate $I + RCG$ to lines of business and to surplus in the insurance expense exhibit. Allocations essentially are in proportion to liabilities for each line.

one assumes that the underlying assumption about investment gains is appropriate? The answer generally will be no.

Theory suggests that break-even premiums would equal the risk-adjusted present value of expected future claim payments plus the present value of all other costs of writing the business, including income taxes or foregone investment returns resulting from cost-reducing tax avoidance.[90] Even if all policies were priced to break even, loss forecasts were perfectly accurate, and investment returns including capital gains were equal to the rate used to discount future costs, the operating ratio generally would not equal 1. The principal reason is the failure to discount losses in insurance accounting (both SAP and GAAP). Lack of discounting is one major reason that accounting profits may differ greatly from economic profits. Another factor is the use of book values rather than market values for bonds.

To illustrate economic profit measurement, let the market value of an insurer's surplus for all business written (old and new) before the statement date, $S_M$, be defined as

$$(A\text{-}8) \qquad S_M = A + B - PVL,$$

where $A$ is the SAP value of assets, $B$ is the market value of bonds less book value, and $PVL$ is the market value of unpaid claims, that is, the present value of unpaid claims discounted at a market-determined rate of interest.[91] The change in $S_M$ is given by

$$(A\text{-}9) \qquad \Delta S_M = [WP - (LP + \Delta PVL) - E - D] - T + IG',$$

where $IG' = IG + \Delta B$, that is, net investment income plus realized and unrealized capital gains on bonds (in excess of bond amortization) and on stocks.

An expression for $\Delta S_M$ that is more comparable to equations A-3 and A-5 can be obtained by defining $PVL'$ as the present value of unpaid claims only for accidents that have occurred by the statement date and by noting that the unearned premium reserve less the adjustment for prepaid acquisition expenses would approximately equal the present

90. See, for example, Myers and Cohn, "Discounted Cash Flow Approach"; and appendix B.

91. $PVL$ includes losses that have already occurred as of the statement date and the value of claims expected to occur after that date for business written before the date. If all expenses were not assumed to be acquisition expenses, the present value of unpaid expenses also would be deducted.

value of unpaid losses for claims that are expected to occur after the statement date for policies written as of the statement date. Using these results gives

(A-10)    $\Delta S_M = [EP - (LP + \Delta PVL') - (E/WP)EP - D]$

$$- T + IG'.$$

The quantity in brackets equals GAAP underwriting profit using discounted losses.

## Appendix B: Calculation of Break-Even Prices

According to the Myers-Cohn model, the break-even premium equals the present value of expected future losses discounted at a risk-adjusted rate plus the present value of income taxes discounted at the risk-free rate. In illustrating their model, Myers and Cohn ignored underwriting expenses, assumed that funds backing policies were invested in taxable risk-free securities, and assumed that tax deductions for losses were taken as the losses were paid. The modification used here considers underwriting expenses. The appropriate treatment of taxes is complex, given that they can be reduced by holding tax-exempt securities.[92] While value-maximizing portfolio decisions may involve tax minimization,[93] questions concerning the allocation of tax costs across business lines and years for multiperiod contracts have barely been raised, let alone answered.

For this reason, it is assumed in this analysis that investment decisions eliminate income taxes over time and that break-even premiums reflect the implicit tax cost that results from holding tax-exempt securities to eliminate taxes. To illustrate the model, assume that break-even premiums, $P$, and underwriting expenses, $E$, for a group of contracts are paid at the beginning of the period of coverage and that the amount of loss paid at time $t = 1, 2, \ldots, n$ equals $\beta_t L$, where $L$ is total expected losses. If no income taxes are paid and all investments are risk-free, break-even premiums are given by

92. See Derrig, "Effect of Federal Taxes on Investment Income."

93. Patric H. Hendershott and Timothy W. Koch, "The Demand for Tax-Exempt Securities by Financial Institutions," *Journal of Finance,* vol. 35 (June 1980), pp. 717–27; and Smith, "Investment Yields and Insurance Underwriting."

(B-1) $$P = E + \gamma_1 L + (r_f - r_p)(P - E + S)(\gamma_2 - \gamma_3),$$

where $S$ is the initial surplus supporting the contracts, $r_f$ is the rate of interest on taxable risk-free securities; $r_p$ is the rate of interest earned on the investment of $P - E + S$; $\gamma_1$ is $\Sigma[\beta_t/(1 + r_f - u)^t]$; $u$ is the adjustment factor for the risk of future losses; $\gamma_2$ is $\Sigma[1/(1 + r_f)^t]$; $\gamma_3$ is $\Sigma[\partial_{t-1}/(1 + r_f)^t]$; and $\partial_t$ is the cumulative proportion of total losses paid through time $t$.[94]

The first two terms in equation B-1 give the discounted values of expenses and losses, respectively. The third term gives the implicit tax on insurance operations in the form of foregone return from holding tax-exempt securities to eliminate taxes. Following Myers and Cohn, the formula assumes that funds invested to back the contracts, and thus implicit taxes, decline in proportion to claims paid.

As discussed in the text, let the break-even price of the contracts be defined as $\lambda = P/(\gamma L)$, where $\gamma$ equals $\Sigma[\beta_t/(1 + r_f)^t]$, that is, the ratio of break-even premiums to the present value of expected future losses discounted at the risk-free rate. Using this definition and equation B-1 gives

(B-2) $$\lambda = \frac{(e/k)(1 - \tau) + \gamma_1}{\gamma[1 - (1 + s)]\tau},$$

where $e = E/P$, $k = L/P$, $s = S/P$, and $\tau = (r_f - r_p)(\gamma_2 - \gamma_3)$.

The accident year loss ratio for general liability for 1981–85 and assumed loss ratios of 70 and 80 percent for 1986 were used for $k$. The remaining variables used to calculate $\lambda$ for each year follow.

Since the accident year loss ratio in year $t$ reflects business primarily written in years $t$ and $t-1$, the average ratio of underwriting expenses to written premiums for years $t$ and $t-1$ was used to obtain a GAAP expense ratio and then substituted for $e$ in equation B-2. The values were 0.300, 0.312, 0.318, 0.311, 0.271, and 0.225 for the years 1981–86, respectively. Data were obtained from *Best's Aggregates and Averages: Property-Casualty, 1986.*

Yields on U.S. government and prime municipal bonds of various maturities for 1977–86 are shown in table 3-15, along with the ratios of tax-exempt to taxable yields. As can be seen, the implicit tax from holding tax-exempt bonds declines with maturity. Property-liability insurance companies invested heavily in long-term taxable and tax-exempt

94. All summations are from $t = 1$ through $t = n$.

Table 3-15. *U.S. Government and Prime Municipal Bond Yields, 1977–86*
Percent unless otherwise specified

| Year | U.S. government bonds | | | | Prime municipal bonds | | | | Ratio of municipal to U.S. government | | | |
|---|---|---|---|---|---|---|---|---|---|---|---|---|
| | one-year | five-year | ten-year | twenty-year | one-year | five-year | ten-year | twenty-year | one-year | five-year | ten-year | twenty-year |
| 1977 | 5.9 | 6.9 | 7.4 | 7.6 | 2.9 | 3.9 | 4.4 | 5.2 | 0.49 | 0.56 | 0.59 | 0.68 |
| 1978 | 8.2 | 8.2 | 8.3 | 8.4 | 4.2 | 4.7 | 4.9 | 5.5 | 0.51 | 0.57 | 0.59 | 0.65 |
| 1979 | 10.5 | 9.4 | 9.3 | 9.2 | 5.3 | 5.4 | 5.5 | 6.0 | 0.50 | 0.57 | 0.58 | 0.64 |
| 1980 | 12.1 | 11.4 | 11.4 | 11.3 | 6.1 | 6.4 | 6.8 | 7.8 | 0.51 | 0.56 | 0.60 | 0.69 |
| 1981 | 14.7 | 14.2 | 13.7 | 13.7 | 7.9 | 8.5 | 9.4 | 10.6 | 0.54 | 0.60 | 0.69 | 0.77 |
| 1982 | 12.4 | 13.1 | 13.2 | 13.1 | 7.1 | 8.7 | 9.9 | 11.1 | 0.58 | 0.66 | 0.75 | 0.85 |
| 1983 | 9.5 | 10.8 | 11.0 | 11.3 | 5.3 | 6.8 | 7.9 | 8.9 | 0.55 | 0.63 | 0.72 | 0.79 |
| 1984 | 10.9 | 12.3 | 12.4 | 12.5 | 6.1 | 7.6 | 8.7 | 9.7 | 0.56 | 0.62 | 0.70 | 0.78 |
| 1985 | 8.5 | 10.3 | 10.7 | 11.0 | 5.1 | 6.9 | 8.0 | 8.9 | 0.60 | 0.67 | 0.75 | 0.80 |
| 1986 | 7.6 | 8.6 | 9.0 | 9.5 | 5.4 | 6.5 | 7.4 | 8.1 | 0.71 | 0.76 | 0.82 | 0.86 |

Source: Salomon Brothers, *An Analytical Record of Yields and Yield Spreads* (New York: Salomon Brothers, 1986), pt. 1, table 1, and pt. 3, table 3. Values for 1977–85 are average values for the year; values for 1986 are for January issues.

Table 3-16. *Paid-Loss Development Factors, 1976–84*[a]

| Accident year (t) | P2t/P1t | P3t/P2t | P4t/P3t | P5t/P4t | P6t/P5t | P7t/P6t | P8t/P7t | P9t/P8t | P10t/P9t |
|---|---|---|---|---|---|---|---|---|---|
| 1976 | 2.215 | 1.544 | 1.404 | 1.301 | 1.207 | 1.157 | 1.089 | 1.062 | 1.045 |
| 1977 | 2.063 | 1.550 | 1.461 | 1.303 | 1.200 | 1.124 | 1.075 | 1.060 | ... |
| 1978 | 2.175 | 1.610 | 1.460 | 1.281 | 1.179 | 1.128 | 1.086 | ... | ... |
| 1979 | 2.214 | 1.616 | 1.441 | 1.289 | 1.185 | 1.121 | ... | ... | ... |
|  | (2.234) | (1.646) | (1.393) | (1.301) | ... | ... |  |  |  |
| 1980 | 2.437 | 1.649 | 1.428 | 1.293 | 1.189 | ... |  |  |  |
|  | (2.354) | (1.632) | (1.432) | (1.290) | (1.183) |  |  |  |  |
| 1981 | 2.510 | 1.736 | 1.431 | 1.273 | ... |  |  |  |  |
|  | (2.387) | (1.730) | (1.421) | (1.271) |  |  |  |  |  |
| 1982 | 2.351 | 1.634 | 1.472 | ... |  |  |  |  |  |
|  | (2.292) | (1.620) | (1.435) |  |  |  |  |  |  |
| 1983 | 2.511 | 1.695 | ... |  |  |  |  |  |  |
|  | (2.362) | (1.685) |  |  |  |  |  |  |  |
| 1984 | 2.615 | ... |  |  |  |  |  |  |  |
|  | (2.441) | ... |  |  |  |  |  |  |  |
| Average | 2.485 | 1.666 | 1.446 | 1.288 | 1.192 | 1.133 | 1.083 | 1.061 | 1.045 |
|  | (2.367) | (1.663) | (1.420) | (1.289) | (1.191) | ... | ... | ... | ... |
| Sum-of-the-years digits | 2.509 | 1.676 | 1.447 | 1.285 | 1.189 | 1.127 | 1.083 | 1.061 | 1.045 |
|  | (2.377) | (1.667) | (1.426) | (1.286) | (1.187) | ... | ... | ... | ... |
| Most recent year | 2.615 | 1.695 | 1.472 | 1.273 | 1.189 | 1.121 | 1.086 | 1.060 | 1.045 |
|  | (2.441) | (1.685) | (1.435) | (1.271) | (1.183) | ... | ... | ... | ... |

Sources: Data for industry calculations are from *Best's Aggregates and Averages: Property-Casualty, 1986*; data for the forty-five-company sample are from Aetna Life and Casualty Company.

a. *Pjt* equals cumulative losses paid through year *j* for accident year *t*. Values in parentheses reflect industry data; remaining values are for the forty-five-company sample. Average and sum-of-the-years digits values are for the most recent five years, using forty-five-company data for the forty-five-company sample, and industry data for the industry when industry data are not available (or the number available for the forty-five-company sample, if smaller), except for *P4t/P3t* for the industry, for which only four years were used.

bonds during this period. Derrig argues that the implicit tax in the Myers-Cohn model should be based on yields available on a portfolio of taxables and tax exempts that matches the duration of assets and liabilities. His argument assumes that all risk of holding long-term investments is borne by shareholders rather than policyholders.[95] This argument may be reasonable, given the existence of guaranty funds.

For simplicity, yields on five-year U.S. government and prime municipal bonds were used to calculate $r_p$. For each year from 1981 to 1985, average yields on issues during years $t$ and $t-1$ were used, since accident year loss ratios reflect business written in years $t$ and $t-1$. The variable, $r_p$, was calculated assuming equal investments in taxable and tax-exempt bonds. For 1986 the yield on January 1986 issues was used. This was the last month for which yields were available in Salomon Brothers, *An Analytical Record of Yields and Yield Spreads*. The values were 0.0265, 0.0250, 0.0215, 0.0215, 0.0200, and 0.0105 for 1981 to 1986, respectively.

For 1981–85, average yields on five-year U.S. government bonds in years $t$ and $t-1$ were used to discount future values. It was assumed that expenses were paid at the beginning of the year and that all loss payments were made at the middle of the year of payment. As described in the text, $\beta_t$ was calculated using the average industry loss development factors shown in table B-2 and assuming development of 1.02 and 1.01 in years eleven and twelve. The resultant $\beta_t$ for years one through twelve was 0.083, 0.114, 0.130, 0.138, 0.134, 0.114, 0.095, 0.067, 0.054, 0.042, 0.019, and 0.010.

A value of 0.5 was used for $s$. This value corresponds to a premium-to-surplus ratio of 2, a common industry benchmark.

95. Derrig, "Effect of Federal Taxes on Investment Income."

Reserve Levels and Reserve Requirements
for Profit-maximizing Insurance Firms

Jörg Finsinger
University of Bern and
International Institute of Management,
Science Center Berlin

Mark Pauly
The Wharton School, University of Pennsylvania, and
International Institute of Management,
Science Center Berlin

I. Introduction

Virtually all western countries regulate the reserves of insurance firms, even when they do not directly regulate the premiums charged. The justification for such reserve requirements is usually based on consumer ignorance; it is alleged to be costly if not impossible for a typical consumer of insurance to determine the level of reserves held by insurance firms from which he buys; consequently, consumers would often be unprepared for insurer default.[1] But even if one accepts the premise of consumer ignorance, the premise only implies that reserves regulation may be useful. To show that regulation will be needed to improve things, two additional propositions must hold: (1) If not regulated, firms will hold levels of reserves that deviate from (usually below) the social optimum. (2) Regulators can determine and enforce a level of reserves that is at least closer to the social optimum than the unregulated level. Crucial to the empirical or theoretical establishment of either of these propositions is a positive model which predicts the level of reserves the unregulated firm will choose in different circumstances.

Construction of such a positive model of insurer choice of reserves is the main task of this paper. In addition, we investigate how those unregulated

---

[1]Sometimes it is assumed that preventing insolvency and safeguarding consumer interests are identical. For example, it has been noted that: "The safeguarding of the insurance consumers' interests is the most important objective of solvency policy. The insurer should not be allowed to reach a state in which he is unable to meet his insurance obligations." (Pentikäinen and Rantala, 1982, Vol. I, p. 1.1-3.)

---

Editor's note: This article is a slightly edited version of the article that appeared in *Lecture Notes in Economics and Mathematical Systems, Vol. 227, Risk and Capital*. Edited by G. Bamberg and K. Spremann. ©Springer-Verlag Berlin Heidelberg 1984.

levels compare with the socially optimal level. This information will help us to know when regulation _can_ do some good. Of course, whether or not actual regulation _will_ improve welfare requires development of a positive model of the regulatory process itself, a task we shall not attempt in this paper.

## II. Reserve Choice in the Literature

Although the literature predominantly contains normative empirical models of what reserves ought to be, based on some assumption about an acceptable probability of insolvency, there have been two distinct approaches to answering the positive question of the unregulated profit maximizing level of reserves.

The answer most common in the literature is based on applying an actuarial theory of the probability of ruin to a model of a firm whose objective is to maximize the present value of the stream of dividends it expects to pay. Borch (1982) has provided the most recent statement of this theory. He concludes that, under empirically plausible assumptions about the form of the distribution of total losses, the ideal level of reserves for such a firm will be positive and finite as long as the premium stream associated with a given portfolio of contracts exceeds a certain level.

A second answer to the question has been recently provided by Munch and Smallwood (1981). They argue that a stockholder expected wealth or discounted dividend maximizing insurance firm will, under reasonable assumptions about the distribution of total losses, set reserves at either of two extremes--either at zero, or at (virtual) infinity. In their model, reserves will _never_ be positive and finite.

In this paper we investigate both of these types of models. We first show how the difference in results depends on differences in assumptions about the nature of regulation, and (less obviously) on the institutional features of the bankruptcy or insolvency process. While each of the models is based on assumptions plausible in some real world situations, many other real world cases are not well represented by either model. We therefore show the consequences of different models based on these other cases.

Both the Borch and the Munch-Smallwood models are models of short run firm equilibrium. That is, they show how the optimal level of reserves is determined by the firm, given the price or demand it faces and given the insurance contracts it can sell. We extend these models to consider the question of long run or zero expected profit equilibrium, with no regulatory restrictions on entry. We determine the long run equilibrium (LRE) premium and level of reserves, and show how they both change as entry costs change and as the cost of holding reserves changes.

Finally we consider how the LRE level of reserves compares with the social optimum. Perhaps not surprisingly, we show that LRE reserves may fall short of socially optimal reserves. We indicate that a movement toward the social optimum which increases reserves may have an unintended consequence: it may raise the LRE price of insurance. But we also show that in some circumstances LRE reserves may be equal to socially optimal reserves. While the real world rarely is exactly in these circumstances, it may sometimes approximate them to a sufficient extent to make reserve regulations unnecessary in some insurance markets. We indicate what those circumstances are.

We adopt the following procedure. We first present the Borch model. We then discuss alternative concepts of firm equilibrium (FE) using that basic model but altered assumptions about regulatory, bankruptcy, or entry processes. Then we illustrate the LRE of the Borch model for several selected sets of assumptions. We follow the same procedure for the Munch-Smallwood model, dealing first with firm equilibrium and then with long run equilibrium. A final section investigates normative models of insurer reserves and compares them with FE and LRE levels.

III.  Restricted Investment Models (Borch)

We first list a set of general assumptions we will maintain throughout most of our discussion of both types of models.

General assumptions:
(G1)  Consumers (incorrectly) believe that firms will always pay insurance contracts at their nominal (contractual) values, regardless of the level of reserves a firm holds and regardless of the price of insurance.
(G2)  All insurance firms are owned by stockholders, and firms set reserves to maximize stockholder welfare.
(G3)  At the end of any period, a firm is financially insolvent if total losses X exceed revenues R plus initial reserves K plus the interest earned for

the period on revenues and reserves.[2] (The rate of return earned, if any, may depend on regulatory rules about the types of assets that can be used as reserves.) It then is required to pay claims pro-rata with the funds available and cannot obtain additional funds.[3]

(G4) If a firm is not financially insolvent in any period, it may adjust its reserve capital only after paying all losses. Losses have claims on premiums and reserves which are prior to those of stockholders.

(G5) Firms sell each customer a standard insurance contract. Any firm which does enter must be of a fixed size, defined by the number of insurance contracts sold.

(G6) There are zero administrative costs to insurance.

Given these general assumptions, Borch developed his model by treating a case in which initial reserve capital is exogenously determined at $K_0$, and firms may only pay nonnegative dividends $d_t$ given by:

$$d_t = K_t + R_t - X_t - K_{t+1}.$$

An implication of this assumption is that reserves and premiums earn zero return when held as assets. He also assumed that, if $X_t$ is greater than $(K_t + R_t)$, the firm is financially insolvent and "the company is not allowed to operate" in the future, in the sense that stockholders cannot invest in this type of insurance business again. Financial insolvency means complete loss of access to any future premium stream. Borch explicitly stated only the portion in quotation marks, but a complete prohibition on reentry will be shown to be necessary to make his firm's objective function consistent with stockholder utility maximization. Borch further assumed that stockholders are risk neutral and have access to an alternative use of wealth which yields annual return r. Finally, he assumed that the firm receives exogenous premium revenues R at the beginning of each period, and accepts a portfolio of risks with probability distribution of cotal claims

---

[2]Financial insolvency is to be distinguished from "bankruptcy," in which no firm or investor is willing to pay the firm's liabilities even if it were permitted to do so, and "regulatory insolvency" in which reserves fall below some regulatory minimum and the firm is not permitted to sell more insurance, even if it has funds to pay current claims.

[3]An implication of this assumption is that there is no possibility of "bailout" for an insolvent firm, even if its stockholders or other investors wished to add cash.

and accepts a portfolio of risks with probability distribution of total claims $F(X)$ and corresponding density function $f(X) = F'(X)$.

Given the assumptions (G1)-(G6) and the additional assumptions of Borch's model, maximization of stockholder welfare is equivalent to maximizing $D$, the present discounted expected value of the stream of dividend payments:

$$D = E \left[ \sum_{t=0}^{\infty} \frac{d_t}{(1 + r)^t} \right]. \tag{1}$$

The only choice variable for the firm is its dividend in each period $t$, $t = 1, 2, \ldots, \infty$. The value of $D$ depends upon the initial capital $K_0$ and the chosen dividend policy. Alternatively, since $d_t$ determines $K_{t+1}$, $D$ can be said to be a function of $R$, of $K_0$, and of the reserve policy $\hat{K} = (K_1, K_2, \ldots)$.[4] Thus the firm's objective can be written:

$$V(K_0, R) = \underset{\hat{K}}{\text{Max}}\ D(\hat{K}). \tag{2}$$

The general solution to this maximization problem takes a complicated form. However, Borch argued that, for empirically plausible claim distributions, a reserve policy of the following kind is optimal for $t = 1, 2, \ldots$

$$K_t = \begin{cases} K^* & \text{if} \quad K_{t-1} + R - X \geq K^* \\ K_{t-1} + R - X & \text{if} \quad K_{t-1} + R - X < K^* \end{cases} \tag{3}$$

where $K^*$ is the optimal reserve target for the firm. This "barrier" policy requires positive dividend payments whenever the firm's capital exceeds the target $K^*$. The larger the target reserves $K^*$, the lower the probability that the firm will go bankrupt over any interval of time. However, there is a "cost" to stockholders of increasing reserves (in addition to the lost interest), since larger reserves mean that more is lost when bankruptcy does occur because $X$ is unusually high. In effect, current reserves protect access to future dividends.

Somewhat surprisingly, it will not necessarily be the case that increasing $R$, given $X$, will necessarily increase $K^*$. This can be shown by R. Bellman's optimality principle of dynamic programming. By this principle, any sequence

---

[4]One could permit the firm to declare a dividend before accepting any premiums or risks, and so adjust $K_0$.

of optimal decisions must also be optimal in the first step(s). One can write $V(K,R)$ as:[5]

$$V(K,R) = \underset{\tilde{K}}{\text{Max}} \left[ K - \tilde{K} + \frac{1}{1+r} \int_0^{\tilde{K}+R} V(\tilde{K} + R - X,R)f(X)dX \right].$$ (4)

$\tilde{K}$ must be chosen so that the initial dividend $K - \tilde{K}$ is optimal. Hence,

$$\frac{d}{d\tilde{K}} \int_0^{\tilde{K}+R} V(\tilde{K} + R - X,R)f(X)dX = 1 + r$$ (5)

or the optimal $K^*$ must fulfill:

$$\int_0^{K^*+R} \frac{\partial V}{\partial K} f(X)dX + V(0,R) = 1 + r.$$ (6)

$K^*$ clearly is a function of R. Comparative statics on (6) indicate:

$$(\frac{dK^*}{dR} + 1) \frac{\partial V}{\partial K} + \int_0^{K^*(R)+R} \frac{\partial^2 V}{\partial K \partial R} f(X)dX + \frac{\partial V}{\partial R} = 0.$$ (7)

or

$$\frac{dK^*}{dR} = - \frac{\frac{\partial V}{\partial K} + \frac{\partial V}{\partial R} + \int_0^{K^*(R)+R} \frac{\partial^2 V}{\partial K \partial R} f(X)dX}{\frac{\partial V}{\partial K}}.$$ (8)

The right hand side may be either positive or negative.

It is indeed intuitively plausible that $K^*$ could fail to increase with R. As R rises from a low level, additional reserves provide access to an increasingly profitable business. As R becomes very large relative to X, the revenue payments themselves provide sufficient protection against insolvency so that additional reserves K become less necessary.[6] However, we have been unable to show that increasing R unequivocally reduces the probability of insolvency in any future time period.

---

[5]See K. Borch (1974), pp. 227-228.

[6]Of course, if firms competed on the basis of service quality and therefore caused the administrative cost loading to be large, this conclusion would not hold.

The Borch model can be thought of as describing a single firm's equilibrium under the given set of assumptions. But since there is the alternative use of capital into which dividends disappear, it is natural to ask whether a particular level of R and F(X) is consistent with equilibrium in a capital market which furnishes the funds for reserves. That is, if we permit the entry and exit of firms (and capital), what level(s) of R for a given F(X) constitute an LRE? Initial reserves are to be thought of as a negative dividend, equal in value to $K^*$.

For a situation to be an LRE two conditions must be satisfied: (1) The reserve policy must be a firm equilibrium policy, i.e., it must be the policy that yields an expected dividend stream with present value $V(K^*)$. (2) Investors must expect the firm to break even, so that $V(K^*) = K^*$. To permit us to focus on the entry and exit of firms, we have assumed that all firms must write portfolios of fixed size. The process by which entry would bid R down until expected profits are zero if there were initial positive rents is not described here, but such a process is assumed to exist.

We now establish the following proposition: If there is a nonzero probability of small claims, more precisely, if $\inf\{X|f(X) > 0\}$, LRE requires $K^* = 0$ and $R = 0$. That is, the only LRE is one in which worthless insurance is sold. This is the lemons model with a vengeance! To show this, we simply note that, for any $R > 0$ and $K = 0$, expected profits are positive. Hence, for the firm equilibrium value $K^*$ profits must be even higher. Consequently, the only LRE values are $K^* = 0$ and $R = 0$.

To get an equilibrium in which real insurance actually exists, we obviously need to add something to the problem. A reasonable assumption is that the firm may initially have to incur some fixed costs C in order to have access to a stream of premiums and revenues. We assume that C is the same for all firms and is both minimum and maximum: paying less than C does no good and paying more than C yields no additional benefit.

The existence of positive entry costs changes the equilibrium condition; now it is required that $V(K^*) = K^* + C$. Such an equilibrium obviously permits R to be greater than zero. We can establish that increases in C will tend to raise R, and that there will generally be a unique set of equilibrium values of R and K for any C.

First note that the "return to an investment in the insurance business," or $V(K^*(R),R) - K^*(R)$, rises with R. This can be shown by noting that for fixed

K the stream of dividends minus K, or $D(K,R) - K$, rises with R. But then, adjusting K optimally,

$$V(K^*(R),R) - K = D(K^*(R),R) - K \tag{9}$$

must rise even more.

Hence it is obvious that

$$\frac{dV}{dR} - \frac{dK^*}{dR} \geq 0. \tag{10}$$

Now, from differentiating $V(K^*) = K^* + C$ we find:

$$\frac{dV}{dR}\frac{dR}{dC} = \frac{dK^*}{dR}\frac{dR}{dC} + 1 \tag{11}$$

or

$$\frac{dR}{dC} = \frac{1}{\dfrac{dV}{dR} - \dfrac{dK}{dR}} \geq 0. \tag{12}$$

We now ask how regulation would affect the LRE level of price or revenue. Suppose the regulator sets the minimum reserve level at $K_m$ and suppose firms would want to hold less than $K_m$. Denote the expected discounted flow of dividends at this reserve level and at price R by $D(K_m,R)$. Then we must have

$$D(K_m,R) = K_m + C. \tag{13}$$

We have

$$\frac{\partial D}{\partial K_m} + \frac{\partial D}{\partial R}\frac{dR}{dK_m} = 1. \tag{14}$$

It is easy to see that in the simple Borch framework $\partial D/\partial K_m = 0$. Why? If the capital of the regulated firm falls below $K_m$, the firm cannot continue business and hence there are no future dividend payments. This is why the stream of dividend payments $\{d_i\}$ is independent of $K_m$:

$$d_i = \begin{cases} R - X & \text{if } X \leq R \\ 0 & \text{if } X > R \end{cases} \tag{15}$$

Hence it follows from (14) that

$$\frac{dR}{dK_m} = \frac{1}{\partial D/\partial R} \geq 0. \tag{16}$$

However, it probably does not make sense to assume that, irrespective of $K_m$, the entire value of the firm is lost just because the firm is in regulatory insolvency. The regulatory authority will recognize that the firm may still have positive assets and arranges a sale or the infusion of new capital. We will discuss such "bailouts" below.

IV. Unrestricted Investment Models (Munch-Smallwood)

To derive the previous results, it was assumed that owners of capital could not add capital (receive negative dividends) in any period except the initial period. However, such a restriction seems unnecessarily strict. In most insurance markets, funds can be added to equity capital for a solvent firm at any time investors (existing stockholders, new investors, other firms) wish to do so. In addition, a firm can be sold at any time so that the value of the firm will reflect its future profit stream.

Under these assumptions, maximization of stockholder welfare is more naturally defined as maximization of the excess of the firm's market value over the amount of funds invested. In a discrete time version of such a process, one can therefore model the stockholders' objective at the beginning of a period as maximization of the net expected value of the firm at the end of the period. Our problem then becomes one of determining the level of reserve capital which maximizes that net value.

Such a model of unrestricted capital infusion has in fact been developed by Munch and Smallwood (MS).[7] They also assume, in contrast to the Borch-type models treated earlier, that insurance firm reserves can earn a positive return. They limit their analysis, however, to the case in which reserves must be held in the form of the risk free asset, which earns for the insurance firm its market rate r, the same rate at which future consumption or income is discounted.

Short run firm equilibrium in the MS model. A stockholder owned insurance firm is assumed to have access to the revenue stream R in return for accepting

---

[7]Actually, in their model investment is not completely unrestricted. They assume, as do we, that all capital must be committed, if it is to be committed at all, before losses are known. "Bailouts" are not permitted.

a portfolio with claims distribution F(X); claims are independent of the return on the market portfolio. Consumers are ignorant of the level of reserves, so that the level of R is unaffected by the level of reserve capital K.

As in the previous model, reserves are only held to stave off insolvency, and so reserves will obviously only be positive if something is lost through insolvency. There are two possible candidates for what is lost. On the one hand, MS assume that insolvency implies loss of access to the revenue stream R (just as in the Borch model). This assumption again raises the difficult question for LRE of how that revenue stream was initially obtained, and why all such "goodwill" should be lost simply because of insolvency. However, a model which has an equivalent firm equilibrium but a more plausible LRE can be constructed by assuming as before that fixed costs C must be incurred to sell any insurance at all, but that these fixed costs are lost in insolvency. The firm can reenter the insurance business and have access to the same R and F(X) as before, but only if it incurs the cost of C again.

We assume that R is sufficiently high that the value of the firm is at least C. That is, we will only consider cases in which expected underwriting profits at least cover the expected value of the loss of C should insolvency occur. It is also assumed that claims and market returns are uncorrelated, and that reserves are only held in a "safe" form for which the interest rate is r. For simplicity, we will assume that r = 0 but that the firm will only exist for a finite number of periods. At the end of any period, the firm will have net tangible assets of

$$\mu = (K + R) - X. \tag{17}$$

If $\mu \geq 0$, the firm continues to exist with tangible capital $\mu$ rather than K. If $\mu < 0$, the firm loses all of its capital, tangible (K) and intangible (C).

For all periods except the last period, the firm's optimal reserve policy in a stationary environment can be described as follows: If $\mu >$ optimal reserves $K^*$, then the owners will withdraw capital (profits) of $\mu - K^*$; if $0 \leq \mu < K^*$, they provide additional capital of $K^* - \mu$. If $\mu < 0$, the firm is declared insolvent and owners are not permitted to provide any additional capital even if they would wish to do so.[8]

---

[8]Obviously, the assumption that capital can be added if $\mu > 0$ but not when $\mu < 0$ is in a sense arbitrary.

The firm must therefore choose $K^*$, and it is assumed that it does so in a way that maximizes the "net" market value of the firm $Z(K)$, defined by:

$$Z(K) = V(K) - K. \tag{18}$$

Let $\delta(K)$ be the critical value of X (given K) at which the firm becomes insolvent. That is

$$\delta(K) = (K + P) \tag{19}$$

so that the firm becomes insolvent, and of zero value, when $X > \delta$. Let $F_\delta = 1 - F[\delta(K)]$ be the probability that a firm with some level of K becomes insolvent during any single period, and let $E_\delta$ be expected claims cost, taking limited liability into account. That is:

$$E_\delta = \int_0^\delta X \, f(X) \, dX. \tag{20}$$

We can then write:

$$V(K) = (P + K + C)(1 - F_\delta) - E_\delta. \tag{21}$$

Substituting (18) and solving for $Z(K)$ gives

$$Z(K) + K = (P + K + C)(1 - F_\delta) - E_\delta, \quad \text{or} \tag{22}$$

$$Z(K) = P(1 - F_\delta) - F_\delta K + C(1 - F_\delta) - E_\delta. \tag{23}$$

Taking the derivative of (23) with respect to K:

$$\frac{\delta Z(K)}{\partial K} = -PF_\delta' - F_\delta - KF_\delta' - CF_\delta' - E_\delta'. \tag{24}$$

But note that $E_\delta' = -(K + P)F_\delta'$. So (24) simplifies to

$$\frac{\partial Z(K)}{\partial K} = -F_\delta - CF_\delta'. \tag{25A}$$

If there is to be an interior solution for K, a necessary condition therefore is:

$$F_\delta = -CF_\delta'. \tag{25B}$$

In effect, $F_\delta$ is the marginal cost of adding a unit of capital to reserves (since $F_\delta$ is the addition to expected losses), whereas $-CF_\delta'$ is the marginal benefit from doing so.

If $C = 0$ (no entry cost), then $\partial Z(K)/\partial K = -F_\delta$, which is always negative for any $K > 0$, and $K^*$ will always be zero. In effect, adding capital only reduces the advantage of limited liability protection during insolvency, but provides no benefit to the firm. If $C > 0$, the term on the right hand side of (25B) is positive or zero because $F_\delta'$ is always nonpositive. But both $F_\delta$ and $|F_\delta'|$ decline as K increases for "well-behaved" probability distributions. In addition, for most empirically plausible distributions,[9] it will be the case that $F_\delta/F_\delta'$ declines continuously, i.e., $F_\delta$ falls faster than $F_\delta'$.

With these assumptions, we can derive the two cases described by MS. Consider the values of $F_\delta$ and $F_\delta'$ at $K = 0$. Suppose first that $F_{\delta(0)} < -CF_{\delta(0)}'$. Then, as shown by the lines labelled $MB^1$ and $MC^1$ in figure 1, both the marginal benefit and the marginal cost of adding reserves eventually decline as $K \to \infty$. But since MB is always greater than MC, $K^* = \infty$.

In contrast, suppose that $F_{\delta(0)} > -CF_{\delta(0)}'$. Then the lines may be as $MB^2$ and $MC^2$ in figure 2, in which case MB - MC is initially negative, so that there is a local optimum at $K^* = 0$. The marginal net benefit from adding reserves, while initially negative, eventually becomes positive and then remains positive (but approaches zero). Hence, there is another possible optimum at $K^* = \infty$. Depending on the magnitudes involved, the global optimum could be at either extreme. (One would need to compare the magnitude of area A with the (asymptotic limit of) area B.) In any of these cases--and this is the fundamental point--it will never happen that $K^*$ is positive but less than infinity.

In order to bring about a more reasonable result, however, we need only assume that there is some opportunity cost to additions to K. (In the case where the interest rate $r > 0$, this could mean a reduction in the net return on reserves to a level below r.) Suppose that this cost is s per dollar of K. Then condition (25B) becomes:

$$F_\delta + s = -CF_\delta'. \tag{26}$$

Consider the case analogous to the one that yielded $K^* = \infty$; that is, suppose $F_{\delta(0)} + s < -CF_{\delta(0)}'$. As before, $F_\delta' \to 0$ as $K \to \infty$, but the left hand side of (26) approaches s. Hence, there must be an interior solution with $0 < K^* < \infty$. Figure 1 also illustrates such an interior solution when the marginal cost $\hat{MC}^1$

---

[9]For example, this is true for the so-called "increasing failure rate" distributions.

includes s; the optimal level of reserves is then $\hat{K}^*$.

We can also easily determine comparative statics properties. If there is an interior solution, the level of optimal reserves will fall as s rises, but will increase as C rises. Hence, the "transactions costs" s play a crucial role in determining the level of reserves. In the case shown in figure 2, there will generally be two local optima, $K^* = 0$ and $K^*$ equal to some K less than infinity. Changes in C can then lead to shifts from zero to large positive K, as MS describe. In addition changes in s can lead to jumps in K between zero and large positive amounts.

The final question is the nature of long run competitive equilibrium in this analysis. The necessary condition for LRE is, as before, zero expected profits or

$$V(K^*) = K^* + C. \tag{27}$$

If $K^*$ takes on a value greater than zero, the <u>net</u> present value of the firm must therefore equal C. It will be the case that the LRE value of $K^*$ will vary positively with C and inversely with s, although one may observe the kind of discrete jumps described above.

The LRE condition can also be interpreted in a single period model. With $r = 0$, the expected cost of engaging in the insurance business for one period is $F_{\delta(K)}(C + K) + sK$. Equilibrium requires that expected gross underwriting surplus equal this amount, or:

$$R - E_{\delta(K)} = F_{\delta(K)}(C + K) + sK. \tag{28}$$

If this condition and (26) hold, LRE prevails.

Since K is nondecreasing in C and since $E_{\delta(K)}$ increases with K, this condition implies that R rises with C. That is, an increase in C simultaneously increases the premium and reduces the likelihood of default.

## V. The Nature of the Opportunity Cost of Reserve Capital

What reasons could there be why additions to reserve capital would carry a positive opportunity cost? One possibility is that a special tax is levied on insurance firm reserves (either on the principal or on the return), something that occurs frequently in the United States. Another, less obvious, possibility is that the management of the insurance firm is less adept than other managers at managing reserves in a way which maximizes the (risk adjusted) return from

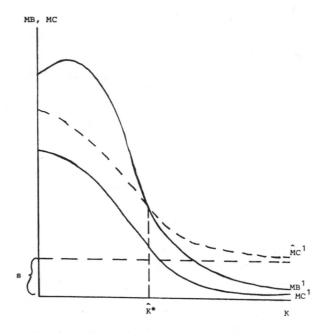

Figure 1

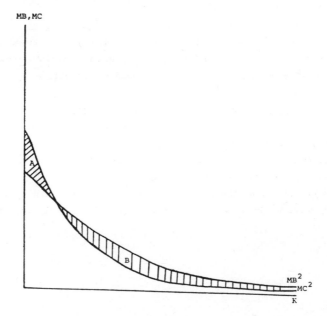

Figure 2

them. This is probably what would, even in a non-intervention environment with very high C, prevent the $K^* = \infty$ outcome. At the margin, at very high K, the net gain from adding reserves, while still positive, is so small that it would be offset by the costs associated with the transaction that pledges assets to the insurance firm.

As the MS discussion suggests, a common regulatory practice that will not necessarily impose an opportunity cost (or at least a much smaller cost than one might suspect) is a regulatory requirement that a firm holds reserves in the form of some safe asset. The reason is that, although the safe asset has a lower return than an unrestricted optimal portfolio, it also carries a lower risk than the alternative. Investors will take both return and risk into account in valuing the insurance firm.

Suppose reserves do not generate a real resource cost due to agency and transactions costs. Is there nevertheless a positive price the capital market would require for reserves because of the greater risk associated with stochastic claims on reserves? That is, will the capital market require a risk premium when a dollar is transferred to reserves, a price that is in excess of the expected value of the increment in claims on reserves?

To answer the question of the market price of risk, it is natural to turn to the capital asset pricing model (CAPM) (e.g., see Copeland and Weston, 1980). There is some inconsistency in doing so, however, since insurance markets would not exist in the ideal CAPM world of complete (spot) financial markets and no agency costs. Every citizen would own part of the portfolio of all risky assets; the loss from the destruction of the house in which one lives or the automobile one drives would already be spread (optimally) across the portfolios of many investors. The loss would affect one's wealth only insofar as the total net value of all assets fluctuated, and only in proportion to the fraction of the total portfolio of risky assets which one owned. So to have an insurance market exist we need to assume exclusive (undiversified) ownership by some individuals of some assets, possibly for agency-incentive reasons that will not be considered further. On the same grounds, one wants to rule out by assumption the possibility that individuals can or will purchase additional insurance against insurer default.

We now attempt to apply the CAPM to the question of the incremental price of reserves. Define Y as the market value of the firm at the end of the period taking limited liability into account, and $\mu$ as the net underwriting profit as before. That is:

$$Y = 0 \qquad \text{if } \mu < 0$$

$$Y = Z(K) + \mu \quad \text{if } \mu \geq 0.$$

Then the value of the firm V(K) under the CAPM is:

$$V(K) = \frac{1}{(1 + R_f)} [E(Y) - \theta \, Cov(Y,U)] \tag{29}$$

where U is the return on the market portfolio of risky assets, $R_f$ is the risk-free interest rate, and $\theta$ is the market price of risk. Now if $Cov(Y,U) = 0$, we note immediately that the cost of adding a dollar of reserves is simply $\partial E(Y)/\partial K$, which equals $F_\delta$. On the other hand, if $Cov(Y,U)$ is not always zero, then increasing K may change the covariance, and alter the value of the firm by more than $F_\delta$. As Munch and Smallwood have noted, the inclusion of a nonzero covariance introduces great complexity. Not only may increasing reserves sometimes cause an increase in the covariance (if actual losses tend to be high, and therefore $\mu$ low, when U is low), but sometimes as well there may be a reduction in covariance (e.g., because automobile accidents are more common in periods of prosperity).

At this point, the most one can do is to describe circumstances in which the covariance is likely to be zero or not. There are two cases in which the covariance will be zero:

(a)     The classic case for the application of the law of large numbers is the case of many small independent risks. However, the issue of regulation of reserves is not very relevant for such cases, since even with small reserves relative to total expected losses, the probability of default will be negligible.

(b)     Losses could have a positive covariance within firms, so that there is a nontrivial possibility of firm default, but could be independent across firms. This case could occur either because a firm happened to insure a set of correlated losses (e.g., a set of houses on the same flood plain) or because the firm underestimated the premium for a set of independent losses (Munch and Smallwood). However, since all investors own a diversified portfolio of stocks, with the stock of any one insurance firm only a small part of the portfolio, this risk is effectively diversified away. Hence, in such a case firms would choose full reserves without regulation if there were no bankruptcy or agency costs and C were large enough.

There are two cases of nonzero covariance that are worthwhile to discuss:

(c) If losses are independent, but the maximum possible loss is large relative to U, then (as Munch and Smallwood note) the covariance will not be zero because insurance firm losses are part of U. Increasing K exposes owners of the firm to larger losses and therefore increases the covariance. Consequently, the insurance firm will choose less reserves than otherwise.

(d) If the losses are not independent of the other components of U, the change in covariance can be either positive or negative. If it is positive, it is like case (c). If it is negative, then reserves may be obtainable at a price below $F_\delta$.

## VI. Bailouts and Optimal Capital

Now we wish to change the nature of the insolvency rule. We suppose that if $\mu < 0$, the firm is permitted to obtain additional capital in the capital market in order to pay off claims X. If it can obtain a "bailout," it avoids insolvency. If it cannot obtain a bailout, it becomes insolvent. A bailout will occur if:

$$C > X - R - K. \qquad (30)$$

In effect, if it is cheaper to save the firm than to start anew, it will be optimal to bail it out.

We now ask, given that bailouts are an option, what is $K^*$? The answer now is that, _regardless_ of the magnitude of C (or s), $K^*$ will always be zero. With K = 0, the firm can always bring about a bailout when it is optimal to do so, but can avoid losing anything if X is so large that a bailout would not pay. Hence, when unlimited bailouts are possible, the firm will never choose to hold any reserves voluntarily. To get positive levels of reserves in the absence of regulation one must assume some restriction or cost to bailing out, compared to the cost of holding higher levels of reserves.

As MS note, the possibility of bailouts faces the regulator with a dilemma. If an insolvent firm would be bailed out, it would not go bankrupt, and insurance purchasers would eventually receive benefits in full. However, permitting bailouts may induce firms to choose no or low reserves, with consequent increases in the frequency with which financial insolvency with no bailout and no partial recovery occurs. Indeed, it is even possible that with bailouts forbidden a firm may set $K^* > C$; the firm might hold infinite reserves to protect a finite entry cost. In such cases a rule against bailouts will make consumers better off.

## VII. Socially Optimal Costly Reserves

The previous sections showed that, if there are positive agency or transactions costs associated with the holding or reserves, firms would not find it optimal to hold full reserves in LRE. How does the level that firms would choose in such a situation compare with the socially optimal level of reserves?

We have shown that, at the firm optimal level of reserves $K^*$, the marginal private costs of reserves $F_\delta + s$ is equated to the marginal private benefit from reserves $-CF_\delta'$. If the setup costs $C$ represent real resources which are lost when insolvency occurs, the marginal social benefit obviously includes the marginal private benefit. However, it will also be the case that an increase in reserves will benefit risk averse insurance purchasers, while insurance firms will not take this benefit into account. Suppose all buyers of insurance have identical risk averse utility functions $U^{Bi}$. Let the marginal utility for person i for an increment in reserves at $K = \delta$ be $EU_K^{Bi}$. Dividing this marginal utility by $\lambda$, the marginal utility of a certain dollar, we can write the marginal conditions for socially optimal reserves when there are N customers for each firm as:

$$ s + F_\delta = -CF_\delta' + \sum_{i=1}^{N} \left( \frac{EU_K^{Bi}}{\lambda} \right). $$

If $EU_K^{Bi}$ is greater than zero, socially optimal reserves $K^{**}$ will exceed the firm optimal reserves $K^*$.

Imposing a reserve requirement will also change the LRE level of price. Hence, the socially optimal level of reserves is <u>not</u> found by only satisfying the first order condition for $K^{**}$; rather, $K^{**}$ and $R^{**}$ must be chosen simultaneously. However, since at any price $EU_K^{Bi} \to 0$ as $K \to \infty$, $K^{**}$ must be less than $\infty$; if $K^* < \infty$ it will never be socially optimal to hold "full" or virtually infinite reserves. Note, however, that the degree of suboptimality will tend to be small if $K^*$ is sufficiently high. One may therefore conjecture that if C is large relative to s, the welfare loss from unregulated reserves would be small.

It is, of course, possible that the costs of insolvency C do not represent real resources lost. For example, C may represent a franchise or license fee paid to the government, which is simply transferred to general government revenues. Since firms treat a reduction in the probability of losing C as a benefit to them, even if it is not a social benefit, it would be possible for $K^*$ to exceed socially optimal reserves. That is, even though firms ignored the benefits of buyers of insurance from reducing the likelihood of bankruptcy, they may overestimate the real value of bankruptcy costs, and hence may choose to hold excessive reserves.

What about the case in which s is zero but there is a positive covariance between X and U? This appears to be a very difficult question to answer; it does, however, appear possible to suggest that socially optimal reserves must be less than full reserves. To see why, note that at full reserves the insured is protected from all losses in all states of the world. If we think of there being only two events as far as the individual insured is concerned--he suffers a loss or he does not suffer a loss--and if $U'_{BL}$ and $U'_{BN}$ are his marginal utility in each of the two states, then at full coverage and full reserves,

$$U'_{BL}/U'_{BN} = 1.$$

However, if the insurer is also risk averse, his ratio of marginal utilities will exceed unity, since his net wealth in the loss state will be lower than his net wealth in the no loss state. Hence, it will be advantageous to both types of person to reduce the insured's wealth in the loss state somewhat, and to increase the insurer's wealth in the loss state. One way to do this is to have less than full reserves. A preferred route would be to maintain full reserves but have all buyers of insurance share in the total loss, whether they suffer individual losses or not; such mutual insurance or assessment features are common but not universal.

VIII. Conclusion

In the case where there is no covariance of firm risk with the market return, agency costs are small, and fixed costs are moderate, regulation of insurer reserves is probably unnecessary, even if consumers are uninformed or imperfectly informed. Where agency costs are high or fixed costs low, so that firms may set reserves at suboptimal level, there is a potential gain from regulation. The ability of real-world regulators to achieve this gain may, however, be questioned, since at present they have little knowledge of agency and bankruptcy costs.

If bailouts are not forbidden, then reserves will be virtually certain to be too low, if not zero. Such a situation may, however, still be consistent with a low likelihood that benefits will not be paid, if the entry costs a bailout can save are sufficiently high.

In the case where there is nonzero covariance of insurance firms returns with returns on the market portfolio, the price of risk generated by the capital market is also relevant, as is the agency, bankruptcy, and risk costs imposed on buyers. Future research should concentrate on obtaining empirical estimates of these concepts.

## References

Beckmann, M., "Optimum Dividend Policy," in H. Göppl and R. Henn, eds., Geld, Banken und Versicherungen, Vol. 1 (Königstein/Ts., 1981), pp. 491-501.

Borch, K., The Mathematical Theory of Insurance (D.C. Heath & Co., 1974).

Borch, K., "Is Regulation of Insurance Companies Necessary?" in H. Göppl and R. Henn, eds., Geld, Banken und Versicherungen, Vol. 2 (Königstein/Ts., 1981), pp. 717-731.

Borch, K., "Optimal Strategies in a Game of Economic Survival," Naval Research Logistics Quarterly, Vol. 29 (March 1982), pp. 19-27.

Copeland, J.E. and J.F. Weston, Financial Theory and Corporate Policy (Addison-Wesley, 1980).

De Finetti, B., "Su una Impostazione Alternativa della Teoria Collettiva del Rischio," Transactions of the XV International Congress of Actuaries, Vol. 2 (1957), pp. 433-443.

Halling, M., "Band Strategies: The Random Walk of Reserves," Blätter der Deutschen Gesellschaft für Versicherungsmathematik (1979), pp. 231-236.

Miyasawa, K., "An Economic Survival Game," Journal of the Operations Research Society of Japan (1962), pp. 95-113.

Morrill, J., "One-Person Games of Economic Survival," Naval Research Logistics Quarterly (1966), pp. 49-69.

Munch, P. and D. Smallwood, "Theory of Solvency Regulation in the Property and Casualty Insurance Industry," in G. Fromm, ed., Studies in Public Regulation (MIT Press, 1981), pp. 119-180.

Pentikäinen, T. and J. Rantala, Solvency of Insurers and Equalization of Reserves, Vol. 1 (Helsinki: Insurance Publishing Company Limited, 1982).

Reprinted from THE BELL JOURNAL OF ECONOMICS
Vol 11, No. 1, Spring 1980

# Solvency regulation in the property-liability insurance industry: empirical evidence

Patricia Munch

and

Dennis E. Smallwood

*This article reports empirical evidence concerning the effects of solvency regulation on the number of companies and frequency of insolvencies. Minimum capital requirements appear to reduce insolvencies by reducing the number of small, domestic firms. This supports the view of capital requirements as a differentially higher tax on small, new firms. Other forms of regulation have ambiguous effects or none. A comparison of the characteristics of insolvent and solvent firms supports the model of insolvency as the (unlucky) outcome of value-maximizing risk-taking.*

## 1. Introduction

■ The objective of this paper is to provide empirical evidence on the effects of solvency regulation of the property and liability insurance industry.[1] Elsewhere, we have developed a theoretical analysis of the insolvency problem and the effects of regulation (Smallwood and Munch, 1979) and discussed in detail the various forms of regulation (Munch and Smallwood, 1979). Our basic premise is that managers adopt those underwriting and investment risks that maximize the value of the firm. Thus, in contrast to previous studies of solvency regulation, we assume that the firm's probability of insolvency is chosen, not determined exogenously by the properties of the distribution of claims and investment returns. Solvency regulation is predicted to be effective only to the extent it modifies the incentives and constraints faced by the firm.

The rationale for solvency regulation is to protect the interests of policyholders, third-party liability claimants and other firms (to whom the obligations of an insolvent firm are shifted by guaranty fund arrangements). The public

---

[1] Property and liability insurance may be roughly defined as all lines other than life, accident, and health. It includes both commercial and personal lines and both third-party (liability) and first-party coverages. Total premium volume in 1977 was $71.7 billion, of which private passenger automobile accounted for over one-third. (*Best's Review, Property-Casualty Insurance Edition*, August 1978). There are over 2,000 firms in the industry. In 1945 the McCarran-Ferguson Act granted the insurance industry immunity from federal antitrust law, provided there is regulation at the state level. Subsequently, all states have enacted regulations relating to rates and to financial condition. Previous empirical studies of the effects of regulation have focused on rate regulation (Joskow, 1973; Ippolito, 1979). Studies of solvency regulation have been primarily prescriptive (Hofflander, 1969; Hammond, 1978).

good aspects of monitoring provide a *prima facie* case for regulation by a single authority. However, questions of feasibility and cost cast doubt on the overall efficiency of regulation in practice. Despite extensive regulation, many aspects of risk-taking necessarily remain uncontrolled, and it is an empirical question whether regulation in fact significantly reduces the frequency of insolvencies.

Against any potential benefits of regulation must be weighed the costs. The administrative costs are obvious.[2] Less evident are the adverse consequences arising from the fact that regulation raises the cost of entry and the minimum efficient scale of operation in the authorized section of the market. This imposes a loss on consumers if small firms provide a specialized and/or lower cost product than larger firms, and if the threat of entry by small firms constitutes an important competitive threat to established firms.[3]

Many of the 2,000 firms in the industry are small, are often organized as mutuals, and write a specific type of coverage for a carefully selected group of policyholders. The fact that such firms survive, when not subjected to a cost disadvantage by regulation, suggests that their apparent disadvantage in terms of diversification of risk is offset by a comparative advantage in selecting and monitoring policyholders. That there should be some advantages of small scale is not surprising in view of the inherent heterogeneity of policyholders and hence the importance of policyholder-specific information in accurately pricing the insurance product. Because the price of the insurance product is set before the cost is known and that cost is influenced by policyholder behavior, accurate information about expected claims cost and monitoring of moral hazard are crucial for successful writing.[4]

With the available data we cannot undertake a full weighing of the costs and benefits of solvency regulation. Our more limited objective is to demonstrate the effects of solvency regulation on the frequency of insolvencies and the number and average size of firms. The evidence presented in Section 2 suggests that minimum capital requirements do reduce the number of insolvencies, but that this is achieved solely by deterring the entry of small, relatively risky firms. We find no effect on the frequency of insolvencies among firms which do enter the market. Thus, the overall evaluation of solvency regulation reduces to the question of whether the net value to consumers of the type of firm that is eliminated is positive and exceeds the administrative cost of regulation.

---

[2] In New York in 1974 regulation of financial condition absorbed over 50 percent of insurance department expenditure (*Regulation of Financial Conditions of Insurance Companies*, New York, 1974).

[3] Since 1975, at least 15 physician-owned mutuals have been formed to write medical mal practice. Other physicians and hospitals have chosen to form captive offshore companies, in part to avoid the regulations on the authorized market.

[4] Furthermore, it would be a mistake to conclude from the large total number of firms in the property-liability insurance industry that potential entry, and hence barriers to entry, are irrelevant to market performance. The industry consists of many submarkets, arising naturally from differences in types of coverage, policyholder characteristics, and, in liability lines, local legal environment. The information necessary to write specific coverages creates inevitable obstacles to the movement of firms among submarkets. Licensure requirements by line and by state impose an additional restriction on entry. At any one time there may be only two or three firms writing a specific line in a particular state. This is particularly true for the small liability lines, such as professional and municipal liability.

In Section 3 we compare the characteristics of a sample of insolvent firms with a matched sample of solvent firms. This evidence supports the theoretical predictions as to the characteristics likely to be associated with a relatively high preferred risk of insolvency.

## 2. Evidence on the effects of solvency regulation

■ The major forms of solvency regulation include minimum capital and surplus requirements, constraints on portfolio choice, the filing of detailed annual statements and triennial examinations. Preserving solvency is one of the stated objectives of rate regulation. In addition, most states have established a guaranty fund, which effectively transfers the obligations of an insolvent firm to other firms in the state.

We have argued elsewhere (Munch and Smallwood, 1979) that some forms of solvency regulation may operate as a differentially higher tax on small, new firms and hence tend to reduce entry to the authorized insurance market, increase minimum efficient firm size, and decrease the number of firms in a market.[5] On the other hand, these regulations (and also guaranty funds) may deter insolvencies, both by eliminating from the market firms which have a higher propensity to go insolvent and by raising the cost of risk taking for firms that do enter. In addition, rate regulation is expected to increase the number and to reduce the average size of firms, but possibly to increase profit margins. Its effect on frequency of insolvencies is uncertain *a priori*.[6] Guaranty funds transfer the incentive to monitor financial conditions from policyholders to other firms. Guaranty funds are therefore expected to decrease the frequency of insolvencies, if other firms are lower cost monitors of financial condition and report imminent insolvencies early enough to forestall them.

In this section we first test the hypothesis that solvency regulation reduces the number of firms and increases minimum efficient size. Because regulation is directed primarily at domestic firms, i.e., firms incorporated or domiciled in the state, we test for differential effects between domestic and nondomestic

---

[5] Minimum capital regulation is likely to impose a binding constraint primarily on small, new firms for several reasons. First, for a given supply price of capital, the optimal level of capital is an increasing function of the number of policyholders and an increasing function of the age of the firm's "intangible capital," presumed to be a nondecreasing function of the age of the firm. Thus, the requirement to hold a specified absolute amount of capital (rather than some proportion of premium volume) is more likely to exceed the desired level for small, new firms.

Second, the supply price of the required amount of capital will be higher for new firms, if confidence in the investment expertise and honesty of management can only be established with experience. The requirement that some absolute amount of capital be held in specific securities is more likely to be a binding constraint on portfolio choice, the smaller the portfolio. Constrained, nonoptimal portfolio choice implies a higher supply price of capital. To the extent that fiduciary risk and constraint on portfolio selection raise the supply price of capital to small, new firms, their desired level of capital is reduced. This increases the likelihood that regulatory constraints will be binding. Binding regulatory constraints on small firms will tend to increase the minimum efficient size of the firm and reduce the number of firms in a market of given size.

[6] It has been argued (Joskow, 1973; Ippolito, 1979) that prior approval rate regulation facilitates cartel pricing by the insurance industry, limits expansion of more efficient firms, and protects small, less efficient firms. To the extent prior approval increases profit margins, it should reduce the frequency of insolvencies. On the other hand, this may be offset to the extent it tends to increase the proportion of small, relatively inefficient firms which are more prone to insolvency.

firms. Second, we test the hypothesis that regulation deters insolvencies and, if it does, whether this results solely from preventing firms which would accept a higher risk of insolvency from entering the market, or whether there is an additional deterrent effect on firms that do enter.

These hypotheses may be stated in terms of the following simultaneous system:

$$C = \alpha_0 + \alpha_1 TPRM + \alpha_2 R + u_1 \tag{1}$$

$$I = \gamma_0 + \gamma_1 C + \gamma_2 R + \gamma_3 X + u_2, \tag{2}$$

where

$$
\begin{aligned}
C &= \text{number of companies,} \\
I &= \text{number of insolvencies,} \\
TPRM &= \text{total premiums (proxy for market size),} \\
R &= \text{vector of measures of regulation,} \\
X &= \text{vector of measures of underwriting experience,} \\
u_1 &\sim N(0,\sigma_1), \\
u_2 &\sim N(0,\sigma_2), \\
E(u_1,u_2) &\neq 0.
\end{aligned}
$$

In estimating the effect of regulation on insolvencies, we control for average underwriting experience.[7] Given the variability of the claims distribution, the probability of insolvency is expected to be inversely related to the average margin between premium level and claims cost. Given the mean underwriting margin, the probability of insolvency is expected to be positively related to the variability of claims, particularly if year-to-year deviations from the mean are positively correlated.[8]

☐ **The data.** Since regulation is state specific, the state is the basic unit of observation.

*Number of companies and number of insolvencies.* The data on the number of companies and insolvencies are from two sources: state insurance departments and *Best's Reports.* Unfortunately, *Best's* data exclude an unknown number of small companies, which are precisely those expected to be most affected by solvency regulation. We use three samples of companies. The first two, domestic companies only and total companies, i.e., domestic and licensed nondomestic companies for 1967 are from insurance department sources and include stocks, mutuals, and other types. The third sample is from *Best's* and is confined to stock companies active during the period 1957–1968. The three insolvency samples consist of two from insurance department sources for the periods 1958–1968 and 1965–1975. The third insolvency sample is confined to stock companies reported in *Best's*, 1957–1968.

*Capital requirements.* Because capital requirements vary by line of insurance, ownership type, state of domicile, years of operation, etc., any simple definition

---

[7] In principle, underwriting experience may itself be endogenous, depending in part on regulation. However, in regressions not reported here, we found no effect of regulation on the mean loss ratio.

[8] If the objective of insurance commissioners is to detect *relatively* risky companies, they may adjust downwards their standards of technical insolvency in years when underwriting results are bad for the industry as a whole. This will mitigate the expected increase in the number of insolvencies in years of generally bad underwriting results.

of capital requirements is necessarily arbitrary and entails measurement error. We consider six measures: the capital plus surplus requirements for writing a single line (casualty where available, automobile otherwise) and for multiple lines for each of three types of company, domestic stocks, domestic mutuals, and foreign mutuals.[9] The capital requirements for multiple lines are shown in Table 1.

*Investments, examinations, etc.* As a proxy for regulatory effort at enforcing all other forms of regulation, we use total expenditure of the insurance department, normalized on the total premium volume of the state.

*Rate regulation.* A binary variable indicates having some form of prior approval regulation as of September, 1973. This is a very imperfect indicator of the stringency of rate regulation. It obscures diversity among states classified as prior approval. Worse, it ignores differences in the timing of the switch to open competition. Sixteen of the 17 states classified as open competition switched from prior approval between 1960 and 1973, i.e., after the period of observation for most of our data. Thus, for the samples that predate the changeover, this variable is intended as a possible indicator of a regulatory environment that was tending toward competition, although nominally prior approval.

*Guaranty funds.* Since guaranty funds were introduced in most states at different times during the period spanned by the second insolvency sample, 1965–1975, the variable used is the number of years of operation of a guaranty fund prior to 1976.

*Subrogation rights under the uninsured motorist provision.* Many states have extended the uninsured motorist coverage (*UM*) to cases where the liable party's insurer becomes insolvent. This affects the incentives of shareholders and creditors to monitor solvency. Specifically, it reduces the number claimants against an insolvent insurer and hence reduces the expected costs of insolvency to shareholders and other creditors, *unless* the victim's insurer has subrogation rights against the insolvent insurer. Assuming that an insurance company is more likely to pursue its subrogation rights than is an individual claimant to pursue a liability claim, the incentives of the owners of a firm to avoid insolvency are higher in states in which insolvency is covered by *UM* coverage *and* the victim's insurer has subrogation rights against the insolvent insurer.

A binary variable takes the value of 1 if insolvency is covered by *UM and* the victim's insurer has subrogation rights against the insolvent insurer.

*Underwriting experience.* Our measure of the average underwriting profit margin is the average over the period 1966–1974 of the statewide average loss ratio, over all companies, for automobile liability insurance, as reported in *Best's*.[10] Among alternative measures of variability, the best fit was obtained with the maximum of a three-year moving average of annual loss ratios. Other

---

[9] Requirements are always the same for domestic and foreign stocks.

[10] For the years 1966–1970 the series is for auto bodily injury, for 1971–1974 it is for auto liability. The mean loss ratio varies from 55 percent to 75 percent.

The loss ratio is losses incurred relative to premium earned, excluding loss adjustment expense, but adjusted for dividends to policyholders. To the extent low expenditure on claims is the result of high expenditure on claims defense, losses and loss adjustment are inversely correlated and the loss ratio is an imperfect measure of profit margin.

TABLE 1

NUMBER OF COMPANIES AND INSOLVENCIES, AND MULTIPLE LINE CAPITAL REQUIREMENTS

| | COMPANIES | | | INSOLVENCIES | | | CAPITAL REQUIREMENTS | |
|---|---|---|---|---|---|---|---|---|
| | TOTAL, STOCK AND MUTUAL, 1967 | DOMESTIC, STOCK, AND MUTUAL, 1967 | DOMESTIC, STOCK, 1958–67 | STOCK, MUTUAL 1967–75 | STOCK, 1958–67 | STOCK AND MUTUAL 1958–68 | MUTUAL | STOCK |
| ALABAMA | 894 | 106 | 18 | 2 | 0 | 0 | 1,000 | 1,000 |
| ALASKA | 448 | 5 | 1 | 0 | 0 | 0 | 400 | 600 |
| ARIZONA | 1,115 | 267 | 3 | 2 | 0 | 0 | 350 | 525 |
| ARKANSAS | 993 | 114 | 20 | 10 | 12 | 6 | 500 | 1,000 |
| CALIFORNIA | 895 | 149 | 89 | 8 | 2 | 3 | 1,000 | 2,000 |
| COLORADO | 841 | 54 | 17 | 4 | 2 | 2 | 750 | 750 |
| DELAWARE | 644 | 47 | 9 | 1 | 2 | 2 | 500 | 750 |
| D.C. | 712 | 31 | 12 | 1 | 1 | 0 | 150 | 300 |
| FLORIDA | 961 | 54 | 21 | 5 | 3 | 3 | 750 | 1,250 |
| GEORGIA | 911 | 68 | 17 | 2 | 1 | 0 | 400 | 600 |
| HAWAII | 415 | 16 | 7 | 0 | 0 | 0 | 500 | 750 |
| IDAHO | 740 | 26 | 2 | 0 | 1 | 0 | 1,300 | 1,300 |
| ILLINOIS | 1,323 | 472 | 93 | 16 | 8 | 17 | 1,000 | 1,500 |
| INDIANA | 1,125 | 183 | 31 | 2 | 3 | 6 | 1,000 | 1,000 |
| IOWA | 1,033 | 237 | 17 | 1 | 0 | 0 | 300 | 500 |
| KANSAS | 811 | 66 | 13 | 0 | 0 | 0 | 300 | 1,000 |
| KENTUCKY | 782 | 60 | 9 | 0 | 0 | 0 | 900 | 1,500 |
| LOUISIANA | 1,025 | 171 | 10 | 2 | 3 | 2 | 1,000 | 1,000 |
| MAINE | 666 | 42 | 5 | 3 | 1 | 1 | 1,000 | 2,000 |
| MARYLAND | 789 | 50 | 19 | 4 | 2 | 3 | 250 | 1,250 |
| MASSACHUSETTS | 524 | 63 | 25 | 3 | 1 | 1 | 1,000 | 1,000 |
| MICHIGAN | 916 | 96 | 19 | 2 | 3 | 3 | 1,000 | 1,500 |
| MINNESOTA | 773 | 230 | 20 | 2 | 2 | 1 | 500 | 1,000 |
| MISSISSIPPI | 990 | 231 | 3 | 0 | 0 | 0 | 300 | 1,000 |
| MISSOURI | 918 | 135 | 25 | 10 | 0 | 8 | 800 | 800 |
| MONTANA | 707 | 8 | 4 | 1 | 0 | 0 | 600 | 800 |
| NEBRASKA | 824 | 115 | 21 | 3 | 2 | 2 | 400 | 600 |
| NEVADA | 836 | 4 | 1 | 1 | 1 | 1 | 400 | 600 |
| NEW HAMPSHIRE | 550 | 27 | 10 | 1 | 0 | 1 | 100 | 1,200 |
| NEW JERSEY | 770 | 66 | 18 | 3 | 0 | 0 | 1,350 | 3,000 |
| NEW MEXICO | 831 | 13 | 1 | 0 | 0 | 0 | 600 | 600 |
| NEW YORK | 724 | 305 | 173 | 8 | 1 | 1 | 6,650 | 3,975 |
| N. CAROLINA | 693 | 74 | 16 | 0 | 0 | 0 | 700 | 1,800 |
| N. DAKOTA | 636 | 55 | 1 | 0 | 0 | 0 | 1,000 | 1,000 |
| OHIO | 1,023 | 217 | 38 | 4 | 1 | 0 | 200 | 1,000 |
| OKLAHOMA | 1,084 | 99 | 26 | 1 | 0 | 0 | 250 | 375 |
| OREGON | 802 | 34 | 5 | 0 | 0 | 0 | 500 | 1,000 |
| PENNSYLVANIA | 1,130 | 372 | 50 | 27 | 2 | 14 | 310 | 1,725 |
| RHODE ISLAND | 580 | 27 | 7 | 1 | 0 | 0 | 450 | 450 |
| S. CAROLINA | 733 | 64 | 29 | 1 | 4 | 1 | 305 | 500 |
| S. DAKOTA | 705 | 71 | 3 | 0 | 1 | 1 | 300 | 800 |
| TENNESSEE | 895 | 76 | 15 | 1 | 1 | 2 | 950 | 1,425 |
| TEXAS | 1,605 | 776 | 93 | 28 | 5 | 4 | 300 | 300 |
| UTAH | 785 | 24 | 1 | 0 | 0 | 0 | 550 | 1,000 |
| VERMONT | 813 | 18 | 4 | 0 | 0 | 0 | 250 | 400 |
| VIRGINIA | 880 | 91 | 5 | 0 | 0 | 0 | 800 | 800 |
| WASHINGTON | 850 | 42 | 9 | 0 | 0 | 0 | 1,300 | 1,300 |
| W. VIRGINIA | 781 | 40 | 8 | 2 | 3 | 3 | 1,125 | 1,125 |
| WISCONSIN | 933 | 264 | 25 | 1 | 0 | 2 | 100 | 2,925 |
| WYOMING | 701 | 9 | 0 | 0 | 0 | 0 | 300 | 600 |

TABLE 2

DEFINITION OF VARIABLES, SOURCES, MEANS AND STANDARD DEVIATIONS

| VARIABLE | DEFINITION AND SOURCE | MEAN | STANDARD DEVIATION |
|---|---|---|---|
| DOMESTIC, STOCK AND MUTUAL COMPANIES, 1967 | HART HEARINGS | 117.4 | 139.4 |
| TOTAL, STOCK AND MUTUAL COMPANIES, 1967 | HART HEARINGS | 842.3 | 210.4 |
| DOMESTIC STOCK COMPANIES 1958–67 | BEST'S INSURANCE REPORTS REPORTED IN NELSON | 21.4 | 30.7 |
| STOCK AND MUTUAL INSOLVENCIES 1967–75 | NATIONAL ASSOCIATION OF INSURANCE COMMISSIONERS | 3.3 | 5.9 |
| STOCK AND MUTUAL INSOLVENCIES 1958–68 | HART HEARINGS | 1.8 | 3.4 |
| STOCK INSOLVENCIES 1958–67 | BEST'S INSURANCE REPORTS REPORTED IN NELSON | 1.4 | 2.2 |
| TOTAL PREMIUM 1967 ($0,000) | INSURANCE INDUSTRY COMMITTEE OF OHIO HART HEARINGS | 106,231 | 139,248 |
| FUNDS/PREMIUM | OPERATING EXPENDITURE OF INSURANCE DEPT. ÷ TOTAL PREMIUM. HART | .00084 | .00036 |
| PRIOR APPROVAL | PRIOR APPROVAL RATE REGULATION, NAIC. 1973. | .74 | .44 |
| ML ($000) | MULTIPLE LINE CAPITAL REQUIREMENTS, NAII. 1968. | 734.8 | 920.7 |
| COMPANY SIZE. ($0,000) | PREMIUM WRITTEN BY DOMESTIC COMPANIES/ # DOMESTIC COMPANIES. 1967. HART. | 248.2 | 374.1 |
| UM X SUBROGATION | UNINSURED MOTORIST COVERS INSOLVENCY AND SUBROGATION RIGHTS AGAINST INSOLVENT INSURER, MAGNUSON. | .5 | .505 |
| GUARANTY FUND | # YEARS OPERATION OF GUARANTY FUND. NCIGF | 4.1 | 1.9 |
| MAXIMUM LOSS RATIO | MAXIMUM 3–YEAR MOVING AVERAGE AUTO LOSS RATIO. BEST'S. 1966–74 | 65.7 | 6.5 |
| MEAN LOSS RATIO | MEAN AUTO LOSS RATIO. BEST'S. 1966–74 | 62.0 | 4.8 |

measures tried were the average absolute deviation around the mean, the variance, and the third moment.

*Market size.* In estimating the effect of regulation on the number of firms, we control for the potential size of the market by including total premium volume written in the state in 1967. A more complete analysis would treat premium volume as endogenous. Potential simultaneous equations bias is discussed below.

Table 2 gives a summary of variables, sources, means and standard deviations.

☐ **Regression results.** *Number of companies.* The first hypothesis to be tested is that solvency regulation creates diseconomies of small size and therefore decreases the number of firms operating in a state. To test whether regulations are more readily enforced against companies domiciled in a state, separate equations are estimated for domestic companies only and for total companies in the 1967 sample. The results are reported in Table 3. To allow for a nonlinear

TABLE 3

NUMBER OF COMPANIES, BY STATE OF DOMICILE, VARIOUS CLASSES, VARIOUS YEARS

| | DOMESTIC, STOCK & MUTUAL, 1967a | | | | TOTAL, STOCK & MUTUAL, 1967a | | | | DOMESTIC, STOCK, 1958–67b | | | |
|---|---|---|---|---|---|---|---|---|---|---|---|---|
| | # COS | | LOGe# COS | | # COS | | LOGe# COS | | # COS | | LOGe# COS | |
| | (1) | (2) | (1) | (2) | (1) | (2) | (1) | (2) | (1) | (2) | (1) | (2) |
| TOTAL PREMIUM | 1.301 | .001** (5.56) | | | 1.25 | .002** (4.90) | | | .880 | .2D–03** (8.26) | | |
| (TOTAL PREMIUM)2 | −1.004 | −.2D–08** (−2.84) | | | −1.116 | −.4D–08** (−2.89) | | | .081 | .041 (.67) | | |
| FUNDS/ PREMIUM | .013 | 5015 (.11) | −.199 | −626 (−2.15) | −.029 | −16770 (−.23) | −.044 | −30.31 (−.35) | .036 | 3065 (.669) | .002 | 8.14 (.03) |
| PRIOR APPROVAL | −.003 | −1.057 (−.03) | .130 | .336 (1.49) | −.058 | −27.407 (−.47) | −.090 | −.05 (−.75) | .002 | .164 (.04) | .097 | .280 (1.26) |
| ML | −.752 | −.114** (−2.59) | | | −.47 | −.108 (−1.50) | | | −.295 | −.013** (−2.84) | | |
| (ML)2 | .93 | 26D–04** (2.62) | | | .535 | .2 D–04 (1.38) | | | .268 | .36D–05** (2.35) | | |
| LOG TOTAL PREMIUM | | | .771 | .765** (7.95) | | | .608 | .131** (4.54) | | | .919 | 1.017** (10.31) |
| LOG ML | | | −.187 | −.288** (−2.05) | | | −.248 | −.083** (−1.96) | | | −.133 | −.304 (−1.52) |
| C | — | 81.78 (1.43) | | −2.092* (−1.68) | | 811.1** (8.61) | | 5.86** (15.7) | — | 7.04 (1.07) | — | |
| R2/ARSQ | .504 | .435 | .668 | .638 | .411 | .329 | .363 | .307 | .895 | .878 | .742 | .719 |
| SEE | 104.7 | | .690 | | 172.4 | | .207 | | 10.73 | | .678 | |

(1) BETA COEFFICIENT.
(2) COEFFICIENT/t–RATIO IN PARENTHESES.
aML = MULTIPLE LINE CAPITAL REQUIREMENT FOR MUTUAL COMPANIES.
bML = MULTIPLE LINE CAPITAL REQUIREMENT FOR STOCK COMPANIES.
 * = SIGNIFICANT AT 10% LEVEL, 2–TAILED TEST.
 ** = SIGNIFICANT AT 5% LEVEL, 2–TAILED TEST.

effect of market size and capital requirements, for each sample we report two specifications, one including squared terms, the other in log linear form.

In the first pair of equations reported in Table 3 (domestic companies, 1967) the negative coefficient on $ML$, the multiple line capital requirement, and positive coefficient on $(ML)^2$ support the hypothesis that capital requirements reduce the number of companies domiciled in a state, with the negative effect diminishing at higher levels of capital requirements.[11] The magnitude of the effect is calculated in Table 4, which shows the change in the number of domestic companies implied by the mean, minimum, and maximum observed $ML$, excluding New York. The minimum, $100,000, has essentially no effect; the mean of $735,000 implies a decrease of 84 domestic companies; the function reaches a maximum at $4,324,000, which eliminates 147 companies; for even higher requirements the predicted effect is positive, because the positive

---

[11] An F-test on the addition of the two capital requirement variables to the estimating equation indicates significance at the .01 percent level.

TABLE 4

PREDICTED EFFECT OF CAPITAL REQUIREMENTS ON NUMBER OF DOMESTIC COMPANIES

| SAMPLE | CAPITAL REQUIREMENTS ($000) | | | | | |
|---|---|---|---|---|---|---|
| | MUTUAL | | | STOCK | | |
| | MIN(100) | MEAN(735) | MAX[1](1350) | MIN(300) | MEAN(1103) | MAX[1](2000) |
| DOMESTIC COMPANIES, STOCK & MUTUAL, 1967 | −1 | −84 | −140 | 0 | −118 | −174 |
| TOTAL COMPANIES, STOCK & MUTUAL, 1967 | −1 | −79 | −133 | | | |
| DOMESTIC COMPANIES STOCK, 1958–67 | | | | 0 | −14 | −20 |

[1]EXCLUDING NEW YORK.

squared term dominates the negative linear term.[12] As can be seen in Table 2 which reports the actual capital requirements by state, all states except New York have requirements of $2,350,000 or less, and thus fall well within the range of negative impact.[13]

Since the minimum, mean, and maximum number of companies in the sample are 4, 117, and 776, respectively, these estimates of the magnitude of the effect of capital requirements seem reasonable. The log linear specification supports the conclusion that the effect of capital requirements on number of domestic companies is negative and nonlinear. The estimated elasticity is −.288.

The next hypothesis is that capital requirements only affect a firm's decision whether to incorporate in a state, not whether to obtain a license to operate in the state. If capital requirements are unenforceable against nondomestic companies, high capital requirements will merely induce the substitution of foreign for domestic incorporation, with no effect on the total number of (licensed) companies.

The second set of equations in Table 3 provides weak evidence against the substitution hypothesis. The coefficients on $ML$ and $(ML)^2$ are similar to the corresponding coefficients in the equation for domestic companies only, but the $t$-statistics are not significant at the 10-percent level.[14] The implied effect on the total number of companies is similar to that for domestic companies: −2 at the minimum, −80 at the mean, and −133 at the maximum, excluding New York.[15] Thus the reduction in total companies is essentially the same as the reduction in domestic companies. This suggests that the capital requirements are

[12] Since $(ML)^2$ is measured in deviations from the mean, the net effect of capital requirements at the point of means is given by the coefficient on $ML$ alone.

[13] At $6,650,000, New York is 6 standard deviations above the mean. Similar results were obtained using the capital requirement for stock companies, for which the range is smaller ($300,000–$3,975,000) and for which New York is only 4 standard deviations above the mean. The implied effects range from essentially zero at the minimum of $300,000 to −118 companies at the mean of $1,103,000 and reach −174 at $2,000,000, with the maximum excluding New York.

[14] The addition to the adjusted $R^2$ from adding the vector of capital requirement variables is not significant at the 10-percent level.

[15] Because the number of total companies typically exceeds the number of domestic companies, elasticities and beta coefficients are larger for domestic than for total companies.

indeed effective only against domestic companies. However, foreign companies do not replace the domestic companies that are eliminated by high entry requirements. A plausible explanation of this absence of substitution is that the type of company which is eliminated by high capital requirements is a small company offering a specialized product which is not readily exported, such as a highly selective mutual. A small firm must offset its comparative disadvantage at diversification by superior efficiency in selecting low risks and providing incentives for loss prevention, i.e., reducing the dead weight loss due to moral hazard and hence the loading charge.[16]

The third sample in Table 3 is domestic stock companies active over the period 1958–1967. The effect of $ML$ is again negative, but nonlinear.[17] The implied reduction in number of domestic stock companies increases from zero at the minimum of \$300,000 to a maximum effect of $-20$ companies at \$2,136,000. The great majority of states fall in the range for which the net effect is an increasing function of requirements.[18] The evidence from this sample confirms that the effect of capital requirements is not confined to mutual companies nor to companies too small to be listed in *Best's*. However, the beta coefficients are smaller for this sample than for the other two samples which include mutuals and many smaller companies. This implies that capital requirements explain less of the across-state variance in the number of larger, stock companies than in the total number of companies, including mutuals and small companies.[19]

Turning to the other variables, we find that the beta coefficients indicate

---

[16] The following table shows the number of fire and casualty companies, by type and place of domicile for Ohio in 1976:

|  | domestic | foreign | alien | total |
|---|---|---|---|---|
| stock | 45 | 327 | 15 | 387 |
| mutual | 24 | 79 | — | 104 |
| reciprocal | 3 | 13 | — | 16 |
| assessment fire | 69 | — | — | 69. |

The difference between the distribution by type of domestic and nondomestic firms is striking. Assessment fire companies are the largest single category of domestic firms, but there are no nondomestic firms of this type (*source*: State of Ohio, Department of Insurance, 110th Annual Report).

[17] For this sample, $ML$ is the multiple line requirement for stock companies.

[18] An $F$-test on the addition of the vector of capital requirements variables shows significance at the 5-percent level.

[19] We tested the hypothesis that the effects of capital requirements increase with the degree of constraint on the type of asset that may be held and on the enforceability of the requirements. For both reasons, security deposits, minimum capital for stock firms and surplus for mutuals, surplus required at licensure, and finally operating surplus for stock companies are expected to be of decreasing degree of stringency. The results for the domestic companies' 1967 sample were weakly in support of the theory, with minimum capital and entry surplus having a larger and more significantly negative effect on the number of companies than operating surplus. For the other samples, however, separate effects of the different requirements were not distinguishable. Other specifications of capital requirements were considered, but provided a worse fit to the data than those reported in Table 3.

The single line requirement, for either stocks or mutuals, was insignificant when added after the multiple line requirement, and had less explanatory power when included alone. Similarly, including both stock and mutual requirements added no explanatory power. The ratio of the single to the multiple line requirement and the requirement for nondomestic mutual companies were insignificant.

that the variable contributing most to variation in the number of companies is premium volume, an imperfect measure of the size of the market.[20]

Of the other regulatory variables, insurance department operating expenditure relative to premium volume is insignificant in all equations except for the log-linear specification for domestic companies in 1967, where it is significantly negative. The theoretical prediction is that if department expenditure operates simply as a tax per premium dollar, it should have no effect on the number of companies, given premium volume.[21] If, on the other hand, examinations, etc., impose a proportionally larger tax on smaller firms because of fixed costs, a negative relation between the number of firms and the department expenditure is predicted. Because each insurance department is responsible primarily for its domestic firms, the negative effect is expected to be stronger on domestic than on total firms. This prediction is supported only by the log-linear specification for the sample that includes small firms.

Prior approval rate regulation has no consistent, significant effect on the number of companies. This is at best weak evidence against the hypothesis that prior approval tends to protect small firms, because our binary variable is an imperfect index of the stringency of rate regulations in 1967.[22]

In conclusion, the evidence seems clear that capital requirements reduce the number of firms writing insurance in a state. The impact falls almost exclusively on domestic companies.[23] With the available data we cannot determine whether this uneven incidence results because regulations are unenforceable against nondomestic companies or because the capital requirements are only binding on small firms and multistate firms typically exceed the critical size.

The elimination of small firms may impose costs on consumers in two ways. First, the range of "quality" of product available may be reduced if small firms provide specialized forms of coverage tailored to the needs of relatively

---

[20] Strictly, premium volume should be treated as an endogenous variable in the system:

$$\Pi = a_0 + a_1 N + a_2 R + a_3 X + e_1 \tag{i}$$

$$N = b_0 + b_1 \Pi + b_2 R + b_c Y + e_2, \tag{ii}$$

where

$\Pi$ = total premium volume,
$N$ = number of firms,
$R$ = vector of regulatory variables,
$X, Y$ = vectors of other exogenous variables, and
$e_1, e_2$ = error terms.

If equation (ii) is estimated by using the observed value of $\Pi$, the coefficients are unbiased provided both $a_1 = 0$, and $u_1$ and $u_2$ are uncorrelated, i.e., premium volume is independent of the number of firms in the market.

[21] In terms of supply and demand for dollars of coverage, the tax implies a vertical shift in the supply schedule which may increase or decrease premium volume, depending on the elasticity of demand. However, the tax has no effect on minimum efficient firm size.

[22] Other studies have reported findings that prior approval regulation tends to decrease the market share of the direct writers (Joskow, 1973; Ippolito, 1979). Thus, to the extent our prior approval variable does reflect differences in the regulatory environment in 1967, the finding of no effect on the number of firms suggests that prior approval tends to increase the average size of bureau firms, rather than permit the proliferation of more small firms.

[23] In regressions reported elsewhere (Munch and Smallwood, 1979), we estimate that capital requirements increase average firm size and decrease the percentage of licensed companies domestically incorporated.

small groups of policyholders. Second, prices, at least to some consumers, may be higher, either because of the relatively low cost of the eliminated firms or because of the reduction in competitive pressure on remaining firms. We lack the data to measure these effects. We can only speculate that these costs will be greatest in lines which are relatively concentrated and where the formation of small companies is potentially cost-effective, as in fire, product liability, and medical malpractice.[24]

*Number of insolvencies.* Capital requirements have been shown to reduce the number of firms in the market, and hence potentially to impose costs on consumers. The next question is whether regulation conveys offsetting benefits by deterring insolvencies and, if it does, whether the effect results simply from having prevented firms which would accept a higher risk of insolvency from entering the market, or whether there is a further, "conditional" deterrent effect on firms that do enter.

The hypothesis that solvency regulation has a conditional deterrent effect is tested in three ways. The first involves estimation of a reduced form equation for the number of insolvencies. Combining equations (1) and (2) above, the reduced form for the number of insolvencies is:

$$I = \gamma_0 + \gamma_1[\alpha_0 + \alpha_1 TPRM + \beta_0 R + u_1] + \beta_1 R + u_2 \qquad (2a)$$

$$= \delta_0 + \delta_1 TPRM + \delta_2 R + \gamma_1 u_1 + u_2.$$

The hypothesis that capital requirements have a deterrent effect over and above the entry effect implies that $\beta_1 < 0$. We can solve for the structural parameters from the estimated coefficient as follows:

$$\hat{\gamma}_1 = \frac{\hat{\delta}_1}{\hat{\alpha}_1} ; \qquad \hat{\beta}_1 = \hat{\delta}_2 - \hat{\gamma}_1 \hat{\beta}_0.$$

Table 5 reports regressions for three samples of insolvencies: stock and mutual companies, 1965–1975; stock and mutual companies, 1958–1968; and stock companies only, 1958–1967. The first equation for each sample is the OLS reduced form. The multiple line capital requirement has a significant negative effect on the number of insolvencies in the first two samples, but an insignificant negative effect in the third sample, which includes only firms large enough to be reported in *Best's*.

To solve for the structural parameters we use the 1967 domestic companies equations from Table 3 and the 1965–1975 stock and mutual insolvency equation from Table 5. The estimated coefficients yield the following estimates of the structural parameters of interest:

$$\hat{\gamma}_1 = \frac{.00004}{.001} = .04$$

$$\hat{\beta}_1 = -.003 + (.04 \times .114)$$

$$= .0016$$

---

[24] For example, although there are over 2,000 firms in the industry nationwide, it is not uncommon for there to be only two or three writers of medical malpractice in a state. Following the malpractice insurance "crisis" in 1975, which was characterized by premium increases of over 300 percent in some states and withdrawal of all commercial carriers in others, a sizeable number of physician-owned mutuals entered the authorized market. However, some physicians and hospitals resorted to the formation of captive, offshore companies, in part to avoid the regulatory requirements of the authorized market.

TABLE 5

NUMBER OF INSOLVENCIES, DOMESTIC COMPANIES; BY STATE OF DOMICILE

| | STOCK & MUTUAL 1965–75a | | | | STOCK & MUTUAL 1958–68a | | | | STOCK 1958–67b | | | |
|---|---|---|---|---|---|---|---|---|---|---|---|---|
| | OLS | | TSLS | | OLS | | TSLS | | OLS | | TSLS | |
| | (1) | (2) | (1) | (2) | (1) | (2) | (1) | (2) | (1) | (2) | (1) | (2) |
| TOTAL PREMIUM | .947 | .4D–04** (6.44) | | | .664 | .2D–04** (3.80) | | | .331 | .5D–05* (1.67) | | |
| COMPANY SIZE | –.170 | –.003 (–1.41) | .203 | .003** (2.19) | –.140 | –.001 (–.98) | .122 | .001 (.89) | –.085 | –.5D–03 (–.49) | –.024 | –.1D–03 (–.15) |
| FUNDS/ PREMIUM | .092 | 1492 (.917) | .086 | 1391 (1.02) | –.108 | –993 (–.91) | –.111 | –1023 (–.89) | .079 | 480 (.55) | .052 | 317 (.37) |
| PRIOR APPROVAL | –.055 | –.73 (–.52) | –.117 | –1.57 (–1.35) | –.182 | –1.378 (–1.46) | –.225 | –1.704* (–1.74) | –.070 | –.351 (–.46) | –.082 | –.409 (–.56) |
| UM X SUB–ROGATION | .344 | 4.03** (3.25) | .149 | 1.752* (1.60) | .420 | 2.789** (3.34) | .281 | 1.867** (2.02) | .380 | 1.661** (2.43) | .374 | 1.635** (2.45) |
| GUARANTY FUND | –.200 | –.621* (–1.85) | –.158 | –.490* (–1.72) | –.167 | –.294 (–1.30) | –.136 | –.239 (–.99) | –.112 | –.129 (–.71) | –.114 | –.132 (–.74) |
| ML | –.485 | –.003** (–3.51) | –.005 | –.3D–04 (–.06) | –.361 | –.001** (–2.20) | –.026 | –.9D–04 (–.19) | –.153 | –.5D–03 (–.79) | –.096 | –.3D–03 (–.53) |
| MAXIMUM LOSS RATIO | .662 | .601** (2.09) | .803 | .730** (3.03) | .583 | .300 (1.55) | .681 | .351* (1.73) | .142 | .048 (.31) | .154 | .052 (.34) |
| MEAN LOSS RATIO | –.527 | –.651* (–1.64) | –.694 | –.856** (–2.58) | –.398 | –.279 (–1.04) | –.514 | –.360 (–1.29) | .075 | .034 (.16) | .064 | .029 (.14) |
| #COMPANIES | | –– | .885 | .038** (8.03) | | –– | .629 | .015** (3.84) | | –– | .252 | .018 (1.38) |
| C | | 2.61 (.26) | | 4.32 (.51) | | .599 (.08) | | 1.236 (.17) | | –4.29 (–.78) | | –4.163 (–.77) |
| R²/ARSQ | .6302 | .5470 | .749 | | .479 | .362 | .441 | | .2147 | .0381 | .266 | |
| SEE | 3.98 | | 3.346 | | 2.68 | | 2.822 | | 2.168 | | 2.104 | |

(1) BETA COEFFICIENT.
(2) COEFFICIENT/t–RATIO.
aML = MULTIPLE LINE CAPITAL REQUIREMENT FOR MUTUAL COMPANIES.
bML = MULTIPLE LINE CAPITAL REQUIREMENT FOR STOCK COMPANIES.
 * = SIGNIFICANT AT 10% LEVEL, 2–TAILED TEST.
 ** = SIGNIFICANT AT 5% LEVEL, 2–TAILED TEST.

This suggests that the negative coefficient on *ML* in the reduced form is attributable to the negative effect of capital requirements on the number of companies. By this test there is no evidence that capital requirements have an additional deterrent effect.

The same conclusion emerges from the second test, in which number of insolvencies is regressed on a predicted value of the number of companies, capital requirements, and other variables by using two stage least squares.[25] This is the second equation in each sample in Table 5. In all cases the coefficient on capital requirements is negative, but not statistically significant.

For the third test the insolvency rate, computed as the ratio of the number of insolvencies to the number of companies, was regressed on capital require-

---

[25] The number of companies is the number of domestic stock and mutual companies in 1967 for the first two samples and the number of domestic stock companies 1958–1967 for the third sample.

ments and other variables. The results are not reported because almost all variables, including capital requirements, were insignificant. Thus all three tests support the same conclusion—there is no evidence that capital requirements have an independent deterrent effect on the number of insolvencies over and above the effect on the number of companies.

The most important variable explaining number of insolvencies is market size, whether measured by the total premium volume or by the predicted number of domestic companies. Of the other regulatory variables, department expenditure has no significant effect. Prior approval regulation has a consistently negative effect, although the significance level is low by conventional standards.

The number of years in which the state has operated a guaranty fund has the predicted negative sign, significant at the 10-percent level, in the 1965–1975 sample of insolvencies. This is consistent with the hypothesis that other companies to whom liability for insolvencies is shifted by creation of a guaranty fund are more efficient monitors of potentially weak companies than are consumers.[26]

To test for the possibility of reverse causation—that guaranty fund laws were passed first in states with relatively low frequency of insolvencies, where industry opposition would presumably be weakest—we included the guaranty fund variable in the estimating equations for the two insolvency samples that predate the passage of guaranty fund laws. The coefficients are indeed negative, but beta coefficients and $t$-ratios are lower than in the 1965–1975 sample. Thus, the correct interpretation of the negative correlation between guaranty funds and the number of insolvencies remains uncertain.

A similar ambiguity of interpretation applies to the uninsured motorist/ subrogation dummy variable. Contrary to predictions, this variable is significantly positive in all three insolvency equations. The most plausible explanation is one of endogeneity—that uninsured motorist laws with subrogation rights have been passed in states with a high frequency of insolvencies. The passage of these laws has not sufficed to reduce the insolvency rate below that in states without such laws. Obviously it is still possible that the laws have reduced the number of insolvencies below what it would otherwise have been.

Persistently adverse underwriting results, measured by the maximum three-year moving average loss ratio, increase the frequency of insolvencies in the two samples that include mutuals and small companies.[27] Controlling for the maximum three-year average, the overall seven-year average loss ratio has a negative effect, which is counterintuitive.[28]

These three samples, drawn from different company populations and different time periods suggest several conclusions on the causes of insolvencies.

---

[26] It is also consistent with the hypothesis that under a guaranty fund, the other companies exert pressure on the Commissioner to use alternatives, such as rehabilitation or reinsurance, in preference to liquidation. This raises the question of the extent to which the frequency of insolvencies is a discretionary variable.

[27] Beta coefficients and $t$-ratios are larger for the sample from the period 1965–1975, to which the loss ratio data corresponds. The significance of the loss ratio variables in the 1958–1968 sample suggests that interstate differences in loss ratios were similar in the two periods.

[28] Included alone, the average loss ratio is insignificant. The addition of both the three-year maximum and the seven years' average is significant at the 10-percent level.

For the sample of stock companies only, which excludes very small companies, interstate differences cannot be explained by either the characteristics of the regulatory environment or the average state-wide underwriting results.[29] The only variable that is statistically significant is the *UM*/subrogation dummy variable, which should itself probably be viewed as endogenous.

The other two samples include both stock and mutual companies, small as well as large, and span almost two decades, 1958–1975. Comparing beta coefficients, the single most important variable explaining the absolute frequency of insolvencies is the number of companies. Abnormal underwriting results, in particular a sustained period of abnormally high loss ratios, increase insolvencies. This is consistent with our underlying hypothesis that insolvencies are at least in part the (unlucky) outcome of calculated risk taking. If fraud were the whole story behind insolvencies, there would be no reason to observe a positive relation between insolvencies and abnormally bad underwriting results.[30]

Regulation through expenditure or examinations, etc., appears to have no effect. Regulation through minimum capital requirements has no effect independent of its effect on reducing the number of companies operating in a state.

Prior approval rate regulation and insolvency guaranty funds are negatively related to insolvencies. However, the mechanism of the former effect is unclear and the latter effect is probably at least in part attributable to reverse causation. Thus, there is little evidence that any of the several forms of solvency regulation has a significant deterrent effect on insolvencies.

## 3. Characteristics of insolvent companies

■ Our analysis of the insurance firm's choice of risk implies that the probability of insolvency is negatively related to its intangible capital, to its underwriting profit margin, and to the sensitivity of demand for its product to its choice of risk, and is positively related to the ease of withdrawing capital, if insolvency becomes imminent and to the supply price of capital. In this section we perform crude tests of this theory by comparing the characteristics of a sample of firms that have been declared insolvent with a matched random sample of solvent firms.

The insolvency sample consists of insolvencies reported by the National Committee on Insurance Guaranty Funds (NCIGF) for the period 1969–1976 which are also listed in *Best's* within one or two years of the date of insolvency, with data on certain key variables. Of the 47 companies listed by NCIGF, complete data are available on 33, probably the larger firms. Corresponding to each insolvent firm, a solvent firm from the same state and listed in the same year was selected at random from *Best's*.[31] Thus the two samples are

---

[29] The adjusted $R^2$ from the OLS regression is only .038.

[30] By "fraud" we mean establishing a firm with the intention of defrauding policyholders. Our findings are consistent with fraud in a more limited sense—it is a strategy which becomes relatively attractive when underwriting results are bad.

[31] For each insolvency we selected the matched firm by taking the volume of *Best's* for the year in which the insolvent firm was last listed, choosing a page by using a table of random numbers, and then proceeding through *Best's* to the first firm domiciled in the same state as the insolvent firm. By matching firms by year of insolvency there is no bias in comparing ages of insolvent and surviving firms.

TABLE 6

COMPARISON OF CHARACTERISTICS OF INSOLVENT COMPANIES WITH A MATCHED
RANDOM SAMPLE OF SOLVENT COMPANIES

| | INSOLVENT COMPANIES | | RANDOM SAMPLE OF COMPANIES | |
|---|---|---|---|---|
| | n | % | n | % |
| I. OWNERSHIP: | (N=37) | | (N=33) | |
| (1) DEFINITELY HOLDING COMPANY SUBSIDIARY | 21 | (56.8) | 12 | (36.4) |
| (2) PROBABLY HOLDING COMPANY SUBSIDIARY | 2 | ( 5.4) | 2 | ( 6.1) |
| (3) INSURANCE GROUP | 6 | (16.2) | 6 | (18.2) |
| (4) MUTUAL | 2 | ( 5.4) | 7 | (21.2) |
| (5) CLOSELY HELD STOCK COMPANY | 6 | (16.2) | 5 | (15.2) |
| (6) WIDELY HELD STOCK COMPANY | 0 | ( 0 ) | 1 | ( 3.0) |
| SIGNIFICANCE: .295 | | | | |
| II. NUMBER OF STATES LICENSED: | (N=37) | | (N=33) | |
| 1 | 9 | (24.3) | 7 | (21.2) |
| 2–5 | 8 | (21.6) | 6 | (18.2) |
| 6–10 | 4 | (10.8) | 1 | ( 3.0) |
| >10 | 16 | (43.2) | 19 | (57.6) |
| SIGNIFICANCE: .499 | | | | |
| III. NUMBER OF LINES WRITTEN: | (N=37) | | (N=33) | |
| 1–5 | 14 | (37.8) | 14 | (42.4) |
| 6–10 | 16 | (43.2) | 9 | (27.3) |
| >10 | 7 | (18.9) | 10 | (30.3) |
| SIGNIFICANCE: .322 | | | | |
| IV. NUMBER OF COMPANIES WRITING AUTO | (N=37) | | (N=33) | |
| | 34 | (91.9) | 23 | (69.7) |
| SIGNIFICANCE: .038 | | | | |
| V. NUMBER OF YEARS IN OPERATION: | (N=5) | | (N=50) | |
| 1–5 | 5 | (13.5) | 3 | ( 9.1) |
| 6–10 | 5 | (13.5) | 2 | ( 6.1) |
| 11–99 | 27 | (73.0) | 26 | (78.8) |
| >99 | 0 | | 2 | ( 6.0) |
| SIGNIFICANCE: .505 | | | | |
| VI. NET PREMIUMS WRITTEN ($000): | (N=36) | | (N=33) | |
| <$2M. | 11 | (30.6) | 14 | (42.4) |
| $2–$5M. | 16 | (44.4) | 3 | ( 9.1) |
| $6–$10M. | 5 | (13.9) | 5 | (15.2) |
| >$10M. | 4 | (11.1) | 11 | (33.3) |
| SIGNIFICANCE: .006 | | | | |
| VII. NUMBER UNDER SAME MANAGEMENT ≤5 | (N=37) | | (N=33) | |
| | 20 | (54.1) | 6 | (18.2) |
| SIGNIFICANCE: .004 | | | | |

matched by year and state. Table 6 presents a comparison of the characteristics
of the insolvent and solvent firms.[32]

Most striking is the almost total absence of the stereotype, self-contained,
widely held stock company. The majority of firms in both samples are either

---

[32] The number of firms in the insolvency sample varies, because for a few firms data
were incomplete.

holding company subsidiaries or members of an insurance group.[33] One reason for the formation of holding companies may be to facilitate the withdrawal of capital if insolvency becomes imminent. This theory would predict a higher frequency of the holding company corporate structure in the insolvency sample. The percentage of firms that are definitely part of a holding company is 56.8 percent for the insolvencies, and 36.4 percent for the solvent firms. However, the test for difference in the overall distribution of ownership types is only significant at the 30-percent level.[34]

The number of states in which a firm is licensed and the number of lines of insurance written are not significantly different between the two samples. Thus insolvencies are not confined to single-state, single-line firms. This conclusion is based on only 79 percent of the insolvencies listed by the NCIGF, and the omitted companies are probably smaller on average. Since the control group is also drawn from *Best's*, the comparison is not necessarily biased. However, in terms of net premiums written, insolvent firms are significantly smaller than surviving firms.[35]

There is no significant difference in the number of years in operation between the two samples. However, since many of the firms changed names and affiliations with other firms since incorporation, years in operation may be a very poor proxy for intangible capital. Interestingly, a much larger percentage of the insolvent firms had undergone a change of management within the last five years. Whether a change of management is a cause rather than an effect of imminent insolvency remains an unanswered question.

Although there is no significant difference in the total number of lines written by firms in the two groups, a much larger fraction of the insolvent firms were writing automobile insurance (92 percent compared with 70 percent). There are at least two possible explanations of this finding. First, automobile insurance is one of the more competitive lines of insurance. The underwriting profit margin is probably lower than in other lines, and hence the firm's optimal probability of insolvency higher. Second, automobile insurance is unique in being compulsory in many states. Policyholders who purchase insurance merely to satisfy requirements are presumably more likely to select a low cost, low quality product, and have relatively low incentives to monitor the quality of the insurer. A compilation by the U.S. Senate Subcommittee on Antitrust and Monopoly listed 109 insolvent property-casualty insurers for the period 1958–1968. Of the total, 108 were providing automobile insurance and 106 were writing high-risk drivers (Olson, 1970). To the extent drivers are correctly categorized as high-risk, this suggests that there is a disproportionate number

---

[33] This precludes use of the ratio of market value to book value as a measure of intangible capital.

The proliferation of separate but connected companies may be in part a response to various regulations, in particular, restrictions on charging discriminatory rates to policyholders and restrictions on writing certain combinations of lines within the same company. In addition, this proliferation may reflect the desire to avoid the application of regulations in the most stringent state to business written in states with less stringent regulation.

[34] Determining the type of ownership from the description in *Best's* involved judgment, so conclusions based on this variable are tentative.

[35] To test for the possibility that this might be a reporting "error" due to the incentives to understate net premiums as insolvency becomes imminent, we also compared net premiums written four years previously. We confirmed the finding that insolvent firms are typically smaller.

TABLE 7

DETERMINANTS OF THE PROBABILITY OF INSOLVENCY

| | LOGIT COEFFICIENT | t–RATIO[a] | PROBIT COEFFICIENT | DERIVATIVE OF PROBABILITY FUNCTION AT MEANS | t–RATIO[a] |
|---|---|---|---|---|---|
| YEARS IN OPERATION | −.000691 | (−.381) | −.00418 | −.00163 | (−.385) |
| HOLDING CO. AFFILIATE[b] | 1.148 | ( 1.769) | .650 | .254 | ( 1.719) |
| NUMBER OF STATES LICENSED | −.029 | (−1.436) | −.0162 | −.00634 | (−1.347) |
| NUMBER OF LINES WRITTEN | .013 | (.153) | .00869 | .00340 | (.182) |
| AUTO[b] | 1.998 | (2.459) | 1.135 | .443 | ( 2.479) |
| NET PREMIUMS WRITTEN | −4.439 D−05 | (−1.515) | −.265 D−04 | −.104 D−04 | −1.449 |
| MANAGEMENT CHANGE WITHIN 5 YEARS[b] | 1.235 | ( 1.777) | .670 | .262 | 1.706 |
| CONSTANT | −1.562 | (−1.566) | −.890 | −.348 | −1.612 |

[a] APPROXIMATE t–RATIO.
[b] BINARY VARIABLE.

of policyholders of insolvent firms who would consciously select a relatively high-risk insurer. This tends to undermine the case for solvency regulation to protect uninformed policyholders, although not necessarily the case for it to attempt to protect claimants against them.

We next tried to measure the contribution of these characteristics to the probability of insolvency. In the equations reported in Table 7, the dependent variable takes the value of one if the firm became insolvent and zero if it survived. Thus the coefficients are to be interpreted as the effect on the probability of insolvency.

Probit and logit estimates are reported.[36] The conclusions are robust under the two alternative specifications. Writing automobile insurance is the single most important variable. Affiliation with a holding company and a recent change of management are also positively associated with the probability of insolvency. Each alone is not highly significant. This partly stems from collinearity between them.

In conclusion, the evidence from this comparison of characteristics of solvent and insolvent firms is consistent in several respects with the theoretical model of insolvency as the unlucky outcome of expected-value-maximizing risk-taking. Insolvent firms are more likely to be writing automobile insurance, a highly competitive line with a disproportionately large percentage of involuntary policyholders. They are more likely to be holding-company affiliates, which may indicate a relatively high preference for risk and ease of withdrawing capital. They have undergone recent management change, which indicates a high cost of capital. Finally, they are relatively small, and hence presumably have a relatively small stock of intangible capital.

---

[36] The logit coefficients are to be interpreted as the effect on the log of the odds ratio.

# References

*Best's Insurance Report—Fire and Casualty*. Oldwick, N.J.: A. M. Best Co., Inc., annually.

*Best's Review—Property/Casualty Insurance Edition*. Oldwick, N.J.: A. M. Best Co., Inc., annually.

IPPOLITO, R.A. "The Effects of Price Regulation in the Automobile Insurance Industry." *Journal of Law and Economics*, forthcoming.

JOSKOW, P. "Cartels, Competition, and Regulation in the Property-Liability Insurance Industry." *Bell Journal of Economics*, Vol. 4, No. 2 (Autumn, 1973).

MAYERSON, A.L. "Ensuring the Solvency of Property and Liability Insurance Companies" in S.L. Kimball and H.S. Denenberg, eds., *Insurance, Government, and Social Policy*, 1969.

MCKINSEY AND CO., INC. *Strengthening the Surveillance System*. National Association of Insurance Commissioners, April 1974.

MEADOR, N.W. AND THORNTON, J.H. "The NAIC Early Warning System: A One-State Review." *Best's Review* (July 1978).

MUNCH, P. AND SMALLWOOD, D.E. "Solvency Regulation in the Property and Liability Insurance Industry: Empirical Evidence." The Rand Corporation, Santa Monica, P-6349. June 1979.

NATIONAL ASSOCIATION OF INDEPENDENT INSURERS. *Capital and Surplus Requirements: Summary of State Laws and Regulation Relating Thereto*. Chicago: 1968.

NATIONAL ASSOCIATION OF INSURANCE COMMISSIONERS. *Monitoring Competition*. Milwaukee: May 1974.

OLSON, D.G. *Insolvencies among Automobile Insurers, U.S. Department of Transportation*. July 1970.

SENATE COMMITTEE ON THE JUDICIARY, SUBCOMMITTEE ON ANTITRUST AND MONOPOLY. U.S. Congress, 91st Session, Hearings on the Insurance Industry, Part 15. Washington, D.C.: 1970. (Hart Committee.)

SENATE COMMITTEE ON COMMERCE. U.S. Congress, 91st Session, Hearings on S.2236, A Bill To Create A Federal Insurance Guaranty Corporation. Washington, D.C.: 1970. (Magnuson Committee.)

SMALLWOOD, D.E. AND MUNCH, P. "Solvency Regulation in the Property and Liability Insurance Industry." NBER 1977, forthcoming.

STATE OF NEW YORK INSURANCE DEPARTMENT. *Regulation of Financial Condition of Insurance Companies*. March 1974.

U.S. DEPARTMENT OF JUSTICE. *The Pricing and Marketing of Insurance*. 1977.

*Reprinted from* THE REVIEW OF ECONOMICS AND STATISTICS, Vol. LXIX, No. 1, Feb. 1987;
*Published for Harvard University by Elsevier Science Publishers*
*Copyright 1987 by the President and Fellows of Harvard College*

# A NOTE ON THE IMPACT OF AUTO INSURANCE RATE REGULATION

## Scott E. Harrington*

*Abstract*—The impact of rate regulation on auto insurance loss ratios during 1976–81 is estimated using cross-state data to determine whether regulation significantly affected rates. The methodology allows for random variation in the impact of rate regulation and no-fault laws on loss ratios. The model controls for the influence of the average expected loss per insured vehicle in a state, and growth rates for the average loss per insured vehicle are analyzed to determine whether unanticipated growth in losses is likely to have affected the estimated mean impact of regulation. The results suggest that regulation reduced rates during the period studied.

Received for publication March 1, 1985. Revision accepted for publication April 2, 1986.

* University of Pennsylvania.

An early version of this paper was presented at the 1984 ARIA Risk Theory Seminar in Los Angeles, California. Thanks are due Howard Kunreuther, Joseph Launie, Harris Schle-singer, and the referees for helpful comments. Beom-ha Jee provided excellent research assistance.

## I. Introduction

Rates in the competitively structured private passenger auto insurance market are subject to some form of prior approval regulation in nearly half of the states. The remainder have competitive rating laws, which allow pricing freedom. A number of studies have attempted to determine whether regulation affects rates by analyzing auto insurance loss ratios (i.e., ratios of losses to premiums). The results generally indicated a positive, but not always significant, impact of regulation on loss ratios (e.g., Ippolito, 1979; the U.S. General Accounting Office (GAO), 1979; Grabowski, Viscusi, and Evans (GVE), 1985; and Pauly, Kleindorfer, and Kunreuther (PKK), 1986).[1]

The motivation for analyzing loss ratios is that the ratio of premiums to expected losses (i.e., the expected value of total losses given information available at the time policies are issued) is an ex ante measure of the average price of insurance. However, since loss ratios reflect actual losses, inferences concerning regulation's impact on ex ante prices may be affected by differences between actual and expected losses.[2] For example, higher loss ratios under regulation might only reflect larger unanticipated growth in losses in regulated states. If so, policy implications would depend on whether regulation contributed to the unanticipated growth. An impact of regulation on expected losses also could affect inferences. If regulation increased expected accident costs, for example, higher loss ratios under regulation would overstate the impact on premiums.

This study's objective is to determine whether regulation has significantly affected auto insurance rates. The study differs from previous work in three principal ways. First, the estimation procedure for the loss ratio model allows for heteroscedasticity that may result from differences in market size and from random variation in the impact of rate regulation and no-fault laws.[3] It also

is used to estimate regulation's effect in individual states. Second, a variable is included to control for the positive relationship between loss ratios and the average expected loss per insured vehicle that could exist regardless of regulation. If regulation is more likely in high cost states, such a relationship could cause loss ratios to be greater in regulated states, other things being equal, even if regulation did not affect rates. Third, growth rates in the average loss per insured vehicle are analyzed to determine whether differences between actual and expected losses may have substantively influenced the estimated average impact of regulation on loss ratios.

## II. Econometric Model

The loss ratios analyzed were for liability, uninsured motorists, and medical payments coverage, as well as for personal injury protection ($PIP$) coverage in states with no-fault laws. The model assumes that variation in loss ratios primarily would result from product and market related cost differences in the absence of rate regulation. Following most previous studies, the model is estimated separately for direct writers and independent agency insurers. Evidence suggests that independent agency insurers have higher operating expenses and lower loss ratios than direct writers (e.g., Joskow, 1973; also see Harrington, 1984b). Whether higher prices for coverage obtained through independent agents are associated with valuable advisory and claims service has been disputed.[4]

Operating expenses and expected loss ratios may depend on the proportion of premiums represented by $PIP$ coverage. Claim settlement costs, for example, may be lower for $PIP$ than for liability. Actual loss ratios may reflect possibly large, unanticipated growth in losses in some no-fault states, and such increases may have been greater in states with low tort thresholds.[5] Loss ratios may be positively related to the average expected loss per insured vehicle if production costs increase less

---

[1] Also see Harrington (1984b). Auto insurance costs usually increased rapidly during the periods studied. A positive impact might be expected given evidence for other industries suggesting that regulated firms often find it difficult to obtain rate increases quickly during periods of rapidly rising costs (e.g., Joskow, 1974).

[2] Estimates of expected losses by state are not available. Insurance companies, regulators, or both estimate future losses for the average driver in a state, but aggregation across policy issue dates and companies would be problematic even if such data were available and insurer and regulatory estimates were in agreement. The impact of purely random differences between actual and expected losses will tend to diminish with increases in either market size or the time period analyzed according to the law of large numbers. The impact of unanticipated changes in structural factors that influence losses, such as changes in liability rules or driving conditions, should diminish as the sample period increases.

[3] The precise nature of the heteroscedasticity is shown later. The effect of rate regulation might vary considerably across

states, as is suggested both by Joskow's (1974) discussion of regulatory lag and by interest group and ideology models of government behavior. Previous work has not completely ignored such variation. The GAO model included a dummy variable for New Jersey. GVE placed Massachusetts, New Jersey, and North Carolina in a "stringent" regulation category based on insurer opinions concerning overall management freedom. See Smallwood (1975) and D'Arcy (1982) for similar procedures.

[4] See Joskow (1973) and PKK. These studies also note that regulation could affect the two types of insurers differently. Lack of knowledge about the relative magnitude of fixed policy issue costs and other aspects of production makes it difficult to predict differences in model parameters for the two groups. The average market share for direct writers was 0.54 in prior approval states and 0.64 in competitive rating states for the coverages and period analyzed.

[5] Growth in losses influenced the modification or repeal of no-fault laws in three states since 1979.

than proportionately with the expected loss per policy.[6] They also may be decreasing in wage rates (see PKK).

Adding a regulatory dummy, the model may be expressed as

$$LR = f(PA, PIP\%, THRESH, LOSS, WAGE, u)$$
(1)

where

$LR$ = statewide dividend–adjusted loss ratio;

$PA$ = 1 if the state had prior approval regulation, 0 otherwise;

$PIP\%$ = $PIP$ premiums divided by total premiums for liability and related first-party coverages if the state had a no-fault law, 0 otherwise;

$THRESH$ = 1 if a no-fault state's threshold for tort action was greater than or equal to \$1,000 of medical expenses or verbally restricted tort action to severe injury cases, 0 otherwise;

$LOSS$ = average expected loss per insured vehicle;

$WAGE$ = average wage rate for production workers;

$u$ = a disturbance term.

To allow for cross-state variation, the impact of prior approval regulation in a state is assumed to equal a mean effect plus a mean-zero random disturbance, $v$. Given the heterogeneity in no-fault laws, the impact of no-fault is assumed to depend linearly on $PIP\%$, $THRESH$, and a mean-zero random disturbance, $w$. Assuming a linear relationship for the remaining variables yields

$$LR = b_0 + b_1 PA + b_2 PIP\% + b_3 THRESH$$
$$+ b_4 LOSS + b_5 WAGE + e$$
(2)

where $b_1$ is the mean effect of regulation, $e = u + vPA + wNF$ is a mean-zero disturbance with variance given by $\text{var}(e) = \text{var}(u) + \text{var}(v)PA + \text{var}(w)NF$, and $NF$ equals one for no-fault states and zero otherwise. Given omitted influences and random variation that should decrease with market size, $\text{var}(u)$ was assumed to depend linearly on a constant and $1/P$ where $P$ is total premiums (in \$100 millions) so that

$$\text{var}(e) = a_0 + a_1 PA + a_2 NF + a_3(1/P)$$
(3)

where $a_1 = \text{var}(v)$ and $a_2 = \text{var}(w)$.[7]

[6] PKK included the proportion of population living in SMSAs ($URBAN$) to provide some control for this influence.

[7] Harrington (1984a) estimated a model similar to (2) that allowed for random variation in each coefficient. The results suggested the constraints reflected in (3). PKK and GVE included per capita income in their models. This variable was superfluous in the present study.

## III. Estimation and Data

Let $b_{1i}$ denote $b_1 + v_i$, the impact of prior approval regulation for state $i$. The best linear unbiased estimator of $b_{1i}$ equals (e.g., Griffiths, 1972):

$$\hat{b}_{1i} = \hat{b}_1 + [\text{var}(v)/\text{var}(e)]\hat{e}$$
(4)

where $\hat{b}_1$ is the GLS estimate of $b_1$ and $\hat{e}$ is the GLS residual from (2). Given the possibility of negative variance estimates with estimated GLS, a maximum likelihood (ML) estimation procedure (assuming normality) was used that constrained each parameter in (3) to be nonnegative. The ML variance estimates and residuals were used to calculate $\hat{b}_{1i}$ for both insurer groups in each prior approval state. Average values of the variables during 1976–81 for all states and the District of Columbia were used for estimation.[8]

$LOSS$ is unobservable and may depend on the effect of regulation on rates. The actual average loss per insured vehicle ($ALOSS$) also contains noise that is correlated with $LR$. $ALOSS$ (in \$100s) was regressed on a set of variables correlated with insured accident frequency and severity, and its predicted value ($ILOSS$) was used as an instrumental variable for $LOSS$.[9] The variables were (1979 or 1980 values were used unless otherwise noted) $URBAN$, population (in 100s) per road mile ($DENS$), proportion of households with money income less than \$10,000 ($POOR$), median household income ($MEDIAN$, in \$1,000s), mass transit vehicle miles per capita ($MASS$), average hospitalization cost (in \$100s) per day during 1976–81 ($HOSP$), adult per capita consumption of distilled spirits ($ALC$), and the proportion of population aged 18 to 24 ($YOUNG$). While a structural model was not specified, these variables were chosen in a rough attempt to provide a reduced form equation that would yield consistent parameter estimates. $REG$ was excluded since rate regulation may be more likely in high cost states. The no-fault variables were excluded for a similar reason.

[8] $PA$ equaled the proportion of years that rates were regulated for the 3 (out of 29) prior approval states that deregulated during the period. The loss ratios were adjusted to mitigate distortions in accounting results between the direct writer and independent agency samples that could arise in the 8 states that had reinsurance facilities or joint underwriting associations for residual market insurers. Several diagnostics were calculated to check for influential observations (see Harrington, 1984a). A listing of data sources is available from the author. The model also was estimated for each year using OLS. The estimates of $b_1$ ranged from 0.02 to 0.04 for both insurer groups.

[9] The data did not permit separate calculation of $ALOSS$ for independent agency insurers and direct writers.

OLS estimates of this model are shown below (absolute $t$-values are in parentheses):[10]

$$ALOSS = -1.363 + 0.550URBAN + 0.213DENS$$
$$(1.19) \quad (3.41) \quad\quad (3.09)$$
$$+ 3.257POOR + 0.083MEDIAN$$
$$(1.91) \quad\quad\quad (2.16)$$
$$- 0.013MASS + 0.036HOSP$$
$$(2.85) \quad\quad\quad (0.42)$$
$$+ 0.675ALC - 3.898YOUNG$$
$$(2.86) \quad\quad (2.14)$$
$$\bar{R}^2 = 0.73.$$

The signs of the coefficients generally seem plausible.[11] $ILOSS$ should be free from correlation with $LR$ that could result from purely random fluctuations in losses. While some of the regressors could be correlated with unanticipated changes in factors that influence losses across states, any correlation between $ILOSS$ and $LR$ due to these factors should be considerably lower than that between $ALOSS$ and $LR$.

## IV. Results

The OLS and ML results (shown in table 1) suggest that the average effect of rate regulation was to increase loss ratios by 0.03 to 0.05. The implied negative impact on average premiums would be slightly greater, but the estimates could overstate the impact on premiums if regulation increased expected losses. The estimated mean impact on loss ratios is larger by 0.017 for the independent agency insurers and by 0.007 for the direct writers using ML, but the policy conclusion would be similar for both estimation methods.

The average annual growth rate in the average loss per insured vehicle was regressed on $PA$, $PIP\%$, $THRESH$, and $WAGE$ using OLS to provide evidence of the potential effect of differences between actual and expected losses on the estimates for $PA$.[12] The resultant estimates indicate the relationship between the variables and total (anticipated and unanticipated) growth in losses. The estimate for $PA$ was 0.011 with a $t$-value of 1.77. If the average anticipated growth rate in prior approval states was at least as large as that for competi-

---

[10] OLS will provide consistent estimates. Although disturbance variance could depend on $1/P$, OLS was felt to be adequate since the purpose was not to make inferences concerning $ALOSS$.

[11] The negative sign for $YOUNG$ might reflect omitted factors, such as population shifts. ($YOUNG$ tended to be greater for southern and western states.) $MEDIAN$ may be associated with higher coverage limits and larger liability and loss of income claims. $POOR$ should be related to the number of uninsured drivers, which tends to increase the average loss per insured driver.

[12] Similar results were obtained when $ILOSS$ was included.

---

TABLE 1.—ESTIMATION RESULTS FOR LOSS RATIO MODEL: 1976–81

| Variable | Independent Agency | | Direct Writer | |
|---|---|---|---|---|
| | OLS | ML | OLS | ML |
| Constant | 0.625 | 0.611 | 0.607 | 0.619 |
| | (11.94) | (13.95) | (13.82) | (15.74) |
| PA | 0.028 | 0.045 | 0.030 | 0.037 |
| | (1.85) | (3.50) | (2.34) | (3.49) |
| PIP% | 0.367 | 0.374 | 0.390 | 0.389 |
| | (3.80) | (4.21) | (5.60) | (5.56) |
| THRESH | -0.034 | -0.020 | -0.050 | -0.050 |
| | (1.13) | (0.63) | (2.16) | (1.92) |
| ILOSS | 0.073 | 0.033 | 0.072 | 0.059 |
| | (2.49) | (1.65) | (2.98) | (2.67) |
| WAGE | -0.014 | -0.008 | -0.007 | -0.007 |
| | (1.84) | (1.38) | (1.08) | (1.31) |
| Log L | 82.29 | 87.40 | 90.96 | 93.27 |
| $\bar{R}^2$ | 0.41 | — | 0.54 | — |

Note: The absolute value of the coefficient estimate divided by its estimated standard error is in parentheses.

---

tive rating states, this figure would provide an estimate of the maximum difference in the average unanticipated growth rate in losses for the two groups of states after controlling the influence of the remaining variables. Its magnitude suggests that the estimates for $PA$ in table 1 primarily reflect an impact of regulation on the ratio of expected losses to premiums.

The estimates for $PIP\%$ are positive and highly significant; those for $THRESH$, $ILOSS$, and $WAGE$ have the expected signs, but are insignificant in some instances. The inclusion of $ILOSS$, as opposed to $URBAN$ or exclusion of both variables, improved the fit but had little influence on the estimates for $PA$, suggesting that prior work has not been greatly affected by failure to control for the effect of $LOSS$.[13]

The ML estimates of (3) for the independent agency insurers were (ratios of estimates to estimated standard errors are in parentheses):

$$\text{var}(e) \times 100 = 0.174PA + 0.173NF + 0.029(1/P).$$
$$(2.10) \quad\quad (1.99) \quad\quad (2.07)$$

The nonnegativity constraint was binding for $a_0$. The estimates suggest significant cross-state variation in the impact of prior approval and no-fault laws, as well as size-related heteroscedasticity. The results for the direct writers suggest much less variation in the effect of rate regulation:

$$\text{var}(e) \times 100 = 0.040 + 0.026PA + 0.159NF$$
$$(1.43) \quad (0.54) \quad\quad (2.22)$$
$$+ 0.024(1/P).$$
$$(1.35)$$

---

[13] OLS regression of $ALOSS$ on $PA$, $PIP\%$, $THRESH$, and $WAGE$ yielded an estimate for $PA$ of $6.09 with a $t$-value of 0.71. The mean average loss for all states was $94.64.

The hypothesis that var($e$) was constant across states would be rejected at the 0.05 level for the independent agency sample using a likelihood ratio test. It would not be rejected at the 0.10 level for the direct writers.

For the independent agency insurers, $\hat{b}_{1i}$ ranged from $-0.008$ to 0.149. The range for direct writers was 0.020 to 0.049.[14] The five states with the largest weighted-average (by premiums) $\hat{b}_{1i}$s for the groups (in parentheses) were New Hampshire (0.111), New Jersey (0.068), North Carolina (0.061), Rhode Island (0.059), and Maine (0.055). The five states with the smallest values were Tennessee (0.007), Arkansas (0.013), New York (0.022), Nebraska (0.022), and Iowa (0.025). Research is needed to explain this variation. It also would be desirable to estimate the effect of rate regulation on expected losses, to examine potential differences in its impact across consumer groups, and to investigate nonprice responses to restrictive rate regulation in this market.

## REFERENCES

D'Arcy, Stephen, "An Economic Theory of Insurance Regulation," Ph.D. dissertation, University of Illinois, 1982.

Grabowski, Henry, W. Kip Viscusi, and William Evans, "The Effects of Regulation on the Price and Availability of Automobile Insurance," paper presented at Nineteenth International Atlantic Economic Conference, Rome, Italy, March 1985.

[14] The correlation between the estimates for the groups was 0.75.

Griffiths, William, "Estimation of Actual Response Coefficients in the Hildreth-Houck Random Coefficient Model," *Journal of the American Statistical Association* 67 (Sept. 1972), 633–635.

Harrington, Scott, "Estimating the Impact of Prior Approval Regulation on Auto Insurance Rates," Working Paper No. 84-3, Center for Research on Risk and Insurance, University of Pennsylvania, July 1984a.

———, "The Impact of Rate Regulation on Prices and Underwriting Results in the Property-Liability Insurance Industry: A Survey," *Journal of Risk and Insurance* 51 (Dec. 1984b), 577–623.

Ippolito, Richard, "The Effects of Price Regulation in the Automobile Insurance Industry," *Journal of Law and Economics* 22 (Apr. 1979), 55–89.

Joskow, Paul, "Cartels, Competition and Regulation in the Property-Liability Insurance Industry," *Bell Journal of Economics and Management Science* 4 (Autumn 1973), 375–427.

———, "Inflation and Environmental Concern: Structural Change in the Process of Public Utility Price Regulation," *Journal of Law and Economics* 17 (Oct. 1974), 291–327.

Pauly, Mark, Paul Kleindorfer, and Howard Kunreuther, "Regulation and Quality Competition in the U.S. Insurance Industry," in J. Finsinger and M. Pauly (eds.), *The Economics of Insurance Regulation* (London: Macmillan Press, 1986).

Smallwood, Dennis, "Competition, Regulation, and Product Quality in the Automobile Insurance Industry," in Almarin Phillips (ed.), *Promoting Competition in Regulated Markets* (Washington, D.C.: The Brookings Institution, 1975).

U.S. General Accounting Office, *Issues and Needed Improvements in State Regulation of the Insurance Business* (Washington, D.C.: U.S. General Accounting Office, 1979).